Garage Sale & Flea Market

ANNUAL

FIFTH EDITION

CASHING IN ON
TODAY'S LUCRATIVE
COLLECTIBLES MARKET

COLLECTOR BOOKS

A Division of Schroeder Publishing Co., Inc.

The current values of this book should be used only as a guide. They are not intended to set prices, which vary from one section of the country to another. Auction prices as well as dealer prices vary and are affected by condition as well as demand. Neither the Editors nor the Publisher assumes any responsibility for any losses that might be incurred as a result of consulting this guide.

Searching for a Publisher?

We are always looking for knowledgeable people considered to be experts within their fields. If you feel that there is a real need for a book on your collectible subject and have a large comprehensive collection, contact Collector Books.

Editorial Staff

Editors
Sharon and Bob Huxford

Research and Editorial Assistants
Michael Drollinger, Nancy Drollinger, Linda Holycross, Donna Newnum, Loretta Woodrow

On the Cover:
Blue Ridge, dinner plate, Spring Song pattern on Candlewick shape, $10.00 – $15.00; Tappan salt and pepper shakers, 4½", $20.00; Coca-Cola sign, cardboard, 22", 1938, $2,000.00; Porcelain Blue Rhapsody Barbie doll, 11½", $740.00; Esso glass block bank, 5", $95.00; Gene Autry comic book, $3.00 – $8.00.

Cover design by Beth Summers
Book layout by Donna Ballard, Michelle Dowling, Kent Henry, Beth Ray, Karen Smith

A Word From The Editor

Psychologists tell us that it's basic to the human spirit to want to make order out of chaos and that confronted with vast amounts of assorted and seemingly unrelated objects, a typical individual will immediately began to lay out a plan whereby he or she can organize these things into groups with certain features in common. I think a collector is simply a person endowed with a motivation particularly supercharged by whatever gene it is that predetermines this characteristic at inception. And, being one myself, I prefer to view such an individual as extremely important in the human social organization, and I personally rate this person high in the pecking order of things. Imagine a world with no collectors. What would society do with it all? Instead of parks, would there be vast wastelands filled with mountains of discarded dinnerware? Would Grand Canyon have become a national garbage dump overflowing with old books and toys? I'm sure you see my point.

Call it rationalization if you will, and well it may be, but on occasion I have to look at our collections and convince myself that we're not crazy. But every cabinet and shelf holds things that are special to us — things we appreciate simply for their esthetics, things that cause us to remember pleasant times and circumstances, or things that we aggressively hunted until we finally found them. Then there are the nice things 'the garage-sale and flea-market gods' sent our way that more than likely we would never have purchased otherwise, like the 'Marie and Julian' vase we told you about a couple of editions ago that we bought for 40¢ (valued today at around $500.00) or the Regal Peek-a-Boo Bunny shakers — the large ones — we paid $2.00 for that 'book' at $500.00. We found those the same day we got a Fiesta Kitchen Kraft fork and spoon in cobalt for 50¢ each, valued at a minimum of $95.00 apiece. There are the Frankoma sculptures — the Garden Girl and the Prancing Pony — bought for $8.00 at an antique mall (collectively worth $225.00); the Roseville Burmese lady-head candle holders I paid $1.00 for (they go for about $300.00 a pair); and the pair of Kay Finch doves found at a southern Oregon flea market for $3.00 (these book at $200.00).

We've made lots of other great buys this summer too. Some items went right into our cabinets (if they were things we already collected), but when we'd run into underpriced merchandise we knew we could make some money on, we'd pick that up too. A friend of ours finds room in her antique shop for a few of our things, and in the fall, we set up at the 'Covered Bridge Festival,' which draws millions of visitors each year to our area. Generally our garage-sale 'junk' will bring in about $2,400.00 over the 10-day period of the festival, and even though we price things well under 'book,' we make a good profit on them, since we pay very little for anything. Now that I reflect on our summer, I guess maybe we're not crazy at all; in fact, I'm beginning to feel a bit smug.

But though we're basically collectors looking to add to our own collections and the things we sell are items we've picked up just because we know they're things we can make a decent profit on, we know dealers who take selling much more seriously than we do and seem to do quite well 'picking' garage sales and some of the smaller local flea markets (where you're more likely to find the sleepers, since the 'extravaganza type' dealers tend to travel about more and often seem to have a better feel for what the market will bear). I spoke with a lady by phone just recently who bought a bagfull of Pez dispensers for $5.00 and sold them for $1,200.00! She isn't a collector of anything, but she studies the market and has been able to earn plenty of extra cash doing something she enjoys very much. So whatever the motivation, the person who's interested enough to work at becoming familiar with what is collectible and what such items are worth can be just as successful as she is.

This book has been drafted with just such a person in mind. Basically we've tried to cover items produced since the 1930s on. Not only are you more apt to find these items at garage sales, but I'd venture to say that no less than 80% of the goods sold on the secondary market today come from that era. Things have made a turnaround during the past ten years or so, and some of the most active areas of trading today revolve around items that were of absolutely no value to collections before. If you'd like to break into working the antique/collectible market, plan on dealing in the more modern collectibles. Antiques are great, but you'll seldom find resale items you don't have to first invest a good deal of money in. Keeping a step ahead of the collectibles market is the key to buying low and selling at a good profit. It's our intent with this publication to add to your understanding of these newer fields of interest, so that you'll be able to recognize what is collectible and have a feel for current values. We'll have some suggestions for holding your own garage sale, where and how to sell those extra goodies you will no doubt accumulate from time to time, and in the back we'll even list names and addresses of hundreds of potential buyers, sorted for you by alphabetized, topical subjects. We'll have some recommendations concerning how to establish yourself as a knowledgeable, reputable dealer, should you desire to become one, what collectibles are 'hot' and which have the best investment potential, and we'll be suggesting additional reading material in nearly every category we cover, so that you will have resources for in-depth information on the subjects you find particularly fascinating. These books, compiled and written by many of today's experts and leading authorities, will help beginners as well as seasoned collectors and dealers to develop a feel for the market. You'll find your money well spent if you begin immediately to build a substantial library on a broad range of subjects.

In addition to studying a book such as this, you'll find that networking with other collectors with similar interests is a great way to learn. As a special feature, we'll list clubs and newsletters that relate to a specific area of collecting right under the opening narrative in each category. Tradepapers are listed in the Directory. If you're not already receiving them, see about getting a sample copy. When the weather hampers outdoor sales as it does here in the Midwest, you'll find a tradepaper such as *The Antique Trader* or *The Depression Glass Daze* a good substitute and very often an even better source for buying if you have a particularly hard-to-find item in mind. They'll have not only buyers and sellers advertisements but show schedules, auction bills, book reviews and informational articles as well.

How To Hold Your Own Garage Sale

Just as we promised we would, here are our suggestions for holding your own garage sale. If you're toying with the idea of getting involved in the business of buying and selling antiques and collectibles but find yourself short of any extra cash to back your venture, this is the way we always recommend you get started. Everyone has items they no longer use; get rid of them! Use them to your advantage. Here's how.

Get Organized. Gather up your merchandise. Though there's not a lot of money in selling clothing, this is the perfect time to unload things you're not using. Kids' clothing does best, since it's usually outgrown before it's worn out, and there's lots of budget-minded parents who realize this and think it makes good sense to invest as little as possible in their own children's wardrobes. Everything should of course be clean and relatively unwrinkled to sell at all, and try to get the better items on hangers. Leave no stone unturned. Clean out the attic, the basement, the garage — then your parent's attic, basement, and garage. If you're really into it, bake cookies, make some crafts. Divide your house plants; pot the starts in attractive little containers — ladies love 'em. Discarded and outgrown toys sell well. Framed prints and silk flower arrangements you no longer use, recipe books and paperbacks, tapes, records, and that kitchen appliance that's more trouble to store than it's worth can be turned into cash to get you off and running!

After you've gathered up your merchandise, you'll need to price it. Realistically, clothing will bring about 25% of what you had to pay for it, if it's still in good, ready-to-wear shape. There's tons of used clothing out there, and no one is going to buy much of anything with buttons missing or otherwise showing signs of wear. If you have good brand-name clothing that has been worn very little, you would probably do better by taking it to a resale or consignment shop. They normally price things at about one-third of retail, with their cut being 30% of that. Not much difference money-wise, but the garage-sale shopper that passes up that $150.00 suit you're asking $35.00 for will probably give $50.00 for it at the consignment shop, simply because like department stores, many have dressing rooms with mirrors so you can try things on and check them for fit before you buy. Even at $35.00, the suit is no bargain if you can't use it when you get it home.

Remember that garage-sale buyers expect to find low prices. Depending on how long you plan on staying open, you'll have one day, possibly two to move everything. If you start out too high, you'll probably be stuck with lots of leftover merchandise, most of which you've already decided is worthless to you. The majority of your better buyers will hit early on; make prices attractive to them and you'll do alright. If you come up with some 'low-end' collectibles — fast-food toys, character glasses, played-with action figures, etc. — don't expect to get much out of them at a garage sale. Your competition down the block may underprice you. But if you have a few things you think have good resale potential, offer them at about half of 'book' price. If they don't sell at your garage sale, take them to a flea market or a consignment shop. You'll probably find they sell better on that level, since people expect to find prices higher there than at garage sales.

You can use pressure-sensitive labels or masking tape for price tags on many items. But *please* do not use either of these on things where damage is likely to occur when they are removed. For instance (as one reader pointed out), on boxes containing toys, board games, puzzles, etc.; on record labels or album covers; or on ceramics or glass with gold trim or unfired, painted decoration. Unless a friend or a neighbor is going in on the sale with you, price tags won't have to be removed; the profit will all be yours. Of course, you'll have to keep tabs if others are involved. You can use a sheet of paper divided into columns, one for each of you, and write the amount of each sale down under the appropriate person's name, or remove the tags and restick them on a piece of poster board, one for each seller. I've even seen people use straight pins to attach small squares of paper which they remove and separate into plastic butter tubs. When several go together to have a sale, the extra help is nice, but don't let things get out of hand. Your sale can get *too* big. Things become too congested, and it's hard to display so much to good advantage.

Advertise. Place your ad in your local paper or on your town's cable TV information channel. It's important to make your ad interesting and upbeat. Though most sales usually start early on Friday or Saturday mornings, some people are now holding their sales in the early evening, and they seem to be having good crowds. This gives people with day jobs an opportunity to attend. You *might* want to hold your sale for two days, but you'll do 90% of your selling during the first two or three hours, and a two-day sale can really drag on. Make signs — smaller ones for street corners near your home to help direct passers-by, and a large one for your yard. You might even want to make another saying 'Clothing ½-Price after 12:00.' (It'll cut way down on leftovers that you'll otherwise have to dispose of yourself.) Be sure that you use a wide-tipped felt marker and print in letters big enough that the signs can be read from the street. Put the smaller signs up a few days in advance unless you're expecting rain. (If you are, you might want to include a rain date in your advertising unless your sale will be held under roof.) Make sure you have lots of boxes and bags, and plenty of change. If you price your items in increments of 25¢, you won't need anything but a few rolls of quarters, maybe ten or fifteen ones, and a few five-dollar bills. Then on the day of the sale, put the large sign up in a prominent place out front with some balloons to attract the crowd. Take a deep breath, brace yourself, and raise the garage door!

What To Do With What's Left. After the sale, pack up any good collectibles that didn't sell. Think about that consignment shop or setting up at a flea market. (We'll talk about that later on.) Sort out the better items of clothing for Goodwill or a similar charity, unless your city has someone who will take your leftovers and sell them on consignment. This is a fairly new concept, but some of the larger cities have such 'bargain centers.'

Learning To Become A Successful Bargain Hunter

Let me assure you, anyone who takes the time to become an informed, experienced bargain hunter will be successful. There is enough good merchandise out there to make it well worthwhile, at all levels. Once you learn what to look for, what has good resale potential, and what price these items will probably bring for you, you'll be equipped and ready for any hunting trip. You'll be the one to find treasures. They are out there!

Garage sales are absolutely wonderful for finding bargains. But you'll have to get up early! Even non-collectors can spot quality merchandise, and at those low, low garage sale prices (unless held by an owner who's done his homework) those items will be the first to move.

In order for you to be a successful garage sale shopper, you have to learn how to get yourself organized. It's important to conserve your time. The sales you hit during the first early-morning hour will prove to be the best nine times out of ten, so you must have a plan before you ever leave home. Plot your course. Your local paper will have a section on garage sale ads and local cable TV channels may also carry garage sale advertising. Most people hold their sales on the weekend, but some may start earlier in the week, so be sure to turn to the 'Garage Sales' ads daily. Write them down and try to organize them by areas — northwest, northeast, etc. At first, you'll probably need your city map, but you'll be surprised at how quickly the streets will become familiar to you. Upper middle-class neighborhoods generally have the best sales and the best merchandise, so concentrate on those areas. When you've decided where you want to start, go early! If the ad says 8:00, be there at 7:00. This may seem rude and pushy, but if you can bring yourself to do it, it will pay off. And chances are when you get there an hour early, you'll not be their first customer. If they're obviously not ready for business, just politely inquire if you may look. If you're charming and their nerves aren't completely frayed from trying to get things ready, chances are they won't mind.

Competition can be fierce during those important early-morning hours. Learn to scan the tables quickly, then move to the area that looks the most promising. Don't be afraid to ask for a better price if you feel it's too high, but most people have already priced garage sale merchandise so that it will sell. Keep a notebook to jot down items you didn't buy the first time around but think you might be interested in if the price were reduced later on. After going through dozens of sales (I've done as many as thirty or so in one morning), you won't remember where you saw what! Often by noon, at least by mid-afternoon, veteran garage sale buyers are finished with their rounds and attendance becomes very thin. Owners are usually much more receptive to the idea of lowering their prices, so it may pay you to make a second pass. In fact some people find it advantageous to go to the better sales on the last day as well as the first. They'll make an offer for everything that's left, and since most of the time the owner is about ready to *pay* someone to take it at that point, they can usually name their price. Although most of the collectibles will normally be gone at this point, there are nearly always some useable household items and several pieces of good, serviceable clothing left. The household items will sell at flea markets or consignment shops, and if there are worthwhile clothing items, take them to a resale boutique. They'll either charge the 30% commission fee or buy the items outright for about half of the amount they feel they can ask, a new practice some resale shops are beginning to follow. Because they want only clothing that is in style, in season, and like new, their prices may be a little higher than others shops, so half of that asking price is a good deal.

Tag sales are common in the larger cities. They are normally held in lieu of an auction, when estates are being dispersed, or when families are moving. Sometimes only a few buyers are admitted at one time, and as one leaves another is allowed to take his place. So just as is true with garage sales, the early bird gets the goodies. Really serious shoppers begin to arrive as much as an hour or two before the scheduled opening time. I know of one who will spend the night in his van and camp on the 'doorstep' if he thinks the sale is especially promising. And he can tell you fantastic success stories! But since it's customary to have tag sale items appraised before values are set, be prepared to pay higher prices. That's not to say, though, that you won't find bargains here. If you think an item is overpriced, leave a bid. Just don't forget to follow through on it, since if it doesn't sell at their asking price, they may end up holding it for you. It's a good idea to check back on the last day of the sale. Often the prices on unsold items may have been drastically reduced.

Auctions can go either way. Depending on the crowd and what items are for sale, you can sometimes spend all day and never be able to buy anything anywhere near 'book' price. On the other hand, there are often 'sleepers' that can be bought cheaply enough to resell at a good profit. Toys, dolls, Hummels, Royal Doultons, banks, cut glass, and other 'high-profile' collectibles usually go high, but white ironstone, dinnerware sets from the twenties through the fifties, silverplated hollowware, books, records, and linens, for instance, often pass relatively unnoticed by the majority of the buyers.

If there is a consignment auction house in your area, check it out. These are usually operated by local auctioneers, and the sales they hold in-house often involve low-income estates. You won't find something every time, so try to investigate the merchandise ahead of schedule to see if it's going to be worth your time to attend. Competition is probably less at one of these than in any of the other types of sales we've mentioned, and wonderful buys have been made from time to time.

Flea markets, I would have to say, are my favorite places to find bargains. I don't like the small ones — not that I don't find anything there, but I've learned to move through them so fast (to beat the crowd), I don't get my 'fix'; I just leave wanting more. If you've never been to a large flea market, you don't know what you're missing. Even if you're not a born-again collector, I guarantee you will love it. And they're excellent places to study the market. You'll be able to see where the buying activity is, you can check and compare prices, talk with dealers and collectors, and do hands-on inspections. I've found that if I first study a particular subject by reading a book or a magazine article, this type of exposure to that collectible really 'locks in' what I have learned.

Because there are many types of flea market dealers, there are plenty of bargains. The casual, once-in-a-while dealer may not always keep up with changing market values. Some of them simply price their items by what they themselves had to pay for it. Just as being early at garage sales is important, here it's a must. If you've ever been in line waiting for a flea market to open, you know that cars are often backed up for several blocks, and people will be standing in line waiting to be admitted hours before the gate opens. Browsers? Window shoppers? Not likely. Competition. So if you're going to have a chance at all, you'd better be in line yourself. Take a partner and split up on the first pass so that you can cover the grounds more quickly. It's a common sight to see the serious buyers conversing with their partners via walkie-talkies, and if you like to discuss possible purchases with each other before you actually buy, this is a good way to do it.

Learn to bargain with dealers. Their prices are usually negotiable, and most will come down by 10% to 20%. Be polite and fair, and you can expect the same treatment in return. Unpriced items are harder to deal for. I have no problem offering to give $8.00 if an item is marked $10.00, but it's difficult for me to have to ask the price and then make a counter offer. So I'll just say 'This isn't marked. Will you take...?' I'm not an aggressive barterer, so this works for me.

There are so many reproductions on the flea market level (and at malls and co-ops), that you need to be suspicious of anything that looks too new! Some fields of collecting have been especially hard hit. Whenever a collectible becomes so much in demand that prices are high, reproductions are bound to make an appearance. For instance, Black Americana, banks, toys of all types, teddy bears, lamps, glassware, doorstops, cookie jars, prints, advertising items, and many other fields have been especially vulnerable. Learn to check for telltale signs — paint that is too bright, joints that don't fit, variations in sizes or colors, creases in paper that you can see but not feel, and so on. Remember that zip codes have been used only since 1963, and this can sometimes help you date an item in question. Check glassware for areas of wavy irregularities often seen in new glass. A publication we would highly recommend to you is called *Antique and Collector Reproduction News*, a monthly report of 'Fakes, Frauds, and Facts.' To subscribe, call 1-800-227-5531. Rates are very reasonable compared to the money you may save by learning to recognize reproductions.

Antique malls and co-ops should be visited on a regular basis. Many mall dealers restock day after day, and traffic and buying competition is usually fierce. As a rule, you won't often find great bargains here; what you do save on is time. And if time is what you're short of, you'll be able to see lots of good merchandise under one roof, on display by people who've already done the leg work and invested *their* time, hence the higher prices. But there are always underpriced items as well, and if you've taken the time to do your homework, you'll be able to spot them right away.

Unless the dealer who rents the booth happens to be there, though, mall and co-op prices are usually firm. But often times they'll run sales — '20% off everything in booth #101.' If you have a dealer's license, and you really should get one, most will give you a courtesy 10% discount on items over $10.00, unless you want to pay with a credit card.

Antique shows are exciting to visit, but obviously if a dealer is paying several hundred dollars to set up for a three-day show, he's going to be asking top price to offset expenses. So even though bargains will be few, the merchandise is usually superior, and you may be able to find that special item you've been looking for.

Mail order buying is not only very easy, but most of the time economical as well. Many people will place an ad in 'For Sale' sections of tradepapers. Some will describe and price their merchandise in their ad, while others offer lists of items they have in exchange for a SASE (stamped, self-addressed envelope). You're out no gas or food expenses, their overhead is minimal so their prices are usually very reasonable, so it works out great for both buyer and seller. I've made lots of good buys this way, and I've always been fairly and honestly dealt with. You may want to send a money order or cashier's check to save time, otherwise (especially on transactions involving larger sums of money) the seller might want to wait until your personal check clears.

Goodwill stores and re-sale shops are usually listed in the telephone book. When you travel, it will pay you to check them out. If there's one in your area, visit it often. You never know what may turn up there.

What's Hot On Today's Market

If you haven't already, you're going to find the nineties to be an exciting time to become involved in collecting. Today's collectibles are 'tomorrow's antiques' and values can only go up. But how much more satisfying (and economical) it is to buy at today's prices and be able to sit back and watch your investments appreciate. The trick is to look for trends; and to ferret them out, you'll have to spend some time. Attend shows; observe. For this, specialized shows are best. Go to toys shows — you'll learn which toys are hot and where the main thrust of interest is concentrated. There are advertising shows, pottery shows, glass shows, Art Deco shows, etc. General shows and sales can be a good arena for buying, but when you have many dealers with the same type of merchandise, you can't as easily mistake personal preferences for solid indications of market activity. Read tradepapers and magazines, and check out the 'antiques and collectibles' isle of your book store. Any type of material that publicizes a collectible serves to draw attention to it and many times that's all it takes to get it off and running.

Co-ops are wonderful for 'trend watching.' These dealers generally have high overheads and to stay in the 'black' must stock merchandise that sells. I've seen several new collectibles show up at co-ops — a few pieces at first, a few months later, a tablefull.

For the most part, the areas we reported as 'hot' last year still are, and to inject other fields here simply for the sake of having new copy would be both inappropriate and inaccurate, we'll just add what we need to and update the remainder.

Ceramics Imported From Japan. Here's what you need to be watching for:

1) Lefton China — exquisite giftware that has been imported since the 1940s. Workmanship is of the highest quality. Most pieces carry either a fired-on trademark or a paper label. In particular, these pieces are good — the Christmas line called 'Green Holly'; animals, angels and figurines; pieces with applied flowers and figures; figural banks; and the kitchenware lines of cookie jars, salt and pepper shakers, teapots, etc., called 'Miss Priss' (the blue kitten), and similar figural designs.

2) Enesco — this is an importer whose goods are really hot! Lots of it is whimsical and funky, and dealers tell us it's the 'off the wall' things that are selling! There are 'Human Beans,' little slug-like bean-people banks, cookie jars, and figurines that sport inscribed messages across their tummies. And they have a license to produce a line of Garfield the Cat items — cookie jars, salt and pepper shakers, bookends, a variety of banks, etc., all of which are bringing very good prices on the secondary market. We told you last year about their 'Kitchen Prayer Ladies,' they're still going strong! The line was originally called 'Mother-in-the-Kitchen,' and they're easily identified by the prayer inscribed on their white aprons. They're often wearing pink dresses, but if you find one in blue, she'll be worth even more. Some pieces are common, but the hard-to-find cookie jars, for instance, are generally priced at a minimum of $250.00. Kitchen Independence with Betsy Ross and George Washington is another of their lines to watch for.

3) Rooster and Roses — a dinnerware line imported by several companies in the forties and fifties. It's quite extensive, and prices are already climbing, indicating much collector interest. You'll recognize it by the design — full-blown roses, yellow borders punctuated by groups of brown slash marks, and, of course, the rooster — yellow breast with black crosshatching, brown head, red crest and waddle. The most common mark you'll find is Ucagco, but ACSON, Norcrest, Py and Lefton imported some as well. This stuff sells the minute it hits our table, and it's fast disappearing from the antique malls as well.

4) Holt Howard. There are several styles of these figural ceramic novelties, and they're hot! From the late 1950s, collectors search for the pixie kitchenware items such as cruets, condiments, etc., all with flat, disk-like pixie heads for stoppers. In the sixties, the company designed and distributed a line of roosters — egg cups, napkin holders, salt and pepper shakers, candle holders, plates and bowls. Items with Christmas themes featuring Santa or angels, for instance, were sold from the fifties through the seventies, and you'll also find a line decorated with comical white cats. There are bobbin'

head banks, desk accessories, and cookie jars. Virtually all are marked and most are dated as well. Be wary of unmarked but very similar items. Copy-cat lines abound. Rare items in particular are becoming very pricey, I've seen such pieces carrying price tags of $100.00 and up!

5) Kreiss Ceramics. Here's a new one! Remember, you heard it here first! This line is full of some of the strangest ceramic items you'll ever care to see. I like the series with the cute little drunk and his pink elephant friend, but there are other lines that dealers tell us are selling very well for them too, for instance, the beatniks and the Psycho Ceramics. Figural banks are always good, and Kreiss's are certainly no exception. Watch for their napkin holder dolls and their salt and pepper shakers as well.

These are only a few highlights in this wide field. Watch for items marked Vandor and Fitz & Floyd. Both are importers of quality merchandise, much of which is figural, some of it character related. Apart from looking for trademarks of companies such as we mentioned, certain categories of Japanese imports are good as well, for instance, napkin ladies, black cat kitchenware, cookie jars, and salt and pepper shakers. The market is ripe for the pickin' right now, and prices are definitely on their way up!

Advertising. In the advertising field, character collectibles maintain a high profile. Some of the most collectible are Poppin' Fresh, Reddy Killowat, Campbell Kids, Big Boy, Mr. Peanut, and Elsie the Cow. But there are scores of others, old and new, that are well worth your attention as well. Even more recent issues are good: watch for Camel Joe items, M & M candy men, and don't forget the Eveready bunny that keeps on going and going — he already has lots of fans. Character radios and telephones are good, so are banks and push-button puppets. You'll find that these promotional items appear with surprising frequency at garage sales, even more so at flea markets. They've been distributed in large numbers, since most of them are very inexpensive to produce. Obviously their values hinge on their advertising appeal rather than their intrinsic worth.

Soda pop memorabilia is coming on strong. Of course, Coca-Cola items are always good, since pieces are easy to find in a price range that suits just about anyone's budget. Pepsi-Cola items are running a close second; and Hires, 7-Up and Orange Crush are also becoming popular. With so much memorabilia of this type around today, you'll need to do lots of research. Here's where a good price guide comes in.

Americans like their beer, and breweriana is a hot subdivision of advertising right now. Many collectors like to decorate their recreation room with neon signs, clocks, rows of glass mugs, thermometers, signs, statuettes, and trays.

Automobilia collectibles are attracting a following, in fact there are huge cataloged auctions where everything for sale is related in some way to automobilia and gasoline and service station collectibles. The decade of the thirties produced the items that are beginning to accelerate in value as well. Paper ephemeral such as brochures and manuals can make an interesting collection in their own right, and they're still not expensive. Motorcycle items have also been in the spotlight this year; we've observed them showing up at shows and auctions all over the country, and there's also been a new book written on the subject. Racing memorabilia is another facet of this field where interest seems to be intensifying. This year, we've included information on all of these categories.

Toys. This field remains at the forefront of activity, though prices appear to leveling off and becoming more reasonable. We've included toys several times in our 'What's Hot' list, and to leave them out this time would be a major omission. They're plentiful at garage sales, and they certainly don't have to be old to have value. Some toys are instant collectibles, made by the producer with the collector in mind — for instance, Ertl banks, the new GI Joes and the Holiday Barbies. Disney movies also generate instant collectibles. Rocketeer, Roger Rabbit and the Nightmare Before Christmas casts already have devoted collector followings, and the PVC figures, dolls, watches, etc., representing these 1990s characters will turn up every once in awhile on your garage-sale tours. Action figures are hugely popular. Marx's 'Best of the West' (Johnny West) line is very good now, with the character figures bringing from $70.00 to more than $300.00, if you can find them in their original box, complete (or nearly so), and in fine condition. Captain Action is another series where prices are soaring — the Action Boy figure with accessories in excellent condition books at about $325.00. Watch for Mego's 'Official World's Greatest Super Heroes'; it's an extensive line with some of the harder-to-find characters in mint condition bringing upwards of $100.00 (much more if their original boxes are present).

Character collectibles still rule the roost, though, whether in the form of windups and battery-ops whose price tags at toy shows are staggering, or less-expensive, easier to access toys of a more recent vintage such as coloring books, board games, paper dolls, bubble bath containers and lunch boxes. Besides the staples such as Disney and Western characters, others areas that are hot right now include vintage TV show titles such as Lost in Space, Flintstones, Bonanza, Addams Family, Howdy Doody, Man From U.N.C.L.E., Charlie's Angels, CHiPs, Munsters, Batman, and I Love Lucy. Star Trek and Star Wars items continue to be in high demand as well. Look for puzzles, playsets, model kits, etc., that were issued with these shows and movies in mind. Board games circa 1960s and '70s routinely go for $25.00 to $50.00, some much higher. And while you might buy a character-related model kit from the same era for under $50.00, on the retail level you can expect to pay as much as $500.00 for a mint-in-the-box James Bond #414 by Aurora.

Lots of really 'cool' stuff came out of the decade of the fifties, like Elvis, '57 Chevys, rock 'n roll, poodle skirts, cherry Cokes, drive-ins, and Barbie dolls. Everything (and everyone) else may be only pleasant memories now, but Barbie's still with us on a grand scale! The market continues to be strong, and prices are constantly on the increase. Watch for these dolls on your garage-sale rounds — even nude Barbies of fairly recent manufacture often sell for $8.00 and up, and you may even find a rare vinage doll, it's certainly not out of the realm of possibility. Look for Ken, Midge, Skipper, Francie, Stacie, Tutti and all the other family members and friends that Mattel created to keep her company, as well as her many pets. They all have value too, though compared to Barbie herself, they attract a much smaller circle of collectors. The most sought-after Barbie items are those made before 1970, and condition is extremely important in establishing their worth. Because they were mass produced in such huge quantities, only mint-in-box items bring the top prices. Once out of the original packaging, you can immediately deduct about half from the mint-in-box value. Dating your Barbies can be complicated, so you need to study reference books to become knowledgeable. For instance, the date on a doll's back may only indicate a copyright date, not the date of issue.

You need to study a good toy price guide to pick up on all the current trends, if you're going to be a successful buyer/seller of toys. Of course, we recommend *Schroeder's Collectible Toys, Antique To Modern*, published by Collector Books. It covers every imaginable field in the toy market to some extent, with particularly large, comprehensive sections on all the areas we've mentioned here as well as many other currently hot categories such as Japanese Windups and Battery-Ops, Fisher-Price, GI Joe, Star Wars, Celebrity Dolls, Diecasts and Disneyana.

American-made Ceramics. An ever-popular field that shows no evidence of waning interest, art pottery made by companies such as Roseville, Weller, and Rookwood has long been recognized as the cream of the crop, and though you seldom run across it at garage sales, it's certainly in the realm of possibility to pick up a piece now and then. Only a few weeks ago, I bought an immaculate pair of candleholder/bookends in Roseville's Burmese line. (They book at about $300.00, my price was $1.00.)

You'll be much more apt to pick up Hall, Hull, McCoy, Pfaltzgraff, Regal, Ceramic Arts Studio, Shawnee, or Royal Haeger, for instance. If you're buying to resell, you'll find a ready market for the wares of any that I've mentioned, and similar manufacturers as well. In fact, if you can find a piece of any marked American pottery at garage-sale prices, you can be sure you've found a bargain. (Unmarked items are good too, but you'll have to do your homework to be able to recognize them.) Virtually any pottery you could mention is seeing a steady growth in value. McCoy has been at the top of the heap for the past several years, and we see no signs of it slowing down. From the nondescript flowerpots and Floraline vases to the top-of-the-line cookie jar, if it's marked McCoy, they want it.

Dinnerware is making a comeback, especially anything by Homer Laughlin. Fiesta and the other colored HLC lines have been good for twenty years, but you'll still find a few pieces now and then. The Virginia Rose lines sell well, and patterns from the fifties are also becoming popular. In Pfaltzgraff, we've found several good pieces of the brown drip they called 'Gourmet Royal' — three corn trays for 25¢ each (worth $15.00 apiece) and a set of the hard-to-find style of canisters for $30.00 (worth at least $80.00.) Their Village pattern has been discontinued, and we're finding it easy to reassemble a set of it for ourselves. We bought a good-size boxfull of blue Russel Wright this summer for $5.00, several pieces of Red Wing, some Homestead by Regal, and a few pieces of Lu Ray.

We found it all sold well at the flea market, and we realized a very tidy profit on it, even though we always price it at 75% of book or less.

You'd have to be from another planet to have missed the furor the California potteries have stirred up! There are many of them, some of them major players, some of them minor. But even the minor companies are attracting more and more of a following. Among the top designer-potters are Kay Finch, Florence, Sascha Brastoff, Marc Bellaire, Cleminson, Howard Pierce, Brayton, and Vernon Kilns. We've dealt with most of these in individual categories, and the others we've touched on in a category called simply California Pottery. You'll do well to become familiar with these companies.

Modern Glassware. Once you learn what to look for, you'll have no trouble spotting these glassware lines, most of which have been made since the 1950s. Moon and Star is at the top of our list; we've done very well at finding it, and it certainly sells for us, though we don't part with many of the red pieces! There were several companies who pressed the glass; two of the largest distributors of this line were L.E. Smith and L.G. Wright. You'll see photographed examples further on back that will serve to identify the pattern for you. Eye Winker is another line of the same time period. It was also sold through the catalogs of L.G. Wright and made in red, green, blue and crystal, similar to some of the Moon and Star colors. We see Fostoria's Coin Glass every now and then at garage sales, as well as some of Fenton's later lines. We buy all we can find, since we know it will usually sell very quickly. The milk glass line called 'Paneled Grape' made by Westmoreland in the 1950s is very collectible, as is their colored glass of the 1960s. Both they and Indiana Glass produced an extensive assortment of iridescent 'carnival' glass in the 1970s, and that too is selling. If you'll take the time to acquaint yourselves with this type of glassware, I promise you it will be time well spent. We'll provide you with the basics, since all of these are included in this guide, and we'll refer you to other sources of information as well.

When viewed in its entirety, granted, the antiques and collectibles market can be overwhelming. But in each line of glassware, any type of pottery or toys, or any other field I could mention, there are examples that are more desirable than others, and these are the ones you need to be able to recognize. If you're a novice, it will probably be best at first to choose a few areas that you find most interesting and learn just what particular examples or types of items are most in demand within that field. Concentrate on the top 25%. This is where you'll do 75% of your business. Do your homework. Quality sells. Obviously no one can be an expert in everything, but gradually you can begin to broaden your knowledge. As an added feature of our guide, information on clubs and newsletters, always a wonderful source of up-to-date information on any subject, is contained in each category when available. (Advisor's names are listed as well. We highly recommend that you exhaust all other resources before you contact them with your inquiries. Their roll is simply to check over our data before we go to press to make sure it is as accurate as we and they can possibly make it for you; they do not agree to answer reader's questions, though some may. If you do write, you must send them an SASE. If you call, please take the time zones into consideration. Some of our advisors are professionals and may charge an appraisal fee, so be sure to ask.)

There are many fields other than those we've already mentioned that are strong and have been for a long time — Depression, elegant and carnival glass; photographica; ephemeral such as valentines and sheet music; good costume jewelry; Fiesta; dolls; Christmas collectibles; and railroadiana. It's impossible to list them all. But we've left very little out of this book; at least we've tried to represent each category to some extent and where at all possible to refer you to a source of further information. It's up to you to read, observe the market and become acquainted with it to the point that you feel confident enough to become a part of today's antiques and collectibles industry, if you haven't already. You don't know what you're missing!

The thousands of current values found in this book will increase your awareness of today's wonderful world of buying, selling, and collecting antiques and collectibles. Use it to educate yourself to the point that you'll be the one with the foresight to know what and how to buy as well as where and how to turn those sleepers into cold, hard cash.

How To Evaluate Your Holdings

In addition to this one, there are several other very fine price guides on the market. One of the best is *Schroeder's Antiques Price Guide*, another is *The Flea Market Trader*. Both are published by Collector Books. *The Antique Trader Antiques and Collectibles Price Guide*, *Warman's Antiques and Collectibles Price Guide*, and *Kovel's Antiques and Collectibles Price List* are others. You may want to invest in a copy of each. Where you decide to sell will have a direct bearing on how you price your merchandise, and nothing will affect an item's worth more than condition.

If you're not familiar with using a price guide, here's a few tips that may help you. When convenient and reasonable, antiques will be sorted by manufacturer. This is especially true of pottery and most glassware. If you don't find the item you're looking for under manufacturer, look under a broader heading, for instance, cat collectibles, napkin dolls, cookie jars, etc. And don't forget to use the index. Most guides of this type have very comprehensive indexes — a real boon to the novice collector. If you don't find the exact item you're trying to price, look for something similar. For instance, if it's a McCoy rabbit planter you're researching, go through the McCoy section and see what price range other animal planters are in. Or if you have a frame-tray puzzle with Snow White and the Seven Dwarfs, see what other Disney frame-trays are priced at. Just be careful not to compare apples to oranges. You can judge the value of a 7" Roseville Magnolia vase that's not listed; just look at the price given for one a little larger or smaller and adjust it up or down. Pricing collectibles is certainly not a science; the bottom line is simply where the buyer and the seller finally agree to do business. Circumstances dictate sale price, and we can only make suggestions, which we base on current sales, market observations, and the expert opinions of our advisors.

Once you've found 'book' price, decide how much less you can take for it. 'Book' price represents a high average retail. A collectible will often change hands many times, and obviously it will not always be sold at book price. How quickly do you want to realize a profit? Will you be patient enough to hold out for top dollar, or would you rather price your merchandise lower so it will turn over more quickly? Just as there are both types of dealers, there are two types of collectors. Many are bargain hunters. They shop around — do the legwork themselves. On the other hand, there are those who are willing to pay whatever the asking price is to avoid spending precious time searching out pieces they especially want, but they represent the minority. You'll often see tradepaper ads listing good merchandise (from that top 25% we mentioned before) at prices well above book value. This is a good example of a dealer who knows that his merchandise is good enough to entice the second type of buyer we mentioned and doesn't mind waiting for him (or her) to come along, and that's his prerogative.

Once you have a price range in mind, the next step is to assess condition. Most people, especially inexperienced buyers and sellers, have a tendency to overlook some flaws and to overrate merchandise. Mint condition means that an item is complete and undamaged, in effect, just as it looked the day it was made. Glassware, china, and pottery may often be found in mint condition, though signs of wear will downgrade anything. Unless a toy is still in its original box and has never been played with, you seldom see a toy in mint condition. Paper collectibles are almost never found without deterioration or damage. Most price guides will list values that apply to glass and ceramics that are mint (unless another condition is specifically indicated within some descriptions). Other items are usually evaluated on the assumption that they are in the best as-found condition common to that area of collecting. Grade your merchandise as though you were the buyer, not the seller. You'll be building a reputation that will go a long way toward contributing to your success. If it's glassware or pottery you're assessing, an item in less than excellent condition will be mighty hard to sell at any price. Just as a guideline (a basis to begin your evaluation, though other things will factor in), use a scale of one to five with Good being a one, Excellent being a three, and Mint being a five. As an example, a beer tray worth $250.00 in mint condition would then be worth $150.00 if excellent and $50.00 if only good. Remember, the first rule of buying (for resale or investment) is 'Don't put your money in damaged goods.' And the second rule should be be, 'If you do sell damaged items, indicate 'as is' on the price tag, and don't price the item as though it were mint.' The Golden Rule applies just as well to us as antique dealers as it does in any other phase of interaction. Some shops and co-ops have poor lighting — your honesty will be greatly appreciated. If you include identification on your tags as well, be sure it's accurate. If you're not positive, it's better to let the buyer decide.

Deciding Where To Best Sell Your Merchandise

Personal transactions are just one of many options. Overhead and expenses will vary with each and must be factored into your final pricing. If you have some especially nice items and can contact a collector willing to pay top dollar, that's obviously the best of the lot. Or you may decide to sell to a dealer who may be willing to pay you only half of book. Either way, your expenses won't amount to much more than a little gas or a phone call.

Classified ads are another way to get a good price for your more valuable merchandise without investing much money or time. Place a 'For Sale' ad or run a mail bid in one of the collector magazines or newsletters, several of which are listed in the back of this book. Many people have had excellent results this way. One of the best to reach collectors in general is *The Antique Trader Weekly* (P.O. Box 1050, Dubuque, Iowa 52004). It covers virtually any and all types of antiques and collectibles and has a very large circulation. If you have glassware, china, or pottery from the Depression era, you should have good results through *The Depression Glass Daze* (Box 57, Otisville, Michigan 48463). If you have several items and the cost of listing them all is prohibitive, simply place an ad saying (for instance) 'Several pieces of Royal Copley (or whatever) for sale, send SASE for list.' Be sure to give your correct address and phone number.

When you're making out your list or talking with a prospective buyer by phone, try to draw a picture with words. Describe any damage in full; it's much better than having a disgruntled customer to deal with later, and you'll be on your way to establishing yourself as a reputable dealer. Sometimes it's wise to send out photographs. Seeing the item exactly as it is will often help the prospective buyer make up his or her mind. Send a SASE along and ask that your photos be returned to you, so that you can send them out again, if need be. A less expensive alternative is to have your item photocopied. This works great for many smaller items, not just flat shapes but things with some dimension as well. It's wonderful for hard-to-describe dinnerware patterns or for showing their trademarks.

If you've made that 'buy of a lifetime' or an item you've hung onto for a few years has turned out to be a scarce, highly sought collectible, a mail bid is often the best way to get top dollar for your prize. This is how you'll want your ad to read. 'Mail Bid. Popeye cookie jar by American Bisque, slight wear (or mint — briefly indicate condition), closing 6/31/95, right to refuse' (standard self-protection clause meaning you will refuse ridiculously low bids), and give your phone number. Don't commit the sale to any bidder until after the closing date, since some may wait until the last minute to try to place the winning bid.

Be sure to let your buyer know what form of payment you prefer. Some dealers will not ship merchandise until personal checks have cleared. This delay may make the buyer a bit unhappy. So you may want to request a money order or a cashier's check.

Be very careful about how you pack your merchandise for shipment. Breakables need to be well protected. There are several things you can use. Plastic bubble wrap is excellent, or scraps of foam rubber such as carpet padding (check with a carpet-laying service or confiscate some from family and friends who're getting new carpet installed). I've received items wrapped in pieces of egg-crate type mattress pads (watch for these at garage sales!). If there is a computer business near you, check their dumpsters for discarded foam wrapping and other protective packaging. It's best not to let newspaper come in direct contact with your merchandise, since the newsprint may stain certain types of items. After you've wrapped them well, you'll need boxes. Find smaller boxes (one or several, whatever best fits your needs) that you can fit into a larger one with several inches of space between them. First pack your well-wrapped items snugly into the smaller box, using crushed newspaper to keep them from shifting. Place it into the larger box, using more crushed paper underneath and along the sides, so that it will not move during transit. Remember, if it arrives broken, it's still your merchandise, even though you have received payment. You may want to insure the shipment; check with your carrier. Some have automatic insurance up to a specified amount.

After you've mailed it out, it's good to follow it up with a phone call after a few days. Make sure the box arrived in good condition and that your customer is pleased with the merchandise. Most people who sell by mail allow a 10-day return privilege, providing their original price tag is still intact. You can simply initial a gummed label or use one of those pre-printed return address labels that most of us have around the house.

For very large or heavy items such as furniture or slot machines, ask your buyer for his preferred method of shipment. If the distance involved is not too great, he may even want to pick it up himself.

Flea market selling can either be lots of fun, or it can turn out to be one of the worst experiences of your life. Obviously you will have to deal with whatever weather conditions prevail, so be sure to listen to weather reports so that you can dress accordingly. You'll see some inventive shelters you might want to copy. Even a simple patio umbrella will offer respite from the blazing sun or a sudden downpour. I've recently been seeing stands catering just to the needs of the flea market dealer — how's that for being enterprising! Not only do they carry specific items the dealers might want, but they've even had framework and tarpaulins for shelters they'll erect right on the spot!

Be sure to have plastic table covering in case of rain and some large clips to hold it down if there's much wind. The type of clip you'll need depends on how your table is made, so be sure to try them out before you actually have need for them. Otherwise your career as a flea market dealer may be cut short for lack of merchandise!

Price your things, allowing yourself a little bargaining room. Unless you want to collect tax separately on each sale (for this you'd need lots of small change), mentally calculate the amount and add this on as well. Sell the item 'tax included.' Everybody does.

Take snacks, drinks, paper bags, plenty of change, and somebody who can relieve you occasionally. Collectors are some of the nicest people around. I guarantee that you'll enjoy this chance to meet and talk them, and often you can make valuable contacts that may help you locate items you're especially looking for yourself.

Auction houses are listed in the back of this book. If you have an item you feel might be worth selling at auction, be sure to contact one of them. Many have appraisal services; some are free while others charge a fee, dependent on number of items and time spent. We suggest you first make a telephone inquiry before you send in a formal request.

In Summation

Whatever the reason you've become interested in the antiques and collectibles field, whether to supplement your income part-time, go into it on a full-time basis, simply because you want to be a wise collector/investor, I'm confident that you will achieve your goals. Aside from monetary gain, it's a wonderful hobby, a real adventure. There's never been a better time to become involved. With study comes knowledge, and knowledge is the key to success. The time you invest in reading, attending shows, talking with experienced collectors, and pursuing understanding of the field in every way you can devise will pay off handsomely as you enjoy the hunt for today's collectibles, tomorrow's antiques.

Abbreviations

dia - diameter	**M** - mint condition	**NM** - near mint	**qt** - quart
EX - excellent	**med** - medium	**oz** - ounce	**sm** - small
G - good	**MIB** - mint in (original) box	**pc** - piece	**VG** - very good
gal - gallon	**MIP** - mint in package	**pr** - pair	**w/** - with
lg - large	**MOC** - mint on card	**pt** - pint	

Abingdon Pottery

You may find smaller pieces of Abingdon around, but it's not common to find many larger items. This company operated in Abingdon, Illinois, from 1934 until 1950, making not only nice vases and figural pieces but some kitchen items as well. Their cookie jars are very well done and popular with collectors. They sometimes used floral decals and gold to decorate their wares, and a highly decorated item is worth a minimum of 25% more than the same shape with no decoration. Some of their glazes also add extra value. If you find a piece in black, bronze, or red, you can add 25% to those as well.

If you talk by phone about Abingdon to a collector, be sure to mention the mold number on the base.

See also Cookie Jars.

Newsletter: *Abingdon Pottery Collectors Newsletter*
Abingdon Pottery Club
Penny Vaughan, President
212 S. Fourth
Monmouth, IL 61462; 309-734-2337

Ashtray, donkey, #510, 5½"	$95.00
Ashtray, elephant, #509, 5½"	$95.00
Bookends, cactus, #370, 6", pr	$65.00
Bookends, dolphin (planter), decorated, #444, 5½", pr	$50.00
Bookends, quill, white, on black base, #595, 8¼", pr	$100.00
Bookends, Russian dancer, #321, 8½", pr	$100.00
Bookends, Scotty dog, black, #650, 7½", pr	$125.00
Bowl, blue, oval, #547	$13.00
Bowl, console; lt blue, #532	$25.00
Bowl, Panel, #460, 8"	$25.00
Bowl, pineapple, #700, 14¼"	$125.00
Bowl, scallop, pink, #564	$12.00
Bowl, scroll, dark blue, #532, med	$26.00
Bowl, shell, pink, #501, med	$20.00
Bowl, soup; round, #341, 5½"	$25.00
Bowl, Streamliner, #544, 9"	$15.00
Box, butterfly, #580, 4¾"	$60.00
Butter dish, #RE4, 1-lb	$20.00
Candle holder, triple, Chain, beige, #404, 3x8½"	$35.00
Casserole, #RE5, 8"	$20.00
Cornucopia, double, blue, #482	$16.00
Cornucopia, pink, #565	$16.00
Cornucopia, white, #474	$16.00
Dish, square, #337, 5"	$25.00
Figurine, goose, black, #571, 5"	$40.00
Figurine, gull, colors other than black, #562, 5"	$50.00
Figurine, kangaroo, solid colors, #605, 7"	$70.00
Figurine, penguin, decorated, #573, 5½"	$40.00
Flowerpot, cattail, #150	$28.00
Goblet, Swedish, green, #322	$50.00
Jar, elephant, #606, 9¼"	$55.00
Jug, water; w/lid, #RE1, 2-qt	$45.00
Leftover, round or square, 4-6", each	$20.00
Nut cup, Daisy, #385, 3½"	$20.00
Pitcher, Fern Leaf, white, #430, 1937-38, 8"	$150.00
Planter, burro, #673, 4½"	$35.00

Planter, donkey, #669, 7½"	$50.00
Planter, fawn, #672, 5"	$35.00
Planter, pooch, $670, 5½"	$35.00
Planter, ram, #671, 4"	$45.00
Plate, round, #343, 12"	$50.00
String holder, Chinese face, #702D, 5½"	$125.00
String holder, mouse, #712, 8½"	$75.00
Tea tile, geisha, #400, 5" square	$50.00
Vase, Barre, #522, 9"	$23.00

Vase, blue, 10", $35.00.

Vase, bowknot, blue, #593, 9"	$25.00
Vase, Classic, #115	$16.00
Vase, Dutch Girl, #470, 8"	$100.00
Vase, Fern Leaf, #421, 8¾"	$40.00
Vase, Gamma Classic, #103	$20.00
Vase, hackney, #659, 8½"	$30.00
Vase, morning-glory, #392, 5½"	$35.00
Vase, oak leaf, #706D, 9½"	$75.00
Vase, shell, oval, #507, 7½"	$25.00
Vase, ship motif, #494, 7"	$25.00
Vase, star, #708D, 9"	$75.00
Vase, swirl, green, #514, lg	$45.00
Vase, Trojan head, black, #499, 7½"	$100.00
Vase, tulip, #604D	$40.00
Vase, wheel handle, white matt, #466, 8"	$30.00
Vase, wreath, #467, 8"	$50.00
Wall pocket, apron, #699, 6"	$50.00
Wall pocket, cherub bracket, #587, 7½"	$65.00
Wall pocket, Tri-Fern, #435, 8"	$135.00
Wall pocket, Triad, #640, 5½", from $40 to	$50.00

Advertising Character Collectibles

The advertising field holds a special fascination for many of today's collectors. It's vast and varied, so its appeal is universal; but the characters of the ad world are its stars right now. Nearly every fast-food restaurant and manufacturer of a consumer product has a character logo. Keep your eyes open on your garage sale outings;

it's not at all uncommon to find the cloth and plush dolls, plastic banks and mugs, bendies, etc., such as we've listed here. There are several books on the market that are geared specifically toward these types of collectibles. Among them are: *Collectible Aunt Jemima* by Jean Williams Turner (Schiffer)*; Advertising Character Collectibles* by Warren Dotz and *Zany Characters of the Ad World* by Mary Jane Lamphier (both published by Collector Books); and *Hake's Guide to Advertising Collectibles* by Ted Hake (Wallace-Homestead). *Huxford's Collectible Advertising* offers a more general overview of the market but nevertheless includes many listings and values for character-related items as well. (It's also published by Collector Books.)

See also Breweriana; Bubble Bath Containers; Cereal Boxes; Character and Promotional Drinking Glasses; Coca-Cola Collectibles; Fast-Food Collectibles; Pez Candy Containers; Pin-Back Buttons; Salt and Pepper Shakers; Soda Bottles; Soda Pop Memorabilia.

Aunt Jemima

One of the most widely recognized ad characters of them all, Aunt Jemima has decorated bags and boxes of pancake flour for more than ninety years. In fact, the original milling company carried her name, but by 1926 it had become part of the Quaker Oats Company. She and Uncle Mose were produced in plastic by the F&F Mold and Die Works in the 1950s, and the salt and pepper shakers, syrup pitchers, cookie jars, etc., they made are perhaps the most sought-after of the hundreds of items available today. Age is a big worth-assessing factor for memorabilia such as we've listed below, of course, but so is condition. Watch for very chipped or worn paint on the F&F products, and avoid buying very soiled cloth dolls.

Advisor: Lynn Burkett (See Directory, Advertising)

Dolls, Aunt Jemima, Uncle Mose, Wade and Diana, stuffed cloth, M, from $100.00 to $150.00 each.

Banner, painted canvas, image of Aunt Jemima w/stack of pancakes, Coming... in Person..., 33x56", NM....**$330.00**

Button, tin pin-back, Aunt Jemima Pancake Club, Pancake Days Are Here Again, image of drummer, black & red, 3", M.......**$45.00**

Button, tin w/fold-down tab, Aunt Jemima Breakfast Club, Eat a Better Breakfast, Adcraft, 1940s, 1¼", M, from $25 to **$30.00**

Candle holders, plastic, primary colors of nursery-rhyme characters, mail-order **$75.00**

Clipboard, New Aunt Jemima Butter Lite, yellow w/5 images of Aunt Jemima down side, for grocery store use, unused, M..**$75.00**

Cookbook, from Aunt Jemima's Junior Chef baking set, 1950s, EX..**$25.00**

Cookie jar, plastic figural, F&F, NM...........................**$400.00**

Coupon, for rag doll family, family illustrated front & back, ca 1917, 3½x2¼", EX **$125.00**

Cup, restaurant china, gray top border, her image inside, made by Wellsville China....................................**$100.00**

Flour bag wrapper, brown paper shipping bag, image w/full bandana in blue, 17x24", NM **$45.00**

Hat, paper, Aunt Jemima'a Pancake Jamboree! w/image of Aunt Jemima, 1950s, VG **$45.00**

Mug, plastic thermal travel type w/lid, black w/yellow & orange paper insert, Aunt Jemima, Free Orange Juice, M.....**$35.00**

Napkin, paper, Aunt Jemima's Pancake Jamboree! yellow w/marching-band border in black & white, EX **$5.00**

Pancake mold, aluminum, round w/4 animal shapes, black wooden handle, 8½" dia.......................................**$145.00**

Pancake shaker, yel plastic figural, F&F, NM.............**$100.00**

Pancake turner, Hooray! It's Aunt Jemima Day! lettered on plastic handle, round slotted metal turner, EX **$45.00**

Pancake-making kit for children, complete w/instructions, dated 1986, EXIB **$60.00**

Paper cup, featuring image of Aunt Jemima & restaurant, w/fold-out handles, 6-oz, M..................................**$50.00**

Paper plate, Aunt Jemima Helps You Make The Finest Pancakes In The World..., white & yellow border, w/1950s image, EX **$30.00**

Place mat, The Story of Aunt Jemima, Yesterday, Today & Now...at Disneyland, from restaurant in Frontierland, 1955, EX...**$25.00**

Recipe book, Cake Mix Miracles, 1950s, EX...............**$50.00**

Recipe book, Magical Recipes, Aunt Jemima Story on back, 28 pgs, 1954, EX..**$20.00**

Salt & pepper shakers, Aunt Jemima & Uncle Mose, F&F, 5", pr...**$75.00**

Salt & pepper shakers, plastic figurals of Aunt Jemima & Uncle Mose, F&F, 3½", pr **$45.00**

Spice shaker, plastic figural, F&F, from set of 6, each ..**$50.00**

Sugar bowl, yellow plastic w/figural handle, F&F **$75.00**

Syrup pitcher, plastic figural, F&F, 5½", from $60 to ..**$70.00**

Tablecard, Oh Happy Snack!, shows steaming stack of pancakes w/sm image of Aunt Jemima, EX...............**$40.00**

Tablecard, red w/plate of pancakes, diecut Aunt Jemima head stands up when folded **$38.00**

Tin, Aunt Jemima advertising w/Pancakes lettered vertically, wood-grain lid w/knob, plastic spoon, dated 1983, 6", EX **$45.00**

Tin, shadow box w/knick-knacks sitting on shelf, Quaker Commemorative Limited Edition, 1983 ....**$55.00**

Big Boy and Friends

Bob's Big Boy, home of the nationally famous Big Boy, the original double-deck hamburger, was founded by Robert C. 'Bob' Wian in Glendale, California, in 1938. He'd just graduated from high school, and he had a dream. With the $300.00 realized from the sale of the car he so treasured, he bought a run-down building and enough basic equipment to open his business. Through much hard work and ingenuity, Bob turned his little restaurant into a multimillion-dollar empire. Not only does he have the double-deck 2-patty burger to his credit, but car hops and drive-in restaurants were his invention as well.

With business beginning to flourish, Bob felt he needed a symbol — something that people would recognize. One day in walked a chubby lad of six, his sagging trousers held up by reluctant suspenders. Bob took one look at him and named him Big Boy, and that was it! It was a natural name for his double-deck hamburger — descriptive, catchy and easy to remember. An artist worked out the drawings, and Bob's Pantry was renamed Bob's Big Boy.

The enterprise grew fast, and Bob added location after location. In 1969 when he sold out to the Marriott Corporation, he had 185 restaurants in California, with franchises such as Elias Big Boy, Frisch's Big Boy, and Shoney's Big Boy in other states. The Big Boy burger and logo was recognized by virtually every man, woman, and child in America, and Bob retired knowing he had made a significant contribution to millions of people everywhere.

Since Big Boy has been in business for over sixty years, you'll find many items and numerous variations. Some, such as the large statues, china, and some menus, have been reproduced. If you're in doubt, go to an experienced collector for help. Many items of jewelry, clothing, and kids promotions were put out over the years, too numerous to itemize separately. Values range from $5.00 up to $100.00. In the listings that follow, prices ranges are given for items from excellent to mint condition.

Advisor: Steve Soelberg (See Directory, Advertising)

Ashtray, ceramic with Big Boy figure on rim, NM, $375.00. (Photo courtesy of Steve Soelberg.)

Ashtray, Big Boy figural, green or maroon, from $500 to.**$700.00**
Ashtray, smoked glass, white & gold image of Big Boy in center w/outline border, curved sides, 1970s, 2x2", M..**$20.00**
Baby bottle, see-through soft vinyl, w/logo (new).......**$3.50**
Bank, figural, vinyl, slender, sm red & white checks, 1970s, MIP...**$35.00**

Bank, figural, vinyl, 1994, MIP.......................................**$15.00**
Bobbin' head doll, Big Boy, from $1,000 to **$1,500.00**
Buttons, employee items, promo items, each, minimum values...**$20.00**
China or glassware w/logo, from $20 to **$50.00**
Comic book #1, from Bob's chain in California........**$200.00**
Cookie jar, Big Boy, ceramic, brown **$500.00**
Cookie jar, Big Boy, ceramic, 1994 edition, glazed full color..**$650.00**
Cookie jar, Big Boy, ceramic, 1995 edition, glazed full color **$300.00**
Display, Big Boy plaster figure, for counter, 14" ...**$1,800.00**
Doll, Big Boy w/hamburger & shoes, Dakin **$100.00**
Doll, Dolly, stuffed printed cloth, hands on hips, dotted dress, 1978, 14", M..**$30.00**
Doll, Nugget the Dog, stuffed printed cloth, side view in seated position, w/collar, 1978, MIP......................**$35.00**
Doll, stuffed printed cloth w/Big Boy lettered on chest, 1978, 14", MIP **$30.00**
Employee items not available to the public, each, from $20 to...**$200.00**
Figurine, Big Boy, hard plastic, w/hamburger on tray .**$5.00**
Figurine, Big Boy, quality pewter, 5" **$35.00**
Game, Big Boy, w/gameboard **$200.00**
Key ring, white enameling w/Big Boy logo (new).......**$2.50**
Kite, paper, Big Boy image...**$250.00**
Lamp, figural, ceramic, w/shade, from $2,000 to ..**$2,500.00**
Lighter, disposable; logo on white (new) **$2.50**
Lighter, tan w/brown Big Boy image, 1960s, 4", EX...**$20.00**
Lighter, Zippo; logo on gold-tone **$18.95**
Matchbook, Coast-To-Coast, 1950s, EX......................**$12.00**
Matchbook, up to 10 locations, from $20 to **$50.00**
Matchbook #1, showing 1st location.........................**$200.00**

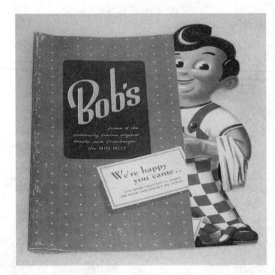

Menu, diecut cardboard, ca 1956, 4 pages, M, $150.00. (Photo courtesy of Steve Soelberg.)

Menu, other early (2nd, 3rd, 4th locations), minimum value **$100.00**
Menu, up to 20 locations, from $20 to **$50.00**
Menu #1, showing original location, minimum value..**$300.00**
Money clip, Zippo; black enamel w/logo on metal ...**$10.00**
Photos, letters, newsletters, old, each, minimum value ..**$20.00**

Playing cards, Big Boy, from $25 to............................**$35.00**
Quill pen, gold on silver-tone **$17.00**
Salt & pepper shakers, Big Boy figural, ceramic, 1960s-70s,
    pr..**$375.00**
Salt & pepper shakers, Big Boy figural, ceramic, 1994, pr.**$30.00**
Salt & pepper shakers, Big Boy figural, ceramic, 1996, pr ..**$10.00**
Sign, restaurant, minimum value **$100.00**
Statue, Big Boy, fiberglass, 60" to 84", from $1,500 to ..**$3,500.00**
Statue, Big Boy, gold 'Oscar,' from $400 to...............**$500.00**
Telephone dialer, plastic figural rotary dialer, Big Boy let-
    tered on hat & hamburger, orange, 1950s, 4½x3½",
    NM **$40.00**
Trading cards, Famous American, 1976, set of 30.......**$75.00**
Trophy or award, employee; minimum value..........**$100.00**
Watches, each, from $50 to.......................................**$100.00**
Wrapper, hamburger; early, from $20 to.....................**$50.00**

Buster Brown and Tige

Created in 1902 by cartoonist Richard Felton, Buster
Brown and his dog Tige have become best known as the
trademark for the Brown Shoe Company, though they've promoted several other consumer products ranging all the way
from hosiery to bread! As toddlers, baby-boomers everywhere
wore Buster Brown shirts and shorts. Millions of premiums
have been issued over the years; you'll find all types — comic
books, pin-back buttons, and scores of noveties. Point-of-sale
items (signs, banners, etc., used on the retail store level) are
often very pricey.

**Balloon inflator, 19x19", EX, $400.00. (Photo
courtesy of Dunbar Gallery.)**

Bank, figural bust images of Buster & Tige atop red molded
    plastic ball shape embossed Buster Brown Bank, 1950s,
    5", M...**$40.00**
Bank, No Parents Allowed, 1980s, 11".........................**$40.00**
Bill hook, Buster Brown w/Tige, copyright 1946, 2¼" dia .**$40.00**
Birthday card, Buster & Tige holding balloons, inside reads
    Wish A Happy Birthday, 1960s, EX.....................**$15.00**
Dealer's sign, 1950s, 15x15", MIB............................**$150.00**
Doll, Buster Brown, stuffed cloth, 1974, 14", NM **$35.00**

Game, Buster Brown Shoe Game, ring toss, complete,
    MIB **$70.00**
Game, Necktie, variation of Pin the Tail on the Donkey,
    w/printed cloth ties, EX **$150.00**
Key chain, 2" brown plastic fob w/embossed image of Buster
    Brown w/Tige, 1950s **$50.00**
Kite, 1940s, NM...**$38.00**
Magic slate, 1950s-60s store giveaway, M...................**$20.00**
Pin-back button, Brown Bilt Club arched above image of
    Buster & Tige, product name below, EX.............**$10.00**
Shoe stretcher, plastic figural images of Buster & Tige, spring-
    operated, 1950s, 7½", NM, from $35 to **$45.00**
Tote bag, 1960s, NM...**$45.00**
Whistle, image of Buster & Tige, rectangular, EX+ **$32.00**
Wrist decoder, Moon Mission Agent, 1950s, NM........**$50.00**

Campbell Kids

It's difficult to imagine a cup of hot Campbell's Soup
without mentally associating the product with its chubby little logo kids. They were created by artist Grace Gebbie
Drayton, and in 1904 they were adopted by the company,
who featured them early on in their *Ladies' Home Journal*
ads. (It's estimated that about 2,000 of these ads were
designed.) Campbell Kids postcards became very popular,
and today these are highly collectible, fetching as much as
$75.00 on today's market. Calenders, prints, mirrors and
placecards were favored in the 1920s and '30s; by the mid-
century mark, toys, kitchen items, silverware, pot holders,
cookbooks and salt and pepper shakers were distributed
nationwide. Several variations of dolls have been issued over
the years; some of the best were made by the American
Character Company and the Horsman Company of New
York. Both of these companies produced their dolls in composition. Later dolls were generally made of cloth, hard plastic and soft rubber; several are listed below.

The values that follow represent typical prices observed
at toy shows and antique shops or malls.

Advisors: David and Micki Young (See Directory,
Advertising)

Club: Soup Collector Club
David and Micki Young, Editors and Founders
414 Country Lane Ct.
Wauconda, IL 60084, 847-487-4917; 6 issues per year for $19
donation per address.

Bank, Campbell's Vegetable Garden, tin w/paper label,
    Money Saving..., w/original contents, 4½", EX **$25.00**
Banner, red felt, running kid illustrated, 18", EX **$135.00**
Calendar, 1989, M **$8.00**
Christmas ornament, glass, 1991, unused, MIB **$8.00**
Clock w/shelf & 2 oven-mitt wall pockets, Burwood, 1991,
    M **$20.00**
Commemorative coin, w/Campbell Kid chef from 1st convention,
    sequentially numbered to 120 only, limited edition......**$20.00**
Commemorative mug, glass, from 1st Campbell's Soup
    Convention **$15.00**

Cup, girl's face, F&F Mold Co, M $25.00
Decals, boy & girl in kitchen, Meyorcord, 6 decals in set, MIP..$20.00
Doll, boy, vinyl, 1975, 10", EX.................................$65.00
Doll, boy, 1976 Bicentennial, MIB, from $60 to..........$70.00
Doll, boy chef, vinyl, 8", EX $50.00
Doll, boy or girl, vinyl, Product People, 1974, 10", EX, each $30.00
Doll, girl cheerleader, vinyl, 1967, 8", EX, from $70 to..$75.00
Dolls, boy & girl, rag type, 1970s, MIB, pr $125.00
Dolls, boy & girl, special edition, 1988, MIB, pr.......$100.00
Fork, child's, kid's head engraved above M-m-m Good on handle, EX...$15.00
Game, Alphabet Soup, kids illustrated on cardboard canister, tin lid, contains red plastic letters, EX...................$22.00

Hotpad holder, painted plaster, recent, 6", M, $12.00.

Jigsaw puzzle, 1986, All Aboard, 28-pc, VG................$25.00
Kitchen timer, can form..$10.00
Lunch box w/thermos, metal, dome top, 1968, rare, VG .$300.00
Menu board, kid w/bowl of soup, Today's Specials, Good & Hearty, lined board below, 23x18", EX.................$55.00
Salt & pepper shakers, plastic, figural kids w/kitchen utensils, 4¼", EX, pr..$65.00
Sign, Captain America & the Campbell Kids, Help Save Energy, 1980, 24x16", EX $18.00
Spoon, yellow porcelain w/Campbell's lettered on handle, kid pictured in bowl, 7", EX $30.00
Squeeze toy, boy, Oak Rubber, ca 1950s, MIB.........$125.00
Squeeze toy, girl, Oak Rubber, 1950s, EX $75.00
Storybook, kids on cover, Rand McNally, 1954, 8x6½", VG...$30.00
Tea set, plastic, kids illustrated, 4 cups, plates, tray, dish & utensils, 1982, MIB...$50.00
Toy garden set, 5 metal & wood tools on display card featuring the Campbell Kids, 1950s, NM...................$50.00
Toy mixer, kids shown on sides, Mirro, 1960s, MIB...$225.00
Toy vacuum cleaner, features the Campbell Kids, aluminum canister type, battery-operated, Pla-Mor/Mirro, 1950s, MIB $85.00

Wall plaques for hanging kitchen utensils, boy & girl figures, sm hook at base, painted plaster, 1940s, 7", pr....$80.00
Warming dish, kids illustrated, signed Grace Drayton, 1930s, G $75.00
Watch, boy, 50th Anniversary, 1982, EX.....................$50.00

Cap'n Crunch

Cap'n Crunch was the creation of Jay Ward, whom you will no doubt remember was also the creator of the Rocky and Bullwinkle show. The Cap'n hails from the '60s, and was one of the first heroes of the pre-sweetened cereal crowd. Jean LaFoote was the villian always scheming to steal the Cap'n's cereal.

Bank, Jean LaFoote figure, molded vinyl, 1975, 7½", M..$90.00
Cars, 1974, 3 different, M...$10.00
Kaleidoscope, paper on cardboard w/lithographed Cap'n Crunch & other characters, Quaker Oats, 1970s, 7", M...........$25.00
Sea Cycle, mail-order premium, M (in shipping bag).....$35.00
Treasure chest, EX $85.00

Charlie Tuna

Poor Charlie, never quite good enough for the Star-Kist folks to can, though he yearns for them to catch him; but since the early 1970s he's done a terrific job working for them as the company logo. A dapper blue-fin tuna in sunglasses and a beret, he's appeared in magazines, done TV commercials, modeled for items as diverse as lamps and banks, but still they deny him his dream. 'Sorry, Charlie.'

Figure, inflatable, Star-Kist, 1980s, EX...........................$20.00
Lamp, painted plaster figure of Charlie, w/metal fixture, Star-Kist, 1970, 12½", no shade, EX+ $75.00
Squeeze toy, vinyl figure, 1973, 7½", M, from $35 to.$40.00
Tie clip & cuff links, gold die-cut figures of Charlie, name engraved on hat, 1970s, EX $45.00
Wristwatch, Star-Kist, 1977, EX $75.00

Colonel Sanders

There's nothing fictional about the Colonel — he was a very real guy, who built an empire on the strength of his fried chicken recipe with 'eleven herbs and spices.' In the 1930s, the Colonel operated a small cafe in Corbin, Kentucky. As the years went by, he developed a chain of restaurants which he sold in the mid-sixties. But even after the sale, the new company continued to use the image of the handsome southern gentlemen as their logo. The Colonel died in 1980.

Bank, plastic figure, no base, white w/black necktie, holding bucket of chicken, 1970s, 8", EX..........................$40.00
Bank, plastic figure w/arm around restaurant building & holding bucket of chicken, white w/red & black, 6", EX..$125.00
Child's tea set, plastic, 1970s, MIB $110.00
Clock, image of the Colonel, square, G $365.00
Finger puppet, white vinyl figure w/black trim, EX...$10.00

Football, rubber, image of the Colonel, 12", M **$15.00**
Jigsaw puzzle, We Fix Sunday Dinner 7 Days a Week, image of bucket of chicken, sealed, 9x7", M **$25.00**
Nodder, painted skin tone w/white suit, black trim, cane & glasses, holds red bucket of chicken, 1960s, 7", EX **$85.00**
Salt & pepper shakers, plastic figural, pr **$40.00**

Bank, white plastic, black bow tie, holding chicken bucket, ca 1970s, 10", EX, $40.00.

Elsie the Cow and Family

She's the most widely recognized cow in the world; everyone knows Elsie, Borden's mascot. Since the mid-1930s, she's been seen on booklets and posters; modeled for mugs, creamers, dolls, etc.; and appeared on TV, in magazines, and at grocery stores to promote their products. Her husband is Elmer (who once sold Elmer's Glue for the same company), and her twins are best known as Beulah and Beauregard, though they've been renamed in recent years (now they're Bea and Beaumister). Elsie was retired in the 1960s, but due to public demand was soon reinstated to her rightful position, and continues today to promote the company's dairy products.

Advisor: Lee Garmon (See Directory, Advertising)

Bank, molded vinyl, Elsie's head w/ring of daisies around her neck, round red base, 1970s, 9", EX **$85.00**
Booklet, Know Your Cheese & How To Sell It, image of Elsie on cover, 60 pgs, 1949, rare, EX **$60.00**
Bottle capper **$15.00**
Butter mold **$20.00**
Cookbook, Bond Wheelright, w/illustrated cover, 1952, EX **$20.00**
Cookie cutter, yellow Beulah & blue Elsie, pr **$50.00**
Cookie jar, ceramic, Elsie-Handle w/Care on barrel base, Elsie as lid, 13", from $400 to **$450.00**
Creamer, ceramic, head form w/yellow daisies along base, horns form spout **$75.00**
Creamer, full figure cow, standing, curled tail as handle, open-mouth spout, unmarked **$135.00**
Creamer & sugar bowl, molded plastic, marked TBC The Borden Co, Made in USA, 3½", from $45 to **$55.00**
Doll, brown plush body w/vinyl head & hooves, VG **$50.00**
Doll, fabric w/rubber head, 1950s **$180.00**

Doll, stuffed plush with vinyl head, 12", EX, $75.00.

Figure, bendable PVC, 3¾", M, from $14 to **$18.00**
Game, Elsie & Her Family, Selchow & Righter Co, 1940s, EXIB **$50.00**
Hand puppet, 1 of the twins, 1950s, EX **$75.00**
Ice cream box, image of Elsie, 1-pt **$10.00**
Matches, Borden's, w/Elsie in color on cover, EX **$10.00**
Milk shake glass, tapered clear glass w/white image of Elsie's head & name, 1950s, 6", EX **$25.00**
Mug, ceramic, head of Elsie w/name lettered below, 1940s, NM **$65.00**
Place mat, image of Elsie w/family, M **$8.00**
Playing cards, image of Elsie, NMIB **$20.00**
Poster, Sale, Elsie Brand Vanilla Ice Cream, ½-Gal...$1.00, image of Elsie, yellow background, EX **$40.00**
Rattle toy, plastic Beauregard figure in diaper sucking on bottle, 1950s, 5", EX **$40.00**
Sugar bowl, ceramic, head form, bow tie at neck, green hat & horns form lid, unmarked **$100.00**
Train, paper, in original package, EX **$165.00**
Tumbler, clear glass w/brown & yellow image of Elsie's head against daisy, 1950s, 5½", from $25 to **$35.00**

Gerber Baby

Since the late 1920s, the Gerber company has used the smiling face of a baby to promote their line of prepared strained baby food. Several dolls and rubber squeeze toys have been made over the years. Even if you're a novice collector, they'll be easy to spot. Some of the earlier dolls hold a can of product in their hand. Look for the Gerber mark on later dolls.

Cup, embossed image of baby & emblem, pink, aqua or yellow, marked Gerber Prod Co, 3¼", EX, each **$5.00**
Doll, in wicker basket w/eyelet pillow, Atlanta Toys, 1979, 12", M (original mailing box) **$50.00**
Doll, rubber w/sculpted hair, Sun Rubber Co, worn letters on bib, 1955, 12" **$45.00**
Doll, stuffed checked body w/vinyl head, 1979, MIB **$80.00**
Doll, vinyl w/molded yellow hair, painted eyes, 1-pc sleeper, Uneeda, 1972, 11", VG **$35.00**

Doll, vinyl w/painted eyes, blue or pink outfit, 1989, MIB..**$15.00**
Doll, w/tub & extra outfit, Atlanta Toys, 1979, 12", MIB .**$50.00**

Green Giant

The Jolly Green Giant has been a well-known ad fixture since the 1950s (some research indicates an earlier date); he was originally devised to represent a strain of European peas much larger than the average-size peas Americans had been accustomed to. At any rate, when Minnesota Valley Canning changed its name to Green Giant, he was their obvious choice. Rather a terse individual himself, by 1974 he was joined by Little Sprout, with the lively white eyes and more talkative personality.

Bank, composition figure of Little Sprout, plays Valley of the Jolly Green Giant, 8½" **$50.00**
Cookie jar, Little Green Sprout, ceramic figure, Taiwan, 1988, from $55.00 to **$75.00**
Doll, doll, stuffed cloth, Green Giant Vegetables, 1966, 16", M (M plastic mailing pouch)................................**$50.00**
Doll, Little Green Sprout, plush w/cloth outfit & felt leaf hair, Green Giant Vegetables, 12", NM **$20.00**
Figure, Little Green Niblet, vinyl, Green Giant Vegetables, 1970s, 6½", EX **$12.00**
Figure, Little Green Sprout, vinyl, Green Giant Vegetables, 1970s, 6½", EX **$12.00**

Figure, Little Sprout, molded vinyl, 1970s, 6½", M, $15.00.

Jump rope, Little Green Sprout, MIB **$30.00**
Salt & pepper shakers, Little Green Sprout, ceramic figures, unmarked, M, pr **$15.00**
Spoon holder, Little Green Sprout, ceramic.................**$18.00**
Squeeze toy, w/movable upper torso, vinyl, Green Giant Vegetables, 1970s, NM+.......................................**$55.00**
Talking alarm clock, Little Green Sprout, M................**$36.00**

Keebler Elf

For more than twenty year, the Keebler Company's choice of spokesman has been Ernie, the Keebler Elf. He's appeared on countless TV commercials and cookie boxes — always dressed in the same red hat, yellow pants and green jacket.

Bank, ceramic, Ernie, seated, holding barrel, recent, from $15 to **$20.00**
Cap, cotton w/elf embroidered on front, NM...............**$7.00**
Cookie jar, Keebler Treehouse w/Ernie, McCoy 350 USA, 1986-87 ....**$60.00**
Cookie jar, Keebler Treehouse w/Ernie, produced by Haeger, from $80 to **$90.00**
Cookie jar, plastic, Ernie's head, F&F Mold, M **$125.00**
Cookie jar & 4 tumblers, plastic jar w/images of the elves making cookies, Louisiana Plastics Inc, M...........**$25.00**
Doll, stuffed plush, 1981, 24", VG+.............................**$45.00**
Figure, vinyl, 1970s, 7", M...**$30.00**
Mug, plastic, head of Ernie, F&F Mold, EX+ **$20.00**
Spoon rest, ceramic, recent, from $12 to.....................**$15.00**

Michelin Man (Bibendum or Mr. Bib)

Perhaps one of the oldest character logos around today, Mr. Bib actually originated in the late 1900s, inspired by a stack of tires that one of the company founders thought suggested the figure of a man. Over the years his image has changed considerably, but the Michelin Tire man continues today to represent his company in many countries around the world.

Ashtray, yellow figure seated on edge of black Bakelite ashtray w/spiral-like rim, 1930s, 4½", EX..................**$65.00**
Clock, white plastic, hexagon, image of running Michelin man on blue ground, 14x16", EX.........................**$135.00**
Display figure, standing, all white w/embossed chest banner, 1980s, 12", EX **$65.00**
Figure, ceramic, standing, white w/black lettering on yellow chest banner, 1990s, 11", NM....................**$30.00**
Figure, vinyl, standing, w/movable head, all white w/embossed banner, 1980s, 14", EX **$60.00**
Jacket patch, image of Mr Bib, blue & white, gold trim, 3x3", EX...**$3.50**
Key ring, green plastic figure, w/metal ring, Michelin lettered on back, 1950s, 1½", EX **$30.00**
Playing cards, image of 2 Michelin men seated at table playing cards, Michelin Tires/Tubes around border, complete, EX **$85.00**
Sign, porcelain, man & tire below product name, yellow w/blue border, V-shaped bottom, 32x24", EX....**$160.00**
Snow dome, Mr Bib in mountains, European issue, MIB ...**$45.00**
Squeeze toy, soft vinyl figure w/baby, French premium, NM **$150.00**
Wind-up toy, MIB **$20.00**

Sign, porcelain, Mr. Bib running beside tire on blue background, 18x15", NM, $275.00.

Mr. Peanut

The personification of the Planters Company, Mr. Peanut has been around since 1916, adding a bit of class and dash to all their advertising efforts. Until the company was sold in 1961, he was a common sight on their product containers and at special promotional events. He was modeled as salt and pepper shakers, mugs, whistles, and paperweights. His image decorated neckties, playing cards, beach towels, and T-shirts. Today he has his own fan club, a collectors' organization for those who especially enjoy this area of advertising memorabilia.

Just about everyone remembers the Planter's Peanut jars, though they're becoming very scarce today. There are more than fifteen different styles and shapes, and some have been reproduced. The earliest, introduced in 1926, was the 'pennant' jar. It was octagonal, and the back panel was embossed with this message: 'Sold Only in Printed Planters Red Pennant Bags.' A second octagonal style carried a paper label instead. Pennant jars marked 'Made in Italy' are reproductions, beware!

Newsletter: *Peanut Papers*
Planter's Peanuts Collectors Club
804 Hickory Grade Rd.
Bridgeville, PA 15017; 412-221-7599

Alarm clock, round metal footed case w/2 bells, image of Mr Peanut w/arms as clock hands on yellow dial, 1960s, EX **$75.00**

Ashtray, metal, Mr Peanut standing in center, marked Planters Peanuts 1906-56, 6x6" dia, EX **$25.00**

Bank, ceramic figural, recent **$30.00**

Blotter, diecut peanut shape w/image of spilled bag of peanuts & Mr Peanut, 1940s, EX **$35.00**

Book, Fun Days With Mr Peanut, image of children on carousel & Mr Peanut, 1960s, EX **$30.00**

Bracelet, Mr Peanut figure on round gold-tone charm w/chain-link bracelet, 1970s, M..........................**$18.00**

Coasters, leather, round w/brown images of Mr Peanut, brown line border, set of 4, 1980s, M...................**$25.00**

Cocktail glasses, plastic, red w/figural Mr Peanut stems, set of 6, 5", EX..**$160.00**

Cookie jar, ceramic, Benjamin & Medwin, recent.......**$65.00**

Cooler, Planters Racing lettered on white & blue molded plastic w/image of Mr Peanut, 1990s, EX **$25.00**

Cooler jug, Planters Corn Chips, blue & white w/image of Mr Peanut, yellow & red lettering, 1970s, M..............**$40.00**

Dart board, wood case w/Planters lettered in yellow above image of Mr Peanut on hinged doors opening to game, 1980s, EX **$20.00**

Display box, cardboard, held 24 5¢ Planters Peanuts bags, white w/red, white & blue logo & Mr Peanut, 1970s, EX..**$15.00**

Drinking glass, clear w/applied yellow & white on blue Planters Cocktail Peanuts label w/Mr Peanut, 1970s, 8-oz, M **$10.00**

Jar, clear glass, slanted front w/painted-on Planters Peanuts lettering, tin screw lid w/Mr Peanut advertising, EX+ **$150.00**

Key ring, plastic #1 shape w/gold lettering & image of Mr Peanut, 1980s, M..**$10.00**

Kitchen tool holder, ceramic figural, recent **$25.00**

Lighter, plastic disposable, image of Mr Peanut above Planters, M..**$20.00**

Napkin holder, ceramic, Mr Peanut embossed on peanut shape, yellow & black, 4x5", M...........................**$25.00**

Night light, cream-colored plastic Mr Peanut figure on round beveled brown base, 10", NM+ **$250.00**

Nut set, lithographed tin, EX, $25.00.

Paperweight, glass, Salted Peanuts, silhouette image of tennis player & detailed Mr Peanut w/text, 1930s, 4x3x1", EX **$75.00**

Playing cards, image of Mr Peanut on white w/blue border, complete, 1980s, EX...**$8.00**

Scoop, plastic, figural Mr Peanut handle, NM **$20.00**

Spoon, silver plate, figural Mr Peanut handle, round spoon bowl, NM...**$20.00**

Spoon rest, ceramic, Mr Peanut shape, yellow & black, 8", from $15 to **$18.00**

Stir sticks, plastic, cream stick w/various colored Mr Peanut figures at top, 8½", 1950s, M, each **$6.00**

Tin, blue, Mixed Nuts, 75th Birthday, image of Mr Peanut on white oval, round w/slip lid, 1991, M....................**$6.00**

Toaster cover, white w/repeated images of Mr Peanut & red, white & blue Planters Peanuts logos, 1970s, M....**$22.00**

Toothpick holder, ceramic, Mr Peanut sitting on peanut behind holder, black, brown & cream, 4", EX ...**$100.00**

Toy truck, red cab w/image of Mr Peanut & Planters Peanuts lettered on white trailer sides, 5½", 1950s-60s, NM..**$90.00**

Tray, blue metal w/yellow lettering & image of Mr Peanut, square w/rounded corners, 1989, EX...................**$20.00**

Pocketknife, flat gold peanut marked Mr. Peanut, Nov. 2nd, 1976, Taylor Cutlery, 2⅞", M, $30.00.

Poppin' Fresh (Pillsbury Doughboy) and Family

Who could be more lovable than the chubby blue-eyed Doughboy with the infectious giggle, introduced by the Pillsbury Company in 1965. Wearing nothing but a neck scarf and a chef's hat, he single-handedly promoted the company's famous biscuits in a tube until about 1971. It was then that the company changed his name to 'Poppin' Fresh' and presented him with a sweet-faced, bonnet-attired mate named Poppie. Many premiums such as dolls, salt and pepper shakers and cookie jars have been produced over the years, but much of what you see at flea markets today is very recent. Most of the new ceramic items will be marked with a date and sometimes 'Made in Taiwan.'

Bank, cardboard biscuit tube w/repeated images of Poppin' Fresh, 1980s, 7", NM..**$15.00**
Bank, Poppin' Fresh, ceramic, 1987, 7½", MIB..........**$25.00**
Cookie jar, glass, Anchor Hocking, 1991 ....**$40.00**
Cookie jar, Poppin' Fresh figure, white w/Cookies & trim in blue, dated 1973, NM **$50.00**
Cookie Jar, Poppin' Fresh figure, 1988, from $35 to...**$45.00**
Display figure, Poppin' Fresh, styrofoam, 1980s, 2-pc, 50", EX, from $200 to...**$225.00**
Doll, Poppin' Fresh, plush, 1982, M...........................**$50.00**
Doll, Poppin' Fresh, white stuffed cloth w/blue-printed features 1970s, 14", VG **$15.00**
Figure, Poppin' Fresh, vinyl w/jointed head, 1972, 7", EX/NM..**$15.00**
Figures, Grandmommer & Grandpopper, soft vinyl, 1970s, EX, pr...**$100.00**
Figures, Poppin' & Poppie Fresh, soft vinyl, movable heads, rectangular bases, 1971-72, 7"/6", NM, pr.............**$35.00**
Finger puppet, Biscuit the Cat, EX.............................**$35.00**
Finger puppet, Flapjack the Dog, EX..........................**$55.00**
Finger puppet, Grandmommer, EX **$50.00**
Finger puppet, Poppie Fresh, vinyl, 3½", EX.............**$15.00**
Flour bin, features the Dough Boy, 1960s, G.............**$15.00**
Gumball machine, Doughboy.....................................**$400.00**
Hand puppet, plastic Poppin' Fresh image w/name, 1972, EX..**$2.50**
Hand puppets, Poppin' or Poppie Fresh pop out of refrigerator can, vinyl & cloth, 1974, EX, each................**$10.00**
Magnet, current, 3", pr...**$6.00**
Mug, ceramic, features Poppin' Fresh, 1979, 5", VG...**$15.00**
Napkin holder, current **$10.00**
Playhouse, vinyl, 1974, w/Bun-Bun, Popper, Poppie & Poppin' Fresh, 14x11x3", EX, from $185 to........**$225.00**
Radio, Poppin' Fresh, plastic, w/headphones, 1985, 6½", EX...**$50.00**
Radio, Poppin' Fresh, plastic, w/headphones, 1985, MIB.**$125.00**
Salt & pepper shakers, Poppin' & Poppie Fresh, white plastic figures w/blue trim, 1974, M **$25.00**
Salt & pepper shakers, Poppin' Fresh, ceramic, 1988, range size, MIB, from $15 to...**$20.00**
Salt & pepper shakers, Poppin' Fresh, white ceramic w/blue details painted over the glaze, 1970s, 3½", pr, EX..**$22.00**
Soap dispenser, current..**$10.00**
Squeeze toy, Poppin' Fresh, vinyl, 1970s, 6½", VG **$12.00**
Standup, Poppin' Fresh, promotional, 1985, from $20 to..**$30.00**
Telephone, Poppin' Fresh, arms extended to hold receiver, 1980s, 14", M...**$90.00**
Utensil holder, Poppin' Fresh, ceramic, 1983, 8".........**$18.00**

Red Goose

At the turn of the century, retail companies became very advertising conscious, and Herman Giesecke, a shoe company owner, was no exception. The pronunciation of his name suggested the choice of a 'goose,' so Herman promptly added a goose logo to his boxes and cartons. An employee unintentionally added the finishing touch when he idly colored in the goose outline with red crayon, and the idea for 'Red Goose Shoes' was conceived.

Bank, plastic, 1960s, 5", M, $15.00. (Photo courtesy of Lee Garmon.)

Bank, red-painted cast-iron figure, 4", EX **$85.00**
Display figure, plaster of Paris, red goose on green base, 11", NM **$100.00**
Floor mirror, 21x14½", NM..**$150.00**
Horn, cardboard w/wooden mouthpiece, Red Goose Shoes, Half the Fun of Having Feet, 6", EX........................**$8.50**
Ring, glow-in-the-dark, w/secret compartment, NM..**$150.00**
School tablet, child & goose on cover, 8x10"..............**$35.00**
String holder, CI goose w/removable side plate, red w/yellow lettering green base, 14½" long, VG............**$475.00**
Thermometer, porcelain, For Boys & Girls, 27x7", EX...**$260.00**
Thermometer, wood, logo above bulb, beveled edge, arched top, 1930s, 21x8", EX...**$200.00**
Top, red- & gold-painted wood w/metal tip, 1930s, 2½x1¾", NM **$55.00**
Whistle, tin, round, 1¼", NM **$20.00**

Reddy Kilowatt

Reddy was developed during the late 1920s and became very popular during the '50s. His job was to promote electric power companies all over the United States, which he did with aplomb! Reddy memorabilia is highly collectible today, with the plastic figures sometimes selling for $200.00 or more. Because of high collector demand, new merchandise is flooding the market. Watch for items such as a round mirror, a small hand-held game with movable squares, a ring-toss game, etc., marked 'Made in China.'

Ashtray, glass, square, EX $10.00
Cigarette lighter, 2 styles, each, from $40 to $50.00
Comic book, Wizard of Light, Story of Thomas Edison, illustrations of Reddy, 1965...................................$25.00
Cookbook...$10.00
Cookie cutter, red plastic diecut, Your Favorite Cookie Cutter lettered on box, 3x3", EX $50.00
Cooking chart, timetables & measurements guide for electric ranges, 3 lg images of Reddy, Ohio Edison Co, 1950s, VG $25.00
Egg separator, yellow plastic, M $8.00

Figure, celluloid, 1950s, 6", M, $200.00. (Photo courtesy of Lee Garmon.)

Figure, plastic Reddy on base, sm head, EX $200.00
Folder, clear plastic, Reddy's image in corner, NM.....$20.00
Hot pad, M (sealed)...$20.00
Jar opener, Magic Gripper, MOC (sealed), from $15 to..$20.00
Litter bag, for car, M $15.00
Measuring spoon, w/image of Reddy, PA Electric $10.00
Night light, plastic plug-in, white w/red trim, EX.......$20.00
Nodder, papier-mache cowboy figure w/name on square base, 1960s, 6½", M.......................................$260.00
Patch, Safety, assorted, each, from $8 to $10.00
Pencil, metal w/pocket clip $17.00
Pin-back button, from $8 to......................................$10.00
Playing cards, double deck, M $40.00
Postcard, 1¢, Reddy in cowboy hat, M $8.00
Recipe book, Reddy's Christmas Recipes, 16 pages, 1950s, NM+ $15.00
Recipe book, The Art of Preparing Salads, 1940s, NM+ ..$15.00
Suction-cup doll, vinyl head w/plush body, Steven Smith, 1980s, EX...$35.00
Tape measure, M $45.00
Tie tac, pewter face, MOC $15.00

Smokey Bear

The year 1994 was the 50th anniversary of Smokey Bear, the spokesbear for the State Foresters, Ad Council, and US Forest Service. After ruling out other mascots (including Bambi), by 1944 it had been decided that a bear was best suited for the job, and Smokey was born. When a little cub was rescued from a fire in a New Mexico national forest in 1950, Smokey's role intensified. Over the years his appearance has evolved from one a little more menacing to the lovable bear we know today.

Advisor: Glen Brady (See Directory, Advertising, Smokey Bear)

Alarm clock, Prevent Forest Fires, Smokey w/shovel on round dial, 2 bells, German, 1960s, 7", EX.........$100.00
Ashtray, ceramic, image of Smokey dousing a fire, Norcrest, 1950s-60s, 6x4x4", from $95 to.....................$125.00
Ashtray, metal bucket for car.....................................$25.00
Bank, ceramic seated bear w/hand to hat, 1 arm through pail, Japan, from $110 to $135.00
Bank, hard plastic figure, 1970s, 8", EX.....................$50.00
Bank, w/2 cubs, white w/gold sponging $65.00
Book, Smokey Finds a Friend, w/Mr Peanut, Whitman, 1973, NM...$30.00
Button, tin pin-back, Join Smokey's Campaign, Prevent Forest Fires, head image on 2-color ground, 1960s, 1½" dia, M $10.00
Button, tin pin-back, Jr Fire Fighter, Please Prevent Forest Fires above head, yellow, brown & red, 1950s, 1½", M $10.00
Coloring book, Whitman, 1960s, EX+ $18.00
Comic book, Smokey March of Comics, restaurant giveaway, 1960s, EX......................................$25.00

Doll, plush with vinyl face, inset eyes, Ideal, MIB, $250.00.

Doll, stuffed cotton, Knickerbocker, 1972, 6", EX+ (original box) $20.00
Doll, Three Bears Inc, 1985, w/original hang tag, 13", M..$20.00
Figure, bendable, Lakeside, 1967, MIP, from $50 to ...$60.00
Mug, ceramic w/figural handle, I Like Milk, 1960s, from $50 to...$60.00
Nodder, composition figure w/shovel on square base lettered Prevent Forest Fires, 1960s, 6", EX $80.00
Pathfinder set, w/compass, whistle, walkie-talkies & cord, Larami, 1978, MIP, from $80 to......................$90.00
Plate, Melmac, Smokey & forest friends, 7".................$25.00
Salt & pepper shakers, ceramic figures w/1 holding bucket & the other holding a shovel, 1960s, 4", M, pr........$30.00
Salt & pepper shakers, 1 w/shovel, 2nd w/pail, pr....$75.00
Songbook, Songs From the Ballad of Smokey Bear, 1966, EX..$25.00

Snap!, Crackle! and Pop!

Rice Krispies, the talking cereal, was first marketed by Kelloggs in 1928. Capitalizing on the sounds the cereal made in milk, the company chose elves named 'Snap!' 'Crackle!' and 'Pop!' as their logos a few years later. The first of the Rice Krispie dolls were introduced in 1948. These were 12" tall, printed on fabric for the consumer to sew and stuff. The same dolls in a 16" size were offered in 1954. Premiums and memorabilia of many types followed over the years, all are very collectible.

Figures, Crackle!, 1984, 5", MIB, $55.00; Snap! and Pop!, loose, M, $25.00 each.

Blotter, figures beside cereal bowl, Vernon Grant art, 1930s, 3½x5¼", EX **$12.00**
Blotter, Kellogg's Rice Krispies, 1940s, EX+ **$40.00**
Coloring book, 50 Years With Snap! Crackle! & Pop!, 1978, NM+ **$30.00**
Display box, 3 figures on front, Kellogg's Rice Krispies, Rockwell illustration on back, 1960, 20x14", EX **$95.00**
Doll, Snap! (only), plastic w/jointed limbs, red hair, 1984, 4½", MIP **$15.00**
Figures, vinyl, Kellogg's Rice Krispies, 1970s, set of 3, 8", EX, from $110.00 to **$125.00**
Friction toy, Snap! (only), Talbot Toys, 1984, M (VG card) .**$18.00**
Push-button puppets, plastic, Kellogg's Rice Krispies, 1984, 4", EX, each **$20.00**
Salt & pepper shakers, pottery, Snap! and Pop! only, 1950s, 2½", pr, from $75 to **$100.00**

Tony the Tiger

Kellogg's introduced Tony the Tiger in 1953, and since then he's appeared on every box of their Frosted Flakes. In his deep rich voice, he's convinced us all that they are indeed 'Gr-r-r-eat'!

Bank, seated figure, hard plastic w/rubber stopper, Kellogg's Frosted Flakes, 1970s, 8½", NM **$50.00**
Bowl, plastic, round w/paws as base, Kellogg's Frosted Flakes, 1981, NM **$25.00**
Doll, stuffed cloth, 1960s, 13", EX **$25.00**
Figure, vinyl w/arms up & wearing red neckerchief, Kellogg's Frosted Flakes, 1974, 7½", NM **$40.00**
Mug, plastic, F & F, 1960s, 8-oz, EX+ **$35.00**

Miscellaneous

Actigall Gall Bladder, squeeze toy, green vinyl gall bladder figure w/facial features, arms & feet, Summit, 1989, 4", M **$40.00**
Baby Ruth, doll, beanbag body w/vinyl head & hands, Hasbro, 1970s, EX..**$35.00**
Betty Crocker, doll, cloth body w/brown suede hair, yarn ponytails, glancing eyes, checked dress, Kenner, 1970s, 13", G **$30.00**
Bonnie Breck, doll, w/accessories & booklet, Breck/Hasbro, 1972, MIB **$35.00**
Boo Berry, figure, vinyl, General Mills, 1975, 7½", M...**$75.00**
Camel Joe, can cooler, molded vinyl head of Camel Joe wearing sunglasses & smoking a cigarette, 1991, 4", M..**$15.00**
Camel Joe, tumbler, plastic, colorful images of Joe at Joe's Place, 1994, 4½", M **$6.00**
Captain Marine, bank, vinyl, Marine Bank, 1980s, M....**$60.00**
Cerasota Boy, doll, printed cloth, name on shirt, Ceresota Flour, 17", EX **$100.00**
Charlie Chocks, doll, printed cloth, Chocks Vitamins, 1970-'71, 20", EX **$25.00**
Chicken of the Sea Mermaid, doll, satin cloth w/painted features, yarn hair, 13", MIP **$12.00**
Chiquita Banana, doll, printed material, uncut, 1950s, 11x17", NM **$45.00**
DollyGram, doll, Congratulations, printed velvet w/raffia hair, Western Union, 6", EX....................................**$6.00**
Dust Beastie, doll, Hoover Vacuum Cleaners, rare, EX...**$60.00**
Dydee Bear, doll, plush in cloth diaper, Curity, EX....**$15.00**
Energizer Bunny, doll, plush, in sunglasses, Eveready Energizer Batteries, 24", M **$50.00**
Energizer Bunny, flashlight, squeezable vinyl, Eveready Energizer Batteries, 1991, MIP (sealed)................**$15.00**

Energizer Bunny, figure, lights up, battery-operated, 3¾", M, $10.00.

Eskimo Pie, doll, stuffed cloth, brown parka w/red & white diamond design, earlier version without name, 1964, 16", MIP..**$25.00**

Esso, see Happy the Esso Oil Drop

Facit Man, figure, vinyl w/jointed arms, red suit w/black trim, black dunce cap w/white name, 1960s, 4", NM....**$30.00**

Fisk Tire Boy, bank, plaster, all white yawning figure standing w/tire & holding candle, Uniroyal, 1970s, 8½", NM.**$130.00**

Franken Berry, figure, vinyl, General Mills, NM..........**$95.00**

Gilbert Giddyup, doll, stuffed printed cloth, orange cowboy outfit w/star badge & holding gun, Hardee's, 1971, EX.**$15.00**

Harry Hood, figure, vinyl, Hood Dairies, NM **$95.00**

Heinz Ketchup Ant, figure, bendable PVC, 4½", EX ..**$10.00**

Helping Hand, glove-like plush figure w/3 fingers & thumb, facial features on palm, Hamburger Helper, 14", M..**$10.00**

Hersheykin, figure, holding candy bar & saw, PVC, 1980s, NM..**$5.00**

Hush Puppies Hound, bank, molded vinyl basset hound seated on round lettered base, 1970s, 8", EX **$30.00**

Jeans Man, doll, Jordache/Mego, 12", MIB **$30.00**

Kool-Aid Kid, doll, 1989, 14", VG **$25.00**

Kraft Cheesasarus Rex, bank, mail-in premium, Kraft Macaroni & Cheese, M...**$35.00**

Lazy Lion, doll, orange plush w/gold mane & white nose, Pillsbury Bundt Cake, 1977, 23", EX **$10.00**

Libby's Girl, stuffed cloth with yarn hair, pull-string talker, Mattel, 1974, talker not working otherwise EX, $35.00. (Photo courtesy of June Moon.)

Little Miss Sunbeam, doll, stuffed printed cloth, Sunbeam Bread, 17", NM...**$20.00**

Little-T, puppet, Tastee Freeze, 1960s-70s, NM **$15.00**

Lucky Lymon, doll, vinyl, talker, Sprite, 1990s, 7½", M ..**$20.00**

Marky Maypo, bank, seated figure, molded vinyl, Maypo Oat Cereal, 1960s, 9", NM **$60.00**

Miss Sunbeam, doll, vinyl w/arms & legs, rooted hair, cotton dress w/white apron, Sunbeam Bread/Eegee, 1959, 17", NM **$40.00**

Miss Tastee Freeze, doll, plastic w/cloth dress & banner, G **$20.00**

Mother Nature, doll, stuffed cloth w/dress, yarn hair, Chiffon Margarine, MIB..**$30.00**

Mr Clean, figure, painted vinyl, Proctor & Gamble, 1961, 8", VG/EX..**$85.00**

Mr Kool-Aid as Awesome Dude, doll, stuffed, w/sunglasses & surfing shorts, MIP...**$10.00**

Nipper, figure, dog seated on round base marked RCA Victor, chalkware, white w/black trim, 1930s, 3", EX.....**$40.00**

Orange Bird, bank, vinyl, Florida Oranges, 1974, MIP .**$35.00**

Oreo Cookie Man, figure, bendable PVC, Nabisco, EX, from $12 to...**$15.00**

Pizza-Pizza Man, doll, plush, Little Ceaser's Pizza, 1990, EX..**$8.00**

Rollupo the Wizard, figure, bendable, Fruit Rollups, 6", EX..**$12.00**

Scrubbing Bubble, bank, ceramic, Dow Bathroom Cleaner, M..**$20.00**

Scrubbing Bubble, squeeze toy, vinyl, Dow Bathroom Cleaner, 1989, 3½" dia, VG **$10.00**

Sleepy Bear, doll, plush, name lettered on hat, no clothing, Travelodge, 1967, 12", EX....................................**$10.00**

Sleepy Bear, squeeze toy, vinyl figure in yellow hat & nightshirt w/black stitching, Travelodge, 1970s, 5½", EX.........**$25.00**

Smilin' Sprite, doll, vinyl, talker, NM.........................**$45.00**

Snuggles the Bear, doll, plush w/glassine eyes, ear button & wrist tag, Snuggle Fabric Softener/Lever Bros, 1986, 16", M..**$35.00**

Swiss Miss, doll, stuffed cloth w/dress & apron, yarn hair, Swiss Miss Chocolate, 1978, 16", EX **$20.00**

Tagamet Tommy, skin-tone stomach figure w/facial features on round base reading Tagamet Brand Of Cimetidine, 1988, 5", M **$20.00**

Taped Crusader, bank, vinyl figure, Curad Bandages, 1975, 7", NM..**$55.00**

Toucan Sam, figure, vinyl, Kellogg's Fruit Loops, 1984, 5", MIB **$45.00**

Tropic-Ana, doll, printed cloth w/grass skirt, name lettered on bowl of oranges on head, Tropicana Orange Juice, 17", EX...**$6.00**

Wally Welch, hand puppet, plastic, Welch's Grape Juice, 9", EX..**$3.00**

Wizard of O's, figure, vinyl, Franco American/Campbell's Soups, 7½", M..**$30.00**

Woodsy Owl, bank, ceramic figure, Give a Hoot...Don't Pollute, US Forest Service, 1970s, 8½", NM+, from $60 to **$75.00**

Yipe Zebra, figure, bendable, Fruit Stripe Gum, scarce, M **$30.00**

24-Hour Bug, bank, green vinyl figure w/spots on chest, pink eyes, Pepto Bismol/Proctor & Gamble, 1970s, 7", NM **$40.00**

Akro Agate

Everybody remembers the 'Aggie' marbles from their childhood; this is the company that made them. They operated in West Virginia from 1914 until 1951, and in addition to their famous marbles they made children's dishes as well as many types of novelties — flowerpots, powder jars with scotty dogs on top, candlesticks, and ashtrays, for instance — in many colors and patterns. Though some of their glassware was made in solid colors, their most popular products were made of the same swirled colors as their marbles. Nearly everything they produced is marked with their logo: a crow flying through the letter 'A' holding an Aggie in its beak and one in each claw. Some children's dishes may be marked 'JP,' and the novelty items may instead carry one of these trademarks: 'JV Co, Inc,' 'Braun & Corwin,' 'NYC Vogue Merc Co USA,' 'Hamilton Match Co,' and 'Mexicali Pickwick Cosmetic Corp.'

In the children's dinnerware listings below, you'll notice that color is an important worth-assessing factor. As a general rule, an item in green or white opaque is worth only about one-third as much when compared to the same item in any other opaque color. Marbleized pieces are about three times higher than solid opaques, and of the marbleized colors, blue is the most valuable. It's followed closely by red, with green about 25% under red. Lemonade and oxblood is a good color combination, and it's generally three times higher item for item than the transparent colors of green or topaz.

For further study we recommend *The Collector's Encyclopedia of Akro Agate Glassware* by Gene Florence and *The Collector's Encyclopedia of Children's Dishes* by Margaret and Kenn Whitmyer.

Newsletter: *The Akro Agate Gem*
Akro Agate Art Association
Joseph Bourque
P.O. Box 758
Salem, NH 03079

Octagonal (large), plate, green, $6.00; Cup, closed handle, pumpkin (rare color), $22.00; Saucer, yellow, $4.00.

Chiquita, boxed set, transparent cobalt, 16-pc **$140.00**
Chiquita, creamer, transparent cobalt, 1½" **$16.00**
Chiquita, plate, green opaque, 3¾" **$3.00**
Chiquita, saucer, other opaque colors, 3⅛" **$5.00**
Chiquita, sugar bowl, baked-on colors, 1½" **$8.00**
Chiquita, tablecloth w/4 napkins, set **$35.00**
Concentric Rib, boxed set, opaque green & white, 10-pc... **$53.00**
Concentric Rib, boxed set, other opaque colors, 8-pc.. **$54.00**
Concentric Rib, saucer, opaque green & white, 2¾" **$2.00**
Concentric Rib, saucer, other opaque colors, 2¾" **$3.00**
Concentric Rib, sugar bowl, other opaque colors, 3⅜" . **$15.00**
Concentric Rib, teapot, w/lid, opaque green & white, 3⅜".. **$12.00**

Concentric Ring, bowl, cereal; transparent cobalt, lg, 3⅜"..**$35.00**
Concentric Ring, boxed set, solid opaque colors, lg, 21-pc **$350.00**
Concentric Ring, creamer, blue marbleized, lg, 1⅜" ...**$50.00**
Concentric Ring, creamer, transparent cobalt, sm, 1¼"..**$35.00**
Concentric Ring, cup, blue marbleized, sm, 1¼" **$35.00**
Concentric Ring, cup, solid opaque colors, lg, 1⅜"....**$30.00**
Concentric Ring, plate, solid opaque colors, sm, 3¼" ..**$6.00**
Concentric Ring, saucer, transparent cobalt, sm, 2¾" ..**$10.00**
Concentric Ring, sugar bowl, transparent cobalt, w/lid, lg, 1⅞" **$55.00**
Concentric Ring, teapot, transparent cobalt, w/lid, lg, 3¾"....**$70.00**
Concentric Ring, teapot, transparent cobalt, w/lid, sm, 3⅜"..**$50.00**
Interior Panel, bowl, cereal; transparent green, lg, 3⅜"..**$15.00**
Interior Panel, boxed set, green & white marbleized, 21-pc, lg **$345.00**
Interior Panel, boxed set, green & white marbleized, 8-pc, sm **$90.00**
Interior Panel, creamer, azure blue or yellow, sm, 1¼"..**$32.00**
Interior Panel, creamer, azure blue or yellow opaque, lg, 1⅜" **$35.00**
Interior Panel, creamer, blue & white marbleized, lg, 1⅜" **$37.00**
Interior Panel, creamer, blue & white marbleized, sm, 1¼" ..**$30.00**
Interior Panel, creamer, green & white marbleized, lg, 1⅜" **$25.00**
Interior Panel, cup, green lustre, sm, 1¼" **$10.00**
Interior Panel, cup, lemonade & oxblood, lg, 1⅜" **$25.00**
Interior Panel, plate, green & white marbleized, sm, 3¾" ..**$10.00**
Interior Panel, plate, pink lustre, sm, 3¾" **$6.00**
Interior Panel, plate, red & white marbleized, lg, 4¼" . **$18.00**
Interior Panel, saucer, blue & white marbleized, sm, 2⅜" ..**$10.00**
Interior Panel, saucer, pink or green lustre, lg, 3⅛" **$4.00**
Interior Panel, saucer, transparent green, lg, 3⅛" **$4.00**
Interior Panel, sugar bowl, pink or green lustre, w/lid, lg, 1⅞" **$32.00**
Interior Panel, sugar bowl, red & white marbleized, w/lid, lg, 1⅞" **$60.00**
Interior Panel, teapot, azure blue or yellow opaque, w/lid, lg, 3¾" **$65.00**
Interior Panel, teapot, blue & white marbleized, w/lid, lg, 3¾" **$75.00**
Interior Panel, teapot, pink lustre, w/lid, sm, 3⅜" **$32.00**
Interior Panel, teapot, red & white marbleized, w/lid, sm, 3⅜" **$50.00**
Interior Panel, teapot, transparent topaz, w/lid, lg, 3¾" ..**$35.00**
JP, boxed set, transparent red or brown, 17-pc A **$400.00**
JP, creamer, transparent red or brown, 1½" **$55.00**
JP, plate, lt blue or crystal, 4¼" **$10.00**
JP, saucer, baked-on colors, 3¼" **$1.50**
JP, sugar bowl, transparent green, w/lid, 1½" **$50.00**
Miss America, creamer, orange & white, forest green or white w/decal, 1¼" **$65.00**
Miss America, cup, white, 1⅝" **$40.00**
Miss America, plate, orange & white, forest green or white w/decal, 4½" **$45.00**
Miss America, saucer, white, 3⅝" **$15.00**
Miss America, sugar bowl, orange & white, forest green or white w/decal, w/lid, 2" **$85.00**
Miss America, teapot, white, w/lid, 3¼" **$85.00**

Octagonal, bowl, cereal; green or white, lg, 3⅜" **$10.00**
Octagonal, creamer, lemonade & oxblood, closed handle, lg, 1½" **$30.00**
Octagonal, cup, dk green, blue or white, sm, 1¼".....**$10.00**
Octagonal, saucer, pink, yellow & other opaques, lg, 3⅜".**$4.00**
Octagonal, saucer, pumpkin, yellow or lime green, sm, 2¾" **$3.50**
Octagonal, tumbler, dk green, blue or white, sm, 2"..**$12.00**
Raised Daisy, cup, green, 1¾" **$18.00**
Raised Daisy, saucer, yellow, 2½" **$10.00**
Raised Daisy, sugar bowl, yellow, 1¼" **$50.00**
Raised Daisy, tumbler, yellow, 2" **$27.00**
Stacked Disc, creamer, opaque green or white, 1¼"..**$10.00**
Stacked Disc, plate, any opaque colors other than green or white, 3¼" **$5.00**
Stacked Disc, tumbler, opaque green or white, 2"........**$8.50**
Stacked Disc & Interior Panel, bowl, cereal; transparent green, lg, 3⅜"...**$22.00**
Stacked Disc & Interior Panel, creamer, blue marbleized, lg, 1¼"...**$45.00**
Stacked Disc & Interior Panel, creamer, transparent cobalt, lg, 1⅜"...**$32.00**
Stacked Disc & Interior Panel, cup, transparent cobalt, sm, 1¼"...**$22.00**
Stacked Disc & Interior Panel, plate, solid opaque colors, lg, 4¾"...**$12.00**
Stacked Disc & Interior Panel, teapot, transparent cobalt, w/lid, lg, 3¾" **$75.00**
Stacked Disc & Interior Panel, teapot, transparent green, w/lid, sm, 3⅜"..**$35.00**
Stippled Band, creamer, transparent green, lg, 1½"....**$25.00**
Stippled Band, creamer, transparent green, sm, 1¼"..**$30.00**
Stippled Band, cup, transparent azure, lg, 1½"...........**$25.00**
Stippled Band, pitcher, transparent amber, sm, 2⅞"...**$18.00**
Stippled Band, plate, transparent amber, lg, 4¼"..........**$8.50**
Stippled Band, saucer, transparent green or amber, sm, 2⅜...**$2.50**
Stippled Band, sugar bowl, transparent amber, w/lid, lg, 1⅞" **$30.00**
Stippled Band, teapot, transparent green, w/lid, sm, 3⅜"..**$22.00**

Aluminum

The aluminum items which have become today's collectibles range from early britecut giftware and old kitchen wares to furniture and club aluminum cooking pans. But the most collectible, right now, at least, is the giftware of the 1930s through the '50s.

There were probably several hundred makers of aluminum accessories and giftware with each developing their preferred method of manufacturing. Some pieces were cast, other products were hammered with patterns created by either an intaglio method or repousse. Machine embossing was utilized by some makers, many used faux hammering, and lightweight items were often decorated with pressed designs. During one period, spun aluminum and colored aluminum became very popular.

As early as the 1940s, collectors began to seek out aluminum, sometimes to add to the few pieces received as wedding gifts. By the late 1970s and early '80s, aluminum giftware was

found in abundance at almost any flea market, and prices of $1.00 or less were normal. As more shoppers became enthralled with the appearance of this lustrous metal and its patterns, prices began to rise and have not yet peaked for the products of some companies. A few highly prized pieces have brought prices of four or five hundred dollars and occasionally even more.

One of the first to manufacture this type of ware was Wendell August Forge, when during the late 1920s they expanded their line of decorative wrought iron and began to use aluminum, at first making small items as gifts for their customers. Very soon they were involved in a growing industry estimated at one point to be comprised of several hundred companies, among them Arthur Armour, the Continental Silver Company, Everlast, Buenilum, Rodney Kent, and Palmer-Smith. Few of the many original companies survived the WWII scarcity of aluminum.

Prices differ greatly from one region to another, sometimes without regard to quality or condition, so be sure to examine each item carefully before you buy. If you're in doubt as to value, we recommend the newsletter *The Aluminist* published by Dannie Woodard, author of *Hammered Aluminum, Hand Wrought Collectibles*. Another good book on the subject is titled *Collectible Aluminum, An Identification and Value Guide*, by Everett Grist (Collector Books).

Advisor: Dannie Woodard (See Directory, Aluminum)

Newsletter: *The Aluminist*
Dannie Woodard
P.O. Box 1347
Weatherford, TX 76086; 817-594-4680

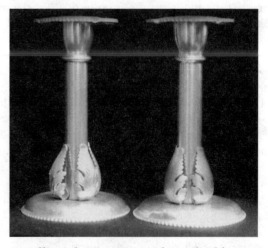

Candlesticks, Continental, applied leaves on stem, 4½", $65.00 for the pair. (Photo courtesy of Dannie Woodard.)

Ashtray, Bruce Fox, square w/horse head, 5½" **$38.00**
Ashtray, unmarked, round dish w/3 extended rests, embossed leaping marlin in center, 4½" dia **$30.00**
Ashtray, Wendell August Forge, square w/4 corner rests, embossed sailboat in center, 4½" **$40.00**
Basket, Continental, square w/rolled-up serrated edges, crimped handle w/applied leaves, chrysanthemum pattern, 8x8" **$20.00**

Basket, Cromwell, round bowl w/fruit & flower design, twisted double handle w/knot in center, 10" dia.........**$15.00**

Basket, Farber & Shlevin, polished w/stamped rose design, double handle w/twisted center, fluted glass insert, 10" **$35.00**

Basket, Farber & Shlevin, polished w/stamped rose pattern, twisted handle, pottery insert, 7"............................**$18.00**

Basket, Hand Forged #29, hammered w/sailing ship, twisted handle, 10" **$12.00**

Basket, Japan, round w/hammered flat rim, serrated edge crimped up on 2 sides, floral center, double loop handle, 10" **$7.00**

Bookends, Everlast, hammered, with applied horseshoe, $85.00 for the pair. (Photo courtesy of Dannie Woodard.)

Bookends, Wendell August Forge, canted corners, hammered w/daisy pattern, pr **$125.00**

Bowl, Buenilum, round, hammered w/bromeliad-type flowers, 9¼" dia **$15.00**

Bowl, Everlast, hammered w/fruit pattern, 12½" dia..**$18.00**

Bowl, Everlast, round w/scalloped rim, hammered w/oak leaves & acorns, 13" dia.......................................**$22.00**

Bowl, Wendell August Forge, round w/flared fluted rim, allover dogwood pattern, 7" dia............................**$30.00**

Bracelet, unmarked, C-type band w/leaf design.........**$15.00**

Bread tray, Continental, hammered w/chrysanthemum design, applied leaves **$20.00**

Bread tray, Everlast, hammered w/anchor design **$18.00**

Brooch, Wendell August Forge, hammered w/pine cone design, 1½x2"..**$45.00**

Butter dish, Buenilum, polished frame w/round glass insert, loop finial on domed lid, undertray w/beaded rim, 6½" **$27.00**

Butter dish, Forman Family, embossed chrysanthemums on lid w/floret finial, pressed glass insert **$15.00**

Candlestick, Buenilum, 3 candles, thick bar w/center loop, hammered, 6x14" **$125.00**

Candlestick, Continental, 1 candle, applied leaves on stem, 4½"..**$30.00**

Candlestick, Everlast, 1 candle, hammered w/scalloped base, 3½"...**$25.00**

Candlestick, Wendell August Forge, 2 candles, hammered w/scrolled band on rectangular base.................**$150.00**

Candy dish, Buenilum, hammered w/flower sprigs & 'spoon-handle' curl on lid, footed etched-glass insert, 6"...**$45.00**

Candy dish, Buenilum, 2 leaf dishes w/upturned & serrated rims connected by single-looped handle, 6x5" leaves........**$25.00**

Candy dish, Cromwell, double bowls w/finely fluted rims, fruit & flower design in bottoms, center loop handle, 13"...**$25.00**

Candy dish, World Hand Forged, simple leaf form w/3-masted sailing ship in center, tall handle w/scrolled end, 8" **$60.00**

Casserole, Arthur Armour, hammered w/2 grooved handles, butterfly, dogwood finial, w/baking dish, 9" dia .**$125.00**

Casserole, Everlast, hammered w/2 square handles, floral band design on lid, daffodil-type floral finial.......**$15.00**

Casserole, Rodney Kent, hammered w/2 curved handles, overlapping serrated lid w/closed tulip finial & ribbons **$20.00**

Chafing dish, Spain, hammered w/black handle & knob..**$12.00**

Chip & dip set, Buenilum, plain bowl w/beaded lip, handle curves up to form round stand for dip bowl, 9" dia..**$15.00**

Cigarette box, Wendell August Forge, hammered w/pine cone design...**$85.00**

Cigarette box, World, hammered w/applied leaves & rosette on lid...**$35.00**

Coaster, unmarked, round w/plain rim, embossed goose in flight..**$3.00**

Coaster, unmarked, round w/turned-up fluted rim, assorted fruit embossed in center...............................**$2.00**

Coaster, unmarked, round w/turned-up plain rim, embossed Scotty dog in center....................................**$8.00**

Coaster set, Continental, round w/serrated rims, allover chrysanthemum pattern, set of 12 in basket holder, 4" dia **$30.00**

Coaster set, Everlast, round w/allover bamboo pattern, 4-footed trivet-type holder, 3½" dia.....................**$25.00**

Cocktail shaker, Buenilum, double-looped finial, 9½".**$85.00**

Compote, unmarked, deep hammered bowl w/flared rolled rim, low pedestal foot, 5x6" dia **$10.00**

Condiment set, Continental, hammered w/center twisted handle, cruets & covered jars w/apple design.....**$55.00**

Condiment set, Rodney Kent, hammered caddy w/center handle in ribbon & flower design, 2 covered jars w/spoons..**$35.00**

Creamer & sugar bowl, World Hand Forged, simple shapes w/hammered pattern, angled elbow handles, flower & leaf finial...**$15.00**

Creamer & sugar bowl (open), unmarked, simple bowl shape w/diagonal line pattern on band around top, scrolled handles **$18.00**

Creamer & sugar bowl w/tray, Everlast, plain creamer & & sugar bowl on hammered tray w/grape pattern ..**$28.00**

Crumber & tray, Everlast, scalloped rims w/leaf design ..**$22.00**

Dresser set, Rodney Kent #403, hammered caddy w/ribbon & flower design on handles, 2 covered glass jars w/tulip finials **$45.00**

Gravy boat, Buenilum, plain w/serrated lip & plate rim, double-strap loop handle **$25.00**

Ice bucket, Continental #504, hammered open style w/chrysanthemum pattern & handles w/leaves ...**$65.00**

Ice bucket, NS Co, plain polished bucket w/upper & lower rib, curled handles, wood knob on plain lid, 8" dia **$20.00**

Ice bucket, unmarked, beehive shape w/hammered pattern, mushroom finial, swing handle, 8x8" dia **$15.00**

Lamp, Wendell August Forge, hammered w/zinnia pattern, silk shade **$650.00**

Lazy Susan, Cromwell, hammered w/fluted rim, fruit-&-flower pattern in well, serrated base, 18" dia.......**$10.00**

Lazy Susan, unmarked, round w/deep well & upturned rim, ivy pattern, loop handles w/applied leaf, plain base, 13" dia **$18.00**

Magazine rack, Wendell August Forge, 2 panels w/side braces & cut-out handles, embossed ducks & cattails, 9x14"............................**$200.00**

Matchbox cover, Everlast, hammered kitchen-size w/bamboo design **$35.00**

Mint dish, Wendell August Forge, round w/allover dogwood pattern, 3-compartment insert, 12" dia **$45.00**

Money clip, DeMarsh Forge, embossed lighthouse **$12.00**

Napkin holder, Everlast, hammered trefoil shape w/rose design **$20.00**

Nut bowl, Cromwell, hammered pedestal bowl w/fruits-&-flowers design, loop handles, w/picks, 10" dia....**$27.00**

Pie or cake server, Buenilum (unmarked), hammered w/twisted double-loop handle.............................**$45.00**

Pitcher, Cellini Craft, hammered & grooved bulbous form w/berry-&-leaf design on handle.........................**$95.00**

Pitcher, Continental, chrysanthemum pattern, applied ice lip, question-mark handle w/applied leaf at bottom, 9" dia **$35.00**

Pitcher, Everlast, tapered hammered pattern w/tall ear-shaped handle, applied ice lip, 8x6" dia **$17.00**

Pitcher, Rodney Kent, hammered w/tulip pattern, ribbon-styled handle, tulip on ice lip **$45.00**

Pitcher, unmarked, slight hammered pattern on sleek bulbous shape w/applied bar handle w/2 beads, plain lip, 7x6" dia......................**$40.00**

Platter, Continental #546, chrysanthemums, handled, slotted insert for dripping juices, 15½x11"......................**$18.00**

Punch bowl, Keystone, hammered w/blue crock liner, ring handles, w/ladle & tray.........................**$150.00**

Salad fork & spoon, Wendell August Forge (unmarked), hammered w/twisted handles......................**$55.00**

Silent butler, Kraftware, hammered pattern w/wheat design, solid hammered handle crimped down at end, 6½" dia **$20.00**

Silent butler, unmarked, hammered w/sunflower on lid, solid hammered handle w/pointed end, 6" dia.............**$20.00**

Teapot, Sona Ware, Art Nouveau design encircles pot, plain upturned applied spout, black plastic handle & finial, 5"..........................**$20.00**

Tidbit tray, Cromwell, square dish w/fruit-&-flower design in 4 divided wells, center handle w/loop finial, 9x9".....**$25.00**

Toast rack, Wendell August Forge #709, hammered w/wheat pattern......................**$75.00**

Toothpick holder, unmarked, tapered w/paneled sides, weighted low pedestal foot, rolled rim, 2½"........**$12.00**

Tray, Arthur Armour, rectangular w/handles, chessman design, 10x16".........................**$45.00**

Tray, Buenilum, round, hammered w/grape cluster design, 14½" dia......................**$8.00**

Tray, Continental #703, round w/fluted rim, twisted handles, hammered wild rose pattern, 13½" dia.................**$20.00**

Tray, Everlast, rectangular w/tab handles, hammered w/tropical fish design, 9x14".........................**$35.00**

Tray, Hand Forged, round w/rod handles wrapped in coiled wire, fruit design, 17" dia......................**$25.00**

Tray, Kensington, rectangular w/raised flat rim, polished w/fox-hunt scenes on tab handles, 14x23"...........**$45.00**

Tray, Keystone, rectangular w/bar handles, hammered w/hunt scene, 13x17".........................**$45.00**

Tray, Russel Wright, round w/raffia-wrapped handles, spun texture, 14½" dia.........................**$65.00**

Tray, unmarked, oval w/fluted rim, smooth finish w/stamped wild roses, 12¼".........................**$10.00**

Tray, unmarked, rectangular w/applied curved handles, hammered pattern w/geometric square design, 12x16"..**$20.00**

Tray, unmarked, rectangular w/raised scalloped rim, wire loop handles, poinsettia design, 11x18"................**$10.00**

Tray, Wendell August Forge, vegetable pattern, 9x14", $85.00. (Photo courtesy of Dannie Woodard.)

American Bisque

This was a West Virginia company that operated there from 1919 until 1982, producing a wide variety of figural planters and banks, cookie jars, kitchenware and vases. It has a look all its own; most of the decoration was done by the airbrushing method, and some pieces were gold trimmed. Collectors often identify American Bisque items by the 'wedges' or dry-footed cleats on the bottom of the ware. The most valuable pieces are those modeled after copyrighted characters like Popeye and the Flintstones. If you'd like more information, refer to *American Bisque, Collector's Guide With Prices*, by Mary Jane Giacomini.

See also Cookie Jars.

Advisor: Mary Jane Giacomini (See Directory, American Bisque)

Ashtray, teepee incised w/heart, club, diamond & spade, smoke rises out of top, airbrushing w/painted trim, 6¼" **$36.00**

Bank, chick w/neck bow, airbrushed trim, unmarked, 6½" **$40.00**

Bank, Chicken Feed, chicken against lg feed sack, unmarked, 4½"..........................**$25.00**

Bank, Fred & Wilma........................**$400.00**

Bank, pig standing w/neck bow, pastel airbrushing, marked USA, 5¼" **$30.00**

Bank, pig w/multicolored indented dots & red neck bow, unmarked, 14" **$95.00**

Bank, Popeye **$450.00**

Bank, rag doll girl or boy, 5", each **$25.00**

Christmas plate, decorated tree shape w/green airbrushing & red cold-paint & gold trim, 14½" **$75.00**

Flower frog, 2 conjoined swans on wavy base, airbrushed, APCO, unmarked, 5¾" **$28.00**

Grease jar, butter churn w/embossed & painted floral design on brown airbrushed background, 6½" **$20.00**

Lamp base, bear seated w/neck bow, black & red cold-painted features & trim, unmarked, 6" **$35.00**

Pitcher, apple, airbrushing w/gold handle & trim, APCO, marked USA, 6" **$75.00**

Pitcher, ball-shaped w/embossed & cold-painted strawberry design, marked USA, 6¾" **$35.00**

Pitcher, pig seated, lg neck bow, airbrushed trim, unmarked, 8½" **$175.00**

Pitcher, pig seated, lg neck bow, cold-painted trim, unmarked, 8" **$125.00**

Planter, bear & rag doll w/blocks & baseball, gold trim, 5½" **$36.00**

Planter, bear & rag-doll clown w/blocks & baseball, no gold, unmarked, 5½" **$24.00**

Planter, bear cubs (2) around tree stump, gold trim, 5½" ..**$24.00**

Planter, bear cubs (2) around tree stump, no gold, unmarked, 5½" **$14.00**

Planter, dog & cat by stump, marked USA, 4½" **$18.00**

Planter, donkey (1 ear up & 1 ear down) sitting upright in front of cart, unmarked, 6½" **$12.00**

Planter, duck face on basket, unmarked, 3¼" **$10.00**

Planter, Dutch boy or girl w/wooden shoe, unmarked, 6", each **$8.00**

Planter, gazelle in leaping pose w/flower on back, unmarked, 5¼" **$26.00**

Planter, hen w/chicks, unmarked, 5¼" **$20.00**

Planter, kitten propped up on toe of shoe, marked USA, 3½x6½" **$16.00**

Planter, kitten sleeping by slipper, unmarked, 2¾", $8.00. (Photo courtesy of Mary Jane Giacomini.)

Planter, lamb pulling cart, unmarked, 4¾" **$10.00**

Planter, paddle boat, unmarked, 9½" **$24.00**

Planter, panther leaning against smooth stump w/leaves at base, unmarked, 5¾" **$24.00**

Planter, parakeet perched on edge of well w/flower vine, unmarked, 6" **$14.00**

Planter, puppy playing w/slipper, unmarked, 5½" **$18.00**

Planter, rabbit w/happy expression hugging cabbage head, unmarked, 5" **$22.00**

Planter, yarn doll w/block, unmarked, 5¾" **$20.00**

Teapot, ball shape w/rose stem embossed over lattice design, underglazed leaves w/red cold-painted rose, APCO, 7¼" **$30.00**

Vase, cornucopia, upright, white w/rose design, gold trim, APCO, unmarked, 5" **$24.00**

Vase, vertical philodendron leaves, gold trim (Shafer), unmarked, 7¼" **$28.00**

Wall pocket, heart shape with bow and flowers, gold trim, APCO, marked USA, 6", $26.00. (Photo courtesy Mary Jane Giacomini.)

Wall pocket, 2 birds in front of birdhouse w/flower, gold trim, 5½" **$32.00**

Wall pockets, creamer & sugar bowl, white swirls w/embossed & painted floral detail, gold trim, unmarked APCO, pr **$28.00**

Autographs

'Philography' is an extremely popular hobby, one that is very diversified. Autographs of sports figures, movie stars, entertainers, and politicians from our lifetime may bring several hundred dollars, depending on rarity and application, while John Adams' simple signature on a document from 1800, for instance, might bring thousands. A signature on a card or photograph is the least valuable type of autograph. A handwritten letter is the most valuable, since in addition to the signature you get the message as well. Depending upon what it reveals about the personality who penned it, content can be very important and can make a major difference in value.

Many times a polite request accompanied by an SASE to a famous person will result in receipt of a signed photo or a short handwritten note that might in several years be worth a tidy sum!

Obviously as new collectors enter the field, the law of supply and demand will drive the prices for autographs upward, especially when the personality is deceased. There are forgeries around, so before you decide to invest in expensive autographs, get to know your dealers.

Advisors: Don and Anne Kier (See Directory, Autographs)

Newsletter: *The Autograph Review*
Jeffrey Morey
305 Carlton Rd.
Syracuse, NY 13207; 315-474-3516

Newsletter: *Autographs and Memorabilia*
P.O. Box 224
Coffeyville, KS 67337; 316-251-5308; Six issues per year on movie and sports memorabilia

Newsletter: *The Pen and Quill*
Universal Autograph Collectors Club
P.O. Box 6181
Washington, DC 20044-6181

Newspaper: *Autograph Times*
Barbara Righam and Ardith Wilson
BARD Enterprises
2303 N 44th St., #225
Phoenix, AZ 85008; 602-947-3112 or Fax 602-947-8363; Subscription: $15 per year for 10 issues

Nat King Cole, signed black and white photo, 'To Randy, Best Wishes...,' matted and framed, 10x8", $250.00.

Aikman, Troy; in-person signed card, 3x5" $10.00
Allison, Davey; signed color photo, kneeling next to race car, 8x10" $75.00
Andretti, Mario; signed card, 3x5" $5.00
Armstrong, Neil; inscribed signed photo in business suit, 8x10" $175.00
Ashe, Arthur; signed photo of action pose, 8x10" $50.00
Bailey, F Lee; signed card, 3x5"................$5.00
Becker, Boris; in-person signed color action photo, 8x10"...$25.00
Belushi, James; inscribed signed photo, 8x10"...........$15.00

Bernstein, Kenny; signed color photo w/race car, 8x10"..$10.00
Blanc, Mel; signed card, 3x5" $20.00
Bowe, Riddick; in-person signed photo, 8x10" $20.00
Bowie, David; signed color photo, 8x10" $65.00
Brooks, Garth; in-person signed card, 3x5" $20.00
Brown, Paul; signed photo as coach, 5x7" $40.00
Bruno, Frank; signed color photo of boxing pose, 5x7"...$15.00
Bundy, King Kong; signed card, 3x5" $5.00
Calhoun, Rory; signed black & white photo, in cowboy hat, 8x10" $20.00
Calloway, Cab; signed album cover................$25.00
Campbell, Glenn; signed black & white portrait, 8x10".$15.00
Candy, John; signed photo, 8x10" $65.00
Carter, Rosalyn; inscribed signed color photo, 8x10" .$30.00
Chamberlain, Wilt; in-person signed card, 3x5" $15.00
Chitwood, Joey Jr; signed card, 3x5" $3.00
Chung, Connie; signed photo, 8x10" $10.00
Clapton, Eric; signed photo, 4x6" $45.00
Coppola, Francis Ford; signed card, scarce, 3x5"........$20.00
Craven, Wes; signed card, 3x5"................$7.00
Crenshaw, Ben; signed card, 3x5" $5.00
Davis, Jim; signed typed letter on Garfield letterhead, color, 5x7" $18.00
De La Hoya, Oscar; signed card, 3x5" $7.00
Dickerson, Eric; in-person signed color photo as Colt, 8x10" $14.00
DiMaggio, Joe; in-person signed card, 3x5" $95.00
Duvall, Robert; signed photo from Lonesome Dove, 8x10" $25.00
Earnhardt, Dale; signed card, 3x5" $10.00
Eastwood, Clint; signed photo, western pose, 8x10"..$30.00
Englund, Robert; signed card matted w/picture as Freddie, 12x16" $25.00
Esiason, Boomer; in-person signed promotional poster, 20x30" $35.00
Fingers, Rollie; in-person signed color photo, pitching, 8x10" $15.00
Flutie, Doug; signed card, 3x5"................$8.00
Foreman, George; signed photo, full length, recent pose, 8x10" $35.00
Foyt, AJ; inscribed signed color photo w/race cars, 8x10"..$18.00
Freleng, Fritz; Pink Panther cartoonist, signed card, scarce 3x5" $35.00
Gallagher, signed photo, smiling, holding hammer, 8x10"..$20.00
Garlits, 'Big Daddy' Don; signed card, 3x5" $5.00
Glenn, John; inscribed signed photo, standing next to space-craft, 8x10"................$20.00
Gordon, Jeff; signed card, 3x5" $10.00
Gurney, Dan; signed card, 3x5"................$5.00
Hammer, MC; color magazine photo signed, 8x10"....$25.00
Harvey, Paul; inscibed signed photo, 8x10" $8.00
Hefner, Hugh; inscribed signed photo, 8x10" $15.00
Hogan, Ben; signed golf gum card $90.00
Holyfield, Evander; signed color photo w/champ's belt, 8x10" $25.00
Howard, Ron; signed card, scarce, 3x5" $15.00
Hull, Bobby; signed card, 3x5" $5.00
Irvan, Ernie; signed color photo w/race car, 8x10" $10.00
Jackson, Jesse; inscribed signed card, 3x5" $15.00

Jackson, Reggie; in-person signed card, 3x5"..............$15.00
Johnson, Dave; signed card, 3x5"........................$5.00
Jones, James Earl; signed vintage Christmas card.......$30.00
Jones, Parnelli; signed card, 3x5"........................$7.00
Joyner, Florence Griffith; signed color photo while running, 8x10"........................$10.00
Kelly, Emmett; signed personal check, 1970...............$75.00
Kelly, Jim; in-person signed Buffalo Bills baseball cap..$50.00
Ketchum, Hank; original facial sketch, signed card, 3x5"..$12.00
King, Larry; signed card, 3x5"........................$10.00
Knievel, Evel; inscribed signed photo, 8x10"............$20.00
Lantz, Walter; original signed sketch of Woody Woodpecker on a 3x5 card........................$155.00
Lee, Spike; in-person signed card, 3x5"........................$7.00
Lemon, Meadowlark; signed card, 3x5"........................$10.00
Leonard, Sugar Ray; inscribed signed color photo in boxing pose, 8x10"........................$18.00
Letterman, David; signed card, 3x5"........................$10.00
Lewis, Lennox; signed card, 3x5"........................$10.00
Mailer, Norman; signed card, 3x5"........................$10.00
Mantle, Mickey; Official American League baseball signed in person........................$150.00
Marino, Dan; in-person signed card, 3x5"...............$12.00
Moore, Clayton; signed photo as Lone Ranger, 8x10"..$25.00
Morgan, Frank; signed album pages in pencil..........$200.00
Mosconi, Willie; signed card, 3x5"........................$15.00
Muldowney, Shirley; signed color photo w/race car, 8x10".$12.00
Namath, Joe; inscribed signed photo, 8x10"............$35.00
Nicklaus, Jack; signed card, 3x5"........................$20.00
Nicks, Stevie; inscribed signed photo, 8x10"...........$25.00
Osborne, Ozzy; signed photo, 8x10"........................$25.00
Parks, Rosa; signed card, scarce, 3x5"........................$20.00
Pippen, Scottie; in-person signed card, 3x5"..............$10.00
Polanski, Roman; signed card, 3x5"........................$15.00
Pollack, Sydney; signed card, 3x5"........................$5.00
Powell, Colin; signed card, 3x5"........................$10.00
Price, Vincent; signed original self-portrait, 8x10"....$100.00
Quayle, Dan; signed card, 3x5"........................$7.00
Roach, Hal; signed card, 3x5"........................$25.00

Roddenberry, Gene; signed card, 3x5"........................$30.00
Rooney, Andy; signed bookplate, scarce...............$10.00
Salk, Dr Jonas; signed photo, 8x10"........................$50.00
Sawyer, Diane; signed color photo, 8x10"...............$10.00
Selleck, Tom; inscribed signed photo, 4x6"............$7.00
Seuss, Dr; signed bookplate........................$55.00
Shavers, Ernie; signed card, 3x5"........................$10.00
Sheen, Charlie; signed photo in aviator jacket, 4x6"..$15.00
Shoemaker, Willie; signed card, 3x5"........................$25.00
Spillane, Mickey; inscribed signed photo of very early pose, 8x10"........................$16.00
Taupin, Bernie; signed card, scarce, 3x5"...............$10.00
Thomas, Clarence; signed card, 3x5"........................$12.00
Tyson, Mike; in-person signed card, 3x5"...............$25.00
Warhol, Andy; inscribed signed photo, 1980, 8x10".......$200.00
Westheimer, Dr Ruth; signed card, 3x5"........................$3.00
Yeager, Chuck; signed color photo in front of jet, 8x10"..$25.00

Automobilia

A specialized field that attracts both advertising buyers and vintage car buffs alike, 'automobilia' is a term collectors use when referring to auto-related items and accessories such as hood ornaments, gear shift and steering wheel knobs, owner's manuals, license plates, brochures, and catalogs. Many figural hood ornaments bring from $75.00 to $200.00 — some even higher. Things from the thirties through the fifties are especially popular right now.

Advisors: Jim and Nancy Schaut (See Directory, Automobilia)

Newsletter: *Automobile License Plate Collectors*
Gary Brent Kincade
P.O. Box 712
Weston, WV 26452; 304-842-3773

Auto Con-Den-So-Meter, cast-iron butterfly shape, reacts when radiator is overheated, 3½x5", EX..............$85.00
Badge, Ford Rouge, heavy pressed metal, badge number above Ford lettered over factory scene, ships below, 1½", EX........................$75.00
Bank, Dodge Dart, America's 1st Fine Economy Car, cardboard & metal barrel shape, cream & orange, 4", VG......$25.00
Bank, Ford, shaggy dog figure w/Ford collar, Florence Ceramics, 1960s, 8", EX........................$45.00
Box, Chevrolet, wooden, bow-tie logo & painted images of money bags & coins, ca 1950s, 5½x8x6¾", VG...$25.00
Brochure, Oldsmobile Six & Eight, shows various Oldsmobiles available w/accessories & service, color, 1930s, 9x10", VG+........................$40.00
Brochure, Royal Blue Line Motor Tours/Boston, blue & white, 1929, EX+........................$15.00
Change purse, leather w/metal top embossed w/driver & passengers in open touring car, twisted design around edge, VG+........................$80.00
Change purse, shaped like leather chauffeur's cap w/metal bill & band embossed w/woman entering early 4-door sedan, EX........................$90.00

Robert Young and the cast of Father Knows Best, signed black and white photo, 10x8", $125.00.

Cigar box, Cadillac, lithographed paper over cardboard, Sweet Tips, 5¢, Very Mild, 2½x9", VG **$150.00**

Cigar box, Ford, wood w/black lettering & graphics, red & cream paper border, 2½x9", VG **$160.00**

Cigarette case, Ford V-8, rectangular w/rounded corners & hinged lid, blue w/silver trim & V-8 emblem, 3¼x2¾", EX **$275.00**

Clock, Cadillac, neon, octagon w/numbers reverse painted on glass front, Cadillac Service & emblem in center, 18", EX **$950.00**

Clock, Genuine Ford Muscle Parts, rectangular metal frame w/plastic face, square clock left of graphics, 11x24", VG **$125.00**

Clock, Official AAA Station, round metal frame w/plastic lens, numbers around oval logo, light-up, 15" dia, VG **$60.00**

Clock, Pontiac Service, round metal frame w/2 glass faces & frosted plastic lens, numbers around logo, 15" dia, VG **$175.00**

Clock, Studebaker Batteries, square metal frame w/glass lens, numbers 12-3-6-9 around name & logo, light-up, 15", G **$75.00**

Coin, 1954 Corvette, Motorama commemorative, gold-tone, EX **$15.00**

Compact, New Jersey Turnpike, round w/image of entrance to turnpike & lettering, 2¾" dia, EX **$20.00**

Display box, Schlaich Locks for the Boyce Moto Meter, tin, frontal view of open car, 9x13", VG+ **$225.00**

Display rack, Ford Color Patch, Cover That Scratch With..., Factory-Matched Colors, 3 stepped shelves w/marquee, 19", G **$100.00**

Display rack, Packard Automotive Cable, metal, black w/red & black lettering on gold marquee, 35½x17½", VG **$50.00**

Fan, cardboard paddle shape w/whip-stiched border, early touring car in countryside w/different models on handle, VG **$85.00**

Fan, Chevrolet, cardboard, 11½x8", EX, $90.00. (Photo courtesy of Dunbar Gallery.)

Fan, Dodge/Plymouth, round steering-wheel shape w/safety phrases, countryside images & car emblems, 1936, VG+ **$45.00**

Fan, First Lessons, vertical cardboard rectangle w/irregular border, man teaching lady to drive, wood handle, VG+ **$40.00**

Game, Dealer's Choice, Wheeling Dealing Used Car Game, Parker Bros, unused, NM **$20.00**

Gearshift knob, glass w/brown & tan swirls, 2" dia, EX .. **$50.00**

Gearshift knob, white plastic funnel shape w/black streaks & specks, 2x1¼" dia, EX **$25.00**

Hood ornament, Ford Mustang, sleek chrome horse figure, box reads Crowning Touch of Beauty!, 5¾", NMIB **$175.00**

Hood ornament, GMC, chrome w/green & black inlay, 3x6½", EX+ **$60.00**

Hood ornament, Mack Jr Truck Bulldog, chrome-plated, early, EX **$75.00**

Jar, Volkswagen, amber glass figural VW Bug w/cork stopper, 6", EX **$40.00**

Key chain, '66 Olds Super Salesman, M **$15.00**

Key chain, Chevrolet, 50 Years, EX **$10.00**

Lighter, Downtown Ford Sales w/1950s-60s emblem, Zippo type , EX **$20.00**

Match holder & ashtray, brass, embossed image of driver in open touring car along countryside on footed ashtray base, VG **$125.00**

Necklace, Buick Riveria, sterling silver vehicle-shaped pendant, Anson, 1963, 1", EXIB **$45.00**

Paperweight, GM Golden Milestones 1908-1958, Forward From Fifty, oval brass token imbedded in Lucite cube, EX. **$45.00**

Pen, Oldsmobile, Golden Anniversary, car floats in pen top, 5", EX **$30.00**

Pin-back button, Pontiac Excitement, 1985, 3" dia, EX .. **$5.00**

Playing cards, Cadillac emblem, double deck in plastic box, EX **$10.00**

Postcard, image of red 1966 Ford GT 2+2 Fastback, EX .. **$8.00**

Postcard, image of 1964 Plymouth Fury 4-door hardtop, VG **$4.00**

Poster, Chrysler Six, Inspired by the Best Design of Ancient Greece, image of early 4-door sedan, framed, 27x20", EX **$10.00**

Poster, Compliments of JC Smyser Auto Co, image of girl in bonet w/bouquet of roses on yellow ground, framed, 23x19", EX **$15.00**

Poster, De Soto...Knee-High to a Parking Meter, lettering above side view of 2-door De Soto w/driver, 1957, 31x68", EX **$45.00**

Poster, 1958 Chevrolet Impala Convertible, paper, side-view image w/driver & beach scene beyond, framed, 18½x32", EX **$100.00**

Radio, Audi, AM-FM transistor, plastic w/repeated logos, retracting antenna & strap, brown, blue & white, 4¼", EX **$15.00**

Shop manual, Packard, 1937 Series, black & white, 71 pages, EX **$55.00**

Sign, American Auto Stores, porcelain, white w/blue lettering, facial image made up of auto parts, 15x20", VG **$50.00**

Sign, Baum's Wonderful Polish, diecut cardboard stand-up, lettering above image of lady driving open car, 13x9", NM **$110.00**

Sign, FoMoCo Genuine Ford Parts, painted metal, red & white, 2-sided, 13½x18", EX **$60.00**

Sign, Genuine Chevrolet Fan Belts Only 85¢, painted metal, sits atop display rack, 1950s-60s, 14x23", EX, from $35 to $45.00

Sign, Hertz Rent A Car, metal case w/glass front, yellow background w/black lettering, light-up, late 1940s, 12x26", EX $210.00

Sign, MG, More Go!, front & side images of MG w/passengers, cardboard on wood w/simulated beveled frame, 14½x30", VG $70.00

Sign, Mirrolike Auto Polish, painted metal, 2 girls in checked outfits flank trademark, ca 1920s, 10x14", EX $185.00

Sign, Plymouth, neon, flag shape w/Plymouth in block lettering, w/transformer, 21½x24½", NM $325.00

Thermometer, Ford Sales & Service, pink keyhole shape w/black lettering & image of early auto above, 8¾x3¼", EX...$85.00

Thermometer, International Trucks/International Harvester Co, metal, blue & black on cream, canted corners, 16", VG $45.00

Thermometer w/chalkboard, Dodge Message Center, painted metal, thermometer & red lettering above chalkboard, VG $65.00

Thermometer/Hygrometer, cast-metal roadster w/dial thermometer & hygrometer in wheels, hanger on back, 4x8", EX...$75.00

Tie tack, Cadillac crest, Certified Craftsman, gold-tone, dated 1951, EX...$25.00

Tire pressure gauge, Buick, round w/chrome frame, logo above tires sizes & pressure amounts, EX+..........$75.00

Tire pressure gauge, Dodge, round w/chrome frame, EX+ $65.00

TV tray, Ford, metal w/folding stand, black w/names of Ford cars & dates in gold, Ford logo in center, 29", EX $15.00

Sign, Genuine Ford Parts, porcelain, white on dark blue, 16x24", NM, $675.00. (Photo courtesy of Dunbar Gallery.)

Autumn Leaf Dinnerware

A familiar dinnerware pattern to just about all of us, Autumn Leaf was designed by Hall China for the Jewel Tea Company who offered it to their customers as premiums. In fact, some people refer to the pattern as 'Jewel Tea.' First made in 1933, it continued in production until 1978.

Pieces with this date in the backstamp are from the overstock that was in the company's warehouse when production was suspended. There are matching pitchers, tumblers, and stemware all made by the Libbey Glass Company, and a set of enameled cookware that came out in 1979. You'll find blankets, tablecloths, metal canisters, clocks, playing cards, and many other items designed around the Autumn Leaf pattern. All are collectible.

Since 1984 the Hall Company has been making items for the National Autumn Leaf Collectors Club. These pieces are listed below, designated as such by 'Club' and the date of issue in each of their descriptions.

Limited edition items (by Hall) are being sold by China Specialties, a company in Ohio; but once you become familiar with the old pieces, these are easy to identify, since the molds have been redesigned or were not previously used for Autumn Leaf production. So far, these are the pieces I'm aware of: the Airflow teapot, the Norris refrigerator pitcher, a square-handled beverage mug, a restyled Irish mug, 'teardrop' salt and pepper shakers, a mustard jar, a set of covered onion soup bowls, sherbets, the automobile teapot, a tankard-shaped beer pitcher, fluted salt and pepper shakers, an oval handled relish, a reamer, a round butterdish, a hurricane lamp with a glass shade, a collector's prayer wall plaque, a Hook Cover teapot, a Fort Pitt baker (6" x 4½" x 1¼"), a 7" square wall clock, a small Melody teapot, a 16-oz. chocolate pot, a display shelf sign, 4-oz. footed demitasse cups, a 'Graeter' bud vase, and a 1-handle (2½-pint) bean pot. In glassware they've issued cruets, water and wine goblets, iced tea and juice tumblers, shot glasses, dessert plates, and beer pilsners. These are crystal (not frosted) and are dated at the base of one of the leaves. Their accessory items include playing cards that are dated in the lower right-hand corner.

For further study, we recommend *The Collector's Encyclopedia of Hall China* by Margaret and Kenn Whitmyer. For information on company products see Jewel Tea.

Advisor: Gwynneth M. Harrison (See Directory, Autumn Leaf)

Club: National Autumn Leaf Collectors' Club
Gwynne Harrison
P.O. Box 1
Mira Loma, CA 91752-0001; 909-685-5434

Newsletter: *Autumn Leaf*
Jim Steele, Treasurer
2415 Brookhaven
Canton, MI 48188, 313-397-8169. Membership: $20 per year

Apron, oilcloth, from $400 to $450.00
Apron, plastic...$550.00
Baker, French; 2-pt..$150.00
Baker, French; 3-pt..$18.00
Baker, individual; Fort Pitt, 12-oz..............................$200.00
Ball jug, #3 ....$40.00
Blanket, Vellux, Autumn Leaf, king-size $220.00
Blanket, Vellux, blue, full-size $175.00

Book, Autumn Leaf Story, from $40 to $60.00
Bowl, fruit; 5½" $6.00
Bowl, New Metal, set of 3 ....$250.00
Bowl, salad; 9" $20.00
Bowl, soup; flat, 8½" $15.00
Bowl, vegetable; Glasbake, milk glass, divided $25.00
Bowl, vegetable; oval, divided, 10½" $90.00
Bowl, vegetable; round, 9" $125.00
Bread box, metal, from $300 to $400.00
Butter dish, regular, ruffled top, ¼-lb, $175 to $200.00
Cake plate, from $15 ....$20.00
Cake plate, metal stand, from $150 to $225.00
Cake safe, metal, top or side motif, from $35 to $40.00
Candle holder, Club, 1989, pair $250.00
Candle holder, Club, Christmas 1994, from $75 to ...$100.00
Candlestick, Douglas, metal, pr $70.00
Candy jar, metal base, from $450 to $500.00
Canister, Douglas, brown & gold, white plastic lid $10.00
Canister, metal, coppertone lid, 4-pc set, from $200 to...$300.00
Carafe, Douglas, glass & metal $175.00
Carrying case, Jewel salesman, from $150 to $300.00
Casserole, Club, 1991, w/lid $125.00
Casserole, Glasbake, round, w/lid, from $25 to $35.00
Casserole, Mary Dunbar, round, 1½-qt, w/clear Heatflow
  lid $75.00

Casserole, round, 2-qt, from $30.00 to $45.00.

Catalog, Jewel, hardbound cover, from $20 to $50.00
Chair, kitchen $550.00
Cleanser can, metal $750.00
Clock, salesman's award, from $300 to $400.00
Coaster, metal, 3⅛", from $5 to $10.00
Coffeepot, Jewel's Best, 30-cup $500.00
Condiment, 3-pc set, from $65 to $80.00
Cookbook, Club, 1984 ....$45.00
Cookbook, Club, 1988 ....$30.00
Cookbook, Mary Dunbar, from $15 to $30.00
Cookware, New Metal, 7-pc set, minimum value $400.00
Creamer & sugar bowl, Melmac, pr $15.00
Creamer & sugar bowl, Rayed, pr, from $60 to $80.00
Creamer & sugar bowl, Ruffled-D, pr, from $25 to.....$45.00
Cup, Oyster, 1992 Annual Meeting, Club.................$200.00
Cup, custard; Mary Dunbar, Heatflow $8.00
Cup, custard; Radiance, from $4 to $6.00

Cup, regular, Ruffled-D...$8.00
Cup & saucer, Melmac $15.00
Fondue set, pot, w/lid, burner assembly & sticks, from $150
  to...$200.00
Gravy boat underplate...$20.00
Hotpad, oval, 10¾", from $12 to $15.00
Hotpad, tin back, 7¼", from $10 to $15.00
Jug, baby ball; Club, 1992, from $60 to $95.00
Jug, Rayed, 2½-pt $20.00
Jug, water; Donut, Club, 1991 ....$100.00
Jug, water; Douglas, ice lip $350.00
Lamp, Douglas, hurricane style, pr $350.00
Magnetic holders, set...$8.00
Mixer cover, Mary Dunbar $50.00
Mug, chocolate; Club, 1992, 4-pc set $90.00
Mug, Irish coffee, from $100 to $120.00
Napkin, muslin, 16" square, from $30 to $35.00
Newsletter, Jewel News, from $10 to $20.00
Percolator, glass, Douglas $225.00
Pickle fork, Jewel Tea $55.00
Pie plate, Mary Dunbar, from $18 to $20.00
Placemat, from $35 to $40.00
Plate, dinner; Melmac, 10" $15.00
Plate, 6"..$5.00
Plate, 9"..$10.00
Platter, Melmac, oval, 14" $35.00
Platter, oval, 13½", from $20 to $25.00
Playing cards, Autumn Leaf, 1943-46, double deck, from $150
  to...$200.00
Pressure cooker, Mary Dunbar, from $150 to...........$225.00
Punch bowl, w/12 cups, Club, 1993 ....$350.00
Salt & pepper shakers, Casper, Ruffled, regular, pr, from $20
  to...$30.00
Salt & pepper shakers, left or right handled, range size, pr.$25.00
Saucepan, Douglas, w/warmer base $150.00
Saucepan, metal, 2-qt, w/lid $80.00
Saucer, regular, Ruffled-D, from $3 to $5.00
Saucer, St Denis, from $6 to $8.00
Shelf paper, pattern on edge, sheet $45.00
Sherbet, gold & frost on clear, Libbey, 6½"...............$55.00
Sifter, metal $400.00
Silverware, place setting pcs, stainless steel, each $25.00
Silverware, serving items, silverplate, each................$90.00
Souffle dish, 4½"...$45.00
Sugar packet holder, Club, 1990..............................$100.00
Tablecloth, sailcloth, 54x54" $100.00
Tablecloth, sailcloth, 54x72", from $110 to..............$125.00
Teakettle, metal & porcelain, from $200 to $250.00
Tea for Two set, Club, 1990 ....$165.00
Tea set, Philadelphia, 1990 ....$200.00
Teapot, Aladdin, from $40 to....................................$50.00
Teapot, Club, New York, 1984 ....$550.00
Teapot, Club, Solo, 1991 ....$85.00
Teapot, Donut, 1993...$125.00
Teapot, French, Club, 1992 ....$85.00
Teapot, Newport, 1970s, from $175 to $200.00
Thermos, metal $350.00
Toaster cover, Mary Dunbar, plastic, from $30 to $40.00
Towel, tea; 16x33", from $50 to................................$60.00

Toy, Jewel truck, green......................................**$150.00**
Toy, Jewel truck, orange...................................**$75.00**
Toy, Jewel van, brown, from $150 to **$300.00**
Trash can, metal, red.......................................**$275.00**
Tray, tidbit; 2-tier, from $75 to........................**$85.00**
Tumbler, frosted band, 5½"...............................**$25.00**
Tumbler, gold & frost on clear, Libbey, 15-oz............**$50.00**
Tumbler, juice; frosted, Libbey, 3¾", from $25 to.......**$30.00**
Tumbler, plastic, insulated **$125.00**
Vase, bud; Club, 1994.......................................**$40.00**
Vase, Club, Edgewater, 1987............................**$275.00**
Warmer, oval **$150.00**

Avon

You'll find Avon bottles everywhere you go! But it's not just the bottles that are collectible — so are jewelry, awards, magazine ads, catalogs, and product samples. Of course, the better items are the older ones (they've been called Avon since 1939 — California Perfume Company before that), and if you can find them mint in box (MIB), all the better. For more information we recommend *Hastin's Avon Collector's Price Guide* by Bud Hastin.

See also Cape Cod.

Advisor: Tammy Roderick (See Directory, Avon)

Newsletter: *Avon Times*
c/o Dwight or Vera Young
P.O. Box 9868, Dept. P
Kansas City, MO 64134; inquiries should be accompanied by LSASE

Club: National Association of Avon Collectors
c/o Connie Clark
6100 Walnut, Dept. P
Kansas City MO 64103; inquiries should be accompanied by LSASE

Somewhere Cologne, Gay '90s Girl, 1974, MIB, $12.50.

ALBEE award, bisque figurine, by Goebel, 1978 ....**$60.00**
Barber Pole Decanter, milk glass w/red & blue striped label, plastic cap, 3-oz, 1974-75, M (no box)...................**$6.50**
Bay Rum Gift Set, glass bottle of after shave w/paper label & black cap along w/talc, 4-oz each, 1964, MIB **$36.00**

Beautiful You Set, moisture cream, skin freshener & moisture suds, 1958, all M in pink & white box.................**$20.00**
Betsy Ross Decanter, white paint over clear glass, 1976, 4-oz, MIB...**$6.00**
Bright Night Beauty Dust, white plastic round box w/gold stars on lid, 1959-61, MIB **$12.50**
Bright Night Cologne Mist, white plastic coating over clear glass, white paper label, gold lid, 3-oz, 1958-61, MIB **$15.00**
Cannonball Express 4-6-0 decanter, black glass, 1976-77, 3¼-oz, MIB..**$12.00**
Captivators Compact, wild animal-skin design plastic oval compact, 1969, MIB **$6.00**
Checker Cab 1926 Decanter, yellow paint over clear w/black plastic details, 1977-78, 5-oz, MIB **$10.00**
Corvette Stingray '65 Decanter, green glass w/plastic cap, 1972, MIB...**$7.00**
Cotillion Bath Oil, pink & white plastic bottle, 1962, 6-oz, M **$6.50**
Country Chicken Decanter, white ceramic bottle w/pump top, 9½-oz, 1987, MIB **$7.50**
Country Peaches Soap Jar & Soaps, glass fruit jar form w/wire bail holds peach-shaped soaps, MIB..........**$8.50**
Crystal Treasure Box, leaded crystal box w/butterfly on lid, 1990, 1¾x2¾x2¾", MIB **$18.00**
Daisies Won't Tell Miss Daisy Set, cologne & beauty dust, 1956, MIB..**$40.00**
Daisies Won't Tell Spray Cologne, pink plastic-coated bottle w/white lid, 1958-60, MIB....................................**$10.00**
Daisies Won't Tell Spray Cologne Mist, bottle coated w/white plastic, blue painted label, white cap, 1962-64, 2-oz, MIB...**$10.00**
Dove in Flight Candlette, clear glass dove figural, 1977-78, MIB...**$8.00**
Ducks of American Wilderness Stein, ceramic w/wildlife scenes in relief, duck finial, 1988, 8¾", MIB **$40.00**
Dune Buggy Decanter, blue glass w/silver motor cap, 1971-73, 5-oz, MIB..**$10.00**
Fielder's Choice Decanter, dark amber glove form w/black cap, 5-oz, 1971-72, MIB.....................................**$10.00**
Gardenia Perfume, glass bottle w/painted label, flowered cap, ⅜-oz, 1948-52, M in round box w/clear plastic lid...**$75.00**
Glistening Star Crystal Candle Holders, leaded crystal, 2x2", 1993, MIB...**$8.00**
Going Steady Set, compact & lipstick in gray hinged purse, 1960, MIB...**$16.50**
Golden Moments Pendant Perfume, antiqued brass pendant opens to hold ⅛-oz perfume, w/32" chain, 1971-72, MIB **$17.50**
Goodyear Blimp Decanter, silvery gray paint over clear glass w/blue lettering, 1979, 2-oz, MIB **$7.50**
Heart-Shaped Cologne Bottle, clear heart-shaped bottle w/fancy stopper top, came in many fragrances, 1964-66, ½-oz, M...**$3.00**
Here's My Heart Cologne Mist, blue plastic-coated glass bottle w/embossed heart, gold cap, 1957-48, M (no box) **$17.50**
Highway King Decanter, green glass tractor form w/white plastic trailer (talc), 1977-79, 4-oz & 6½-oz, MIB.**$15.00**

Hobnail Decanter, white opalescent cruet form w/hobnails, stopper top, 5-oz, 1972-74, MIB **$5.00**

Imperial Garden Cologne Mist, white Oriental-style bottle w/orange flowers & gold trim, 3-oz, 1973-77, M ...**$1.50**

Jeep Renegade Decanter, black glass w/decals, tan plastic top, 1981-82, 3-oz, MIB **$10.00**

King Pin Decanter, milk glass bowling pin w/red label, 1969-70, 4-oz, MIB **$5.00**

Lady Spaniel Decanter, white opalescent glass w/plastic head, 1½-oz, 1974-76, MIB **$5.00**

Patterns Tray, black plastic w/gold trim, 1969-70, 10", MIB.**$4.50**

Pheasant Decanter, brown glass w/green plastic head that removes, 1972-74, M (no box) **$7.50**

Precious Lamb Baby Lotion Decanter, white plastic lamb figural w/blue painted bow, 1975-76, 6-oz, MIB........**$4.50**

Pretty Cat Decanter, white glass cat form, head removes, 1½-oz, 1988, MIB **$5.00**

Reggie Raccoon Hair Brush & Comb, plastic raccoon figural brush w/tan plastic comb, 1973, MIB **$5.00**

Snoopy Comb & Brush Set, Snoopy figural brush w/white comb, 1971-75, MIB..**$6.00**

Snowmobile Decanter, blue glass w/yellow plastic details, 1974-75, 4-oz, MIB...**$10.00**

Somewhere Perfume, glass bottle w/jewels along base, pink jeweled lid w/4 butterflies, 1-oz, 1961-63, MIB....**$75.00**

Sparkling Jewel Stackable Candles, blue glass, 1984, pr, MIB **$7.50**

Spirit of St Louis Decanter, silver paint on clear glass, 1970-72, 5-oz, 7½" long, MIB **$12.50**

Sports Rally Bracing Lotion, glass bottle w/blue lid, 1966-68, 4-oz, MIB **$4.50**

Strawberry Porcelain Sugar Shaker & Talc, white porcelain shaker & box of talc, 1979, MIB...........................**$10.00**

Tai Winds Gift Set, green glass bottle w/green lid & yellow ribbon, 5-oz, along w/5-oz embossed soap, 1971-72, MIB **$16.00**

Tall Ships Stein, ceramic w/sailing ships in relief, rope handle, w/8-oz red plastic cologne, 1977, MIB..........**$37.50**

To a Wild Rose Cologne, white milk glass bottle w/paper label, pink ball cap, 1957, 2-oz, M.....................**$17.50**

To a Wild Rose Sweethearts Set, bath powder tied w/ribbon & 4-oz cologne, 1955, MIB **$60.00**

Touch of Roses Perfumed Soap, set of 3 rose-shaped pink soaps, 1972-77, MIB...**$5.00**

Western Boot Decanter, amber glass boot w/silver lid & spurs, 5-oz, 1973-75, MIB...**$7.50**

Barbie and Her Friends

Here's a good example of the rapid appreciation some collectibles achieve. Last year we reported that the #1 Barbie issued in 1959, was valued at $4,500.00 mint in box. One year later, the same doll books for $9,000.00 – 10,000.00 if she happens to be a brunette! Of course, original Barbie dolls are hard to find, especially in this condition, but even dolls made more recently can be pricey! For instance, the 1988 Holiday Barbie (never removed from the box) books for $750.00, and even the Kool-Aid Barbie from 1993, first in the series, already goes for $195.00.

Barbie was first introduced in 1959, and soon Mattel found themselves producing not only dolls but tiny garments, fashion accessories, houses, cars, horses, books, and games as well. Today's Barbie collectors want them all. Though the early Barbie dolls are very hard to find, there are many of her successors still around. The trend today is toward Barbie exclusives — Holiday Barbie dolls and Bob Mackies are all very 'hot' items. So are special-event Barbie dolls.

When buying the older dolls, you'll need to do lots of studying and comparisons to learn to distinguish one Barbie from another, but this is the key to making sound buys and good investments. Remember, though, collectors are sticklers concerning condition; compared to a doll mint in box, they'll often give an additional 20% if that box has never been opened! If you want a good source for study, refer to one of these fine books: *A Decade of Barbie Dolls and Collectibles, 1981–1991*, by Beth Summers; *The Wonder of Barbie* and *The World of Barbie Dolls* by Paris and Susan Manos; *The Collector's Encyclopedia of Barbie Dolls and Collectibles* by Sibyl DeWein and Joan Ashabraner; *Barbie Fashions* by Sarah Sink Eames; *Barbie Exclusives, Books I and II*, by Margo Rana; *The Barbie Doll Boom, 1986–1995*, and *Collector's Encyclopedia of Barbie Doll Exclusives and More* by J. Michael Augustyniak; *The Barbie Years, 1959 to 1995*, by Patrick C. Olds; *The Story of Barbie* by Kitturah Westenhouser; *Barbie, The First 30 Years, 1959 Through 1989*, by Stefanie Deutsch; and *Schroeder's Collectible Toys, Antique to Modern* (Collector Books).

Barbie, 1991, Holiday, NRFB, $200.00. (Photo courtesy of Lee Garmon.)

Dolls

Barbie, 1960, #4, brunette, original swimsuit, NM...........**$425.00**

Barbie, 1961, Bubble-Cut, blond hair, MIB................**$450.00**

Barbie, 1961, Bubble-Cut, blond, original swimsuit, EX........**$175.00**

Barbie, 1961, Bubble-Cut, brunette hair, replica swimsuit, NM...**$250.00**

Barbie, 1963, Fashion Queen, molded brunette hair, complete w/3 wigs & stand, NRFB **$500.00**

Barbie, 1963, Fashion Queen, molded brunette hair, complete w/3 wigs & stand, NM...............................**$150.00**

Barbie, 1972, Miss America, brunette hair, original outfit, no roses otherwise complete, NM......................**$95.00**

Barbie, 1975, Deluxe Quick Curl, department-store special, NRFB.......................................**$50.00**

Barbie, 1979, Italian, NRFB **$200.00**

Barbie, 1981, Scottish, Dolls of the World series, NRFB...**$140.00**

Barbie, 1983, Angel Face, MIB **$45.00**

Barbie, 1983, Ballerina, department-store special, NRFB...**$75.00**

Barbie, 1983, Eskimo, Dolls of the World series, NRFB..**$120.00**

Barbie, 1984, Irish, Dolls of the World series, NRFB ..**$135.00**

Barbie, 1986, Dreamglo, original outfit, VG **$15.00**

Barbie, 1986, Greek, Dolls of the World series, NRFB..**$85.00**

Barbie, 1987, California Dream, department-store special, NRFB.......................................**$45.00**

Barbie, 1987, German, Dolls of the World series, NRFB.**$110.00**

Barbie, 1988, Holiday, NRFB **$750.00**

Barbie, 1989, Golden Greetings, FAO Schwarz, department-store special, NRFB...............**$250.00**

Barbie, 1989, Holiday, NRFB **$300.00**

Barbie, 1989, Ice Capades, NRFB **$30.00**

Barbie, 1989, Mexican, Dolls of the World series, NRFB...**$75.00**

Barbie, 1990, Brazilian, Dolls of the World series, NRFB ..**$35.00**

Barbie, 1990, Holiday, NRFB **$150.00**

Barbie, 1991, American Beauty Queen, NRFB **$55.00**

Barbie, 1991, Ballroom Beauty, Wal-Mart Special, NRFB .**$40.00**

Barbie, 1991, Holiday (Black), MIB.......................**$125.00**

Barbie, 1991, Night Sensation, FAO Schwarz, department-store special, NRFB.................**$225.00**

Barbie, 1991, Platinum, Bob Mackie, NRFB, from $600 to..**$700.00**

Barbie, 1991, Starlight Splendor, Bob Mackie, NRFB, from $700 to...............................**$750.00**

Barbie, 1992, Benefit Ball, NRFB **$150.00**

Barbie, 1992, Dazzlin' Date, Target special, NRFB......**$35.00**

Barbie, 1992, Empress Bride, Bob Mackie, NRFB, from $950 to.................................**$1,000.00**

Barbie, 1992, English, Dolls of the World series, NRFB.**$50.00**

Barbie, 1992, Holiday, NRFB **$125.00**

Barbie, 1992, Holiday (Black), MIB......................**$100.00**

Barbie, 1992, Holiday Hostess, NRFB **$60.00**

Barbie, 1992, Neptune Fantasy, Bob Mackie, MIB...**$1,000.00**

Barbie, 1993, Australian, Dolls of the World series, NRFB ..**$25.00**

Barbie, 1993, Egyptian Queen, NRFB **$65.00**

Barbie, 1993, Holiday, NRFB **$125.00**

Barbie, 1993, Masquerade Ball, Bob Mackie, NRFB .**$400.00**

Barbie, 1993, Silver Screen, FAO Schwarz, department-store special, NRFB **$200.00**

Barbie, 1994, Dance 'N Twirl, department-store special, NRFB.......................................**$65.00**

Barbie, 1994, Holiday (Black), MIB......................**$125.00**

Barbie, 1994, Scarlett, Hollywood Legend Series, red dress, NRFB.......................................**$75.00**

Barbie, 1995, Busy Gal, NRFB **$100.00**

Barbie, 1995, Goddess of the Sun, Bob Mackie, NRFB .**$200.00**

Barbie, 1995, Holiday Memories, department-store special, NRFB.......................................**$75.00**

Barbie as Scarlett, 1994, Hollywood Legend series, red dress, NRFB.......................................**$75.00**

Christie, 1970, Twist 'N Turn, NRFB **$250.00**

Christie, 1976, Superstar, department-store special, NRFB .**$55.00**

Christie, 1980, Golden Dream, department-store special, NRFB.......................................**$40.00**

Courtney, 1990, Cool Tops, department-store special, NRFB.**$30.00**

Courtney, 1991, Pet Pals, department-store special, NRFB.......................................**$35.00**

Francie, 1966, blond hair, original striped swimsuit, bendable legs, NM.......................................**$90.00**

Francie, 1966, brunette hair, straight legs, MIB.........**$450.00**

Francie, 1970, Malibu, original outfit, VG **$45.00**

Ken, 1961, flocked blond hair, straight legs, NRFB ..**$350.00**

Ken, 1972, Busy, department-store special, NRFB **$35.00**

Ken, 1975, Free Moving, painted hair, original outfit & accessories, EX+.......................................**$35.00**

Ken, 1979, Sport 'N Shave, NRFB.......................**$35.00**

Ken, 1980, Western, department-store special, NRFB .**$35.00**

Ken, 1994, Rhett Butler, Hollywood Legend Series, NRFB..**$65.00**

Midge, 1963, blond hair, nude, NM......................**$85.00**

Midge, 1963, blond hair, straight legs, MIB **$200.00**

Midge, 1963, blond hair, straight legs, no freckles, MIB...**$500.00**

Midge, 1965, titian hair, original swimsuit, replaced hair ribbon, bendable legs, NM.......................**$250.00**

Ricky, 1965, MIB.......................................**$125.00**

Skipper, 1965, blond hair, bendable legs, NRFB.......**$400.00**

Skipper, 1970, titian hair, straight legs, EX+ **$60.00**

Skipper, 1975, Growing Up, original outfit, VG **$35.00**

Skipper, 1982, Horse Lovin', NRFB **$50.00**

Skooter, 1965, brunette hair, original swimsuit, straight legs, NM **$65.00**

Stacey, 1967, Talking, titian hair, NRFB **$450.00**

Stacey, 1967, Talking, titian hair, original swimsuit, NM ..**$165.00**

Steffie, 1972, Walk Lively, brunette hair, bendable legs, original outfit, NM.......................................**$125.00**

Tuttie, 1966, blond or brunette hair, NRFB, each **$150.00**

Accessories

Barbie, 1994, Queen of Hearts, Bob Mackie, NRFB, $275.00. (Photo courtesy of Lee Garmon.)

Furniture, Barbie Bedroom Accents Grandfather Clock, #2372, 1985, NRFB.......................................**$5.00**

Furniture, Barbie Dream Canopy Bed, #5641, 1987, NRFB.**$15.00**

Furniture, Barbie Dream Furniture Vanity & Stool, #2469, 1978, NRFB..**$15.00**

Furniture, Barbie Dream House Finishing Touches Bedroom Set, #3769, MOC..**$6.00**

Furniture, Barbie Dream House Finishing Touches Living Room Set, #3769, MOC..**$6.00**

Furniture, Barbie Kitchen Accents Microwave, #2373, 1985, NRFB..**$10.00**

Furniture, Barbie Living Room Set, white wicker, 1983, NRFB..**$20.00**

Furniture, Superstar Barbie Piano Concert, 1990, NRFB ..**$25.00**

Outfit, Barbie, Beverly Hills Fashions, #3298, 1987, NRFB..**$35.00**

Outfit, Barbie, Career Girl, #954, complete, NM+.....**$110.00**

Outfit, Barbie, Cheerleader, #876, complete, EX.........**$55.00**

Outfit, Barbie, Color Kick, #3422, bodysuit only, NM...**$25.00**

Outfit, Barbie, Fancy Frills, #3183, MOC......................**$5.00**

Outfit, Barbie, Fashion Favorites, #3789, silver robe, 1981, MIP **$5.00**

Outfit, Barbie, Fashion Luncheon, #1656, dress only, EX ..**$95.00**

Outfit, Barbie, Finishing Touches, 1984, MOC **$5.00**

Outfit, Barbie, Friday Night Date, #979, complete, NM ..**$85.00**

Outfit, Barbie, Heavenly Holidays, #4277, 1982, NRFB, $75.00.

Outfit, Barbie, Jump Into Lace, #1823, complete, EX .**$45.00**

Outfit, Barbie, Knitting Pretty, #957, blue, complete, NM..**$75.00**

Outfit, Barbie, Paris Pretty, #1911, 1988, NRFB...........**$30.00**

Outfit, Barbie, Tennis Anyone?, #941, complete, NM+ .**$45.00**

Outfit, Barbie, Western Fashions, w/boots & hat, 1983, MIP **$25.00**

Outfit, Francie, #1256, complete, EX+......................**$65.00**

Outfit, Francie, Dance Party, #1257, dress only, EX ...**$10.00**

Outfit, Francie, Gold Rush, #1222, complete, EX+......**$65.00**

Outfit, Francie, Leather Limelight, #1269, complete, NM+..**$125.00**

Outfit, Francie, Pretty Frilly, #3366, EX **$25.00**

Outfit, Ken, Cheerful Chef Fashion Pak, VG **$50.00**

Outfit, Ken, College Student, #1416, complete, NM+ .**$300.00**

Outfit, Ken, Dream Boat, #785, complete, NM...........**$45.00**

Outfit, Ken, Goin' Hunting, #1409, complete, EX+.....**$45.00**

Outfit, Ken, In Training, #780, complete, M...............**$18.00**

Outfit, Ken, Night Scene, #1496, complete, NM.........**$35.00**

Outfit, Ken, Rally Days, #788, complete, NM.............**$35.00**

Outfit, Ken, Sleeper Set, #781, blue, complete, NM....**$40.00**

Outfit, Skipper, Chilly Chums, #1973, complete, M **$40.00**

Outfit, Skipper, Fashion Collectibles, #1943, coat, 1980, MIP **$4.00**

Outfit, Skipper, Happy Birthday, #1919, dress only, G **$12.00**

Outfit, Skipper, Ice Cream 'N Cake, #1970, complete, M.**$35.00**

Outfit, Skipper, Red Sensation, #1901, complete, EX..**$40.00**

Vehicle, Classy Corvette, #9612, 1976, NRFB.............**$35.00**

Vehicle, Country Camper, #4994, 1970, NRFB............**$35.00**

Vehicle, Ferrari, #3564, 1988, white, MIB.................**$50.00**

Vehicle, Star Cycle, #2149, 1978, MIB **$20.00**

Vehicle, Travelin' Trailer, #5489, NRFB **$25.00**

Gift Sets

Army Barbie & Ken, department-store special, 1993, NRFB..**$45.00**

Barbie Denim Fun, #4893, 1989, MIB **$50.00**

Barbie Dream Wedding, 1993, NRFB **$45.00**

Beach Fun at McDonalds, department-store special, 1993, NRFB..**$35.00**

Dance Magic Barbie & Ken, #5409, 1990, MIB **$45.00**

Disney Barbie & Friends, 1991, NRFB **$65.00**

Disney Weekend Barbie & Ken, 1993, NRFB **$65.00**

Dolls of the World, 1995, NRFB **$65.00**

Rollerblade Barbie Snack 'N Surf, 1992, NRFB...........**$45.00**

Superstar Barbie Piano Concert, 1990, NRFB **$25.00**

Miscellaneous

Wallet, red vinyl, 1962, NM, $55.00. (Photo courtesy of June Moon.)

Autograph book, Barbie, 1961, unused, M..................**$95.00**

Book, Barbie's New York Summer, Random House, 1962, EX+ **$30.00**

Booklet, Fashion & Play Accessories by Mattel, EX....**$25.00**

Booklet, World of Barbie Fashions, #1, EX **$10.00**

Coin purse, Skipper, 1964, blue, EX...........................**$30.00**

Coloring book, Barbie Busy Fun Book, Barbie w/short hair, Whitman, 1973, G **$10.00**

Doll box, Ken, 1963, VG..**$50.00**

Doll box, Skipper, 1963, G **$35.00**

Figurine, 1961 Ballerina, Danbury Mint, 1993, NRFB .**$30.00**

Jewelry box, red, 1963, EX **$50.00**
Magazine, Barbie Bazaar, March/April, 1992, EX **$25.00**
Picture Maker, complete w/6 cards to draw scenes, Mattel, 1969, NMIB..**$60.00**
Postcards, set of 12, M (in original envelope)............**$40.00**
Powder-puff mitt, Barbie, 1961, MIB **$125.00**
Sheet set, Barbie, Stevens, 1991, twin-size, MIP.........**$25.00**
Tea set, Barbie's 35th Anniversary, 1994, NRFB..........**$45.00**
Wallet, Skipper in Masquerade, blue, 1964, EX............**$30.00**

Barware

Our economy may be 'on the rocks,' but cocktail shakers are becoming the hot new collectible of the nineties. These micro skyscrapers are now being saved for the enjoyment of future generations, much like the 1930s buildings saved from destruction by landmarks preservation committees of today.

Cocktail shakers — the words just conjure up visions of glamour and elegance. Seven hard shakes over your right shoulder and you can travel back in time, back to the glamour of Hollywood movie sets with Fred Astaire and Ginger Rogers and luxurious hotel lounges with gleaming chrome; the world of F. Scott Fitzgerald and *The Great Gatsby*; *The Thin Man* movie showing William Powell instructing a bartender on the proper way to shake a martini — the reveries are endless.

An original American art form, cocktail shakers reflect the changing nature of various styles of art, design, and architecture of the era between WWI and WWII. We see the graceful lines of Art Nouveau in the early twenties being replaced by the rage for jagged geometric modern design. The geometric cubism of Picasso that influenced so many designers of the twenties was replaced with the craze for streamline design of thirties. Cocktail shakers of the early thirties were taking the shape of the new deity of American architecture, the skyscraper, thus giving the appearance of movement and speed in a slow economy.

Cocktail shakers served to penetrate the gloom of depression, ready to propel us into the future of prosperity like some Buck Rogers rocket ship — both perfect symbols of generative power, of our perpetration into better times ahead.

Cocktail shakers and architecture took on the aerodynamically sleek industrial design of the automobile and airship. It was as Norman Bel Geddes said: 'a quest for speed.' All sharp edges and corners were rounded off. This trend was the theme of the day, as even the sharp notes of jazz turned into swing.

Cocktail shakers have all the classic qualifications of a premium collectible. They are easily found at auctions, antique and secondhand shops, flea markets, and sales. They can be had in all price ranges. They require little study to identify one manufacturer or period from another, and lastly they are not easily reproduced.

The sleek streamline cocktail shakers of modern design are valued by collectors of today. Those made by Revere, Chase, and Manning Bowman have taken the lead in this race. Also commanding high prices are those shakers of unusual design such as penguins, zeppelins, dumbells, bowling pins, town crier bells, airplanes, even ladies' legs. They're all out there — waiting, waiting to be found, waiting to be recalled to life, to hear the clank of ice cubes, and to again become the symbol of elegance.

For more information we recommend *Vintage Bar Ware, An Identification and Value Guide*, by Stephen Visakay (Collector Books).

Advisor: Steve Visakay (See Directory, Barware)

Cocktail napkin, brown linen w/cocktail shaker design, ca 1930s, set of 6 ....**$40.00**
Cocktail napkin, linen w/recipe & cocktail glass design, set of 6, from $20 to...**$30.00**
Cocktail napkin, linen w/rooster motif, ca 1930s, 4x6", each, from $1 to..**$2.00**
Cocktail shaker, aluminum, anodized gold, silver or red, stamped Mirro, ca 1950s, 8¼", each, from $8 to..**$10.00**
Cocktail shaker, amber glass, footed, silverplated top w/juicer, ca 1930s, from $45 to **$75.00**

Cocktail shaker, chrome with yellow Bakelite handle, top knob and spout, Krome Kraft, Farber Bros, ca 1937, from $45.00 to $65.00. (Photo courtesy of Steve Visakay.)

Cocktail shaker, chrome cylinder w/black horizontal stripes, stamped Chase, ca 1930s, from $45 to..................**$55.00**
Cocktail shaker, chrome cylinder w/blue Bakelite ball top, stamped Chase, ca 1930s, from $55 to..................**$75.00**
Cocktail shaker, chrome cylinder w/white plastic knob at top, stamped Chase, ca 1930s, from $65 to..........**$75.00**
Cocktail shaker, clear glass, pink & black silkscreened rooster design, anodized-gold aluminum top, from $75 to....**$95.00**
Cocktail shaker, clear glass w/silkscreened elephant design, chrome top, from $65 to **$75.00**
Cocktail shaker, clear glass w/silkscreened gold & recipe design, ca 1950s, from $35 to **$45.00**
Cocktail shaker, cobalt glass w/silkscreened angelfish, Sportsman Series, Hazel Atlas, from $45 to..........**$55.00**

Cocktail shaker, cobalt glass w/silkscreened dancing sailor, Sportsman Series, Hazel Atlas, chrome top, from $125 to **$140.00**

Cocktail shaker, cobalt glass w/silkscreened horse & rider, Sportsman Series, Hazel Atlas, chrome top, from $45 to **$65.00**

Cocktail shaker, cobalt glass w/silkscreened sailboat design, Sportsman Series, Hazel Atlas, chrome top, from $65 to **$75.00**

Cocktail shaker, cobalt glass w/silkscreened windmill design, Sportman Series, Hazel Atlas, chrome top, from $45 to **$55.00**

Cocktail shaker, cobalt or ruby glass w/chrome top, ca 1930s-40s, each, from $45 to **$75.00**

Cocktail shaker, frosted glass w/red plastic top, top-pouring style, Libbey Glass, ca 1940, from $25 to **$45.00**

Cocktail shaker, hammer tone & plain finish chrome, black composite handle, Krome Kraft, party size, 15", from $75 to **$95.00**

Cocktail shaker, pottery base w/chrome & Bakelite recipe-dial top, marked Epcolite, Trenton NJ, from $80 to....**$120.00**

Cocktail shaker, pressed glass w/diamond pattern, red, green or yellow plastic recipe-dial top, each, from $25 to **$35.00**

Cocktail shaker, ruby glass w/chrome top, silkscreened recipe design, ca 1930s, from $45 to **$65.00**

Cocktail shaker, skyscraper-styled chrome, top pouring, stamped Revere...**$200.00**

Cocktail shaker, skyscraper-styled chrome w/walnut top, stamped Manning Bowman, from $65 to..............**$75.00**

Cocktail shaker, skyscraper-styled chrome w/yellow Bakelite top, stamped Manning Bowman, from $75 to......**$85.00**

Cocktail shaker, teapot-styled chrome, stamped Farberware, 1930s, from $25 to **$30.00**

Cocktail shaker, teapot-styled chrome w/red plastic handle, unmarked & stamped chrome, from $25 to **$35.00**

Ice bucket, aluminum, anodized apple shape, ca 1950s, 8x8", from $15 to...**$30.00**

Ice bucket, clear glass w/silkscreened pink elephants ..**$20.00**

Ice bucket, cobalt glass w/silkscreened angelfish, windmill, horse & rider, Sportsman Series, Hazel Atlas, from $35 to **$55.00**

Ice bucket, cobalt glass w/silkscreened sailboat or dancing sailor, Sportsman Series, Hazel Atlas, each, from $35 to..**$55.00**

Ice bucket, frosted glass w/silver bands, ca 1930s, 4½x5" dia, from $20 to...**$30.00**

Ice bucket, pressed glass w/chrome handle, 1930s, 5x5¼" dia, from $25 to **$35.00**

Ice bucket, ruby or cobalt glass w/silver-overlay bands, 1930s, from $35 to **$45.00**

Martini glass, clear, ca 1940s-50s, each, from $1 to **$3.00**

Martini glass, cobalt, ca 1930s, 4½", from $20 to........**$25.00**

Martini glass, frosted w/applied silver bands, each, from $3 to **$5.00**

Recipe book, Here's How, by WC Whitfield, wood covers, 1941, from $12 to..**$17.00**

Recipe book, Just Cocktails, by WC Whitfield, wood covers, 1939, from $12 to..**$17.00**

Bauer Pottery

Undoubtedly the most easily recognized product of the Bauer Pottery Company who operated from 1909 until 1962 in Los Angeles, California, was their colorful 'Ring' dinnerware (made from 1932 until sometime in the early sixties). You'll recognize it by its bright solid colors: Jade Green, Chinese Yellow, Royal Blue, Light Blue, Orange-Red, Black and White, and by its pattern of closely aligned ribs. They made other lines of dinnerware as well. They're collectible, too, although by no means as easily found.

Bauer also made a line of Gardenware vases and flowerpots for the florist trade. To give you an idea of their values, a 12" vase from this line would bring about $75.00 to $100.00.

To further your knowledge of Bauer, we recommend *The Collector's Encyclopedia of California Pottery* by Jack Chipman.

Al Fresco, casserole, speckled, green, or gray, w/lid, 1½-qt..**$30.00**

Al Fresco, cup & saucer, coffee brown or Dubonnet.**$18.00**

Brusche Al Fresco, vegetable bowl, speckled colors, 9½" ..**$15.00**

El Chico, cup & saucer, any color..............................**$45.00**

El Chico, plate, any color, 9" **$35.00**

La Linda, gravy boat, any color **$20.00**

La Linda, pitcher, green, yellow, or turquoise, w/ice lip, 2-qt..**$65.00**

La Linda, ramekin bowl, burgundy or dark brown.....**$10.00**

La Linda, tumbler, burgundy or dark brown, 8-oz......**$20.00**

Monterey, fruit bowl, white, 6"..................................**$22.00**

Monterey, plate, any color, 6".....................................**$8.50**

Monterey, platter, all colors but white, oval, 12" **$30.00**

Monterey Moderne, butter dish, all colors but black, round..**$45.00**

Monterey Moderne, dessert bowl, black, 5" **$25.00**

Monterey Moderne, grill plate, round.........................**$20.00**

Plain, bean pot, all colors but black, no handle, 1-pt ..**$45.00**

Plain, coffee server, all colors but black, open...........**$40.00**

Plain, sugar bowl, all colors but black, w/lid..............**$45.00**

Ring, ashtray, black, 3" dia...**$75.00**

Ring, coffeepot, bright orange, 8x9", from $100.00 to $150.00. (Photo courtesy Michael John Verlangieri.)

Ring, cookie jar, yellow, jade green, or light blue....**$200.00**

Ring, mixing bowl, olive, chartreuse or red-brown, #24, 1-qt..**$30.00**

Ring, pickle dish, all colors but black.........................**$45.00**

Ring, sherbet, orange-red, dark blue, or burgundy **$50.00**

Ring, tumbler, black, cylinder w/no handle, 6-oz.......**$45.00**

Ring, tumbler, light blue or olive, raffia-wrapped handle, 6-oz **$35.00**

Beatles Collectibles

Possibly triggered by John Lennon's death in 1980, Beatles fans, recognizing that their dreams of the band ever reuniting were gone along with him, began to collect memorabilia of all types. Recently some of the original Beatles material has sold at auction with high-dollar results. Handwritten song lyrics, Lennon's autographed high school textbook, and even the legal agreement that was drafted at the time the group disbanded are among the one-of-a-kind multi-thousand dollar sales recorded.

Unless you plan on attending sales of this caliber, you'll be more apt to find the commercially produced memorabilia that literally flooded the market during the sixties when the Fab Four from Liverpool made their unprecedented impact on the entertainment world. A word about their 45 rpm records: they sold in such mass quantities that unless the record is a 'promotional,' made to send to radio stations or for jukebox distribution, they have very little value. Once a record has lost much of its originial gloss due to wear and handling, becomes scratched, or has writing on the label, its value is minimal. Even in near-mint condition, $4.00 to $6.00 is plenty to pay for a 45 rpm (much less if it's worn), unless the original picture sleeve is present. (An exception is the white-labeled Swan recording of 'She Loves You/I'll Get You'.) A Beatles picture sleeve is usually valued at $30.00 to $40.00, except for the rare 'Can't Buy Me Love,' which is worth ten times that amount. (Beware of reproductions!) Albums of any top recording star or group from the fifties and sixties are becoming very collectible, and the Beatles are among the most popular. Just be very critical of condition! An album must be in at least excellent condition to bring a decent price.

See also Celebrity Dolls; Movie Posters; Records; Sheet Music.

Advisor: Bojo/Bob Gottuso (See Directory, Character and Personality Collectibles)

Newsletter: *Beatlefan*
P.O. Box 33515
Decatur, GA 30033; Send SASE for information

Newsletter: *The Working Class Hero*
3311 Niagara St.
Pittsburgh, PA 15213-4223; Published 3 times per year; send SASE for information.

Beatles Buddies, set of 4 prints, Beatles Fan Club Membership card on header, MIP (sealed)...........**$80.00**
Brooch, George's photo on plastic guitar, VG (original card)..**$35.00**
Cake decorations, miniature replicas of the Revell dolls, 3", EX...**$60.00**
Charms, black plastic records w/faces & labels, from gumball machine, ¾", set of 4 ....**$30.00**
Coin holder, black rubber squeeze type w/black & white head shots w/first names, EX **$45.00**
Diary, vinyl w/black & white photos, 1965, 3x4", EX...**$30.00**

Doll, George w/instrument, inflatable purple vinyl, 13", EX **$30.00**

Dolls, Applause, 1988, complete set in Sgt. Pepper costumes with original stands and tags, 22", M, $385.00. (Photo courtesy of June Moon.)

Figures, hand-painted resin, set of 4, 1985 recast, 6", NM...**$150.00**
Figures, lead, set of 4 in snow-scene pose from the movie Help!, NM **$90.00**
Frisbee, Rock 'N Roll Music LP promo, 1976, 9" dia, VG...**$35.00**
Hairbrush, Genco, 1964, MIP.......................................**$40.00**
Handkerchief, With Love From Me to You, United Kingdom, 8½", VG **$35.00**
Hangers, black & white diecut cardboard shoulder images of George or Ringo, w/inserts, VG+, each.............**$130.00**
Headband, Love the Beatles, Better Wear, MIP, from $55 to..**$70.00**
Iron-on transfers, set of 4, Star Trip, 1975, 3" dia, MIP (sealed)...**$25.00**
Key chain, Come Together, new, M............................**$15.00**
Key chain, Yellow Submarine, 1968, 6x2½", VG **$35.00**
Locket, plastic over front photo w/11 black & white photos inside, brass ribbon & pin top, NM **$100.00**
Mobile, punch-out characters from Yellow Submarine w/hanging string, Sunshine Art Studios, MIP (sealed)................**$160.00**
Mobile, 4 punch-out portraits w/stage, Whitman, EX..**$150.00**
Music box, All My Loving, laminated black box w/glossy color photo on front, 2½x4½x6½", EX................**$40.00**
Pencil case, yellow vinyl w/group image & autographs, zipper closure, EX **$140.00**
Pennant, I Love the Beatles w/hearts on red background, 29", VG+..**$110.00**
Playing cards, green w/gold trim on white border, Apple Records, unused, M (hard plastic case) **$120.00**
Police, puffy stickers, set of 5, EX................................**$5.00**
Pop-Out Art Decorations, Yellow Submarine, King Features, 1968, M **$35.00**
Ring, gold metal w/group photo, EX............................**$45.00**
Rings, flasher type, blue, set of 4, EX (beware of reproductions)...**$65.00**
Scrapbook, stickers in corner, Whitman, G **$35.00**

Stage for Sgt Pepper dolls, multicolored cardboard, Applause, EX......**$50.00**

Stationery, Yellow Submarine, set of 20 w/matching envelopes, Flying Horseman, MIB (sealed)......**$45.00**

Stick pin, hand-painted diecut Yellow Submarine, 1", EX..**$35.00**

Switchplate, Yellow Sumarine Snapping Turk, MIP (sealed)......**$25.00**

Tote bag, plastic w/handle, original hang tag, Japan, 1966, 14x13", VG......**$125.00**

Wallet, bifold, brown vinyl w/pictures under plastic, Florida on back, EX......**$200.00**

Wallpaper, single panel, 1964, 21x21", VG+......**$30.00**

Watercolor set, complete w/Yellow Submarine pictures & paint, lg, M (VG+ box)......**$135.00**

Wig, Lowell Toys, M (VG+ card)......**$110.00**

Beer Cans

In the mid-1930s, beer came in flat-top cans that often carried instructions on how to use the triangular punch-type opener. The 'cone-top' can was patented about 1935, and in the 1960s both types were replaced by the aluminum beer can with the pull-tab opener. There are hundreds of brands and variations available to the collector today. Most are worth very little, but we've tried to list a few of the better ones to help you get a feel for the market.

Condition is very, very important! Collectors grade them as follows: 1) rust-free, in 'new' condition; 2) still no rust, but a few scratches or tiny dents are acceptable; 3) a little faded, minor scratching, maybe a little rusting; 4) all of the above only more pronounced. The numbers you'll see at the end of our description lines refer to these grading numbers. The letters 'IRTP' in some lines stand for 'Internal Revenue Tax Paid.'

Advisor: Steve Gordon, G&G Pawnbrokers (See Directory, Beer Cans and Breweriana)

Newsletter: *Beer Cans and Brewery Collectibles*
Beer Can Collectors of America
747 Merus Ct.
Fenton, MO 63026-2092; phone or Fax 314-343-6486; Subscription: $30 per year for US residents; includes 6 issues and right to attend national CANvention®

Club: National Association Breweriana Advertising
2343 Met-To-Wee Lane
Wauwatosa, WI, 53226; 414-257-0158. Membership: $20 (U.S.), $30 (Canada), $40 (Overseas); Publishes *The Breweriana Collector* and membership Directory; Holds annual convention

Acme Englishtown Brand Ale, gold can w/horse & rider, IRTP, flat-top, 12-oz, 1......**$125.00**

Anoka Halloween Festival 1978, orange & black, pull tab, 12-oz, 1, from 50¢ to......**$1.00**

Billy Falls City, pull tab, from 50¢ to......**$1.00**

Bilow New Year 1979, pull tab, 1, from 50¢ to......**$1.00**

Bix, white w/brown letters, 2 labels, pull tab, 12-oz, 1, from 50¢ to......**$1.00**

Blatz, pull tab, 1, from 50¢ to......**$1.00**

Blatz Bock Beer, flat top, new lid, 12-oz, 1......**$15.00**

Bobs, gold & black, pull tab, 1......**$.50**

Brew 102 Beer, pull tab, 16-oz, 1......**$5.00**

Brown Derby Pilsener Beer, flat top, w/instructions on how to open, 12-oz, 3+......**$20.00**

Budweiser Big Size, flat top, 16-oz, 1......**$15.00**

Budweiser Lager, white can w/red letters, flat top, 16-oz, 1......**$1.00**

Budweiser Lager Beer, gold w/white stars, IRTP, flat top, 1......**$20.00**

Budweiser Lager Beer, Withdrawn Free of Revenue Tax, gold w/white stars, flat top, 1......**$70.00**

Bull Dog Ale, white label on metallic green, flat top, 1...**$30.00**

Bull Dog Malt Liquor, black, red & white, flat top, 12-oz, 1......**$18.00**

Busch Bavarian Beer, Aged Slow Cold, blue & white can w/mountain scene, flat top, 12-oz, 1......**$8.00**

Chippewa Falls 1st Annual Water Days, pull tab, 2......**$1.00**

Coors Export Lager Beer, flat top, 12-oz, 1......**$100.00**

Drewery's Lager Beer, flat top, IRTP, w/instructions on how to open, 12-oz, 2+......**$20.00**

Eagles, multicolor w/single label, pull tab, 12-oz, 1.....**$1.00**

Eastside Beer, cone top, IRTP, 12-oz, 1......**$45.00**

Ebling, crowntainer, IRTP, silver & red on silver, 12-oz, 1......**$35.00**

Elder Brau Beer, Grace Brothers Brewing Co, red seal on white, flat top, 12-oz, 1......**$60.00**

Falls City Beer, flat top, w/instructions on how to open, 12-oz, 4......**$15.00**

**Falstaff, cone top,
12-oz, VG, $40.00.**

Falstaff Draft, gold & maroon shield on white w/Draft on blue ribbon, pull tab, 12-oz, 1......**$7.50**

Fisher Beer, pull tab, 6 for $1.29 encircled above red label on white, 16-oz......**$5.00**

Fitzgerald's Beer, crowntainer, IRTP, white & black on white, 12-oz, 2+......**$15.00**

Fox Head 400 Beer, red fox's head & black lettering on cream-color can, flat top, 12-oz, 1......**$25.00**

Franken Muth Beer, 'Mel-O-Dry,' flat top, 12-oz, 1.....**$20.00**

Garrison, orange w/white label, pull tab, 12-oz, 1......**$1.00**

GB Beer, flat top, blue & gold, 12-oz, 1......**$95.00**

Gennessee Beer, red lettering on white label surrounded in black on gold can, flat top, 12-oz, 1.....................$15.00

Grain Belt Premium, cone top, 1 ....$15.00

Hanley Lager Beer, green can w/single label, tab top, 12-oz, 1 ....$2.50

Harley Milwaukee 1988, aluminum, 1......................$1.00

Holstein Centennial, black w/white label, pull tab, 12-oz, 1 ....$1.00

Huber, cone top, white & red on white, gold trim, 12-oz, 2+ $30.00

Hunderjahriges Jubilaum, white w/blue letters & covered wagon, pull tab, 12-oz, 1 ....$1.00

Iron City Beer, black & white on red background, cone top, 1 ....$125.00

Iron City Penguins, stainless steel, 1 ....$1.00

Jaguar Beer, red label on spotted can that resembles jaguar markings, punch top, 12-oz, EX $25.00

Jax, 'Go Texan,' red & yellow, pull tab, 1................$100.00

Jax, white w/red letters & gold bands, pull tab, 12-oz, 1 ..$3.00

JB, red & white w/single label, pull tab, 12-oz............$1.00

King Turkey, red w/single label, pull tab, 12-oz, 1 ......$1.00

Knickerbocker Beer, New York's Famous Beer, flat top, 16-oz, 1...$35.00

Krewes Premium Light, light blue w/blue tiger & red letters, pull tab, 12-oz, 1..$1.00

Meister Brau Lite Brand, white w/blue letters & yellow trim, pull tab, 12-oz, 1..$3.00

Meister Brau Real Draft, woodgrain w/white label & Draft in red letters, flat top, 12-oz, 1..............................$8.00

Michelob Beer, embossed gold can w/2 labels & vertical ribbons, pull tab, 12-oz, 1................................$4.50

Milwaukee Brand Premium Beer, white w/red letters & gold trim, pull tab, 1 ....$1.00

Munich Light Beer, white w/blue label & gold trim, pull tab, 12-oz $3.00

Munich Light Lager, white w/blue label & gold trim, pull tab, stainless steel, 1..$2.00

Narragansett Beer, flat top, 16-oz, 2+ $15.00

Narragansett Beer, pull tab, 1964, 16-oz, 1...............$10.00

National Bohemian Pale Beer, flat top, new top & bottom, 16-oz, 1-..$35.00

Neuwiler Light Lager Beer, bank top, 8-oz, 1- $20.00

O'Keenan's St Patrick's 1979, stainless steel, 1 ....$1.00

Oertels '92 Lager Beer, crowntainer, 12-oz, 1-...........$35.00

Old Chicago Lager, yellow w/red label & gold trim, pull tab, 12-oz, 1 ....$3.00

Old German Beer, black w/white letters, cone top, 12-oz, 1-...$125.00

Old German Beer, red, white & yellow, cone top, IRTP, 12-oz, 1 ....$30.00

Olde English 600 Malt Liquor, pull tab, full, 16-oz, 1.$40.00

Olde Virginia Special, cone top, 12-oz, 1-...................$60.00

Pabst Blue Ribbon, white can w/red ribbon, flat top, 12-oz, from $1 to $2.00

Peter Hand Extra Light, white w/blue letters, pull tab, 12-oz, 1 ....$3.00

Pfeiffer Famous Beer, woodgrain w/metallic gold bands, pull tab, 12-oz, 1..$3.00

Pikes Peak Malt Liquor, flat top, 8-oz, 1-...................$20.00

Point Bicentennial, stainless steel, 1...........................$1.00

Prior Beer, red, white & black, flat top, 12-oz, 2+......$28.00

Railfans Special, multicolor photo of train, pull tab, 12-oz, 1 ....$3.50

Rainier Beer Not-So-Light, flat top, lower case script letters at bottom, 12-oz, 1..$25.00

Rainier Beer Special Export, flat top, 12-oz, 1 ....$100.00

Rainier Old Stock Ale, flat top, lettering within decorative oval border, 12-oz, 1-..................................$25.00

Red Fox Beer, cone top, 12-oz, 4..............................$38.00

Schell's, It's a Grand Old Beer on maroon, pull tab, 12-oz, 1 ....$3.00

Schell's Hunters Special, multicolored w/pheasant, pull tab, 12-oz, 1..$1.00

Schlitz Malt Liquor, pull tab, 1975, 24-oz, 1................$2.00

Schlitz Tall Boy, flat top, 1969, 24-oz, 2+ $4.00

Schmidt Betsy Ross 1976, 1, from 50¢ to....................$1.00

Schmidt Draft Beer, white w/red label, pull tab, 12-oz ..$2.00

Schmidt Extra Special Beer, yellow w/black label, pull tab, 12-oz, 1 ....$3.00

State Flag, shows Ohio state flag, pull tab, 12-oz, 1.....$1.00

State Line, white w/2 labels, pull tab, 12-oz, 1 ....$.50

Sunshine Premium Beer, cone top, full, 12-oz, 2........$60.00

Tavern Pale Beer, red logo on silver, flat top, scratches & light rust, 12-oz, 3..$10.00

Tropical Extra-Fine Ale, gold w/white label, pull tab, 12-oz, 1 ....$10.00

Walter's Beer, red, white & black, flat top (new lid), 12-oz, 2...$3.00

Walter's Light Ale 1976, stainless steel, 1 ....$1.00

Wildcat, red w/label, pull tab, 12-oz, 1........................$1.00

Wilmington Catfish Days, red w/1 label, pull tab, 12-oz, 1 ....$.50

Wooden Shoe Lager Beer, cone top, 12-oz, 1-............$50.00

Xmas Brew Beer, yellow, pull tab, 12-oz, 1 ....$1.00

Zodiac Malt Liquor, silver w/blue emblem, pull tab, 12-oz, 1, from $1 to...$2.00

Bells

Bell collectors claim that bells rank second only to the wheel as being useful to mankind. Down through the ages bells have awakened people in the morning, called them to meals and prayers, and readied them to retire at night. We have heard them called rising bells, Angelus Bells (for deaths), noon bells, Town Crier bells (for important announcements), and curfew bells. Souvenir bells are often the first type collected, with interest spreading to other contemporaries then on to the old, valuable bells. As far as limited edition bells are concerned, the fewer made per bell, the better. (For example a bell made in an edition of 25,000 will not appreciate as much as one from an edition of 5,000.)

For further information we recommend *World of Bells #5, Bell Tidings, Lure of Bells, Collectible Bells, More Bell Lore,* and *Bells Now and Long Ago* by Dorothy Malone Anthony.

Advisor: Dorothy Malone Anthony (See Directory, Bells)

Newsletter: *The Bell Tower*
The American Bell Association
Charles Blake
P.O. Box 172
Shoreham, VT 05770

Ormolu, stork and wolf handle (from La Fontaine poem), nodder type, 4½", $425.00. (Photo courtesy of Dorothy Malone Anthony.)

Brass, lady figural, ruffled skirt, 6x3½" **$75.00**
Brass, school type, 6" **$35.00**
Brass, sleigh, 30 graduated bells on leather strap.....**$290.00**
Brass, sleigh, 4 on arched metal strap **$40.00**
Brass, St Peter's cross atop, 7x4⅛" **$200.00**
Brass, warrior's head embossed each side, 4" **$60.00**
Cast iron, upright farm type, Crystal Metal #2..........**$125.00**
Copper, cow bell, lg, EX **$12.50**
Enamel over silver, Chinese, oval base, 4½" **$85.00**
Glass, custard w/smocking pattern, original clapper..**$90.00**
Glass, pressed crystal w/hexagonal metal handle, glass clapper **$25.00**
Silver, cherub figural, hallmark................................**$150.00**

Birthday Angels

Not at all hard to find and still reasonably priced, birthday angels are fun to assemble into 12-month sets, and since there are many different series to look for, collecting them can be challenging as well as enjoyable. Generally speaking, angels are priced by the following factors: 1) company — look for Lefton, Napco, Norcrest, and Enesco marks or labels (unmarked or unknown sets are of less value); 2) application of flowers, bows, gold trim, etc. (the more detail, the more valuable); 3) use of rhinestones (which will also increase the price); 4) age; and 5) quality of the workmanship involved, detail and accuracy of paint.

Advisors: Denise and James Atkinson (See Directory, Birthday Angels)

#1194, angel of the month series, white hair, 5", each, from $18 to..**$20.00**
#1294, angel of the month, white hair, 5", each, from $18 to.**$20.00**
#1300, boy angels, wearing suit, white hair, 6", each, from $22 to..**$25.00**

#1600 Pal Angel, month series of both boy & girl, 4", each, from $10 to..**$15.00**
Enesco, angels on round base w/flower of the month, gold trim, each, from $15 to..........................**$18.00**
High Mountain Quality, colored hair, 7", each, from $30 to..**$32.00**
Kelvin, C-230, holding flower of the month, 4½", each, from $15 to..**$20.00**
Kelvin, C-250, holding flower of the month, 4½", each, from $15 to..**$20.00**
Lefton, #1323, angel of the month, bisque, each, from $18 to..**$22.00**
Lefton, #2600, birthstone on skirt, 3¼", each, from $25 to..**$30.00**
Lefton, #3332, bisque, w/basket of flowers, 4", each, from $18 to..**$22.00**
Lefton, #489, holding basket of flowers, 4", each, from $25 to..**$30.00**
Lefton, #556, boy w/blue wings, 5", each, from $28 to..**$32.00**
Lefton, #574, day of the week series (like #8281 but not as ornate), each, from $25 to **$28.00**
Lefton, #6224, applied flower/birthstone on skirt, 4½", each, from $18 to..**$20.00**
Lefton, #627, day of the week series, 3½", each, from $28 to..**$32.00**
Lefton, #6883, square frame, day of the week & months, 3¼x4", each, from $20 to................................**$25.00**
Lefton, #6949, day of the week series in oval frames, 5", each, from $28 to..**$32.00**
Lefton, #8281, day of the week series, applied roses, each, from $30 to..**$35.00**
Lefton, #985, flower of the month, 5", each, from $25 to..**$30.00**
Lefton, AR-1987, w/ponytail, 4", each, from $18 to....**$22.00**
Lefton, 1987J, w/rhinestones, 4½", each, from $25 to ..**$30.00**
Napco, A1360-1372, angel of the month, each, from $20 to..**$25.00**
Napco, A1917-1929, boy angel of the month, each, from $20 to..**$25.00**
Napco, A4307, angel of the month, sm, each, from $22 to..**$25.00**
Napco, C1361-1373, angel of the month, each, from $20 to..**$25.00**
Napco, C1921-1933, boy angel of the month, each, from $20 to..**$25.00**
Napco, S1291, day of the week 'Belle,' each, from $22 to..**$25.00**
Napco, S1307, bell of the month, each, from $22 to..**$25.00**
Napco, S1361-1372, angel of the month, each, from $20 to..**$25.00**
Napco, S1392, oval frame angel of the month, each, from $25 to..**$30.00**
Napco, S401-413, angel of the month, each, from $20 to..**$25.00**
Napco, S429, day of the week angel (also available as planters), each, from $25 to................................**$30.00**
Norcrest, F-120, angel of the month, 4½", each, from $18 to..**$22.00**
Norcrest, F-15, angel of the month, on round base w/raised pattern on dress, 4", each, from $18 to................**$22.00**

Norcrest, F-167, bell of the month, 2¾", each, from $8 to **$12.00**

Norcrest, F-210, day of the week angel, 4½", each, from $18 to **$22.00**

Norcrest, F-23, day of the week angel, 4½", each, from $18 to **$22.00**

Norcrest, F-340, angel of the month, 5", each, from $20 to **$25.00**

Norcrest, F-535, angel of the month, 4½", each, from $20 to **$25.00**

Relco, 4¼", each, from $15 to **$18.00**

Relco, 6", each, from $18 to......................................**$22.00**

SR, angel of the month, w/birthstone & 'trait' of the month (i.e. April - innocence), each, from $20 to **$25.00**

TMJ, angel of the month, w/flower, each, from $20 to ..**$25.00**

Ucagco, white hair, 5¾", from $12 to **$15.00**

Wales, wearing long white gloves, white hair, Made in Japan, 6⅜", each, from $25 to..**$28.00**

Arnart Kewpies, in choir robes, with rhinestones, 4½", from $12.00 to $15.00 each. (Photo courtesy of Denise and James Atkinson.)

Black Americana

There are many avenues one might pursue in the broad field of Black Americana and many reasons that might entice one to become a collector. For the more serious, there are documents such as bills of sales for slaves, broadsides, and other historical artifacts. But by far, most collectors enjoy attractive advertising pieces, novelties and kitchenware items, toys and dolls, and Black celebrity memorabilia.

It's estimated that there are at least 50,000 collectors around the country today. There are large auctions devoted entirely to the sale of Black Americana. The items they feature may be as common as a homemade pot holder or a magazine or as rare as a Lux Dixie Boy clock or a Mammy cookie jar that might go for several thousand dollars. In fact, many of the cookie jars have become so valuable that they're being reproduced; so are salt and pepper shakers, so beware.

For further study, we recommend *Black Collectibles Sold in America* by P.J. Gibbs, and *Black Dolls, An Identification and Value Guide 1820 - 1991,* by Myla Perkins.

See also Advertising, Aunt Jemima; Condiment Sets; Cookie Jars; Salt and Pepper Shakers; Sheet Music; Postcards; String Holders.

Advisor: Judy Posner (See Directory, Black Americana)

Advertising store display, diecut cardboard stand-up, Golly It's Good!, animated golliwog w/glancing eyes, 10", EX.**$175.00**

Apron, golliwog in vinyl pinafore, 1950s, adult sz, NM..**$125.00**

Art plate, Tobacco Fields (from Bits of the Old South Series), family on cabin porch, Vernon Kilns, 1940, scarce, EX ...**$65.00**

Ashtray, boy & alligator, ceramic, EX..........................**$65.00**

Ashtray, clear glass, Mammy's Shanty Restaurant, Atlanta Georgia, image of Mammy in center, round w/3 rests, M........**$65.00**

Bank, watermelon slice, painted plaster, 1940s, EX....**$65.00**

Birthday card, Ah Wishes Yo' De Best Birthday That You Ever Had!, girl chef presenting cake to boy w/dog, 1940s, M...**$18.00**

Birthday card, Ah's Bringing You A Trunkful of Birthday Cheer, porter carrying trunk, EX............................**$20.00**

Book, Here Comes Golly, Gyles Brandreth, illustrated by Sara Silcock, 1979, EX **$75.00**

Book, Little Black Sambo, 1st edition, Grosset Dunlap, illustrated by Robert Moore, 21 pages, 1942, EX.......**$110.00**

Book, Rufty Tufty Flies High, Ruth Ainsworth, illustrated by DG Valentine, Heinemann Publishing, 1959, EX..**$90.00**

Book, The Story of Little Black Sambo, linen, color & black & white illustrations, 10 pages, Whitman, 1937, 7x9", EX...**$70.00**

Canister, ceramic, head shaped w/Coffee lettered on hair (lid) of tan-skinned girl w/pixie look, glancing eyes, 5", M...**$95.00**

Canister, tin, Uncle Ben's Rice, 40th-anniversary limited edition, 1943-1983, portrait w/name & colorful border, 8", EX...**$45.00**

Christmas card, It Would Be a Complete Washout if I Couldn't Wish You a Merry Christmas, Mammy at clothesline, 1930s, EX..**$25.00**

Cigar holder, painted plaster figure of boy holding box & hat flanked by match & cigar holders, early 1900s, 6", EX **$200.00**

Cigarette box, wooden w/roll top that exposes fellow jumping up w/cigarette, 1940s, EX..............................**$125.00**

Clothes brush, purse size, lady's head atop gold-tone lipstick-type tube, base twists to expose brush, 1930s, 2¾", EX...**$85.00**

Coffee tin, Luzianne, 5¼", EX......................................**$75.00**

Dice toy, wooden man in top hat unscrews to reveal miniature dice for crap shooting, marked Kobe (Japan), 1930s, EX **$150.00**

Dinner bell, ceramic, brown-skinned Mammy figure, by Carolina, Laguna Beach, 1940s, EX **$65.00**

Dish towel, banjo player sits on porch while boy & girl dance in yard, floral & watermelon border, 1930s, M **$50.00**

Dish towel, off-white cotton, embroidered image of waiter running w/dome-covered tray, EX........................**$30.00**

Doll, golliwog boy, black skin tone w/plush hair, hard plastic eyes, red corduroy pants & yellow shirt, 11", EX ..**$60.00**

Doll, Golly, Combex, squeak type, molded rubber w/nappy hair, 7" **$95.00**

Doll, slender Mammy w/straw-stuffed body & celluloid face, multipatterned short dress & scarf, long legs, earrings, EX...**$35.00**

Drinking glass, clear glass w/applied Art Deco design featuring stylized musicians, 1930s, 4¾", EX **$45.00**

Egg cup, golliwog, bright multicolor on white ceramic, 3" **$95.00**

Egg timer, diecut wooden Mammy figure w/painted red dress & bandana, white apron, 1930s, EX.....................**$95.00**

Fight program, Joe Louis vs Jersey Joe Walcott, June 23, 1943, EX **$175.00**

Figurine, celluloid, wide-eyed standing drummer wearing red jacket & blue pants, blue bow tie, 1930s, 9", EX..**$110.00**

Figurine, ceramic, brown-skinned boy w/hands behind back appears to be whistling, eyes looking up, 1930s, 4½", EX **$65.00**

Figurine, ceramic, Snowflake (Walter Lantz character), black skin, green shorts, white shirt & brown shoes, 1940s, 5", M...**$225.00**

Figurine, choir boy w/candle, bisque face w/shiny hair, glancing eyes, white robe w/gold trim, Japan, 1940s, 5", M...**$40.00**

Figurines, composition, Uncle Mose seated playing the banjo & Mammy dancing, 1930s, 2½" & 3¼", EX, pr.....**$155.00**

Get well card, Hurry Honey & Get Well, Mammy at crystal ball, 1930s, EX..**$22.00**

Handkerchief, cotton, white w/tan & brown wavy lines around edge & repeated images of dancing golliwog, 1940s, EX...**$100.00**

Hat, paper, Sambo's Restaurant logo, Cellucap, 1960s, EX **$85.00**

Humidor, terra cotta, barrel shape w/brown-skinned gent in top hat & fancy neck tie on lid, 8", EX..............**$325.00**

Iron-on transfers, Aunt Martha's #3341, complete, 1930s, M..**$60.00**

Label, Ole Vir-Gin-A Biscuit Baker, image of Mammy's face over a pan of biscuits, 1930s, 6x10", EX..............**$40.00**

Lamp, ceramic, Mammy sweeping in front of cabin shape w/airbrushed highlights, light beams through cabin windows, 5", EX..**$250.00**

Marionette, clown, composition head w/smiling face & side-glancing eyes, multipatterned cloth clothing, EX..**$100.00**

Marionette, clown, plastic head, dapper suit & hat, EX **$95.00**

Matchbook, Sambo's Restaurant, red & blue, unused, M..**$35.00**

Menu, Sambo's Restaurant, 1967, 15x6¾", EX.............**$85.00**

Menu, Thanksgiving, for Black army soldiers, 1930, EX..**$100.00**

Menu pad holder, Remember Cream of Wheat, oval image of the Cream of Wheat chef, EX **$95.00**

Mug, china, image of a golliwog atop Santa's full sack of toys, gold rim, 4", EX...**$75.00**

Napkin caddy, wooden female figure w/brown skin & basket of fruit atop head, blue skirt w/pink blouse, 6¼", EX **$85.00**

Noisemaker, metal, round w/5 different caricatures, wooden handle, 1930s, EX **$50.00**

Noisemaker, metal, shows brown-skinned dancing fellow in blue jacket & red & yellow checked pants, 1940s, EX..**$45.00**

Paperweight, cast-iron jockey figure w/brass ring, black skin in white pants & shirt, red vest & hat, 1940s, 3½", EX..**$85.00**

Patch, cloth, embroidered head images of Amos 'N Andy, Check-Double Check in script below, 1930s, 4¾" dia, EX **$100.00**

Pencil sharpener, cast-metal image of man's head w/sharpener in mouth, black skin, red lips, white eyes, 1920s, EX **$125.00**

Pillow cover, yellow w/fringe, Mammy selling pralines, Uncle Mose playing banjo & whistling boy, souvenir, 1930s, EX...**$80.00**

Pin, carved wooden image of soldier w/hand-painted features, brown skin w/khaki uniform, yellow tie, 1940s, 4", EX **$85.00**

Pincushion, velvet and cotton, ca 1920s, 4½", EX, $65.00.

Pipe stand, molded Syrocco-type material, man in white serving jacket stands between woodgrain rests, 1930s, 6", EX, A..**$125.00**

Pitcher, earthenware, repeated images of Little Black Sambo around center, painted scallop design on rim, 1930s, 3", EX **$125.00**

Planter, ceramic, black man resting on logs w/leaves, majolica, VG..**$125.00**

Plate, ceramic, In the Evening by the Moonlight arched above minstrel trio & musical notes on ivory, 1940s, 6" dia, EX **$40.00**

Plate, Golly clock series, ceramic, 8" **$60.00**

Print, Chesapeake & Ohio Railroad, linen, porter checking berth & discovering Chessie the cat asleep, 1930s, 20x19", EX..**$125.00**

Puzzle, Golly In the Strawberry Garden/Robertson's Jam Factory, 6½x8", EX **$125.00**

Puzzle, jigsaw, Beloved Belindy Diner, shows train engine marked Nice Brown Pancakes w/dining car, 1940s, 7x18", EX..**$85.00**

Recipe cards, Southern Recipe Notes, brown-skinned Mammy serving cake on box cover, dated 1954, 9x5½" box, EX **$55.00**

Record album, Little Black Sambo, 78 rpm, 2-record set, Columbia Records, 1940s, G (w/jacket)...............**$85.00**

Record album, Uncle Remus, 78 rpm, 2-record set, 1940s, EX (EX jacket & inside covers illustrated by Barnes) ..**$125.00**

Salt dip server, ceramic, brown-skinned fisherman sitting & smoking a pipe, 1940s, 5½", EX........................**$225.00**

Salt dip spoon, sterling silver, detailed full figure of boy (Johnny Griffin) eating watermelon on handle, 2¼", EX...**$85.00**

Scouring pad holder, airbrushed ceramic, dish shaped as bust of a wide-eyed Mammy, Coventry, 1940s, 5", EX ..**$95.00**

Sheet music, Melon Time Dixieland, 3 sheets separate of spine, Leo Feist Inc, 1931, EX....................**$40.00**

Sheet music, When He Plays Jazz He's Got Hot Lips, 1922, EX **$35.00**

Shopping reminder list, wooden plaque w/2 columns of foods listed, bust image of Mammy thinking above, 1940s, 9x6", EX **$90.00**

Spice rack, wooden shelf holds 6 ceramic containers painted as chefs w/black skin, glancing eyes, white & yellow, EX **$95.00**

Squeeze toy, golliwog-type boy standing w/hands up & thumbs under lapels, vinyl w/painted clothing, 1950s, 7", EX....................**$20.00**

Teapot, pottery, brown figural face w/yellow hat lid & bow tie, rosy cheeks, gold wire bail handle, 1940s, EX.......**$85.00**

Toast rack, dapper golliwogs at both ends, artist signed JB, Clarice Cliff Pottery, England, 1930s, 3½x4", M.**$200.00**

Toast rack, golliwog on motorcycle, 4"....................**$37.00**

Toothpick holder, ceramic black-skinned boy w/watermelon slice next to pot-shaped holder on wood base w/bark, EX....................**$95.00**

Towel, hand-size w/appliqued Mammy & boy, EX....**$45.00**

Toy, Bobbin' Sam, celluloid roly-poly, It Floats, It Rattles, It Rocks, LA Goodman, 1930s, MIB **$65.00**

Wall plaques, diecut wooden figures of Little Black Sambo w/open umbrella & tiger beneath palm tree, 1930s, 7¾", EX....................**$90.00**

Yo-yo, wood, red w/image of golliwog w/arms & legs spread, by Lumar Yo-Yos & Beginners, EX **$95.00**

Black Cats

Kitchenware, bookends, vases, and many other items designed as black cats were made in Japan during the 1950s and exported to the United States where they were sold by various distributors who often specified certain characteristics they wanted in their own line of cats. Common to all these lines were the red clay used in their production and the medium used in their decoration — their features were applied over the glaze with 'cold (unfired) paint.' The most collectible is a line marked (or labeled) Shafford. Shafford cats are plump and pleasant looking. They have green eyes with black pupils; white eyeliner, eyelashes, and whiskers; and red bow ties. The same design with yellow eyes was marketed by Royal, and another fairly easy-to-find 'breed' is a line by Wales with yellow eyes and gold whiskers. You'll find various other labels as well. Some collectors buy only Shafford, while others like them all.

When you evaluate your black cats, be critical of their paint. Even though no chips or cracks are present, if half of the paint is missing, you have a half-price item. Remember this when using the following values which are given for cats with near-mint to mint paint.

Ashtray, flat face, Shafford, hard to find, 3¾" **$30.00**

Ashtray, flat face, Shafford, 4¾" **$18.00**

Ashtray, head shape, not Shafford, several variations, each, from $12 to....................**$15.00**

Ashtray, head shape w/open mouth, Shafford, 3" **$18.00**

Bank, seated cat w/coin slot in top of head, Shafford .**$125.00**

Bank, upright cat, Shafford-like features, marked Tommy, 2-part, from $150 to....................**$175.00**

Cigarette lighter, Shafford, 5½", from $150 to **$175.00**

Cigarette lighter, sm cat stands on book by table lamp..**$65.00**

Condiment set, pair of 4-sided cruets with yellow-eyed embossed cat faces and pair of matching shakers in wire rack, $75.00.

Condiment set, upright cats, yellow eyes, 2 bottles & pr of matching shakers in wireware stand, row arrangement **$85.00**

Condiment set, 2 joined heads, J&M bows w/spoons (intact), Shafford, 4"....................**$75.00**

Condiment set, 2 joined heads, yellow eyes (not Shafford) **$65.00**

Cookie jar, cat's head, fierce expression, yellow eyes, brown-black glaze, heavy red clay body, lg, rare..........**$250.00**

Cookie jar, lg cat head, Shafford **$85.00**

Creamer & sugar bowl, cat-head lids are salt & pepper shakers, yellow eyes variations, 5⅜" **$50.00**

Creamer & sugar bowl, Shafford **$45.00**

Cruet, slender form, gold collar & tie, tail handle **$12.00**

Cruet, upright cat w/yellow eyes, open mouth, paw spout **$30.00**

Cruets, oil & vinegar; cojoined cats, Royal Sealy, 1-pc (or similar items w/heavier yellow-eyed cats), 7¼"........**$40.00**

Cruets, upright cats, she w/V eyes for vinegar, he w/O eyes for oil, Shafford, pr, from $50 to **$60.00**

Decanter, long cat w/red fish in his mouth as stopper...**$50.00**

Decanter, upright cat holds bottle w/cork stopper, Shafford, from $40 to....................**$50.00**

Decanter set, upright cat, yellow eyes, +6 plain wines ..**$35.00**

Decanter set, upright cat, yellow eyes, +6 wines w/cat faces **$45.00**

Demitasse pot, tail handle, bow finial, Shafford, 7½"...**$95.00**

Desk caddy, pen forms tail, spring body holds letters, 6½" **$8.00**

Egg cup, cat face on bowl, pedestal foot, Shafford **$30.00**

Grease jar, sm cat head, Shafford, scarce, from $65 to..**$75.00**

Ice bucket, cylindrical w/embossed yellow-eyed cat face, 2 sizes, each **$75.00**

Measuring cups, 4 sizes on wooden wall-mount rack w/painted cat face, Shafford, rare **$300.00**

Mug, Shafford, scarce, 4"..**$65.00**

Mug, Shafford, 3½"...**$50.00**

Paperweight, cat's head on stepped chrome base, open mouth, yellow eyes, rare...**$75.00**

Pincushion, cushion on cat's back, tongue measure ..**$25.00**

Pitcher, milk; seated upright cat, ear forms spout, tail handle, Shafford, 6" or 6½", each, from $85 to **$100.00**

Pitcher, squatting cat, pour through mouth, Shafford, rare, 5", 14½" circumference **$75.00**

Pitcher, squatting cat, pour through mouth, Shafford, scarce, 4½", 13" circumference...**$65.00**

Pitcher, squatting cat, pour through mouth, Shafford, very rare, 5½", 17" circumference, from $150 to........**$200.00**

Planter, cat & kitten in a hat, Shafford-like paint........**$25.00**

Planter, cat sits on knitted boot w/gold drawstring, Shafford-type paint, Elvin, 4¼x4½"...................................**$25.00**

Planter, upright cat, Shafford-like paint, Napco label, 6"....**$20.00**

Pot holder caddy, 'teapot' cat, 3 hooks, Shafford.....**$125.00**

Salad set, spoon & fork, funnel, 1-pc oil/vinegar cruet & salt & pepper shakers on wooden wall-mount rack, Royal Sealy **$200.00**

Salt & pepper shaker, long cat lying on back, yellow eyes, shaker each end, 10½"...**$60.00**

Salt & pepper shaker, long crouching cat, shaker in each end, Shafford, 10", from $75 to.......................................**$85.00**

Salt & pepper shakers, range size; upright cats, Shafford, scarce, 5", pr, from $40 to.......................................**$50.00**

Salt & pepper shakers, round-bodied 'teapot' cat, Shafford, pr, from $40 to...**$50.00**

Salt & pepper shakers, seated, blue eyes, Enesco label, 5¾", pr..**$15.00**

Salt & pepper shakers, upright cats, Shafford, 3¾" (watch for sightly smaller set as well), pr **$25.00**

Spice set, triangle, 3 rounded tiers of shakers, 8 in all, in wooden wall-mount triangular rack, very rare...**$350.00**

Spice set, 4 upright cat shakers hook onto bottom of wire-ware cat-face rack, Shafford, rare.......................**$350.00**

Spice set, 6 square shakers in wooden frame, Shafford...**$145.00**

Spice set, 6 square shakers in wooden frame, yellow eyes **$125.00**

Stacking tea set, mamma pot w/kitty creamer & sugar bowl, yellow eyes...**$65.00**

Stacking tea set, yellow eyes, 3 cats w/red collar, w/gold ball, 3-pc...**$65.00**

Sugar bowl/planter, sitting cat, red bow w/gold bell, Shafford-like paint, Elvin, 4" **$25.00**

Teapot, bulbous body, head lid, green eyes, Shafford, med sizes, from $40 to...**$45.00**

Teapot, bulbous body, head lid, green eyes, Shafford, 4-4½"...**$30.00**

Teapot, bulbous body, head lid, green eyes, Shafford, 7"..**$75.00**

Teapot, cat face w/double spout, Shafford, scarce, 5"...**$125.00**

Teapot, cat's face, yellow hat, blue & white eyes, pink ears, lg from $40 to **$50.00**

Teapot, crouching cat, paw up to right ear is spout, inset green jewel eyes, 8½" long.................................**$60.00**

Teapot, panther-like appearance, gold eyes, sm........**$20.00**

Teapot, upright, slender cat (not ball-shaped), lift-off head, Shafford, rare, 8"..**$175.00**

Teapot, upright cat w/paw spout, yellow eyes & red bow, Wales, 8¼"...**$60.00**

Teapot, yellow eyes, 1-cup.......................................**$30.00**

Teapot, yellow-eyed cat's face embossed on front of standard bulbous teapot shape, wire bale, from $50 to...**$60.00**

Thermometer, cat w/yellow eyes stands w/paw on round thermometer face...**$30.00**

Toothpick holder, cat by vase atop book, Occupied Japan...**$12.00**

Tray, flat face, wicker handle, Shafford, lg..............**$125.00**

Utensil (fork, spoon or strainer), wood handle, Shafford, rare, each...**$90.00**

Utensil rack, flat-backed cat w/3 slots for utensils, cat only...**$90.00**

Wall pocket, flat-backed 'teapot' cat, Shafford............**$95.00**

Wine, embossed cat's face, green eyes, Shafford, sm..**$20.00**

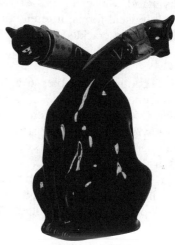

Cruets, oil and vinegar; cojoined cats, Royal Sealy, 1-pc (or similar items with heavier yellow-eyed cats), 7¼", $40.00.

Blair Dinnerware

American dinnerware has been a popular type of collectible for several years, and the uniquely styled lines of Blair Ceramics, who operated in Ozark, Missouri, for a few years from the mid-forties until the early fifties are especially appealing, though not often seen except in the Midwest. Gay Plaid, recognized by its squared-off shapes and brush-stroke design (in lime, brown, and dark green on white), is the one you'll find most often. Several other lines were made as well. You'll be able to recognize them easily enough, since most pieces (except for the smaller items) are marked.

Bowl, Rick Rack, round **$12.00**

Bowl, vegetable; Bird, divided, rectangular w/tab handles..**$32.00**

Casserole, Gay Plaid, rope handles...........................**$25.00**

Creamer, Bamboo, pitcher form, rope handle.............**$17.50**
Cup & saucer, Gay Plaid, rope handle......................**$12.00**
Mug, Gay Plaid, from $15 to....................................**$18.00**
Nut dish, Autumn Leaf..**$8.00**
Pitcher, Gay Plaid, rope handle, ice lip **$45.00**
Plate, Bamboo, 8" square **$8.00**
Plate, Bird, 6" **$17.50**
Plate, Bird, 9¾"..**$16.00**
Plate, Gay Plaid, 9¾"..**$12.00**
Platter, Yellow Plaid, divided, w/3 sections, oval **$25.00**
Salt & pepper shakers, Bird, pr **$15.00**
Salt & pepper shakers, Gay Plaid, pr........................**$12.50**
Sugar bowl, Bamboo, rope handle, w/lid **$17.50**
Tumbler, Gay Plaid, from $10 to..............................**$14.00**

Blenko

Blenko glass has been made in Milton, West Virginia, since the 1920s. Even today, all glassware produced there is made entirely by hand. Characteristics of Blenko glass are vibrant colors and unusual forms. It often contains seed-like bubbles, or it may have a crackled appearance.

See also Crackle Glass.

Ashtray, med blue, controlled bubbles, 6½" dia **$10.00**
Bookends, owl, green, w/labels, pr **$30.00**
Candlestick, green w/crystal woven stem...................**$35.00**
Pitcher, deep blue w/seed bubbles, #361P.................**$25.00**
Plate, blue w/crimped rim, 12" **$25.00**
Punch cup, crystal w/colored handle **$10.00**
Tumbler, iced tea; deep amethyst, footed **$15.00**
Tumbler, Rosette, light blue, #445, 2½", 8 for............**$50.00**
Vase, amethyst w/optic ribs, flared, footed, 11½".......**$55.00**

Blue Ridge Dinnerware

Blue Ridge has long been popular with collectors, and prices are already well established, but that's not to say there aren't a few good buys left around. There are! It was made by a company called Southern Potteries, who operated in Erwin, Tennessee, from sometime in the latter thirties until the mid-fifties. They made literally hundreds of patterns, all hand decorated. Some collectors prefer to match up patterns, while others like to mix them together for a more eclectic table setting.

One of the patterns most popular with collectors (and one of the most costly) is called French Peasant. It's very much like Quimper with simple depictions of a little peasant fellow with his staff. They made many lovely floral patterns, and it's around these where most of the buying and selling activity is centered. You'll also find roosters, plaids, and simple textured designs, and in addition to the dinnerware, some vases and novelty items as well.

Nearly every piece is marked 'Blue Ridge,' though occasionally you'll find one that isn't. Watch for a similar type of ware often confused with Blue Ridge that is sometimes (though not always) marked Italy.

The values suggested below are for the better patterns. To evaluate the French Peasant line, double these figures; for the simple plaids and textures, deduct 25% to 50%, depending on their appeal.

If you'd like to learn more, we recommend *The Collector's Encyclopedia of Blue Ridge Dinnerware, Identification and Values*, by Betty and Bill Newbound.

Advisors: Bill and Betty Newbound (See Directory, Dinnerware)

Newsletter: *National Blue Ridge Newsletter*
Norma Lilly
144 Highland Dr.
Blountsville, TN 37617; Subscription: $12 (6 issues) per year

Pitcher, Sculptured Fruit, china, $80.00.

Ashtray, advertising, Railroad.......................................**$75.00**
Ashtray, w/rest (ears) **$20.00**
Basket, aluminum edge, 7"..**$14.00**
Bonbon, Charm House, china **$85.00**
Bonbon, flat, shell shape, china **$65.00**
Bowl, cereal/soup; Premium, 6" **$15.00**
Bowl, fruit; 5¼" **$6.00**
Bowl, mixing; lg sizes **$35.00**
Bowl, mixing; med sizes **$20.00**
Bowl, salad; 10½x11½" **$50.00**
Bowl, vegetable; w/lid **$70.00**
Box, cigarette; square...**$75.00**
Box, pearlized, Rose Step **$70.00**
Box, Seaside, china **$100.00**
Butterdish, Woodcrest...**$60.00**
Cake tray, Maple Leaf, china..**$55.00**
Celery, leaf shape, china **$35.00**
Coffeepot, ovoid shape..**$100.00**
Creamer, Charm House, china..**$55.00**
Creamer, demitasse; earthenware...................................**$35.00**
Cup & saucer, Holiday **$40.00**
Cup & saucer, jumbo size **$40.00**
Cup & saucer, regular..**$10.00**
Deviled egg dish...**$35.00**
Dish, baking; plain, 8x13" **$25.00**
Dish, child's divided; deep sides **$35.00**
Gravy boat, Premium **$30.00**
Gravy boat..**$25.00**
Jug, batter; w/lid...**$75.00**

Lazy Susan base, wooden, 16-18" dia $80.00
Mug, child size...$25.00
Pie baker $30.00
Pitcher, Antique, china, 5" $75.00
Pitcher, fancy, china $95.00
Pitcher, Grace, china $85.00
Plate, advertising, lg $350.00
Plate, aluminum edge, 12" $25.00
Plate, dinner; Premium, 10½" $45.00
Plate, dinner; 9½" $15.00

Plate, French Peasant, 9½", $50.00.

Plate, party; w/cup well & cup $30.00
Plate, round, 6" $5.00
Plate, salad; Bird $65.00
Plate, Square Dance, 14" $85.00
Plate, Thanksgiving Turkey.................................$70.00
Plate, 11½" $40.00
Platter, regular patterns, 11" $15.00
Platter, regular patterns, 15" $30.00
Ramekin, w/lid, 7½" $35.00
Relish tray, heart shape $45.00
Relish tray, loop handles, china $80.00
Relish tray, shell shape, deep, china......................$60.00
Salt & pepper shakers, Apple, 1¾", pr $12.00
Salt & pepper shakers, Blossom Top, pr $35.00
Salt & pepper shakers, footed, china, tall, pr.............$50.00
Salt & pepper shakers, regular, short, pr $15.00
Sugar bowl, Charm House, china.............................$40.00
Sugar bowl, rope handle, w/lid.............................$20.00
Tea Tile, round or square, 3" $25.00
Teapot, chevron handle $90.00
Teapot, demitasse; china..................................$125.00
Teapot, demitasse; earthenware $95.00
Tidbit, 2-tier...$25.00
Tumbler, juice; glass $12.00
Vase, boot, 8" $80.00
Vase, bud..$90.00

Blue Willow Dinnerware

Blue Willow dinnerware has been made since the 1700s, first by English potters, then Japanese, and finally American companies as well. Tinware, glassware, even paper 'go-withs' have been produced over the years — some fairly recently, due to on-going demand. It was originally copied from the early blue and white wares made in Nanking and Canton in China. Once in awhile you'll see some pieces in black, pink, red, or even multicolor.

Obviously the most expensive will be the early English wares, easily identified by their backstamps. You'll be most likely to find pieces made by Royal or Homer Laughlin, and even though comparatively recent, they're still collectible, and their prices are very affordable.

For further study we recommend *Blue Willow Identification and Value Guide* by Mary Frank Gaston.

See also Homer Laughlin; Royal China.

Advisor: Mary Frank Gaston (See Directory, Dinnerware)

Newsletter: *American Willow Report*
Lisa Kay Henze, Editor
P.O. Box 900
Oakridge, OR 97463; Bimonthly newsletter, subscription: $15 per year, out of country add $5 per year

Newsletter: *The Willow Word*
Mary Berndt, Publisher
P.O. Box 13382
Arlington, TX 76094; Send SASE for information about subscriptions and the International Willow Collector's Convention

Baking dish, Two Temples II Simplified pattern w/line border, marked Hall China, 3x8"...................$25.00
Biscuit jar, Two Temples II w/Traditional border, cane handle, marked Adderly, 4½" $175.00
Bone dish, crescent shape, marked Wood & Sons, 7½x4½" $45.00
Bowl, covered vegetable; scalloped edge, interior pattern, marked Buffalo Pottery, 9x5½".............$250.00
Bowl, covered vegetable; stacking set of 4, Moriyama mark, 9" dia $300.00
Bowl, covered vegetable; Variant pattern decals on sides & on lid, marked Limoges China Co, 11x8½".........$55.00

Bowl, cream soup; with 7" underplate, unmarked, $30.00.

Bowl, reversed Traditional center pattern, unmarked Japan, 15" dia................................$200.00
Bowl, salad; unmarked Japan, 3½x10", w/matching ceramic & wood fork & spoon..................$125.00

Bowl, vegetable; Allerton, 10", $235.00.

Bowl, vegetable; rectangular, w/handles, unmarked English, 8¾x7"...$75.00

Bowl, vegetable; round w/scalloped edge, marked Allerton, 8"...$65.00

Bowls, mixing; unmarked (Heritage Marketing), plastic lids, set of 3...$15.00

Butter dish, round open style w/Butter embossed on side, Traditional center pattern w/Butterfly border, unmarked, 6½"..$80.00

Cake plate, Mandarin center pattern w/Dagger border, marked Shore & Coggins, 9½" square...................$60.00

Candle holders, Two Temples II Simplified pattern w/Pictorial border, multicolored, unmarked, 5½", pr............$250.00

Canister set, square shape, 7" flour, 5½" sugar, 5" coffee, 4½", unmarked...$100.00

Cheese dish, Burleigh pattern, Scroll & Flower border, marked Burleigh Ware................................$200.00

Chocolate pot, Two Temples II pattern w/Butterfly border, marked Hammersley's China, England, 8"..........$175.00

Coffeepot, marked Japan, 7".............................$100.00

Cookie jar, pitcher form w/Willow medallion on side, McCoy, 9"...$60.00

Creamer, marked Made in Japan, 3½".............$12.50

Creamer & sugar bowl, gold trim, w/lid, unmarked Japan, 3½"...$50.00

Crisper, marked Blue Magic Krispy Kan...South Norwalk Conn, 10"..$35.00

Cup, often called a Texas cup due to its size, marked Japan, 5½x8½"...$80.00

Cup & saucer, demitasse; restaurant ware, Pictorial border, marked Buffalo China..........................$45.00

Cup & saucer, Father printed between 2 birds on interior rim, marked Japan...$40.00

Cup & saucer, porcelain, Pictorial border pattern, Noritake mark...$35.00

Ginger jar, w/lid, marked Arthur Wood, England, 5"..$35.00

Gravy, boat, marked Shenango China, 6" long...........$45.00

Gravy bowl w/attached underplate, scalloped edge, Dudson, Willcox & Till mark, 6½".................................$90.00

Hot pot, borderless, marked Japan, 6"...................$40.00

Mug, milk glass w/silk-screened pattern, Fire-King by Anchor Hocking...$6.00

Mug, Two Temples II w/Line border, hotel ware, marked Sebring Pottery, 3½"......................................$10.00

Mustard pot, w/lid & spoon, marked Shenango China, 2½"..$45.00

Pitcher, printed pattern on carnival-type glass, Jeannette, ca 1949, 8"..$125.00

Pitcher, reversed Two Temples II pattern w/Butterfly border, marked Wedgwood & Co Ltd, 4¾".......................$75.00

Pitcher, Simplified Traditional pattern w/Pictorial border, scalloped rim, unmarked, 8"..................................$60.00

Pitcher, Two Temples II pattern w/Butterfly border, cylindrical w/rope-style handle, unmarked, 9¾"...........$150.00

Plate, grill; Traditional center & border pattern, 3-compartment, Made in Japan...$25.00

Plate, reversed & simplified Two Temples II pattern, unmarked American, 8"...................................$10.00

Plate, Traditional center & border patterns, scalloped edge, marked Buffalo Pottery, 9½"............................$45.00

Plate, Traditional pattern, reticulated rim, unmarked English, 7¼"..$150.00

Platter, Canton pattern, somewhat octagonal, marked Greenwood China, 10x7"....................................$55.00

Platter, reversed & simplified Two Temples II pattern w/Floral border, unmarked American, 12x9"........$35.00

Relish, ribbed surface & scalloped edge, unmarked, 8¼" long..$60.00

Sherbet, Two Temples II center pattern w/Butterfly border, footed, marked Made in Japan, 3½x3¼"..............$35.00

Snack set, Traditional center & border patterns, plate w/raised edge holds cup, marked Japan..............$30.00

Spoon rack, rolling-pin shape w/open planter pocket at top, unmarked Japan, 9½"..................................$75.00

Tea tile, cane border, unmarked Japan, 7½" square...............$75.00

Teapot, marked North Staffordshire Pottery Co Ltd, ca 1940s, 4-cup..$60.00

Teapot, musical type, unmarked Japan....................$120.00

Toothpick holder, marked Buffalo China, 2¼"............$45.00

Tumbler, Willow pattern on frosted glass, unmarked, 5¼".$15.00

Wall pocket, pitcher form, simplified Traditional pattern w/Floral border, Japan, 6"...................................$40.00

Bookends

You'll find bookends in various types of material and designs. The more inventive their modeling, the higher the price. Also consider the material. Cast-iron examples, especially if in original polychrome paint, are bringing very high prices right now. Brass and copper are good as well, though elements of design may override the factor of materials altogether. If they are signed by the designer or marked by the manufacturer, you can about triple the price. Those with a decidedly Art Deco appearance are often good sellers.

Abraham Lincoln, seated, bronze paint on cast lead, 6½", pr..$70.00

Ann Hathaway's Cottage, copper paint on cast iron, pr...$75.00

Asters, cast iron w/worn original paint, pr.................$155.00

Boy in armchair, NuArt, EX, pr...............................$80.00

Bust of lady, Frankart, pr.......................................$180.00

Cactus, copper, Craftsman.......................................$30.00

Cocker spaniel, gilt metal, white onyx base, pr..........$70.00

Diana & the hounds, cast iron w/VG paint, pr.........**$235.00**

Duck in flight, copper paint on cast iron, full figure, pr.**$125.00**

Dutch children kissing, cast iron w/original EX paint, Hubley #332, pr **$335.00**

Fish, copper paint on cast iron, full figure, pr..........**$235.00**

Flamenco dancer, Deco style, signed Herzel, pr.......**$185.00**

Flower vase, painted cast iron, Hubley, EX, pr **$145.00**

German shepherd, brass, old, pr..............................**$65.00**

German shepherd, bronze paint on cast iron, pr **$45.00**

Hartford Fire Insurance Co, metal with embossed elk, 5½", $65.00.

Homer & Dante, copper paint on cast iron, Bradley & Hubbard, pr..**$140.00**

Horse & foal, metal on wooden base, pr **$70.00**

Inn & Stagecoach, multicolor paint on cast iron, EX, pr...**$325.00**

Irish setter, full figure, painted cast iron, Hubley #363, pr.**$260.00**

Lincoln Memorial, gold paint on cast iron, Bradley & Hubbard, pr..**$135.00**

Lovebirds, painted cast iron, Acorn #600, pr **$125.00**

Monk, reading from crouched position, cast iron, Bradley & Hubbard, pr..**$135.00**

Nude, painted cast iron, Nouveau style, pr **$85.00**

Nude in shell, painted chalkware, EX, pr...................**$45.00**

Oil lamp w/books, brown & brass paint on cast iron, pr..**$125.00**

Owls w/book, painted cast iron, pr............................**$70.00**

Pointer dog, bronze paint on cast iron, 8", pr **$80.00**

Quotes by Pope & Young, copper paint on cast iron, Bradley & Hubbard, pr **$125.00**

Sailing ships, painted cast iron, Bradley & Hubbard, pr..**$135.00**

Scottie, recumbent, black paint on cast iron, pr **$75.00**

Scottie dog, Frankart, EX, pr...................................**$150.00**

Shakespeare, bronze paint on cast iron, 1920s, pr **$50.00**

Shakespeare, copper paint on cast iron, Bradley & Hubbard, pr **$165.00**

Ship's wheel, metal, Jennings Brothers, pr **$60.00**

Sphinx, cast iron w/VG paint, Bradley & Hubbard, pr..**$150.00**

Spirit of Freedom, painted cast iron, pr....................**$200.00**

Wire-haired Terrier, bronze, EB Parsons, 6x8" **$250.00**

Books

Books have always fueled the imagination. Before television lured us out of the library into the TV room, everyone enjoyed reading the latest novels. Western, horror, and science fiction themes are still popular to this day — especially those by such authors as Louis L'Amour, Steven King, and Ray Bradbury, to name but a few. Edgar Rice Burrough's Tarzan series and Frank L. Baum's Wizard of Oz books are regarded as classics among today's collectors. A first edition of a popular author's first book (especially if it's signed) is especially sought after, so is a book that 'ties in' with a movie or television program.

Dick and Jane readers are fast becoming collectible. If you went to first grade during the 1930s until the mid-1970s, you probably read about their adventures. They were used allover the United States and in military base schools over the entire world. They were published here as well as in Canada, the Philippine Islands, Australia, and New Zealand; there were special editions for the Roman Catholic parochial schools and the Seventh Day Adventists', and even today they're in use in some Mennonite and Amish schools.

On the whole, ex-library copies and book club issues (unless they are limited editions) have very low resale values.

For further information we recommend *Huxford's Old Book Value Guide* by Sharon and Bob Huxford. This book is designed to help the owners of old books evaluate their holdings, and it also lists the names of prospective buyers.

Newsletter: Martha's Kidlit Newsletter
Box 1488A
Ames, IA 50010; A bimonthly publication for children's books collectors. Subscription $25 per year

Newsletter: *National Book Collector*
National Book Collectors Society
65 High Ridge Rd., Suite 349
Stamford, CT 06095; Annual dues: $20 (includes 6 issues) per year in USA; $25 in Canada and foreign countries; sample copy: $2

Magazine: *AB Bookman's Weekly*
P.O. Box AB
Clifton, NJ 07015; 201-772-0020 or FAX 201-772-9281; $80 per year bulk mail USA ($80 per year Canada or Foreign). $125 per year 1st class mail (USA, Canada, and Mexico). Foreign Air Mail: Inquire. Sample copies: $10. AB Bookman's Yearbook: $25. All advertising and subscriptions subject to acceptance

Big Little Books

The Whitman Publishing Company started it all in 1933 when they published a book whose format was entirely different than any other's. It was very small, easily held in a child's hand, but over an inch in thickness. There was a cartoon-like drawing on the right-hand page, and the text was printed on the left. The idea was so well accepted that very soon other publishers — Saalfield, Van Wiseman, Lynn, World Syndicate, and Goldsmith — cashed in on the idea as well. The first Big Little Book hero was Dick Tracy, but soon every radio cowboy, cartoon character, lawman, and space explorer was immortalized in his own adventure series.

When it became apparent that the pre-teen of the fifties preferred the comic-book format, Big Little Books were finally phased out; but many were saved in boxes and stored in attics, so there's still a wonderful supply of them around. You need to watch condition carefully when you're buying or selling. For further information we recommend *Big Little Books, A Collector's Reference and Value Guide*, by Larry Jacobs.

Newsletter: *Big Little Times*
Big Little Book Collectors Club of America
Larry Lowery
P.O. Box 1242
Danville, CA 94526; 415-837-2086

Air Fighters of America, #1448, Whitman, 1948, EX ...**$18.00**
Allen Pike of the Parachute Squad, #1481, Whitman, 1941, G **$10.00**
Andy Panda & the Pirate Ghosts, #1459, Whitman, 1949, NM **$40.00**
Bambi, #1489, Whitman, Walt Disney's, 1942, EX.......**$35.00**
Big Chief Wahoo, #1443, Whitman, 1938, EX, from $20 to .**$30.00**
Blondie, Cookie & Daisy's Pups, #1492, Whitman, 1943, EX **$20.00**
Blondie & Baby Dumpling, #1429, Whitman, 1937, NM...**$40.00**
Blondie or Life Among the Bumsteads, #1466, 1944, VG .**$15.00**
Brer Rabbit, Song of the South, #1426, Whitman, Walt Disney, movie tie-in, EX........................**$40.00**
Buck Jones, The Rough Riders, #1486, Whitman, 1943, NM **$45.00**
Buck Jones, 1934, EX **$50.00**
Buck Jones & the Killers of Crooked Butte, #1451, Whitman, EX+ **$35.00**
Buck Rogers & the Super-Dwarf of Space, #1490, Whitman, 1943, EX..**$65.00**
Bugs Bunny, All Pictures Comics, #1435, VG..............**$30.00**
Bugs Bunny & His Pals, #1496, Whitman, 1945, EX...**$40.00**
Captain Easy Behind Enemy Lines, #1474, Whitman, NM..**$25.00**

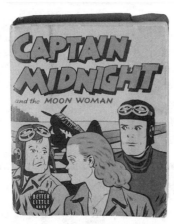

Captain Midnight and the Moon Woman, #1452, EX, $60.00.

Captain Midnight vs Terror of the Orient, #1458, Whitman, 1942, G **$20.00**
Charlie McCarthy & Edgar Bergen, #1456, Whitman, 1938, EX+ **$45.00**
Chester Gump in the Pole to Pole Flight, #1402, Whitman, 1937, EX................................**$25.00**

David Copperfield, #1149, Whitman, 1934 Metro-Goldwin-Mayer movie tie-in w/WC Fields on the cover, EX **$15.00**
Dick Tracy & the Phantom Ship, #1434, Whitman, 1940, VG..**$20.00**
Dick Tracy on Voodoo Island, #1478, Whitman, 1944, NM .**$55.00**
Don Winslow of the Navy & the Secret Enemy Base, #1453, Whitman, G **$10.00**
Donald Duck & His Misadventures, Silly Symphony, #1441, Whitman, Walt Disney, 1937, NM........................**$90.00**
Donald Duck Forgets To Duck, #1434, Whitman, Walt Disney, 1939, EX............................**$45.00**
Ellery Queen, Adventure of the Last Man Club, #1406, Whitman, 1940, EX+ **$45.00**
Felix the Cat, #1439, Whitman, 1945, EX+..................**$70.00**
Flash Gordon & the Perils of Mongo, #1423, Whitman, 1940, EX..**$50.00**
Flash Gordon on the Planet of Mongo, #1110, Whitman, 1934, G **$25.00**
G-Man & the Gun Runners, #1469, Whitman, 1940, G..**$5.00**
Gene Autry & the Hawk of the Hills, #1493, Whitman, 1942, EX..**$40.00**
Green Hornet Cracks Down, #1480, Whitman, 1942, EX...**$75.00**
Invisible Scarlet O'Neil Vs the King of the Slums, #1406, Whitman, 1948, NM **$45.00**
Jackie Cooper in Gangster's Boy, #1402, Whitman, 1939, G **$10.00**
Ken Maynard in Western Justice, #1430, Whitman, 1938, EX..**$20.00**
Junior Nebb Joins the Circus, 31470, Whitman, 1939, VG .**$25.00**
Last Days of Pompeii, #1132, Whitman, Feature Movie Book, oversize, EX..**$40.00**
Little LuLu, Alvin & Tubby, #1429, Whitman, 1947, G..**$15.00**
Little Orphan Annie & the Haunted Mansion, #1482, Whitman, 1937, VG................................**$25.00**
Lone Ranger & the Great Western Span, #1477, Whitman, 1942, EX..**$30.00**
Lone Ranger & the Silver Bullets, #1498, Whitman, 1946, EX..**$25.00**
Mandrake the Magician & the Flame Pearls, #1418, Whitman, 1946, NM **$55.00**
Mickey Mouse & the Lazy Daisy Mystery, #1433, Whitman, Walt Disney, 1947, EX **$45.00**
Mickey Mouse & the 7 Ghosts, #1475, Whitman, Walt Disney, 1940, EX+ **$65.00**
Myra North Special Nurse & Foreign Spies, #1497, Whitman, 1938, NM **$30.00**
Peggy Brown & the Mystery Basket, #1411, Whitman, 1941, NM **$30.00**
Popeye & Castor Oyl the Detective, #1497, Whitman, EX..**$35.00**
Popeye & the Deep Sea Mystery, #1499, Whitman, 1939, VG **$25.00**
Red Ryder & Little Beaver on Hoofs of Thunder, #1400, Whitman, 1939, EX **$30.00**
Roy Rogers & the Mystery of the Lazy M, #1462, Whitman, 1949, NM **$55.00**
Shadow & the Ghost Makers, #1495, Whitman, 1942, EX...**$90.00**
Smilin' Jack & the Escape From Death Rock, #1445, Whitman, 1943, VG **$25.00**

Spike Kelly of the Commandos, #1467, Whitman, 1943, EX...**$20.00**

Tailspin Tommy Hunting for Pirate Gold, #1172, Whitman, 1935, G **$15.00**

Tarzan Lord of the Jungle, #1407, Whitman, 1946, NM ...**$45.00**

Tarzan the Terrible, #1453, Whitman, 1942, VG **$25.00**

Texas Ranger, VG, $35.00; Radio Patrol Trailing the Safeblowers, #1173, 1937, VG, $35.00.

Tim McCoy in The Westerner, #1193, Whitman, 1936 Columbia movie tie-in, EX......................................**$30.00**

Tom Swift & His Giant Telescope, #1485, Whitman, 1939, EX...**$25.00**

Wells Fargo, #1471, Whitman, 1938 Paramount movie tie-in, NM **$40.00**

Zane Grey's King of the Royal Mounted & the Great Jewel Mystery, #1486, Whitman, EX **$20.00**

Children's Miscellaneous Books

Adventures of Paddy the Beaver, Thornton W Burgess, Grosset Dunlap, 1945, w/dust jacket, NM **$25.00**

Animal Babies, John Bellairs, Donohue, Jacob Bates Abbott illustrator, 1949, w/dust jacket, VG........................**$8.00**

Animal Story Book, Watty Pipper, Platt Munk, ca 1954, W Dennis illustrator, VG **$25.00**

Baby Animals, Susan Jeffers, Random, 1989, 1st edition, w/dust jacket, VG **$10.00**

Boy Scout's Hike Book, Edward Cave, Doubleday, 1920, cloth cover w/picture, 243 pages, VG...................**$25.00**

Child's Garden of Verses, Robert Lewis Stevenson, Childrens' Classics, 1985, JW Smith illustrator, w/dust jacket, NM..**$9.00**

Child's Garden of Verses, Tony Brice, Rand McNally Jr Elf Book, 1942, EX **$7.00**

Emily's Runaway Imagination, Beverly Cleary, Morrow, 1st edition, Beth/Joe Krush illustrators, 1961, 221 pages, VG **$35.00**

Exploding Frog & Other Fables From Aesop, John McFarland, Little Brown, 1981, 1st edition, J Marshall illustrator, NM.......**$25.00**

Golden Circus: A Fuzzy Golden Book, Kathryn Jackson, Simon Schuster, 1950, probable 1st edition, w/dust jacket, EX.**$50.00**

Grimm's Fairy Tales, Grimm & Grimm, Pantheon, 1945, w/dust jacket, NM...**$20.00**

How Peter Cottontail Got His Name, Thornton W Burgess, Wonder Book, 1957, EX **$7.00**

Just So Stories, Rudyard Kipling, Weathervane, 2nd edition, w/dust jacket, VG **$10.00**

Kidnapped, Robert Louis Stevenson, Scribner Classic, 1941, NC Wyeth illustrator, VG.....................................**$40.00**

Little Black Sambo, Helen Bannerman, Whitman Tell-A-Tale, 1950, VG **$15.00**

Little Brother & Sister, Barbara Cooney, Doubleday, 1982, 1st edition, w/dust jacket, NM.....................................**$60.00**

Little Lost Lamb, Margaret Wise Brown, Doubleday, 1945, 1st edition, VG **$75.00**

Little Red Ferry Boat, Russell Potter, Holt, 1947, 50 pages, VG **$10.00**

Moko & Koko in the Jungle, V Kubasta, London, 1961, mechanical pop-up, picture boards, VG **$20.00**

Mr Penny's Circus, Marie Hall Ets, Viking, 1961, picture paper boards, VG...**$7.50**

Night Before Christmas, Clement C Moore, Derrydale, 1992, JW Smith illustrator, NM **$5.00**

Paddington Bear, Michael Bond, Random, 1973, 1st American edition, picture boards, VG+..............................**$12.00**

Pooh Craft Book, Carol S Friedrichsen, Dutton, 1976, 1st edition, w/just jacket, NM **$35.00**

Pooh Get-Well Book, Virginia H Ellison, Dutton, 1972, 3rd printing, w/dust jacket, M **$25.00**

Pooh's Counting Book, AA Milne, Dutton, 1982, 1st edition, Shepard illustrator, NM **$20.00**

Pop-Up Minnie Mouse, Disney Studios, Applewood, 1993, 1st edition, EX...**$10.00**

Present for Auntie, Emma Brock, Knopf, 1939, 1st edition, cloth cover w/picture, w/dust jacket, NM **$45.00**

Socks, Beverly Cleary, Morrow, 1st edition, Beatrice Darwin illustrator, 1972, 156 pages, VG **$30.00**

Story of Sambo & the Twins, Helen Bannerman, Chato Windus, 1971, picture paper boards, VG.............**$40.00**

Three Little Pigs, Altemus, JK Neill illustrator, 1904, EX, $48.00.

Timmy Mouse, Tony Brice, Rand McNally Jr Elf Books #8019, 1959, EX...**$6.00**

Walt Disney's Story of Minnie Mouse, Disney Studios, Whitman, 1938, 92 pages, VG **$50.00**

Wonderful Storybook, Margaret Wise Brown, Giant Golden Book #1577-1, B edition, EX................................**$20.00**

Young Readers' Science Fiction Stories, Richard M Elam, Grosset Dunlap, no date, VG................................**$5.00**

Dell Fast Action Books

Adventures of Andy Panda, EX+ **$65.00**

Bugs Bunny & the Secret of Storm Island, G..............**$25.00**

Captain Marvel, The Return of the Scorpion, EX......**$150.00**

Charlie McCathy & Edgar Bergen, EX.......................**$65.00**

Dick Tracy & the Blackmailers, EX **$85.00**

Dick Tracy & the Chain of Evidence, G **$45.00**

Donald Duck & the Ducklings, G **$60.00**

Dumbo the Flying Elephant, G...................................**$45.00**

Flash Gordon & the Ape Men of Mor, G....................**$45.00**

Gene Autry in Gun Smoke, EX **$80.00**

Little Orphan Annie in Rags to Riches, NM............**$140.00**

Smilin' Jack & the Border Bandits, EX......................**$60.00**

Spy Smasher & the Red Death, G **$40.00**

Tarzan the Avenger, G...**$65.00**

Tom Mix Avenges the Dry Gulched Range King, G...**$50.00**

Walt Disney's Mickey Mouse & Pluto, G **$45.00**

Juvenile Series Books

Beverly Gray Reporter, Clair Blank, Grosset Dunlap, 1st edition, 1940, w/dust jacket, VG **$25.00**

Beverly Gray Sophomore, Clair Blank, AL Burt, 1934, w/dust jacket, VG...**$75.00**

Beverly Gray's Quest, Clair Blank, Grosset Dunlap, 1942, 1st edition, green cloth cover, w/dust jacket, VG......**$40.00**

Beverly Gray's Scoop, Clair Blank, McLoughlin, 1954, VG .**$15.00**

Beverly Gray's Scoop (#24), Clair Blank, 1951, Grosset Dunlap, 253 pages, w/dust jacket, VG.................**$22.50**

Beverly Gray's Surprise, Clair Blank, McLoughlin, 1955, glossy picture board, G+ **$20.00**

Bobbsey Twins at Mystery Mansion, Laura Lee Hope, Grosset Dunlap, undated reprint, w/dust jacket, VG+ **$17.50**

Bobbsey Twins at School, Laura Lee Hope, Grosset Dunlap, 1913, w/dust jacket, VG **$35.00**

Bobbsey Twins at School (#4), Grosset Dunlap, 1941, NM **$15.00**

Bobbsey Twins at the County Fair (#15), Laura Lee Hope, Grosset Dunlap, 1922, 1st edition, w/dust jacket, VG **$50.00**

Bobbsey Twins at the Seashore (#3), Laura Lee Hope, Grosset Dunlap, 1950, w/dust jacket, NM **$15.00**

Bobbsey Twins in the Country, Laura Lee Hope, Grosset Dunlap, undated reprint, w/dust jacket, VG+ **$12.50**

Bobbsey Twins in Washington, Laura Lee Hope, Grosset Dunlap, 1919, green cloth cover, VG...................**$10.00**

Bobbsey Twins on a Ranch, Laura Lee Hope, Grosset Dunlap, 1935, w/dust jacket, VG...........................**$15.00**

Bobbsey Twins on an Airplane Trip, Laura Lee Hope, Grosset Dunlap, 1933, w/dust jacket, VG...........................**$35.00**

Bobbsey Twins Treasure Hunting, Laura Lee Hope, Grosset Dunlap, thicker edition w/paper dolls on dust jacket, 1920, VG...**$20.00**

Bomba & the Lost Explorers, Roy Rockwood, Grosset Dunlap, no date, VG **$12.00**

Bomba the Jungle Boy in the Abandoned City, Roy Rockwood, Cupples Leon, 1st edition, 1927, VG..**$15.00**

Bronc Burnett: Seven in Front, Wilfred McCormick, Grosset Dunlap, 1965, picture boards, 179 pages, EX.......**$20.00**

Cherry Ames Army Nurse, Helen Wells, Grosset Dunlap, w/dust jacket, VG **$6.00**

Cherry Ames Cruise Nurse, Helen Wells, Grosset Dunlap, VG **$5.00**

Cherry Ames Senior Nurse, Helen Wells, Grosset Dunlap, w/dust jacket, VG **$8.00**

Cherry Ames Student Nurse, Helen Wells, Grosset Dunlap, w/dust jacket, VG **$8.00**

Cherry Ames' Book of First Aid & Home Nursing, Helen Wells, Grosset Dunlap, 1959, cloth cover, w/dust jacket, EX...**$32.00**

Chip Hilton: Backboard Fever, Clair Bee, Grosset Dunlap, 1953, cloth cover, w/dust jacket, VG **$22.00**

Chip Hilton: Championship Ball, Grosset Dunlap, later edition, 1948, w/dust jacket, VG **$16.00**

Chip Hilton: Freshman Quarterback, Clair Bee, 1952, 212 pages, cloth cover, w/dust jacket, VG...................**$18.00**

Chip Hilton: Home Run Feud, Clair Bee, Grosset Dunlap, 1964, VG...**$110.00**

Dana Girls: Clue of the Rusty Key, Carolyn Keene, Grosset Dunlap, 1942, purple cloth cover, w/dust jacket, EX..**$22.00**

Dana Girls: Mystery at the Crossroads, Carolyn Keene, Grosset Dunlap, 1954, green binding, VG.............**$8.00**

Dana Girls: Mystery at the Crossroads, Carolyn Keene, Grosset Dunlap, hardcover, decorated boards, 1954, VG **$8.00**

Dana Girls: Mystery of the Bamboo Bird, Carolyn Keen, Grosset Dunlap, hardcover, decorated boards, 1960, VG..........**$8.00**

Dana Girls: Secret of the Jade Ring, Carolyn Keene, Grosset Dunlap, 1953, w/dust jacket, NM **$22.50**

Dick & Jane, Elson Gray Basic Readers-Primer, Scott Foresman, 4 stories, 1936, G.................................**$70.00**

Dick and Jane, Friends and Neighbors, Scott Foresman, 1941, EX, $45.00.

Dick & Jane, Fun w/Our Friends, Scott Foresman, cloth cover, 1962, VG..**$25.00**

Dick & Jane, Guess Who, hardcover, 1951, VG..........**$35.00**

Dick & Jane, New Fun w/Dick & Jane, hardcover, 1951, VG **$35.00**

Dick & Jane, Our New Friends, Scott Foresman, 191 pages, 1946, VG...**$45.00**

Dick & Jane, The New Our New Friends, Scott Foresman, cloth binding, 1956, VG+ **$40.00**

Dick & Jane, The New We Come & Go, Scott Foresman, 1956, 3rd/last primer, VG **$30.00**

Dick & Jane, Think-And-Do Book, workbook, softcover, 1962, 8x11", unused...**$20.00**

Dick & Jane, We Come & Go, Scott Foresman, 3rd/last primer, 1956, VG..**$30.00**

Hardy Boys: Deathgame, Franklin W Dixon, Archway #69375, 6th printing, VG **$4.00**

Hardy Boys: Detective Handbook, Franklin W Dixon, Grosset Dunlap, 1959, VG **$10.00**

Hardy Boys: Figure in Hiding, Franklin W Dixon, Grosset Dunlap, 1937, 212-page, partial dust jacket, VG ..**$100.00**

Hardy Boys: Great Airport Mystery, Franklin W Dixon, Grosset Dunlap, 1930, brown cloth cover, w/dust jacket, EX...**$70.00**

Hardy Boys: In Self-Defense, Franklin W Dixon, Archway #70042, 1990, VG **$4.00**

Hardy Boys: Missing Chums, Franklin W Dixon, Grosset Dunlap, 1942, w/dust jacket, VG............................**$60.00**

Hardy Boys: Mystery of the Chinese Junk (#39), Franklin W Dixon, Grosset Dunlap, 1st edition, 1960, w/dust jacket, NM **$40.00**

Hardy Boys: Mystery of the Desert Giant, Franklin W Dixon, Grosset Dunlap, 1st edition, 1961, w/dust jacket, VG **$40.00**

Hardy Boys: Secret of Pirates' Hill, Franklin W Dixon, Grosset Dunlap, 1st edition, 1956, w/dust jacket, VG.......**$45.00**

Hardy Boys: Secret of the Caves, Franklin Dixon, Grosset Dunlap, 1929, w/dust jacket, EX+ **$22.50**

Hardy Boys: Short-Wave Mystery, Franklin W Dixon, Grosset Dunlap, thin edition, 1945, w/dust jacket, VG **$25.00**

Hardy Boys' Detective Handbook, Franklin W Dixon, Grosset Dunlap, 1959, VG **$10.00**

Home Run Series, Batter Up!, Harold M Sherman, Grosset Dunlap, 1930, w/dust jacket, VG............................**$20.00**

Home Run Series, Strike Him Out, Harold M Sherman, Goldsmith, later printing, 1932, w/dust jacket, VG ..**$15.00**

Jerry Todd & the Purring Egg (#6), Leo Edwards, Grosset Dunlap, 1926, cloth cover, w/dust jacket, EX **$45.00**

Judy Bolton: Ghost Parade, Margaret Sutton, Grosset Dunlap, 1933, green cloth cover, w/dust jacket, EX **$30.00**

Ken Holt: Mystery of the Vanishing Magician, Bruce Campbell, Grosset Dunlap, 1956, 1st edition, w/dust jacket, VG **$22.00**

Little Dancer, Lorna Hill, Thomas Nelson, 1957, 1st American edition, cloth cover, w/dust jacket, EX **$14.00**

Lone Ranger, Fran Striker, Grosset Dunlap, 1938, w/dust jacket, VG...**$15.00**

Lone Ranger & the Bitter Spring Fued (#15), Fran Striker, Grosset Dunlap, 1953, cloth cover, w/dust jacket, EX **$35.00**

Lone Ranger & the Gold Robbery, Fran Striker, Grosset Dunlap, 1939, ragged dust jacket, VG **$35.00**

Lone Ranger & the Outlaw Stronghold, Fran Striker, Grosset Dunlap, 1939, w/dust jacket, EX **$20.00**

Lone Ranger in Wild Horse Canyon, Fran Striker, Grosset Dunlap, 1950, 1st edition, w/dust jacket, VG.......**$22.00**

Lone Ranger Rides Again, Fran Striker, Grosset Dunlap, 1943, thick edition, 1943, w/dust jacket, VG.................**$35.00**

Lone Ranger Rides at the Haunted Gulch, Fran Striker, Grosset Dunlap, 1941, w/dust jacket, NM **$20.00**

Lone Ranger Traps the Smugglers, Fran Striker, Grosset Dunlap, 1941, 1st edition, w/dust jacket, VG.......**$45.00**

Lone Ranger: Mystery Ranch, Fran Striker, Grosset Dunlap, 1938, w/dust jacket, EX+.......................................**$15.00**

Nancy Drew Ghost Stories, Carolyn Keene, Wanderer #45458, 1983, VG **$3.50**

Nancy Drew: Clue of the Tapping Heels (#16), Carolyn Keene, Grosset Dunlap, ca 1950, w/dust jacket, VG **$30.00**

Nancy Drew, The Double Jinx Mystery, #50, Grosset Dunlap, 1973, EX, $5.00.

Nancy Drew: Hidden Window Mystery, Carolyn Keene, Grosset Dunlap, no date, w/dust jacket, VG........**$10.00**

Nancy Drew: Secret in the Old Attic, Carolyn Keene, Grosset Dunlap, 1st edition, 1944, w/dust jacket, VG.......**$55.00**

Nancy Drew: Secret of Red Gate Farm, Carolyn Keen, Grosset Dunlap, hardcover, 1931, VG................................**$12.50**

Oz: Dorothy & the Wizard in Oz, Frank L Baum, Reilly Briton, 1st edition, 1980, EX **$570.00**

Oz: Emerald City of Oz, Frank L Baum, Rand McNally, 1939, G **$10.00**

Oz: Emerald City of Oz, Frank L Baum, Reilly Lee, Neill illustrator, 1920, picture on tan cloth cover, G..........**$100.00**

Oz: Glinda of Oz, Frank L Baum, Reilly Lee, 1st edition, 1920, tan cloth cover, G **$250.00**

Oz: Lost Princess of Oz, Frank L Baum, Reilly Lee, early reprint, ca 1920, blue cloth cover, G....................**$95.00**

Oz: Magic of Oz, Frank L Baum, Reilly Lee, 1st edition, Neill illustrator, 1920, picture on green cloth cover, G...**$150.00**

Oz: Road to Oz, Frank L Baum, Reilly Lee, Neill illustrator, 1965, white cloth cover w/picture, VG **$17.50**

Oz: Road to Oz, Frank L Baum, Reilly Lee, Neill illustrator, ca 1965, picture on white cloth cover, VG **$17.50**

Oz: Tin Woodsman...Original Story, Frank L Baum, Reilly Lee, Ulrey illustrator, ca 1955, cloth cover, w/dust jacket, VG........**$20.00**

Oz: Wizard of Oz, Frank L Baum, Jelly Bean, 1st edition, Santore illustrator, 1991, w/dust jacket, EX.............**$8.50**

Oz: Woodsman of Oz...An Original Story, Frank L Baum, Reilly Lee, cloth cover, ca 1955, VG.....................**$20.00**

Penny Parker: Danger at the Drawbridge, Mildred A Wirt, red cloth cover, w/dust jacket, VG **$30.00**

Radio Boys at Mountain Pass (#4), Allen Chapman, Grosset Dunlap, 1922, w/dust jacket, VG...........................**$32.00**

Radio Boys in Gold Valley, Allen Chapman, NY, 1st edition, 1927, w/dust jacket, VG **$45.00**

Rover Boys at Big Bear Lake, Arthur M Winfield, Grosset Dunlap, 1923, brown cloth cover, w/dust jacket, VG **$25.00**

Ted Scott: Brushing the Mountain Top, Franklin W Dixon, Grosset Dunlap, 1st edition, 1934, w/dust jacket, VG................**$40.00**

Ted Scott: South of the Rio Grande, Franklin W Dixon, Grosset Dunlap, no date, VG...................................**$8.00**

Ted Scott: Through the Air to Alaska, Franklin W Dixon, Grosset Dunlap, hardcover, VG **$6.00**

Tom Swift & Big Dirigible, Victor Appleton, Grosset Dunlap, 1st edition, 1930, w/dust jacket, VG **$65.00**

Tom Swift & His Atomic Earth Blaster, Victor Appleton, Grosset Dunlap, no date, VG....................................**$8.00**

Tom Swift & His Chest of Secrets, Victor Appleton, Grosset Dunlap, #38, w/dust jacket, VG **$50.00**

Tom Swift & His Chest of Secrets (#28), Victor Appleton, Grosset Dunlap, 219 pages, w/dust jacket, VG....**$50.00**

Tom Swift & His Electric Locomotive, Victor Appleton, Grosset Dunlap, 1922, w/dust jacket, VG.............**$45.00**

Tom Swift & His Electronic Retroscop, Victor Appleton II, Grosset Dunlap, hardcover, VG............................**$10.00**

Tom Swift & His Giant Robot, Victor Appleton II, Grosset Dunlap, hardcover, VG......................................**$5.00**

Tom Swift & His Jetmarine, Victor Appleton, Grosset Dunlap, 1954, w/dust jacket, VG **$20.00**

Tom Swift & His Motorboat (#2), Victor Appleton, Grosset Dunlap, 1910, 2 dust jackets, VG **$35.00**

Tom Swift & His Outpost in Space, Victor Appleton, Grosset Dunlap, 1955, w/dust jacket, VG...........................**$20.00**

Tom Swift & His Space Solartron, Victor Appleton, Grosset Dunlap, no date, VG **$10.00**

Tom Swift & His Submarine Boat, Victor Appleton, Grosset Dunlap, 1910, w/dust jacket, VG...........................**$50.00**

Tom Swift & His Triphibian Atomicar, Victor Appleton II, Grosset Dunlap, hardcover, decorated boards, VG **$10.00**

Tom Swift & His Ultrasonic Cycloplan, Victor Appleton, Grosset Dunlap, no date, VG...................................**$8.00**

Tom Swift & His 3-D Telejector, Victor Appleton II, Grosset Dunlap, hardcover, decorated boards, VG **$15.00**

Tom Swift in the Race to the Moon, Victor Appleton II, Collins, hardcover, decorated boards, VG **$20.00**

Little Golden Books

Everyone has had a few of these books in their lifetime; some we've read to our own children so many times that we still know them word for word, and today they're appearing in antique malls and shops everywhere. The first were printed in 1942. These are recognizable by their blue paper spines (later ones had gold foil). Until the early 1970s, they were numbered consecutively; after that they were unnumbered.

First editions of the titles having a 25¢ or 29¢ cover price can be identified by either a notation on the first or second pages, or a letter on the bottom right corner of the last page (A for 1, B for 2, etc.). If these are absent, you probably have a first edition.

Condition is extremely important. To qualify as mint, these books must look just as good as they looked the day they were purchased. Naturally, having been used by children, many show signs of wear. If your book is only lightly soiled, the cover has no tears or scrapes, the inside pages have only small creases or folded corners, and the spine is still strong (though its cover may be missing), it will be worth about half as much as one in mint condition. Additional damage would of course lessen the value even more.

A series number containing an 'A' refers to an activity book, while a 'D' number identifies a Disney story. Our values are for examples in excellent condition.

For more information, we recommend *Collecting Little Golden Books* by Steve Santi (who provided us with our narrative material).

Advisor: Ilene Kayne (See Directory, Books)

Newsletter: *The Pokey Gazette*
Steve Santi
19626 Ricardo Ave.
Hayward, CA 94541; 501-481-2586; a *Little Golden Book* collector newsletter

Adventures of Tom Sawyer, #1058, Saalfield, 1934, G..**$15.00**

Aristocats, #D122, 1st edition, VG/EX.........................**$12.00**

Bambi, #7, Walt Disney, 1948, NM...............................**$12.00**

Big Bird's Red Book, #157, 3rd edition, VG/EX............**$3.00**

Black Beauty, #1057, Saalfield, 1934, G **$4.00**

Brick Bradford & the City Beneath the Sea, #1059, Saalfield, VG **$16.00**

Broken Arrow, 1957 ....**$15.00**

Bugs Bunny & the Indians, #120, C edition, VG/EX ..**$12.00**

Burn 'Em Up Barnes, #1321, Saalfield, 1935, VG........**$12.50**

Circus Time, #31, 1st edition, VG/EX...........................**$20.00**

Cowboy Millionaire, #1106, Saalfield, VG....................**$20.00**

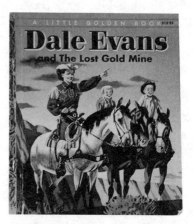

**Dale Evans and the Lost Gold Mine,
#213, A edition, EX, $18.00.**

Donald Duck & the Witch Next Door, #102-44, Q edition, VG/EX..**$2.00**

Fuzzy Duckling, #78, C edition, VG/EX.........................**$9.00**

Golden Book of Birds, #13, 4th edition, VG/EX.........**$12.00**

Grandpa Bunny, #D21, A edition, VG/EX...................**$24.00**

Hockey Spare, #1125, Saalfield, 1937, VG **$10.00**

Hymns, #34, C edition, VG/EX.....................................**$12.00**

I Think About God, #111, 6th edition, VG/EX.............**$5.00**

Ken Maynard in Strawberry Roan, #1090, Saalfield, G .**$10.00**

Law of the Wild, #1092, Saalfield, 1935, EX...............**$22.50**

Let's Go Shopping w/Peter & Penny, #33, B edition, VG/EX..**$15.00**

Magic Next Door, #106, 4th edition, VG/EX.................**$6.00**

Mr Ed, #483, A edition, VG/EX.....................................**$17.00**

Night Before Christmas #20, 31st edition, red cover, VG/EX.**$1.50**

Pete's Dragon, #105-44, I edition, VG/EX....................**$3.00**

Popeye's Ark, #1117, Saalfield, 1935, VG **$26.00**

Prayers for Children, 35, S edition, VG/EX.................**$10.00**

Robin Hood, #D126, 1st edition, VG/EX **$12.00**

Stan Kent, Captain, #1132, Saalfield, 1937, G **$6.00**

Story of Jesus, #27, D edition, VG/EX **$12.00**

Story of Will Rogers, #1096, Saalfield, VG **$15.00**

Three Bears, #47, 38th edition, VG/EX........................**$8.00**

Uncle Remus, #D6, D edition, VG/EX **$6.00**

What Am I?, #58, B edition, VG/EX **$10.00**

Woody Woodpecker Takes a Trip, #445, A edition, VG/EX...**$9.00**

Movie and TV Tie-Ins

A Many-Splendored Thing, Han Suylin, Signet #D1183, 1955, 2nd printing, VG+...............................**$3.00**

Alfie, Bill Naughton, Ballantine #U5061, 1966, Michael Caine, EX...**$4.00**

All the President's Men, Bernstein & Woodward, Warner #89-093, 1976, 2nd printing, EX....................**$2.50**

Alvarez Kelly, Friend, Gold Medal #K1732, 1966, William Holden & Richard Widmark, VG+.............**$6.00**

Anastasia, Maurette, Signet #S1356, Bergman & Brynner, VG **$3.00**

At the Earth's Core, Edgar Rice Burroughs, Ace #03325, no date, VG..**$2.00**

Banyon, William Hohnston, Warner #74-285, 1972, 2nd printing, VG...**$2.00**

Batman Vs 3 Villains of Doom, Winston Lyon, Signet #D2940, 1966, VG **$3.00**

Battlestar Galactica: The Photostory, Larson, Berkley #04139, 1979, EX..**$5.00**

Bells of St Mary's, Martin, Bantam #103, 1947, Ingrid Bergman & Bing Crosby, VG **$4.00**

Billy Jack, Frank & Teresa Christina, Avon #N458, 1973, photos, VG+..**$3.00**

Blade Runner, Stan Lee, Marvel #02839, 1982, VG **$2.50**

Bonnie & Clyde, Hirschfeld, Lancer #73-684, 1967, Warren Beatty & Faye Dunaway, VG+ **$6.00**

Bus Stop, William Inge, Bantam #1518, 1956, Marilyn Monroe, VG **$8.00**

Cape Fear, Crest #S520, John D MacDonald, new edition, 1962, EX...**$12.00**

Charlie Brown Christmas, Schultz, Signet #P3258, 1967, EX **$5.00**

Chase, Horton Foote, Signet #P2818, 1966, Marlon Brando, EX..**$5.00**

Chisum, Sam Bowie, Ace #10470, 1970, John Wayne, VG+...**$8.00**

Christine, Steven King, Signet #AE2838, 2nd printing, 8 pages of photos, VG.....................................**$3.00**

Clash of the Titans, Alan Dean Foster, Warner #95-829-8, 1981, photos, EX.......................................**$3.00**

Cocoon, David Saperstein, Jove #08400, 1985, VG+.....**$2.00**

Conan the Barbarian, De Camp & Carter, Bantam #22544, 1982, EX..**$3.00**

Crack in the Mirror, Marcel Haedrich, Dell First Edition #B160, 1960, VG **$3.00**

Creature From the Black Lagoon, Dreadstone, Berkley #03464, 1977, photos, EX...........................**$12.00**

Devil in Davos, Gil Brewer, ACE #37598, 1969, It Takes a Thief #1, EX......................................**$8.00**

Do Not Disturb, Marvin H Albert, Dell #2117, 1965, Doris Day, VG+..**$3.50**

Flower Drum Song, CY Lee, Dell #F175, 1961, new edition, VG+..**$4.00**

For a Few Dollars More, Millard, Award #A919x, no date, Clint Eastwood, EX..............................**$3.50**

Guns of Navarone, Alistair MacLean, Perma #M4089, 1961, 3rd printing, VG+..................................**$3.00**

Haunted Strangler, John C Cooper, Ace #D359, 1959, EX...**$17.50**

High Wind in Jamaica, Hughes, Signet #P2648, 1965, Anthony Quinn, EX......................................**$5.00**

Hondo, Louis L'Amour, Gold Medal #347, 1953, John Wayne, VG **$25.00**

I Can Get It for You Wholesale, Weldman, Avon #356, 1951, Susan Hayward, VG...........................**$5.00**

I Could Go On Singing, JD MacDonald, Gold Medal #K1291, 1963, Judy Garland, VG **$20.00**

Indiana Jones & the Temple of Doom, James Kahn, Ballantine, #31457, 1984, photos, EX **$3.50**

It Started in Naples, Cooper, Gold Medal #1017, 1960, Clark Gable & Sophia Loren, EX **$7.50**

Jaws-The Revenge, Hank Searls, Berkley #10546, 1987, EX **$2.50**

Jerk, Steve Martin & Carl Gottlieb, Warner #92-523, 1979, photos, EX...**$3.00**

Judgment at Nuremberg, Abby Mann, Signet #D2025, 1961, photos, VG+...**$5.00**

King Solomon's Mines, Haggard & Webb, Dell #433, 1950, Stewart Granger & Deborah Kerr, VG.....**$8.00**

Lady Takes a Flyer, Ronns, Avon #T228, 1958, Lana Turner & Jeff Chandler, EX...........................**$7.50**

Lieutenant Robin Crusoe USN, Bill Ford, Tempo #T138, 1966, Dick Van Dyke, VG.......................**$3.00**

Love at First Bite, Fotonovel #006, 1979, G+.................**$3.00**

Lucille Ball Story, James Gregory, Signet #W5833, 1974, photos, EX...**$5.00**

Marjorie Morningstar, Wouk, Signet #T1454, 1957, Gene Kelly & Natalie Wood, VG **$3.50**

Master of the World, Jules Verne, Ace #D504, 1961, Vincent Price, VG..**$5.00**

My Naughty Naughty Life, Century #001, Mamie Van Doren, 32 photo pages, 1964, EX **$25.00**

Raiders of the Lost Ark, Campbell Black, Ballantine #29490, 1981, Harrison Ford, EX **$2.50**

Red River, Borden Chase, Bantam #205, 1948, John Wayne, VG **$6.00**

Sgt Bilko Joke Book, Ballantine #289k, 1959, Phil Silvers, VG **$5.00**

Solomon & Sheba, Williams, Bantam #A1958, 1959, Yul Brynner & Gina Lollobrigida, VG **$2.50**

Some Like It Hot, Wilder & Diamond, Signet #S1656, Marilyn Monroe, VG..**$12.00**

Splintered Sunglasses Affair, Leslie, Ace #G752, 1968, Man From UNCLE, EX..**$6.00**

Star Is Born, Edwards, Warner #84-214, 1976, Streisand & Kristofferson, EX **$2.50**

Star Trek Log One, Alan Dean Poster, Ballantine #24014, 1974, VG **$3.00**

Star Trek Quiz Book, Andrews & Dunning, Signet #W7497, 1977, EX..**$6.00**

Star Wars: The Empire Strikes Back, Glut, Del Rey #28392, 1980, VG+...**$3.00**

Swamp Thing, Houston & Wein, Tor #48-039-3, 1982, Adrienne Barbeau, EX **$6.00**

Sweathog Trail, Johnston, Tempo #12406, 1976, Welcome Back Kotter, VG **$2.00**

Sweet Smell of Success, Lehman, Signet #S1413, 1957, Lancaster & Curtis, VG **$3.50**

James Bond, Diamonds Are Forever, paperback, Permabook edition, 1st printing, 1957, NM, $30.00. (Photo courtesy of June Moon.)

Terror in the Sun, Avallone, Signet #P3994, 1969, Hawaii Five-O #2, VG **$3.00**

They Came to Cordura, Swarthout, Signet #D1679, 1959, VG **$3.00**

Those Daring Young Men in Their Jaunty Jalopies, Hildick, Berkley #S1699, 1969, EX...............................**$4.00**

Thousand Coffins Affair, Avallone, Ace #G553, 1965, Man From UNCLE, VG **$3.00**

Trouble w/Tribbles, Gerrold, Ballantine, 323402, 1973, Star Trek, EX **$6.50**

Twilight Zone: The Movie, Robert Bloch, Warner #30840, 1982, photos, VG **$3.00**

Visit to a Small Planet, Vidal, Signet #S1799, 1960, Jerry Lewis, VG **$3.00**

Who Gets the Drumstick?, Bantam #H3675, 1968, Lucille Ball & Henry Fonda, VG **$2.00**

Young Dillinger, Stuart, Belmont #92-636, 1965, Nick Adams & Mary Ann Mobley, VG.........................**$4.00**

Bottle Openers

A figural bottle opener is one where the cap lifter is an actual feature of the subject being portrayed — for instance, the bill of a pelican or the mouth of a 4-eyed man. Most are made of painted cast-iron or aluminum; others were chrome or brass plated. Some of the major bottle-opener producers were Wilton, John Wright, L&L, and Gadzik. They have been reproduced, so beware of any examples with 'new' paint. Condition of the paint is an important consideration when it comes to evaluating an opener.

For more information, read *Figural Bottle Openers, Identification Guide*, by the Figural Bottle Opener Collectors. Number codes in our descriptions correlate with their book.

Advisor: Charlie Reynolds (See Directory, Bottle Openers)

Club: Figural Bottle Opener Collectors
Donna Kitzmiller
117 Basin Hill Road
Duncannon, PA 17020

Newsletter: *Just for Openers*
John Stanley
3712 Sunningdale Way
Durham, NC 27707-5684; 919-419-1546. Quarterly newsletter covers all types of bottle openers and corkscrews

Alligator, F-135, cast iron w/multicolor paint, open mouth, EX **$125.00**

Bar Bum, F-190, no tools, aluminum **$22.50**

Bear head, F-426, cast iron w/EX original multicolor paint, wall mount **$95.00**

Bear head, F-426, repainted cast iron, wall mount.....**$25.00**

Billy goat, F-74, aluminum...**$15.00**

Caddy, F-44, painted cast iron or brass, each **$300.00**

Cowboy w/guitar, F-27, painted cast iron, EX **$110.00**

Donkey, F-60, painted cast iron, EX **$40.00**

Double-eyed man, F-414, cast iron, EX **$45.00**

Drunk at Lamppost, F-1, cast iron w/poor paint...........**$4.00**

Drunk at Sign Post, F-11, cast iron, VG **$25.00**

Drunk at Sign Post, F-11, marked New York City, mounted on ashtray, EX..**$40.00**

Elephant, F-48, brass, trunk up....................................**$15.00**

False teeth, cast iron w/pink & white paint, wall mount, Wilton, EX **$95.00**

Flamingo, F-119, bright original paint, hollow mold ..**$175.00**

Iroquois Indian, F-197, copper, Iroquois head band ..**$37.50**

Lion, F-430, cast iron, wall mount **$1,200.00**

Lobster, F-168, cast iron w/EX red & black paint **$35.00**

Mademoiselle Lamp Post, F-4, painted cast iron, EX..**$75.00**

Mallard Duck, F-106, cast iron w/multicolor paint, VG ...**$75.00**

Miss Four Eyes, cast iron w/multicolor paint, wall mount, Wilton Products **$115.00**

Negro, F-402, brass, indented pupils, wall mount **$40.00**

Negro, F-402, repainted cast iron, wall mount...........**$40.00**

Pelican, F-131, cast iron w/multicolor paint, John Wright ..**$215.00**

Pheasant, F-104, cast iron w/EX multicolor paint.....**$150.00**

Rooster, F-97, cast iron w/EX multicolor paint............**$75.00**

ea horse, cast iron w/original multicolor paint, John Wright, 4⅛"...**$140.00**

ea horse, brass, 5x1⅛"..**$25.00**

hovel, F-221, brass, EX..**$22.50**

quirrel, F-91, cast iron w/multicolor paint...............**$150.00**

Lion wall mount, F-430, cast iron, $1,200.00. (Photo courtesy of Charlie Reynolds.)

Boyd Crystal Art Glass

After the Degenhart glass studio closed (see the Degenhart ection for information), it was bought out by the Boyd family, who added many of their own designs to the molds they acquired from the Degenharts and other defunct glasshouses. They are located in Cambridge, Ohio, and the glass they've been pressing in the more than 225 colors they've developed since they opened in 1978 is marked with their 'B in diamond' logo. Since 1988, a line has been added under the diamond. All the work is done by hand, and each piece is made in a selected color in limited amounts — a production run lasts only about six weeks or less. Items in satin glass or an exceptional slag are especially collectible, so are those with hand-painted details.

Advisor: Joyce Pringle (See Directory, Boyd)

Club: Boyd's Art Glass Collectors Guild
P.O. Box 52
Hatboro, PA 19040-0052

Airplane, Nile Green..**$18.00**
Bernie the Eagle, Capri Blue................................**$8.00**
Bernie the Eagle, Cardinal Red Carnival............**$10.00**
Boyd Airplane, Heather Gray..............................**$21.00**
Bulldog Paperweight, Blue Swirl.........................**$12.50**
Bunny Salt, Classic Black Slag.............................**$10.00**
Cat on Pillow, Persimmon....................................**$35.00**
Cat Slipper, Buckeye..**$10.00**
Cat Slipper, Chocolate...**$18.50**
Chick Salt, Golden Delight, 1".............................**$18.00**
Chick Salt, Waterloo...**$7.50**
Christmas Bell, Rubina...**$20.00**
Chuckles the Clown, Ebony.................................**$10.00**
Debbie Duck & Ducklings, Cobalt, set................**$22.50**
Debbie Duck & Ducklings, Mint Green, set.........**$22.50**

Duck Salt, Cobalt..**$12.00**
Elephant Head Toothpick, Chocolate, 1980........**$35.00**
Forget-Me-Not Toothpick, Cardinal Red..............**$10.00**
Forget-Me-Not Toothpick, Elizabeth 2 (rare color).....**$25.00**
Freddie the Clown, Cobalt..................................**$10.00**
Heart Jewel Box, Persimmon...............................**$18.50**
Heart Toothpick, Rubina......................................**$16.00**
Hen-on-Nest Covered Dish, Spinnaker Blue, 5".........**$25.00**
Horse Joey, Flame...**$40.00**
Horse Joey, Persimmon..**$20.00**
Horse Joey, Vaseline Carnival.............................**$35.00**
Horse Joey, Zack Boyd Slag.................................**$17.50**
JB Scotty, Cashmire Pink.....................................**$12.00**
JB Scotty, Cornsilk...**$10.00**
JB Scotty, Crystal...**$10.00**
JB Scotty, Pocono Blue..**$20.00**
Laced Heart Bonbon, Helitrope............................**$8.00**
Logo Paperweight, Impatient...............................**$12.50**
Louise Bell, Holly Green, 2nd Annual, 1980........**$50.00**
Louise Doll, Pink Champagne...............................**$45.00**
Lucky Unicorn, Touch of Pink..............................**$10.00**
Owl Bell, crystal..**$12.50**
Sammy Squirrel, Spinnaker Blue.........................**$10.00**
Sleigh, Nile Green..**$20.00**
Teardrop Wine, Willow Blue.................................**$8.00**
Zak the Elephant, Crown Tuscan.........................**$30.00**
Zak the Elephant, Flame......................................**$45.00**
Zak the Elephant, Lilac..**$17.00**
Zak the Elephant, Sandpaper...............................**$17.00**

Brastoff, Sascha

Sascha Brastoff's friend, Nelson Rockefeller, built a showplace complex to incorporate the various items Sascha created. It did not seem to matter if it was dinnerware, artware, resins, textiles, paintings, enamels, or jewelry, Sascha mastered all of them. In the early years (1947–1952) pieces were signed 'Sascha B.' or with a 'Sascha Brastoff' full signature. When the factory/studio operated sometime after 1952 and before 1962, pieces done by Sascha's employees were marked 'Sascha B'; and more often than not, the mark included the Chanticleer backstamp. The 'Sascha B.' mark with an 'R' in a circle was used after 1962. Sascha left the company in 1963, and ten years later the business closed. Of all the marks, the Chanticleer has to be the one that confuses collectors most. Some people believe that because Sascha's full signature is below the Chanticleer, they have a 'full signature' piece and price it accordingly. This is not the case. The full signature is almost always his first and last name, just as an autograph would be, and is not embellished with any other designs. The Chanticleer mark has Sascha's full name below it and is almost always done in gold.

During Brastoff's career, he created hand-painted china with names such as La Jolla, Night Song, and Roman Coin. He also designed a pottery dinnerware line which he named Surf Ballet. It was a combination of real gold or platinum and colors such as blue, pink or yellow. The 'dipping' into the gold or platinum created a wavy effect. Its simplicity made it an attractive line. Artware lines had various names, but Rooftops and Star

Steed were among the most popular. Sascha Brastoff died on February 4, 1993.

For simplification, entries in this category have the 'Sascha B.' mark unless otherwise noted.

For more information we recommend *The Collector's Encyclopedia of California Pottery* by Jack Chipman, and *The Collectors Encyclopedia of Sascha Brastoff* by Steve Conti, A. DeWayne Bethany, and Bill Seay.

Advisor: Susan Cox (See Directory, California Pottery)

Ashtray, Alaska, Eskimo face, green & white, 7x5" **$75.00**
Ashtray, angular free-form, #F3, 9¾" **$35.00**
Ashtray, enamel ware, hooded, 5½" **$40.00**
Ashtray, free-form, Mosaic design, 8½" **$40.00**
Ashtray, lg pipe form w/8" cigarette holder, green w/gold trim **$135.00**
Ashtray, orange w/flowers, 6" square **$25.00**
Ashtray, Rooftops design, 13x5" **$50.00**
Ashtray, Rooftops design, 15½x7" **$65.00**
Ashtray, Star Steed design, rectangular, #05, 7"..........**$45.00**
Bowl, Alaska, walrus, gray, footed, 3½" **$45.00**
Bowl, blue w/horse, rounded rectangular shape, 9" ..**$60.00**
Bowl, cereal; Night Song, Sascha Brastoff Fine China stamped mark, 6" **$35.00**
Bowl, Rooftops design, 10" **$65.00**
Bowl, Star Steed design, 5½" square.........................**$55.00**
Bowl, 3-footed, 2¼x10"...**$100.00**
Box, free-form, Jewel Bird design, w/lid, 7" **$80.00**
Box, Rooftops design, w/lid **$55.00**
Candle holder, resin, green, round............................**$45.00**
Canister, tea; Treetops design, w/lid, 10½" **$250.00**
Cigarette lighter, Mosaic design, round......................**$30.00**
Compote, Alaska, w/native, footed, 8".......................**$65.00**
Compote, Mayan Aztec design, #061, 9x9".................**$85.00**
Cup & saucer, Star Steed design, 3½x5½"..................**$45.00**
Dish, Alaska, footed, oblong, 2¼x7½".......................**$55.00**
Dish, Alaska, 3½" square **$40.00**
Dish, free-form, #F-42, 10"..**$60.00**
Dish, Pagoda design, #C-2 ....**$50.00**
Figure, poodle, satin-matt crackle glaze, 7x9"...........**$200.00**
Figurine, horse head, satin-matt crackle glaze, 7½" .**$250.00**
Gravy boat, Surf Ballet design, w/attached underplate, 9½" **$30.00**
Mug, Alaska, white & brown, #055C...........................**$45.00**
Mug, fruit design, 5" **$50.00**
Native wall mask, black & gold, 1 of a series, 9½"..**$210.00**
Nut dish, Vanity Fair design, #01, 3" **$50.00**
Obelisk, Rooftops design, w/lid, 22".........................**$315.00**
Obelisk, Stripes design, w/lid, full signature, 22" **$715.00**
Pitcher, Abstract design, blue & white w/gold trim..**$150.00**
Pitcher, Fruit design, dark brown, 6" **$110.00**
Planter, floral on light blue, 4x5"..............................**$50.00**
Plate, dinner; Winrock, porcelain, Sascha Brastoff Fine China stamped marks, 11" **$45.00**
Plate, Leaf design, full signature, 1959, 6" **$425.00**
Plate, Percheron horse, crackle gray, full signature, 11"...**$700.00**
Plate, salad; Night Song, porcelain, Sascha Brastoff Fine China stamped mark, 9" **$35.00**

Plate, Star Steed design, hand decorated, full signature, 1959, 10½"...**$250.00**
Plate, Surf Ballet design, blue w/platinum **$22.00**
Platter, Surf Ballet design, 3 sections, pink w/gold, 21"...**$80.00**

Sketch, framed, 20x17", $875.00.

Smoke set, w/ashtray, cigarette lighter & holder, rooster (Chanticleer) mark, 3-pc **$110.00**
Tray, Alaska, walrus on dark blue background, 11x15"..**$135.00**
Tray, white w/platinum & gold, #F-3, 9¾" **$40.00**
Vase, Abstract design, 12" **$125.00**
Vase, Alaska, #082, 8"...**$75.00**
Vase, Alaska, 13½"...**$150.00**
Vase, enamel & copper, 5".......................................**$70.00**
Vase, peacock, #066, 9" **$85.00**
Vase, Star Steed design, #047, 8" **$75.00**
Vase, Surf Ballet design, 5" **$68.00**

Brayton Laguna

In 1927 Durlin E. Brayton began a business in Laguna Beach, California, that today ranks in the top ten in terms of desirability among collectors. He created a variety of lines that appeal to widely diverse tastes. Disney characters and the Childhood series are very popular, and their values reflect this. A white crackle finish sometimes overall and sometimes in combination with other glazes is just now beginning to catch the collectors' eye. Webton Ware is fast becoming *the* line. This may be due to the country trend that is sweeping the United States. Be it American, Swedish, Romanian or others, Webton Ware is decorated in an appealing motif of flowers, farmers, dancers, etc., all in colorful blues, rusts, browns and greens. This line is inexpensive now compared to other Brayton lines. Several reasons may account for this, but the most prominent one may be that the mark was erroneously shown in a book on the subject as 'Welton,' which only served to confuse the novice Brayton collector. Of course, there is no Welton line. 'Webton' was named for Ellen (Webb) Webster Grive, Durlin's wife and business partner. It is a late line which may also account for the fact that it has gone relatively unnoticed by collectors until now.

Due to the imports that were being introduced into the United States after World War II, Brayton ceased production in 1968.

For further study, read *The Collector's Encyclopedia of California Pottery* by Jack Chipman.

Advisor: Susan Cox (See Directory, California Pottery)

Candle holders, Blackamoor, 5", pr	$150.00
Candy jar, Gypsy Woman	$425.00
Creamer & sugar bowl, eggplant glaze, 2½"	$65.00
Figurine, abstract man w/cat, satin-matt black, in-mold mark, ca 1957, 21"	$295.00
Figurine, Ann, seated child, Childhood series, 4"	$135.00
Figurine, baby leaning against pillow, 6x6"	$75.00
Figurine, bear, seated, 3½", from $18 to	$22.00
Figurine, Blackamoor, w/bowl	$70.00
Figurine, Blackamoor series, kneeling man holds vase, pastel jewels, gold trim, 14½", from $295 to	$325.00
Figurine, Chinese boy	$60.00
Figurine, Chinese girl w/child on her back	$95.00
Figurine, Donald Duck	$275.00
Figurine, duck, glossy green face, textured white body, 5"	$65.00
Figurine, Fifi & Mimi, fancy cats, 9", pr	$200.00
Figurine, Gay Nineties, bartender & 2 customers at bar, 9x9"	$130.00
Figurine, Gay Nineties, Honeymoon, couple in bathing suits, from $100 to	$135.00
Figurine, monkey & organ grinder	$85.00
Figurine, monkey female, woodtone w/white crackle face, 12"	$145.00
Figurine, mule, brown, w/blinders, yoke & purple collar, 7¼x10"	$100.00
Figurine, owl, woodtone w/white crackle, 6"	$45.00
Figurine, Pedro, yellow sombrero, multicolored scarf, pink shirt & white pants, Childhood series, stamped mark, 6½"	$80.00
Figurine, penguin, 7"	$55.00
Figurine, Pluto, howling; Walt Disney line, from $175 to	$190.00
Figurine, Pluto, sniffing; Walt Disney line, 3¼x6"	$175.00
Figurine, St Bernard, brown & white, standing, late 30s	$100.00
Figurine, toucan, polychrome high glaze, in-mold marks, 50s-60s, 9"	$125.00
Figurines, cow family: purple bull, cow & calf, 3-pc	$350.00
Figurines, dancing man & lady, Carol Safholm design, pr	$275.00
Flower holder, Sally, apron holds flowers	$35.00
Flower holder, Swedish Maid	$75.00
Pitcher, dark blue over light blue, loop-handled, incised marks, handmade by Durlin Brayton, 7¼"	$150.00
Pitcher, maroon, handmade by Durlin Brayton, 5"	$100.00
Planter, Provincial wheelbarrow	$20.00
Planter, Webton Ware, white w/blue peasants, 4"	$25.00
Planter, woodtone finish, green interior, oblong	$20.00
Plate, solid pink or maroon, early, 10½"	$40.00
Salt & pepper shakers, Dutch couple, pr	$125.00
Teapot, brown stain w/white crackle decor, CX-35	$50.00
Teapot, light blue, wide bottom, incised mark, handmade, 5"	$200.00
Teapot, Webton Ware, white w/blue peasants	$40.00
Tile, fancy tree w/dark purple background, handmade, incised mark, ca 1928, 6½"	$150.00
Tile, 2 black cats on multicolored patchwork roof, yellow background, handmade, incised mark, ca 1928, 4½"	$100.00
Vase, bud; Provincial design	$30.00
Vase, Hawaiian lady, half body, topless, head to side, eyes closed	$225.00
Vase, orange/yellow drip glaze, round, incised mark, 5½"	$100.00
Wall plaque, Blackamoor	$175.00

Breweriana

'Breweriana' is simply a term used by collectors to refer to items (usually freebies) given away by breweries to advertise their products. Some people prefer pre-prohibition era bottles, pocket mirrors, foam scrapers, etched and enameled glasses, mugs, steins, playing cards, postcards, pin-back buttons, and the like; but many collectors like the more available items from the past few decades as well. Some specialize either in breweries from a particular state, specific items such as foam scrapers (used to clean the foam off the top of glasses or pitchers of beer), or they might limit their buying to just one brewery.

The books we recommend for this area of collecting are *Back Bar Breweriana* by George J. Baley and *Huxford's Collectible Advertising* (Collector Books).

See also Beer Cans.

Club: National Association of Breweriana Advertising
Robert E. Jaeger, Executive Secretary
2343 Met-To-We Ln.
Wauwatosa, WI 53226, 414-257-0158; Annual dues: $20 US, $30 Canada, $40 overseas; with paid membership receive Membership Directory and certificate as well as 2 recent issues of *Breweriana Collector*

Ashtray, Ballantine Beer, round metal w/3-circle logo in center, 2 rests, 3½" dia, NM+	$15.00
Ashtray, Kaier's Special Beer, cast iron, figure of man on base, 4 rests, 1940s, EX	$45.00
Ashtray, Old Faithful Beer, round w/tin rim, glass bottom, frothy glass in center, G+	$80.00
Bank, Hamm's Beer, ceramic Hamm's bear posed w/head turned & eyes closed holding sign, Red Wing Mfg, VG	$355.00
Bottle opener, Grand Prize Lager Beer, wall-mount, 1950s, G+	$10.00
Bottle opener, Schlitz Beer, wood & metal bottle shape, pre-prohibition, NM+	$12.00
Bottle topper, Knickerbocker Beer, diecut image of young colonial man holding tray w/bottle & pilsner glass, 11x5", VG+	$20.00
Bridge set, Anheuser-Busch, score pad & 2 decks of cards in leather-type Amity folding case, 1973 sales convention, VG+	$50.00

Brochure, Tropical Beer, Welcome to Cuba, unfolds to colorful image of fort on Cuban coast w/2 palm trees, G+ ..**$30.00**

Calendar, Acme, 1944, easel-back desk type image of lady smiling at glass of Acme above full pad, EX........**$35.00**

Calendar, Pabst, 1936, Old Tankard Ale above tavern scene, product can & calendar pad below, framed, 19x15", VG+ **$135.00**

Charger, Falstaff Beer, metal, interior tavern scene w/ladies & gents at fireside table, 23" dia, NM **$60.00**

Clock, Budweiser, mantel-type clock atop see-through base showing 12-team Clydesdale wagon w/driver, 16x17", EX **$90.00**

Clock, Reading Premium, plastic & metal square shape w/Reach for Reading Premium 'The Friendly Beer...,' no numbers, EX+..**$60.00**

Clock, Schlitz Malt Liquor, plastic, square clock at right of image of bull w/name above & below, framed, 13x23", EX...**$35.00**

Clothes brush, Tivoli Brewing Co, decaled scene of man in knickers pouring glass of beer, 7", VG **$35.00**

Coaster, Hampden on Tap & Lager, Porter, Ale & Mild Ale lettered around bartender holding up tray, red & black, EX+ **$85.00**

Cookie jar, Budweiser, barrel shape w/painted image of the Clydesdale team pulling beer wagon, knob lid, 10", NM **$85.00**

Display, Blatz, 3-D pot metal figures of a baseball umpire calling runner safe as catcher catches ball, VG+ **$175.00**

Display, Bud Light, molded plastic light-up image of Spuds MacKenzie, dated, May 1987, EX **$100.00**

Display, Burgermeister Beer, gold-painted plaster chest-length statue of the Burgie man holding frothy mug, 16x14", EX **$125.00**

Display, Frankenmuth Beer & Ale, plaster image of seated dachshund on lettered base, 6x7", VG+................**$25.00**

Display, Goebel Beer, red & yellow plaster chicken tipping hat to beer bottle, green beveled base, 8x10", EX **$100.00**

Display, Hamm's, plastic bear holding Good Friends Meet Here sign, Hamm's Big Beer/Bear Drinking Brotherhood, 16", M **$100.00**

Display, Hunter, First Over the Bars, pot-metal statue of rider & horse jumping fence, lettered oval base, 15x14", EX.**$145.00**

Display, Lucky Lager, plaster elf holding a barrel next to beer bottle on rectangular base, 11x7", VG **$175.00**

Display, Pabst, What'll You Have? on bonnet of 3-D plaster bust of a woman, logo & Finest Beer Served... on base, VG+..**$115.00**

Drinking glass, Bartholomy Beer & Ale, clear glass barrel shape w/applied white pebble-grain logo, M **$20.00**

Drinking glass, Budweiser, fluted clear glass pilsner w/red & black applied label, 8½", M **$25.00**

Drinking glass, Schlitz, fluted clear glass mug w/pebble-grain screened design, M...**$30.00**

Drinking glass, Schmidt's City Club, fluted clear glass mug w/etched name, NM **$75.00**

Foam scraper, Ruppert Knickerbocker Beer, red & blue on white, NM **$10.00**

Foam scraper holder, Tru-Age Beer Special Light, gold plastic base w/enameled insert, blue glass holder, EX+ .**$110.00**

Lamp, Schlitz, stained-glass hanger shaped like a carousel top w/name on every 4th panel, 14" dia, VG+, A.......**$45.00**

Lighter, Jax Beer, red, blue & yellow pocket type, Smooth Mellow Jax on reverse, MIB..................................**$35.00**

Match safe, Lotos Export/Adam Scheidt Brewing Co, celluloid, brands listed on reverse, EX **$110.00**

Menu board, Old Reading Beer, tin, It's Wonderful Good! & Old Reading Beer logo above board, floral trim, 27x19" EX **$30.00**

Menu board, Pennsylvania Dutch Old German Beer, tin name above blackboard w/bottle & glass, A Real Treat 27x16", G **$40.00**

Mug, Budweiser, CS-57, 3rd Holiday, 50th Anniversary, M.**$40.00**

Mug, Burgie!, man holding sign, 2-sided, Ceramarte, M ...**$60.00**

Mug, Hamm's Beer, M, $15.00.

Note holder, brass, w/A & eagle logo, 6x4", EX **$40.00**

Patch, Ballantine Beer, for shirt, ovoid shape w/wide top 7x7", EX+ **$8.00**

Playing cards, Old Style Lager, image of cavalier holding up frothy glass, unopened, MIB..............................**$20.00**

Playing cards, Pearl Lager Beer, w/US tax stamp, EX...**$10.00**

Print, Blackhawk Brewing Co, profile portrait of Chief Blackhawk, embossed to resemble oil painting, framed 24x22", VG+ **$265.00**

Salt & pepper shakers, Coors, wooden barrels w/Coors in script, EX **$50.00**

Salt & pepper shakers, Koppitz Beer, bottle shape, NM+ pr..**$20.00**

Sign, Budweiser, reverse-painted glass, We Feature Budweiser Draught Beer Preferred Everywhere, framed 8x14", EX **$150.00**

Sign, Pabst, neon, ribbon logo w/Pabst on Tap in center, red & white, VG **$75.00**

Sign, Schlitz, composition, No Bitterness, Just the Kiss of Hops, bottle & hops image on woodgrain ground, 17x11", EX ...**$75.00**

Sign, Schlitz Malt Liquor, tin, The Bull lettered above image of a bull crashing through brick wall, 34x23", EX......**$60.00**

Sign, Schmidt's, neon, Schmidt's (of Philadelphia) Beer Sold Here, VG **$130.00**

Sign, Schmitd's City Club Beer, celluloid over tin hanger, name & logo in red & silver on black, round, 9" dia, EX......**$100.00**

Sign, Simon Pure Beer & Ale, plaster buffalo head mounted atop composition simulated wood plaque, 1950s, 12x14" VG+..**$60.00**

Sign, Sterling, tin hanger, We Serve Sterling Super-Bru above bottle image, vertical pennant shape, 17½x9", VG+......**$115.00**

Sign, Tam o' Shanter, reverse-painted glass, Ale Sir! Tam o' Shanter on Tap, back lit, 1930s-40s, rectangular, VG+.............**$75.00**

Spinner, Schmidt's, No Sugar No Glucose No Fattening Syrups on reverse, EX **$30.00**

Stein, Anheuser-Busch Inc, CS-64, A & eagle logo above name on scrolled banner w/leaf & hops design, metal cone lid, M **$100.00**

Stein, Budweiser, 1980 Holiday, Clydesdales, 5", from $80 to **$95.00**

Stein, Lone Star, #991, The Lone Star Is on the Rise Again, metal cone lid, 1988, M **$100.00**

Tap knob, Bud Lite, name on rectangular knob w/cut-out image of Spuds MacKenzie atop, 7x4", NM **$75.00**

Tap knob, Lucky Premium Lager, wooden U-shaped backing w/engraved brass badge-shaped nameplate, VG **$45.00**

Tap knob, PON Feigenspan, black ball shape w/white, gold & red on green enameled insert, VG+ **$30.00**

Tap knob, Schlitz, black ball shape w/name on cream insert, celluloid cover, EX **$155.00**

Thermometer, Fitger's Beer, metal, Everybody Here Likes... above pilsner glass, rectangular w/rounded corners, 12", VG+ **$50.00**

Thermometer, Ortlieb's, round dial-type w/glass lens, Drink Ortlieb's, Brewers for 100 Years, 10" dia, EX **$75.00**

Tip tray, Grand Prize Beer, yellow & chrome, 6x4", VG+ **$30.00**

Tip Tray, National Beer, purple & chrome, rectangular, 6x4", EX+ **$25.00**

Tray, Atlantic, ...The Beer of the South above visitors at southern mansion entrance, red wavy rim, 13½x18½", EX **$100.00**

Tray, Budweiser, Ask Your Customers To Make the ...Test, glass, bottle & can images, address below, deep rim, 13" dia, A . **$45.00**

Tray, Falstaff Beer, features 1978 Indy 500, elongated, 21", EX+ **$60.00**

Tray, Iroquois Indian Head Beer & Ale, lettering & profile image of Indian on white, deep orange rim, 12" dia, EX+ **$35.00**

Tray, Jacob Ruppert Beer-Ale, name above hand-held mugs toasting on woodgrain ground, 1930s-40s, oval, 14½", EX **$35.00**

Tray, Schlitz, For Great Occasions lettered diagonally & flanking bottle image, deep gold rim, 13" dia, VG+ **$20.00**

Tray, Stegmaier's Gold Medal Beer Ale-Porter, white & gold lettering on brown, deep straight rim, 12" dia, G **$15.00**

Breyer Horses

Breyer horses have been popular children's playthings since they were introduced in 1952, and you'll see several at any large flea market. Garage sales are good sources as well. The earlier horses had a glossy finish, but after 1968 a matt finish came into use. You'll find smaller domestic animals too. They are evaluated by condition, rarity, and desirability; some of the better examples may be worth a minimum of $150.00.

For more information and listings, see *Schroeder's Collectible Toys, Antique to Modern* (Collector Books).

Action Stock Horse Foal, matt chestnut, 1984-86, Traditional scale **$22.00**

Andalusian Foal, matt dark chestnut, 1979-93, Classic scale **$15.00**

Andalusian Mare, matt alabaster, Sears, 1984, Classic scale **$25.00**

Andalusian Stallion, matt dapple gray, Sears, 1984, Classic scale **$25.00**

Arabian Mare, matt chestnut, 1973-91, Classic scale ... **$15.00**

Arabian Stallion, matt sorrel, 1973-91, Classic scale.... **$15.00**

Black Beauty, matt black, 1980-93, Classic scale **$15.00**

Black Stallion, matt black, 1983-93, Classic scale........ **$15.00**

Bucking Bronco, matt gray, 1961-67, Traditional scale .. **$200.00**

Duchess, matt bay, 1980-93, Classic scale **$15.00**

Five-Gaiter, matt sorrel w/red & white ribbons, 1963-86, Traditional scale **$35.00**

Ginger, matt chestnut, 1980-93, Classic scale **$15.00**

Halla, matt bay, 1977-85, Traditional scale **$50.00**

Hobo (on base), matt buckskin, w/book & carrying case, 1975-80, Traditional scale **$55.00**

Jet Run, matt bay, 1980-93, Classic scale **$15.00**

Johar, matt alabaster, 1983-93, Classic scale **$15.00**

Keen, matt chestnut, 1980-93, Classic scale.................. **$15.00**

Kelso, matt or semigloss bay, 1975-90, Classic scale .. **$30.00**

Lipizzan Stallion, matt alabaster, 1975-80, Classic scale .. **$50.00**

Man O'War, matt red chestnut, 1973-90, Classic scale .. **$30.00**

Merrylegs, matt dapple gray, 1980-93, Classic scale ... **$10.00**

Mesteno, charging; matt dark buckskin, 1995-present, Classic size **$15.00**

Mesteno, fighting; matt dark buckskin, 1994-present, Classic scale **$15.00**

Mesteno, matt dark buckskin, 1992-present, Classic scale **$15.00**

Mesteno the Foal, matt light dun, 1993-present, Classic scale **$7.00**

Mesteno's Mother, matt buskskin, 1993-present, Classic scale **$15.00**

Might Tango, matt dapple gray, 1980-91, Classic scale ... **$20.00**

Morgan, matt black w/diamond star, 1965-87, Traditional scale **$40.00**

Mustang Foal, matt chestnut, 1976-90, Classic scale ... **$10.00**

Mustang Mare, matt chestnut pinto, 1976-90, Classic scale **$20.00**

Mustang Stallion, matt chestnut, 1976-90, Classic scale... **$20.00**

Old Timer, #200, alabaster, Traditional scale, 1966-76, missing hat, $40.00. (Photo courtesy of Carol Karbowiak Gilbert.)

Polo Pony (on base), matt bay, 1976-82, Traditional scale **$75.00**

Quarter Horse Foal, matt light bay, 1974-93, Classic scale...**$15.00**

Quarter Horse Mare, matt bay, 1974-93, Classic scale ..**$25.00**

Quarter Horse Stallion, matt palomino, 1974-93, Classic scale...**$25.00**

Racehorse, matt woodgrain, 1958-66, Traditional scale...**$200.00**

Rearing Stallion, matt palomino, 1965-85, Classic scale ...**$30.00**

Rojo, matt red dun, 1995-present, Classic scale **$15.00**

Ruffian, matt dark bay, 1977-90, Classic scale.............**$30.00**

Secretariat, matt chestnut, 1987-95, Traditional scale..**$20.00**

Silky Sullivan, matt brown, 1975-90, Classic scale **$30.00**

Sombra, matt grulla, 1994-present, Classic scale **$15.00**

Swaps, matt chestnut, 1975-90, Classic scale...............**$30.00**

Terrang, matt dark brown, 1975-90, Classic scale.......**$30.00**

Western Pony, glossy black, 1956-63, Traditional scale ..**$70.00**

British Royal Commemoratives

While seasoned collectors may prefer the older pieces using circa 1840 (Queen Victoria's reign) as their starting point, even present-day souvenirs make a good inexpensive beginning collection. Ceramic items, glassware, metalware, and paper goods have been issued on the occasion of weddings, royal tours, birthdays, christenings, and many other celebrations. Food tins are fairly easy to find, and range in price from about $30.00 to around $75.00 for those made since the 1950s.

For more information, we recommend *British Royal Commemoratives* by Audrey Zeder.

Advisor: Audrey Zeder (See Directory, British Royalty Commemoratives)

Loving cup, Queen Elizabeth II Coronation, June 2, 1953, Royal Doulton, #254 from limited edition of 1,000, 10¾", rare, $550.00.

Ashtray, Elizabeth 1953 coronation, portrait, white on blue, Wedgwood **$45.00**

Beaker, George V coronation, multicolor portrait, Foley, child size, 3¼" **$65.00**

Bell, William 1982 birth, 6-sided shape, Aynsley **$45.00**

Booklet, Elizabeth 1977 jubilee, pictorial record, heavy stock, EX+ **$15.00**

Bookmark, William 1982 birth, woven in original card, Cashs, NM **$20.00**

Calendar, Elizabeth II, 1949, complete.....................**$35.00**

Compact, Elizabeth 1953 coronation, multicolor royal regalia, 3½" **$50.00**

Covered dish, William 1982 birth, screw lid, Coalport .**$50.00**

Cup & saucer, Princess Margaret 1958 Canada visit, Aynsley...**$125.00**

Doll, William 1982 birth, Royal Doulton, MIB **$225.00**

Ephemera, Edward VII cigar band, multicolor w/gold, 1900 ....**$12.00**

First Day cover, Charles 21st birthday, young prince stamp **$15.00**

Magazine, Field, Charles & Diana 1981 wedding, w/cover, August 1981...**$35.00**

Magazine, Illustrated London News, Elizabeth 1953 Royal Tour, November 1953 ....**$25.00**

Magazine, Radio Times, Charles/Diana 1981 wedding, July 1981 ....**$15.00**

Magnet, Elizabeth II 1994 Russia visit, multicolor, 2½", pr ..**$10.00**

Miniature, Charles/Diana/William/Henry album, 15 photos, 1¼x1" **$30.00**

Miniature, William 1982 birth, multicolor, Caverswall, 2¼x1" **$35.00**

Mug, Charles 1969 investiture, sepia photo portrait ...**$35.00**

Mug, Elizabeth II 1953, multicolor portrait, barrel shape, Royal Winton...**$45.00**

Mug, Prince William 1982 birth, gold profiles, Kilncraft...**$35.00**

Plate, Charles/Diana 1992 separation, pressed blue glass, 3½" **$30.00**

Plate, Diana w/1-year-old William, multicolor, Danbury, 8" **$85.00**

Plate, Elizabeth II 1953 coronation, black portrait, shield shape, 5" **$25.00**

Plate, Queen Mother 1980 birthday, Doulton, 8¼".....**$75.00**

Postcard, Diana 1995 Tokyo visit, limited edition of 500..**$5.00**

Postcard, Queen Mother 85th birthday, limited edition, numbered, Carousel **$15.00**

Spoon, Prince William 1982 birth, silverplate w/enameled bowl...**$25.00**

Stamps, Prince William birth, 6-stamp block...............**$15.00**

Textile, Charles/Diana 1981 wedding towel, multicolor portrait, linen **$35.00**

Textile, Elizabeth II 1977 jubilee shopping bag, official design **$15.00**

Thimble, Charles/Diana wedding, multicolor enameling, gold rim, Spode **$35.00**

Thimble, Elizabeth II 1992 Australia visit, multicolor portrait, China...**$25.00**

Tin, Elizabeth II 1977 jubilee, multicolor portrait, match striker, 2x2" **$30.00**

Tin, Prince William 1982 birthday, hinged, upright, 4x3x3" **$45.00**

Toby mug, Diana, hand painted, Kevin Francis, limited edition...**$300.00**

Tray, Anne, 1973 wedding, riding horseback, oval, melamine...**$65.00**

Tray, Prince William 1982 birth, embossed design on copper, 11" dia..**$50.00**

Vehicle, Diana 1981 miniature Austin Metro car, Corgi Mettoy **$40.00**

Bubble Bath Containers

By now, you're probably past the state of being incredulous at the sight of these plastic figurals on flea market tables with price tags twenty time higher than they carried when new and full. (There's no hotter area of collecting today than items from the fifties through the seventies that are reminiscent of early kids' TV shows and hit movies.) Most of these were made in the 1960s. The Colgate-Palmolive Company produced the majority of them — they're the ones marked 'Soaky' — and these seem to be the most collectible. Each character's name is right on the bottle. Other companies followed suit; Purex also made a line, so did Avon. Be sure to check for paint loss, and look carefully for cracks in the brittle plastic heads of the Soakies. For more information, we recommend *Schroeder's Collectible Toys, Antique to Modern* (Collector Books).

Advisors: Matt and Lisa Adams (See Directory, Bubble Bath Containers)

Baloo Bear (Jungle Book), Colgate-Palmolive, slipover only, 1960s, NM **$25.00**
Bambi, EX...**$30.00**
Barney Rubble, Purex, 1960s, NM................................**$30.00**
Batman, Avon, MIB..**$25.00**
Beatles, Paul McCartney, Colgate-Palmolive, EX.......**$110.00**
Big Bad Wolf, Tubby Time, 1960s, NM........................**$35.00**
Bozo the Clown, VG **$25.00**
Bugs Bunny, Colgate-Palmolive, w/cap ears, 1960s, NM...**$30.00**
Bugs Bunny, leaning against eggs, VG **$15.00**
Creature From the Black Lagoon, NM..........................**$95.00**
Dum Dum, VG..**$25.00**
Fred Flintstone, Colgate-Palmolive, EX **$20.00**
Fred Flintstone, Purex, 1960s, NM...............................**$30.00**
Goofy, Colgate-Palmolive, 1960s, NM **$25.00**
Gravel Truck, Colgate-Palmolive, 1960s, NM..............**$40.00**
Gumby, No More Tears/Perma Toy, 1987, M (sealed).....**$20.00**
King Louie (Jungle Book), Colgate-Palmolive, slipover only, 1960s, NM..**$25.00**
Lippy the Lion, Purex, 1960s, EX **$55.00**
Magilla Gorilla, Purex, 1960s, NM **$60.00**
Mousketeer Girl, Colgate-Palmolive, 1960s, NM.........**$25.00**
Mummy, Colgate-Palmolive, 1960s, NM......................**$100.00**
Mush Mouse, EX..**$50.00**
Oil Truck, Colgate-Palmolive, 1960s, NM **$40.00**
Panda Bear, Tubby Time, 1960s, NM...........................**$30.00**
Pebbles Flintstone, Purex, 1960s, NM **$35.00**
Rocky Squirrel, Soaky, 1960s, EX **$35.00**
Santa Claus, EX..**$15.00**
Simon (Chipmunks), Colgate-Palmolive, 1960s, NM...**$30.00**
Smokey Bear, w/contents, NM **$15.00**
Snagglepuss, Purex, 1960s, NM **$50.00**
Snow White, Colgate-Palmolive, bank, 1960s, NM **$30.00**

Spouty the Whale, w/original tag, M **$25.00**
Squiddly Diddly, Purex, 1960s, NM............................**$60.00**
Tennesse Tuxedo, 1960s, NM......................................**$30.00**
Three Little Pigs, Tubby Time, 1960s, NM.................**$35.00**
Tidy Toy Race Car, NM **$50.00**
Wally Gator, Purex, 1960s, NM...................................**$50.00**

Wendy the Witch, Colgate-Palmolive, 1960s, M, with original packaging, $50.00.

Wendy Witch, Colgate-Palmolive, 1960s, NM **$30.00**
Wolfman, VG..**$85.00**
Yakky Doodle Duck, 1976, w/original tag, M.............**$25.00**

Calculators

It is difficult to picture the days when a basic four-function calculator cost hundreds of dollars, especially when today you get one free by simply filling out a credit application. Yet when they initially arrived on the market in 1971, the first of these electronic marvels cost from $300.00 to $400.00. All this for a calculator that could do no more than add, subtract, multiply, and divide.

Even at that price there was an uproar by consumers as calculating finally became convenient. No longer did you need to use a large mechanical monster adding machine or a slide rule with all of its complexity. You could even put away your pencil and paper for those tough numbers you couldn't 'do' in your head.

With prices initially so high and the profit potential so promising, several hundred companies jumped onto the calculator bandwagon. Some made their own; many purchased them from other (often overseas) manufacturers, just adding their own nameplate. Since the product was so new to the world, most of the calculators had some very different and interesting body styles.

Due to the competitive nature of all those new entries to the market, prices dropped quickly. A year-and-a-half later, prices started to fall below $100.00 — a magic number that caused a boom in consumer demand. As even more calculators became available and electronics improved, prices continued to drop, eventually forcing many high-cost makers (who could not compete) out of business. By 1978 the number of major calculator companies could be counted on both hands. Fortunately calculators are still available at almost every garage sale or flea market for a mere pittance — usually 25¢ to $3.00.

For more information refer to *A Guide to HP Handheld Calculators and Computers* by Wlodek Mier-Jedrzejowicz and *Collector's Guide to Pocket Calculators* by Guy Ball and Bruce Flamm (both published by Wilson/Barnette), and *Personal Computers and Pocket Calculators* by Dr. Thomas Haddock.

Advisor: Guy D. Ball (See Directory, Calculators)

Club: International Association of Calculator Collectors
P.O. Box 345
Tustin, CA 92681

Bowmar MX-20, MIB	**$42.00**
Bowmar MX-35	**$12.00**
Bowmar 901	**$45.00**
Canon F-5	**$20.00**
Casio CQ-2	**$16.00**
Eldorado 8KB	**$20.00**
Hewlett Packard HP-01 Calculator Watch, red LED type	**$750.00**
Hewlett Packard HP-25	**$40.00**
Hewlett Packard HP-35, 1st scientific pocket model	**$90.00**
Hewlett Packard HP-38E	**$60.00**
Hewlett Packard HP-67	**$160.00**
KingsPoint SC-20	**$25.00**
Lloyds E650, MIB	**$25.00**
Miida 8	**$18.00**
Omron 86M	**$25.00**
Pico Mini PA80D	**$18.00**
Sharp EL-8, 1st portable model	**$45.00**
Sound Design 8309	**$20.00**
Texas Instruments SR-50	**$28.00**
Texas Instruments 1680	**$12.00**
Texas Instruments 1680, MIB	**$25.00**
Unitrex CB8SL, MIB	**$28.00**

California Potteries

This is a sampling of the work of several potteries and artists who operated in California ca. 1940–1960. Today good examples of this genre are among the most highly collectible pottery items on the market. Some of the more renowned companies are listed elsewhere in this book.

For more information we recommend *The Collector's Encyclopedia of California Pottery* by Jack Chipman.

See also Sascha Brastoff; Brayton, Laguna; Kay Finch; Brad Keeler; Howard Pierce; Hedi Schoop; Twin Winton; and Weilware.

Advisors: Pat and Kris Secor (See Directory, California Pottery)

Adams, Matthew; bowl, Alaska in gold, bear scene on bright yellow, pedestal foot, w/lid, signed, 5" H **$185.00**
Adams, Matthew; lighter, walrus on light blue, rounded top, signed Matthew Adams, #183, 5½" **$115.00**
Adams, Matthew; planter, polar bear on green & white, 4½" **$95.00**

Adams, Matthew; salt & pepper shakers, Eskimo design on bright blue w/gold trim, bulbous, 4", pr **$65.00**
Adams, Matthew; vase, polar bear design, blue & white, curved bulbous top, #1262, 8½" **$265.00**
Bellaire, Marc; ashtray, Mardi Gras, triangular, 8½" **$165.00**
Bellaire, Marc; bird, long neck, body forms large bowl, black, pink & blue w/gold trim, 17" **$315.00**
Bellaire, Marc; birds, tan w/green leaf design, gold trim, pr **$195.00**
Block, planter, dog, seated, w/open back, white w/pastel flowers, 4½" **$24.00**
Brock of California, baker, skillet shape, w/lid..........**$30.00**
Brock of California, bowl, divided vegetable..........**$35.00**
Brock of California, bowl, soup; 6¾"..........**$9.00**
Brock of California, condiment set, 3 jars w/lid **$35.00**
Brock of California, cup & saucer....................**$10.00**
Brock of California, pitcher, 3-footed..........**$45.00**
Brock of California, plate, dinner; 11" **$10.00**
Brock of California, sugar bowl, w/lid..........**$18.00**
Brock of California, tureen, soup; w/lid..........**$50.00**
DeForest of California, condiment jar, American **$50.00**
DeForest of California, condiment jar, Italian Jam **$45.00**
DeForest of California, pitcher, water; pig face, lg, rare...**$265.00**

Kaye, figurine, Black mailman tipping hat, 8½", $110.00. (Photo courtesy of Pat and Kris Secor.)

Kaye, figurine, blond in strapless gown w/applied roses, arms behind her head, #311, 12", from $70 to.....**$85.00**
Lane & Co of Van Nuys, snack tray, weiner dog center, 1958, 15x20" **$50.00**
Modglin, figurine, brown bear w/yellow flowers, 3½" ..**$45.00**
Modglin, figurine, girl, tan w/embossed flowers, 9"...**$80.00**
S-Quire, figurine, lady Spanish dancer, blue dress w/brown floral design, signed Zaida, #102, 11" **$75.00**
S-Quire, figurines, Dutch boy & girl in blue w/tulips, signed Zaida, 7", pr..........**$55.00**
Treasure Craft, figurine, horses, wood tone & white crackle, 8x10", pr **$70.00**
Treasure Craft, figurine, male & female, wood tone & white crackle, 11", pr..........**$70.00**
Ward, Kim; figurine, boy w/flower, green pants, hat, #45, 8" **$65.00**

Ward, Kim; figurine, girl holds skirt to form large bowl & heavy base, pink & blue flowers, rosy cheeks, 13x12x6"...**$125.00**

West Coast Pottery, figurine, Hawaiian lady, topless, pink floral skirt, applied flowers in hair, sticker/#302D, 17¼"...**$275.00**

Ynez, figurine, girl w/cat **$55.00**

Yona, figurine, angel, Be Kind to Animals, 5" **$28.00**

Yona, figurine, Chinese man w/basket, 12" **$20.00**

Yona, figurine, European couple, white, blue clothes, man in cape, lady w/bucket, 8¾", pr **$75.00**

Yona, figurine, girl holding bouquet, applied flowers, brown & white dress **$55.00**

Yona, nut/mint dish, red & white stripe w/striped handle .**$32.00**

California Raisins

Since they starred in their first TV commercial in 1986, the California Raisins have attained stardom through movies, tapes, videos, and magazine ads. Today we see them everywhere on the secondary market — PVC figures, radios, banks, posters — and they're very collectible. The PVC figures were introduced in 1987. Originally there were four, all issued for retail sales — a singer, two conga dancers, and a saxophone player. Before the year was out, Hardee's, the fast-food chain, came out with the same characters, though on a slightly smaller scale. A fifth character, Blue Surfboard (horizontal), was created, and three 5½" Bendees with flat pancake-style bodies appeared.

In 1988 the ranks had grown to twenty-one: Blue Surfboard (vertical), Red Guitar, Lady Dancer, Blue/Green Sunglasses, Guy Winking, Candy Cane, Santa Raisin, Bass Player, Drummer, Tambourine Lady (there were two styles), Lady Valentine, Boy Singer, Girl Singer, Hip Guitar Player, Sax Player with Beret, and four Graduates (styled like the original four, but on yellow pedestals and wearing graduation caps). And Hardee's issued an additional six: Blue Guitar, Trumpet Player, Roller Skater, Skateboard, Boom Box, and Yellow Surfboard.

Still eight more characters came out in 1989: Male in Beach Chair, Green Trunks with Surfboard, Hula Skirt, Girl Sitting on Sand, Piano Player, AC, Mom, and Michael Raisin. They made two movies and thereafter were joined by their fruit and vegetable friends, Rudy Bagaman, Lick Broccoli, Banana White, Leonard Limabean, and Cecil Thyme. Hardee's added four more characters in 1991: Anita Break, Alotta Style, Buster, and Benny.

All Raisins are dated with these exceptions: those issued in 1989 (only the Beach Scene characters are dated, and they're actually dated 1988), and those issued by Hardee's in 1991.

For more information we recommend *Schroeder's Collectible Toys, Antique to Modern* (Collector Books).

Applause, Captain Toonz, w/blue boom box, yellow sunglasses & sneakers, Hardee's 2nd Promotion, 1988, M.....**$3.00**

Applause, FF Strings, w/blue guitar, orange sneakers, Hardee's 2nd Promotion, 1988, M **$3.00**

Applause, Michael Raisin (Jackson), w/silver microphone & studded belt, Special Edition, 1989, M **$20.00**

Applause, Rollin' Rollo, w/roller skates & yellow sneakers, hat marked H, Hardee's 2nd Promotion, 1988, M..**$3.00**

Applause, Waves Weaver 1 or 2, surfboard connected or not connected to foot, Hardee's 2nd Promotion, 1988, M........**$4.00**

CALRAB, Guitar, red guitar, 1st Commercial Issue, 1988, M **$8.00**

CALRAB, Hip Band Guitarist (Jimmy Hendrix), w/headband & yellow guitar, 2nd Key Chains, 1988, M **$35.00**

CALRAB, Microphone, Graduate w/right hand pointing up & microphone in left, Graduate Key Chains, 1988, M ..**$35.00**

CALRAB, Microphone, right hand formed into fist w/microphone in left, Post Raisin Bran Issue, 1987, M.......**$6.00**

CALRAB, Microphone, right hand points up w/microphone in left hand, Hardee's 1st Promotion, 1987, M............**$3.00**

CALRAB, Santa, red cap & green sneakers, Christmas Issue, 1988, M **$9.00**

CALRAB, Saxophone, gold sax, no hat, Hardee's 1st Promotion, 1987, M..**$3.00**

CALRAB, Saxophone, inside of sax painted black, Post Raisin Bran Issue, 1987, M **$4.00**

CALRAB, Sunglasses, Graduate w/index fingers touching face, Graduate Key Chains, 1988, M **$35.00**

CALRAB, Sunglasses, holding candy cane, green sunglasses, red sneakers, Christmas Issue, 1988, M..................**$9.00**

CALRAB, Sunglasses 1, eyes visible, aqua sunglasses & sneakers, 1st Commercial Issue, 1988, M **$16.00**

CALRAB, Sunglasses 2, eyes not visible, aqua sunglasses & sneakers, 1st Commercial Issue, 1988, M...............**$8.00**

CALRAB, Winky, hitchhiking & winking, 1st Commercial Issue, 1988, M **$8.00**

CALRAB-Applause, AC, 'Gimme-5' pose w/tall pompadour & red sneakers, Meet the Raisins 2nd Edition, 1989, M.......**$85.00**

CALRAB-Applause, Alotta Style, w/purple boom box & pink boots, Hardee's 4th Promotion, 1991, M...............**$12.00**

CALRAB-Applause, Anita Break, w/Hardee's bags, Hardee's 4th Promotion, 1991, MIP **$12.00**

CALRAB-Applause, Benny, w/bowling ball & orange sunglasses, Hardee's 4th Promotion, 1991, MIP **$12.00**

CALRAB-Applause, Boy w/Surfboard, purple board, brown base, Beach Theme Edition, 1988, M....................**$10.00**

CALRAB-Applause, Drummer, black hat w/yellow feather, 2nd Commercial Issue, 1988, M............................**$8.00**

CALRAB-Applause, Girl Singer, w/bracelet & reddish purple shoes, 2nd Commercial Issue, 1988, M **$12.00**

CALRAB-Applause, Girl w/Boom Box, purple sunglasses, green shoes, brown base, Beach Theme Edition, 1988, M...**$10.00**

CALRAB-Applause, Hip Band Guitarist (Jimmy Hendrix), w/headband & yellow guitar, 3rd Commercial Issue, 1988, M **$22.00**

CALRAB-Applause, Hip Band Microphone (Female), w/bracelet & yellow shoes, 2nd Key Chains, 1988, M **$25.00**

CALRAB-Applause, Hip Band Microphone (Male), left hand extended w/open palm, 3rd Commercial Edition, 1988, M **$9.00**

CALRAB-Applause, Hip Band Saxophone, black beret & blue eyelids, 3rd Commercial Issue, 1988, M................**$15.00**

CALRAB-Applause, Hula Girl, green skirt w/yellow shoes & bracelet, Beach Theme Edition, 1988, M **$10.00**

CALRAB-Applause, Piano, blue piano, red hair & green sneakers, Meet the Raisins 1st Edition, 1989, M...**$15.00**

CALRAB-Applause, Saxophone, black beret, blue eyelids, 2nd Key Chains, 1988, small, M, $35.00. (Photo courtesy Larry DeAngelo.)

CALRAB-Applause, Valentines (Be Mine/I'm Yours), male or female holding hearts, Special Lovers issue, 1988, each..............**$8.00**
Claymation-Applause, Cecil Thyme, carrot-like figure, Meet the Raisins 2nd Edition, 1989, M **$85.00**
Claymation-Applause, Lick Broccoli, w/guitar, green, black, red & orange, Meet the Raisins 1st Edition, 1989, M......**$12.00**
Claymation-CALRAB, Saxophone, Graduate on yellow base, Post Raisin Bran Issue, 1988, M............................**$40.00**
Claymation-CALRAB, Sunglasses, Graduate on yellow base, Post Raisin Bran Issue, 1988, M............................**$40.00**

Miscellaneous

AM/FM Radio, Nasta, poseable arms and legs, MIB, from $150.00 to $175.00. (Photo courtesy of Larry DeAngelo.)

Air Freshener, various styles, M, each............................**$5.00**
Book tote, w/tag, M **$30.00**
Bookmarks, diecut U or punched hole at top, different styles, M, each **$5.00**
Colorforms, MIB (sealed) **$30.00**
Computer game, IBM, M...**$22.00**
Doorknob hangers, 6 different styles, M, each..............**$6.00**

Erasers, set of 2, MOC...**$15.00**
Paper plates, MIP...**$15.00**
Party invitations, M..**$15.00**
Pen, orange, white & black ballpoints w/PVC figures at top, set of 3, M **$25.00**
Sandwich music box, any figure, CALRAB, 1987, M...**$25.00**
Scarf, Raisin Chorus Line printed on fabric, M...........**$20.00**
Trading cards, World Tour Series #1, complete set, M .**$15.00**
Wrapping paper, M...**$15.00**
Wristwatch, w/second hand, EX+.................................**$35.00**

Camark Pottery

Camark Pottery was manufactured in CAMden, ARKansas, from 1927 to the early 1960s. The pottery was founded by Samuel J. 'Jack' Carnes, a native of east central Ohio familiar with Ohio's fame for pottery production. Camark's first wares were made from Arkansas clays shipped by Carnes to John B. Lessell in Ohio in early to mid-1926. Lessell was one of the associates responsible for early art pottery making. These wares consisted of Lessell's lustre and iridescent designs based on similar ideas he pioneered earlier at Owens, Weller, and other potteries. The variations made for Camark included Weller Marengo, LaSa, and Lamar. These early pieces were signed only with the 'Lessell' signature. When Camark began operations in the spring of 1927, the company had many talented, experienced workers including Lessell's wife and step-daughter (Lessell himself died unexpectedly in December, 1926), the Sebaugh family, Frank Long, and Boris Trifonoff. This group produced a wide range of art pottery finished in glazes of many types including lustre and iridescent (signed LeCamark), crackle, and two-color drips. Art pottery manufacture continued until the early 1930s when emphasis changed to industrial castware (molded wares) with single-color, primarily matt glazes.

Some of Camark's designs and glazes are easily confused with the wares of other companies. For instance, Lessell decorated and signed a line in his lustre and iridescent glazes for Fraunfelter, but these were done in porcelain, not pottery. Camark's drip glazes (green over pink and green over mustard/brown) closely resemble Muncie's, but Muncie's clay is generally white while Camark used a cornmeal-colored clay for its drip-glaze pieces. Muncie's are marked with a letter/number combination, and the bottoms are usually smeared with the base color. Camark's bottoms have a more uniform color application.

For more information, we recommend the *Collector's Encyclopedia of Camark Pottery* (Collector Books) by David Edwin Gifford, Arkansas pottery historian and author of *Collector's Encyclopedia of Niloak Pottery*. (Autographed editions available from the author at the address below.)

Advisor: David Edwin Gifford (See Directory, Niloak)

Club: National Society of Arkansas Pottery Collectors
c/o David Edwin Gifford
P.O. Box 7617
Little Rock, Arkansas 72217

Art Ware

Ashtray, frog, olive green drip, marked w/block letter, 2¾" **$75.00**
Ashtray, green/brown drip, brown Arkansas sticker, 1¾x4¼" **$40.00**
Ashtray set, green/brown drip, marked w/block letter, 3½", 2-pc **$55.00**
Flower bowl, yellow, green-blue & blue drip, marked Arkansas w/die stamp, 5¼" **$175.00**
Humidor, glossy black, marked w/block letter, 5½" ... **$50.00**
Humidor, green & pink drip, marked w/block letter, 7½" . **$100.00**
Lamp base, glossy black w/lustre design, no mark, 14" . **$550.00**
Pitcher, w/stopper, olive green drip, marked w/block letter, 7" **$125.00**
Vase, green & blue drip, ring handles, brown Arkansas sticker, 6" **$100.00**
Vase, lustre design of palm trees, signed Lessell, 8" .. **$400.00**
Vase, pink & green drip, ribbed, marked w/block letter, 6¼" **$75.00**
Vase, white crackle design, gold Arkansas ink stamp, 8" .. **$250.00**

Hand-painted Ware

Bowl, console; blue iris, Arkansas inventory sticker: shape 804, finish R, (original) price $3.50, 14½" **$90.00**
Candlesticks, double; pink roses, marked Camark/269/USA (in the mold), 5", pr **$60.00**
Ewer, rose-pink iris, marked Camark/800/USA (in the mold), 13¼" **$100.00**
Vase, blue roses, w/handles, marked Camark/810/USA (in the mold), 7½" **$60.00**
Wall pocket, yellow iris, no mark, 9" **$125.00**

Vase, yellow and blue iris, 8½", $50.00.

Industrial Castware

Ashtray, blue, petal design, marked w/block letter, 2½" .. **$20.00**
Ashtray, stove, burgundy, blue Arkansas sticker, 3½" .. **$10.00**
Bowl, green, marked Camark/624/USA (in the mold), 9x3" **$35.00**
Box, cigarette; green, marked w/block letter, 4½x5" . **$40.00**
Candlesticks, ivory, marked w/block letter, 3", pr **$40.00**
Cat, climbing, white, marked Camark/058/USA (in the mold), 15" **$100.00**
Dogs, Pointer & Setter, burgundy, no mark, 2¾" **$30.00**
Elephant, free-standing, burgundy, no mark, 3¾" **$20.00**
Ewer, blue, marked Camark/268/USA (in the mold), 10" . **$35.00**
Fishbowl, cat sits aside, white, marked w/block letter, 9" ... **$75.00**
Flowerpot, pink, marked Camark/992/USA (in the mold), 6" **$15.00**
Pitcher, gold, marked Camark/791/USA (in the mold), 8" wide **$25.00**

Pitcher, Pelican, green, 5¾", $35.00.

Rabbit, cotton dispenser, white, Camark black ink stamp, 4" **$25.00**
Rooster, black, marked Camark/323/USA (in the mold), 8½" **$30.00**
Salt & pepper shakers, ball shape w/S & P handles, green, blue Arkansas sticker, pr **$20.00**
Salt & pepper shakers, S & P shapes, free-standing, pink, no mark, pr **$20.00**
Sugar bowl & creamer, brown, marked Camark/830/USA (in the mold) **$20.00**
Vase, cream, w/rope handles, Arkansas inventory sticker: Shape 568, finish S, (original) price 50¢, 7" **$35.00**
Vase, green, marked Camark/953/USA (in the mold), 14" .. **$60.00**
Vase, pink, fan shape, marked Camark/811/USA (in the mold), 6" **$15.00**
Vase, pink, fan shape, marked Camark/829/USA (in the mold), 5" **$15.00**
Vase, pink, w/handles, marked Camark/404/USA (in the mold), 7" **$25.00**
Vase, yellow, fan shape w/3 openings, marked Camark/403/USA (in the mold), 7" **$20.00**
Wall pocket, handkerchief, blue Arkansas sticker, 7" . **$20.00**

Cambridge Glassware

If you're looking for a 'safe' place to put your investment dollars, Cambridge glass is one of your better options. But as with any commodity, in order to make a good investment, knowledge of the product and its market is required. There are two books we would recommend for your study, *Colors in Cambridge Glass,* put out by the National Cambridge Collectors Club, and *The Collector's Encyclopedia of Elegant Glass* by Gene Florence.

The Cambridge Glass Company (located in Cambridge, Ohio) made fine quality glassware from just after the turn of the century until 1958. They made thousands of different items in hundreds of various patterns and colors. Values hinge on rarity of shape and color. Of the various marks they used, the 'C in triangle' is the most common. In addition to their tableware, they also produced flower frogs representing ladies and children and models of animals and birds that are very valuable today. To learn more about them, you'll want to read *Glass Animals and Figural Flower Frogs From the Depression Era* by Lee Garmon and Dick Spencer.

Advisor: Debbie Maggard (See Directory, Elegant Glassware)

Newsletter: *The Cambridge Crystal Ball*
National Cambridge Collectors, Inc.
P.O. Box 416
Cambridge, OH 43725-0416; Dues: $15 for individual member and $3 for associate member of same household

Apple Blossom, crystal, comport, fruit cocktail; 4" **$12.50**
Apple Blossom, crystal, pitcher, loop handle, 67-oz...**$135.00**
Apple Blossom, crystal, sugar bowl, tall, footed.........**$15.00**
Apple Blossom, pink or green, bonbon, 2-handled, 5¼"...**$25.00**
Apple Blossom, pink or green, bowl, low footed, 11"..**$90.00**
Apple Blossom, pink or green, bowl, 13" **$75.00**
Apple Blossom, pink or green, stem, water; #3135, 8-oz...**$20.00**
Apple Blossom, pink or green, tumbler, footed, #3155, 5-oz...**$25.00**

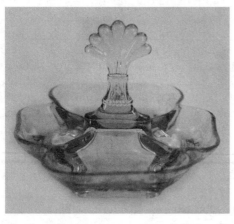

Apple Blossom, green, relish, 4-part, 9", $90.00.

Apple Blossom, yellow or amber, bowl, finger; w/plate, footed, #3025 ....**$47.50**
Apple Blossom, yellow or amber, bowl, flat, 12"........**$60.00**
Apple Blossom, yellow or amber, bowl, fruit/oyster cocktail; #3025, 4½-oz **$22.50**
Apple Blossom, yellow or amber, plate, dinner; square ..**$65.00**
Apple Blossom, yellow or amber, saucer, AD.............**$15.00**
Apple Blossom, yellow or amber, stem, tall sherbet; #3130, 6-oz **$22.00**
Apple Blossom, yellow or amber, tumbler, #3025, 4-oz ..**$17.00**
Candlelight, crystal, bowl, footed, 2-handled, #3900/28, 11½" **$65.00**
Candlelight, crystal, icer, cocktail; 2-pc, #968 ....**$65.00**
Candlelight, crystal, lamp, hurricane; w/bobeche, #1613.**$265.00**
Candlelight, crystal, plate, dinner; #3900/24, 10½" **$65.00**
Candlelight, crystal, plate, torte; 4-toed, #3900/33, 13".**$65.00**

Candlelight, crystal, relish tray, divided, 2-handled, #3900/124, 7"...**$35.00**
Candlelight, crystal, relish tray, 5-part, #3900/120, 12".....**$65.00**
Candlelight, crystal, stem, oyster cocktail; #3776, 4½-oz .**$29.00**
Candlelight, crystal, stem, water; #3111, 10-oz............**$30.00**
Candlelight, crystal, tumbler, iced tea; #3776, 12-oz...**$29.00**
Candlelight, crystal, tumbler, juice; footed, #3111, 5-oz .**$27.50**
Candlelight, crystal, vase, footed, #6004, 8" **$45.00**
Caprice, blue or pink, bonbon, 2-handled, square, #154, 6"..**$35.00**
Caprice, blue or pink, bowl, relish; 3-part, #124, 8"...**$55.00**
Caprice, blue or pink, candlestick, w/prism, #70, 7", each...**$75.00**
Caprice, blue or pink, celery/relish dish, 3-part, #124, 8½" **$40.00**
Caprice, blue or pink, creamer, #141, lg.....................**$25.00**
Caprice, blue or pink, saucer, #17...............................**$12.00**
Caprice, blue or pink, stem, cocktail; blown, #300, 3-oz.**$49.00**
Caprice, blue or pink, tumbler, footed, #10, 10-oz.....**$40.00**
Caprice, blue or pink, tumbler, juice; footed, #300, 5-oz..**$39.00**
Caprice, crystal, ashtray, #215, 4" **$7.00**
Caprice, crystal, bonbon, footed, square, #133, 6"......**$15.00**
Caprice, crystal, bowl, fruit; #18, 5" **$30.00**
Caprice, crystal, bowl, 4-footed, square, #58, 10" **$35.00**
Caprice, crystal, candlestick, keyhole shape, #646, 5", each **$20.00**
Caprice, crystal, cigarette box, w/lid, #208, 4½x3½"..**$22.00**
Caprice, crystal, creamer, #38, med.............................**$11.00**
Caprice, crystal, salt & pepper shakers, individual, ball shape, #90, pr...**$45.00**
Caprice, crystal, stem, fruit cocktail; #7, 4½-oz...........**$30.00**
Caprice, crystal, tray, oval, #42, 9" **$22.00**
Caprice, crystal, tumbler, juice; blown, #301, 5-oz......**$13.00**
Caprice, crystal, vase, ball shape, #238, 6½" **$40.00**
Cascade, crystal, bowl, celery; 3-part, 10" **$18.00**
Cascade, crystal, bowl, relish; 6½" **$13.00**
Cascade, crystal, plate, salad; 8½" **$7.50**
Cascade, crystal, plate, 21"...**$50.00**
Cascade, crystal, stem, sherbet **$10.00**
Cascade, crystal or green, creamer.............................**$18.00**
Cascade, green or yellow, sugar bowl.........................**$18.00**
Cascade, green or yellow, vase, 9½" **$65.00**
Chantilly, crystal, bottle, salad dressing **$90.00**

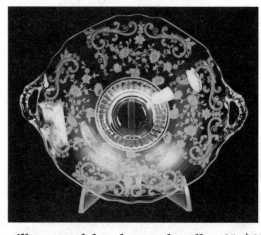

Chantilly, crystal, bowl, open handles, 9", $50.00.

Chantilly, crystal, bowl, relish/pickle; 7".....................$30.00

Chantilly, crystal, candlestick, fleur-de-lis, 2-light, 6"..$40.00

Chantilly, crystal, creamer, individual, scalloped edge, #3900...$15.00

Chantilly, crystal, mustard, w/lid...............................$65.00

Chantilly, crystal, plate, bonbon; footed, tab handled, 8"..$20.00

Chantilly, crystal, stem, cordial; #3600, 1-oz................$55.00

Chantilly, crystal, stem, low sherbet; #3625, 7-oz........$18.00

Chantilly, crystal, stem, tall sherbet; #3775, 6-oz..........$22.00

Chantilly, crystal, stem, water; #3600, 10-oz................$25.00

Chantilly, crystal, stem, wine; #3600, 2½-oz................$35.00

Chantilly, crystal, tumbler, juice; footed, #3600, 5-oz..$20.00

Chantilly, crystal, vase, flower; high footed, 8"............$40.00

Chantilly, crystal, vase, flower; pedestal foot, 11".......$65.00

Cleo, blue, bowl, fruit; 5½"......................................$25.00

Cleo, blue, bowl, oval, 11"..$95.00

Cleo, blue, plate, 7"..$15.00

Cleo, blue, platter, 12"..$125.00

Cleo, blue, tumbler, footed, #3022, 12-oz..................$75.00

Cleo, blue, tumbler, footed, #3077, 5-oz....................$50.00

Cleo, pink, green, yellow or amber, bowl, oval, 11½"..$50.00

Cleo, pink, green, yellow or amber, bowl, relish; 2-part...$35.00

Cleo, pink, green, yellow or amber, server, center handle, 12"...$45.00

Cleo, pink, green, yellow or amber, stem, fruit; #3115, 6-oz..$20.00

Cleo, pink, green, yellow or amber, tumbler, flat, 12-oz..$35.00

Decagon, pastel colors, basket, 2-handled, upturned sides, 7"...$15.00

Decagon, pastel colors, bowl, cranberry; flat rim, 3¾"..$15.00

Decagon, pastel colors, bowl, relish; 2-part, 9"..........$18.00

Decagon, pastel colors, plate, bread & butter; 6¼"......$5.00

Decagon, pastel colors, saucer..................................$2.00

Decagon, pastel colors, server, center handle............$30.00

Decagon, pastel colors, tray, service; oval, 15"..........$35.00

Decagon, red or blue, bonbon, 2-handled, 5½".........$25.00

Decagon, red or blue, bowl, cream soup; w/liner.....$27.50

Decagon, red or blue, bowl, vegetable; round, 11"...$30.00

Decagon, red or blue, cup..$12.00

Decagon, red or blue, plate, service; 12½"................$25.00

Decagon, red or blue, saucer....................................$5.00

Decagon, red or blue, stem, water; 9-oz...................$30.00

Decagon, red or blue, tray, center handled, 12".........$25.00

Decagon, red or blue, tumbler, footed, 5-oz..............$18.00

Diane, crystal, bonbon, 2-handled, 5¼".....................$18.00

Diane, crystal, bowl, celery/relish; 3-part, 9"..............$30.00

Diane, crystal, bowl, finger; w/liner, #3106................$35.00

Diane, crystal, bowl, 4-footed, oval, 12"....................$45.00

Diane, crystal, candelabrum, keyhole shape, 3-light..$50.00

Diane, crystal, candy box, w/lid, round.....................$85.00

Diane, crystal, lamp, hurricane; candlestick base.....$200.00

Diane, crystal, plate, bonbon; footed, 2-handled, 8"..$17.50

Diane, crystal, salt & pepper shakers, flat, pr............$32.00

Diane, crystal, sugar bowl, scroll handle, #3400........$22.50

Diane, crystal, tumbler, footed, #3106, 3-oz..............$25.00

Elaine, crystal, bowl, ear handled, 4-footed, oval, 12"..$40.00

Elaine, crystal, candlestick, 3-light, 6".......................$35.00

Elaine, crystal, ice bucket, w/chrome handle.............$65.00

Elaine, crystal, plate, bonbon; tab handled, 8"...........$22.50

Elaine, crystal, plate, 2-handled, 6"...........................$18.00

Elaine, crystal, salt & pepper shakers, footed, pr........$30.00

Elaine, crystal, stem, cocktail; #3104, 3½-oz..............$60.00

Elaine, crystal, stem, cocktail; #3500, 3-oz................$25.00

Elaine, crystal, stem, tall sherbet; #3121, 6-oz............$17.50

Elaine, crystal, stem, water; #3500, 10-oz..................$20.00

Elaine, crystal, tumbler, tea; footed, #3500, 12-oz......$27.50

Elaine, crystal, tumbler, water; footed, #3121, 10-oz..$20.00

Figurine, Bashful Charlotte, flower frog, green, 6½"..$150.00

Figurine, bridge hound, ebony, 1¾"...........................$35.00

Figurine, lion, bookend, each..................................$125.00

Figurine, Scottie, frosted, hollow...............................$75.00

Figurine, swan, emerald green, 3½".............................$35.00

Gloria, crystal, bowl, fruit; square, 5"........................$10.00

Gloria, crystal, bowl, relish; 3-handled, 2-part, 8"......$18.00

Gloria, crystal, creamer, footed.................................$15.00

Gloria, crystal, ice pail, metal handle, w/tongs...........$55.00

Gloria, crystal, stem, cocktail; #3035, 3-oz................$17.50

Gloria, crystal, stem, tall sherbet; #3120, 6-oz...........$15.00

Gloria, crystal, tumbler, footed, #3115, 10-oz............$18.00

Gloria, green, pink or yellow, bonbon, 2-handled, 5½"..$21.00

Gloria, green, pink or yellow, bowl, relish; 3-handled, 3-part, 8"...$34.00

Gloria, green, pink or yellow, bowl, salad; tab handled, 9"...$55.00

Gloria, green, pink or yellow, creamer, footed, tall....$25.00

Gloria, green, pink or yellow, plate, salad; tab handled, 10"...$32.00

Gloria, green, pink or yellow, stem, low sherbet; #3035, 6-oz..$16.00

Gloria, green, pink or yellow, stem, water; #3130, 8-oz..$30.00

Gloria, green, pink or yellow, tumbler, footed, #3130, 5-oz..$20.00

Gloria, green, pink or yellow, vase, keyhole base, flared rim, 12"...$110.00

Imperial Hunt Scene, colors, ice bucket......................$85.00

Imperial Hunt Scene, colors, ice tub...........................$85.00

Imperial Hunt Scene, colors, stem, parfait; #3085, 5½-oz..$60.00

Imperial Hunt Scene, colors, sugar bowl, footed........$30.00

Imperial Hunt Scene, crystal, bowl, 8".......................$30.00

Imperial Hunt Scene, crystal, mayonnaise, w/liner.....$35.00

Imperial Hunt Scene, crystal, stem, sherbet; #1402, 7½"..$35.00

Imperial Hunt Scene, crystal, stem, tomato; #1402, 6-oz..$40.00

Imperial Hunt Scene, crystal, tumbler, flat, tall, #1402, 10-oz..$30.00

Mt Vernon, amber or crystal, ashtray, oval, #71, 6x4½"..$12.00

Mt Vernon, amber or crystal, bottle, toilet; square, #18, 7-oz..$65.00

Mt Vernon, amber or crystal, bowl, bell shape, #128, 11½"...$30.00

Mt Vernon, amber or crystal, bowl, flared, #44, 12½"..$35.00

Mt Vernon, amber or crystal, bowl, ivy ball or rose; footed, #12, 4½"..$27.50

Mt Vernon, amber or crystal, bowl, salad; #120, 10½"..$25.00

Mt Vernon, amber or crystal, bowl, sweetmeat; 2-handled, 4-part, #105, 8½"...$32.00

Mt Vernon, amber or crystal, candlestick, #35, 8".......$25.00

Mt Vernon, amber or crystal, celery, #98, 11"..............$17.50

Mt Vernon, amber or crystal, comport, #97, 6½"........$17.50

Mt Vernon, amber or crystal, creamer, footed, #8.......**$10.00**

Mt Vernon, amber or crystal, stem, cocktail; #26, 3½" .**$9.00**

Mt Vernon, amber or crystal, stem, tall sherbet; #2, 6½" .**$10.00**

Mt Vernon, amber or crystal, tray, for individual creamer & sugar bowl, #4 ....**$10.00**

Mt Vernon, amber or crystal, tumbler, old fashioned; #57, 7-oz **$15.00**

Mt Vernon, amber or crystal, vase, crimped, #119, 6" ..**$20.00**

Mt Vernon, amber or crystal, vase, squat, #107, 6½" .**$27.50**

Portia, crystal, bowl, cranberry; square, 3½" **$22.50**

Portia, crystal, bowl, relish; 3-part, 6½" **$18.00**

Portia, crystal, comport, blown, 5⅜" **$35.00**

Portia, crystal, mayonnaise, divided, w/liner & 2 ladles ..**$40.00**

Portia, crystal, plate, dinner; 10½" **$65.00**

Portia, crystal, stem, brandy; low footed, #3126, 1-oz ..**$45.00**

Portia, crystal, stem, cocktail; #3121, 3-oz **$25.00**

Portia, crystal, stem, cordial; #3121, 1-oz...................**$65.00**

Portia, crystal, stem, low sherbet; #3124, 7-oz **$14.00**

Portia, crystal, stem, tall sherbet; #3130, 7-oz..............**$16.50**

Portia, crystal, tumbler, bar; #3121, 2½-oz.................**$30.00**

Portia, crystal, tumbler, juice; #3126, 5-oz **$17.50**

Portia, crystal, vase, footed, 6"...................................**$45.00**

Portia, crystal, vase, pedestal footed, 11"....................**$65.00**

Rosalie, amber, candlestick, keyhole shape, 5" **$25.00**

Rosalie, amber, ice tub **$60.00**

Rosalie, amber, sugar bowl, footed **$15.00**

Rosalie, blue, pink or green, bowl, console; 13" **$50.00**

Rosalie, blue, pink or green, bowl, soup; 8½"...........**$40.00**

Rosalie, blue, pink or green, bowl, 11" **$40.00**

Rosalie, blue, pink or green, creamer, footed **$17.00**

Rosalie, blue, pink or green, plate, bread & butter; 6¾" ..**$10.00**

Rosalie, blue, pink or green, vase, footed, 5½" **$45.00**

Rose Point, crystal, ashtray, #3500/124, 3¼" **$32.50**

Rose Point, crystal, basket, 11", minimum value $700.00.

Rose Point, crystal, basket, 2-handled, #3400/1182, 6" .**$35.00**

Rose Point, crystal, bonbon, footed, 2-handled, #3500/54, 6"..**$35.00**

Rose Point, crystal, bowl, finger; #3106, w/liner.........**$90.00**

Rose Point, crystal, bowl, flared, #3400/168, 10½" **$65.00**

Rose Point, crystal, bowl, handled, #3500/49, 5" **$35.00**

Rose Point, crystal, bowl, nut; 4-footed, #3400/71, 3" ..**$70.00**

Rose Point, crystal, candelabrum, 2-light, #3500/94....**$95.00**

Rose Point, crystal, candlestick, #3500/108, 2½".........**$30.00**

Rose Point, crystal, candlestick, keyhole shape, 2-light, #3400/647, 6"...**$45.00**

Rose Point, crystal, candlestick, 3-tiered light, #1338, 6"..**$65.00**

Rose Point, crystal, candy box, w/lid, 3-part, #3500/57, 8".**$85.00**

Rose Point, crystal, celery/relish dish, 3-part, #3900/125, 9"..**$50.00**

Rose Point, crystal, comport, blown, #3500/101, 5⅜"...**$62.50**

Rose Point, crystal, comport, 4-footed, #3400/13, 6" ..**$37.50**

Rose Point, crystal, creamer, individual, pie crust edge, #3500/15 ....**$32.50**

Rose Point, crystal, cruet, ball shape, w/stopper, #3400/96, 2-oz **$75.00**

Rose Point, crystal, hot plate, or trivet......................**$95.00**

Rose Point, crystal, ice bucket, w/chrome handle, #3900/671 ....**$135.00**

Rose Point, crystal, pitcher, #3900/115, 76-oz **$195.00**

Rose Point, crystal, pitcher, ball shape, #3900/116, 80-oz **$225.00**

Rose Point, crystal, plate, rolled edge, #1397, 13½" ...**$80.00**

Rose Point, crystal, plate, salad; #3900/22, 8" **$20.00**

Rose Point, crystal, plate, 2-handled, #3400/35, 11" ...**$50.00**

Rose Point, crystal, relish tray, 4-part, $65.00.

Rose Point, crystal, salt & pepper shakers, flat, w/chrome tops, #3900/1177, pr **$40.00**

Rose Point, crystal, stem, high sherbet; #3106, 7-oz....**$30.00**

Rose Point, crystal, stem, sherbet; low footed, #3500, 7-oz **$25.00**

Rose Point, crystal, stem, tall sherbet; #3121, 6-oz **$28.00**

Rose Point, crystal, sugar bowl, footed, #3900/41 ......**$25.00**

Rose Point, crystal, tumbler, #3900/115, 13-oz............**$49.00**

Rose Point, crystal, tumbler, footed, #3106, 3-oz **$25.00**

Rose Point, crystal, tumbler, water; low footed, #3121, 10-oz **$27.50**

Rose Point, crystal, vase, #1309, 5" **$67.50**

Rose Point, crystal, vase, flower; high footed, #6004, 8"..**$55.00**

Rose Point, crystal, vase, footed, #6004, 10" **$75.00**

Square, crystal, ashtray, #3797/151, 3½"......................**$8.00**

Square, crystal, bowl, dessert; #3797/16, 4½" **$11.00**

Square, crystal, candle holder, block base, #3797/495, 3¾", pr **$27.50**

Square, crystal, comport, #37397/54, 6" **$25.00**

Square, crystal, lamp, hurricane; 2-pc, #3797/68.........**$42.00**

Square, crystal, plate, bread & butter; #3797/20, 6" **$8.00**

Square, crystal, relish, 3-part, #3797/125, 8" **$22.50**

Square, crystal, saucer, tea; #3797/15 ....**$5.00**

Square, crystal, sugar bowl, individual, #3797/40 ....**$10.00**

Square, crystal, tumbler, juice; #3797, 5-oz.................**$12.50**

Square, crystal, vase, belled shape, #3797/92, 5"........**$22.50**
Valencia, crystal, ashtray, round, #3500/126, 4" **$14.00**
Valencia, crystal, bowl, handled, #3500/49, 5" **$18.00**
Valencia, crystal, bowl, salad dressing; divided, #1402/95 ....**$40.00**
Valencia, crystal, creamer, individual, #3500/15 ....**$17.50**
Valencia, crystal, plate, salad; #3500/167, 7½" **$10.00**
Valencia, crystal, stem, claret; #1402 ....**$35.00**
Valencia, crystal, stem, cocktail; #1402.......................**$20.00**
Valencia, crystal, sugar bowl, individual, #3500/15.....**$17.50**
Valencia, crystal, tumbler, #3400/115, 14-oz...............**$22.00**
Wildflower, crystal, basket, footed, 2-handled, #3400/1182, 6" **$25.00**
Wildflower, crystal, bonbon, 2-handled, #3900/130, 7"...**$20.00**
Wildflower, crystal, bowl, pickle (corn); footed, #477, 9½" **$35.00**
Wildflower, crystal, bowl, 4-footed, flared, #3400/4, 12"..**$40.00**
Wildflower, crystal, comport, blown, #3121, 5⅜".......**$40.00**
Wildflower, crystal, ice bucket, w/chrome handle, #3900/671 ....**$65.00**
Wildflower, crystal, salt & pepper shakers, #3400/77, pr..**$35.00**
Wildflower, crystal, stem, cocktail; #3121, 3-oz..........**$22.50**
Wildflower, crystal, sugar bowl, individual, #3900/40...**$20.00**
Wildflower, crystal, vase, flower; footed, #6004, 6" **$35.00**

Cameras

Camera collecting as a hobby or investment has undergone a considerable change in the past few years due largely to the numerous camera shows that emphasize both user and classic collectible cameras. Also the influence of foreign investors in classic cameras has been evident in prices; and some types of cameras that were, in the past, high on collectors' want lists are now priced at levels putting them in the investment category. Therefore a person must consider from the start if he is going into camera collecting as a hobby or as an investment and plan his collecting accordingly. This is an extremely interesting hobby, including not only the cameras themselves, but all items associated with photography. One can get involved in collecting at all levels of prices, from expensive to low-level value collections.

There are many distinct types of cameras to consider: large format, medium format, early folding and box styles, 33mm single-lens-reflex (SLR), 35mm range finders, twin-lens-reflex (TLR), miniature or sub-miniature, novelty, and other types — including the more recent Polaroid types and movie cameras. To date, there are only a few collectors of old movie cameras as compared to still cameras. Most pre-1900 cameras will be found in the large-format view camera or studio camera types. The 1900 to 1930 era turned out millions of folding- and box-type cameras, which make good collector items. Most have fairly low values because of their vast numbers. Many of the more expensive classics were manufactured in the 1930 through 1955 period and primarily include the range-finder type of camera and those with the first

built-in meters. The most prized of these are of German or Japanese manufacture, due to their innovative designs and great optics. The key to collecting these types of cameras is to find a mint-condition item or one still in the original box. In camera collecting, quality is the most important aspect. But just owning a particular model can be a joy, and there's always the anticipation of finding a better example just around the corner.

This brief listing includes only a few of the various categories and models of cameras along with average prices for working models with average wear. The same item in mint condition or mint with its original box may be valued much higher, while a very worn example with defects (scratches, dents, torn covers, poor optics, non-working meters or range finders) would be valued far less.

Note: Some models such as Canon Range Finder J-Series, Nikon Range Finder (I, M, S, S2, S3, S4), Rolleicord and Rolleiflex TLR, and Tower Series (sold by Sears and made by various well-known manufacturers) will have a wide range of prices. Please consult the advisor for more information on these models.

Advisor: Gene's Cameras (See Directory, Cameras)

Agfa B2 Speedex, 85mm-f4.5 lens.................................**$25.00**
Agfa Karat; Art Deco front, Igestar f6.3 lens................**$35.00**
Ansco Rediflex, TLR...**$12.00**
Ansco Sure Shot Jr, 1948 box camera, 120 size...........**$10.00**
Argoflex TLR, 75mm-f4.5 lens, black or chrome.........**$15.00**
Argus C3, 50mm-f3.5 lens, black, w/case, flash..........**$15.00**
Argus C4, 50mm-f2.8 lens, case, flash.......................**$30.00**
Asahi Pentax, Original '57, w/50mm lens...................**$200.00**
Asahiflex I, 1st Japanese 35mm SLR..........................**$400.00**
Bolsey B2, 44mm-f3.2 lens, case **$25.00**
Bolsey Jubilee, Steinheil 45mm-f2.8 lens, case...........**$35.00**
Contax II, w/various lenses **$250.00**
Contax S, D, F models of East German Manufacture .**$100.00**
Contax 1a, w/various lenses **$600.00**

Coronet 3-D Binocular Viewer, ca 1954, from $65.00 to $75.00. (Photo courtesy of Gene's Cameras.)

Exa, by Exakta, Meritar 50mm-f2.8 lens......................**$70.00**
Exakta, Original 1933 model **$300.00**
Exakta II, ca 1949-50, various lenses **$130.00**
Exakta RTL1000, ca 1970...**$90.00**

Exakta V Varex, w/interchangeable finder, lens........**$120.00**
Falcon, Miniature Deluxe **$7.00**
Foldex 20, folding 120 camera **$12.00**
Graflex, many models & sizes, mostly lg format type w/variety of lenses, from $50 to **$500.00**
Hit Cameras, Japanese novelty sub-miniatures............**$15.00**
Ikoflex 1, Novar 75mm-f3.5 lens **$100.00**
Kodak, folding 2-A Autographic Brownie....................**$20.00**
Kodak, folding 2-A Cartridge Premo 116....................**$15.00**
Kodak Autographic Vest Pocket, rectilinear.................**$35.00**
Kodak Baby Brownie, early..**$15.00**
Kodak Baby Brownie Special, 1939-54 ....**$5.00**
Kodak Bantam, Anastar 48mm-f4.5 lens **$20.00**
Kodak Brownie Flash Camera, black Bakelite...............**$8.00**
Kodak Brownie Hawkeye Box Camera **$10.00**
Kodak Dualflex, TLR..**$5.00**
Kodak Jiffy Six-16..**$15.00**
Kodak Jiffy Vest Pocket **$25.00**
Kodak Medalist I or II **$175.00**
Kodak No 2 Bull's Eye Box Camera **$25.00**
Kodak No 2 folding Brownie, maroon bellows **$15.00**
Kodak Retina Automatic...**$50.00**
Kodak Retina I, various models, average **$65.00**
Kodak Retina II, various models, average **$100.00**
Kodak Retina IIIC (lg C)..**$300.00**
Kodak Retina IIIc (little c) **$150.00**
Kodak Retina Reflex S...**$120.00**

Kodak Signet 3.5, Ektar lens, 1951-58, from $15.00 to $30.00. (Photo courtesy of Gene's Cameras.)

Kodak 35mm, w/range finder, f3.5 lens......................**$25.00**
Konica III, 1956-59 range finder, f2 lens....................**$60.00**
Konica Range Finder 1948-54, f2.8 or f3.5 lens...........**$80.00**
Mamiya 6, 1940-50, folding bed, 120 film, f3.5 lens ...**$90.00**
Mamiyaflex, TLR, 75mm-f3.5 lens..............................**$100.00**
Mamiyaflex C, Professional TLR, 80mm-f2.8 lens......**$175.00**
Mercury, mid-1940s, half-frame camera **$30.00**
Minolta, ca 1933, strut-folding, f4.5...........................**$300.00**
Minolta A, 1955-57, 45mm-f3.5 lens **$50.00**
Minolta AL, 1961-65, 45mm-f2 lens **$40.00**
Minolta Autocord, TLR, (w/o meter, $125), w/meter **$150.00**
Minolta SR-1, 1964, w/attached CdS meter & standard lens **$65.00**
Minolta 35, range finder, various models A, B, C, D, E, F, from $250 to **$500.00**

Minox, Sub-miniature Spy, some Special models exceed...**$500.00**
Minox, Sub-miniature Spy cameras, standard model, from $50 to..**$200.00**
Nikkormats, various models, from $50 to..................**$200.00**
Olympus Flex BI, ca 1952, 1st Olympus TLR, 75mm-f2.8 lens...**$190.00**
Olympus Pen Half-Frame Cameras, many models made, from $35 to **$200.00**
Olympus Six, ca 1939, folding bellows, 120 size......**$180.00**
Olympus Six IV, ca 1954, folding bellows w/range finder.**$140.00**
Pearlette, 1925-46, folding, 127 size, f4.5 lens............**$85.00**
Pentax Spotmatics, only recently considered collectibles, from $50 to...**$150.00**
Petri Flex V, 55mm-f2 lens..**$60.00**
Polaroid, 100, 101, 102, 103, 104, 125, 850, or 900.......**$7.00**
Polaroid 110, 110A, 110B or 120 ....**$35.00**
Polaroid 95 or 95A...**$10.00**
Poloroid SX-70 ....**$25.00**
Poloroid 180, 195 Professional models, Tominon 114-f3.8.**$300.00**
Praktica FX, Victar 50mm-f2.8 lens.............................**$40.00**
Pressman 4x5", Ektar f4.7 lens, press camera............**$200.00**
Robot 11a, 38mm-f3 lens, sm German spring-wound camera **$150.00**
Seneca View Camera, 1905-25, 5x7", w/lens, wooden body **$150.00**
Voigtlander Bessa, early folding camera, f6.3 lens **$35.00**
Voigtlander Bessamatic, 50mm-f2.8 Skopar lens **$125.00**
Voigtlander Prominent 35mm, Nokton 50mm-f1.5 lens....**$225.00**
Voigtlander Vitessa L, Ultron 50mm-f2 lens..............**$175.00**
Voigtlander Vito, 50mm-f3.5 lens.................................**$45.00**
Wirgin Edixa, 43mm-f2.8 lens **$30.00**
Yashica Lynx 1000, 45mm-f1.8 lens, meter..................**$40.00**
Yashicamat TLR, series of cameras w/various features, from $35 to...**$225.00**
Zeiss-Ikon, Box Tengor, series of box cameras, from $30 to **$100.00**
Zeiss-Ikon Contaflex I, Tessar 45mm-f2.8 lens............**$75.00**
Zeiss-Ikon Contaflex IV, w/standard lens **$120.00**
Zeiss-Ikon Contaflex Super B **$150.00**
Zeiss-Ikon Contarex Special..**$800.00**
Zeiss-Ikon Contessa 35..**$200.00**
Zeiss-Ikon Contina I, 45mm-f3.5 lens.........................**$50.00**
Zeiss-Ikon Super Ikonta B, 80mm-f2.8 lens..............**$200.00**

Mercury II CX, 35/f.27 lens, 1945, from $30.00 to $50.00. (Photo courtesy of Gene's Cameras.)

Candlewick Glassware

This is a beautifully simple, very diverse line of glassware made by the Imperial Glass Company (a division of Lenox Inc., Bellaire, Ohio) from 1936 until the company closed in 1982. It was named Candlewick because its design suggested the tufted needlework called Candlewicking done by the colonial ladies in early America. Rows of small crystal balls surround rims of bowls and plates, foot rings of tumblers, and decorate the handles of pitchers. Some pieces have stems of stacked balls. Though most was made in crystal, a few pieces were made in color, and others had a gold wash. Imperial made two etched lines, Floral and Valley Lily, that utilized the Candlewick shapes. Both are very scarce.

Among the hardest-to-find items are the desk calendars that were made as gifts for company employees and customers, the chip-and-dip set, and the dresser set containing a cologne bottle, powder jar, clock, and mirror.

There were more than 740 items in all, and collectors often use the company's mold numbers to help identify all those variations and sizes. Gene Florence's *Collector's Encyclopedia of Elegant Glassware* has a chapter that gives this line very good coverage.

From the 1940s through the sixties, Hazel Atlas produced sherbets, cocktail glasses, wines, and water goblets that are being mistaken for Candlewick, so beware. You'll find these in malls and antique shops, priced and labeled as Candlewick. They were made with a crystal, green, amber, or ruby top on a crystal foot ringed with small glass balls. But the flared part of the foot is ribbed, unlike any Candlewick foot, so you can tell the difference. These are becoming very collectible in their own right, but they're certainly not worth Candlewick prices, and you won't want them in your collection. Gene Florence calls them 'Boopie' and indicates values in the $3.00 to $7.00 range for crystal and in the $7.00 to $15.00 range for colors.

Newsletter: *The Candlewick Collector*
Virginia R. Scott
275 Milledge Terrace
Athens, GA 30306; 404-548-5966

Ashtray, heart form, #400/172, 4½"	**$9.00**
Ashtray, oblong, #400/134/1, 4½"	**$6.00**
Bell, #400/108, 5"	**$85.00**
Bowl, #400/5F, 7"	**$22.00**
Bowl, #400/7F, 8"	**$37.50**
Bowl, #400/92B, 12"	**$40.00**
Bowl, belled (console base), #400/127B, 7½"	**$45.00**
Bowl, centerpiece; mushroom, #400/92L, 13"	**$50.00**
Bowl, handles, #400/42B, 4¾"	**$10.00**
Bowl, heart w/hand, #400/49H, 5"	**$18.00**
Bowl, mint; w/hand, #400/51F, 6"	**$20.00**
Bowl, nappy, 4-footed, #400/74B, 8½"	**$45.00**
Bowl, relish; #400/60, 7"	**$25.00**
Bowl, relish; oval, handles, #400/217, 10"	**$40.00**
Bowl, relish; 3-section, #400/256, 10½"	**$30.00**
Bowl, sauce; deep, #400/243, 5½"	**$35.00**
Bowl, 3-toed, #400/205, 10"	**$135.00**

Bowl, #400/10F, 9"	**$42.50**
Butter dish, beaded top, #400/161, ¼-lb	**$30.00**
Candle holder, flower (epergne inset), #400/40CV, 5"	**$95.00**
Candle holder, flower w/2-bead stem, #400/66F, 4"	**$45.00**
Candle holder, 2-light, #400/100	**$20.00**
Candle holder, 3-light on circular beaded center, #400/147	**$25.00**
Candy box, #400/245, 6½" sq w/round lid	**$150.00**
Cigarette holder, beaded foot, #400/44, 3"	**$40.00**
Compote, low, plain stem, #400/66B, 5½"	**$18.00**
Creamer, beaded handle, #400/30, 6-oz	**$8.00**
Creamer, plain foot, #400/31	**$9.00**
Cruet, oil; beaded base, #400/164, 4-oz	**$55.00**
Cruet, oil; bulbous, #400/275, 6½"	**$55.00**
Cup, coffee; #400/37	**$7.50**
Cup, tea; #400/35	**$8.00**
Deviled egg server, center handle, #400/154, 12"	**$100.00**
Fork & spoon set, #400/75	**$35.00**
Icer, seafood/fruit cocktail; #400/53/3, 2-pc	**$95.00**
Ladle, marmalade; 3-bead stem, #400/130	**$10.00**
Ladle, mayonnaise, #400/135, 6¼"	**$10.00**
Marmalade jar, w/lid, spoon & saucer, #400/89	**$42.50**
Mayonnaise, w/ladle & tray, #400/52/3, 3-pc	**$45.00**
Pitcher, plain, #400/416, 20-oz	**$40.00**
Pitcher, plain, #400/419, 40-oz	**$40.00**
Pitcher, short, round, #400/330, 14-oz	**$125.00**

Pitcher, 64-oz., $55.00; Tumbler, beaded foot, 5", $16.50.

Plate, #400/34, 4½"	**$6.00**
Plate, canape; off-center indent, #400/36, 6"	**$11.00**
Plate, crimped rim, handles, #400/145C, 12"	**$32.50**
Plate, handles, #400/52D, 7½"	**$10.00**
Plate, handles, sides upturned, #400/62E, 8½"	**$25.00**
Plate, serving; cupped rim, #400/92V, 13½"	**$37.50**
Plate, torte; #400/20D, 17"	**$45.00**
Plate, torte; handles, #400/113D, 14"	**$30.00**
Plate, w/indent, #400/50, 8"	**$11.00**
Salt & pepper shakers, bulbous w/beaded stems, plastic lids, #400/116, pr	**$42.50**
Salt & pepper shakers, straight sides, beaded feet, chrome lids, #400/247, pr	**$16.00**
Salt cellar, #400/61, 2"	**$9.00**
Saucer, AD; #400/77AD	**$5.00**
Stem, cocktail, #400/190, 4-oz	**$18.00**
Stem, cordial, #3800, 1-oz	**$42.50**

Stem, sherbet, #400/190, 6-oz......................................**$14.00**
Stem, sherbet, low, #3400, 5-oz....................................**$10.00**
Stem, tea, #4000, 12-oz...**$20.00**
Sugar bowl, bridge; individual, #400/122 ....**$6.00**
Tidbit set, #400/18TB, 3-pc..**$165.00**
Tray, #400/29, 6½"...**$15.00**
Tray, celery; oval, handles, #400/105, 13½" **$30.00**
Tumbler, #400/19, 10-oz..**$12.00**
Tumbler, footed, #3400, 9-oz **$10.00**
Tumbler, juice; #400/18, 5-oz **$37.50**
Tumbler, water; #400/18, 9-oz......................................**$40.00**
Tumbler, wine, footed, #400/19, 3-oz **$16.00**
Vase, flat, crimped edge, #400/287C, 6"......................**$20.00**
Vase, fluted rim w/beaded handles, #400/87C, 8" **$27.50**
Vase, ivy bowl, #400/74J, 7"...**$50.00**
Vase, mini bud; beaded foot, #400/107, 5¾"..............**$40.00**

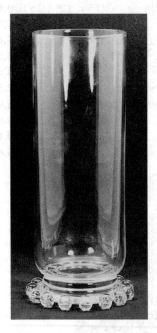

Vase, straight sides, beaded foot, 10", $140.00.

Candy Containers

Most of us can recall buying these glass toys as a child, since they were made well into the 1960s. We were fascinated by the variety of their shapes then, just as collectors are today. Looking back, it couldn't have been we were buying them for the candy, though perhaps as a child those tiny sugary balls flavored more with the coloring agent than anything else were enough to satisfy our 'sweet tooth.'

Glass candy containers have been around since our country's centennial celebration in 1876 when the first two, the Liberty Bell and the Independence Hall, were introduced. Since then they have been made in hundreds of styles, and some of them have become very expensive. The leading manufacturers in the East — Westmoreland, Victory Glass, J.H. Millstein, Crosetti, L.E. Smith, Jack Stough, T.H. Stough, and West Bros. — made perhaps 90% of them and collectors report finding many in the Pennsylvania area. Most are clear, but you'll find them in various other colors as well.

If you're going to deal in candy containers, you need a book that will show you all the variations available. *The Compleat*

American Glass Candy Containers Handbook by Eikelberner and Agadjaninian (recently revised by Adele Bowden) uses a numbering system that has become universal among collectors. Numbers in our listings refer to this book, except for the few 'L' numbers which correspond with Jenny Long's *Album of Candy Containers*, published in 1978–83.

Because of their popularity and considerable worth, many of the original containers have been reproduced. Beware of any questionable glassware that has a slick or oily touch. Among those that have been produced are: Amber Pistol (#283), Auto (#48 and #33), Carpet Sweeper (#132 and #133), Chicken on Nest (#149), Display Case (#177), Dog (#179), Drum Mug (#543), Fire Engine (#213), Independence Hall (#342), Jackie Coogan (#345), Kewpie (#539), Mail Box (#521), Mantel Clock (#164), Mule and Waterwagon (#539), Peter Rabbit (#618), Piano (#577), Rabbit Pushing Wheelbarrow (#601), Rocking Horse (#651), Safe (#661), Santa (#674), Santa's Boot (#111), Station Wagon (#567), Uncle Sam's Hat (#303). Others are possible.

Our values are given for candy containers that are undamaged, in good original paint, and complete (with all original parts and closure). Repaired or repainted containers are worth much less.

See also Christmas; Easter; Halloween.

Advisor: Doug Dezso (See Directory, Candy Containers)

Newsletter: *The Candy Gram*
Candy Container Collectors of America
Douglas Dezso
864 Paterson, Ave.
Maywood, NJ 07607; 201-845-7707

Club: Candy Container Collectors of America
P.O. Box 352
Chelmsford, MA 01824-0352

Peter Rabbit, E&A #618, $30.00.

Basket, #81, floral design **$30.00**
Black Cat, papier-mache, fur covered, glass eyes, 7½"
  EX **$635.00**
Bulldog #2, #186, cardboard closure............................**$45.00**
Car, Electric Coupe #2, #47, closure.............................**$60.00**
Car, Ribbed-Top Sedan, #32, closure **$25.00**
Chicken in Sagging Basket, #148.................................**$75.00**
Chicken on Oblong Basket, #147, closure, green.......**$50.00**
Circus Dog w/Hat, L#478...**$30.00**

Dog, #22, #181, w/glass hat..................................**$25.00**
Dog, Mutt, #194 ....**$55.00**
Fairy Pups, #193..**$75.00**
Foxy Doctor, L#657..**$125.00**
Gun, Kolt #1, #285, screw cap **$125.00**
Horn, Millstein, #311 ....**$25.00**
Jeep Scout Car, #350...**$35.00**
Lantern, #403, w/brass cap **$20.00**
Lantern, Crossette-Little One, #386.........................**$20.00**
Lantern, #426, barn type #2 ....**$75.00**
Locomotive, #496, rectangular windows, w/closure ...**$85.00**
Lynn Doll Nurser, #550..**$32.00**
Model Cruiser, #98, original closure.........................**$25.00**
Poodle, L#471, glass head.....................................**$20.00**
Rabbit in Eggshell, #608, gold paint........................**$85.00**
Rabbit Nibbling Carrot, #609...................................**$35.00**
Rabbit w/Layed-Back Ears, #616, EX paint...............**$100.00**
Rooster Crowing, #151, original paint.......................**$250.00**
Santa Claus, #674, plastic head..............................**$65.00**
Telephone, Stough's #3, L#308, #751 ....**$40.00**

Stop and Go, E&A #706, lever missing, 4½", $250.00.

Cape Cod by Avon

You can't walk through any flea market or mall now without seeing volumes of this ruby red glassware. It has been issued by Avon since the seventies, the small cruet and tall candlesticks, for instance, filled originally with one or the other of their fragrances, the wine and water goblets filled with scented candlewax, and the dessert bowl with guest soap. Many 'campaigns' since then have featured accessory tableware items such as plates, cake stands, and a water pitcher, and obviously the line was very good seller for them, judging from the sheer volume of it around. Until very recently it was still featured in their catalogs, but it has now been discontinued, and you can look for interest in it to increase.

I've found some nice pieces at garage sales, so I've bought it with an eye to the future. The glassware is of good quality, there's a nice assortment of items in the line, and it's readily available. Even at mall prices, it's not expensive. That's about all it takes to make a collectible.

Bell, marked Christmas 1979 on bottom, 6½", from $20 to .**$25.00**
Bowl, dessert; 1978-80, 5" **$12.00**
Bowl, serving; 1986, 8¾" **$25.00**
Bowl, soup/cereal; 1991, 7½" dia...........................**$13.00**

Butter dish, 1983-84, MIB, from $20.00 to $25.00.

Candle holder, hurricane type w/clear chimney, 1985 .**$25.00**
Candle holders, squat form, 1983-84, 2½x3¾" dia, pr, from $15 to..**$18.00**
Candlestick, 1975-80, 5-oz, from $7 to....................**$9.00**
Candlesticks, 8½", pr, from $25 to **$30.00**
Candy dish, footed, 1987, 3½x6" dia, from $12 to **$15.00**
Condiment dish, divided, rectangular, 1985, from $12 to..**$15.00**
Creamer, footed, 1981-84, 4"................................**$12.50**
Cruet, 1975-80, 4", from $10 to.............................**$13.00**
Cup & saucer, 1990, 3½", from $9 to......................**$12.00**
Decanter, w/stopper, 1977-80, 16-oz, from $18 to......**$22.00**
Dessert server, wedge-shape stainless steel, red plastic handle, 1981-84, 8" long, from $12 to.....................**$15.00**
Goblet, champagne; 1991, 5¼"...............................**$12.50**
Goblet, water; 1976-90, 6".....................................**$9.00**
Goblet, wine; 1992, 5¼", from $4 to.......................**$6.00**
Heart box, 1989, 4" wide, from $20 to.....................**$25.00**
Mug, pedestal foot, 1982-84, 5" **$10.00**
Napkin rings, set of 4, 1989...................................**$20.00**
Pie plate, server, 1991, 11" dia, from $35 to.............**$40.00**
Pitcher, water; footed, 1984, 8¼", from $35 to...........**$40.00**
Plate, bread & butter; 1992, 5¾" dia **$8.50**
Plate, cake; footed, 1991, 3¼x10¾" dia....................**$50.00**
Plate, dessert; 1980, 7¼"......................................**$6.50**

Plate, dinner; 1982-83, 11", MIB, from $15.00 to $18.00.

Platter, 1986, 10¾x13½"..**$24.00**
Relish, 9¼x5½" **$20.00**
Salt & pepper shakers, marked May 1978 on bottom, pr, from $18 to...**$22.00**
Sauce boat, footed, 1988, 8" long...........................**$25.00**
Sugar bowl, footed, 1980-83, 3½" **$12.50**

Tidbit tray, 2-tier, brass handle, 1987, 9¾", from $30 to ..**$35.00**
Tumbler, footed, 1988, 3¾"...**$7.50**
Tumbler, straight sided, 1990, 5½", from $8 to **$10.00**
Vase, footed, 1985, 8", from $20 to **$25.00**
Wine glass, footed, 5"..**$7.50**

Cardinal China Company

This was the name of a distributing company who had their merchandise made to order and sold it through a chain of show-rooms and outlet stores in several states from the late 1940s through the 1950s. (Although they made some of their own pottery early on, we have yet to find out just what they themselves produced.) They used their company name to mark cookie jars (some of which were made by the American Bisque Company), novelty wares and kitchen items, many of which you'll see as you make your flea market rounds. Their primary colors were yellow and green, and their spoon holders came complete with colorful plastic measuring spoons. *The Collector's Encyclopedia of Cookie Jars* by Joyce and Fred Roerig shows a page of their jars.

See also Cookie Jars.

Measuring spoon holder, flowerpot shape with basketweave base, with spoons, $15.00; Spoon rest, yellow flower, $6.00; Salt and pepper shakers, Chinese man and lady, green and yellow, $22.00 for the pair.

Condiment jar, Onion lettered on hat of sad clown head, unmarked, 5¼"..**$65.00**
Dresser dish, Doxie-dog..**$18.00**
Flower holder, doughnut shape, turquoise on white, 7" ..**$8.00**
Measuring spoon holder, flowerpot shape, basketweave base, w/spoons **$15.00**
Measuring spoon holder, flowerpot shape, plain base, w/spoons..**$12.00**
Measuring spoon holder, shaped to look like a window sill planter..**$15.00**
Salt & pepper shakers, Chinese man & lady, green & yellow, pr..**$22.00**
Scissors holder, nest w/chicken figural **$25.00**
Spoon holder, cottage w/peaked roof, applied thermometer..**$15.00**
Spoon rest, yellow flower **$6.00**
String holder, nest w/chicken figural **$25.00**
Tray, dresser; dachshund **$16.00**

Carnival Chalkware

From about 1910 until in the fifties, winners of carnival games everywhere in the United States were awarded chalk-ware figures of Kewpie dolls, the Lone Ranger, Hula girls, comic characters, etc. The assortment was vast and varied. The earliest were made of plaster with a pink cast. They ranged in size from about 5" up to 16".

They were easily chipped, so when it came time for the carnival to pick up and move on, they had to be carefully wrapped and packed away, a time consuming, tedious chore. When stuffed animals became available, concessionists found that they could simply throw them into a box without fear of damage, and so ended an era.

Today the most valuable of these statues are those modeled after Disney characters, movie stars, and comic book heroes.

Chalkware figures are featured in *The Carnival Chalk Prize, Vols I and II,* written by Thomas G. Morris, who has also included a fascinating history of carnival life in America.

See also Cat Collectibles.

Advisor: Tom Morris (See Directory, Carnival Chalkware)

Air Raid Warden holding US flag, ca 1940s, 14" **$85.00**
American buffalo lamp, ca 1930-40, figure: 8½x10".**$140.00**
Betty Boop, painted details, several variations, ca 1930-40, 14½"...**$265.00**
Black boy eating watermelon, marked By Buelah, ca 1930-40, 7½"...**$80.00**
Cat w/flat back, ca 1940-50, 6" **$10.00**
Charlie McCarthy, sitting, ca 1940-50, 7¼" **$25.00**

Charlie McCarthy, standing, hand painted, several sizes and variations, 1930-40, $75.00.

China girl, ca 1930-40, 5½" **$40.00**
Dog, begging, Have a Heart, dated 1920 on back, 6½" ..**$45.00**
Dog, lg soulful eyes, long ears, flat back, ca 1940-50, 6½"..**$8.00**
Donald Duck, head bank, ca 1940-50, 10½" **$80.00**
Donald Duck's Uncle Scrooge, ca 1940-50, 8" **$40.00**
Girl in horseshoe, marked Baby Luck & signed Riverview Park, Chicago July 1947, 10½"...............................**$80.00**
Little Lady, hand-painted details, jointed arms, mohair wig, crepe-paper dress, ca 1920-30, 12"......................**$165.00**

Little Sheba, hand painted, original feathers, made in several variations, ca 1920s, 13" **$155.00**
Lone Ranger & Silver, painted details, ca 1938-50, 10½"...**$75.00**
Mae West w/parasol, ca 1930-40, 14"..........................**$95.00**
Nude bust lamp, Deco-style bust, ca 1930-40, 8½" ..**$120.00**
Nude lamp, sitting, ca 1940-50, figure size: 6½x7"...**$145.00**
Penguin in top hat, glass eyes, ca 1935-45, 7¼".........**$40.00**
Pluto, seated, ca 1930-40, 6" **$35.00**
Popeye, ca 1930-50, 13½" or 15½", each **$95.00**
Sailor girl, ca 1930-40, 9¾" **$25.00**
Three Little Pigs, 1930s-50s, 5x5½" **$20.00**

Cat Collectibles

Cat collectibles continue to grow in popularity as cats continue to dominate the world of household pets. Cat memorabilia can be found in almost all categories, and this allows for collections to grow rapidly! Most cat lovers/collectors are attracted to all items and to all breeds, though some do specialize. Popular categories include Siamese, black cats, Kitty Cucumber, Kliban, cookie jars, teapots, books, plates, postcards, and Louis Wain.

Because cats are found throughout the field of collectibles and antiques, there is some 'crossover' competition among collectors. For example: Chessie, the C&O Railroad cat, is collected by railroad and advertising buffs; Felix the Cat, board games, puppets, and Steiff cats are sought by toy collectors. A Weller cat complements a Weller pottery collection just as a Royal Doulton Flambe cat fits into a Flambe porcelain collection.

Since about 1970 the array and quality of cat items have made the hobby explode. And, looking back, the first half of the 20th century offered a somewhat limited selection of cats — there were those from the later Victorian era, Louis Wain cats, Felix the Cat, the postcard rage, and the kitchen-item black cats of the 1950s. Prior to 1890, cats were few and far between, so a true antique cat (100-years old or more) is scarce, much sought after, and when found in mint condition, pricey. Examples of such early items would be original fine art, porcelains, and bronzes.

There are several 'cat' books available on today's market; if you want to see great photos representing various aspects of 'cat' collecting, you'll enjoy *Cat Collectibles* by Pauline Flick, *Antique Cats for Collectors* by Katharine Morrison McClinton, *American Cat-alogue* by Bruce Johnson, and *The Cat Made Me Buy It* and *The Black Cat Made Me Buy It* by Muncaster and Yanow.

See also Black Cats; Character Collectibles; Cookie Jars; Lefton.

Advisor: Marilyn Dipboye (See Directory, Cat Collectibles)

Newsletter: *Cat Talk*
Marilyn Dipboye, President
33161 Wendy Dr.
Sterling Hts., MI 48130; 810-264-0285; Subscription $20 per year US or $27 Canada

Bank, Persian, Royal Doulton, made for Royal Society for Prevention of Cruelty to Animals, c 1913........**$1,200.00**
Chalkware, carnival prize cat, white & brown w/blue bow & ball, 7¼" **$20.00**
Chalkware, cat sitting upright w/pipe in mouth, 9½"...**$125.00**

Chalkware, Oriental black sleeping cat, 11½", M **$110.00**
Chalkware, Oriental sleeping tabby, shaded brown w/collar, 11" **$95.00**
Decanter, cat, Jim Beam, 1967, any of 3 color variations, 11½"..........................**$30.00**
Decanter, Katz, black & white cat, Jim Beam, 1963, 14¾" ..**$50.00**
Figurine, cat, breeds other than Persian, Shafford, each, from $38 to..........................**$40.00**
Figurine, gray tabby w/tail in air, Goebel & marked w/Germany in block letters, 5½" **$65.00**
Figurine, kitten, Boehm, 1971-1981, any of 3 color variations, 4½", each..........................**$250.00**

Figurine, Red Persian Tabby, Shafford (Japan), 1967, 10", $45.00. (Photo courtesy of Marilyn Dipboye.)

Figurine, Siamese, Bing & Grondahl, marked B&B #2308, 5¼" **$240.00**
Figurine, Siamese, Royal Doulton, 1960-1985, in pose #2655, #2660 or #2662, each..........................**$155.00**
Jewelry box, various colored plastic bases, lids w/embossed cats, each..........................**$28.00**
Kitty Cucumber, cookie jar, Kitty Cucumber Clown, 1991-?.**$50.00**
Kitty Cucumber, music box, plays September Song, #330133, 1988-?..........................**$38.00**
Kitty Cucumber, music box, plays White Christmas, #330026, 1988-89 ....**$48.00**
Kitty Cucumber, ornament, KC & JP on tricycle, #333264 ..**$12.00**
Kliban, apron, shows cat playing guitar, M **$15.00**
Kliban, bank, Kliban on stool, sm, from $50 to..........**$70.00**
Kliban, bookends, pr..........................**$185.00**
Kliban, coffeepot **$225.00**

Kliban, cookie jar, cat in long pants, Sigma, from $150.00 to $175.00. (Photo courtesy of Marilyn Dipboye.)

Kliban, cookie jar, cat playing guitar, Sigma, from $150 to...**$175.00**
Kliban, cookie jar, cat sitting upright w/kitten, marked Taste Setter Sigma..........................**$475.00**
Kliban, cookie jar, cat w/long pants, Sigma, from $150 to..**$175.00**

Kliban, cookie jar, Mom cat, Sigma, from $325 to **$350.00**
Kliban, cup, skating...**$25.00**
Kliban, mug, figural cat, from $28 to.........................**$30.00**
Kliban, mug, I Love LA, MIB **$8.00**
Kliban, mug, w/picture of cat playing guitar, from $15 to ..**$18.00**
Kliban, plate, 1995..**$35.00**
Kliban, salt & pepper shakers, cat w/red shoes, composition
    material, pr..**$125.00**
Kliban, teapot, cat in blue airplane, from $225 to **$250.00**
Kliban, teapot, cat in tuxedo, from $175 to **$200.00**
Lamp, cat 'n fiddle, ceramic, table style, 15" **$60.00**
Lamp, TV; 2 Siamese, ceramic, eyes glow when bulb is
    turned on, ca 1950s, 12"...................................**$85.00**
Linens, calendar towel, NM, from $7 to.......................**$8.00**
Linens, dresser scarf, embroidered or cross-stitched scene
    w/cat at each end, from $20 to **$30.00**
Linens, handkerchief, Chessie, Peake & babies shown, some
    stains **$10.00**
Linens, handkerchief, w/cat design, NM, from $5 to....**$7.00**
Linens, towel, hand-stitched days-of-the-week pictures on
    linen, set of 7, M...**$65.00**
Plate, Christmas Rose, Royal Copenhagen, 1970.........**$37.00**
Plate, Uncle Tad's Cats, 1979, set of 4, from $700 to..**$800.00**
Plate, Uncle Tad's Holiday Cats, 1982, set of 4.........**$600.00**
Salt & pepper shakers, black & white cats, porcelain, marked
    Made in Czechoslovakia, pr.................................**$15.00**
Tin, Droste-Haarlem Holland, 4 tabbies shown on lid, 6¾"
    long..**$25.00**
Tin, Sharps, Christmas picture on lid, 5¼" square......**$12.00**
Tin, Tornes Toffee, 6 kittens shown on lid, 10x4"......**$14.00**
Toy, Felix, jointed wood, marked Patented June 23, 1925, Pat
    Sullivan c 1922, 1924 on bottom of foot, 4".......**$275.00**

Toy, litho tin cat with leather ears, push tail down and cat moves forward, marked MARX Toys, Made in the United States of America, New York, NY, $85.00. (Photo courtesy of Marilyn Dipboye.)

Cat-Tail Dinnerware

    Cat-tail was a dinnerware pattern popular during the late twenties until sometime in the forties. So popular, in fact, that ovenware, glassware, tinware, even a kitchen table was made to coordinate with it. The dinnerware was made primarily by Universal Potteries of Cambridge, Ohio, though a catalog from Hall China circa 1927 shows a 3-piece coffee service, and there may have been others. It was sold for years by Sears Roebuck and Company, and some items bear a mark with their name.

    The pattern is unmistakable: a cluster of red cattails (usually six, sometimes one or two) with black stems on creamy white. Shapes certainly vary; Universal used at least three of their standard mold designs, Camwood, Old Holland, Laurella, and possibly others. Some Cat-tail pieces are marked Wheelock on the bottom. (Wheelock was a department store in Peoria, Illinois.)

    If you're trying to decorate a forties vintage kitchen, no other design could afford you more to work with. To see many of the pieces that are available and to learn more about the line, read *The Collector's Encyclopedia of American Dinnerware* by Jo Cunningham.

Advisors: Barbara and Ken Brooks (See Directory, Dinnerware)

Casserole, with lid, $30.00. (Photo courtesy of Barbara and Ken Brooks.)

Batter jug, metal top...**$80.00**
Bowl, Old Holland shape, marked Wheelock, 6" **$6.00**
Butter dish, w/lid, 1-lb **$45.00**
Cake cover & tray, tinware **$30.00**
Canister set, tinware, 4-pc **$45.00**
Coffeepot, 3-pc **$65.00**
Cookie jar **$85.00**
Cracker jar, barrel shape **$75.00**
Creamer, Laurella shape **$16.00**
Custard cup **$7.00**
Gravy boat, w/liner **$35.00**
Jug, refrigerator; w/handle **$30.00**
Jug, side handle, cork stopper **$32.00**
Kitchen scales, tinware **$37.00**
Match holder, tinware **$35.00**
Pie plate..**$25.00**
Pie server, hole in handle for hanging, marked Universal
    Potteries **$25.00**
Pitcher, ice lip; glass...**$100.00**
Pitcher, utility or milk...**$25.00**
Plate, dinner; Laurella shape, from $12 to...................**$15.00**
Plate, dinner; 3-compartment....................................**$25.00**
Plate, salad or dessert; round.....................................**$5.00**
Plate, serving; early, marked Universal Potteries-Oven Proof,
    Cambridge Ohio, from $30 to.............................**$35.00**
Platter, oval...**$25.00**

Salad set (fork, spoon & bowl) $50.00
Salt & pepper shakers, different styles, pr.........$15.00
Saucer, Old Holland shape, marked Wheelock............$6.00
Shaker set, salt, pepper, flour & sugar shakers, glass, on red
    metal tray...$40.00
Stack set, 3-pc w/lids................................$40.00
Sugar bowl, 2-handled, w/lid $16.00
Tablecloth..$85.00
Teapot, w/lid, from $30 to............................$35.00
Tumbler, iced tea; glass..............................$35.00
Tumbler, marked Universal Potteries, scarce...........$65.00
Tumbler, water; glass.................................$30.00

Waste can, tinware, oval, $30.00. (Photo courtesy of Barbara and Ken Brooks.)

Catalin Napkin Rings

Plastic (Catalin) napkin rings topped with heads of cartoon characters, animals, and birds are very collectible, especially examples in red and orange; blue is also good, and other colors can be found as well.

Band, lathe turned, amber, red or green, 1¾" $10.00
Band, plain, amber, red, or green, 2", each...........$8.00
Band, plain, colors, 2", set of 6, MIB $40.00
Camel, inlaid eye rod $72.00
Chicken, no inlaid eyes...............................$30.00
Donald Duck, w/decal, from $65 to $80.00
Duck, no inlaid eyes $30.00
Elephant, ball on head................................$35.00
Elephant, no ball on head $30.00

Fish, Duck and Elephant, $30.00 each.

Mickey Mouse, w/decal, from $70 to....................$85.00

Rabbit, inlaid eye rod................................$40.00
Rabbit, no inlaid eyes................................$30.00
Rocking horse, inlaid eye rod.........................$72.00
Schnauzer dog, no inlaid eyes.........................$30.00
Scotty dog, inlaid eye rod............................$40.00

Catalogs

Right now, some of the most collectible catalogs are those from the the fifties, sixties, and seventies, especially those Christmas 'wish books.' They're full of the toys that are so sought after by today's collectors — battery-ops, Tonkas, and of course, GI Joes and Barbies. No matter what year the catalog was printed, its value will hinge on several factors: subject, illustrations and the amount of color used, collector demand, size, rarity, and condition (grade them carefully and be sure to adjust their values accordingly). Generally, manufacturers' catalogs are more valuable than those put out by a jobber.

Aldens, 1974, Fall/Winter, NM $32.00
Aldens, 1978, Spring/Summer, EX $22.00
Bailey's, 1969, beauticians' supplies, 126 illustrated pages,
    M $32.00
Bella Hess, 1956, Spring/Summer, NM..................$28.00
Black & Decker Electrical Power Tools, 1947, 64 illustrated
    pages, EX..$20.00
Busch Jewelers, 1937, Christmas, 32 illustrated pages,
    w/inserts & envelope, VG.........................$12.50
Butterick Home Catalog, 1950, Fall, patterns, 60 illustrated
    pages, NM..$15.00
Chicago Hair Goods, 1957, beauticians' supplies, 140 illustrated pages, NM......................................$32.00
Colt Firearms, 1978, pistols, 20 illustrated pages, EX..$15.00
Edmund Scientific Co, 1974, scientific-related goods & optics,
    164 illustrated pages, EX........................$18.00
FAO Schwarz, 1949, Christmas, 96 color-illustrated pages,
    VG $27.50
Fuller Brush #69A, 1950, housewares, EX $20.00
Fuller Brushes for Health, Beauty & Home, 1937, 16 pages
    w/2 inserts, VG+.................................$25.00
Gambles, 1955, Spring/Summer, general merchandise, 128
    illustrated pages, NM............................$27.50
Gifts for the Entire Family, 1948, Mayfair Gifts, New York, 64
    pages, VG $10.00
Hanover House, 1969, Christmas, 64 illustrated pages, M..$22.00
Hayes, 1950, Half-Size Fashions for Ladies, Spring/Summer,
    68 color-illustrated pages, NM $15.00
Heathkit, 1970, electronics, 116 illustrated pages, NM..$15.00
Herters, 1955, hunting & fishing equipment, 546 illustrated
    pages, EX..$32.00
JC Penney, 1968, Spring/Summer, EX $20.00
JC Penney, 1989, Christmas, NM $20.00
Jewel Tea, 1955, Spring/Summer, clothing & general merchandise, 100 illustrated pages, EX $27.50
John Plain, 1954, jewelry, silver, general line, 650 illustrated
    pages, EX..$70.00
Koantry Klub Sportswear, 1942, clothing & golf accessories,
    23 illustrated pages, EX.........................$20.00

Lana Labell Fashions for Juniors/Misses, 1962, Summer, 80 color-illustrated pages, NM **$18.00**

Lane Bryant Fashions for Larger Ladies, 1971, Winter, 40 color-illustrated pages, M **$12.00**

Lane Bryant Fashions for Stout Ladies, 1943, Spring/Summer, 84 illustrated pages, EX **$35.00**

Lee Wards, 1964, Spring/Summer, crafts & supplies, 64 illustrated pages, NM...............................**$15.00**

Majestic, 1961, jewelry, gifts & general merchandise, 482 illustrated pages, NM **$50.00**

Marklin, 1966, toy trains and cars, 72 color-illustrated pages, M **$45.00**

Monogram, 1959, toy models, 32 color-illustrated pages, NM.......................................**$70.00**

Montgomery Ward, 1950, electrical power tools, 48 illustrated pages, EX **$20.00**

Montgomery Ward, 1950, Spring/Summer, NM **$50.00**

Montgomery Ward, 1959, hunting & fishing equipment & accessories, NM.......................................**$35.00**

Montgomery Ward, 1966, Fall/Winter, NM.................**$35.00**

Montgomery Ward, 1976, farm-related merchandise, NM..**$15.00**

Montgomery Ward, 1980, Spring/Summer, EX **$22.00**

Murray Wheel Goods, 1956, pedal vehicles including cars, tractors and bikes, 8 color-illustrated pages, w/price list, NM...............................**$30.00**

National Bella Hess, 1969, Christmas, NM.................**$32.00**

Neiman Marcus, 1983, Christmas, NM.........................**$22.00**

Power of Play, 1967, Creative Playthings, Princeton NJ, 8½x11", VG **$30.00**

Remington Firearms, 1947, Fall, ammunition, 28 pages, EX+......................................**$22.50**

Roman's Ladies' Fashions, 1974, Spring/Summer, EX ..**$15.00**

Sears, 1944, Mid-Winter, 88 pages, EX.........................**$10.00**

Sears, 1948, farm equipment, fencing & garden needs, 196 illustrated pages, NM...............................**$20.00**

Sears, 1951, wallpaper, NM...**$18.00**

Sears, 1952, Craftsman tools, 48 illustrated pages, EX ..**$20.00**

Sears, 1959, Christmas, EX **$85.00**

Sears, 1963, Fall/Winter, EX **$35.00**

Sears, 1972, Fall/Winter, NM..............................**$30.00**

Sears, 1984, Christmas, NM **$30.00**

Sears, 1984, Spring/Summer, NM.........................**$20.00**

Sears, 1991, Spring/Summer, M **$10.00**

Selmer Showbook Catalog #14, 1948, musical accessories, 17 pages, EX......................................**$22.50**

Skylark Originals, 1956, ladies' clothing, 48 illustrated pages, EX **$16.00**

South Carolina Mills, 1955, Spring/Summer, clothing, 68 illustrated pages, EX......................................**$15.00**

Spiegel's, 1972, Spring/Summer, NM.........................**$30.00**

Sporting Firearms, 1980, Marlin Firearms Co, 32 pages, 8½x11", VG **$10.00**

Top Value Stamps, 1958, 50 pages, VG **$15.00**

Top Value Stamps, 1965, redemption book w/Rockwell Cover, 170 pages, M **$35.00**

Transogram, 1949, toys, games & craft sets, 36 color-illustrated pages, NM......................................**$28.00**

United Jewelers, 1972, jewelry, gifts, sporting goods, toys, etc, 336 illustrated pages, M..................................**$40.00**

Wally Frank, 1951, pipes & tobacco, 30 illustrated pages, EX......................................**$18.00**

Walter Field Gifts, 1958, Winter Fashions, 60 illustrated pages, EX......................................**$15.00**

Walter Fields, 1949, Fall/Winter, fashions & gifts, 52 illustrated pages, NM......................................**$17.50**

Wilson Restricted Line Golf Equipment, 1942, 47 illustrated pages, EX......................................**$55.00**

Ceramic Arts Studio

American-made figurines are very popular now, and these are certainly among the best. They have a distinctive look you'll soon learn to identify with confidence, even if you happen to pick up an unmarked piece. They were first designed in the forties and sold well until the company closed in 1955. (After that, the new owner took the molds to Japan and produced them over there for a short time.) The company's principal designer was Betty Harrington, who modeled the figures and knicknacks that so many have grown to love. In addition to the company's mark, 'Ceramic Arts Studios, Madison Wisconsin,' some of the character pieces she designed also carry their assigned names on the bottom.

The company also produced a line of metal items to accessorize the figurines; these were designed by Liberace's mother, Zona.

Though prices continue to climb, once in awhile there's an unmarked bargain to be found, but first you must familiarize yourself with your subject! BA Wellman has compiled *The Ceramic Arts Studio Price Guide* as well as an accompanying video tape that we're sure you'll enjoy if you'd like to learn more.

Advisor: BA Wellman (See Directory, Ceramic Arts Studio)

Catalog Reprints: BA Wellman
88 State Rd. W, Homestead Farms #2
Westminster, MA 01473-1435

Newsletter/Club: CAS Collectors Association
CAS Collector bimonthly newsletter
P.O. Box 46
Madison, WI 53701; 608-241-9138; Newsletter $15; Annual membership, $15. Inventory record and price guide listing 800+ works, $12 postage paid

Figurines, Autumn Andy and Summer Sue, 5", from $55.00 to $65.00 each.

Ashtray, Peek-a-boo pixie, 5" wide $60.00
Bank, paisley pig, 3"..$70.00
Bell, Winter Belle, 5¼", from $65 to $75.00
Figurine, Al, hunter w/gun $75.00
Figurine, Archibald the Dragon, 8" $200.00
Figurine, Autumn Andy, 5", from $55 to...................$65.00
Figurine, Bobby, black boy, pulling his ear, white diaper,
  3¼"...$140.00
Figurine, Collie puppy playing, 2¼" $22.00
Figurine, Cupid on flower, brown hair, yellow wings &
  flower...$75.00
Figurine, Dachshund, 3½" long $40.00
Figurine, drummer girl, 4¼"......................................$55.00
Figurine, FiFi, 3"...$50.00
Figurine, Gremlin boy, standing $90.00
Figurine, guitar boy, 5"...$65.00
Figurine, Gypsy tambourine girl, 7" $75.00
Figurine, Hansel & Gretel, 1-pc, 4½", from $45 to $50.00
Figurine, kitten, playing w/ball of yarn, 2"...............$30.00
Figurine, Lu-Tang on bamboo bud (vase) $50.00
Figurine, mermaid baby, seated $50.00
Figurine, Miss Muffet, bowl in hand (3 variations), from $50
  to $95.00
Figurine, My Lady of Fatima $90.00
Figurine, Pioneer Susie, w/broom, 5" $50.00
Figurine, Polish girl, 6"...$45.00
Figurine, Poncho, Mexican boy, sitting playing banjo, 3¾",
  from $45 to $50.00
Figurine, squirrel w/jacket, 2¼"................................$45.00
Figurine, square dance boy, 6½"................................$55.00
Figurine, St George on Charger, 8½" $175.00
Figurine, Wee Scotch boy & girl, 3¼", pr $45.00

Figurines, Comedy and Tragedy, 10", $150.00 for the pair.

Flowerpot, square...$30.00
Jug, Adam & Eve, boy & girl w/apple, hourglass form..$60.00
Jug, horse head...$60.00
Salt & pepper shakers, covered wagon & oxen, 3" long each,
  pr $80.00
Salt & pepper shakers, fish, upright tails, 4", pr.........$65.00
Salt & pepper shakers, frog under toadstool, 3" & 2",
  pr...$55.00
Salt & pepper shakers, Hindu boys, set $110.00

Salt & pepper shakers, Paul Bunyon & tree, pr.........$95.00
Salt & pepper shakers, snuggle type; dog & doghouse,
  pr $75.00
Salt & pepper shakers, snuggle type; kitten & pitcher, 2½",
  pr $85.00
Salt & pepper shakers, snuggle type; mother & baby cow,
  5½" & 2½", pr...$85.00
Salt & pepper shakers, snuggle type; mother & baby monkey,
  4¾" & 2½", pr...$60.00
Salt & pepper shakers, snuggle type; mother & baby rabbit,
  running, pr $95.00
Salt & pepper shakers, snuggle type; mouse & cheese wedge,
  3", pr $30.00
Salt & pepper shakers, snuggle type; Thai & Thai Thai,
  Siamese cats, 4¾" & 5", pr....................................$125.00
Salt & pepper shakers, Suzette on Pillow, white poodle, 4",
  pr $85.00
Salt & pepper shakers, Wee Eskimos, boy & girl, 3" & 3¼",
  pr $75.00
Shelf sitter, boy w/puppy, 4¼"..................................$65.00
Shelf sitter, canary, head up or down, each...............$45.00
Shelf sitter, cowgirl, 4¾"...$65.00
Shelf sitter, Nip 'n Tuck, 4¼", pr...............................$50.00
Shelf sitter, Pete & Polly parrots, 7½", pr $125.00
Shelf sitter, Willy, holding ball down, white diaper..$135.00
Shelf sitter, Young Love boy & girl, 4½", pr...............$95.00

Figurines, Little Miss Muffet and Little Jack Horner, #2, 4½", $55.00 each.

Cereal Boxes

Yes, cereal boxes — your eyes aren't deceiving you. But think about it. Cereal boxes from even the sixties have to be extremely scarce. The ones that are bringing the big bucks today are those with a well-known character emblazoned across the front. Am I starting to make more sense to you? Good. Now, say the experts, is the time to look ahead into the future of your cereal box collection. They recommend going to your neighborhood supermarket to inspect the shelves in the cereal aisle today! Choose the ones with Batman, Quisp, Ninja Turtles, or some other nineties' phenomenon. Take them home and (unless you have mice) display them unopened, or empty them out and fold them up along the seam lines. If you want only the old boxes, you'll probably have to find an old long-abandoned grocery store or pay prices somewhere around those in our listings when one comes up for sale.

Store displays and advertising posters, in-box prizes or 'send-a-ways,' coupons with pictures of boxes, and shelf signs and cards are also part of this field of interest.

Our values are based on recent selling prices. If you want to learn more about this field of collecting, we recommend *Toys of the Sixties* by Bill Bruegman and *Cereal Box Bonanza, The 1950s, ID and Values,* by Scott Bruce.

Advisor: Scott Bruce (See Directory, Cereal Boxes and Premiums)

Newsletter: *FLAKE, The Breakfast Nostalgia Magazine*
P.O. Box 481
Cambridge, MA 02140; 617-492-5004

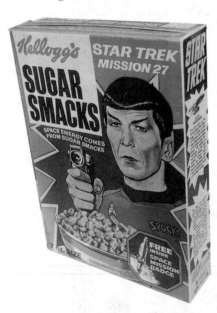

Sugar Smacks, British, Mr. Spock, 1969, $1,000.00. (Photo courtesy of Scott Bruce.)

Addams Family, portrait on back, flat, EX $10.00
Apple Cinnamon, Bugs Bunny's 50th Anniversary Magic Motion sticker premium, flat, EX $12.00
Boo Berry, treasure club offer, flat, EX $15.00
Cap'n Crunch, Sea Creeper premium, Canadian, flat, EX . $15.00
Cap'n Crunch Crunch Berries, breakfast fun & games on box back, flat, EX $10.00
Chrunceroos, dinosaur skeleton cutout on box back, Canadian, 1991, flat, EX $15.00
Cinnamon Toast Crunch, Wendell cookie premium, flat, EX $12.00
Cocoa Krispies, fossil factory premium, flat, EX $15.00
Cocoa Krispies, River Run game on box back, flat, 1991, EX $15.00
Cocoa Pebbles, free bowling premium on box back, flat, 1989, EX $8.00
Cookie Crisp, Teenage Mutant Ninja Turtles collector cards on box back, w/bowl, flat, EX $20.00
Cookie Crisp, Teenage Mutant Ninja Turtles collector cards on box back, 1989, flat, EX $12.00

Corn Flakes, Duck Tales mask premium on box back, flat, EX $10.00
Corn Flakes, Superman Satellite launcher offer, 1956 .. $460.00
Corn Flakes, Yogi Bear birthday party, 1962 .... $420.00
Corn Pops, Mexican, flat, 1980s, EX $15.00
Count Chocula, Big Foot on box back, flat, EX $22.00
Count Chocula, cartoon box on back, flat, EX $15.00
Count Chocula, flicker eye cover, door sign on box back, 1988, EX $15.00
Count Chocula, glow-in-the-dark picture on box back, flat, EX $15.00
Count Chocula, Mystery Drawing Disk premium, flat, EX $15.00
Count Chocula, spooky shape-maker, flat, EX $15.00
Crisp Crunch, laugh mask on box back, flat, 1991, EX . $10.00
Crispy Rice, Thunder & Lightning on box back, flat, EX .. $15.00
Deep Sea Crunch, Deep Sea fact or fiction on box back, flat, 1994, EX $12.00
Frankenberry, flicker eyes box front, door sign on box back, flat, 1988, EX $15.00
Frankenberry, spooky shape-maker premium, flat, EX .. $15.00
Frankenberry, Spooky Trail notebook cover offer, flat, EX $15.00
Frosted Flakes, Tony Tiger Bites Recipe on box back, flat, EX $15.00
FrostyO's, Dudley DoRight, 1970 .... $600.00
Fruit & Frosted O's, flat, 1990s, EX $15.00
Fruit Brute, flat, 1977 .... $300.00
Fruit Islands, contest on box back, flat, 1987, EX $25.00
Fruit Loops, Disney Gummi Bears Stamper premium, flat, 1991, EX $15.00
Holiday Lucky Charms, gift tags on box back, flat, EX .. $12.00
Honey Smacks, Dig'em mask on box back, flat, EX .. $15.00
Hot Wheels, car premium, flat, EX $12.00
Hot Wheels, Super Changer Contest, flat, 1989, EX $10.00
Huckleberry Hound All Stars, flat, 1966, EX $300.00
Jetsons, hologram sticker premium, 1990s, flat, EX $10.00
Kellogg's Cinnamon Mini Buns, w/cassette offer on box back, flat, 1991, EX $10.00
Kellogg's Corn Pops, table-top soccer game on box back, flat, 1991, EX $10.00
Kellogg's Frosted Krispies, finger twister game on box back, flat, 1990, EX $15.00
Kellogg's Fruity Marshmallow Krispies, finger twister game on box back, flat, 1990, EX $15.00
Kellogg's Honey Smacks, ghost detector premium, flat, 1989, EX $20.00
Kellogg's Smacks, 'La Conquista Del Mar' on box back, Spanish, flat, EX $10.00
Kellogg's Sugar Corn Pops, secret decoder premium, digital watch offer, flat, 1983, EX $10.00
Life, Dick Tracy pencil case offer, flat, 1990, EX $15.00
Morning Funnies, 3rd Collectors Edition, flat, 1988, EX . $15.00
Nabisco Rice Honeys, Frontier hero medal, full, never opened, 1960, EX $100.00
New Pink Panther Flakes, flat, 1971 .... $500.00
Nintendo, hologram box, flat, 1988, EX $15.00
Pacman, free foam flyer offer, Canadian, flat, EX $25.00
Pep, Space Cadet cast photo on front, 1952 .... $375.00

Post Crispy Critters, Crispy Critters counting game on box back, flat, 1990, EX......................................**$12.00**
Punch Crunch, flat, 1975....................................**$300.00**
Quake, ring offer, flat, 1966............................**$900.00**
Quaker Harvest, glow-in-the-dark badge premium, English, flat, 1990, EX......................................**$22.00**
Quisp, Space trivia box, flat, 1990, EX..............**$10.00**
Quisp, Vote Quake Out of Business, flat, 1970............**$4.00**
Real Ghostbusters, glow-in-the-dark door hanger on box back, flat, EX......................................**$12.00**
Real Ghostbusters, hologram box, flat, EX................**$15.00**
Rice Chex, Charlie Brown After School Mix Recipe on box back, flat, 1990, EX......................................**$6.00**
Rice Chex, Charlie Brown in Chef hat holding bowl, flat, 1990, EX......................................**$6.00**
Storybook Twinkles, early 1960s............................**$325.00**
Sugar Golden Crisp, coins from around the World premium, flat, EX......................................**$15.00**
Sugar Smacks, British, Mr Spock, 1969..................**$1,000.00**
Super Golden Crisp, Sugar Bear adventure game on box back, flat, 1990, EX......................................**$15.00**
Teddy Grahams Breakfast Bears Graham Cereal, Eddy mask on box back, flat, EX......................................**$12.00**
Teenage Mutant Ninja Turtles, Pizza Flyer Flip 'n Toss game on box back, flat, EX......................................**$10.00**
Weetabix Wheetos Wheat Hoops, Wheets whirly top premium, English, flat, 1990, EX......................................**$10.00**
Wheaties, Michael Jordan, flat, EX **$15.00**

Character and Promotional Drinking Glasses

In any household, especially those with children, I would venture to say, you should find a few of these glasses. Put out by fast-food restaurant chains or by a company promoting a product, they have for years been commonplace. But now, instead of glass, the giveaways are nearly always plastic. If a glass is offered at all, you'll usually have to pay 99¢ for it.

You can find glasses like these for small change at garage sales, and at those prices, pick up any that are still bright and unfaded. They will move well on your flea market table. Some are worth more than others. Among the common ones are Camp Snoopy, B.C. Ice Age, Garfield, McDonald's, Smurfs, and Coca-Cola. The better glasses are those with super heroes, characters from Star Trek and thirties movies such as 'Wizard of Oz,' sports personalities, and cartoon characters by Walter Lantz and Walt Disney. Some of these carry a copyright date, and that's all it is. It's not the date of manufacture.

Many collectors are having a good time looking for these glasses. If you want to learn more about them, we recommend *The Collector's Guide to Cartoon and Promotional Drinking Glasses* by John Hervey, and *Collectible Drinking Glasses, Identification and Values,* by Mark Chase and Michael Kelly (Collector Books).

There are some terms used in the descriptions that may be confusing. 'Brockway' style refers to a thick, heavy glass that tapers in from top to bottom. 'Federal' style, on the other hand, is thinner, and the top and bottom diameters are the same.

Advisors: Mark Chase and Michael Kelly (See Directory, Character and Promotional Drinking Glasses)

Newsletter: *Collector Glass News*
P.O. Box 308
Slippery Rock, PA 16057; 412-946-8126 or 412-794-6420

Al Capp, Dog Patch, Sneaky Pete's Hot Dogs, Brockway, 6 different, 4", each (except Joe Btsfplk) from $40 to......**$80.00**
Al Capp, Dog Patch, 1975, Brockway, 6 different, 6", each (except Joe Btsfplk) from $30 to......................**$50.00**
Al Capp, Joe Btsfplk, Sneaky Pete's Hot Dogs, 4", from $60 to......................................**$90.00**
Al Capp, Joe Btsfplk, 1975, Brockway, 6", from $40 to....**$60.00**
Archies, Betty & Veronica Give a Party, Welch's, 1971, 4¼", NM, from $2 to......................................**$4.00**
Atlanta Falcons, McDonald's/Dr Pepper, 1981, 4 different, each from $4 to......................................**$6.00**
Batgirl, DC Comics Super Heroes (Moon) Series, Pepsi, 1976, 6½", from $12 to......................................**$15.00**
Battlestar Galactica, Universal Studios, 1979, 4 different, each from $7 to......................................**$10.00**
BC Ice Age, Arby's, 1981, 6 different, each from $3 to ..**$5.00**
Beaky Buzzard, Cool Cat & the Kite, Interaction Series, Warner Bros/Pepsi, 1976, Brockway, from $8 to....................**$10.00**
Blue Fairy (Pinocchio), blue image w/verse on back, 1940, 4⅜"......................................**$20.00**

Bugs Bunny, 50th Anniversary, Ultramar/Canadian, from $5.00 to $7.00 each. (Photo courtesy of Collector Glass News.)

Bugs Bunny, Static Pose Series (white lettering), Warner Bros/Pepsi, 1973, Federal, from $6 to..................**$10.00**
Bugs Bunny & Marvin Martian & the Ray Gun, Interaction Series, Warner Bros/Pepsi, 1976, Brockway, from $45 to......**$65.00**
Bullwinkle, Bicentennial Series, Arby's, 1976, 6", from $10 to......................................**$12.00**
Bullwinkle, Static Pose Series, PAT Ward/Pepsi, late 1970s, 5", from $25 to......................................**$30.00**
Burger Chef & Jeff, Friendly Monster Series, Burger Chef, 1976, 6 different, each from $25 to......................**$35.00**
Burger Chef & Jeff, Now We're Glassified!, Burger Chef, from $15 to......................................**$25.00**
Care Bears, Friend Bear or Good Luck Bear, Pizza Hut, 1983, each from $7 to......................................**$10.00**
Care Bears, Pizza Hut, 1983, 6 different, each (except Good Luck Bear or Friend Bear)......................**$1.00**

Cool Cat, Static Pose Series (logo on side w/black lettering), Warner Bros/Pepsi, 1973, Federal, from $8 to......**$12.00**

Davy Crockett, Welch's, 6 different, from $7 to..........**$10.00**

Dick Tracy, Domino's Pizza, 1970s, Brockway, 16-oz, from $100 to..**$125.00**

Dudley Do-Right, Action Scene, PAT Ward/Pepsi, late 1970s, Brockway, 12-oz, from $8 to **$10.00**

Elmer Fudd, Static Pose Series, Warner Bros/Pepsi, 1973, Federal, from $5 to **$8.00**

Empire Strikes Back, Burger King/Coca-Cola, 1980, 4 different, each from $5 to **$7.00**

ET, Army & Air Force Exchange Service, 1982, 4 different, each from $5 to...**$10.00**

ET, Collector's Series, Pizza Hut/Pepsi, 1982, 4 different, each from $2 to **$3.00**

Flash, DC Comics Super Heroes, Pepsi, 1978, Brockway, 6¼", from $8 to **$12.00**

Flintstones Kids, Pizza Hut, 1986, 4 different, each from $2 to **$3.00**

Gasoline Alley, Sunday Funnies, 1976, from $8 to **$15.00**

Go-Go Gophers, Leonardo TTV/Pepsi, 6", from $15 to..**$20.00**

Great Muppet Caper, McDonald's, 1989, 4 different, each from $1 to **$2.00**

Green Lantern, DC Comics Super Heroes (Moon) Series, Pepsi, 1976, from $35 to **$50.00**

Holly Hobbie, Happy Talk Series, Coca-Cola, undated, 6 different, each from $2 to **$5.00**

Howard the Duck, Marvel Comics Super Heroes Series, 7-Eleven, 1977, from $15 to **$18.00**

Huckleberry Hound & Yogi Bear, Hanna-Barbera/Pepsi, 1977, from $20 to..**$30.00**

Incredible Hulk, Marvel Comics Super Heroes Series, 7-Eleven, 1977, from $20 to **$25.00**

Indiana Jones & the Temple of Doom, 7-Up, 1984, 4 different, each from $8 to **$12.00**

James Bond 007, Collector Series (Roger Moore movies), 1985, 4 different, each from $10 to **$15.00**

Josie & the Pussycats, Hanna-Barbera/Pepsi, 1977, from $20 to..**$30.00**

Jungle Book, Bagheera, WDP/Pepsi, late 1970s, from $60 to...**$90.00**

Jungle Book, Canadian, 3 from a set of 6, from $35.00 to $50.00 each. (Photo courtesy of Collector Glass News.)

King Kong, Coca-Cola, 1976, 4 different, each from $5 to....**$8.00**

Little Orphan Annie, Sunday Funnies, 1976, from $8 to ...**$15.00**

McDonaldland, Action Series, McDonald's, 1977, 6 different, each from $3 to...**$5.00**

McDonaldland, Adventure Series, McDonald's, 1980, 6 different, each from $10 to **$15.00**

Mickey Mouse, Happy Birthday, WDP/Pepsi, 1978, from $6 to...**$8.00**

Mickey Mouse Through the Years, Sunoco, 1988, 6 different, each from $5 to...**$7.00**

Minnie Mouse, Disney/Hooks Drugs, 1984, from $12 to..**$15.00**

Natasha, Static Pose Series, PAT Ward/Pepsi, late 1970s, 5", from $10 to..**$15.00**

Norman Rockwell, Saturday Evening Post Series, Arby's, early 1980s, 6 different, each from $2 to **$4.00**

Norman Rockwell, Summer Scenes Series, Arby's, 1987, 4 different, each from $3 to..**$5.00**

Nursery Rhymes, Big Top Peanut Butter, 1950s, each from $3 to...**$5.00**

Pac-Man, Arby's, 1980, 4½", from $2 to........................**$4.00**

Peanuts, Camp Snoopy Series, McDonald's, 1983, 5 different, each from $1 to...**$2.00**

Peanuts, Kraft Jelly, 1988, 4 different, each **$2.00**

Petunia Pig, Static Pose Series (logo under name), Warner Bros/Pepsi, 1973, Federal, 15-oz, minimum value ..**$50.00**

Petunia Pig, Static Pose Series (side logo), Warner Bros/Pepsi, 1973, Brockway or Federal, 16-oz, from $6 to **$8.00**

Pittsburgh Steelers Superbowl 13, McDonald's, 1978, 4 different, each from $5 to...**$8.00**

Popeye, Kollect-A-Set Series, Coca-Cola 1975, 6 different, each from $6 to...**$8.00**

Porky Pig, Static Pose Series (logo under name), Warner Bros/Pepsi, 1973, Federal, 15-oz, from $15 to......**$20.00**

Road Runner, Static Pose Series, Warner Bros/Pepsi, 1973, Brockway, from $5 to...**$10.00**

Snoopy, Sports Series, Dolly Madison, 4 different, each..**$5.00**

Speedy Gonzales, Static Pose Series (black letters), Warner Bros/Pepsi, 1973, Federal, from $6 to...................**$10.00**

Star Trek, Dr Pepper, 1976, 4 different, each from $15 to **$20.00**

Star Trek III: The Search for Spock, Taco Bell/Coca-Cola, 1984, 4 different, each from $3 to **$5.00**

Star Wars, Burger King/Coca-Cola, 1977, 4 different, each from $10 to...**$15.00**

Supergirl, DC Comics Super Heroes (Moon) Series, Pepsi, 1976, each from $10 to.......................................**$15.00**

Superman the Movie, DC Comics, 1978, 6 different, each from $5 to...**$10.00**

Sylvester, Tweety & the Limb, Interaction Series, Warner Bros/Pepsi, 1973, Brockway, from $5 to................**$7.00**

Tasmanian Devil, Static Pose Series (side logo), Warner Bros/Pepsi, 1973, Brockway or Federal, 16-oz, from $15 to **$20.00**

Winnie the Pooh, Disney World Souvenirs Series, WDP/Sears, 1970s, scarce, from $15 to................**$25.00**

Winnie the Pooh for President, WDP/Sears, 1970s, from $10 to...**$15.00**

Wizard of Id, Arby's, 1983, 6 different, each from $7 to....**$10.00**

Wizard of Oz, Swift & Co, 3 sets of 6 different w/3 different bottoms, each from $12 to **$18.00**

Wonder Woman, DC Comics Super Heroes Series (round bottom), Pepsi, 1978, from $10 to **$15.00**

Woody Woodpecker, Walter Lantz/Pepsi, 1970s, Brockway, from $10 to...**$20.00**

Underdog, Action Series, Leonardo TTV/Pepsi, 5", from $15.00 to $20.00.

Plastic Mugs

For over forty years, children's plastic cups have been a favorite of advertisers as well as children at the breakfast table. In the 1950s the Wander Company, makers of Ovaltine, offered Beetleware plastic cups depicting comic characters such as Howdy Doody, Little Orphan Annie, and Captain Midnight. They were very popular and sold in large quantities, and good examples can still be found today.

In the 1960s other companies such as Walt Disney Studios, Kellogg's, Pillsbury, and Planters, to name only a few, found this a successful form of advertising for their products and many thousands of cups found their way into homes through special offers on cereal boxes and through other promotions. The cups were designed after the likenesses of favorite cartoon or advertising characters. Few children would eat breakfast without first having their cup at the table by them.

Look at the bottoms of these cups and you will see the imprints of manufacturers such as F&F Mold and Die Works Company of Dayton, Ohio; Deka of Elizabeth, New Jersey; Beacon Plastics; and others. Some have dates; others don't.

Advisors: Lee and Cheryl Brown (See Directory, Character and Personality Collectibles)

Club/Newsletter: Children's Cups America
Cheryl and Lee Brown
7377 Badger Ct.
Indianapolis, IN 46260

Bugs Bunny, F&F, Warner Bros, VG **$18.00**

Campbell Kid, Campbell Soup Co, EX.....................**$24.00**

Cowboy Boot, E-Z Por Corp, M **$12.00**

Cowboy Pistol, E-Z Por Corp, M **$18.00**

Dennis the Menace, F&F, Hall Syn, VG **$35.00**

Dough Boy, Pillsbury Co, 1979, M............................**$18.00**

Dukes of Hazzard, Deka, Warner Bros, 1981, EX.......**$11.00**

Flintstones, all, Deka, Hanna-Barbera, 1978, EX.........**$12.00**

Flintstones, Bamm-Bamm, F&F, Vitamins, Hanna-Barbera, 1972, M..**$18.00**

Flintstones, Dino, F&F, Hanna-Barbera, 1968, M **$24.00**

Flintstones, Fred, F&F, Vitamins, Hanna-Barbera, 1968, G..**$18.00**

Flintstones, Pebbles, F&F, Vitamins, Hanna-Barbera, 1972, M **$18.00**

Frosty the Snowman, F&F, G **$15.00**

Gerber Baby, Gerber Products, pink, M **$9.00**

Incredible Hulk, Deka, Marvel Comics, 1977, G.........**$15.00**

Indianapolis 500, Whirley Ind, G................................**$9.00**

Jiminy Cricket, Walt Disney Productions, flickering eyes, M..**$38.00**

Keebler Elf, F&F, Keebler Co, 1972, M **$26.00**

Kool Aid, F&F, clear, General Foods, M **$28.00**

Kool Aid, F&F, frosted, General Foods, M...................**$35.00**

Kool Aid, unmarked, red, M......................................**$7.00**

Masters of the Universe, Deka, Mattel Inc, 1983, G....**$18.00**

Mickey Mouse, Walt Disney Productions, flickering eyes, rare, EX..**$55.00**

Mickey Mouse Club, Deka, Walt Disney Productions, EX .**$14.00**

Mr Peanut, no handle, brown, rare **$48.00**

Nestles Quik Bunny, Nestles Co, VG **$12.00**

Pilgrim, F&F, Quaker Oats, G **$35.00**

Popeye, Deka, King Features Syn, 1971, G **$11.00**

Porky Pig, Eagle, blue, M...**$35.00**

Quaker Oats, F&F, 3¾", $18.00.

Roy Rogers 'King of the Cowboys,' F&F, EX..............**$60.00**

Smurfs, Deka, SEPP, 1980, EX....................................**$10.00**

Snoopy, Knickerbocker, United Features, 1958, G......**$50.00**

Star Trek, The Motion Picture, Deka, Paramount Pictures Corp, 1979, VG **$24.00**

Star Wars, Deka, 20th Century Fox, 1977, G **$22.00**

Strawberry Shortcake, Deka, American Greetings, 1980, EX...**$7.00**

Tony the Tiger, F&F, Kellogg's, 1964, EX....................**$37.00**

Woody Woodpecker, F&F, WLP, 1965, G **$18.00**

Wyler's Choo Choo Cherry, F&F, Pillsbury Co, 1969, M ..**$32.00**

Wyler's Goofy Grape, F&F, Pillsbury Co, 1969, M **$32.00**

Wyler's Lefty Lemon, F&F, Pillsbury Co, 1969, M........**$32.00**

Wyler's Silly Strawberry, F&F, Pillsbury Co, 1969, EX.**$24.00**

Yogi Bear, F&F, Hanna-Barbera, 1961, VG **$28.00**

Character Clocks and Watches

There is growing interest in the comic character watches and clocks produced from about 1930 into the fifties and beyond. They're in rather short supply simply because they were made for children to wear (and play with). They were cheaply made with pin-lever movements, not worth an expensive repair job, so many were simply thrown away. The original packaging that today may be worth more than the watch itself was usually ripped apart by an excited child and promptly relegated to the wastebasket.

Condition is very important in assessing value. Unless a watch is in like-new condition, it is not mint. Rust, fading, scratching, or wear of any kind will sharply lessen its value, and the same is true of the box itself. Good, excellent, and mint watches can be evaluated on a scale of one to five, with excellent being a three, good a one, and mint a five. In other words, a watch worth $25.00 in good condition would be worth five times that amount if it were mint ($125.00). Beware of dealers who substitute a generic watch box for the original. Remember that these too were designed to appeal to children and (99% of the time) were printed with colorful graphics.

Some of these watches have been reproduced, so be on guard. For more information, we recommend *Comic Character Clocks and Watches* by Howard S. Brenner, and *Schroeder's Collectible Toys, Antique to Modern* (Collector Books).

Advisor: Howard Brenner (See Directory, Character Clocks and Watches)

Clocks

Pluto alarm clock, Baynard/France, 1964, blue case, 5", EX, $250.00. (Photo courtesy of Dunbar Gallery.)

Batman & Robin, alarm, action pose on dial, 1980s, 4½", M **$25.00**
Batman & Robin, talking alarm, multicolored plastic w/Batman & Robin in Batmobile before city, Janex, 1974, 7x7", EX.......................................**$100.00**
Bugs Bunny, talking alarm, shows Bugs saying Eh Wake Up Doc, Janex, 1974.......................................**$100.00**
C-3PO & R2-D2, talking alarm, Bradley, 1980, MIB .**$100.00**
Cinderella, France, 1940, Cinderella in coach w/moving donkey's head, round dial, white case, 6", EX.........**$120.00**
Donald Duck, alarm, Donald holding pointers for hands, round dial, blue case, Bayard/France, MIB **$250.00**

Donald Duck, pendulum, w/moving eyes, 1960s, MIB ..**$150.00**
Howdy Doody, alarm, It's Howdy Doody Time, numbers & Howdy's head at 12-3-6-9, round dial, 2 bells, 6", EX...**$75.00**
Mickey Mouse, alarm, lg face of Mickey on dial, black tin figural ears atop, red case, German, 1960, 5", NM...**$50.00**
Mickey Mouse, alarm, Mickey flanked by name on oval dial, red case, 2 yellow bells, 3½", EX.........................**$60.00**
Minnie Mouse, alarm, Minnie w/lg red hands, round dial, yellow case, 2 red bells, 7", EX..................................**$90.00**
Mr Magoo, alarm, Mr Magoo w/fishing pole in 1 hand & trying to grab fish w/other, China, 5", EX..............**$100.00**
Smurfs, alarm, Have a Smurfy Day!, shows a Smurf & blue numbers on yellow dial, 2 yellow bells, 6½", EX ..**$25.00**
Snoopy, alarm, playing baseball, round dial, United Features Syndicate, 1958, 5", EX...**$55.00**
Snoopy doghouse, alarm, LED, Salton, 6", M.............**$40.00**
Tom Mix, alarm, name & bust image w/red numbers on round dial, gold-tone case, German, 1950s, 3½", EX **$75.00**

Pocket Watches

Hopalong Cassidy, Hoppy's image in center of black dial w/white numbers, chrome case, unmarked, 1969, 2" dia, EX **$150.00**
Marilyn Monroe, portrait on black dial, 2" dial, M......**$65.00**
Mighty Mouse, image of Mighty Mouse flexing muscles on dial, 2" dia, EX **$100.00**
Roy Rogers, w/chain attached coin, Ingraham, 1959, MIB..**$250.00**
Three Stooges, image of Moe pulling Curley's tooth w/pliers, nickel-plated case, marked FTCC, 2", EX.............**$80.00**

Wristwatches

Aladdin, battery, image of Genie, MIB **$10.00**
Archie, image of Betty & Veronica orbiting Archie, plastic case & band, Cheval/Hong Kong, 1989, MIB.......**$30.00**
Bart Simpson, LCD, multicolored plastic, 5-function, Nelsonics, MOC...**$12.00**
Batman, quartz, image of running Batman, gold-tone w/chrome back, brown leather band, Fossil/DC Comics, 1989, M **$75.00**
Batman & Robin, face flashes from Batman to Robin, Binky Flasher, 1960s-70s, NM+ **$20.00**
Beauty & the Beast, quartz, log on dial, gold-tone w/black leather strap, limited edition, Disney, 1994, M.......**$150.00**
Boris & Natasha, quartz, second hand, chrome case, A&M Hollywood/PAT Ward, 1984, VG **$100.00**
Bozo the Clown, 1971, MOC **$20.00**
Chucky (Child's Play), MOC **$35.00**
Dick Tracy, digital, Omni, 1981, NM (original cardboard police car box w/movable plastic wheels).........**$100.00**
Dick Tracy, New Haven, 1947, VG+ **$125.00**
Donald Duck, Birthday Watch, w/image, blue band, Bradley/WDP, w/warranty, unused, NMIB **$180.00**
Dukes of Hazzard, LCD, stainless steel band, Unisonic, 1981, NRFB **$40.00**

Flash Gordon, Swiss movement, chrome case, second hand, Bradley/King Features, 1979, MIB......................$200.00

Hopalong Cassidy, Good Luck From Hoppy on back, round chrome case w/original band, US Time/William Boyd, VG...$80.00

Hopalong Cassidy, 100th Anniversary, MIB $100.00

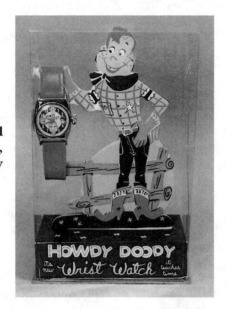

Howdy Doody, Ideal Watch Company, M, on original display stand, $175.00.

James Bond 007, Swiss movement, world time dial w/lg cyclolac case, velcro band, Gilbert-Eon/Glidrose Prod, 1965, VG..$165.00

Jughead, image of burger & soda orbiting Jughead, plastic case & band, Cheval/Hong Kong, 1989, MIB.......$30.00

Little Orphan Annie & Sandy, comic-strip image on dial, gold-tone band, 1970s, M.....................................$30.00

Little Rascals, LCD, MOC..$30.00

Madonna, MOC...$35.00

Mickey as Sorcerer, leather strap, limited edition of 5000, Disney Credit Card Exclusive, 1993, MIB $100.00

Mickey as Sorcerer, w/broom, limited edition of 3000, Disneyana Convention Walt Disney World, 1994, MIB (wood)..$75.00

Mickey Mouse, image of Mickey painting self-portrait, silver case, Classic Moments, Bulova/WD, 1991, MIB ...$90.00

Minnie Mouse, image on dial, yellow band, complete w/celluloid plaque, Timex, 1958, MIB $355.00

New Kids on the Block, metal w/leather band, EX....$12.00

Real Ghostbusters, flasher type, M.............................$10.00

Rocketeer, LCD, gold-tone case w/blue vinyl band, Hope/WD Co, 1991, MOC $35.00

Roy Rogers & Trigger, expansion band, Ingraham, 1951, scarce, NM+ (EX+ box)...$225.00

Six Million Dollar Man, Swiss movement, gold-tone w/blue leather band, Berger/Universal, 1976, VG $75.00

Snow White & Dopey, Snow White at 10 & Dopey at 4, round chrome case w/replaced leather band, Timex/WDP, 1958, VG.......................................$65.00

Snow White & the Seven Dwarfs, battery, 1993, MIP.$12.00

Tom & Jerry, quartz, Looney Tunes 3-D Series, oversized black acrylic case & band, Armitron/Warner Bros, 1991, MIB $30.00

Character Collectibles

Any popular personality, whether factual or fictional, has been promoted through the retail market to some degree. Depending on the extent of their success, we may be deluged with this merchandise for weeks, months, even years. It's no wonder, then, that the secondary market abounds with these items or that there is such wide-spread collector demand for them today. There are rarities in any field, but for the beginning collector, many nice items are readily available at prices most can afford. Disney characters, Western heroes, TV and movie personalities, super heroes, comic book characters, and sports greats are the most sought after.

For more information, we recommend *Character Toys and Collectibles* by David Longest; *Toys of the Sixties* and *Superhero Collectibles: A Pictorial Price Guide,* both by Bill Bruegman; *Collector's Guide to TV Memorabilia, 1960s and 1970s,* by Greg Davis and Bill Morgan; and *Howdy Doody* by Jack Koch. *Schroeder's Collectible Toys, Antique to Modern,* published by Collector Books contains extensive listing of character collectibles with current market values.

See also Advertising Characters; Beatles Collectibles; Bubble Bath Containers; California Raisins; Character and Promotional Drinking Glasses; Character Watches; Cookie Jars; Cowboy Character Collectibles; Disney Collectibles; Dolls, Celebrity; Elvis Presley Memorabilia; Paper Dolls; Pez Candy Containers; Pin-Back Buttons; Premiums; Puzzles; Rock 'n Roll Memorabilia; Shirley Temple; Star Trek Memorabilia; Star Wars; Toys; TV Shows and Movies; Vandor.

Advisor: Adrienne Warren, Garfield (See Directory, Character and Personality Collectibles)

Club: Smurf Collectors
24ACH, Cabot Rd. W
Massapequa, NY 11758; Membership includes newsletter; LSASE required for information

Club/Newsletter: Garfield Collector Society
c/o David L. Abrams, Editor
744 Forester Ridge Rd.
Germantown, TN 38138-7036; 901-753-1026

Alf, doll, stuffed, 17", EX..$8.00

Alvin & the Chipmunks, soap dispenser, Helm Products, 1984, MIB $10.00

Alvin & the Chipmunks, Curtain Call Theater, Ideal, 1983, MIB .$25.00

Alvin & the Chipmunks, doll, Simon, inflatable, Ideal, 1964, 16", unused, NMIP...$20.00

Alvin & the Chipmunks, On Tour Van, Ideal, 1983, MIB..$30.00

Alvin & the Chipmunks, outfit for 10" doll, Ideal, 1983, EX..$10.00

Andy Panda, mug, ceramic, figural, Walter Lantz, 1974 ....$65.00

Archie, promotion brochure, cover shows Archie, Betty & Veronica in malt shop, Archie Comic Pub Inc, 1986, 12x9", EX+ $20.00

Archie, tattoos, Topps, 1969, MIP..............................$20.00

Baby Huey, hand puppet, cloth body w/vinyl head, Gund, 1960, 10", EX+ $20.00

Bamm-Bamm & other Flintstones characters, see Flintstones

Banana Splits, tambourine, MIP.....................................$35.00

Bart Simpson & other Simpsons characters, see Simpsons

Batman, air freshener, multicolored diecut, 1970s, unused, MIP...$6.00

Batman, charm bracelet, 5 muticolored character charms on gold-tone chain, DC Comics, 1966, EX.................$50.00

Batman, Colorforms, 1966, NMIB..............................$40.00

Batman, lamp, plastic, Vanity Fair Industries, 7½" wide with expandable arm for light, EX, $135.00.

Batman, mittens, blue plastic w/raised full-figure illustration of Batman & logo, 1973, NM.................................$15.00

Batman, party hat, cardboard, Amscan/Canada, 1972, 7", unused, M...$10.00

Batman, patch, Batman or Robin, 1966, EX, each......$35.00

Batman, sleeping bag, 1975, EX+.................................$50.00

Batman, spoon & fork, stainless steel w/raised image, marked Batman, Imperial Knife/NPPI, 1966, unused, NM (EX+ card)..$65.00

Beetle Bailey, nodder, NM..$125.00

Big Bird, bank, w/toy chest, ceramic, Applause.........$15.00

Boo Boo, doll, stuffed cloth, Mighty Star, 1979, 12", NM..$25.00

Bozo, bank, full-color hard plastic bust, Play Pal, 1972, EX..$25.00

Bozo, Press-Out Book, Whitman, 1966, 12x8", unused, EX+..$18.00

Bozo, toy pocket watch, plastic, tin & paper, Larry Harman/Japan, 1960s, MIP.................................$10.00

Buck Rogers, matchbook cover, EX.............................$15.00

Buck Rogers, pencil box, embossed w/12 characters & spaceships including names on side panel, Dille, 1935, 10", M...$85.00

Bugs Bunny, bank, multicolored vinyl, Homecraft, 1972, 13", EX..$25.00

Bugs Bunny, canister, ceramic, Warner Bros..............$45.00

Bugs Bunny, coloring book, Private Eye, Bugs as Sherlock Holmes, Whitman, 1957, 7x6", unused, EX..........$15.00

Bugs Bunny, cookie mold, 1978, EX..............................$5.00

Bugs Bunny, jack-in-the-box, Mattel, 1970s, VG.........$15.00

Bugs Bunny, pencil case, vinyl, 1975, EX...................$15.00

Bugs Bunny, tray, metal, 1982, 12x17", EX.................$10.00

Bullwinkle, see Rocky & Bullwinkle

Captain Action, flicker ring, premium, 6 different, EX, each..$50.00

Captain Marvel, figure, Flying Captain Marvel, uncut paper, premium, Fawcett, 1944, M (with envelope).......$40.00

Captain Marvel, greeting card, inside blank for own message, Third Eye, 1971, M (w/envelope)..........................$10.00

Captain Midnight, book, Trick & Riddle, premium, EX+..$35.00

Captain Midnight, wings, Mystro-Magic Weather, premium, NM...$30.00

Captain Video, Mini Space Map, glow-in-the-dark, premium, EX..$30.00

Captain Video, ring, Flying Saucer, 1951, EX...........$150.00

Casper the Friendly Ghost, bank, plastic w/decals, 1970s, EX..$20.00

Casper the Friendly Ghost, figure, bendable, 1970s, EX.....$12.00

Casper the Friendly Ghost, lamp shade, EX...............$50.00

Casper the Friendly Ghost, doll, plush w/Casper sweater, 1960s, VG...$20.00

Charlie McCarthy, figure, diecut cardboard w/lever on back for eye & mouth movement, Chase & Sanborn premium, 18", NM..$135.00

Charlie McCarthy, spoon, silver-plated, 1940s, EX+....$22.00

Daffy Duck, bank, ceramic, Warner Bros.....................$25.00

Daffy Duck, place mat, Warner Bros/Pepsi, EX............$8.00

Dennis the Menace, figure, vinyl, Hall Syndicate, 1959, 8", EX..$85.00

Dennis the Menace, night light, $30.00; Dennis the Menace, record, Golden, 78rpm, $10.00; Margret, hand puppet, $25.00. (Photo courtesy of Cindy Sabulis.)

Deputy Dawg, bagatelle game, Imperial Toy, 1978, NM....$8.00

Deputy Dawg, Colorforms, M (VG box).....................$30.00

Dick Darling, manual, New Bag of Tricks, 1934, premium, EX..$25.00

Dick Tracy, badge, Girl's Division, premium, EX........$45.00

Dick Tracy, Christmas-tree light bulb, multicolored glass, 1940s, 3¼", EX+...$65.00

Dick Tracy, Colorforms Adventure Kit, 1962, NMIB...$65.00

Dick Tracy, Crime Stoppers set, complete, Laramie, 1967, EX+ (original bubble pack)....................................$35.00

Dick Tracy, Decoder Card, Post Cereal premium, early 1950s, NM...$40.00

Dick Tracy, flashlight, Secret Service, green, pocket size, VG..$20.00

Donald Duck, bank, toy sack, ceramic......................$30.00

Dr. Dolittle, bank, plastic, pink with blue and black detail, NM, $50.00. (Photo courtesy of Matt and Lisa Adams.)

Dr Seuss, book bag, features Cat in the Hat, cloth, 1970s-80s, 9x11", NM..$12.00

Dr Seuss, doll, Morton the Elephant, sitting on elf & nest, w/original tag, M...$50.00

Dr Seuss, jack-in-the-box, Cat in the Hat, plays For He's a Jolly Good Fellow, 1970, EX+............................$125.00

Elmer Fudd, pencil holder, diecast figure, 1940s, NM.$125.00

ET, bank, ceramic, 1983...................................$20.00

ET, Colorforms, 1982, MIB (sealed)......................$25.00

ET, doll, plush, Showtime, 1982, 8", NM..................$6.00

ET, figure, jointed arms, necks extends, 4", MOC.......$10.00

ET, ring, 1982, EX...$5.00

ET, sticker, Stick-On Fuzzies, 1982, MOC.................$6.00

ET, tray, metal, 1982, 17x12", EX.........................$15.00

Felix the Cat, bank, ceramic, Applause...................$38.00

Felix the Cat, dish, china, 2 illustrations of Felix, unmarked, 1930s, 5" dia, EX...$25.00

Felix the Cat, figure, cardboard, Felix holding fish in arms, 1950s, EX...$20.00

Flash Gordon, photo, Buster Crabbe, Dixie, NM........$65.00

Flintstones, bank, Fred, Homecraft, 1973, NM...........$35.00

Flintstones, bowl, plastic, 1978, EX......................$15.00

Flintstones, cake decorations, plastic, set of 4, 1960s-70s, 2", M (NM sealed package).................................$25.00

Flintstones, clothes hanger, Bamm-Bamm, 1975, EX..$20.00

Flintstones, dinnerware set, 3-pc Melamine, 1986, MIB (sealed)..$25.00

Flintstones, doll, Barney, vinyl w/fur outfit, Knickerbocker, 17", EX..$40.00

Flintstones, doll, Dino, plush w/vinyl head, Knickerbocker, 1960s, NM...$85.00

Flintstones, doll, Pebbles, stuffed cloth body w/vinyl head, arms & legs, Mighty Star Ltd, 1982, 12", MIB.......$55.00

Flintstones, figure, Barney w/lawnmower, Mattel, 1993, MOC..$5.00

Flintstones, hand puppet, Bamm-Bamm, cloth body w/vinyl head, Ideal, 1964, 10", EX+.............................$20.00

Flintstones, night light, Barney Rubble Electroid, 1979, MOC..$6.00

Flintstones, tablecloth, 1974, MIB (sealed)..............$12.00

Flintstones, wall plaque, Bedrock, 1976, EX..............$20.00

G-Man, tin star, premium, EX.............................$35.00

Garfield, air freshener, standing w/mouth open & tongue out, MIP..$1.00

Garfield, Art Plas figure, on crutches, Get Well Soon, no box...$5.00

Garfield, bank, bowling...................................$65.00

Garfield, bank, Garfield w/blue & red cap, holding bat, ceramic..$35.00

Garfield, bank, in chair, ceramic, Enesco, from $110 to..$125.00

Garfield, bank, on skis, ceramic, Enesco.................$70.00

Garfield, bank, vinyl, San Diego Chargers, MIB.........$16.00

Garfield, book, Scary Tales, Grosset Dunlap..............$4.00

Garfield, Christmas ornament, on star, Hallmark, 1991, MIB..$20.00

Garfield, Christmas ornament, Tweet Greetings, Garfield hanging on side of birdcage, Enesco #564044, 1990, MIB..$35.00

Garfield, cookie tin, Garfield tangled in lights.............$6.00

Garfield, door chime, wood, face w/3 chimes, 2 are teeth & 1 is nose, Enseco #651060, 10x9".....................$20.00

Garfield, figurine, as Humphrey Bogart..................$20.00

Garfield, figurine, Class of '84, from $10 to..............$15.00

Garfield, figurine, Odie in bunny suit w/basket of eggs, ceramic..$15.00

Garfield, gift bag w/handles, Garfield hanging upside down in fireplace..$2.00

Garfield, lamp, ceramic, party shade, Prestigeline, MIB...$40.00

Garfield, lunch bag, Keep Your Claws Off My Lunch..$2.50

Garfield, mug, Ho Ho Ho, Garfield as Santa, standing beside toy sack...$5.00

Garfield, musical birthday candle, Garfield in purple shirt, plays Happy Birthday to You, Hallmark, MIB......$15.00

Garfield, night light, Off the Wall, Prestigeline PT-5658.$15.00

Garfield, party hat, lavender & pink stripes, Carousel #1127, MIP..$1.00

Garfield, pencil topper, Garfield in Hawaiian shirt.......$1.50

Garfield, pin, cloisonne, Garfield sitting.................$2.00

Garfield, plush doll, shirt w/G on front & football helmet..$8.00

Garfield, poster, Being a Superstar Isn't a Pretty Job..., Garfield in sunglasses....................................$3.00

Garfield, PVC figure, in duck innertube..................$3.50

Garfield, stickers, 4 sheets, multiple pictures, Hallmark, MIP...$2.50

Garfield, switch plate, Garfield in a tree throwing apples to Odie, Prestigeline PT-5658.............................$15.00

Garfield, tile, I Hate Mondays, ceramic..................$12.00

Garfield, trinket box, Be My Valentine, ceramic, Enesco...$30.00

Garfield, wacky wind-up, Cake Walkin', MIP.............$6.00

Garfield, water dome, I Want You, dressed as Uncle Sam, #55974...$7.00

Garfield & Odie, bookends, ceramic, Enesco, pr, from $100 to...$125.00

Gloria Vanderbilt Cat, teapot, ceramic, Sigma, from $50 to...$60.00

Goldilocks, doll, Storybook Small Talk, Mattel, MIB ..**$85.00**

Heckle & Jeckle, bagatelle game, Imperial Toy, 1978, NM...**$10.00**

Herman & Catnip, 3-D paint set, framed 3-D picture w/6 paints, water bowl & brush, Pressman, 1961, 11x14", unused, EXIB **$60.00**

Hong Kong Phooey, tablecloth, 1975, MIP..................**$15.00**

Howdy Doody, bubble pipe, Clarabell, plastic, 5", NM..**$35.00**

Howdy Doody, Doodle Slate, Stickless Corp./Kagran, 9x10", NM, $155.00. (Photo courtesy of Dunbar Gallery.)

Howdy Doody, keychain, puzzle style, M...................**$45.00**

Howdy Doody, pencil topper, vinyl, Leadworks, 1988, 1½", M **$5.00**

Howdy Doody, shower curtain, plastic w/circus scenes, EX **$75.00**

Huckleberry Hound, Cartoon Kit, Colorforms, 1960, complete w/booklet, EX+ (EX+ box)...........................**$50.00**

Huckleberry Hound, charm bracelet, metal, Hanna-Barbera, 1959, MOC...**$60.00**

Huckleberry Hound, pencil box, cardboard, Hanna-Barbera, 1960s, VG+ **$45.00**

Huckleberry Hound & Friends, birthday paper plate, features all the Hanna-Barbera characters, unused, EX+ **$12.00**

Incredible Hulk, contact paper, comic-book format, 1978, 8x18" roll, M (original shrink wrap).....................**$65.00**

Incredible Hulk, figure, hand-painted ceramic, Marvel Comics, 1979, 3", M **$5.00**

Incredible Hulk, paint-by-number set, 2 pictures & 6 vials of paint, Hasbro, 1982, unused, MIB.......................**$15.00**

Incredible Hulk, playing cards, plastic coated, Marvel Comics, 1979, MIB **$5.00**

Jetsons, bank, ceramic, sleep scene, from $175.00 to...**$225.00**

Jetsons, cap, EX **$8.00**

Jetsons, magic slate, w/plastic stylus, Watkins/Strathmore, 1962, unused, EX+..**$30.00**

Jetsons, socks, features Elroy, 1980, EX, pr.............**$10.00**

Jetsons, Space Vehicle bank, ceramic, Hanna-Barbera, MIB...**$265.00**

Joker (Batman), doll, stuffed body w/vinyl head, 13", EX..**$40.00**

Joker (Batman), make-up kit, 1989, MIB **$8.00**

Koko (Betty Boop), honey jar, ceramic, Leeds...........**$20.00**

Lariat Sam, magic slate, w/plastic stylus, Lowe, 1962, VG+ **$15.00**

Little Orphan Annie, coloring book, cover shows Annie w/paint palette & Sandy, Artcraft, 1974, 11x8", unused, M **$12.00**

Little Red Riding Hood & Wolf, bank, ceramic, Adrian, 12"...**$55.00**

Mammy & Pappy Yokum, bank, multicolored composition figure, Capp Enterprises Inc/Dogpatch USA, 1975, 7¼", M **$100.00**

Masters of the Universe, tray, metal, 1982, 12x17", EX ..**$12.00**

Mickey Mouse, bank, driving armored truck, ceramic....**$70.00**

Mickey Mouse, toothbrush holder, ceramic, Leeds **$60.00**

Mighty Mouse, sticker book, Whitman, 1967, 1 page partially used o/w EX+ **$15.00**

Minnie Mouse, bank, Minnie w/Christmas Tree, ceramic....**$29.00**

Mork and Mindy, activity book, $10.00; Mork, doll with talking backpack, Mattel, 1979, $25.00. (Photo courtesy of Cindy Sabulis.)

Mother Goose, jack-in-the-box, Mattel, 1971, EX+......**$25.00**

Muppet Babies, squeak toy, Fozzie, yellow outfit w/polka-dot bow tie, Tommee Tippee, 5", G **$4.00**

Muppets, bank, Miss Piggy, ceramic, Sigma, from $40 to ..**$55.00**

Muppets, box, Miss Piggy Valentine w/Kermit's Picture, Sigma **$40.00**

Muppets, mug, Fuzzy **$18.00**

Muppets, mug, Miss Piggy **$18.00**

Muppets, oven mitt, Miss Piggy, 1981, EX...................**$8.00**

Muppets, planter, Kermit..**$40.00**

Muppets, planter, Miss Piggy, Sigma **$20.00**

Muppets, tissue cover, Miss Piggy, Sigma...................**$40.00**

Muppets, vehicle, Miss Piggy, Tomy, 1983, EX **$6.00**

Olive Oyl, hand puppet, cloth body w/vinyl head, Gund, 1950s, 10", VG+...**$25.00**

Olive Oyl, ponytail holder, King Features, 1958, MOC..**$30.00**

Paddington Bear, bank, ceramic, Enesco, from $30 to ..**$40.00**

Paddington Bear, bookends, ceramic, Schmid, MIB ...**$80.00**

Peanuts, bank, Snoopy on rainbow, ceramic, Enesco ..**$15.00**

Peanuts, bank, Snoopy on soccer ball, ceramic, 1960s, NM...**$20.00**

Peanuts, bank, Snoopy's doghouse, papier-mache, Korea, 6", EX **$10.00**

Peanuts, bank, Woodstock, ceramic................................**$35.00**

Peanuts, bicycle horn, Snoopy, 1958, NM **$20.00**

Peanuts, bicycle license plate, Powered by Woodstock lettered on red, MOC...**$10.00**

Peanuts, bookends, Snoopy, ceramic, Enesco............**$24.00**

Peanuts, bookends, Snoopy, red plastic hearts, Hong Kong, EX..**$18.00**

Peanuts, cake pan, Charlie Brown, aluminum w/plastic face, Wilton, M..**$25.00**

Peanuts, charm bracelet, gold-tone w/5 cloisonne charms, Applause, M...**$20.00**

Peanuts, doll, Linus, vinyl, 1950s, 9"......................**$40.00**

Peanuts, doll, Snoopy, rag-type w/plastic nose, blue jeans & red shirt, Ideal #1410, VG................................**$10.00**

Peanuts, doll, Snoopy as China Beach Beagle, w/blue visor, Applause, M...**$20.00**

Peanuts, doormat, Snoopy & Woodstock, white & yellow on gray, 14x26", M..**$15.00**

Peanuts, egg, Snoopy, ceramic, I Feel Free, Enesco...**$12.00**

Peanuts, jack-in-the-box, Snoopy, NMIB.....................**$75.00**

Peanuts, nodder, any character, square black base, Lego, lg, NM, each...**$75.00**

Peanuts, nodder, any character as baseball player, ceramic, Japan, 1970s, NM, each......................................**$75.00**

Peanuts, nodder, Snoopy as Flying Ace, Joe Cool or in Christmas outfit, no base, sm, NM, each..............**$40.00**

Peanuts, paperweight, Snoopy holding Woodstock, ceramic, sm..**$16.00**

Peanuts, soap dish, soft vinyl Snoopy figure lying on his back, Avon, 1968, 7", EX+................................**$12.00**

Penguin (Batman), bank, bust figure, Mego, w/original sticker, NM...**$60.00**

Penguin (Batman), doll, vinyl, Applause, 10", M........**$10.00**

Penguin (Batman), pencil topper, NM.........................**$2.00**

Pepe Le Pew, vase, ceramic, Warner Bros..................**$30.00**

Peter Potamus, bank, 12", EX.....................................**$65.00**

Phantom, iron-on transfer, w/logo & classic pose, ca 1965, unused, NM..**$20.00**

Pink Panther, clip-on toy, plush, w/original hang tag, Mighty Star, 5", EX...**$8.00**

Pink Panther, jewelry set, 1989, MOC.......................**$12.00**

Pixie & Dixie, cereal bowl, plastic, white w/color image, Melmac 1960, 5" dia, EX...............................**$12.00**

Popeye, cereal bowl, plastic, 1979, EX......................**$8.00**

Popeye, flashlight, pocket type, Larami, 1983, MOC..**$16.00**

Popeye, knapsack, multicolored canvas, w/tags, 1979, M...**$12.00**

Popeye, pop-up spinach can, lid pops up to reveal Popeye's head, Mattel, 1957, VG+...................................**$20.00**

Popeye, trinket box, hand-painted ceramic Popeye on spinach crate, 1980, M...**$30.00**

Popeye & Friends, coloring & paint book, Whitman, 1951, 48 pages, 11x8", unused, VG+...........................**$50.00**

Popeye & Olive Oyl, bank, sitting on spinach can, ceramic, VG..**$8.00**

Porky Pig, bank, figural, 1972, 16", EX......................**$25.00**

Porky Pig, bank, That's All Folks, ceramic..................**$16.00**

Porky Pig, cookie mold, 1978, EX..............................**$5.00**

Porky Pig, hand puppet, talker, cloth body w/vinyl head, Mattel, 1964, nonworking o/w EX.......................**$12.00**

Quick Draw McGraw, Magic Rub-Off Picture Set, Whitman, 1960, used, EXIB...**$25.00**

Raggedy Andy, doll, Playskool, 1987, 12", MIB..........**$12.00**

Raggedy Ann, bank, vinyl figure in sitting position, 1972, EX...**$20.00**

Raggedy Ann, coat rack, wall type, 18x20", EX..........**$18.00**

Raggedy Ann, doll, Hasbro, 1983, 17", MIB...............**$25.00**

Raggedy Ann, doll, Knickerbocker, 1970s, 14", NM, $30.00. (Photo courtesy of June Moon.)

Raggedy Ann, figure, bisque, 1988, 4", M...................**$15.00**

Ricochet Rabbit, plate, Melmac, 1960s, 8", EX............**$25.00**

Rocky & Bullwinkle, magic slate, w/stylus, Whitman, 1972, EX...**$30.00**

Rocky & Bullwinkle, marbles, 1988, MIP....................**$4.00**

Rocky & His Friends, sewing cards, 1 each of Rocky & Bullwinkle, 1961, EX...**$25.00**

Rocky Squirrel, figure, painted ceramic, 2½", NM......**$45.00**

Scooby Doo, bank, vinyl w/felt vest, NM....................**$25.00**

Scooby Doo, stamper, Hanna-Barbera, 1983, MOC......**$5.00**

Sesame Street, tray, 1971, metal, 17x12", EX..............**$12.00**

Simpsons, airwalker, Anagram International, MIP........**$12.00**

Simpsons, crayon-by-number, w/6 pictures & numbered crayons, Rose Art, MIB...**$6.00**

Simpsons, doll, Bart, stuffed body w/vinyl head, arms & legs, Dandee, 16", MIB...**$15.00**

Simpsons, doll, Bubble Blowin' Lisa, w/4-oz bubble solution, Mattel, 18", MIB...**$35.00**

Simpsons, figures, bendable, 5 different, Jesco, MOC..**$5.00**

Simpsons, frisbee, white w/Radical Dude, Betras Plastics, MIP...**$5.00**

Simpsons, paper plates, package of 8, Chesapeake, 9", MIP...**$5.00**

Smokey the Bear, see Advertising category

Smurfs, alarm clock, Have a Smurf Day!, A Smurf & blue numbers on round yellow dial, 2 yellow bells, 6½", EX...**$20.00**

Smurfs, bicycle license plate, I (Heart) Smurfs, pink w/Smurf offering Smurfette flowers, W Berrie, 1983, EX......**$6.00**

Smurfs, doll, Smurfette, stuffed, 1981, EX...................**$10.00**

Smurfs, record player, 1982, EX.................................**$20.00**

Smurfs, wind-up toy, Smurfette, Galoob, 1982, EX......**$4.00**

Smurfs, zipper pull, Brainy or Smurfette, hard plastic, w/clip, 2½", NM, each...**$5.00**

Snoopy & other Peanuts characters, see Peanuts

Snow White, bank, ceramic, Leeds, from $160 to.....**$195.00**

Snow White, planter, ceramic, Leeds, from $110 to.**$125.00**

Snydley Whiplash, figure, bendable, Wham-O, 1971, MOC $28.00

Speedy Gonzales, doll, cloth, Mighty Star, 1971, EX+...$20.00

Spider-Man, book bag, canvas, EX $12.00

Spider-Man, coloring book, The Arms of Doctor Octopus, Marvel Books, 1983, 22x17", unused, M $22.00

Spider-Man, comb & brush set, 1970s, MIB $45.00

Spider-Man, iron-on transfer, The Amazing Spider-Man above crouched image ready to leap, black & red, ca 1965, unused, M $30.00

Spider-Man, pencil sharpener, Masta, 1980, MOC (sealed) ..$5.00

Spider-Man, roller skates, red, black & blue plastic, 1979, EX $15.00

Spider-Man, Scissors, figural handle w/metal blades, Nasta, 1980, 3½", MOC (sealed)..$5.00

Spider-Man, TV tray, skyline background w/Spider-Man lurking on the rooftops, Cadence Industries 1979, 12x17", EX+ $25.00

Strawberry Shortcake, figurine trinket box, ceramic ...$17.50

Super Heroes, beach tote bag, 1978, EX $15.00

Super Heroes, Colorforms, Marvel Comics, 1983, NMIB..$12.00

Super Heroes, contact paper, w/various characters, covers 50 square feet, DC Comics, 1975, MIP $25.00

Super Heroes, postcard book, shows various characters, perforated, DC Comics, 1981, EX+ $10.00

Super Heroes, stamp set, set of 8 w/stamp pad, Fleetwood, 1978, MIP (sealed) $8.00

Superman, bank, bust, ceramic, Enesco, 1987, from $100 to $125.00

Superman, doll, stuffed, Mego, 1978, 18", EX $30.00

Superman, iron-on transfers, black & red image, 1950s, 14x9", EX $35.00

Superman, kite, 1971, MIP $22.00

Superman, party hat, 1977, EX $6.00

Superman, pencil sharpeners, set of 5, 1980, M $30.00

Superman, tote bag, 1982, EX $12.00

Superman, wallet, brown leather, 1976, M $10.00

Sweet Pea, hand puppet, cloth body w/vinyl head, Gund, 1950s, 10", VG+..$25.00

Sylvester, doll, velour, 5", VG $8.00

Sylvester, figure, inflatable, 1970, 8", EX................$8.00

Sylvester, rattle, 1975, EX $6.00

Sylvester & Tweety Bird, bowl, plastic, EX.................$5.00

Tarzan, magic slate, 1968, EX $20.00

Tarzan, tennis bag, 1975, EX $30.00

Tasmanian Devil, doll, stuffed, 1980, 13", EX.............$12.00

Thor, flashlight, Marvel Comics, 1978, 3½", MIP (sealed) ..$3.00

Thor, wind-up figure, plastic, Marvel Comics/Marx, 1968, 4", scarce, unused, M (NM window box).................$140.00

Tom & Jerry, squeak toy, Jerry as cowboy, Lanco, 1960s, NM $20.00

Tom Corbett Space Cadet, binoculars, blue metal w/decals, Sport Glass, 1950s, M $135.00

Tom Corbett Space Cadet, book bag, 1950s, EX.......$150.00

Tommy Tortoise & Moe Hare, coloring book, Saalfield, 1966, 11x8", minor coloring o/w EX $12.00

Tweety & Sylvester, butter dish, ceramic, Warner Bros.....$25.00

Tweety & Sylvester, Christmas Tree platter, ceramic, Warner Bros..$35.00

Tweety & Sylvester, teapot, ceramic, Warner Bros......$35.00

Tweety Bird, coloring book, Whitman, 1955, 7x6", partially colored o/w EX..$20.00

Tweety Bird, doll, stuffed, Mighty Star, 1971, EX........$15.00

Underdog, harmonica, plastic, embossed Simon Bar Sinister of Underdog at each end, 8", NM+ $15.00

Underdog, pillow, inflatable vinyl, EX....................$25.00

Wile E Coyote, bank, coyote on rocket, ceramic, rare...$300.00

Wolfman, eraser top, 1960s, 1", NM $12.00

Wolfman, green plastic bust w/sharpener base, UP CO 1960s, 3", NM $25.00

Wonder Woman, music box, ceramic, 1978, working NM..$50.00

Woody Woodpecker, bank, ceramic, Applause $30.00

Yogi Bear, camera, 1960s, MIB, from $50.00 to $60.00. (Photo courtesy of June Moon.)

Yogi Bear, chair, inflatable vinyl, 1980, MIP (sealed)..$20.00

Yogi Bear, doll, stuffed felt, 5", EX..............................$8.00

Yogi Bear, squeeze toy, vinyl figure of Yogi sitting on log & straightening his tie, Dell, 1960, 6", EX.................$30.00

Yogi Bear, 3-D glasses, Kellogg's Rice Krispies premium picturing Snap!, Crackle! & Pop! w/Yogi, 1991, EX.....$2.00

Yogi Bear & Friends, birthday napkins, bag of 20 w/Yogi leading the parade & Pixie & Dixie carrying cake, Reed 1962, NM $20.00

Yosemite Sam, doll, stuffed, 1971, 17", EX...............$15.00

Ziggy, bank, w/dog on safe, ceramic $12.00

Christmas Collectibles

Christmas is nearly everybody's favorite holiday, and it's a season when we all seem to want to get back to time-honored traditions. The stuffing and fruit cakes are made like Grandma always made them, we go caroling and sing the old songs that were written two hundred years ago, and the same Santa that brought gifts to the children in a time long forgotten still comes to our house and yours every Christmas Eve.

So for reasons of nostalgia, there are thousands of collectors interested in Christmas memorabilia. Some early Santa figures are rare and may be very expensive, especially when dressed in a color other than red. Blown glass ornaments and Christmas tree bulbs were made in shapes of fruits and vegetables, houses, Disney characters, animals and birds. There are Dresden ornaments and candy containers from Germany, some of which were made prior to the 1870s, that have been lovingly preserved and handed down to our generation. They were made of cardboard that sparkled with gold and silver trim.

Artificial trees made of feathers were produced as early as 1850 and as late as 1950. Some were white, others blue, though most were green, and some had red berries or clips to hold candles. There were little bottle-brush trees, trees with cellophane needles, and trees from the sixties made of aluminum.

Collectible Christmas items are not necessarily old, expensive, or hard to find. Things produced in your lifetime have value as well. To learn more about this field, we recommend *Christmas Collectibles* by Margaret and Kenn Whitmyer, and *Christmas Ornaments, Lights and Decorations* by George Johnson.

Bank, chalkware Santa seated on cardboard chimney, red & white suit w/black boots & mittens, 11", EX........**$35.00**

Bank, plaster Santa w/bag of toys, red & white w/green bag, black & gold trim, marked Copr L Mori, 1949, 12½", EX **$60.00**

Candy container, boot, red plastic w/white fur trim, blue draw-string bag atop, EX.......................................**$35.00**

Candy container, house, cardboard, roof lifts off, 6x6", EX **$25.00**

Candy container, Santa box, diecut cardboard image of Santa w/green toy bag, red & white w/black boots & belt, 11", EX..**$20.00**

Candy container, Santa by chimney holding bag open, cardboard, American, 1940-50s, 10" **$55.00**

Candy container, Santa in car w/tree & gifts, celluloid, red & green on white, 3½", EX.......................................**$65.00**

Candy container, Santa on sleigh w/tree & toys, celluloid, multicolored, 3¼", EX..**$65.00**

Candy container, Santa on sleigh w/tree & toys, celluloid, red & white, 3¼", EX..**$50.00**

Candy container, Santa w/open bag on back, papier-mache, white w/hint red & green airbrushing & red-painted trim, 8", EX..**$55.00**

Decoration, Santa in sleigh, all white w/shredded satin beard on vinyl face, satin suit, wood sleigh, 1940s-50s, 12", EX..**$80.00**

Decoration, Santa in sleigh w/single reindeer, celluloid, red, white & green, 4¾", EX.......................................**$75.00**

Decoration, Santa in sleigh w/single reindeer, celluloid, waving pose, white w/red & brown airbrushing, 10", EX......**$55.00**

Decoration, Santa on sleigh, ceramic, red & white w/black boots, white sleigh w/holly & gold trim, NAPCo, 1960s, 6", EX..**$20.00**

Display, Santa, flocked diecut figure w/lg bag of toys lettered Want List, Whitman, 21", EX **$40.00**

Display, Santa, painted papier-mache head w/gold glitter, 18", EX..**$80.00**

Figure, Santa, cardboard body, plastic face w/fur beard, red & white cloth suit, black boots, Japan, 1950s-60s, 13", EX **$20.00**

Figure, Santa w/gifts & holding bag over shoulder, celluloid, red & white, 5", EX..**$55.00**

Figurine, girl in long white dress, green coat & wide-brimmed hat w/red gloves carrying gold-trimmed gifts, NAPCo, NM **$40.00**

Figurine, Santa w/bag over shoulder on round base, painted ceramic, red & white w/blue pants & mittens, 1960s, 7", EX...**$30.00**

Gift tag, green wreath w/Santa head, red ribbon atop, silver holly leaves below, stapled to card, Flower Products, EX...**$15.00**

Head vase, girl's head w/brown hair, holly-trimmed red hat & bodice w/white collar & black-dotted muff, Lefton, EX...**$50.00**

Lamp, plastic & tin Santa half-figure w/glancing eyes, 1 eyebrow up & 1 down, arms open, Glo-Light Corp, 1950s, 9", NM...**$15.00**

Lamp, red & white plastic Santa figure wearing crown & pointing while holding green tree on round base, electric, 6", NM...**$12.00**

Lamp, Santa holding bubble light, plastic, 1950s, 8", minimum value $45.00. (Photo courtesy of Margaret and Kenn Whitmyer.)

Lantern, full-figure Santa on round base w/handle, late 1940s-early 1950s, EX..**$45.00**

Lantern, green wreath w/red bow & Noel lettered in center on red round base & handle, battery-op, EX.......**$60.00**

Light bulb, bubble, common base, 1940s, EX.............**$10.00**

Light bulb, bubble, rocket base, 1940s, EX **$20.00**

Light bulb, flower, various colors, Japan, 1930s-50s, EX..**$40.00**

Light bulb, fruit basket, EX......................................**$30.00**

Light bulb, Japanese lantern, various shapes & colors, EX...**$15.00**

Light bulb, lion gent holding pipe & dressed in jacket, pants & vest, EX...**$55.00**

Light bulb, lion holding tennis racket, EX...................**$30.00**

Light bulb, parrot, various colors, Japan, 1930s-50s, EX ..**$30.00**

Light bulb, Santa figure, ball-shaped body w/head & arms, no legs or feet, red w/white beard & trim, Japan, 3", EX........**$45.00**

Light bulb, Santa head, realistic shape & features, red hat & lips, white beard, dotted eyes, rosy cheeks, Japan, 2", EX...**$40.00**

Light bulb, seashell, various colors, 3", EX..................**$40.00**

Light bulb, snow-covered house, various colors & shapes, Japan, 1930s-50s, EX..**$20.00**

Light bulb, songbird, various colors, 1930s-50s, EX....**$25.00**

Light reflectors, Mirostar Christmas Lights, set of 8 plastic stars of various colors, NOMA Electric Corp, EXIB **$75.00**

Light shades, Popeye-Cheers, set of 8 colored domes w/various characters, Royal Electric, c 1929, EXIB......**$155.00**

Nodder, Santa holding candy cane on green base, painted ceramic, red & white, spring neck, 8", EX............**$40.00**

Ornament, blown glass, crane standing on 1 leg, blue body w/orange beak & legs, 4½", EX **$55.00**

Ornament, blown glass, silver reindeer w/black antlers, 1930s, 4½", EX...**$60.00**

Ornament, blown glass, white fox figure on spring clip, black-dotted eyes, 3", EX **$55.00**

Ornament, cardboard village pcs, brightly painted & mica-coated church or houses, Czech, 1½", EX, each..**$28.00**

Ornament, celluloid, Christmas tree w/round bottom, green w/white ornaments, 4", EX **$10.00**

Ornament, celluloid, little girl, red dress, hat & shoes w/white trim, delicately painted features, Japan, 4", EX **$60.00**

Ornament, chenille, Santa w/clay face & holding single tree branch, Occupied Japan, 6", EX **$25.00**

Ornament, chenille, Santa w/scrap face, ribbon bow atop, 4", EX...**$15.00**

Ornament, chenille, wreath w/silver foil candle, 4" dia, EX **$12.00**

Ornament, glass, candle w/clip, 1940s, 3½", VG **$22.00**

Ornament, glass, clown head, silver face w/black & red features, red cone-type hat w/white band & collar, 1930s, 3", EX...**$45.00**

Ornament, glass, clown w/hands in pockets, pearl white costume w/red hat & shoes, green collar, gold buttons, 4½", EX..**$40.00**

Ornament, glass, doll head w/red hat, metallic-gold hair, black brows & eyes, red lips, rosy cheeks, 1930s-40s, 2", EX...**$90.00**

Ornament, glass, grape cluster, deep metallic red, white leaves sprinkled w/red, 1950s, 3½", EX...............**$15.00**

Ornament, glass, helicopter, blue body w/figure in clear ball-shaped cockpit, Italian, 8", EX...............................**$60.00**

Ornament, glass, horn w/loop, silver w/painted floral decoration, 1930s, 6½", VG...**$25.00**

Ornament, glass, icicle w/swirled design, various colors, 1950s, 14", EX **$38.00**

Ornament, glass, Indian corn, red w/green leaves, 2", VG..**$60.00**

Ornament, glass, peacock, blue body w/red dots on white wings & fanned-out tail w/blue shading, EX **$35.00**

Ornament, glass, peacock on spring clip, rose body w/white & metallic gold fanned-out tail & wings, 4", EX ..**$25.00**

Ornament, glass, Santa head, silver face w/stern expression, blue eyes, red hat w/white trim, gold beard, 1950s, 5", EX...**$70.00**

Ornament, glass, Santa holding tree, blue suit & hat w/white beard & trim, white tree w/gold accents, 1930s, 3", EX.........**$50.00**

Ornament, glass, space Santa, blue suit w/white trim, red nose, clear dome helmet, Italian, 1950s-70s, 6", EX..........**$45.00**

Ornament, glass, teapot, pink w/white grape & green leaf design, 2½", EX...**$30.00**

Ornament, glass beads, butterfly, solid body w/silver-beaded outline of wings w/pink interior rows, Czech, EX..**$40.00**

Ornament, glass beads, cross, beaded outline w/lg green beads down center, Occupied Japan, 1950s, EX..**$30.00**

Ornament, pressed cotton, bell, 1½", EX....................**$22.00**

Ornament, pressed cotton, peach w/leaf, 3", EX........**$38.00**

Ornament, pressed cotton, turnip, 4", EX...................**$25.00**

Ornament, spun glass & scrap, Santa in blue robe w/toy bag & tree against spun-glass background, 3" dia, EX **$50.00**

Outdoor candle, red candle w/repeated holly design & white drips on black Bakelite base, beige flame, 42", NM .**$25.00**

Pin, clear rhinestone profile outline of deer head w/red & green rhinestone antlers, red nose & blue-stone eye, NM **$30.00**

Pin, gold-tone Santa head w/red stones for eyes & mouth, green stones dot full beard, NM..........................**$35.00**

Pin, 3 red & white Santas singing on gold log w/green holly trim, NM..**$40.00**

Place-card holder, snowman w/shovel & wearing hat standing on green base, celluloid, 3", EX....................**$40.00**

Stir sticks, Santa head, plastic, set of 8, EXIB.............**$10.00**

Toy, Santa figure waving, squeeze rubber, red & white w/white boots & mittens, black belt w/gold buckle, Sanitoy, 9", EX...**$12.00**

Toy, Santa figure waving, squeeze rubber, red & white w/black boots, mittens & belt, gold buckle, Rempel, 12", EX...**$15.00**

Tree, aluminum branches & needles w/star-burst tips, tripod stand, 1960s, 18", EX **$30.00**

Tree, bubble lights on full tree w/green cellophane needles, round plastic base, 1950s, 19", EX........................**$80.00**

Tree, music-box base, wire branches w/green vinyl needles, 1960s-on, 19", EX..**$35.00**

Tree, plastic-coated cardboard needles, beige tone w/square beveled plastic base, Japan, 1960, 9", EX **$50.00**

Tree, 10 feather branches, red wood pot, 10½", EX..**$150.00**

Tree, 6 feather branches, red wood pot, 7", EX.........**$95.00**

Village, mica-coated cardboard w/beaded roofs & trim, church & 2 houses, multicolored, EX, 3-pc set....**$45.00**

Village, painted & flocked cardboard, farm, 3 houses & store on square bases, Japan, 3½" to 6½", EX, 5-pc set ..**$75.00**

Wind-up toy, painted celluloid boy figure lying on green metal sled, Occupied Japan, 1950s, EX................**$70.00**

Wind-up toy, painted celluloid Santa driving green metal sleigh w/single white reindeer, Occupied Japan, 1950s, 7", EX...**$85.00**

Wreath, chenille w/electric candle light in center, applied holly decoration, post WWII, EXIB.....................**$20.00**

Cigarette Lighters

Collectors of tobacciana tell us that cigarette lighters are definitely hot! Look for novel designs (figurals, Deco styling and so forth), unusual mechanisms (flint and fuel, flint and gas, battery, etc.), those made by companies now defunct, those with advertising, and quality lighters made by Ronson, Dunhill, Evans, Colibri, Zippo, and Ronson. For more information we recommend *Collector's Guide to Cigarette Lighters, Vols. I and II,* by James Flanagan.

Newsletter: *On the Lighter Side*
Judith Sanders
Route 3, 136 Circle Dr.
Quitman, TX 75783; 903-763-2795; SASE for information

Bakelite, table-top, black w/yellow swirls, engraved initials, 1940s, 6" $100.00

Beau-Lite Delux, musical (plays Dixie), Civil War soldier on side, Confederate flag, Made in Japan $40.00

Cartier, wavy design on gold-tone, butane burning, Swiss made & numbered, 2¾" $55.00

Colby, brushed chromium, sm flat center opens to light, ca 1935, 2⅜x1⅛" $75.00

Elgin, brass w/brushed finish, engraved Anaconda Copper Mining lettering & trademark, 1959, EX $35.00

Evans, chromium w/red leather insert band, ca 1934, 2x1½" $35.00

Evans, lighter & cigarette case combination, copper w/nickel plate, engraved design, 4x2½", EX $45.00

Evans, silverplated, linear decor, ca 1934, 2x1½" $35.00

Figural, bird shape, brushed & smooth chromium finish, ca 1958, 1½x2⅛" $25.00

Figural, camel on knees, painted metal, lift-arm lighter on howdah, mid-1930s, 2½x4¾" $40.00

Figural, camera, chromium, Made in Occupied Japan, ca 1948, 1¾x2½" $45.00

Figural, cowboy boot, Evans, table-top, ca 1948, 5x5" .$25.00

Figural, dog w/paws on fence looking at a book (lighter), Made in Occupied Japan, ca 1948, 2⅝x2⅜" $100.00

Figural, elephant, Ronson, table-top, shiny chromium, ca 1935, 5x3¾" $125.00

Figural, gold clubs & bag, butane burning, Germany, ca 1990, 2⅞x1⅜" $25.00

Figural, hand grenade, chromium, butane burning, PGL, ca 1960, 4¼x2½" $20.00

Figural, horse rearing, chromium, butane burning, Japan, ca 1988, 7x4½" $25.00

Figural, horse, table-top, ceramic, Japan, 1955, 5½", from $15.00 to $25.00. (Photo courtesy of James Flanagan.)

Figural, hound dog, table-top, shiny chromium, ca 1934, 4½x4" $50.00

Figural, match, plastic strike-type, head of match comes off to light, mid-1930s, 4x½" dia, EX $20.00

Figural, Model-T Ford, table-top, ceramic, ca 1964, 3¼x4" ..$20.00

Figural, motorcycle, table-top, chromium, butane burning, mid-1980s, 3½x6" $35.00

Figural, saxophone, butane burning, Germany, ca 1990, 3½x2" $15.00

Figural, steamship, chromium w/red plastic, Made in Occupied Japan, ca 1950, 2x5" $55.00

Figural, tiger w/head up & mouth open, metal, ca 1935, 1¾x2⅜" $20.00

Figural, wooden shoe, souvenir of Holland, 1940s, 2⅛x4½" ..$35.00

Figural, 8-ball, table-top, plastic, mid-1960s, 3x2½" $12.50

Ronson, Adonis, blue enamel w/ivory cherubs, 1954, 1¾x2⅛", MIB $25.00

Ronson, lighter & cigarette case combination, polished chrome w/black floral enamel, engraved initials, 4x2½" $15.00

Ronson, Penciliter, black w/chrome, w/instructions, MIB ..$125.00

Ronson, table-top, oak wood body w/chrome-plated details, 1950s, 3x2¾", M $20.00

Ronson, table-top, Queen Anne, silverplated finish, 1950s, NMIB..............................$150.00

Ronson, touch-tip table-top style, heavy metal w/dark bronzed finished, chrome top, 3½x2½" dia $45.00

Ronson, Varaflame, polished finish w/linear decoration, butane burning, MIB $22.00

Zippo, black leather covered w/silver linear design, gold mark on bottom, ca 1950 ....$75.00

Zippo, brushed finish w/Ford emblem, 1950s, VG.....$25.00

Zippo, brushed finish w/man snowmobiling, ca 1977 .$15.00

Zippo, brushed finish worn to brass w/enameled Masonic emblem, 1950s, G $20.00

Zippo, brushed finish w/gold-tone Colt revolver affixed on side, 1966, EX $55.00

Zippo, green simulated reptile leather cover, 3-barrel hinge, ca 1953..............................$90.00

Zippo, polished finish w/bust of Jeff Gordon (racer) & facsimile signature, M..............................$25.00

Zippo, Skelly trademark enameled on brushed finish, ca 1970 ....$60.00

Zippo, Slim Line, polished finish w/enameled United States Lines logo, 1963, VG $22.00

Zippo, Slim Line, polished finish w/Winchester & cowboy on horse in red enamel, EX..............................$35.00

Zippo, Slim Line, 10k gold filled, 1957 mark, M in original case $200.00

Zippo, table-top, Corinthian, polished chrome w/white enameling, 1960s $150.00

Zippo, table-top, polished gold-tone finish w/New England Dragway design, 1960s, 3¼", NM..............................$160.00

Zippo, United States Steel, brushed finish w/enameled emblem, 1958, MIB..............................$50.00

Cleminson Pottery

One of the several small potteries that operated in California during the middle of the century, Cleminson was a family-operated enterprise that made kitchenware, decorative items and novelties that are beginning to attract a considerable amount of interest. At the height of their productivity, they employed 150 workers, so as you make your rounds, you'll be very likely to see a piece or two offered for sale just about anywhere you go. Prices are not high; this may be a 'sleeper.'

They marked their ware fairly consistently with a circular ink stamp that contains the name 'Cleminson.' But even if you find an unmarked piece, with just a little experience you'll easily be able to recognize their very distinctive glaze colors. They're all strong, yet grayed-down, dusty tones. They made a line of bird-shaped tableware items that they marketed as 'Distlefink' and several plaques and wall pockets that are decorated with mottoes and Pennsylvania Dutch-type hearts and flowers.

In Jack Chipman's *The Collector's Encyclopedia of California Pottery,* you'll find a chapter devoted to Cleminson Pottery. Roerig's *The Collector's Encyclopedia of Cookie Jars* has some more information.

See also Clothes Sprinkler Bottles.

Advisor: Robin Stine (See Directory, California Pottery)

Bank, Here's Hoping treasure chest, white w/blue floral trim **$45.00**
Bowl, cereal; clown in center, from $60 to **$80.00**
Bowl, Gala Gray, heart form **$22.00**
Butter dish, Distlefink, brown, w/lid..........................**$40.00**
Butter dish, lady figure, 2-pc **$65.00**
Canister, marked Flour, white w/blue flowers **$65.00**
Cleanser shaker, girl figure, 5 holes, w/card explaining use, 6½"...**$32.00**
Creamer & sugar bowl, Distlefink, pr **$30.00**
Creamer & sugar bowl, King & Queen, pr, scarce, from $75 to **$85.00**
Cup, clown w/hat lid, 2-pc, from $60 to **$80.00**
Cup, My Best Gal, lg **$20.00**
Cup & saucer, Make Mine Strong...............................**$28.00**
Cup & saucer, There's Something About a Soldier **$28.00**
Darn-It (sock-darner lady), bright blue w/ribbon in hair..**$30.00**
Denture dish, Pop's, w/lid **$28.00**
Egg cup, double, painted as lady w/spoon & apron, early .**$25.00**
Figurine, Dopey...**$380.00**
Gravy boat, Distlefink, brown, from $30 to.................**$40.00**
Hair receiver, girl w/folded hands, 2-pc, from $35 to ..**$40.00**
Head vase, girl w/freckles **$80.00**
Luncheon set, plate w/cup, white w/brown leaf design ..**$15.00**
Marmalade, green-dotted flowerpot base, strawberry finial on lid...**$28.00**
Match holder, butler **$55.00**

Match holder, inscribed 'Smokes,' with image of burning cigarette, $40.00.

Matchbox holder, wall type, white w/red cherries, from $38 to **$40.00**
Mug, Morning After, w/lid **$30.00**
Mug, Special Achievement..**$32.00**

Pancake server, Big Top Circus, juvenile, from $60 to .**$80.00**
Pie bird, rooster **$20.00**
Pipe holder, singing quartet, 4 pipes **$150.00**
Pitcher, Distlefink, brown, 9", from $60 to **$65.00**
Pitcher, Gala Gray, 7"...**$30.00**
Pitcher, marked Batter, white w/gray & pink design..**$40.00**
Pitcher, marked Syrup, cherries.................................**$40.00**
Planter, blue bathtub w/pink flowers, 7" long **$50.00**
Plaque, clock w/gold trim...**$95.00**
Plaque, flowers, pastel, 5¾", pr.................................**$28.00**
Plaque, Gay Nineties man & lady, pr.........................**$25.00**
Plaque, heart form w/pansies.....................................**$18.00**
Plaque, man inside, deep edges, oval, 4" **$15.00**
Plaque, white w/pears & blue-plaid design, 8"...........**$15.00**
Plate, crowing rooster, radiating yellow-striped rim, 9½" ...**$30.00**
Plate, Pennsylvania Dutch...**$22.00**

Ring holder, bulldog, $25.00.

Ring holder, elephant w/head back & trunk up **$45.00**
Ring holder, hand w/fingers spread, flower at wrist ..**$45.00**
Salt & pepper shakers, cherries, 6", pr......................**$25.00**
Salt & pepper shakers, Distlefink, brown, pr, from $20 to..**$30.00**
Sprinkler, Chinese boy **$35.00**
Tea tile, white w/blue flowers & design, 7" **$30.00**
Toothbrush holder, baby's face **$55.00**
Toothbrush holder, Pinocchio, from $60 to **$75.00**
Toothpick holder, English Bobby, w/hat, from $25 to ..**$30.00**
Trivet, pink & purple flowers, 7", from $20 to............**$25.00**
Wall pocket, coffeepot w/bail handle, Let's Have Another, from $20 to...**$30.00**
Wall pocket, frying pan...**$26.00**
Wall pocket, kitchen motto...**$36.00**
Wall pocket, mortgage bank, from $25 to **$30.00**
Wall pocket, pink diaper, from $15 to **$20.00**
Wall pocket, puppy **$75.00**

Clothes Sprinkler Bottles

With the invention of the iron, clothes were sprinkled with water, rolled up to distribute the dampness, and pressed. This created steam when ironing, which helped to remove wrinkles. The earliest bottles were made of hand-blown clear glass. Ceramic figurals were introduced in the 1920s; these had a metal sprinkler cap with a rubber cork.

Later versions had a true cork with an aluminum cap. More recent examples contain a plastic cap. A 'wetter-downer' bottle had no cap, but contained a hole in the top to distribute water to larger items such as sheets and tablecloths. Water was filled through a large opening in the bottom and plugged with a cork. Some 'wetter-downers' are mistaken for shakers and vice versa. In the end, with the invention of more sophisticated irons that produced their own steam (and later their own sprayers), the sprinkler bottle was relegated to the attic or, worse yet, the trash can.

The variety of subjects depicted by figural sprinkler bottles runs from cute animals to laundry helpers and people who did the ironing. Because of their whimsical nature, their scarcity, and desirability as collectibles, we have seen a rapid rise in the cost of these bottles over the last couple of years.

See also Kitchen Prayer Ladies.

Advisor: Ellen Bercovici (See Directory, Clothes Sprinkler Bottles)

Cat, marble eyes, ceramic, American Bisque, from $150 to **$195.00**
Cat, Siamese, tan, ceramic, from $100 to.................**$125.00**
Cat, variety of designs & colors, homemade ceramic, from $50 to...**$60.00**
Chinese man, Sprinkle Plenty, white, green & brown, holding iron, ceramic, from $125 to **$145.00**
Chinese man, Sprinkle Plenty, yellow & green, ceramic, Cardinal China Co, from $20 to **$30.00**
Chinese man, variety of designs & colors, homemade ceramic, from $30 to.......................................**$60.00**
Chinese man, white & aqua, ceramic, Cleminson, from $30 to **$40.00**
Chinese man, white & aqua w/paper shirt tag, ceramic, Cleminson's, from $65 to **$75.00**
Clothespin, aqua, yellow & pink w/smiling face, ceramic, from $100 to.....................................**$125.00**
Clothespin, hand decorated, ceramic, from $50 to **$60.00**
Clothespin, red, yellow & green plastic, from $15 to .**$25.00**

Dearie Is Weary, ceramic, Enesco, minimum value $200.00. (Photo courtesy of Ellen Bercovici.)

Dutch boy, green & white, ceramic, from $125 to ...**$145.00**
Dutch girl, white w/green & pink trim, wetter downer, ceramic, from $125 to **$145.00**

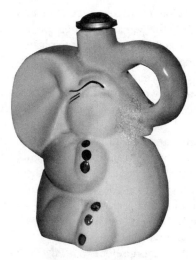

Elephant, ceramic, trunk forms handle, American Bisque, from $225.00 to $250.00. (Photo courtesy of Ellen Bercovici.)

Elephant, pink & gray, ceramic, from $45 to **$55.00**
Elephant, white & pink w/shamrock on tummy, ceramic, from $65 to..**$75.00**
Emperor, variety of designs & colors, homemade ceramic, from $50 to..**$100.00**
Iron, blue flowers, ceramic, from $50 to **$60.00**
Iron, green ivy, ceramic, from $30 to **$40.00**
Iron, green plastic, from $15 to **$25.00**
Iron, lady ironing, ceramic, from $60 to.....................**$70.00**
Iron, man & woman farmer, ceramic, from $100 to .**$125.00**
Iron, souvenir of Aquarena Springs, San Marcos, Texas, ceramic, from $100 to **$125.00**
Iron, souvenir of Florida, pink flamingo, ceramic, from $85 to **$95.00**
Iron, souvenir of Wonder Cave, ceramic, from $85 to..**$95.00**
Mammy, ceramic, possibly Pfaltzgraff, from $225 to ..**$250.00**
Mary Maid, all colors, plastic, Reliance, from $15 to ..**$35.00**
Mary Poppins, ceramic, Cleminson, from $150 to **$175.00**
Myrtle, ceramic, Pfaltzgraff, from $195 to **$225.00**
Poodle, gray & pink or white, ceramic, from $125 to ..**$150.00**
Queen or King, ceramic, Tilso, Japan, from $100 to ..**$125.00**
Rooster, red & green, ceramic, from $100 to **$125.00**

Clothing and Accessories

Vintage clothing shops are everywhere. Have you noticed? And what's especially fascinating to buyers today are fashion items from the fifties, sixties, and even the seventies. Hawaiian shirts have been hot for some time, and when padded shoulders became fashionable for women, thirties and forties clothing became very trendy.

Levi jeans and jackets made circa 1971 and before have a cult following, especially in Japan. Among the most sought-after denim Levi items are jeans with a capitol 'E' on a *red* tab or back pocket. The small 'e' jeans are collectible as well; these were made during the late 1960s until about 1970 (with two rows of single stitching inside the back pocket) and in the 'red line' style of the eighties (these have double-stitched back pockets). Other characteristics to look for in vintage Levis are visible rivets inside the jeans, and single pockets and silver-colored buttons on jackets with vertical pleats. From the same circa, Lee, Wrangler, Bluebell, J.C. Penney, Oxhide, Big Yanks, James Dean, Doublewear, and Big Smith denims are collectible as well. The values we've listed here for Hawaiian shirts and denims are prices realized from a large, cataloged auction.

Running and basketball shoes from the 1980s such as Nike 'Air Jordans' and 'Terminators' are becoming popular as well. Look for an orange logo on the tongue, 'NIKE' in block letters on the heel, or a date inside the shoe.

While some collectors buy with the intent of preserving their clothing and simply enjoy having it, many buy it to wear. If you do wear it, be very careful how you clean it. Many fabrics become fragile with age.

For more information, refer to *Vintage Clothing, 1880–1980*, 3rd edition, by Maryanne Dolan (Books Americana) and *Antique and Vintage Clothing* by Diane Snyder-Haug (Collector Books).

Newsletter: *Costume Society of America*
55 Edgewater Dr.
P.O. Box 75
Earleville, MD 21919; Phone 301-275-2329 or FAX 301-275-8936

Apron, linen w/embroidered flowers & butterfly on bib, snap straps, EX...**$6.00**
Apron, pink dimity w/blue lace trim & applied flowers on pocket & bib **$6.50**
Apron, pink organdy w/white crochet edge & swirls, pocket, long **$6.50**
Apron, tea; fine cotton, top pins to blouse, much lace, double-pointed pocket, embroidered rosettes **$7.00**
Apron, unbleached muslin, long & wide w/appliqued fruit & leaves on bib & pocket **$3.00**
Apron, white crochet, lacy corners, ribbon at waistband & pocket **$6.00**
Bed jacket, floral print on pink rayon w/eyelet lace on puffed sleeves, collar & front, 1940s **$8.50**
Bed jacket, peach rayon, elbow-length sleeves, placket front, scalloped lace at ruffled neck.................................**$7.00**
Belt, nickel links in sun ray & arrowhead designs on octagonal medallions & rings **$4.00**
Blouse, gold satin w/sequins & beads allover, scoop neck, sleeveless, fancy gold beaded 2" border...............**$32.00**
Blouse, ivory rayon w/jabot-style ruffle w/lace edge, no collar or sleeves, 1940s, EX......................................**$5.00**
Blouse, orange crochet, see-through type w/long sleeves, draw-string neck **$10.00**
Blouse, sheer cotton print, multicolored flowers on black & white stripes, long sleeves **$5.00**
Blouse, sheer pink w/pleated button-down front, collar w/lace edge, elbow-length sleeves, 1950s **$7.50**
Blouse, sheer rayon, V neck, long sleeves, 3" pleated panels, Wardles of Nottingham, 1940s **$8.00**
Blouse, white rayon, self-tie collar, short sleeves, 1940s, EX.**$4.00**
Blue jean jacket, Lee Stormrider, corduroy collar, blanket lining, 1950s, EX **$100.00**
Blue jean jacket, Levi Second Edition, Big-E label, 1960s, some wear & fading **$150.00**

Blue jean jacket, Levi western tux type, 1940s, EX **$50.00**
Blue jean jacket, Levi's, tab cut, EX **$50.00**
Blue jean jacket, Maverick Blue Bell, brass buttons, EX..**$55.00**

Blue jean jacket, Ranchcraft, J.C. Penney, snaps, little wear, $85.00.

Blue jean jacket, snap front, Ranchcraft JCP Co, EX...**$55.00**
Blue jeans, bell bottoms, Levi's Sta-Prest, Big-E label, 1950s, M...**$55.00**
Blue jeans, Levi's Boot-Cut Saddleman, original paper tags, 1970s, M..**$60.00**
Blue jeans, Levi's Super Slims, 1960s, NM **$50.00**
Bonnet, Amish ecru net bonnet w/ribbon ties, EX.....**$40.00**
Boots, lady's white go-go style, zippered side w/buckle, man-made materials, Italy, 1960s, NM.................**$25.00**
Caftan, Morroccan type, royal blue w/brown braid trim, hand made & signed label, floor length.......................**$32.00**
Camisole, off-white w/fine thread crochet straps & yoke.**$8.50**
Camisole, peach nylon trico w/thin straps & drawstring top, plain **$2.00**
Cape, crochet in lavender & purple zigzag pattern, button front **$8.00**
Cape, organza, black 20" circle w/applied 6" white leaves, pearls **$16.00**
Coat, man's, gray wool w/satin lining, plastic buttons, ¾-length, 1940-50s, EX...**$35.00**
Collar, cotton, long triangular lapels w/tiny eyelets, 1" lace band **$2.50**
Collar, crochet boucle, fine rose-rust thread, fancy lace stitch, 3½" wide **$5.00**
Collar, nylon organza, 1½" machine lace border, 6" wide ..**$2.00**
Collar, pink eyelet, floral design, 5" wide bib w/1" ruffled eyelet edge **$2.00**
Collar, satin w/allover pearls & beading, 1950s, from $10 to **$15.00**
Collar, white cotton w/1½" lace ledge & 3-D petals on front, 3" wide **$4.00**
Corset, pink lace-up, 1930s-40s, EX **$35.00**
Dress, black rayon & velvet in alternate bands, sleeveless, A-line short skirt, 1940s, EX.......................................**$30.00**
Dress, black rayon crepe, squared scoop neck w/boat back, back zipper, cap sleeves, lined, draped front, 1940s..........**$15.00**
Dress, evening; aqua moire faille w/white satin tie, short cuffed sleeves, A-line skirt, 1940-50s, EX.............**$30.00**
Dress, evening; black sheath, black net sleeves w/beadwork on full flowing cuffs, full length, 1930s **$100.00**

Dress, evening; black silk w/heavy black satiny poppies, no sleeves, high scoop front, V back, straight skirt...**$28.00**

Dress, evening; metallic paisley on red & green paisley-printed blue chiffon, long sleeves, belt, scoop neck, 1950s **$25.00**

Dress, evening; rayon crepe print over pink rayon, long sleeves w/cuffs, back zipper, ruffled neck, long skirt **$20.00**

Dress, evening; rayon satin w/floral beads, slitted long skirt w/red lining, no sleeves, heart V neck, scoop back, '50s..**$40.00**

Dress, evening; red chiffon w/gathers over bust, strap goes behind neck, floor length A-line skirt, 1960s **$38.00**

Dress, evening; red satin w/black velvet cording, strapless, mid-calf length, EX **$35.00**

Dress, Hawaiian, black & gold palm trees on green cotton, short sleeves, black band trim & 4 frogs, long w/slit sides **$30.00**

Dress, knitted boucle w/openwork vertical striped top, long waist, cuffs, collar, Miss Joan, 1940s **$20.00**

Dress, pink linen sheath, sleeveless, cutwork & embroidered flowers, scalloped neck **$15.00**

Dress, ribbon-crocheted sheath w/gold metallic & olive thread, oriental closure, no sleeves, handmade, 1950s...........**$15.00**

Dress, wedding; antique white satin, gathered bust w/beaded shoulders & bodice, gathered bust, long train, 1940s, EX **$185.00**

Fur cape, brown mink, short, arm slits, lined, Fashion Furs, EX **$125.00**

Fur coat, Persian lamb, wide gray fur collar & lapel, ¾-length **$125.00**

Fur collar, black fox, 14x5" **$15.00**

Fur collar, brown mink, 27x5" **$15.00**

Fur collar, brown seal, boomerang shape, 40x20" **$10.00**

Fur collar, raccoon, lapel notches, 42x6" **$20.00**

Fur hat, black mink, pelts sewn on stiff mesh in Robinson-Crusoe style **$10.00**

Fur hat, sheared beaver..**$10.00**

Fur jacket, seal, hip length, long sleeves, ca 1950s, EX..**$75.00**

Gloves, beaded, white, short style, ca 1950, pr **$22.50**

Gloves, crochet, off-white & gold in alternating vertical bands, pr...**$5.00**

Gloves, leather, black, 10" long **$8.00**

Gloves, leather, bone, midarm length, pr...................**$15.00**

Gloves, suede, 9½" long, pr **$8.00**

Hat, beige straw, wide brim w/brown ribbon around crown & bow in back, 1930s-40 ....**$55.00**

Hat, hot pink w/black silk tie running around crown & down back, Lilli Dache, 1960s, sm, EX............................**$35.00**

Hat, Kelly green w/purple flowers, lg floppy brim in front but none in back, Faillot label, 1940s, EX **$30.00**

Hat, navy straw w/netting & pink flowers, 3" brim, 1940s **$30.00**

Hat, red velvet beanie style w/black cording, Bergdorf Goodman label, ca 1940s...**$20.00**

Jacket, boy's, brown & white rayon & wool, Rugby Knitting Mills, 1940s, EX...**$37.50**

Jacket, boy's winter, red & gray, zippered, Lakeland, 1940s-50s, NM..**$27.50**

Jacket, child's, Harley-Davidson, black leather, zippered front, 1960s, EX...**$85.00**

Jacket, crocheted wool cardigan in shell stitch, long sleeves **$8.00**

Jacket, gold brocade w/stand-up collar, satin lining, sm, EX **$30.00**

Jacket, hunter's, green cotton w/brown corduroy collar & cuff linings, leather shoulder pads, game pockets, 1950s, NM **$100.00**

Jacket, stadium; blue wool, knit cuffs, collar & waist band, white leather trim, 1960s, NM...............................**$70.00**

Jacket, tailored style w/padded shoulders (Joan Crawford style), 2 tones of brown, 1940s, EX **$30.00**

Nightgown, heavy white cotton w/crochet yoke & wide straps, Victorian style...**$28.00**

Nightgown, pink nylon, shirred & embroidered top, cap sleeves **$7.00**

Panties, peach rayon w/½" lace trim **$4.00**

Pants, Hanover Brand regulation uniform, tan cotton, 1940s, EX..**$25.00**

Pants, Levi's, fawn-color corduroy, Big-E paper label, 1960s, M..**$55.00**

Poncho, crocheted red & navy stripes, open stitch, 21" long w/3" fringe..**$7.00**

Shawl, bright pink netting w/ruching, black bugle beads along fringe, ca 1920s, 120" long **$115.00**

Shirt, boy's, multicolor squares, Fruit of the Loom, 1940s .**$22.00**

Shirt, chambray, Sweet-Orr label, 1950s, M................**$50.00**

Shirt, Hawaiian, paradise flowers on black cotton, Highlight California, NM...**$130.00**

Shirt, Hawaiian, waterfall design on rayon crepe, bamboo buttons, Iolani label, 1940s................................**$125.00**

Shirt, Hawaiian cotton print, short sleeves, pearl buttons, Swim Mates USA, 1970s, NM **$30.00**

Shirt, Western style, black w/much embroidery work, long sleeves, ca 1950s-60s, EX.................................**$25.00**

Shoes, lady's platform, white woven vinyl uppers w/burlap covered 3" platforms, Spain, EX **$85.00**

Shoes, lady's platform, wood w/leather uppers & woven cord, Carole King, India, EX................................**$30.00**

Shoes, man's, tan leather w/rubber soles, slip-ons, 2" heels, Wayfarer, 1960s, EX **$40.00**

Shoes, Nike high-top sneakers, white & blue, 1980, M ..**$50.00**

Skirt, Mexican style, beads and sequins in stenciled pattern on red & green flannel...**$40.00**

Skirt, royal blue velvet circle style, 1950s, EX............**$40.00**

Skirt & sweater set, green & black knit, pleated front & back on skirt, 1940s..**$35.00**

Slip, black taffeta w/4 layers of ruching, 1940s, VG...**$25.00**

Slip, black w/scalloped lace bottom, unlined stretch lace in top, Barbizon..**$10.00**

Slip, half, white cotton w/lace trim, side button placket ..**$25.00**

Slip, half, white rayon taffeta, w/net between layers, lace hem **$9.00**

Slip, pink nylon w/lace **$5.00**

Sweater, black wool, 2-pocket cardigan style, Varsity Sport Shop, 1950s, EX...**$20.00**

Sweater, boy's, dark & light blue w/leather buttons, Deluxe Knit Sportsware, 1940s, sm...................................**$45.00**

Sweater, lined beige wool w/seed pearl flowers at neck, waist, cuffs & down front **$30.00**

Sweater, lined ivory wool tiny white beads & pearls at neck, down front, on cuffs, hook & eye closure **$28.00**

Sweater, mother-of-pearl sequined scrolls w/bugle beads & pearls on light blue, pearl buttons **$24.00**

Sweater, navy blue wool w/blue buttons, 2 pockets, Stadium Brand by Shaker Sweater Co, 1950s.....................**$20.00**

Sweater, wool, angora & nylon blend, fully lined, beadwork on neck, front, waist & cuffs **$30.00**

Coca-Cola Collectibles

Coca-Cola was introduced to the public in 1886. Immediately an advertising campaign began that over the years and to the present day has literally saturated our lives with a never-ending variety of items. Some of the earlier calendars and trays have been known to bring prices well into the four figures. Because of these heady prices and the extremely wide-spread collector demand for good Coke items, reproductions are everywhere, so beware! Some of the items that have been reproduced are pocket mirrors (from 1905, 1906, 1908–11, 1916, and 1920), trays (from 1899, 1910, 1913–14, 1917, 1920, 1923, 1926, 1934, and 1937), tip trays (from 1907, 1909, 1910, 1913–14, 1917, and 1920), knives, cartons, bottles, clocks, and trade cards. Currently being produced and marketed are an 18" brass 'button,' a 24" brass bottle-shaped thermometer, cast-iron toys and bottle-shaped door pulls, Yes Girl posters, a 12" 'button' sign (with one round hole), a rectangular paperweight, a 1949-style cooler radio, and there are others. Look for a date line.

In addition to reproductions, 'fantasy' items have also been made, the difference being that a 'fantasy' never existed as an original. Don't be deceived. Belt buckles are 'fantasies.' So are glass doorknobs with an etched trademark, bottle-shaped knives, pocketknives (supposedly from the 1933 World's Fair), a metal letter opener stamped 'Coca-Cola 5¢,' a cardboard sign with the 1911 lady with fur (9" x 11"), and celluloid vanity pieces (a mirror, brush, etc.).

When the company celebrated its 100th anniversary in 1986, many 'centennial' items were issued. They all carry the '100th Anniversary' logo. Many of them are collectible in their own right, and some are already high priced.

If you'd really like to study this subject, we recommend these books: *Goldstein's Coca-Cola Collectibles* by Sheldon Goldstein; *Huxford's Collectible Advertising* by Sharon and Bob Huxford; *Collector's Guide to Coca-Cola Items, Vols I and II*, by Al Wilson; *Collectible Coca-Cola Toy Trucks* by Gael and Lara de Courtivron; *Petretti's Coca-Cola Collectibles Price Guide* by Allan Petretti; and B. J. Summer's *Guide to Coca-Cola*.

Club: Coca-Cola Collectors Club International
P.O. Box 49166
Atlanta, GA 30359; Annual dues: $25

Information Hotline: 941-355-COLA or 941-359-COLA

Ashtray, glass, round w/white Coca-Cola on red bottom, white border, M **$15.00**

Ashtray, metal, red, Drink Coca-Cola Enjoy That Refreshing New Feeling, 1960, EX **$4.00**

Ashtray, metal woodgrain, Enjoy That Refreshing New Feeling, 1960, EX **$3.00**

Bank, red can shape w/white diamond reading Coca-Cola, Canadian, 1960, VG **$100.00**

Bank, wooden early-style van w/stamped Drink Coca-Cola logo, w/driver & cases of bottles, Toystalgia Inc, 1980s, 7", M...**$30.00**

Banner, Be Really Refreshed, Coca-Cola Around the Clock!, image of clock at right of seafood barbecue & bottle, 1950s, M..**$45.00**

Banner, Have a Coke lettered on double diamonds flanking Drink Coca-Cola fishtail logo, corrugated cardboard, 20x56", M...**$20.00**

Banner, Take Coke Home in green & red above image of wooden case & price spot on yellow & white, canvas, 9-ft, NM..**$175.00**

Blotter, Coke Knows No Season, snow scene w/hand-held bottle, 1948, NM+ **$12.00**

Blotter, Cold Refreshment, Drink Coca-Cola on diamond at left of tilted bottle, 1937, EX+ **$18.00**

Blotter, Friendliest Drink on Earth & Drink Coca-Cola on pennant at left of hand-held bottle against globe, 1956, EX **$10.00**

Blotter, I Think It's Swell, image of girl lying on her stomach, red disk logo upper left, 1942, M...........................**$12.00**

Blotter, Wholesome Refreshment, image of 2 Boy Scouts enjoying bottles from cooler, 1942, EX **$6.00**

Blotter, 58 Million a Day, 1957, NM **$5.00**

Book, 100 Best Posters, hardcover, 1941, EX+............**$45.00**

Bottle carrier, aluminum w/wooden handle, holds 6 bottles, 1950s, VG **$25.00**

Bottle carrier, cardboard, 6 for 25 Cents, holds 6 bottles, 1950s, NM...**$40.00**

Bottle carrier, wood w/wooden grip on wire handle, Drink Coca-Cola, 1930s-40s, VG **$60.00**

Bottle opener, metal, Shirts for the Coke Set lettered on solid handle, EX+ **$30.00**

Bottle opener, plastic & metal turtle shape w/Enjoy Coke & Trade Mark on turtle's shell, NM **$25.00**

Bottle opener/spoon, Happy Days stamped on spoon, 1930, EX+ **$225.00**

Bottle topper, plastic, 1950s, NM, $725.00. (Photo courtesy of Gary Metz.)

Bracelet, Rock 'N Roll Charm Bracelet, Things Go Better With Coke logo, 4 charms, 1965, MIB **$50.00**

Calendar, 1932, The Old Oaken Bucket, boy seated at edge of well w/bucket full of Cokes, dog watches, complete, NM **$575.00**

Calendar, 1942, Thirst Knows No Season, image of couple building snowman, disk logo lower left, complete, EX **$275.00**

Calendar, 1948, image of girl w/bottle, red disk logo, complete, EX+ **$150.00**

Calendar, 1954, image of girl putting on skates while being offered a bottle of Coke, complete, VG **$100.00**

Calendar, 1959, The Pause That Refreshes, basketball scene w/girl being offered a bottle of Coke, complete, VG+ **$80.00**

Calendar, 1967, For the Taste That You Never Get Tired Of, complete, NM **$35.00**

Calendar, 1973, linen w/Lillian Nordica image at top, 12 months shown below, M **$12.00**

Clock, Drink Coca-Cola, plastic light-up w/square face above 2 rows of repeated designs, EX **$115.00**

Clock, Enjoy Coke, brown molded plastic case w/square clock above contour logo on panel below, 1970s, 18x12", EX **$30.00**

Clock, Gilbert regulator, reproduction, Coca-Cola on face, Delicious & Refreshing at bottom, battery-operated, NM+ **$200.00**

Clock, pocket watch w/Coca-Cola dial, brass finish, 1994, 15x11½", NM **$35.00**

Clock, Things Go Better With Coke in place of 10 & 11, disk logo at 4 & 5, plastic & metal, 16x16", NM **$110.00**

Coasters, Santa in different poses, set of 6, 1990, 4¼" square, MIB **$10.00**

Cookie jar, polar bear, ceramic, 1994, M **$25.00**

Cookie jar, syrup jug replica, ceramic, 1990, M **$30.00**

Cooler, red picnic-style w/decal showing hand-held bottle, lg swing handle, sm lid handle, 1940s, 13x12", VG . **$125.00**

Cooler, red vinyl picnic box w/folding top & strap, white fishtail logo, ...Refreshing New Feeling, 1960s, NM **$50.00**

Cups, plastic, set of 4 Santa cups, 1960s, NMIB (box reading Things Go Better w/Coke) **$65.00**

Decal, Enjoy Coca-Cola, foil, 1960s, 6x13", M **$10.00**

Decal, Things Go Better With Coke (receding words), 1960s, NM **$18.00**

Display, cardboard, Free Easy Recipe Ideas, Take One & Pick Up the Fixins', Enjoy Coke..., 1957, 14x20", NM .. **$30.00**

Display bottle, plastic, red base, ca 1953, 20", NM+ .. **$175.00**

Doll, Buddy Lee, plastic, in uniform w/hat, 1950s, EX+ .. **$550.00**

Door plate, porcelain, Iced Here in yellow flanks Coca-Cola in white, red background, 31", EX+ **$150.00**

Door plate, tin, Drink Coca-Cola contour logo above bottle on white, square corners, 1970s, 20x4", EX+ **$100.00**

Door push bar, porcelain, Come In! Have a Coca-Cola, yellow & white on red, yellow border, 1930s, 4x11½", EX+ .. **$285.00**

Door push bar, porcelain, Ice Coca-Cola Here in yellow & white on red, 1950s, 3x30", EX+ **$175.00**

Fan, Drink Coca-Cola above bottle against yellow dot on 2-color background, Sprite boy on reverse, 1930s, EX+ **$65.00**

Festoon, Icicles, The Pause That Refreshes..., 5 pcs, 1930s, EX (w/envelope) **$700.00**

Frame, for cardboard sign, gold, reproduction, 16x27", M **$75.00**

Frame, for cardboard sign, gold, 1940s, 20x36", EX .. **$225.00**

Game, Bingo, complete, VG+ (original box) **$50.00**

Game, Shanghai, MIB **$20.00**

Game, Streamlined Darts, EX+ (original box) **$40.00**

Game, Table Tennis, complete, EXIB **$65.00**

Ice pick, Drink Coca-Cola on wooden handle, 1960s, NMIB (Drink Coca-Cola Delicious & Refreshing on box) **$25.00**

Key ring, glass bottle, 1992, 3", M **$5.00**

Knife, bone & plastic handle chrome ends, 3 blades & opener, Krusius/Germany, 1960s-70s, NM+ **$40.00**

Lighter, flip top, silver w/embossed bottle, MIB **$60.00**

Lighter, silver w/red logo, given as an executive's award, 1984, NM **$30.00**

Matchbook, Coke Adds Life to Everything, M **$1.50**

Mechanical pencil, Coca-Cola lettered on side, w/pocket clip & eraser tip, early, NM **$110.00**

Menu board, cardboard stand-up, Refreshing You Best flanked by 2 bottles below, Drink... marquee above, 1950s, NM **$200.00**

Menu board, tin, Drink Coca-Cola on panel above chalkboard, Delicious & refreshing w/silhouette girl below, 1940, EX+ **$285.00**

Nail clippers, sample set w/advertising clip-ons, MIB .. **$30.00**

Napkin dispenser, metal, Have a Coke, 1950s style, white & red center strip w/lettering, chrome ends, 1992, 7", M **$25.00**

Night light, bottle shape, 1994, 6½", MIB **$18.00**

No-Drip Protector, So Refreshing With Food, 1944, NM .. **$5.00**

Paper cup, Things Go Better With Coke in red on white square center, red background, 1960s, 3½", NM+ .. **$4.00**

Pennant, Official Soft Drink of Hockey, Wayne Gretzsky facsimile signature, felt, EX **$12.00**

Pin-back button, club pin depicting hand-held bottle, G+ .. **$15.00**

Playing cards, Coke Refreshes You Best!, image of girl holding bottle & score pad, complete, NMIB **$85.00**

Playing cards, cowgirl with bottle or party girl with bottle, 1951, complete, MIB, $125.00 each. (Photo courtesy of Gary Metz.)

Playing cards, double deck, Betty/Coca-Cola Girl by Hamilton King, 1977, complete, M **$45.00**

Playing cards, Enjoy Coke, red & white, 1980s, M (in plastic case) **$5.00**

Playing cards, It's the Real Thing, image of girl sitting in field, contour logo, complete, 1971, MIB (sealed) **$35.00**

Playing cards, Sign of Good Taste, close-up image of girl in pool w/bottle, complete, 1959, NMIB.................**$100.00**

Pocket mirror, diecut cardboard cat's head opens to round mirror & red bottle w/logo, NM+.......................**$450.00**

Pocket mirror, The Coca-Cola Girl, 1910, oval, VG+ ..**$225.00**

Puzzle, jigsaw; 2000 pcs, a collage of Coke items including bottle, fan, toy truck, can, cup, sign, etc, NMIB.....**$20.00**

Puzzle, jigsaw; 700 pcs in tin w/multiple advertising images, 1994, 12x34" puzzle/6x5" dia tin, M......................**$12.00**

Radio, AM/FM stereo w/cassette, red 1950s-style vending machine w/Drink Coca-Cola in bottles, 1994, 15x7", M............**$60.00**

Radio, upright vending machine, red Drink Coca-Cola on white upper panel, red lower panel, w/antenna, 1950s, EX **$175.00**

Record, Buy the World a Coke, by the New Seekers, 45 rpm, M **$15.00**

Salt & pepper shakers, replicas of Coca-Cola Vendo 44 machines, w/holder, 1994, M, pr **$10.00**

Sheet music, Rum & Coca-Cola, EX+ **$25.00**

Sign, arrow, tin, Sold Here Coca-Cola Ice Cold, embossed, 1990, 27", M...**$10.00**

Sign, button, Coca-Cola lettered over bottle, red porcelain, 1950s, 36" dia, NM.......................................**$600.00**

Sign, cardboard, diecut, Always Coca-Cola, Always lettered on arched panel attached to button w/bottle, 1993, 15" dia, M...**$30.00**

Sign, cardboard, diecut, Greetings From Coca-Cola, image of Santa w/bottle, 1946, 12", EX **$150.00**

Sign, cardboard, diecut, Take Home Enough! on panel w/ribbon border above hand-held bottle, 1952, NM..**$160.00**

Sign, cardboard, diecut hanger, Serve Coca-Cola on circle behind bells w/Regular Size & Sign Of Good Taste, 1950s, M.**$25.00**

Sign, cardboard, diecut stand-up, A Merry Christmas Call for Coke, image of Santa in chair w/elves, 1950s, EX+ **$180.00**

Sign, cardboard, Face the Sun Refreshed, image of girl w/bottle shielding her face from sun, 1937, 50x29", EX+.......**$375.00**

Sign, cardboard, Home Refreshment, image of girl with bottle and tulips, 1949, 20x36", NM, $375.00. (Photo courtesy of Gary Metz.)

Sign, cardboard, They All Want Coca-Cola, image of waitress w/tray of burgers, 1940s, 20x36", VG+ **$150.00**

Sign, cardboard, Things Go Better With Coke, 2-sided, skating couple/girl in captain's hat, 1964, 27x16", EX+ **$100.00**

Sign, celluloid, Delicious & Refreshing Coca-Cola, red w/gold border, 1940s, 9" dia, EX........................**$180.00**

Sign, flange, Enjoy That Refreshing New Feeling, red fishtail logo on white panel w/green lines, 1952, 15x18", NM **$275.00**

Sign, flange, Have a Coca-Cola, yellow & white on red, yellow border, 1941, 18x18", EX+ **$350.00**

Sign, light-up, Drink Coca-Cola on disk w/metal wall basket, 1950, NM **$300.00**

Sign, neon, Coke With Ice, shaped like soda glass w/Coke lettered vertically, With Ice arched above, 1980s, NM **$275.00**

Sign, paper, Take Along Coke In 12-oz Cans, Buy a Case left of diamond can & men in boat, 1960s, 19x35", NM **$150.00**

Sign, plastic, Delicious With Ice-Cold Coca-Cola, image of overflowing popcorn box, 7x24", EX...................**$40.00**

Sign, porcelain, Coca-Cola Sold Here Ice Cold, white & yellow on red, yellow border, 1940s, 12x29", EX...**$160.00**

Sign, porcelain, Drink Coca-Cola Ice Cold on image of fountain dispenser w/full glass, 1950s, 28x28", EX+ .**$750.00**

Sign, tin, Drink Coca-Cola on red field pointed toward bottle on white field, silver self-frame, 1950s, 18x54", EX+...**$175.00**

Sign, tin, Enjoy...All the Year Round, image of Earth & hand-held bottle above swimmer & ice skater, 1982, 33x24", NM+ **$75.00**

Sign, tin, Pause, Drink Coca-Cola on red w/tilted bottle on yellow dot, self-framed, 1930s, 54x18", EX+ **$300.00**

Sign, wood, Ye Who Enter Here... on rustic board w/bottle, emblem below, Kay Displays, 1940s, 11x39", rare, EX+ **$650.00**

Squeeze bottle w/straw, plastic, Drink Coca-Cola Classic, red on white w/red lid & straw, EX.............................**$4.00**

Syrup keg, wooden w/paper label, 1930s, VG **$100.00**

Thermometer, dial, Coca-Cola lettered over bottle on red button surrounded by degrees on square backing, 1993, 12", M **$20.00**

Thermometer, dial, Drink 5¢ Enjoy Thirst lettered next to image of bottle, 1990s, 12" dia, MIB **$20.00**

Thermometer, dial, Things Go Better With Coke, 1960s, 12" dia, NM...**$200.00**

Thermometer, tin bottle shape marked Coca-Cola w/sm Trade Mark, 1958, 30", NM **$60.00**

Tip tray, 1914, Betty in a bonnet, green w/gold decorative border, oval, 6x4", EX+ **$265.00**

Tip tray, 1916, Elaine leaning on hand looking over her shoulder while holding glass, oval, 6x4", EX+ ...**$100.00**

Tote bag, plastic-lined mesh, Can't Beat the Feeling!, 14x21", M **$6.00**

Toy Bang Gun, Dayton Bottling Co, 1950s, EX...........**$35.00**

Toy bus, Sweetcentre, 1980s, cardboard double-decker w/contour logo front & back, M **$25.00**

Toy car, Ford Sedan, red & white tin w/Refresh With Zest lettered on sides, friction, 9", EX+........................**$200.00**

Toy train set, Lionel, 1970s-80s, 027-gauge, cars feature various Coke products, electric, NMIB....................**$250.00**

Toy transformer robot, can shape w/contour logo, 1986, MIB **$50.00**

Toy truck, Buddy L #5215, Ford, 1970s, 7½", NM **$30.00**

Toy truck, Buddy L #5426, 1965-69, Ford style, steel, yellow w/chrome grille & bumper, whitewall tires, EX.**$150.00**

Toy truck, Marx #21, 1954-56, tin, yellow w/red trim & stripe on hood, open divided double-decker bay, 12½", NM..**$275.00**

Toy truck, Matchbox, 1978, Super King, tractor-trailer, NMIB **$35.00**

Toy truck, Smith-Miller, 1947-53, GMC, red metal cab w/Coke bottle decals & logo on wooden open bed, 14", G **$500.00**

Toy truck set, Buddy L, 1981, Brute Coca-Cola Set, 5 pcs, NMIB...**$50.00**

Tray, commemorative tray featuring Bobby Knight and the Hoosiers, 1976 NCAA Champions and Big Ten Champions 1973-76 on back, M, from $10.00 to $15.00.

Tray, 1930, Meet Me at the Soda Fountain, image of girl on phone, vertical, VG.................................**$175.00**

Tray, 1936, image of girl in white silky gown leaning back on chair w/glass in hand, vertical, EX+....................**$345.00**

Tray, 1940, image of fishing girl on dock enjoying a bottle of Coke, horizontal, NM **$325.00**

Tray, 1950, image of girl holding bottle w/white-gloved hand against screened background, vertical, NM+......**$125.00**

Tray, 1953-60, menu girl w/bottle of Coke resting chin on hand, vertical, VG+...**$40.00**

Tray, 1976, Bobby Knight, round, EX-...........................**$8.00**

Tray, 1988, When Friends Drop In, w/Santa, round, EX ..**$8.00**

Tray, 1989, Coca-Cola Collector's Club 15th Convention, image of Los Angeles bottling plant, horizontal, EX.........**$12.00**

Tray, 1989, Drive Refreshed, image of silhouette girl & car, elongated horizontal, EX **$8.00**

Tray, 1990, Santa standing w/bunny, vertical, EX.........**$8.00**

Tray, 1991, Travel Refreshed, image of silhouette cowboy & western scene, elongated, horizontal, NM...........**$10.00**

Tray, 1993, Always Cool above close-up image of polar bear w/bottle, vertical, NM...**$10.00**

Tray, 1993, Everything Coming Up Springtime, image of girl gardening, horizontal, EX.......................................**$10.00**

Wallet, gold-stamped Whenever You See an Arrow Think of Coca-Cola encircled by arrow, snap closure, rare, NM **$165.00**

Whistle, plastic, Merry Christmas, Coca-Cola Bottling Memphis TN, 1950s, EX **$18.00**

Whistle, wood cylinder w/flared mouthpiece, Pure As Sunlight & Coca-Cola logo, 1930s, NM **$150.00**

Comic Books

Though just about everyone can remember having stacks and stacks of comic books as a child, few of us ever saved them for more than a few months. At 10¢ a copy, new ones quickly replaced the old, well-read ones. We'd trade them with our friends, but very soon, out they went. If we didn't throw them away, Mother did. So even though they were printed in huge amounts, few survive, and today they're very desirable collectibles.

Factors that make a comic book valuable are condition (as with all paper collectibles, extremely important), content, and rarity, but not necessarily age. In fact, comics printed between 1950 and the late 1970s are most in demand by collectors who prefer those they had as children to the earlier comics. They look for issues where the hero is first introduced, and they insist on quality. Condition is first and foremost when it comes to assessing worth. Compared to a book in excellent condition, a mint issue might be worth six to eight times as much, while one in only good condition should be priced at less than half the price of the excellent example. We've listed some of the more collectible (and expensive) comics, but many are worth very little. You'll really need to check your bookstore for a good reference book before you actively get involved in the comic book market.

Advisor: Larry Curcio, Avalon Comics (See Directory, Comic Books)

A Date With Millie, #4, VG+ **$13.00**

Action, #129, VG+ **$100.00**

Adventure, #144, VG- **$80.00**

Adventure Into Mystery, #6, VG+ **$23.00**

Adventures Into Terror, #14, G+ **$20.00**

Adventures Into Weird Worlds, #25, G+ **$13.00**

Adventures of Rex the Wonder Dog, #14, VG+ **$32.00**

All-American Men of War, #5, VG **$82.00**

All-Star, #50, G **$115.00**

All-True Crime, #44, G...**$7.00**

Amazing Adventures, #8, VG+ **$8.00**

Amazing Spider-Man, #12, VG+ **$92.00**

Animal Man, #1, NM **$9.00**

Annie Oakley & Tagg, Dell #4, 1955, EX....................**$40.00**

Anthro, #2, G..**$2.50**

Astonishing, #40, VG **$18.00**

Astonishing Tales, #22, VG **$1.50**

Atom, #7, VG- **$50.00**

Avengers, #54, EX **$15.00**

Batman, #28, VG- **$200.00**

Battle, #66, VG+ **$17.00**

Battle Front, #34, VG **$9.00**

Black Magic, #2, NM...**$4.00**

Blackhawk, #66, VG+ **$40.00**

Boy Commandos, #36, VG...**$4.00**

Brave & the Bold, #41, VG **$30.00**

Captain America, #41, VG-................................$250.00
Captain Marvel, #24, EX.................................$7.00
Captain Savage, #14, EX+..............................$4.00
Challenges of the Unknown, #4, VG- $75.00
Congo Bill, #3, G+..$80.00
Creatures on the Loose, #10, VG...................$6.50
Danger Trail, #1, G......................................$110.00
Daredevil, #9, VG+..$25.00

Dark Shadows, Gold Key #15, 1972, EX, $10.00.

Demon, #1, NM-..$21.00
Detective, #178, G+..$60.00
Doctor Strange, #173, VG- $10.00
Doom Patrol, #19, NM+ $12.00
Fantastic Four, #35, VG $14.00
Flash, #125, G+...$15.00
Frankenstein, #3, NM......................................$9.00
Ghost Rider, #4, 1990 series, NM+ $12.00
GI Combat, #40, VG+......................................$20.00
Godzilla, #1, NM...$6.00
Green Lantern, #7, VG-...................................$39.00
Hawk & Dove, #4, G+.....................................$6.00
Hero for Hire, #1, VG.....................................$9.00
House of Mystery, #30, VG-...........................$25.00
House of Secrets, #25, VG-............................$13.00
Hulk, #371, NM $4.00
Invaders, #5, NM...$6.00
Iron Fist, #5, EX..$6.50
Jimmy Olsen, #20, VG+..................................$45.00
Journey Into Mystery, #89, VG+ $58.00
Journey Into Unknown Worlds, #52, VG+......$21.00
Justice, #16, VG-...$10.00
Justice League, #11, G $20.00
Leave It to Binky, #22, VG-............................$8.00
Lois Lane, #36, VG+..$8.50
Love Romances, #68, VG+..............................$5.00
Man Comics, #5, VG $16.00
Marvel Feature, #3, VG-..................................$6.00
Marvel Mystery, #91, EX.................................$80.00
Marvel Premiere, #22, EX+............................$4.00
Marvel Super-Heroes, #12, VG+ $28.00
Marvel Tales, #154, VG+.................................$27.00
Marvel Team-up, #55, NM...............................$7.00
Millie the Model, #18, VG+............................$23.00
Miss America, #83, VG+..................................$5.00

Mister Miracle, #10, NM.................................$5.00
Mutt & Jeff, #27, VG $19.00
My Greatest Adventure, #35, G+ $10.00
My Love Story, #7, EX.....................................$12.00
Mystery in Space, #54, VG+............................$90.00
Mystery Tales, #46, VG-..................................$21.00
Mystic, #54, VG+...$28.00
Navy Action, #8, EX-.......................................$14.00
New Adventures of Charlie Chan, #4, G........$25.00
New Mutants, #86, NM+..................................$13.00
Nova, #12, EX+..$4.00
Our Army at War, #38, VG+............................$40.00
Our Fighting Forces, #39, VG-........................$13.00
Pat Boone, #4, G+...$33.00
Patsy & Hedy, #50, VG+..................................$6.00
Patsy Walker, #70, EX.....................................$11.00
Power Man & Iron Fist, #78, VG+ $3.00
Robin Hood Tales, #14, G+.............................$27.00
Sensation, #79, G+..$38.00
Sgt Fury, #14, VG..$9.00
Shadow, #4, NM...$11.00
Shazam, #1, NM+..$7.00
Showcase, #41, G+ $18.00
Spellbound, #33, EX..$90.00
Star Spangled Banner, #99, G+ $50.00
Star Spangled War Stories, #58, VG-..............$9.00
Stories of Romance, #9, G+............................$3.50
Strange Adventures, #34, VG..........................$60.00
Strange Sport Stories, #1, NM+......................$6.00
Strange Tales, #47, VG+..................................$45.00
Sugar & Spike, #56, G.....................................$8.50
Superboy, #82, VG+...$13.50
Superman, #87, G+..$60.00

Superman's Girlfriend Lois Lane, DC Comics #2, 1958, NM, $195.00.

Suspense, #12, VG+...$34.00
Tales of Justice, #36, VG+..............................$40.00
Tales of the Unexpected, #36, G+..................$15.00
Tales To Astonish, #33, VG.............................$40.00
Teen Titans, #2, VG-.......................................$15.00
Thor, #166, VG+..$11.00
Tomb of Dracula, #14, EX+............................$9.00
Uncanny Tales, #25, VG-.................................$22.00
Venus, #6, VG $85.00
Wanted, #7, VG+...$1.50

Warlock, #4, VG+ **$2.50**
Warlord, #12, NM **$3.00**
Web of Spider-man, #7, NM **$3.50**
Weird Wonder Tales, #12, EX+ **$3.00**
Wonder Woman, #72, G **$26.00**
World of Fantasy, #1, G **$29.00**
World of Suspense, VG- **$19.00**
Worlds Unknown, #1, NM+ **$5.00**
X-Factor, #63, NM **$4.00**
X-Men, #4, VG- **$70.00**
Yellow Claw, #2, VG- **$75.00**

Compacts and Carryalls

Very new to the collectibles scene, compacts are already making an impact. When 'liberated' women entered the workforce after WWI, cosmetics, previously frowned upon, became more acceptable, and as as result the market was engulfed with compacts of all types and designs. Some went so far as to incorporate timepieces, cigarette compartments, coin holders, and money clips. All types of materials were used, mother-of-pearl, petit point, cloisonne, celluloid, and leather among them. There were figural compacts, those with wonderful Art Deco designs, souvenir compacts, and some with advertising messages.

Carryalls were popular from the 1930s to the 1950s. They were made by compact manufacturers and were usually carried with evening wear. They contained compartments for powder, rouge and lipstick, often held a comb and mirror, and some were designed with a space for cigarettes and a lighter. Other features might have included a timepiece, a tissue holder, a place for coins or stamps, and some even had music boxes.

For further study, we recommend *Vintage Ladies' Compacts* and *Vintage Vanity Bags and Purses* by Roselyn Gerson; and *Collectors Encyclopedia of Compacts, Carryalls and Face Powder Boxes* by Laura Mueller.

Advisor: Roselyn Gerson (See Directory, Compacts)

Newsletter: The Compacts Collector Chronicle
Powder Puff
P.O. Box Letter 40
Lynbrook, NY 11563; Subscription: $25 (4 issues, USA or Canada) per year

Carryalls

Marhill, mother-of-pearl carryall, painted peacock & glitter on lid, from $150 to **$200.00**
Unmarked, gunmetal book form carryall w/4 faux amethysts on lid, 4 compartments & pencil, mini, from $200 to ...**$225.00**

Compacts

Coro, half-moon gold-tone case w/enameled Persian design on lid, from $40 to...**$60.00**
Coty, gold-tone metal w/Coty trademark of white puffs on orange background, from $60 to.........................**$80.00**

Coty, octagonal polished nickel-finish vanity, upper lid for rouge, lower opening for powder, from $60 to ...**$80.00**
Coty, Sub-Deb, red & white plastic, 1940s, from $25 to ..**$40.00**
Divine, lavender-striped enameling w/white silhouette, mini, from $30 to...**$50.00**
Dorothy Gray, oval gold-tone case w/black enamel Harlequin mask on lid, 1940s, from $80 to........**$100.00**
Elgin, stylized heart shape w/enameling, Give Me Your Answer Do! on lid, 1940s-50s, from $80 to........**$120.00**
Elgin American, 4-color enamel swirls on gold-tone metal, GE Color TV logo on lid, from $125 to.............**$175.00**
Evans, blue enamel tango chain vanity w/painted cloisonne lid, powder & rouge compartments, from $150 to.......**$200.00**
Evans, gold-tone basketweave heart shape w/pink & yellow enameling, ca 1946, from $150 to **$225.00**
Evans, gold-tone case, double access w/rose & gold-tone ribs, wrist chain, ca 1952, 1x6¾x3¼", from, $150 to ...**$175.00**
Evans, silver-tone standard, rectangular w/snake wrist chain, 2x5½x3⅛", from $150 to **$175.00**
Evans, silvered-metal compact/watch combination, 1950s, from $100 to..**$150.00**
Evans, Sunburst, gold-tone square metal case, no lighter, from $75 to...**$100.00**
Glamour, mother-of-pearl & abalone shell in checked pattern, snake wrist chain, mirror, 1⅛x4x3", from $75 to **$90.00**
K&K, polished satin-finish compact/bracelet combination, hinged style, from $200 to **$250.00**

Karess, gold-tone with girl, rose and star on lid, silver-tone bottom lid, 1¾" dia, from $80.00 to $150.00. (Photo courtesy of Roselyn Gerson.)

Kigu, blue enameling w/Limoges-type locket centered on lid, 1940-50s, from $60 to **$100.00**
Kigu, Cherie, gold-tone heart shape w/jeweled crown on lid, 1940-50s, from $50 to **$80.00**
Lady Vanity, oval blue leather case w/snap closure, from $40 to..**$60.00**
Lesco Bond Street, green alligator covering, sm, from $70 to **$90.00**
Lin-bren, green leather w/envelope-motif coin holder on lid, 1940s, from $70 to **$100.00**
Marathon, gold-tone metal w/heart on lid, lid opens to reveal locket, open by pressing side panels, from $60 to **$80.00**
Rex, gilt mesh vanity pouch w/mini white plastic beads, 1930s, from $40 to **$60.00**

Rex Fifth Avenue, 2 pink enameled flamingos on turquoise background, from $75 to **$100.00**

Richard Hudnut, gilt metal w/raised tulip design, lipstick encased in lid cover, from $40 to.........................**$60.00**

Rowenta, oval enameled petit-point, from $30 to.......**$50.00**

Shagreen, tango chain style w/initial set w/marcasites, 1930s, from $250 to...**$300.00**

Silvaray, Art Nouveau red enameling on metal, from $80 to **$100.00**

Stratton, gold-tone metal w/scenic transfer on lid, 1950s, from $40 to...**$60.00**

Unmarked, blue leather, 1-pc horse shape, from $40 to..**$60.00**

Unmarked, crystal Lucite w/polished metal cutout of Mexican man sleeping beside a cactus plant, 1940s, from $60 to......**$80.00**

Unmarked, Damascene black matt inlaid w/gilt Egyptian scene, from $75 to...**$100.00**

Unmarked, gold-tone case designed as hand mirror w/decorated & engraved lid, from $80 to.......................**$100.00**

Unmarked, gold-tone heart shape w/brocade lid, 1930s, from $40 to..**$60.00**

Unmarked, gold-tone metal triangular enameled compact w/2 green birds in flight on light blue, finger ring chain, from $80 to...**$120.00**

Unmarked, gold-tone metal w/scenes of Paris mounted on lid, from $80 to **$100.00**

Unmarked, gold-tone metal w/2 pink & gray simulated feathered birds enclosed in a plastic dome, from $100 to.......**$150.00**

Unmarked, gold-tone oval w/blue plastic lid set w/faux gems, from $40 to...**$60.00**

Unmarked, gunmetal mesh vanity type w/finger ring chain, mini, from $150 to...**$200.00**

Unmarked, lavender cloisonne silver-metal vanity type w/blue flowers, powder sifter, rouge compartment, from $100 to...**$150.00**

Unmarked, lizard-covered case designed to resemble suitcase w/carrying handles, from $125 to...............**$175.00**

Unmarked, mother-of-pearl checkerboard case, 1940s, 5" dia, from $150 to...**$200.00**

Unmarked, navy blue & white vanity type w/nautical motif on lid, powder & rouge compartments, ca 1940s, from $40 to..**$60.00**

Unmarked, nickel-silver w/red & black enameling, metal mirror, compartments, finger ring on chain, 1920s, from $125 to **$150.00**

Unmarked, oval red plastic case set w/rhinestones, carrying cord & tassel, ca 1920s, from $250 to.................**$350.00**

Unmarked, oval simulated tortoise-shell plastic w/raised vintage design on lid, sterling catches, 1940s, from $60 to ...**$80.00**

Unmarked, petit-point half-moon-shaped gold-tone vanity, powder & rouge compartments, sliding lipstick, 1930s, from $100 to...**$150.00**

Unmarked, plastic cigarette/compact combination, metal cutout of Scottie on lid, 1940s, from $80 to.......**$100.00**

Unmarked, silver-plated heart shape w/engraved decor, w/carrying chain, from $75 to.............................**$100.00**

Unmarked vanity, black & white mother-of-pearl, attached lipstick, 1930s, from $50 to...................................**$75.00**

Volupte, gold-tone basketweave rectangle w/red stones on lid, sliding lipstick, 1940s, from $50 to **$60.00**

Volupte, gold-tone hand shape, 1940s, from $100 to ..**$150.00**

Volupte, gold-tone metal w/Cub Scout, Den Mother emblem, from $60 to..**$80.00**

Wadsworth, gold-tone metal w/hand-painted yellow enameling on fan shape, 1950s, from $80 to **$100.00**

Yardley, gold-tone vanity w/red, white & blue embossed design on lid, powder & rouge compartments, 1940s, from $60 to..**$75.00**

Zell Fifth Avenue, black enameling w/incised intersecting lines, double access, 1¼x4x3", from $75 to **$90.00**

Condiment Sets

Whimsical styling makes these sets lots of fun to collect. Any species of animals or plant, that ever existed and many that never did or ever will are represented, so an extensive collection is possible, and prices are still reasonable. These sets are usually comprised of a pair of salt and pepper shakers and a small mustard pot on a tray, though some sets never had a tray, and others were figurals that were made in three parts. For more information, we recommend *Salt and Pepper Shakers, Vols I through IV,* by Helene Guarnaccia, and *Collectors Encyclopedia of Salt and Pepper Shakers, Figural and Novelty,* by Melva Davern.

See also Black Americana.

Apples hanging from tree w/bird in nest, ceramic, Japan...**$40.00**

Beehives on a tray, ceramic, 3 white round beehives w/honey-colored bees on footed white tray........**$35.00**

Bowl of fruit, ceramic, minimum value $35.00. (Photo courtesy of Melva Davern.)

British telephone booth & mailboxes on a tray, ceramic, cream booth w/blue & red trim, 2 red & black mailboxes, 1950...**$80.00**

Cabbage heads in basket, ceramic, 3 realistic green cabbage heads in yellow basket w/handle..........................**$35.00**

Cats & goldfish bowl on a tray, ceramic, lg cat attached to fishbowl w/2 smaller cats, fish handle on spoon .**$75.00**

Chef w/2 covered pots on brick oven, ceramic, chef in white hat & flower on lapel attached to oven w/pot shakers, Japan..**$80.00**

Chickens on a tray, ceramic, 3 gold chickens w/black tail feathers & dotted chests, red combs & waddles, grassy tray....**$40.00**

Children w/gramophone on tray, ceramic, multicolored seated boy & girl flank gramophone on green tray, Japan, 1950 ....**$100.00**

Dachshund, ceramic, black 3-pc dog w/head & middle as shakers, rear as mustard, 1960s............................**$22.00**

Dogs playing football, ceramic, lg dog attached to football w/bee atop, 2 smaller dog shakers, dog handle on spoon...**$75.00**

Donkey cart, ceramic, fruit baskets hang from donkey pulling 2-wheeled cart w/fruit motif **$25.00**

Drum majors & drum on tray, ceramic, honey gold figures standing at attention in front of lg brown & gold drum, 1960s **$30.00**

Egg shakers w/mustard pot on tray, porcelain, white w/gold floral design & banded trim **$25.00**

English houses on tray, ceramic, 3 half-timbered houses w/reddish brown roofs on green tray w/tab handles........**$65.00**

Fish, lustre, top fin is lid to mustard body w/tail fin & top of head as shakers, white & blue w/silver lustre ...**$120.00**

Fish on a tray, ceramic, fish shakers & mustard on fish-shaped tray, white w/black trim, 1950.................**$60.00**

Fort w/2 cannons on a tray, ceramic, brown fort w/2 green cannons on green brick-wall tray, 1950.............**$100.00**

Galleon, lustre, 3 sails are shakers & mustard, blue & honey w/gold trim, marked State Capitol Albany NY, Japan..**$90.00**

Gardener w/2 watering cans on tray, ceramic, gardener in blue overalls, tray w/2 end handles, Japan, 1950s **$90.00**

Girls w/valise seated on trunk, ceramic, 2 girls wearing red hats & blue dresses w/brown valise on black trunk **$50.00**

Gondola w/2 men, lustre, 2 seated men flank building on honey-colored gondola **$110.00**

Heads on a tray, ceramic, pouting & winking heads in red & green hats flank yelling head in black hat, German, 1950s ...**$80.00**

Horse-drawn coach on a tray, 2 horses w/green coach, black trim, cobblestone tray, 1950s **$100.00**

Humpty Dumptys on a tray, 2 Humpty Dumpty shakers looking up at Humpty Dumpty mustard, brick-wall tray, 1950s-60s **$120.00**

Indian at drum w/2 teepees, lustre, no tray...............**$50.00**

Indian couple seated in front of teepee, white w/multicolored accents, chief w/hand out.............................**$35.00**

Indian couple seated in front of teepee on tray, ceramic, tray marked Wisconsin Dells.......................................**$30.00**

Jugs on a tray, ceramic, floral design on 3 white jugs w/loop handles & tray, 4-pc set **$12.00**

Millhouse, ceramic, water wheel & shed flank house on base, white w/gold trim...**$65.00**

Monks on a tray, ceramic, 3 different monks in brown robes w/yellow rope belts on white rectangular tray, English, 1950s **$60.00**

Native boys & hut on tray, ceramic, brown-skinned boys seated by grass hut on green grassy tray, Japan, 1950..**$90.00**

Native boys beating drum on tray w/palm tree, ceramic, Japan, 1950..**$100.00**

Native boys w/watermelon on tray, ceramic, black-skinned w/pink lips, watermelon w/flat top, Japan **$120.00**

Pagodas, ceramic, 6-sided shakers w/square mustard, maroon, yellow & green, no tray **$30.00**

Pig, ceramic, stacked, white head w/pink ears & mouth, black eyes & nose, blue body w/black dots **$65.00**

Pussy Cat, Pussy Cat, Where Have You Been? on a tray, ceramic, girl & cat shakers w/house mustard, 1950-60..**$120.00**

Sailors & pot on a tray, 2 milk-glass sailors w/light blue plastic hats looking at pot on blue plastic tray, 1930s........**$45.00**

Three Wise Monkeys, ceramic, See No Evil, Speak No Evil & Hear No Evil on green marked tray, 1950s **$120.00**

Train engine w/tender & caboose, ceramic, engine w/smiling face, tender & caboose marked Salt & Pepper, multicolored...**$45.00**

Windmills on a tray, ceramic, blue airbrushed tops, green & honey accents, green airbrushed tray, Japan........**$25.00**

Windmills on a tray, ceramic, 3 windmills in a row on elongated tray...**$25.00**

Woman & 2 children in boat, lustre, woman & children in green w/yellow & red trim, blue & honey boat, Japan, 1930s...**$80.00**

Cookbooks and Recipe Leaflets

If you've ever read a 19th-century cookbook, no doubt you've been amused by the quaint way the measurements were given. Butter the size of an egg, a handful of flour, a pinch of this or that — sounds like a much more time-efficient method, doesn't it? They'd sometimes give household tips or some folk remedies, and it's these antiquated methods and ideas that endear those old cookbooks to collectors, although examples from this era are not easily found.

Cookbooks from the early 20th century are scarce too, but even those that were printed thirty and forty years ago are well worth collecting. Food and appliance companies often published their own, and these appeal to advertising buffs and cookbook collectors alike, especially if they illustrate kitchen appliances pre-1970. Some were die-cut to represent the product, perhaps a pickle or a slice of bread. Cookbooks that focus on unusual topics and those that have ethnic or regional recipes are appealing, too. The leaflets we list below were nearly all advertising giveaways and premiums. Condition is important in any area of paper collectibles, so judge yours accordingly. Some were issued with dust jackets. Without them, such cookbooks hold little interest for the collector.

For further study, we recommend *A Guide to Collecting Cookbooks* by Colonel Bob Allen, and *Price Guide to Cookbooks and Recipe Leaflets* by Linda Dickenson. Our values are based on cookbooks in excellent condition.

Club/Newsletter: *Cookbook Gossip*
Cookbook Collectors Club of America, Inc.
Bob and Jo Ellen Allen
231 E James Blvd., P.O. Box 85
St. James, MO 65559; 314-265-8296

Newsletter: *The Cookbook Collector's Exchange*
Sue Erwin
P.O. Box 32369
San Jose, CA 95152-2369; Subscription: $15 per year for 6 issues

After 50 Cookbook, D Hamilton, 1974, 365 pages **$12.00**

America's Cook Book, Home Institute, NY, 1937, hard-bound, 1006 pages..**$18.00**

Armour Star, Just a Few Armour Star Recipes, leaflet, 1930..**$4.00**

Art of Italian Cooking, M Pinto, 1948, 177 pages..........**$8.00**

Aunt Sammy's Radio Recipes Revised, 1931, 142 pages, G.**$10.00**

Ball Blue Book, Russel, 1930, paperback, 56 pages ...**$16.00**

Berks County Cookbook, Pennsylvania Dutch Recipes, ca 1945, paperback, 48 pages.......................................**$7.00**

Better Homes & Gardens Cookbook, 1968, hard-bound, 80 pages...**$12.00**

Betty Crocker's Cookie Carnival, Gold Medal Flour, 1957, 38 pages, G...**$6.00**

Blue Bonnet Margarine, Economy Recipes, 1939, leaflet..**$2.00**

Borden, Elsie's Cookbook, hard-bound, 374 pages....**$10.00**

Borden's Eagle Brand Magic Recipes, 1946, 28 pages, VG **$10.00**

Calumet Baking Book, 1931, paperback, 31 pages.......**$5.00**

Campus Survival Cookbook, J Wood, 1973, paperback, 160 pages...**$5.00**

Carnation Milk, 100 Glorified Recipes, 1930, paperback ..**$4.00**

Clabber Girl Baking Book, undated, 15 pages, G.........**$8.00**

Clementine Paddleford's Cook Young Cookbook, 1966, paperback, 124 pages.......................................**$5.00**

Cow Baking Powder, Good Things To Eat, 1936, 32 pages **$4.00**

Culinary Arts, Seafoods, 1955, paperback, 68 pages.....**$4.00**

Diamond Walnuts, Menu Magic in a Nutshell, 1941, 30 pages, VG **$6.00**

Duncan Hines Food Odyssey, 1955, hard-bound, 274 pages.**$7.00**

Encyclopedia of Cookery, W Wise, 1948, hard-bound, 1269 pages...**$22.00**

Evaporated Milk Association, Why Evaporated Milk Makes Good Food Better, 1934, 38 pages, VG **$8.00**

Fannie Farmer, Boston Cooking-School Cookbook, 1942, hard-bound, 838 pages.......................................**$15.00**

Fondue Cookbook, Ed Callahan, 1968, 104 pages........**$5.00**

Frigidaire Frozen Delights, 1927, 47 pages, VG **$12.00**

GE, How To Enjoy Better Meals With Your New 1949 GE Space Maker Refrigerator, 36 pages, G **$6.00**

Good Housekeeping, Book of Cookies, 1958, paperback, 68 pages...**$7.00**

Good Housekeeping, Quick & Easy, 1958, paperback, 68 pages...**$3.00**

Heinz Book of Meat Cookery, 1930, paperback, 54 pages..**$5.00**

Hershey's Index Recipe Book, 1934, 48 pages, VG....**$11.00**

Hummingbirds & Radishes, F Hoffman, 1953, 214 pages...**$5.00**

Incredible Edibles, Lake Forest Park, Washington, 1979, paperback, 124 pages...**$5.00**

James Beard, American Cookery, 1972, hard-bound, 877 pages...**$32.00**

Jell-O, New Jell-O Book of Surprises, 1930, leaflet, 18 pages.**$6.00**

Jell-O, What Mrs Dewey Did With the New Jell-O!, 1933, 23 pages, $15.00.

Jell-O, What You Can Do With Jell-O, 1933, 26 pages, G...**$12.00**

Kerr Home Canning Book, National Nutrition Edition, 1943, 56 pages, G **$12.00**

Knox Gelatin, Presenting Knox Cookies, 1938, paperback, 23 pages...**$2.00**

Lowney's Cook Book, Lowney's Chocolate, 1912, hard-bound, 421 pages **$25.00**

Ma's Cookin' Mountain Recipes, 1966, paperback, 55 pages...**$3.00**

Metropolitan Cookbook, 1914, paperback, 65 pages....**$6.00**

Mexican Cookery for American Homes, Gebhardt's, 1923, 32 pages, VG **$6.00**

Morton Salt Co, Meat Curing Made Easy, 1934, 40 pages, G-..**$6.00**

National Biscuit Co, The Whole Wheat Way to Better Meals, 1940, tab indexed, VG..**$12.00**

New York Times 60-Minute Gourmet, P Franey, 1979, 339 pages...**$6.00**

Pillsbury Bake-Off, 1st edition, paperback **$65.00**

Pillsbury Bake-Off, 13th edition, paperback.................**$5.00**

Pillsbury's Best Flour, A Book for a Cook, 1905, 128 pages, $25.00.

Premier Coffee, Aladdin's Lamp at Mealtime, 1927, leaflet, 47 pages...**$2.00**

Queen Is in the Kitchen, McCarthy, 1954, hard-bound, 232 pages...**$5.00**

Quick 'N Easy Riceland Rice, ca 1950, leaflet...............**$2.00**

Royal Baker & Pastry Cook, 1911, 46 pages, G **$16.00**

Rumford Complete Cook Book, L Wallace, 1946, hard-bound, 213 pages...**$8.00**

Season To Taste Spices & How To Use Them, HJ Mayer & Sons Co, 1939, paperback, 48 pages.......................**$5.00**

Snoopy Doghouse Cookbook, 1979, 125 pages............**$8.00**

Sunkist Lemons Bring Out the Flavor, California Fruit Growers Exchange, 1939, 32 pages, VG...............**$10.00**

Sunsweet Prunes, Visions of Sugarplums, 1959, leaflet ..**$2.00**

Tasty Dairy Dishes, Iowa Dairy Industry Commission, 1950s, 17 pages, VG **$6.00**

Time-Life Recipes, America, 1969, paperback, any.......**$6.00**

Towel's Log Cabin Syrup, set of 24 recipe cards **$35.00**

Wesson Oil, Salad Dressings, 1925, 27 pages, G.........**$10.00**

Wonder Bread Cookbook, 1930, paperback.................**$5.00**

Cookie Cutters

Cookie cutters have come into their own in recent years as worthy kitchen collectibles. Prices on many have risen astronomically, but a practiced eye can still sort out a good bargain. Advertising cutters and product premiums, especially in plastic, can still be found without too much effort. Aluminum cutters with painted wood handles are usually worth several dollars each, if in good condition. Red and green are the usual handle colors, but other colors are more highly prized by many. Hallmark plastic cookie cutters, especially those with painted backs, are always worth considering, if in good condition.

Be wary of modern tin cutters being sold for antique. Many present-day tinsmiths chemically antique their cutters, especially if done in a primitive style. These are often sold by others as 'very old.' Look closely because most tinsmiths today sign and date these cutters.

Molds, instead of cutting the cookie out, impressed a design into the dough. To learn more about both (and many other old kitchenware gadgets as well), we recommend *300 Years of Kitchen Collectibles* by Linda Campbell Franklin and *Kitchen Antiques, 1790 to 1940*, by Kathryn McNerney. Also read *The Cookie Shaper's Bible* by Phyllis Wetherill and our advisor, Rosemary Henry.

Advisor: Rosemary Henry (See Directory, Cookie Cutters)

Newsletter: *Cookies*
Rosemary Henry
9610 Greenview Ln.
Manassas, VA 20109-3320; Subscription: $10 per year for 6 issues

Newsletter: *Cookie Crumbs*
Cookie Cutter Collectors Club
Ruth Capper
1167 Teal Rd. SW
Dellroy, OH 44620; 216-735-2839 or 202-966-0869

Animal Snacks, yellow plastic lion, elephant, hippo & zebra, w/impression lines, back & handle, Hallmark, 1978, MIP **$15.00**
Animals, tan plastic w/number, when assembled form 3-D cookies, Crisco, set of 8 w/instructions **$20.00**
Betty Crocker Gingerbread Boy, various plastic colors w/back & handle, marked Betty Crocker Gingerbread Mix, Made in USA **$3.00**
Calumet Snap-Together Cutters, aluminum pastry, cookie & biscuit cutters, 4", 3", 7¾", set of 3 ....**$12.00**
Formay Rabbit, sitting pose, machine-formed metal w/self handle, ca 1930, 6", G **$10.00**
Gingerbread Queen, metal outline, Progress Works, 1977, MOC...**$7.00**
Gingerbread Twins, hot pink boy & orange girl, w/impression lines, backs & handles, Hallmark, set of 2, MIP.....**$10.00**
Hershey Chocolate Bar, white plastic w/brown-painted back, 1980..**$6.00**

Indian maiden, white plastic w/blue-painted back, Minnegasco, 1969...**$12.00**
Jack Frost Sugar Elf, white plastic w/impression lines, M..**$2.00**
Kellogg's Rice Krispies Easter Duck, pastel yellow, 1982 ..**$1.50**
Kiddie Kreetures Halloween Set, orange plastic children in costumes, Aluminum Specialty Co (Chilton), set of 7, MIB **$15.00**
MGM cartoon character, red transparent plastic w/impression lines, marked Copyright Loew's Incorporated, 1956, set of 6..**$20.00**
Planters Peanuts' Mr Peanut, white plastic w/painted back, no handle, 1990 ....**$4.00**
Rudolf the Red-Nosed Reindeer, plastic w/impression lines, Dial Soap Christmas premium, 1981, from set of 4..**$3.00**
San Diego Zoo, lion, white plastic w/gold-painted back, Monogram Products, MOC....................................**$8.00**
Santa Claus, plastic w/impression lines, Dial Soap Christmas premium, 1981, from set of 4 ....**$3.00**
Snoopy What's Cookin'?, yellow plastic w/impression lines, back & handle, Hallmark, G **$9.00**
Vampire, light blue plastic w/impression lines & painted back, Hallmark, 1979...**$9.00**

Snowman or Gingerbread boy, 2-in-1, metal, 8", MIB, $8.00. (Photo courtesy of Rosemary Henry.)

Cookie Jars

This is an area that for years saw an explosion of interest that resulted in some very high prices. Rare cookie jars sell for literally thousands of dollars. Even a common jar from a good manufacturer will fall into the $40.00 to $100.00 price range. At the top of the list are the Black-theme jars, then come the cartoon characters such as Popeye, Howdy Doody, or the Flintstones. In fact, any kind of a figural jar from an American pottery is extremely collectible right now.

The American Bisque company was one of the largest producers of these jars from 1930 until the 1970s. Many of their jars have no marks at all; those that do are simply marked 'USA,' sometimes with a mold number. But their airbrushed colors are easy to spot, and collectors look for the molded-in wedge-shaped pads on their bases — these say 'American Bisque' to cookie jar buffs about as clearly as if they were marked.

The Brush Pottery (Ohio, 1946–71) made cookie jars that were decorated with the airbrush in many of the same colors used by American Bisque. These jars are strongly holding their values, and the rare ones continue to climb in price. McCoy was probably the leader in cookie-jar production. Even some of their very late jars bring high prices. Abingdon, Shawnee, and Red Wing all manufactured cookie jars as well, and there are lots of wonderful jars by many other companies. Joyce and Fred Roerig's books *The Collector's Encyclopedia of Cookie Jars, Vols I and II*, cover them all beautifully, and you won't want to miss Ermagene Westfall's *An Illustrated Value Guide to Cookie Jars II*. All are published by Collector Books.

Warning! The marketplace abounds with reproductions these days. Roger Jensen of Rockwood, Tennessee, is making a line of cookie jars as well as planters, salt and pepper shakers, and many other items which he marks McCoy. Because the 'real' McCoys never registered their trademark, he was able to receive federal approval to begin using this mark in 1992. Though he added '#93' to some of his pieces, the majority of his wares are undated. He is using old molds, and novice collectors are being fooled into buying the new for 'old' prices. Here are some of his reproductions that you should be aware of: McCoy Mammy, Mammy With Cauliflower, Clown Bust, Dalmatians, Indian Head and Rocking Horse; Hull Little Red Riding Hood; Pearl China Mammy; and the Mosaic Tile Mammy. Several Brush jars have been reproduced as well (see *Schroeder's Antiques Price Guide* for information), and there are others.

Cookie jars from California are getting their fair share of attention right now, and then some! We've included several from companies such as Brayton Laguna, Treasure Craft, Vallona Star, and Twin Winton. Roerig's books have information on all of these.

Advisors: Phil and Nyla Thurston, Fitz & Floyd (See Directory, Figural Ceramics); Mike Ellis, Twin Winton (See Directory, California Pottery); Bernice Stamper, Vallona Star (See Directory, California Pottery)

Newsletter: *The Cookie Jar Collector's Club News*
c/o Louise Messina Daking
595 Cross River Road
Katonah, NY 10536; 914-232-0383 or FAX 914-232-0384

Newsletter: *The Cookie Jar Express Newsline*
Paradise Publications
P.O. Box 221
Mayview, MO 64071-0221; Subscription: $30 per year for 12 monthly issues by first-class mail

Newsletter: *Cookie Jarrin' With Joyce*
R.R. 2, Box 504
Walterboro, SC 29488

Abingdon, Clock, 1949 ....**$85.00**
Abingdon, Daisy, #677, 1949 ....**$45.00**

Abingdon, Fat Boy, #495, minimum value **$350.00**
Abingdon, Girl (Cooky), #693, from $75 to **$100.00**
Abingdon, Hippo, decorated, 1942, from $225 to **$250.00**
Abingdon, Hobby Horse, #602, from $200 to **$225.00**

Abingdon, Humpty Dumpty, #663, $250.00.

Abingdon, Jack-in-the-Box, #611, from $250 to **$275.00**
Abingdon, Little Old Lady, #471, green, rare **$195.00**
Abingdon, Miss Muffett, #622, from $225 to **$250.00**
Abingdon, Money Bag, #588, 1947.............................**$70.00**
Abingdon, Pineapple, #664, from $75 to **$95.00**
Abingdon, Pumpkin, 1949 ....**$310.00**
Abingdon, Three Bears, #696, from $90 to **$120.00**
Abingdon, Wigwam, from $500 to **$700.00**
Advertising, Aramis Bear, no mark, from $50 to.........**$75.00**
Advertising, Avon Bear from $40 to **$60.00**
Advertising, Blue Bonnet Sue, from $40 to **$50.00**
Advertising, Century 21 House, current (no 'Real Estate' on sign), minimum value...**$250.00**
Advertising, Coke Can, McCoy, current, from $65 to **$75.00**
Advertising, Green Sprout, Benjamin & Medwin, from $55 to..**$75.00**
Advertising, Harley-Davidson Gas Tank, from $85 to..**$95.00**
Advertising, Jim Beam, San Joaquin Valley, from $120 to..**$145.00**
Advertising, Mrs Fields Sack, from $45 to...................**$65.00**
Advertising, Nabisco Chips Ahoy **$85.00**
Advertising, Nestle's Toll House, from $50 to **$65.00**
Advertising, Nestle's Toll House, w/gold trim, from $100 to **$150.00**
Advertising, Pepperidge Farm Cookie Sack, from $65 to .**$80.00**

Advertising, Pillsbury Doughboy, marked Pillsbury Company 1973, from $50.00 to $65.00.

Advertising, Pillsbury Flour Sack, from $30 to **$40.00**
Advertising, President's Choice Bear, from $100 to ..**$125.00**
Advertising, Sunshine Cookies, from $60 to...............**$70.00**
Advertising, Tony the Tiger, plastic, from $80 to......**$100.00**
Advertising, US Soccer Ball..**$45.00**
American Bisque, Bear & Beehive, from $350 to **$375.00**
American Bisque, Bear w/Visor Cap, from $75 to......**$85.00**
American Bisque, Blackboard Girl, from $325 to **$350.00**
American Bisque, Cat, w/indented dots, from $75 to.**$85.00**
American Bisque, Collegiate Owl, from $75 to...........**$85.00**
American Bisque, Cookie Girl w/Braids, from $85 to ..**$95.00**
American Bisque, Cookie RR Locomotive, marked USA..**$75.00**
American Bisque, Cookie Time Clock, marked USA 203, from
 $65 to...**$75.00**
American Bisque, Cookies Sack, #307, airbrushed, cookies
 on lid, marked Cardinal USA #307 ....**$60.00**
American Bisque, Cookies Sack, cold paint, knob lid, marked
 USA 201...**$40.00**
American Bisque, Graduate, from $100 to **$125.00**
American Bisque, Ice Cream Freezer, from $225 to ..**$250.00**
American Bisque, Jack-in-the-box, marked USA, 1958 ..**$125.00**
American Bisque, Kitten on Ball of Yarn....................**$70.00**
American Bisque, Kitten on Beehive, marked USA, 1958...**$45.00**
American Bisque, Liberty Bell, from $90 to...............**$110.00**
American Bisque, Majorette, from $225 to **$250.00**
American Bisque, Picnic Basket, from $300 to **$325.00**
American Bisque, Pig in Cookie Sack, marked USA, 1958...**$75.00**
American Bisque, Poodle, marked USA, 1959...........**$125.00**
American Bisque, Puppy in a Pot, from $60 to...........**$75.00**
American Bisque, Schoolhouse, from $65 to..............**$75.00**
American Bisque, Sea Bag, from $150 to **$175.00**
American Bisque, Seal on Igloo, from $250 to **$275.00**
American Bisque, Spool of Thread, marked USA **$140.00**
American Bisque, Train, Smiley Face, from $125 to ..**$135.00**
American Bisque, Treasure Chest, marked USA.......**$175.00**
American Bisque, Yarn Doll **$120.00**

American Bisque, Yogi Bear, Better Than the Average Cookies, marked Hanna-Barbera Productions Inc. 1979, minimum value $400.00.

American Pottery, Pig, turnabout **$175.00**
Applause, '57 Chevy, from $85 to **$100.00**
Applause, Bugs Miranda **$55.00**
Applause, Cinderella & Fairy Godmother...................**$55.00**
Applause, Tasmanian Devil, in can **$40.00**
Artistic Potteries, Black Chef, minimum value **$400.00**
Brayton Laguna, Calico Dog.......................................**$595.00**

Brayton Laguna, Christina (Swedish Maiden)............**$425.00**
Brayton Laguna, Gingerbread House.........................**$250.00**
Brayton Laguna, Mammy, green or blue dress, minimum
 value..**$1,000.00**
Brayton Laguna, Mammy, red dress, minimum value...**$800.00**
Brayton Laguna, Mammy, yellow dress, minimum value..**$1,200.00**
Brayton Laguna, Matilda, blue & green skirt.............**$475.00**
Brayton Laguna, Provincial Lady **$295.00**
Brayton Laguna, Wedding Ring Granny (Grandma), not
 reproduction...**$500.00**
Brush, Antique Touring Car, minimum value............**$700.00**
Brush, Cinderella Pumpkin, #W32 ....**$200.00**
Brush, Clown, yellow pants..**$250.00**
Brush, Cookie House, #W31.......................................**$85.00**
Brush, Cow w/Cat on Back, brown............................**$110.00**
Brush, Cow w/Cat on Back, purple, minimum value...**$1,000.00**
Brush, Donkey w/Cart, ears down, gray, #W33 ....**$400.00**
Brush, Elephant w/Baby Bonnet & Ice Cream Cone..**$500.00**
Brush, Formal Pig, green hat & coat (watch for reproduc-
 tions)...**$300.00**
Brush, Granny, pink apron, blue dots on skirt.........**$325.00**
Brush, Granny, plain skirt, minimum value **$400.00**
Brush, Happy Bunny, #W25 ....**$225.00**
Brush, Hen on Basket, 1969 ....**$125.00**
Brush, Humpty Dumpty, #W18 USA, 1956-61.........**$275.00**
Brush, Laughing Hippo, #W27 ....**$650.00**
Brush, Nite Owl, #W40, 1967 ....**$125.00**
Brush, Old Shoe, #W23..**$95.00**
Brush, Peter, Peter Pumpkin Eater, #W24...............**$300.00**
Brush, Raggedy Ann, #W16 ....**$350.00**
Brush, Smiling Bear, #W64 ....**$350.00**
Brush, Stylized Owl..**$250.00**
Brush, Teddy Bear, feet apart....................................**$250.00**
Brush, Teddy Bear, feet together...............................**$200.00**
Brush, Three Bears **$100.00**
Brush, Treasure Chest, #W28, 1962..........................**$150.00**
California Originals, Big Bird on Nest, marked copyright
 Muppets Inc 976, from $50 to **$60.00**
California Originals, Circus Wagon, w/lion, from $75 to ..**$95.00**
California Originals, Cookie Monster, marked copyright
 Muppets Inc 970, from $45 to **$65.00**
California Originals, Cookie Safe w/Sitting Cat, marked 2630.**$35.00**
California Originals, Crocodile, from $80 to..............**$100.00**
California Originals, Eeyore, minimum value............**$450.00**
California Originals, Elf Schoolhouse, from $40 to.....**$50.00**
California Originals, Frog w/Bow Tie, USA #2645, from $45
 to **$55.00**
California Originals, Gumball Machine, from $50 to ..**$65.00**
California Originals, Juggler Clown, from $90 to......**$125.00**
California Originals, Oscar the Grouch, marked copyright
 Muppets Inc 972 ....**$75.00**
California Originals, Owl on Stump **$30.00**
California Originals, Rabbit w/Cookie, from $35 to....**$50.00**
California Originals, Sheriff on Cookie Safe **$50.00**
California Originals, Shoe House, mouse in door.......**$40.00**
California Originals, Train Engine, from $40 to...........**$60.00**
California Originals, Yawning Lion, from $225 to.....**$250.00**
Cardinal, Cookie Safe, USA #309..............................**$110.00**
Cardinal, Cookieville Bus Co, school bus, from $325 to..**$350.00**

Cardinal, Garage (Free Parking for Cookies), USA #306, from $85 to...$95.00
Cardinal, Sad Clown...$225.00
Cardinal, Soldier (Drum Major)................................$200.00
Cardinal, Telephone, USA #311, $65 to $75.00
Carol Gifford, Mammy w/Pancake, 1987.................$130.00
Certified Int'l, Barney Rubble.....................................$40.00
Certified Int'l, Bugs Bunny..$40.00
Certified Int'l, Road Runner $45.00
Certified Int'l, Tasmanian Devil.................................$45.00
Certified Int'l, Yosemite Sam......................................$40.00
Clay Art, Wizard of Oz 50th Anniversary.................$65.00
Cleminson, Card King, rare.......................................$600.00
Cleminson, Cookie Book $95.00
Cleminson, Cookie Box..$85.00
Cleminson, Cookie Canister, Cherries $65.00
Cleminson, Cookie Canister, Gala Gray.....................$65.00
Cleminson, Gingerbread House...................................$85.00
Cleminson, Mother's Best..$225.00

Cleminson, Potbellied Stove, from $80.00 to $100.00.

Cleminson, Yellow Heart $300.00
Dan Brechner, Donald Duck $450.00
Dept 56, Mirage Cactus, lg green body w/yellow base & red blossom finial on lid...$40.00
Dept 56, Someone's Kitchen Mammy, from $125 to ..$150.00
Doranne of California, Bloodhound, yellow $50.00
Doranne of California, Brown Bagger $40.00
Doranne of California, Camel, marked J8 USA, from $75 to.$90.00
Doranne of California, Cookie Cola, marked CJ68 USA, 1984, from $40 to..$50.00
Doranne of California, Cow Jumping Over the Moon, yellow, marked J2 USA, late 1950s...................................$250.00
Doranne of California, Fancy Cat w/Bow Tie, marked J5 USA, from $40 to $55.00
Doranne of California, Green Pepper, marked CJ 30 USA..$35.00
Doranne of California, Lion, marked, KO3 USA, from $40 to.$50.00
Doranne of California, Lunch Bucket, from $45 to.....$55.00
Doranne of California, Seal, marked USA 17 ....$40.00
Doranne of California, Walrus, from $50 to................$70.00
Dorrane of California, Dog w/Bow............................$60.00
Enesco, Betsy Ross $225.00
Enesco, Bulldog Cookie Guard, w/hydrant, from $35 to..$45.00
Enesco, Circus Elephant...$85.00
Enesco, Circus Wagon $95.00
Enesco, Coke Machine $58.00

Enesco, Cookie Monster...$70.00
Enesco, Human Bean, Kids Love Cookies, 1981, from $50 to.$85.00
Enesco, Ice Cream Shop $48.00
Enesco, Mickey Mouse w/Straw Hat.........................$75.00
Fitz & Floyd, Black Boy in Turban $600.00
Fitz & Floyd, Bunny Bloomers, from $150 to $175.00
Fitz & Floyd, Bunny Bonnet......................................$110.00
Fitz & Floyd, Bunny Hop Pink Cadillac...................$295.00
Fitz & Floyd, Car w/Flat Tire...................................$275.00
Fitz & Floyd, Cat Holding Fish $65.00
Fitz & Floyd, Caterine the Great, Reigning Cats & Dogs Series 1990..$125.00
Fitz & Floyd, Cinderella Fairy Godmother...............$100.00
Fitz & Floyd, Cookie Factory $85.00
Fitz & Floyd, Dot Kangaroo.....................................$175.00
Fitz & Floyd, Famous Amos, signed $150.00
Fitz & Floyd, Halloween Hoedown Witch, w/cauldron, cat & lizard, from $100 to...$140.00
Fitz & Floyd, Halloween Witch, black robe, basket on arm, from $100 to..$130.00
Fitz & Floyd, Harvest Farm Piggly Pig....................$135.00
Fitz & Floyd, Hat Box Bunnies.................................$160.00
Fitz & Floyd, Hat Party Bear....................................$175.00
Fitz & Floyd, Hippo Limpix, from $60 to $85.00
Fitz & Floyd, Holiday Leaves Deer $160.00
Fitz & Floyd, Jungle Elephant...................................$250.00
Fitz & Floyd, Kittens of Knightsbridge.....................$100.00
Fitz & Floyd, Man Playing Bass Viol (older jar)........$195.00
Fitz & Floyd, Mother Rabbit, from $70 to...................$90.00
Fitz & Floyd, Old Woman in Shoe, from $85 to $110.00
Fitz & Floyd, Paint Party Hedda Gobbler Turkey $80.00
Fitz & Floyd, Panda w/plaid scarf & holly-decorated red hat...$150.00
Fitz & Floyd, Parrots...$15.00
Fitz & Floyd, Petting Zoo, Hippo.............................$150.00
Fitz & Floyd, Pink Dinosaur, from $120 to...............$140.00
Fitz & Floyd, Plaid Teddy (figural bear) $175.00
Fitz & Floyd, Polka-Dot Witch, from $250 to...........$325.00
Fitz & Floyd, Prunella Pig..$125.00
Fitz & Floyd, Queen of Hearts $175.00
Fitz & Floyd, Rolls Royce, Christmas, Signature collection 1986 ....$895.00
Fitz & Floyd, Santa & Reindeer in Rolls Royce, lg....$875.00
Fitz & Floyd, Santa in Airplane, lg, from $1,800 to .$2,000.00
Fitz & Floyd, Santa in Sleigh, from $150 to.............$175.00
Fitz & Floyd, Santa on Motorcycle, from $500 to $600.00
Fitz & Floyd, Scarlet O'Hare, from $100 to $125.00
Fitz & Floyd, Sheriff, black & white full figure, minimum value $450.00
Fitz & Floyd, Southwest Santa, from $500 to $575.00
Fitz & Floyd, The Runaway (older jar) $475.00
Fitz & Floyd, Three Little Kittens.............................$175.00
Fitz & Floyd, Wanda the Witch................................$190.00
Fitz & Floyd, Woodland Santa Centerpiece $475.00
Fitz & Foyd, Old Woman in a Shoe $85.00
Fredericksburg Art Pottery Co, Bear, marked FAPCo..$55.00
Fredericksburg Art Pottery Co, Hen w/Chick on Back, marked FAPCo, from $45 to..$55.00
Fredericksburg Art Pottery Co, Windmill, marked FAPCo...$35.00

Gilner, Rooster, #622, from $50 to...............................$65.00

Hasbro, Transformer, Portugal.................................$125.00

Hearth & Home Designs, Birdhouse, marked (c) H&HD...$40.00

Hearth & Home Designs, Butch Calfidy, from $50 to...$75.00

Hearth & Home Designs, Cat w/Kittens, marked (c) H&HD, from $35 to...$45.00

Hearth & Home Designs, Elephant, from $50 to........$65.00

Hearth & Home Designs, School Bus, from $50 to....$60.00

Holiday Designs, Elephant.......................................$65.00

Holiday Designs, Lion w/Crown, green.....................$42.00

Holiday Designs, Orange, marked #9045 ....$25.00

Holiday Designs, Owl..$38.00

Holt Howard, Apple..$40.00

Holt Howard, Mice...$50.00

Holt Howard, Santa, 3-pc.......................................$145.00

Italy, Dog w/Dog Biscuit, marked.............................$65.00

Japan, Alice in Wonderland, from $100 to $125.00

Japan, Cookie Time Clock w/Mouse Finial.................$20.00

Japan, Cookies Can w/Raccoon.................................$20.00

Japan, Grandma (If All Else Fails Ask Grandma).........$20.00

Japan, Hippo w/Baseball Cap, from $25 to.................$35.00

Japan, Horse Mechanic, from $35 to..........................$45.00

Japan, Ice Cream Cone..$24.00

Japan, Pear w/Smiling Face, marked 6 C 30 ....$20.00

Japan, Raggedy Ann Seated, Cookies lettered on hat...$45.00

JC Miller, Grandma Bell...$80.00

Lane, Churn, marked USA...$38.00

Lane, Clown w/Umbrella, 1950 ....$200.00

Lane, Cowboy (watch for reproductions), minimum value $500.00

Los Angeles Pottery, Bakery, marked Made in USA...XX95, 1956 ....$45.00

Los Angeles Pottery, Christmas Tree, marked ...(c) 58 made in USA XX99..$40.00

Los Angeles Pottery, Owl, marked, Calif USA #81 (c) 62...$35.00

Maddux, Cat Dressed for Shopping $150.00

Maddux, Chipmunk on Stump, #2110 ....$140.00

Maddux, Clown..$395.00

Maddux, Humpty Dumpty, #2113 ....$300.00

Maddux, Queen #2104 or King #2103, each $140.00

Maddux, Rabbit Dressed for Shopping, from $150 to...$175.00

Maddux, Raggedy Andy $300.00

Marcia Ceramics, Bear w/Beehive on Stump $40.00

Marcia Ceramics, Bear w/Cookie, marked (c) 84........$40.00

Marcia Ceramics, Love Hippy Hippo $45.00

Marcia Ceramics, Mushroom House...........................$35.00

Marcia Ceramics, Pig Conductor..............................$25.00

Marcia Ceramics, Sheriff, marked, KJ 5 USA $45.00

Marcia Ceramics, Snowman w/Candy Cane, marked (c) 84.$100.00

Marcia Ceramics, Tortoise & the Hare.......................$30.00

Maurice of California, Cookie Clown, 1976.............$225.00

Maurice of California, Fruit Basket, marked USA FR211 ...$30.00

Maurice of California, Indian Scout, from $50 to.......$75.00

McCoy, Animal Crackers, from $100 to $120.00

McCoy, Apple, 1950-64, $50 to.................................$65.00

McCoy, Apple on Basketweave, from $60 to $70.00

McCoy, Asparagus..$50.00

McCoy, Bananas, from $100 to.................................$125.00

McCoy, Baseball Boy...$225.00

McCoy, Basket of Eggs, from $40 to $60.00

McCoy, Basket of Potatoes, from $30 to.....................$50.00

McCoy, Bear w/Cookie in Vest, no 'Cookies,' from $75 to..$95.00

McCoy, Bicentennial Milk Can, silver or brown, each..$30.00

McCoy, Blue Willow Pitcher $50.00

McCoy, Bobby Baker, from $80 to.............................$100.00

McCoy, Bugs Bunny, cylinder $225.00

McCoy, Burlap Sack, from $25 to.............................$35.00

McCoy, Caboose $165.00

McCoy, Cat on Coal Scuttle $200.00

McCoy, Chairman of the Board, minimum value......$400.00

McCoy, Chef, from $125 to $140.00

McCoy, Chinese Lantern...$75.00

McCoy, Chipmunk, from $125 to $150.00

McCoy, Clown (Little), from $80 to...........................$100.00

McCoy, Clown Bust, smiling.....................................$85.00

McCoy, Coca-Cola Can, from $75 to $100.00

McCoy, Coca-Cola Jug, from $60 to $85.00

McCoy, Coffee Grinder...$45.00

McCoy, Coffee Mug...$40.00

McCoy, Cookie Barrel...$40.00

McCoy, Cookie Cabin, from $100 to $125.00

McCoy, Cookie Log, from $65 to...............................$75.00

McCoy, Cookie Safe...$65.00

McCoy, Cookstove, black, from $25 to $50.00

McCoy, Corn, from $150 to $200.00

McCoy, Dog on Basketweave.....................................$85.00

McCoy, Duck on Basketweave, from $75 to............$100.00

McCoy, Dutch Boy..$55.00

McCoy, Dutch Boy & Girl, image on each side, rare .$150.00

McCoy, Dutch Treat Barn, from $65 to......................$75.00

McCoy, Eagle on Basket..$35.00

McCoy, Elephant...$200.00

McCoy, Fireplace (Colonial)......................................$95.00

McCoy, Football Boy $225.00

McCoy, Frog on Stump $45.00

McCoy, Frontier Family $50.00

McCoy, Gingerbread Boy, cylindrical........................$75.00

McCoy, Grandfather Clock..$85.00

McCoy, Granny, from $90 to $120.00

McCoy, Granny, gold trim $125.00

McCoy, Green Pepper, from $35 to............................$45.00

McCoy, Happy Face $75.00

McCoy, Kangaroo, blue...$300.00

McCoy, Keebler Tree House, from $75 to $95.00

McCoy, Kittens on Basketweave, $90.00.

McCoy, Lemon $50.00
McCoy, Mushrooms on Stump, from $25 to $40.00
McCoy, Oaken Bucket...$35.00
McCoy, Picnic Basket, from $75 to $85.00
McCoy, Potbellied Stove, black, from $25 to.............$50.00
McCoy, Rabbit on Stump $45.00
McCoy, Red Bird on Burlap Sack...........................$40.00
McCoy, Snoopy on Doghouse...............................$295.00
McCoy, Spaniel in Doghouse, pup finial.................$295.00
McCoy, Squirrel on Stump $40.00
McCoy, Strawberry, 1955-57..................................$55.00
McCoy, Strawberry, 1971-75..................................$55.00
McCoy, Timmy the Tortoise....................................$40.00
McCoy, Two Kittens in Basket $700.00
McCoy, Upside Down Bear, panda $60.00
Metlox, Apple, red, from $75 to $100.00
Metlox, Bear as Ballerina $140.00
Metlox, Bear on Roller Skates, from $100 to............$130.00
Metlox, Bird on Pine Cone, stain finish.....................$80.00
Metlox, Bucky Beaver, from $175 to $250.00
Metlox, Calf, says Moo, minimum value...................$375.00
Metlox, Cat, calico design, cream w/blue ribbon $150.00
Metlox, Clown, yellow $150.00
Metlox, Cookie Boy, from $325 to $350.00
Metlox, Daisy Topiary $75.00
Metlox, Dina-Stegosarus Dinosaur, any color except lavender
    (experimental) $175.00
Metlox, Dog, gingham design, cream w/blue collar..$150.00
Metlox, Drummer Boy, minimum value $500.00
Metlox, Dutch Girl w/Mixing Bowl.........................$190.00
Metlox, Goosey Lucy, from $160 to $175.00
Metlox, Humpty Dumpty, seated, w/feet, from $250 to ..$275.00
Metlox, Katy Kat, from $95 to $110.00
Metlox, Koala Bear, from $110 to..........................$135.00
Metlox, Mouse Chef, from $100 to $125.00
Metlox, Owl, blue, from $65 to $75.00
Metlox, Owl (Snow) $65.00
Metlox, Panda Bear, no lollipop.............................$100.00
Metlox, Panda Bear, w/lollipop, minimum value......$350.00
Metlox, Pinocchio, minimum value.........................$350.00
Metlox, Pretty Anne, from $175 to $200.00
Metlox, Pretzel Barrel..$125.00
Metlox, Rabbit on Cabbage....................................$175.00
Metlox, Raggedy Ann, Poppytrail, from $125 to $175.00
Metlox, Shock of Wheat, from $100 to $125.00
Metlox, Sir Francis Drake, from $40 to $60.00
Metlox, Slenderella Pig, standing on scale $150.00
Metlox, Sombrero Bear, from $140 to......................$165.00
Metlox, Squirrel on Pine Cone, decorated, from $90 to...$110.00
Metlox, Walrus, brown & white, from $350 to $375.00
Morton, Poodle Head, white w/green trim.................$75.00
NAPCo, Cinderella $250.00
NAPCo, Little Bo Peep $250.00
NAPCo, Woody Woodpecker...................................$400.00
National Silver, Mammy, from $200 to.....................$250.00
Newcor, Cookie Monster...$45.00
Norcrest, Elephant $55.00
Norcrest, Emmet Kelly..$90.00
Norcrest, Goose $60.00

Norcrest, Owl...$60.00
North American Ceramics, Cadillac, pink w/whitewalls...$175.00
Omnibus, Cowboy, from $50 to.............................$60.00
Pfaltzgraff, Chef, white outfit & hat, French-style mustache &
    goatee $200.00
Pfaltzgraff, Old Woman in a Shoe, from $200 to $250.00
Pfaltzgraff, USS Enterprise, from $60 to $85.00
Pottery Guild, Balloon Lady, from $100 to...............$125.00
Pottery Guild, Girl Holding Chest $135.00
Pottery Guild, Rooster $75.00
Red Wing, Bob White $125.00
Red Wing, Chef (Pierre), brown $195.00
Red Wing, Crock, white $60.00
Red Wing, Dutch Girl, yellow w/brown trim............$140.00
Red Wing, Friar Tuck, yellow.................................$175.00
Red Wing, Grapes...$225.00
Red Wing, Pineapple, yellow $200.00
Regal China, Churn Boy, from $275 to $295.00
Regal China, Davy Crockett Bust, from $550 to........$585.00
Regal China, Diaper Pin Pig, from $500 to $600.00
Regal China, Hobby Horse $250.00
Regal China, Humpty Dumpty, on yellow wall $450.00
Regal China, Humpty Dumpty, red wall..................$325.00
Regal China, Kraft Bear $150.00
Regal China, Miss Muffett.......................................$385.00
Regal China, Quaker Oats Canister..........................$125.00
Regal China, Three Bears.......................................$285.00
Regal China, Tulip...$300.00
Robinson Ransbottom, Cow Jumped Over the Moon...$250.00
Robinson Ransbottom, Dutch Boy, from $250 to $265.00
Robinson Ransbottom, Dutch Girl, from $250 to......$265.00
Robinson Ransbottom, Sailor Jack...........................$195.00

Robinson Ransbottom, Wise Owl, from $55.00 to $75.00.

Robinson Ransbottom, Wise Owl, w/gold trim, from $150
to $175.00
Roman Ceramics, Monk $80.00
Roman Ceramics, R2-D2, from $125 to.....................$145.00
Sears, Sunbonnet Baby, 1972..................................$75.00
Shawnee, Basketweave, hexagon shape, marked USA, mini-
    mum value $50.00
Shawnee, Dutch Boy, decals & gold trim, marked USA, min-
    imum value $250.00
Shawnee, Dutch Boy, double stripes, marked USA, minimum
    value $175.00
Shawnee, Dutch Boy, patches, gold trim, marked USA, min-
    imum value $275.00

Shawnee, Dutch Girl, cold paint, marked USA, minimum value **$75.00**

Shawnee, Dutch Girl, tulips, marked USA, minimum value **$100.00**

Shawnee, Elephant, pink, marked 60, minimum value .**$150.00**

Shawnee, Elephant Sitting, cold paint, marked USA, minimum value..**$75.00**

Shawnee, Fernware, octagonal shape, marked, USA, minimum value...**$75.00**

Shawnee, Fruit Basket, gold trim, #84, minimum value...**$200.00**

Shawnee, Little Chef, brown cold paint, marked USA, minimum value...**$60.00**

Shawnee, Owl, gold trim, marked USA, minimum value .**$225.00**

Shawnee, Puss 'N Boots, minimum value **$150.00**

Shawnee, Smiley the Pig, shamrock w/gold trim, marked USA, minimum value...**$400.00**

Shawnee, Smiley the Pig, shamrocks w/gold trim, marked USA, minimum value...**$325.00**

Shawnee, Winnie the Pig, blue collar, marked USA, minimum value **$225.00**

Shawnee, Winnie the Pig, red collar w/gold trim, minimum value **$350.00**

Sierra Vista, Canister, w/rooster, square......................**$75.00**

Sierra Vista, Circus Wagon, 1957, from $125 to **$140.00**

Sierra Vista, Clown Bust...**$80.00**

Sierra Vista, Poodle, 1956, from $225 to....................**$250.00**

Sierra Vista, Squirrel, from $100 to.............................**$140.00**

Sierra Vista, Stagecoach...**$250.00**

Sierra Vista, Telephone, from $50 to.............................**$75.00**

Sierra Vista, Train Engine...**$115.00**

Sigma, Circus Fat Lady, from $225 to **$250.00**

Sigma, Fireman Beaver, from $235 to **$285.00**

Sigma, Kabuke Dancer, from $150 to **$175.00**

Sigma, Puppy Is a Rabbit...**$385.00**

Taiwan, Mammy, patterned after cast-iron bank.........**$35.00**

Treasure Craft, Baseball Boy.......................................**$60.00**

Treasure Craft, Bunny in Straw Hat, from $50 to........**$60.00**

Treasure Craft, Cactus...**$40.00**

Treasure Craft, Carousel...**$55.00**

Treasure Craft, Castle, from $50 to.............................**$70.00**

Treasure Craft, Cat, Stitch in Time, from $45 to..........**$65.00**

Treasure Craft, Cat Holding Rose, marked Susan-Marie...USA **$45.00**

Treasure Craft, Clock, marked copyright Made in USA ..**$45.00**

Treasure Craft, Clown, from $75 to.............................**$95.00**

Treasure Craft, Conductor Bear, from $50 to.............**$70.00**

Treasure Craft, Cookie Barn.......................................**$45.00**

Treasure Craft, Cookie Chef, marked copyright USA, from $45 to **$55.00**

Treasure Craft, Cookie Van, marked Made in USA **$70.00**

Treasure Craft, Cookieville House, marked copyright Made in USA **$45.00**

Treasure Craft, Covered Wagon, from $55 to **$85.00**

Treasure Craft, Dinosaur, Cookiesaurus **$75.00**

Treasure Craft, Dog on Sled..**$60.00**

Treasure Craft, Eight Ball, marked Made in USA, from $45 to **$70.00**

Treasure Craft, Famous Amos Sack **$85.00**

Treasure Craft, Farmer Pig, from $40 to.....................**$65.00**

Treasure Craft, Football, marked Made in USA **$42.00**

Treasure Craft, Football House, Rose Petal Series, David Kirschner **$325.00**

Treasure Craft, Golf Ball, from $35 to.........................**$50.00**

Treasure Craft, Granny, from $50 to **$70.00**

Treasure Craft, Hobo, from $45 to **$65.00**

Treasure Craft, Ice Wagon, from $50 to......................**$70.00**

Treasure Craft, Jukebox (Wurlitzer), marked Made in USA **$115.00**

Treasure Craft, Leopard, from $50 to **$65.00**

Treasure Craft, Lila Lamb, from $50 to........................**$70.00**

Treasure Craft, Mickey or Minnie Mouse, each..........**$85.00**

Treasure Craft, Mrs Owl, from $40 to **$50.00**

Treasure Craft, Mrs Potts, from $60 to **$70.00**

Treasure Craft, Pig, pink head & feet w/glass-bowl middle **$75.00**

Treasure Craft, Potbellied Stove, marked Made in USA, from $40 to...**$60.00**

Treasure Craft, Rocking Horse, marked copyright Made in USA, from $45 to.............................**$60.00**

Treasure Craft, Sailor Elephant, from $60 to..............**$75.00**

Treasure Craft, Snowman **$60.00**

Treasure Craft, Sweetheart Cat, from $45 to..............**$65.00**

Treasure Craft, Teddy Bear, from $40 to.....................**$60.00**

Treasure Craft, Victorian House.................................**$80.00**

Twin Winton, Apple w/Worm, wood stain w/painted details..**$120.00**

Twin Winton, Bambi w/Squirrel Finial, wood stain w/painted detail..**$175.00**

Twin Winton, Barrel of Cookies (no mouse), wood stain w/painted detail..**$75.00**

Twin Winton, Barrel of Cookies w/Mouse Finial, wood stain w/painted detail **$75.00**

Twin Winton, Butler, wood stain w/painted detail, minimum value..**$300.00**

Twin Winton, Cookie Barn, Collector Series, fully painted...**$175.00**

Twin Winton, Cookie Barn, wood stain w/painted detail or gray, each...**$80.00**

Twin Winton, Cookie Catcher, wood stain w/painted detail or gray, each..**$100.00**

Twin Winton, Cookie Elf, Collector Series, fully painted....**$250.00**

Twin Winton, Cookie House, wood stain w/painted detail **$175.00**

Twin Winton, Cop, wood stain w/painted detail or gray, each **$100.00**

Twin Winton, Cop (Policeman), Collector Series, fully painted...**$250.00**

Twin Winton, Dinosaur, wood stain w/painted detail, minimum value..**$900.00**

Twin Winton, Dog w/Lg Bow, wood stain w/painted detail or gray, each...**$125.00**

Twin Winton, Donkey w/Cart, wood stain w/painted detail, avocado green, pineapple yellow or orange, each..**$90.00**

Twin Winton, Donkey w/Straw Hat, Collector Series, fully painted...**$175.00**

Twin Winton, Dutch Girl, Collector Series, fully painted..**$250.00**

Twin Winton, Dutch Girl, wood stain w/painted detail .**$100.00**

Twin Winton, Elf Bakery, wood stain w/painted detail....**$90.00**

Twin Winton, Elf on Stump, wood stain w/painted detail, avocado green, pineapple yellow or orange, each..............$65.00

Twin Winton, Fire Truck, wood stain w/painted detail..$85.00

Twin Winton, Foo Dog, wood stain w/painted detail, avocado green, pineapple yellow, orange or red, each.......$85.00

Twin Winton, Gorilla, wood stain w/painted detail, minimum value......................$350.00

Twin Winton, Grandma w/Bowl of Cookies (Lg), wood stain w/painted detail......................$110.00

Twin Winton, Grandma w/Bowl of Cookies (Sm), wood stain w/painted detail......................$80.00

Twin Winton, Gunfighter Rabbit, Collector Series, fully painted......................$200.00

Twin Winton, Hen on Nest, wood stain w/painted detail..$125.00

Twin Winton, Hobby Horse, Collector Series, fully painted......................$250.00

Twin Winton, Jack-in-the-Box, wood stain w/painted detail, minimum value......................$350.00

Twin Winton, Lamb, Collector Series, fully painted .$175.00

Twin Winton, Lighthouse, wood stain w/painted detail.$250.00

Twin Winton, Mother Goose, Collector Series, fully painted......................$275.00

Twin Winton, Ole King Cole, wood stain w/painted detail, minimum value......................$450.00

Twin Winton, Owl, Collector Series, fully painted ...$100.00

Twin Winton, Peanut Man, wood stain w/painted detail......................$1,000.00

Twin Winton, Pear w/Worm, wood stain w/painted detail, avocado green, pineapple yellow, orange or red, each......................$120.00

Twin Winton, Persian Cat, wood stain w/painted detail..$140.00

Twin Winton, Pirate Fox, Collector Series, fully painted..$250.00

Twin Winton, Pirate Fox, wood stain w/painted detail ..$85.00

Twin Winton, Pot O' Cookies, wood stain w/painted detail, avocado green, pineapple yellow or orange, each $40.00

Twin Winton, Potbellied Stove, wood stain w/painted detail, avocado green, pineapple yellow, orange or red, each......................$85.00

Twin Winton, Raggedy Andy (Flopsy), Collector Series, fully painted......................$200.00

Twin Winton, Raggedy Ann (Mopsy), Collector Series, fully painted......................$200.00

Twin Winton, Ranger Bear, Collector Series, fully painted..$100.00

Twin Winton, Rooster, Collector Series, fully painted...$100.00

Twin Winton, Sailor Elephant, Collector Series, fully painted......................$125.00

Twin Winton, Sailor Mouse, Collector Series, fully painted $250.00

Twin Winton, Sheriff Bear, Collector Series, fully painted $200.00

Twin Winton, Sheriff Bear, wood stain w/painted detail $75.00

Twin Winton, Snail w/Elf Finial, wood stain w/painted detail......................$175.00

Twin Winton, Squirrel w/Acorns, wood stain w/painted detail or gray, each......................$75.00

Twin Winton, Teddy Bear, wood stain w/painted detail ..$85.00

Twin Winton, Tug Boat, wood stain w/painted detail....$250.00

Twin Winton, Ye Olde Cookie Bucket, wood stain w/painted detail......................$60.00

Vallona Starr, Peter Pumpkin Eater, Design Pat copyright 49 Ct 49 California......................$425.00

Vallona Starr, Peter, Peter Pumpkin Eater, orange w/hand-painted details, minimum value $375.00

Vallona Starr, Squirrel on Stump, #86......................$75.00

Vallona Starr, Winkie, original pink & yellow w/blush (mold was sold, beware of other colors), from $600 to..$900.00

Vandor, Betty Boop, as cook......................$75.00

Vandor, Betty Boop, standing, minimum value.........$600.00

Vandor, Betty Boop Head, marked Copyright, 1983 KFS, w/paper label, from $75 to......................$100.00

Vandor, Betty Boop Holiday 1994......................$125.00

Vandor, Betty Boop Holiday 1995......................$50.00

Vandor, Betty Boop Kitchen......................$40.00

Vandor, Cowboy, from $60 to......................$80.00

Vandor, Fred Flintstone, standing......................$125.00

Vandor, Howdy Doody Bumper Car, 1988, minimum value......................$325.00

Vandor, Howdy Doody Bust, winks eye, w/paper label, minimum value......................$375.00

Vandor, Jukebox, booth style......................$150.00

Vandor, Jukebox, 1985......................$125.00

Vandor, Mona Lisa......................$65.00

Vandor, Popeye Head, w/winking eye, marked 1980 King Features Syndicate, from $400 to $450.00

Vandor, Radio, from $80 to......................$95.00

Vandor, Socks, from $50 to......................$65.00

Wisecarver, Indian Chief......................$180.00

Wisecarver, Indian Maid......................$180.00

Wisecarver, Saturday Bath......................$265.00

Yona, clown head, rare......................$295.00

Yona, elephant w/clown......................$650.00

Coors Rosebud Dinnerware

Golden, Colorado, was the site for both the Coors Brewing Company and the Coors Porcelain Company, each founded by the same man, Adolph Coors. The pottery's beginning was in 1910, and in the early years they manufactured various ceramic products such as industrial needs, dinnerware, vases, and figurines, but their most famous line and the one we want to tell you about was 'Rosebud.'

The Rosebud 'Cook 'n Serve' line was introduced in 1934. It's very easy to spot, and after you've once seen a piece, you'll be able to recognize it instantly. It was made in solid colors — rose, blue, green, yellow, ivory, and orange. The rose bud and leaves are embossed and hand-painted in contrasting colors. There are nearly fifty different pieces to collect, and bargains can still be found; but prices are accelerating, due to increased collector interest. For more information we recommend *Collector's Encyclopedia of Colorado Pottery, Identification and Values,* written by Carol and Jim Carlton.

Note: To evaluate pieces in ivory, add 10% to the prices listed.

Advisor: Rick Spencer (See Directory, Regal)

Newsletter: *Coors Pottery Newsletter*
Robert Schneider
3808 Carr Pl. N
Seattle, WA 98103-8126

Baker, deep, 4x6"..	**$35.00**
Bowl, batter; handled, no lid, 3½-pint........................	**$65.00**
Bowl, cereal; 6", from $25 to.................................	**$30.00**
Bowl, cream soup; 4"...	**$30.00**
Bowl, mixing; no Rosebud, 9".................................	**$65.00**
Bowl, pudding; tab handles, 5"..............................	**$35.00**
Casserole, triple service, 2-pt, w/lid.......................	**$65.00**
Creamer	**$35.00**
Cup & saucer	**$35.00**
Egg cup	**$60.00**
French casserole, 7½" dia, w/lid............................	**$80.00**
Honey pot, no spoon, w/lid, from $150 to...................	**$170.00**
Loaf pan, $40 to...	**$55.00**
Pantry jar, Deluxe, tab handles, hand painted, 8-pt ...	**$80.00**
Pie plate, from $35 to......................................	**$50.00**

Pitcher, water; English, $150.00.

Pitcher, w/lid, lg	**$150.00**
Plate, soup; 8"...	**$35.00**
Plate, 10"...	**$30.00**
Plate, 7"...	**$20.00**
Plate, 7"...	**$12.00**
Platter, 9x12"	**$40.00**
Salt & pepper shakers, range size, pr, from $35 to.....	**$50.00**
Shirred egg dish, 6½".....................................	**$35.00**
Sugar shaker, from $50 to..................................	**$60.00**
Teapot, 6-cup..	**$145.00**
Tumbler, footed or handled, from $100 to................	**$125.00**

Cottage Ware

Made by several companies, cottage ware is a line of ceramic table and kitchen accessories, each piece styled as a cozy cottage with a thatched roof. At least four English potteries made the ware, and you'll find pieces marked 'Japan' as well as 'Occupied Japan.' From Japan you'll also find pieces styled as windmills and water wheels, though the quality is inferior. The better pieces are marked 'Price Brothers' and 'Occupied Japan.' They're compatible in coloring as well as in styling, and values run about the same. Items marked simply 'Japan' are worth considerably less.

Bowl, salad; English	**$65.00**
Butter dish, English.......................................	**$45.00**
Butter pat, embossed cottage, rectangular, Occupied Japan...	**$17.50**
Chocolate pot, English.....................................	**$135.00**
Condiment set, 2 shakers & mustard on tray, Occupied Japan...	**$45.00**
Cookie jar, pink, brown & green, square, Japan, 8½x5½" ..	**$65.00**
Cookie jar/canister, cylindrical, English	**$85.00**
Creamer, windmill, Occupied Japan, 2⅝"..................	**$15.00**
Creamer & sugar bowl, English, 2½", 4½"	**$45.00**
Creamer & sugar bowl, w/lid, on tray, Occupied Japan...	**$65.00**
Cup & saucer, English, 2½", 4½"..........................	**$45.00**
Demitasse pot, English.....................................	**$100.00**
Dish w/cover, Occupied Japan, sm..........................	**$35.00**
Grease jar, Occupied Japan.................................	**$35.00**
Marmalade, English...	**$40.00**
Mug, Price Bros...	**$50.00**
Pin tray, English, 4" dia	**$20.00**
Pitcher, water; English.....................................	**$150.00**
Salt & pepper shakers, windmill, Occupied Japan, pr ..	**$20.00**
Sugar bowl, windmill, w/lid, Occupied Japan, 3⅞"....	**$25.00**
Sugar box, for cubes, English, 5¾" long....................	**$45.00**
Tea set, child's, Japan, serves 4...........................	**$150.00**
Teapot, English or Occupied Japan, 5".....................	**$45.00**
Teapot, English or Occupied Japan, 6½"...................	**$50.00**
Toast rack, English, $65 to.................................	**$75.00**
Tumbler, Occupied Japan, 3½".............................	**$10.00**

Cowboy Character Memorabilia

When we come across what are now called cowboy character toys and memorabilia, it rekindles warm memories of childhood days for those of us who once 'rode the range' (often our backyards), with these gallant heroes. Today we can really appreciate them for the positive role models they were. They sat tall in the saddle, reminded us never to tell an un-truth, to respect 'women-folk' as well as our elders, animal life, our flag, our country, and our teachers; to eat all the cereal placed before us in order to build strong bodies; to worship God, and have (above all else) a strong value system that couldn't be compromised. They were Gene, Roy, and Tex, along with a couple of dozen other names, who rode beautiful steeds such as Champion, Trigger, and White Flash.

They rode into a final sunset on the silver screen only to return and ride into our homes via television in the 1950s. The next decade found us caught up in more western adventures such as Bonanza, Wagon Train, The Rifleman, and many more. These set the stage for a second wave of toys, games, and western outfits.

Annie Oakley was one of only a couple of cowgirls in the corral; Wild Bill Elliott used to drawl, 'I'm a peaceable man'; Ben Cartwright, Adam, Hoss, and Little Joe provided us with thrills and laughter. Some of the earliest collectibles are represented by Roy's and Gene's 1920s predecessors — Buck Jones, Hoot Gibson, Tom Mix, and Ken Maynard. There were so many others, all of whom were very real to us in the 1930s–'60s, just as their memories and values remain very real to us today.

Remember that few items of cowboy memorabilia have survived to the present in mint condition. When found, mint or near-mint items bring hefty prices, and they continue to escalate every year. Our values are for examples in good to very good condition.

For more information we recommend these books: *Roy Rogers, Singing Cowboy Stars, Silver Screen Cowboys, Hollywood Cowboy Heroes,* and *Western Comics: A Comprehensive Reference* by Robert W. Phillips.

Advisor: Robert W. Phillips, Phillips Archives (See Directory, Character and Personality Collectibles)

Club/Newsletter: Roy Rogers-Dale Evans Collectors Association
Nancy Horsley
P.O. Box 1166
Portsmouth, OH 45662-1116; Annual membership: $15 per year, includes free admission to annual convention

Club/Newsletter: Hopalong Cassidy Fan Club International and *Hopalong Cassidy Newsletter*
Laura Bates, Editor
6310 Friendship Dr.
New Concord, OH 4362-9708; 614-826-4850; Subscription: $15 US, $20 Canadian; includes quarterly newsletter and information about annual festival

Newsletter: *Gene Autry Star Telegram*
Gene Autry Development Association
Chamber of Commerce
P.O. Box 158
Gene Autry, OK 73436

Newsletter: *The Lone Ranger Silver Bullet*
P.O. Box 553
Forks, WA 98331; 206-327-3726; Subscription: $12 per year

Annie Oakley, book, Ghost Town Secret, Whitman #1538:49, 1957, 6x8" $20.00
Annie Oakley, bread label, black & white photo image on yellow background, Wonder Bread, EX $35.00
Annie Oakley, soap, Shooting Gallery, Pure Castile, 2 rows of soap ducks, unused, NMIB $100.00
Annie Oakley & Tagg, comic book, Dell No 4, 1955 .$40.00
Annie Oakley & Tagg, gun & holster set, Daisy, 1955, boxed $225.00
Bat Masterson, cane, chrome-looking plastic handle w/embossed name, 1958, 30", EX+ $25.00
Bat Masterson, cane, chrome-looking plastic handle w/embossed name, instruction booklet, 1958, 30", NM (original mailer) $90.00

Bonanza, cup, lithographed tin, EX, $15.00.

Bonanza, double holster set w/cap pistols, Halpern, 1965 ....$200.00
Bonanza, lunch box & thermos, Aladdin, 1965, M, $150 to $200.00
Broken Arrow, book, Little Golden, Simon & Schuster, 1957, 6½x8" $15.00
Buck Jones, book, Big Little Book, Whitman, 1934, 4¾x5¼" $50.00
Buck Jones, sheet music, Hidden Valley, 1936, 9x12" ..$40.00
Buffalo Bill, 5¢ weekly pulp, Buffalo Bill Stories, #467, April 23, 1948 ....$25.00
Buffalo Bill Jr, ring, 1950s, VG................................$45.00
Cheyenne, cap gun & double holster set, Daisy, 1959, NMIB $250.00
Cheyenne, cap gun & double holster set, Daisy, 1959, no box..$125.00
Cisco Kid, movie poster, In Old Mexico, 1945, 27x41"..$150.00
Cisco Kid, photograph, black & white, Butternut Bread, 1956, 8x10" $40.00
Cochise, doll, w/outfit & accessories, Excel, 9½", NM .$30.00
Dale Evans, comic book, Dell No 1 (Four Color No 479), photo cover, 1953 ....$80.00
Dale Evans, comic book, National Per Pub (DC) No 1, photo cover, 1948 ....$300.00
Dale Evans, fan, cardboard, 1950s, VG................$15.00
Dale Evans, outfit, red & tan skirt w/fringe, blue vest, EX $100.00
Dale Evans, outfit, 11-pc set, 1952, NMIB $500.00
Dale Evans, outfit, 11-pc set, 1952, no box..............$200.00
Dale Evans, record, Guitar Song, Varsity Records #8035, 78 rpm, 1930s..$20.00
Dale Evans, school bag, Queen of the West, Acme Brief Case Co, 1952 ....$150.00
Dale Evans, sheet music, I Dream of Jeanie, 1939, 9¼x12" $25.00
Daniel Boone, wallet, Fess Parker image, 1964, EX ...$35.00
Davy Crockett, belt, leather w/Frontierland illustration & lg metal buckle, child-size, EX................................$25.00
Davy Crockett, guitar, circular decal picturing Davy, EC/France, 24", EXIB..$350.00
Davy Crockett, night light, glass bust of Davy, Kupper, 1950s, 2", M (EX box) $75.00
Davy Crockett, suitcase, King of the Wild Frontier, raised image of Davy on horse, WDP, 7", EX................$85.00

Deputy, board game, Milton Bradley, 1960, 9½x19x2"..**$50.00**

Durango Kid, photograph, Dixie Ice Cream, 1937, 8x10"..**$45.00**

Gene Autry, book, Gene Autry & Champion, Little Golden #267, Simon & Schuster, 1950s **$20.00**

Gene Autry, book, Red Bandit's Ghost, Better Little Book #1461, Whitman, 1940s..........................**$45.00**

Gene Autry, cap pistol, gold-tone metal, Leslie Henry, 9".**$150.00**

Gene Autry, comic book, Dell No 115, 1957 ....**$15.00**

Gene Autry, guitar, plastic, w/instruction booklet, Emenee Industries, 1955, NMIB **$300.00**

Gene Autry, guitar, plastic, w/instruction booklet, Emenee Industries, 1955, no box..........................**$100.00**

Gene Autry, iron-on transfer, 1940s **$30.00**

Gene Autry, photo plaque, color, laminated, 1940s, 5½x4"...**$30.00**

Gene Autry, postcard, real photo, Sturditoy/Gene Autry Shirts, M.......................................**$18.00**

Gene Autry, poster, for personal appearance in Albany NY area, 1951, 9x6", EX...........................**$35.00**

Gene Autry, poster, Valley of Fire, 1951, 27x41".........**$75.00**

Gene Autry, record, Nine Little Reindeer, Republic No 2001, 45 rpm, multicolored photo sleeve, 1950s............**$12.00**

Gene Autry, ring, w/face, M...........................**$100.00**

Gene Autry, ring, w/flag, EX **$50.00**

Gunsmoke, magazine ad, L&M cigarettes, 1950s, full page..**$15.00**

Have Gun Will Travel, TV Guide, May 10, 1958.........**$25.00**

Hoot Gibson, leather holster & belt (no gun), 1930s .**$75.00**

Hopalong Cassidy, ad card, Bond Bread, NM.............**$18.00**

Hopalong Cassidy, bath towel, 20x38", faded **$25.00**

Hopalong Cassidy, board game, Milton Bradley, ca 1950, 9½x19"...**$100.00**

Hopalong Cassidy, cowboy hat, black felt, VG...........**$85.00**

Hopalong Cassidy, cup, 1950, 3"........................**$25.00**

Hopalong Cassidy, Dixie Ice Cream Cup lid, 1930s ...**$25.00**

Hopalong Cassidy, magazine, Life, June 12, 1950, Hoppy cover **$50.00**

Hopalong Cassidy, newspaper supplement cover, Colorama, Philadelphia Inquirer, February 21, 1954 ....**$75.00**

Hopalong Cassidy, pencil, gold letters on green, unused, VG **$15.00**

Hopalong Cassidy, photograph, reproduction publicity shot **$5.00**

Hopalong Cassidy, pulp magazine, Hopalong Cassidy's Western, #1 (Fall), 1950.........................**$150.00**

Hopalong Cassidy, ring, Bar-20, 1950s, VG.............**$50.00**

Hopalong Cassidy & Topper, figures, plastic, Ideal, 1950, 5"..**$125.00**

John Wayne, poster, Paradise Canyon, Hollywood Cowboy Heroes series, color reproduction, 1993 ....**$20.00**

John Wayne, puzzle, frame-tray jigsaw, Saalfield, 1951, 11½x15"..**$100.00**

Johnny Mack Brown, comic book, Dell No 6, 1951 ...**$30.00**

Ken Maynard, book, Whitman Penny Book/Whitman Publishing, 1938, 2½x3½"..........................**$30.00**

Ken Maynard, exhibit card, 1930s, 3½x5½" **$15.00**

Lash Larue, knife, plastic w/color illustration, Smoky Mountains Knife Works, 1990s..........................**$10.00**

Lash Larue, photo, facsimile signature, 1940s, 8x10"..**$70.00**

Lone Ranger, ballpoint pen, silver-tone metal, Everlast Pen Corp, 1950s, EXOC.................................**$165.00**

Lone Ranger, bandana, Cheerios cereal premium, 1940...**$75.00**

Lone Ranger, blotter, Bond Bread, 1940s, NM............**$20.00**

Lone Ranger, bolo tie, Half a Century, M...................**$22.00**

Lone Ranger, coloring book, Whitman, 1939, 14x11".**$75.00**

Lone Ranger, Deputy Kit, Cherrios, 1980, NM (original mailer) **$40.00**

Lone Ranger, doll, complete, Gabriel Ind Inc, 1973, 10", VG **$12.00**

Lone Ranger, exhibit card, 1930s, 3½x5½".................**$15.00**

Lone Ranger, key chain, silver bullet, Hamilton #P2875, MIB..**$15.00**

Lone Ranger, mask, cut from cereal box, EX.............**$35.00**

Lone Ranger, paperweight, Lucite silver bullet, M......**$15.00**

Lone Ranger, photocopy of newspaper comic strip, signed by Lone Ranger writer Paul S Newman or artist Tom Gill, 1990s...**$20.00**

Lone Ranger, publicity photo, color, signed by Clayton Moore, 1980s...**$40.00**

Lone Ranger, radio, white plastic case, Majestic, 1950s, 5x6x7½"..**$1,000.00**

Lone Ranger, target game, tin, Marx, 1938, NMIB **$125.00**

Lone Ranger, tattoo transfers, set of 4, Swell (bubble gum), 1960s, NM..**$25.00**

Lone Ranger, wallet, Hidecraft, 1948, EX, $125.00.

Matt Dillon, vest & badge, NMOC.............................**$145.00**

Matt Dillon, writing tablet, 1950s, unused, EX **$10.00**

Pancho (Cisco Kid), mask, paper, Tip Top Bread, 1950s, NM...**$15.00**

Range Rider, coloring book, Abbott Publishing Co, 1956 ..**$40.00**

Range Rider, comic book, Dell No 9, 1955 ....**$30.00**

Red Ryder, book, The Fighting Westerner, Better Little Book, Whitman, 1939 ....**$60.00**

Red Ryder, book, The Thunder Trail, Whitman No 1547:49, laminated lithographed hardback, 1956, 8x5½" ...**$25.00**

Red Ryder, Sunday comic strip, color, 1944 ....**$20.00**

Rex Allen, photo, Dixie Ice Cream, color, 1950s, 8x10"..**$25.00**

Rifleman, comic book, Dell No 5, 1960......................**$55.00**

Rifleman, hat, felt, Tex-Felt Co, 1958 ....**$70.00**

Rin-Tin-Tin, doll, stuffed dog, Ideal, EX....................**$70.00**

Rin-Tin-Tin & Rusty, belt buckle, EX **$65.00**

Roy Rogers, alarm clock, Ingraham, 1951, EX **$300.00**

Roy Rogers, cap gun, Shootin' Iron, Kilgore, 1953, 8"..**$150.00**

Roy Rogers, comic book, Official Roy Rogers Riders' Club, premium, 1952, 7x10"..**$100.00**

Roy Rogers, cup, head portrait w/signature, Quaker Oats premium, 1950, 4½"..**$50.00**

Roy Rogers, gun & double-holster set, Classy Products, 1955...**$400.00**

Roy Rogers, magazine, Life, July 12, 1943, Roy & Trigger cover..**$50.00**

Roy Rogers, paint set, 1950s, unused, NMIB............**$125.00**

Roy Rogers, pencil set, cardboard box w/pull-out drawer containing various items, lid shows Roy on Trigger, 6x9", EX..**$55.00**

Roy Rogers, TV Guide, December 28, 1951, New England (pre-national issue)....................................**$175.00**

Roy Rogers, TV Guide, July 17, 1954, Roy cover........**$60.00**

Roy Rogers & Dale Evans, paper dolls, Whitman, 1953, uncut...**$100.00**

Roy Rogers & Trigger, camera, Herbert George, 1950s, NMIB **$150.00**

Roy Rogers & Trigger, bandana, 1950s.....................**$100.00**

Straight Arrow, bandana, 1949, 17x17" **$75.00**

Sunset Carson, writing tablet, 1950 ....**$35.00**

Tales of Wells Fargo, book, Whitman, laminated lithographed hardcover, 1958..**$20.00**

Tex Ritter, record, Capitol Records, 78 rpm, w/10½x12" sleeve...**$40.00**

Tom Mix, blotter, Tom Mix Circus, color image, 1930s, 3x6", NM **$65.00**

Tom Mix, lobby card, The Miracle Rider, scene from movie, 1935, 11x14"...**$100.00**

Tom Mix, photograph, Dixie Ice Cream, 1930s **$125.00**

Tom Mix, title card, The Miracle Rider, 1935, 11x14" .**$350.00**

Wagon Train, playset, Marx Toys, 1950s, 15x21x5" box...**$500.00**

Wagon Train, TV Guide, April 11, 1959, Ward Bond cover...**$30.00**

Wild Bill Elliot, Dixie Ice-Cream Cup lid, 1940s **$20.00**

Wild Bill Elliot, exhibit card, 1940s, 3½x5½" **$12.00**

Wild Bill Hickok, guns w/holster set, mid-1950s......**$200.00**

Zorro, book, Little Golden, Simon & Schuster, 1958 ..**$15.00**

Zorro, gloves, 1958, EX, pr...**$50.00**

Zorro, pinwheel, black, red & silver w/Zorro graphics, WDP, 1950s-60s, 18", EX...**$30.00**

Zorro, travel bag, vinyl, 1960, 12x7x4" **$75.00**

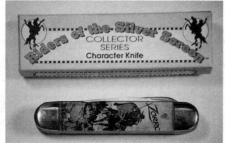

Zorro, pocketknife, Riders of the Silver Screen Collector Series, MIB, $45.00.

Miscellaneous

Book, Jim Babcock's Buckaroo, Log Cabin Syrup/Treasure Chest Publishers, 1936, 6x9" **$25.00**

Book, Little Tex in the Midst of Trouble, Samuel Lowe N 582, 1949, 3½x4¼ **$15.0**

Book, Silver Screen Cowboys, Gibbs-Smith Publishing, w/si ver bullet intact, 1993, 7¼x8¾" **$25.0**

Magazine, Madison Square Garden Rodeo Magazine, 17t Annual, 1942 ....**$40.0**

Magazine, The Buffalo Bill Stories No 467, April 12, 191 weekly issue, original 5¢ price **$25.0**

Magazine, Zane Grey's Western Magazine, Vol 2, No 2, Apr 1948 ....**$15.0**

Crackle Glass

At the height of productivity from the 1930s throug the 1970s, nearly five hundred companies created crackl glass. As pieces stayed in production for several years, da ing items may be difficult. Some colors such as ruby rec amberina, cobalt and cranberry were more expensive t produce. Smoke gray was made for a short time, an because quantities are scarce, prices on these pieces ten to be higher than on some of the other colors, amethys green, and amber included. Crackle glass is still in pr duction today by the Blenko Glass Company, and it being imported from Taiwan and China as well. For furthe information on other glass companies and values we rec ommend *Crackle Glass, Identification and Value Guide*, b Stan and Arlene Weitman (Collector Books).

Advisors: Stan and Arlene Weitman (See Director Crackle Glass)

Bottle, scent; light blue w/matching flower stoppe unknown origin, 4½"...**$55.0**

Candle holder, light sea green, bulbous shape w/holder top Blenko, 1960s, 5¼" **$55.0**

Candy bowl, topaz, ruffled rim, attributed to Blenk 5x8" **$60.0**

Candy dish, tangerine, ruffled rim, footed, Pilgrim, 1949-6 5½"...**$110.0**

Cruet, blue w/ruffled rim & matching pulled-back handl blue 3-ball stopper, Rainbow, late 1940s-60s, 6½".**$55.0**

Cruet, sea green w/ruffled top & ball stopper, Pilgrim, 194 69, 6"..**$55.0**

Decanter, amberina, stick neck, red teardrop stoppe Blenko, 1960s, 13" **$110.0**

Decanter, charcoal (w/blue tint), flared cylinder w/cryst teardrop stopper, Blenko, 1960s, 11¾" **$85.0**

Decanter, sea green gourd shape w/matching stemmed tea drop stopper (6"), Rainbow, late 1940s-60s, 12½" ..**$110.0**

Decanter, topaz, apothecary jar style, attributed to Blenk 9¼"..**$75.0**

Decanter, topaz, bulbous, Blenko, 1963, 8¾" **$65.0**

Decanter, topaz, ribbed crystal drop-over handle, Pilgrim 1949-69, 6¼", pr..**$100.0**

Decanter, topaz, waisted form w/ball stopper, Rainbow 1940s-60s, 14"...**$85.0**

Fruit, apple, cobalt blue w/applied stem & leaf, Blenk 1950s-60s, 4½"..**$65.0**

ruit, pear, pale sea green w/applied leaf, Blenko, 1950s-60s, 5" **$65.00**

ig, blue, crystal drop-over handle, Pilgrim, 1949-69, 4" ..**$32.00**

ig, topaz, crystal drop-over handle, Pilgrim, 1949-69, 6¾" **$65.00**

itcher, amberina, waisted form w/drop-over handle, Pilgrim, 1949-69, 3½" **$30.00**

Pitcher, amethyst, Pilgrim, 1949-69, 3¼", from $35.00 to $40.00. (Photo courtesy of Stan and Arlene Weitman.)

itcher, blue, flared cylinder w/clear drop-over handle & square top, unknown maker & date, 4" **$40.00**

itcher, blue w/ruffled top, clear angular handle, Pilgrim, 1949-69, 3½" **$35.00**

itcher, cobalt waisted form w/clear pulled-back handle, flared rim, unknown maker & date, 4¼" **$65.00**

itcher, crystal bulbous shape w/drop-over handle, Pilgrim, 1949-69, 3¼" **$25.00**

itcher, dark amber flared shape w/sm top, dark amber drop-over handle, Blenko, 1949-50, 17" **$125.00**

itcher, olive green, ewer form w/ruffled top, clear drop-over handle, Pilgrim, 1949-69, 4¼" **$35.00**

itcher, ruby w/long cylindrical neck, ruffled top, clear pulled-back handle, Pilgrim, 1949-69, 4½" **$30.00**

itcher, tangerine, flared cylinder w/amber pulled-back handle, Pilgrim, 1949-69, 4" **$30.00**

itcher, topaz w/trumpet neck, ribbed crystal drop-over handle, Pilgrim, 1949-69, 3¾" **$35.00**

alt & pepper shakers, crystal w/metal tops, 4", pr **$40.00**

op hat, topaz, Blenko, 1940s-50s, 2¾" **$35.00**

umbler, crystal w/dark amber drop-over handle, unknown maker or date, 5¼" **$40.00**

umbler, emerald green w/green drop-over handle, unknown maker or date, 5¼" **$40.00**

umbler, sea green, pinched sides, Blenko, late 1940s-50s, 5¾" **$60.00**

ase, amberina, classic shape, unknown maker & date, 5½" **$75.00**

ase, amberina, pinched rim, Pilgrim, 1949-69, 4" **$65.00**

ase, blue w/applied decoration along waist, ruffled rim, Pilgrim, 1949-1969, 3½" **$35.00**

ase, dark amber, cylindrical w/slightly ruffled rim, Pilgrim, 1949-69, w/original paper label, 4½" **$50.00**

Vase, emerald green, double-neck style, Blenko, late 1940s-50s, 4" **$65.00**

Vase, emerald green, stick neck bottle form, Hamon, late 1940s-70s, 9¾" **$65.00**

Vase, orange, stick neck, ruffled rim, unknown maker & date, 8" **$40.00**

Vase, ruby, flared rim, bulbous base, Rainbow, late 1940s-70s, 5¼" **$65.00**

Vase, sea green, bulbous base w/flared rim, unknown maker & date, 4¼" **$30.00**

Vase, sea green, pinched rim, Blenko, late 1940s-50s, 3¾" **$65.00**

Cuff Links

Cuff links are one of the fastest-growing areas of interest on the collectibles market today. And while prices are rapidly increasing for the precious metal and gemstone varieties, plenty of good buys are still available at flea markets, garage sales, thrift shops, and estate sales. Cuff link collectors tend to specialize. One of the most popular areas of specialization is advertising. These include cuff links containing logos, mottos, and product images. Cuff link collectors are not the only hobbyists chasing this category of specialization. Advertising cuff links are also sought by individuals and companies who collect every medium containing logos and other product identifiers.

Cameos are another growing area of cuff link specialization. While antique (pre-1900) cameo cuff links are highly prized, contemporary cameo cuff links of bone, ivory, and even plastic are also in demand. Intaglios, a reverse cameo design, are also increasing in popularity. Some cuff link collectors fear that many of the cameos are being converted into rings, earrings, and other jewelry items.

Some other areas of specialization are age, brand, size, era (Art Deco, Victorian, etc.), gold, sterling, and marcasite. Some cuff link enthusiasts limit their collections to certain states or countries of manufacture. According to the National Cuff Link Society, there are more than three hundred recognized areas of specialization. But novices and veteran collectors agree: few collectibles offer more variety, affordability, or availability than cuff links. For further information we recommend the National Cuff Link Society and our advisor, Gene Klompus.

Advisor: Gene Klompus

Club: The National Cuff Link Society

Newsletter: *The Link*
Gene Klompus, President
P.O. Box 346
Prospect Hts., IL 60070-0346; Phone or Fax: 847-816-0035

Anson, hand-in-circle peace sign, 1970, G **$45.00**

Chance, cuff buttons, separable adaption, mother-of-pearl insets, 1925, G w/original box **$100.00**

Coca-Cola, toggle closure, Made in Australia, 1970, M w/original box..**$65.00**

Dice, w/matching tie tac, removable closure enables use of dice, 1955 ....**$90.00**

Krementz, gold-colored plating, w/4 matching studs, 1935, G **$95.00**

Marcasite, initial G w/matching key chain, 1950 ....**$80.00**

S&S, sterling, barbell shape, 1902, ¾" long, M **$150.00**

Shields, turquoise stone, silver-colored base, swivel closure, 1975, original box...**$25.00**

Snap-Link, separable (Snappers), octagon w/mother-of-pearl inset, 1925 ....**$40.00**

SWANK, imitation tiger eye, w/tie tac, 1970, set.........**$30.00**

SWANK, initial F, w/tie bar, 1965, NM w/original box..**$6.00**

Other Accessories

Collar button, Airplane brand, metal boomerang shape, 1898...**$75.00**

Collar pin, ornate key design, 14k gold, 1960, 2".......**$90.00**

Shirt studs, Hayward, silver w/red stone insert, 1955, set of 4..**$35.00**

Shirt studs, Montclair, sterling posts w/black onyx faces, 1950, set of 4..**$90.00**

Tie bar, sterling, Chinese bamboo motif w/initials HK, security chain, 1960, original box..............................**$100.00**

Tie tack, watch inset, 1970, NM **$30.00**

Czechoslovakian Glass and Ceramics

Established as a country in 1918, Czechoslovakia is rich in the natural resources needed for production of glassware as well as pottery. Over the years it has produced vast amounts of both. Anywhere you go, from flea markets to fine antique shops, you'll find several examples of their lovely pressed and cut glass scent bottles, Deco vases, lamps, kitchenware, tableware and figurines.

More than thirty-five marks have been recorded; some are ink stamped, some etched, and some molded in. Paper labels have also been used. *Czechoslovakian Glass and Collectibles* by Diane and Dale Barta and *Made in Czechoslovakia* by Ruth Forsythe are two books we highly recommend for further study.

Ceramics

Basket, green bow garland design on orange, dresser type, 4¼"...**$45.00**

Creamer, bird figure w/open beak spout, multicolor w/black rim & details, 4½"...**$50.00**

Creamer, bright red round body w/white spout & handle, 4"...**$35.00**

Creamer, brown wood barrel design w/black bands, 3⅝"..**$35.00**

Creamer, cow in sitting position, white w/rust spots, open mouth spout, black handle, 4¾" **$50.00**

Creamer, moose head w/open mouth spout, antlers along rim, rust & brown to white to blue-gray base, 3½" **$60.00**

Creamer, white swan w/black & orange details, neck of swan forms handle, green pearl lustre background, 3¼"..**$50.00**

Figurine, white goose w/gold trim & details, glossy, 5¼"...**$45.00**

Flower arranger, parakeet by stump, multicolor, 5¼"..**$45.00**

Pitcher, bright Deco-style flowers on cream w/black trim handle, 5¾"..**$60.00**

Pitcher, floral design on green, brown handle, ewer form 7¼"...**$60.00**

Pitcher, purple & orange flowers w/green leaves on white w/orange at rim & handle, 5½"............................**$50.00**

Pitcher, ram figural, red & black details on cream, horns form handle, Erphila, 8¼"...............................**$175.00**

Planter, purple mottling, square w/indented sides, 2⅝"..**$30.00**

Plate, majolica, dark green and brownish yellow leaves with dark brown vine, 7", from $40.00 to $50.00.

Pitcher, multicolor Deco-style flowers w/black accents on cream, wide ewer-like top, 5¾" **$180.00**

Sugar bowl, pink & white variegated petal design w/green leaves along base, green vine handle, 4" **$55.00**

Sugar bowl, white pearl lustre shell design w/4 raised feet ear-shaped handle, 2¼"...**$55.00**

Vase, black, orange & yellow wedge-like design over blue beaded ring, red & black flared base, 7¾"...........**$95.00**

Vase, cream lustre w/X design, blue rim & handles, 5¼"..**$35.00**

Vase, integral flower frog at top, orange, yellow & black stylized flowers on green, 8" **$85.00**

Vase, multicolor flowers on dark brown w/light green to tan design at top, angle handles, 7" **$55.00**

Vase, peacock figural, green base, multicolored tail, 6"..**$65.00**

Vase, pearl gray lustre, black rim & handles, white interior waisted form, 5½"...**$30.00**

Vase, purple & orange flowers among dark green vining leaves on white, black trim at rim & base, classic shape, 6" **$40.00**

Vase, red high gloss, 6-sided, 4⅞".............................**$25.00**

Glassware

Bottle, perfume; amber cut 4-footed base w/amber intaglio cut drop stopper, 5¾" overall............................**$130.00**

Bottle, perfume; black opaque base w/jewels, black stopper 3"..**$90.00**

Bottle, perfume; clear cut short domed base, amethyst drop stopper w/intaglio decor, 6¾" overall.................$175.00

Bowl, black w/red interior, wide flared rim, 5".........$80.00

Bowl, mottled autumn colors, inverted rim, footed, cased, 4½"..$60.00

Candlestick, brown tones, slim form w/wide round foot, 8½"...$80.00

Candy dish, 4-color mottle w/applied black 4-footed pedestal base, w/lid, 8"..$130.00

Figural ashtray, Western man laying in curled position, blue shirt, red bandana, black pants, ca 1950, 3½"......$90.00

Figure, boy walking in snow w/axe, standing beside ever-greens, purple coat & green scarf, ca 1950, 6" ..$145.00

Figure, doctor in long white smock, blue pants, hand up touching forehead, ca 1950, 7½"........................$155.00

Figure, dwarf night watchman w/lantern, blue clothes, red hat, ca 1950, 5½"...$120.00

Figure, man sitting & working w/tool, blue coat, red neck tie, black hat & shoes, ca 1950, 5½".......................$215.00

Figure, trumpet player, blue hat & pants, red vest, yellow-green trumpet, ca 1950, 8½"...............................$125.00

Perfume bottles: Crystal cut base with etched flowers on fan-shaped stopper, 5", $100.00; Pressed crystal, faceted brass cap with brass decoration and 2 white elephants dangling from chain, 2½", $60.00.

Pitcher, cobalt & red mottle w/applied cobalt handle, scalloped rim, flared foot, cased, 9"..........................$120.00

Pitcher, orange w/applied cobalt rim & handle, scalloped rim, cased, 5"..$85.00

Vase, blue variegated design on clear, lamp-chimney shaped neck on bulbous body, 8½" $175.00

Vase, bud; orange w/black flared foot, cased, 8"........$65.00

Vase, exotic bird enameled on black w/silver rim, classic shape, cased, 7¼"...$145.00

Vase, lavender, blue & green mottled, bulbous, footed, cased, 4" $75.00

Vase, pale green w/red & brown overlay, slightly bulbous, 7"..$145.00

Vase, pink w/white spiraling overlay, scalloped form, footed, cased, 8½" $115.00

Vase, red & white mottle w/applied black serpentine decor, black trim at ruffled rim, red cased, 8" $100.00

Vase, silver bird painted on yellow, cylindrical, cased, 10" $90.00

Vase, varicolored autumn colors, slim cylinder w/4 clear feet, cased, 11¾" $80.00

Vase, varicolored blues w/red splotches, bulbous top on slim form, applied blue handles, cased, 8⅜"................$95.00

Vase, varicolored w/red & blues, long slim neck, cased, 7½"..$90.00

Vase, variegated colors, gourd shape, cased, 4½" $65.00

Vase, yellow, white & blue mottle w/jet rim, fan shape, cased, 8¼" $135.00

Dairy Bottles

Between the turn of the century and the 1950s, milk was bought and sold in glass bottles. Until the twenties, the name and location of the dairy was embossed in the glass. After that it became commonplace to pyro-glaze (paint and fire) the lettering onto the surface. Farmers sometimes added a cow or some other graphic that represented the product or related to the name of the dairy.

Because so many of these glass bottles were destroyed when paper and plastic cartons became popular, they've become a scarce commodity, and today's collectors have begun to take notice of them. It's fun to see just how many you can find from your home state — or try getting one from every state in the union!

What makes for a good milk bottle? Collectors normally find the pyro-glaze decorations more desirable, since they're more visual. Bottles from dairies in their home state hold more interest for them, so naturally New Jersey bottles sell better there than they would in California, for instance. Green glass examples are unusual and often go for a premium; so do those with the embossed baby faces. (Watch for reproductions here!) Those with a 'Buy War Bonds' slogan or a patriotic message are always popular, and cream tops are good as well.

Some collectors enjoy adding 'go-alongs' to enhance their collections, so the paper pull tops, advertising items that feature dairy bottles, and those old cream-top spoons will interest them as well. The spoons usually sell for about $6.00 to $10.00 each.

For more information, we recommend *Udderly Delightful* by John Tutton, whose address may be found in the Directory under Bottles.

Newsletter: *The Milk Route*
National Association of Milk Bottle Collectors, Inc.
Thomas Gallagher
4 Ox Bow Rd.
Westport, CT 06880-2602; 203-277-5244

Newsletter: *Creamers*
Lloyd Bindscheattle
P.O. Box 11
Lake Villa, IL 60046-0011; Subscription: $5 for 4 issues

All Jersey, Gamage Farms Augusta ME, cow's head on orange & red painted label, tall & square, qt.....................$8.50

Asgard Dairy, Rockwell Kent, Ausable Forks, cow & figure, green pyro, round, ½-pt..$9.00

Ashland Farms Milk Co, Holbrook MA, mother nursing baby, red pyro, round, qt..$8.00

Atzke Dairy, farm scene, Try our Heavy Cream, red pyro, square, qt..$6.50

Avondale Farm, Luxenburg MA, orange pyro, qt..........**$9.00**

Boyles Dairy Quality Dairy Products, white pyro on amber, square, qt................................**$10.00**

Cloverdale Farms, Milk Is Your Best Food Buy, red pyro w/dacro top for plastic snap cap, cream top, square, qt..........**$18.00**

Cloverleaf, Stockton CA, orange pyro, cream top, qt ..**$22.50**

Cloverleaf, Stockton CA, red pyro label, modern-style cream top.............................**$27.50**

Cloverleaf Store Bottle, Drive Safely, red pyro, cream top..**$25.00**

Cream Crest Milk Products, General Ice Cream Corp Springfield MA, embossed letters, round, 10-oz.....**$6.50**

Ellerman Dairy, Athens WI, red pyro, tall, round, qt..**$16.00**

Estey's Farm Fairy, orange pyro, square, qt.................**$5.00**

Excelsior Sanitary Dairy, Chas F Rothenhoefer, Bottle Is Not Sold....Frederick MO, embossed letters, ½-pt.......**$12.00**

Farm Fresh, white pyro on amber, rectangular, ½-gal..**$8.00**

Ferndale, Grand Ledge MI, white pyro on amber, square, qt.....................................**$10.00**

Fisher Dairy, Crystal Falls MI, lady's portrait, black pyro..**$18.00**

Frank's Dairies Store Bottle, red pyro, square, qt **$5.00**

Frederick's Farm Dairy Conyngham PA & Ayrshire cow, brown pyro, tall, pt **$17.50**

Gibbs Dairy, Rochester MA, embossed letters, round, pt ..**$7.50**

Heiss & Sons Dairy Rochelle Park NJ, orange pyro, tall, round, qt.................................**$12.50**

HP Hood & Sons Boston 1925, embossed letters, round, pt..**$7.50**

Indian Hill Farm Dairy, Indian chief's portrait, Greeneville ME, orange pyro, tall & round, qt **$25.00**

Inwood Farms Inc Harrison NY, White Plains NY, Perfectly Pasteurized, embossed letters, round, qt **$12.00**

Ipswich Diary, embossed script letters, round, ½-pt **$6.50**

It's Hood's, cow's head logo, red pyro, ½-pt..............**$10.00**

JF McAdams & Bros, Chelsea MA, embossed script letters, ½-pt.................................**$7.50**

Joe Bernard, Dartmouth St, embossed lettering, round, qt...**$12.50**

John Mello Light Cream Dairy, red pyro, 1-pint, $10.00.

Marshall Dairy, Ithaca New York, ice cream sundae, red pyro, tall, round, qt **$17.50**

McIntire Dairy Farm, Bridgewater, orange pyro, square, ½-pt.................................**$7.50**

Paiva's Farm Dairy, red pyro, cream top, round, qt ...**$22.50**

Ruff's Dairy, girl beside safety slogan, St Clair MI, orange pyro, qt...........................**$7.50**

Schiller Park Dairy, Syracuse NY, embossed letters, round, qt.....................................**$10.00**

Seneca Indian, Syracuse NY, orange pyro, square, qt ..**$10.00**

Shadow Lawn Dairy, East Providence RI, red pyro, pt..**$15.00**

Smith's Dairy Farm, Erie PA, round, ½-pt.....................**$8.50**

Superior Ruda's Dairy Product, embossed letters, quilted, round, ½-pt **$6.50**

Thatcher Farm, Milton MA, maroon pyro label, square body w/cream top, qt **$17.50**

United Farmer's, red pyro, ½-pt **$5.00**

Universal 5" Store Bottle, embossed, round, qt.............**$7.50**

Vermont Country Milk, cow w/bell, Shelburne VT, green pyro, square, qt................................**$8.50**

Wauregan Dairy, children w/glasses of milk & rhyme, red & black pyro label, cream top, pt **$35.00**

Weiler-Sterling Farms Co, Boston, Where Purity Rules Supreme, black pyro, round, qt.........................**$12.50**

White Bros, That Creamy Milk, baby's portrait, black pyro, ½-pt.................................**$7.50**

Whiting Milk Companies in triangular logo, embossed, round qt **$15.00**

Wroblinksi Farm Dairy, Acushnet MA, cow & barn, boy & girl, orange pyro, round, pt **$12.00**

Dakin

Dakin has been in the toy-making business since the 1950s and has made several lines of stuffed and vinyl dolls and animals, but the Dakins that collectors are most interested in today are the licensed characters and advertising figures made from 1968 through the seventies. Originally there were seven Warner Brothers characters, each with a hard plastic body and a soft vinyl head, all under 10" tall. The line was very successful and eventually expanded to include more than fifty cartoon characters and several more that were advertising related. In addition to the figures, there are banks that were made in two sizes. Some Dakins are quite scarce and may sell for over $100.00 (a few even higher), though most will be in the $30.00 to $60.00 range.

Condition is very important, and if you find one still in the original box, add about 50% to its value. Figures in the colorful 'Cartoon Theatre' boxes command higher prices than those that came in a clear plastic bag or package (MIP). More Dakins are listed in *Schroeder's Collectible Toys, Antique to Modern*, published by Collector Books.

Advisor: Jim Rash (See Directory, Dakins)

Baby Puss, Hanna-Barbera, 1971, EX+ **$100.00**

Bambi, Disney, 1960s, MIP **$35.00**

Bamm-Bamm, Hanna-Barbera, w/club, 1970, EX **$35.00**

Banana Splits, Fleegle, 1970, 7", NM...........................**$75.00**

Benji, name embossed on brass tag, 10", VG..............**$15.00**

Big Foot Sasquatch Savings, bank, 10", EX **$65.00**

Bob's Big Boy, w/hamburger, 1974, EX+ **$190.00**

Bozo the Clown, Larry Harmon, 1974, EX...............**$35.00**

Bugs Bunny, Warner Bros, 1971, MIP **$30.00**

Bull Dog, Dream Pet, EX **$15.00**

Cool Cat, Warner Bros, w/beret, 1970, EX+ **$40.00**

Daffy Duck, Warner Bros, 1968, EX.........................**$30.00**

Deputy Dawg, Terrytoons, 1977, EX.........................**$40.00**

Diaparene Baby, Sterling Drug Company, 1980, EX...**$40.00**

Dino Dinosaur, Hanna-Barbera, 1970, EX **$40.00**

Donald Duck, Jay Ward, 1976, MIB (cartoon theater box) .**$75.00**

Dumbo, Disney, cloth collar, 1960s, MIB **$25.00**

Elmer Fudd, hunting outfit, 1968, EX, $125.00.

Elmer Fudd, Warner Bros, in tuxedo, 1968, EX **$30.00**

Foghorn Leghorn, Warner Bros, 1970, EX+ **$75.00**

Freddie Fast, 1976, M **$95.00**

Glamour Kitty, white or black w/gold crown, 1977, EX, each **$150.00**

Goofy, Disney, 1960s, EX **$20.00**

Goofy Gram, Fox, Wanna See My Etchings?, EX.........**$20.00**

Goofy Gram, kangaroo, World's Greatest Mom!, EX ..**$20.00**

Hawaiian Hound, Dream Pet, w/original tag & surfboard, EX.**$25.00**

Hokey Wolf, Hanna-Barbera, 1971, EX+ **$250.00**

Hoppy Hopperoo, Hanna-Barbera, 1971, EX+.........**$100.00**

Huckleberry Hound, Hanna-Barbera, 1970, EX+ **$75.00**

Jack-in-the-Box, bank, 1971, EX+ **$25.00**

Kernal Renk, American Seeds, 1970, rare, EX+.........**$350.00**

Li'l Miss Just Rite, 1965, EX+.................................**$75.00**

Lion in the Cage, bank, 1971, EX.............................**$25.00**

Merlin the Magic Mouse, Warner Bros, 1970, NM, $25.00.

Mickey Mouse, Disney, cloth clothes, 1960s, EX **$20.00**

Mighty Mouse, Terrytoons, 1978, EX **$100.00**

Miss Liberty Belle, w/hat, 1975, MIP.........................**$75.00**

Monkey on a Barrel, bank, 1971, EX.........................**$25.00**

Oliver Hardy, Larry Harmon, 1974, EX+ **$30.00**

Opus, cloth, 1982, 12", EX **$15.00**

Pepe Le Peu, Warner Bros, 1971, EX+ **$75.00**

Pink Panther, Mirisch-Freleng, 1971, EX+ **$50.00**

Pinocchio, Disney, 1960s, cloth clothes, EX..............**$20.00**

Popeye, King Features, cloth clothes, 1974, MIP **$50.00**

Porky Pig, Warner Bros, 1968, EX+...........................**$30.00**

Quasar Robot, bank, 1975, NM **$150.00**

Ren & Stimpy, water squirters, Nickelodeon, 1993, EX, each..**$10.00**

Road Runner, Warner Bros, 1968, EX+ **$30.00**

Sambo's Boy, 1974, EX+ **$75.00**

Sambo's Tiger, 1974, EX+.....................................**$125.00**

Scooby Doo, Hanna-Barbera, 1982, EX+ **$75.00**

Seal on a Box, bank, 1971, EX...............................**$25.00**

Second Banana, Warner Bros, 1970, EX **$35.00**

Smokey Bear, 1974, MIP **$20.00**

Snagglepuss, Hanna-Barbera, 1971, EX **$100.00**

Stan Laurel, Larry Harmon, 1974, EX+ **$30.00**

Sylvester, Warner Bros, 1968, EX+...........................**$20.00**

Tasmanian Devil, Warner Bros, 1978, EX (fun farm bag)...**$400.00**

Tiger in a Cage, bank, 1971, EX...............................**$25.00**

Tweety Bird, Warner Bros, 1966, EX+........................**$20.00**

Tweety Bird, Warner Bros, 1976, MIB (carton theater box) **$40.00**

Uncle Bugs Bunny, Warner Bros, 1975, EX+..............**$50.00**

Underdog, Jay Ward, 1976, MIB (cartoon theater box)..**$150.00**

Wile E Coyote, Warner Bros, 1968, MIB **$30.00**

Woodsy Owl, 1974, MIP...**$60.00**

Yogi Bear, Hanna-Barbera, 1970, EX..........................**$60.00**

Yosemite Sam, Warner Bros, 1968, MIB....................**$30.00**

Decanters

The first company to make figural ceramic decanters was the James Beam Distilling Company. Until mid-1992 they produced hundreds of varieties in their own US-based china factory. They first issued their bottles in the mid-fifties, and over the course of the next twenty-five years, more than twenty other companies followed their example. Among the more prominent of these were Brooks, Hoffman, Lionstone, McCormick, Old Commonwealth, Ski Country, and Wild Turkey. In 1975, Beam introduced the 'Wheel Series,' cars, trains, and fire engines with wheels that actually revolved. The popularity of this series resulted in a heightened interest in decanter collecting.

There are various sizes. The smallest (called miniatures) hold two ounces, and there are some that hold a gallon! A full decanter is worth no more than an empty one, and the absence of the tax stamp doesn't lower its value either. Just be sure that all the labels are intact and that there are no cracks or chips. You might want to empty your decanters as a safety precaution (many collectors do) rather than risk the possibility of the inner glaze breaking down and allowing the contents to leak into the porous ceramic body.

All of the decanters we've listed are fifths unless we've specified 'miniature' within the description.

See also Elvis Presley Collectibles.

Advisor: Art and Judy Turner, Homestead Collectibles (See Directory, Decanters)

Newsletter: *Beam Around the World*
International Association of Jim Beam Bottle and Specialties Club
Shirley Sumbles, Secretary
2015 Burlington Ave.
Kewanee, IL 61443; 309-853-3370

Newsletter: *The Ski Country Collector*
1224 Washington Ave.
Golden, CO 80401

Aesthetic Specialist (ASI), 1909 Stanley Steamer, green ..**$39.00**
Aesthetic Specialist (ASI), 1910 Oldsmobile, black **$69.00**
Aesthetic Specialist (ASI), 1910 Oldsmobile, gold.....**$125.00**
Beam, Casino Series, Barney's Slot Machine **$25.00**
Beam, Casino Series, Binion's Horseshoe, from $9 to ..**$12.00**
Beam, Casino Series, Circus Circus Clown **$50.00**
Beam, Casino Series, Golden Gate, 1969.....................**$80.00**
Beam, Casino Series, Golden Nugget, 1969.................**$50.00**
Beam, Casino Series, Harvey Hotel.............................**$10.00**
Beam, Casino Series, Horseshoe Club..........................**$9.00**
Beam, Casino Series, Reno...**$9.00**
Beam, Casino Series, Smith's North Shore **$10.00**
Beam, Centennial Series, Alaskan Purchase.................**$9.00**
Beam, Centennial Series, Antioch................................**$9.00**
Beam, Centennial Series, Blue Hen............................**$15.00**
Beam, Centennial Series, Civil War, North.................**$20.00**
Beam, Centennial Series, Civil War, South.................**$30.00**
Beam, Centennial Series, Colorado Springs **$9.00**
Beam, Centennial Series, Dodge City...........................**$9.00**
Beam, Centennial Series, Edison Light Bulb, from $15 to..**$19.00**
Beam, Centennial Series, Fox (Runner) **$10.00**
Beam, Centennial Series, Indy Sesquicentennial **$10.00**
Beam, Centennial Series, Key West **$15.00**
Beam, Centennial Series, New Mexico Bicentennial...**$10.00**
Beam, Centennial Series, Riverside Central **$15.00**
Beam, Centennial Series, Santa Fe **$95.00**
Beam, Centennial Series, Statue of Liberty, 1975 ....**$20.00**
Beam, Centennial Series, Statue of Liberty, 1985 ....**$34.00**
Beam, Club Series, Beam Pot.....................................**$15.00**
Beam, Club Series, Blue Hen.....................................**$15.00**
Beam, Club Series, California Mission Bell.................**$10.00**
Beam, Club Series, Evergreen Club..............................**$9.00**
Beam, Club Series, Five Seasons Club **$10.00**
Beam, Club Series, Fox, blue......................................**$50.00**
Beam, Club Series, Fox, Distillery, red **$750.00**
Beam, Club Series, Fox, white coat.............................**$20.00**
Beam, Club Series, Milwaukee Stein **$25.00**
Beam, Club Series, Republic of Texas.........................**$10.00**
Beam, Club Series, Twin Bridges **$25.00**
Beam, Convention Series, Buccaneer, gold **$39.00**
Beam, Convention Series, Bucky Beaver......................**$35.00**
Beam, Convention Series, Chicago, 1978.....................**$10.00**
Beam, Convention Series, Cowboy, beige or color, each ..**$29.00**
Beam, Convention Series, Denver, 1971 ....**$10.00**
Beam, Convention Series, Detroit, 1973.......................**$10.00**
Beam, Convention Series, Las Vegas...........................**$45.00**

Beam, Convention Series, Louisville **$45.00**
Beam, Convention Series, Mermaid, blond or brunette, each...**$39.00**
Beam, Convention Series, Minuteman, color or pewter, each.**$49.00**
Beam, Convention Series, Sacramento, 1975..............**$10.00**
Beam, Convention Series, Showgirl, blond or brunette, each..**$39.00**
Beam, Convention Series, St Louis **$55.00**
Beam, Convention Series, Waterman, Pewter.............**$29.00**
Beam, Customer Series, ABC Florida **$12.00**
Beam, Customer Series, Armanette Flower Vase **$9.00**
Beam, Customer Series, Bohemian Girl **$19.00**
Beam, Customer Series, Delco Battery.........................**$25.00**
Beam, Customer Series, Foremost, gray.....................**$225.00**
Beam, Customer Series, Harley-Davidson Eagle **$250.00**
Beam, Customer Series, Harley-Davidson 85th Anniversary Stein **$200.00**
Beam, Customer Series, Herre Brothers.......................**$25.00**
Beam, Customer Series, Jewel T Man, 50th Anniversary .**$75.00**
Beam, Customer Series, Marina City **$10.00**
Beam, Customer Series, Osco Drugs...........................**$15.00**
Beam, Customer Series, Ponderosa Ranch...................**$15.00**
Beam, Customer Series, Ralph's Market **$10.00**
Beam, Customer Series, Ramada Inn **$10.00**
Beam, Customer Series, Spencers Grotto.....................**$20.00**
Beam, Customer Series, Travelodge Bear **$15.00**
Beam, Customer Series, Zimmerman's Art Institute **$9.00**
Beam, Customer Series, Zimmerman's Blue Beauty ...**$10.00**
Beam, Customer Series, Zimmerman's Cherub.............**$9.00**
Beam, Customer Series, Zimmerman's Vase, green.......**$9.00**
Beam, Executive Series, Antique Pitcher, 1982............**$20.00**
Beam, Executive Series, Bowl, 1986............................**$25.00**
Beam, Executive Series, Cherub, gray, 1957 ....**$125.00**
Beam, Executive Series, Fantasia, 1971.......................**$15.00**
Beam, Executive Series, Flower Basket, 1962 ....**$24.00**
Beam, Executive Series, Golden Jubilee, 1977 ....**$15.00**
Beam, Executive Series, Italian Marble Urn, 1985.......**$15.00**
Beam, Executive Series, Majestic, 1966 ....**$18.00**
Beam, Executive Series, Marbled Fantasy, 1965..........**$29.00**
Beam, Executive Series, Mother of Pearl, 1979 ....**$15.00**
Beam, Executive Series, Presidential, 1968 ....**$15.00**
Beam, Executive Series, Reflections, 1975, from $12 to..**$15.00**
Beam, Executive Series, Regency, 1972 ....**$15.00**
Beam, Executive Series, Royal Di Monte, 1957 ....**$35.00**
Beam, Executive Series, Royal Gold Diamond, 1964..**$24.00**
Beam, Executive Series, Royal Rose, 1963..................**$24.00**
Beam, Executive Series, Texas Rose, 1978...................**$15.00**
Beam, Executive Series, Twin Doves, 1987 ....**$15.00**
Beam, Foreign Series, Australia, Hobo........................**$24.00**
Beam, Foreign Series, Australia, Kangaroo.................**$15.00**
Beam, Foreign Series, Australia, Koala........................**$15.00**
Beam, Foreign Series, Australia, Magpie.....................**$20.00**
Beam, Foreign Series, Boystown, Italy........................**$10.00**
Beam, Foreign Series, Colin Mead **$149.00**
Beam, Foreign Series, Fiji Islands, from $7 to **$9.00**
Beam, Foreign Series, Queensland..............................**$21.00**
Beam, Foreign Series, Richard Hadlee........................**$95.00**
Beam, Foreign Series, Samoa......................................**$9.00**
Beam, Opera Series, Aida w/base...............................**$95.00**
Beam, Opera Series, Carmen, w/base & paperweight..**$125.00**
Beam, Opera Series, Figaro, w/base & paperweight..**$125.00**

Beam, Opera Series, Madame Butterfly, w/base & paper-weight.................$195.00

Beam, Opera Series, Mephistopheles, w/base & paper-weight.................$150.00

Beam, Opera Series, Nutcracker, w/paperweight.......$95.00

Beam, Organization Series, Amvets.................$9.00

Beam, Organization Series, Beverage Association, NLBA.$9.00

Beam, Organization Series, Blue Goose Order.............$9.00

Beam, Organization Series, Devil Dog.................$35.00

Beam, Organization Series, Ducks Umlimited #10, Mallard, 1984.................$95.00

Beam, Organization Series, Ducks Unlimited #12, Redhead, 1986.................$50.00

Beam, Organization Series, Ducks Unlimited #16, Canadian Goose, 1990.................$49.00

Beam, Organization Series, Ducks Unlimited #2, Wood Duck, 1975.................$45.00

Beam, Organization Series, Ducks Unlimited #20, Cinnamon Teal, 1993.................$125.00

Beam, Organization Series, Ducks Unlimited #5, Canvasback Drake, 1979.................$45.00

Beam, Organization Series, Ducks Unlimited #8, Wood Ducks, 1982.................$65.00

Beam, Organization Series, Elks.................$9.00

Beam, Organization Series, Kentucky Colonel.............$9.00

Beam, Organization Series, Marine Corps.................$35.00

Beam, Organization Series, Pearl Harbor 1972.................$15.00

Beam, Organization Series, Shriner, Indiana.................$9.00

Beam, Organization Series, Shriner, Moila w/Camel...$15.00

Beam, Organization Series, Shriner, Rajah Temple.....$24.00

Beam, Organization Series, Sigma Nu, Kentucky........$10.00

Beam, Organization Series, Telephone #2, Desk Set, 1897..$29.00

Beam, Organization Series, Telephone #4, Dial, 1919..$45.00

Beam, Organization Series, Telephone #6, Battery.....$40.00

Beam, Organization Series, VFW.................$9.00

Beam, Organization Series, Yuma Rifle Club.................$20.00

Beam, People Series, Bob Devaney.................$15.00

Beam, People Series, Buffalo Bill.................$15.00

Beam, People Series, Charley McCarthy.................$30.00

Beam, People Series, Emmet Kelley.................$35.00

Beam, People Series, George Washington.................$19.00

Beam, People Series, Hank Williams Jr.................$25.00

Beam, People Series, Indian Chief.................$25.00

Beam, People Series, Martha Washington.................$14.00

Beam, People Series, Paul Bunyan.................$14.00

Beam, People Series, Santa Claus, w/paperweight...$150.00

Beam, People Series, Viking.................$10.00

Beam, Political Series, Boxer Elephant, 1964.............$19.00

Beam, Political Series, Clown Donkey, 1968.................$19.00

Beam, Political Series, Drum Donkey, 1976.................$19.00

Beam, Political Series, Election Democrat, 1988........$29.00

Beam, Political Series, Football Elephant, 1972.................$19.00

Beam, Political Series, Republican Convention, gold, 1972, w/plate.................$400.00

Beam, Political Series, Superman Elephant or Donkey, 1980, ea.................$19.00

Beam, Sports Series, Baseball.................$29.00

Beam, Sports Series, Bing Crosby 30th, 1971.............$19.00

Beam, Sports Series, Bing Crosby 34th, 1975.............$65.00

Beam, Sports Series, Bowling Pin.................$10.00

Beam, Sports Series, Chicago Cubs.................$85.00

Beam, Sports Series, College Football Bowls.............$55.00

Beam, Sports Series, Glen Campbell.................$24.00

Beam, Sports Series, Hawaiian Open, Pineapple........$15.00

Beam, Sports Series, Indianapolis 500, 1970, from $15.00 to $20.00.

Beam, Sports Series, Kentucky Derby 95th, pink........$19.00

Beam, Sports Series, Louisville Downs.................$14.00

Beam, Sports Series, Mile Racetrack, red.................$19.00

Beam, Sports Series, Mint 400, china stopper, 1970....$95.00

Beam, Sports Series, PGA.................$15.00

Beam, Sports Series, Sahara Golf.................$15.00

Beam, Sports Series, US Open.................$24.00

Beam, States Series, Colorado.................$25.00

Beam, States Series, Idaho.................$39.00

Beam, States Series, Illinois.................$14.00

Beam, States Series, Kentucky, black, brown or white head, each.................$24.00

Beam, States Series, Maine.................$9.00

Beam, States Series, New Hampshire.................$9.00

Beam, States Series, New Mexico.................$14.00

Beam, States Series, Oregon.................$29.00

Beam, States Series, South Carolina.................$15.00

Beam, States Series, Wyoming.................$55.00

Beam, Trophy Series, Armadillo.................$15.00

Beam, Trophy Series, Bird, Cardinal Male.................$25.00

Beam, Trophy Series, Bird, Duck.................$15.00

Beam, Trophy Series, Bird, Sierra Eagle.................$24.00

Beam, Trophy Series, Blue Jay.................$10.00

Beam, Trophy Series, Dog, Labrador.................$30.00

Beam, Trophy Series, Dog, Setter.................$21.00

Beam, Trophy Series, Eagle.................$10.00

Beam, Trophy Series, Fish, Bass.................$19.00

Beam, Trophy Series, Fish, Crappie.................$19.00

Beam, Trophy Series, Fish, Walleye '77.................$19.00

Beam, Trophy Series, Horse, Appaloosa.................$15.00

Beam, Trophy Series, Horse, brown, 1962.................$19.00

Beam, Trophy Series, Horse, white, 1962.................$15.00

Beam, Trophy Series, Jaguar.................$20.00

Beam, Trophy Series, Ram.................$40.00

Beam, Wheel Series, Ambulance.................$70.00

Beam, Wheel Series, Bass Boat.................$29.00

Beam, Wheel Series, Circus Wagon.............................$25.00

Beam, Wheel Series, Duesenberg Convertible, cream..$150.00

Beam, Wheel Series, Duesenberg Convertible, light blue..$110.00

Beam, Wheel Series, Ernie's Flower Cart.....................$25.00

Beam, Wheel Series, Ford International Delivery Wagon, black or green, each..$95.00

Beam, Wheel Series, Ford Model A, Parkwood Supply..$150.00

Beam, Wheel Series, Golf Cart, from $35 to................$45.00

Beam, Wheel Series, Grant Locomotive, $90.00.

Beam, Wheel Series, Olsonite Eagle Racer.................$65.00

Beam, Wheel Series, State Trooper, blue.....................$75.00

Beam, Wheel Series, Tractor Trailer, yellow or orange, each..$65.00

Beam, Wheel Series, Train, Box Car, brown $65.00

Beam, Wheel Series, Train, Caboose, red or gray, each, from $65 to...$75.00

Beam, Wheel Series, Train, Combination Car..............$40.00

Beam, Wheel Series, Train, Dining Car.......................$85.00

Beam, Wheel Series, Train, Log Car...........................$75.00

Beam, Wheel Series, Train, Lumber Car $50.00

Beam, Wheel Series, Train, Passenger Car..................$50.00

Beam, Wheel Series, Train, Tank Car..........................$50.00

Beam, Wheel Series, Train, Vendome Wagon $35.00

Beam, Wheel Series, Train, Water Tower.....................$45.00

Beam, Wheel Series, Train, Wood Tender....................$95.00

Beam, Wheel Series, Volkswagon, red.........................$75.00

Beam, Wheel Series, 1903, Ford Model A, red.............$50.00

Beam, Wheel Series, 1913 Ford Model T, black or green, each $55.00

Beam, Wheel Series, 1917 Mack Fire Truck $125.00

Beam, Wheel Series, 1929 Ford Woodie Wagon $75.00

Beam, Wheel Series, 1930 Ford Paddy Wagon $175.00

Beam, Wheel Series, 1934 Ford Fire Chief $65.00

Beam, Wheel Series, 1935 Ford Fire Pumper Truck ...$90.00

Beam, Wheel Series, 1935 Ford Pickup Truck $50.00

Beam, Wheel Series, 1935 Ford Police Tow Truck $60.00

Beam, Wheel Series, 1955 Chevy Corvette, copper $85.00

Beam, Wheel Series, 1956 Ford T-Bird, black.............$95.00

Beam, Wheel Series, 1956 Ford T-Bird, yellow or green, each $110.00

Beam, Wheel Series, 1957 Chevy, red $85.00

Beam, Wheel Series, 1957 Chevy Convertible, turquoise...$50.00

Beam, Wheel Series, 1957 Chevy Corvette, black.......$60.00

Beam, Wheel Series, 1957 Chevy Corvette, blue $495.00

Beam, Wheel Series, 1957 Chevy Hot Rod, yellow.....$90.00

Beam, Wheel Series, 1959 Cadillac, pink....................$50.00

Beam, Wheel Series, 1963 Chevy Corvette, red $65.00

Beam, Wheel Series, 1963 Chevy Corvette, silver.......$70.00

Beam, Wheel Series, 1964 Ford Mustang, white $80.00

Beam, Wheel Series, 1969 Chevy Camaro, blue $50.00

Beam, Wheel Series, 1969 Chevy Camaro Pace Car ...$90.00

Beam, Wheel Series, 1970 Dodge Challenger, plum...$40.00

Beam, Wheel Series, 1970 Dodge Hot Rod, lime......$125.00

Beam, Wheel Series, 1974 Mercedes, Australia, silver .$95.00

Beam, Wheel Series, 1974 Mercedes, gold $50.00

Beam, Wheel Series, 1978 Chevy Corvette, white.......$55.00

Beam, Wheel series, 1978 Chevy Corvette Pace Car .$225.00

Beam, Wheel Series, 1984 Chevy Corvette, black.......$95.00

Beam, Wheel Series, 1984 Chevy Corvette, white.......$49.00

Beam, Wheel Series, 1986 Chevy Corvette, bronze $90.00

Black & White, Scotties, 1st edition, pr $125.00

Brooks, American Legion Convention Miami $5.00

Brooks, Automotive & Transportation Series, Indy Racer Penske #2 ....$75.00

Brooks, Automotive & Transportation Series, 1957 Corvette, blue or yellow...$125.00

Brooks, Bulldog, red $39.00

Brooks, Foremost Astronaut...$25.00

Brooks, Foremost Man $19.00

Brooks, Whitetail Deer $9.00

Budweiser, Bill Elliott, signature...............................$149.00

Budweiser, Jim Beam 1983 Convention, brown........$125.00

Budweiser, Joe Louis $59.00

Budweiser, Sea World, dolphin....................................$29.00

Budweiser, Sport's Legend—Babe Ruth $54.00

Davis County, IML Tractor Trailer $65.00

Davis County, Wheel Series, Jeep CJ-7, red $45.00

Dickel, powder horn, qt..$9.00

Famous First, Automotive & Transportation Series, Duesenberg $95.00

Famous First, Automotive & Transportation Series, Marmon Wasp, gold...$19.00

Famous First, Automotive & Transportation Series, Mustang Airplane $95.00

Famous First, Automotive & Transportation Series, National Racer #8..$49.00

Famous First, Automotive & Transportation Series, Renault Racer #3..$49.00

Famous First, Automotive & Transportation Series, Robert E Lee Riverboat...$49.00

Famous First, Automotive & Transportation Series, Spirit of St Louis Airplane $75.00

Famous First, Automotive & Transportation Series, 1953 Corvette $95.00

Federal, Fireman #2, Are You Ok.................................$75.00

Hoffman, Lucky Lindy...$95.00

Kingston Classics, Fire Truck $95.00

Kingston Classics, Shotgun Shell $39.00

Lionstone, Automotive & Transportation Series, Corvette, white, 1.75-liter $95.00

Lionstone, Automotive & Transportation Series, Delco Oil Filter..$75.00

Lionstone, Bartender.................................$15.00
Lionstone, Boxers $65.00
Lionstone, Football Players $39.00
Lionstone, Frontiersmen, set of 6............$125.00
Lionstone, Saturday Night Bath $65.00
McCormick, Calamity Jane $19.00
McCormick, Elvis, See Elvis Presley category

McCormick, Gunfighter Series, Black Bart, $35.00.

McCormick, Jeb Stuart..............................$65.00
McCormick, Jefferson Davis......................$65.00
McCormick, JR Ewing...............................$49.00
McCormick, Muhammad Ali, from $150 to.........$175.00
McCormick, Train, Locomotive..................$15.00
McCormick, Weary Willie Clown................$95.00
Michter, Pennsylvania Fireman Association, 100th
    Anniversary..$65.00
Mike Wayne, Christmas Tree, white $75.00
Mike Wayne, John Wayne, bust.................$65.00
Mike Wayne, John Wayne Statue, bronze.................$125.00
Mount Hope, Always Ready, 1987 ....$65.00
Mount Hope, Fireman & Soldier $39.00
Mount Hope, Fireman #1 Pennsylvania Volunteer, 1980 .$75.00
Mount Hope, Fireman #2 Firefighter, 1981 ....$49.00
Mount Hope, Korean Vet $65.00
Old Commonwealth, Fireman #2, Volunteer, 1978 .....$65.00
Old Commonwealth, Fireman #3, On Call, red, 1983.$85.00
Old Commonwealth, Fireman #4, Fallen Comrade.....$75.00
Old Commonwealth, Fireman #5, Harmony...............$75.00
Old Commonwealth, Fireman #6, Breaking Through.$59.00
Pacesetter, Mack Distillery Truck...............$115.00
Pacesetter, 1978 Corvette, gold, mini $49.00
Pacesetter, 1978 Corvette, yellow $35.00
Ski Country, Ahrens Fox Firetruck, gold $175.00
Ski Country, Arhens Fox Firetruck, red & white.......$125.00
Ski Country, Ladies of Leadville $25.00
Ski Country, Muskie..................................$25.00
Ski Country, Pelican $35.00
Ski Country, Stephen Foster.......................$50.00
Ski Country, Tom Thumb, mini $15.00
Wild Turkey, #1, In Flight...........................$95.00
Wild Turkey, #10, w/Coyote, mini $39.00

Wild Turkey, #11, w/Falcon........................$85.00
Wild Turkey, #3, Flying Turkey, 1973, mini $15.00
Wild Turkey, #5, w/Raccoon, from $75 to $90.00
Wild Turkey, #6, w/Poults, from $75 to $90.00
Wild Turkey, #7, w/Fox, mini, from $40 to..............$50.00
Wild Turkey, #8, w/Owl.............................$79.00
Wild Turkey, #9, w/Bear Cubs, from $85 to $90.00
Wild Turkey, Flask....................................$9.00
Wild Turkey, Habitat #1, 1988....................$85.00
Wild Turkey, Spirit of 1976, 1975...............$25.00
Wild Turkey, Turkey on Log, 1972 ....$110.00
Wild Turkey, Turkey on Log, 1972, mini.................$15.00

Degenhart

John and Elizabeth Degenhart owned and operated the Crystal Art Glass Factory in Cambridge, Ohio. From 1947 until John died in 1964 they produced some fine glassware; John himself was well known for his superior paperweights. But the glassware that collectors love today was made after '64, when Elizabeth restructured the company, creating many lovely molds and scores of colors. She hired Zack Boyd, who had previously worked for Cambridge Glass, and between the two of them, they developed almost 150 unique and original color formulas.

Complying with provisions she had made before her death, close personal friends at Island Mould and Machine Company in Wheeling, West Virginia, took Elizabeth's molds and removed the familiar 'D in heart' trademark from them. She had requested that ten of her molds be donated to the Degenhart Museum, where they remain today. Zack Boyd eventually bought the Degenhart factory and acquired the remaining molds. He has added his own logo to them and is continuing to press glass very similar to Mrs. Degenhart's.

For more information, we recommend *Degenhart Glass and Paperweights* by Gene Florence, published by the Degenhart Paperweight and Glass Museum, Inc., Cambridge, Ohio.

Club: Friends of Degenhart
Degenhart Paperweight and Glass Museum
P.O. Box 186
Cambridge, OH 43725; Individual membership: $5 per year; membership includes newsletter, *Heartbeat*, a quarterly publication and free admission to the museum

Beaded Oval toothpick holder, Mulberry, $25.00.

Baby Shoe Toothpick, Caramel Custard Slag	$25.00
Baby Shoe Toothpick, Lemon Custard	$30.00
Basket Toothpick, Cobalt	$18.00
Basket Toothpick, Sparrow Slag	$25.00
Beaded Oval Toothpick, Concord Grape	$30.00
Bicentennial Bell, Bluebell	$15.00
Bicentennial Bell, Jade	$30.00
Bicentennial Bell, Sea Foam	$15.00
Bird Salt, Autumn	$25.00
Bird Salt, Brown	$25.00
Bird Salt, Holly Green	$25.00
Bird Salt, Pigeon Blood	$50.00
Bird Salt & Pepper, Antique Blue	$44.00
Bird Salt & Pepper, Nile Green	$44.00
Bird Salt & Pepper, Vaseline	$30.00
Bird Toothpick, Bernard Boyd's Ebony	$44.00
Bird Toothpick, Teal	$18.00
Blown Bootie, Custard or Milk White	$25.00
Blown Darner, Milk Blue	$30.00
Bow Slipper, Blue Jay Slag	$30.00
Bow Slipper, End of Blizzard	$25.00
Bow Slipper, Willow Green	$30.00
Buzz Saw Wine, Buttercup	$36.00
Buzz Saw Wine, Desert Sun	$44.00
Buzz Saw Wine, Gold	$25.00
Chick Covered Dish, Aqua, 2"	$37.00
Chick Covered Dish, Pink, 2"	$30.00
Coaster, Amberina	$20.00
Coaster, Shamrock	$10.00
Colonial Drape Toothpick, Amber	$18.00
Daisy & Button Creamer & Sugar Bowl, Cobalt	$115.00
Daisy & Button Creamer & Sugar Bowl, Pine Green	$95.00
Daisy & Button Hat, Nile Green	$25.00
Daisy & Button Hat, Off White	$18.00
Daisy & Button Hat, Pink Opalescent	$20.00
Daisy & Button Hat, Rubina	$57.00
Daisy & Button Salt, Delft Blue	$18.00
Daisy & Button Salt, Heliotrope	$30.00
Daisy & Button Toothpick, Apple Green	$25.00
Daisy & Button Toothpick, Elizabeth's Lime Ice	$25.00
Daisy & Button Wine, Cobalt Carnival	$36.00
Daisy & Button Wine, Milk Blue	$50.00
Elephant Head Toothpick, Amethyst	$30.00
Elephant Head Toothpick, Honey Amber	$30.00
Forget-Me-Not Toothpick, Amethyst w/White	$57.00
Forget-Me-Not Toothpick, Baby Pink Slag	$30.00
Forget-Me-Not Toothpick, Blue Fire	$25.00
Forget-Me-Not Toothpick, Dogwood	$50.00
Forget-Me-Not Toothpick, Lavender Marble Slag	$30.00
Gypsy Pot Toothpick, Bloody Mary	$63.00
Gypsy Pot Toothpick, Golden Glo	$18.00
Gypsy Pot Toothpick, Lemon Chiffon	$44.00
Hand, Bluebell	$18.00
Hand, Fog	$25.00
Hand, Frosty Jade	$18.00
Heart & Lyre Cup Plate, Blue Green	$15.00
Heart Jewel Box, Baby Green	$30.00
Heart Jewel Box, Gun Metal	$36.00
Heart Paperweight, Crystal or Vaseline	$30.00
Heart Toothpick, Blue Jay	$30.00
Heart Toothpick, Tomato	$63.00
Hen Covered Dish, Apple Green, 5"	$80.00
Hen Covered Dish, Blue Green, 3"	$50.00
Hen Covered Dish, Honey, 3"	$25.00
Hen Covered Dish, Lemon Custard, 5"	$95.00
Hen Covered Dish, Taffeta, 5"	$75.00
High Boots, Champagne	$18.00
High Boots, Milk Blue	$30.00
Hobo Shoe Toothpick, Blue Carnival	$25.00
Kat Slipper, Bloody Mary	$63.00
Kat Slipper, Canary	$30.00
Kat Slipper, Ivory	$50.00
Kat Slipper, Pine Green	$44.00
Lamb Covered Dish, Canary	$43.00
Lamb Covered Dish, Red	$95.00
Mini Slipper w/out Sole, Lime Ice	$30.00
Mini Slipper w/out Sole, Sapphire	$18.00
Mini Slipper w/Sole, Milk Blue	$44.00
Owl, April Day	$50.00
Owl, Caramel Opal	$63.00
Owl, Dark Amethyst	$36.00
Owl, Desert Sun	$63.00
Owl, Indigo	$125.00
Owl, Orchid	$44.00
Owl, Snow White	$30.00
Owl, Tiger	$50.00
Pitcher, Chocolate Slag, mini	$25.00
Pitcher, Fawn, mini	$25.00
Pooch, Baby Green	$25.00
Pooch, Charcoal	$25.00
Pooch, Gray Tomato	$44.00
Pooch, Milk Blue	$18.00
Pooch, Powder Blue Slag	$57.00
Pottie Salt, Blue & White Slag	$18.00
Pottie Salt, Fog	$18.00
Pottie Salt, Sunset	$15.00
Priscilla, Bittersweet	$185.00
Priscilla, Fawn	$122.00
Robin Covered Dish, Emerald Green	$68.00
Robin Covered Dish, Pink	$75.00
Roller Skate, Aqua	$50.00
Roller Skate, Custard Slag	$95.00
Seal of Ohio Cup Plate, Crystal	$12.50
Star & Dew Drop Salt, Burnt Persimmon	$18.00
Star & Dew Drop Salt, Heatherbloom	$50.00
Star & Dew Drop Salt, Lavender Marble Slag	$44.00
Stork & Peacock, Child's Mug, Amber	$25.00
Stork & Peacock, Child's Mug, Gold	$25.00
Texas Boot, Mint Green Opal Slag	$30.00
Texas Boot, Willow Blue	$25.00
Texas Creamer & Sugar Bowl, Cambridge Pink	$57.00
Texas Creamer & Sugar Bowl, Red	$125.00
Tomahawk, Custard Maverick	$95.00
Tomahawk, Dichromatic	$57.00
Turkey Covered Dish, Bloody Mary	$125.00
Turkey Covered Dish, Peach Blo	$63.00
Wildflower, Candle Holder, Cobalt	$30.00
Wildflower, Candle Holder, Ruby	$50.00

Wildflower, Candy Dish, Crown Tuscan $37.00
Wildflower, Candy Dish, Persimmon...........................$30.00

deLee Art Pottery

Jimmie Lee Adair Kohl founded her company in 1938. She was the inspiration, artist, and owner of the company for the 20 years it was in business. The name deLee means 'of or by Lee' and is taken from the French language. She trained as an artist at the San Diego Art Institute and UCLA where she also earned an art education degree. She taught art and ceramics at Belmont High School in Los Angeles while getting her ceramic business started. In 1996 she turned 90 years old and is still a working artist, doing commissioned pieces and other creations for fun.

The deLee line included children, adults, animals, birds, and specialty items such as cookie jars, banks, wall pockets, and several licensed Walter Lantz characters. Skunks were a favorite subject, and more of her pieces were modeled as skunks than any other single animal. Her figurines are distinctive for their design, charm and excellent hand painting; when carefully studied, they can be easily recognized. Jimmie Lee modeled almost all the pieces — more than 350 in all.

The beautiful deLee colors were mixed by her and remained essentially the same for 20 years. The same figurine may be found painted in different colors and patterns. Figurines were sold wholesale only. Buyers could select from a catalog or visit the deLee booth in New York and Los Angeles Gift Marts. All figurines left the factory with name and logo stickers. The round Art Deco logo sticker is silver with the words 'deLee Art, California, Hand Decorated.' Many of the figures are incised 'deLee Art' on the bottom.

The factory was located in Los Angeles during its 20 years of production and in Cuernavaca, Mexico, for 4 years during WWII. Production continued until 1950, when Japanese copies of her figures caused sales to decline. For further study we recommend deLee Art by Joanne and Ralph Schaefer and John Humphries.

Advisors: Joanne and Ralph Schaefer (See Directory, deLee)

Bank, bunny w/purse, 9", from $65 to $100.00
Cookie jar, girl or boy, 12", each, from $150 to........$300.00
Figurine, adult Cuban couple, Panchita dancing & Pedro
    playing bongos, 8" & 12", pr, from $175 to........$250.00
Figurine, Annie, w/basket & planter, 10", from $75 to ..$150.00
Figurine, Chinese couple, Oh Boy & Oh Joy, 8½", pr, from
    $60 to...$85.00
Figurine, Hank, boy standing & leaning against planter, 7½",
    from $30 to...$40.00
Figurine, Hattie, girl in long skirt w/fan and planter, 7½",
    from $25 to..$35.00
Figurine, Nina, girl w/long skirt & bandana, apron/planter,
    6½", from $25 to...$35.00
Figurine, pigs, Grunt & Groan, 3½" & 4", pr, from $50 to ..$60.00
Figurine, skunks, Squirt, Phew or Stinkie, 4½", each, from
    $20 to...$25.00
Head vase, woman, 3½", from $50 to $75.00
Salt & pepper shakers, pigs, 3½", pr, from $35 to......$50.00
Wall pocket, skunk, DeStinker, 6", from $25 to $35.00

Depression Glass

Since the early sixties, this has been a very active area of collecting. Interest is still very strong, and although values have long been established, except for some of the rarer items, Depression glass is still relatively inexpensive. Some of the patterns and colors that were entirely avoided by the early wave of collectors are now becoming popular, and it's very easy to reassemble a nice table setting of one of these lines today.

Most of this glass was produced during the Depression years. It was inexpensive, mass produced, and available in a wide assortment of colors. The same type of glassware was still being made to some extent during the fifties and sixties, and today the term 'Depression glass' has been expanded to include the later patterns as well.

Some things have been reproduced, and the slight variation in patterns and colors can be very difficult to detect. For instance, the Sharon butter dish has been reissued in original colors of pink and green (as well as others that were not original); and several pieces of Cherry Blossom, Madrid, Avocado, Mayfair, and Miss America have also been reproduced. Some pieces you'll see in 'antique' malls and flea markets today have been recently made in dark uncharacteristic 'carnival' colors, which, of course, are easy to spot.

For further study, Gene Florence has written several informative books on the subject, and we recommend them all: *The Pocket Guide to Depression Glass*, *The Collector's Encyclopedia of Depression Glass*, and *Very Rare Glassware of the Depression Years*.

Publication: *Depression Glass Daze*
Teri Steel, Editor/Publisher
Box 57
Otisville, MI 48463; 810-631-4593; the nation's marketplace for glass, china, and pottery

Adam, green, ashtray, 4½" $25.00
Adam, green, butter dish, w/lid $310.00
Adam, green, coaster, 3¼" $20.00
Adam, green, lamp $275.00
Adam, green, plate, dinner; square, 9" $28.00
Adam, green, shakers, footed, 4" $100.00
Adam, green, sugar bowl/candy jar lid only $40.00
Adam, pink, bowl, no lid, 9" $30.00
Adam, pink, candlesticks, 4", pr $85.00
Adam, pink, plate, sherbet; 6" $9.00
Adam, pink, platter, 11¾" $28.00
Adam, pink, saucer, round, 6" $75.00
Adam, pink, sugar bowl..$17.50
Adam, pink, vase, 7½" $250.00
Adam, pink or green, bowl, cereal; 5¾".....................$40.00
Adam, pink or green, bowl, oval, 10".........................$30.00
Adam, yellow, cup $100.00
American Pioneer, amber, bowl, handled, 5" $40.00
American Pioneer, amber, pitcher, urn shaped, w/lid, 7"..$300.00
American Pioneer, crystal, pink or green, pilsner, 11-oz,
    5¾"..$100.00
American Pioneer, crystal or pink, bowl, w/lid, 8¾"..$95.00
American Pioneer, crystal or pink, candy jar, w/lid, 1-lb..$85.00
American Pioneer, crystal or pink, creamer, 2¾" $25.00

American Pioneer, crystal or pink, dresser set **$375.00**
American Pioneer, crystal or pink, plate, handle, 6"...**$12.50**
American Pioneer, crystal or pink, sherbet, 4¾" **$32.50**
American Pioneer, crystal or pink, tumbler, 8-oz, 4" ..**$30.00**
American Pioneer, green, bowl, console; 10¾"...........**$65.00**
American Pioneer, green, cheese & cracker set, platter & comport **$60.00**
American Pioneer, green, goblet, wine; 3-oz, 4" **$45.00**
American Pioneer, green, plate, handled, 11½" **$20.00**
American Pioneer, green, vase, 4 styles, 7" **$100.00**
American Pioneer, red, bowl, console; 18"...............**$850.00**
American Sweetheart, blue, plate, salver; 12" **$185.00**
American Sweetheart, blue, saucer...............................**$25.00**
American Sweetheart, blue, sugar bowl, open, footed .**$115.00**
American Sweetheart, cremax, bowl, cereal; 6" **$10.00**
American Sweetheart, lamp shade, cremax...............**$450.00**
American Sweetheart, monax, bowl, soup; flat, 9½" ..**$75.00**
American Sweetheart, monax, plate, salad; 8" **$8.00**
American Sweetheart, monax, shakers, footed..........**$325.00**
American Sweetheart, monax, sherbet, footed, design inside or outside, 4¼" **$18.00**
American Sweetheart, monax, tidbit, 3-tier, 8", 12" & 15½" ..**$275.00**
American Sweetheart, pink, cup..................................**$17.50**
American Sweetheart, pink, plate, salver; 12" **$20.00**
American Sweetheart, pink, platter, oval, 13" **$50.00**
American Sweetheart, pink, sherbet, footed, 3¾" **$20.00**
American Sweetheart, pink, sugar bowl, open, footed..**$12.00**
American Sweetheart, red, plate, salad; 8"................**$65.00**
American Sweetheart, red, plate, server; 15½"..........**$300.00**
American Sweetheart, red, tidbit, 2-tier, 8" & 12"......**$195.00**
American Sweetheart, smoke & other trims, bowl, berry; round, 9"...**$150.00**
American Sweetheart, smoke & other trims, creamer, footed **$85.00**
American Sweetheart, smoke & other trims, plate, bread & butter; 6" **$18.00**
American Sweetheart, smoke & other trims, plate, luncheon; 9" **$37.50**
American Sweetheart, smoke & other trims, platter, oval, 13" **$175.00**
American Sweetheart, smoke & other trims, sherbet, footed, design inside or outside, 4¼" **$70.00**
Aunt Polly, blue, bowl, berry; 4¾"..............................**$17.50**
Aunt Polly, blue, bowl, pickle; oval, handled, 7¼" **$40.00**
Aunt Polly, blue, candy jar, footed, 2-handled...........**$30.00**
Aunt Polly, blue, plate, luncheon; 8" **$20.00**
Aunt Polly, blue, sugar bowl **$30.00**
Aunt Polly, green, bowl, 1-handle, 5½".......................**$14.00**
Aunt Polly, green, butter dish, w/lid.........................**$225.00**
Aunt Polly, green, creamer **$30.00**
Aunt Polly, green, plate, sherbet; 6"..............................**$6.00**
Aunt Polly, green, vase, footed, 6½"...........................**$30.00**
Aurora, cobalt or pink, bowl, deep, 4½".......................**$40.00**
Aurora, cobalt or pink, creamer, 4½"............................**$22.50**
Aurora, cobalt or pink, plate, 6½".................................**$12.00**
Aurora, green, bowl, cereal; 5⅜".....................................**$7.00**
Aurora, green, cup...**$7.50**
Aurora, green, saucer **$2.50**
Avocado, crystal, bowl, 2-handled, 5½".......................**$10.00**

Avocado, crystal, bowl, 3¼x9½" **$22.00**
Avocado, crystal, plate, luncheon; 8¼" **$7.00**
Avocado, crystal, sugar bowl, footed **$12.00**
Avocado, green, bowl, oval, 2-handled, 8"..................**$27.50**
Avocado, green, pitcher, 64-oz..............................**$1,000.00**
Avocado, green, saucer, 6⅜".......................................**$24.00**
Avocado, pink, bowl, preserve; handled, 7"................**$20.00**
Avocado, pink, cup, footed, 2 styles............................**$30.00**
Avocado, pink, plate, cake; 2-handled, 10¼" **$35.00**
Avocado, pink, sherbet..**$50.00**
Avocdao, pink, plate, sherbet; 6⅜"...............................**$14.00**
Beaded Block, blue, bowl, square, 5½" **$11.00**
Beaded Block, blue or vaseline, plate, square, 7¾" ...**$10.00**
Beaded Block, crystal or green, bowl, jelly; 2-handled, 4⅞" to 5"...**$7.50**
Beaded Block, crystal or green, creamer....................**$16.00**
Beaded Block, crystal or green, vase, bouquet; 6" **$12.00**
Beaded Block, crystal or pink, bowl, pickle; 2-handled, 6½"...**$13.00**
Beaded Block, iridescent or milk white, bowl, round, plain edge, 7½"...**$23.00**
Beaded Block, pink or amber, bowl, handled, 5½"......**$7.50**
Beaded Block, pink or amber, bowl, round, flared, 7¼" ...**$11.50**
Beaded Block, pink or amber, stemmed jelly, 4½".......**$9.50**
Beaded Block, red or milk white, sugar bowl.............**$25.00**
Beaded Block, red or opalescent, bowl, round, unflared, 6¾"..**$17.00**
Beaded Block, vaseline, bowl, round, 6¼" **$16.50**
Block, Optic, pink or green, bowl, console; rolled edge, 11¾"..**$60.00**
Block Optic, green, bowl, berry; lg, 8½"......................**$25.00**
Block Optic, green, bowl, 1½x4½"...............................**$27.50**
Block Optic, green, bowl, 1⅜x4½"..................................**$8.00**
Block Optic, green, butter dish, w/lid, 3x5"................**$47.50**
Block Optic, green, candy jar, w/lid, 6¼" **$55.00**
Block Optic, green, ice/butter tub, open.....................**$45.00**
Block Optic, green, pink or yellow, sherbet, 6-oz, 4¾" ..**$15.00**
Block Optic, green, sandwich server, center handle ..**$65.00**
Block Optic, green, sherbet, 5½-oz, 3¼".......................**$6.00**
Block Optic, green, tumbler, flat, 12-oz, 4⅞" **$25.00**
Block Optic, pink, bowl, cereal; 5¼".............................**$25.00**
Block Optic, pink, candlesticks, 1¾", pr......................**$75.00**
Block Optic, pink, goblet, wine; short, 3½"...............**$400.00**
Block Optic, pink, plate, luncheon; 8".............................**$5.00**
Block Optic, pink, whiskey, 1-oz, 1⅝"...........................**$40.00**
Block Optic, yellow, candy jar, w/lid, 2¼"...................**$60.00**
Block Optic, yellow, goblet, thin, 9-oz, 7¼" **$35.00**
Block Optic, yellow, plate, dinner; 9"...........................**$40.00**
Block Optic, yellow, plate, sherbet; 6"...........................**$3.00**
Block Optic, yellow or pink, shakers, footed, pr.......**$75.00**
Bowknot, green, bowl, berry; 4½"................................**$16.00**
Bowknot, green, cup..**$8.00**
Bowknot, green, sherbet, low footed **$16.00**
Bowknot, green, tumbler; 10-oz, 5"..............................**$20.00**
Cameo, crystal, decanter, w/stopper, 10"..................**$195.00**
Cameo, crystal, ice bowl, 3x5½" **$250.00**
Cameo, crystal, jam jar, w/lid, 2"...............................**$160.00**
Cameo, crystal, relish, footed, 3-part, 7½".................**$150.00**
Cameo, crystal, tumbler, water; 9-oz, 4".......................**$9.00**

Cameo, green, bowl, berry; lg, 8¼" $35.00
Cameo, green, bowl, cream soup; 4¾"..............$115.00
Cameo, green, butter dish, w/lid..............$200.00
Cameo, green, domino tray, w/3" indention, 7" $130.00
Cameo, green, plate, sandwich; 10" $13.00
Cameo, green, shakers, footed, pr $67.50
Cameo, green, sherbet, 4⅞"..............$34.00
Cameo, green, vase, 5¾" $185.00
Cameo, pink, bowl, cereal; 5½" $150.00
Cameo, pink, comport, mayonnaise; 5"..............$195.00
Cameo, pink, cup, 2 styles..............$75.00
Cameo, pink, goblet, wine; 4" $200.00
Cameo, pink, plate, cake; flat, 10½" $150.00
Cameo, yellow, bowl, vegetable; oval, 10"..............$40.00
Cameo, yellow, candy jar, w/lid, low, 4" $75.00
Cameo, yellow, creamer, 3¼" $20.00
Cameo, yellow, plate, grill; 10½"..............$6.00
Cameo, yellow, plate, luncheon; 8" $11.00
Cameo, yellow, saucer, 6" $3.00
Cameo, yellow, tumbler, flat, 11-oz, 5"..............$47.50
Cherry Blossom, bowl, cereal; 5¾" $37.50
Cherry Blossom, delphite, bowl, berry; round, 8½" ...$50.00
Cherry Blossom, delphite, creamer $18.00
Cherry Blossom, delphite, plate, sherbet; 6" $10.00
Cherry Blossom, delphite, platter, oval, 11"..............$40.00
Cherry Blossom, delphite, tumbler, allover pattern, footed, 4-oz, 3¾" $20.00
Cherry Blossom, green, bowl, 2-handled, 9" $65.00
Cherry Blossom, green, coaster $13.00
Cherry Blossom, green, cup..............$19.00
Cherry Blossom, green, tumbler, allover pattern, footed, 9-oz, 4½" $33.00
Cherry Blossom, pink, bowl, berry; 4¾" $15.00
Cherry Blossom, pink, butter dish, w/lid..............$72.50
Cherry Blossom, pink, pitcher, allover pattern, scalloped or round bottom, 36-oz, 6¾" $55.00
Cherry Blossom, pink or green, pitcher, pattern at top, flat, 42-oz, 8"..............$52.50
Cherry Blossom, pink or green, plate, grill; 9"............$25.00

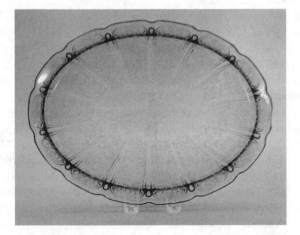

Cherry Blossom, pink or green, platter, 13", $65.00.

Cherry Blossom, pink or green, sherbet $6.00
Cherry Blossom, pink or green, tray, sandwich; 10½"...$25.00
Cherryberry, crystal, bowl, berry; 4"..............$6.50

Cherryberry, crystal, butter dish, w/lid $145.00
Cherryberry, crystal, creamer, lg, 4⅝" $15.00
Cherryberry, crystal, pitcher, 7¾" $160.00
Cherryberry, crystal, sherbet $6.50
Cherryberry, pink or green, bowl, salad; deep, 6½" ..$20.00
Cherryberry, pink or green, creamer, sm..............$17.00
Cherryberry, pink or green, olive dish, handled, 5" ...$15.00
Cherryberry, pink or green, plate, sherbet; 6" $9.00
Cherryberry, pink or green, sugar bowl, lg..............$25.00
Chinex Classic, castle decal, bowl, vegetable; 9" $35.00
Chinex Classic, castle decal, plate, dinner; 9¾" $20.00
Chinex Classic, castle decal, sherbet, low footed.......$17.50
Chinex Classic, decal decorated, bowl, soup; 7¾" $20.00
Chinex Classic, decal decorated, butter dish, w/lid $75.00
Chinex Classic, decal decorated, cup $6.50
Chinex Classic, decal decorated, sugar bowl, open......$9.00
Chinex Classic, ivory, bowl, cereal; 5¾" $5.50
Chinex Classic, ivory, bowl, 11" $17.00
Chinex Classic, ivory, plate, sandwich; 11½" $7.50
Circle, green or pink, bowl, 5¼" $10.00
Circle, green or pink, bowl, 9⅜" $18.00
Circle, green or pink, decanter, handled $45.00
Circle, green or pink, pitcher, 60-oz $32.00
Circle, green or pink, plate, sherbet/saucer; 6" $1.50
Circle, green or pink, plate, 9½" $12.00
Circle, green or pink, saucer, w/cup ring..............$2.50
Circle, green or pink, sherbet, 4¾" $6.00
Circle, green or pink, tumbler, flat, 15-oz..............$20.00
Circle, green or pink, tumbler, water; 8-oz, 4" $9.00
Cloverleaf, black, ashtray, match holder in center, 4"..$67.50
Cloverleaf, black, shakers, pr..............$85.00
Cloverleaf, black, sherbet, footed, 3" $20.00
Cloverleaf, green, bowl, cereal; 5" $27.50
Cloverleaf, green, plate, sherbet; 6"..............$5.00
Cloverleaf, green, tumbler, footed, 10-oz, 5¾"............$22.50
Cloverleaf, pink, cup $7.00
Cloverleaf, pink, saucer..............$4.00
Cloverleaf, yellow, bowl, dessert; 4" $25.00
Cloverleaf, yellow, plate, luncheon; 8" $14.00
Cloverleaf, yellow, sugar bowl, footed, 3⅝" $17.50
Colonial, crystal, bowl, soup; low, 7" $25.00
Colonial, crystal, goblet, claret; 4-oz, 5¼" $18.00
Colonial, crystal, pitcher, cream/milk; 16-oz, 5"..........$17.50
Colonial, crystal, platter, oval, 12" $15.00
Colonial, crystal, sugar bowl, 5" $10.00
Colonial, crystal, tumbler, lemonade; 15-oz..............$45.00
Colonial, green, bowl, cereal; 5½" $85.00
Colonial, green, butter dish bottom only..............$32.50
Colonial, green, goblet, cocktail; 3-oz, 4" $25.00
Colonial, green, plate, dinner; 10"..............$60.00
Colonial, green, sherbet, 3⅜"..............$15.00
Colonial, green, tumbler, footed, 5-oz, 4"..............$40.00
Colonial, green, tumbler, 11-oz, 5⅛"..............$42.00
Colonial, pink, bowl, berry; 3¾" $45.00
Colonial, pink, bowl, vegetable; oval, 10"..............$32.00
Colonial, pink, cup..............$12.00
Colonial, pink, plate, sherbet; 6" $6.00
Colonial, pink, tumbler, juice; 5-oz, 3"..............$18.00
Colonial, pink or green, shakers, pr $135.00

Colonial Block, pink or green, bowl, 4" $6.50
Colonial Block, pink or green, butter dish, w/lid.......$45.00
Colonial Block, pink or green, candy jar, w/lid..........$37.50
Colonial Block, pink or green, pitcher $40.00
Colonial Block, pink or green, sherbet.........................$9.00
Colonial Block, white, creamer...................................$7.00
Colonial Block, white, sugar bowl, w/lid $10.00
Colonial Flute, green, bowl, berry; lg, 7½" $16.00
Colonial Flute, green, bowl, berry; 4" $6.00
Colonial Flute, green, bowl, salad; 2½x6½".................$20.00
Colonial Flute, green, cup..$5.00
Colonial Flute, green, plate, sherbet; 6" $2.50
Colonial Flute, green, sherbet.......................................$6.00
Columbia, crystal, bowl, cereal; 5" $16.00
Columbia, crystal, bowl, salad; 8½" $18.00
Columbia, crystal, butter dish, w/lid..........................$20.00
Columbia, crystal, plate, chop; 11"............................$10.00
Columbia, crystal, tumbler, juice; 4-oz, 2⅞"..............$20.00
Columbia, pink, plate, luncheon; 9½".........................$30.00
Columbia, pink, saucer..$10.00
Coronation, green, bowl, no handles, 8"..................$150.00
Coronation, pink, bowl, berry; 4¼"..............................$4.50
Coronation, pink, pitcher, 68-oz, 7¾"........................$500.00
Coronation, pink, sherbet...$4.50
Coronation, royal ruby, bowl, nappy; 6½".................$12.00
Coronation, royal ruby, cup...$6.50
Coronation, royal ruby, plate, luncheon; 8½" $8.00
Crow's Foot, black or blue, bowl, square, 11"...........$70.00
Crow's Foot, black or blue, bowl, 6" $35.00
Crow's Foot, black or blue, cheese stand, 5" $30.00
Crow's Foot, black or blue, gravy boat, pedestal $140.00
Crow's Foot, black or blue, saucer, round, 6" $3.00
Crow's Foot, colors other than red, black or blue, bowl, con-
    sole; round, 3-footed, 11½".................................$42.50
Crow's Foot, colors other than red, black or blue, bowl,
    square, 2-handled, 8½".......................................$27.50
Crow's Foot, colors other than red, black or blue, candle
    holder, round base, tall $37.50
Crow's Foot, red, bowl, cream soup; footed or flat....$20.00
Crow's Foot, red, bowl, square, 4⅞"...........................$25.00
Crow's Foot, red, candlestick, 5¾"..............................$25.00
Crow's Foot, red, creamer, flat....................................$12.50
Crow's Foot, red, cup, footed or flat...........................$10.00
Crow's Foot, red, plate, round, 8" $9.00
Crow's Foot, red, relish tray, 3-part, 11".....................$85.00
Crow's Foot, red, sugar bowl, footed..........................$11.00
Cube, green, bowl, salad; 6½".....................................$14.00
Cube, green, candy jar, w/lid, 6½"..............................$30.00
Cube, green, coaster, 3¼"..$7.50
Cube, pink, bowl, dessert; 4½".....................................$6.50
Cube, pink, cup $7.50
Cube, pink, plate, luncheon; 8" $6.50
Cube, pink or green, butter dish, w/lid.......................$20.00
Cube, pink or green, saucer $3.00
Cupid, green or pink, bowl, center-handled, 9¼" $165.00
Cupid, green or pink, comport, 6¼"............................$75.00
Cupid, green or pink, creamer, footed, 4½"...............$90.00
Cupid, green or pink, ice bucket, 6".........................$190.00
Cupid, green or pink, plate, cake; 11¾".....................$150.00

Cupid, green or pink, plate, 10½"..............................$100.00
Cupid, green or pink, sugar bowl, footed, 5" $90.00
Diamond Quilted, blue or black, bowl, cereal; 5" $15.00
Diamond Quilted, blue or black, bowl, crimped edge, 7" ..$18.00
Diamond Quilted, blue or black, candlesticks, 2 styles, pr.$50.00
Diamond Quilted, blue or black, creamer..................$17.50
Diamond Quilted, blue or black, plate, salad; 7".........$9.00
Diamond Quilted, blue or black, sandwich server, center
    handle $50.00
Diamond Quilted, blue or black, sugar bowl..............$17.50
Diamond Quilted, blue or black, vase, fan shape, dolphin
    handles $75.00
Diamond Quilted, pink or green, bowl, cream soup;
    4¾"...$10.00
Diamond Quilted, pink or green, bowl, 1-handle, 5½"..$7.50
Diamond Quilted, pink or green, cake salver, tall, 10"
    dia...$55.00
Diamond Quilted, pink or green, compote, 6x7¼"....$45.00
Diamond Quilted, pink or green, goblet, champagne; 9-oz,
    6" $11.00
Diamond Quilted, pink or green, goblet, cordial; 1-oz...$12.00
Diamond Quilted, pink or green, pitcher, 64-oz.........$50.00
Diamond Quilted, pink or green, plate, luncheon; 8" ..$6.00
Diamond Quilted, pink or green, saucer.......................$3.00
Diamond Quilted, pink or green, tumbler, water; 9-oz.$9.00
Diana, amber, bowl, console fruit; 11".......................$17.50
Diana, amber, coaster, 3½" $10.00
Diana, amber, plate, 9"..$9.00
Diana, amber, saucer..$2.00
Diana, crystal, ashtray, 3½"...$2.50
Diana, crystal, bowl, scalloped edge, 12" $7.00
Diana, crystal, plate, sandwich; 11¾".........................$5.00
Diana, pink, bowl, cream soup; 5½".........................$22.00
Diana, pink, candy jar, w/lid, round..........................$40.00
Diana, pink, cup & saucer, demitasse.........................$45.00
Diana, pink, platter, oval, 12"....................................$27.00
Diana, pink, tumbler, 9-oz, 4⅛".................................$42.00
Dogwood, green, bowl, berry; 8½".............................$100.00
Dogwood, green, creamer, flat, thin, 2½"...................$45.00
Dogwood, green, saucer..$8.00
Dogwood, green, sugar bowl, thin, flat, 2½" $45.00
Dogwood, green, tumbler, decorated, 10-oz, 4" $85.00
Dogwood, green, tumbler, decorated, 12-oz, 5" $100.00
Dogwood, pink, cup, thick...$17.00
Dogwood, pink, plate, bread & butter; 6" $8.00
Dogwood, pink, plate, cake; heavy, solid footed, 13" ..$110.00
Dogwood, pink, plate, dinner; 9½"............................$35.00
Dogwood, pink, sherbet, low footed..........................$35.00
Dogwood, pink, sugar bowl, thick, footed, 3¼".........$18.00
Dogwood, pink, tumbler, decorated, 5-oz, 3½"........$260.00
Dogwood, pink, tumbler, moulded band $20.00
Dogwood, pink or green, bowl, cereal; 5½".................$30.00
Doric, delphite, bowl, berry; lg, 8¼".........................$125.00
Doric, delphite, candy dish, 3-part..............................$8.00
Doric, delphite, sherbet, footed...................................$6.00
Doric, green, butter dish, w/lid..................................$85.00
Doric, green, pitcher, flat, 32-oz, 5½" $40.00
Doric, green, plate, salad; 7" $20.00
Doric, green, relish tray, 4x4".......................................$8.50

Doric, green, saucer...**$4.50**
Doric, pink, bowl, berry; 4½"............................**$7.00**
Doric, pink, candy dish, w/lid, 8".....................**$35.00**
Doric, pink, creamer, 4"......................................**$12.00**
Doric, pink, plate, grill; 9"................................**$15.00**
Doric, pink, plate, sherbet; 6"............................**$4.00**
Doric, pink, shakers, pr..**$32.50**
Doric, pink, tray, handled, 10"...........................**$12.50**
Doric, pink or green, bowl, 2-handled, 9"........**$15.00**
Doric, pink or green, plate, cake; 3 legs, 10"...**$21.00**
Doric & Pansy, pink, bowl, berry; lg, 8"..........**$20.00**
Doric & Pansy, pink, cup......................................**$9.00**
Doric & Pansy, pink, plate, dinner; 9"..............**$7.50**
Doric & Pansy, pink, plate, sherbet; 6"............**$7.50**
Doric & Pansy, pink, sugar bowl, open.............**$65.00**
Doric & Pansy, ultramarine, bowl, berry; 4½"...**$17.50**
Doric & Pansy, ultramarine, bowl, salad; 7"....**$35.00**
Doric & Pansy, ultramarine, butter dish, w/lid........**$450.00**
Doric & Pansy, ultramarine, tumbler, 9-oz, 4½"........**$80.00**
English Hobnail, ice blue, ashtray, 4½".............**$22.50**
English Hobnail, ice blue, plate, round, 10"......**$65.00**
English Hobnail, ice blue, stem, sherbet; square, footed, high..**$35.00**
English Hobnail, ice blue, stem, wine; square, footed, 2-oz..**$60.00**
English Hobnail, pink or green, ashtray, 3".......**$20.00**
English Hobnail, pink or green, bonbon, handled, 6½"..**$25.00**
English Hobnail, pink or green, bottle, toilet; 5-oz.....**$45.00**
English Hobnail, pink or green, bowl, celery; 12"......**$32.50**
English Hobnail, pink or green, bowl, cereal; 9"........**$30.00**
English Hobnail, pink or green, finger bowl; square, footed, 4½"..**$15.00**
English Hobnail, pink or green, finger bowl; 4½"......**$15.00**
English Hobnail, pink or green, bowl, footed, 8".......**$45.00**
English Hobnail, pink or green, bowl, grapefruit; 6½".**$20.00**
English Hobnail, pink or green, bowl, nappy; round, 7".**$22.00**
English Hobnail, pink or green, bowl, nappy; square, 6"..**$16.00**
English Hobnail, pink or green, bowl, rose; 4".........**$45.00**
English Hobnail, pink or green, candy jar, w/lid, cone shaped, ½-lb..**$40.00**
English Hobnail, pink or green, cigarette jar, w/lid, round.**$60.00**
English Hobnail, pink or green, compote, honey; footed, round, 6"..**$30.00**
English Hobnail, pink or green, creamer, footed, hexagonal...**$45.00**
English Hobnail, pink or green, cup, demitasse........**$50.00**
English Hobnail, pink or green, ice tub, 5½"..........**$100.00**
English Hobnail, pink or green, marmalade, w/lid.....**$40.00**
English Hobnail, pink or green, pitcher, rounded, 23-oz.**$145.00**
English Hobnail, pink or green, plate, round, 5½".....**$9.50**
English Hobnail, pink or green, plate, round, 8"........**$12.50**
English Hobnail, pink or green, puff box, w/lid, round, 6".**$27.50**
English Hobnail, pink or green, stem, water goblet; square, footed, 8-oz.....................................**$30.00**
English Hobnail, pink or green, tumbler, iced tea; 10-oz.**$25.00**
Floral, delphite, bowl, salad; 7½"......................**$60.00**
Floral, green, butter dish, w/lid.........................**$87.50**
Floral, green, coaster, 3¼"....................................**$10.00**
Floral, green, ice tub, oval, 3½"..........................**$875.00**

Floral, green, pitcher, cone shape, 32-oz, 8"..............**$35.00**
Floral, green, plate, grill; 9"..............................**$175.00**
Floral, green, sherbet...**$18.00**
Floral, green, tumbler, juice; footed, 5-oz, 4"............**$21.00**
Floral, jadite, canister set, coffee, tea, cereal & sugar, 5¼" tall, each...**$50.00**
Floral, pink, bowl, berry; 4"................................**$16.00**

Floral, pink, bowl, vegetable; with lid, 8", $45.00.

Floral, pink, creamer, flat....................................**$13.00**
Floral, pink, relish dish, 2-part oval...................**$16.00**
Floral, pink, shakers, flat, 6", pr.........................**$47.50**
Floral & Diamond Band, green, bowl, berry; lg, 8"....**$13.50**
Floral & Diamond Band, green, sugar bowl, sm........**$11.00**
Floral & Diamond Band, green, tumbler, iced tea; 5".**$38.00**
Floral & Diamond Band, pink, bowl, berry; 4½"........**$7.50**
Floral & Diamond Band, pink, butter dish, w/lid.....**$130.00**
Floral & Diamond Band, pink, compote, 5½"...........**$15.00**
Floral & Diamond Band, pink, sherbet......................**$6.50**
Floral & Diamond Band, pink, sugar bowl, 5½".........**$14.00**
Florentine No 1, cobalt blue, comport, ruffled, 3½"...**$60.00**
Florentine No 1, cobalt blue, saucer.......................**$17.00**
Florentine No 1, crystal, green or pink, sherbet, footed, 3-oz...**$10.00**
Florentine No 1, crystal, green or pink, sugar bowl, ruffled..**$35.00**
Florentine No 1, crystal or green, ashtray, 5½".........**$22.00**
Florentine No 1, crystal or green, bowl, berry; 5".....**$11.00**
Florentine No 1, crystal or green, bowl, vegetable; w/lid, oval, 9½"..**$50.00**
Florentine No 1, crystal or green, pitcher, flat, 48-oz, 7½"..**$70.00**
Florentine No 1, crystal or green, plate, salad; 8½"...**$7.50**
Florentine No 1, crystal or green, tumbler, footed, 4-oz, 3¼"..**$16.00**
Florentine No 1, pink, ashtray/coaster, 3¾"............**$25.00**
Florentine No 1, pink, bowl, cream soup; 5"............**$18.00**
Florentine No 1, pink, creamer.................................**$17.00**
Florentine No 1, pink, plate, grill; 10"..................**$18.00**
Florentine No 1, pink, tumbler, ribbed, 9-oz, 4".......**$22.00**
Florentine No 1, yellow, cup...................................**$10.00**
Florentine No 1, yellow or pink, butter dish..............**$85.00**
Florentine No 1, yellow or pink, plate, dinner; 10"...**$22.00**
Florentine No 1, yellow or pink, sugar bowl..............**$12.00**
Florentine No 1, yellow or pink, tumbler, iced tea; footed, 12-oz, 5¼"..**$30.00**

Florentine No 1, yellow or pink, tumbler, juice; 5-oz, 3¾" **$22.00**

Florentine No 2, cobalt blue, tumbler, water; 9-oz, 4" ..**$65.00**

Florentine No 2, crystal, green & pink, plate, salad; 8½" **$8.50**

Florentine No 2, crystal, green or pink, platter, oval, 11" ...**$16.00**

Florentine No 2, crystal, green or pink, tumbler, juice; 5-oz, 3⅜" **$12.00**

Florentine No 2, crystal, green or yellow, plate, grill; 10¼" **$12.00**

Florentine No 2, crystal or green, bowl, berry; 4½" ...**$12.00**

Florentine No 2, crystal or green, bowl, flat, 9" **$25.00**

Florentine No 2, crystal or green, coaster/ashtray, 5½" ..**$17.50**

Florentine No 2, crystal or green, plate, sherbet; 6" **$4.00**

Florentine No 2, crystal or green, relish dish, 3-part or plain, 10" **$19.00**

Florentine No 2, crystal or green, tumbler, blown, 6-oz, 3⅝" **$18.00**

Florentine No 2, crystal or green, tumbler, tea; 12-oz, 5" **$33.00**

Florentine No 2, pink, bowl, cream soup; 4¾" **$16.00**

Florentine No 2, pink, coaster, 3¼" **$16.00**

Florentine No 2, pink, comport, ruffled, 3½" **$14.00**

Florentine No 2, pink, pitcher, 48-oz, 7½" **$115.00**

Florentine No 2, pink, relish dish, 3-part or plain, 10" **$25.00**

Florentine No 2, pink, tumbler, footed, 5-oz, 3¼" **$16.00**

Florentine No 2, yellow, bowl, shallow, 7½" **$85.00**

Florentine No 2, yellow, butter dish, w/lid **$140.00**

Florentine No 2, yellow, custard cup **$80.00**

Florentine No 2, yellow, saucer **$5.00**

Florentine No 2, yellow, sugar bowl **$11.00**

Florentine No 2, yellow, tumbler, footed, 5-oz, 4" **$17.00**

Flower Garden w/Butterflies, amber or crystal, candlesticks, 4", pr **$42.50**

Flower Garden w/Butterflies, amber or crystal, comport, fits 10" plate **$20.00**

Flower Garden w/Butterflies, amber or crystal, plate, 7" ..**$16.00**

Flower Garden w/Butterflies, amber or crystal, tray, oval, 5½x10" **$50.00**

Flower Garden w/Butterflies, black, bonbon, w/lid, 6⅝" dia **$250.00**

Flower Garden w/Butterflies, black, bowl, orange; footed, 11" **$225.00**

Flower Garden w/Butterflies, black, comport, 5⅝x10" ..**$225.00**

Flower Garden w/Butterflies, blue or canary yellow, candy jar, w/lid, cone-shaped, 7½" **$165.00**

Flower Garden w/Butterflies, pink, green or blue-green, candy jar, w/lid, flat, 6" **$155.00**

Flower Garden w/Butterflies, pink, green or blue-green, cologne bottle, w/stopper, 7½" **$185.00**

Flower Garden w/Butterflies, pink, green or blue-green, comport, 4¾x10¼" **$65.00**

Flower Garden w/Butterflies, pink or green, creamer..**$70.00**

Flower Garden w/Butterflies, pink or green, cup.......**$65.00**

Flower Garden w/Butterflies, pink or green, plate, 10" ..**$42.50**

Flower Garden w/Butterflies, pink or green, powder jar, flat, 3½" **$75.00**

Flower Garden w/Butterflies, pink or green, saucer ..**$27.50**

Flower Garden w/Butterflies, pink or green, sugar bowl.**$65.00**

Flower Garden w/Butterflies, pink or green, vase, 6¼" .**$125.00**

Fortune, pink or crystal, bowl, berry; 4" **$3.50**

Fortune, pink or crystal, bowl, berry/salad;, lg, 7¾" ..**$14.00**

Fortune, pink or crystal, bowl, handled, 4½" **$4.50**

Fortune, pink or crystal, plate, sherbet; 6" **$3.00**

Fortune, pink or crystal, saucer **$3.00**

Fortune, pink or crystal, tumbler, water; 9-oz, 4" **$10.00**

Fruits, green, bowl, berry; 5" **$25.00**

Fruits, green, saucer..**$5.50**

Fruits, green, sherbet..**$8.00**

Fruits, green, tumbler, 1-fruit design, 4" **$17.50**

Fruits, green or pink, plate, luncheon; 8" **$6.50**

Fruits, pink, cup..**$7.00**

Fruits, pink, tumbler, juice; 3½" **$20.00**

Fruits, pink, tumbler, 12-oz, 5" **$90.00**

Georgian, green, bowl, berry; 4½" **$8.00**

Georgian, green, bowl, deep, 6½" **$62.50**

Georgian, green, bowl, vegetable; oval, 9" **$60.00**

Georgian, green, butter dish, w/lid **$70.00**

Georgian, green, creamer, footed, 3" **$11.00**

Georgian, green, cup..**$9.00**

Georgian, green, plate, dinner; 9¼" **$25.00**

Georgian, green, plate, sherbet; 6" **$6.00**

Georgian, green, platter, closed handles, 11½" **$62.50**

Georgian, green, sherbet..**$12.00**

Georgian, green, sugar bowl, footed, 4" **$11.00**

Georgian, green, tumbler, flat, 9-oz, 4" **$55.00**

Hex Optic, pink or green, bowl, berry; ruffled, 4½" **$5.50**

Hex Optic, pink or green, bowl, mixing; 8¼" **$17.50**

Hex Optic, pink or green, ice bucket, metal handled ..**$18.00**

Hex Optic, pink or green, plate, luncheon; 8" **$5.50**

Hex Optic, pink or green, sherbet, footed, 5-oz...........**$4.50**

Hex Optic, pink or green, sugar bowl, 2 styles of handles...**$5.50**

Hex Optic, pink or green, tumbler, footed, 7" **$12.00**

Hex Optic, pink or green, tumbler, 12-oz, 5" **$7.00**

Hobnail, crystal, bowl, cereal; 5½" **$4.00**

Hobnail, crystal, goblet, water; 10-oz...........................**$7.00**

Hobnail, crystal, sherbet..**$3.00**

Hobnail, crystal, tumbler, iced tea; 15-oz.....................**$7.00**

Hobnail, crystal, whiskey, 1½-oz..................................**$6.00**

Hobnail, pink or crystal, cup **$4.50**

Hobnail, pink or crystal, plate, luncheon; 8½"............**$3.50**

Hobnail, pink or crystal, plate, sherbet; 6" **$2.00**

Homespun, pink or crystal, bowl, closed handles, 4½" .**$10.00**

Homespun, pink or crystal, coaster/ashtray **$6.50**

Homespun, pink or crystal, cup...................................**$10.00**

Homespun, pink or crystal, platter, closed handles, 13"..**$15.00**

Homespun, pink or crystal, saucer.................................**$4.00**

Homespun, pink or crystal, tumbler, footed, 15-oz, 6⅜" ...**$27.50**

Homespun, pink or crystal, tumbler, iced tea; 13-oz, 5¼".**$30.00**

Homespun, pink or crystal, tumbler, straight, 6-oz, 3⅞"..**$20.00**

Indiana Custard, ivory, bowl, berry; lg, 1¾x9"..........**$30.00**

Indiana Custard, ivory, bowl, berry; 5½" **$8.00**

Indiana Custard, ivory, plate, bread & butter; 5¾" **$6.50**

Indiana Custard, ivory, plate, dinner; 9¾" **$25.00**

Indiana Custard, ivory, plate, salad; 7½" **$15.00**

Indiana Custard, ivory, saucer **$8.00**

Indiana Custard, ivory, sugar bowl, w/lid **$30.00**

Indiana Ivory, bowl, berry; 5½".....................................**$8.00**

Iris, all crystal: Goblet, 5½", $25.00; Wine, 4½", $16.00; Pitcher, 9½", $40.00.

Iris, crystal, bowl, berry; beaded edge, 4½" $40.00
Iris, crystal, bowl, fruit; ruffled, 11½" $15.00
Iris, crystal, candlesticks, pr $40.00
Iris, crystal, fruit/nut set $65.00
Iris, crystal, goblet, cocktail; 4-oz, 4½" $25.00
Iris, crystal, plate, dinner; 9" $50.00
Iris, crystal, tumbler, footed, 6½" $34.00
Iris, crystal or iridescent, creamer, footed.................$12.00
Iris, crystal or iridescent, sugar bowl, w/lid $23.00
Iris, iridescent, bowl, soup; 7½" $57.50
Iris, iridescent, butter dish, w/lid..............................$40.00
Iris, iridescent, goblet, 4-oz, 5½" $125.00
Iris, iridescent, plate, sherbet; 5½" $13.00
Iris, iridescent, saucer...$11.00
Jubilee, pink, bowl, 3-footed, 5⅛x8" $250.00
Jubilee, pink, plate, salad; 7" $22.50
Jubilee, pink, sugar bowl..$35.00
Jubilee, pink or yellow, bowl, 3-footed, 11½" $250.00
Jubilee, pink or yellow, candlesticks, pr $185.00
Jubilee, yellow, creamer...$20.00
Jubilee, yellow, plate, sandwich; 13½" $50.00
Jubilee, yellow, stem, 3-oz, 4⅞"................................$135.00
Jubilee, yellow, tumbler, juice; footed, 6-oz, 5" $95.00
Jubilee, yellow, vase, 12"...$350.00
Laced Edge, blue or green, bowl, fruit; 4⅜"-4¾"........$30.00
Laced Edge, blue or green, bowl, 5" or 5⅞" $37.50
Laced Edge, blue or green, candlesticks, double, pr..$150.00
Laced Edge, blue or green, cup $35.00
Laced Edge, blue or green, plate, bread & butter; 6½" ..$18.00
Laced Edge, blue or green, plate, dinner; 10" $85.00
Laced Edge, blue or green, saucer.............................$15.00
Laced Edge, blue or green, sugar bowl......................$40.00
Laced Edge, blue or green, tumbler, 9-oz.................$60.00
Lake Como, white, bowl, cereal; 6" $22.00
Lake Como, white, bowl, soup; flat $95.00
Lake Como, white, cup, regular $30.00
Lake Como, white, plate, salad; 7¼" $18.00
Lake Como, white, platter, 11"...................................$65.00
Lake Como, white, saucer...$11.00
Lake Como, white, sugar bowl, footed........................$30.00
Laurel, blue, creamer, tall..$30.00
Laurel, blue, platter, oval, 10¾"..................................$37.00

Laurel, blue or green, bowl, berry; lg, 9" $45.00
Laurel, blue or green, candlesticks, 4", pr.................$30.00
Laurel, green, bowl, berry; 4¾".................................$6.50
Laurel, green, plate, salad; 7½".................................$14.00
Laurel, green, sherbet...$10.00
Laurel, ivory, bowl, 3 legs, 6"...................................$15.00
Laurel, ivory, sugar bowl, short..................................$9.00
Lincoln Inn, blue or red, ashtray $17.50
Lincoln Inn, blue or red, bowl, crimped, 6"...............$13.00
Lincoln Inn, blue or red, bowl, footed, 10½".............$50.00
Lincoln Inn, blue or red, cup $16.50
Lincoln Inn, blue or red, plate, 6" $7.50
Lincoln Inn, blue or red, sandwich server, center handled..$95.00
Lincoln Inn, blue or red, tumbler, footed, 9-oz...........$26.00
Lincoln Inn, colors other than blue or red, bowl, fruit; 5" ..$8.50
Lincoln Inn, colors other than blue or red, comport..$14.50
Lincoln Inn, colors other than blue or red, finger bowl....$12.50
Lincoln Inn, colors other than blue or red, goblet, wine ..$16.50
Lincoln Inn, colors other than blue or red, plate, 9¼" ..$11.50
Lincoln Inn, colors other than blue or red, sherbet, cone
     shape, 4½"...$11.50
Lincoln Inn, colors other than blue or red, vase, 9¾" ..$75.00
Lorain, crystal or green, bowl, cereal; 6" $40.00
Lorain, crystal or green, bowl, vegetable; oval, 9¾"...$40.00
Lorain, crystal or green, plate, dinner; 10¼" $40.00
Lorain, crystal or green, plate, sherbet; 5½" $7.50
Lorain, crystal or green, saucer.................................$4.50
Lorain, yellow, bowl, berry; deep, 8" $140.00
Lorain, yellow, cup...$15.00
Lorain, yellow, plate, salad; 7¾" $15.00
Lorain, yellow, platter, 11½".......................................$42.00
Lorain, yellow, sugar bowl, footed.............................$22.00
Madrid, amber, bowl, cream soup; 4¾".......................$15.00
Madrid, amber, butter dish, w/lid...............................$70.00
Madrid, amber, plate, dinner; 10½"............................$37.50
Madrid, amber, sugar bowl $7.50
Madrid, amber or green, plate, sherbet; 6" $4.00
Madrid, amber or pink, tumbler, 9-oz, 4¼" $15.00
Madrid, blue, bowl, vegetable; oval, 10" $38.00
Madrid, blue, jam jar, 7" $35.00
Madrid, blue, plate, luncheon; 8⅞"............................$18.00
Madrid, blue, shakers, footed, 3½", pr $135.00
Madrid, green, bowl, salad; 8"...................................$17.50
Madrid, green, creamer, footed..................................$11.00
Madrid, green, platter, oval, 11½"...............................$16.00
Madrid, green, tumbler, footed, 10-oz, 5½" $38.00
Madrid, pink, candlesticks, 2¼", pr $20.00
Madrid, pink, pitcher, square, 60-oz, 8" $35.00
Madrid, pink, plate, relish; 10¼" $12.50
Madrid, pink or green, bowl, sauce; 5".......................$6.50
Madrid, pink or green, saucer....................................$5.00
Manhattan, crystal, ashtray, round, 4" $11.00
Manhattan, crystal, bowl, sauce; handles, 4½" $9.00
Manhattan, crystal, candy dish, w/lid.........................$37.50
Manhattan, crystal, plate, dinner; 10¼".....................$20.00
Manhattan, crystal, saucer/sherbet plate $7.00
Manhattan, crystal or pink, comport, 5¾" $32.00
Manhattan, crystal or pink, tumbler, footed, 10-oz $17.00
Manhattan, pink, bowl, berry; w/handles, 5⅜" $18.00

Manhattan, pink, bowl, fruit; open handles, 9½".......**$32.00**
Manhattan, pink, bowl, salad; 9" **$19.00**
Manhattan, pink, pitcher, tilted, 80-oz **$60.00**
Mayfair (Federal), amber, bowl, sauce; 5" **$8.50**
Mayfair (Federal), amber, creamer, footed................**$13.00**
Mayfair (Federal), amber, plate, dinner; 9½".............**$14.00**
Mayfair (Federal), amber, tumbler, 9-oz, 4½" **$27.50**
Mayfair (Federal), amber or green, bowl, vegetable; oval, 10"..**$30.00**
Mayfair (Federal), crystal, bowl, cream soup; 5"........**$11.00**
Mayfair (Federal), crystal, saucer **$2.50**
Mayfair (Federal), green, plate, salad; 6¾" **$9.00**
Mayfair (Federal), green, platter, oval, 12"................**$30.00**
Mayfair (Open Rose), blue, bowl, vegetable; oval, 9½" .**$67.50**
Mayfair (Open Rose), blue, pitcher, 37-oz, 6" **$147.50**
Mayfair (Open Rose), blue, plate, cake; footed, 10"...**$70.00**
Mayfair (Open Rose), blue, plate, grill; 9½"..............**$52.50**
Mayfair (Open Rose), blue, plate, 5¾".....................**$25.00**
Mayfair (Open Rose), blue, sherbet, flat, 2¼"..........**$115.00**
Mayfair (Open Rose), blue, tumbler, juice; 5-oz, 3½"..**$115.00**
Mayfair (Open Rose), blue, vase, sweet pea............**$110.00**

Mayfair (Open Rose), candy dish, blue, $265.00.

Mayfair (Open Rose), green, bowl, low flat, 11¾" **$40.00**
Mayfair (Open Rose), green, sandwich server, center handle **$37.50**
Mayfair (Open Rose), green or yellow, tumbler, water; 11-oz, 4¾"...**$200.00**
Mayfair (Open Rose), pink, bowl, cereal; 5½"...........**$24.00**
Mayfair (Open Rose), pink, butter dish, w/lid **$65.00**
Mayfair (Open Rose), pink, celery dish, 10"...............**$40.00**
Mayfair (Open Rose), pink, creamer, footed **$27.50**
Mayfair (Open Rose), pink, goblet, cocktail; 3-oz, 4" ..**$72.50**
Mayfair (Open Rose), pink, goblet, water; 9-oz, 5¾" ..**$57.50**
Mayfair (Open Rose), pink, plate, luncheon; 8½" **$25.00**
Mayfair (Open Rose), pink, relish tray, non-partitioned, 8⅜"..**$210.00**
Mayfair (Open Rose), pink, sugar bowl, footed..........**$28.00**
Mayfair (Open Rose), pink, whiskey, 1½-oz, 2¼" **$65.00**
Mayfair (Open Rose), yellow, bowl, vegetable; 7" ...**$125.00**
Mayfair (Open Rose), yellow, platter, open handles, oval, 12" **$115.00**
Miss America, crystal, bowl, fruit; straight, deep, 8¾".**$35.00**
Miss America, crystal, celery dish, oblong, 10½" **$15.00**

Miss America, crystal, goblet, juice; 5-oz, 4¾" **$27.00**
Miss America, crystal, pitcher, 65-oz, 8".....................**$46.00**
Miss America, crystal, relish tray, 4-part, 8¾".............**$11.00**
Miss America, crystal, sherbet **$8.00**
Miss America, green, bowl, berry; 4½" **$12.00**
Miss America, green, plate, salad; 8½".......................**$9.50**
Miss America, green, tumbler, water; 10-oz, 4½"........**$18.00**
Miss America, pink, bowl, cereal; 6¼".......................**$22.00**

Miss America, pink, celery dish, 6½x10½", $26.00.

Miss America, pink, creamer, footed...........................**$18.00**
Miss America, pink, pitcher, w/ice lip, 65-oz, 8½" ...**$135.00**
Miss America, pink, plate, cake; footed, 12" **$42.00**
Miss America, pink, shakers, pr..................................**$58.00**
Miss America, pink, tumbler, juice; 5-oz, 4" **$45.00**
Miss America, royal ruby, saucer................................**$65.00**
Moderntone, amethyst, creamer **$10.00**
Moderntone, amethyst, plate, sandwich; 10½"...........**$40.00**
Moderntone, amethyst, saucer **$4.00**
Moderntone, amethyst, tumbler, 12-oz........................**$85.00**
Moderntone, amethyst, tumbler, 5-oz..........................**$30.00**
Moderntone, cobalt, bowl, berry; lg, 8¾" **$50.00**
Moderntone, cobalt, bowl, cream soup; 4¾" **$20.00**
Moderntone, cobalt, plate, luncheon; 7¾"..................**$12.50**
Moderntone, cobalt, plate, sherbet; 5⅞".......................**$6.50**
Moderntone, cobalt, platter, oval, 12" **$75.00**
Moderntone, cobalt, sugar bowl...................................**$11.00**
Moderntone, cobalt, whiskey, 1½-oz **$40.00**
Moderntone, cobalt or amethyst, bowl, cereal; 6½" ...**$70.00**
Moondrops, colors other than red or blue, bowl, console; 3-footed, round, 12"....................................**$32.00**
Moondrops, colors other than red or blue, bowl, pickle; 7½" **$14.00**
Moondrops, colors other than red or blue, candles, sherbet style, 4½", pr...**$20.00**
Moondrops, colors other than red or blue, decanter, lg, 11¼"..**$50.00**
Moondrops, colors other than red or blue, plate, salad; 7⅛" **$10.00**
Moondrops, colors other than red or blue, powder jar, 3-footed...**$110.00**
Moondrops, colors other than red or blue, tumbler, handled, 9-oz, 4⅞"...**$16.00**
Moondrops, colors other than red or blue, tumbler, shot; 2-oz, 2¾" **$10.00**

Moondrops, red or blue, ashtray.................................$32.00

Moondrops, red or blue, bowl, ruffled, 3-legged, 9½" ..$65.00

Moondrops, red or blue, butter dish bottom only $62.50

Moondrops, red or blue, candlesticks, triple light, 5¼", pr $110.00

Moondrops, red or blue, comport, 4" $27.50

Moondrops, red or blue, creamer, regular, 3¾" $16.00

Moondrops, red or blue, goblet, wine; metal stem, 3-oz, 5⅛"..$16.00

Moondrops, red or blue, goblet, 5-oz, 4¾" $24.00

Moondrops, red or blue, mug, 12-oz, 6⅞"...................$40.00

Moondrops, red or blue, pitcher, no lip, 53-oz, 8⅛" ..$185.00

Moondrops, red or blue, plate, sandwich; round, 14" ..$38.00

Moondrops, red or blue, sherbet, 4½".........................$26.00

Moondrops, red or blue, tumbler, 5-oz, 3⅝" $15.00

Mt Pleasant, amethyst, black or cobalt, bowl, fruit; scalloped, 10"...$40.00

Mt Pleasant, amethyst, black or cobalt, bowl, 2-handled, square, 6"...$18.00

Mt Pleasant, amethyst, black or cobalt, cup $12.00

Mt Pleasant, amethyst, black or cobalt, mint dish, center handle, 6"...$22.00

Mt Pleasant, amethyst, black or cobalt, plate, grill; 9" ..$12.00

Mt Pleasant, amethyst, black or cobalt, sandwich server, center handle $38.00

Mt Pleasant, pink or green, bonbon, rolled-up edge, handled, 7"..$16.00

Mt Pleasant, pink or green, bowl, 2-handled, square, 8" ..$19.00

Mt Pleasant, pink or green, candlesticks, double, pr..$26.00

Mt Pleasant, pink or green, mayonnaise, 3-footed, 5½".....$18.00

Mt Pleasant, pink or green, plate, cake; 2-handled, 10½"..$16.00

Mt Pleasant, pink or green, plate, scalloped or square, 8"..$10.00

Mt Pleasant, pink or green, shakers, 2 styles, pr $24.00

Mt Pleasant, pink or green, sherbet, 2 styles...............$10.00

New Century, any color, pitcher, 60-oz, 7¾"...............$35.00

New Century, any color, tumbler, 5-oz, 3½" $12.00

New Century, green or crystal, ashtray/coaster, 5⅜" ..$28.00

New Century, green or crystal, bowl, cream soup; 4¾" ..$20.00

New Century, green or crystal, decanter, w/stopper ..$55.00

New Century, green or crystal, goblet, cocktail; 3¼-oz.$22.00

New Century, green or crystal, plate, breakfast; 7⅛"....$9.00

New Century, green or crystal, plate, salad; 8½".........$10.00

New Century, green or crystal, platter, oval, 11" $18.00

New Century, green or crystal, sugar bowl $8.00

New Century, green or crystal, whiskey, 1½-oz, 2½"...$18.00

New Century, pink, cobalt or amethyst, cup................$19.00

New Century, pink, cobalt or amethyst, saucer $7.50

New Century, pink, cobalt or amethyst, tumbler, 10-oz, 5"..$16.00

Newport, amethyst, platter, oval, 11¾".......................$35.00

Newport, amethyst, sugar bowl....................................$14.00

Newport, cobalt, bowl, berry; 4¾".............................$18.00

Newport, cobalt, cup..$12.00

Newport, cobalt, plate, luncheon; 8½" $14.00

Newport, cobalt or amethyst, bowl, cream soup; 4¾" .$18.00

Newport, cobalt or amethyst, plate, dinner; 8¾" $30.00

Newport, cobalt or amethyst, saucer...........................$5.00

No 610 Pyramid, crystal, bowl, berry; 4¾"..................$11.00

No 610 Pyramid, crystal, ice tub..................................$55.00

No 610 Pyramid, pink, tumbler, footed, 11-oz $45.00

No 610 Pyramid, pink or green, bowl, oval, 9½" $30.00

No 610 Pyramid, pink or green, bowl, pickle; 9½x5¾"..$30.00

No 610 Pyramid, pink or green, sugar bowl...............$25.00

No 610 Pyramid, yellow, tray for creamer & sugar bowl..$50.00

No 612 Horseshoe, green, bowl, berry; 4½" $25.00

No 612 Horseshoe, green, bowl, vegetable; oval, 10½" .$22.50

No 612 Horseshoe, green, plate, sherbet; 6" $8.00

No 612 Horseshoe, green, tumbler, 9-oz, 4¼" $150.00

No 612 Horseshoe, green or yellow, bowl, vegetable; 8½"..$30.00

No 612 Horseshoe, green or yellow, plate, grill; 10⅜"..$85.00

No 612 Horseshoe, green or yellow, platter, oval, 10¾"..$25.00

No 612 Horseshoe, green or yellow, saucer.................$5.00

No 612 Horseshoe, yellow, creamer, footed.............$18.00

No 612 Horseshoe, yellow, tumbler, footed, 12-oz ..$150.00

No 616 Vernon, crystal, cup..$8.00

No 616 Vernon, crystal, sugar bowl, footed $11.00

No 616 Vernon, green or yellow, creamer, footed......$25.00

No 616 Vernon, green or yellow, plate, sandwich; 11½"..$25.00

No 616 Vernon, green or yellow, saucer $5.50

No 616 Vernon, green or yellow, tumbler, footed, 5".$35.00

No 618 Pineapple & Floral, amber or red, bowl, cereal; 6"..$20.00

No 618 Pineapple & Floral, amber or red, plate, sherbet; 6"..$6.00

No 618 Pineapple & Floral, amber or red, platter, closed handles, 11" $18.00

No 618 Pineapple & Floral, amber or red, tumbler, 8-oz, 4¼" $25.00

No 618 Pineapple & Floral, crystal, amber or red, saucer .$5.00

No 618 Pineapple & Floral, crystal, ashtray, 4½".......$17.50

No 618 Pineapple & Floral, crystal, creamer, diamond shaped $7.50

No 618 Pineapple & Floral, crystal, plate, w/indentation, 11½"...$25.00

Nora Bird, pink or green, candlesticks, pr $80.00

Nora Bird, pink or green, cup......................................$55.00

Nora Bird, pink or green, saucer.................................$15.00

Nora Bird, pink or green, tumbler, 10-oz, 5¼" $60.00

Nora Bird, pink or green, tumbler, 3-oz, 2¼" $35.00

Normandie, amber, bowl, berry; 5"...............................$6.00

Normandie, amber, pitcher, 80-oz, 8".........................$75.00

Normandie, amber, plate, grill; 11"..............................$14.00

Normandie, amber, tumbler, juice; 5-oz, 4" $30.00

Normandie, iridescent, sherbet $7.00

Normandie, pink, bowl, vegetable; oval, 10" $35.00

Normandie, pink, plate, salad; 7¾"..............................$11.00

Normandie, pink, shakers, pr $75.00

Normandie, pink, tumbler, water; 9-oz, 4¼" $50.00

Old Cafe, crystal, candy jar w/ruby lid, 5½" $15.00

Old Cafe, crystal or pink, bowl, berry; 3¾" $3.00

Old Cafe, crystal or pink, lamp $20.00

Old Cafe, crystal or pink, pitcher, 36-oz, 6" $70.00

Old Cafe, crystal or pink, plate, sherbet; 6"..................$2.50

Old Cafe, royal ruby, bowl, cereal; 5½" $10.00

Old Cafe, royal ruby, sherbet, low footed $10.00

Old Cafe, royal ruby, tumbler, water; 4"......................$18.00

Old Colony (Lace Edge), crystal, fishbowl, 1-gal 8-oz..$30.00

Old Colony (Lace Edge), pink, bonbon, w/lid...........$65.00

Old Colony (Lace Edge), pink, bowl, cereal; 6⅜" **$22.00**

Old Colony (Lace Edge), pink, bowl, plain, 9½" **$24.00**

Old Colony (Lace Edge), pink, butter dish, w/lid.......**$65.00**

Old Colony (Lace Edge), pink, candy jar, w/lid, ribbed ..**$45.00**

Old Colony (Lace Edge), pink, plate, grill; 10½" **$20.00**

Old Colony (Lace Edge), pink, platter, 12¾" **$32.50**

Old Colony (Lace Edge), pink, saucer **$11.00**

Old Colony (Lace Edge), pink, tumbler, flat, 9-oz, 4½" ..**$18.00**

Old English, crystal, egg cup **$8.00**

Old English, pink, green or amber, bowl, flat, 4" **$17.50**

Old English, pink, green or amber, compote, 2-handled, 3½x6⅜" **$22.50**

Old English, pink, green or amber, pitcher **$65.00**

Old English, pink, green or amber, sandwich server, center handle **$55.00**

Old English, pink, green or amber, tumbler, footed, 4½" **$22.50**

Old English, pink, green or amber, vase, fan type, 5⅜x7" ..**$47.50**

Old English, pink green or amber, candlesticks, 4", pr..**$32.50**

Orchid, red, black or cobalt blue, comport, 3¼x6¼" ..**$40.00**

Orchid, red, black or cobalt blue, vase, 10" **$135.00**

Orchid, yellow, green, amber or pink, bowl, square, 4⅞"..**$20.00**

Orchid, yellow, green, amber or pink, creamer **$30.00**

Ovide, black, creamer **$6.50**

Ovide, black, saucer **$3.50**

Ovide, decorated white, bowl, berry; 4¾" **$7.00**

Ovide, decorated white, plate, dinner; 9" **$20.00**

Ovide, decorated white, tumbler **$16.50**

Ovide, green, candy dish, w/lid **$22.00**

Ovide, green, cup **$3.50**

Oyster & Pearl, bowl, 1 handle, 5½" **$13.00**

Oyster & Pearl, crystal or pink, bowl, heart-shaped, 1 handle, 5¼" **$8.00**

Oyster & Pearl, crystal or pink, relish dish, divided, oblong, 10¼" **$10.00**

Oyster & Pearl, royal ruby, candle holders, 3½", pr...**$50.00**

Parrot, amber, bowl, vegetable; oval, 10" **$65.00**

Parrot, amber, creamer, footed **$60.00**

Parrot, amber, jam dish, 7" **$35.00**

Parrot, amber, platter, oblong, 11¼" **$70.00**

Parrot, amber, tumbler, 10-oz, 4¼" **$100.00**

Parrot, green, bowl, berry; 5" **$24.00**

Parrot, green, butter dish, w/lid **$350.00**

Parrot, green, cup **$40.00**

Parrot, green, plate, dinner; 9" **$50.00**

Parrot, green, sherbet, cone shape, footed **$24.00**

Patrician, amber, crystal or green, pitcher, applied handle, 75-oz, 8¼" **$150.00**

Patrician, amber, crystal or green, sugar bowl lid only ...**$55.00**

Patrician, amber or crystal, bowl, cream soup; 4¾" ...**$16.00**

Patrician, amber or crystal, cookie jar, w/lid **$85.00**

Patrician, amber or crystal, plate, sherbet; 6" **$10.00**

Patrician, amber or crystal, tumbler, 9-oz, 4¼" **$28.00**

Patrician, any color, saucer **$9.50**

Patrician, green, bowl, vegetable; oval, 10" **$35.00**

Patrician, green, butter dish, w/lid **$110.00**

Patrician, green, tumbler, footed, 8-oz, 5¼" **$55.00**

Patrician, pink, bowl, berry; lg, 8½" **$25.00**

Patrician, pink, plate, dinner; 10½" **$35.00**

Patrician, pink or green, cup **$11.00**

Patrician, pink or green, platter, oval, 11½" **$25.00**

Patrician, pink or green, sherbet **$14.00**

Patrick, pink, bowl, fruit; handled, 9" **$175.00**

Patrick, pink, mayonnaise set, 3-pc **$195.00**

Patrick, pink, plate, salad; 7½" **$25.00**

Patrick, pink, saucer **$20.00**

Patrick, pink or yellow, candlesticks, pr..................**$150.00**

Patrick, yellow, cup **$37.50**

Patrick, yellow, sugar bowl **$37.50**

Peacock & Wild Rose, all colors, bowl, flat, 8½" **$75.00**

Peacock & Wild Rose, all colors, bowl, footed, 10½" ...**$95.00**

Peacock & Wild Rose, all colors, candy dish, w/lid, 7" ..**$150.00**

Peacock & Wild Rose, all colors, ice bucket 4¾" **$135.00**

Peacock & Wild Rose, all colors, vase, 2 styles, 10".**$110.00**

Peacock Reverse, all colors, bowl, square, 4⅞" **$35.00**

Peacock Reverse, all colors, candlesticks, square base, 5¾", pr **$125.00**

Peacock Reverse, all colors, comport, 4¼x7⅜" **$75.00**

Peacock Reverse, all colors, plate, sherbet; 5¾" **$22.50**

Peacock Reverse, all colors, saucer **$20.00**

Peacock Reverse, all colors, server, center handled ...**$75.00**

Petalware, cremax, monax florette, fired-on decorations, platter, oval, 13" **$25.00**

Petalware, crystal w/decorated bands, pitcher, 80-oz.**$25.00**

Petalware, pink, bowl, cream soup; 4½" **$12.00**

Petalware, pink, plate, sherbet; 6" **$2.50**

Petalware, plain monax, bowl, berry; lg, 9" **$18.00**

Petalware, plain monax, plate, salver; 12" **$18.00**

Petalware, red trim floral, sugar bowl, footed **$32.50**

Primo, yellow or green, bowl, 4½" **$15.00**

Primo, yellow or green, creamer **$12.00**

Primo, yellow or green, cup **$12.00**

Primo, yellow or green, plate, cake; 3-footed, 10" **$25.00**

Primo, yellow or green, plate, dinner; 10" **$20.00**

Primo, yellow or green, saucer **$3.00**

Primo, yellow or green, sugar bowl **$12.00**

Princess, green, ashtray, 4½" **$70.00**

Princess, green, candy dish, w/lid **$60.00**

Princess, green, pink, topaz or apricot, tumbler, juice; 5-oz, 3" **$28.00**

Princess, green, pitcher, 37-oz, 6" **$50.00**

Princess, green, spice shakers, 5½", pr...................**$40.00**

Princess, green, topaz or apricot, creamer, oval **$14.00**

Princess, green or pink, butter dish, w/lid **$90.00**

Princess, green or pink, pitcher, 60-oz, 8" **$90.00**

Princess, green or pink, plate, grill; 9½" **$14.00**

Princess, green or pink, plate, salad; 8" **$14.00**

Princess, green or pink, saucer **$10.00**

Princess, pink, bowl, cereal/oatmeal; 5" **$25.00**

Princess, pink, cookie jar, w/lid **$65.00**

Princess, pink, plate, grill; closed handles, 10½" **$12.00**

Princess, pink, topaz or apricot, tumbler, iced tea; 13-oz, 5¼" **$28.00**

Princess, topaz or apricot, bowl, hat shaped, 9½" ...**$120.00**

Princess, topaz or apricot, relish, plain, 7½" **$150.00**

Princess, topaz or apricot, sugar bowl **$8.50**

Princess, topaz or apricot, tumbler, footed, 10-oz, 5¼" .**$21.00**

Queen Mary, crystal, bowl, cereal; 6" **$6.50**

Queen Mary, crystal, bowl, 1 handle, 4" **$3.50**

Queen Mary, crystal, celery/pickle dish, 5x10" **$9.00**
Queen Mary, crystal, cup, lg..**$5.50**
Queen Mary, crystal, plate, dinner; 9¾" **$15.00**
Queen Mary, crystal, relish tray, 4-part, 14" **$12.00**
Queen Mary, crystal, sugar bowl, oval...........................**$4.50**
Queen Mary, pink, ashtray, oval, 2x3¾".......................**$5.00**
Queen Mary, pink, bowl, berry; lg, 8¾" **$16.00**
Queen Mary, pink, bowl, berry; 5" **$10.00**
Queen Mary, pink, candy dish, w/lid **$35.00**
Queen Mary, pink, creamer, footed **$37.50**
Queen Mary, pink, serving tray, 14" **$20.00**
Queen Mary, pink, sherbet; footed **$9.00**
Queen Mary, pink, tumbler, footed, 10-oz, 5"............**$60.00**
Radiance, amber, bowl, crimped, 12"..............................**$27.50**
Radiance, amber, bowl, pickle; 7".....................................**$15.00**
Radiance, amber, comport, 6"..**$22.00**
Radiance, amber, cup, footed **$12.00**
Radiance, amber, shakers, pr..**$50.00**
Radiance, ice blue or red, bonbon, w/lid, 6" **$95.00**
Radiance, ice blue or red, bowl, flared, 10" **$42.00**
Radiance, ice blue or red, bowl, nut; 2-handled, 5" ...**$20.00**
Radiance, ice blue or red, bowl, punch; 9"..............**$190.00**
Radiance, ice blue or red, candlesticks, 2-light, pr ...**$110.00**
Radiance, ice blue or red, lamp, 12"............................**$110.00**
Radiance, ice blue or red, sugar bowl **$25.00**
Raindrops, green, bowl, berry; 7½"...............................**$40.00**
Raindrops, green, bowl, fruit; 4½" **$6.00**
Raindrops, green, plate, luncheon; 8" **$5.50**
Raindrops, green, sherbet..**$6.50**
Raindrops, green, sugar bowl **$7.50**
Raindrops, green, tumbler, 10-oz, 5"..............................**$9.00**
Raindrops, green, tumbler, 2-oz, 2⅛".............................**$5.00**
Ribbon, black, bowl, berry; lg, 8" **$35.00**
Ribbon, black, shakers, pr **$45.00**
Ribbon, green, bowl, berry; 4" **$20.00**
Ribbon, green, creamer, footed **$15.00**
Ribbon, green, plate, luncheon; 8" **$5.00**
Ribbon, green, plate, sherbet; 6¼" **$2.50**
Ribbon, green, sherbet, footed **$5.50**
Ribbon, green, tumbler, 10-oz, 6"....................................**$27.50**
Ring, crystal, bowl, berry; 5"..**$3.50**
Ring, crystal, cup...**$4.50**
Ring, crystal, goblet, wine; 3½-oz, 4½" **$13.00**
Ring, crystal, plate, sandwich; 11¾".................................**$7.00**
Ring, crystal, sugar bowl, footed **$4.50**
Ring, crystal, tumbler, 12-oz, 5⅛".....................................**$7.00**
Ring, decorated, bowl, berry; lg, 8" **$12.00**
Ring, decorated, decanter, w/stopper **$40.00**
Ring, decorated, pitcher, 80-oz, 8½" **$33.00**
Ring, decorated, saucer **$2.00**
Ring, decorated, tumbler, 5-oz, 3½" **$6.50**
Ring, decorated, vase, 8"..**$35.00**
Rock Crystal, colors other than crystal or red, lamp, electric..**$300.00**
Rock Crystal, colors other than crystal or red, vase, footed, 11"...**$110.00**
Rock Crystal, colors other than red or crystal, cup, 7-oz ..**$27.50**
Rock Crystal, crystal, bonbon, scalloped edge, 7½" ...**$20.00**
Rock Crystal, crystal, comport, 7"..................................**$35.00**

Rock Crystal, crystal, ice dish, 3 styles........................**$35.00**
Rock Crystal, crystal, pitcher, scalloped edge, 1-qt **$165.00**
Rock Crystal, crystal, plate, dinner; scalloped edge, lg center design, 10½"...**$47.50**
Rock Crystal, crystal, relish dish, 2-part, 11½" **$30.00**
Rock Crystal, crystal, saucer...**$7.50**
Rock Crystal, crystal, syrup w/lid.................................**$150.00**
Rock Crystal, red, bowl, pickle; 7".................................**$65.00**
Rock Crystal, red, candelabra, 2-light, pr...................**$250.00**
Rock Crystal, red, plate, bread & butter; scalloped edge, 6"..**$20.00**
Rock Crystal, red, stem, wine; 3-oz................................**$52.50**
Rock Crystal, red, tumbler, concave or straight, 12-oz..**$67.50**
Rose Cameo, bowl, cereal; 5" **$15.00**
Rose Cameo, green, bowl, straight sides, 6"...............**$20.00**
Rose Cameo, green, plate, salad; 7".................................**$12.00**
Rosemary, amber, bowl, cream soup; 5" **$15.00**
Rosemary, amber, platter, oval, 12" **$15.00**
Rosemary, green, bowl, vegetable; oval, 10".............**$26.00**
Rosemary, green, saucer..**$5.00**
Rosemary, pink, cup...**$10.00**
Rosemary, pink, tumbler, 9-oz, 4¼" **$47.50**
Rosemary, plate, dinner...**$14.00**
Roulette, crystal, bowl, fruit; 9"..**$9.50**
Roulette, crystal, plate, luncheon; 8½"...........................**$5.00**
Roulette, crystal, tumbler, juice; 5-oz, 3¼"....................**$7.00**
Roulette, crystal, whiskey, 1½-oz, 2½" **$8.00**
Roulette, pink or green, pitcher, 65-oz, 8".................**$35.00**
Roulette, pink or green, saucer...**$3.50**
Roulette, pink or green, tumbler, water; 9-oz, 4⅛".....**$22.00**
Round Robin, green, creamer, footed **$7.50**
Round Robin, green or iridescent, bowl, berry; 4" **$5.00**
Round Robin, green or iridescent, plate, sherbet; 6" **$2.50**
Round Robin, green or iridescent, saucer......................**$2.00**
Round Robin, green or iridescent, sugar bowl.............**$6.00**
Roxana, yellow, bowl, cereal; 6" **$15.00**
Roxana, yellow, bowl, 4½x2⅜"...**$11.00**
Roxana, yellow, sherbet, footed **$10.00**
Royal Lace, blue, cup..**$33.00**
Royal Lace, blue, platter, oval, 13" **$50.00**
Royal Lace, crystal, bowl, cream soup; 4¾" **$12.00**

Royal Lace, crystal, butter dish, $65.00.

Royal Lace, crystal, pitcher, 64-oz, 8"...........................**$45.00**
Royal Lace, crystal, tumbler, 12-oz, 5⅜" **$25.00**

Royal Lace, green, bowl, berry; round, 10" $30.00
Royal Lace, green, candlesticks, ruffled edge, pr........$70.00
Royal Lace, green, plate, dinner; 9⅞" $27.00
Royal Lace, pink, bowl, vegetable; oval, 11"............$140.00
Royal Lace, pink, bowl, 3-legged, straight edge, 10"..$35.00
Royal Lace, pink, candlesticks, straight edge, pr........$55.00
Royal Lace, pink, pitcher, 96-oz, 8½"........................$95.00
Royal Lace, pink, sherbet, footed.............................$18.00
S Pattern, crystal, bowl, cereal; 5½"..........................$5.00
S Pattern, crystal, plate, grill..................................$6.50
S Pattern, crystal, tumbler, 5-oz, 3½".......................$45.00
S Pattern, yellow, amber or crystal w/trims, plate, dinner;
  9¼"...$9.00
S Pattern, yellow, amber or crystal w/trims, tumbler, 10-oz,
  4¾"..$7.50
Sandwich (Indiana), amber or crystal, bowl, 6" $4.00
Sandwich (Indiana), amber or crystal, creamer............$9.00
Sandwich (Indiana), amber or crystal, decanter, w/stop-
  per...$22.00
Sandwich (Indiana), amber or crystal, shapes of playing
  cards suits, each $3.25
Sandwich (Indiana), amber or crystal, tumbler, iced tea; foot-
  ed, 12-oz...$10.00
Sandwich (Indiana), pink or green, bowl, console; 11½"..$50.00
Sandwich (Indiana), pink or green, cruet, w/stopper, 6½-
  oz $160.00
Sandwich (Indiana), pink or green, sandwich server, center
  handled..$30.00
Sandwich (Indiana), red, plate, luncheon; 8⅜"..........$20.00
Sandwich (Indiana), red, sugar bowl, lg....................$45.00
Sandwich (Indiana), teal blue, bowl, hexagonal, 6" ...$14.00
Sandwich (Indiana), teal blue, plate, sherbet; 6"..........$7.00
Sharon, amber, bowl, berry; 5" $8.50
Sharon, amber, jam jar, 7½".....................................$37.50
Sharon, amber, plate, cake; footed, 11½"...................$25.00
Sharon, amber, platter, oval, 12½" $18.00
Sharon, green, bowl, berry; lg, 8½"...........................$32.00
Sharon, green, creamer, footed.................................$20.00
Sharon, green, sugar bowl..$15.00
Sharon, pink, bowl, fruit; 10½" $37.50
Sharon, pink, pitcher, w/lip, 80-oz...........................$145.00
Sharon, pink, tumbler, footed, 15-oz, 6½"..................$47.50
Sharon, pink, tumbler, thin, 9-oz, 4⅛".......................$40.00
Sharon, pink or green, bowl, cereal; 6" $25.00
Sharon, pink or green, saucer $12.00
Ships, blue/white, cocktail shaker.............................$32.50
Ships, blue/white, pitcher, w/lip, 86-oz $47.50
Ships, blue/white, saucer $17.00
Ships, blue/white, tumbler, roly poly; 6-oz $10.00
Ships, blue/white, tumbler, water; 9-oz, 4⅝" $11.00
Ships, blue/white, tumbler, whiskey; 3½" $27.50
Sierra, green, bowl, vegetable; oval, 9¼" $110.00
Sierra, green, cup...$14.00
Sierra, green, serving tray, 2-handled, 10¼" $18.00
Sierra, pink, bowl, cereal; 5½" $12.00
Sierra, pink, creamer $18.00
Sierra, pink, plate, dinner; 9"....................................$18.00
Sierra, pink, platter, oval, 11"...................................$40.00
Sierra, pink, sugar bowl, w/lid..................................$34.00

Sierra, pink or green, shakers, pr...............................$37.50
Spiral, green, bowl, berry; 4¾"..................................$5.00
Spiral, green, bowl, mixing; 7"..................................$8.50
Spiral, green, cup...$5.00
Spiral, green, pitcher, 58-oz, 7⅝".............................$30.00
Spiral, green, platter, 12"..$27.50
Spiral, green, preserve, w/lid....................................$30.00
Spiral, green, sandwich server, center handle.............$25.00
Spiral, green, sherbet..$4.00
Spiral, green, tumbler, footed, 5⅞".............................$15.00
Spiral, green, tumbler, juice; 5-oz, 3" $4.50
Starlight, crystal or white, bowl, cereal; closed handles,
  5½"..$7.00
Starlight, crystal or white, bowl, salad; 11½"..............$20.00
Starlight, crystal or white, creamer, oval $5.00
Starlight, crystal or white, plate, luncheon; 8½"..........$5.00
Starlight, crystal or white, saucer..............................$2.00
Starlight, crystal or white, sugar bowl, oval................$5.00
Starlight, pink, bowl, closed handles, 8½" $15.00
Starlight, pink, plate, sandwich; 13".........................$15.00
Strawberry, crystal or iridescent, bowl, berry; 4" $6.50
Strawberry, crystal or iridescent, olive dish, 1-handle, 5"..$8.50
Strawberry, crystal or iridescent, pitcher, 7¾"...........$160.00
Strawberry, crystal or iridescent, sugar bowl, open, sm.$12.00
Strawberry, pink or green, bowl, 2x6½".....................$65.00
Strawberry, pink or green, butter dish, w/lid............$150.00
Strawberry, pink or green, creamer, sm......................$17.50
Strawberry, pink or green, plate, salad; 7½" $13.00
Strawberry, pink or green, tumbler, 8-oz, 3⅝"...........$30.00
Sunburst, crystal, bowl, berry; 4¾"............................$6.00
Sunburst, crystal, candlesticks, double, pr.................$30.00
Sunburst, crystal, cup...$6.00
Sunburst, crystal, plate, sandwich; 11¾"...................$12.00
Sunburst, crystal, tumbler, flat, 9-oz, 4"....................$17.50
Sunflower, green, cup $14.00
Sunflower, green, tumbler, footed, 8-oz, 4¾".............$30.00
Sunflower, pink, plate, dinner; 9"..............................$15.00
Sunflower, pink, saucer..$8.00
Sunflower, pink or green, plate, cake; 3-legged, 10"..$15.00
Swirl, delphite, bowl, salad; 9"..................................$28.00
Swirl, delphite, candle holders, single branch, pr.....$115.00
Swirl, delphite, platter, oval, 12"...............................$35.00
Swirl, pink, bowl, console; footed, 10½"....................$19.00
Swirl, pink, butter dish, w/lid.................................$180.00
Swirl, pink, coaster, 1x3¼".......................................$9.50
Swirl, pink, plate, sherbet; 6½"..................................$4.50
Swirl, pink, sugar bowl, footed $10.00
Swirl, ultramarine, bowl, closed handles, footed, 10".$28.00
Swirl, ultramarine, plate, dinner; 9¼".........................$18.00
Swirl, ultramarine, tumbler, 9-oz, 4" $32.00
Swirl, ultramarine, vase, 2 styles, footed, 8½"............$26.00
Swirl, ultramarine or delphite, saucer $5.00
Tea Room, green, finger bowl....................................$50.00
Tea Room, green, bowl, vegetable; oval, 9½"..............$62.50
Tea Room, green, creamer & sugar bowl on tray, 4".$75.00
Tea Room, green, lamp, electric; 9"............................$85.00
Tea Room, green, pitcher, 64-oz $140.00
Tea Room, green, shakers, pr.....................................$55.00
Tea Room, green, sugar bowl, w/lid, 3".....................$100.00

Tea Room, green, tray, center handled......................$195.00
Tea Room, green, tumbler, footed, 11-oz...................$45.00
Tea Room, green, vase, ruffled edge, 11".................$175.00
Tea Room, green or pink, creamer, 3¼".....................$26.00
Tea Room, pink, bowl, celery; 8¼"............................$26.00

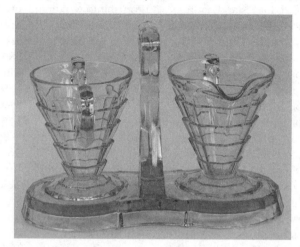

Tea Room, pink, creamer and sugar bowl on tray, $75.00.

Tea Room, pink, goblet, 9-oz $60.00
Tea Room, pink, mustard jar, w/lid $125.00
Tea Room, pink, plate, luncheon; 8¼" $30.00
Tea Room, pink, sherbet, low, flared edge $26.00
Tea Room, pink, sugar bowl, w/lid, flat.....................$160.00
Tea Room, pink, tumbler, flat, 8-oz, 4⅛"...................$85.00
Tea Room, pink, vase, ruffled edge, 6½" $90.00
Thistle, green, cup, thin $24.00
Thistle, green, plate, grill; 10¼".................................$22.00
Thistle, pink, bowl, cereal; 5½"..................................$20.00
Thistle, pink, plate, luncheon; 8"...............................$14.00
Thistle, pink or green, saucer $9.50
Tulip, amber, crystal or green, candy dish, w/lid $30.00
Tulip, amber, crystal or green, ice tub, 3x4⅞" $20.00
Tulip, amber, crystal or green, saucer.......................$2.00
Tulip, amber, crystal or green, tumbler, whiskey........$16.00
Tulip, amethyst or blue, bowl, 6"...............................$12.50
Tulip, amethyst or blue, cup.......................................$12.00
Tulip, amethyst or blue, plate, 7¼"............................$7.50
Tulip, amethyst or blue, sugar bowl $14.00
Twisted Optic, blue or yellow, basket, 10" $75.00
Twisted Optic, blue or yellow, candlesticks, 2 styles, 3", pr .$40.00
Twisted Optic, blue or yellow, plate, salad; 7" $6.00
Twisted Optic, blue or yellow, sandwich server, 2-handled .$18.00
Twisted Optic, blue or yellow, tumbler, 2-handled, rolled
   edge, 7¼" $50.00
Twisted Optic, pink, green or amber, bowl, salad; 7"..$10.00
Twisted Optic, pink, green or amber, candy jar, w/lid, flat,
   flange edge...$30.00
Twisted Optic, pink, green or amber, mayonnaise jar..$20.00
Twisted Optic, pink, green or amber, plate, sandwich; 10" ...$9.00
Twisted Optic, pink, green or amber, sherbet..............$6.00
US Swirl, green, bowl, berry; 4⅜" $5.50
US Swirl, green, creamer..$14.00
US Swirl, green, plate, salad; 7⅞"...............................$5.50
US Swirl, green or pink, bowl, oval, 8⅜"...................$50.00
US Swirl, green or pink, butter dish, w/lid $110.00

US Swirl, green or pink, tumbler, 8-oz, 3⅝"..............$10.00
US Swirl, pink, bowl, berry; lg, 7⅞".........................$16.00
US Swirl, pink, sherbet, 3¼" $5.00
US Swirl, pink, vase, 6½"...$20.00
Victory, amber, pink or green, bonbon, 7"................$11.00
Victory, amber, pink or green, bowl, rolled edge, 11" .$28.00
Victory, amber, pink or green, creamer.....................$15.00
Victory, amber, pink or green, plate, bread & butter; 6" ..$6.00
Victory, amber, pink or green, plate, dinner; 9".........$19.00
Victory, black or blue, bowl, flat edge, 12½"..............$65.00
Victory, black or blue, bowl, soup; flat, 8½"...............$45.00
Victory, black or blue, cup $33.00
Victory, black or blue, plate, salad; 7" $20.00
Victory, black or blue, saucer....................................$12.00
Vitrock, bowl, vegetable; 9½"....................................$14.00
Vitrock, white, bowl, berry; 4".....................................$4.50
Vitrock, white, bowl, fruit; 6".......................................$5.50
Vitrock, white, creamer, oval......................................$4.50
Vitrock, white, plate, dinner; 10".................................$8.50
Vitrock, white, plate, salad; 7¼"..................................$2.50
Vitrock, white, saucer...$2.50
Waterford, crystal, ashtray, 4"....................................$7.50
Waterford, crystal, coaster, 4"....................................$19.00
Waterford, crystal, goblet, Miss America style, 5½" $35.00
Waterford, crystal, plate, salad; 7⅛"...........................$6.00
Waterford, crystal, plate, sherbet; 6"..........................$3.00
Waterford, crystal, saucer $3.00
Waterford, pink, bowl, berry; lg, 8¼"..........................$20.00
Waterford, pink, cup...$14.00
Waterford, pink, plate, sandwich; 13¾".......................$25.00
Waterford, pink, sugar bowl $10.00
Waterford, pink, tumbler, footed, 10-oz, 4⅞"...............$20.00
Windsor, crystal, ashtray, 5¾".....................................$13.50
Windsor, crystal, creamer $4.50
Windsor, crystal, plate, dinner; 9"...............................$5.00
Windsor, crystal, shakers, pr......................................$16.00
Windsor, crystal, tumbler, 5-oz, 3¼"............................$8.00
Windsor, green, bowl, cereal; 5⅛"...............................$22.00
Windsor, green, bowl, vegetable; oval, 9½" $25.00
Windsor, green, coaster, 3¼" $18.00
Windsor, green, plate, sherbet; 6"...............................$8.00
Windsor, green, platter, oval, 11½"..............................$22.00
Windsor, green, tray, square, w/handles, 4"...............$12.00
Windsor, pink, bowl, pointed edge, 5".........................$18.00
Windsor, pink, bowl, 2-handled, 8"..............................$16.00
Windsor, pink, butter dish, 2 styles............................$50.00
Windsor, pink, cup $9.50
Windsor, pink, plate, sandwich; closed handle, 10" ...$22.00
Windsor, pink, sherbet, footed $11.00
Windsor, pink, tray, w/handles, 4⅛x9".........................$10.00
Windsor, tumbler, footed, 7¼"......................................$15.00

Disney

The largest and most popular area in character collectibles is without doubt Disneyana. There are clubs, newsletters, and special shows that are centered around this hobby. Every aspect of the retail market has been thoroughly saturated with Disney-related merchandise over the years, and today collectors are able to find many good examples at garage sales and flea markets.

Disney memorabilia from the late twenties until about 1940 was marked either 'Walt E. Disney' or 'Walt Disney Enterprises.' After that time, the name was changed to 'Walt Disney Productions.' Some of the earlier items have become very expensive, though many are still within the reach of the average collector.

During the thirties, Mickey Mouse, Donald Duck, Snow White and the Seven Dwarfs, and the Three Little Pigs (along with all their friends and cohorts) dominated the Disney scene. The last of the thirties' characters was Pinocchio, and some 'purists' prefer to stop their collections with him.

The forties and fifties brought many new characters with them — Alice in Wonderland, Bambi, Dumbo, Lady and the Tramp, and Peter Pan were some of the major personalities featured in Disney's films of this era.

Even today, thanks to the re-releases of many of the old movies and the popularity of Disney's vacation 'kingdoms,' toy stores and department stores alike are full of quality items with the potential of soon becoming collectibles.

If you'd like to learn more about this fascinating field, we recommend *Stern's Guide to Disney Collectibles, First and Second Series*, by Michael Stern; *The Collector's Encyclopedia of Disneyana* by Michael Stern and David Longest; *Character Toys and Collectibles* and *Toys, Antique and Collectible*, both by David Longest; and *Schroeder's Collectible Toys, Antique to Modern*. All are published by Collector Books.

See also Character and Promotional Drinking Glasses; Character Watches; Cowboy Character Memorabilia; Dolls, Mattel; Games; Pencil Sharpeners; Pin-Back Buttons; Puzzles; Salt and Pepper Shakers; Toys; TV Shows and Movies; Valentines.

Note: In the following listings, many of the characters have been sorted by the name of the feature film in which they appeared.

Advisor: Judy Posner (See Directory, Character and Personality Collectibles)

Club: The Mouse Club East
P.O. Box 3195
Wakefield, MA 01880; Family membership of $25 includes 2 newsletters and 2 shows per year

Newsletter: National Fantasy Fan Club
Dept. AC, Box 19212
Irvine, CA 92713; Membership: $20 per year, includes newsletters, free ads, chapters, conventions, etc.

Aladdin, pin, figural, from Disney store, 1993, M.......**$12.00**
Alice in Wonderland, bank, ceramic, standing, pastel airbrushing w/painted eyes, Leeds/marked WD Prod, 6¼", M...**$165.00**
Alice in Wonderland, coloring book, Whitman, 1951, EX+ **$18.00**
Alice in Wonderland, figure, March Hare, vinyl, Gund/WDP, 14", EX **$25.00**
Alice in Wonderland, planter, pottery, double style, Leeds/WDP, 7", NM **$135.00**

Babes in Toyland, Colorforms, WDP, 1961, unused, NMIB, from $20 to **$30.00**
Babes in Toyland, printer set, 6 stamps, ink pad & paper, Colorforms, 1960, EXIB, from $20 to **$30.00**
Bambi, bank, Flower, chalkware, figural skunk, EX...**$50.00**
Bambi, bank, standing figure, airbrushing w/painted eyes & nose, Leeds/marked Walt Disney Productions, 7½"..**$65.00**
Bambi, bank, Thumper, 1 ear up & 1 ear down, airbrushing w/painted eyes & trim, Leeds, 6¾" **$80.00**
Bambi, figure, ceramic, Shaw, 1940s, 7¾", M, minimum value **$150.00**
Bambi, friction toy, Linemar, 1950s, EX+ **$50.00**
Bambi, milk pitcher, ceramic, Shaw, 1940s, M..........**$175.00**
Bambi, planter, Flower, airbrushing w/painted eyes, Leeds/marked w/name & Walt Disney, 4¼", M ...**$65.00**
Bambi, plate, Disneyland souvenir w/multicolored graphics, Beswick, 1955, 7", M **$125.00**
Bambi, shoe polish, Baby Shoe White, EXIB **$15.00**
Bambi, wall pocket, Bambi & Thumper by tree stump, airbrushing w/painted features, marked Bambi, Leeds, 8" **$65.00**
Beauty & the Beast, pin, cloisonne Beast face, 1990s, NM ..**$10.00**
Black Hole, activity book, 1979, unused, NM **$15.00**
Black Hole, press-out book, 1979, EX **$10.00**
Black Hole, wastebasket, litho metal, 1979, 11x6½", G..**$12.00**
Chip & Dale (Rescue Rangers), carryall bag, images of Chip & Dale on red vinyl, premium, M **$20.00**
Chip & Dale (Rescue Rangers), shoelace snappers, Hope Industries, MIP **$12.00**
Chitty-Chitty Bang-Bang, car, Husky, 1960s, EX..........**$30.00**
Chitty-Chitty Bang-Bang, coloring & activity book, wipe-off type, w/crayons, Golden Books, 1960s, NM **$30.00**
Cinderella, bank, standing, holding wand, pink & blue airbrushing, Leeds/marked Cinderella USA Walt Disney 1950, 6½" **$165.00**
Cinderella, doll, Effanbee, 1985, MIB..........................**$50.00**
Cinderella, mold set, complete, Model Craft, 1950s, EX.**$85.00**
Cinderella, pattern for apron, early, unused, M..........**$25.00**
Daisy Duck, figure, bendable, Applause, 5½", MIP......**$6.00**
Disney, coloring book, It's a Small World, Whitman, 1966, NM **$12.00**

Disney, sand pail, features Mickey at drink stand, Ohio Art, 1936, 3", NM, from $200.00 to $300.00.

Disney, sand pail, features Mickey, Minnie, Donald & Pluto, Happynak, 1940s, 4", EX+.......................................**$90.00**

Disney, tray, Disney's Wonderful World of Color, lithographed metal, 1961, 17x12", EX...........................**$30.00**

Disney, tray, litho metal w/characters watching Professor Von Drake on TV, 17x12", VG+.................................**$30.00**

Disney, yo-yo, features, Mickey, Donald & Pluto, 1980s Festival, MIP **$10.00**

Disneyland Tea Set, 1950s, MIB, $250.00. (Photo courtesy of Dunbar Gallery.)

Donald Duck, bank, ceramic, cross-eyed head, bright cold-painted features, Leeds, 7", M.......................**$200.00**

Donald Duck, bank, ceramic, seated looking up & holding coin, airbrushing w/painted eyes, Leeds, 6¼", M.**$200.00**

Donald Duck, bank, ceramic, seated looking up & holding coin, cold-painted detail, Leeds/marked Walt Disney, 7½", M **$200.00**

Donald Duck, bank, ceramic, standing cowboy figure, airbrushed details, Leeds, 7", M.....................**$160.00**

Donald Duck, bank, vinyl w/articulated arms that drop coins into pig, 9", NM......................................**$50.00**

Donald Duck, cake-pan mold, head only, Wilton, 1970s, EX+ **$35.00**

Donald Duck, figure, bendable, Applause, 5", MIP **$6.00**

Donald Duck, planter, ceramic, Donald holding flower, white w/painted details, Leeds/marked Walt Disney USA, 6¾", M **$80.00**

Donald Duck, planter, ceramic, Donald on ABC blocks, airbrushing w/black-painted eyes, Leeds/marked WDP, 5x6½", M **$100.00**

Donald Duck, squeeze toy, Donald as baby, vinyl, 1986, 7", EX..**$8.00**

Donald Duck, suspenders, Flying Cadet All Elastic Kiddie Braces, w/metal clips, 1950s, NMOC **$75.00**

Donald Duck, swim goggles, Auburn Rubber, 1950s-60s, M (EX card) **$35.00**

Donald Duck, xylophone, litho tin, letters of the notes incised on each musical bar, w/original stick, WDP, 4x10", EX..**$65.00**

Donald Duck & 3 Nephews, wall plaques, WDP, 15" Donald, 10" Nephews, VG/EX **$20.00**

Donald Duck's Nephews, gelatin mold, 5x7x2", EX.....**$8.00**

Duck Tales, figure, Baggy Beagle, bendable, Justoys, 6", MIP...**$6.00**

Duck Tales, figure, Scrooge McDuck, bendable, Justoys, 4½", MIP...**$6.00**

Duck Tales, gumball machine bank, Scrooge McDuck, Superior/WD, 1989, 9½", MIB **$20.00**

Duck Tales, sticker book & stickers, complete set, Panini, 1987, NM **$30.00**

Dumbo, bank, ceramic, seated, white w/pink & yellow airbrushing, black-painted eyes, Leeds/marked Walt Disney, 7", M...................................**$90.00**

Dumbo, bank, ceramic, seated w/coin on forehead, yellow airbrushing & black-painted detail, gold trim, Leeds, 6¼", M...**$115.00**

Dumbo, bank, metal figure, 1950s, M.......................**$25.00**

Dumbo, candy mold, 2-part figure, Wilton, 1972, 6x4x2", EX...**$20.00**

Dumbo, figure, blue vinyl, 1960s, NM **$20.00**

Dumbo, figure, painted plaster, 1950s, 2½", EX..........**$40.00**

Ferdinand the Bull, figure, rubber, Seiberling, EX+ **$65.00**

Goofy, doll, Pop-A-Part, Multiple, 1965, 9", MIP.......**$50.00**

Goofy, nodder, arms folded, square white base, Disney World, NM...**$75.00**

Goofy, nodder, painted ceramic, driving car, 1960s, EX.**$125.00**

Goofy, squeak toy, vinyl, 8", EX................................**$8.00**

Hook, Flintlock Knife & Compass Set, 1991, MIB........**$8.00**

Jamboree Bear, bank, brown ceramic, WDP, 1960s, 11", EX..**$50.00**

Jungle Book, doll, Baloo Bear, vinyl head w/plush body, Knickerbocker, 1960s, 14", VG **$30.00**

Lady & the Tramp, coloring book, Whitman, 1954, EX..**$25.00**

Lady & the Tramp, figure, Lady, ceramic, 1970s, EX..**$45.00**

Lion King, pin, Simba, cloisonne & enamel, 1994, M..**$20.00**

Lion King, playset, Once Upon a Time, 4 PVC figures & 5 different scenes w/carrying case, Mattel, 1994, MIB ..**$15.00**

Little Meramid, figure, Sebastian, bendable, Justoys, 3", MIP...**$5.00**

Little Mermaid, doll, Flounder, stuffed, Tyco, MIB......**$20.00**

Little Mermaid, doll, Sebastian, stuffed, Tyco, MIB.....**$20.00**

Little Mermaid, figure, Ariel, bendable, Justoys, 6", MIP..**$5.00**

Ludwig Von Drake, squeeze toy, Dell, 1950s-60s, 7½", VG **$50.00**

Ludwig Von Drake, umbrella, NM.............................**$75.00**

Mary Poppins, charm bracelet, multicolored charms on gold-tone metal, 1960s, EX.................................**$85.00**

Mary Poppins, coloring book, Mary Poppins Merry-Go-Round, 1964, M..**$15.00**

Mary Poppins, transfers, Rub-Ons, set of 3, Hasbro 1964, NM (EX+ box) **$22.00**

Mickey Mouse, bank, Armored Car, Enesco.............**$65.00**

Mickey Mouse, bank as cowboy, airbrushed w/black cold-painted eyes & nose, gold trim, Leeds, 6½".......**$200.00**

Mickey Mouse, belt buckle, metal, round, EX............**$65.00**

Mickey Mouse, birthday card, shows Mickey as sailor, Hall Bros, 1930s, EX+......................................**$75.00**

Mickey Mouse, cake-pan mold, head only as band leader, Wilton, 1970s, 14", EX+...............................**$35.00**

Mickey Mouse, doll, as baseball player, w/suction cups, Playskool, 1988, 12", MIB.............................**$15.00**

Mickey Mouse, doll, as Sorcerer, plush, Applause, 1990, 16", M..**$30.00**

Mickey Mouse, magic slate, 1970s, MOC..................**$20.00**

Mickey Mouse, marbles, 1970s, MOC **$20.00**

Mickey Mouse, necklace, embossed image of Mickey on round pendant, WDP, 1¼" dia, EX......................**$10.00**

Mickey Mouse, nodder, painted wood, head & hands on springs, Disneyland, 1960s, 3¾", EX.....................**$65.00**

Mickey Mouse, pin, enameled Mickey w/attached initial, 1990s, NM...**$5.00**

Mickey Mouse, pistol, Mickey Mouse Bubble Buster, Kilgore, 1930s, 7", NM, $275.00. (Photo courtesy of Dunbar Gallery.)

Mickey Mouse, push-button puppet, Kohner, 1970, 5", MIB..**$45.00**

Mickey Mouse, tray, litho tin, 11" dia, EX **$12.00**

Mickey Mouse, wall plaque, as Sherlock Holmes, WDP, 14", EX..**$25.00**

Mickey Mouse & Donald Duck, hangers, plastic, 1970s, MIP **$20.00**

Mickey Mouse & Goofy, crossword puzzles, 1982, unused, M.**$8.00**

Mickey Mouse & Minnie, key chain, flashes w/Mickey & Minnie kissing, 1980s, NM.......................................**$8.00**

Mickey Mouse Club, album, group picture on front, 1975, M (sealed) **$55.00**

Mickey Mouse Club, bank, tin & plastic, Mattel, 1957, EX.**$75.00**

Mickey Mouse Club, name plate, plastic, w/Mickey Mouse Club member & personalized first name, 1950s, 2x4", each .**$5.00**

Minnie Mouse, bank, vinyl figure w/pink outfit & yellow umbrella, Illco Toys, 1970s, 11", NM.....................**$15.00**

Minnie Mouse, doll, Twinkle Twinkle Little Star plays when doll is hugged, lights flash, Mattel, 1991, 16", MIB **$45.00**

Minnie Mouse, hand puppet, cloth body, WDP, EX...**$15.00**

Minnie Mouse, purse, Pretty Minnie, 1970s, MIP **$18.00**

Minnie Mouse, ring, silver face, 1930s, EX................**$100.00**

Minnie Mouse, ring, silver face, 1980s **$20.00**

Nightmare Before Christmas, doll, Boogie, glow-in-the-dark mouth, makes noise, M **$50.00**

Nightmare Before Christmas, dolls, Sally and Jack Skellington, MIB, $350.00 (for Sally); $225.00 (for Jack). (Photo courtesy of June Moon.)

Nightmare Before Christmas, figures, PVC, set of 5, M..**$20.00**

Nightmare Before Christmas, kite, M **$10.00**

Nightmare Before Christmas, pencil topper, figural, EX, each...**$6.00**

Nightmare Before Christmas, postcard book, M.........**$15.00**

Peter Pan, hand puppet, Captain Hook, cloth body w/vinyl head, Gund, 1950s, 10", EX **$35.00**

Peter Pan, hand puppet, cloth body w/vinyl head, Gund, 1950s, 10", VG+...**$35.00**

Peter Pan, hand puppet, Tinkerbell, Disney, EX+ **$45.00**

Peter Pan, plate, Tinkerbell flying over castle, Disneyland, 1960s, 4" dia, NM..**$20.00**

Pinocchio, bank, vinyl bust, Play Pal, 1971, EX..........**$60.00**

Pinocchio, doll, vinyl head w/beanbag body, early 1960s, VG **$20.00**

Pinocchio, figure, ceramic, 1940s, 2½", EX **$40.00**

Pinocchio, figure, Jiminy Cricket, pink plastic, 1960s, 5", EX **$20.00**

Pinocchio, mask, Figaro, Gillette Blue Blade premium, 1939, VG+..**$18.00**

Pinocchio, mask, Geppetto, Gillette Blue Blade premium, 1939, EX+ **$18.00**

Pinocchio, night light, Jiminy Cricket, hand-painted, EXIB **$25.00**

Pinocchio, pencil sharpener, Bakelite, round, 1940s, EX.**$55.00**

Pinocchio, rug, w/Jiminy Cricket & other characters, 40x19", EX...**$95.00**

Pinocchio, wallet, Jiminy Cricket, leather, EX, $30.00.

Pinocchio & Jiminy Cricket, wall plaques, WDP, 15" Pinocchio, 8" Jiminy Cricket, VG/EX....................**$25.00**

Pluto, bank, composition figure, MIB **$65.00**

Pluto, bank, vinyl figure w/articulated arm that drops coin into doghouse, 1970s, 9", EX **$50.00**

Pluto, doll, vinyl head w/beanbag body, early 1960s, EX....**$25.00**

Pluto, figure, bendable, 1960s-70s, 6", EX **$22.00**

Pluto, hand puppet, cloth body w/vinyl head, squeaker, Gund, 1950s, NM **$35.00**

Pluto, jump rope, 1970s, MOC **$12.00**

Pluto, nodder, round green base, 1970s, NM **$75.00**

Pluto, wall pocket, Pluto seated w/2 wheeled cart, airbrushing w/painted features, Leeds/marked Walt Disney Prod, 7", M **$120.00**

Rescuers Down Under, figure, Bernard, bendable, Applause, 2", MIP **$4.00**

Rescuers Down Under, figure, Bernard, bendable, Justoys, 5",
  MIP..**$6.00**
Rescuers Down Under, figure, Bianca, bendable, Applause,
  2'" MIP..**$4.00**
Rescuers Down Under, figure, Bianca, bendable, Justoys, 5",
  MIP..**$6.00**
Robin Hood, watering can, figural, 1973, NMIB **$50.00**
Rocketeer, beach towel, AMC Theatres promotion, 2 designs,
  M, each..**$25.00**
Rocketeer, candy container, plastic helmet, Topps, 2½", M.**$4.00**
Rocketeer, doll, Applause, NM **$18.00**
Rocketeer, Fan Club Membership Card, M **$10.00**
Rocketeer, figure, bendable, Justoys/Disney, 1991, 6", MOC .**$5.00**
Rocketeer, figure, standing, vinyl, Applause, 9", EX ..**$20.00**
Rocketeer, notebook, Mead, 4 different, M, each **$5.00**
Rocketeer, pencil, helmet, M...**$3.00**
Rocketter, slumber bag, NM..**$50.00**
Sleeping Beauty, Magic Bubble Wand, Gardner, 1959,
  NMIP **$25.00**
Sleeping Beauty, squeeze toy, kneeling w/forest animals,
  rubber, Dell, 1959, EX+ **$45.00**
Snow White, bank, Enesco...**$175.00**
Snow White, bank, standing holding up skirt, airbrushed
  dress w/painted hair & features, Leeds, 6" **$165.00**
Snow White, figure, ceramic, holds sides of skirt, G, Leonard,
  12", VG **$50.00**
Snow White & the Seven Dwarfs, calendar, 1994, 16-month,
  Day Dream Calendars, MIP.....................................**$14.00**
Snow White & the Seven Dwarfs, cereal bowl, red graphics
  on milk glass, WDE, 1930s, 5" dia........................**$75.00**
Snow White & the Seven Dwarfs, doll, Bashful, stuffed cloth
  w/painted features, Chad Valley, 1939, original tag, 7",
  EX **$125.00**
Snow White & the Seven Dwarfs, doll, Doc, stuffed cloth w/paint-
  ed features, original tag, Chad Valley, 1939, 7", EX+ .**$125.00**
Snow White & the Seven Dwarfs, lamp base, Dopey figure, airbrush-
  ing w/painted eyes, Leeds/marked WDP, 6½", M..........**$150.00**
Snow White & the Seven Dwarfs, napkins, beverage or lun-
  cheon, Beach Products, 1994, 16-ct, MIP, each **$4.00**
Snow White & the Seven Dwarfs, rubber stamp, Dwarfs form-
  ing pyramid w/Dopey on top, Rubber Stampede, 1994,
  MIP..**$6.00**
Snow White & the Seven Dwarfs, squeeze toy, Dopey, paint-
  ed rubber, 1960s, 4", EX..**$45.00**
Snow White & the Seven Dwarfs, table cover, plastic, Beach
  Products, 1994, MIP **$6.00**
Snow White & the Seven Dwarfs, toy ironing board, litho
  metal, Wolverine, 24", EX.......................................**$35.00**
Three Little Pigs, ashtray, lustreware, shows musical scene,
  M **$100.00**
Who Framed Roger Rabbit, doll, Roger Rabbit, stuffed, 18",
  M...**$55.00**
Who Framed Roger Rabbit, figure, Baby Herman, ceramic,
  Disney store item, M **$50.00**
Who Framed Roger Rabbit, figure, Jessica, bendable, LJN, 6",
  MOC...**$35.00**
Who Framed Roger Rabbit, figure, Judge Doom, bendable,
  LJN, 6", MOC **$6.00**
Winnie the Pooh, ceiling light cover, EX...................**$40.00**

Winnie the Pooh, doll, stuffed velvet, 1960s, 6", NM .**$65.00**
Winnie the Pooh, night light, ceramic, shows characters
  sleeping under lg mushroom, EX..........................**$40.00**
Winnie the Pooh, switch plate, WDP, EX+ **$6.00**
Winnie the Pooh, toy box, vinyl, 16x30x15", EX **$35.00**
101 Dalmatians, coloring book, Whitman, 1960, EX+...**$16.00**
101 Dalmatians, poster, 1972, 41x27", NM...................**$15.00**
101 Dalmatians, squeeze toy, EX+ **$25.00**

Dog Collectibles

Dog lovers appreciate the many items, old and new, that are modeled after or decorated with their favorite breeds. They pursue, some avidly, all with dedication, specific items for a particular accumulation or a range of objects, from matchbook covers to bronzes.

Perhaps the Scottish Terrier is one of the most highly sought-out breeds of dogs among collectors; at any rate, Scottie devotees are more organized than most. Both the Aberdeen and West Highland Terriers were used commercially; often the two are found together in things such as magnets, Black & White Scotch Whiskey advertisements, jewelry, and playing cards, for instance. They became a favorite of the advertising world in the 1930s and 1940s, partly as a result of the public popularity of President Roosevelt's dog, Fala.

Poodles were the breed of the 1950s, and today items from those years are cherished collectibles. Trendsetter teeny-boppers wore poodle skirts, and the 5-&-10¢ stores were full of pink poodle figurines with 'coleslaw' fur. For a look back at these years, we recommend *Poodle Collectibles of the '50s and '60s* by Elaine Butler (L-W Books).

Many of the earlier collectibles are especially prized, making them expensive and difficult to find. Prices listed here may vary as they are dependent on supply and demand, location, and dealer assessment.

Advisor: Donna Palmer, Scotties (See Directory Scottie Dog Collectibles)

Newsletter: *Canine Collectibles Quarterly*
Patty Shedlow, Editor
736 N Western Ave., Ste. 314
Lake Forest, IL 60045; Subscription: $28 per year

Newsletter: *Collectively Speaking!*
Joan L. Neidhardt, Editor
428 Philadelphia Rd.
Joppa, MD 21085; 410-679-7224; Specializing in 'old, new, Lassie too — anything collies; Subscription $20 per year

Newsletter: *Scottie Sampler*
David Bohnlein
P.O. Box 2597
Winchester, VA 22604-2597

Magazine: *Great Scots Magazine*
Tartan Scottie
1028 Girard NE
Albuquerque, NM 87106

Afghan, decanter, McCormick, 1976...........................**$25.00**

Basset Hound, figurine, Norcrest, 1960s, 6", from $18 to...**$22.00**

Basset Hound, figurines, Hagen-Renaker, 1995, sm, set of 3.**$15.00**

Borzoi, bookends, brass, pr...**$85.00**

Boston Terrier, playing cards, pinochle, 1940s, MIB...**$35.00**

Boxer, salt & pepper shakers, realistic paint, Japan, pr..**$25.00**

Cocker Spaniel, figurine, crouching puppy w/ball, Franklin Mint, 3x5"..**$15.00**

Collie, decanter, Garner Liquors, 1972.........................**$25.00**

Dachshund, letter holder, ceramic w/spring body, Japan, 3½x10½"...**$15.00**

Dachshund, table lighter, Ronson, ca 1940, 4x9", from $125 to...**$200.00**

Doberman, belt buckle, enamelled brass head, 3x2½"..**$15.00**

English Sheep Dog, salt & pepper shakers, Norcrest, 1990s, pr, from $8 to..**$12.00**

German Shepherd, figurine, standing pose, marked Giftcraft/Japan, 5x7"...**$8.00**

German Shepherd, toy, stuffed plush, Dakin, 1974, M w/original tag..**$15.00**

Great Dane, decanter, Limestone................................**$35.00**

Great Dane, figurine, recumbent, Norcrest.................**$65.00**

Irish Wolfhound, calendar, 1953, boy w/young dog, 13½x9", M..**$15.00**

Japanese Chin, bookends, bronze, pr........................**$165.00**

Old English Sheepdog, plate, enamelled copper, marked Valleau, 5½" dia...**$25.00**

Poodle, ashtray, figure w/coleslaw & hand-painted detail on shell-formed base, unmarked................................**$15.00**

Poodle, bank, coleslaw bust w/rhinestone eyes, Poodle Bank at base in gold, from $20 to....................................**$25.00**

Poodle, bookends, black w/red & white trim, Japan, pr, from $10 to...**$15.00**

Poodle, clothes hamper, pink & white painted black vinyl, clear Lucite handles, from $60 to..........................**$75.00**

Poodle, figurine, graduate w/Pedigree book, coleslaw & hand-painted details, marked Thames Hand-Painted Japan.**$20.00**

Poodle, lint brush, hand-painted ceramic figural handle w/brush across back, Japan.....................................**$20.00**

Poodle, plaque, pink & aqua on black ground, marked Helen DeTar, pr, from $40 to..**$50.00**

Poodle, purse, wicker w/plastic handles, framed scene on side, marked Princess Charming Atlas Hollywood Fla, from $20 to...**$25.00**

Poodle, wall plaque, w/white poodle, Norcrest..........**$15.00**

Poodle, wastebasket, lithographed metal, unmarked, from $25 to..**$30.00**

Pug, inkwell, brass plated, 4½x3½".............................**$75.00**

Saluki, Dessert Hunter, Bosson..................................**$95.00**

Scottie, bank, black metal, slot in head for coins, bottom lock w/key, 4¼"...**$95.00**

Scottie, book, The Book of the Scottish Terrier, by Fayette C Ewing, revised edition, Orange Judd, 1952..........**$60.00**

Scottie, bookends, heavy hollow glass, front feet raised on block, ears cocked w/1 down, Cambridge, pr...**$275.00**

Scottie, bootscraper, cast iron on bar w/standing Scottie profile, cut-out eye, 7½x8½".................................**$125.00**

Scottie, brush holder set, carved wood w/glass eyes, sitting pose w/brushes between legs & in back, w/hanger, 7x2½".**$40.00**

Scottie, buttons, brown Bakelite, Scottie profile in standing pose, set of 5...**$50.00**

Scottie, chocolate mold, metal, sitting pose, Hans Bruhn & Co, Germany, 4½x3½"......................................**$175.00**

Scottie, cookie cutter, aluminum w/green painted knob, standing pose, 2½x2¾"......................................**$15.00**

Scottie, cup, chrome w/solid black metal Scottie attached to side, red eyes, marked Made in Japan, pre-WWII, 2x2"..**$60.00**

Scottie, decanter, glass w/2 reverse-painted standing black Scotties & red stripes, round stopper, Czechoslovakia..........**$175.00**

Scottie, figurine, crystal, standing pose, Heisey, 4x2".**$125.00**

Scottie, figurine, hollow cast bronze, 1 sitting & 1 standing w/ears cocked, 6½" & 7½", pr.........................**$195.00**

Scottie, figurine, black, standing w/tail up, eyes & ears alert, Royal Doulton #1016...**$145.00**

Scottie, lamps, white glass w/3-step base, white cube shade, 4 black painted Scotties, 10", pr......................**$195.00**

Scottie, pencil sharpener, black, sitting dog & sharpener hole on chrome lid, black painted base, crimped sides, 5x3".**$75.00**

Scottie, pin, 14k gold, standing profile, sm..............**$175.00**

Scottie, pipe holder, metal dog and holder on wooden base, 4½x4" dia base, EX, $18.00.

Scottie, place card holder, sterling w/standing cut-out profile on tray, pr...**$75.00**

Scottie, playing cards, sitting pose w/tam & bow, red w/black or blue w/white, double deck, Hamilton, MIB..............**$20.00**

Scottie, print, by Gladys Emerson Cook, head portrait w/eyes looking straight ahead, 16½x12¾".....................**$150.00**

Scottie, print, Friendship, w/poem, sitting pose, Buzza, 1926...**$35.00**

Scottie, print, Scottish Terriers, by Lucy Dawson, depicts sitting Scottie & Westie, red frame, 14½x13".........**$125.00**

Scottie, radio, black case w/sm white Scottie cutout on bottom, Remler, 1940s...**$175.00**

Scottie, rug, sm reversible throw type, depicts 2 Scotties on leashes w/ball, gray on gray, 11½x27½"..............**$75.00**

Scottie, towels, guest; printed paper w/green Scotties, instructions & Use It, 36 in box w/original ribbon ties......**$30.00**

Scottie, tray, 3 mirror Scotties on black ground, black & mirror-checked border, chrome edges & black wood handles.**$85.00**

St Bernard, fan, boy & dog on raft, Faithful Guardian & advertising **$30.00**

St Bernard, marmalade jar, Norcrest, 1970s, 4½", from $25 to **$30.00**

Terrier, figurine, black & white celluloid, standing pose, 6x4½" **$15.00**

Terrier, thimble, pewter w/hand-painted dog at top, marked England...**$20.00**

Dollhouse Furniture

Some of the mass-produced dollhouse furniture you're apt to see on the market today was made by Renwal and Acme during the forties and Ideal in the 1960s. All three of these companies used hard plastic for their furniture lines and imprinted most pieces with their names. Strombecker furniture was made of wood, and although it was not marked, it has a certain recognizable style to it. Remember that if you're lucky enough to find it complete in the original box, you'll want to preserve the carton as well.

Advisor: Marian Schmuhl (See Directory, Dollhouse Furniture and Accessories)

Ideal Petite Princess, boudoir chaise lounge, #4408-1, pink, MIB, $25.00.

Acme, Ferris wheel, 4 yellow chairs w/green seats on red wheel, blue base...**$45.00**

Acme, rocker, yellow w/red trim...................................**$4.00**

Acme, stroller, pink...**$6.00**

Acme, wagon, green w/red wheels & handle.............**$20.00**

Allied, highboy, red...**$3.00**

Allied, refrigerator, white...**$3.00**

Allied, sink, white...**$3.00**

Allied, table, white..**$3.00**

Allied, vanity w/bench, red...**$5.00**

Best, cradle, pink..**$6.00**

F&F, refrigerator, turquoise, ½" scale..........................**$2.00**

F&F, stove, white, ½" scale...**$2.00**

F&F, trash compactor, light brown, ½" scale................**$2.00**

Ideal, bed, turquoise spread...**$6.00**

Ideal, buffet, dark brown...**$10.00**

Ideal, chair, dining; brown w/yellow seat.....................**$5.00**

Ideal, china cupboard, dark marbelized maroon........**$10.00**

Ideal, hamper, ivory..**$4.00**

Ideal, refrigerator, ivory w/black trim.........................**$15.00**

Ideal, sink, bathroom; yellow or blue..........................**$35.00**

Ideal, table, coffee; brown..**$8.00**

Ideal, vacuum cleaner, green upright w/red base, yellow handle, no bag..**$20.00**

Ideal Petite Princess, buffet, #4419-8, no accessories....**$12.00**

Ideal Petite Princess, chair, dining; #4414-9.............**$10.00**

Ideal Petite Princess, chair, dining; #4423-1...............**$8.00**

Ideal Petite Princess, table, pedestal; #4427-1...........**$22.00**

Ideal Petite Princess, tea cart, #4424-8......................**$25.00**

Ideal Young Decorator, armoire, reddish-brown swirl..**$25.00**

Ideal Young Decorator, bed, white w/rose spread.....**$35.00**

Ideal Young Decorator, diaper pail, yellow & blue....**$25.00**

Ideal Young Decorator, sofa, straight section, rose.....**$10.00**

Jaydon, buffet, reddish brown.......................................**$4.00**

Jaydon, sofa, red w/brown trim...................................**$10.00**

Marx, bathroom set w/corner tub, toilet, sink & hamper, hard plastic, ivory, ¾" scale...........................**$20.00**

Marx, bathroom set w/tub, toilet, sink & chair, soft plastic, blue...**$16.00**

Marx, bathtub, hard plastic, ivory, ½" scale.................**$2.00**

Marx, chair, armless; hard plastic, pale blue, ½" scale.**$2.00**

Marx, chair, captain's; soft plastic, red, ½" scale..........**$3.00**

Marx, chair, kitchen; hard plastic, ivory w/red painted seat, ¾" scale...**$5.00**

Marx, china cupboard, hard plastic, dark brown, ½" scale.**$2.00**

Marx, dining room set, soft plastic, brown, 6-pc set, ¾" scale...**$18.00**

Marx, dresser, hard plastic, pink, ½" scale...................**$2.00**

Marx, hamper, hard plastic, peach, ¾" scale................**$5.00**

Marx, highboy, hard plastic, yellow, ½" scale...............**$2.00**

Marx, highboy, hard plastic, yellow, ¾" scale...............**$5.00**

Marx, nightstand, hard plastic, ivory, ¾" scale.............**$5.00**

Marx, playpen, hard plastic, blue, ¾" scale..................**$5.00**

Marx, sink, bathroom; hard plastic, blue, ¾" scale.......**$5.00**

Marx, sofa, hard plastic, blue, ¾" scale........................**$5.00**

Marx, sofa, hard plastic, green, ½" scale......................**$2.00**

Marx, sofa, soft plastic, red, ¾" scale...........................**$3.00**

Marx, table, step end; hard plastic, red, ¾" scale.........**$5.00**

Marx, TV/phonograph combination, hard plastic, blue, ¾" scale..**$5.00**

Marx Little Hostess, chair, bedroom; ivory w/bright pink trim...**$8.00**

Marx Little Hostess, vanity w/3-way mirror, ivory......**$12.00**

Mattel, chair, kitchen...**$3.00**

Mattel Littles, armoire..**$8.00**

Mattel Littles, dresser..**$8.00**

Mattel Littles, sofa..**$8.00**

Plasco, baby crib, dark peach......................................**$25.00**

Plasco, buffet w/top, dark maroon................................**$8.00**

Plasco, chair, dining; brown...**$3.00**

Plasco, fireplace w/andirons, brown & ivory..............**$12.00**

Plasco, hamper, pink...**$4.00**

Plasco, sink, bathroom; pink...**$4.00**

Plasco, stove, white w/blue base...................................**$5.00**

Plasco, table, patio; blue w/ivory legs, no umbrella.....**$4.00**

Plasco, vanity, round mirror, w/bench, pink.................**$8.00**

Renwal, bedroom set: dresser, $20.00; beds, $8.00 each; night stand, $4.00; lamp, $8.00; vanity, $18.00; bench, $3.00. (Photo courtesy of Judith Mosholder.)

Renwal, buffet, #D55, brown **$8.00**
Renwal, chair, teacher's; #35, blue **$15.00**
Renwal, clock, kitchen; #11, ivory or red, each..........**$20.00**
Renwal, desk, student; #33, red **$10.00**
Renwal, desk, teacher; #34, brown **$20.00**
Renwal, doll, baby, #8..**$8.00**
Renwal, doll, father, #42..**$28.00**
Renwal, doll, mother, #43, flesh, no paint...................**$25.00**
Renwal, doll, mother, #43, rose dress **$55.00**
Renwal, ironing board, #32, blue **$7.00**
Renwal, night stand, #884, pink **$4.00**
Renwal, radio, floor model, #79, brown **$8.00**
Renwal, radio, table model, #16, brown.......................**$12.00**
Renwal, stool, #12, red w/ivory seat **$12.00**
Renwal, table, cocktail; #72, light reddish brown **$8.00**
Renwal, table, folding; #108, turquoise.........................**$15.00**
Renwal, washing machine, #31, blue w/decal **$30.00**
Strombecker, bed, pink, ¾" scale...................................**$12.00**
Strombecker, nightstand, pink, ¾" scale **$5.00**
Strombecker, sink, bathroom; light green, ¾" scale......**$8.00**
Strombecker, tub, light green, ¾" scale **$8.00**
Superior, hutch, pink, ¾" scale......................................**$5.00**
Superior, tub, blue, ¾" scale..**$5.00**
Thomas, doll, baby w/diaper...**$4.00**
Thomas, doll, girl w/raised hand....................................**$4.00**
Tomy Smaller Homes, bathtub..**$8.00**
Tomy Smaller Homes, dresser, w/3 hangers **$14.00**
Tomy Smaller Homes, refrigerator, 3 drawers.............**$12.00**
Tootsietoy, cupboard, ivory **$20.00**
Tootsietoy, table, dining; ivory **$15.00**
Tootsietoy, vanity, w/3 mirrors, pink............................**$25.00**

Dolls

Doll collecting is one of the most popular hobbies in the United States. Since many of the antique dolls are so expensive, modern dolls have come into their own and can be had at prices within the range of most budgets. Today's thrift-shop owners know the extent of 'doll mania,' though, so you'll seldom find a bargain there. But if you're willing to spend the time, garage sales can be a good source for your doll buying. Granted most will be in a 'well loved' condition, but as long as they're priced right, many can be redressed, rewigged, and cleaned up. Swap meets and flea markets may sometimes yield a good example or two, often at lower-than-book prices.

Modern dolls, those made from 1935 to the present, are made of rubber, composition, magic skin, synthetic rubber, and many types of plastic. Most of these materials do not stand up well to age, so be objective when you buy, especially if you're buying with an eye to the future. Doll repair is an art best left to professionals, but if yours is only dirty, you can probably do it yourself. If you need to clean a composition doll, do it very carefully. Use only baby oil and follow up with a soft dry cloth to remove any residue. Most types of wigs can be shampooed with wig shampoo and lukewarm water. Be careful not to mat the hair as you shampoo, and follow up with hair conditioner or fabric softener. Comb gently and set while wet, using small soft rubber or metal curlers. Never use a curling iron or heated rollers.

In our listings, unless a condition is noted in the descriptions, values are for dolls in excellent condition.

For further study, we recommend these books by Patricia Smith: *Patricia Smith's Doll Values, Antique to Modern; Modern Collector's Dolls* (eight in the series); *Vogue Ginny Dolls, Through the Years With Ginny;* and *Madame Alexander Collector's Dolls.* Patsy Moyer's books, *Modern Collectible Dolls* and *Doll Values* are also highly recommended. Patikii Gibbs has written the book *Horsman Dolls, 1950–1970,* and Estelle Patino is the author of *American Rag Dolls, Straight From the Heart;* both contain a wealth of information on those particular subjects. Myla Perkins has written *Black Dolls: 1820–1991* and *Black Dolls, Book II; Chatty Cathy Dolls* is by Kathy and Don Lewis; and Judith Izen is the author of *Collector's Guide to Ideal Dolls.* All these references are published by Collector Books.

See also Barbie and Her Friends; Shirley Temple; Toys (Action Figures and GI Joe); Trolls.

Annalee

Barbara 'Annalee' Davis was born in Concord, N.H., on February, 11, 1915. She started dabbling at doll-making at an early age, often giving her creations to friends. She married Charles 'Chip' Thorndike in 1941 and moved to Meredith, N.H., where they started a chicken farm and sold used auto parts. By the early 1950s, with the chicken farm failing, Annalee started crafting her dolls on the kitchen table to help make ends meet. She designed her dolls by looking into the mirror, drawing faces as she saw them, and making the clothes from scraps of material.

The dolls she developed are made of wool felt with 'hand-painted' features and flexible wire frameworks. The earlier dolls from the 1950s had a long white red-embroidered tag with no date. From 1959 to 1964, the tags stayed the same except there was a date in the upper right-hand corner. From 1965 to 1970, this same tag was folded in half and sewn into the seam of the doll. In 1970 a transition period began. The company changed its tag to a white satiny tag with a date preceded by a copyright symbol in the upper right-hand corner. In 1975 they made another change to a long white cotton strip with a copyright date. In 1982 the white tag was folded over, making it shorter. Many people mistake the copyright date as the date the doll was made — not so! It wasn't until 1986 that they finally began to date the tags with the year of manufacture, making it much easier for collectors to identify their dolls. Besides the red-lettered white Annalee tags, numerous others were used in the 1990s, but all reflect the year the doll was actually made.

The company has held an annual auction on the premises in June since 1983. Recently they have added a second fall auction, which they hold in selected areas around the East Coast. Annalee's signature on a doll increases its value by as much as $300.00, sometimes more. The dolls that are signed can only be purchased at their June auction.

Remember, these dolls are made of wool felt. To protect them, store them with moth balls, and avoid exposing them to too much sunlight, since they will fade. Our advisor has been a collector for fifteen years and a secondary market dealer since 1988. Most of these dolls have been in her collection at one time or another. She recommends 'If you like it, buy it, love it, treat it with care, and you'll have it to enjoy for many years to come.'

Our values are suggested for dolls in very good to excellent condition, not personally autographed by Annalee herself. For more reading and photographs, you won't want to miss *Teddy Bears, Annalees and Steiff Animals,* by Margaret Fox Mandel.

Advisor: Jane Holt (See Directory, Dolls)

Newsletter: *The Collector*
Annalee Doll Society
P.O. Box 1137, 50 Reservoir Rd.
Meredith, NH 03253-1137; 1-800-433-6557

1957, boy building boat, 10"	$800.00
1964, choir boy, red robe, bandage on nose, 10"	$200.00
1964, friar, red robe, 10"	$225.00
1966, flat-face reindeer, 36"	$575.00
1966, Yum Yum bunny, numerous colors, 7"	$300.00
1966, Yum Yum bunny, numerous colors, 12"	$550.00
1968, brown horse w/hearts, 10"	$425.00
1969, Mr & Mrs Tuckered, 1969, 7", pr	$150.00

1970, Country cousin boy and girl, 7", $225.00 each. (Photo courtesy of Jane Holt.)

1971, Santa on ski-bob w/sack, 7"	$150.00
1972, choir girl, 18"	$175.00
1972, Mrs Snowman (missing broom), 29"	$450.00
1974, reindeer w/red nose, 18"	$175.00
1975, elf, in red (Christmas), 10"	$40.00
1976, Bicentennial boy & girl mice, 7", pr	$300.00
1976, gnome, 18"	$275.00
1978, boy or girl golfer mouse (produced many years), 7", each	$35.00
1978, gnome, red, white or green, 12", each	$225.00
1979, leprechaun, 10"	$70.00
1979, snowman, 10"	$70.00
1979, white caroller mouse (made in white 1 year only), 12"	$125.00
1980, bride & groom frogs, 10", pr	$300.00
1980, clown, 10"	$95.00
1980, clown, 18"	$175.00
1980, clown, 42"	$600.00
1980, jogger mouse, 7"	$40.00
1980, mouse in nightshirt, 7"	$35.00
1980, Mr & Mrs Claus w/potbelly stove (made 1 year), 7"	$150.00
1980, Mr & Mrs Santa mice (made many years), 12", pr	$100.00
1980, Mr & Mrs Santa w/potbelly stove, 7"	$150.00
1981, boy or girl on sled (made for 4 years), 18", each	$100.00
1982, equestrienne mouse, 7"	$100.00
1982, I'm #10 Girl (1 year in production), 7"	$95.00
1982, mouse on skis, 7"	$65.00
1982, windsurfer mouse, Annalee birthdate on sail, 7"	$150.00
1983, drummer boy, 7"	$45.00
1983, quilting mouse, 7"	$75.00
1984, angel w/slingshot, 12"	$125.00
1984, angel w/star, 7"	$50.00
1984, bowling mouse, 7"	$75.00
1984, country girl (1 year in production), 7"	$75.00
1984, devil mouse (1 year in production), 12"	$150.00
1984, gardener, 7"	$75.00
1984, Halloween witch mouse (produced many years), 7"	$35.00
1984, Santa w/reindeer, 5"	$85.00
1984, teacher, 7"	$75.00
1984, 1985, 1986 & 1987, cardholder Santa (made for many years w/different fabric), 18", each	$50.00
1985, cat w/Valentine, 18"	$125.00
1986, hobo cat, 18"	$125.00
1986, Mark Twain in dome, Folk Hero series, 10"	$400.00
1986, raincoat duck, 5"	$50.00
1986, Santa in rocking chair, 18"	$75.00
1986, skier, 10"	$75.00
1986, skier boy, 3"	$40.00
1987, caroller boy or girl on stand, 3", each	$35.00
1987, duck in Santa hat, 5"	$40.00
1987, elf, Fall orange, brown, or moss green (made for several years), 10", each	$40.00
1987, Indian boy & girl, 7", pr	$75.00
1988, bear on sled, 10"	$65.00
1988, Christmas goose, 10"	$40.00
1988, St Nicholas w/plaque, 10"	$95.00
1988, toy soldier, 10"	$65.00

1989, artist bunny, 18"...$100.00
1989, caroller girl or boy, 1989, 7", each.....................$35.00
1989, Eskimo bear, 10"...$85.00
1989, kitten w/mittens, 10"...$50.00
1989, Santa chef, 18"...$60.00
1989, witch mouse, 12"..$70.00
1990, angel on sled, 7"...$40.00
1990, elf, pink or yellow, 20", each............................$75.00
1990, ghost, 7"...$55.00
1991, ballerina girl on music box, 7"..........................$50.00

1991, Desert Storm mouse, 7", $70.00.

1991, Indian man or woman, 1991, 10", each.............$50.00
1991, Santa w/potbelly stove, 12"................................$70.00
1992, gnome w/mushroom, 7".....................................$50.00
1993, baby New Year, 7"..$50.00
1993, Mrs Victorian Santa, 7".....................................$35.00
1993, scarecrow boy, 12"...$75.00
1994, hobo clown, 10"...$50.00
1994, soccer player, 10"...$50.00

Aurora Dolls by Tonka

The advertising theme of Aurora's #6700 line of Aurora dolls was 'the future looks beautiful.' Their bodies were made of colored, shiny metal-like material, and their faces are flesh-colored with colored rhinestone eyes. Hair colors are blond, pink, purple or blue. There appear to be four dolls in this series; all are made to stand alone, and they each came with a styling brush. Dolls are marked 'Creata-1984.' Boxes are marked with the Tonka logo and are dated 1987. Note that Mattel made similar dolls in 1986 — but they had no rhinestone eyes and tinsel was sprinkled through their hair. Loose dolls in excellent condition are worth only $8.00 to $10.00 each.

Aurora, flesh-colored face w/amber rhinestone eyes, gold body, long blond hair, MIB...................................$25.00
Crysta, flesh-colored face w/pink rhinestone eyes, silver body, pink hair, MIB $25.00
Lustra, flesh-colored face w/purple rhinestone eyes, silver body, purple hair, MIB $25.00
Mirra, flesh-colored face w/blue rhinestone eyes, silver body, long blue hair, MIB..$25.00

Betsy McCall

The tiny 8" Betsy McCall doll was manufactured by the American Character Doll Company from 1957 through 1963. She was made from high-quality hard plastic with a bisque-like finish and hand-painted features. Betsy came in four hair colors — tosca, red, blond and brunette. She had blue sleep eyes, molded lashes, a winsome smile, and a fully-jointed body with bendable knees. On her back there is an identification circle which reads McCall Corp. The basic doll wore a sheer chemise, white taffeta panties, nylon socks, and Maryjane-style shoes and could be purchased for $2.25.

There were two different materials used for tiny Betsy's hair. The first was a soft mohair sewn into fine mesh. Later the rubber scullcap was rooted with saran which was more suitable for washing and combing.

Betsy McCall had an extensive wardrobe with nearly one hundred outfits, each of which could be purchased separately. They were made from wonderful fabrics such as velvet, taffeta, felt, and even real mink. Each ensemble came with the appropriate footwear and was priced under $3.00. Since none of Betsy's clothing was tagged, it is often difficult to indentify other than by its square snap closures (although these were used by other companies as well).

Betsy McCall is a highly collectible doll today but is still fairly easy to find at doll shows. The prices remain reasonable for this beautiful clothes horse and her many accessories.

Advisor: Marci Van Ausdall (See Directory, Dolls)

Newsletter: *Betsy McCall's Fan Club*
Marci Van Ausdall
P.O. Box 946
Quincy, CA 95971; Subscription $12.50 per year or send $3 for sample; e-mail: DREAMS707@aol.com

American Character, dress not original, 8", $50.00. (Photo courtesy of Cindy Sabulis.)

American Character, extra joints at ankles, knees, waist & wrists, marked McCall 1961, all original, 29", minimum value $400.00

American Character, hard plastic, jointed knees, original ball-gown, 1958, 8", M, minimum value **$200.00**

American Character, hard plastic, jointed knees, original bathing suit or romper, 1958, 8", M **$100.00**

American Character, hard plastic, jointed knees, original street dress, 1958, 8", M **$165.00**

American Character, hard plastic, jointed knees, riding habit, 1958, 8", M **$200.00**

American Character, vinyl, rooted hair, all original, 36", M, minimum value **$550.00**

American Character, vinyl, rooted hair, medium high heels, sleep eyes, marked McCall 1958 (made in '61), 14", M, minimum value **$265.00**

American Character, vinyl, rooted hair, slim limbs, 20" (allow higher value for flirty eyes), M **$300.00**

American Character, vinyl, rooted hair, 29-30", M.....**$400.00**

American Character (unmarked), extra joints at waist, ankles, wrists & knees, all original, 22", M....................**$250.00**

Horsman, marked BMC Horsman 1971, all original, 29", M **$175.00**

Horsman Dolls, Inc 1967 on head, 13", M................**$65.00**

Ideal, marked McCall 1959, all original, 36", minimum value **$550.00**

Ideal, Sandy McCall, marked McCall 1959, all original, 39", M, minimum value **$650.00**

Ideal, vinyl & hard plastic, rooted hair, marked P-90 on body, all original, 14", minimum value........................**$250.00**

Ideal, vinyl & plastic, extra joints, 22", M, minimum value..**$275.00**

Uneeda (unmarked), vinyl & plastic, brown sleep eyes, reddish rooted hair, all original, 11½", M..................**$95.00**

Celebrity Dolls

Celebrity and character dolls have been widely collected for many years, but they've lately shown a significant increase in demand. Except for rarer examples, most of these dolls are still fairly easy to find at doll shows, toy auctions, and flea markets, and the majority are priced under $100.00. These are the dolls that bring back memories of childhood TV shows, popular songs, favorite movies and familiar characters. Mego, Mattel, Remco and Hasbro are among the largest manufacturers.

Condition is a very important worth-assessing factor, and if the doll is still in the original box, so much the better! Should the box be unopened (NRFB), the value is further enhanced. Using mint as a standard, add 50% for the same doll mint in the box and 75% if it has never been taken out. On the other hand, dolls in only good condition or poorer condition drop at a rapid pace.

Advisor: Henri Yunes (See Directory, Dolls)

Andy Gibb, w/disco dancing stand, Ideal, 1979, 7½", M (EX box) **$50.00**

Angie Dickinson (as Pepper Martin from Police Woman), Horsman, 1976, MIB **$40.00**

Beatles, John, Paul, George or Ringo, Remco, MIB, each .**$200.00**

Beverly Johnson, Real Models Collection, Matchbox #54613, 1989, 11½", NRFB **$35.00**

Brooke Shields, 1st issue, sweater outfit, LJN, 1982, 11½", MIB **$50.00**

Brooke Shields, Prom Party, 3rd issue, LJN, 1983, rare, 11½", MIB, $100.00. (Photo courtesy of Henri Yunes.)

Cher, 1st issue, pink dress, Mego, 1976, 12", NRFB....**$45.00**

Cher, 2nd issue, w/growing hair, Mego, 1976, 12", M (EX+ box) **$65.00**

Cheryl Tiegs, Real Models Collection, Matchbox #54612, 1989, NRFB..**$35.00**

Christie Brinkley, Real Models Collection, Matchbox #54611, 1989, 11½", NRFB..**$35.00**

Diahann Carroll (Julia), 1st issue, straight red-brown hair, 2-pc nurse's outfit, Mattel, 1969, 11½", NRFB **$200.00**

Diahann Carroll (Julia), 1st issue, talker, straight red-brown hair, gold & silver jumpsuit, 11½", NRFB **$250.00**

Diahann Carroll (Julia), 2nd issue, regular or talker, dark Afro hair, Mattel, 1970-71, 11½", each.........................**$175.00**

Dolly Parton, red gown, World Doll, 1987, 18", NRFB .**$90.00**

Elvis Presley, Burning Love, World Doll, 1984, 21", VG+ .**$110.00**

Farrah Fawcett (as Jill from Charlie's Angels), jumpsuit & scarf, Hasbro, 1977, 8½", MOC............................**$35.00**

Farrah Fawcett (as Jill from Charlie's Angels), white jumpsuit, Mego, 1976, 12", MIB **$50.00**

Flip Wilson (Geraldine), Shindana, 1976, 16", MIB.....**$65.00**

Jaclyn Smith (Charlie's Angels), Hasbro, 1977, 8½", MOC, $35.00. (Photo courtesy of June Moon.)

James Dean, Rebel Rouser or City Streets outfit, DSI, 1994, NRFB, each..**$75.00**

John Travolta (Superstar), Chemtoy, 1977, 12", MIB...**$55.00**

John Wayne, 1st issue, Legend Series, Spirit of the West Cowboy outfit, 1981, 17", MIB..........................**$125.00**

Kate Jackson (as Sabrina from Charlie's Angels), jumpsuit & scarf, Hasbro, 1977, 8½", MOC..........................**$35.00**

Linda Carter (as Wonder Woman), 2nd issue, Mego, 1977, 12", MIB **$60.00**

Linda Carter (as Wonder Woman/Diana Prince), 1st issue, w/military uniform, 12", MIB **$85.00**

Madonna (as Breathless Mahoney from Dick Tracy), black evening gown w/gold trim & heels, Applause, 1990, 10", MIB **$50.00**

Marie Osmond, Mattel, 1976, 11", MIB **$50.00**

Marie Osmond, Mattel, 1976, 30", MIB **$115.00**

Marilyn Monroe, issued in 4 different outfits, Tri-Star, 1982, 16", MIB, each......................**$110.00**

Marilyn Monroe, issued in 6 different outfits, DSI, 1993, 11½", NRFB, each......................**$60.00**

Marilyn Monroe, issued in 8 different outfits, Tri-Star, 1982, 11½", NRFB, each **$75.00**

Michael Jackson, issued in 4 different outfits, LJN, 1984, NRFB, each......................**$50.00**

Mr T, 1st issue, overalls outfit, Galoob, 1983, 12", MIB ..**$50.00**

Mr T, 2nd issue, talker, jeans & vest outfit w/accessories, Galoob, 1983, 12", MIB **$65.00**

New Kids on the Block, 1st issue, Hangin' Loose, 5 different, 1990, 12", MIB, each......................**$15.00**

Patty Duke (Patty/Cathy Lane from The Patty Duke Show), red sweater & pants w/phone, Horsman, 1965, 12½", rare, NRFB **$400.00**

Prince Charles, wedding attire, Peggy Nesbit/England, 1984, 8", MIB......................**$100.00**

Princess Diana, wedding dress, Peggy Nesbit/England, 1984, 8", M **$100.00**

Rex Harrison (as Dr Doolittle), 3rd issue, talker, Mattel, 1969, 24", MIB......................**$130.00**

Robert Vaughn (as Napoleon Solo from Man From UNCLE), w/accessories, Gilbert, 1965, 12½", MIB............**$215.00**

Roger Moore (as James Bond from Moonraker), Mego, 1979, 12", MIB......................**$100.00**

Sally Field (as Flying Nun), Hasbro, 1967, 5", MIB.....**$80.00**

Sarah Stimson (as Little Miss Marker), Ideal, 1980, 12", MIB......................**$40.00**

Shirly Temple, Glad Rags to Riches outfit, Ideal, 1984, 16", MIB **$125.00**

Sonny Bono, white shirt & jeans, Mego, 1976, 12", MIB .**$65.00**

Sonny and Cher, Mego, 1975, 12", M, from $25.00 to $35.00 each. (Photo courtesy of Cindy Sabulis.)

Soupy Sales, Knickerbocker, 1966, VG+ **$80.00**

Vanilla Ice, issued in 3 different outfits, THQ (Toy Headquarters), 1991, 12", NRFB, each **$25.00**

Jem

The glamorous life of Jem mesmerized little girls who watched her Saturday morning cartoons, and she was a natural as a fashion doll. Hasbro saw the potential in 1985 when they introduced the Jem line of 12" dolls representing her, the rock stars from Jem's musical group, the Holograms, and other members of the cast, including the only boy, Rio, Jem's road manager and Jerrica's boyfriend. Each doll was poseable, jointed at the waist, head and wrists, so that they could be positioned at will with their musical instruments and other accessory items. Their clothing, their makeup, and their hairdos were wonderfully exotic, and their faces were beautifully modeled. The Jem line was discontinued in 1987 after being on the market for only two years.

Aja, blue hair, complete w/accessories, MIB **$40.00**

Ashley, curly blond hair, w/stand, 11", MIB..............**$20.00**

Clash, straight purple hair, complete, MIB **$40.00**

Danee, straight black waist-length hair, w/stand, MIB...**$20.00**

Danse, pink & blond hair, invents dance routines, MIB..**$40.00**

Jem, Roll 'N Curl, 12", MIB (sealed)..........................**$25.00**

Jem/Jerrica, Glitter & Gold, w/accessories, MIB **$50.00**

Jetta, black hair w/silver streaks, complete, MIB........**$40.00**

Kimber, red hair, w/stand, cassette, instrument & poster, 12½", MIB......................**$40.00**

Krissie, dark skin w/dark brown curly hair, w/stand, 11", MIB **$20.00**

Pizzaz from Misfits, chartreuse hair, complete, MIB ...**$40.00**

Raya, pink hair, complete, MIB **$40.00**

Rio, Glitter & Gold, complete, 12½", MIB **$50.00**

Roxy, blond hair, complete, MIB..........................**$40.00**

Shana, of Holograms Band, purple hair, complete, EX, $30 to......................**$40.00**

Stormer, curly blue hair, complete, MIB **$40.00**

Liddle Kiddles

These tiny little dolls ranging from ¾" to 4" tall were made by Mattel from 1966 until 1979. They all had poseable bodies and rooted hair that could be restyled, and they came with accessories of many types. Some represented storybook characters, some were flowers in perfume bottles, some were made to be worn as jewelry, and there were even spacemen 'Kiddles.'

Serious collectors prefer examples that are still in their original packaging and will often pay a premium of about 30% over the price of a doll in excellent condition with all her original accessories. A doll whose accessories are missing is worth from 65% to 70% less. Our prices range from excellent and complete to mint with no packaging.

For more information, we recommend *Liddle Kiddles* by Paris Langford and *Schroeder's Collectible Toys, Antique to Modern* (both published by Collector Books).

Advisor: Dawn Parrish (See Directory, Dolls)

Club: Liddle Kiddle Klub
Laura Miller
3639 Fourth Ave.
La Crescenta, CA 91214

Alice in Wonder-liddle, #3533, missing storybook otherwise complete and EX, $100.00. (Photo courtesy of Cindy Sabulis.)

Anabelle Autodiddle, auburn hair, shorts set & cap, w/Autodiddle car & skediddler/pusher, 1968-70, 4", from $35 to.....**$45.00**

Beat-a-Diddle, Sears Exclusive, long blond hair, floral top & bell-bottoms, guitar & microphone, 3½", 1966-67, from $150 to..**$175.00**

Calamity Jiddle, blond w/ponytail, cowgirl outfit, hat, rocking horse, lasso, comb & brush, 1966-67, from $40 to.....**$50.00**

Cinderiddle, blond or white hair, ragged dress, scarf, broom, white gown, earrings & storybook, 1968, 3½", from $85 to.**$100.00**

Dainty Deer, 2-pc brushed nylon deer suit, orange ears & yarn bands, pipe-cleaner antlers, 1969-70, 2", from $25 to..**$35.00**

Flower necklace, blond hair, orange cloth dress, 1", in flower-shaped case pendant, gold-tone chain, 1969-70, from $85 to..**$100.00**

Funny Bunny Kiddle, 2-pc bunny suit, 1968-69, 3¾", from $15 to **$25.00**

Heart pin, blond hair w/crown, painted-on swimsuit, banner across chest, 1", in heart-shaped case pin, 1968-70, from $15 to...**$25.00**

Liddle Diddle, blond baby in sleeper, pink crib, pillow & blanket, yellow plastic ducky, brush & comb, 1966-67, from $50 to...**$60.00**

Liddle Middle Muffet, auburn pony tail, peach jumpsuit, w/tuffet, spider, spoon, bowl, & book, 1967-68, 3½", from $75 to..**$85.00**

Lois Locket, Black doll w/2 ponytails, green & white dress, green-framed locket w/jewels, 1968-69, from $25 to............**$35.00**

Lola Locket, platinum or blond hair w/flower headband, pink top & flower skirt, gold-framed locket, 1967, from $15 to **$25.00**

Luscious Lime Kola Kiddle, green hair, yellow cap w/green leaf, green dress, w/5" bottle, 1968-69, 2", from $35 to.....**$45.00**

Rapunzel & the Prince, 2 figures complete w/pendant necklace, 2 stands & storybook, 1969-70, each 2", from $65 to **$75.00**

Rosemary Roadster, blond w/lg bun, jacket & skirt, roadster w/steering wheel, 1969-70, 2⅞", from $45 to **$55.00**

Sleeping Biddle, blond w/tiara, velvet gown, w/chaise lounge & storybook, 1968, 3½", from $75 to.......**$85.00**

Swingy Skediddle, blond updo, pink outfit & purse, orange skediddler/pusher, 1969-70, 4", from $50 to........**$60.00**

Teeter-Time Baby, yellow yarn bands, pink & white outfit, yellow duck-shaped rocker, 1970, 2½", from $50 to..**$75.00**

Tessie Tractor, blond braids, blue denim-look jumper, w/orange tractor and skediddler/pusher, 4", 1969-70, from $55 to...**$65.00**

Trikey Triddle, red pigtails, playdress w/attached panties, w/balloon, trike, comb & brush, 1967, 2½", from $40 to **$55.00**

Littlechaps

In 1964 Remco Industries created a family of four fashion dolls that represented an upper-middle class family. The Littlechaps family consisted of the father, Dr. John Littlechap, his wife, Lisa, and their two children, Judy and Libby. Their clothing and fashion accessories were made in Japan and are of the finest quality. Because these dolls are not as pretty as other fashion dolls of the era and their size and placement of arms and legs made them hard to dress, children had little interest in them at the time. This lack of interest during the 1960s has created shortages of them for collectors of today. Mint and complete outfits or outfits never-removed-from-box are especially desirable to Littlechap collectors.

Advisor: Cindy Sabulis (See Directory, Dolls)

Doctor John, MIB (sealed) **$60.00**
Judy, MIB (sealed) **$65.00**
Libby, MIB (sealed) **$45.00**
Lisa, MIB (sealed) **$60.00**

Remco's Littlechap Family: Libby (front), Judy (left), John (back), and Lisa (right), EX, from $15.00 to $20.00 each. (Photo courtesy of Cindy Sabulis.)

Mattel

One of the largest manufacturers of modern dolls is the Mattel company, the famous maker of the Barbie doll. But besides Barbie, there are many other types of Mattel's dolls that have their own devotees, and we've tried to list a sampling of several of their more collectible lines.

Next to Barbie, the all-time favorite doll was Mattel's Chatty Cathy. She was first made in the 1960s, in blond and brunette variations, and much of her success can be attributed to that fact that she could talk! By pulling the string on her back, she could respond with eleven different phrases. The line was expanded and soon included Chatty Baby, Tiny Chatty Baby and Tiny Chatty Brother (the twins), Charmin' Chatty, and finally Singing' Chatty. They all sold successfully for five years, and although Mattel reintroduced the line in 1969 (smaller and with a restyled face), it was not well received. For more information we recommend *Chatty Cathy Dolls, An Identification & Value Guide,* by our advisors, Kathy and Don Lewis.

In 1960 Mattel introduced their first line of talking dolls. They decided to take the talking doll's success even further by introducing a new line — cartoon characters that the young TV viewers were already familiar with.

Below you will find a list of the more popular dolls and animals available. There are two prices listed with each doll/toy. The lower price is for a played-with nontalking doll/toy and the other price is for a mint-in-box (MIB) item. Most MIB toys found today are mute, but this should not detract from the listed price. If the doll still talks, you may consider adding a few more dollars to the price.

Advisors: Kathy and Don Lewis (See Directory, Dolls)

Animal Yacker, Bernie Bernard, from $25 to **$200.00**
Animal Yacker, Chester O'Chimp, from $35 to **$300.00**
Animal Yacker, Crackers the Talking Plush Parrot, from $100 to..**$350.00**
Baby, Bye-Bye Diapers, uses potty chair & claps hands, 1981, MIB (sealed)..**$25.00**
Baby, Dancerella, 1978, 17", MIB (sealed)..................**$35.00**
Baby, Li'l Drowsy Beans, blond hair, 11", MIB (sealed).**$20.00**
Baby, Magic Baby Tenderlove, 1978, 14", MIB **$30.00**
Baby, Tender Love & Kisses, 1976, 14", MIB **$25.00**
Baby Brother Tenderlove, anatomically correct, 16", MIB..**$35.00**
Baby Grows Up, 1978, grows from 16" to 18", MIB...**$35.00**

Buffy and Mrs. Beasley, M, $75.00. (Photo courtesy of Cindy Sabulis.)

Larry the Talking Plush Lion, from $20 to.................**$175.00**
Storybook Small-Talk, Cinderella, from $10 to...........**$85.00**
Storybook Small-Talk, Goldilocks, from $10 to...........**$85.00**

Storybook Small-Talk, Little Bo Peep, from $10 to **$85.00**
Storybook Small-Talk, Snow White, from $10 to **$85.00**
Talk Up, Casper, from $15 to......................................**$75.00**
Talk Up, Funny Talk, from $10 to...............................**$75.00**
Talk Up, Mickey Mouse, from $10 to **$125.00**
Talk Up, Silly Talk, from $5 to **$75.00**
Talk Up, Tweety Bird, from $5 to **$75.00**
Talker, Baby First Step, from $25 to..........................**$150.00**
Talker, Baby Say 'n See, from $30 to........................**$125.00**
Talker, Baby Secret, $20 to **$125.00**
Talker, Baby Small Talk, from $10 to **$75.00**
Talker, Black Chatty Baby, M **$325.00**
Talker, Black Chatty Cathy, pageboy-style hair, M....**$600.00**
Talker, Black Chatty Cathy, w/pigtails, M..................**$700.00**
Talker, Black Drowsy, from $10 to **$100.00**
Talker, Black Tiny Chatty Baby, M............................**$300.00**
Talker, Bozo the Clown, from $10 to.........................**$150.00**
Talker, Bozo the Clown hand puppet, from $10 to..**$100.00**
Talker, Buffy & Mrs Beasley, from $50 to **$250.00**
Talker, Bugs Bunny, from $10 to **$200.00**
Talker, Bugs Bunny hand puppet, from $10 to **$100.00**
Talker, Casper the Friendly Ghost, from $25 to........**$225.00**
Talker, Cat in the Hat, rag & plush, from $100 to **$300.00**
Talker, Cecil the Seasick Serpent, from $45 to..........**$300.00**
Talker, Charmin' Chatty, auburn or blond hair, blue eyes, 1 record, M **$95.00**
Talker, Chatty Baby, brunette, red pinafore over white romper, MIB **$200.00**
Talker, Chatty Baby, early, blond hair, blue eyes, ring around speaker, M **$90.00**
Talker, Chatty Baby, early, brunette hair, blue eyes, M...**$85.00**
Talker, Chatty Baby, early, brunette hair, brown eyes, M **$125.00**
Talker, Chatty Baby, open speaker, blond hair, blue eyes, M **$75.00**
Talker, Chatty Baby, open speaker, brunette hair, blue eyes, M **$90.00**
Talker, Chatty Baby, open speaker, brunette hair, brown eyes, M **$125.00**
Talker, Chatty Cathy, brunette hair, brown eyes, M .**$150.00**
Talker, Chatty Cathy, later issue, open speaker grille, blond hair, blue eyes, M **$130.00**
Talker, Chatty Cathy, later issue, open speaker grille, brunette hair, blue eyes, M **$150.00**
Talker, Chatty Cathy, later issue, open speaker grille, brunette hair, brown, eyes, M............................**$175.00**
Talker, Chatty Cathy, mid-year or transitional, brunette hair, brown eyes, M **$135.00**
Talker, Chatty Cathy, mid-year or transitional, brunette hair, blue eyes, M..**$125.00**
Talker, Chatty Cathy, mid-year or transitional, open speaker, blond hair, blue eyes, M **$120.00**
Talker, Chatty Cathy, Patent Pending, brunette hair, blue eyes, M **$130.00**
Talker, Chatty Cathy, Patent Pending, cloth over speaker or ring around speaker, blond hair, blue eyes, M ..**$150.00**
Talker, Chatty Cathy, porcelain, 1980, MIB **$650.00**
Talker, Doctor Doolittle, from $10 to........................**$150.00**
Talker, Doctor Doolittle hand puppet, from $25 to..**$150.00**

Talker, Herman Munster hand puppet, from $50 to.	**$250.00**
Talker, King Kong & Bobby Bond, rag & plush, from $50 to	**$275.00**
Talker, King Kong & Bobby Bond hand puppet, from $25 to	**$200.00**
Talker, Larry Lion hand puppet, from $10 to	**$150.00**
Talker, Linus the Lionhearted, from $10 to	**$100.00**
Talker, Monkees finger puppet, from $75 to	**$300.00**
Talker, Mother Goose, rag & plush, from $5 to	**$125.00**
Talker, Mrs Beasley, rag & plush, from $5 to	**$175.00**
Talker, Off To See the Wizard finger puppet, from $50 to.	**$300.00**
Talker, Patootie, rag & plush, from $10 to	**$300.00**
Talker, Scooby-Doo, from $35 to	**$175.00**
Talker, Shrinkin' Violette, from $40 to	**$175.00**
Talker, Singin' Chatty, blond hair, M	**$100.00**
Talker, Singin' Chatty, brunette hair, M	**$125.00**
Talker, Sister Belle the Talking Doll, from $25 to	**$200.00**
Talker, Tatters, from $10 to	**$100.00**
Talker, Timey Tell, from $5 to	**$100.00**
Talker, Tiny Chatty Baby, blond hair, blue eyes, M	**$75.00**
Talker, Tiny Chatty Baby, brunette hair, blue eyes, M	**$90.00**
Talker, Tiny Chatty Baby, brunette hair, brown eyes, M	**$125.00**
Talker, Tom & Jerry, rag & plush, from $25 to	**$175.00**

Strawberry Shortcake and Friends

Strawberry Shortcake came on the market with a bang around 1980. The line included everything to attract small girls — swimsuits, bed linens, blankets, anklets, underclothing, coats, shoes, sleeping bags, dolls and accessories, games, and many other delightful items. Strawberry Shortcake and her friends were short lived, lasting only until the mid-1980s.

Advisor: Geneva Addy (See Directory, Dolls)

Newsletter: *Berry-Bits*
Strawberry Shortcake Collector's Club
Peggy Jimenez
1409 72nd St.
N Bergen, NJ 07047

Orange Blossom and Marmalade Painting a Picture, MIB, $25.00.

Almond Tea, 5½", MIB	**$25.00**
Apple Dumpling, cloth, 12", G	**$25.00**

Cafe Ole, 5½", MIB	**$25.00**
Merry Berry Worm, MIB	**$20.00**
Mint Tulip, 5½", MIB	**$25.00**
Strawberry Shortcake, strawberry scented, 12", MIB (sealed)	**$25.00**
Strawberry Shortcake, 15", NM	**$35.00**

Tammy and Friends

In 1962 the Ideal Novelty and Toy Company introduced their teenage Tammy doll. Slightly pudgy and not quite as sophisticated looking as some of the teen fashion dolls on the market at the time, Tammy's innocent charm captivated consumers. Her extensive wardrobe and numerous accessories added to her popularity with children. Tammy had a car, a house, and her own catamaran. In addition, a large number of companies obtained licenses to issue products using the 'Tammy' name. Everything from paper dolls to nurses' kits were made with Tammy's image on them. Her success was not confined to the United States; she was also successful in Canada and several other European countries. For further information we recommend *Collector's Guide to Tammy, The Ideal Teen,* by Cindy Sabulis and Susan Weglewski (Collector Books).

Advisor: Cindy Sabulis (See Directory, Dolls)

Magazine: *Doll Castle News*
37 Belvidere Ave., P.O. Box 247
Washington, NJ 07882; 908-689-7042 or Fax 908-689-6320;
Subscription $16.95 per year

Newsletter: Doll Collectors of America
14 Chestnut Rd.
Westford, MA 01886; 617-692-8392

Newsletter: *Doll Investment Newsletter*
P.O. Box 1982
Centerville, MA 02632

Newsletter: *Doll News*
United Federation of Doll Clubs
P.O. Box 14146
Parkville, MO 64152

Newsletter: *Modern Doll Club Journal*
Jeanne Niswonger
305 W Beacon Rd.
Lakeland, FL 33803

Black Tammy, MIB	**$225.00**
Dodi, suntan version, 1977, 9", MIB	**$40.00**
Grown-Up Tammy, MIB	**$55.00**
Patty, Montgomery Ward's Exclusive, MIB	**$125.00**
Pepper, slim body, 1965, MIB	**$50.00**
Pepper, 1963, 9", MIB	**$40.00**
Pos'n Dodi, MIB	**$75.00**
Pos'n Pepper, original clothes, 1964, 9", VG	**$20.00**
Pos'n Pete, MIB	**$80.00**
Pos'n Salty, MIB	**$80.00**

Pos'n Tammy & Her Phone Booth, MIB.....................**$65.00**
Tammy's Dad, MIB **$50.00**
Tammy's Mom, MIB...**$50.00**
Ted, re-dressed, 12½", VG **$25.00**
Ted, 1964, 12½", MIB **$50.00**

Tammy, MIB, from $45.00 to $50.00. (Photo courtesy of Cindy Sabulis.)

Door Knockers

Though many of the door knockers you'll see on the market today are of the painted cast-iron variety (similar in design to doorstop figures), they're also found in brass and other metals. Most are modeled as people, animals and birds; and baskets of flowers are common. All items listed are cast iron unless noted otherwise. Prices shown are suggested for examples without damage and in excellent original paint.

Advisor: Craig Dinner (See Directory, Door Knockers)

Buster Brown & Tige, cream shirt & blue pants, cream dog w/black spots, #200, 4¾x2" **$450.00**
Butterfly, multicolored w/pink rose, cream & purple backplate, 3½" **$115.00**
Butterfly on flower, yellow, red & blue wings, multicolored flowers, 4x2½" **$240.00**
Cardinal, female w/berries on branch, cream & green backplate, 5x3" **$180.00**
Cardinal, w/berries on branch, red w/black details, oval backplate, 5" **$200.00**
Colonial man, marked WS in triangle, Pat Apld For, 4⅜x2½" **$150.00**
Colonial woman, Waverly Studio, Wilmette Ill, 4¾x2½" ..**$150.00**
Cottage, white w/peaked red roof, 2 chimneys & trees on cream, 3½" **$285.00**
Cupid, blond hair, flesh body, w/purple scarf & pink roses on blue background, #618 & 622, 4x3" **$500.00**
Flower basket, multicolored w/3-color backplate, marked Hubley #205, 4x2".................................**$95.00**

Flower basket, pink & blue flowers in white basket w/yellow ribbon, 4x2½"......................................**$95.00**
Ivy in basket, shaded green & yellow, white backplate, 4¼x2½"...**$125.00**
Morning-glory, single purple-blue flower w/bud, leaf backplate, 3x3"...**$210.00**
Owl, yellow, brown, white & black w/cream & green backplate **$200.00**
Parrot, holding branch, pink, blue & yellow w/cream & green backplate, 3x3".................................**$400.00**
Peacock, black body w/spread multicolored feathers, white backplate, 3x3".......................................**$400.00**
Redheaded woodpecker, pink flowers w/leaves on brown tree backplate...**$100.00**
Snow owl, white w/black details, cream & green backplate, 4¾x3"...**$225.00**

Castle, large, cream with green sky and single red, white and blue flag, gold trim, #630 & #631, 2¾x4", $190.00; Ship, 3-masted, cream-colored sails & boat, w/flags, blue-green ocean and blue sky, gold trim, 2¾x3¾", $175.00; Castle (right), smaller version, cream with green mountains, 3 red, white and blue flags, #630 and #632, $190.00. (Photo courtesy of Craig Dinner.)

Doorstops

There are three important factors to consider when buying doorstops — rarity, desirability, and condition. Desirability is often a more important issue than rarity, especially if the doorstop is well designed and detailed. Subject matter often overlaps into other areas, and if they appeal to collectors of Black Americana and advertising, for instance, this tends to drive prices upward. Most doorstops are made of painted cast iron, and value is directly related to the condition of the paint. If there is little paint left or if the figure has been repainted or is rusty, unless the price has been significantly reduced, pass it by.

Be aware that Hubley, one of the largest doorstop manufacturers, sold many of their molds to the John Wright Company who makes them today. Watch for seams that do not fit properly, grainy texture, and too-bright paint.

The doorstops we've listed here are all of the painted cast-iron variety unless another type of material is mentioned in the description. Values are suggested for examples in near-mint condition and paint and should be sharply reduced if heavy wear is apparent. For further information, we recommend *Doorstops, Identification and Values*, by Jeanne Bertoia.

Club: Doorstop Collectors of America
Jeanne Bertoia
2413 Madison Ave.
Vineland, NJ 08630; 609-692-4092; Membership $20 per year, includes 2 *Doorstopper* newsletters and convention. Send 2-stamp SASE for sample.

Newsletter: *Doorstopper*
Jeanne Bertoia
2413 Madison Ave.
Vineland, NJ 08630; 609-692-4092; Membership $20.00 per year, includes 2 newsletters and convention. Send 2-stamp SASE for sample.

Basket of Flowers, multicolor pastel flowers in graceful woven-look basket, Hubley, 7x5" **$125.00**
Bloodhound, tall & thin stylized shape, wedge, 15¼x⅜"..**$250.00**
Bobby Blake, child holding teddy bear, Hubley, 9½x5¼"...**$450.00**
Cape Cod Cottage, brown roof, flowers along sides, 5¾x8¾" **$150.00**
Cat, black paint, full figure, 6¾x3½" **$260.00**

Cinderella's Carriage, 19" long, from $150.00 to $200.00.

Cottage in the Woods, red roof, surrounded by trees, 8¼x7¼" **$275.00**
Cottage w/Fence, dormer window, many flowers surrounding cottage, National Foundry, 5¾x8".................**$145.00**
Daisy Bowl, multicolor flowers in footed bowl vase, Hubley, 7½x5⅛" **$115.00**
Duck, head up, full figure, 11¼x7"...........................**$200.00**
Fireplace, lady at spinning wheel beside fireplace in interior scene, Eastern Specialty, 6¼x8"..........................**$250.00**
Fireside Cat, striped recumbent full-figure cat, Hubley, 5⅝x10¾"...**$200.00**
Flower Basket, multicolor flowers, Bradley & Hubbard, 8⅝x5"...**$250.00**
French Bulldog, full figure, sitting, head up, 7⅝x6¾".**$150.00**
Fruit Bowl, mixed fruit in footed bowl, Hubley, 6⅞x 6⅝"..**$145.00**
Geese, white w/orange bills & feet, Hubley, 8x8"....**$400.00**
Gladiolas, pink w/assorted other flowers in urn, Hubley, 10x8" **$150.00**
Kitten, green bow at neck, 8x6"................................**$165.00**
Lantern, red & black w/bail handle, 13x5"................**$175.00**
Little Colonial Woman, bonnet & full skirt, full figure, 4¾x2⅝" **$100.00**
London Royal Mail Coach, 2 horses pulling coach w/driver & footman, 7x12¼" **$80.00**

Marigolds, multicolor flowers, Hubley, marked Made in USA, 7½x8" **$150.00**
Nasturtiums, multicolor flowers, Hubley, 7¼x6½"....**$125.00**

Owl, 10", from $150.00 to $200.00.

Parrot in Medallion, supported on fancy scrolling base, 9¼x5"...**$135.00**
Penguin w/Top Hat, full figure, Hubley, 10½x3¾", NM.**$325.00**
Persian Cat, seated w/head turned, full figure, Hubley, 8½x6½" **$175.00**
Petunias & Asters, multicolor flowers, Hubley, 9½x6½", VG **$135.00**
Poppies & Cornflowers, multicolor flowers in striped vase, Hubley, 7¼x6½" **$155.00**
Poppy, red flowers in cream vase, Hubley, 10⅝x7⅛"..**$150.00**
Putting Golfer, red jacket, short brown pants, Hubley, 8¾x7"...**$325.00**
Rooster, multicolor figure on green leafy base, full figure, 7x5½"..**$245.00**
Rose Basket, multicolor flowers in basket w/pink bow at top of handle, Hubley 121, 11x8" **$200.00**
Rose Vase, pink flowers, Hubley, 10⅛x8"................**$160.00**
Russian Wolfhound, facing left, full figure, repainted, 9x16" **$145.00**
Sunbonnet Girl, facing left, 6¼x3⅞" **$115.00**
Terrier w/Bushes, marked copt c 1929 PAL, 8x7".....**$200.00**
Tiger Lilies, 3 lg white lilies w/green leaves, Hubley, 10½x6", VG...**$175.00**
Tropical Woman, lady in apron holds bowl of fruit on her head, 12x6¼" **$250.00**
Tulip Pot, multicolor flowers, National Foundry, 8¼x7"..**$195.00**
Tulip Pot, red w/green leaves, LA-CS 770, 10½x5⅞".........**$250.00**
Tulip Vase, multicolor, Hubley, 10x8"......................**$150.00**
Turkey, multicolored paint, 13x11" **$650.00**
Victorian House on Hill, copper-tone paint, Bradley & Hubbard, 8¼x9¾" **$450.00**
Wolfhound, black & white w/narrow red collar, wedge base, Spencer, 6½x3½" **$200.00**
Woman Holding Flower Baskets, prim bonnet, flower at waist, 8x4¾" **$250.00**

Duncan and Miller Glassware

Although the roots of the company can be traced back to as early as 1865 when George Duncan went into business in Pittsburgh, Pennsylvania, the majority of the glassware that collectors are interested in was produced during the twentieth century. The firm became known as Duncan and Miller in 1900. They were bought out by the United States Glass Company, who continued to produce many of the same designs through a separate operation which they called the Duncan and Miller Division.

In addition to crystal, they made some of their wares in a wide assortment of colors including ruby, milk glass, some opalescent glass, and a black opaque glass they called Ebony. Some of their pieces were decorated by cutting or etching. They also made a line of animals and bird figures. For information on these, see *Glass Animals of the Depression Era* by Lee Garmon and Dick Spencer, as well as specific glass manufacturers in this book as Fenton, Fostoria, Heisey, etc.

Astaire, cocktail, crystal	$6.00
Astaire, cordial, red	$45.00
Astaire, finger bowl, red	$35.00
Astaire, plate, red, 7½"	$12.50
Canterbury, ashtray, crystal, 3"	$6.00
Canterbury, bowl, blue, deep, 6¼"	$30.00
Canterbury, bowl, crystal, oval, 9"	$20.00
Canterbury, candlesticks, crystal, etched, pr	$30.00

Canterbury, mayonaise set, crystal, 3-piece, $45.00.

Canterbury, candy dish, crystal, 3-part, w/lid	$32.50
Canterbury, relish, crystal, 2-part, 2-handled, 7"	$15.00
Canterbury, relish, crystal, 3-part, 3-handled	$17.50
Canterbury, relish, crystal w/silver overlay, 3-part	$30.00
Canterbury, tumbler, iced tea; crystal, footed, 7"	$15.00
Canterbury, tumbler, juice; crystal, footed	$10.00
Canterbury, vase, blue opalescent, crimped rim, 5½x4"	$35.00
Caribbean, bowl, blue, 5"	$35.00
Caribbean, cake plate, blue, scalloped rim	$29.00
Caribbean, candy dish, blue, flat	$97.00
Caribbean, cocktail, blue, 3¾-oz, 4⅛"	$45.00
Caribbean, goblet, water; blue	$38.00
Caribbean, plate, blue, handles, 6"	$18.00
Caribbean, relish, blue, 2-part, 6" dia	$30.00
Diamond, relish, amber, oval, 2-part	$18.00

Early American Hobnail, bowl, crystal, flared, 12"	$25.00
Early American Hobnail, goblet, cocktail; crystal	$8.00
Figurine, dove, head down, 11½" long	$175.00
Figurine, goose, fat, 6x6"	$275.00
Figurine, swan, open, 7"	$45.00
Figurine, swan, solid, 5"	$30.00
Figurine, tropical fish, ashtray, pink opal, 3½"	$50.00
First Love, candlestick, crystal, #30, 2-light, 6"	$40.00
First Love, cordial, crystal	$75.00
First Love, decanter, crystal, 32-oz	$295.00
First Love, nappy, crystal, scalloped, handles, 6½"	$25.00
First Love, salt & pepper shakers, crystal, pr	$40.00
First Love, sugar bowl, crystal	$15.00
First Love, urn vase, crystal, square base, 7"	$65.00
Flower holder, crown form, crystal, 5"	$22.00
Hilton, goblet, water; crystal w/blue stain, 5½"	$55.00
Indian Tree, nappy, crystal, triangular, handled	$20.00
King Arthur, punch set, 10-pc	$110.00
Language of Flowers, bowl, crystal, flared, 12"	$37.50
Language of Flowers, mayonnaise, crystal, 3-pc	$37.50
Language of Flowers, sugar bowl, crystal	$18.00
Mardi Gras, creamer, crystal, individual	$12.00
Mardi Gras, foot for punch bowl, crystal	$90.00
Mardi Gras, punch bowl, crystal, 2-gal	$150.00
Mardi Gras, salt cellar, crystal, oval, flat	$4.75
Mardi Gras, vase, milk glass, footed, 10½"	$30.00
Murano, nappy, crystal, ruffled rim, 6"	$20.00
Nautilus, marmalade, red, sterling lid	$110.00
Pall Mall, swan, crystal, 3"	$30.00
Pall Mall, swan, crystal, 5"	$35.00
Pall Mall, swan, crystal, 7", from $35 to	$45.00
Puritan, compote, pink w/silver overlay, 5¼x7"	$40.00
Puritan, cup & saucer, demitasse; pink	$12.00
Puritan, lemon/mint tray, green, center handle	$25.00
Puritan, plate, dinner; crystal w/floral cutting, 10¼"	$24.00
Sandwich, basket, amber, flat w/loop handle, 6½"	$90.00
Sandwich, basket, crystal, handled, 6"	$70.00
Sandwich, bowl, console; amber, 9"	$30.00
Sandwich, bowl, fruit salad; crystal, 6"	$17.00
Sandwich, bowl, grapefruit; green, 7¼"	$20.00
Sandwich, cake salver, crystal, pedestal foot, fluted edge, 13"	$90.00
Sandwich, candlesticks, crystal, bobeches/prisms, 10", pr	$250.00
Sandwich, candlesticks, crystal, 4", pr, from $28 to	$32.00
Sandwich, candy dish, crystal, footed, w/lid	$60.00
Sandwich, coaster, crystal, 4½"	$12.00
Sandwich, compote, crystal, low, crimped rim, 5½"	$25.00
Sandwich, creamer & sugar bowl on tray, crystal, individual	$32.00
Sandwich, cup & saucer, crystal, from $14 to	$18.00
Sandwich, deviled egg plate, crystal	$90.00
Sandwich, goblet, wine; crystal	$20.00
Sandwich, goblet, wine; red	$30.00
Sandwich, nut dish, crystal	$14.00
Sandwich, plate, amberina, 8"	$15.00
Sandwich, plate, crystal, 13"	$55.00
Sandwich, plate, crystal, 7¼"	$9.00
Sandwich, plate, crystal, 8"	$16.00

Sandwich, plate, green, 6"..............................**$8.50**
Sandwich, plate, green, 8" **$15.00**
Sandwich, relish, crystal, 3-compartment, oblong, 10"..**$30.00**
Sandwich, tumbler, crystal, flat, 4½" **$14.00**
Sandwich, vase, crystal, footed, 10", from $65 to **$85.00**
Sanibel, celery/relish, pink opalescent, 13" **$45.00**
Sanibel, flower bowl, blue opalescent, 14"................**$90.00**
Sanibel, plate, salad; pink opalescent, 8½" **$32.00**
Seahorse Etch, whiskey, red/crystal, footed, 2-oz.......**$45.00**
Spiral Flutes, compote, green, tall **$30.00**
Spiral Flutes, creamer, green, oval............................**$8.00**
Spiral Flutes, cup & saucer, pink...............................**$15.00**
Spiral Flutes, nut dish, green, footed, individual, 2"...**$12.00**
Spiral Flutes, sherbet, pink, low **$15.00**
Sylvan, relish, cobalt, 3-part, handled **$35.00**
Sylvan, swan, crystal, 7"...**$40.00**
Tear Drop, butter dish, crystal, silver lid, ¼-lb, from $24
   to **$28.00**
Tear Drop, canape plate w/indent, 6¼" **$10.00**
Tear Drop, cheese compote, crystal...........................**$20.00**
Tear Drop, claret, crystal, 5½" **$16.00**
Tear Drop, cup, footed...**$6.00**
Tear Drop, goblet, crystal, 9-oz, 7"............................**$12.00**
Tear Drop, marmalade, crystal....................................**$27.00**
Tear Drop, mayonnaise, crystal, footed, w/spoon **$24.00**
Tear Drop, pitcher, crystal w/silver overlay, ½-gal.....**$90.00**
Tear Drop, plate, crystal, 8" **$6.00**
Tear Drop, relish, crystal, oblong, 3-part, 12", from $24 to ..**$28.00**
Tear Drop, sherbet/champagne, crystal, tall...............**$12.00**
Tear Drop, tumbler, crystal, 5¾"................................**$12.00**
Terrace, ashtray, red, square......................................**$35.00**
Terrace, plate, cobalt, handles, 5" **$30.00**
Terrace, relish, crystal, 5-part....................................**$35.00**
Terrace, tumbler, water; red.......................................**$37.50**
Three Feathers, cornucopia vase, crystal...................**$145.00**
Three Feathers, cruet, crystal **$22.50**
Three Feathers, goblet, water; crystal **$14.00**
Venetian, vase, crystal, crimped rim, 8" **$35.00**

Viking Ship, crystal, 12" long, $225.00.

Easter Collectibles

The egg (a symbol of new life) and the bunny rabbit have long been part of Easter festivities; and since early in the twentieth century, Easter has been a full-blown commercial event. Postcards, candy containers, toys, and decorations have been made in infinite varieties. In the early 1900s, many holiday items were made of papier-mache and composition and imported to this country from Germany. Rabbits were made of mohair, felt, and velveteen, often filled with straw, cotton, and cellulose.

Figures, rabbits, boy and girl, plastic, 6½", $25.00 each.

Candy container, papier-mache, chick in top hat, Germany, 1950s, 7", EX **$65.00**
Candy container, papier-mache, chick w/egg-shaped body, Germany, 1950s, 6½", EX.........................**$45.00**
Candy container, papier-mache, duck w/egg-shaped body, 6½", EX...**$45.00**
Candy container, papier-mache, hen on nest, Germany, 1950s, 6", EX **$50.00**
Candy container, papier-mache, rabbit w/basket, Germany, 1950s, 4¾", EX **$40.00**
Chicken pulling wagon, celluloid, chicks & multicolored eggs in wagon w/red wheels, early, 3½", EX............**$120.00**
Decoration display, heavy cardboard stand-up, diecut rabbit in striped suit jumping over egg in tulip bed, 8", EX..**$95.00**
Egg, lithographed tin, yellow w/image of rabbits painting eggs, Chein, 5½", EX............................**$110.00**
Egg w/chicken, lithographed tin, chicken atop yellow egg w/image of grass & flowers, Chein, 5", EX+ **$95.00**
Nodder, composition, rabbit w/toothache standing on round candy box, Germany, 8½", EX **$245.00**
Rattle, celluloid, girl dressed in beige bunny suit w/pink ears & green bow tie, 4", EX **$75.00**

Puzzles, wood, made in England, 1940s, 4½", $15.00 each.

Egg Cups

Egg cups were once commonplace kitchen articles that were often put to daily use. Recent trends include changes in dietary patterns that have caused egg cups to follow butter pats and salt dishes into relative obscurity. These small egg holders were commonly made in a variety of shapes from many metals, wood, plastic, and ceramics. They were used as early as ancient Rome and were very common on Victorian tables. Many were styled like whimsical animals or made in other shapes that would specifically appeal to children. Some were commemorative or sold as souvenirs. Still others were part of extensive china or silver services.

They're easy to find today, and though most are inexpensive, some are very pricey! Single egg cups with pedestal bases are the most common, but shapes vary and include doubles, egg hoops, buckets, and sets of many types. Pocillivists, as egg cup collectors are known, are increasing in numbers every day. For more extensive listings we recommend *Schroeder's Antiques Price Guide* (Collector Books).

Newsletter: *Egg Cup Collector's Corner*
Dr. Joan George, Editor
67 Stevens Ave.
Old Bridge, NJ 08857; Subscription $18 per year for 4 issues; sample copies available at $5 each

Boy, marked Occupied Japan, 2⅜", $15.00.

Bucket shape, white w/tiny applied flowers, Elfinware .**$95.00**
Bunny stands before holder, tan lustre & multicolor, shiny, Japan mark, 3¼", from 18 to **$26.00**
Chick figural, yellow luster w/multicolor details, Japan mark, 2¼", from $15 to **$20.00**
Chick figural, yellow lustre, Japan mark, 2¾", from $16 to..**$25.00**
Chicken, wings support cup, milk glass w/painted details.**$15.00**
Chicken figural, tan & yellow lustre, Japan mark, 2½", from $16 to..**$23.00**
Duck beside lg half egg, multicolor & white, shiny, Japan mark, 2", from $18 to **$15.00**
Duck figural, multicolor, shiny, Japan mark, 3", from $18 to..**$26.00**
Girl bunny stands beside flower cup, orange lustre w/multi-colored matt, Japan mark, 3", from $15 to **$20.00**
Goose w/cup on back, multicolor matt, Japan mark, 2½", from $15 to...**$20.00**
Holly Hobbie at kitchen counter w/cat, Japan, 1960s ..**$15.00**

Mountain scenic, tan lustre & multicolored, shiny, red Japan mark, 3", from $11 to **$18.00**
Pelican beside lg half egg, multicolor & white, shiny, Japan mark, 2", from $8 to **$15.00**
Swan figural, orange & white lustre, Japan mark, 2½", from $12 to...**$18.00**
2 boy bunnies support tan lustre cup, multicolor & white shiny figures, Japan mark, 3", from $15 to **$20.00**
2 bunnies support teal lustre basket on backs, multicolor shiny figures, Japan mark, 2½", from $15 to........**$18.00**
2 chickens stand at sides of half ear of white corn, multicolor lustre & matt, Japan mark, 2½", from $16 to...**$26.00**

Chick pulling cart, Japan mark, 2", $15.00.

Egg Timers

Egg timers are comprised of a little glass tube, pinched in the center and filled with sand, attached to a figural base, usually between 3" and 5" in height. They're all the rage today among collectors. Most figural egg timers reached their heyday in the 1940s. However, Germany produced many beautiful and detailed timers much earlier. Japan followed suit by copying many German designs. Today, one may find timers from the United Kingdom as well as many foreign ports. The variety of subjects represented by these timers is endless. Included are scores of objects, animals, characters from fiction, and people in occupational or recreational activities. Timers have been made in many materials including bisque, china, ceramic, chalkware, cast iron, tin, brass, wood, and plastic.

Although they were originated to time a 3-minute egg, some were also used to limit the duration spent on telephone calls as a cost-saving measure. Frequently a timer is designed to look like a telephone or a phone is depicted on it.

Since the glass tubes were made of thin, fine glass, they were easily broken. You may recognize a timer masquerading as a figurine by the empty hole that once held the tube. Do not pass up a good timer just because the glass is missing. These can be easily replaced by purchasing a cheap egg timer with a glass tube at your local grocery story.

Listings are for timers in excellent to mint condition with their glass tubes attached.

Advisor: Ellen Bercovici (See Directory, Egg Timers)

Bear dressed as chef w/towel over arm, ceramic, Japan, 4" **$65.00**

Bellhop, green, ceramic, Japan, 4½" **$60.00**

Bellhop on phone, ceramic, Japan, 3" **$40.00**

Black chef sitting w/raised right hand holding timer, ceramic, many sizes & shadings, German, from $95 to......**$120.00**

Black chef standing w/fry pan in right hand, chalkware, Japan, 5½" **$125.00**

Black chef standing w/lg fish, timer in fish's mouth, ceramic, Japan, 4¾" **$125.00**

Boy, Mexican playing guitar, ceramic, German, 3½" ..**$45.00**

Boy skiing, ceramic, German, 3" **$65.00**

Boy stands on head (plastic) which fills w/sand, ceramic, Cooley Lilley sticker, 3¾" **$35.00**

Boy w/black cap stands & holds black bird, ceramic, unmarked, 3½" **$50.00**

Boy w/black cloak & cane, ceramic, German, 3¾" **$65.00**

Boy w/red cap, stands & holds different glass tubes in both hands, wooden, unmarked, 4½" **$20.00**

Cat, standing by base of grandfather clock, ceramic, German, 4¾" **$65.00**

Cat with orange ribbon around neck, Occupied Japan, 2⅝", $25.00.

Chef, standing in blue w/white apron, towel over right arm, timer in jug under left, ceramic, Japan, 4½".........**$35.00**

Chef holding plate w/hole to hold timer which removes to change, ceramic, Japan, 3¾" **$35.00**

Chef in white on blue base holding spoon, ceramic, German, 4" **$60.00**

Chef in yellow pants, white jacket, blue trim, holds platter of food, ceramic, Japan, 3½" **$35.00**

Chef winking, white clothes, timer in back, turn upside-down to tip sand, ceramic, 4" **$35.00**

Chicken, wings hold tube, ceramic, German, 2¾"......**$50.00**

Chicken on nest, green plastic, England, 2½" **$15.00**

Chimney sweep carrying ladder, ceramic, German, 3¼" ..**$65.00**

Clown on phone, standing, yellow suit, ceramic, Japan, 3¾" **$50.00**

Clown sitting w/legs to side, timer in right hand, ceramic, German, 3¼" **$65.00**

Colonial lady w/bonnet, variety of dresses & colors, ceramic, German, 3¾" **$65.00**

Colonial man in knickers, ruffled shirt, waistcoat hides hat, ceramic, Japan, 4¾" **$65.00**

Dutch boy kneeling, ceramic, Japan, 2½" **$40.00**

Dutch boy standing, ceramic, German, 3½"...............**$65.00**

Dutch girl on phone, standing, blue & white, ceramic, Japan, 3¾"..**$50.00**

Dutch girl w/flowers, walking, chalkware, unmarked, 4½"...**$45.00**

Geisha, ceramic, German, 4½" **$65.00**

Goebel, double, chefs, man & woman, ceramic, German, 4" **$100.00**

Goebel, double, Mr Wicket, green, ceramic, German, 4"...**$150.00**

Goebel, double, rabbits, various color combinations, ceramic, German, 4½"...**$100.00**

Goebel, double, roosters, various color combinations, ceramic, German, 4" **$100.00**

Goebel, single chimney sweep, ceramic, German, 4¼"..**$70.00**

Goebel, single Friar Tuck, ceramic, German, 4" **$70.00**

Golliwog, bisque, England, 4½", minimum value.....**$150.00**

Leprechaun, shamrock on base, brass, Ireland, 3¼" ..**$30.00**

Lighthouse, blue, cream & orange lustreware, ceramic, German, 4½" **$65.00**

Mammy, tin, lithographed picture of her cooking, pot holder hooks, unmarked, 7¾" **$95.00**

Mouse, yellow & green, chalkware, Josef Originals, Japan, 1970s, 3¼" **$35.00**

Newspaper boy, ceramic, Japan, 3¾" **$50.00**

Parlor maid w/cat, ceramic, Japan, 4" **$50.00**

Penguin, chalkware, England, 3¾"............................**$50.00**

Pixie, ceramic, Enesco, Japan, 5½" **$40.00**

Sailor, blue, ceramic, German, 4" **$65.00**

Sailor w/sailboat, ceramic, German, 4" **$65.00**

Santa Claus w/present, ceramic, Sonsco, Japan, 5½" .**$60.00**

Scotsman w/bagpipes, plastic, England, 4½" **$50.00**

Sultan, Japan, 3½", $50.00.

Telephone, black glaze on clay, Japan, 2"..................**$20.00**

Telephone, candlestick type on base w/cup for timer, wooden, Cornwall Wood Prod, So Paris, Maine...........**$25.00**

Veggie man or woman, bisque, Japan, 4½" **$60.00**

Welsh woman, ceramic, German, 4½" **$65.00**

Windmill, yellow w/bird on top, ceramic, unmarked, 4"..**$60.00**

Windmill w/dog on base, ceramic, Japan, 3¾"...........**$60.00**

Elvis Presley Memorabilia

Since he burst upon the fifties scene wailing 'Heartbreak Hotel,' Elvis has been the undisputed 'King of Rock 'n Roll.' The fans that stood outside his dressing room for hours on end, screamed themselves hoarse as he sang, or simply danced to his music till they dropped are grown-up collectors today. Many of their children remember his comeback performances, and I'd venture to say that even their grandchildren know Elvis on a first-name basis.

There has never been a promotion in the realm of entertainment to equal the manufacture and sale of Elvis merchandise. By the latter part of 1956, there were already hundreds of items that appeared in every department store, drugstore, specialty shop, and music store in the country. There were bubble gum cards, pin-back buttons, handkerchiefs, dolls, guitars, billfolds, photograph albums, and hundreds of other items. You could even buy sideburns from a coin-operated machine. Look for the mark 'Elvis Presley Enterprises' (along with a 1956 or 1957 copyright date); you'll know you've found a gold mine. Items that carry the 'Boxcar' mark are from 1974 to 1977, when Elvis's legendary manager, Colonel Tom Parker, promoted another line of merchandise to agument their incomes during the declining years. Upon his death in 1977 and until 1981, the trademark became 'Boxcar Enterprises, Inc., Lic. by Factors ETC. Bear, DE.' The 'Elvis Presley Enterprises, Inc.' trademark reverted back to Graceland in 1982, which re-opened to the public in 1983.

Due to the very nature of his career, paper items are usually a large part of any 'Elvis' collection. He appeared on the cover of countless magazines. These along with ticket stubs, movie posters, lobby cards, and photographs of all types are sought after today, especially those from before the mid-sixties.

Though you sometime see Elvis 45s with $10.00 to $15.00 price tags, unless the record is in excellent condition, this is just not realistic, since they sold in such volume. In fact, the picture sleeve itself (if it's in good condition) will be worth more than the record. The exceptions are, of course, the early Sun label records (he cut five in all) that collectors often pay in excess of $500.00 for. In fact, at a recent auction, a near-mint copy of 'That's All Right' (his very first Sun recording) realized $2,800.00! And some of the colored vinyls, promotional records, and EPs and LPs with covers and jackets in excellent condition are certainly worth researching further. For instance, though his *Moody Blue* album with the blue vinyl record can often be had for under $25.00, depending on condition; if you find one of the rare ones with the black record you can figure on about ten times that amount! For a thorough listing of his records as well as the sleeves, refer to *Official Price Guide to Elvis Presley Records and Memorabilia* by Jerry Osborne.

For more general information and an emphasis on the early items, refer to *Elvis Collectibles* and *Best of Elvis Collectibles* by Rosalind Cranor, P.O. Box 859, Blacksburg, VA 24063. ($19.95+$1.75 postage each volume.)

Special thanks to Art and Judy Turner, Homestead Collectibles (see Directory, Decanters) for providing information on decanters.

See also Dolls, Celebrity; Movie Posters; Pinback Buttons; Records; Sheet Music.

Advisor: Lee Garmon (See Directory, Elvis Presley)

Binder, white leather with zipper closure, Elvis Presley Enterprises, 1956, 14x10", NM, $1,000.00; Pillow, pink with sketched image of Elvis, Elvis Presley Enterprises, 1956, 10½x10½", NM, $365.00.

Ashtray, glass, horseshoe-shaped w/image of Elvis, EX .**$20.00**
Balloon, advertises Kid Galahad, unused, M..............**$50.00**
Beach hat, w/original photo hang tag, 1956, EX, from $110
   to **$125.00**
Book, Meet Elvis Presley, softbound, Scholastic, 1971,
   EX **$10.00**
Bracelet, double photo of Elvis, Boxcar, M (sealed) ..**$25.00**
Bracelet, lady's dog tag on original card, Elvis Presley
   Enterprises, M...**$30.00**
Calendar, 1978, EX...**$12.00**
Catalog, RCA, Elvis Records & Tapes, 1972, black & white
   cover, 3x10½"..**$10.00**
Catalog, RCA, Elvis Records & Tapes, 1973, color cover,
   3x10½"...**$20.00**
Charm bracelet, 1956, MOC, from $220 to **$260.00**

Cologne with white teddy bear, Be My Teddy Bear, marked Elvis Fragrances, Inc. Atlanta, GA (fragrance made in USA, teddy bear made in Hong Kong), 7½" plastic container, M, $45.00. (Photo courtesy of Lee Garmon.)

Coloring sheet, unused in contest to promote the film Girls!
   Girls! Girls!, 1962, EX...**$30.00**
Concert ticket, Terre Haute IN, August, 26, 1977, unused ..**$35.00**
Decanter, McCormick, 1978, Elvis '77, plays 'Love Me
   Tender'..**$85.00**
Decanter, McCormick, 1978, Elvis Bust, no music box, 750
   ml **$65.00**

Decanter, McCormick, 1979, Elvis '55, plays 'Loving You,' 750 ml **$75.00**

Decanter, McCormick, 1979, Elvis '77 Mini, plays 'Love Me Tender,' 50 ml **$45.00**

Decanter, McCormick, 1979, Elvis Gold, plays 'My Way,' 750 ml **$150.00**

Decanter, McCormick, 1980, Elvis '55 Mini, plays 'Loving You,' 50 ml **$45.00**

Decanter, McCormick, 1980, Elvis '68, plays 'Can't Help Falling in Love,' 750 ml **$75.00**

Decanter, McCormick, 1980, Elvis Silver, plays 'How Great Thou Art,' 750 ml **$125.00**

Decanter, McCormick, 1981, Aloha Elvis, plays 'Blue Hawaii,' 750 ml **$150.00**

Decanter, McCormick, 1981, Elvis '68 Mini, plays 'Can't Help Falling in Love,' 50 ml **$45.00**

Decanter, McCormick, 1981, Elvis Designer I (Joy), plays 'Are You Lonesome Tonight,' 750 ml **$125.00**

Decanter, McCormick, 1982, Aloha Elvis Mini, plays 'Blue Hawaii,' 50 ml **$150.00**

Decanter, McCormick, 1982, Elvis Designer II (Love), plays 'It's Now or Never,' 750 ml **$125.00**

Decanter, McCormick, 1982, Elvis Karate, plays 'Don't Be Cruel,' 750 ml **$250.00**

Decanter, McCormick, 1983, Elvis Designer III (Reverence), plays 'Crying in the Chapel,' 750 ml **$250.00**

Decanter, McCormick, 1983, Elvis Gold Mini, plays 'My Way,' 50 ml **$125.00**

Decanter, McCormick, 1983, Elvis Silver Mini, plays 'How Great Thou Art,' 50 ml **$95.00**

Decanter, McCormick, 1983, Sgt Elvis, plays 'GI Blues,' 750 ml **$295.00**

Decanter, McCormick, 1984, Elvis & Rising Sun, plays 'Green, Green Grass of Home,' 750 ml **$495.00**

Decanter, McCormick, 1984, Elvis Designer I Gold, plays 'Are You Lonesome Tonight,' 750 ml **$125.00**

Decanter, McCormick, 1984, Elvis Designer II Gold, plays 'It's Now or Never,' 750 ml **$195.00**

Decanter, McCormick, 1984, Elvis Karate Mini, plays 'Don't Be Cruel,' 50 ml **$125.00**

Decanter, McCormick, 1984, Elvis on Stage, plays 'Can't Help Falling in Love,' 50 ml **$195.00**

Decanter, McCormick, 1984, Elvis w/Stage, 50 ml **$450.00**

Decanter, McCormick, 1984, Elvis 50th Anniversary, plays 'I Want You, I Need You, I Love You,' 750 ml **$495.00**

Decanter, McCormick, 1984, Sgt Elvis Mini, plays 'GI Blues,' 50 ml **$95.00**

Decanter, McCormick, 1985, Elvis Designer I White Mini, plays 'Are You Lonesome Tonight,' 50 ml **$125.00**

Decanter, McCormick, 1985, Elvis Designer III Gold, plays 'Crying in the Chapel,' 750 ml **$250.00**

Decanter, McCormick, 1985, Elvis' Teddy Bear, plays 'Let Me Be Your Teddy Bear,' 750 ml **$695.00**

Decanter, McCormick, 1986, Elvis & Gates of Graceland, plays 'Welcome to My World,' 750 ml **$150.00**

Decanter, McCormick, 1986, Elvis & Rising Sun Mini, plays 'Green, Green Grass of Home,' 50 ml **$250.00**

Decanter, McCormick, 1986, Elvis Designer I Gold Mini, plays 'Are You Lonesome Tonight,' 50 ml **$150.00**

Decanter, McCormick, 1986, Elvis Designer I Silver Mini, plays 'Are You Lonesome Tonight,' 50 ml **$135.00**

Decanter, McCormick, 1986, Elvis Hound Dog, plays 'Hound Dog,' 750 ml **$695.00**

Decanter, McCormick, 1986, Elvis Season's Greetings, plays 'White Christmas,' 375 ml **$195.00**

Decanter, McCormick, 1986, Elvis Teddy Bear Mini, plays 'Let Me Be Your Teddy Bear,' 50 ml **$295.00**

Decanter, McCormick, 1986, Elvis 50th Anniversary Mini, plays 'I Want You, I Need You, I Love You,' 50 ml **$250.00**

Decanter, McCormick, 1987, Elvis Memories, plays variety of songs, 750 ml **$695.00**

Doll, Eugene, 1984, issued in 6 different outfits, 12" MIB, each from $60 to **$65.00**

Doll, Hasbro, Teen Idol, Jail House Rock or '68 special, 12", MIB, each **$40.00**

Doll, World Doll, 1984, Burning Love, vinyl, 21", VG/EX ..**$110.00**

Doll, World Dolls, 1984, Joyce Christofer designer, rooted hair, 21", from $400 to **$500.00**

Doubloon (coin thrown from floats at Mardi Gras in 1981), Elvis image, 'Beloved American,' red, blue, or silver, each, from $25 to **$30.00**

Figures, pewter, Legend Lives On, 3 in series: Early Years, Movies, Vegas Years, artist signed, Boxcar Ent, 1977, 5", each **$150.00**

Film, 8mm, Change of Habit **$150.00**

Guitar, plastic, Lapin Productions, 1984, M (EX card), lg ...**$65.00**

Guitar, plastic, Lapin Productions, 1984, M (EX card), sm .**$45.00**

Hat, brown paper, GI Blues, RCA Victor/Paramount, 5x12", EX **$100.00**

Key chain, flasher type w/full figure on yellow background, M **$18.00**

Lipstick tube, Hound Dog Orange, comes w/copy of original card, 1956, rare, EX **$340.00**

Magazine, Keyhole Mystery, Great EP Mystery Case, April 1960, EX **$50.00**

Magazine, Life, Collectors Edition, February 10, 1995, 60th Birthday **$3.00**

Menu, Las Vegas souvenir, 10¾" dia, EX **$40.00**

Necktie, silk blue or red w/image of Elvis, EX, each .**$15.00**

Ornament, Elvis, brass-look figure, Hallmark, 1992, MIB ...**$20.00**

Paint-by-number set, Elvis Presley Enterprises, 1956, EX **$1,800.00**

Pen, Tickle Me promotion w/feathers atop, NM **$18.00**

Pencil sharpener, Elvis Presley Enterprises, 1956, EX ..**$210.00**

Photo album, souvenir sold at 1956 concerts, EX **$175.00**

Picture, glow-in-the-dark, 1957, EX **$150.00**

Pin, guitar shape, 1960s, rare, EX **$35.00**

Pin-back button, portrait, Sincerely Elvis, black & white flasher type, 1956, 2¾" **$30.00**

Pin-back button, The King Forever, Elvis; Boxcar, 1977, 3" **$5.00**

Pin-back button, You Ain't Nothing But a Hound Dog, from bubble gum machine, 1956, 1" **$30.00**

Plate, Melmac, July 1969, EX **$25.00**

Playing cards, The Best of Elvis, MIB (sealed) **$5.00**

Pocket mirror, image of Elvis w/his parents, 1956, EX ...**$15.00**

Postcard, black & white photo of Elvis on motorcycle, Germany, NM **$15.00**

Promo Kit, Tickle Me, w/feather **$65.00**

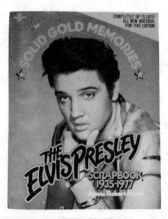

Scrapbook, Solid Gold Memories, Ballantine Books, 1977, $25.00.

Songbook, Jukebox, Fan Club Edition, 1956, EX........**$50.00**
Standee, Love Me Tender, 72", EX.........................**$1,000.00**
Stir stick, King of Rock 'N Roll, EX **$4.00**
Sweater clip, silver-tone w/image of Elvis, EX............**$18.00**
Tape measure, heart shaped, original issue w/white printing, from 1977 concert....................................**$25.00**
Tapestry, lg black & white image of Elvis, EX............**$20.00**
Teddy Bear, Elvis Presley Enterprises, 1957, 24", NM.**$450.00**
Tip tray, plastic, assorted photos, EX...........................**$5.00**
Towels, Sincerely Elvis Presley, 4-pc set, EX..............**$15.00**
Wine, Collectors Series #1, Blanc D'oro, 'Always Elvis' neckband, 1978 Boxcar Enterprises Inc, Lic by Factors ETC Inc..**$125.00**
Wine, Collectors Series #2, Blanc D'oro, 'Portrait of Elvis' neckband, 1979 Boxcar Enterprises Inc, Lic by Factors ETC **$125.00**

Enesco

Enesco is an importing company based in Elk Grove, Illinois. They're distributors of ceramic novelties made for them in Japan.

One of their most collectible lines, Mother-in-the-Kitchen, or as collectors refer to it, Kitchen Prayer Ladies, has become so popular that it's been given its own category later on in this guide, but several other groupings are starting to catch on, and we'll list them here. One is Kitchen Independence which features George Washington with the Declaration of Independence scroll held at his side, and Betsy Ross wearing a blue dress and holding a large flag. Another line is called Snappy the Snail, then there's the winking-eye cat, the Dutch boy and girl, and several others. You'll find them turning up as kitchen wares such as teapots, salt and pepper shakers, cookie jars, and spoon rests, as well as banks and other novelties.

Advisor: April Tvorak (See Directory, Figural Ceramics)

Bank, clown head, wide ruffed collar, from $25 to....**$30.00**
Bank, This Is a Retired Human Being, Human Beans, 1981, from $15 to...**$20.00**
Condiment, Winking Eye Cat, yellow **$95.00**

Cookie jar, Kitchen Independence, Betsy Ross, sm, minimum value **$200.00**
Cookie jar, Snappy the Snail.....................................**$150.00**
Cutting board plaque, girl on right, boy on left, 'Kissin' Don't Last, Cookin' Do'..**$45.00**
Figurine, Human Bean series, Moms Are Special, 1981..**$12.00**
Jar, Headache Pills, man's head w/lid.........................**$15.00**
Napkin holder, Kitchen Independence, George, from $18 to **$22.00**
Pincushion, Kitchen Independence, Betsy w/velvet cushion on her left, 4½"..**$65.00**
Salt & pepper shakers, Dutch shoes, boy on 1, girl on other, kissing, sm, pr...**$25.00**
Salt & pepper shakers, Kitchen Independence, Betsy & George, pr...**$20.00**
Salt & pepper shakers, Snappy the Snail, pr.............**$16.00**
Salt & pepper shakers, Winking Eye Cat, pr.............**$20.00**

Spoon holders, Mary Poppins, from $50.00 to $75.00; and Kitchen Independence, Betsy Ross, $22.00 each. (Photo courtesy of Pat Duncan.)

Spoon rest, Busy Body...**$30.00**
Spoon rest, Granny in hat, white gloves & purse, 6¾".**$18.00**
Spoon rest, Snappy the Snail......................................**$12.00**
Tape measure/pincushion, Winking Eye Cat, yellow .**$38.00**
Tea bag holder, Snappy the Snail.................................**$6.00**
Tea set, Dutch boy & girl, girl as pot, boy as handle, girl sugar bowl, boy creamer, trimmed in blue roses, 3-pc **$125.00**
Toothpick holder, Kitchen Independence, George (drummer), scarce..**$35.00**
Toothpick holder, Winking Eye Cat **$20.00**
Wall plaque w/key hooks, Fairy Godmother **$100.00**

Eye Winker

Designed along the lines of an early pressed glass pattern by Dalzell, Gilmore and Leighton, Eye Winker was one of several attractive glassware assortments featured in the catalogs of L. G. Wright during the sixties and seventies. The line was extensive and made in several colors: amber, blue, green, crystal, and red. It was probably pressed by Fostoria, Fenton, and Westmoreland, since we know these are the companies who made Moon and Star for Wright, who was not a glass manufacturer but simply a distributing company. Red and green are the most desirable colors and are priced higher than the others we mentioned. The values given here are for red and green, deduct about 20% for examples in clear, amber, or light blue.

Advisor: Sophia Talbert (See Directory, Eye Winker)

Goblet, plain rim and foot, 6¼", $18.00; Sherbet, plain rim and foot, 4½", $12.00.

Ashtray, allover pattern, 4½" dia $12.00
Bowl, 4 toes, 2½x5" $15.00
Butter dish, allover pattern, 4½" dia lid, 6" base $38.00
Candy dish, allover pattern, disk foot, w/lid, 5¼x5½" .$25.00
Candy dish, oval, 4-toed, 5x3½" $18.00
Celery or relish, ruffled rim, oblong, 9½x5", from $22 to.$25.00
Compote, allover pattern except for plain flared rim, patterned lid, 10½x6"+finial $50.00
Compote, allover pattern except for plain flared rim & foot, patterned lid, 7x5" w/lid $35.00
Compote, allover pattern except for plain flared rim & foot, 7x7" $25.00
Compote, ruffled rim, plain foot, 4-sided, 7x6"...........$30.00
Compote, ruffled rim, 4-sided, 6x10" $42.00
Creamer & sugar bowl, allover pattern, disk foot, sm, 3¼", from $35 to...$45.00
Fairy lamp, allover pattern, disk foot, 2-pc $35.00
Jelly dish, patterned lid, plain foot & rim, 6¼x3½" $32.00
Marmalade, w/lid, 5¼x4" $32.00
Pickle tray, scalloped edge, 9½" $32.00
Pitcher, ruffled rim, plain foot, 1-qt, 7¼", from $40 to..$45.00

Salt and pepper shakers, allover pattern with metal lids, 3¾", $22.00 for the pair.

Salt cellar, allover pattern, ruffled rim, 1¾" $9.00
Toothpick holder, allover pattern, ruffled rim, 2¼" $10.00
Tumbler, 8-oz..$12.00
Vase, ruffled rim, 3-sided, 3-toed, 7¾"..........................$40.00
Vase, 3-footed, scalloped, 6"..$32.00

Farber Brothers Krome Kraft

Louis and Harry Farber established Farber Brothers in 1915 in New York City. They specialized in metalcrafting and in the early days produced hollowware pieces in a variety of finishes. Some were nickel or silverplated, while others were made of solid brass. Fruit bowls, smoking articles, and accessory items of all types were popular.

When chromium plating was developed in the late twenties, the company began to use the new material to a very large extent. They patented a special type of snap-on fastener that allowed metal holders to be used with glass and china inserts. The inserts could be replaced with ease in case of accidental breakage. Their innovations met with immediate approval, and their line of products sold well for years through leading department and gift shops all across the country. But fashion is fickle. By the fifties, the market for chromium-plated ware had fallen off dramatically, and the public once again showed a preference for silverplating. The glass industry had suffered as well during this time, and few companies remained to supply them with their inserts. By 1965, the Farber Brothers Company had closed.

Nearly every piece was marked, but even the few that weren't should be easy to identify once you become familiar with their patterns. Most of the glassware inserts were made by the Cambridge Company, though several other glass companies were involved on a much smaller scale.

When you buy, check for signs of deterioration to the clip-on as well as to the surface. Replating, though it can be done, is often very expensive. If you need to clean a piece, take note of the finish and use an appropriate cleaning product.

Basket, amethyst insert in chrome frame w/handle, #5563, from $48 to..$58.00
Bitters bottle, cobalt insert in chrome frame, 5⅞" $95.00
Butter dish, colored insert in chrome holder w/domed lid & loop handle, 4½x5½" $45.00
Cocktail, amber insert in chrome frame, #6018, 4¼" ..$15.00
Cocktail, crystal insert in chrome frame, #6018...........$18.00
Compote, amber insert in chrome holder, #5562, 5½"..$37.50
Compote, amethyst insert in chrome holder, #5569, 7½"...$55.00
Compote, red Fenton insert in chrome holder, #5785 ..$75.00
Condiment set, w/2 cruets & stoppers, salt & pepper shakers on tray, amber inserts in chrome frames, #5454 ....$130.00
Cordial, amethyst insert in chrome holder, #1900, 1-oz..$20.00
Cordial, cobalt insert in chrome holder, 2⅞"..............$35.00
Creamer & sugar bowl, colored Cambridge inserts in chrome holder w/lid, 4" & 3", from $32 to $38.00

Decanter, amber insert w/chrome frame & stopper, #3400/133, 55-oz..**$85.00**

Decanter, red insert in chrome frame, #3400/92, 32-oz ..**$165.00**

Mustard jar, cobalt insert w/frame base & lid **$45.00**

Oil, amethyst w/amethyst handle, 3-oz **$40.00**

Pitcher, amethyst w/chrome mounts, #6124, 76-oz, 8½"..**$135.00**

Relish, amethyst in chrome holder, 4-part, #5784 ....**$47.50**

Relish, clear insert w/center handle sits in chrome frame, 2x5½" **$38.00**

Relish, clear 3-compartment insert in chrome base, #3500/69, 6½" **$25.00**

Relish, clear 3-compartment insert in chrome Duchess Filigree tray, 12" dia...**$35.00**

Relish, forest green insert in chrome frame, #5782.....**$35.00**

Salt & pepper shakers, amber inserts in chrome frame, #5450, pr..**$35.00**

Salt & pepper shakers, amber inserts in chrome frames, #5874, pr..**$35.00**

Salt & pepper shakers, amethyst inserts in chrome frames, #5450, pr..**$35.00**

Sherbet, amethyst insert in chrome frame, #5462 ....**$27.50**

Sherbet, red insert in chrome frame, #5462.................**$32.00**

Sugar bowl, amethyst w/chrome mounts, w/lid, #3400..**$37.50**

Tumbler, amethyst insert in chrome frame, #5633, 12-oz .**$30.00**

Tumbler, cobalt insert in chrome frame, #5614, 3½"..**$35.00**

Tumbler, forest green insert in chrome frame, #5633, 12-oz.**$27.50**

Tumbler, red insert in chrome frame, #5633, 12-oz....**$32.50**

Wine, amethyst insert in chrome holder, #3400/92, 2½-oz ..**$16.50**

Fast-Food Collectibles

Since the late 1970s, fast-food chains have been catering to their very young customers through their kiddie meals. The toys tucked in each box or bag have made a much longer-lasting impression on the kids than any meal could. Today it's not just kids but adults (sometimes entire families) who're clammoring for them. They're after not only the kiddie meal toys but also boxes, promotional signs used by the restaurant, the promotional items themselves (such as Christmas ornaments you can buy for 99¢, collector plates, glass tumblers, or stuffed animals), or the 'under 3' (safe for children under 3) toys their toddler customers are given on request.

There have been three kinds of promotions: 1) national — every restaurant in the country offering the same item, 2) regional, and 3) test market. While, for instance, a test market box might be worth $20.00, a regional box might be $10.00, and a national, $1.00. Supply dictates price.

To be most valuable, a toy must be in the original package, just as it was issued by the restaurant. Beware of dealers trying to 'repackage' toys in plain plastic bags. Most original bags were printed or contained an insert card. Vacuform containers were quickly discarded, dictating a premium price of $10.00 minimum. Toys without the original packaging are worth only about one-half to two-thirds as much as those mint in package.

Toys representing popular Disney characters draw cross-collectors, so do Star Trek, My Little Pony, and Barbie

toys. It's not always the early items that are the most collectible, because some of them may have been issued in such vast amounts that there is an oversupply of them today. At the same time, a toy only a year or so old that might have been quickly withdrawn due to a problem with its design will already be one the collector will pay a good price to get.

As I'm sure you've noticed, many flea market dealers are setting out huge plastic bins of these toys, and no one can deny they draw a crowd. It's going to be interesting to see what develops here! If you'd like to learn more about fast-food collectibles, we recommend *Tomart's Price Guide to Kid's Meal Collectibles* by Ken Clee; *The Illustrated Collector's Guide to McDonald's® Happy Meal® Boxes, Premiums and Promotions©*, *McDonald's Happy Meal Toys in the USA*, *McDonald's Happy Meal Toys Around the World*, and *Illustrated Collector's Guide to McDonald's McCAPS*, all by Joyce and Terry Losonsky; and *Schroeder's Collectible Toys, Antique to Modern* (Collector Books).

See also California Raisins.

Club: McDonald's® Collector Club
c/o Joyce and Terry Losonsky
7506 Summer Leave Ln.
Columbia, MD 21046-2455; 301-381-3358

Club: McDonald's® Collector's Club, SUNSHINE Chapter
c/o Bill and Pat Poe
220 Domica Cir. E
Niceville, FL 32578-4068; 904-987-4163 or FAX 904-897-2606.
Annual membership is $10 per individual or $15 per family (includes 6 newsletters and 2 McDonald's Only shows)

Newsletter: *Collecting Tips*
Meredith Williams
Box 633
Joplin, MO 64802; Send SASE for information

Newsletter: *McDonald's® Collector Club*
c/o Tenna Greenberg
5400 Waterbury Rd.
Des Moines, IA 50312; 515-279-0741

Burger King, Goof Troop Bowlers, Max, 1992, MIP, $3.00.

Arby's, Babar's World Tour License Plates, 1990, each.**$2.00**

Arby's, Looney Tunes Car Tunes, 1989, 6 different, each..**$3.00**

Arby's, Looney Tunes Characters, standing, 1988, 6 different, each...**$3.00**

Arby's, Looney Tunes Fun Figures, 1989, each **$4.00**

Burger King, Archies, 1991, 4 different, MIP, each........**$4.00**

Burger King, Beauty & the Beast, 1991, 4 different, MIP, each...**$4.00**

Burger King, Beetlejuice, 1990, 6 different, each..........**$2.00**

Burger King, Bone Age, 1989, 4 different, each............**$5.00**

Burger King, Dino Crawlers, 1994, 5 different, MIP, each .**$2.00**

Burger King, Gargoyles, 1995, MIP, each from $2 to....**$3.00**

Burger King, Lion King Characters, 1994, 7 different, MIP, each...**$4.00**

Burger King, Lion King Finger Puppets, 1995, 6 different, MIP, each...**$3.00**

Burger King, Little Mermaid, 4 different, 1993, MIP, each...**$3.00**

Burger King, McGruff Cares for You songbooks & tapes, 1991, 4 different sets, MIP, each **$6.00**

Burger King, Mini Sports Games, 1993, 4 different, MIP, each...**$3.00**

Burger King, Nerfuls Characters, 1989, 3 different, MIP, each...**$4.00**

Burger King, Pinocchio Summer Inflatables, 1992, 5 different, MIP, each...**$4.00**

Burger King, Pocahontas, 1995, 8 different, MIP, each.**$3.00**

Burger King, Pranksters, 1994, 5 different, MIP, each...**$3.00**

Burger King, Save the Animals, 1993, 4 different, MIP, each...**$4.00**

Burger King, Silverhawk, 1987, pencil topper, M..........**$5.00**

Burger King, Simpsons, 1990, 4 different, each.............**$2.00**

Burger King, Surprise Celebration Parade, 1992, 4 different, MIP, each...**$4.00**

Burger King, Thundercats, Snarf, 1986.......................**$5.00**

Dairy Queen, Baby's Day Out Books, 4 different, M, each .**$12.00**

Dairy Queen, Radio Flyer Miniature Wagon, 1991, M ..**$5.00**

Denny's, Flinstones Rock 'N Rollers, 1992, each, M **$4.00**

Denny's, Flintstones Fun Squirters, 1991, 5 different, MIP, each...**$4.00**

Denny's, Jetsons Space Travel Fun Books, 1992, 6 different, M, each **$3.00**

Denny's, Jetsons Space-Age Puzzle Ornaments, 1992, MIP, each...**$3.00**

Frish's Big Boy, Racers, 1992, each **$5.00**

Frish's Big Boy, Sports Figures, 1990, each **$5.00**

Hardee's, Apollo 13 Rocket, 1995, 3 different, MIP, each..**$4.00**

Hardee's, Days of Thunder Racers, 1990, 4 different, MIP, each...**$5.00**

Hardee's, Dinosaur in My Pocket, 1993, 4 different, MIP, each...**$3.00**

Hardee's, Fender Bender 500 Racers, 1990, 5 different, MIP, each...**$3.00**

Hardee's, Flintstone First 30 Years, 1991, 5 different, MIP, each...**$5.00**

Hardee's, Gremlin Adventures Read-Along Book & Record Set, 1984, 5 different, M, each **$6.00**

Hardee's, Kazoo Crew Sailors, 1991, 4 different, MIP, each.**$3.00**

Hardee's, Marvel Super Heroes in Vehicles, 1990, 4 different, MIP, each **$3.00**

Hardee's, Mickey's Christmas Carol, 1984, 5 different, M, each...**$6.00**

Hardee's, Nicktoons Cruisers, 1994, 8 different, MIP, each...**$3.00**

Hardee's, Pound Puppies, stuffed plush, 1986, 4 different, each...**$5.00**

Hardee's, Smurf's Funmeal Pack, 1990, 6 different, each..**$3.00**

Hardee's, Tune-A-Fish Whistles, 1994, 4 different, MIP, each **$3.00**

Hardee's, Waldo's Straw Buddies, 1991, 4 different, MIP, each **$3.00**

Hardee's, X-Men, 1995, 6 different, MIP, each..............**$3.00**

Jack-in-the Box, Bendable Buddies, 1994, 5 different, MIP, each...**$6.00**

Jack-in-the-Box, Star Trek the Next Generation, figures, 6 different, MIP, each from $4 to **$5.00**

Long John Silver's, Free Willy 2, 5 different, each **$4.00**

Long John Silver's, Sea Watchers Miniature Kaleidoscope, 1991, MIP...**$5.00**

Long John Silver's, Treasure Trolls pencil toppers, 1992, each...**$3.00**

Long John Silver's, Water Blasters, 1990, 4 different, each..**$4.00**

McDonald's, Amazing Wildlife, 1995, 8 different, MIP, each...**$3.00**

McDonald's, American Tale Storybook, 1986, each **$2.00**

McDonald's, Barbie/Hot Wheels, 1994, any Barbie except Camp Teresa or under-age-3, MIP, each **$5.00**

McDonald's, Barbie/Hot Wheels, 1994, any Hot Wheels, MIP, each...**$4.00**

McDonald's, Barnyard (Old McDonald's Farm), 1986, 6 different, each...**$8.00**

McDonald's, Beach Toys, 1990, 8 different, MIP, each .**$1.50**

McDonald's, Berenstain Bears Books, 1990, 8 different, each...**$2.00**

McDonald's, Cabbage Patch Kids, Lindsay Elizabeth and Mimi Kristina, 1992, MIP, $3.00. each.

McDonald's, Crazy Creatures w/Popoids, 1985, 4 different, each...**$5.00**

McDonald's, Dinosaur Days, 1981, 6 different, each **$2.00**

McDonald's, Flintstones, Rocking Dino, under age 3, 1994, MIP **$5.00**

McDonald's, Flintstones Kids, 1988, 4 different, MIP, each from $6 to...**$8.00**

McDonald's, Fun w/Food, 1989, 4 different, MIP, each .**$8.00**

McDonald's, Halloween Pails, 1990, each.....................**$2.00**

McDonald's, Hook, 1991, 4 different, MIP, each **$3.00**

McDonald's, Jungle Book characters, 1990, 4 different, MIP, each..**$4.00**

McDonald's, Little Golden Books, 1982, 5 different, EX, each..**$3.00**

McDonald's, Little Mermaid, 1989, 4 different, MIP, each .**$5.00**

McDonald's, Mickey's Birthdayland, 1988, any of 6 different except under age 3, each........................**$2.00**

McDonald's, Movables, 1988, 6 different, each from $8 to..**$9.00**

McDonald's, Muppet Workshop, 1995, 4 different, MIP, each..**$1.50**

McDonald's, New Archies, 1988, 6 different, each........**$8.00**

McDonald's, 101 Dalmatians, Cruella Deville, 1991, MIP, $4.00.

McDonald's, Potato Heads, 1992, 8 different, each.......**$4.00**

McDonald's, Power Rangers, 1995, 5 different, MIP, each from $3 to..**$4.00**

McDonald's, Runaway Robots, 1987, 6 different, each .**$3.00**

McDonald's, Space Rescue, 5 different except under age 3, MIP, each **$4.00**

McDonald's, 101 Dalmatians, 1991, 4 different, MIP, each...**$4.00**

Pizza Hut, Beauty & the Beast hand puppets, 1992, rubber, 4 different, MIP, each **$5.00**

Pizza Hut, Fievel Goes West, Fievel or Cat R Waul, 1991, each..**$5.00**

Pizza Hut, Pagemaster, 4 different, MIP, each **$4.00**

Pizza Hut, Squirt Toons, 5 different, MIP, each.............**$5.00**

Roy Rogers, Beakman's World, 4 different, MIP, each ..**$5.00**

Roy Rogers, Space Meals, 4 different, MIP, each...........**$4.00**

Roy Rogers, Tootin' Jammers, 4 different, MIP, each **$5.00**

Subway, Battle Balls, 4 different, MIP, each **$3.00**

Subway, Cone Heads, 1993, 4 different, MIP, each.......**$4.00**

Subway, Monkey Trouble, 1994, 5 different, MIP, each..**$3.00**

Taco Bell, Milk Caps, MIP, each **$3.00**

Taco Bell, Pebble & the Penguin, 3 different, MIP, each ..**$5.00**

Wendy's, All Dogs Go to Heaven, 1989, 6 different, MIP, each..**$4.00**

Wendy's, Ballsasaurus, 1992, 4 different, MIP, each......**$4.00**

Wendy's, Glo-Friends, 1989, 12 different, each **$2.00**

Wendy's, Potato Head II, 1988, 5 different, each **$4.00**

Wendy's, Rocket Writers, 1992, 5 different, each..........**$2.00**

Wendy's, Wacky Windups, 1991, 5 different, MIP, each from $3 to..**$4.00**

White Castle, Blue Beany Bow Biter, 1989, MIP **$5.00**

White Castle, Camp White Castle, 1990, MIP, each.......**$4.00**

White Castle, Glow-in-the-Dark Monsters, 3 different, MIP, each..**$4.00**

Fenton Glass

Located in Williamstown, West Virgina, the Fenton Company is still producing glassware just as they have since the early part of the century. Nearly all fine department stores and gift shops carry an extensive line of their beautiful products, many of which rival examples of finest antique glassware. The fact that even their new glassware has collectible value attests to its fine quality.

Over the years they have made many lovely colors in scores of lines, several of which are very extensive. Paper labels were used exclusively until 1970. Since then some pieces have been made with a stamped-in logo.

Numbers in the descriptions correspond with catalog numbers used by the company. Collectors use them as a means of identification as to shape and size. If you'd like to learn more about the subject, we recommend *Fenton Glass, The Second Twenty-Five Years*, by William Heacock; and *Fenton Art Glass, 1907 to 1939*, by Margaret and Kenn Whitmyer.

Advisor: Ferill J. Rice (See Directory, Fenton Glass)

Club: Fenton Art Glass Collectors of America, Inc. Williamstown, WV 26187

Club: Pacific Northwest Fenton Association
8225 Kilchis River Rd.
Tillamook, OR 97141; $20 per year for quarterly newsletters; annual glass show, convention; annual special edition collector glass; covering old to new Fenton

Newsletter: *The Fenton Flyer*
National Fenton Glass Society
P.O. Box 4008
Marietta, OH 45750

Baskets

Hobnail, French opalescent with dusty rose handle and crest, $95.00.

Basketweave, blue carnival, rare color **$35.00**

Big Cookies, black, hat form (no handle), #1681 ....**$85.00**

Big Cookies, ruby, #1681, new wicker handle, 10½".**$75.00**

Black Rose, #7237, 7½"...**$130.00**

Burmese, plain, 7" **$40.00**

Burmese, w/roses hand painted by N Gribble, deep, rare, #7238RB..**$250.00**

Coin Dot, cranberry, #1434CC **$35.00**

Coin Dot, French opalescent, 1925, 6".....................**$60.00**

Cranberry opalescent stripes, #7237, 1978 convention ..**$50.00**

Hobnail Swirl, cranberry opalescent, 8½"..................**$32.50**

Lily of the Valley, Cameo opalescent, oval, #9437CO..**$25.00**

Ming crystal, #1616, 10x7".......................................**$65.00**

Rose overlay, hand-painted roses, 1968.....................**$65.00**

Thumbprint, Colonial Green, 8½" **$32.00**

Vasa Murrhina cased w/teal iridescent, Connisseur Collection, #3132OT, 1988...............................**$65.00**

Wisteria Lane, hand painted by D Fredrick, limited edition, #3749JW **$90.00**

Bells

Anticipation, limited edition....................................**$32.50**

Aurora, ivory w/Burnished Rose edges, shiny, 7".......**$15.00**

Bicentennial, chocolate, cameos of Washington, Adams, Jefferson & Franklin, 7" **$45.00**

Bicentennial, Patriot Red Slag **$45.00**

Cameo Satin, hand-painted daisies, Medallion #8267, 7" ..**$25.00**

Christopher Columbus, crystal carnival, 7" **$20.00**

Currier & Ives, brown & white **$40.00**

Custard, hand-painted pink flowers, Petite, 4½".........**$15.00**

Custard w/hand-painted roses **$30.00**

Daisy & Button, blue satin..**$25.00**

Daisy & Button, teal carnival, Gracious Touch, 1988, 6"....**$25.00**

Daisy & Button, teal opalescent **$25.00**

Faberge, pink carnival, 7"...**$18.00**

Faberge, purple carnival, #8466................................**$35.00**

Faberge, rosalene, #8466RE **$30.00**

Famous Women Connoisseur Collection, red carnival, cameo of Seton, Keller & Earhart **$35.00**

Mary Gregory, Petite...**$17.00**

Mother's Day, w/bird, 1980 ....**$24.00**

Paisley, black, 7"...**$17.00**

Paisley, floral decor **$27.50**

Ruby, hand-painted white roses, 4½" **$35.00**

Sables Arch, red carnival, 6" **$28.00**

Silver Crest, Spanish Lace..**$20.00**

Teal, cross handle, 6"..**$17.00**

Temple, red carnival..**$35.00**

Temple, Sage Green opaque, 7" **$30.00**

Velva Rose, 75th Anniversary....................................**$35.00**

Carnival Glass

Note: Carnival glass items listed here were made after 1970.

Bowl, Cherries & Orange Tree, purple, lg..................**$40.00**

Bowl, Fentonia, marigold, 3-footed, ca 1913-15.........**$72.50**

Bowl, Hearts & Vines, purple, ruffled rim..................**$30.00**

Compote, Persian Medallion, cobalt, ruffled pie-crust edge.**$37.50**

Compote, Roses, purple, footed, lg............................**$40.00**

High shoe, Daisy & Button, amber **$22.00**

Rose bowl, Orange Tree, purple **$25.00**

Tobacco jar, Grape & Cable, red................................**$250.00**

Crests

Aqua, comport, 4x5"..**$35.00**

Blue, comport, low footed, #7228, 6".........................**$22.50**

Emerald, tidbit tray, 2-tier, #630, 11½".......................**$45.00**

Flame, bonbon, 8" **$45.00**

Flame, comport, footed, #7429FC, 6"........................**$37.50**

Flame, comport, low foot, #7329FC **$40.00**

Gold, bonbon, #36, 6"...**$15.00**

Gold, compote, double-crimped rim, footed, #7249, 6¼x8¼"...**$35.00**

Peach, shell bowl, #9020, ca 1955-64.........................**$65.00**

Rose, basket, deeply crimped rim, looped handle, 9x5x5" square **$80.00**

Rose, bowl, double-crimped rim, 4x10½" **$55.00**

Silver, banana boat, low footed.................................**$47.50**

Silver, basket, #1523, 11"...**$85.00**

Silver, bonbon, ruffled, center metal handle, 8"..........**$30.00**

Silver, bowl, hand-painted roses & aqua stars w/gold trim, double-crimped rim, 3¾x7" **$35.00**

Silver, bowl, shallow, #7316, 10½" **$40.00**

Silver, bowl, 7½"..**$16.00**

Silver, cake stand, crimped rim, 5x13" **$30.00**

Silver, comport, ruffled, 6x8", from $18 to..................**$23.00**

Silver, iced tea, scarce **$58.00**

Silver, relish dish, heart shape, #7333SC.....................**$35.00**

Silver, vase, #7254, 4½"..**$25.00**

Silver, vase, cornucopia form, pr................................**$70.00**

Silver, vase, melon ribbed, beaded bulbous base, double-crimped rim, #711, 6½" **$15.00**

Silver/Spanish Lace, cake stand, #3510SC, 11" **$48.00**

Snow, pinch vase, emerald green, #3152, 8½"...........**$65.00**

Figurines and Novelties

Hat, Coin Dot, opalescent cranberry, ruffled rim, 3½", $75.00.

Alley cat, dark carnival, 10½" **$75.00**

Bear, crystal, sitting on font **$38.00**

Bear, milk glass w/hand-painted lilacs, sitting **$25.00**

Bear, Polar; Golden Flax on cobalt **$23.00**

Bird, blue, short tail, 25th Anniversary **$20.00**

Bird, Meadow Blossom, short tail **$23.00**

Bird, Rose Garden, short tail......................................**$24.00**

Bunny, light blue **$16.00**

Butterfly, amethyst carnival, design on wings, #5170.**$20.00**
Butterfly on stand, blue slag...............................**$30.00**
Butterfly on stand, red slag................................**$20.00**
Cane, ruby, #5090..**$180.00**
Cat, sitting, custard w/hand-painted roses..................**$25.00**
Cat, sitting, Lime Sherbet..................................**$22.00**
Duck, custard w/hand-painted orange rose **$34.00**
Duckling, Optic Pastel Blue..............................**$15.00**
Eagle, paperweight, Patriot Red **$40.00**
Egg on pedestal, custard w/hand painting, signed.....**$25.00**
Egg on pedestal, tulips on pearlized iridescent opalescent, #5140TL **$30.00**
Fish, paperweight, purple carnival.........................**$30.00**
Fish, paperweight, red carnival, limited edition.........**$65.00**
Happiness Bird, custard w/hand-painted decor, artist signed **$25.00**
Happiness Bird, red, 6½"...................................**$28.00**
Hat, plated amberina, 1984 Connoisseur Collection, #3193..**$150.00**
Hat, Spiral, French opalescent, smooth brim, #1923...**$25.00**
Kitten slipper, red carnival...............................**$22.00**
Lion, Pink Pearl..**$27.00**
Lovebirds, paperweight, deep red carnival **$35.00**
Owl, ring holder, carnival glass, signed Shelley Fenton, 1988 ....**$25.00**
Praying boy & girl, black, #5100, pr **$88.00**
Praying boy & girl, Crystal Velvet, pr...................**$32.00**

Rabbit, iridescent blue, hollow, 1971-72, 5½", $85.00.

Raccoon, hand-painted Hearts & Flowers...................**$24.00**
Scale of Justice, cranberry opalescent, #7100.............**$35.00**
Slipper, Daisy & Button, topaz **$20.00**
Slipper, Hobnail, topaz, #3995...........................**$22.00**
Wise Owl Decision Maker, black, #5180 ....**$32.50**

Hobnail

Ashtray, Colonial Amber, #3610CA, set of 3...............**$12.00**
Banana basket, plum opalescent...........................**$450.00**
Basket, French opalescent, #3837, 7" **$30.00**
Basket, milk glass, #3735, 5½"...........................**$18.00**
Basket, plum opalescent, original label, #3837PO, ca 1960-62 ....**$150.00**
Bowl, blue opalescent, flared crimped edge, sm........**$17.50**

Bowl, blue pastel, double crimped, #3924, 10"...........**$20.00**
Bowl, cranberry opalescent, #3927CR.....................**$32.50**
Bowl, topaz opalescent, ruffled rim, #389, ca 1941-43, 9"..**$70.00**
Candle holder, milk glass, cornucopia form, #3874, lg.**$20.00**
Candlesticks, cranberry opalescent, handled, #3870CR, pr **$130.00**
Candy dish, milk glass, w/lid, #3887.....................**$30.00**
Canoe planter, milk glass, #3698, 10"....................**$36.00**
Comport, pink, 8-crimp, #3920, 5½".......................**$22.50**
Creamer & sugar bowl, milk glass, #3901 ....**$15.00**
Cruet, milk glass, #3863.................................**$35.00**
Cruet, milk glass, ribbed, w/stopper, 8".................**$22.50**
Epergne, blue opalescent, 8½" dia........................**$85.00**
Epergne, milk glass, 1-horn, #3704 ....**$42.00**
Ivy ball, milk glass, #3726..............................**$10.00**
Jam set, cranberry opal, #3903CR.........................**$100.00**
Jam set, milk glass, #3903, 3-pc.........................**$30.00**
Jug, blue opalescent, handled, uncrimped top, 5½"..**$30.00**
Lamp, fairy; blue satin..................................**$30.00**
Lamp, fairy; Colonial Green..............................**$25.00**
Lamp, fairy; Colonial Orange.............................**$25.00**
Lavabo set, milk glass, #3867MI, 3-pc....................**$50.00**
Nut dish, milk glass, footed, w/hobs on stem, #3629.**$12.00**
Plate, dessert; French opalescent, square **$16.00**
Plate, French opalescent, 8" dia, 3 for **$25.00**
Relish, divided, #3740, 12" **$35.00**
Relish, milk glass, heart shape w/handle, #3733.........**$27.50**
Relish, milk glass, 3-part w/straight dividers, #3822, 7½".**$23.50**
Salt & pepper shakers, cranberry opalescent, #3806, pr ..**$60.00**
Salt & pepper shakers, French opalescent, #3806, pr..**$20.00**
Spooner, milk glass, #3612...............................**$45.00**
Syrup jug, cranberry opalescent, 33762CR.................**$52.50**
Vase, blue opalescent, crimped rim, #389 ....**$25.00**
Vase, blue opalescent, fan form, 8"......................**$75.00**
Vase, bud; blue opalescent **$35.00**
Vase, bud; Lime Sherbet..................................**$30.00**
Vase, bud; plum opalescent, 8" **$45.00**
Vase, flip; topaz opalescent, #389, 8½"..................**$180.00**
Vase, French opalescent, flared, deeply ruffled, 5½x5½"..**$16.00**
Vase, green opalescent, #3850, 5½" **$50.00**
Vase, milk glass, #3657, 7" **$20.00**
Vase, milk glass, ruffled edge, #3952, 4"................**$8.00**
Vase, plum opalescent, #3756, 8" **$32.50**
Vase, swung; blue opalescent, 9" **$32.50**
Vase, swung; milk glass, #3652, tall **$22.00**
Wedding jar, milk glass, #3780...........................**$20.00**

Lamps

Fairy, All Things Are Possible w/God painted on white satin **$45.00**
Fairy, Birds in Winter, Downy Woodpecker, limited edition **$55.00**
Fairy, burmese w/decaled maple leaves, 2-pc **$85.00**
Fairy, custard, shiny, no paint **$20.00**
Fairy, custard w/hand-painted pink flowers...............**$40.00**
Fairy, custard w/hand-painted 1980 Christmas............**$48.00**
Fairy, Heart, rosalene, #846RE, 1976 ....**$75.00**

Fairy, log cabin hand painted on custard, 150th Chesterhill, OH, 1934-1984 ....**$60.00**
Fairy, Old Virginia, amber, 2-pc **$24.00**
Fairy, owl, blue satin, #5108A **$25.00**
Fairy, owl, Lime Sherbet, #5108LS **$12.50**
Fairy, owl, rosalene, #5106 ....**$35.00**
Fairy, Persian Medallion, blue, glossy, 3-pc **$37.50**
Fairy, Persian Medallion, custard, 3-pc **$25.00**
Fairy, Strawberry, Crystal Velvet **$25.00**
Fairy lamp, red carnival, Santa, 2-pc, from $35 to **$50.00**
Gone With the Wind, rosalene striped, #2602 ....**$400.00**
Hurricane, Dot Optic, blue, milk glass base, #170, 11" .**$52.50**
Hurricane, Spiral, blue opalescent, milk glass base **$75.00**
Hurricane, Spiral, green opalescent, milk glass base, #170, 11" **$60.00**

Pancake lamp, light pink with cut decoration, #G-70, $250.00.

Student, custard w/hand-painted scene, #7411, 21" .**$500.00**
Student, lime green opalescent Hobnail font, milk glass shade w/painted roses, NM **$60.00**
Table, Moonstone, etched, ginger jar form, #893, 20" .**$200.00**
Table, rose burmese, replaced cloth shade, #7405 ...**$650.00**

Louise Piper Decorated Pieces

Basket, daisies on custard, #7237DC, 1979, 7" **$55.00**
Bell, brown rabbits & daisies on custard satin **$60.00**
Bell, white swans & water lilies on custard satin, #7504, 1981 ....**$75.00**
Bird, lily of the valley on lavender satin, #5163, 1978, sm. .**$70.00**
Box, blue flowers & butterfly on blue satin, w/lid, #7484, 1979 ....**$85.00**
Clown sitting on base, pansies on glossy milk glass, #5111 ....**$110.00**
Cookie tray, red cardinals on Silver Crest **$150.00**
Happiness Bird, blue & white daisies on blue satin, #5197 ....**$120.00**
Happiness Bird, holly & bell on custard satin, #5197 ..**$120.00**
Student lamp, roses on burmese, #7410 ....**$350.00**
Vase, bud; pansy & butterfly on Cameo Satin, #9056, 1979 ....**$60.00**
Vase, daisies on custard, tri-crimp, #7252DC, 1976 .....**$32.50**

Vase, log cabin on custard satin, #7254LC, 1977 ....**$55.00**
Vase, white coralene doves w/ribbon & flowers on dusty rose satin, #7660FE, 1985 ....**$80.00**

Plates

Birthplace of Liberty, purple carnival, Christmas 1975 ..**$35.00**
Christmas 1973, purple carnival **$40.00**
Currier & Ives seasons, signed, set of 4 ....**$150.00**
Lafayette & Washington at Valley Forge, chocolate, 8" ..**$50.00**
Mother's Day, Madonna of the Rose Hedge, red carnival, signed Tom Fenton **$95.00**
Shoemaker, purple carnival, 1973 ....**$35.00**

Miscellaneous

Ashtray, Beatty Rib, blue opalescent, square **$14.00**
Atomizer, DeVilbiss Diamond pattern, blue opalescent ..**$40.00**
Bowl, Basketweave, Lime Sherbet, #8222 ....**$14.00**
Bowl, Coin Dot, cranberry opalescent, double-crimped rim, #1522, 10" **$90.00**
Bowl, console; Swirl, green opalescent, #1522, 9½" ...**$50.00**
Bowl, cranberry opalescent stripes, #7237, 1978 convention **$27.50**
Bowl, Dolphin, black, crimped, #1502, 9" **$90.00**
Bowl, Petal, ebony, points of petals curve out, 8" **$25.00**
Bowl, planter; Lime Sherbet, octagonal, #8336 ....**$40.00**
Bowl, Water Lily, Crystal Velvet, footed, #8423VE **$55.00**
Candle holder, butterfly, ruby iridized, 1989 FAGCA souvenir, lg **$37.50**
Candle holders, crystal iridescent, 8½", pr **$17.50**
Candy box, Beaded Melon, cased Ivy Green (rare color), w/lid **$60.00**
Candy box, burmese w/hand-painted roses by H Biggs, #7284RB **$400.00**
Candy box, Cameo Satin w/hand-painted chocolate roses, #7484DR **$20.00**
Candy box, Chessie, purple carnival, 1970, made for Chessie Employees only **$300.00**
Candy box, Chessie, rosalene **$250.00**
Candy box, Chessie, teal carnival **$60.00**
Candy box, Strawberry, #9068CN **$30.00**
Candy box, Water Lily, rosalene, 1976 ....**$60.00**
Candy dish, Strawberry, Pekin Blue, footed, w/lid **$95.00**
Candy jar, plated amberina, shiny, #1680, w/lid **$120.00**
Comport, Bicentennial, Jefferson, Patriot Red, w/lid, #8476 ....**$140.00**
Comport, Bicentennial, Jefferson, white satin, #8476VW ..**$95.00**
Comport, Colonial Amber, #9222CA, 8" **$9.00**
Cordial, Lincoln Inn, crystal **$35.00**
Cruet, blue burmese satin, hand-painted butterfly w/flowers, #07359OL **$180.00**
Decanter, ruby w/silver overlay, 1934, w/6 shots **$240.00**
Epergne, Diamond Lace, green opalescent, 1985 Connoisseur Collection, #4809GO **$175.00**
Ewer, blue burmese satin, hand-painted lilies of the valley, #07368OL **$120.00**
Ginger jar, blue satin w/hand-painted blue roses, 3-pc ..**$130.00**
Ivy ball, green Thumbprint, on milk glass base, #1021 ..**$80.00**

Jug, Melon, pink overlay, 6" $30.00

Mug, Butterfly, burmese or rosalene, made for FAGCA, each $65.00

Mug, Butterfly, topaz opalescent or Celeste Blue, made for FAGCA, each $50.00

Pitcher, burmese, hand-painted roses by G Finn, #7461RB $50.00

Rose bowl, Cactus, aqua opalescent $48.00

Rose bowl, Coin Dot, cranberry opalescent, #1425CR..$40.00

Rose bowl, Tiara, Ivy Green, #711, 4" $22.50

Rose bowl, Water Lily, Lime Sherbet, #8329...............$22.00

Sherbet, Lincoln Inn, crystal............................$17.50

Sherbet/wine, Thumbprint, Colonial Pink, #4441 .....$150.00

Stein, Bicentennial, Independence Blue, #8446 ....$55.00

Stein Bicentennial, chocolate, #8446CK $30.00

Tobacco jar, Grape & Cable, black, #9188BK................$60.00

Tumbler, Georgian, ruby, footed, #1611, 8-oz, pr......$20.00

Vase, amberina overlay, 6-crimp, #7460, 6" $42.50

Vase, Black Rose, crimped, #1456, 6" $75.00

Vase, bud; Ebony Thumbprint w/white daisies, #4453WD, 17½" $30.00

Vase, bud; rosalene, paneled, footed, 8" $30.00

Vase, Coin Dot, blue, crimped, #1450, 5½" $42.50

Vase, Coin Dot, cranberry opalescent, #1448, 5".........$40.00

Vase, Coin Dot, lime green, crimped, #1454, 4½" $40.00

Vase, cranberry swirl, ruffled rim, 6", $95.00.

Vase, cream opalescent w/decals, signed Mike Fenton ..$80.00

Vase, Diamond Optic, aquamarine, fan form w/dolphin handles, #1532, 5" $47.50

Vase, Diamond Optic, cranberry, handled jug form, #192, 4½" $45.00

Vase, Dolphin, Jade Green, footed fan form w/dolphin handles, 6x7" $48.00

Vase, Dot Optic, blue opalescent, tri-top, #1454, 4½" ..$20.00

Vase, Empress, Jade, #8256JA, 8"................................$50.00

Vase, Jacqueline, blue, #9156..................................$32.50

Vase, Love Bird, Lime Sherbet, #8358 ....$30.00

Vase, Moonstone, fan form, #857, 8"..........................$70.00

Vase, peachblow, shade style, 10"............................$60.00

Vase, Pink Mist, fan form, 7" $120.00

Vase, Rose, Blue Marble, handkerchief form, #9254...$12.00

Vase, Spiral, cranberry opalescent, #3161CR, 11".......$42.50

Vase, Vasa Murrhina, #6455GB, 5½"..........................$35.00

Vase, Velva Rose stretch/Dolphin, fan form $30.00

Vase, Violets in the Snow, fan form, 6" $42.00

Water set, Coin Dot, blue, 7-pc................................$350.00

Whimsey, cruet, blue burmese, w/stopper, #7369UB.$120.00

Fiesta

You still can find Fiesta, but it's hard to get a bargain. Since it was discontinued in 1973, it has literally exploded onto the collectibles scene, and even at today's prices, new collectors continue to join the ranks of the veterans.

Fiesta is a line of solid-color dinnerware made by the Homer Laughlin China Company of Newell, West Virginia. It was introduced in 1936 and was immediately accepted by the American public. The line was varied. There were more than fifty items offered, and the color assortment included red (orange-red), cobalt, light green, and yellow. Within a short time, ivory and turquoise were added. (All these are referred to as 'original colors.')

As tastes changed during the production years, old colors were retired and new ones added. The colors collectors refer to as 'fifties' colors are dark green, rose, chartreuse, and gray, and today these are very desirable. Medium green was introduced in 1959 at a time when some of the old standard shapes were being discontinued. Today, medium green pieces are the most expensive. Most pieces are marked. Plates were ink stamped, and molded pieces usually had an indented mark.

In 1986, Homer Laughlin reintroduced Fiesta, but in colors different than the old line: white, black, cobalt, rose (bright pink), and apricot. Many of the pieces had been restyled, and the only problem collectors have had with the new colors is with the cobalt. But if you'll compare it with the old, you'll see that it is darker. Turquoise, periwinkle blue, yellow, and Seamist green were added next, and though the turquoise is close, it is a little greener than the original. Lilac and persimmon were made for sale exclusively through Bloomingdale's department stores. Production was limited on lilac (not every item was made in it), and now that it's been discontinued, collectors are already clammoring for it, often paying several times the original price. The newest color is sapphire blue. It's also a Bloomingdale's exclusive and the selection will be limited. Probably another 'instant collectible' in the making!

Items that have not been restyled are being made from the original molds. This means that you may find pieces with the old mark in the new colors (since the mark is an integral part of the mold). When an item has been restyled, new molds had to be created, and these will have the new mark. So will any piece marked with the ink stamp. The new ink mark is a script 'FIESTA' (all letters upper case), while the old is 'Fiesta.' Compare a few, the difference is obvious. Just don't be fooled into thinking you've found a rare cobalt juice pitcher or individual sugar and creamer set, they just weren't made in the old line.

For further information, we recommend *The Collector's Encyclopedia of Fiesta, 7th Edition,* by Sharon and Bob Huxford.

Newsletter: *Fiesta Club of America*
P.O. Box 1583
Loves Park, IL 61132-5383

Newsletter: *Fiesta Collector's Quarterly*
China Specialties, Inc.
19238 Dorchester Circle
Strongville, OH 44136. $12 (4 issues) per year

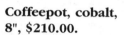
Coffeepot, cobalt,
8", $210.00.

Note: The term 'original colors' in the following listings refers to light green, yellow and turquoise.

Ashtray, '50s colors	$85.00
Ashtray, original colors	$42.00
Ashtray, red, cobalt or ivory	$60.00
Bowl, covered onion soup; cobalt or ivory	$675.00
Bowl, covered onion soup; red	$700.00
Bowl, covered onion soup; turquoise	$3,000.00
Bowl, covered onion soup; yellow or light green	$575.00
Bowl, cream soup; '50s colors	$70.00
Bowl, cream soup; med green, minimum value	$4,000.00
Bowl, cream soup; original colors	$40.00
Bowl, cream soup; red, cobalt or ivory	$60.00
Bowl, dessert; '50s colors, 6"	$52.00
Bowl, dessert; med green, 6"	$450.00
Bowl, dessert; red, cobalt or ivory, 6"	$52.00
Bowl, fruit; '50s colors, 4¾"	$32.00
Bowl, fruit; '50s colors, 5½"	$35.00
Bowl, fruit; med green, 4¾"	$450.00
Bowl, fruit; med green, 5½"	$70.00
Bowl, fruit; original colors, 11¾"	$250.00
Bowl, fruit; original colors, 4¾"	$24.00
Bowl, fruit; original colors, 5½"	$25.00
Bowl, fruit; red, cobalt or ivory, 11¾"	$285.00
Bowl, fruit; red, cobalt or ivory, 4¾"	$30.00
Bowl, fruit; red, cobalt or ivory, 5½"	$32.00
Bowl, individual salad; med green, 7½"	$105.00
Bowl, individual salad; red, turquoise or yellow, 7½"	$85.00
Bowl, nappy; '50s colors, 8½"	$60.00
Bowl, nappy; med green, 8½"	$140.00
Bowl, nappy; original colors, 8½"	$40.00
Bowl, nappy; original colors, 9½"	$52.00
Bowl, nappy; red, cobalt or ivory, 8½"	$52.00
Bowl, nappy; red, cobalt or ivory, 9½"	$65.00
Bowl, salad; original colors, footed	$265.00
Bowl, salad; red, cobalt or ivory, footed	$330.00

Bowl, Tom & Jerry; ivory w/gold letters	$250.00
Candle holders, bulbous, original colors, pr	$95.00
Candle holders, bulbous, red, cobalt or ivory, pr	$130.00
Candle holders, tripod, original colors, pr	$465.00
Candle holders, tripod, red, cobalt or ivory, pr	$595.00
Carafe, original colors	$220.00
Carafe, red, cobalt or ivory	$275.00
Casserole, '50s colors	$300.00
Casserole, French; yellow	$275.00
Casserole, med green	$700.00
Casserole, original colors	$140.00
Casserole, red, cobalt or ivory	$195.00
Coffeepot, '50s colors	$345.00
Coffeepot, demitasse; original colors	$340.00
Coffeepot, demitasse; red, cobalt or ivory	$435.00
Coffeepot, original colors	$195.00
Coffeepot, red, cobalt or ivory	$245.00
Compote, red or cobalt, 12"	$180.00
Compote, sweets; original colors	$75.00
Compote, sweets; red, cobalt or ivory	$90.00
Creamer, '50s colors	$38.00
Creamer, individual; red	$230.00
Creamer, individual; turquoise	$345.00
Creamer, individual; yellow	$70.00
Creamer, med green	$80.00
Creamer, original colors	$20.00
Creamer, original colors, stick handled	$45.00
Creamer, red, cobalt or ivory	$35.00
Creamer, red, cobalt or ivory, stick handled	$62.00
Cup, demitasse; '50s colors	$350.00
Cup, demitasse; original colors	$60.00
Cup, demitasse; red, cobalt or ivory	$75.00
Egg cup, '50s colors	$155.00
Egg cup, original colors	$55.00
Egg cup, red, cobalt or ivory	$70.00
Marmalade, original colors	$230.00
Marmalade, red, cobalt or ivory	$280.00
Mixing bowl #1, original colors	$165.00
Mixing bowl #1, red, cobalt or ivory	$200.00
Mixing bowl #2, original colors	$110.00
Mixing bowl #2, red, cobalt or ivory	$125.00
Mixing bowl #3, original colors	$115.00
Mixing bowl #3, red, cobalt or ivory	$130.00
Mixing bowl #4, original colors	$130.00
Mixing bowl #4, red, cobalt or ivory	$150.00
Mixing bowl #5, original color	$155.00
Mixing bowl #5, red, cobalt or ivory	$172.00
Mixing bowl #6, original colors	$200.00
Mixing bowl #6, red, cobalt or ivory	$240.00
Mixing bowl #7, original colors	$280.00
Mixing bowl, #7, red, cobalt or ivory	$325.00
Mug, Tom & Jerry; '50s colors	$90.00
Mug, Tom & Jerry; ivory w/gold letters	$65.00
Mug, Tom & Jerry; red, cobalt or ivory	$75.00
Mustard, original colors	$200.00
Mustard, red, cobalt or ivory	$250.00
Pitcher, disk juice; gray, minimum value	$2,500.00
Pitcher, disk juice; red	$450.00
Pitcher, disk water; '50s colors	$275.00

Pitcher, disk water; med green..................$1,150.00
Pitcher, disk water; original colors..................$112.00
Pitcher, disk water; red, cobalt or ivory..................$165.00
Pitcher, ice; original colors..................$125.00
Pitcher, ice; red, cobalt, or ivory..................$150.00
Pitcher, jug; 2-pt, '50s colors..................$145.00
Pitcher, jug; 2-pt, original colors..................$78.00
Pitcher, jug; 2-pt, red, cobalt or ivory..................$112.00
Plate, '50s colors, 10"..................$50.00
Plate, '50s colors, 6"..................$9.00
Plate, '50s colors, 7"..................$13.00
Plate, '50s colors, 9"..................$22.00
Plate, cake; original colors..................$750.00
Plate, cake; red, cobalt or ivory..................$885.00
Plate, calendar; 1954-1955, 10"..................$45.00
Plate, calendar; 1955, 9"..................$50.00
Plate, chop; '50s colors, 13"..................$90.00
Plate, chop; '50s colors, 15"..................$112.00
Plate, chop; med green, 13"..................$270.00
Plate, chop; original colors, 13"..................$35.00
Plate, chop; original colors, 15"..................$45.00
Plate, chop; red, cobalt or ivory, 13"..................$50.00
Plate, compartment; '50s colors, 10½"..................$78.00
Plate, compartment; original colors, 10½"..................$40.00
Plate, compartment; original colors, 12"..................$52.00
Plate, compartment; red, cobalt or ivory, 12"..................$60.00
Plate, deep; '50s colors..................$55.00
Plate, deep; original colors..................$38.00
Plate, deep; red, cobalt or ivory..................$52.00
Plate, med green, 10"..................$108.00
Plate, med green, 6"..................$20.00
Plate, med green, 7"..................$32.00
Plate, med green, 9"..................$45.00
Plate, original colors, 10"..................$30.00
Plate, original colors, 6"..................$5.00
Plate, original colors, 7"..................$9.00
Plate, original colors, 9"..................$12.00
Plate, red, cobalt or ivory, 6"..................$7.00
Plate, red, cobalt or ivory, 7"..................$10.00
Plate, red, cobalt or ivory, 9"..................$18.00
Plate, red, cobalt or ivory, 10"..................$40.00
Platter, '50s colors..................$55.00
Platter, med green..................$140.00
Platter, original colors..................$32.00
Platter, red, cobalt or ivory..................$44.00
Salt & pepper shakers, '50s colors, pr..................$40.00
Salt & pepper shakers, med green, pr..................$140.00
Salt & pepper shakers, original colors, pr..................$20.00
Salt & pepper shakers, red, cobalt or ivory, pr..................$28.00
Sauce boat, '50s colors..................$78.00
Sauce boat, med green..................$155.00
Sauce boat, original colors..................$45.00
Sauce boat, red, cobalt or ivory..................$68.00
Saucer, '50s colors..................$6.00
Saucer, demitase; original colors..................$16.00
Saucer, demitasse; '50s colors..................$95.00
Saucer, demitasse; red, cobalt or ivory..................$20.00
Saucer, med green..................$10.00
Saucer, original colors..................$4.00

Saucer, red, cobalt or ivory..................$5.00
Sugar bowl, '50s colors, w/lid, 3¼x3½"..................$72.00
Sugar bowl, individual; turquoise, w/lid..................$350.00
Sugar bowl, individual; yellow, w/lid..................$115.00
Sugar bowl, med green, w/lid, 3¼x3½"..................$158.00
Sugar bowl, original colors, w/lid, 3¼x3½"..................$44.00
Sugar bowl, red, cobalt or ivory, w/lid, 3¼x3½"..................$55.00
Syrup, original colors..................$320.00
Syrup, red, cobalt or ivory..................$380.00
Teacup, '50s colors..................$35.00
Teacup, med green..................$58.00
Teacup, original colors..................$25.00
Teacup, red, cobalt or ivory..................$32.00
Teapot, '50s colors, med..................$305.00

Teapot, medium, rose, $305.00.

Teapot, med green, med..................$870.00
Teapot, original colors, lg..................$180.00
Teapot, original colors, med..................$155.00
Teapot, red, cobalt or ivory, lg..................$220.00
Teapot, red, cobalt or ivory, med..................$195.00
Tray, figure-8; cobalt..................$82.00
Tray, figure-8; turquoise..................$275.00
Tray, figure-8; yellow..................$275.00
Tray, relish; mixed colors, no red..................$270.00
Tray, utility; original colors..................$35.00
Tray, utility; red, cobalt or ivory..................$42.00
Tumbler, juice; Harlequin yellow, dark green or chartreuse, each..................$460.00
Tumbler, juice; original colors..................$40.00
Tumbler, juice; red, cobalt or ivory..................$45.00
Tumbler, juice; rose..................$62.00
Tumbler, water; original colors..................$60.00
Tumbler, water; red, cobalt or ivory..................$74.00
Vase, bud; original colors..................$78.00
Vase, bud; red, cobalt or ivory..................$100.00
Vase, original colors, 10"..................$710.00
Vase, original colors, 12"..................$940.00
Vase, original colors, 8"..................$550.00
Vase, red, cobalt, or ivory, 12", minimum value....$1,200.00
Vase, red, cobalt or ivory, 10", minimum value..................$800.00
Vase, red, cobalt or ivory, 8", minimum value..................$600.00

Kitchen Kraft

Bowl, mixing; light green or yellow, 10"..................$85.00
Bowl, mixing; light green or yellow, 6"..................$55.00

Bowl, mixing; red or cobalt, 10" **$95.00**
Bowl, mixing; red or cobalt, 6" **$65.00**
Bowl, mixing; red or cobalt, 8" **$82.00**
Casserole, individual; red or cobalt.........................**$145.00**
Casserole, light green or yellow, 7½" **$75.00**
Casserole, light green or yellow, 8½" **$90.00**
Casserole, red or cobalt, 8½"...................................**$100.00**
Covered jar, light green or yellow, lg.....................**$250.00**
Covered jar, light green or yellow, med...................**$220.00**
Covered jar, light green or yellow, sm.....................**$225.00**
Covered jar, red or cobalt, lg................................**$275.00**
Covered jar, red or cobalt, med..............................**$240.00**
Covered jar, red or cobalt, sm **$250.00**
Covered jug, red or cobalt.....................................**$220.00**
Fork, light green or yellow **$90.00**
Fork, red or cobalt **$100.00**
Plate, cake; green **$48.00**
Plate, cake; red or cobalt **$52.00**
Plate, pie; light green or yellow, 9"..........................**$40.00**
Plate, pie; red or cobalt, 10" **$45.00**
Plate, pie; red or cobalt, 9".....................................**$45.00**
Salt & pepper shakers, light green or yellow, pr........**$85.00**
Salt & pepper shakers, red or cobalt, pr...................**$95.00**
Server, cake; light green or yellow..........................**$100.00**
Server, cake; red or cobalt **$120.00**
Spoon, light green or yellow **$95.00**
Spoon, red or cobalt **$110.00**
Stacking refrigerator lid, light green or yellow............**$58.00**
Stacking refrigerator lid, red or cobalt **$68.00**
Stacking refrigerator unit, light green or yellow **$40.00**
Stacking refrigerator unit, red or cobalt....................**$45.00**

Finch, Kay

Wonderful ceramic figurines signed by artist-decorator Kay Finch are among the many that were produced in California during the middle of the century. She modeled her line of animals and birds with much expression and favored soft color combinations, often with vibrant pastel accents. Some of her models were quite large, but generally they range in size from 12" down to a tiny 2". She made several animal 'family groups' and some human subjects as well. After her death a few years ago, prices for her work began to climb.

She used a variety of marks and labels, and though most pieces are marked, some of the smaller animals are not; but you should be able to recognize her work with ease, once you've seen a few marked pieces.

For more information, we recommend *Collectible Kay Finch* by Richard Martinez, Devin Frick and Jean Frick; *The Collector's Encyclopedia of California Pottery* by Jack Chipman (both by Collector Books); and *Kay Finch Ceramics, Her Enchanted World*, by Mike Nickel and Cindy Horvath (Schiffer).

Club/Newsletter: *Kay Finch Collectors Club*
Mike Nickel and Cindy Horvath
P.O. Box 456
Portland, MI 48875; 517-647-7646; Dues $25 per year includes
4 issues of full color newsletter and free ads

Bowl, swan, #4956, green interior, 6", from $125 to...**$150.00**
Dish, #5004, light green shell form **$45.00**
Figurine, Afghan, playing, #5555, sm......................**$350.00**
Figurine, angel, #114, pink, 4¾"...............................**$65.00**
Figurine, angel, #114, white w/sm blue flowers & wings.**$60.00**
Figurine, angels, 1 kneeling, 1 standing, #4909/#4910, 2-
    pc..**$200.00**
Figurine, birds, Mr & Mrs Bird, #453/454, pink & purple, 4",
    pr...**$175.00**
Figurine, cat, Jezebel, #179, pastel colors, from $250 to.**$275.00**
Figurine, cherub head, #212, from $65 to **$75.00**

Figurine, cat, Mehitable, #181, pink with vibrant pastel accents, 8½", $450.00.

Figurine, choir boy, kneeling, #211.............................**$85.00**
Figurine, Cocker Spaniel, #5260, 4½" **$300.00**
Figurine, cottontail bunny, #152, 2½", from $85 to **$95.00**
Figurine, donkey w/baskets, #4769, sm, from $90 to..**$100.00**
Figurine, doves, #5101/5102, white w/black details, 8x5",
    pr...**$200.00**
Figurine, duck, Mama, #472, 4" **$225.00**
Figurine, ducks, Peep & Jeep, #178A/B, 4", pr, from $100
    to...**$125.00**
Figurine, elephant, Mumbo, #4804, 5", from $160 to..**$175.00**

Figurine, Elephant, Peanuts, #191, pastel colors, $225.00.

Figurine, elephant, Popcorn, #192, 6¾", from $195 to ..**$235.00**
Figurine, fish, #5008, plain green, 7"..........................**$85.00**
Figurine, Godey Lady, #160, cream & blue, 7½" **$75.00**
Figurine, kittens, Muff & Puff, #182/183, pr..............**$150.00**

Figurine, lamb, #136, kneeling, white w/pink trim.....**$50.00**
Figurine, owl, Hoot, #187, 8¾" **$200.00**
Figurine, owl, Toot, #188, 5¾", from $100 to **$125.00**
Figurine, owl, Tootsie, #189, 3¾", from $45 to **$60.00**
Figurine, penguin, Polly, #467, 4¾" **$180.00**
Figurine, pig, Sassy, #166, 3½", from $85 to **$100.00**
Figurine, pig, Smiley, #164, 7x8", from $250 to **$300.00**
Figurine, rooster, Chanticleer, #129, 11" **$395.00**
Figurine, rooster & hen, Butch & Biddy, #176/177, 8½", 5½",
    pr, from $220 to..**$250.00**
Figurine, Scandy Girl, #126, 5¼", from $50 to **$75.00**
Figurine, Squirrel, 1¾" **$45.00**
Lapel pin, Afghan head, #5081 ....**$300.00**
Mug, Santa on white, from $80 to............................**$100.00**
Planter, baby bassinette, #104B, pink **$95.00**
Planter, block w/blue bear, Baby's First Series, #B106 .**$125.00**
Plaque, pomeranian, #4955, square, 4¾", from $50 to ...**$60.00**
Vase, flared oval, white w/green ivy, 10½x10x6" **$125.00**
Vase, lavender, footed, straight taper to top, incised mark,
    9" **$60.00**

Fire-King

This is an area of collecting interest that you can enjoy without having to mortgage the home place. In fact, you'll be able to pick it up for a song, if you keep your eyes peeled at garage sales and swap meets.

Fire-King was a trade name of the Anchor Hocking Glass Company, located in Lancaster, Ohio. As its name indicates, this type of glassware is strong enough to stand up to high oven temperatures without breakage. From the early forties until the mid-seventies, they produced kitchenware, dinnerware, and restaurant ware in a variety of colors. (We'll deal with two of the most popular of these colors, peach lustre and Jad-ite, later on in the book.) Blues are always popular with collectors, and Anchor Hocking made two, turquoise blue and azur-ite (light sky blue). They also made pink, forest green, ruby (popular in the Bubble pattern), gold-trimmed lines, and some with fired-on colors. During the late sixties they made Soreno in avocado green to tie in with home-decorating trends.

Bubble (made from the thirties through the sixties) was produced in just about every color Anchor Hocking ever made. You may also hear this pattern refered to as Provincial or Bullseye.

Alice was a mid-forties to fifties line. It was made in Jad-ite and a white that was sometimes trimmed with blue or red. Cups and saucers were given away in boxes of Mother's Oats, but plates had to be purchased (so they're scarce today).

In the early fifties, they produced a 'laurel leaf' design in peach and 'Gray Laurel' lustres (the gray is scarce), followed later in the decade and into the sixties with several lines made of white glass decorated with decals — Honeysuckle, Fleurette, Primrose, and Game Bird, to name only a few.

Anchor Hocking made ovenware in many the same colors and designs as their dinnerware. Their most extensive line (and one that is very popular today) was made in Sapphire Blue, clear glass with a blue tint, in a pattern called Philbe. Most pieces are still very reasonable, but some are already worth in excess of $50.00, so now is the time to start your collection. These are the antiques of the future! If you'd like to study more about Anchor Hocking and Fire-King, we recommend *Collectible Glassware of the 40s, 50s, and 60s*, by Gene Florence, and *Fire-King Fever '97* by April Tvorak.

See also Jad-ite Kitchen Collectibles.

Advisor: April Tvorak (See Directory Fire-King)

Newsletter: *The '50s Flea!!!*
April and Larry Tvorak
P.O. Box 126
Canon City, CO 81215-0126; 719-269-7230; Subscription: $5 per year for 1 yearly postwar glass newsletter; includes free 30-word classified ad

Alice, cup & saucer, blue trim **$12.00**
Alice, cup & saucer, white or ivory.............................**$8.00**
Alice, plate, dinner; blue trim.....................................**$24.00**
Alice, plate, dinner; white or ivory **$20.00**
American Artware, bowl, console; fired-on color, 10½" .**$22.00**
American Artware, jewel box, fired-on color, ivory rose
    lid **$20.00**
American Artware, leaf & blossom dessert set, fired-on
    color **$9.00**
Apple Blossom, bowl, cereal; 5"..................................**$6.00**
Apple Blossom, cake pan, round **$14.00**
Apple Blossom, casserole, round w/clear lid, 1-pt **$12.00**
Apple Blossom, custard cup **$4.00**
Apple Blossom, mug **$7.00**
Apple Blossom, refrigerator jar, 4x8".........................**$12.00**
Bubble, bowl, cereal; forest green or ruby red, 5¼" ..**$10.00**
Bubble, bowl, vegetable; crystal or white **$10.00**
Bubble, cup & saucer, sapphire blue, forest green or ruby
    red..**$8.00**
Bubble, plate, dinner; crystal or white.........................**$6.00**
Bubble, plate, dinner; forest green or ruby red **$20.00**
Bubble, platter, oval, forest green or ruby red...........**$18.00**
Bubble, tumbler, water; forest green or ruby red, 9-oz ...**$9.00**
Charm, bowl, serving; Azur-ite or Forest Green **$16.00**
Charm/Square, bowl, dessert; Azur-ite or Forest Green ..**$7.00**
Charm/Square, creamer & sugar bowl, Azur-ite or Forest
    Green **$14.00**
Charm/Square, cup & saucer, Azur-ite or Forest Green...**$3.00**
Charm/Square, plate, dinner; Azur-ite or Forest Green.....**$16.00**
Charm/Square, plate, luncheon; Azur-ite or Forest Green..**$7.00**
Charm/Square, plate, salad; Azur-ite or Forest Green ..**$5.00**
Charm/Square, platter, rectangular, Azur-ite or Forest
    Green **$20.00**
Decal Dinnerware, bowl, cereal; 5"..............................**$6.00**
Decal Dinnerware, bowl, serving.................................**$14.00**
Decal Dinnerware, creamer & sugar bowl, w/lid **$14.00**
Decal Dinnerware, cup & saucer...................................**$5.00**
Decal Dinnerware, plate, dinner; 9⅛" **$5.00**
Decal Dinnerware, snack set (cup & tray)....................**$6.00**
Distlefink, casserole, oval..**$25.00**
Fishscale, bowl, deep cereal; ivory or ivory w/trim, 5½" ..**$9.00**
Fishscale, bowl, soup; ivory or ivory w/trim, 7½" **$15.00**
Fishscale, plate, dinner; ivory or ivory w/trim, 9¼"......**$9.00**

Fruit, bowl, cereal; 5" $8.00
Fruit, utility pan, rectangular............$15.00
Gray Laurel, bowl, serving............$18.00
Gray Laurel, creamer & sugar bowl $12.00
Gray Laurel, cup & saucer $8.00
Gray Laurel, plate, dinner $8.00
Honeysuckle, creamer, 1958-1960 ....$8.00
Honeysuckle, plate, dinner; 1958-1960, 9⅛"............$5.00
Honeysuckle, sugar bowl, open, 1958-1960 ....$3.00
Jane Ray, bowl, deep-flanged cereal; Vitrock............$18.00
Jane Ray, bowl, sauce; ivory............$15.00
Jane Ray, cup & saucer, demitasse; white w/gold trim...$20.00
Jane Ray, cup & saucer, ivory............$15.00
Jane Ray, cup & saucer, Vitrock $12.00
Jane Ray, plate, dinner; ivory $15.00
Jane Ray, plate, dinner; Vitrock $12.00
Laurel, bowl, cereal; ivory............$12.00
Laurel, bowl, sauce $7.50
Laurel, bowl, serving; oval, ivory $22.00
Laurel, bowl, soup; ivory $16.00
Laurel, cup & saucer, ivory $8.00
Laurel, plate, dessert or sherbet; ivory............$8.00
Laurel, plate, dinner; Fire-King $8.00
Laurel, plate, dinner; ivory $8.00
Laurel, plate, grill; ivory, 3-compartment............$12.00
Laurel, plate, salad; ivory $10.00
Laurel, platter, ivory, oval, minimum value............$25.00
Laurel, salt & pepper shakers, ivory, footed, scarce, pr, minimum value............$45.00
Laurel, sherbet, ivory $8.00

Mugs, all 3½": Jad-ite, game bird or blue, $8.00 each.

Peach Luster, plate, serving; 11" dia............$12.00
Peach Lustre, bowl, cereal; swirled rim $5.00
Peach Lustre, bowl, soup............$9.00
Peach Lustre, mug, household............$3.00
Peach Lustre, plate, dinner............$6.00
Sheaf of Wheat, cup & saucer, crystal............$8.00
Sheaf of Wheat, plate, dinner; crystal $10.00
Soreno, bowl, deep, Avocado Green, deep, 5⅞"............$3.00
Soreno, butter dish, Avocado Green $12.00
Soreno, salt & pepper shakers, Avocado Green............$9.00
Swirl/Flat, bowl, cereal; Sunrise (ivory w/red-orange trim)............$9.00
Swirl/Flat, bowl, sauce; ivory............$5.00
Swirl/Flat, bowl, soup; ivory............$14.00
Swirl/Flat, creamer & sugar bowl, ivory, w/lid............$12.00
Swirl/Flat, creamer & sugar bowl, w/lid, Anniversary (white w/gold trim) $6.00

Swirl/Flat, cup & saucer, ivory............$8.00
Swirl/Flat, plate, dinner; ivory $7.00
Swirl/Flat, plate, salad; Azur-ite $6.00
Turquoise Blue, bowl, cereal; 5" $9.00
Turquoise Blue, bowl, mixing; Splash Proof, 4-qt, 9½" ..$15.00
Turquoise Blue, bowl, mixing; Splash Proof, 8½" $12.00
Turquoise Blue, bowl, teardrop mixing; 1-qt $20.00
Turquoise Blue, bowl, teardrop mixing; 3-qt $30.00
Turquoise Blue, bowl, vegetable............$12.00
Turquoise Blue, egg plate, gold trim $12.00
Turquoise Blue, plate, dinner; 9"............$8.00
Turquoise Blue, relish dish, 3-part, gold trim............$8.00

Fishbowl Ornaments

Mermaids, divers, and all sorts of castles have been devised to add interest to fishbowls and aquariums, and today they're starting to attract the interest of collectors. Many were made in Japan and imported decades ago to be sold in 5-&-10¢ stores along with the millions of other figural novelties that flooded the market after the war.

Boy on dolphin, brown hair & yellow suit w/brown trim on white dolphin, blue wave, 3¾" $28.00
Castle, blue castle (red cone-shaped tower roofs) bridged w/tan castle (flat tower roofs), green base, 3¾" ..$20.00
Castle, double rust & black roofs over tan & white arched opening w/trees on sides, 3¼"............$20.00
Castle, white fortress w/blue accents & rust roof on tan rock formation w/oval opening, 2¼"............$20.00
Castle, 2 towers connected by bridge, white w/tan & blue wash, 3", VG............$5.00
Diver, orange suit & helmet w/blue circular eyes, black & brown trim, 3¼"............$22.00
Diver holding dagger, white suit & helmet, blue gloves, brown boots, black airpack, 4¾"............$22.00
Fish, 2 white fish w/black & yellow eyes & black & tan accents on deep-blue wave base, 3¼"............$22.00
Mermaid, reclining on side w/hands behind head, brown hair w/green lower body, 4¾"............$45.00
Mermaid on snail, brown hair & blue lower body, white snail w/pink & blue wash, semi-gloss, 4"............$45.00
Mermaid on 2 seashells, reclining w/1 hand up to head & other resting on shell, blond hair w/blue lower body, 3½"............$10.00
Ornamental archways, tall slightly fanned archway connected to lower archway on wavy base, multicolor on white, 5", VG............$10.00
Pagoda, center tower w/orange knob atop blue roof connected to 2 smaller towers w/orange & green roofs, no base, 4"............$20.00
Pagoda, pink, roof over yellow & white archway next to yellow roof over blue archway on green grassy base w/tree, 4½"............$20.00
Pagoda, rust & black roof over white building w/steps leading to arched opening on rocky base w/palm tree, 3½"......$20.00
Torii gate, blue wave in between cream-colored gate, 3¾"............$20.00

Fisher-Price

Probably no other toy manufacture is as well known among kids of today than Fisher-Price. Since the 1930s they've produced wonderful toys made of wood covered with vividly lithographed paper. Plastic parts weren't used until 1949, and this can sometimes help you date your finds. These toys were made for play, so very few older examples have survived in condition good enough to attract collectors. Watch for missing parts and avoid those that are dirty. Edge wear and some paint dulling is normal and to be expected. Our values are for toys with minimum signs of such wear.

For more information we recommend *Modern Toys, American Toys, 1930-1980,* by Linda Baker; *Fisher-Price, A Historical, Rarity Value Guide,* by John J. Murray and Bruce R. Fox (Books Americana); and *Schroeder's Collectible Toys, Antique to Modern*, published by Collector Books.

Advisor: Brad Cassidy (See Directory, Toys)

Club: Fisher-Price Collector's Club
Jeanne Kennedy
1442 N Ogden
Mesa, AZ 85205; Monthly newsletter with information and ads; send SASE for more information

Snoopy Sniffer, #181, 1971, MIB, $50.00. (Photo courtesy of Doug Dezso.)

Adventure People & Their Wilderness Patrol, complete, #0307, 1975-79 ....$20.00
Adventure People Daredevil Sports Van, complete, #0316, 1978-82 ....$15.00
Adventure People Turbo Hawk, complete, #0367, 1982-83 ..$8.00
Bouncy Racer, #0008, 1960 ....$40.00
Bunny Bell Cart, #0604, 1954 ....$100.00
Bunny Cart, #0005, 1948 ....$75.00
Bunny Egg Cart, #0028, 1950..$75.00
Cash Register, 3 wooden coins, #0729, 1960..............$50.00
Chick Cart, #0407, 1950..$50.00
Cookie Pig, #0476, 1967..$50.00
Crackling Hen, white, #0120, 1958.............................$40.00
Cry Baby Dear, #0711, 1967-69....................................$40.00
Dollhouse w/lights, 3 stories w/5 rooms, has battery compartment & 7 outlets, #0280, 1981.......................$30.00
Fred Flintstone Xylophone, Sears only, #0712, 1962 ..$250.00
Humpty Dumpty, plastic, #0736, 1972-79 ....$8.00

Jack-in-the-Box Puppet, #0138, 1970-73 ....$30.00
Jenny Doll, vinyl face & hands w/cloth body, removable skirt, #0201, 1974-78...$40.00
Jiffy Dump Truck, squeeze bulb & dump moves, #0156, 1971-73 ....$30.00
Joey Doll, vinyl face & hands w/cloth body, w/jacket, lace & tie sneakers, #0206, 1975 ....$40.00
Kitchen Appliances, oven range w/exhaust, refrigerator & sink, #0252, 1978, each $2.00
Lady Bug, #0658, 1961-62 ....$55.00
Little People Main Street, w/figures & accessories, #2500, 1986-90 ....$40.00
Little People Playground, w/2 figures & accessories, #2525, 1986-90 ....$15.00
Mini Copter, blue litho, #0448, 1971-83 ....$25.00
Mother Goose, #0164, 1964-66 ....$40.00
Music Box, Teddy Bear's Picnic, plastic, #0792, 1980-81...$15.00
Music Box Iron, #0125, 1967-69 ....$50.00
Offshore Cargo Base, 3 platforms, 4 figures & accessories, #0945, 1979-80 ....$50.00
Oscar the Grouch, #0177, 1977-84 ....$30.00
Patch Pony, #0616, 1963 ....$50.00
Perky Penguin, #0786, 1973-75....................................$30.00
Pick-Up & Peek Puzzle, #0500, 1972-86 ....$10.00
Picture Disk Camera, 5 picture disks, #0112, 1968-71 ..$40.00
Piggy Bank, pink plastic, #0166, 1981-82 ....$20.00
Play Family Camper, 4 figures & accessories, #0994, 1973-76 ....$75.00
Play Family Circus Train, 1st version, w/figures, animals & gondola car, #0991, 1973-78.................................$25.00
Play Family Farm, 1st version, 4 wooden figures, plastic animals & accessories, #0915, 1968-91.....................$30.00
Play Family Hospital, w/figures & accessories, #0931, 1976-78 ....$115.00
Play Family Merry-Go-Round, plays Skater's Waltz, w/4 figures, #0111, 1972-76...$40.00
Play Family Pull-A-Long Lacing Shoe, 6 figures & 50" round lace, #0146, 1970-75...$45.00
Pocket Radio, Mulberry Bush, wood & plastic, #0758, 1970-72 ....$20.00
Pocket Radio, Whistle a Happy Tune, wood & plastic, #0763, 1978 ....$20.00
Push Pullet, 16" push stick, #0194, 1971-72................$25.00
Queen Buzzy Bee, red litho, #0444, 1959 ....$40.00
Roly Raccoon, waddles side to side, tail bobs & weaves, #0172, 1980-82...$15.00
Safety School Bus, Fisher-Price Club logo, 6 figures, #0983, 1959 ....$250.00
Sesame Street Characters, #0940, 1977, each.............$3.00
Smokie Engine, black litho, #0642, 1960 ....$75.00
Talky Parrot, #0698, 1963..$100.00
Teddy Zilo, #0734, 1964-66 ....$45.00
Timmy Turtle, green shell, #0150, 1953....................$100.00
Tote-A-Tune Radio, Toyland, #0795, 1984-91 ....$10.00
Tow Truck & Car, wood & plastic, #0718, 1969-70.....$30.00
Tractor, #0627, 1962..$50.00
Tuggy Turtle, #0139, 1959..$100.00
Woodsey's Airport, airplane, hanger, figure & 32-page book, #0962, 1980..$40.00

Fishing Lures

There have been literally thousands of lures made since the turn of the century. Some have bordered on the ridiculous, and some have turned out to be just as good as the manufacturers claimed. In lieu of buying outright from a dealer, try some of the older stores in your area — you just might turn up a good old lure. Go through any old tackle boxes that might be around, and when the water level is low, check out the river banks.

If you have to limit your collection, you might want to concentrate just on wooden lures, or you might decide to try to locate one of every lure made by a particular company. Whatever you decide, try to find examples with good original paint and hardware. Though many lures are still very reasonable, we have included some of the more expensive examples as well to give you an indication of the type you'll want to fully research if you think you've found a similar model. For such information, we recommend *Fishing Lure Collectibles* by Dudley Murphy and Rick Edmisten (Collector Books).

Advisor: Dave Hoover (See Directory, Fishing Lures)

Club: NFLCC Tackle Collectors
HC 3, Box 4012
Reeds Spring, MO 65737; Send SASE for more information about membership and their publications: *The National Fishing Lure Collector's Club Magazine* and *The NFLCC Gazette*

Pflueger Swimming Mouse, MIB, $25.00.

Creek Chub Crawdad #300, green body, black or red bead eyes, 2 treble hooks, 1916, 2¾"..............................**$25.00**
Creek Chub Fin Tail Shiner #2100, metal dorsal fin & fluted tail, spinners for pectoral fins, 2 treble hooks, 1930, 4"..**$175.00**
Creek Chub Giant Jointed Pikie Minnow #800, glass eyes, yellow 2-pc body, 3 treble hooks, 1957, 14"............**$55.00**
Creek Chub Husky Musky #600, multicolored metallic body, 2 treble hooks, 1925, 5"..**$85.00**
Creek Chub Pikie Minnow #700, red body, double line tie, hand-painted gill marks, 3 treble hooks, 1920, 4¼"...........**$25.00**
Heddon's Baby Crab Wiggler #1900, U-shaped collar, inch-worm line tie, 2 double hooks, 1916, 3⅛" **$75.00**
Heddon's Deep-O-Diver #7000, nail head on back for pork rind strip, 1 double hook, 1921, 2½" **$55.00**
Heddon's Dowagiac #210, collar attached by 3 screws, 2 double hooks, 1920, 3½"..**$25.00**

Heddon's Dowagiac Minnow #100, brass hardware, 3 belly weights, 3 treble hooks, 1905, 2¾"......................**$650.00**
Heddon's Dowagiac Minnow #100, fat body style, 2-pc toilet seat & surface rig, 3 treble hooks, 1917, 2⅝".......**$85.00**
Heddon's Killer #450, sm body, brass hardware, unmarked propellers, 3 treble hooks, 1905, 2⅝" **$275.00**
Heddon's Musky Surfusser #300, wire-through line tie & tail hanger, 6 treble hooks, 1939, 3¾"......................**$300.00**
Heddon's Musky Vamp #7600, lg box swivel line tie, lg body, 3 lg treble hooks, 1925, 8"..................................**$200.00**
Heddon's Salt Water Minnow #700, deep belly, many belly weights, heavy duty hardware, 3 treble hooks, 1911, 5"..........**$650.00**
Heddon's Spin-Diver #3000, diving lip & front prop combined w/fishtail body is unique, 3 treble hooks, 1918, 4½".**$450.00**
Heddon's Sucker Minnow #1300, cup rig or L-rig, 3 treble hooks, 1911, 5¾" **$950.00**
Jamison's Twin Spinner Bucktail, 1932 ....**$20.00**
Lure, Tad Poly, Heddon, perch finish, 1920s, 70% original paint, hooks are rusty, G **$37.00**
Millsite Paddle Bug, 1937, 2" **$15.00**
Millsite Wig Wag, 1946, 3"...**$15.00**
Moonlight Crawfish, hanging belly weight, rubber legs, painted tack eyes, 1 fixed double hook, 1929, 2¾"...**$125.00**
Moonlight Feather Minnow #1500, flat sloping back, feathered tail, 1 single hook, 1926, 1½".......................**$75.00**
Moonlight Zig-Zag, flat cup hardware, angled front, 3 treble hooks, 1914, 3½" **$40.00**
Paw Paw Bullfrog, diver, painted tack eyes, screw eye, cup hook hardware, 2 treble hooks, 1930, 2½" **$150.00**
Paw Paw Croaker Frog, real frog skin covering, 2 treble hooks, 1940, 3" **$55.00**
Paw Paw Natural Hair Mouse, deer hair body, 1 treble hook, 1930, 2½"..**$65.00**
Pflueger Baby Scoop #9300, sm glass eyes, 3 bladed props, 2 treble hooks, short wire leader, 1935, 3" **$35.00**
Pflueger Floating Monarch Minnow, bow-tie prop, see-through hook hangers, 2 treble hooks, 1906, 2¾" **$300.00**
Pflueger Flocked Mouse, lip of Mustang & tail of Wizard Wiggler, 2 treble hooks, 1950, 2¾" **$175.00**
Pflueger Kent Floater, raised painted wood eyes, Neverfail hook hardware, marked props, 3 treble hooks, 1915, 2¾".**$525.00**
Pflueger Live-Wire #7600, raised dorsal fin, faceted red glass eyes, marked pointed props, 3 treble hooks, 1931, 4¾".....**$40.00**
Pflueger Muskallonge, metal fins, wire-through construction, 3 lg single hooks, molded rubber, 1895, 7"........**$450.00**
Pflueger Peerless Minnow, tack/washer eyes, screw eye hook hangers, floppy front prop, 2 treble hooks, 1907, 3½".**$20.00**
Pflueger Simplex Minnow, bow-tie type prop, 1 treble hook w/bucktail hair, painted gills, 1907, 1¾"...............**$65.00**
Pflueger Soft Rubber Frog, hand-painted finish, loop end weed guards, 2 single hooks, 1907, 2⅞" **$65.00**
Shakespeare's Albany Floating Bait #64, no eyes, flat plate-hook hangers, 5 treble hooks, 1913, 5½"...........**$400.00**
Shakespeare's Frog Skin Jr #6505-S, real frog skin stretched over wood, 1 treble & 1 double hook, 1930, 3" .**$65.00**
Shakespeare's Musky Minnow #64, pointed props, flat plate hook hangers, 5 treble hooks, 1918, 5¼".........**$550.00**
Shakespeare's Pikie Kazoo #637, glass eyes, marked lip, hand-painted gill marks, 3 treble hooks, 1925, 4½"........**$65.00**

Shakespeare's Rhodes Rubber Frog, hand painted, flexible legs, 1 double & 2 single hooks, 1909, 3¼" **$225.00**

Shakespeare's Shiner #23, wire clip hook hangers, nose prop & feathered tail hook, 3 treble hooks, 1911, 2½" **$125.00**

Shakespeare's Slim Jim #52, belly hooks, scale-like finish, lg glass eyes, 3 treble hooks, 1930, 4½" **$80.00**

Shakespeare's Submerged Wooden Minnow #33, yellow glass eyes, wire clip hook hangers, 3 treble hooks, 1907, 2¾" **$125.00**

Shakespeare's Surface Wonder #42, collared, screw eye hardware, 3 treble hooks, 1910, 4" **$65.00**

Shakespeare's Waukazoo Surface Spinner #6555, pear-shape body, front prop, 2 treble hooks, 1930, 2½" **$65.00**

South Bend Fish-Oreno, NMIB, $30.00.

South Bend's Midget Lunge-Oreno #965, wire-through construction, tack eyes, stainless prop, 2 treble hooks, 1936, 3¾" **$65.00**

South Bend's Min-Oreno #926, tack eyes, cup rigged, flat body, metal lip w/wire leader, 2 treble hooks, 1933, 3" **$25.00**

South Bend's Minnow #999, glass eyes, tail cap, weighted nose, 2 treble hooks, 1929, 4" **$55.00**

Fitz & Floyd

If you've ever visited a Fitz & Floyd outlet store, you know why collectors find this company's products so exciting. Steven Speilberg has nothing on their designers when it comes to imagination. Much of their production is related to special holidays, and they've especially outdone themselves with their Christmas lines. But there are wonderful themes taken from nature featuring foxes, deer, birds, or rabbits, and others that are outrageously and deliberately humorous. Not only is the concept outstanding, so is quality.

Prices for Fitz & Floyd are on the rise due to the uncertainty of the company's future.

See also Cookie Jars.

Advisors: Phil and Nyla Thurston (See Directory, Figural Ceramics)

Bank, Cheshire Cat **$55.00**
Bank, Dinosaur, pink, green & white **$140.00**
Bank, Dracula **$45.00**
Bank, Platypus Duck **$45.00**
Bank, Porky Pig **$55.00**
Bank, Rolls Royce, ceramic, 1978 ....**$65.00**
Bookends (go w/Hershel Hippo) **$85.00**
Box, Christmas package, lid w/standing Santa on green bow **$50.00**

Candle holder, Kitchen Witch, each **$25.00**
Candy jar, Butler Cat **$35.00**
Candy jar, Christmas Car, w/Santa driver, marked FF 1987, 6" **$175.00**
Candy jar, Dancing Cats, 1992 ....**$35.00**
Candy jar, Frog w/Crown **$35.00**
Candy jar, Halloween Witch, 1988 ....**$50.00**
Candy jar, Santa & reindeer in Rolls Royce **$125.00**
Candy jar, Santa in airplane, from $195 to **$225.00**
Candy jar, sleeping pigs on lid, 1977 ....**$25.00**
Centerpiece, Sugar Plum Vase **$275.00**
Cookie jar, Runaway **$375.00**
Creamer, Purrdinand de Creme, Reigning Cats & Dogs series, 1990 ....**$45.00**
Lamp, Berenstein Bear **$30.00**
Lamp, Care Bear, blue **$25.00**
Mug, Polka Dot Witch **$55.00**
Pencil holder, cannon w/little boy holding ears, 1977 ..**$30.00**
Pitcher, Louis Cattorze, Reigning Cats & Dogs series, 1990 .**$75.00**
Pitcher, Snowman, marked FF 1¾ Qt, w/paper label **$80.00**
Planter, Santa figural **$30.00**
Salt & pepper shakers, Catnap, pr **$35.00**
Salt & pepper shakers, Courting Kitty Kottage, pr, from $25 to **$35.00**
Salt & pepper shakers, dinosaur, necks twist together, pr **$75.00**
Salt & pepper shakers, ear of corn, pr **$12.00**
Salt & pepper shakers, Halloween Hoedown Witch, 1992, pr **$25.00**
Salt & pepper shakers, Hershel Hippo, pr **$35.00**
Salt & pepper shakers, Kittens of Knightsbridge, pr, from $35 to **$45.00**
Salt & pepper shakers, leprechauns, pr **$75.00**
Salt & pepper shakers, mice, pr **$20.00**
Salt & pepper shakers, mice w/garlic, pr **$12.00**
Salt & pepper shakers, Owl & Pussy Cat, in boat, pr, from $65 to **$75.00**
Salt & pepper shakers, parrots, pr **$75.00**
Salt & pepper shakers, Polka-Dot Witch, pr, from $75 to.**$125.00**
Salt & pepper shakers, The Cat's Pajamas, pr, from $35 to..**$40.00**
String holder, Cat Snip, 1977 ....**$85.00**
Sugar bowl, Queen Isabulla de Mastiff, Reigning Cats & Dogs series, 1990 ....**$45.00**
Sugar bowl & creamer set, pig & rooster, 1987 ....**$65.00**

Teapot, cat holding fish, $75.00.

Teapot, Chips $65.00	Montgomery Wards, FL................................$24.00
Teapot, Cookie Factory $45.00	Schlitz, beer bottle shape $10.00
Teapot, Hippo Limpix, from $55 to..............$65.00	USA Lite Red Head, red glass ring behind lens $52.00
Teapot, Mad Hatter......................................$90.00	Winchester, 20-gauge shotgun shell....................$52.00

Teapot, Marie Catoinette, Reigning Cats & Dogs series, 1990..**$85.00**
Teapot, Miss Kitty, Kittens of Knightsbridge, from $65 to..**$75.00**
Teapot, Paw De Deux, Reigning Cats & Dogs series, 1990...**$85.00**
Teapot, Platypus Duck **$150.00**
Teapot, Polka Dot Witch................................**$175.00**
Teapot, Rio Rita, from $150 to......................**$165.00**
Teapot, Santa in Volkswagon, marked FF 32-oz on bottom..**$150.00**
Teapot, Snowman, green scarf forms handle, broom-handle spout...**$75.00**
Trinket box, Catnap......................................**$45.00**
Utensil holder, mouse w/mixing bowl........................**$35.00**

Flashlights

The Acme Electric Lamp was the first known electric device to use the D battery which was introduced in 1896. The flashlight was invented in 1898 and produced by the Eveready Company for 98 years. Eveready dominated the flashlight market for most of that period but more than 125 other US flashlight companies have come and gone to provide competition along the way. Add to that number over 35 known foreign flashlight manufacturers and you have over 1,000 different models of flashlights to collect. Flashlights come in a wide variety of styles, shapes and sizes. The flashlight field includes tubular, lanterns, figural, novelty, litho, etc. At present, over 45 categories of collectible flashlights have been identified.

Advisor: Bill Utley (See Directory, Flashlights)

Club/Newsletter: Flashlight Collector Club and Newsletter
Bill Utley
P.O. Box 4095
Tustin, CA 92781; 714-730-1252 or Fax 714-505-4067; Subscription: $12 for 4 issues per year

Acme Lamp Comp, lantern, 1896..............................$325.00
Bright Star, watch flashlight $75.00
Embury, lantern, patent 1-10-24 ....$24.00
Eveready, Baby flashlight, 2-C cell, 1902..................$175.00
Eveready, Ceiling Projection clock............................$400.00
Eveready, Masterlite, table model................................$55.00
Eveready, pistol style, gun-metal color, 1914 ....$36.00
Eveready, puzzle light, Is That You Santa?, ...$75.00
Eveready, vest-pocket style, sterling, 1904 ....$150.00
Eveready, Wood lantern, 1911 ....$65.00
Eveready, 3-D, 'Glove Catch' switch, 3 patent dates ..$75.00
Franco, pistol style, patented 1-7-08, made ca 1913...$45.00
Franco, vest-pocket style, green glass button switch..$25.00
Fumalux, Flashlight 400, combination flashlight & cigarette lighter..$22.00
Jack Armstrong, black case $35.00
Jenks, Railroad lantern, brass, July 25, 1911................$75.00

Florence Ceramics

During the forties, Florence Ward began modeling tiny ceramic children as a hobby at her home in Pasadena, California. She was so happy with the results that she expanded, hired decorators, and moved into a larger building where for two decades she produced the lovely line of figurines, wall plaques, busts, etc., that have become so popular today. The 'Florence Collection' featured authentically detailed models of such couples as Louis XV and Madame Pompadour, Pinkie and Blue Boy, and Rhett and Scarlett. Nearly all of the Florence figures have names which are written on their bases.

Many figures are decorated with 22k gold and lace. Real lace was cut to fit, dipped in a liquid material called slip, and fired. During the firing it burned away, leaving only hardened ceramic lace trim. The amount of lacework that was used is one of the factors that needs to be considered when evaluating a 'Florence.' Size is another. Though most of the figures you'll find today are singles, a few were made as groups, and once in awhile you'll find a lady seated on a divan. The more complex, the more expensive.

If you'd like to learn more about the subject, we recommend *The Collector's Encyclopedia of California Pottery* by Jack Chipman; and *The Florence Collectibles, An Era of Elegance,* by Doug Foland.

Advisor: Doug Foland (See Directory, Florence Ceramics)

Eugenia, teal with gold, 9", from $300.00 to $350.00.

Abigail, blue or green, 8½", each, from $175 to.......**$200.00**
Angel, 7", from $80 to..**$100.00**
Bea, from $150 to..**$175.00**
Beth, 7¼", from $175 to..**$200.00**
Boy, modern, bust form, 9¾", from $250 to **$275.00**
Boy, w/ice cream cone, 7½", from $250 to..............**$300.00**
Camille, w/card in hand, 8½", from $350 to............**$400.00**
Catherine, seated at settee, 8x7", from $600 to........**$650.00**

Charmaine, white, 9", from $275 to $300.00
Chinese couple, flower holders, black & white, 8", pr..$150.00
Cindy, fancy, 8", from $175 to...............................$200.00
Clarissa, gold trim, 8", from $175 to.....................$200.00
David, white w/gold trim, 7½", from $225 to $250.00
Delia, gold trim, 7½", from $190 to $225.00
Doralee, white, 8½", from $300 to...........................$375.00
Emily, flower holder, 8", from $40 to.......................$50.00
Eugenia, wine w/gold, 9", from $300 to...................$350.00
Girl in pinafore, 7", from $150 to............................$175.00
Irene, white, 6", from $150 to.................................$175.00
Jim, 6¼"..$90.00
John Alden, 9¼", from $250 to.................................$300.00
Josephine, blue, 9", from $150 to............................$200.00
June, planter...$50.00
Karla, ballerina, 9¾", from $300 to $425.00
Lillian, pink, 8", from $125 to.................................$200.00
Linda Lou, 8", from $125 to $200.00
Madeline, gray, 9", from $250 to.............................$375.00
Madonna, white w/gold, from $175 to $225.00
Marilyn, w/hat box, pink, 8½", from $175 to...........$300.00
Mimi, planter...$50.00
Musette, red, 9", from $200 to $250.00
Nancy, bud vase..$50.00
Pamela, youth figure, w/basket, 7¼", from $150 to .$175.00
Patsy, planter, 6"..$50.00
Peasant girl, w/2 baskets, 8¾"..................................$70.00
Peasant man, flower holder, w/flower cart, lg, from $175
    to...$225.00
Pin box, sm, from $125 to $175.00
Planter, swan form, matt white, 12", from $300 to ...$375.00
Prima Donna, maroon, from $300 to $425.00
Prom girl, 9", from $300 to $400.00
Richard, w/white cape, 8¼", from $200 to...............$300.00
Roberta, moss, 8½", from $200 to $275.00
Scarlett, articulated fingers, ornate, red w/gold, 9", from $300
    to...$375.00
Sue, white w/gold, from $125 to..............................$150.00
Vase, cornucopia, pink, from $95 to.........................$125.00

Victor, maroon and white, 10", $250.00.

Victoria, burgundy dress, gray sofa, 8½x7", from $350
    to...$400.00
Vivian, green, 9½", from $300 to $375.00

Wendy, planter, 6"...$50.00
Wynken, 5½", from $125 to.......................................$150.00

Flower Frogs

Nearly every pottery company and glasshouse in America produced their share of figural flower 'frogs,' and many were imported from Japan as well. They were probably most popular from about 1910 through the 1940s, coinciding not only with the heyday of American glass and ceramics, but with the gracious, much less hectic style of living the times allowed. Way before a silk flower or styrofoam block was ever dreamed of, there were fresh cut flowers on many a dining room sideboard or table, arranged in shallow console bowls with matching frogs such as we've described in the following lines.

See also specific pottery and glass companies.

Advisor: Nada Sue Knauss (See Directory, Flower Frogs)

Bird, black w/white face & breast, orange beak, on forked
    tan stump, lustre finish, Japan, 4½" $28.00
Bird, red w/black mask & beak, white under his tail, on blue
    stump, lustre & glossy finish, Japan, 5¼" $28.00
Bird, red w/yellow breast & orange beak on irregular 2½" dia
    base, Made in Japan, 3¼" $12.00
Bird, wings outstretched, aqua semi-matt, 4x3¼", in 8x10"
    leaf-motif bowl marked Camark..........................$38.50
Birds, row of 3, blue lustre w/yellow breasts, orange &
    white on face, on blue lustre branch, Made in Japan,
    4x3¾x2"..$20.00
Birds, 1 blue & white, 1 white, both w/orange beaks, on tan
    stump w/ivy & berries, lustre finish, Japan, 5¾"..$28.00
Blue jay, blue lustre w/yellow breast, on orange lustre logs, +7½"
    bowl w/floral & bird decor, Hand-painted Japan.......$45.00
Crane pr on perch, +lotus bowl, white semi-matt, Camark,
    11" $50.00
Dancing lady, 6½", attached scalloped 5" dia bowl, white
    w/hint of yellow on sides, from $15 to $25.00
Duck pr, white w/orange bills on tan stump, lustre finish,
    Japan, 5" $28.00
Flower bud, yellow w/blue center w/2 green leaves on blue
    base, lustre & glossy finish, Japan, 2½" $22.00
Frog, blue lustre w/yellow belly, front legs on pink flower,
    orange lustre base, hand-painted, Made in Japan,
    3x2¾"..$15.00
Lotus bud, cupped in 2 rings of green petals, glossy finish,
    Japan, 4½" $18.00
Oriental lady, 13", lime green, on 3½" dia base, ca 1940-
    50s...$15.00
Pelican, yellow lustre body, orange glossy wings & crest, blue
    lustre stump, Made in Japan, 3x2½", from $8 to........$10.00
Pelican, yellow w/orange & black wings & turquoise crest atop
    tied log pylon, glossy finish, Made in Japan, 4".......$12.00
Penguin pr, blue lustre w/pale yellow breasts, on pearl lustre
    ice/snow base, marked Made in Japan, 4¾x3¾" $25.00
Rosebud, pink w/yellow edges on blue leaf & stem, +3-lobed
    yellow & blue lustre bowl w/candle holders, Japan, 6",
    $35 to $45.00

Rosebud, pink w/yellow edges on blue leaf & stem, tan base, lustre finish, Japan, 2½" **$22.00**

Scarf dancer, Deco, lime green, 9", on 4¾x3½" base, from $15 to...**$25.00**

Scarf dancer, nude, white semi-matt, 6½", on 2½x3½" oval base, from $15 to...**$25.00**

Scarf dancer, teal, 7½", w/attached 6x4½" scalloped bowl, Yankoware, ca 1920s, 7½" **$20.00**

Scarf dancer, white semi-matt, 6¼x4¾", from $15 to .**$25.00**

Songbird, blue lustre w/pale yellow breast & red beak sitting on orange lustre stumps, 3x2¼x1⅞", from $8 to.**$12.00**

Turtle on rock, glossy terra-cotta red finish, Rushmore Pottery, 3½"..**$35.00**

Water lily, orange & yellow, green leaves on side, on irregular square base, Japan, 2½x3¼x2¼", from $10 to.**$12.00**

Water lily leaf, dark green, old, 1½x4x4" **$22.50**

Rosebud, pastel colors with lustre finish, 3-lobed bowl with candle holder, Japan, 6" dia, from $35.00 to $45.00.

Fostoria

This was one of the major glassware producers of the twentieth century. They were located first in Fostoria, Ohio, but by the 1890s had moved to Moundsville, West Virginia. By the late thirties, they were recognized as the largest producers of handmade glass in the world. Their glassware is plentiful today and, considering its quality, not terribly expensive.

Though the company went out of business in the mid-eighties, the Lancaster Colony Company continues to use some of the old molds — herein is the problem. The ever-popular American and Coin Glass patterns are currently in production, and even experts have trouble distinguishing the old from the new. Before you invest in either line, talk to dealers. Ask them to show you some of their old pieces. Most will be happy to help out a novice collector. Read *Elegant Glassware of the Depression Era* by Gene Florence; *Fostoria, An Identification and Value Guide,* by Ann Kerr; and *Fostoria Stemware, The Crystal for America,* by Milbra Long and Emily Seate. If there is a Fostoria outlet within driving distance, it will be worth your time just to see what is being offered there.

You'll be seeing lots of inferior 'American' at flea markets and (sadly) antique malls. It's often priced as though it is American, but in fact it is not. It's been produced since the 1950s by Indiana Glass who calls it 'Whitehall.' Watch for pitchers with only two mold lines, they're everywhere. (Fostoria's had three.) Remember that Fostoria was handmade, so their pieces were fire polished. This means that if the piece you're examining has sharp, noticeable mold lines, be leery. There are other differences to watch for as well. Fostoria's footed pieces were designed with a 'toe,' while Whitehall feet have a squared peg-like appearance. The rays are sharper and narrower on the genuine Fostoria pieces, and the glass itself has more sparkle and life. And if it weren't complicated enough, the Home Interior Company sells 'American'-like vases, covered bowls, and a footed candy dish that were produced in a foreign country, but at least they've marked theirs.

Coin Glass was originally produced in crystal, red, blue, emerald green, olive green, and amber. It's being reproduced today in crystal, green (darker than the original), blue (a lighter hue), and red. Though the green and blue are 'off' enough to be pretty obvious, the red is close. Beware. Here are some (probably not all) of the items currently in production: bowl, 8" diameter; bowl, 9" oval; candlesticks, 4½"; candy jar with lid, 6¼"; creamer and sugar bowl; footed comport; wedding bowl, 8¼". Know your dealer!

Numbers included in our descriptions were company-assigned stock numbers that collectors use as a means to distinguish variations in stems and shapes.

Advisor: Debbie Maggard (See Directory, Elegant Glassware)

Newsletter/Club: *Facets of Fostoria*
Fostoria Glass Society of America
P.O. Box 826
Moundsville, WV 26041; Membership: $12.50 per year

American, crystal, ashtray, oval, 3⅞"...........................**$12.00**
American, crystal, bowl, boat shape, 12".....................**$17.50**
American, crystal, bowl, vegetable; oval, 9" **$25.00**
American, crystal, candlestick, octagon footed, 6".....**$25.00**
American, crystal, cigarette box, w/lid, 4¾" **$37.50**
American, crystal, comport, 5¼x9½"............................**$35.00**
American, crystal, creamer, individual, 4¾-oz.............**$9.00**
American, crystal, hat, tall, 3" **$25.00**
American, crystal, napkin ring......................................**$10.00**
American, crystal, nappy, 4½" **$12.00**
American, crystal, pitcher, flat, 1-pt, 5⅜" **$35.00**
American, crystal, plate, bread & butter; 6"...............**$12.00**
American, crystal, plate, torte; 14"..............................**$30.00**
American, crystal, saucer..**$3.00**
American, crystal, syrup, w/drip-proof top.................**$45.00**
American, crystal, tumbler, juice; footed, #2056, 5-oz, 4¾"..**$12.00**
American, crystal, vase, flared rim, 6½".......................**$15.00**
American, crystal, vase, straight side, 10" **$90.00**
American, sugar bowl, handled, 3¼" **$12.00**
Baroque, blue, bowl, flared, 12"...................................**$40.00**
Baroque, blue, bowl, square, 6"...................................**$20.00**
Baroque, blue, mayonnaise, w/liner, 5½"....................**$55.00**
Baroque, blue, stem, water; 9-oz, 6¾" **$27.50**
Baroque, crystal, bowl, handled, 8½" **$14.00**
Baroque, crystal, plate, torte; 14" **$13.00**
Baroque, crystal, plate, 6" **$3.00**
Baroque, yellow, bowl, handled, 4 styles, 4".............**$20.00**

Baroque, yellow, candle, holder, 8-lustre, 7¾" $75.00
Baroque, yellow, creamer, individual, 3¼" $25.00
Baroque, yellow, tumbler, cocktail; footed, 3½-oz, 3"..$15.00
Buttercup, crystal, ashtray, individual, #2364, 2⅝".....$20.00
Buttercup, crystal, bowl, baked apple; #2364, 6"........$16.00
Buttercup, crystal, bowl, fruit; #2364, 13" $65.00
Buttercup, crystal, bowl, salad; #2364, 11" $55.00
Buttercup, crystal, candlestick, #2364, 6"...................$27.50
Buttercup, crystal, candlestick, duo; #6023, 5½".........$32.50
Buttercup, crystal, cheese stand, #2364, 5¾x2⅞"........$20.00
Buttercup, crystal, comport, #2364, 8" $35.00
Buttercup, crystal, cup, footed, #2350½ $15.00

Buttercup, crystal, pitcher, 8½", $250.00.

Buttercup, crystal, plate, #2337, 6" $7.00
Buttercup, crystal, plate, #2337, 8½"..........................$17.50
Buttercup, crystal, plate, crescent salad; #2364, 7¼x4½"...$40.00
Buttercup, crystal, plate, torte; #2364, 14" $45.00
Buttercup, crystal, relish, 2-part, #2364, 6½x5" $22.50
Buttercup, crystal, shaker, #2364, 2⅝" $32.50
Buttercup, crystal, stem, claret/wine; #6030, 3½-oz, 6"....$32.50
Buttercup, crystal, stem, low sherbet; #6030, 6-oz, 4⅜"...$17.50
Buttercup, crystal, sugar bowl, footed, #2350, 3⅛".....$13.00
Buttercup, crystal, vase, footed, #6021, 6" $65.00
Camelia, crystal, bonbon, 3-footed, 7¼".....................$25.00
Camelia, crystal, bowl, flared, 12" $52.50
Camelia, crystal, bowl, handled, 4½"..........................$15.00
Camelia, crystal, bowl, lily pond; 9"...........................$35.00
Camelia, crystal, bowl, salad; 10½"............................$47.50
Camelia, crystal, candlestick, triple; 7¾"....................$45.00
Camelia, crystal, cruet, w/stopper, 5-oz $50.00
Camelia, crystal, ice bucket......................................$75.00
Camelia, crystal, plate, bread & butter; 6½" $7.00
Camelia, crystal, plate, cracker; 10¾"..........................$30.00
Camelia, crystal, plate, dinner; 10¼"...........................$40.00
Camelia, crystal, platter, 12"......................................$47.50
Camelia, crystal, salt & pepper shakers, 3⅛", pr.........$40.00
Camelia, crystal, stem, high sherbet; #6036, 6-oz, 4¾" ..$15.00
Camelia, crystal, stem, oyster cocktail; #6036, 4-oz, 3¾"...$17.50
Camelia, crystal, sugar bowl, individual......................$10.00
Camelia, crystal, tray, for individual creamer & sugar bowl, 7⅛" $20.00
Camelia, crystal, tumbler, juice; footed, #6036, 5-oz, 4⅝"....$20.00
Camelia, crystal, vase, footed, #4143, 6".....................$65.00

Camelia, crystal, vase, footed, #5092, 8" $65.00
Century, crystal, ashtray, 2¾"....................................$10.00
Century, crystal, bowl, flared, footed, 10¾" $35.00
Century, crystal, bowl, flared, 12" $35.00
Century, crystal, bowl, fruit; 5" $14.00
Century, crystal, bowl, salad; 8½"..............................$25.00
Century, crystal, bowl, serving; oval, 9½" $32.50
Century, crystal, bowl, 3-footed, triangular, 7⅛".........$15.00
Century, crystal, candlestick, 4½"...............................$17.50
Century, crystal, ice bucket.......................................$65.00
Century, crystal, pitcher, 48-oz, 7⅛"...........................$97.50
Century, crystal, plate, cracker; 10¾" $30.00
Century, crystal, plate, dinner; 10½" $32.00
Century, crystal, plate, party; w/indent for cup, 8".....$25.00
Century, crystal, preserve, w/lid, 6" $35.00
Century, crystal, salt & pepper shakers, 3⅛", pr.........$20.00
Century, crystal, stem, cocktail; 3½-oz, 4⅛"................$20.00
Century, crystal, stem, sherbet; 5½-oz, 4½" $12.00
Century, crystal, sugar bowl, individual.......................$9.00
Century, crystal, tray, for individual creamer & sugar bowl, 7⅛"..$14.00
Century, crystal, tumbler, juice; footed, 5-oz, 4¾" $22.50
Chintz, crystal, bonbon, #2496, 7⅝"............................$32.50
Chintz, crystal, bowl, finger; #869, 4½" $55.00
Chintz, crystal, bowl, footed, #6023 ....$40.00
Chintz, crystal, bowl, fruit; #2496, 5" $30.00
Chintz, crystal, bowl, vegetable; #2496, 9½" $70.00
Chintz, crystal, candlestick, #2496, 4"........................$18.00
Chintz, crystal, candlestick, double; #6023 ....$37.50
Chintz, crystal, comport, cheese; #2496, 3¼" $25.00
Chintz, crystal, creamer, footed, #2496, 3¾"...............$20.00
Chintz, crystal, pickle dish, #2496, 8".........................$35.00
Chintz, crystal, plate, cake; handled, #2496, 10½"........$45.00
Chintz, crystal, platter, #2496, 12"..............................$95.00
Chintz, crystal, relish dish, 2-part, square, #2496, 6" ..$33.00
Chintz, crystal, relish dish, 5-part, #2419 ....$40.00
Chintz, crystal, sauce boat liner, oblong, #2496, 8" $30.00
Chintz, crystal, saucer, #2496 ....$5.00
Chintz, crystal, stem, water goblet; #6026, 9-oz, 7⅝" ..$32.50
Chintz, crystal, sugar bowl, footed, #2496, 3½" $16.00
Chintz, crystal, tray, for individual creamer & sugar bowl, #2496½, 6½"..$22.00
Chintz, crystal, vase, #4108, 5"...................................$85.00
Coin, amber, ashtray, center coin design, #1372/119, 7½"..$20.00
Coin, amber, ashtray, 5" $17.50
Coin, amber, bowl, oval, 9" $30.00

Coin, amber, cake stand, 110.00.

Coin, amber, candy box, w/lid, #1372/354, 4⅛" $30.00

Coin, amber, creamer, #1372/680 ....$11.00

Coin, amber, cruet, w/stopper, 7-oz............................$65.00

Coin, amber, lamp, chimney; courting, #1372/461......$50.00

Coin, amber, nappy, handled, #1372/499, 5⅜" $20.00

Coin, amber, pitcher, 32-oz..$50.00

Coin, amber, salt & pepper shakers, w/chrome tops, #1372/652, 3¼", pr $30.00

Coin, amber, sugar bowl, w/lid.....................................$35.00

Coin, amber, vase, bud; #1372/799, 8".......................$22.00

Coin, blue, ashtray, #1372/124, 10"............................$50.00

Coin, blue, cigarette box, w/lid, #1372/374, 5¾x4½"...$75.00

Coin, blue, jelly dish, #1372/448.................................$25.00

Coin, blue, pitcher, #1372/453, 32-oz, 6⅜"..............$105.00

Coin, blue, sugar bowl, w/lid, #1372/673...................$45.00

Coin, crystal, ashtray, #1372/110, 3"..........................$25.00

Coin, crystal, cigarette urn, footed, #1372/381, 3⅜" ...$20.00

Coin, crystal, lamp, patio; electric, #1372/466, 16⅝".$125.00

Coin, crystal, nappy, #1372/495, 4½"..........................$18.00

Coin, crystal, plate, #1372/550, 8" $20.00

Coin, crystal, punch cup, #1372/615 ....$30.00

Coin, crystal, salver, footed, tall, #1372/630, 6½".......$90.00

Coin, crystal, tumbler, double old fashioned; #1372/23, 10-oz, 5⅜"...$22.00

Coin, crystal, tumbler, iced tea/high ball; #1372/64, 12-oz, 5⅛"...$35.00

Coin, crystal, tumbler, juice/old fashioned; #1372/81, 9-oz, 3⅝"...$27.50

Coin, crystal, vase, footed, #1372/818, 10" $45.00

Coin, green, bowl, footed, #1372/199, 8½"...............$100.00

Coin, green, cruet, w/stopper, #1372/531, 7-oz $150.00

Coin, green, nappy, w/handle, #1372/499, 5⅜".........$40.00

Coin, green, urn, w/lid, footed, #1372/829, 12¾".....$200.00

Coin, olive, bowl, oval, #1372/189, 9" $30.00

Coin, olive, condiment tray, #1372/738, 9⅝"..............$75.00

Coin, olive, stem, goblet; #1372/2, 10½" $45.00

Coin, olive, stem, wine; #1372/26, 5-oz, 4" $45.00

Coin, ruby, candle holder, #1372/316, 4½", pr $50.00

Coin, ruby, creamer, #1372/738....................................$16.00

Coin, ruby, plate, #1372/550, 8" $40.00

Coin, ruby, stem, sherbet; #1372/7, 9-oz, 5¼" $60.00

Colony, crystal, bowl, handled, 5"................................$10.00

Colony, crystal, bowl, pickle; 9½".................................$15.00

Colony, crystal, bowl, round, 4½".................................$7.00

Colony, crystal, candlestick, 3½"..................................$12.50

Colony, crystal, cup, footed, 6-oz.................................$7.50

Colony, crystal, plate, bread & butter; 6".....................$4.00

Colony, crystal, saucer..$2.00

Colony, crystal, tumbler, footed, 12-oz, 5¾" $17.00

Corsage, crystal, bonbon, 3-footed, #2496, 7⅜".........$15.00

Corsage, crystal, bowl, finger; #869.............................$29.00

Corsage, crystal, bowl, handled, #2484, 10" $55.00

Corsage, crystal, candelabra, 2-light w/prisms, #2527...$65.00

Corsage, crystal, candlestick, duo; Flame, #2425, 6¾"..$37.50

Corsage, crystal, candy dish, w/lid, 3-part, #2496.......$85.00

Corsage, crystal, comport, #2496, 5½" $22.50

Corsage, crystal, cup, #2440...$18.00

Corsage, crystal, mayonnaise, 3-pc, #2496½ $45.00

Corsage, crystal, plate, #2337, 6½".............................$8.00

Corsage, crystal, plate, #2337, 9½" $37.50

Corsage, crystal, plate, #2364, 16" $75.00

Corsage, crystal, plate, cake; handled, #2496, 10" $32.50

Corsage, crystal, relish dish, 3-part, #2440................$35.00

Corsage, crystal, relish dish, 4-part, #2496................$37.50

Corsage, crystal, sauce tray, oval, #2440, 8½"............$35.00

Corsage, crystal, stem, claret; #6014, 4-oz, 7⅞"........$35.00

Corsage, crystal, stem, high sherbet; #6014, 5½-oz, 5⅜"..$22.00

Corsage, crystal, stem, oyster cocktail; 4-oz, #6014, 3¾"..$17.50

Corsage, crystal, tidbit, 3-footed, #2496 ....$15.00

Corsage, crystal, tumbler, water; footed, #6014, 9-oz, 5½"..$21.00

Figurine, bird, crystal, candle holder, 1½"..................$15.00

Figurine, cat, light blue, 3¾".......................................$35.00

Figurine, dolphin, blue, 4¾" $25.00

Figurine, duckling, walking, crystal, (beware of repro-ductions)..$15.00

Figurine, penguin, crystal, 4⅝".....................................$75.00

Figurine, squirrel, amber, running...............................$35.00

Figurine, whale, crystal $20.00

Heather, crystal, bowl, flared, 8" $32.50

Heather, crystal, bowl, handled, 4½" $12.00

Heather, crystal, bowl, salad; 10½"..............................$45.00

Heather, crystal, bowl, snack; footed, 6¼"..................$14.50

Heather, crystal, candlestick, 4½" $18.00

Heather, crystal, candy dish, w/lid, 7" $32.50

Heather, crystal, creamer, 4½" $10.00

Heather, crystal, ice bucket..$70.00

Heather, crystal, plate, dinner; sm, 9½" $30.00

Heather, crystal, plate, salad; 7½"................................$11.00

Heather, crystal, platter, 12" $52.50

Heather, crystal, relish dish, 2-part, 7⅜"......................$20.00

Heather, crystal, saucer $5.00

Heather, crystal, stem, cocktail; #6037, 4-oz, 5" $20.00

Heather, crystal, sugar bowl, footed, 4".......................$12.50

Heather, crystal, tidbit, upturned edge, 3-footed, 8⅛"..$30.00

Heather, crystal, tray, muffin; handled, 9½" $35.00

Heather, crystal, vase, #4121, 5"..................................$45.00

Heather, crystal, vase, handled, 7½" $75.00

Jamestown, amber or brown, bowl, dessert; #2719/421, 4½"...$8.50

Jamestown, amber or brown, butter dish, w/lid, #2719/3000, ¼-lb...$24.00

Jamestown, amber or brown, jelly dish, w/lid, #2719/447, 6⅛"...$32.50

Jamestown, amber or brown, plate, torte; #2719/567, 14".$26.00

Jamestown, amber or brown, sauce dish, w/lid, #2719/635, 4½"...$18.00

Jamestown, amber or brown, tray, muffin; handled, #2719/726, 9⅜"...$26.00

Jamestown, amber or brown, tumbler, tea; #2719/63, 11-oz, 6"...$10.00

Jamestown, amethyst, crystal or green, bowl, salad; #2719/211, 10"..$37.50

Jamestown, amethyst, crystal or green, celery dish, #2719/360, 9¼"..$32.50

Jamestown, amethyst, crystal or green, pitcher, ice jug; #2719/456, 48-oz, 7⅜"...$95.00

Jamestown, amethyst, crystal or green, stem, goblet; #2719/2, 5⅞"...$16.00

Jamestown, amethyst, crystal or green, stem, wine; #2719, 4-oz, 4⅜" **$20.00**

Jamestown, amethyst, crystal or green, tumbler, juice; #2719/88, 5-oz, 4¾" **$21.00**

Jamestown, blue, pink or ruby, bowl, serving; 2-handled, #2719/648, 10" **$55.00**

Jamestown, blue, pink or ruby, creamer, footed, #2719/681, 3½" **$24.00**

Jamestown, blue, pink or ruby, plate, #2719/550, 8" ..**$19.00**

Jamestown, blue, pink or ruby, salver, #2719/630, 7x10" .**$100.00**

Jamestown, blue, pink or ruby, stem, sherbet; #2719, 6½-oz, 4¼" **$16.00**

Jamestown, blue, pink or ruby, sugar bowl, footed, #2719/679, 3½" **$24.00**

June, crystal, bowl, cereal; 6" **$25.00**

June, crystal, goblet, wine; 3-oz, 5½" **$25.00**

June, crystal, plate, chop; 13" **$30.00**

June, pink or blue, creamer, footed **$25.00**

June, pink or blue, high sherbet, 6-oz, 6" **$35.00**

June, pink or blue, plate, salad; 7½" **$15.00**

June, yellow, candlestick, Grecian, 3" **$30.00**

June, yellow, plate, canape **$20.00**

June, yellow, sweetmeat **$25.00**

Lido, crystal, bowl, handled, square, 4" **$13.00**

Lido, crystal, bowl, 2-handled, 10½" **$45.00**

Lido, crystal, bowl, 3-footed, cupped, 6¼" **$20.00**

Lido, crystal, candlestick, duo; Flame, #2545, 6¾" **$37.50**

Lido, crystal, candlestick, duo; 4½" **$32.50**

Lido, crystal, comport, 4¾" **$17.50**

Lido, crystal, creamer..**$10.00**

Lido, crystal, cup, footed..**$15.00**

Lido, crystal, jelly dish, w/lid, 7½" **$55.00**

Lido, crystal, pickle dish, 8" **$17.50**

Lido, crystal, plate, cake; handled, 10" **$30.00**

Lido, crystal, plate, 7½" **$9.00**

Lido, crystal, relish dish, 3-part, 10" **$30.00**

Lido, crystal, stem, oyster cocktail; #6017, 4-oz, 3⅝" ..**$20.00**

Lido, crystal, stem, water; #6017, 9-oz, 7⅜" **$22.50**

Lido, crystal, stem, wine; #6017, 3-oz, 5½" **$27.50**

Lido, crystal, tidbit, 3-footed, flat, 8¼" **$20.00**

Lido, crystal, tumbler, old fashioned; #4132, 7½-oz, 3⅛" ..**$15.00**

Lido, crystal, tumbler, sham; #4132, 7-oz, 4⅛" **$12.00**

Lido, crystal, tumbler, water; footed, #6017, 9-oz, 5½" ..**$18.00**

Mayflower, crystal, bonbon, 3-footed, #2560, 7¼" **$22.50**

Mayflower, crystal, bowl, crimped, #2560, 11½" **$55.00**

Mayflower, crystal, bowl, finger; #869 ....**$20.00**

Mayflower, crystal, bowl, salad; #2560, 10" **$40.00**

Mayflower, crystal, candlestick, #2560½, 4" **$27.50**

Mayflower, crystal, candlestick, duo; #2560, 5⅛" **$35.00**

Mayflower, crystal, celery, #2560, 11" **$25.00**

Mayflower, crystal, cup, footed, #2560........................**$17.00**

Mayflower, crystal, olive dish, #2560, 6¾" **$15.00**

Mayflower, crystal, plate, #2560, 6" **$6.00**

Mayflower, crystal, plate, #2560, 7½" **$10.00**

Mayflower, crystal, plate, torte; #2560, 14" **$40.00**

Mayflower, crystal, saucer, #2560..................................**$5.00**

Mayflower, crystal, stem, claret; #6020, 5½-oz, 6⅛" ..**$35.00**

Mayflower, crystal, stem, oyster cocktail; #6020, 4-oz, 3¾" .**$20.00**

Mayflower, crystal, stem, wine; #6020, 3½-oz, 5⅜" **$30.00**

Mayflower, crystal, tray, muffin; handled, #2560, 10x8¼" ..**$32.50**

Mayflower, crystal, tumbler, iced tea; footed, #6020, 12-oz, 6⅜" **$25.00**

Mayflower, crystal, vase, footed, Flame, #2545, 10" ..**$125.00**

Meadow Rose, crystal, bowl, flared, handled, 5" **$18.50**

Meadow Rose, crystal, bowl, floating garden; oval, 10" .**$50.00**

Meadow Rose, crystal, bowl, handled, square, 4"......**$12.50**

Meadow Rose, crystal, candlestick, 5½" **$27.50**

Meadow Rose, crystal, candy dish, w/lid, 3-part **$100.00**

Meadow Rose, crystal, creamer, footed, 4¾"..............**$22.50**

Meadow Rose, crystal, ice bucket, 4⅜" **$100.00**

Meadow Rose, crystal, pickle dish; 8"..........................**$27.50**

Meadow Rose, crystal, plate, bread & butter; 6" **$11.00**

Meadow Rose, crystal, plate, cake; handled, 10" **$47.50**

Meadow Rose, crystal, relish dish, 2-part, square, 6"..**$32.50**

Meadow Rose, crystal, salt & pepper shakers, footed, #2375, 3½", pr..**$95.00**

Meadow Rose, crystal, saucer..**$6.00**

Meadow Rose, crystal, stem, low sherbet; #6016, 6-oz, 4⅜".**$24.00**

Meadow Rose, crystal, sugar bowl, individual **$16.00**

Meadow Rose, crystal, tray, for individual creamer & sugar bowl, #2496½, 6½" **$22.00**

Meadow Rose, crystal, tumbler, tea; footed, #6016, 13-oz, 5⅞" **$30.00**

Meadow Rose, crystal, vase, #4128, 5" **$75.00**

Navarre, blue or pink, dinner bell................................**$80.00**

Navarre, blue or pink, stem, saucer champagne; #6016, 6-oz, 5⅝" **$35.00**

Navarre, blue or pink, tumbler, tea; footed, #6106, 13-oz, 5⅞" **$40.00**

Navarre, crystal, bottle, salad dressing; #2083, 6½" ..**$225.00**

Navarre, crystal, bowl, finger; #869, 4½" **$45.00**

Navarre, crystal, bowl, footed, #2470½, 10½" **$57.50**

Navarre, crystal, bowl, nut; 3-footed, #2496, 6¼" **$18.50**

Navarre, crystal, candlestick, double; #2496, 4½" **$35.00**

Navarre, crystal, candlestick, double; Flame, #2545, 6¾" ...**$50.00**

Navarre, crystal, celery dish, #2496, 11" **$40.00**

Navarre, crystal, ice bucket, #2496, 4⅜" **$110.00**

Navarre, crystal, pickle dish, #2496, 8" **$27.50**

Navarre, crystal, plate, cake; oval, #2440, 10½" **$50.00**

Navarre, crystal, plate, cracker; #2496, 11" **$42.50**

Navarre, crystal, plate, salad; #2440, 7½" **$15.00**

Navarre, crystal, relish dish, 2-part, square, #2496, 6" ..**$32.50**

Navarre, crystal, relish dish, 5-part, #2419, 13¼" **$87.50**

Navarre, crystal, saucer, #2440....................................**$5.00**

Navarre, crystal, stem, cocktail/sherry; #6016, 6-oz, 6¼"..**$37.50**

Navarre, crystal, stem, oyster cocktail; #6016, 4-oz, 3⅝" ...**$27.50**

Navarre, crystal, stem, water; #6016, 10-oz, 7⅝".........**$30.00**

Navarre, crystal, sugar bowl, individual, #2496...........**$20.00**

Navarre, crystal, tumbler, water; footed, #6106, 10-oz, 5⅜".**$25.00**

Romance, crystal, ashtray, individual, #2364, 2⅝" **$12.50**

Romance, crystal, bowl, lily pond; #2364, 12"............**$45.00**

Romance, crystal, bowl, salad; #2364, 9" **$37.50**

Romance, crystal, bowl, shallow, oblong, #2596, 11".**$47.50**

Romance, crystal, candlestick, #2324, 4" **$17.50**

Romance, crystal, cigarette holder, blown, #2364, 2"..**$37.50**

Romance, crystal, comport, #2364, 8" **$40.00**

Romance, crystal, ice tub, #4132, 4¾" **$67.50**

Romance, crystal, plate, #2337, 6" **$8.00**

Romance, crystal, plate, sandwich; #2364, 11" $45.00
Romance, crystal, plate, torte; #2364, 16" $75.00
Romance, crystal, relish dish, 3-part, #2364, 10" $25.00
Romance, crystal, saucer, #2350..............................$5.00
Romance, crystal, stem, goblet; #6017, 9-oz, 7⅜" $25.00
Romance, crystal, stem, wine; #6017, 3-oz, 5½" $30.00
Romance, crystal, tumbler, footed, #6017, 12-oz, 6" ...$27.50
Romance, crystal, tumbler, oyster cocktail; footed, #6017, 4-oz, 3⅝" $17.50
Romance, crystal, vase, #2614, 10" $75.00
Romance, crystal, vase, footed, #4143, 6" $50.00
Starburst, crystal, plate, dinner $12.00
Trojan, pink, bowl, fruit; #2375, 5".........................$25.00
Trojan, pink, creamer, footed, #2375.....................$22.50
Trojan, pink, plate, chop; #2375, 13" $50.00
Trojan, pink, stem, oyster cocktail; footed, #5099.......$30.00
Trojan, pink, tumbler, footed, #5099, 5-oz, 4½".........$30.00
Trojan, yellow, bowl, bouillon; footed, #2375............$25.00
Trojan, yellow, bowl, centerpiece; footed, #2394, 12" ..$40.00
Trojan, yellow, bowl, whipped cream; #2375 ....$25.00
Trojan, yellow, grapefruit, #5282½.........................$45.00
Trojan, yellow, plate, bread & butter; #2375, 6"..........$5.00
Trojan, yellow or pink, saucer, AD; #2375.................$7.50
Versailles, blue, comport, #5099/2400, 6" $59.00
Versailles, blue, plate, dinner; #2375, sm, 9½" $40.00
Versailles, pink, green or yellow, parfait, #5098 or #5099...$40.00
Versailles, pink, green or yellow, plate, sauce boat; #2375...$25.00
Versailles, pink or green, bowl, cream soup; footed, #2375...$30.00
Versailles, pink or green, candlestick, scroll design, #2395½, 5"...$30.00
Versailles, pink or green, vase, #4100, 8" $110.00
Versailles, yellow, bowl, baker; #2375, 10"................$40.00

Franciscan Dinnerware

Franciscan is a trade name of Gladding McBean, used on their dinnerware lines from the mid-thirties until it closed its Los Angeles-based plant in 1984. They were the first to market 'starter sets' (four-place settings), a practice that today is commonplace.

Two of their earliest lines were El Patio (simply styled, made in bright solid colors) and Coronado (with swirled borders and pastel glazes). In the late thirties, they made the first of many hand-painted dinnerware lines. Some of the best known are Apple, Desert Rose, and Ivy. From 1941 to 1977, 'Masterpiece' (true porcelain) china was produced in more than 170 patterns.

Many marks were used, most included the Franciscan name. An 'F' in a square with 'Made in U.S.A.' below it dates from 1938, and a double-line script F was used in more recent years.

For further information, we recommend *The Collector's Encyclopedia of California Pottery* by Jack Chipman.

Advisors: Mick and Lorna Chase, Fiesta Plus (See Directory, Dinnerware)

Apple, ashtray, individual $22.00
Apple, bowl, batter...$395.00
Apple, bowl, fruit...$14.00
Apple, bowl, rimmed soup $31.00
Apple, bowl, straight sides, med $45.00
Apple, butter dish $45.00
Apple, celery dish, 3-part...$75.00
Apple, coffeepot $125.00
Apple, creamer, regular..$22.00
Apple, egg cup $35.00
Apple, jam jar..$80.00
Apple, jam jar, redesigned $135.00
Apple, napkin ring..$40.00

Apple, platter, oval, 14", $70.00.

Apple, salt & pepper shakers, rose bud, pr $29.00
Apple, teapot $100.00
Apple, tumbler, juice; 6-oz...$38.00
Autumn, creamer & sugar bowl $20.00
Autumn, cup & saucer $10.00
Autumn, pitcher, water...$30.00
Autumn, tidbit server..$6.00
Cafe Royal, bell, dinner..$90.00
Cafe Royal, bowl, vegetable; 8"..................................$22.00
Cafe Royal, cup & saucer, tall....................................$32.00
Cafe Royal, tea canister...$155.00
Coronado, bowl, cereal...$12.00
Coronado, bowl, vegetable; serving, oval.....................$20.00
Coronado, candlesticks, pr..$28.00
Coronado, cigarette box..$40.00
Coronado, cup & saucer, demitasse.............................$22.00
Coronado, nut cup, footed...$16.00
Coronado, plate, chop; 14"...$35.00
Coronado, plate, 6½"...$8.00
Coronado, plate, 8½"...$12.00
Coronado, platter, 15½"..$35.00
Coronado, salt & pepper shakers, pr $15.00
Desert Rose, ashtray, individual $20.00
Desert Rose, Bell, Danbury Mint.................................$125.00
Desert Rose, bowl, mixing; sm....................................$125.00
Desert Rose, bowl, vegetable; divided.........................$45.00
Desert Rose, bowl, vegetable; 8"................................$32.00
Desert Rose, box, heart shape....................................$165.00
Desert Rose, bud vase..$75.00
Desert Rose, compote, lg..$75.00

Desert Rose, creamer, regular.....................................$22.00
Desert Rose, cup & saucer, tea...............................$18.00
Desert Rose, gravy boat $32.00

Desert Rose, grill plate, $125.00.

Desert Rose, jam jar...$125.00
Desert Rose, mug, barrel shape, 12-oz $50.00
Desert Rose, piggy bank $295.00
Desert Rose, plate, chop; 12"..................................$75.00
Desert Rose, plate, divided; child size $195.00
Desert Rose, plate, 10½"..$25.00
Desert Rose, platter, 12¾"..$45.00
Desert Rose, teapot $125.00
Desert Rose, tumbler, juice; 6-oz $35.00
El Patio, bowl, fruit...$12.00
El Patio, creamer...$10.00
El Patio, plate, bread & butter $7.00
El Patio, saucer...$4.00
El Patio, sherbet..$10.00
Forget-Me-Not, bowl, soup/cereal...........................$25.00
Forget-Me-Not, platter, 11½" $36.00
Fresh Fruit, bowl, vegetable; 9" $48.00
Fresh Fruit, mug, 7-oz $30.00
Fresh Fruit, plate, salad; 8"......................................$21.00
Ivy, bowl, fruit $15.00
Ivy, compote, lg..$125.00
Ivy, pitcher, water...$175.00
Ivy, plate, 6½"...$12.00
Meadow Rose, pitcher, water; 2½-qt.........................$110.00
Meadow Rose, sherbet $22.00

October, platter, 14", $65.00; Creamer, $24.00; Sugar bowl, $30.00.

Poppy, gravy boat $90.00
Poppy, plate, chop; 12"...$100.00
Starburst, bonbon/jelly dish $22.00

Starburst, bowl, cereal $8.00
Starburst, bowl, divided, 8".......................................$25.00
Starburst, bowl, fruit..$7.00
Starburst, bowl, oval, 8"...$22.00
Starburst, bowl, salad; individual.............................$25.00
Starburst, bowl, salad; 12", from $80 to....................$100.00
Starburst, bowl, soup...$15.00
Starburst, butter dish...$45.00
Starburst, candlesticks, pr, $175 to $200.00
Starburst, casserole, med..$65.00
Starburst, chop plate, from $55 to.............................$65.00
Starburst, coffeepot...$135.00
Starburst, creamer, from $10 to.................................$15.00
Starburst, cup & saucer, from $8 to...........................$9.00
Starburst, gravy boat, from $20 to.............................$25.00
Starburst, ladle, from $25 to.....................................$35.00
Starburst, mug...$30.00
Starburst, pepper grinder, from $150 to....................$175.00
Starburst, pitcher, 7½", from $50 to...........................$65.00
Starburst, plate, dinner; from $10 to $12.00
Starburst, plate, 6½", from $5 to................................$6.00
Starburst, plate, 7½", from $6 to................................$8.00
Starburst, platter, 15", from $40 to............................$50.00
Starburst, relish, 3-part...$35.00
Starburst, salt & pepper shakers, sm, pr, from $18 to...$22.00
Starburst, salt & pepper shakers, tall, pr, from $22 to ..$28.00
Starburst, sugar bowl, w/lid......................................$20.00
Starburst, tumbler, 6-oz, from $40 to.........................$50.00
Starburst, TV tray, from $60 to $75.00
Strawberry Time, butter dish $55.00
Wildflower, ashtray, individual $40.00
Wildflower, casserole, 1½-qt......................................$350.00

Frankoma Pottery

This pottery has operated in Oklahoma since 1933, turning out dinnerware, figurines, novelties, vases, bicentennial plates and plaques, and political mugs in various lovely colors.

Their earliest mark was 'Frankoma' in small block letters; but when fire destroyed the pottery in 1938, all of the early seals were destroyed, so new ones had to be made. The new mark was similar, but slightly larger, and the 'O' (rather than being perfectly round) was elongated. Some of their early wares (1936–38) were marked with a 'pacing leopard'; these are treasured by collectors today. By the mid-1950s the mark was no longer impressed by hand but instead became part of the mold. Paper labels have been used since the late forties, and since 1942 nearly every item has had an impressed mold number.

The early clay was a light golden brown color; it was mined near the town of Ada, and collectors refer to this type of clay as 'Ada' to distinguish it from the red-firing Sapulpa clay that has been used since 1954, when Frankoma began digging their clay from another area of the neighboring countryside.

Their glazes have varied over the years due in part to the change in the color of the clay, so with a knowledge of the marks and color variances, you can usually date a piece with a fair amount of accuracy. If you'd like to learn more, we recommend *Frankoma Pottery, Value Guide and More*, by Susan Cox; and *Frankoma and Other Oklahoma Potteries* by Phyllis and Tom Bess.

Advisor: Susan Cox (See Directory, Frankoma)

Newsletter: *Frankoma Family Collectors Association*
c/o Nancy Littrell
P.O. Box 32571
Oklahoma City, OK 73123-0771
Membership dues: $20; includes newsletter and annual convention

Baker w/lid, Mayan Aztec, White Sand, 2-qt, #7V	**$24.00**
Bookends, Dreamer Girl, Prairie Green, Ada clay, pr	**$375.00**
Bowl, dogwood form, Prairie Green, 12"	**$22.00**
Bowl, willow leaf form, Jade Green, #225, 7"	**$22.00**
Bowl, willow leaf form, Prairie Green, #226, 11"	**$12.00**
Bowl & pitcher, Woodland Moss, #F30A/B, 5½", set	**$23.00**
Candelabrum, Rosetone, Ada clay, holds 5 candles, #306	**$100.00**
Candle holder, double cactus form, Prairie Green	**$22.00**
Canteen, Thunderbird, Red Bud, leather thong, #59, 6"	**$38.00**
Creamer, Wagon Wheel, Desert Gold, #94A	**$9.00**
Cup, Mayan Aztec, Woodland Moss, #7C	**$8.00**
Cup, Wagon Wheel, Desert Gold, #94C	**$10.00**
Cup & saucer, Mayan Aztec, Woodland Moss, #7C/E, set	**$13.00**
Cup & saucer, Wagon Wheel, Prairie Green, #94C/E, set	**$11.00**
Figurine, Circus Horse, Prairie Green, Ada clay, #138, 6"	**$125.00**
Figurine, English Setter, Ivory, #141, 8"	**$175.00**
Figurine, Farmer Boy, blue belted pants	**$95.00**
Figurine, Gardener Girl, yellow dress	**$90.00**
Figurine, swan, Black Onyx, #168, 3"	**$45.00**

Figurines, elephants, pink or green, 3", from $45.00 to $50.00 each.

Jar, Prairie Green, Ada clay, carved decor, #70, 5¼"	**$45.00**
Jug w/stopper, Prairie Green, pot & leopard mark, #86, 2-qt	**$140.00**
Mug, Elephant, Nixon-Agnew, Desert Gold, 1973	**$53.00**
Mug, Elephant, Nixon-Agnew, Flame, 1969	**$70.00**
Mug, Plainsman, Desert Gold, #5CL, 12-oz	**$5.00**
Pitcher, Fireside, Ada clay, #77Z, 17"	**$120.00**
Planter, cork bark treatment, Peach Glow, #B3, 4½"	**$17.00**
Planter, swan, Desert Gold, #228, 7½"	**$35.00**
Plaque, Bicentennial, White Sand, 1975, 8½"	**$55.00**
Plaques, Comedy & Tragedy, flat black, #118C/T, pr	**$95.00**
Plate, Christmas, 1969, Laid in a Manger, 8½"	**$80.00**
Plate, Christmas 1968, Flight Into Egypt, 8½"	**$85.00**
Plate, Christmas 1970, King of Kings, 8½"	**$85.00**
Plate, Easter, Oral Roberts, 1972	**$10.00**
Plate, Mayan Aztec, Woodland Moss, #7G, 7"	**$5.50**
Plate, Plainsman, Woodland Moss, #5GS, 6½"	**$5.00**
Platter, Wagon Wheel, Desert Gold, #94P, 16"	**$28.00**
Salt shaker, Wagon Wheel, Desert Gold, #94H	**$5.00**
Sugar bowl, Mayan Aztec, Desert Gold, tab handles	**$12.00**
Sugar bowl w/lid, Mayan Aztec, Woodland Moss	**$15.00**
Trivet, cattle brands, Desert Gold, Ada clay, #94TRC	**$14.00**
Trivet, horseshoes, Peach Glow, #94TRH, 6"	**$20.00**
Trivet, rooster, Woodland Moss, #94TR, 6"	**$14.00**
Tumbler, Ada clay, #80C, 4¾"	**$19.00**
Vase, Cactus, Desert Gold, Ada clay, #5, 6¾"	**$35.00**
Vase, fan shell shape, turquoise, Ada clay, #54, 6"	**$30.00**
Vase, free-form, Red Bud, Ada clay, #7, 7"	**$25.00**
Vase, Grecian, Prairie Green, Ada clay, #78, pot & leopard mark	**$145.00**
Vase, leaf handle, Ada clay, #71, 10"	**$100.00**
Wall pocket, acorn shape, Jade Green, #190	**$35.00**

Furniture

A piece of furniture can often be difficult to date, since many 17th- and 18th-century styles have been reproduced. Even a piece made early in the 20th century now has enough age on it that it may be impossible for a novice to distinguish it from the antique. Sometimes cabinetmakers may have trouble identifying specific types of wood, since so much variation can occur within the same species; so although it is usually helpful to try to determine what kind of wood a piece has been made of, results are sometimes inconclusive. Construction methods are usually the best clues. Watch for evidence of 20th-century tools — automatic routers, lathes, carvers, and spray guns.

For further information we recommend *Collector's Guide to Oak Furniture* by Jennifer George; *Heywood-Wakefield Modern Furniture* by Steven Rouland and Roger Rouland; *Collector's Encyclopedia of American Furniture, Vol I and II*, and *Furniture of the Depression Era* both by Robert and Harriett Swedberg; and *American Oak Furniture* by Katherine McNerney. All are published by Collector Books.

Bookcase, refinished walnut, cutout feet and scrolled apron, doubledoors with 8 panes of glass in each, cove molded cornice, 77", $1,100.00.

Armchair, Baroque style, early 1900s, 56" **$220.00**

Armchair, Boston style, oak w/spindle back, top & center slats, turned legs & front stretchers, 42" **$125.00**

Armchair, Chippendale-style wingback, blue & white floral upholstery (worn), reproduction, 39" **$165.00**

Armchair, Country ladderback, hardwood w/old refinishing, repairs to arm & spindles, replaced rush seat, 44x15"................**$95.00**

Armchair, Country ladderback, 4 arched slats, turned feet & stretcher, paper seat...**$275.00**

Armchair, Mission-style oak, even-arm cube, 3-slat sides, 33", VG..**$650.00**

Armchair, Mission-style oak, restored silk upholstery seat, 38" **$185.00**

Armchair, original mohair upholstery, Kroehler, 1930s, 33x35"...**$150.00**

Armchair, Queen Anne-style wingback, carved ball & claw feet, creweled linen upholstery, reproduction, 50½" **$330.00**

Armchair, upholstered shell (easy) type, hardwood frame w/carved designs, 1930s, 35x32" **$250.00**

Armchair, youth's, oak w/pressed back (horse design) in crest, 6 spindles, 38"...**$100.00**

Armchair rocker, maple, 4-slat back, turned finial, repainted, 44" **$110.00**

Armchair rocker, Windsor, bamboo scroll, shaped seat, 40½"..**$225.00**

Armchairs, Chippendale style, carved mahogany frames, yellow silk reupholstery (minor wear only), 39", pr.......**$2,200.00**

Armchairs, Sheraton style, walnut finish w/gold plush upholstery, modern reproduction, 38", pr....................**$185.00**

Bed, brass frame, polished finish, castors missing, 60x72x55"..**$60.00**

Bed, bunk; maple w/old finish, simple styling, Conant-Ball, late 1940s, 81x42" **$300.00**

Bed, day; Jenny Lind, walnut w/old dark finish, original rails, fitted as a couch w/cushions & bolster back, 28x72x31" **$200.00**

Bed, day; refinished maple & cherry, turned posts, spindles & rails, 25x60¾x24"..**$135.00**

Bed, figured walnut veneer w/bird's-eye maple overlay, router lines, hardwood frame, 1930s, 52x57" **$250.00**

Bed, mahogany veneer, 4-poster, incised lines & applied decor, 1930s, 50" headboard, 56" wide...............**$135.00**

Bed, Mission-style oak, 3 wide slats in head- & footboards, original finish **$200.00**

Bed, pencil-post style, birch w/pine headboard, refinished, 83x74x38"..**$250.00**

Bed, Sheraton canopy, birch & pine, tall posts, reproduction, single size..**$450.00**

Bedroom set, Baroque style, walnut burl veneer w/carved detail, bed+dresser+chest+stand+2 mirrors+dresser chair, 1950s...**$1,200.00**

Bedroom set, mahogany veneer, side swell drawer fronts, full bed+vanity w/round mirror+bench+chest, 1940s....**$600.00**

Bedroom set, Oriental walnut veneer & 2-tone diamond-matched zebrawood, waterfall top, late 1930s, full bed+vanity+chest **$600.00**

Bedroom set, solid walnut, late 1940s, full bed+vanity+vanity stool+chest-on-chest...................................**$850.00**

Bookcase, Art Deco, quarter-sawn white oak, 4 glass doors w/decorative hinges, open shelves, 59x74x13" **$88.00**

Bookcase, Country, refinished walnut, cut-out feet, scrolled apron, double 8-pane doors w/arched top panes, cornice, 77" **$1,100.00**

Bookcase, Golden Oak Era, leaded glass doors (1 cracked), 50x54x12½" **$500.00**

Bookcase, mahogany w/alligatored varnish, 4 stacking sections w/attached base & cornice, short cabriole legs, 52x35x12" **$440.00**

Bookcase, walnut, Victorian Eastlake with burl veneer, 3-shelf, 63x31x12" **$250.00**

Bookcase/desk combination, convex glass, swell top drawer over 3, 73x39x13" **$800.00**

Bookcase/desk combination, convex glass swell drawer, applied (grotesque) decor, 73x42x15"...............**$850.00**

Bookcase/desk combination, oak w/applied decorations, 3 scroll feet, inset mirror in top, 3 drawers, 72x37x12".........**$350.00**

Breakfast set, oak w/painted designs on table top & chair backs, 43x32" table+4 chairs...............................**$350.00**

Breakfast set, table w/porcelain top & white painted wooden base, 32x40x25"+leaf extensions, 1940s, +4 painted chairs **$185.00**

Cabinet, curio; French style, dark green-stained wood w/ormolu trim, glass shelves, mirror back, lighted interior, 56".**$440.00**

Cabinet, kitchen; Art Moderne, refinished natural oak w/porcelain work top, replaced pulls, 73x40x26"...............**$425.00**

Cabinet, sewing; plain-cut walnut veneer w/waterfall front, sides & drawer fronts of walnut-stained hardwoods, 24x16x12"...**$155.00**

Chair, bentwood balloon curved back (ice cream-parlor style), ca 1920s, 33" **$65.00**

Chair, Chippendale-style wingback, brocade upholstery (worn), square molded legs w/H stretcher, modern reproduction, 40" **$200.00**

Chair, desk; oak pressed back w/6 turned spindles, swivel seat on 4 casters, 45"...**$175.00**

Chair, kitchen; plain & quarter-sawn oak, arrowback w/stiles continuing from crest into side braces, 38" **$70.00**

Chair, side; Country Queen Anne, maple w/layers of old paint, turned legs, vase splat, yoke crest, rush seat, 38"....**$140.00**

Chair, side; English Chippendale style, carved walnut frame, upholstered seat, 39½" **$220.00**

Chair, side; English Country Queen Anne style, oak w/old dark finish, turned legs & front stretcher, 42" **$65.00**

Chair, side; mahogany veneer, vase splat, turned legs, upholstered seat, Rockford, 1920s, 43"...............................**$55.00**

Chair, side; maple w/curl, sabre legs, replaced cane seat, repaired frame..**$65.00**

Chair, side; oak, 7-spindle back w/shaped crest, depressed seat, 39" **$140.00**

Chair, side; oak bentwood style w/replaced round vinyl removable seat, 33"..**$90.00**

Chair, side; plain & quarter-sawn oak w/vase splat, no carvings, turned spindles, legs & stretchers 38" **$75.00**

Chair, side; Windsor, bamboo, 7-spindle back, repaired seat, 36½", G..**$60.00**

Chair, side; Windsor, 7-spindle bow-back, molded crest rail, saddle seat, old refinishing, 35½"......................**$200.00**

Chair, side; 4-pc matching burl walnut splat & walnut stained hardwoods, 1940s, 36".............**$65.00**

Chair, vanity; golden oak, low back, replaced cane seat, 28½".............**$125.00**

Chairs, dining; 3 flat slats, turned legs, upholstered seat, 1920s, 40", 4 for.............**$325.00**

Chairs, kitchen side; Windsor, old dark green (black) repaint, 32½", set of 4.............**$325.00**

Chairs, side; arrowback w/original dark brown paint, yellow stripes & floral decor, minor touchups, 33", 4 for..**$465.00**

Chairs, side; Chippendale style, mahogany w/old finish, carved backs, upholstered seats (worn), 35½", pr.............**$500.00**

Chairs, side; ladderback w/4 graduated slats, rush seats, 41", pr.............**$165.00**

Chairs, side; quarter-sawn oak, vase splats w/carvings, serpentine front legs, 39½", 4 for.............**$895.00**

Chairs, side; Queen Anne style, mahogany, modern reproductions, 39", pr.............**$330.00**

Chairs, side; Windsor, bamboo w/cage backs & medallions, old black repaint, JE Shores brands, 33¾", 3 for .**$330.00**

Chairs, side; Windsor, bamboo w/step-down crest, old dark green repaint w/white striping, 35½".............**$115.00**

Chaise lounge, French style, carved frame w/white crewel upholstery, 2-pc, modern reproduction.............**$225.00**

Chest, cedar; bleached mahogany w/waterfall front, marked Roos Chest, Forest Park, Illinois, 21x44x19".......**$225.00**

Chest, cedar; walnut & Oriental wood V-matched veneered waterfall, 1940s, 25x45x19".............**$200.00**

Chest, George Nelson, manufactured by Herman Miller, 5 vertical drawers in primavera finish on ebonized wooden legs, worn pulls, 39x40", VG, $800.00.

Chest, Sheraton, curly maple w/mahogany veneer facade, bow-front w/4 dovetailed drawers, repairs, 40x39x21"...**$660.00**

Chest of drawers, Country Sheraton, refinished cherry, turned legs, scalloped apron, 4 dovetailed drawers, 44x38x22" **$770.00**

Chest of drawers, Empire, figured mahogany veneer w/old finish, 5 dovetailed drawers, minor repairs, 42x44x22".............**$495.00**

Chest of drawers, oak, 3 drawers w/original brass hardware, 1920s, 32x40x18".............**$225.00**

Chest-on-chest, refinished maple, 5 drawers w/applied decor on second, ca 1938, 47x31x17".............**$365.00**

Chifferobe, Mission-style oak, 4 drawers, rectangular mirror, 74x45x20".............**$275.00**

Chifferobe, Oriental V-matched & walnut veneer w/cedar-lined section on left, 3 drawers, 1940s, 62x34x19".........**$250.00**

Chifforette, burl mahogany veneer & burl walnut veneer, 3 pull-out drawers behind doors, 50x34x19".........**$250.00**

China buffet, oak w/convex glass bow front, swell-front base drawer, claw feet, 38x44x20".............**$500.00**

China cabinet, Golden Oak Era, quarter-sawn oak w/curved glass side panels, interior shelves, 67x47x15" **$825.00**

China cabinet, mahogany veneer, double 1-pane doors over 4 bow-front drawers, narrow band trim, 1930s, 71x35x17" **$500.00**

China cabinet, oak w/convex glass side panels, swell drawer at base front, applied decor, claw feet, 74x49x15".....**$650.00**

China cabinet, oak w/many press-carvings, curved glass front, mirror, lg.............**$1,250.00**

China cabinet, Oriental walnut veneer w/curly maple overlay, 2 glass doors over drawer over 2 doors, 1920s, 68x36x15".............**$350.00**

China cabinet, walnut veneer w/hardwood base, applied decorations, 2-drawer base, 1920s, 69x40x18" ...**$345.00**

China closet, Golden Oak Era, quarter-sawn oak veneer w/old finish, mirror above top shelf, minor damage to crest, 69".............**$415.00**

China closet, Golden Oak Era, relief-carved stylized foliage decor on door & crest, 58½ (+gallery & crest)x32x14".......**$475.00**

Commode, Country, poplar w/old dark finish, 3 dovetailed drawers, scalloped base & crest, 33(+crest)x33x17".........**$220.00**

Cupboard, corner; Country, refinished cherry, paneled doors, molded cornice, 1-pc, replaced hinges, 81x48" ..**$1,485.00**

Cupboard, corner; figured mahogany veneer pediment & door fronts, hardwood frame, cornice, 1930s, 70x29x13".**$525.00**

Cupboard, curly maple, open wall type, reproduction, 74¼x56x20".............**$715.00**

Cupboard, hanging, poplar w/black paint, 1 drawer & single door, handmade reproduction w/some age, 24x13½x12"....**$85.00**

Cupboard, pine, curved shelves w/spoon cutouts, restored, 41".............**$600.00**

Cupboard, poplar w/dark grainpainting, dovetailed w/molding, 36", EX.............**$500.00**

Cupboard, poplar w/dark stain, simple cut-out feet, paneled door, 38x27".............**$265.00**

Desk, Chippendale style, mahogany w/worn finish, slant front, 42x36x22".............**$465.00**

Desk, knee-hole; English Gothic style, paneled doors w/carving, 2 drawers, late reproduction, crest missing, 28x46x19".............**$220.00**

Desk, knee-hole; hard rock maple by Heywood-Wakefield, 1950s, 29x44x18".............**$350.00**

Desk, oak roll-top, well fitted, 4 drawers each side of base, 45" wide.............**$1,650.00**

Dresser, ash w/incised lines, flower designs & rectangular swing mirror, 3 drawers, 77x40x19".............**$275.00**

Dresser, Princess style, quarter-sawn & plain oak veneer w/solid oak frame, hinged mirror, 3 drawers, 74x40x21" **$425.00**

Dry sink, refinished poplar w/copper lining (replaced), simple cut-out feet, paneled doors, 2 drawer, 34x45x24".**$415.00**

Footstool, Country Windsor, old green repaint, splayed turned legs, oval upholstered top, 12" **$50.00**

Footstool, pine, worn green paint, simply made, 18" wide.**$75.00**

Footstool, Windsor style, splay base, reupholstered, not period, 7x14" **$175.00**

Highchair, oak w/pressed back, hinged tray, 42x15"..**$240.00**

Lowboy, Chippendale style, mahogany w/block front, handmade reproduction, 30x32x20" **$440.00**

Lowboy, Chippendale style, mahogany w/cabriole legs & carved fan, reproduction, 30x36x20"....................**$440.00**

Mirror, console; beveled glass, burnished gold frame, 1930s, 30x16" **$185.00**

Mirror, Hepplewhite style, mahogany w/inlay & gilded swags, brass eagle & urn finials, modern reproduction, 52x25½" **$220.00**

Patio set, repainted wicker, silk upholstery & throw pillows, sofa+2 armchairs......................................**$600.00**

Patio set, white wicker w/print pillows & cushions, modern 3-pc set, 65" couch+2 armchairs..........................**$225.00**

Piano bench, oak w/lift lid & cabriole legs w/paw feet, 20x36x15"..**$275.00**

Pie safe, butternut & poplar, 6 star-punched tin panels, 60", EX **$725.00**

Pie safe, Country, poplar w/cherry finish, double doors w/6 punched tins, 1 drawer at top, 57x36x16".......**$1,000.00**

Rocker, armchair; Country, 4-slat ladderback, rush seat, old dark finish, 37½".....................................**$110.00**

Rocker, armchair; golden oak w/pressed crest & 7 spindles, curved armrests, factory made, 40" **$175.00**

Rocker, child's armchair; oak & hardwood w/old finish, crest w/cat & 4 kittens, cane seat, 28" **$165.00**

Rocker, child's armchair; spindle back, old refinish, 21"...**$95.00**

Rocker, child's captain's chair; turned spindles, old refinish, 16" **$95.00**

Rocker, figured maple, tall 4-slat ladderback **$550.00**

Rocker, folding type, maple w/slat seat, natural finish, 1920s, 39" **$110.00**

Rocker, maple w/natural finish, 4-slat ladderback, replaced splint seat w/minor damage, 42½".........................**$75.00**

Rocker, oak w/pressed crest, 6-spindle back, caned seat (replaced), 40½" **$235.00**

Rocker, youth's armchair; hardwood & oak w/pressed back, 31½" **$140.00**

Secretary, ash w/fall front, bookcase top, 94x44x18" .**$1,350.00**

Secretary, Country, refinished poplar, 2 glazed doors over pigeon holes over 2 doors, EX..........................**$575.00**

Secretary, oak w/fall front, carved design on drop lid, bookcase top, 83x38x19"...**$1,300.00**

Settee, Windsor, spindle back, plank seat, refinished, 40" .**$800.00**

Shelf, corner, walnut w/old finish, cut-out sides w/curving shapes, 2-shelf, wall mount, 36x25"....................**$385.00**

Shelf, hardwood, 3 step-back shelves w/turned posts, varnished, wall mount, 21x23"...................................**$60.00**

Sideboard, Hepplewhite style, mahogany w/inlay, Williamsburg reproduction by Kittinger, 43x61x24½"................**$1,480.00**

Smoking stand, figured walnut veneer top, sides & door panel, hardwood base, painted flower design on door, 1930s, 30" **$165.00**

Smoking stand, V-matched mahogany door front, mahogany & hardwood body, late 1930s, 24x14x12" **$165.00**

Sofa, Chippendale style, camel back, red velvet upholstery w/tufted back & seat, 59" **$100.00**

Sofa, Duncan Phyfe style, carved and reeded mahogany frame with satin wood veneer blocks at feet, red striped satin upholstery has minor wear, 72", $440.00.

Sofa, Duncan Phyfe style, carved mahogany frame w/brass paw feet, reupholstered in silk brocade, 20th century, 78"..**$250.00**

Sofa & armchair, Baroque Revival, highly carved wooden frames w/silk brocade upholstery, 81" sofa, VG..**$550.00**

Stand, bedside; walnut w/old finish, turned spool legs, H stretcher w/dovetailed drawer, replaced mahogany top, 22x17"..**$140.00**

Stand, Country, cherry w/dovetailed drawer, scalloped base shelf, replaced top, 20x21"..............................**$200.00**

Stand, Country, refinished cherry w/turned maple legs, 1 dovetailed drawer, replaced 3-board top, 29½x17x17½" ..**$165.00**

Stand, Country, refinished curly maple, 1 dovetailed drawer, turned legs, 2-board top, 29x21x21" **$660.00**

Stand, drop leaf; Country, walnut w/old finish, turned legs, 2 dovetailed drawers, repairs, 29x24x19"+2 11" leaves..........**$275.00**

Stool, cast-iron base w/old gold repaint, worn upholstery, 14x10½" **$250.00**

Table, coffee; mahogany w/leather top, 1940s, 17x30" dia **$145.00**

Table, coffee; Queen Anne style, mahogany w/drop leaves, cabriole legs, 1930s, 18x48x16+10" drop leaves...**$175.00**

Table, coffee; 4-pc matched crotch walnut veneer top w/inlaid designs & applied decor, ball & claw feet, 20x36x18"...**$165.00**

Table, console; hand-painted floral designs on apron & legs, 1930s, 30x39x22"..**$185.00**

Table, corner; hard rock maple by Heywood-Wakefield, 1950s, 22x32x32" **$125.00**

Table, credenza; Hepplewhite style by Kittinger, mahogany w/inlay, demilune top, 34x68x19"....................**$635.00**

Table, dining; contemporary style w/chrome cradle base & smoked plate-glass top w/rounded corners, 39x65½x36" **$425.00**

Table, dining; Duncan Phyfe style, mahogany veneer w/cross-band inlay on top, modern reproduction, extends to 127x48" **$800.00**

Table, dining; Duncan Phyfe style w/double pedestal base, expandable 1-board top, modern reproduction, 62" w/18" leaf **$225.00**

Table, dining; maple artificially grained as oak, pedestal base w/claw feet, 46" dia, w/5 leaves **$750.00**

Table, drop leaf; Duncan Phyfe, mahogany veneer & mahogany-stained hardwoods, 30x41x24"+2 16" leaves...........**$275.00**

Table, drop leaf; Duncan Phyfe style, cherry, modern reproduction, 29x32x14½"+2 14" leaves **$80.00**

Table, drop-leaf kitchen; porcelain top w/enamel decor, drawer each end, wood base, 1930s, 31x40x24".........**$210.00**

Table, drop-leaf; Chippendale, refinished mahogany, swing legs support leaves, 2 center stationary legs, 29x49x19"..**$195.00**

Table, end; hard rock maple by Heywood-Wakefield, 1950s, 22x30x21" **$95.00**

Table, end; mahogany w/oval mirror top, 1940s, 23x20x16" **$150.00**

Table, hutch; round top, high-quality handmade reproduction w/red repaint, 30x45¾" **$425.00**

Table, occasional; black lacquer finish w/gold & floral design, Quaint Furniture...Stickley Brothers..., 24x19x13" ..**$210.00**

Table, occasional; plain-cut walnut veneer top & gallery, hardwood lyre base, Mersman, 26x24x18" **$210.00**

Table, occasional; plain-cut walnut veneer top & selected hardwood base, 1940s, 27x18x15" **$165.00**

Table, occasional; 4-pc walnut matched veneer & inlay design on top, carved apron, French legs, 1930s, 30x30x20" ..**$265.00**

Table, tea; Queen Anne style, mahogany w/tray top & pull-out candle shelves, Kittinger reproduction, 27x29x18"..**$990.00**

Table, tilt-top; solid mahogany w/scalloped top & router lines, restored finish, 27x25" dia..........................**$300.00**

Table desk, straight-cut walnut veneer top & antique white base, 2 sm drawers, curved legs, 1940s, 30x48x12" **$425.00**

Vanity, walnut w/applied & incised decor, swing mirror, 7 drawers, carved fruit pulls, 1940s, 66x47x18".....**$625.00**

Washstand, Country, refinished poplar, paneled doors, 2 dovetailed drawers, replaced crest, 28½"+crest .**$165.00**

Washstand commode, oak w/attached towel bar rack, 1 lg drawer over 2 drawers & door, 54x32x17".........**$300.00**

Games

Games from the 1870s to the 1970s and beyond are fun to collect. Many of the earlier games are beautifully lithographed. Some of their boxes were designed by well-known artists and illustrators, and many times these old games are appreciated more for their artwork than for their entertainment value. Some represent a historical event or a specific era in the social development of our country. Characters from the early days of radio, television, and movies have been featured in hundreds of games designed for children and adults alike.

If you're going to collect games, be sure that they're reasonably clean, free of water damage, and complete. Most have playing instructions printed inside the lid or on a separate piece of paper that include an inventory list. Check the contents, and remember that the condition of the box is very important too.

If you'd like to learn more about games, we recommend *Toys, Antique and Collectible*, by David Longest; *Toys of the Sixties* by Bill Bruegman; *Board Games of the '50s, '60s & '70s* by Stephanie Lane; *Baby Boomer Games* by Rick Polizzi; and *Schroeder's Collectible Toys, Antique to Modern.*

Club: American Game Collectors Association
49 Brooks Ave.
Lewiston, ME 04240

Newsletter: *Game Times*
Joe Angiolillo
4628 Barlow Dr.
Bartlesville, OK 74006

$20,000 Pyramid TV Game, Milton Bradley, 1974, EX (EX box) **$30.00**

Across the Board, MPH, 1975, G (M box).................**$27.00**

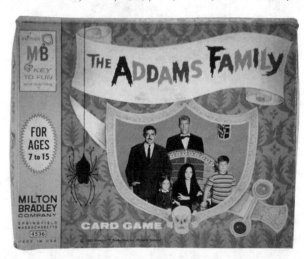

Addams Family Card Game, Milton Bradley, 1965, MIB, $45.00.

Adventures of Indiana Jones, TSR, 1984, VG (EX box).**$30.00**

All the King's Men, Parker Bros, 1979, EX (EX box)..**$30.00**

Amoeba Wars, Avalon Hills, 1981, VG (EX box).........**$30.00**

Archie Bunker's Card Game, Milton Bradley, 1972, NM (NM box), from $15 to...**$20.00**

Astrology, Dynamic, 1972, VG (EX box) **$33.00**

Baretta, Milton Bradley, 1976, EX (EX box), from $20 to ..**$30.00**

Bash, Milton Bradley, 1965, EX (VG box) **$25.00**

Battlestar Galactica, Parker Bros, 1978, VG (EX box).**$27.00**

Beverly Hillbillies Card Game, Milton Bradley, 1963, EX (EX box) **$43.00**

Big League Baseball, Milton Bradley, 1967, EX (EX box)..**$45.00**

Boggle, Parker Bros, 1977, EX (EX box) **$27.00**

Booby Trap, Parker Bros, 1965, NM (EX box)...........**$33.00**

Breakthru, 3M, 1965, VG (EX box) **$31.00**

Broadside, Milton Bradley, 1962, VG (EX box)..........**$40.00**

Call It, Ideal, 1978, VG (EX box)................................**$29.00**

Careers, Parker Bros, 1955, VG (EX box)...................**$35.00**

Cavalcade, Selchow & Righter, 1953, VG (EX box) **$60.00**

Charades, Selchow & Righter, 1968, VG (EX box)......**$25.00**

Chick in the Coop, Gabriel, 1950, EX (EX box)..........**$45.00**

Chutzpah, Cadaco, 1967, VG (EX box).......................**$43.00**

Clever Endeaver, Mind Games, 1989, EX (EX box) **$30.00**

Clue, Parker Bros, 1963, VG (VG box).......................**$39.00**

Conflict, Parker Bros, 1960, VG (EX box) **$60.00**

Cootie, Schaper, 1949, G (EX box)............................**$31.00**

Cross Up, Milton Bradley, 1974, VG (EX box)...........**$25.00**

Dead Stop, Milton Bradley, 1979, VG (EX box).........**$23.00**

Dig, Parker Bros, 1940, VG (EX box) **$30.00**

Dispatcher, Avalon Hill, 1958, VG (EX box) **$110.00**

Dragnet, Game of; Transogram, 1955, VG (EX box) ..**$65.00**

Dungeon Dice, Parker Bros, 1977, EX (EX box).........**$25.00**

East Front, Control Box, 1976, contents zippered (EX box)..**$55.00**

Ecology, Urban Systems, 1970, EX (EX box)...............**$47.00**

Emergency, Milton Bradley, 1974, NM (VG box)........**$30.00**

Espionage, MPH, 1973, EX (EX box) **$45.00**

Facts in 5, 3M, 1971, EX (EX box) **$30.00**

Feeley Meeley, Milton Bradley, 1967, NMIB, $50.00. (Photo courtesy of June Moon.)

Finance, Parker Bros, 1962, EX (EX box)....................**$35.00**

Flying Circus, SPI, 1972, EX (EX box).........................**$45.00**

Force, Invicta, 1977, EX (EX box) **$25.00**

Frogger, Milton Bradley, 1982, EXC (EX box).............**$33.00**

Game of the States, Milton Bradley, 1960, VG (EX box), from $20 to...**$28.00**

Gamma World, TSR, 1978, EX (EX box) **$25.00**

Globe-Trotters, Selchow & Righter, 1948, G (VG box) ..**$35.00**

Golden Girl, Parker Bros, 1985, VG (EX box) **$27.00**

Group Therapy, 1969, VG (EX box) **$29.00**

Hearthrob, Milton Bradley, 1988, EX (EX box) **$30.00**

High Hand, ES Lowe, 1984, EXIB **$30.00**

Hobbit Game, Milton Bradley, 1978, VG (EX box).....**$35.00**

House Divided, GDW, 1989, VG (M box) **$31.00**

Hunt for Red October, TSR, 1988, EXIB **$35.00**

Input, Milton Bradley, 1984, EX (EX box) **$27.00**

Jeopardy, 8th edition, Milton Bradley, 1964, EX (EX box) **$25.00**

Journey Through Europe, Ravensburger, 1982, EXIB .**$45.00**

Keyboard, Parker Bros, 1953, VG (VG box) **$27.00**

King Kong, Ideal, 1976, MIB.......................................**$55.00**

Kreskin's ESP, Milton Bradley, 1967, NM (EX box), from $30 to...**$40.00**

Laverne & Shirley, Parker Bros, 1977, NM (EX box) ..**$30.00**

Liz Taylor: Hollywood Starlet, Ideal, 1963, M (envelope) ..**$55.00**

Magnificent Race, Parker Bros, 1975, VG (EX box)....**$30.00**

Marble Bingo, Wolverine Supply, 1930s, G (EX box).**$75.00**

Mating Game, NBC/Hasbro, 1969, EX (EX box) **$35.00**

Mid-Life Crisis, Game Works, 1982, EX (EX box) **$27.00**

Minutemen, SPI, 1976, EX (EX box) **$45.00**

Mork & Mindy, Parker Bros, 1979, NMIB, from $20 to..**$28.00**

Mysto Magic, Gilbert, 1950s, VG (VG box) **$45.00**

Napoleon, Avalon Hill, 1977, EX (EX box).................**$45.00**

Nine Men's Morris, Transogram, 1956, EX (EX box) ..**$31.00**

Outdoor Survival, Avalon Hill, 1972, EX (EX box) **$25.00**

Pass It On, Selchow & Righter, 1978, EX (EX box) **$25.00**

Password, Milton Bradley, 1962, NM (EX box), from $15 to..**$22.00**

Perquacky, Lakeside, 1970, EX (EX box), from $12 to ..**$20.00**

Pity, Parker Bros, 1964, EX (EX box)...........................**$31.00**

Plaza, Parker Bros, 1947, G (EX box)...........................**$47.00**

Probe, Parker Bros, 1964, EX (EX box), from $20 to ..**$30.00**

Qubic, Parker Bros, 1965, EX (EX box)........................**$28.00**

Rack-O, Milton Bradley, 1961, NM (EX box), from $20 to..**$25.00**

Rat Race, Waddingtons, 1974, EX (EX box).................**$28.00**

Red Rover Game, Cadaco, 1963, EX (EX box).............**$40.00**

Rich Uncle, Parker Bros, 1959, EX (EX box)...............**$50.00**

Robin Hood, Parker Bros, 1960, G (VG box)...............**$35.00**

Ruffhouse, Parker Bros, 1980, EX (EX box) **$27.00**

Scarne's Challenge, 1947, G (EX box) **$27.00**

Scrabble, Selchow & Righter, 1953, NM (EX box) **$35.00**

Shell Shock, Victory Games, 1989, MIB.......................**$40.00**

Shogun, Epoch, 1976, VG (EX box).............................**$33.00**

Skunk, Schaper, 1953, VG (VG box)............................**$25.00**

Snatch, Gopher Games, 1954, EX (EX box).................**$33.00**

Sorry, Parker Bros, 1972, EX (EX box) **$24.00**

Space Shuttle, Rockwell/Media, 1978, EX (EX box) ..**$35.00**

Spelling Match, Cadaco-Ellis, 1954, EX (EX box)........**$33.00**

Starsky & Hutch, Milton Bradley, 1977, EX (EX box).**$30.00**

Stay Alive, Milton Bradley, 1978, EX (EX box)...........**$25.00**

Stock Market Game, Avalon Hill, 1970, EX (EX box).**$35.00**

Stratego, Milton Bradley, 1962, EX (EX box)...............**$29.00**

Sunken Treasure, Parker Bros, 1948, VG (EX box) **$49.00**

Tank Battle, Milton Bradley, 1975, VG (EX box) **$50.00**

Tennis, Parker Bros, 1975, EXIB..................................**$30.00**

Thinking Man's Golf, 3, 1967, VG (VG box)...............**$30.00**

Total Depth, Orc Production, 1984, EXIB....................**$70.00**

Treasure Hunt, 13th edition, Cadaco-Ellis, 1941, EX (EX box) **$30.00**

Tripoly, Cadaco-Ellis, 1942, VG (VG box) **$25.00**

Tune Din, Friends Across, 1988, MIB...........................**$35.00**

Twenty Questions, Pressman, 1988, VG (EX box)......**$25.00**

Upwords, Milton Bradley, 1983, EX (EX box)............**$30.00**

Voltron, Parker Bros, 1985, VG (EX box) **$22.00**

Voyage to the Bottom of the Sea Card Game, Milton Bradley, 1964, NMIB, $70.00.

Waterworks, Parker Bros, 1972, EX (EX box) **$29.00**

What's Up?, Selchow & Righter, 1969, VG (EX box) ..**$30.00**

Who Can Beat Nixon?, Dynamic, 1971, EX (EX box).**$60.00**

Whosit?, Parker Bros, 1976, EX (EX box) **$25.00**

Wizard of Oz, Cadaco, 1974, EX (EX box)..................**$35.00**
Word Yahtzee, Milton Bradley, 1980, VG (EX box)....**$20.00**
Wrestle Around Game, Ideal, 1969, EX (EX box).......**$43.00**
3-D Tic Tac Toe, Milton Bradley, 1990, MIB...............**$25.00**

Gas Station Collectibles

Items used and/or sold by gas stations are included in this specialized area of advertising memorabilia. Collector interest is strong here, due to the crossover attraction of these items to both advertising fans and automobilia buffs as well. Over the past few years, there have been several large auctions in the East that featured gasoline-related material, much of which brought very respectable selling prices.

If you're interested in learning more about these types of collectibles, we recommend *Huxford's Collectible Advertising* by Sharon and Bob Huxford and *Gas Station Memorabilia* by B.J. Summers and Wayne Priddy, both published by Collector Books.

Newsletter: *Petroleum Collectors Monthly*
Scott Benjamin and Wayne Henderson, Publishers
411 Forest St.
LaGrange, OH 44050; 216-355-6608. Subscription: $29.95 per year (Samples: $5).

Ashtray, Sunoco, metal plate shape w/blue & yellow logo in center, knobs make up 3 rests, 7¾" dia, EX.........**$20.00**
Ashtray, Texaco, Division Sales Meeting, china plate shape w/4 rests, image of Division Office, 1968, 6¾" dia, EX+...**$45.00**
Ashtray/thermometer, Texaco/Crosby-Whipple Oil Corp, metal bowl w/2 rests attached to round dial thermometer, 3½", VG..**$70.00**
Bank, Altas, tin, shaped like battery w/slip-lid top, 3x3x2", VG...**$20.00**
Bank, Atlantic Premium, tin gas pump, red, white & blue, 5", EX..**$60.00**
Bank, Blue Sunoco 200X, tin gas pump, blue, yellow & red, VG...**$50.00**
Bank, Quaker State Motor Oil, cardboard can, EX.......**$8.00**
Bank, Sinclair H-C, tin gas pump, green, red & cream, 4", EX...**$100.00**
Bank, Sinclair Power-X, tin gas pump, red & white, EX..**$100.00**
Banner, Seasons Greetings/World Oil Co 24-Hr Service, image of Santa's head & holly, 35x58", EX+.........**$30.00**
Banner, We Recommend Eveready Prestone Anti-Freeze, red, white & blue, 35x57", NM+....................................**$30.00**
Brush, Atlantic Gasoline, round w/wooden base embossed metal top showing showing early station & car, 4" dia, EX..**$85.00**
Brush, Socony Gasoline/Polarine Oil & Greases, elongated red-stained wood back w/decal, mohair bristles, 3x7", VG+..**$60.00**
Can, Locktite Radiator Cement, shaped like radiator w/screw cap, gold w/black & red lettering, 5x4", VG......**$100.00**
Can, Sunoco, 5 Gallons Liquid, milk-can shape w/embossed lettering, small screw lid, single grip handle, 25x10" dia, VG..**$45.00**

Candy container, plastic gas pump w/Candy Pump lettered on round globe, 1-oz, 6", VG.................................**$5.00**
Cigarette box, Firestone Supreme Batteries, composition battery shape w/hinged lid, 3x3½x2¼", VG................**$5.00**
Clock, Havoline, plastic square w/cardboard face, lines & T logos around name, red, gold, white on black, 11x11", EX...**$10.00**
Clock, Penzoil Sound Your 'Z,' round metal body w/glass lens, numbers around name, orange & black on white, 20" dia, VG..**$230.00**
Clock, Tydol Flying A Gasoline, round white plastic face w/black numbers around name, light-up, 15" dia, VG **$200.00**
Cookbook, Esso, Aunt Julia's Cook Book, lettering & image of serviceman over checked background, 32 pages, EX...**$40.00**
Display, Champion Spark Plugs, diecut cardboard stand-up, globe w/Champion banner, plane & spark plug, 37½", VG...**$200.00**
Display cabinet, Sohio Recorded Point By Point Lubrication, w/18 charts for 1936-42 autos, 26x19", NM........**$500.00**
Display case, AC Spark Plugs, blue round metal container w/interior rotating dispenser, gold AC graphic, 11x10" dia, EX..**$125.00**
Display case, Bowes Tirepair Center, red & tan metal box, front opens to 7 compartments, 14x13x10", VG **$20.00**
Display case, Union Auto Fuses, yellow metal box w/5 partitioned sections & marquee, green trim, 10x9x7½", VG...**$15.00**
Display rack, Quaker State Motor Oil, green metal w/white lettering, vertical w/4 shelves, 35½x16x14", VG...**$115.00**
Fan, Cities Service/Maron Oil Co, cardboard paddle shape w/image of The Last Supper & Bible verse, loop handle, G **$15.00**
Fan, Fleetwing Gasoline, cardboard, Swing Along With..., image of sailing ship on reverse, cut-out circular handle, EX...**$50.00**
First-aid kit, Shell Oil Co, brown steel cabinet, M **$75.00**
Flag, Gilmore Gasoline, cloth, leaping lion on red, white & black checked background, 22x36", NM **$400.00**
Game, Standard Oil Checkers, EXIB......................**$100.00**
Globe, Conoco, round green plastic body w/red logo on white lens, 13½" dia, EX....................................**$135.00**
Globe, Mobilgas, red round metal body w/glass lens, Mobilgas lettered in blue w/red line above & below, 16½" dia, EX **$425.00**
Globe, Sinclair Gasoline, round 1-pc milk glass, white lettering around green & white striped center, 16" dia, EX **$475.00**
Globe, Standard Oil 1-pc red & white painted glass crown shape w/metal base, 17", EX+..............................**$255.00**
Globe, Visible Gas, milk glass ball shape w/red etched lettering & scroll design, 14" dia, EX **$375.00**
Globe, Wolf's Head, round 3-pc glass w/Gill body, lettering & image in red & green, 13½" dia, EX..............**$400.00**
Grease pail, Panther Oil & Grease Co, name on band around growling panther, red, black & silver, bail handle, 10-lb, VG..**$40.00**

**Hat, Mobil, brown with cream patch bordered
in blue, red horse, all original, NM, $175.00.**

Hat, Standard Service, attendant's cloth cap w/patch & leather bill, snaps on front for badge, VG............**$50.00**

Lamp, Texaco, 2 cast-iron Scotty dogs w/Listen embossed on base, pleated shade, 1930s, NM **$450.00**

Lighter, Sunoco/DX, Zippo, NMIB **$40.00**

Map holder, Gulf Tourgide (sic) Service, slanted metal base w/wire holders, includes maps, 16½x9", NM (original box) **$100.00**

Map holder, Texaco Touring Service, green metal wall box w/red & white shield & You're Welcome below, 9x4", EX **$120.00**

Mask, Texaco Fire Chief, diecut cardboard image of Ed Win from the nose up in Chief's hat, 12x15", EX **$50.00**

Matchbook cover, Union 76, EX...........................**$4.00**

Mug set, Star Case Pump Mugs, ceramic gas pumps w/nozzle handles, marked Decaffe & Regular Java, 1994, NMIB, pr...**$15.00**

Night light/Alarm clock, battery-operated plastic gas pump w/round light-up globe, digital time, Marksman, 9", MIB..**$40.00**

Oil can, 1-gal, Amoco Motor Oil, Medium, cream & red on green, screw cap & handle, 8¾x9½", VG.............**$75.00**

Oil can, 1-gal, Gargoyle Mobiloil 'A,' cream & red w/image of gargoyle, square w/corner screw cap & handle, 10x5x5", EX **$130.00**

Oil can, 1-gal, Polarine Imperial Oil Limited, Extra Heavy Body, polar bear graphic, gold ground, 13x8x3", VG **$35.00**

Oil can, 1-qt, Air Race Motor Oil/Deep Rock, Air Race Motor Oil & 4-engine plane on white above Deep Rock on gray, VG+ **$160.00**

Oil can, 1-qt, Penzoil, Be Oil Wise, owl family atop oval Penzoil logo, yellow, red & black, bell on reverse, NM+ **$50.00**

Oil can, 1-qt, Phillips 66 HDS Motor Oil, black & white, EX+ **$30.00**

Oil can, 1-qt, Quaker Maid Motor Oil, name above & below bust image of Quaker girl, yellow, green & black, full, NM **$40.00**

Oil can, 1-qt, Texaco Motor Oil, name on white ground above star & T logo on red, back is reversed, pre-1941, EX+......**$30.00**

Oil can, 1-qt, Trojan Motor Oil/Cities Service, white silhouette of Trojan soldier above name on red & black, EX+......**$35.00**

Oil can, 1-qt, Veedol Motor Oil, name above winged V logo, cream, orange & black, EX **$40.00**

Oil can, 2-gal, Marathon Motor Oil, pictures marathon runners, screw cap & handle, black, gold & orange, VG.......**$85.00**

Oil can, 2-gal, Penn City Motor Oil, oval image of Quaker man w/name, company below, screw cap, red, white & blue, EX...**$45.00**

Oil can, 2-gal, Rocket Motor Oil, image of rocket w/lettering, red, white & blue, 11x8", EX **$30.00**

Oil can, 5-gal, Champlin Motor Oil, oval image of race car above Motor Oil on striped ground, yellow, red & black, VG..**$130.00**

Oil can, 5-gal, Gulfpride Oil above orange & blue Gulf logo, square shape w/corner screw top & handle, 15½x9x9", VG..**$55.00**

Oil can, 5-gal, ISO=Vis 'D' Motor Oil/Standard Oil Co, red, white & blue round drum, 13½x11" dia, VG **$45.00**

Oil can, 5-gal, Pennzoil Safe Lubrication, beige w/black lettering w/brown bell on 2 sides, square, 15x9x9", VG+ **$70.00**

Oil pour can, Castrol Motor Oil, The Masterpiece in Oils, handled can w/tall spout, green w/red & cream logo, 11", VG+ **$65.00**

Oil rack, Havoline, wire w/stick legs, coiled handle, holds 8 clear glass bottles w/red & green metal cone caps, VG+ **$375.00**

Oil-can opener, cast iron, shaped liked pelican's beak, CLM lettered on side, 6", EX.......................................**$75.00**

Oiler bottle, 1-qt, Enarco, metal cone-shaped spout, 14", NM **$130.00**

Oiler bottle, 1-qt, Handy Oiler Co, metal inner tube attached to cone-shaped spout, NM....................................**$45.00**

Oiler bottle, 1-qt, McCall-Frontenac Oil Co, embossed image of Indian in profile, metal cone-shaped spout, NM ...**$200.00**

Pin-back button, I'm Fast!, Union 76 man in running pose above lettering, white, orange & blue on orange, 2⅛" dia, NM..**$180.00**

Pin-back button, Standard Oil's red crown on off-white center w/leaf design on gold border, 2¼" dia, EX **$60.00**

Plate, Mobil, white w/red winged horse w/inner & outer blue bands, Shenango China, 6" dia, EX+.....................**$90.00**

Pocket mirror, Socony Motor Gasoline, red, white & blue, 3½" dia, NM..**$150.00**

Pocketknife, Cities Service Petroleum Products, opalescent pearl handle w/green lettering, 1 blade missing, VG **$25.00**

Poster, Quaker State Motor Oil, Keep 'Em Rolling... above close-up image of policeman directing traffic, 34x58", NM..**$150.00**

Pump plate, Dynafuel, diecut porcelain, yellow elongated diamond w/dark & light blue lettering, 8x14½", NM ..**$130.00**

Pump plate, Jenny Arrow, porcelain, rectangular w/bowed top & bottom, name in center, red & blue on cream, 9x12", EX+ **$100.00**

Pump plate, Mobilgas, white porcelain 5-point shield w/winged horse above name, dated 1954, 12x12", NM...**$165.00**

Pump plate, Texaco Fire Chief Gasoline, w/T logo & hat, dated 3-10-62, 12x8", EX+...................................**$175.00**

Puzzle, Phillips 66, shield logo & lettering on cream plastic tiles w/Puzzled? lettered on beige frame, 4½x4", NM........**$6.00**

Restroom key tags, Texaco, Men/Ladies, paddle shape w/5-sided Texaco & star logo, red & black on white, 5½", M, pr **$135.00**

Salt & pepper shakers, Conoco, plastic gas pumps w/decals, 2½", VG+..**$40.00**

Salt and pepper shakers, Texaco, plastic gas pumps, red and yellow, 3", NMIB, $65.00.

Shirt, Esso, gray & white pinstripe w/red, white & blue oval Esso patch, size M, EX $25.00

Sign, Bowes Seal Fast Tire & Tube Repairs, diecut tin, lettering over tire image, 1930s-40s, 22x27", EX........$425.00

Sign, Esso, plastic, Esso in red raised lettering on white oval w/blue border, light-up, 13½x18½", EX............$225.00

Sign, Gulf Executive Men's Room, pressed board key shape, gold w/black lettering, blue, orange & cream logo, 43x21", G..$100.00

Sign, Mobiloil, curb, 2-sided porcelain rectangle on pedestal stand, name above winged horse & chevron design, 50", EX $225.00

Sign, Oilzum Motor Oil, painted tin, triangle w/white & black name above Oilzum man on orange, dated 4-49, 21x19", EX+ $360.00

Sign, Purolator Oil Filter/Valvoline Oil, diecut cardboard stand-up, For Best Engine Protection, serviceman w/cans, NM $180.00

Sign, Texaco Motor Oil, porcelain flange, Clean/ Clear/Golden & T logo w/image of pouring oil, name below, 23x18", EX $350.00

Sign, Texaco Sky Chief Marine, porcelain, 18x12", NM, $650.00. (Photo courtesy of Dunbar Gallery.)

Thermometer, Gulf No-Wax Gasoline & Gulfpride Oil, The Best In Any Season, orange & blue metal, rounded corners, 27", G+ $85.00

Thermometer, Prestone Anti-Freeze, You're Safe...And You Know It, gray, blue & white porcelain, embossed, 36", EX+ $85.00

Thermometer, Standard, plastic pole sign w/oval emblem, proprietor's name & address on bottom plaque, 6¾", EX $30.00

Thermometer, Sunoco, plastic pole sign w/oval Sunoco logo atop, proprietor's name plaque below, 6¾", EX ..$70.00

Thermometer, Texaco, plastic pole sign w/round T logo atop, Your Car's Best Friend on bottom plaque, 6¾", VG+ .$40.00

Tin, Benford's Monarch Golden Giant Spark Plug, 24k Gold Plated, blue, yellow & white, slip lid, 5x2x2", VG ..$15.00

Tip tray, Jenny Aero Gasoline, orange, black & white, 4" dia, NM $275.00

Gaudy Italian

I'm sure you've seen these ceramic items around, marked on the bottom with only 'Italy,' usually handwritten in ink. The ware (circa mid-fifties through the seventies) is hand-made and may be decorated with applied flowers and leaves that have been formed a section at a time by the decorator, whose palm prints are sometimes visible. It's hand painted as well, and some of the floral designs remind you of Blue Ridge. Fruit and animal designs were evidently also popular. Just recently collectors have started to show some interest in this type of pottery, which they have christened 'Gaudy Italian' (and most of it is!). Though many items can still be found for $5.00 and under, we've listed values for some of the more interesting pieces below.

Advisor: April Tvorak (See Directory, Fire-King)

Basket, lg, 10" to 8", from $20 to $22.00
Basket, med, 6" to 8", from $10 to $15.00
Basket, sm, 4", from $6 to...$8.00

Bowl, 10½" dia, $15.00.

Bowl, vegetable; 9"...$10.00
Bowl, vegetable; w/lid $15.00
Box, ring; sm..$5.00
Cigarette box, square..$15.00
Lamp, bedroom; sm, from $20 to $35.00
Lamp, living room; lg, minimum value.....................$45.00
Plate, dinner $8.00

Geisha Girl China

During the decade before the turn of the century, Western interest in Oriental and Japanese artwork, home fur-

furnishings, and accessories had increased to the point that imports were unable to keep pace with demand. In the country of Japan, years of internal strife and the power struggle that resulted had diverted the interests of the feudal lords away from the fine porcelains that had been made there for centuries, and many of the great kilns had closed down. As a result, many tiny household kilns sprang up around the country, worked by both skilled artisans and common laborers, all trying to survive in a depressed economy.

The porcelain they designed to fill the needs of this market was decorated with scenes portraying the day-to-day life of the Japanese people. There were hundreds of different patterns, some simple and others very detailed, but common to each were the geishas. So popular was the ware on the American market that its import continued uninterrupted until WWII. Even after the war, some of the kilns were rebuilt, and a few pieces were manufactured during the Occupied Japan period.

Each piece of this porcelain has a border of a particular color. Some colors are connected with certain time periods, and collectors often use this as a method of dating their pieces. For instance, red, maroon, cobalt blue, and light and Nile green borders were early. Pine green, blue-green, and turquoise were used after about 1917 or so, and in the late 1920s and thirties, a light cobalt was popular. Some pieces from the Occupied era have a black border. Most of our descriptions contain a reference to border color and design.

Even if you're not sure of the name of your pattern, you can use the following listings as a general guide.

Hatpin holder, Garden Bench, 4", $40.00.

Bowl, Bamboo Trellis, 3 ladies kneel at water's edge w/peony-covered trellis beyond, light green w/gold, footed, 7½"...**$42.00**

Bowl, berry; Boat Festival, elaborately decorated boats, pale cobalt blue, #35, individual.....................**$13.00**

Bowl, berry; Fan A, 5 ladies w/fans crossing bridge, scalloped, brick red, cobalt & gold, scalloped, Japan mark...**$25.00**

Bowl, Boy's Processional, 2 sm boys walk off into distance, iris garden in foreground, red-orange w/yellow, 9½"...**$55.00**

Bowl, Cat, kneeling lady plays w/cat while 2nd looks on, 3 reserves, 9-lobed, mint green w/gold, 2¾x8¾"..........**$85.00**

Bowl, Chinese Coin, geisha reserves & stylized coins, ruffled, pierced handle, 10"...**$95.00**

Bowl, dessert; Garden Bench H, lady w/fan on bench, surrounded by lanterns & screens, cobalt blue, 3 reserves.......**$15.00**

Bowl, Footbridge B, ladies stroll through gardens on flat planks over water, red w/yellow, 8".....................**$30.00**

Bowl, mayonnaise; Temple A, ladies in garden, temple complex beyond, w/underplate, multicolor, hexagonal..........**$42.00**

Bowl, salad; Court Lady, lady in floral headdress & ornate kimono kneels on mat, red w/yellow stripes, 4-lobed...............**$35.00**

Bowl, serving; Samurai Dance, geisha w/drum at footbridge, dancing samurai, samisen player, birds in flight, shallow, 7"...**$30.00**

Butter pat, Flower Gathering B, ladies standing & kneeling, flowers in hands, red-orange, 3¼".....................**$10.00**

Cookie jar, Temple Vase, ladies on balcony beside ikebana in vase, cobalt blue w/gold & red............................**$85.00**

Creamer, Feeding the Carp, 2 ladies & young rirl feeding fish at bridge, mother & infant along bank, red w/gold, 4"...**$20.00**

Creamer, Garden Bench B, 2 ladies sit on bench, others stroll in chrysanthemum garden, red, ribbed, 4"...........**$10.00**

Creamer, Lantern A, lady & child among butterflies & oversized ornate lanterns, red......................................**$17.50**

Creamer & sugar bowl, Ribbon & Fan Dance, 4 dancers, red-orange w/gold, melon ribs **$30.00**

Cup, Boy w/Doll, mother w/sm boy holding on to doll, girl at cabinet, 2 reserves, toy, 2".............................**$12.00**

Cup & saucer, Basket B, ladies gathering cockle shells in purple baskets, red w/gold buds & violet chrysanthemums **$24.00**

Cup & saucer, cocoa; Child's Play, lady in garden w/children, cobalt blue w/gold buds.....................................**$12.00**

Cup & saucer, cocoa; Meeting B, 2 ladies accompanied by 1 or 2 children, cobalt blue w/gold, fluted bottom.**$15.00**

Cup & saucer, cocoa; Writing A, lady at writing table on porch, ladies in garden beyond, orange-red w/gold buds...**$60.00**

Cup & saucer, demitasse; Bamboo Trellis, 3 ladies at water's edge w/peony-covered trellis beyond, red-orange w/gold .**$18.00**

Cup & saucer, demitasse; Butterfly Dancers, 2 ladies in multicolor costumes, red w/gold.................................**$30.00**

Cup & saucer, Doll's Tea Party, ladies & trees above a stenciled diaper pattern w/words Doll's Tea Party.....**$30.00**

Cup & saucer, Kite A, 2 ladies flying kites w/aid of child, brown w/gold..**$14.00**

Cup & saucer, Origami, 2 ladies folding paper, man watching, cobalt blue w/gold...**$18.00**

Cup & saucer, tea; Boo Hoo (Singing Bird of Heavan), cobalt bird on tree, strolling ladies...................................**$18.00**

Cup & saucer, tea; Drums, ladies playing sm hand-held drums, blue-green w/gold, multicolored chrysanthemums & gold...**$32.00**

Cup & saucer, tea; Flower Gathering A, 3 ladies in chrysanthemum garden, cherry blossom tree beyond, blue w/gold...**$22.00**

Demitasse pot, Fan Dance A, stencil of 2 ladies dancing w/open fans, hand-painted background, pattern in reserve...**$95.00**

Egg cup, Child Reaching for Butterfly, 2 ladies in garden, child trying to catch butterfly, red w/gold, single **$10.00**

Egg cup, Mother & Son A, mother among peonies, boy w/arms outstretched, blue-green, double **$20.00**

Hair receiver, Boat Dance, 2 lady musicians on boat, 3rd dances w/open fan, flower-lined shore, green w/gold, ribbed **$28.00**

Jug, Garden Bench Q, lady on bench, child to left, geometric red-orange, pine, mint green & gold border, 4½"....**$20.00**

Marmalade, Cloud A, ladies & children among stylized clouds, red-orange w/yellow, melon ribs, Japanese mark, 5".**$55.00**

Match holder, Garden Bench A, lady sitting on bench, 2nd kneels, iris garden, blue-green, hanging................**$35.00**

Mustard jar, Child Reaching for Butterfly, 2 ladies in garden, child trying to catch butterfly, red........................**$18.00**

Mustard jar, Long-Stemmed Peony, boy w/long-stemmed peony accompanied by 2 ladies, 1 w/parasol, red, 3⅝x2¾"......................**$18.00**

Napkin ring, Flower Gathering C, lady w/chrysanthemums & child in garden, red, semicircular **$25.00**

Pancake server, So Big, red and gold edge with floral border, $135.00.

Pin tray, Dutch Watching B, lady & child left of stream, lady on bench on right, all watching ducks, green & white...**$13.00**

Plate, Battledore, ladies & children playing battledore, butterflies overhead, red-orange, scalloped & swirled, 6¼"........**$13.00**

Plate, Bird Cage, lady & child w/birdcage in garden, pine green w/white, toy **$15.00**

Plate, Fan A, 5 ladies w/fans crossing bridge, thin red-orange, modern mark, 7" **$8.00**

Plate, Flute & Koto, lady w/kite, lady on porch playing koto & third w/lantern & child, red, scalloped, 6" **$10.00**

Plate, Parasol K: Parasol & Basket, lady w/open parasol, 2nd w/long-handled basket, cobalt blue w/gold, scalloped, 7"......................................**$20.00**

Puff box, Field Laborers, ladies in long white hats working, red w/gold......................................**$15.00**

Relish, River's Edge, many figures among river's edge looking & talking, multicolor border, fluted edge **$40.00**

Salt & pepper shakers, Bouncing Ball, 2 ladies w/ball between them, kettle & pots beyond, blue-green, pr **$26.00**

Teapot, Fan A, 5 ladies w/fans crossing bridge, diamond-shaped spout, pedestal foot, gold trim, 4-lobed, Japan mark..**$145.00**

Teapot, Torii (entranceway to Shinto shrine), lady & child in garden, Mt Fuji & birds, pagoda, w/creamer & sugar bowl..**$48.00**

Toothpick holder, Court Lady, lady in floral headdress & ornate kimono kneels on mat, 5-sided, melon ribbed, coralene..**$42.00**

Toothpick holder, Garden Bench F, 2 ladies leaving bench, 1 seeking her son by the water, hand painted, 3-handled..**$40.00**

Tray, dresser; Parasol D: Processional Parasol, 6 ladies w/flowers, center figure w/parasol, multicolor, rectangular **$70.00**

Tray, Geisha in Sampan B, ladies in sampan w/manservant, pagoda-shape, wide gold border, 4" **$25.00**

Trivet, Prayer Ribbon, 3 ladies in garden, 1 w/prayer ribbon dangling from string, red.......................................**$18.00**

GI Joe

The first GI Joe was introduced by Hasbro in 1964. He was 12" tall, and you could buy him with blond, auburn, black or brown hair in four basic variations: Action Sailor, Action Marine, Action Soldier, and Action Pilot. There was also a Black doll as well as representatives of many other nations. By 1967, GI Joe could talk, all the better to converse with the female nurse who was first issued that year. The Adventure Team series (1970–1976) included Black Adventurer, Talking Astronaut, Sea Adventurer, Talking Team Commander, Land Adventurer, and several variations. At this point, their hands were made of rubber, making it easier for them to hold onto the many guns, tools, and other accessories that Hasbro had devised. Playsets, vehicles and articles of clothing completed the package, and there were kid-size items designed specifically for the kids themselves. The 12" dolls were discontinued by 1976.

Brought out by popular demand, Hasbro's 3¾" GI Joes hit the market in 1982. Needless to say, they were very well accepted. In fact, these smaller GI Joes are thought to be the most successful line of action figures ever made. Loose (removed from the original packaging) figures are very common, and even if you can locate the accessories that they came out with, most are worth only about $3.00 to $10.00. It's the mint-in-package items that most interest collectors, and they pay a huge premium for the package. There's an extensive line of accessories that go along with the smaller line as well. Many more are listed in *Schroeder's Collectible Toys, Antique to Modern,* and *Collector's Guide to Dolls in Uniform* by Joseph Bourgeois, both published by Collector Books.

12" Figures and Accessories

Air Cadet jacket, VG+.....................................**$40.00**
Armband, Medic, EX...**$15.00**
Backpack, Rescue Raft, EX in VG box........................**$25.00**
Bear trap, EX...**$5.00**
Belt, tan, plastic, EX..**$4.00**
Billy club, EX **$2.00**
Binoculars, red, EX...**$2.00**
Canteen, w/cover, EX.......................................**$12.00**

Cobra Rifle Range Set, complete, 1985, EX **$6.00**
Communications Field Set, #7703, MOC.....................**$85.00**
Diver's gloves, EX, pr **$6.00**
Diver's weighted belt, EX...**$24.00**

Figure, Action Marine, MIB, $325.00. (Photo courtesy of Cindy Sabulis.)

Figure, Astronaut, complete w/accessories, silver space suit, NM **$175.00**
Figure, Combat Soldier, Army sweater, trousers, boots, beret, rifle, belt, M in VG box.........................**$95.00**
Figure, Crash Crew, complete w/accessories, EX **$180.00**
Figure, Deep Freeze, complete w/accessories, VG...**$210.00**
Figure, Deep Sea Diver, complete w/accessories, VG ..**$160.00**

Figure, Duke, Hall of Fame, Desert Storm fatigues, MIB, $70.00.

Figure, Green Beret, complete w/accessories, VG ...**$220.00**
Figure, Landing Signal Officer, complete w/accessories, VG **$230.00**
Figure, Man of Action, nearly complete, EX in EX+ box..**$150.00**
Figure, Marine Demolition, complete w/accessories, EX.....**$150.00**
Figure, Race Car Driver, replaced strap on goggles, VG..**$150.00**
Figure, Sea Adventurer, dog tag, shoulder holster & pistol, EX in VG box...**$130.00**
Figure, Space Ranger Patroller, complete w/accessories, M in VG box **$50.00**
Footlocker, green, w/tray & inner lid illustration, no writing, EX...**$39.00**
Goggles, for Desert Patrol jeep, yellow tinted, EX **$25.00**
Grease gun, EX...**$14.00**
Green Beret pants..**$20.00**
Grenade launcher, w/lugar, silencer & removable stock, MOC...**$30.00**
Gun, M-1 Carbine, w/strap, EX **$12.00**

Hat, fatigue, green, EX **$5.00**
Ice pick/climbing tool, EX **$5.00**
Jacket, from the White Tiger Hunt, green, EX............**$7.00**
Jacket, Military Police, brown, VG **$25.00**
Jet Pac Accessories Pack, fits around waist, EX **$8.00**
Marine dress cap, EX..**$7.00**
Mess kit, EX...**$8.00**

Missile Recovery, GI Joe Adventure Team, #7348, MIB, $40.00.

Mortar launch base, VG+ **$4.00**
Pants, Airbourne Military Police, tan, VG+ **$25.00**
Poncho, camouflage **$15.00**
Raft, orange, EX **$5.00**
Rifle, Green Beret M-16, w/strap, EX **$20.00**
Rifle w/scope, black, EX **$8.00**
Royal Air Force Set, complete w/accessories (no doll), M in EX box..**$70.00**
Russian light machine gun, w/bipod & ammo disc, Action Man, MOC **$45.00**
Sabotage Set, no doll, #7516, EX in VG photo box..**$725.00**
Sand bag, EX..**$4.00**
Scabbard, West Point Cadet, EX **$25.00**
Scuba flippers, black or orange, EX...........................**$2.00**
Scuba tanks, Navy Frogman, #7606, MOC.................**$45.00**
Sea Rescue Set, no doll, #7601, MIB........................**$650.00**
Searchlight, battery-operated, MIB **$19.00**
Shell, for Jeep Cannon, EX **$50.00**
Shirt, Man of Action, green, EX **$3.00**
Shorts, camouflage, VG+ **$4.00**
Shoulder holster, brown, EX **$18.00**
Shovel, from Mummy's Tombs Set, EX **$4.00**
Sledge hammer, diver's, EX.......................................**$12.00**
Snow shoes, white, pr **$12.00**
Stethoscope, EX **$8.00**
Telephone, Marine Field, camouflage, vinyl, EX.......**$12.00**
Tent, Army, green, complete, EX **$35.00**
Walkie-talkie, EX..**$5.00**
West Point Cadet uniform, complete ....:..**$150.00**
Wire roll, black, EX...**$5.00**

3¾" Figures and Accessories

Armadillo Mini Tank, 1984, EX...................................**$8.00**
Cobra Rifle Range Set, complete, EX **$6.00**
Figure, Buzzer, 1985, MIP **$35.00**
Figure, Clutch, complete w/accessories, 1988, EX......**$18.00**
Figure, Cobra Stinger Driver, w/ID card, 1982, M **$12.00**
Figure, Crimson Guard, 1985, MIP............................**$42.00**

Figure, D-Day, 1995, MIP $7.00
Figure, Deep Six, 1989, MIP $14.00
Figure, Doc, complete w/accessories, 1983, EX..........$16.00
Figure, Dr Mindbender, complete w/accessories, 1986, EX.$9.00
Figure, Duke, 1984, MIP $105.00
Figure, Dusty, 1985, MIP $40.00
Figure, Dynomite, 1995, MIP $7.00
Figure, Eels, complete w/accessories, 1985, EX..........$15.00
Figure, Firefly, complete w/accessories, 1984, EX $18.00
Figure, Flash, complete w/accessories, 1982...............$17.00
Figure, Flint, 1985, MIP $55.00
Figure, Frag Viper, 1989, MIP $14.00
Figure, Gen Flagg, 1992, MIP...$6.00
Figure, Gung Ho, complete w/accessories, 1983, EX.$16.00
Figure, Interrogator, complete w/accessories, 1991, EX....$6.00
Figure, Jinx, w/ID card, 1987, M in factory bag..........$12.00
Figure, Lamprey, complete w/accessories, 1985, EX ..$10.00
Figure, Leatherneck, 1983-85, MIP $32.00
Figure, Lowlight, complete w/accessories, 1986, EX ..$10.00
Figure, Mainframe, 1986, MIP $32.00
Figure, Maverick, 1988, MIP..$27.00
Figure, Mega Monster Monstro-Viper, 1993, MIP $15.00
Figure, Metal-Head, 1990, MIP......................................$15.00
Figure, Monkey Wrench, complete w/accessories, 1986, EX.$7.00
Figure, Night Creeper, complete w/accessories, 1990, EX ..$6.00
Figure, Payload, complete w/accessories, 1987, EX ...$23.00
Figure, Psyche-Out, 1987, MIP.......................................$22.00
Figure, Raptor, complete w/ID card & accessories, 1987, EX.$8.00
Figure, Roadblock, complete w/accessories, 1984, EX ...$16.00
Figure, Rock 'N Roll, complete w/ID card & accessories, 1989,
    EX $7.00
Figure, Scarlett, complete w/accessories, 1982, EX.....$25.00
Figure, Sci-Fi, 1991, MIP..$9.00
Figure, Scoop, 1989, MIP $15.00
Figure, Shipwreck, complete w/ID card & accessories, 1985,
    EX...$14.00
Figure, Shipwreck, w/parrot, 1985, MIP $60.00
Figure, Short Fuse, complete w/accessories, 1982, EX ..$20.00
Figure, Snake Eyes, complete w/ID card & accessories, 1989,
    EX...$7.00
Figure, Snow Job, complete w/accessories, 1984, EX.$15.00
Figure, Snow Serpent, complete w/accessories, 1985, EX.$14.00
Figure, Stretcher, 1990, MIP $15.00
Figure, Tele-Viper, 1989, MIP..$13.00
Figure, Tiger Force Duke, complete w/accessories, 1988,
    EX...$12.00
Figure, Torpedo, 1983, MIP $10.00
Figure, Tunnel Rat, 1987, MIP $25.00
Figure, Wild Bill, 1992, MIP $5.00
Figure, Wild Weasel, complete w/accessories, 1984, EX..$15.00
Flame thrower, EX $5.00
Gun, Cobra Pom Pom, 1983, EX $12.00
Machine gun, EX..$5.00
Motorized battle wagon, 1991, MIP..............................$35.00
Mountain Climber Motorized Action Pack, 1986, EX $4.00
Rope Crosser Action Pack, 1987, MOC $5.00
Space Force Battle Gear, Action Force, MIP.................$3.00
Vehicle, Bomb Disposal, no accessories, 1986, EX.......$3.00
Whirlwind twin battle gun, 1983, EX............................$15.00

Glass Knives

Popular during the Depression years, glass knives were made in many of the same colors as the glass dinnerware of the era — pink, green, light blue, crystal, and once in awhile even amber, forest green or white. Some were decorated by hand with flowers or fruit. Collectors will accept reground, resharpened blades as long as the original shape has been maintained. By their very nature, they were naturally prone to chipping, and mint condition examples are scarce.

Prices are volatile and inconsistent across the country. These knives were distributed more heavily throughout the West Coast (many were sold at the San Francisco World's Fair), so prices are generally lower there.

Advisor: Adrienne Escoe (See Directory, Glass Knives)

Club: Glass Knife Collector Club
Wilber Peterson
711 Kelly Dr.
Lebanon, TN 37087; 615-444-4303

Club: *Glass Knife Collector's Club*
Adrienne Escoe
448 Ironwood Ave.
Seal Beach, CA 90740

Aer-Flo (Grid), pink, 7½" $45.00
Block, green...$30.00
Block, pink, Atlantic City engraving, 8¼" $30.00

Block, vaseline, rare color, $70.00.

Butter, green/crystal, 6¼" $25.00
Dur-X (3-Leaf), crystal, 8½" $12.00
Dur-X (5-Leaf), blue, 9¼"...$20.00
Dur-X (5-Leaf), crystal, 8½" $12.00
Plain handle, light pink, 9" $25.00
Thumbguard, crystal, M in plain box...........................$20.00
Vitex (3-Star), blue, 9¼", MIB.......................................$32.00
Vitex (3-Star), crystal, 8½" $10.00
Vitex (3-Star), pink, 9¼"...$25.00

Griswold Cast-Iron Cooking Ware

Late in the 1800s, the Griswold company introduced a line of cast-iron cooking ware that was eventually distributed on a large scale nationwide. Today's collectors appreciate the variety of skillets, cornstick pans, Dutch ovens, and griddles available to them, and many still enjoy using them to cook with.

Several marks have been used, most contain the Griswold name, though some were marked simply 'Erie.'

If you intend to use your cast iron, you can clean it safely by using any commercial oven cleaner. (Be sure to re-season it before you cook in it.) A badly pitted, rusty piece may leave you with no other recourse than to remove what rust you can with a wire brush, paint the surface black, and find an alternate use for it around the house. For instance, you might use a kettle to hold a large floor plant or some magazines. A small griddle or skillet would be attractive as part of a wall display in a country kitchen.

For more information, we recommend *Griswold Cast Collectibles* by Bill and Denise Harned.

Advisors: Bill and Denise Harned (See Directory, Griswold)

Corn Cake Pan, #262, 7-stick, $80.00. (Paper wrapper, fair condition, from $10.00 to $20.00.)

Cake mold, lamb, #866	**$185.00**
Cornstick pan, #21, 7-stick	**$100.00**
Cornstick pan, #22	**$40.00**
Cornstick pan, #273	**$115.00**
Dutch oven, #10, Tite Top, lg emblem	**$75.00**
Dutch oven, #13, glass lid	**$175.00**
Dutch oven, #7, w/trivet	**$135.00**
Egg pan, #129, square	**$40.00**
Griddle, #14, Erie	**$50.00**
Griddle, #8, bail handle	**$120.00**
Loaf pan, #877	**$150.00**
Muffin pan, #10	**$45.00**
Muffin pan, #17	**$75.00**
Platter, #34	**$20.00**
Popover pan, #10, USN, 11-cup	**$75.00**
Popover pan, Griswold #18	**$75.00**
Roaster, #5, oval	**$120.00**
Skillet, #0, lg emblem, no smoke ring	**$85.00**
Skillet, #11, block logo, w/heat ring	**$150.00**
Skillet, #14, bail handle	**$150.00**
Skillet, #2, sm emblem	**$65.00**
Skillet, #3	**$20.00**
Skillet, #7	**$20.00**
Skillet, #8, chicken fryer, smooth bottom, w/lid	**$65.00**
Skillet, #9, slant letters	**$37.50**
Vienna roll pan, #2	**$95.00**
Waffle iron, #11, sq	**$150.00**
Waffle iron, #8, low base, 1910	**$125.00**
Wheat stick pan, #262, mini	**$95.00**
Wheat stick pan, #27	**$185.00**
Wheat/cornstick pan, #280, Erie	**$200.00**

Hall China Company

Hall China is still in production in East Liverpool, Ohio, where they have been located since around the turn of the century. They have produced literally hundreds of lines of kitchen and dinnerware items for both home and commercial use. Several of these in particular have become very collectible.

They're especially famous for their teapots, some of which were shaped like automobiles, basketballs, donuts, and footballs. Each teapot was made in an assortment of colors, often trimmed in gold. Many were decaled to match their dinnerware lines. Some are quite rare, and collecting them all would be a real challenge.

During the 1950s, Eva Zeisel designed dinnerware shapes with a streamlined, ultra-modern look. Her lines, Classic and Century, were used with various decals as the basis for several of Hall's dinnerware patterns. She also designed kitchenware lines with the same modern styling. They were called Casual Living and Tri-Tone. All her designs are popular with today's collectors.

Although some of the old kitchenware shapes and teapots are being produced today, you'll be able to tell them from the old pieces by the backstamp. To identify these new issues, Hall marks them with the shaped rectangular 'Hall' trademark they've used since the early 1970s.

For more information, we recommend *The Collector's Encyclopedia of Hall China* by Margaret and Kenn Whitmyer.

Newsletter: *Hall China Collector's Club Newsletter*
P.O. Box 360488
Cleveland, OH 44136

Acacia, bowl, Radiance, 9"	**$22.00**
Acacia, custard, Radiance	**$9.00**
Acacia, salt & pepper shakers, handled, each	**$16.00**
Arizona, bowl, celery; Tomorrow's Classic, oval	**$13.00**
Arizona, bowl, cereal; Tomorrow's Classic, 6"	**$5.50**
Arizona, cup, Tomorrow's Classic	**$6.00**
Arizona, marmite w/lid, Tomorrow's Classic	**$22.00**
Arizona, saucer, Tomorrow's Classic	**$1.50**
Beauty, bowl, salad; 12"	**$35.00**
Beauty, casserole, Thick Rim	**$45.00**
Blue Blossom, ball jug, #3	**$110.00**
Blue Blossom, casserole, #77, round	**$60.00**
Blue Blossom, creamer, morning set	**$45.00**
Blue Blossom, shirred egg dish	**$65.00**
Blue Blossom, syrup, Sundial	**$145.00**
Blue Bouquet, baker, French; fluted	**$18.00**
Blue Bouquet, bowl, flared, 7¾"	**$35.00**
Blue Bouquet, bowl, fruit; D-style, 5½"	**$7.50**
Blue Bouquet, bowl, Radiance, 6"	**$14.00**
Blue Bouquet, bowl, vegetable; D-style, round, 9¼"	**$30.00**
Blue Bouquet, canister, metal	**$12.00**
Blue Bouquet, casserole, Radiance	**$35.00**
Blue Bouquet, coffee dispenser, metal	**$25.00**
Blue Bouquet, creamer, modern	**$12.00**
Blue Bouquet, custard, Thick Rim	**$13.00**
Blue Bouquet, jug, Medallion, #3	**$18.00**

Blue Bouquet, pie baker..$32.00
Blue Bouquet, plate, D-style, 6"..................................$5.00
Blue Bouquet, plate, D-style, 9".................................$14.00
Blue Bouquet, salt & pepper shakers, handled, each.$17.00
Blue Bouquet, saucer, D-style......................................$2.50
Blue Bouquet, sugar bowl, w/lid, Boston..................$22.00
Blue Crocus, bowl, straight-sided, 9"........................$27.00
Blue Crocus, bowl, Thick Rim, 7½"............................$22.00
Blue Floral, bowl, 6¼"...$12.00
Blue Floral, casserole...$30.00
Blue Garden, ball jug, #3...$70.00
Blue Garden, casserole, Sundial, #4..........................$25.00
Blue Garden, creamer, morning set............................$35.00
Blue Garden, custard, Thick Rim................................$13.00
Blue Garden, sugar bowl, w/lid, New York...............$35.00
Blue Willow, ashtray..$10.00
Blue Willow, bowl, finger; 4".......................................$27.00
Blue Willow, casserole, 5"..$45.00
Bouquet, bowl, celery; Tomorrow's Classic, oval.......$18.00
Bouquet, bowl, fruit; Tomorrow's Classic, 5¾".............$6.00
Bouquet, candlestick, Tomorrow's Classic, 4½".........$30.00
Bouquet, cup, Tomorrow's Classic..............................$9.00
Bouquet, gravy boat, Tomorrow's Classic..................$25.00
Bouquet, plate, Tomorrow's Classic, 11"....................$15.00
Bouquet, saucer, Tomorrow's Classic..........................$2.50
Bouquet, vase, Tomorrow's Classic.............................$32.00
Buckingham, bowl, vegetable; Tomorrow's Classic, open, 8¾" square $16.00
Buckingham, candlestick, Tomorrow's Classic, 4½" ...$25.00
Buckingham, egg cup, Tomorrow's Classic.................$30.00
Buckingham, ladle, Tomorrow's Classic......................$20.00
Buckingham, platter, Tomorrow's Classic, 12¼".........$22.00
Cactus, ball jug, #3...$95.00
Cactus, casserole, Radiance...$50.00
Cactus, creamer, New York...$22.00
Cactus, salt & pepper shakers, handled, each.............$20.00
Cactus, sugar bowl, w/lid, Viking...............................$27.00
Cameo Rose, bowl, cereal; E-style, 6¼"........................$9.50
Cameo Rose, bowl, soup; E-style, flat, 8"...................$12.00
Cameo Rose, creamer, E-style..$9.00
Cameo Rose, cup, E-style...$9.00
Cameo Rose, plate, E-style, 6½"....................................$4.00
Cameo Rose, platter, E-style, oval, 11¼"....................$16.00
Cameo Rose, saucer, E-style...$1.50

Cameo Rose, soup bowl, E-style, flat, 8", $12.00.

Cameo Rose, sugar bowl, w/lid, E-style......................$16.00
Caprice, bowl, cereal; Tomorrow's Classic, 6"............$6.00
Caprice, candlestick, Tomorrow's Classic, 4½"..........$18.00
Caprice, casserole, Tomorrow's Classic, 2-qt.............$27.00
Caprice, cup, Tomorrow's Classic................................$6.00
Caprice, ladle, Tomorrow's Classic............................$12.00
Carrot/Golden Carrot, bowl, Five Band, 6"...............$18.00
Carrot/Golden Carrot, casserole, #65, 5¾"................$37.00
Carrot/Golden Carrot, custard, #351½.......................$15.00
Carrot/Golden Carrot, jug, Radiance, #5....................$40.00
Carrot/Golden Carrot, syrup, Five Band...................$110.00
Clover, bowl, Thick Rim, 6"...$12.00
Clover, casserole, Radiance...$55.00
Clover/Golden Clover, bowl, Radiance, 6"................$18.00
Clover/Golden Clover, jug, Five Band, 1½-pt...........$55.00
Clover/Golden Clover, salt & pepper shakers, Novelty Radiance, each $32.00
Crocus, bowl, cereal; D-style, 6"................................$14.00
Crocus, bowl, Radiance, 6"..$12.00
Crocus, cake plate..$27.00
Crocus, cake safe, metal...$30.00
Crocus, creamer, Art Deco...$22.00
Crocus, cup, St Denis..$40.00
Crocus, mug, flagon style...$47.00
Crocus, plate, D-style, 6"...$6.00
Crocus, plate, D-style, 8¼"..$9.00
Crocus, platter, D-style, oval, 11¼"...........................$22.00
Crocus, salt & pepper shakers, handled, each...........$18.00
Crocus, salt & pepper shakers, Teardrop, each.........$17.00
Crocus, saucer, D-style...$2.50
Crocus, saucer, St Denis...$10.00
Crocus, soap dispenser, metal.....................................$30.00
Crocus, sugar bowl, w/lid, modern.............................$25.00
Eggshell, baker, dot design, fish-shape, 13½"...........$40.00
Eggshell, bowl, Ribbed, dot design, 6".......................$13.00
Eggshell, bowl, Ribbed, plaid or swag patterns, 7¼".$20.00
Eggshell, custard, plaid or swag patterns..................$10.00
Eggshell, mug, Tom & Jerry; dot design.....................$11.00
Eggshell, mustard, plaid or swag patterns................$37.00
Fantasy, bowl, fruit; Tomorrow's Classic, 5¾".............$5.00
Fantasy, bowl, Thick Rim, 6".......................................$22.00
Fantasy, casserole, Sundial, 4"....................................$37.00
Fantasy, casserole, Tomorrow's Classic, 2-qt............$27.00
Fantasy, creamer, New York...$25.00
Fantasy, egg cup, Tomorrow's Classic........................$22.00
Fantasy, marmite, w/lid, Tomorrow's Classic............$25.00
Fantasy, sugar bowl, w/lid...$14.00
Fantasy, sugar bowl, w/lid, morning set.....................$37.00
Fantasy, vinegar bottle, Tomorrow's Classic.............$25.00
Fern, ashtray, Century...$6.00
Fern, butter dish, Century..$30.00
Fern, cup, Century..$5.00
Fern, gravy boat, Century...$14.00
Fern, ladle, Century...$10.00
Fern, platter, Century, 15"..$22.00
Five Band, bowl, batter; red or cobalt........................$55.00
Five Band, bowl, colors other than red or cobalt, 7¼".$12.00
Five Band, casserole, red or cobalt, 8".......................$35.00
Five Band, jug, colors other than red or cobalt, 6¼".$18.00

Five Band, syrup, red or cobalt..................................$65.00

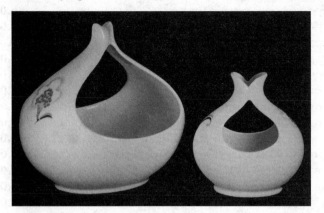

Flair, gravy boat, $35.00; Candle holder, $25.00.

Flamingo, casserole, Five Band $55.00
Flamingo, creamer, Viking $28.00
Flamingo, salt & pepper shakers, Five Band, each.....$22.00
Flareware, bowl, Gold Lace, 6".....................................$7.00
Flareware, casserole, Radial, 3-pt $8.00
Flareware, coffee server, Gold Lace, 15-cup...............$35.00
Flareware, cookie jar, Autumn Leaf............................$19.00
Floral Lattice, bowl, Five Band, 6" $14.00
Floral Lattice, casserole, #99, oval $45.00
Floral Lattice, syrup, Five Band $45.00
French Flower, ball jug, #3 ....$75.00
French Flower, creamer, Boston $22.00
Frost Flower, bowl, onion soup; w/lid, Tomorrow's
    Classic..$27.00
Frost Flower, bowl, salad; Tomorrow's Classic, lg, 14½"...$22.00
Frost Flower, cup, AD; Tomorrow's Classic..................$7.50
Frost Flower, sugar bowl, w/lid, Tomorrow's Classic .$14.00
Frost Flower, vinegar bottle, Tomorrow's Classic........$25.00
Gold Label, beaker, French...$14.00
Gold Label, coffeepot, Terrace $37.00
Golden Glo, ashtray, shell shape....................................$6.00
Golden Glo, baker, French, 8½"...................................$12.00
Golden Glo, jug, Five Band $22.00
Golden Glo, mug, Irish coffee......................................$20.00
Harlequin, ashtray, Tomorrow's Classic $7.00
Harlequin, butter dish, Tomorrow's Classic................$65.00
Harlequin, egg cup, Tomorrow's Classic $25.00
Harlequin, platter, Tomorrow's Classic, 12¼".............$18.00
Heather Rose, bowl, salad; E-style, 9".........................$16.00
Heather Rose, creamer, E-style $9.00
Heather Rose, cup, E-style $6.50
Heather Rose, mug, Irish coffee, E-style.....................$16.00
Heather Rose, pie baker, E-style..................................$18.00
Heather Rose, plate, E-style, 10"...................................$7.50
Heather Rose, saucer, E-style $2.00
Holiday, bowl, fruit; Tomorrow's Classic, 5¾" $5.50
Holiday, bowl, vegetable; Tomorrow's Classic, open, 8¾"
    square...$14.00
Holiday, coffeepot, Tomorrow's Classic, 6-cup $50.00
Holiday, ladle, Tomorrow's Classic $13.00
Holiday, plate, Tomorrow's Classic, 6"..........................$3.00
Holiday, platter, Tomorrow's Classic, 15"...................$19.00
Holiday, vinegar bottle, Tomorrow's Classic $22.00

Homewood, creamer, Art Deco.....................................$22.00
Homewood, cup, D-style $7.00
Lyric, ashtray, Tomorrow's Classic................................$6.00
Lyric, bowl, celery; Tomorrow's Classic, oval............$13.00
Lyric, bowl, onion soup; w/lid, Tomorrow's Classic...$25.00
Lyric, creamer, AD; Tomorrow's Classic........................$8.00
Lyric, platter, Tomorrow's Classic, 17".......................$27.00
Meadow Flower, ball jug, #1 or #2 ....$100.00
Meadow Flower, bowl, Thick Rim, 6".........................$18.00
Meadow Flower, casserole, Radiance...........................$40.00
Meadow Flower, custard, Thick Rim............................$14.00
Medallion, bowl, Chinese red, #5, 8½".......................$18.00
Medallion, bowl, lettuce, #3, 6" $9.00
Medallion, custard, Chinese Red....................................$9.00
Medallion, drip jar, lettuce $14.00
Medallion, jug, w/ice lip, ivory, 4-pt............................$9.00
Medallion, stack set, ivory..$27.00
Morning Glory, bowl, straight-sided, 5"......................$20.00
Morning Glory, custard, straight-sided, 3½" $11.00
Mulberry, bowl, coupe soup; Tomorrow's Classic, 9"...$9.50
Mulberry, candlestick, Tomorrow's Classic, 8" $25.00
Mulberry, gravy boat, Tomorrow's Classic..................$15.00
Mulberry, sugar bowl, AD; Tomorrow's Classic, open..$8.00
Mums, bowl, fruit; D-style, 5½".....................................$5.50
Mums, bowl, salad; 9"..$22.00
Mums, creamer, Art Deco..$18.00
Mums, creamer, New York...$16.00
Mums, cup, D-style...$12.00
Mums, jug, Medallion, #3...$30.00
Mums, pie baker...$30.00
Mums, plate, D-style, 9"...$10.00
Mums, salt & pepper shakers, handled, each.............$16.00
Mums, saucer, D-style..$2.50
Mums, sugar bowl, w/lid, New York $22.00
No 488, bowl, salad; 9"...$22.00
No 488, casserole, Radiance $32.00
No 488, creamer, Art Deco $16.00
No 488, jug, Rayed $35.00
No 488, mug, Tom & Jerry...$16.00
No 488, plate, D-style, 7" $9.00
No 488, salt & pepper shakers, Teardrop, each..........$18.00
No 488, saucer, D-style..$2.50
Orange Poppy, bowl, fruit; C-style, 5½" $7.00
Orange Poppy, bowl, Radiance, 9" $22.00
Orange Poppy, bread box, metal $30.00
Orange Poppy, cake plate $25.00
Orange Poppy, cup, C-style...$16.00
Orange Poppy, pie baker...$32.00
Orange Poppy, salt & pepper shakers, handled, each ..$16.00
Orange Poppy, wastebasket, metal...............................$45.00
Pastel Morning Glory, bowl, fruit; D-style, 5½" $6.00
Pastel Morning Glory, bowl, salad; 9"..........................$18.00
Pastel Morning Glory, cake plate $22.00
Pastel Morning Glory, creamer, Art Deco $18.00
Pastel Morning Glory, custard......................................$11.00
Pastel Morning Glory, pie baker...................................$30.00
Pastel Morning Glory, plate, D-style, 9".......................$10.00
Pastel Morning Glory, saucer, St Denis $7.50
Pastel Morning Glory, sugar bowl, w/lid, modern.......$22.00

Peach Blossom, bowl, cereal; Tomorrow's Classic, 6" ..**$7.50**
Peach Blossom, bowl, fruit; Tomorrow's Classic, footed, lg.**$32.00**
Peach Blossom, egg cup, Tomorrow's Classic............**$30.00**
Peach Blossom, marmite, w/lid, Tomorrow's Classic .**$27.00**
Peach Blossom, vase, Tomorrow's Classic..................**$32.00**
Pert, bowl, straight-sided, Chinese Red, 6" **$12.00**
Pert, custard, straight-sided, Cadet **$5.00**
Pert, jug, Chinese Red, 6½" **$22.00**
Pert, salt & pepper shakers, Cadet, each **$5.00**
Pinecone, bowl, coupe soup; Tomorrow's Classic, 9" ..**$11.00**
Pinecone, butter dish, Tomorrow's Classic.................**$55.00**
Pinecone, cup, E-style **$11.00**
Pinecone, cup, Tomorrow's Classic **$9.00**
Pinecone, jug, Tomorrow's Classic, 3-qt **$25.00**
Pinecone, mug, Tomorrow's Classic............................**$25.00**
Pinecone, plate, E-style, 9¼"..**$8.50**
Pinecone, platter, Tomorrow's Classic, 15" **$24.00**

Poppy and Wheat, dripolator, $140.00.

Primrose, bowl, cereal; E-style, 6¼" **$5.50**
Primrose, bowl, fruit; E-style, 5¼" **$4.50**
Primrose, cake plate, E-style.......................................**$15.00**
Primrose, creamer, E-style **$8.00**
Primrose, pie baker, E-style **$22.00**
Primrose, plate, E-style, 6½"...**$2.50**
Primrose, saucer, E-style...**$1.50**
Radiance, bowl, red or cobalt, #3, 6"...........................**$11.00**
Radiance, canister, ivory, 2-qt **$20.00**
Radiance, drip jar, red or cobalt **$27.00**
Red Poppy, ball jug, #3...**$45.00**
Red Poppy, bowl, soup; flat, D-style, 8½"...................**$18.00**
Red Poppy, cake safe, metal **$35.00**
Red Poppy, custard..**$11.00**
Red Poppy, plate, cake **$22.00**
Red Poppy, plate, D-style, 6" **$5.00**
Red Poppy, recipe box, metal **$35.00**
Red Poppy, soap dispenser, metal **$40.00**
Red Poppy, sugar bowl, w/lid, modern......................**$22.00**

Red Poppy, tea-pot, $95.00.

Red Poppy, toaster cover, plastic **$24.00**
Red Poppy, tumbler, frosted glass, 2-styles **$22.00**
Ribbed, bowl, onion soup; w/lid, russet/red...............**$30.00**
Ribbed, bowl, salad; russet/red, 9"..............................**$18.00**
Ribbed, ramekin, russet/red, 6-oz...............................**$7.50**
Rose Parade, bowl, salad; 9"..**$32.00**
Rose Parade, drip jar, w/lid, tab-handled **$27.00**
Rose Parade, jug, Pert, 5"..**$25.00**
Rose White, bowl, Medallion, 6" **$16.00**
Rose White, bowl, straight-sided, 6"............................**$12.00**
Rose White, creamer, Pert...**$14.00**
Royal Rose, bowl, salad; 9"...**$30.00**
Royal Rose, bowl, straight-sided, 9" **$22.00**
Royal Rose, bowl, Thick Rim, 8½".................................**$22.00**
Royal Rose, custard, straight-sided **$13.00**
Rx, casserole...**$25.00**
Rx, saucer...**$3.00**
Sear's Arlington, bowl, fruit; E-style, 5¼".....................**$4.00**
Sear's Arlington, creamer, E-style................................**$9.00**
Sear's Arlington, cup, E-style.......................................**$5.00**
Sear's Arlington, pickle dish, E-style, 9"......................**$5.00**
Sear's Arlington, plate, E-style, 8"...............................**$4.50**
Sear's Arlington, saucer, E-style..................................**$1.50**
Sear's Fairfax, bowl, cereal; E-style, 6¼".......................**$6.00**
Sear's Fairfax, plate, E-style, 10" **$7.00**
Sear's Monticello, bowl, soup; E-style, flat, 8"............**$11.00**
Sear's Monticello, creamer, E-style.............................**$9.00**
Sear's Monticello, gravy boat, w/underplate, E-style ..**$18.00**
Sear's Monticello, platter, E-style, oval, 11¼" **$13.00**
Sear's Monticello, sugar bowl, w/lid, E-style.............**$14.00**
Sear's Mount Vernon, bowl, fruit; E-style, 5¼" **$6.00**
Sear's Mount Vernon, creamer, E-style **$9.00**
Sear's Mount Vernon, pickle dish, E-style, 9" **$8.00**
Sear's Mount Vernon, plate, E-style, 10".......................**$9.00**
Sear's Richmond/Brown-Eyed Susan, bowl, fruit; 5¼" .**$4.50**
Sear's Richmond/Brown-Eyed Susan, gravy boat, w/under-
    plate **$18.00**
Sear's Richmond/Brown-Eyed Susan, pickle dish, 9"....**$5.00**
Sear's Richmond/Brown-Eyed Susan, plate, 10" **$7.50**
Serenade, bowl, fruit; D-style, 5½".................................**$5.50**
Serenade, creamer, modern **$11.00**
Serenade, cup, D-style..**$9.00**
Serenade, pie baker..**$25.00**
Serenade, plate, D-style, 6" **$4.00**
Serenade, saucer, D-style...**$2.00**
Shaggy Tulip, bowl, Radiance, 6"..................................**$16.00**
Shaggy Tulip, casserole, Radiance...............................**$32.00**
Shaggy Tulip, custard, Radiance..................................**$11.00**
Silhouette, bowl, salad; 9"..**$18.00**
Silhouette, canister set, metal, 4-pc............................**$50.00**
Silhouette, creamer, modern **$15.00**
Silhouette, cup, D-style **$14.00**
Silhouette, cup, St Denis **$35.00**
Silhouette, gravy boat, D-style.....................................**$30.00**
Silhouette, pie baker..**$30.00**
Silhouette, saucer, St Denis **$10.00**
Silhouette, sifter **$55.00**
Silhouette, silverware box..**$65.00**
Silhouette, sugar bowl, w/lid, modern........................**$22.00**

Spring, bowl, fruit; Tomorrow's Classic, 5¾".................$5.00
Spring, bowl, salad; Tomorrow's Classic, lg, 14½"......$19.00
Spring, candlestick, Tomorrow's Classic, 8"................$27.00
Spring, creamer, Tomorrow's Classic............................$9.00
Spring, gravy boat, Tomorrow's Classic.......................$22.00
Spring, plate, Tomorrow's Classic, 8".........................$6.50
Spring, vase, Tomorrow's Classic...............................$25.00
Springtime, ball jug, #3...$55.00
Springtime, bowl, D-style, oval..................................$20.00
Springtime, bowl, fruit; D-style, 5½"..........................$5.50
Springtime, cup, D-style..$7.50
Springtime, custard..$7.00
Springtime, gravy boat, D-style.................................$22.00
Springtime, salt & pepper shaker, handled, each........$14.00
Springtime, saucer, D-style.......................................$2.50
Stonewall, bowl, Radiance, 9".....................................$25.00
Stonewall, custard, Radiance.....................................$12.00
Stonewall, leftover, square...$60.00
Stonewall, salt & pepper shakers, Novelty Radiance, each..$32.00
Sundial, casserole, #2, 5¼".......................................$30.00
Sundial, syrup, red or cobalt $110.00
Sunglow, bowl, soup; Century, 8"...............................$9.00
Sunglow, bowl, vegetable; divided, Century..............$15.00
Sunglow, creamer, Century...$8.00
Sunglow, ladle, Century..$10.00
Sunglow, plate, Century, 8"...$4.50
Sunglow, saucer, Century...$1.50
Tulip, bowl, fruit; D-style, 5½" $6.50
Tulip, creamer, modern...$12.00
Tulip, cup, D-style...$13.00
Tulip, custard $10.00
Tulip, plate, D-style, 7"..$7.00
Tulip, salt & pepper shakers, handled, each...............$15.00
Tulip, saucer, D-style...$2.50
Wild Poppy, baker, rectangular $95.00
Wild Poppy, bowl, Radiance, 9"................................$27.00
Wild Poppy, casserole, #103, oval............................$110.00
Wild Poppy, casserole, Sundial, #4 ....$40.00
Wild Poppy, creamer, Hollywood $30.00
Wild Poppy, custard, Radiance..................................$16.00
Wild Poppy, drip jar, #1188, open $40.00
Wild Poppy, shirred egg dish, 5¼" $40.00
Wild Poppy, tea tile, 6"..$50.00
Wildfire, bowl, cereal; D-style, 6"..............................$10.00
Wildfire, bowl, salad; 9"...$16.00
Wildfire, cake plate...$22.00
Wildfire, cup, D-style...$14.00
Wildfire, custard..$9.00
Wildfire, pie baker..$30.00

Wildfire, plate, D-style, 7"...$7.50
Wildfire, platter, D-style, oval, 11¼".........................$22.00
Yellow Rose, bowl, fruit; D-style, 5½".........................$5.50
Yellow Rose, bowl, onion soup..................................$32.00
Yellow Rose, cup, D-style..$9.00
Yellow Rose, custard $10.00
Yellow Rose, gravy boat, D-style................................$25.00
Yellow Rose, plate, D-style, 9"....................................$9.00
Yellow Rose, saucer, D-style.......................................$2.00
Yellow Rose, sugar bowl, w/lid, Norse.......................$22.00

Halloween

Halloween is an American holiday born of Scottish and Germanic folklore. It is a harvest and mating holiday, a night for wooing, fortune telling, and trick or treating. All religious connections are so remote in history that they are no more a reality than witches flying through the air on a broom stick. Halloween is a gala event which originated with wealthy society families and agrarian centers, integrated, and spread to all those who enjoy the festivities of a night of fun and fantasy. Halloween collectibles have become the most coveted of any of the holidays, for their fantasy figures are endearing. Due to hard use, many items, especially lanterns and costumes, are scarce with examples in collectible condition being difficult to find.

Advisor: C.J. Russel and Pamela E. Apkarian-Russell (See Directory, Halloween)

Newsletter: *Trick or Treat Trader*
P.O. Box 499
Winchester, NH 03470; 603-239-8875; Subscription: $15 per year for 4 quarterly issues

Candy container, witch, cardboard, Germany, 1940s, 8½", NM, $200.00. (Photo courtesy of Dunbar Gallery.)

Candle, white Spooky figure w/chin in hand & holding trick-or-treat bag on green base w/pumpkin, unused, NM..$10.00
Candle, witch, Gurley MFG, 1940s, 8", EX $50.00
Candle holder for cakes, black plastic witch on broom, 3½", NM $18.00
Candy container, smiling pumpkin man in clothes & hat seated on green watermelon, composition, Germany, 4½", EX...$285.00

Wildfire, pitcher, $65.00.

Candy container, witch holding black cat, composition, Germany, 4½", EX **$365.00**

Candy container, witch holding broom, composition face w/cotton hair, red crepe cape & green skirt, Japan, 5½", EX **$215.00**

Candy container, witch standing on round box, composition, Germany, 3½", EX **$265.00**

Costume, Alfred E Neuman, mask only, 1960s, NM ...**$50.00**

Costume, Alien, mask only, unused, M **$10.00**

Costume, Aquaman, Ben Cooper, 1967, NMIB...........**$75.00**

Costume, Aquaman, bodysuit only, green & yellow w/painted image of Aquaman, Ben Cooper, 1967, unused, M...**$25.00**

Costume, Banana Splits, yellow & red 1-pc bodysuit w/images of characters, name & musical notes, Ben Cooper, 1969, M...**$30.00**

Costume, Bart Simpson, Ben Cooper, 1989, MIB........**$15.00**

Costume, Batgirl, 1977, mask & jumpsuit, EX+ **$28.00**

Costume, Batman, Ben Cooper, 1970, EXIB.............**$100.00**

Costume, Batman, DC Comics, 1989, EX+ **$50.00**

Costume, Bullwinkle, mask only, Ben Cooper, 1970, EXIB.**$25.00**

Costume, Cinderella, Ben Cooper, EX+ (EX box).......**$30.00**

Costume, Daffy Duck, Collegeville, 1960s, EXIB **$40.00**

Costume, Daniel Boone, cloth, Ben Cooper, EX........**$50.00**

Costume, Dick Tracy, mask only, plastic w/hinged jaw, 1960s, NM...**$45.00**

Costume, Doctor Doom, yellow & green 1-pc bodysuit, Ben Cooper, 1967, M (in original poly bag) **$100.00**

Costume, Dr Doolittle, Ben Cooper, NMIB.................**$50.00**

Costume, Evil Knevil, late 1960s, EX.........................**$55.00**

Costume, Howdy Doody, 1960s, EX+ **$15.00**

Costume, King Kong, Ben Cooper, 1976, MIB **$20.00**

Costume, Krazy Kat, 1960s, stiff glow-in-the-dark plastic mask w/jumpsuit, NM **$20.00**

Costume, Lassie, EX...**$110.00**

Costume, R2-D2, Ben Cooper, NMIB **$25.00**

Costume, Snoopy, 1960s, G......................................**$35.00**

Costume, Spider-Man, Ben Cooper, 1972, MIB **$35.00**

Costume, Superman, Ben Cooper, 1970s, EXIB **$35.00**

Decoration, black cat against lg moon, diecut, Dennison, 4", EX+ **$10.00**

Decoration, devil holding fork across chest, embossed diecut, 15", EX...**$85.00**

Decoration, magpie, black & orange diecut paper, Dennison, 9", M...**$22.00**

Decoration, Snoopy & Woodstock w/broom, centerpiece, Hallmark, 16", MIP **$6.00**

Decoration, witch, crepe paper, 4", EX, $40.00. (Photo courtesy of Pamela Apkarian-Russell.)

Decoration, witch on broom, diecut paper, 5", EX.....**$25.00**

Eyeglasses, witches atop jack-o'-lantern frames, plastic, Hong Kong, EX **$28.00**

Figure, jack-o'-lantern w/happy face, orange- & green-painted plaster, 3", EX **$35.00**

Figure, witch on motorcycle, hard plastic, 7", EX.......**$95.00**

Figure, witch on rocket, hard plastic, 4", EX.............**$50.00**

Figure, witch w/broom on oval base, painted plaster, 3½", EX...**$55.00**

Jack-o'-lantern, vegetable person, Germany, 1920s, 6½", EX, $175.00. (Photo courtesy of Dunbar Gallery.)

Lantern, cat w/fence-post bottom, papier-mache, orange or black, 1940s, 7½", EX, each.................................**$125.00**

Lantern, devil w/scowling face, molded nose, replaced insert, papier-mache, 5½", EX..**$285.00**

Lantern, jack-o'-lantern, happy face w/closed nose, papier-mache, 5", EX **$85.00**

Lantern, jack-o'-lantern w/angry face, paper insert, papier-mache, 7", EX...**$110.00**

Lantern, jack-o'-lantern w/happy face, open nose, w/replaced insert, papier-mache, 7½", EX **$110.00**

Lantern, skull on base, metal & plastic, battery-op, Hong Kong, M...**$45.00**

Light bulb, round milk glass w/black-line image of a skull & cross-bones, fits in Christmas string, Occupied Japan..........**$35.00**

Lollipop holder, cowboy, orange, hard plastic, Rosen Co, EX **$45.00**

Lollipop holder, witch, hard plastic, Rosen Co, EX **$40.00**

Mobile, Casper & Friends, fold-out card w/5 punch-out figures & their haunted house, Hallmark, 1965, unused, 4", M.**$20.00**

Nodder, composition figure w/orange smiling jack-o'-lantern head holding hat in front, blue coat, Germany, 5", EX......**$285.00**

Noisemaker, cylinder shape w/witch behind fence & owl peering at 2 happy jack-o'-lanterns, w/handle, EX **$32.00**

Noisemaker, frying-pan shape w/jack-o'-lantern, tin, VG .**$12.00**

Noisemaker, horn shape w/Halloween figures, tin, VG....**$12.00**

Noisemaker, round rattle shape w/Halloween images, tin, VG **$7.00**

Nut cup, orange jack-o'-lantern w/green features, EX..**$25.00**

Nut-cup decoration, black paper cat w/bow tie, early, 5", M **$18.00**

Party hat, fairy riding in pumpkin cart pulled by black cat, paper, Beistle, NM+ **$65.00**

Party hat, smiling jack-o'-lantern w/fringe on checkered band, paper, Beistle, NM+....................................**$65.00**

Salt & pepper shakers, half-figure devils, red-painted plaster, Japan, 3", EX, pr **$55.00**

Salt & pepper shakers, witch & jack-o'-lantern figures, pr..**$15.00**

Sipping cup, green witch's head w/black hat & removable sunglasses marked Malibu, orange straw, molded plastic, EX..**$15.00**

Spinner, sexy witch on broom flying by moon & cityscape, EX..**$35.00**

Stickers, black-cat head w/yellow & orange pointed hat & bow tie, complete set, Gibson, 1", EXIB.............**$20.00**

Stickers, ear of corn w/happy jack-o'-lantern face, complete set, Gibson, 1", EXIB................................**$20.00**

Tambourine, costumed children dancing around winking pumpkin, litho tin, sm, EX................................**$40.00**

Tambourine, face of black cat on orange background, lg, EX..**$50.00**

Wall sconces, witch & moon design, tin, NM, pr......**$125.00**

Harker Pottery

Harker was one of the oldest potteries in the country. Their history can be traced back to the 1840s. In the thirties, a new plant was built in Chester, West Virginia, and the company began manufacturing kitchen and dinnerware lines, eventually employing as many as three hundred workers.

Several of these lines are popular with collectors today. One of the most easily recognized is Cameoware. It is usually found in pink or blue decorated with white silhouettes of flowers, though other designs were made as well. Colonial Lady, Red Apple, Amy, Mallow, and Pansy are some of their other lines that are fairly easy to find and reassemble into sets.

If you'd like to learn more about Harker, we recommend *The Collector's Encyclopedia of American Dinnerware* by Jo Cunningham and *The Collector's Guide to Harker Pottery* by Neva Colbert, both published by Collector Books.

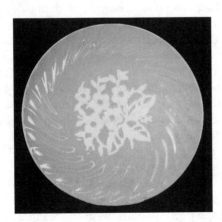

Cameoware, plate, 9½", $15.00.

Aladdin, plate, dinner; teal rose **$10.00**
Aladdin, teapot, gray, no backstamp..........................**$22.00**
Amy, casserole, w/lid **$36.00**
Amy, plate, embossed edge, 6" **$5.00**
Antique Auto, cup & saucer, jumbo..........................**$22.00**
Antique Auto, plate, dinner **$10.00**

Basket of Flowers, bowl, vegetable **$15.00**
Basket of Flowers, range set, Skyscraper, grease jar & shakers, 3-pc..**$17.00**
Black-Eyed Susan, cup **$5.00**
Black-Eyed Susan, plate, 6"..**$5.00**
Black-Eyed Susan, tidbit tray, 1-tier..........................**$6.00**
Bridal Rose, bowl, vegetable; swirled.....................**$11.00**
Bridal Rose, plate, dinner..**$10.00**
Calendar plate, 1907, Christmas................................**$80.00**
Calendar plate, 1915, Panama Canal..........................**$25.00**
Calendar plate, 1960, on Heritance shape **$5.00**
Cherry Blossom, dresser tray................................**$20.00**
Cherry Blossom, plate, dinner **$10.00**
Chesterton, bowl, fruit; gray, 5"................................**$5.00**
Chesterton, chop plate, yellow, 10"..........................**$13.00**
Chesterton, cup, gray w/pink interior.....................**$5.00**
Chesterton, cup & saucer, teal................................**$10.00**
Chesterton, plate, dinner; gray **$10.00**
Chesterton, plate, luncheon; teal..........................**$8.00**
Chesterton, plate, white w/gold edge, 6" **$5.00**
Chesterton, platter, teal, lg................................**$20.00**
Colonial Lady, cup & saucer................................**$10.00**

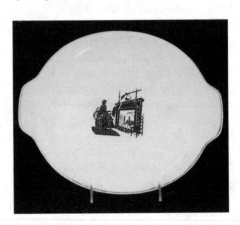

Colonial Lady, plate, gold trim, 9½", $10.00.

Colonial Lady, platter, 12" **$20.00**
Colonial Lady, syrup jug, Modern Age **$18.00**
Dainty Flower, cup & saucer, swirled.....................**$10.00**
Dainty Flower, platter, swirled................................**$22.00**
Dainty Flower, salt & pepper shakers, Modern Age, pr..**$17.00**
Deco Dahlia, high-rise jug **$40.00**
Deco Dahlia, platter, oval, 11"................................**$5.00**
Deco Dahlia, salt & pepper shakers, Skyscraper, pr...**$22.00**
Game Birds, gadroon ashtray, 6" dia..........................**$6.00**
Game Birds, plate, luncheon **$8.00**
Heritance, plate, dinner................................**$5.00**
Heritance, saucer, 6"..**$2.00**
Ivy, bowl, divided vegetable, green, plain **$5.00**
Ivy, cup & saucer..**$7.00**
Ivy, soup, plain, oval..**$5.00**
Modern Tulip, creamer, Modern Age **$12.00**
Modern Tulip, custard..**$10.00**
Monterey, casserole, w/lid................................**$36.00**
Monterey, cheese tray, Zephyr **$40.00**
Oriental Poppy, platter, Melrose, 15"..........................**$25.00**
Oriental Poppy, vase, florist's **$15.00**

Petit Fleurs, cup & saucer	**$7.00**
Petit Fleurs, plate, dinner	**$10.00**
Petit Point, fork or spoon, each	**$20.00**
Petit Point, plate, dinner	**$10.00**
Petit Point, rolling pin	**$120.00**
Poppy, spoon	**$45.00**
Red Apple, cheese plate, Zephyr	**$44.00**
Red Apple, drip jar, Skyscraper	**$18.00**
Red Apple, saucer, jumbo	**$5.00**
Rooster, tidbit tray, 1-tier	**$6.00**
Shadow Rose, bowl, vegetable	**$11.00**
Shadow Rose, cup & saucer	**$9.00**
Shadow Rose, plate, luncheon	**$8.00**
Spring Time, plate, luncheon	**$3.00**
Spring Time, tidbit tray, 1-tier	**$6.00**
Tulip, custard	**$10.00**
Tulip, pie baker	**$25.00**
Tulip, syrup jug	**$18.00**
White Rose, bowl, vegetable; round	**$15.00**
White Rose, creamer & sugar bowl	**$12.00**
White Rose, plate, dinner; 10½"	**$6.00**
White Rose, plate, 6"	**$2.00**
White Ware, bowl, fluted	**$20.00**
White Ware, plate, dinner	**$10.00**
Wood Song, butter dish	**$8.00**
Wood Song, cup & saucer, tea	**$10.00**

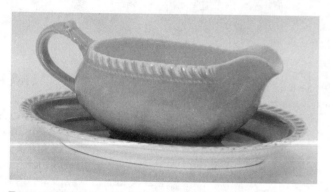

Pate sur Pate, gravy boat and underplate, $15.00.

Hartland Plastics, Inc.

The Hartland company was located in Hartland, Wisconsin, where during the fifties and sixties they made several lines of plastic figures: Western and Historic Horsemen, Miniature Western Series, and the Hartland Sport Series of Famous Baseball Stars. Football and bowling figures and religious statues were made as well. The plastic, virgin acetate, was very durable and the figures were hand painted with careful attention to detail. They're often marked.

For more information, there is a chapter on Hartland in *Collecting Toys* by Richard O'Brien (Books Americana). See also *Schroeder's Collectible Toys, Antique to Modern* (Collector Books).

Advisor: James Watson, Sports Figures (See Directory, Hartland)

Advisors: Judy and Kerry Irvin, Western (See Directory, Hartland)

Newsletter: *Hartland Newsletter*
Gail Fitch
1733 N Cambridge Ave., #109
Milwaukee, WI 53202; Send SASE for information

Sports Figures

In our listings, mint to near-mint condition values are for figures that are white or near-white in color; excellent values are for those that are off-white or cream-colored.

Babe Ruth, NM/M, from $200 to	**$250.00**
Dick Groat, EX, from $800 to	**$1,000.00**
Dick Groat, NM/M, from $1,200 to	**$1,400.00**
Don Drysdale, EX, from $275 to	**$300.00**
Duke Snider, EX, from $300 to	**$325.00**
Duke Snider, M, from $600 to	**$675.00**
Eddie Mathews, NM/M, from $125 to	**$150.00**
Ernie Banks, EX, from $200 to	**$225.00**
Ernie Banks, NM/M, from $250 to	**$350.00**
Harmon Killebrew, NM/M, from $400 to	**$500.00**
Henry Aaron, EX, from $150 to	**$175.00**
Henry Aaron, NM/M, from $200 to	**$250.00**
Little Leaguer, 6", EX, from $100 to	**$125.00**
Little Leaguer, 6", NM/M, from $200 to	**$250.00**
Louie Aparacio, EX, from $200 to	**$225.00**
Louie Aparacio, NM/M, from $250 to	**$350.00**
Mickey Mantle, NM/M, from $250 to	**$350.00**
Minor Leaguer, 4", EX, from $50 to	**$75.00**
Minor Leaguer, 4", NM/M, from $100 to	**$125.00**
Nellie Fox, NM/M, from $200 to	**$250.00**
Rocky Colavito, NM/M, from $600 to	**$800.00**
Roger Maris, EX, from $300 to	**$350.00**
Roger Maris, NM/M, from $350 to	**$400.00**
Stan Musial, EX, from $150 to	**$175.00**
Stan Musial, NM/M, from $200 to	**$225.00**
Ted Williams, NM/M, from $225 to	**$300.00**
Warren Spahn, NM/M, from $150 to	**$175.00**
Willie Mays, EX, from $150 to	**$200.00**
Willie Mays, NM/M, from $225 to	**$275.00**
Yogi Berra, w/mask, EX, from $150 to	**$175.00**
Yogi Berra, w/mask, NM/M, from $175 to	**$250.00**
Yogi Berra, w/o mask, NM/M, from $150 to	**$175.00**

Western Figures With Horses

Annie Oakley, NM	**$275.00**
Bill Longley, NM	**$600.00**
Brave Eagle, NM	**$200.00**
Bret Maverick, NM	**$75.00**
Buffalo Bill, NM	**$300.00**
Bullet, NM	**$45.00**
Cactus Pete, NM	**$150.00**
Champ Cowgirl, NM	**$150.00**
Cheyenne, w/tag, NM	**$190.00**
Chris Colt, NM	**$150.00**
Clay Holister, NM	**$225.00**
Cochise, NM	**$150.00**
Commanche Kid, NM	**$150.00**

Dale Evans, gr, NM	**$125.00**
Dan Troop, NM	**$400.00**
Davy Crockett, NM	**$550.00**
Gil Favor, prancing, NM	**$800.00**
Gil Favor, semi-rearing, NM	**$600.00**
Hoby Gillman, NM	**$225.00**
Jim Hardy, NM	**$150.00**
Jockey, NM	**$150.00**
Josh Randle, NM	**$650.00**
Lone Ranger, NM	**$150.00**
Paladin, NM	**$400.00**
Seth Adams, NM	**$275.00**
Tom Jeffords, NM	**$175.00**
Tonto, NM	**$150.00**
Tonto, rare semi-rearing, NM	**$650.00**
Wyatt Earp, NM	**$200.00**

Head Vases

These are fun to collect, and prices are still reasonable. You've seen them at flea markets — heads of ladies, children, clowns, even some men and a religious figure now and then. A few look very much like famous people — there's a Jackie Onassis vase by Inarco that leaves no doubt as to who it's supposed to represent!

They were mainly imported from Japan, although a few were made by American companies and sold to florist shops to be filled with flower arrangements. So if there's an old flower shop in your neighborhood, you might start your search with their storerooms.

If you'd like to learn more about them, we recommend *Head Vases, Identification and Values*, by Kathleen Cole.

Newsletter: *Head Hunters Newsletter*
Maddy Gordon
P.O. Box 83H
Scarsdale, NY 10583, 914-472-0200; Subscription: $20 per year for 4 issues

American Indian, unmarked, full headdress, 8" **$57.50**
Baby, Inarco, #E3156, blond w/pink bow in hair, ruffled collar, 5½" **$42.50**
Baby, Napco, #C2634B, blond baby in white bonnet & bodice, much gold trim, 1956, 5½" **$42.50**
Baby, unmarked, short brown curls emerging from blue & white knit cap, lg brown eyes, 5" **$32.50**
Baby boy, Relpo, #6744, blond in blue cap, dressed in blue w/white collar, 5½" **$42.50**
Boy in fireman's hat, Inarco (paper label), holds hose in left hand, 5" **$32.50**
Clown, Inarco, #D-5071, white face w/red nose & mouth, sm black hat on side of bald head, 4½" **$22.50**
Geisha, Lee Wards (paper label), dressed in black w/gold trim, 5" **$37.50**
Girl, Inarco, #E1579, blond girl praying, eyes downcast, 1964, 6" **$32.50**
Girl, Inarco, #2523, blue head scarf over blond hair w/braids, expressive brown eyes, 5½" **$37.50**

Girl, Japan, blond dressed in pink w/applied flowers on hat, holds sm gift in white-gloved hands, gold trim, 5½" ..**$47.50**
Girl, Japan, brown ponytail & eyes, holds fan wide, yellow flowers along bodice & fan, 3" **$22.50**
Girl, Napco, #CX2348B, blond dressed in red & white Christmas costume, holds package w/decorated w/holly, 1956, 5½" **$47.50**
Girl, Napco, #C4556B, brown hair w/bands, dressed in white w/yellow trim, hands rest on chin, 1960, 5" **$32.50**
Girl, Parma (paper label), blond w/2 lg flowers in hair, lg brown eyes, sm pouty mouth, 6" **$32.50**
Girl, Reliable Glassware, #K679C, blond in pigtails, green bonnet & dress, hand up as if waving, 1956, 6" ..**$32.50**
Girl, unmarked, blond upswept hair held by blue bow, holds kitten in hands, 5½" **$42.50**

Girl with parasol, unmarked, 4¼", $60.00.

Head vase, nun, 8" **$195.00**
Lady, Inarco, #E2104, flower in brown curly hair, gloved hand to face, pearl necklace, 7" **$42.50**
Lady, Inarco, #E6210, youthful blond w/hair over left shoulder, pearl drop earrings, blue bodice, 6½" **$65.00**
Lady, Japan, flat-brimmed bonnet, holds parasol in left hand, 5½" **$52.50**
Lady, Napco (paper label), #S93A, wide-eyed blond w/pink flower in hair, flowers along neck of bodice, 5"..**$42.50**
Lady, Napcoware, #C348, black bonnet w/holes along rim, black gloved hand to face, pearl drop earrings, 7"..**$42.50**
Lady, Napcoware, #C5677, long curls, flat white hat, ruffled bodice, hand to face, 5½" **$42.50**
Lady, Napcoware, #C7314, youthful blond w/fancy curls, fancy necklace & drop earrings, black bodice, 9"............**$150.00**
Lady, Parma (paper label), #A448, youthful blond w/fancy curls, ruffled white collar on green bodice, pearl necklace, 7" **$62.50**
Lady, RB (paper label), blond w/flip hairdo, pearl necklace, flower on left shoulder of bodice, 5½" **$37.50**
Lady, Relpo, A-1229, pink flowered hat, white-gloved hands up, 6½" **$38.00**
Lady, Rose, brunette in wide-brimmed hat, brown & peach tones, dated 1978, 7½" **$36.50**
Lady, Rubens, #4104, blond hair held by orange band, matching dress w/ruffled collar, pearl earrings & necklace, 6½"..**$22.50**
Lady, Rubens, #483, blond w/side-swept hair, pearl necklace & drop earrings, hand to face, 6½" **$32.50**

Lady, Rubens, #497/M, blond w/flower in hair, leafy bodice, pearl necklace & earrings, 6½"..............$48.00

Lady, Rubens, #499B, brown bonnet w/blue flower at band, flowers along bodice, 6"........................$42.50

Lady, unmarked, blond in blue ruffled hat w/bow tied to side, 5½"...$42.50

Lady Aileene, Inarco, #E1756, blond w/green-jeweled tiara & necklace, 1964, 5½".............................$37.50

Mexican lady, Conchita, white sombrero, sm flat striped scarf around neck, thick eyelashes lowered, 6"............$50.00

Native lady, Japan, golden brown skin, hair wrapped in yellow, gold loop earrings, molded pearl 3-strand necklace, 5"..$42.50

Snow White, Walt Disney Productions, red bow in hair, bird on shoulder, 5½"................................$225.00

Teenage girl, Inarco, #E3548, blond girl in yellow holds black phone receiver, 5½".............................$32.50

Teenage girl, Japan, blond hair pulled to right side, lg dark brown eyes, pearl earring in left ear, 7"..............$47.50

Teenage girl, Rubens (paper label), #4137, blond w/2 ponytails, pearl drop earrings, ruffled collar w/sm gold bow, 7"..$67.50

Lady in green lustre hat and bodice, gold neck band, 7", $30.00.

Heisey Glass

From just before the turn of the century until 1957, the Heisey Glass Company of Newark, Ohio, was one of the largest, most successful manufacturers of quality tableware in the world. Though the market is well established, many pieces are still reasonably priced; and if you're drawn to the lovely patterns and colors that Heisey made, you're investment should be sound.

After 1901 much of their glassware was marked with their familiar trademark, the 'Diamond H' (an H in a diamond), or a paper label. Blown pieces are often marked on the stem instead of the bowl or foot.

Numbers in the listings are catalog reference numbers assigned by the company to indicate variations in shape or stem style. Collectors use them, especially when they buy and sell by mail, for the same purpose. Many catalog pages (showing these numbers) are contained in *The Collector's Encyclopedia of Heisey Glass* by Neila Bredehoft. This book

and *Elegant Glassware of the Depression Era* by Gene Florence are both excellent references for further study.

Advisor: Debbie Maggard (See Directory, Elegant Glassware)

Newsletter: *The Heisey News*
Heisey Collectors of America
169 W Church St.
Newark, OH 43055; 612-345-2932

Charter Oak, crystal, bowl, floral; oak leaf decor, #116, 11"..$30.00

Charter Oak, green, candlestick, oak leaf decor, #116, 3"..$35.00

Charter Oak, green, stem, saucer champagne; #3362, 6-oz...$20.00

Charter Oak, marigold, stem, cocktail; #3362, 3-oz....$40.00

Charter Oak, marigold, tumbler, flat, #3362, 10-oz.....$30.00

Charter Oak, orchid, comport, low footed, #3362, 6".$70.00

Charter Oak, orchid, tumbler, flat, #3362, 12-oz.......$400.00

Charter Oak, pink, bowl, finger; #3362......................$17.50

Charter Oak, pink, stem, oyster cocktail; low footed, #3362, 3½-oz...$10.00

Charter Oak, plate, luncheon/salad; acorn & leaves decor, #1246, 7"..$8.00

Chintz, crystal, bowl, Nasturtium, 7½".....................$16.00

Chintz, crystal, bowl, pickle/olive; 2-part, 13"............$15.00

Chintz, crystal, bowl, preserve; handled, footed, 5½"..$15.00

Chintz, crystal, mayonnaise, dolphin footed, 5½".......$35.00

Chintz, crystal, plate, hors d'oeuvre; 2-handled, 13"...$20.00

Chintz, crystal, plate, luncheon; square, 8"................$10.00

Chintz, crystal, stem, sherbet; #3389, 5-oz................$8.00

Chintz, yellow, bowl, finger; #4107..........................$15.00

Chintz, yellow, plate, bread; square, 6"......................$15.00

Chintz, yellow, stem, cocktail; #3389, 3-oz................$35.00

Chintz, yellow, stem, parfait; #3389, 5-oz..................$35.00

Chintz, yellow, stem, water; #3389, 9-oz...................$30.00

Chintz, yellow, tumbler, iced tea; #3389, 12-oz...........$30.00

Chintz, yellow, tumbler, juice; footed, #3389, 5-oz.....$22.00

Crystolite, crystal, ashtray/coaster, round, 4"................$6.00

Crystolite, crystal, bottle, syrup; w/drip-cut top..........$85.00

Crystolite, crystal, bowl, conserve; handled, 2-part, 8".$16.00

Crystolite, crystal, bowl, dessert/nappy; 4½"...............$8.00

Crystolite, crystal, bowl, nut; individual, swan shape, 2"..$18.00

Crystolite, crystal, bowl, preserve; 2-handled, 6".......$13.00

Crystolite, crystal, candle block, 1-light, swirl decor...$15.00

Crystolite, crystal, cigarette box, w/lid, 4"..................$17.00

Crystolite, crystal, cigarette holder, round..................$17.50

Crystolite, crystal, coaster, 4"..................................$6.00

Crystolite, crystal, creamer, individual......................$17.00

Crystolite, crystal, cup, punch or custard....................$7.00

Crystolite, crystal, mayonnaise ladle..........................$9.00

Crystolite, crystal, plate, sandwich; 12".....................$35.00

Crystolite, crystal, plate, shell; 7".............................$24.00

Crystolite, crystal, plate, underliner for 1000 Island dressing bowl...$10.00

Crystolite, crystal, salad dressing set, 3-pc.................$38.00

Crystolite, crystal, saucer.......................................$5.00

Crystolite, crystal, sugar bowl, individual..................$15.00

Crystolite, crystal, tray, relish; 5-part, round, 10" **$35.00**
Crystolite, crystal, tumbler, pressed, #5003, 8-oz.........**$60.00**
Crystolite, crystal, urn, flower; 7" **$75.00**
Empress, alexandrite, bowl, cream soup **$65.00**
Empress, alexandrite, creamer, dolphin footed.........**$215.00**
Empress, cobalt, ashtray......................................**$250.00**
Empress, cobalt, candlestick, dolphin footed, 9" **$260.00**
Empress, green, creamer, individual **$40.00**
Empress, green, cup, custard or punch, 4-oz..............**$30.00**
Empress, green, plate, 8"..**$24.00**
Empress, pink, bonbon, 6"..**$20.00**
Empress, pink, bowl, mint; dolphin footed, 6" **$20.00**
Empress, pink, bowl, nappy; 4½" **$8.00**
Empress, pink, bowl, nappy; 8".................................**$35.00**
Empress, pink, bowl, vegetable; oval, 10"..................**$35.00**
Empress, pink, tray, celery; 10" **$16.00**
Empress, pink or yellow, plate, 4½" **$6.00**
Empress, yellow, bowl, dessert; oval, 2-handled, 10".**$60.00**
Empress, yellow, bowl, floral; rolled edge, 9" **$38.00**
Empress, yellow, bowl, nut; individual, dolphin footed.**$26.00**
Empress, yellow, bowl, pickle/olive; 2-part, 13" **$30.00**

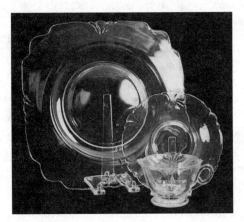

**Empress, yellow, dinner plate, 10",
$150.00; cup and saucer, yellow, $50.00.**

Empress, yellow, vase, flared, 8" **$90.00**
Figurine, crystal, colt, rearing **$195.00**
Figurine, crystal, colt, standing................................**$90.00**
Figurine, crystal, elephant, sm................................**$400.00**
Figurine, crystal, goose, wings down.........................**$95.00**
Figurine, crystal, piglet, standing or sitting, each......**$100.00**
Figurine, crystal, ringneck pheasant, 11¾" **$140.00**
Figurine, crystal, Scotty **$100.00**
Greek Key, crystal, bottle, oil; w/#6 stopper, 4-oz **$80.00**
Greek Key, crystal, bowl, banana split; flat, 9" **$30.00**
Greek Key, crystal, bowl, jelly; low footed, shallow, 4½".**$16.00**
Greek Key, crystal, bowl, nappy; 4" **$20.00**
Greek Key, crystal, bowl, straight sided, low footed, 7"..**$50.00**
Greek Key, crystal, creamer......................................**$35.00**
Greek Key, crystal, jar, horseradish; w/lid, sm...........**$65.00**
Greek Key, crystal, plate, butter; individual **$35.00**
Greek Key, crystal, plate, 4½" **$12.00**
Greek Key, crystal, plate, 6½" **$20.00**
Greek Key, crystal, sherbet, low footed, 6-oz **$13.00**
Greek Key, crystal, sherbet, straight sided, footed, 4½-oz...**$15.00**
Greek Key, crystal, sugar bowl..................................**$35.00**

Greek Key, crystal, tumbler, straight sided, 12-oz......**$40.00**
Greek Key, crystal, tumbler, straight sided, 5-oz.........**$20.00**
Ipswich, cobalt, bowl, floral; footed, 11"..................**$250.00**
Ipswich, crystal, plate, square, 8" **$20.00**
Ipswich, crystal, stem, oyster cocktail; footed, 4-oz....**$22.00**
Ipswich, green, sherbet, knob in stem, footed, 4-oz..**$35.00**
Ipswich, pink, candy jar, w/lid, ½-lb **$225.00**
Ipswich, pink, creamer..**$50.00**
Ipswich, pink, plate, square, 7".................................**$40.00**
Ipswich, yellow, bowl, finger; w/underplate..............**$60.00**
Ipswich, yellow, candlestick, 1-light, 6" **$150.00**
Ipswich, yellow, tumbler, soda; footed, 5-oz **$40.00**
Lariat, crystal, bowl, camellia; 9½"..........................**$22.00**
Lariat, crystal, bowl, cream soup; 2-handled **$40.00**
Lariat, crystal, bowl, floral or fruit; 12".....................**$30.00**
Lariat, crystal, bowl, floral; oval, 13" **$50.00**
Lariat, crystal, bowl, mayonnaise; 2-part, 7" **$20.00**
Lariat, crystal, cheese dish, w/lid, footed, 5" **$40.00**
Lariat, crystal, creamer..**$15.00**
Lariat, crystal, mayonnaise set, bowl (5"), plate (7"), w/ladle
    3-pc set **$55.00**
Lariat, crystal, plate, demi-torte; rolled edge, 12"........**$27.00**
Lariat, crystal, plate, finger bowl liner; 6" **$7.00**
Lariat, crystal, platter, oval, 15"...............................**$50.00**
Lariat, crystal, stem, blown, 10-oz **$20.00**
Lariat, crystal, stem, cocktail; blown, 3½-oz.............**$15.00**
Lariat, crystal, tumbler, iced tea; blown, footed, 12-oz ..**$18.00**
Lodestar, Dawn, bowl, #1565, 6¾"..........................**$45.00**
Lodestar, Dawn, bowl, floral; deep, 12".....................**$75.00**
Lodestar, Dawn, bowl, sauce dish; #1626, 4½" **$35.00**
Lodestar, Dawn, creamer, w/handle...........................**$85.00**
Lodestar, Dawn, plate, 14" **$85.00**
Lodestar, Dawn, sugar bowl, w/handle **$85.00**
Minuet, crystal, bowl, jelly; 2-handled, footed, 6".......**$20.00**
Minuet, crystal, bowl, relish; 3-part, 7" **$35.00**
Minuet, crystal, bowl, salad; shallow, 13½"................**$75.00**
Minuet, crystal, creamer, individual, #1511, Toujours.**$37.50**
Minuet, crystal, mayonnaise, footed, #1511, Toujours ..**$45.00**
Minuet, crystal, plate, mayonnaise liner; 7" **$10.00**
Minuet, crystal, plate, salad; #1511, Toujours, 7" **$12.00**
Minuet, crystal, saucer **$10.00**
Minuet, crystal, stem, sherbet; #5010, 6-oz................**$15.00**
Minuet, crystal, stem, wine; #5010, 2½-oz.................**$70.00**
Minuet, crystal, tray, for individual creamer & sugar
    bowl **$25.00**
Minuet, crystal, vase, #4192, 10"..............................**$95.00**
Minuet, crystal, vase, urn; #5012, 6"..........................**$70.00**

Moongleam, green, candlestick, 6", $150.00.

New Era, crystal, bowl, floral; 11".............$35.00
New Era, crystal, pilsner, 12-oz $30.00
New Era, crystal, plate, 9x7"......................$25.00
New Era, crystal, saucer $5.00
New Era, crystal, stem, goblet; 10-oz..........$15.00
New Era, crystal, stem, high cocktail; 3½-oz...........$10.00
New Era, crystal, stem, oyster cocktail; 3½-oz...........$10.00
New Era, crystal, tray, celery; 13"...............$30.00
New Era, crystal, tumbler, soda; footed, 8-oz...........$10.00
Octagon, crystal, basket, #500, 5"..............$85.00
Octagon, crystal, creamer, #500 ....$7.00
Octagon, crystal, cup, after dinner.............$15.00
Octagon, green, plate, cream soup liner.........$9.00
Octagon, marigold, bowl, nut; individual, 2-handled..$65.00
Octagon, orchid, bowl, grapefruit; 6½" $35.00
Octagon, orchid, plate, muffin; sides up, #1229, 10"..$40.00
Octagon, pink, bowl, mint; #1229, 6"..........$15.00
Octagon, pink, candlestick, 1-light, 3" $25.00
Octagon, pink or yellow, plate, 6" $8.00
Octagon, pink or yellow, saucer, after dinner.............$6.00
Octagon, yellow, bonbon, sides up, #1229, 6"...........$15.00
Octagon, yellow, plate, sandwich; #1229, 10"...........$25.00
Octagon, yellow or green, tray, celery; 12" $17.00
Old Colony, crystal, bowl, cream soup; 2-handled.....$12.00
Old Colony, crystal, bowl, nappy; 4½" $7.00
Old Colony, crystal, bowl, 3-handled, 9".......$36.00
Old Colony, crystal, mayonnaise, dolphin footed, 5½"...$36.00
Old Colony, crystal, plate, round, 12"..........$31.00
Old Colony, green, bowl, grapefruit; footed, #3380 ...$20.00
Old Colony, green, bowl, jelly; 2-handled, footed, 6" ..$32.50
Old Colony, green, plate, square, 6"...........$15.00
Old Colony, green, stem, champagne; #3380, 6-oz $17.00
Old Colony, green, tray, celery; 10"...........$30.00
Old Colony, green, vase, footed, 9"............$175.00
Old Colony, marigold, stem, short soda; #3380, 10-oz ...$30.00
Old Colony, marigold, tumbler, tea; footed, #3380, 12-oz...$35.00
Old Colony, pink, bowl, finger; #4075 ....$15.00
Old Colony, pink, bowl, salad; 2-handled, square, 10" ..$45.00
Old Colony, pink, cup, after dinner.............$25.00
Old Colony, pink, plate, sandwich; 2-handled, square, 13"...$40.00
Old Colony, pink, stem, tall soda; #3380, 10-oz $21.00
Old Colony, pink, tumbler, soda; footed, #3380, 8-oz $21.00
Old Colony, pink or yellow, stem, parfait; #3380, 5-oz..$15.00
Old Colony, yellow, bowl, grapefruit; 6".......$30.00
Old Colony, yellow, bowl, 3-part, 7" $25.00
Old Colony, yellow, saucer, round or square $10.00

Old Colony, yellow, sherbet, $32.00.

Old Sandwich, cobalt, ashtray, individual...........$45.00
Old Sandwich, crystal, bowl, finger $12.00
Old Sandwich, crystal, floral block, #22 ....$15.00
Old Sandwich, green, pilsner, 8-oz $38.00
Old Sandwich, green, sundae, 6-oz $35.00
Old Sandwich, pink, bowl, floral; footed, round, 11".$85.00
Old Sandwich, pink, plate, ground bottom, square, 6" .$20.00
Old Sandwich, pink or yellow, saucer...........$15.00
Old Sandwich, yellow, candlestick, 6" $90.00
Orchid, crystal, bowl, fruit or salad; footed, 9".........$125.00
Orchid, crystal, bowl, jelly; footed, Waverly, 6½".......$40.00
Orchid, crystal, bowl, nappy; Queen Ann, 4½" $37.50
Orchid, crystal, butter dish, w/lid, Waverly, 6" $170.00
Orchid, crystal, candlestick, 2-light, Trident, 5"...........$50.00
Orchid, crystal, mayonnaise, footed, 5½" $40.00
Orchid, crystal, plate, Queen Ann, 15½" $95.00
Orchid, crystal, plate, sandwich; handled, round, 12" .$50.00
Orchid, crystal, plate, 6".........................$12.50
Orchid, crystal, stem, oyster cocktail; #5022 or #5025, 4-oz ..$57.50
Orchid, crystal, stem, sherbet; #5022 or #5025, 6-oz ..$25.00
Orchid, crystal, vase, fan; footed, 7" $85.00
Pleat & Panel, crystal, bowl, grapefruit/cereal; 6½"......$5.00
Pleat & Panel, crystal, bowl, nappy; 4½"........$5.00
Pleat & Panel, crystal, plate, 6"..................$4.00
Pleat & Panel, crystal, saucer....................$3.00
Pleat & Panel, crystal, sherbet, footed, 5-oz.............$4.00
Pleat & Panel, green, bowl, chow chow; 4"...........$12.00
Pleat & Panel, green, creamer, hotel size $30.00
Pleat & Panel, green, tumbler, ground bottom, 8-oz ..$15.00
Pleat & Panel, pink, plate, bread; 7"...........$8.00
Pleat & Panel, pink, saucer.......................$5.00
Pleat & Panel, pink, stem, 8-oz $20.00
Pleat & Panel, pink, tumbler, tea; ground bottom, 12-oz.$17.50
Pleat & Panel, pink or green, plate, bouillon underliner; 6¾".............$8.00
Provincial, crystal, bowl, floral; 12"...........$30.00
Provincial, crystal, bowl, nut/jelly; individual.............$15.00
Provincial, crystal, creamer, footed.............$20.00
Provincial, crystal, plate, bread; 7".............$10.00
Provincial, crystal, stem, sherbet/champagne; 5-oz.......$7.00
Provincial, limelight green, bowl, nappy; tricorner, 5½"..$55.00
Provincial, limelight green, bowl, nappy; 4½" $60.00
Provincial, limelight green, tumbler, footed, 9-oz $65.00
Queen Ann, crystal, bowl, floral; footed, 2-handled, 8½"..$30.00
Queen Ann, crystal, bowl, relish; 3-part, 10".............$20.00
Queen Ann, crystal, bowl, relish; 3-part, 7" $12.50
Queen Ann, crystal, comport, footed, 6" $25.00
Queen Ann, crystal, creamer, dolphin footed $15.00
Queen Ann, crystal, cup, after dinner...........$15.00
Queen Ann, crystal, ice tub, w/metal handles $40.00
Queen Ann, crystal, mustard jar, w/lid $30.00
Queen Ann, crystal, plate, sandwich; 2-handled, 12" .$25.00
Queen Ann, crystal, plate, 6" $5.00
Queen Ann, crystal, plate, 9" $12.00
Queen Ann, crystal, saucer $3.00
Queen Ann, crystal, tray, celery; 13".............$16.00
Ridgeleigh, crystal, ashtray, square...............$4.00
Ridgeleigh, crystal, basket, bonbon..............$11.00
Ridgeleigh, crystal, bowl, floral; oval, 12"....$35.00

Ridgeleigh, crystal, bowl, nappy; straight, 5".................**$6.50**
Ridgeleigh, crystal, bowl, nut; individual.....................**$9.00**
Ridgeleigh, crystal, candle block, #1469½, 3" **$20.00**
Ridgeleigh, crystal, cigarette holder, round.................**$7.50**
Ridgeleigh, crystal, comport, flared, low footed, 6"....**$16.00**
Ridgeleigh, crystal, plate, round, 6".........................**$7.00**
Ridgeleigh, crystal, plate, round, 8".......................**$17.50**
Ridgeleigh, crystal, saucer **$5.00**
Ridgeleigh, crystal, stem, cocktail; blown, 3½-oz **$30.00**
Ridgeleigh, crystal, stem, oyster cocktail; pressed.......**$15.00**
Ridgeleigh, crystal, stem, tall, 8-oz **$30.00**
Ridgeleigh, crystal, tray, for individual creamer & sugar bowl...**$12.50**
Ridgeleigh, crystal, tumbler, pressed, #1469½, 10-oz .**$30.00**
Ridgeleigh, crystal, vase, 8"..................................**$55.00**
Rose, crystal, bowl, dressing; oval, 2-part, Waverly, 6½".**$65.00**
Rose, crystal, bowl, finger; #3309.........................**$95.00**
Rose, crystal, bowl, floral; crimped, Waverly, 9½"......**$65.00**
Rose, crystal, bowl, jelly; footed, Waverly, 6½" **$45.00**
Rose, crystal, bowl, jelly; footed, 2-handled, Queen Ann, 6"...**$42.50**
Rose, crystal, candlestick, 1-light, #112.................**$40.00**
Rose, crystal, cigarette holder, #4035 ....**$95.00**
Rose, crystal, comport, low footed, Waverly, 6½" **$60.00**
Rose, crystal, cup, Waverly **$65.00**
Rose, crystal, mayonnaise, 2-handled, Waverly, 5½" ..**$55.00**
Rose, crystal, plate, mayonnaise; Waverly, 7"............**$20.00**

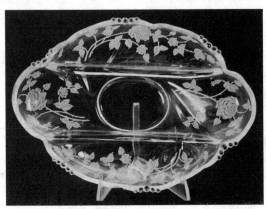

Rose, crystal, relish, 3-part, 11", $85.00.

Rose, crystal, stem, oyster cocktail; footed, #5072, 3½-oz..**$32.50**
Rose, crystal, stem, sherbet; #5072, 6-oz.....................**$27.50**
Rose, crystal, sugar bowl, footed, Waverly **$22.50**
Rose, crystal, tumbler, tea; footed, #5072, 12-oz.........**$55.00**
Saturn, crystal, bowl, baked apple **$7.00**
Saturn, crystal, bowl, floral; 13".................................**$37.00**
Saturn, crystal, bowl, nappy; 4½".................................**$5.00**
Saturn, crystal, bowl, salad; 11"..................................**$40.00**
Saturn, crystal, bowl, whipped cream; 5".......................**$15.00**
Saturn, crystal, creamer **$17.00**
Saturn, crystal, mayonnaise **$8.00**
Saturn, crystal, plate, luncheon; 8"..............................**$7.00**
Saturn, crystal, plate, 6"..**$3.00**
Saturn, crystal, saucer **$5.00**
Saturn, crystal, stem, 10-oz.......................................**$5.00**
Saturn, crystal, sugar shaker (pourer) **$80.00**

Saturn, crystal, tumbler, old-fashioned; 7-oz.............**$10.00**
Saturn, crystal, vase, flared or straight, 8½".............**$25.00**
Saturn, limelight green, bowl, fruit; flared rim, 12" ..**$100.00**
Saturn, limelight green, plate, 6" **$35.00**
Saturn, limelight green, stem, sherbet; 4½-oz **$70.00**
Saturn, limelight green, tumbler, 10-oz **$70.00**
Stanhope, crystal, bowl, finger; blown or plain, #4080 ..**$5.00**
Stanhope, crystal, bowl, mint; 2-handled, w/ or w/out round knobs, 6"...**$15.00**
Stanhope, crystal, creamer, 2-handled, w/ or w/out round knobs **$25.00**
Stanhope, crystal, stem, cocktail; pressed, 3½-oz **$10.00**
Stanhope, crystal, stem, wine; pressed, 2½-oz............**$20.00**
Stanhope, crystal, tumbler, soda; #4083, 5-oz.............**$20.00**
Twist, crystal, bonbon **$5.00**
Twist, crystal, bowl, jelly; 2-handled, 6" **$7.00**
Twist, crystal, cheese dish, 2-handled, 6" **$5.00**
Twist, crystal, plate, cream soup liner......................**$5.00**
Twist, crystal, tumbler, soda; flat bottom, 5-oz.........**$4.00**
Twist, green, bowl, floral; oval, 4-footed, 12" **$50.00**
Twist, green, bowl, grapefruit; footed.......................**$35.00**
Twist, green, bowl, nut; individual **$27.50**
Twist, green, plate, sandwich; 2-handled, 12"............**$50.00**
Twist, green, sugar bowl, footed..............................**$37.50**
Twist, pink, bowl, floral; 9"...................................**$35.00**
Twist, pink, mayonnaise **$40.00**
Twist, pink, saucer...**$5.00**
Twist, pink, sugar bowl, w/lid, zigzag handles...........**$27.00**
Twist, yellow, bowl, nappy; 4"..................................**$17.00**
Twist, yellow, creamer, oval, hotel size **$50.00**
Twist, yellow, plate, muffin; 2-handled, turned sides, 12" ..**$65.00**
Twist, yellow, sugar bowl, oval, hotel size **$50.00**
Twist, yellow, tumbler, iced tea; footed, 12-oz **$50.00**
Victorian, crystal, bottle, French dressing **$65.00**
Victorian, crystal, bowl, finger **$15.00**
Victorian, crystal, butter dish, ¼-lb **$65.00**
Victorian, crystal, cigarette box, 6" **$75.00**
Victorian, crystal, creamer.......................................**$25.00**
Victorian, crystal, plate, liner for finger; 6" **$10.00**
Victorian, crystal, stem, claret; 3-oz..........................**$20.00**
Victorian, crystal, stem, goblet; 1 ball, 9-oz................**$20.00**
Victorian, crystal, tumbler, soda; straight or curved edge, 5-oz...**$15.00**
Victorian, crystal, vase, 4".......................................**$25.00**
Waverly, crystal, bowl, floral; sea horse footed, 11" ...**$65.00**
Waverly, crystal, bowl, ice; 2-handled, 6½".................**$50.00**
Waverly, crystal, candle epergnette, 6½" **$10.00**
Waverly, crystal, creamer & sugar bowl, individual, w/ tray **$47.00**
Waverly, crystal, plate, luncheon; 8" **$8.00**
Waverly, crystal, saucer **$3.00**
Waverly, crystal, stem, sherbet/champagne; #5019, 5½-oz..**$7.00**
Waverly, crystal, tumbler, juice; footed, blown, #5019, 5-oz **$17.00**
Waverly, crystal, vase, footed, 7"..............................**$25.00**
Yeoman, crystal, bowl, cream soup; 2-handled **$12.00**
Yeoman, crystal, cigarette box/ashtray.....................**$25.00**
Yeoman, crystal, plate, bouillon underliner; 6" **$3.00**
Yeoman, crystal, plate, oyster cocktail; 8" or 9" **$9.00**

Yeoman, crystal, stem, cocktail; 3-oz **$10.00**
Yeoman, crystal, tumbler, cupped rim, 10-oz **$4.00**
Yeoman, green, cruet, oil; 4-oz **$65.00**
Yeoman, green, plate, cheese; 2-handled **$15.00**
Yeoman, green, plate, relish; 4-part, 11" **$32.00**
Yeoman, green, plate, 6" **$10.00**
Yeoman, green, stem, soda; 5-oz **$12.00**
Yeoman, green, tray, celery; 9" **$15.00**
Yeoman, marigold, bowl, lemon; round, 5" **$25.00**
Yeoman, orchid, bowl, nappy; 4½" **$15.00**
Yeoman, orchid, bowl, preserve; oval, 6" **$27.00**
Yeoman, orchid, parfait, 5-oz **$30.00**
Yeoman, pink, ashtray, handled, bow-tie shape, 4" ...**$20.00**
Yeoman, pink, comport, shallow, high footed, 5" **$25.00**
Yeoman, pink, green, orchid or marigold, sugar bowl, w/lid **$40.00**
Yeoman, pink, plate, relish; 4-part, 11" **$27.00**
Yeoman, pink, plate, 6" **$6.00**
Yeoman, pink, tray, celery; 9" **$14.00**
Yeoman, pink, tray insert, 3½x4½" **$6.00**
Yeoman, pink or yellow, creamer **$20.00**
Yeoman, yellow, bowl, berry; 2-handled, 8½" **$25.00**
Yeoman, yellow, bowl, finger...................................**$17.00**
Yeoman, yellow, stem, cocktail; 3-oz........................**$17.00**
Yeoman, yellow, tray, relish; 3-part, 13" **$32.00**
Yeoman, yellow, tumbler, 8-oz **$17.00**
Yeoman, yellow or green, stem, soda; 5-oz **$12.00**

Holt Howard

Here's one of today's newest collectibles, and dealers from all over the country tell us it's catching on fast! Now's the time to pick up those kitchenware items (cruets, salt and peppers, condiments, etc.) and novelty banks, ashtrays, and planters marked Holt Howard. There's a wide variety of items and decorative themes; those you're most likely to find will be from the rooster (done in golden brown, yellow and orange), white cat, Santa and pixie lines. They're not only marked but dated as well; you'll find production dates from the 1950s through the seventies. Beware of unmarked copy-cat lines!

Advisor: April Tvorak (See Directory, Figural Ceramics)

Christmas

Airwick, holly girl figural **$38.00**
Angel, cardboard cone body covered w/pink feathers, ceramic head **$22.00**
Ashtray, Santa, med **$25.00**
Bell, holly decoration **$15.00**
Candle holders, angel & fawn, pr **$30.00**
Candle holders, angel figures, pr **$35.00**
Candle holders, Santa w/climbing mouse, pr.............**$35.00**
Candlestick, Santa handle **$22.00**
Demitasse pot, inverted fluting, flared cylinder, white matt w/applied holly & berries, from $50 to **$65.00**
Mug, Santa, $10 to **$12.00**

Pitcher, juice; winking Santa, naturalistic modeling, +6 sm mugs, from $55 to **$65.00**
Pitcher, juice; winking Santa, stylized fan-like beard, +6 sm mugs, from $70 to **$85.00**
Salt & pepper shakers, Santa's head is salt, stacks on pepper body, from $30 to **$40.00**

Pixie Ware

Cherries jar, flat head finial on lid, w/cherry pick or spoon, from $65 to...**$80.00**
Chili sauce, scarce, from $150 to.............................**$170.00**
Honey, very rare, from $175 to **$190.00**
Hors d'oeurve, head on body pierced for toothpicks, exaggerated tall hairdo, saucer base, from $120 to...**$145.00**
Instant coffee jar, brown-skinned blond head finial, from $150 to **$175.00**
Jam & jelly jar, flat-head finial on lid, from $45 to **$60.00**
Ketchup jar, orange tomato-like head finial on lid, from $45 to **$60.00**
Mayonnaise jar, winking head finial on lid, from $45 to...**$60.00**
Mustard jar, yellow head finial on lid, from $45 to **$60.00**
Olive jar, winking green head finial on lid, from $65 to....**$75.00**
Onion jar, flat onion-head finial on lid, 1958, from $65 to **$75.00**
Salt & pepper shakers, pr, from $55 to.......................**$65.00**

Rooster

Bud vase...**$22.00**
Butter dish, embossed rooster, ¼-lb **$35.00**
Candle holders, figural rooster, pr, from $20 to **$25.00**
Coffeepot, electric, from $65 to...............................**$75.00**
Coffeepot, embossed rooster, from $70 to..................**$85.00**
Cookie jar, embossed rooster, from $75 to **$85.00**
Creamer & sugar bowl, embossed rooster..................**$45.00**
Egg cup, double; figural rooster...............................**$18.00**
Jam & jelly jar, embossed rooster.............................**$35.00**
Ketchup jar, embossed rooster **$35.00**
Mug, embossed rooster **$15.00**
Mustard jar, embossed rooster.................................**$35.00**
Napkin holder, from $15 to **$20.00**
Pitcher, embossed rooster, from $40 to......................**$50.00**
Plate, embossed rooster, 8½", from $10 to **$12.00**
Platter, embossed rooster, oval **$25.00**
Salt & pepper shakers, embossed rooster, pr.............**$10.00**
Salt & pepper shakers, figural rooster, tall, pr, from $25 to **$30.00**
Spoon rest, figural rooster, from $30 to **$35.00**

White Cat

Ashtray, cat on square plaid base, 4 corner rests, from $60 to...**$75.00**
Bud vase, cat in plaid cap & neckerchief, from $65 to .**$75.00**
Butter dish, cats peeking out on side, ¼-lb, rare **$150.00**
Cookie jar, head form, from $40 to...........................**$50.00**
Cottage cheese keeper, cat knob on lid, from $45 to.**$55.00**
Letter holder, cat w/coiled-wire back **$25.00**

Memo pad, full-bodied, legs cradle note pad, from $85 to..**$95.00**

**Salt and pepper shakers, cat figures,
meow when shaken, $20.00 for the pair.**

Salt & pepper shakers, cat's head, pr, from $15 to **$20.00**
Salt & pepper shakers, tall cats, pr..............................**$20.00**
Salt & pepper shakers, 4 individual cat heads stacked on
    upright dowel, from $90 to.................................**$120.00**
Scouring powder shaker, full-bodied lady cat, wearing apron,
    w/broom, from $75 to...**$95.00**
Sewing box, figural cat w/tape-measure tongue on lid, from
    $65 to...**$75.00**
String holder, head only, from $35 to **$45.00**
Sugar shaker, cat in apron carries sack lettered 'Pour,' shaker
    holes in hat, side pour spout formed by sack, rare.**$145.00**
Wall pocket, cat's head, from $35 to...........................**$45.00**

Miscellaneous

Ash receiver, comical man in yellow shirt & blue pants, open-
    ing/cigarette rest in stomach, from $100 to **$125.00**
Bank, Coin Clown, bobbing head, from $150 to......**$185.00**
Bank, Dandy Lion, bobbing head, from $140 to **$160.00**
Bank, full-bodied kangaroo, lettered Kangaroo Bank ..**$85.00**
Candle holder, baby chick, from $20 to **$25.00**
Candle holder, boy on shoe **$22.00**
Candle holder, kneeling girl, 2-light............................**$15.00**
Cherry jar, Cherries If You Please lettered on sign held by
    butler **$260.00**
Child's dish, Braille ABCs...**$25.00**
Desk set, figural chickens in white gold & brown, sharpener,
    pencil holder & pen holder, 3-pc set...................**$95.00**
Lipstick holder, ponytail girl, from $60 to **$75.00**
Note pad holder, 3-dimensional lady's hand..............**$45.00**
Plant feeder, bird form **$35.00**
Planter, camel...**$15.00**
Planter, girl **$15.00**
Planter, mother deer & fawn, white w/gold bow, from
    $22 to...**$28.00**
Plate, Rake 'N Spade, MIB **$20.00**
Playing card holder, on base w/3-dimensional bust of granny
    holding playing cards, from $45 to **$55.00**
Russian dressing bottle, stopper is head of man in beret-style
    hat, from $100 to **$125.00**
Salt & pepper shakers, bunnies in wicker baskets, pr..**$45.00**
Salt & pepper shakers, mice in wicker baskets, pr.....**$35.00**
Salt & pepper shakers, ponytail girl, pr......................**$45.00**

Salt & pepper shakers, Rock & Roll, head on springs, pr, from
    $70 to...**$90.00**
Salt & pepper shakers, tomatoes, pr...........................**$15.00**
Snack set, tomato, 1 cup & 1 plate, 1962 ....**$14.00**

Homer Laughlin China Co.

Since well before the turn of the century, the Homer Laughlin China Company of Newell, West Virginia, has been turning out dinnerware and kitchenware lines in hundreds of styles and patterns. Most of their pieces are marked either 'HLC' or 'Homer Laughlin.' As styles changed over the years, they designed several basic dinnerware shapes that they used as a basis for literally hundreds of different patterns simply by applying various decals and glaze treatments. A few of their most popular lines are represented below. If you find pieces stamped with a name like Virginia Rose, Rhythm, or Nautalis, don't assume it to be the pattern name; it's the shape name. Virginia Rose, for instance, was decorated with many different decals. If you have some you're trying to sell through a mail or a phone contact, it would be a good idea to send the prospective buyer a zerox copy of the pattern.

For further information see *The Collector's Encyclopedia of Homer Laughlin Pottery* and *American Dinnerware, 1880s to 1920s*, both by Joanne Jasper. *The Collector's Encyclopedia of Fiesta* by Sharon and Bob Huxford has photographs and prices of several of the more collectible lines we mentioned above.

Note: For Harlequin, the high range of values should be used to price maroon, gray, and spruce green; chartreuse, dark green, rose, red, light green, and mauve blue will run about 10% less. The low range is for evaluating turquoise and yellow. For medium green Harlequin, double the high side of the high range of values.

See also Fiesta.

Newsletter: *The Laughlin Eagle*
c/o Richard Racheter
1270 63rd Terrace South
St. Petersburg, FL 33705; published quarterly

Amberstone

Bowl, jumbo salad; from $30 to **$40.00**
Bowl, vegetable; from $12 to.......................................**$15.00**
Creamer, from $6.50 to...**$7.50**
Mug, jumbo; rare, from $18 to **$22.00**
Pie plate, from $30 to...**$35.00**
Relish tray, center handle, from $22 to........................**$28.00**
Tea server, from $40 to **$50.00**

Conchita

Bowl, fruit; 5", from $9 to..**$12.00**
Bowl, mixing; Kitchen Kraft, 8", from $28 to **$32.00**
Casserole, Kitchen Kraft, 8½", from $65 to..................**$75.00**
Pie plate, Kitchen Kraft, from $28 to...........................**$32.00**
Plate, 9", from $15 to..**$20.00**

Platter, square well, 15", from $30 to $40.00
Platter, 10", from $15 to..................................$20.00
Salt & pepper shakers, Kitchen Kraft, pr, from $45 to.$50.00
Sugar bowl, w/lid, from $22 to $28.00
Tumbler, fired-on design, 6-oz, from $9 to $12.00

Epicure

Bowl, cereal/soup; from $20 to $25.00
Creamer, from $15 to......................................$18.00
Ladle, 5½", from $38 to...................................$42.00
Plate, 10", from $18 to...................................$22.00
Plate, 6½", from $6 to....................................$8.00
Salt & pepper shakers, pr, from $16 to....................$22.00
Teacup & saucer, from $18 to..............................$22.00

Harlequin

Ashtray, basketweave, low range, from $28 to $32.00
Bowl, cream soup; high range, from $22 to.............$26.00
Bowl, cream soup; low range, from $16 to..............$20.00
Bowl, oval baker, high range, from $30 to.............$32.00
Butter dish, ½-lb, low range, from $85 to $95.00
Creamer, high range, individual, from $28 to............$32.00
Cup, demitasse; high range, from $85 to..............$100.00
Cup, demitasse; low range, from $30 to................$38.00
Egg cup, double, low range, from $12 to................$16.00
Pitcher, service water; low range, from $55 to.........$65.00
Plate, high range, 10", from $25 to.....................$30.00

Pitcher, service water; maroon (high range), $60.00.

Plate, high range, 6", from $4 to.......................$5.50
Plate, low range, 10", from $15 to......................$18.00
Salt & pepper shakers, high range, pr, from $15 to....$20.00
Sauce boat, low range, from $18 to $22.00
Teacup, high range, from $9 to..........................$11.00
Tumbler, low range, from $35 to $40.00

Jubilee

Bowl, fruit; from $4 to.................................$5.00
Coffeepot, from $30 to..................................$35.00
Egg cup, from $7 to.....................................$11.00
Nappy, 8½", from $7 to..................................$9.00
Plate, 10", from $8 to..................................$10.00
Plate, 7", from $3 to...................................$4.50
Platter, 13", from $9 to................................$12.00
Sugar bowl, w/lid, from $7 to $10.00

Teapot, from $32 to..................................$40.00

Kraft

Plate, 9", $8.00; creamer, $8.00; sugar bowl with lid, $10.00; teapot, $25.00. (Photo courtesy of Darlene Nossaman.)

Laughlin Art China

Bonbon, Flow Blue, gold trim, from $130 to $150.00
Bowl, orange; Currant, w/handles, 12", from $150 to...$175.00
Mug, Monk, from $150 to...............................$175.00
Plate, Currant, ruffled, 2x10", from $125 to..........$150.00
Plate, Currant, 7", from $30 to.......................$40.00
Stein, White Pets, from $210 to $230.00

Max-i-cana

Bowl, lug soup; 4½", from $30 to.......................$35.00
Butter dish, ½-lb, from $100 to $125.00
Egg cup, rolled edge, from $30 to $40.00
Plate, deep, 8", from $18 to...........................$22.00
Platter, oval well, 13½", from $40 to..................$50.00
Sauce boat, from $28 to................................$32.00
Tumbler, fired-on design, 8-oz, from $12 to............$16.00

Mexicana

Bowl, deep, 2½x5", from $35 to $40.00
Bowl, vegetable; 8½", from $22 to......................$25.00
Cake plate, Kitchen Kraft, 10½", from $28 to...........$32.00
Creamer, from $15 to...................................$18.00
Jar, w/lid, lg, from $120 to..........................$135.00
Plate, 7", from $9 to..................................$12.00
Platter, oval well, 11½", from $28 to..................$32.00
Tumbler, fired-on design, 10-oz, from $15 to...........$18.00
Underplate, 9", from $32 to $38.00

Rhythm

Bowl, cereal/chowder; footed, from $9 to $12.00
Casserole lid, from $40 to.............................$50.00
Cup & saucer, from $8 to...............................$10.00
Plate, 9", from $7 to..................................$9.00
Sauce boat, cobalt, from $16 to........................$20.00
Sugar bowl, w/lid, from $12 to $15.00
Tidbit tray, 3-tier, from $32 to.......................$38.00

Riviera

Bowl, baker; 9", from $16 to $20.00
Bowl, cream soup; w/ivory liner, from $60 to $70.00
Butter dish, ½-lb, from $85 to.......................$115.00
Nappy, 7¼", from $18 to..............................$22.00
Plate, 9", from $12 to...............................$15.00
Platter, closed handles, 11¼", from $18 to $20.00
Sugar bowl, w/lid, from $14 to $17.00
Tumbler, handled, from $52 to.........................$75.00

Serenade

Bowl, lug soup; from $15 to...........................$20.00
Casserole, from $55 to................................$65.00
Creamer, from $7 to...................................$9.00
Pickle dish, from $9 to...............................$12.00
Plate, 10", from $9 to................................$12.00
Platter, 12½", from $10 to............................$14.00
Salt & pepper shakers, pr, from $10 to................$13.00
Sauce boat, from $12 to...............................$15.00
Sugar bowl, w/lid, from $9 to.........................$12.00
Teacup & saucer, from $8 to...........................$10.00
Teapot, from $50 to...................................$65.00

Virginia Rose

Bowl, deep, 5", from $12 to $15.00
Bowl, mixing; Kitchen Kraft, 10", from $30 to $35.00
Butter dish, ½-lb, from $80 to.......................$100.00
Cake plate, Kitchen Kraft, from $40 to $50.00
Cup & saucer, from $9 to..............................$10.00
Mug, coffee; from $25 to..............................$35.00
Plate, 10", from $10 to...............................$12.00
Plate, 7", from $8 to.................................$10.00

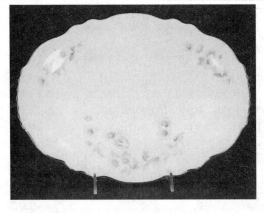

Platter, from $20.00 to $25.00.

Platter, 13", from $20 to.............................$25.00
Platter/gravy liner, 9", from $20 to $25.00
Sugar bowl, w/lid, from $15 to $20.00

Wells Art Glaze

Bowl, cream soup; from $18 to.........................$22.00
Casserole, from $45 to................................$55.00
Creamer, from $15 to..................................$18.00
Cup & saucer, from $12 to.............................$16.00

Nut dish/butter pat, from $8 to $10.00
Plate, 10", from $15 to...............................$18.00
Sauce boat, from $15 to...............................$20.00
Teapot, from $60 to...................................$65.00

Horton Ceramics

Mr. Horace Horton and his wife, Gerry, began production of ceramics in 1949 in Eastland, Texas. All designs were from original sculptures that had been made by Gerry. They continued to produce vases, planters, figurines, and novelty items for florists, variety stores, hardware stores, and gift shops all over the United States until they sold the business in 1961. Pieces are usually marked Horton Ceramics in script on the bottom and may also have a mold number.

Advisor: Darlene Nossaman (See Directory, Horton Ceramics)

Ashtray, painted fruit, #KS-120 ....$4.00
Ashtray, raspberry, white, chartreuse, #A5, 5"........$3.00
Ashtray, rooster, black, turquoise, #1910, 9".........$3.00
Ashtray, Thunderbird, turquoise, white & black, 8" wide..$10.00
Ashtray, 2 rearing horses, Western, 12x7"............$25.00
Planter, #912, mustard, green, pink, 11".............$12.00
Planter, baby bassinet, pink or blue, 5".............$5.00

Planter, brown horse with black mane and tail, W-88, oval, 6", $7.50; Pitcher, rearing horse with black mane and tail, 1-quart, $18.00.

Planter, elephant, 8"................................$5.00
Planter, lady's head, 6" $30.00
Planter, nut bowl, green, lime, yellow, H-4, 7" long.....$7.00
Planter, squirrel on log, brown, 12" $10.00
Planter vase, cat, 7½"..............................$5.00
Planter vase, elephant, 8"..........................$5.00
Planter vase, flower motif, green, lime, yellow, #206...$5.00
Planter vase, free-form, green, lime, #505, 5" wide $4.00
Planter vase, free-form, green, lime, burgundy, mustard, #505..$3.00
Planter vase, hat box, black & white, marked HB, 4" ..$4.00
Planter vase, kangaroo, 7½"..........................$5.00
Planter vase, penguin, 7"...........................$5.00
Planter vase, skunk, 6½"............................$5.00
Planter/vase, plain, green, lime, yellow, HH-1, 7" $3.00
Vase, football player, B-9, 10" $16.00

Vase, pink, blue, yellow, green, C-9, 8½"......................**$6.00**
Vase, swan figural, 10" **$10.00**

Hull Pottery

Hull has a look of its own. Many lines were made in soft, pastel matt glazes and modeled with flowers and ribbons, resulting in a very feminine appeal.

The company operated in Crooksville (near Zanesville), Ohio, from just after the turn of the century until they closed in 1985. From the thirties until the plant was destroyed by fire in 1950, they preferred the soft matt glazes so popular with today's collectors, though a few high gloss lines were made as well. When the plant was rebuilt, modern equipment was installed which they soon found did not lend itself to the duplication of the matt glazes, so they began to concentrate on the production of glossy wares, novelties, and figurines.

During the forties and fifties, they produced a line of kitchenware items modeled after Little Red Riding Hood. Some of this line was sent to Regal China, who decorated Hull's whiteware. All of these pieces are very expensive today. (See also Little Red Riding Hood.)

Hull's Mirror Brown dinnerware line made from about 1960 until they closed in 1985 was very successful for them and was made in large quantities. Its glossy brown glaze was enhanced with a band of ivory foam, and today's collectors are finding that its rich colors and basic, strong shapes just as attractive now as they were back then. In addition to table service, there are novelty trays shaped like gingerbread men and fish, canisters and cookie jars, covered casseroles with ducks and hens as lids, vases, ashtrays, and mixing bowls. It's easy to find, and though you may have to pay 'near book' prices at co-ops and antique malls, because it's just now 'catching on,' the bargains are out there. It may be marked Hull, Crooksville, O; HPCo; or Crestone.

If you'd like to learn more about this subject, we recommend *The Collector's Encyclopedia of Hull Pottery* by Brenda Roberts and *Collector's Guide to Hull Pottery, The Dinnerware Lines*, by Barbara Loveless Gick-Burke.

Advisor: Brenda Roberts (See Directory, Hull)

Advisor, Mirror Brown: Jo-Ann Bentz (See Directory, Hull)

Basket, Blossom Flite, 6", $115.00.

Ashtray, Butterfly, turquoise butterfly on ivory heart shape, #B3, 7" **$45.00**

Ashtray, deer embossed in yellow center, 8" **$25.00**
Ashtray, free-form w/2 oval wells connected by rests, dark brown w/brown mottling, unmarked, 13" **$55.00**
Ashtray, white heart shape w/6 rests, #18, 7" **$24.00**
Bank, Corky Pig, Jumbo; Mirror Brown, #197, from $125 to **$150.00**
Bank, Corky Pig, Mirror Brown, 5", from $60 to **$75.00**
Bank, Corky Pig, pastel, 5" **$105.00**
Bank, pig, pink bow, underglazed, unmarked, 14"..**$190.00**
Bank, Sitting Pig, Mirror Brown, #196, from $55 to....**$60.00**
Base, triple bulbs, yellow shaded to dark green, #107, 3¼x7"..**$35.00**
Basket, Continental, deep orange w/paler stripes, stylized handle, #55, 12½"...**$210.00**
Basket, Dogwood, yellow to green w/pink flower, circle handle attached at sides of rim & base, #501, 7½"..**$375.00**
Basket, Ebb Tide, open shell form, E-11, 16½" **$230.00**
Basket, Magnolia Matt, dusty rose & yellow, #10, 10½", from $360 to...**$400.00**
Basket, Parchment & Pine, scrolls & pine cones on ivory, S-8, 16½" long..**$210.00**
Basket, Sunglow, pink flowers on bright yellow, #84, 1952, 6½"..**$90.00**
Basket, Tropicana, Caribbean figure on white, black trim on handle, #55, 12½"..**$850.00**
Basket, Tuscany, green grapes on milky white, #11, 10½"...**$145.00**
Bowl, Banded Kitchenware, A-1, 7½"..........................**$35.00**
Bowl, mixing; Blossom, yellow flower on white, #20, 9½".**$75.00**
Candle holder, Bow-Knot, blue to green w/pastel multicolor flowers, B-17, 4" **$120.00**
Candle holder, Ebb Tide, shell form, E-13, 2¾".........**$32.00**
Candle holder, Iris, pink to blue, #411, 5"................**$110.00**
Centerpiece, Imperial, swan, #F71, Mirror Brown, from $65 to **$70.00**
Cookie jar, Floral, yellow flowers on ivory w/narrow brown band on lid, yellow finial, #48, 1952-53, 8¾".....**$145.00**
Cornucopia, Dogwood, yellow to green w/pink flower, #522, 3¾"...**$100.00**

Cornucopia, Parchment and Pine, 12", $125.00.

Cornucopia, Rosella, white flowers w/green leaves on white, R-13, 8½" **$140.00**
Cornucopia, Royal Woodland, turquoise w/gray accents, #W10, 11" **$75.00**
Cornucopia, Woodland, Dawn Rose w/pink hand-painted flower, W-2, 5½" **$75.00**
Creamer, Ebb Tide, shell form, E-15, 4".....................**$85.00**

Creamer, Open Rose, pink w/yellow rose, squatty, ring handle, #111, 5" **$125.00**

Creamer, Water Lily, Apricot to Walnut w/lg white flower, L-19, 5" **$80.00**

Ewer, Butterfly, gold butterfly & handle, blue & pink flowers on ivory, #B15, 13½" **$235.00**

Ewer, Royal Woodland, slim form, pink w/brown accents, #W24, 13½" **$175.00**

Ewer, Serenade, Sunlight Yellow w/songbirds on branch, S-2, 6½" **$95.00**

Ewer, Wildflower, yellow to pink w/yellow, white & pink flowers w/green leaves, W-19, 13½" **$450.00**

Figurine, Dancing Girl, flared ruffled skirt, #955, 7" ...**$60.00**

Figurine, Imperial, frog caricature, #F70, Mirror Brown, from $65 to **$70.00**

Flowerpot, Sunglow, bright yellow w/pink flowers, simple shape w/flared rim, #97, 5½" **$40.00**

Grease jar, Floral, bright yellow flowers on white, yellow finial, #43, 5¾" **$45.00**

Grease jar, Floral, yellow flowers on ivory w/narrow brown band at top, #43, 1952-53, 5¾" **$45.00**

Jardiniere, multicolor splotches, turquoise at rim w/embossed decor, H in circle mark, 6½" **$105.00**

Jardiniere, Water Lily, pink to yellow w/lg yellow flower, sm handles, L-23, 5½" **$125.00**

Lavabo, Butterfly, turquoise butterfly on cream w/turquoise & pink flowers, top marked B25, base marked B24, 16" **$210.00**

Leaf dish, Tuscany, green grapes on milky white, #19...**$50.00**

Pitcher, Blossom, yellow flower on white, bulbous, #29, 16-oz **$50.00**

Pitcher, multicolor mottled stripes, turquoise at rim, ivory at base & on handle, stoneware, H in circle mark, 6½" **$350.00**

Planter, Bandana Duck, maroon & dark green body w/ivory head, #75, 5x7" **$65.00**

Planter, dog w/yarn, yellow, brown & ivory, #88, 5½x8"..**$32.00**

Planter, giraffe among green leafy plant, #115, 8" **$55.00**

Planter, Imperial, duck, #F69, Mirror Brown, from $35 to...**$40.00**

Planter, kitten beside vase, pink ribbon, #61, 7½"......**$45.00**

Planter, Lovebirds, shaded pink airbrushing, #93, 6"..**$45.00**

Planter, parrot pulling cart, pink, green & yellow, #60, 6x9½"..**$45.00**

Planter, Regal, white footed-bowl form w/geen at rim, #301, 3½"..**$15.00**

Planter, Siamese cats, sm kitten at mother's side, brown tones on ivory, #63, 5¾" tall **$95.00**

Planter, swan, high-gloss yellow spray w/hand-painted details, #69, 8½" **$65.00**

Planter, twin geese, green & white, #95, 7¼" **$60.00**

Planter, upright poodle beside leaves forming planter, burgundy & dark green, #114, 8"..........................**$55.00**

Planter, yellow flower form w/green leafy base, #118, 10¼" **$35.00**

Sugar bowl, Magnolia Gloss, blue flowers on transparent pink, w/lid, H-22, 3¾".......................................**$40.00**

Sugar bowl, Rosella, white flowers w/green leaves on white, lg handles, R-4, 5½"......................................**$65.00**

Teapot, Magnolia Matte, dusty rose & yellow, #23, 6½" ..**$210.00**

Vase, Bow-Knot, blue to pink w/bow forming foot, pastel flowers embossed on sides, B-2, 5" **$160.00**

Vase, Continental, dark green w/light green stripes, #53, 8½" **$45.00**

Vase, double bud; Woodland, bright yellow to deep pink w/pink flower, W-15, 8½"...................................**$120.00**

Vase, Early Art, wide red & blue stripes on turquoise, sm beaded handles, stoneware, unmarked, 5½"........**$70.00**

Vase, Iris, cream, handles, #403, 4¾" **$95.00**

Vase, Magnolia Gloss, blue flowers on transparent pink, shaped rim, handles, footed, H-9, 8½" **$125.00**

Vase, Magnolia Gloss, pink flower on transparent pink, urn shape w/flared rim, H-6, 6½" **$85.00**

Vase, Magnolia Matte, dusty rose & yellow, flared rim, curled handles, footed, #13, 4¾".................................**$50.00**

Vase, Magnolia Matte, dusty rose & yellow, low handles, #1, 8½" **$150.00**

Vase, Mardi Gras/Granada, creamy white, low handles, #49, 9" **$55.00**

Vase, Open Rose, pink & yellow roses on pink, bulbous, footed, w/handles, #123, 6½" **$135.00**

Vase, Open Rose, pink swan form w/yellow & pink roses low on body of swan, #118, 6½" **$175.00**

Vase, Open Rose, pink w/pink rose, fancy handles, footed, #131, 4¾" **$90.00**

Vase, Poppy, green to pink w/pink & yellow poppies, sm angular handles, #607, 6½" **$150.00**

Vase, Sunglow, Carnation Pink w/bright yellow flowers, handles, #89, 5½"...**$40.00**

Vase, Sunglow, flowers on dark pink gloss, sm ring handles, #100, 1952, 6½" **$60.00**

Vase, Tokay, pink grapes on pink shaded to green, brown vine handles, #4, 8¼" **$95.00**

Vase, tri-lobed, maroon shading to ivory to dark green, #110, 9¼" **$38.00**

Vase, Tropicana, Caribbean woman on white, #54, 12½" .**$495.00**

Vase, Wildflower, pink to yellow w/yellow flowers, flared rim, handles, footed, W-1, 5½".........................**$50.00**

Vase, Wildflower (Number Series), pink w/yellow & pink flowers on pink, handles, footed, #78, 8½" **$150.00**

Vase, Woodland, bright yellow to green w/pink flowers, low handles, W-16, 8½"..**$195.00**

Vases, poodle head, #55; pig head, #39, $80.00 each.

Wall pocket, Bow-Knot, pitcher form, pink to blue, multicolor flowers, B-26, 6"..**$260.00**

Wall pocket, goose figural, dark green & maroon high-gloss blend, #67, 6½"............................**$65.00**

Wall pocket, Poppy, pink to blue cornucopia shape w/pink & yellow poppies, #609, 9"................................**$400.00**

Wall pocket, Royal Woodland, shell form, pink w/brown accents, #W13, 7½"...............................**$105.00**

Wall pocket, Sunglow, cup & saucer, #80, 6¼" **$100.00**

Window box, black w/pink squiggles, $82, 12½" long ..**$35.00**

Dinnerware

Avocado, bean pot, w/lid, 2-qt...........................**$28.00**

Avocado, coffeecup (mug), 9-oz **$5.00**

Avocado, jug, 2-pt..**$25.00**

Avocado, plate, dinner; 10¼".................................**$8.00**

Avocado, salt shaker, mushroom, 3¾" **$15.00**

Avocado, salt shaker, w/cork, 3¾" **$6.00**

Avocado, steak plate, oval, 11¾x9"......................**$12.00**

Centennial, bean pot, w/lid, 7x9".....................**$110.00**

Centennial, creamer, unmarked, 4½"....................**$50.00**

Centennial, pitcher, milk; unmarked, 7½" **$110.00**

Centennial, salt shaker, unmarked, 3"...................**$30.00**

Country Belle, baker, square, white w/blue flower & bell stencil..**$18.00**

Country Belle, bowl, white w/blue flower & bell stencil, 6"..**$18.00**

Country Belle, coffee cup, white w/blue flower & bell stencil..**$7.00**

Country Belle, coffeepot, white w/blue flower & bell stencil **$50.00**

Country Belle, gravy boat w/tray, white w/blue flower & bell stencil..**$28.00**

Country Belle, plate, salad; white w/blue flower & bell stencil..**$8.00**

Country Squire, coffee cup (mug), green agate w/white trim, 9-oz...**$6.00**

Country Squire, cookie jar, green agate w/white trim, 94-oz **$45.00**

Country Squire, plate, dinner; green agate w/white trim, 10¼" **$9.00**

Country Squire, salt shaker, green agate w/white trim, w/cork, 3¾" **$8.00**

Country Squire, steak plate, oval, green agate w/white trim, individual, 11¾x9" **$15.00**

Country Squire, teapot, green agate w/white trim, 5-cup ..**$30.00**

Country Squire, water jug, green agate w/white trim, 80-oz...**$32.00**

Crestone, bowl, vegetable/salad; turquoise, 9¾" **$28.00**

Crestone, carafe, turquoise, 2-cup...........................**$40.00**

Crestone, casserole, turquoise, w/lid, 32-oz..............**$25.00**

Crestone, gravy boat, turquoise, 10-oz....................**$20.00**

Crestone, plate, dessert; turquoise, 7½".....................**$7.00**

Crestone, salt & pepper shakers, turquoise, 3¾", pr ..**$18.00**

Gingerbread Depot Cookie Jar, #801G, Mirror Brown, from $275 to...**$300.00**

Gingerbread Man, child's bowl, #325, Mirror Brown, from $90 to...**$110.00**

Gingerbread Man, child's cup, #324, Mirror Brown, from $90 to...**$110.00**

Gingerbread Man, coaster, #199, gray, 5x5" **$30.00**

Gingerbread Man, coaster, #299, sand, 5x5"..............**$30.00**

Gingerbread Man, coaster, #399, Mirror Brown, 5x5", from $35 to...**$40.00**

Gingerbread Man, cookie jar, #123, gray.................**$225.00**

Gingerbread Man, cookie jar, #223, sand **$225.00**

Gingerbread Man, cookie jar, #323, Mirror Brown, from $295 to...**$325.00**

Gingerbread Man, tray, Mirror Brown, $75.00.

Heartland, casserole, brown heart stencil on ivory w/yellow trim, w/lid, #428....................................**$40.00**

Heartland, coffee cup, brown heart stencil on ivory w/yellow trim..**$7.00**

Heartland, creamer, brown heart stencil on ivory w/yellow trim..**$15.00**

Heartland, custard cup, brown heart stencil on ivory w/yellow trim...**$8.00**

Heartland, plate, dinner; brown heart stencil on ivory w/yellow trim...**$12.00**

Heartland, salt & pepper shakers, brown heart stencil on ivory w/yellow trim, handles, pr **$32.00**

Mirror Almond, baker, sq, 3-pt............................**$10.00**

Mirror Almond, creamer, 8-oz................................**$14.00**

Mirror Almond, custard cup, 6-oz..........................**$8.00**

Mirror Almond, fish platter, 11" **$35.00**

Mirror Almond, mug, 9-oz....................................**$6.00**

Mirror Almond, plate, luncheon; 9⅜"........................**$9.00**

Mirror Almond, sugar bowl, 12-oz **$14.00**

Mirror Brown, ashtray, w/deer imprint, #563, 8", from $20 to...**$22.00**

Mirror Brown, bake 'n serve, #589, round, 6½", from $8 to.**$10.00**

Mirror Brown, bake 'n serve dish, #573, 1980s, 9½-oz, from $9 to...**$10.00**

Mirror Brown, bake 'n serve dish, #574, oval, 16-oz, from $9 to...**$11.00**

Mirror Brown, baker, #568, square, 3-pt, from $10 to ..**$12.00**

Mirror Brown, baker, rectangular, #534, 7-pt.............**$40.00**

Mirror Brown, baker, rectangular, #567, 1980s, from $30 to.**$35.00**

Mirror Brown, baker, w/chicken lid, #560, from $150 to..**$175.00**

Mirror Brown, baker, w/rooster imprint, #558, 3" deep, from $50 to...**$60.00**

Mirror Brown, bean pot, #510, 2-qt, from $30 to........**$35.00**

Mirror Brown, bean pot, individual; #524, 12-oz, w/lid, from $5 to..**$7.00**

Mirror Brown, beer stein, #526, 16-oz, from $10 to....**$12.00**

Mirror Brown, bowl, fruit; #503, 5¼", from $4 to **$5.00**

Mirror Brown, bowl, fruit; #533, 6", from $6 to **$7.00**

Mirror Brown, bowl, mixing; #536, 6", from $7 to........**$8.00**

Mirror Brown, bowl, mixing; #537, 7", from $9 to......**$10.00**

Mirror Brown, bowl, mixing; #538, 8"..........................**$12.00**

Mirror Brown, bowl, mixing; Provincial Mold, #850H, 5¼", from $8 to..**$10.00**

Mirror Brown, bowl, mixing; Provincial Mold, #851H, 6¾", from $9 to..**$12.00**

Mirror Brown, bowl, mixing; Provincial Mold, #852H, 8¼", from $12 to..**$15.00**

Mirror Brown, bowl, onion soup; #535, 1980s, 12-oz, w/lid, from $8 to..**$9.00**

Mirror Brown, bowl, salad; w/rooster imprint, #508, oval, from $40 to..**$45.00**

Mirror Brown, bowl, soup or salad; #569, 6½", from $6 to..**$8.00**

Mirror Brown, bowl, spaghetti or salad; #545, 10¼", from $25 to..**$27.00**

Mirror Brown, bud vase, #870H, 9", from $14 to........**$18.00**

Mirror Brown, butter dish, #561, ¼-lb, from $11 to ...**$15.00**

Mirror brown, canister set, #556/557/558/559, hard to find in mint condition, 4-pc, from $350 to **$550.00**

Mirror Brown, canister set, stacking, #360, 1980s, 4-pc, from $150 to..**$175.00**

Mirror Brown, carafe, #505, 2-cup, from $50 to..........**$65.00**

Mirror Brown, casserole, #314, round, 1980s, w/lid, from $12 to..**$14.00**

Mirror Brown, casserole, #507, 32-oz, w/lid, from $20 to..**$25.00**

Mirror Brown, casserole, #543, open, 2-pt, 7x11", from $5 to..**$8.00**

Mirror Brown, casserole, #544, oval, w/lid, 2-pt, from $18 to..**$20.00**

Mirror Brown, casserole, #548, 2-qt, oval, w/lid, from $25 to **$30.00**

Mirror Brown, casserole, Provincial Mold, #853H, w/lid, from $20 to..**$22.00**

Mirror Brown, casserole, w/chicken cover, #5850, oval, 2-qt, from $55 to..**$60.00**

Mirror Brown, casserole, w/duck lid, #5770, 2-qt, from $65 to..**$75.00**

Mirror Brown, cheese server, #582, from $30 to........**$32.00**

Mirror Brown, chip 'n dip, #583, 3-section, from $60 to....**$70.00**

Mirror Brown, chip 'n dip, #586, 2-pc, 12x11", from $110 to..**$135.00**

Mirror Brown, chip 'n dip leaf, #521, 15", from $20 to...**$30.00**

Mirror Brown, chip 'n dip leaf, #591, 9x12¼", from $30 to .**$35.00**

Mirror Brown, coffee cup, #597, 7-oz, from $3 to........**$4.00**

Mirror Brown, coffee cup/mug, #502, 9-oz, from $4 to..**$5.00**

Mirror Brown, coffeepot, #522, 8-cup, from $30 to....**$35.00**

Mirror Brown, condiment set, #871H, from $75 to...**$100.00**

Mirror Brown, cookie jar, #523, from $25 to..............**$30.00**

Mirror Brown, corn-serving dish, #573, 9" long, from $40 to..**$50.00**

Mirror Brown, creamer, #518, 8-oz, from $4 to.............**$6.00**

Mirror Brown, custard cup, #576, 6-oz, from $7 to.......**$9.00**

Mirror Brown, deviled egg plate, w/rooster imprint, #591, from $45 to..**$50.00**

Mirror Brown, Dutch oven, #565, 3-pt, 2-pc, from $30 to...**$35.00**

Mirror Brown, French casserole, #513, individual, from $3 to..**$5.00**

Mirror Brown, French casserole, #527, 1980s, w/lid, from $6 to..**$7.00**

Mirror Brown, French casserole, #562, stick handle, 9-oz, from $6 to..**$7.00**

Mirror Brown, French casserole, #579, stick handle, w/lid, 9-oz, from $6 to..**$7.00**

Mirror Brown, French casserole, #979, w/lid & warmer, 3-pt, from $75 to..**$90.00**

Mirror Brown, garlic cellar, #3505, 1980s, 13-oz, from $30 to..**$35.00**

Mirror Brown, gravy boat, #511.................................**$14.00**

Mirror Brown, gravy boat & liner, #540, from $25 to .**$28.00**

Mirror Brown, gravy boat liner, #512.........................**$8.00**

Mirror Brown, hen on nest, #592, from $65 to **$70.00**

Mirror Brown, ice jug, 2-qt, #514, from $22 to **$26.00**

Mirror Brown, jam/mustard jar, #550, w/lid, 1980s, 13-oz, from $8 to..**$10.00**

Mirror Brown, jam/mustard jar, #551, w/lid, 12-oz, from $8 to..**$10.00**

Mirror Brown, jug, #525, 2-pt, from $15 to **$17.00**

Mirror Brown, jug, ice; #514, 2-qt, from $22 to **$26.00**

Mirror Brown, jug, water; #509, 80-oz, from $25 to ...**$30.00**

Mirror Brown, leaf dish, #590, 7¼x4¼", from $7 to **$9.00**

Mirror Brown, leaf serve-all, #540, 7½x12", from $26 to...**$28.00**

Mirror Brown, mug, #302, 1980s, 10-oz, from $3 to **$5.00**

Mirror Brown, mug, Continental; #571, 10-oz & 12-oz, each, from $18 to..**$20.00**

Mirror Brown, oil server, #584, from $30 to **$32.00**

Mirror Brown, pie plate, #566, 9½", from $20 to........**$25.00**

Mirror Brown, plate, dinner; #500, 10¼" **$8.00**

Mirror Brown, plate, luncheon, #599, 9¼", from $7 to.**$9.00**

Mirror Brown, plate, luncheon; #531, 8½", from $7 to.**$9.00**

Mirror Brown, plate, salad; #501, 6½", from $4 to........**$5.00**

Mirror Brown, plate, steak; #541, oval, 9x11¾", from $10 to..**$12.00**

Mirror Brown, plate, steak; w/well & tree, #593, oval, 14x10", from $25 to..**$28.00**

Mirror Brown, platter, fish; #596, 11", from $40 to **$50.00**

Mirror Brown, platter, w/chicken cover, #559, from $150 to..**$175.00**

Mirror Brown, platter, w/rooster imprint, #557, oval, from $50 to..**$60.00**

Mirror Brown, quiche dish, #508, 1980s.....................**$25.00**

Mirror Brown, ramekin, #600, 1980s, 2½-oz, from $10 to...**$12.00**

Mirror Brown, roaster, #535, rectangular, 7-pt, w/lid..**$90.00**

Mirror Brown, salad server, #583, rectangular, 6½x11", from $20 to..**$22.00**

Mirror Brown, salt & pepper shakers, #515/516, w/corks, 3¾", pr, from $12 to **$18.00**

Mirror Brown, salt & pepper shakers, #596, table size, pr, from $18 to..**$20.00**

Mirror Brown, salt & pepper shakers, mushroom form, #587/588, 3¾", pr, from $15 to............................**$18.00**

Mirror Brown, sauce bowl for chip 'n dip, #584, from $50 to..**$60.00**

Mirror Brown, saucer, #598, 6", from $3 to **$4.00**

Mirror Brown, server, #873H, w/handle, from $70 to.**$85.00**

Mirror Brown, serving dish, #577, double, scalloped, from $50 to...**$60.00**
Mirror Brown, serving set, #872H, from $75 to........**$100.00**
Mirror Brown, skillet, #595, from $15 to.....................**$17.00**
Mirror Brown, snack set, tray #554 & mug #553, from $18 to **$20.00**
Mirror Brown, souffle dish, #517, 1980s **$28.00**
Mirror Brown, spaghetti dish, individual; #581, oval, 10¾x8¼", from $15 to...**$20.00**
Mirror Brown, spoon rest, #594, w/Spoon Rest imprint, from $25 to...**$35.00**
Mirror Brown, stein, jumbo; #572, 32-oz, from $35 to..**$40.00**
Mirror Brown, sugar bowl, #519, 12-oz, w/lid, from $5 to .**$7.00**
Mirror Brown, teapot, #549, from $15 to **$17.00**
Mirror Brown, tidbit tray, 2-tier, #592, from $60 to.....**$70.00**
Mirror Brown, tray for chip 'n dip set, #584, from $60 to..**$75.00**
Mirror Brown, vegetable dish, #542, divided, 7x10¾", from $12 to...**$14.00**
Mirror Brown, vinegar server, #585, from $30 to **$32.00**
Provincial, baking dish, brown w/white trim, 3-pt **$22.00**
Provincial, cookie jar, brown w/white trim, 94-oz......**$55.00**
Provincial, plate, salad; 6½"...**$11.00**
Provincial, water jug, brown w/white trim, 90-oz **$45.00**
Ridge, bowl, gray or sand, 2½x5½"................................**$6.00**
Ridge, creamer, gray or sand, 8-oz.............................**$10.00**
Ridge, cup, brown, 10-oz...**$5.00**
Ridge, plate, salad; gray or sand, 7¼"..........................**$5.00**
Ridge, tray, gray or sand, 9½x7" **$16.00**
Ridge, vegetable server, brown, 2½x7½", 32-oz **$9.00**
Ring, bowl, mixing; brown, 8"......................................**$15.00**
Ring, bowl, salad/soup; brown, 12-oz **$9.00**
Ring, coffeepot, brown..**$50.00**
Ring, creamer, brown **$12.00**
Ring, pitcher, brown, 36-oz...**$35.00**
Ring, plate, salad; brown...**$7.00**
Tangerine, bowl, salad/soup; 6½" **$7.00**
Tangerine, casserole, oval, w/lid, 2-pt **$22.00**
Tangerine, coffee cup (mug), 9-oz................................**$6.00**
Tangerine, cookie jar, 94-oz...**$45.00**
Tangerine, ice jug, 2-qt...**$28.00**
Tangerine, mug, soup; 11-oz **$8.00**
Tangerine, plate, salad; 6½"...**$5.00**
Tangerine, sugar bowl, w/lid, 12-oz **$12.00**

Imperial Glass

Organized in 1901 in Bellaire, Ohio, the Imperial Glass Company made carnival glass, stretch glass, a line called NuCut (made in imitation of cut glass), and a limited amount of art glass within the first decade of the century. In the mid-thirties, they designed one of their most famous patterns (and one of their most popular with today's collectors), Candlewick. Within a few years, milk glass had become their leading product.

During the fifties, they reintroduced their NuCut line in crystal as well as colors, marketing it as 'Collector's Crystal.' In the late fifties they bought molds from both Heisey and Cambridge. Most of the glassware they reis-

sued from these old molds was marked 'IG,' one letter superimposed over the other. When Imperial was bought by Lenox in 1973, an 'L' was added to the mark. The company changed hands twice more before closing altogether in 1984.

In addition to tableware, they made a line of animal figures, some of which were made from Heisey's molds. *Glass Animals of the Depression Years* by Lee Garmon and Dick Spencer is a wonderful source of information and can help you determine the value and the manufacturer of your figures.

Numbers in the listings were assigned by the company and appeared on their catalog pages. They were used to indicate differences in shapes and stems, for instance. Collectors still use them.

For more information on Imperial we recommend *Imperial Glass* by Margaret and Douglas Archer; *Elegant Glassware of the Depression Era* by Gene Florence; *Imperial Carnival Glass* by Carl O. Burns; and *Imperial Glass Encyclopedia, Vol I A-Cane*, edited by James Measell. See also Candlewick.

Advisor: Joan Cimini (See Directory, Imperial)

Club: National Imperial Glass Collectors' Society, Inc. P.O. Box 534 Bellaire, OH 43906; Dues: $15 per year (+$1 for each additional member of household), quarterly newsletter: *Glasszette*, convention every June

Newsletter: *The Glass Post* P.O. Box 205 Oakdale, IA 52319-0205; Phone or FAX 319-626-3216. Twelve issues per year, $25; ads free to subscribers

Box, sweetmeat; Cathay Crystal, signed, #5022, $250.00.

Ashtray, Cape Cod, crystal, 4"......................................**$14.00**
Ashtray, Heart, ruby red slag, satin or glossy.............**$20.00**
Basket, Crocheted Crystal, 9".......................................**$37.50**
Basket, Herringbone, jade slag w/milk glass handle..**$45.00**
Bell, caramel slag, #720..**$45.00**
Bell, Hobnail, amber carnival, #42340 ....**$45.00**
Bell, Hobnail, peacock carnival...................................**$25.00**
Bell, Suzanne, white carnival, IG mark, 6".................**$40.00**
Bowl, Everglades, Aurora Jewels (cobalt carnival), 3-toed, 10"...**$95.00**
Bowl, fruit; Cape Cod, crystal, footed, 9" **$62.50**
Bowl, Grape, rubigold carnival, crimped edge, #47C, 9"..**$40.00**
Bowl, Grape, rubigold carnival, 4¾"............................**$20.00**

Bowl, jelly; Cape Cod, crystal, 3" $12.00
Bowl, Pansy, amber carnival, oval $30.00
Bowl, Pansy, rubigold carnival, oval..............................$25.00
Bowl, ram's head, Aurora Jewels (cobalt carnival), 9"..$95.00
Bowl, salad; Grape, Helios (green carnival), 11½" $65.00
Bowl, Scroll, Sunset Ruby (red carnival), 3-toed, #329..$65.00
Box, Beaded Jewel, amber carnival, 6½" $40.00
Box, Beaded Jewel, rubigold carnival, #975..............$30.00
Butter dish, Cape Cod, crystal, ¼-lb $45.00
Butter dish, Lustre Rose, amber carnival $45.00
Butter dish, ruby red slag, glossy $75.00
Cake plate, Cape Cod, low footed, square, 10" $95.00

Cake stand, Crocheted Crystal (company name: Lace Edge), #780, from $25.00 to $35.00.

Candle holder, Crocheted Crystal, 2-light, 4½"............$17.50
Candle holders, Grape, rubigold carnival, pr..............$30.00
Candle holders, rose, Horizon Blue carnival or pink carnival, LIG mark, pr..$30.00
Candlestick, Dolphin, crystal $30.00
Candlesticks, ram's head, Aurora Jewels (cobalt carnival), pr..$75.00
Candlesticks, Rose, red slag, glossy, 3½", pr..............$30.00
Candy dish, caramel slag, glossy, marked Heisey, w/lid, #1519/59 ....$55.00
Candy dish, Herringbone, red slag, glossy, w/lid.......$45.00
Candy jar, Dolphin handle, caramel slag, glossy, footed, #1519/140 ....$95.00
Celery, Cape Cod, crystal, #160/189, 10½" $65.00
Champagne, Cape Cod, amber, #1602 ....$20.00
Champagne, Cape Cod, verde green, #1602 ....$16.50
Coaster, Cape Cod, crystal, square, #160/85, 3" $18.00
Cocktail, Crocheted Crystal, 4½", 3½-oz....................$12.50
Compote, Imperial Lace Edge, rubigold carnival, #749B, 6½" $25.00
Compote, Saddle, caramel slag, glossy, #48, 7"...........$90.00
Compote, Zodiac, Peacock carnival, Heisey mold, w/lid .$45.00
Covered dish, duck on nest, jade green slag, glossy..$45.00
Creamer, Crocheted Crystal..$12.50
Creamer & sugar bowl, Cape Cod, crystal, #160/30 ...$20.00
Creamer & sugar bowl, Everglades, Sunset Ruby (red carnival), #3800/27..$65.00
Cup, coffee; Cape Cod, crystal, #160/37 ....$7.00
Decanter, wine; Grape, rubigold carnival, w/6 wines...$150.00
Decanter, wine; Grape, ruby, Helios (green carnival), w/stopper $85.00

Dish, swan w/open back, caramel slag, IG mark, 8" .$85.00
Figurine, Asiatic pheasant, amber $325.00
Figurine, Champ Terrier, caramel slag, glossy............$90.00
Figurine, chick w/head down, milk glass....................$10.00
Figurine, colt, standing, amber....................................$140.00
Figurine, cygnet, caramel slag $55.00
Figurine, donkey, caramel slag....................................$55.00
Figurine, elephant, caramel slag, med $65.00
Figurine, elephant, caramel slag, sm..........................$65.00
Figurine, filly, head backward, verde green..............$145.00
Figurine, Hootless Owl, caramel slag, glossy $45.00
Figurine, mallard, wings up, caramel slag $35.00
Figurine, mallard w/wings down, light blue satin $22.50
Figurine, Parlor Pup, amethyst carnival $35.00
Figurine, Plug Horse, pink, HCA, 1978......................$45.00
Figurine, rooster, fighting, pink..................................$175.00
Figurine, Scottie, milk glass, 3½"................................$40.00
Figurine, swan, milk glass, 4½" $20.00
Figurine, wood duckling, standing, Sunshine Yellow satin ..$15.00
Figurine, woodchuck, caramel slag, glossy $45.00
Goblet, Cape Cod, red, wafer stem..............................$22.00
Goblet, Crocheted Crystal, 7⅛"....................................$14.00
Goblet, Grape, ruby..$25.00
Goblet, Kite & Panel, Aurora Jewels (cobalt carnival), #29/9 ..$40.00
Jar, Hobstar, rubigold carnival, Collector's Crystal, footed, w/lid, #425 ....$40.00
Jar, rubigold carnival, w/lid, Collector's Crystal #282, w/lid, lg...$60.00
Jar, rubigold carnival, 4-toed, #176, w/lid $35.00
Ladle, mayonnaise; Crocheted Crystal, plain $8.00
Lamp, oil; Hobnail, amber carnival shade, crystal base, #42990 ....$150.00
Marmalade, Cape Cod, crystal, #160/89, 4-pc $45.00
Mug, Eagle & Stars, peacock carnival, made for Rose Presznick's Carnival Glass Museum, 1969.............$50.00
Mug, Robin, red slag, glossy..$45.00
Mug, Robin, Sunset Ruby (red carnival) $35.00
Mug, Story book, elephant handle, Aurora Jewels (cobalt carnival), Heisey mold..$45.00
Mug, Story Book, elephant handle, jade slag, glossy, Heisey mold..$55.00
Nappy, Pansy, rubigold carnival, handled, #478, 5½" ..$25.00
Pitcher, Cape Cod, crystal, #160/240, milk size, 16-oz..$45.00
Pitcher, Grape, dark amber carnival, water size..........$90.00
Pitcher, Grape, peacock carnival, #473, water size, 3-pt.$75.00
Pitcher, Grape, rubigold carnival, #473, milk size, 1-pt ..$40.00
Pitcher, Grape, rubigold carnival, water size, w/6 tumblers ..$140.00
Pitcher, Hobnail, marigold carnival, IG mark & etched Levay (made for Levay in 1978), water size, w/6 tumblers..$295.00
Pitcher, Lustre Rose, peacock carnival, IG mark, water size, w/6 tumblers..$190.00
Pitcher, Mayflower or #678, peacock carnival, water size, w/6 tumblers..$190.00
Pitcher, Robin, Sunset Ruby (red carnival), water size, w/6 tumblers..$225.00
Pitcher, Roses, Sunburst (yellow carnival), ALIG mark, water size, w/6 tumblers $255.00
Pitcher, Tiger Lily, pink carnival, water size, w/6 tumblers ..$165.00
Pitcher, Williamsburg, cobalt blue, water size, 2-qt $55.00
Pitcher, Williamsburg, nut brown, water size, 2-qt $45.00

Pitcher, Windmill, peacock carnival, water size, w/6 tumblers $190.00
Pitcher, Windmill, pink carnival, water size, w/6 tumblers ..$175.00
Pitcher, Windmill, red slag, glossy, #240, 1-pt $55.00
Pitcher, Windmill, rubigold carnival, water size, w/6 tumblers $185.00
Plate, Cape Cod, red, #160/5D, 8" $24.00
Plate, Caprice, teal blue, made for National Cambridge Collectors, Cambridge logo in center, 1970 ....$45.00
Plate, Crocheted Crystal, 14" $22.50
Plate, Crocheted Crystal, 8" $7.50
Plate, torte; Cape Cod, crystal, cupped, 13" $35.00
Plate, 1776 Coin, crystal satin, IG mark $25.00
Punch bowl, Crocheted Crystal, 14" $65.00
Relish, Cape Cod, crystal, divided, #160/56, 9½" $35.00
Salt & pepper shakers, Cape Cod, fern green, #160/117, pr..$75.00
Salt cellar, red slag, 4-toed, #61 ....$18.00
Salt shaker, Cape Cod, crystal, #160/238 ....$24.00
Salz & Pfeffer set, Aurora Jewels (cobalt carnival) $55.00

Spider, Cape Cod, divided, with handle, #160/187, 6½", $48.00.

Toothpick holder, rubigold carnival, Collector's Crystal, #505 ....$12.00
Toothpick holder, top hat, Aurora Jewels (cobalt carnival) ..$30.00
Toothpick holder, 3 in 1 Diamond, red slag, glossy, #1 .$15.00
Tumbler, iced tea; Crocheted Crystal, footed, 7⅛" $15.00
Tumbler, juice; Cape Cod, amber, footed, #1602, 5-oz ..$20.00
Tumbler, Tiger Lily, pink carnival $18.00
Vase, Beaded Block, cobalt opal, 6" $75.00
Vase, Crocheted Crystal, 8" $17.50
Vase, flip; Cape Cod, crystal, footed, #160/21, 11½" ..$65.00
Vase, Lace Edge, rubigold carnival, 4-toed, 5" $25.00
Vase, Mayflower, red carnival, #474 ....$55.00
Vase, Rose, Labelle, rubigold carnival, #181, 6¼" $40.00
Vase, 3 Swans, Aurora Jewels (cobalt carnival), #27/7526, 8¾" $120.00
Wine/cigarette holder, Eagle, red slag, glossy or satin ..$35.00

Indiana Glass

From 1972 until 1978, Indiana Glass Company produced a line of iridescent 'new carnival' glass, much of which was embossed with grape clusters and detailed leaves in a line they called Harvest. It was made in blue, gold, and lime, and was evi-

dently a good seller for them, judging from the amount around today. They also produced a line of 'press cut' iridescent glass called Heritage, which they made in amethyst and Sunset (amberina). Collectors always seem to gravitate toward lustre-coated glassware, whether it's old or recently made, and there seems to be a significant amount of interest in this line.

There was also a series of four Bicentennial Commemorative plates made in both blue and gold carnival: American Eagle, Independence Hall, Liberty Bell, and Spirit of '76. They're valued at $12.00 for the gold and $15.00 for the blue, except for the American Eagle plate, which is worth from $12.00 to $15.00 regardless of color.

This glass is a little difficult to evaluate, since you see it in malls and at flea markets with such a wide range of 'asking' prices. On one hand, you'll have sellers who themselves are not exactly sure what it is they have but since it's 'carnival' assume it should be fairly pricey. On the other hand, you have those who've just 'cleaned house' and want to get rid of it. They may have bought it new themselves and know it's not very old and wasn't expensive to start with. This is what you'll be up against if you decide you want to collect it.

In addition to the iridescent glass lines, Indiana produced colored glass baskets, vases, etc., as well as a line called Ruby Band Diamond Point, a clear diamond-faceted pattern with a wide ruby-flashed rim band. We've listed some of the latter below; our values are for examples with the ruby flashing in excellent condition.

Over the last ten years, the collectibles market has changed. Nowadays, some shows' criteria regarding the merchandise they allow to be displayed is 'if it's no longer available on the retail market, it's OK.' I suspect that this attitude will become more and more widespread. At any rate, this is one of the newest interests at the flea market/antique mall level, and if you can buy it right (and like its looks), now is the time!

Advisor: Ruth Grizel (See Directory, Westmoreland)

Iridescent Amethyst Carnival Glass (Heritage)

Basket, footed, 9x5x7" $35.00
Butter dish, 5x7½" dia $35.00
Candle holder, 5½", each $30.00
Center bowl, 4¾x8½", from $35 to $40.00
Goblet, 8-oz $17.50
Pitcher, 8¼" $55.00
Punch set, 10" bowl & pedestal, 8 cups, & ladle, 11-pc ..$95.00
Swung vase, slender & footed w/irregular rim, 11x3" ..$30.00

Iridescent Blue Carnival Glass

Basket, Canterbury, waffled pattern, flared sides drawn in at handle, 11x8x12" $45.00
Basket, Monticello, allover faceted embossed diamonds, square, 7x6" $35.00
Butter dish, Harvest, embossed grapes, ¼-lb, 8" long $25.00
Candlesticks, Harvest, embossed grapes, footed bowl shape, 4x4½" dia, pr $35.00
Candy box, Harvest, embossed grapes w/lace edge, w/lid, 6½" $30.00

Candy box, Princess, diamond-point bands, pointed faceted finial, 6x6" dia, from $20 to **$25.00**

Canister/Candy jar, Harvest, embossed grapes, 7" **$30.00**

Canister/Cookie jar, Harvest, embossed grapes, 9" **$45.00**

Canister/Snack jar, Harvest, embossed grapes, 8" **$35.00**

Center bowl, Harvest, embossed grapes w/paneled sides, 4-footed, 4½x8½x12" **$35.00**

Cooler (iced tea tumbler), Harvest, embossed grapes, 14-oz, set of 4, from $35 to..................................**$40.00**

Creamer & sugar bowl on tray, Harvest, embossed grapes, 3-pc **$30.00**

Egg/Hors d'oeuvre tray, sectioned w/off-side holder for 8 eggs, 12¾" dia, from $30 to................................**$35.00**

Garland bowl (comport), paneled, 7½x8½" dia **$35.00**

Goblet, Harvest, embossed grapes, 9-oz, set of 4, from $25 to..**$30.00**

Hen on nest, from $25 to...**$30.00**

Hostess plate, Canterbury, allover diamond facets, flared crimped rim, 10" **$35.00**

Pitcher, Harvest, embossed grapes, 10½" **$50.00**

Plate, Bicentennial; American Eagle, from $12.00 to $15.00.

Punch set, Princess, 26-pc..**$65.00**

Tidbit, allover embossed diamond points, shallow w/flared sides, 6½" **$18.00**

Wedding bowl, Harvest, embossed grapes, footed, w/lid, 10x6¾" **$35.00**

Wedding bowl (sm comport), Thumbprint, footed, 5x5" ..**$25.00**

Iridescent Gold Carnival Glass

Basket, Canterbury, waffle pattern, flaring sides drawn in at handle terminals, 9½x11x8½", from $35 to..........**$40.00**

Basket, Monticello, lg faceted allover diamonds, square, 7x6" **$25.00**

Candy box, Harvest, embossed grapes, lace edge, footed, 6½x5¾" **$20.00**

Canister/Candy jar, Harvest, embossed grapes, 7" **$25.00**

Canister/Cookie jar, Harvest, embossed grapes, 9" **$35.00**

Canister/Snack jar, Harvest, embossed grapes, 8" **$30.00**

Center bowl, Harvest, oval w/embossed grapes & paneled sides, 4½x8½x12" **$20.00**

Console set, wide naturalistic leaves form sides, 9" bowl w/pr 4½" bowl-type candle holders, 3-pc **$30.00**

Cooler, iced tea tumbler, Harvest, 14-oz.......................**$7.50**

Egg relish plate, 11"...**$15.00**

Goblet, Harvest, embossed grapes, 9-oz........................**$7.00**

Hen on nest, 5½", from $20 to.....................................**$25.00**

Pitcher, Harvest, embossed grapes, 10½" **$45.00**

Plate, hostess; diamond embossing, shallow w/crimped & flared sides, 10" **$18.00**

Punch set, Princess, 6-qt bowl w/12 cups, 12 hooks & ladle, 26 pcs **$50.00**

Relish tray, Vintage, 6 sections, 9x12¾"......................**$20.00**

Salad set, Vintage, embossed fruit, apple-shaped rim w/applied stem, 13", w/fork & spoon, 3-pc.........**$25.00**

Wedding bowl, Harvest, embossed grapes, pedestal foot, 8½x8", from $25 to..**$35.00**

Wedding bowl (sm comport), 5x5" **$12.00**

Candy dish, Harvest, embossed grapes, lace edge, footed, 6½", $20.00.

Iridescent Lime Carnival Glass

Candy box, Harvest, embossed grapes w/lace edge, w/lid, 6½x5¾"..**$25.00**

Canister/Candy jar, Harvest, embossed grapes, 7" **$25.00**

Canister/Cookie jar, Harvest, embossed grapes, 9" **$35.00**

Canister/Snack jar, Harvest, embossed grape, 8".........**$30.00**

Center bowl, Harvest, embossed grapes, paneled sides, 4-footed, 4½x8½x12", from $25 to **$30.00**

Compote, Harvest, embossed grapes, 7x6".................**$30.00**

Console set, Harvest, embossed grapes, 10" comport w/pr comport-shaped candle holders, 3 pcs **$30.00**

Cooler (iced tea tumbler), Harvest, embossed grapes, 14-oz ..**$7.50**

Creamer & sugar bowl on tray, Harvest, embossed grapes, 3-pc **$25.00**

Egg/Relish tray, 12¾" **$20.00**

Goblet, Harvest, embossed grapes, 9-oz.......................**$6.00**

Hen on nest **$25.00**

Pitcher, Harvest, embossed grapes, 10½" **$35.00**

Plate, Hostess; allover diamond points, flared crimped sides, 10" **$20.00**

Punch set, Princess, 26-pc..**$50.00**

Salad/Fruit bowl set, Vintage, embossed fruit, apple-shaped rim w/applied stem, 13", w/fork & spoon, 3 pcs..**$35.00**

Snack set, Harvest, embossed grapes, 4 cups & 4 plates, 8 pcs **$25.00**

Iridescent Sunset (Amberina) Carnival Glass (Heritage)

Basket, footed, 9x5x7"...**$50.00**

Basket, squared, 9½x7½", from $55 to.......................**$65.00**

Bowl, crimped, 3¾x10"..**$50.00**

Butter dish, 5x7½" dia...**$45.00**

Cake stand, 7x14" dia $65.00
Center bowl, 4¾x8½" $50.00
Creamer & sugar bowl $65.00
Dessert set, 8½" bowl, 12" plate................$75.00
Goblet, 8-oz..$20.00
Pitcher, 7¼" $65.00
Pitcher, 8¼" $75.00
Plate, rim w/4 lg & 4 sm opposing lobes, 2x14" $65.00
Punch set, 10" bowl, pedestal, 8 cups, & ladle, 11-pc..$135.00
Rose bowl, 6½x6½", from $35 to $45.00
Sauce set, 4½" bowl, 5½" plate, w/spoon, 3-pc $35.00
Swung vase, slender, footed, w/irregular rim, 11x3" ..$40.00
Tumbler, 3½"...$17.50

Patterns

Canterbury, basket, waffle pattern, Lime, Sunset, or Horizon Blue, 5½x12", from $35 to $55.00
Monticello, basket, lg embossed faceted diamonds overall, Lemon, Lime, Sunset, or Horizon Blue, square, 7x6", from $25 to...$35.00
Monticello, basket, lg faceted diamonds overall, Lemon, Lime, Sunset, or Horizon Blue, 8¾x10½", from $35 to........$45.00
Monticello, candy box, lg faceted allover diamonds, w/lid, Lemon, Lime, Sunset, or Horizon Blue, 5¼x6", from $20 to $25.00

Ruby Band Diamond Point, butter dish, $28.00.

Ruby Band Diamond Point, chip & dip set, 13" dia ...$25.00
Ruby Band Diamond Point, comport, 14½" dia $20.00
Ruby Band Diamond Point, cooler (iced tea tumbler), 15-oz $7.50
Ruby Band Diamond Point, creamer & sugar bowl, 4¼" .$15.00
Ruby Band Diamond Point, creamer & sugar bowl, 4¾", on 6x9" tray...$22.00
Ruby Band Diamond Point, goblet, 12-oz $4.00
Ruby Band Diamond Point, On-the-Rocks, 9-oz...........$4.00
Ruby Band Diamond Point, pitcher, 8".......................$12.00
Ruby Band Diamond Point, plate, hostess; 12", from $12 to..$18.00
Ruby Band Diamond Point, relish tray, 3-part, 12" dia..$15.00
Ruby Band Diamond Point, salt & pepper shakers, 4", pr..$20.00

Indianapolis 500 Racing Memorabilia

You don't have to be a Hoosier to know that unless the weather interferes, this famous 500-mile race is held in Indianapolis every Memorial day and has been since 1911.

Collectors of Indy memorabilia have a plethora of race-related items to draw from and can zero in on one area or many, enabling them to build extensive and interesting collections. Some of the special areas of interest they pursue are autographs, photographs or other memorabilia related to the drivers; pit badges; race programs and yearbooks; books and magazines; decanters and souvenir tumblers; and model race cars.

Advisor: Eric Jungnickel (See Directory, Indy 500 Memorabilia)

Ashtray, Indianapolis Motor Speedway '500s,' white china w/gold trim & colorful winged wheel $20.00
Ashtray, Indianapolis Speedway, black, 2" dia............$10.00
Bobbin' head, driver standing w/blue shirt, 'Indianapolis 500' in gold on chest...$300.00
Bobbin' head, driver w/yellow helmet seated in white & red car, 'Indianapolis 500' on car..........................$500.00
Book, Andretti, by Bill Libby, Tempo Books, paperback, 1970 ....$15.00
Book, Marlboro Salute to 75th Anniversary of Indy 500, hardback, 1986 ....$20.00
Book, Wall Smaker, by Peter DePaolo, 1st edition, 4th printing, author signed, hardback, 1938, EX $95.00
Decanter, Al Unser, Johnny Lightning, blue racer w/gold, #2, M $75.00
Decanter, Indy 500 1971, white racer, #2, Garnier, M...$50.00
Decanter, Mario Andretti, red racer, #9, Old Mr Boston, M.$50.00
First day cover, Indianapolis Stamp Club, postmark w/checkers, dated May 30, 1970, NM $5.00
Flag, black & white checks, signed 1955 winner, Bob Sweikert...$500.00
Folder, Indy 500, 1965 qualifying record, GC Murphy Stores Special #67 ....$15.00
Game, Champion Spark Plugs Auto Race, premium, 1934, M..$60.00
Glass, 1951, Indy winners through 1950 listed, winged wheel logo..$30.00
Glass, 1953, winged wheel logo................................$25.00
Glass, 1968, Indy logo on front, winners on back, Tony Hulman facsimile signature $20.00
Glass, 1972, short...$15.00

Glass, 1981, features Johnny Rutherford, $10.00.

Glasses, 1960s-era rear-engine cars in gold, set of 6 ..$15.00
Hatpin, Craftsman 1993 Team Member.........................$5.00

Magazine, Sports Illustrated, 5/25/59, Indy preview cover, EX/M...$25.00

Magazine, Sports Illustrated, 5/26/56, Bob Sweikert cover, EX/M...$30.00

Magazine, Sports Illustrated, 5/27/57, Jimmy Brian cover, EX/M...$30.00

Magazine, Sports Illustrated, 6/5/78, 'Unser's 3rd' cover, EX/M...$10.00

Media guide, driver biographies, car builders' info, stats, historical information, 1958 ....$35.00

Mug, frosted glass w/wood handle, marked 1954 Bill Vukovich, 130.840 mph on side, brass replica of #14 car at front.$40.00

Pennant, Indianapolis Motor Speedway, black felt w/white lettering, #7 car pictured left, 1929, M.............$800.00

Pennant, Indianapolis Motor Speedway, blue felt w/white lettering, '40s-era cars pictured, M..............$250.00

Pennant, Indianapolis Motor Speedway, tan felt w/multicolored graphic of race car, 26x8½", EX.............$75.00

Pennant, Indy 500, colorful, dated 1984, M.................$10.00

Pennant, 500 Miles Auto Race, Indianapolis 1914, gray & red felt stitched together, letters & date stitched on, M....$1,500.00

Pennant, 500 Miles Speedway Race, Indianapolis 1913, green felt w/yellow car #3, driver & mechanic in car, M......$1,500.00

Pillow sham, Souvenir of Indianapolis Speedway, pink silk w/race scene $30.00

Pit badge, 1951, bronze $140.00

Pit badge, 1952, bronze $120.00

Pit badge, 1953, bronze $100.00

Pit badge, 1954, bronze......................................$80.00

Pit badge, 1955, bronze......................................$68.00

Pit badge, 1959, bronze......................................$56.00

Pit badge, 1978, bronze......................................$48.00

Pit badge, 1979, bronze......................................$40.00

Pit badge, 1981, bronze......................................$40.00

Plate, 1982 Collector Series, pewter, Indy logo on front...$10.00

Playing cards, black & white checks w/Indy 500 on black & gold banner, single deck, MIB.......................$5.00

Postcard, Indianapolis 500, race cars & pace car at start of race, linen....................................$15.00

Postcard, shows cars at start, Cord (?) pace car, linen..$15.00

Postcard, Wally Dallenback & #6 Sugaripe car, autographed, 1967-77 stats, 5x7" $15.00

Program, May 30, 1947......................................$100.00

Program, PPB/Indy Car World Series Yearbook, 1981..$6.00

Program, 1932, some writing, EX.............................$150.00

Program, 1934, some soiling, EX.............................$150.00

Program, 1936, soiled & writing, EX.........................$100.00

Program, 1939, EX..$80.00

Program, 1939, torn back cover, VG..........................$60.00

Program, 1940, EX/M...$90.00

Program, 1948, w/lap score sheet, EX.......................$100.00

Program, 1951, EX..$45.00

Program, 1961, 50th Anniversary, EX.........................$42.50

Program, 1976, 120 pages, NM.................................$15.00

Program, 1982-1990, any, EX...................................$10.00

Promotional race car, metal, marked Wilbur Sales, Indianapolis Speedway, 1946, 8"...............$575.00

Seat cushion, Indianapolis 500 Speedway, '70s-era car, black & white checks $25.00

Ticket, pictures '84 winner Rick Mears & car, 1985....$10.00

Toy, ARCOR (Auburn Rubber Corp) Indy-style racer, red w/white rubber tires, EX/NM................................$25.00

Toy, Aurora T-jet slot car, 1950s-style racer, EX..........$40.00

Tumbler, white & black silkscreen listing winners through 1967, gold trim, set of 6, MIB..............................$65.00

Watch fob, Harroun's Marmon Wasp, brass color.......$25.00

Yearbook, 1955, Floyd Clymer Publishing...................$55.00

Yearbook, 1981 Indy Car World Series, color photos & info, 144 pgs $10.00

Yearbook, 1984, 224 pages, $15.00.

Italian Glass

Throughout the century, the island of Murano has been recognized as one of the major glassmaking centers of the world. Companies including Venini, Barovier, Aureliano Toso, Barvini, Vistosi, AVEM, Cenedese, Cappellin, Seguso and Archimede Seguso have produced very fine art glass, examples of which today often bring several thousand dollars on the secondary market — superior examples much more. Such items are rarely seen at the garage sale and flea market level, but what you will be seeing are the more generic glass clowns, birds, ashtrays and animals, generally referred to as Murano glass. Their values are determined by the techniques used in their making more than size alone. For instance, an item with gold inclusions, controlled bubbles, fused glass patches, or layers of colors is more desirable than one that has none of these elements, even though it may be larger. For more information concerning the specific companies mentioned above, see *Schroeder's Antiques Price Guide* (Collector Books.)

Candlesticks, pink w/gold-washed base, vase-shaped standard, Venetian, 12", pr.......................................$230.00

Console bowl, clear with gold inclusions, applied red dots, w/pr of candlesticks $600.00

Cruet, cased blue satin w/applied red cherries, footed, 8½" $125.00

Cruet, cased pink w/applied trumpet flower, footed, 10".$125.00

Cup & saucer, pink w/gold striping, figural dolphin handle, Venetian..$90.00

Ewer, multicolor stripes of white, pink, yellow, blue, green & gold, Venetian, 12"..$150.00

Figurine, bird, blue & white body, on clear pedestal base, 8"..$40.00

Figurine, bird, light gray, stylized, signed Seguso, 12", pr ..**$400.00**
Figurine, duck, red w/silver mica, Murano, 9" **$60.00**
Figurine, duck, turquoise w/internal gold flakes, 8", pr **$75.00**
Figurine, duck w/spread wings, green w/gold beak, 12" ..**$75.00**

Figurine, elephant, clear with internal blue and yellow stripes and silver mica, 7x5", $45.00.

Figurine, fish, blue body on clear base, 13" **$75.00**
Figurine, fish, clear & black w/internal bubbles, Venetian, 6", pr **$150.00**
Figurine, horse, blue, 10" **$40.00**
Figurine, horse, blue, 4" **$28.00**
Figurine, lady, in blue gown w/gold flakes, lg hat, Venetian, 12" **$250.00**
Figurine, pheasant, crystal w/blue sections, 15½" **$135.00**
Figurine, ram, blue, 8" **$35.00**
Figurine, rooster, clear & opaque w/gold & multicolor applications, 7" **$110.00**
Figurine, rooster, green body w/internal bubbles on clear base, 9" **$50.00**
Figurine, sailfish, yellow & orange on white base, 15", pr ..**$100.00**
Pitcher, pig form, clear w/cobalt tail, ears & eyes, Murano, 8x7" **$85.00**
Rose bowl, cased pink w/applied trumpet flower, 4½" ...**$90.00**
Vase, amber w/internal bubbles, 5-disk handles, footed cone form, Murano, 7" **$700.00**
Vase, clear w/blue powders & gold leaf, pinched sides, Murano, 9" **$160.00**
Vase, melon-colored w/dense bubbles, rim handles, Murano, 6x6" **$250.00**

Jad-ite Glassware

For the past few years, Jad-ite has been one of the fastest-moving types of collectible glassware on the market. It was produced by several companies from the 1940s through 1965. Many of Anchor Hocking's Fire-King lines were available in the soft opaque green Jad-ite, and Jeannette Glass as well as McKee produced their own versions.

It was always very inexpensive glass, and it was made in abundance. Dinnerware for the home as well as restaurants and a vast array of kitchenware items literally flooded the country for many years. Though a few rare pieces have become fairly expensive, most are still reasonably priced, and there are still bargains to be had.

For more information we recommend *Fire-King Fever '97* by April and Larry Tvorak; and *Kitchen Glassware of the Depression Years* and *Collectible Glassware of the '40s, '50s, and '60s,* both by Gene Florence.

Advisor: April Tvorak (See Directory, Fire-King)

Beater bowl, w/beater, Jeannette **$30.00**
Bowl, cereal; Laurel, Fire-King **$12.00**
Bowl, cereal; Swirl/Shell, Fire-King.............................**$10.00**
Bowl, dessert; Charm/Square, Fire-King, 4¾" **$7.50**
Bowl, embossed horizontal ribs & multicolor floral decoration, Jeannette, 9¾" **$35.00**
Bowl, flange soup; Jane-Ray, Fire-King, Anchor Hocking .**$45.00**
Bowl, flanged grapefruit/cereal; Restaurant Ware, Fire-King.**$12.00**
Bowl, flat soup; Jane-Ray, Fire-King, Anchor Hocking ...**$14.00**
Bowl, oatmeal; Jane-Ray, Fire-King, Anchor Hocking ..**$10.00**
Bowl, rolled lip; Restaurant Ware, Fire-King, 15-oz **$12.00**
Bowl, sauce; Jane-Ray, Fire-King, Anchor Hocking **$5.00**
Bowl, sauce; Laurel, Fire-King....................................**$7.50**
Bowl, sauce; Restaurant Ware, Fire-King **$4.50**
Bowl, sauce; Sheaf of Wheat, Fire-King......................**$20.00**
Bowl, sauce; Swirl/Shell, Fire-King.............................**$5.00**
Bowl, serving; Jane-Ray, Fire-King, Anchor Hocking ..**$14.00**
Bowl, serving; Laurel, Fire-King **$22.00**
Bowl, serving; Swirl/Shell, Fire-King...........................**$12.00**
Bowl, soup; Laurel, Fire-King **$16.00**

Bowls, horizontal ribs with flower vines, Jeannette, 9¾", from $30.00 to $35.00; 7½", $25.00.

Butter dish, dark green, rectangular, Jeannette **$45.00**
Butter dish, light green, Jeannette **$40.00**
Canister, black lettering, square w/matching square lid, Jeannette, 48-oz, 5½" **$45.00**
Canister, coffee; metal screw-on lid, light or dark green, round, Jeannette...**$70.00**
Canister, square, Jeannette, 48-oz, 5½" **$45.00**
Canister, vertical ribs, silver paper label, matching glass lid, 47-oz **$50.00**
Charm/Square, bowl, soup **$22.00**
Creamer & sugar bowl, Jane-Ray, w/lid, Fire-King, Anchor Hocking **$16.00**
Cup & saucer, Alice, Fire-King....................................**$5.00**
Cup & saucer, Charm/Square, Fire-King **$8.00**
Cup & saucer, Jane-Ray, Fire-King, Anchor Hocking....**$3.50**
Cup & saucer, Laurel, Fire-King...................................**$8.00**
Cup & saucer, Restaurant Ware, Fire-King **$6.50**
Cup & saucer, Sheaf of Wheat, Fire-King **$25.00**
Cup & saucer, Swirl/Flat, Fire-King **$15.00**
Cup & saucer, Swirl/Shell, Fire-King **$6.00**
Cup/mug, Ranson handle, Restaurant Ware, Fire-King.**$7.00**

Dessert set, Leaf and Blossom, Fire-King, $15.00.

Dish, refrigerator; floral lid, Jeannette, 10x5" **$40.00**
Dish, refrigerator; Hall style, McKee, 4x6" **$16.00**
Egg cup, McKee..**$12.00**
Ice bucket, metal handle, Fenton................................**$55.00**
Jar, drippings; McKee, 4x5" **$85.00**
Jar, Epsom Salt; Jeannette...**$75.00**
Jug, batter; w/lid, Jeannette **$250.00**
Measuring pitcher, light green, sunflower in bottom, Jeannette, 2-cup **$18.00**
Mug, chocolate, slim w/flared top, Restaurant Ware, Fire-King **$15.00**
Mug, coffee; Restaurant Ware, Fire-King, lightweight, 8-oz....**$7.00**
Napkin holder, Serv-All **$175.00**
Pitcher, ball form, Restaurant Ware, Fire-King, 80-oz .**$185.00**
Plate, bread & butter; Restaurant Ware, Fire-King, 5½" ..**$4.50**
Plate, dinner; Alice, Fire-King.......................................**$22.00**
Plate, dinner; Jane-Ray, Fire-King, Anchor Hocking **$5.00**
Plate, dinner; Restaurant Ware, Fire-King, 9" **$8.00**
Plate, dinner; Sheaf of Wheat, Fire-King.....................**$30.00**
Plate, dinner; Swirl/Shell, Fire-King...............................**$8.00**
Plate, grill; Laurel, Fire-King **$12.00**
Plate, grill; Laurel, 3 compartments, Fire-King **$12.00**
Plate, grill; 3-compartment, Restaurant Ware, Fire-King..**$14.00**
Plate, grill; 5-compartment, Restaurant Ware, Fire-King..**$18.00**
Plate, luncheon; Charm/Square, Fire-King....................**$7.00**
Plate, luncheon; Restaurant Ware, Fire-King, 8" **$15.00**
Plate, pie/salad; Restaurant Ware, Fire-King, 6¾" **$4.50**
Plate, salad; Charm/Square, Fire-King, 6⅝" **$7.50**
Plate, salad; Jane-Ray, Fire-King, Anchor Hocking........**$6.00**
Plate, salad; Laurel, Fire-King **$10.00**
Plate, salad; Swirl/Shell, Fire-King................................**$6.00**
Plate, Swirl/Flat, Fire-King...**$35.00**
Platter, Jane-Ray, oval, Fire-King, Anchor Hocking.....**$15.00**
Platter, Laurel, oval, Fire-King, minimum value **$25.00**
Platter, oval, partitioned, Restaurant Ware, Fire-King..**$38.00**
Platter, oval, Swirl/Shell, Fire-King **$28.00**
Platter, rectangular, Charm/Square, Fire-King..............**$20.00**
Platter, Restaurant Ware, Fire-King, 9½" or 11½", each ..**$20.00**
Salt & pepper shakers, Laurel, footed, Fire-King, scarce, pr, minimum value **$45.00**
Sauce pan, 2-spout, Restaurant Ware, Fire-King..........**$65.00**
Shaker, Salt embossed, McKee....................................**$45.00**
Shaker, toiletry; Jeannette, each **$150.00**
Shakers, souvenir; Jeannette, pr **$125.00**
Sherbet, Laurel, Fire-King **$6.50**
Sugar shaker, black lettering, silver-metal lid **$35.00**
Tumbler, Jeannette, 12-oz **$15.00**
Vase, Jeannette...**$15.00**

Japan Ceramics

This category is narrowed down to the inexpensive novelty items produced in Japan from 1921 to 1941 and again from 1947 until the present. Though Japanese ceramics marked Nippon, Noritake, and Occupied Japan have long been collected, some of the newest fun-type collectibles on today's market are the figural ashtrays, pincushions, wall pockets, toothbrush holders, etc., that are marked 'Made in Japan' or simply 'Japan.' In her book called *Collector's Guide to Made in Japan Ceramics*, Carole Bess White explains the pitfalls you will encounter when you try to determine production dates. Collectors refer to anything produced before WWII as 'old,' and anything made after 1952 as 'new.' Backstamps are inconsistent as to wording and color, and styles are eclectic. Generally, items with applied devices are old, and they are heavier and thicker. Often they were more colorful than the newer items, since fewer colors mean less expense to the manufacturer. Lustre glazes are usually indicative of older pieces, especially the deep solid colors. When lustre was used after the war, it was often mottled with contrasting hues.

Imaginative styling and strong colors are what give these Japanese ceramics their charm, and they also are factors to consider when you make your purchases. You'll find all you need to know to be a wise shopper in the book we recommended above.

See also Blue Willow; Cat Collectibles; Condiment Sets; Enesco; Flower Frogs; Geisha Girl; Holt-Howard; Kreiss; Lamps; Lefton; Napkin Dolls; Occupied Japan Collectibles; Toothbrush Holders.

Ashtray, applied duck & bird perched on rim of round green bowl w/1 rest, glossy finish, 2" dia **$25.00**
Ashtray, green frog w/banjo seated on white fanned-out playing cards, orange trim, lustre, 1¾" **$18.00**
Ashtray, Indian wrapped in blanket & holding peace pipe seated on edge of rectangular tray w/oval opening, lustre, 5" **$45.00**
Ashtray/Pin tray, scouting Indian seated in blue & tan canoe, lustre finish, 3" **$45.00**

Ashtray, Satsuma-style with tan lustre glaze, 3¼", from $10.00 to $20.00. (Photo courtesy of Carole Bess White.)

Bank, Art Deco figural cat w/chiseled features seated upright, blue glossy finish, 4¼" **$20.00**

Bank, Hummel-type girl w/open umbrella & white duck on base marked Save for Raining Day, multicolored matt finish, 5" **$20.00**

Bank, white money-bag form w/embossed gold-trimmed dollar sign tied at neck w/orange tie, opalescent finish, 4½" **$20.00**

Basket, footed tulip shape w/handle, Art Deco floral motif on orange, blue & tan w/lustre finish, 6¼"............**$55.00**

Bell, figural colonial lady, glossy w/matt china-painted finish, labeled Seattle Washington at hem of dress, 4¾" ..**$20.00**

Bell, half-figure of Chinese lady w/long black hair, blue bodice w/yellow collar, brown buttons & black trim, glossy, 5" **$35.00**

Bird feeder, 2 birds embossed on branch against white dome w/blue stripes, glossy finish, 3¼".........................**$25.00**

Biscuit jar, green barrel cactus shape w/floral decor, reed handle, glossy finish, 7" **$50.00**

Biscuit jar, white Dutch windmill w/brown, blue & green trim, reed handle, glossy finish, 6½"....................**$50.00**

Biscuit jar, yellow bucket w/embossed playing-card decor & green squirrel finial, swing handle, glossy finish, 5½" **$60.00**

Bookends, Mexican figures in sombreros taking a siesta on L-shaped bases, tan & red glossy & lustre finishes, 4", pr...**$40.00**

Bookends, pheasants in realistic colors on blue-green grassy L-shaped bases, glossy finish, 5", pr.....................**$18.00**

Bookends, sailboat forms L-shaped waves, red, yellow, white & black boats, waves in blue wash, glossy finish, 4¾"...**$35.00**

Bowl, irregular shape w/blue stylized cat handle, floral motif on white w/lustre finish, 7"...................................**$40.00**

Bowl, octagon w/reed handle, red, yellow, green & black kaleidoscopic design on white w/blue border, lustre finish, 8" **$25.00**

Bowl, oval w/cut-out handles, house & landscape scene w/back view of lady in yellow bonnet, tan rim, lustre finish, 8" **$40.00**

Bowl, ridged middle w/flat bottom, butterflies & flowers applied at scalloped rim, blue w/tan interior, lustre, 6½" **$40.00**

Candlestick, trumpet shape in blue semi-matt glaze, multicolored bird motif w/budding branch, 9¾"..............**$40.00**

Candlesticks, blue trumpet shape w/allover multicolored flower, berry & leaf design, flat round cups, glossy, 7½", pr **$130.00**

Candy dish, blue cat figure in pouncing position on round tan base, lustre finish, 6¾"..................................**$100.00**

Candy dish, round, white w/multicolored floral design around embossed bust image of court jester, blue lustre trim, 6" **$40.00**

Candy dish, round w/repeated closed-lotus motif around middle & lid, orange & tan w/black trim, matt finish, 3¼"...**$40.00**

Cigarette box, rectangular w/black dog finial on lid, marbleized green & white w/glossy finish, 3" **$30.00**

Cigarette box, white rectangular shape w/yellow cowboy hat & brown chaps on lid, gun embossed on side, glossy, 5¼"...**$20.00**

Cigarette/Candy box, white elephant w/orange, yellow & black howdah & base, glossy finish, 6¾"............**$40.00**

Clothes brush, white bristles wrapped in blue satin around ceramic dog's head, 8" **$45.00**

Creamer & sugar bowl, flat-sided duck shape in 2-tone blue & tan w/yellow bill, lustre finish, 3¼" **$55.00**

Figurine, blond girl seated on black suitcase w/lg red hat cocked on side of head holding black umbrella, glossy, 4¾"...**$30.00**

Figurine, hitchhiking bird couple w/suitcases, multicolored glossy finish, 3¼", each...**$20.00**

Figurine, monkey in bent-over position scratching head on oval base, white w/green wash & black circle eyes, glossy, 5" **$25.00**

Figurine, Spanish lady holding skirt out, yellow bodice and orange and yellow skirt with shiny glaze, 6¾", from $45.00 to $55.00. (Photo courtesy of Carole Bess White.)

Flask, All Scotch lettered in black on box w/white dog being served by Scottish girl, gold-tone stopper, tan luster, 5"............**$50.00**

Flask, Here's to Both of You! lettered in black above drunk under leaning lamppost w/facial features, tan lustre, 5"...**$50.00**

Hatpin holder, blue peacock w/multicolored accents on black round base, glossy finish, 3¾"....................**$40.00**

Incense burner, Oriental man on elephant, blue, tan & orange black trim, lustre finish, 6¼" **$40.00**

Incense burner, seated buddha in tan lustre w/black hair & trim, 4¼" **$25.00**

Incense burner, 2-pc 6-sided pagoda in blue, tan & orange w/gold-tone finial, lustre finish, 6¼"....................**$20.00**

Lemon server, applied lemon w/painted green leaves & white blossoms on round blue bowl, gold rim, lustre, 6"....**$40.00**

Lemon server, square w/canted corners, center handle, multicolored floral center on white w/zigzag design on rim, 5¾"...**$30.00**

Liquor decanter, figural multicolored clown holding 2 shot glasses w/2 more on base, glossy finish, 9" **$65.00**

Liquor decanter red bellhop figure w/gold trim holding 4 shot glasses w/2 in pockets, glossy finish, 11"...**$155.00**

Match holder, orange, blue & tan Oriental man in gold-tone hat w/blue lustre bowl, glossy finish, 5" **$25.00**

Mayonnaise, footed bowl on round plate w/spoon, white w/multicolored flowers on blue swagged design, lustre finish, 6"...**$50.00**

Napkin ring, girl figure in red hat w/white band, white bow w/black stripes & black shoes, glossy finish, 4¼"..**$20.00**

Nut cup, blue basket w/multicolored floral motif at base of handle, lustre finish, 3¼" **$20.00**

Nut cup, white bunny applied to burnt-orange cup w/tan interior, glossy finish, 1¾"......................................**$20.00**

Pincushion, tan camel w/floral decor on howdah, yellow blanket w/blue border, lustre finish, 4" **$35.00**

Pincushion, tan donkey pulling 2-wheeled white barrel w/blue bands, lustre finish, 1½"........................**$15.00**

Pincushion, white cartoon-like dog w/multicolored trim (1 ear up & 1 ear down) seated next to tan lustre basket, 3¼"...**$25.00**

Pitcher, green palm-tree motif on orange bulbous body w/flat bottom, tan rim & ear-shaped handle, lustre finish, 8½"...**$75.00**

Pitcher, white cartoon-like dog w/brown trim, tail is handle & mouth is spout, glossy finish, 2¾" **$25.00**

Planter, 'stuffed' yellow, blue & white elephant w/floral decor & black stitch marks, 5¼"...........................**$15.00**

Planter, pixie in yellow suit w/black hat holding white bunny & kneeling next to brown tree-trunk pot, glossy, 3" **$20.00**

Planter, white horse w/brown trim standing next to Mexican cowboy in blue, green & tan taking a siesta, glossy, 7"...**$20.00**

Planter, 2 frogs hugging water lily, glossy multicolored finish, 4½"...**$25.00**

Planter, 3 stylized gents in top hats on base w/ribbed pot, green, yellow & pink airbrushing w/black trim, glossy, 5"...**$25.00**

Planter, yellow with bluebird and tulips, shiny glaze, 3½", from $10.00 to $18.00. (Photo courtesy of Carole Bess White.)

Powder box, round tan lustre box w/3 yellow chicks embossed on sides & yellow chick finial on lid, 3¼"...............**$20.00**

Powder/Candy box, white colonial couple w/gold trim, 6¾"..**$20.00**

Relish dish, 3-compartment heart shape in green crackle glaze, applied floral decor in center, 7½"............**$20.00**

Ring holder, blue footed basket w/applied pink flower on side, glossy finish, 2¼"............................**$10.00**

Shoe, applied & embossed multicolored floral decor on maroon high heel w/white polka dots, 2½"........**$15.00**

Shoe, white mice w/black spots playing on man's tan shoe, 2½"...**$15.00**

Thermometer, clown in white w/multicolored polka dots lying atop gray lustre column encasing thermometer, 4¾"..**$30.00**

Toast rack, 5 tan bamboo-type arched holders on blue rectangular base, lustre finish, 5¼" **$40.00**

Toothpick holder, blue dog w/wide-open mouth trimmed in red, lustre finish, 3" **$25.00**

Vase, blue fluted cylinder on round beveled base w/white embossed sailboat design, glossy finish, 7¾".......**$20.00**

Vase, blue pedestaled urn w/white horizontal curved handles, semi-gloss finish, 7½"................................**$30.00**

Vase, blue tree trunk w/tan & black dog barking at owl on black branch, lustre finish, 7" **$65.00**

Vase, blue urn w/Golden Gate Bridge in moriage motif, white interior, semi-gloss finish, 5"......................**$40.00**

Vase, cowboy boot decorated in German beer-stein style, glossy finish w/tan lustre trim, 8¼"......................**$50.00**

Vase, footed fan-shaped basket w/applied handles, multicolored floral motif on blue w/tan interior, lustre finish, 4" **$30.00**

Vase, hippo w/head drawn back & mouth wide open, white & blue w/crosshatch & 3-dot design, red-trimmed mouth, glossy, 3" **$25.00**

Vase, yellow frog pulling lg 2-wheeled blue tulip-type flower w/green leaves, glossy w/tan lustre, 3¾" **$30.00**

Jewel Tea Company

At the turn of the century, there was stiff competition among door-to-door tea-and-coffee companies, and most of them tried to snag the customer by doling out coupons that could eventually be traded in for premiums. But the thing that set the Jewel Tea people apart from the others was that their premiums were awarded to the customer first, then 'earned' through the purchases that followed. This set the tone of their business dealings which obviously contributed to their success, and very soon in addition to the basic products they started out with, the company entered the food-manufacturing field. They eventually became one of the country's largest retailers. Today their products, containers, premiums and advertising ephemera are all very collectible.

Advisors: Bill and Judy Vroman (See Directory, Jewel Tea)

Baking powder, Jewel, script logo w/white letters, round cylindrical tin, 1950s-60s, 1-lb, from $20 to..........**$30.00**

Baking powder, logo & letters in white on red, red cylindrical tin w/red lid, from $20 to **$30.00**

Coffee, Jewel Blend, white logo & letters on orange, shaded orange to brown ground, 1948, 2-lb, from $25 to .**$35.00**

Coffee, Jewel Blend, white logo & letters on orange & gold paper..**$40.00**

Coffee, Jewel Private Blend, white letters on brown, 1-lb, from $15 to..**$25.00**

Coffee, Jewel Special Blend, white & orange letters on brown circle, brown stripes on white ground, 2-lb, from $15 to...**$25.00**

Coffee, Royal Jewel, brown & white on yellow, 1-lb, from $20 to **$35.00**

Coffee, West Coast, white letters on orange & brown w/bell at top center, 1960s, 2-lb, from $25 to **$35.00**

Extract, Jewel Imitation Vanilla, orange & white letters on brown rectangular box, 1960s, 4-oz, from $20 to ..**$30.00**

Extract, Jewel Lemon, orange, blue & white, 1916-19, from $40 to......................................**$50.00**

Flour sifter, lithographed metal, EX, $485.00. (Photo courtesy of Bill and Judy Vroman.)

Laundry product, Daintiflakes, marked Soft Feathery Flakes of Pure Mild Soap, blue & pink box, from $25 to......**$30.00**

Laundry product, Grano Granulated Soap, marked Made For General Cleaning, blue & white box, 2-lb, from $25 to **$30.00**

Laundry product, Pure Gloss Starch, teal & white box, from $25 to...**$30.00**

Mints, Jewel Mints, round green tin, 1920s, 1-lb, from $30 to **$40.00**

Mix, Jewel Sunbrite Mix, paper label on Mason jar w/metal screw-on lid, 1960s, 26-oz, from $15 to................**$25.00**

Mix, Jewel Tea Coconut Dessert, brown & white logo & letters on round tan tin, 1930s, 14-oz, from $30 to..**$40.00**

Mix, Jewel Tea Devil's Food Cake Flour, 1920s, 10-oz, from $30 to **$40.00**

Mix, Jewel Tea Prepared Tapioca, logo & brown letters on orange w/brown stripes, tall & square tin, 1930s, from $25 to...**$35.00**

Mixer, Mary Dunbar, white, electric, w/stand, bowl & original hang tag...**$100.00**

Napkins, paper w/printed pattern, box of 200 ....**$25.00**

Prepared food, Jewel Mix Nuts, orange & brown letters on brown-striped ground, round tin, 1960s, 1-lb, from $15 to **$20.00**

Prepared food, Jewel Quick Oats, white & orange letters on round cylindrical box, from $40 to **$50.00**

Prepared food, Jewel Tea Cocoa or Jewel Cocoa, various boxes, each, from $25 to..**$40.00**

Prepared food, Jewel Tea Jellied Spiced Drops, orange & white letters on orange rectangular box, from $20 to........**$30.00**

Prepared food, Jewel Tea Peanut Butter, multicolored paper label on glass jar w/screw-on lid, 1930s, 1-lb, from $30 to.**$40.00**

Prepared product, Jewel Tea Bags, gold & brown logo w/brown letters, green dragon to side, 1948, EX...**$65.00**

Sweeper, Jewel Little Bissell, from $40 to....................**$50.00**

Sweeper, Jewel Suction Sweeper, letters on lg wood case, hand-push style w/wood handle, early 1900s, lg .**$150.00**

Sweeper, Jewel Sweeper, gold letters on black, 1930s-40s, from $80 to...**$100.00**

Sweeper, Jewel Sweeper, tan letters on dark tan, 1930s-40s, from $80 to...**$100.00**

Tea Bags box, 1948, EX, $65.00. (Photo courtesy of Bill and Judy Vroman.)

Jewelry

Today's costume jewelry collectors may range from nine to ninety and have tastes as varied as their ages, but one thing they all have in common is their love of these distinctive items of jewelry, some of which were originally purchased at the corner five-&-dimes, others from department stores.

Costume jewelry became popular, simply because it was easily affordable by the average woman. Today jewelry made before 1954 is considered to be 'antique,' while the term 'collectible' jewelry generally refers to those pieces made after that time. 1954 was the year that costume jewelry was federally recognized as an American art form, and the copyright law was passed to protect the artists' designs. The copyright mark (c in a circle) found on the back of a piece identifies a post-1954 'collectible.'

Quality should always be the primary consideration when shopping for these treasures. Remember that pieces with colored rhinestones bring the higher prices. (A 'rhinestone' is a clear, foil-backed, leaded glass crystal — unless it is a 'colored rhinestone' — while a 'stone' is not foiled.) Complete sets increase in value by 20% over the total of their components. Check for a manufacturer's mark, since a signed piece is worth 20% more than one not signed. Some of the best designers are Miriam Haskell, Eisenberg, Trifari, Hollycraft and Weiss.

Early plastic pieces (Lucite, Bakelite and celluloid, for example) are very collectible. Some Lucite is used in combination with wood, and the figural designs are especially desirable.

There are several excellent reference books available if you'd like more information. Lillian Baker has written several: *Art Nouveau and Art Deco Jewelry; Twentieth Century Fashionable Plastic Jewelry; 50 Years of Collectible Fashion Jewelry;* and *100 Years of Collectible Jewelry.* Books by other authors include *Collecting Rhinestone Colored Jewelry* by Maryanne Dollan; *The Art and Mystique of Shell Cameos* by Ed Aswad and Michael Weinstein; *Christmas Pins* by Jill Gallina; and *Collecting Antique Stickpins* by Jack and 'Pet' Kerins.

Advisors: Marcia Brown (See Directory, Jewelry)

Bracelet, Bakelite, expandable plastic w/metallic spacers strung on elastic, ca 1950......................**$75.00**

Bracelet, Bakelite bangle, carved rope pattern, wide, ca 1935 ....**$100.00**

Bracelet, Bakelite bangles, simple thin style w/no carving, mottled colors, set of 5.......................**$75.00**

Bracelet, Beau, etched & engraved sterling leaves join at stem & tips to form links, ca 1940 ....**$50.00**

Bracelet, cast sterling, open-mouth faces alternate w/rings forming links, hand finished, ca 1950.........**$100.00**

Bracelet, celluloid bangle, French ivory color w/snake motif...**$50.00**

Bracelet, Chanel, avacodo green plastic thermoset stones in gold-tone links, ca 1960 ....**$50.00**

Bracelet, Coro, 3 rows of Aurora Borealis stones, gold electroplated, Art Modern design, ca 1950................**$30.00**

Bracelet, Eisenberg, rhinestones in rhodium, wide style, ca 1950 ....**$135.00**

Bracelet, Eisenberg, rhinestones set in individual links, flexible, wide style, ca 1960.......................**$120.00**

Bracelet, Eisenberg, rhodium & rhinestones w/3 lg rhinestones, narrow style, special patented safety clasp, ca 1940 ....**$115.00**

Bracelet, Jewel Art, sterling chain w/heart-shaped, finely engraved charm, ca 1940 ....**$60.00**

Bracelet, Kramer of New York, wide flexible cuff of rhodium w/cupped & prong-set rhinestones, 1950..........**$250.00**

Bracelet, Napier, gold-electroplated flexible mesh, molded faux jade stone clasp, ca 1950 ....**$50.00**

Bracelet, plastic, hinged wrap-around style accented w/rhinestones, ca 1935-60 ....**$100.00**

Bracelet & earrings, Trifari, white enamel & blue composition stones, gold electroplating, cast mounting, 1955-60..**$55.00**

Bracelet, rhinestone, marked Eisenberg Original, with guard chain, ¾" wide, $245.00.

Brooch, Bakelite, carved red flower, lg **$150.00**

Brooch, Boucher, Blackamoor, black enameling on gold-tone w/faux gemstones, ca 1960..................**$90.00**

Brooch, Boucher, brushed antique-finished leaf w/rhinestones, ca 1960.....................................**$60.00**

Brooch, Boucher, swirling leaf design, rhodium w/pave-set baguette rhinestones, ca 1960.............................**$40.00**

Brooch, BSK, leaf shape, Aurora Borealis, gold-tone, 1960 ....**$30.00**

Brooch, Castlecliff, simulated pink baroque pearl set in coral branch of heavy gold electroplate, ca 1960..........**$55.00**

Brooch, Coro, marked Pat Pend, crown shape set w/rhinestones, ca 1940.....................................**$65.00**

Brooch, Coro, multicolored faux gemstones on heads of floral spray, ca 1940......................................**$45.00**

Brooch, Coro, topaz-colored rhinestones, star shape, ca 1960..**$40.00**

Brooch, Danecraft, leaf form, sterling repousse, 1950s..**$50.00**

Brooch, De Nicola, pink quartz stone w/rhinestones, gold-tone filigree design, ca 1960 ....**$55.00**

Brooch, Emmons, 'Dearest' spelled in simulated gemstones, diamond for D, emerald for E, etc, on fan shape, ca 1950 ....**$35.00**

Brooch, Emmons, antique auto, rhinestones in rhodium, ca 1970 ....**$30.00**

Brooch, Emmons, crown shape, rhinestones w/faux cabachons, patented, gold-tone, ca 1960 ....**$80.00**

Brooch, Emmons, Rainbow Star, Aurora Borealis stones & cultured pearl, gold-tone star shape, ca 1950.......**$30.00**

Brooch, Hobe, swirled flower form, rhinestones on gold-tone......................................**$300.00**

Brooch, Hollycraft, stemmed flower tied w/bow, shades of green rhinestones, antiqued gold finish, dated 1953............**$55.00**

Brooch, Jomaz, faux teardrop emerald surrounded by rhinestones in ornate gold-tone design, ca 1955..........**$85.00**

Brooch, Kramer, wired simulated pearls among gold electroplated flower shapes, ca 1950 ....**$45.00**

Brooch, Kramer of New York, lavender to white opaque stones, hand set, circular, 2½" **$200.00**

Brooch, Ledo, pave-set pear-shaped & baguette-cut faux yellow & dark amber gemstones in gold-tone basket shape, 1962 ....**$30.00**

Brooch, Lisner, red stones in leafy swirl, gilt-metal, 2¼" long **$100.00**

Brooch, Mazer, gold vermeil sterling, star shape, simulated pearl center, rhinestones, ca 1940 ....**$40.00**

Brooch, Mimi di, ribbon design, prong-set rhinestones, ca 1960 ....**$40.00**

Brooch, Miriam Haskell, blue glass faux lapis cabachons & rhinestones, open filigree mounting, ca 1945-60 .**$90.00**

Brooch, Miriam Haskell, gilt brass flower form w/movable tassels, ca 1945.......................................**$85.00**

Brooch, Miriam Haskell, stemmed flower w/simulated mount-set pearls, antiqued gilt, ca 1950 ....**$60.00**

Brooch, plastic, red flower shape, prong-set rhinestones, ca 1950 ....**$20.00**

Brooch, Sarah Coventry, slender stylized lily w/pronged amber glass center & rhinestones, gold-tone, ca 1950 ....**$75.00**

Brooch, Symmetalic, 14k gold vermeil w/simulated moonstones, Art Nouveau floral shape, ca 1960 ....**$115.00**

Brooch, Trifari, anchor form, blue enameling, gold electroplated, ca 1955.....................................**$40.00**

Brooch, Trifari, feather w/rhinestones, marked Patented, ca 1940 ....**$200.00**

Brooch, Weiss, Christmas tree, multicolored rhinestones, ca 1960 ....**$40.00**

Brooch & earrings, Boucher, bamboo, white enameling, gold electroplating, clip-on backs, ca 1950 ....**$55.00**

Brooch & earrings, Eisenberg, lg flower shape, rhinestones in rhodium, sm swirl-shaped clip-on earrings, ca 1950 ....**$100.00**

Brooch & earrings, Emmons, painted blue enamel flowers w/faux turquoise stones, rhodium, ca 1960 ....**$40.00**

Brooch & earrings, Emmons, simulated pearls, rhinestones, gold-tone, clip-on backs, ca 1960.........................**$40.00**

Brooch & earrings, Hollycraft, bow design, blue Aurora Borealis & 3 sizes of pale blue rhinestones, rhodium, dated 1957..**$65.00**

Brooch & earrings, Hollycraft, floral spray w/lg amethyst stones, sm pink & purple rhinestone flowers, dated 1954 ....**$225.00**

Brooch & earrings, Hollycraft, teardrop & pastel rhinestones, screw-back drop earrings, antiqued gold-tone, dated 1951 ....**$95.00**

Brooch & earrings, Sarah Coventry, Snowflake, smoky faceted glass center & rhinestones, clip-on backs, 1960 ....**$70.00**

Critter, Bakelite brooch, bird in flight, glass eye, enameled **$150.00**

Critter, Bakelite brooch, carved red parrot w/hand-painted beak, ca 1935...**$195.00**

Critter, Boucher brooch, fish figural w/blue & green enamel stripes on gold-tone, ca 1955.................................**$65.00**

Critter, Brooks brooch, bird in flight, gilt brass w/rhinestone center, ca 1960 ....**$65.00**

Critter, BSK brooch, stylized cat, hand-cast gold-tone w/enamel details, ca 1960......................................**$30.00**

Critter, BSK brooch, stylized lion, cast gold-tone w/enamel details, ca 1960...**$40.00**

Critter, butterfly brooch, multicolored rhinestones, ca 1950...**$125.00**

Critter, Catalin brooch, ivory goldfish, glass eye, ca 1936-41 ....**$200.00**

Critter, Coro brooch, eagle w/folded wings, burnished gold-tone mountings, ca 1950 ....**$60.00**

Critter, Coro brooch, peacock on perch, tail down, multicolor enamel on electroplate, ca 1950 ....**$65.00**

Critter, Emmons brooch, Glamour Puss, Art Moderne cat w/simulated stone eyes, ca 1967........................**$20.00**

Critter, Emmons brooch, Lambkin, stylized lamb, oxidized brass, black enamel, ca 1960 ....**$12.50**

Critter, Kramer brooch, butterfly w/multicolor blue sets in gold-tone, ca 1960 ....**$55.00**

Critter, Trifari brooch, bird in Art Moderne style, pave-set rhinestones, ca 1955-65 ....**$40.00**

Critter, Trifari brooch, dragonfly, yellow enamel on gold-tone **$50.00**

Critter, Trifari brooch, elephant, sterling vermeil, cast mounting, cut Bohemian crystal & rhinestone accents, ca 1940 ....**$85.00**

Critter, Weiss brooch, butterfly, prong-set rhinestones (predominately green), ca 1950-60.............................**$90.00**

Earrings, Alice Caviness, wired pink & lavender beads form slender shape, clip-on backs, ca 1970 ....**$50.00**

Earrings, Bakelite, red carved floral design, long shape, clip-on backs **$40.00**

Earrings, Castlecliff, resembling butterflies, finely cast pierced work, rhodium, ca 1950-60 ....**$80.00**

Earrings, Christian Dior/Germany, faux jade & sapphire jewels in 6-sided shape, clip-on backs, ca 1967 ....**$60.00**

Earrings, Eisenberg Ice, blue & pink rhinestones, clip-on backs, ca 1960...**$60.00**

Earrings, Emmons, 3 simulated pearls set in rhodium, clip-on backs, ca 1960...**$15.00**

Earrings, gold arched rope design in gold electroplate, clip-on backs, ca 1950..**$20.00**

Earrings, Hattie Carnegie, Art Moderne geometric shape w/pave-set rhinestones in rhodium, ca 1945.......**$85.00**

Earrings, Hattie Carnegie, bezel-set faux sapphires in gold-tone setting, ca 1960...**$85.00**

Earrings, Hobe, bezel-set blue zircons, amethyst, peridot & topaz gemstones, gold-tone 1x1½" mounting, screw backs **$75.00**

Earrings, Hobe, multicolor genuine gemstones swirl around blue central stone, screw-backs, ca 1940, 1¼x1"..**$100.00**

Earrings, Jomaz, 7 blue glass cabachons surrounded w/rhinestones, circular shape, clip-on backs, ca 1940......**$75.00**

Earrings, KJL (Kenneth Jay Lane), faux coral & emeralds w/seed pearls, round, ca 1970...............................**$95.00**

Earrings, Lisner, red & green molded plastic leaves, gold-tone...**$30.00**

Earrings, Lucite, green w/rhinestones, lg button shape, clip-on backs, 1950s...**$40.00**

Earrings, Lucite, red teardrops, lg, pierced style, ca 1935 ..**$30.00**

Earrings, Miriam Haskell, wired turquoise & blue glass stones w/gilt filigree mounting, ca 1940..........................**$55.00**

Earrings, Mosell, fan-shaped shell design w/pink hand-painted enameling & gold electroplating, clip-on backs, ca 1960 ....**$30.00**

Earrings, Mosell, slim shell design, hand painted & gold electroplated, clip-on backs, ca 1960.........................**$30.00**

Earrings, plastic, molded flowers w/rhinestone centers, buttons style, screw-on backs, ca 1960 ....**$20.00**

Earrings, plastic, red button set w/rhinestones, clip-on backs **$40.00**

Earrings, rhinestone w/faux turquoise stone drop, clip-on backs, ca 1950-60 ....**$60.00**

Earrings, starburst style, marked Emmons, $35.00.

Earrings, Trifari, apple shape, baguette rhinestones, rhodium, clip-on backs, ca 1950...**$40.00**

Earrings, Trifari, classic-style horseshoes, rhodium, clip-on backs, 1950..**$30.00**

Earrings, Trifari, faux Persian turquoise cabachons set in gold-tone, ca 1960 ....**$100.00**

Earrings, Weiss, multifaceted faux gemstones & Aurora Borealis stones, gold-tone, clip-on backs, ca 1960-65 ....**$40.00**

Hair ornament, celluloid, fan-shaped comb set w/blue rhinestones, 6½x7"...**$65.00**

Hair ornament, celluloid, 2 hairpins, pave rhinestones w/cut metal work, Art Deco..**$45.00**

Hair ornament, celluloid, 2 rhinestone doves, 5½" wide, 4" high comb **$110.00**

Hair ornament, Juliette Cap, Art Moderne open ornamental vine accented w/pearl flowers, cast-metal circlet, 6" dia ...**$85.00**

Hair ornament, Sarah Coventry, barrette, Florentine gold-tone w/sm cultured pearl on bar shape, ca 1950, pr **$30.00**

Necklace, Austrian Aurora Borealis beads, 4-strand, ca 1960..**$125.00**

Necklace, bracelet & earrings, Jomaz, light blue opaque stones w/rhinestones on silvery metal, 16" choker, clip-on backs **$165.00**

Necklace, Coro, gold-plated w/square blue stones & lg blue stone drop **$75.00**

Necklace, DeMario, multicolor blue beads on chain, 3-strand, 1960 ....**$85.00**

Necklace, Emmons, Regency cross, antiqued rhodium filigree w/applied beading, ca 1977....................................**$35.00**

Necklace, KJL, Angel Skin, pink molded plastic flowers w/rhinestone trim, 1960-90 ....**$300.00**

Necklace, Miriam Haskell, red glass beads w/rhinestone rondels, disk closure, 18"..**$225.00**

Necklace, Sarah Coventry, chain links joined to resemble rope, rhodium **$10.00**

Necklace, sterling, shamrock charm w/hallmarked casing, ca 1950-60 ....**$40.00**

Necklace & earrings, Emmons, cabachon glass & faux pearls on gold-tone, tassels detach, clip-on backs, ca 1960 ....**$65.00**

Necklace & earrings, Sarah Coventry, blue stones & rhinestones, silver metal, 1950s....................................**$95.00**

Pin, rhinestones in diamond configuration, marked Hattie Carnegie, $145.00.

Ring, Emmons, Aurora Borealis pave diamond shape, gold-tone, ca 1970...**$30.00**

Ring, Florenza, blue Aurora Borealis w/pink & purple rhinestones, glass novelty stone center, antiqued silver..**$45.00**

Ring, Hollycraft, shades of blue rhinestones, adjustable, antiqued gold-tone, dated 1955............................**$55.00**

Ring, KJL, domed lg blue cabachon encircled w/rhinestones, gold-tone, ca 1970 ....**$145.00**

Johnson Bros.

There is a definite renewal of interest in dinnerware collecting right now, and a good percentage of what you find in shops and malls today was made by this Staffordshire company. They made many scenic patterns, and these are among the most popular with collectors. Though Friendly Village, among others, is still being produced, the line is no longer as extensive as it once was, so the secondary market is being tapped to replace broken items that are are not available anywhere else.

On addition to their company logo, their dinnerware is also stamped with the pattern name. Today they're a part of the Wedgwood group.

Coaching Scenes, bowl, vegetable; round, 8", from $20 to..**$25.00**

Coaching Scenes, cup & saucer, from $10 to **$15.00**

Coaching Scenes, plate, dinner; 10", from $10 to **$15.00**

Coaching Scenes, plate, 6", from $6 to **$7.50**

Coaching Scenes, platter, oval, 14"..............................**$55.00**

Coaching Scenes, sugar bowl, w/lid **$25.00**

Coaching Scenes, teapot, from $55 to..........................**$60.00**

English Chippendale, bowl, oval, 10", from $25 to **$35.00**

English Chippendale, cup & saucer, from $10 to........**$15.00**

English Chippendale, gravy boat, fast-stand, from $65 to..**$75.00**

English Chippendale, plate, 7½", from $8 to..............**$10.00**

English Chippendale, platter, 14"................................**$35.00**

Friendly Village, bowl, cereal; 6"................................**$6.00**

Friendly Village, bowl, fruit..**$4.00**

Friendly Village, bowl, rim soup; from $9 to **$12.00**

Friendly Village, bowl, square, 6", from $10 to..........**$12.50**

Friendly Village, bowl, vegetable; oval, from $18 to ..**$22.00**

Friendly Village, bowl, vegetable; round, from $15 to .**$20.00**

Friendly Village, bowl, vegetable; w/lid, from $40 to...**$50.00**

Friendly Village, butter dish, from $25 to **$35.00**

Friendly Village, coaster **$15.00**

Friendly Village, coffeepot, from $45 to **$55.00**

Friendly Village, creamer...**$18.00**

Friendly Village, cup & saucer, from $7 to **$9.00**

Friendly Village, gravy boat stand **$12.00**

Friendly Village, gravy boat w/stand, from $30 to.....**$40.00**

Friendly Village, milk pitcher, 5½", from $25 to **$30.00**

Friendly Village, mug, from $9 to...............................**$12.00**

Friendly Village, plate, bread & butter; from $3 to **$4.00**

Friendly Village, plate, dinner.....................................**$8.00**

Friendly Village, plate, salad **$5.00**

Friendly Village, plate, snack; w/cup well, square **$18.00**

Friendly Village, plate, square, 7", from $6 to.............**$9.00**

Friendly Village, plate, 9", from $6 to **$9.00**

Friendly Village, platter, turkey.................................**$125.00**

Friendly Village, platter, 11½", from $18 to................**$20.00**

Friendly Village, platter, 13½", from $25.00 to $30.00.

Friendly Village, platter, 15", from $35 to **$45.00**
Friendly Village, salt & pepper shakers, pr, from $15 to...**$20.00**
Friendly Village, soup tureen, from $125 to **$140.00**
Friendly Village, sugar bowl, w/lid, from $18 to **$25.00**
Friendly Village, teapot, from $40 to...........................**$45.00**
Merry Christmas, bowl, vegetable; round, 8", from $25 to..**$35.00**
Merry Christmas, creamer & sugar bowl, w/lid, from $20
    to **$30.00**
Merry Christmas, cup & saucer, from $10 to **$15.00**
Merry Christmas, gravy boat & undertray, from $40 to .**$50.00**
Merry Christmas, relish, 8", from $30 to **$40.00**
Merry Christmas, sugar bowl w/lid, from $30 to **$40.00**
Merry Christmas, mug, from $15 to.............................**$20.00**
Old Britain Castles, bowl, berry; 5", from $5.50 to **$7.50**
Old Britain Castles, bowl, cereal; 6", from $7 to.........**$10.00**
Old Britain Castles, bowl, vegetable; oval, from $20 to **$25.00**
Old Britain Castles, bowl, vegetable; round, from $16 to ..**$20.00**
Old Britain Castles, bowl, vegetable; w/lid, from $55 to....**$65.00**
Old Britain Castles, coffeepot, from $50 to **$65.00**
Old Britain Castles, creamer **$18.00**
Old Britain Castles, cup & saucer, from $10 to **$14.00**
Old Britain Castles, gravy boat, from $25 to **$35.00**
Old Britain Castles, gravy stand..................................**$14.00**
Old Britain Castles, plate, dinner; 10", from $10 to **$14.00**
Old Britain Castles, plate, salad **$6.00**
Old Britain Castles, plate, 6" **$4.00**
Old Britain Castles, platter, lg, 15", from $40 to..........**$50.00**
Old Britain Castles, platter, med, 13½", from $30 to ..**$35.00**
Old Britain Castles, platter, sm, 12", from $20 to **$25.00**
Old Britain Castles, soup tureen, from $160 to.........**$180.00**
Old Britain Castles, sugar bowl, w/lid **$25.00**
Old Britain Castles, teapot **$50.00**
Rose Chintz, bowl, cereal; coupe, from $8 to **$12.00**
Rose Chintz, bowl, vegetable; oval, from $20 to **$30.00**
Rose Chintz, bowl, vegetable; round, from $20 to **$30.00**
Rose Chintz, chop plate, 12", from $55 to **$65.00**
Rose Chintz, coffeepot, from $60 to............................**$90.00**
Rose Chintz, cup & saucer, demitasse; from $7 to........**$8.50**
Rose Chintz, cup & saucer, from $8 to **$12.00**
Rose Chintz, egg cup, single, from $5.50 to **$6.50**
Rose Chintz, gravy boat, from $25 to...........................**$35.00**
Rose Chintz, mug, from $12 to **$15.00**
Rose Chintz, pitcher, 5½", from $35 to **$45.00**
Rose Chintz, plate, dinner; from $8 to **$12.00**
Rose Chintz, plate, salad; 8", from $6 to........................**$8.00**
Rose Chintz, platter, 11½", from $20 to **$25.00**
Rose Chintz, sugar bowl, w/lid, from $25 to **$30.00**
Rose Chintz, teapot, from $65 to..................................**$75.00**

**Rose Chintz, plat-
ter, 8", $17.50.**

Josef Originals

Figurines of lovely ladies, charming girls and whimsical animals marked Josef Originals were designed by Muriel Joseph George of Arcadia, California, from 1945 to 1985. Until 1960, they were produced in California. But production costs were high, and copies of her work were being made in Japan. To remain competitive, she and her partner, George Good, found a company in Japan to build a factory and produce her designs to her satisfaction. Muriel retired in 1982; however, Mr. Good continued production of her work and made new designs of his staff's creation. The company was sold in late 1985, and the name is currently owned by Applause; a limited number of figurines bear this name. Those made during the ownership of Muriel are the most collectible. They can be recognized by these characteristics: the girls have a high-gloss finish, black eyes, and most are signed. Brown-eyed figures date from 1982 through 1985; Applause uses a red-brown eye. The animals were nearly always made with a matt finish and were marked with paper labels. Later animals have a flocked coat. Our advisors, Jim and Kaye Whitaker have two books which we recommend for further study: *Josef Originals, Charming Figurines*; and *Josef Originals, A Second Look*. Their address is in the Directory.

See also Birthday Angels.

Advisors: Jim and Kaye Whitaker (See Directory, Josef Originals)

Newsletter: *Josef Original Newsletter*
Jim and Kay Whitaker
P.O. Box 475 Dept. GS
Lynnwood, WA 98046; Subscription (4 issues): $10 per year

A Warm Hello To Bring Us Closer, Thinking of You series, Japan, 5", $35.00. (Photo courtesy of Jim and Kaye Whitaker.)

Angel, character cat, Japan, 3¼"..................................**$20.00**
Anna Victoria, California, 5"..**$50.00**
Buggy Bugs series, wire antenna, Japan, 3¼", each...**$15.00**
Cherie & Choco, California, 3¾", 3¼", each **$35.00**
Country Girl, music box, Japan, 6½" **$45.00**
First Date, Japan, 9"...**$110.00**
God Bless America, music box, Japan, 6" **$85.00**
Hawaiian Wedding Song, music box, Japan, 6" **$85.00**
Hunter, horse, Japan, 6" **$25.00**
Love Bundle, mouse, Japan, 2¾" **$12.00**

Pixies, green, various poses, 3", each $18.00
Poodle, Kennel Club series, Japan, 3½" $15.00
Recipe Girls, various poses, Japan, 3¾", each $30.00
Ruby, Little Jewels series, Japan, 3½" $30.00
Santa w/kiss on forehead, Japan, 4¾" $55.00
Secret Pal, California, 3½" $30.00
Sleeping Beauty, California, 2¼" $45.00
Story angel, various poses, Japan, 5½", each.............$45.00
Wee Folk, various poses, Japan, 4½", each.................$20.00
Yvonne, XVIII Century French series, Japan, 7"..........$85.00

The Voice, Sweet Memories series, Japan, 5¾", $85.00. (Photo courtesy of Jim and Kaye Whitaker.)

Kanawha

This company operated in Dunbar, West Virginia, until 1986. They're noted for a line of slag (End of Day) glass made during the early seventies, some crackle glass, and a line of cased glass called Peachblow. The quality of the glass is good, and it's starting to show up at flea markets and malls, so if you like its looks, now is the time to start looking for it. You can easily spot their Pastel Blue and Green slag glass, since no other company's colors match Kanawha's exactly. Their 'red' is actually a reddish-orange.

Advisor: Ruth Grizel (See Directory, Westmoreland)

Crackle Glass

Pitcher, amberina, tall swollen upper body on ovoid base, applied handle w/curlique at base, paper label, 5½"...............$65.00
Candy dish, ruffled rim, 3x5", from $40 to $50.00
Miniature hat, amberina, 2", from $35 to.....................$40.00
Mug, amberina, rounded body, applied handle, 2¼", from $25 to..$40.00
Pitcher, amberina, rim swoops up to extremely extended pouring spout, flared shape, 13" $80.00
Pitcher, blue, long flared top over bun-shaped body, lobed lip w/pinched spout, applied handle, 4", from $25 to...$30.00
Pitcher, blue, straight sides w/flared top, applied handle w/curlique at base, 4", from $25 to....................$30.00
Pitcher, ruby, waisted w/funnel-shape top, ovoid body, applied handle, 3¼", from $30 to.........................$35.00

Syrup, amethyst (very collectible color), 6" $60.00
Syrup, blue, w/label, 6"..$50.00
Vase, amberina, flared 3-lobe rim elongated ovoid body, 5½", from $50 to..$55.00

Peachblow (cased glass with colored lining)

Basket, embossed grapes, white w/peachblow lining, bulbous w/crimped rim, 9½", from $50 to $60.00
Basket, Hobnail, white w/peachblow lining, wide crimped rim, 7", from $35 to $40.00
Basket, waffle pattern, white w/peachblow lining, wide crimped rim, 8", from $35 to $40.00
Bowl, Hobnail, white w/lemon lining, wide ruffled & crimped rim, 6", from $25 to $30.00
Pitcher, embossed grapes, white w/lemon lining, cylinder neck, bun body, footed, 9", from $45 to $55.00
Pitcher, embossed grapes, white w/peachblow lining, bulbous neck & body, waisted, 7"............................$45.00
Pitcher, embossed grapes, white w/sapphire blue lining, 3¾"..$25.00
Pitcher, embossed grapes, white w/sapphire blue lining, 6½"..$35.00
Pitcher, lobed, red to yellow (peachblow) w/white lining, waisted neck, bulbous body, 4½" $30.00
Vase, embossed grapes, white w/sapphire blue lining, wide ruffled rim, 6½"...$40.00

Vase, embossed grapes, yellow interior, ruffled rim, 9", from $45.00 to $55.00. (Photo courtesy of Frank Grizel.)

Vase, Hobnail, blue w/white lining, elongated slender neck w/angled rim, low applied blue handle, 14"......$125.00
Vase, waffle pattern, white w/sapphire blue lining, flaring toward base, wide ruffled & crimped rim, 5½" $35.00

Slag Glass

Pastel Blue, ashtray, Hobnail, shallow bowl form w/4 rests, 6½" dia, from $15 to...$20.00
Pastel Blue, basket, Hobnail, shallow, scalloped rim, 7½", from $45 to...$55.00
Pastel Blue, candle holders, Hobnail, dome base, 2-knob stem, 5", pr..$40.00
Pastel Blue, creamer & sugar bowl w/lid, Hobnail, scalloped lip, 6½", from $45 to $50.00
Pastel Blue, cruet, Hobnail, 6" $25.00
Pastel Blue, salt & pepper shakers, Hobnail, 5", pr....$35.00

Pastel Blue, salt dip, bird form, 3¼" **$15.00**
Pastel Blue, slipper, Daisy & Button, 5½"...................**$35.00**
Pastel Green, basket, Hobnail, flared crimped rim, 7", from $40 to.........................**$45.00**
Pastel Green, candle holder bowl, Moon & Stars, footed, scalloped rim, interior candle well, 5".......................**$25.00**
Pastel Green, hen on nest, 8", from $85 to **$95.00**
Pastel Green, spoon holder, skillet shape w/embossed eagle, 7½".......................**$30.00**
Pastel Green, toothpick holder, Hobnail, 3 scroll feet extend up sides, 2½", from $10 to.......................**$15.00**
Pastel Green, vase, Moon & Stars, footed, 'swung' top, 10".......................**$25.00**
Red, bird, round base, 5" **$25.00**
Red, bonbon, Hobnail, leaf shape w/handle, scalloped rim, 6", from $25 to **$30.00**
Red, bowl, Hob Star, incurvate w/serrated lobed rim, 7½", from $40 to **$45.00**
Red, compote, Hobnail, flared crimped & ruffled rim, 5½", from $30 to.......................**$35.00**

Red, figurine, lady in bonnet and long dress, large, $150.00. (Photo courtesy of Frank Grizel.)

Red, pitcher, Hobnail, long neck, 3-lobe rim, 8½" **$45.00**
Red, praying hands, 5", from $65 to **$75.00**
Red, slipper, Rose, 6", from $35 to.............................**$40.00**
Red, toothpick holder, Strawberry, 4-footed, 2½".......**$15.00**
Red, vase, diamonds in relief at base, 'swung' top, 11", from $20 to.......................**$25.00**
Red, vase, Hobnail, long neck, flared crimped rim, 8½"....**$45.00**

Keeler, Brad

Keeler is one of the California ceramicists responsible for designing many of the figurines that are now so collectible. He worked circa 1939 to 1950s, producing striking birds and animals which he decorated with the airbrush and enhanced with hand-painted details. *The Collector's Encyclopedia of California Pottery* by Jack Chipman includes more information on his company.

Advisors: Pat and Kris Secor (See Directory, California Pottery)

Biscuit jar, rooster **$250.00**
Bowl, shell form, 9".......................**$18.00**
Dish, leaf base w/tomato lid, #881.............................**$35.00**
Figurine, cat, Siamese, 4x6" **$50.00**
Figurine, cat, Siamese w/yarn, lg **$75.00**

Figurine, cat, 10".......................**$42.50**
Figurine, deer, recumbent, pr.......................**$30.00**
Figurine, flamingo, wings flared up, head up, pink, incised mark, 12".......................**$95.00**
Figurine, flamingos, #902, stamped mk, 8½", 6", pr..**$115.00**
Figurine, Lil' Red Riding Hood, w/original label........**$60.00**
Figurine, pheasants, pr.......................**$150.00**

Figurine, sea gull, in-mold mark #29, 10½", from $60.00 to $80.00.

Figurine, Wee Willie Winkie, w/original label............**$60.00**
Lobster dish, divided, lg.......................**$65.00**
Lobster dish, w/lid.......................**$55.00**
Plate, chicken form, 7-color, 7".......................**$35.00**
Plate, rooster form, multicolor, lg.......................**$45.00**
Tray, tomato form.......................**$38.00**

Kentucky Derby Glasses

Since the 1940s, every running of the Kentucky Derby has been commemorated with a drinking glass. Race fans have begun to collect them, and now some of the earlier glasses are worth several hundred dollars.

Advisor: Betty L. Hornback (See Directory, Kentucky Derby and Horse Racing)

1941, aluminum **$800.00**
1941, plastic Beetleware, from $3,000 to................**$4,000.00**
1945, short **$1,200.00**
1945, tall **$425.00**
1946 ....**$100.00**
1947 ....**$100.00**
1948 ....**$180.00**
1948, frosted bottom **$200.00**
1949 ....**$180.00**
1950 ....**$350.00**
1951 ....**$450.00**
1952 ....**$180.00**
1953 ....**$135.00**
1954 ....**$165.00**
1955 ....**$135.00**
1956, 4 variations, from $175 to **$400.00**
1957 ....**$110.00**
1958, Gold Bar.......................**$175.00**
1958, Iron Liege **$175.00**
1959 ....**$80.00**

1960	$80.00
1961	$100.00
1962	$65.00
1963	$47.00
1964	$50.00
1965	$55.00
1966	$50.00
1967	$47.00
1968	$47.00
1969	$45.00
1970	$55.00
1971	$45.00
1972	$37.50
1973	$37.50
1974, Federal	$125.00
1974, mistake	$18.00
1974, regular	$16.00
1975	$12.00
1976	$14.00
1976, plastic	$10.00
1977	$10.00
1978	$12.00
1979	$12.00

1980, $18.00.

1981	$10.00
1982	$10.00
1983	$9.00

1984, $7.00.

1985	$9.00
1986	$8.00
1986 ('85 copy)	$18.00
1987	$8.00
1988	$8.00
1989	$6.00
1990	$6.00

1991	$6.00
1992	$4.50
1993	$4.50
1994	$4.50
1995	$3.00
1996	$3.00

Festival Glasses

1968	$95.00
1984	$20.00
1987-88	$16.00
1989-90	$12.00
1991-92	$10.00
1993, very few made	$75.00
1994-95	$10.00
1996-97	$6.00

Shot Glasses

1945	$1,000.00
1987, clear, 1½-oz	$200.00
1987, frosted, 1½-oz	$225.00
1987, red, 3-oz	$700.00
1987, black, 3-oz	$500.00
1988, 1½-oz	$40.00
1988, 3-oz	$60.00
1989, 1½-oz	$35.00
1989, 3-oz	$45.00
1990, 1½-oz	$35.00
1991, 1½-oz & 3-oz, each, from $35 to	$40.00
1992, 1½-oz & 3-oz, each, from $20 to	$25.00
1993, 1½-oz & 3-oz, each, from	$15.00
1994, 1½-oz & 3-oz, each	$12.00

King's Crown Thumbprint Line

Back in the late 1800s, this pattern was called Thumbprint. It was first made by the U.S. Glass Company and Tiffin, one of several companies who were a part of the US conglomerate, through the 1940s. U.S. Glass closed in the late fifties, but Tiffin reopened in 1963 and reissued it. Indiana Glass bought the molds, made some minor changes, and during the 1970s, they made this line as well. Confusing, to say the least! Gene Florence's *Collectible Glassware of the '40s, '50s, and '60s,* explains that originally the thumbprints were oval, but at some point Indiana changed theirs to circles. And Tiffin's tumblers were flared at the top, while Indiana's were straight. Our values are for the later issues of both companies, with the ruby flashing in excellent condition.

Ashtray, 5¼" square	$14.00
Bowl, crimped rim, 4½x11½"	$65.00
Bowl, finger	$17.50
Bowl, mayonnaise; 4"	$16.00
Bowl, salad; 9¼"	$56.00
Candle holder, sherbet type	$25.00
Candy dish, platinum trim, 6"	$24.00

Cheese stand	$17.50
Compote, flat, sm.	$18.00
Creamer	$22.50
Cup	$8.00
Cup, punch	$8.00
Goblet, water	$10.00

Pitcher, $120.00.

Pitcher, milk	$80.00
Pitcher, water	$120.00
Plate, dinner; 10"	$35.00
Plate, salad; 7⅜"	$12.00
Plate, torte; 14½"	$50.00
Snack plate & cup	$12.00
Stem, cocktail	$9.00
Stem, goblet, wine; 3½"	$8.00
Stem goblet, wine; ultramarine	$7.00
Sugar bowl	$22.50
Sundae or sherbet, 5½-oz	$10.00
Tumbler, iced tea; flat, 11-oz	$16.00
Tumbler, juice; flat, 4½-oz	$14.00
Vase, bud; 9"	$30.00

Kitchen Collectibles

If you've never paid much attention to old kitchen appliances, now is the time to do just that. Check in Grandma's basement — or your mother's kitchen cabinets, for that matter. As styles in home decorating changed, so did the styles of appliances. Some have wonderful Art Deco lines, while others border on the primitive. Most of those you'll find still work, and with a thorough cleaning you'll be able to restore them to their original 'like-new' appearance. Missing parts may be impossible to replace, but if it's just a cord that's gone, you can usually find what you need at any hardware store.

Even larger appliances are collectible and are often used to add the finishing touch to a period kitchen. Please note that prices listed here are for appliances that are free of rust, pitting or dents and in excellent working condition.

During the 19th century, cast-iron apple peelers, cherry pitters, and food choppers were patented by the hundreds, and because they're practically indestructible, they're still around today. Unless parts are missing, they're still usable and most are very efficient at the task they were designed to perform.

Lots of good vintage kitchen glassware is still around and can generally be bought at reasonable prices. Pieces vary widely from custard cups to refrigerator dishes to canister sets and cookie jars. There are also several books available for further information and study. If this area of collecting interests you, you'll enjoy *300 Years of Kitchen Collectibles* by Linda Campbell and *Kitchen Antiques, 1790-1940*, by Kathryn McNerney. Other books include: *Kitchen Glassware of the Depression Years* by Gene Florence; *Collector's Encyclopedia of Fry Glassware* by H.C. Fry Glass Society; *The '50s and '60s Kitchen, A Collector's Handbook and Price Guide*, by Jan Lindenberger; and *Fire-King Fever* and *Pyrex History and Price Guide*, both by April Tvorak.

See also Aluminum; Fire-King; Glass Knives; Griswold; Jewel Tea; Porcelier; Reamers.

Advisor: Jim Barker, Appliances (See Directory, Appliances; feel free to contact)

Newsletter: *The '50s Flea!!!*
April and Larry Tvorak
P.O. Box 126
Canon City, CO 81215-0126; 719-269-7230; Subscription: $5 per year for 1 yearly postwar glass newsletter; includes free 30 word classified ad

Newsletter: *Kitchen Antiques and Collectibles News*
KOOKS (Kollectors of Old Kitchen Stuff)
Dana and Darlene DeMore
4645 Laurel Ridge Dr.
Harrisburg, PA 17110; 717-545-7320; Annual $24 membership includes 6 issues of newsletter

Appliances

Blender, #K-M 20-9	$30.00
Blender, Oster, chrome base	$40.00
Blender, Waring	$35.00
Cigarette lighter, Vidro, electric	$45.00
Coffee urn set, Alum Cont Silver	$75.00
Coffee urn set, Royal Rochester #17168	$75.00
Coffee urn set, Royal Rochester Floral	$95.00
Coffee urn set, Royal Rochester Poppy #17054	$125.00
Coffee urn set, Universal #W81804	$75.00
Coffeepot, #C-20	$35.00
Heater, #K-M 340-9	$35.00
Heater, General Electric, bulb type	$45.00
Mixer, General Electric, green stripe	$55.00
Mixer, Sunbeam Mix Master	$60.00
Popcorn maker, #K-M 6-9	$45.00
Popcorn maker, General Electric	$40.00
Toaster, Dominion, single slice	$150.00
Toaster, Dominion #367	$45.00
Toaster, General Electric #119T46	$55.00
Toaster, General Electric #119T48	$35.00
Toaster, General Electric #129T75	$45.00
Toaster, General Electric #25T83	$60.00
Toaster, Great Northern	$145.00
Toaster, Handy Hot	$35.00

Toaster, Hotpoint #T159T33 ....$55.00
Toaster, Manning Bowman #K-64.........................$45.00
Toaster, Royal Rochester #E6412 ....$45.00
Toaster, Royal Rochester #1340 ....$55.00
Toaster, Royal Rochester #13520.........................$35.00

Toaster, Son Chief Electrics #650, $85.00. (Photo courtesy of Jim Barker.)

Toaster, Sunbeam #T-1-C..$75.00
Toaster, Universal #E7211..$45.00
Toaster, Universal #E7212..$70.00
Toaster, Universal #E7822..$75.00
Toaster, Universal #E9411 ....$250.00
Toaster, Universal #E947 ....$75.00
Toaster, Westinghouse #T0-71..................................$45.00
Toaster, Westinghouse #3965 ....$65.00
Toaster, Westinghouse #5422, white..........................$65.00
Waffle iron, Colman...$95.00
Waffle iron, Dominion...$55.00
Waffle iron, Manning Bowman Twin O'Matic $85.00
Waffle iron, Royal Rochester Pheasant.........................$85.00
Waffle iron, Superlectric $85.00
Waffle iron, Universal E2024......................................$35.00

Gadgets and Miscellaneous Items

Churn, Dazey #40, 4-quart, $110.00.

Angel food cake pan, Swan's Down Cake Flour $17.50
Apple corer, T-shape, tin, handmade...........................$22.00
Beater, Ladd, green glass bowl w/crank metal top, green
    handles $35.00
Beater bowl, pink bowl w/metal crank beater top w/red han-
    dle $35.00

Biscuit cutter, Forbes Quality Baking Powder, tin.......$10.00
Biscuit cutter, Kreamer, strap handle............................$8.00
Can & cap bottle opener, A&J in diamond trademark, cast
    steel w/brass ferrule, wood handle, 1920s, 6"......$15.00
Can opener, Pet Milk, tin $12.50
Canning jar funnel, gray tin, for wide-mouth canning
    jars $14.00
Cheese slicer, iron w//wire 'blade,' 1920s, 6⅞" long..$18.00
Churn, Dazey, #10, 1-qt...$1,250.00
Churn, Dazey #30, 3-qt $165.00
Churn, Dazey #40, 4-qt $110.00
Churn, Lightning, 2-qt $95.00
Churn, Universal, tin, 2-qt..$375.00
Corkscrew, simple style w/green painted wood handle,
    5½"...$35.00
Cream whip, Fries, tin w/looped legs, side handles & crank,
    from $85 to...$100.00
Cream whip, Horlick, black wire w/tin plate, 2" wide beat-
    ers, 9½"...$32.00
Cream whip/egg beater, Dover patent, rotary action turns
    blades, green wooden handle grip & knob..........$22.00
Crimper, tin wheel, shaped wooden handle, 6¾".......$35.00
Cutter, biscuit/doughnut; aluminum w/painted wood handle,
    1930s, 1¼" dia...$12.00
Cutter, doughnut; gray tin, stamped out, fluted sides, made
    w/no handle...$12.50
Cutter, tea biscuit; tin, varied shapes, green painted wooden
    handle, ca 1930s, approximately 2½" dia $6.00
Cutter/slicer, vegetable; fluted metal blade, green painted
    wooden handle, 7" $15.00
Egg beater, Aluminum Beauty, rotary crank, Pat'd April 20,
    1920, 10½"..$15.00
Egg beater, hand held, plastic handle $5.00
Egg beater, Whipwell...USA Pat Mch 23, 1920, rotary crank
    w/wooden handle, 11" $20.00
Egg separator, JA Frost Grocer, tin $12.50
Egg separator, Town Talk Flour, tin $15.00
Flatware, green marbleized Bakelite w/black sides, marked
    stainless steel, each pc, from $4 to........................$6.00
Flatware, red marbleized Bakelite handles, marked Sta-Brite,
    each pc, from $2 to $4.00
Flatware, 2-tone yellow Bakelite handles, marked Perma-
    Brite, each pc, from $5 to $7.00
Flour scoop, Dover, tin hooded shape w/stick handle...$30.00
Flour scoop, Jenny Wren Ready Mixed Flour, tin $10.00

Flour sifter, Hand-i-Sift, $12.00.

Flour sifter, original paint, rotary handle, unmarked, EX ..**$20.00**

Flour sifter, Rumford Baking Powder, late 1940s, EX ..**$75.00**

Food chopper, clear glass w/metal plunger/chopper attached to lid **$12.00**

Food/rice press, cast-iron handles press perforated cup, 1930s, 10¾" long.................**$18.00**

Fork, stainless steel w/2 prongs, green painted handle w/white stripe, 14½" **$8.00**

Grater, punched tin, half-circle shape **$35.00**

Ice cream disher, cast aluminum w/wooden handle, thumb-press action, 1930s-40s, 8½" **$20.00**

Ice pick, heavy metal w/green painted wood handle ..**$12.00**

Juice extractor, Handy Andy, clear measuring cup sits on base below crank-style extractor **$35.00**

Juice extractor, Ser-mor Juice Extractor Pat, green measuring pitcher w/metal crank-type extractor top w/green handle **$60.00**

Knife sharpener, steel-roller sharpening action, green painted wooden handle, 1930s, w/metal case **$18.00**

Masher, twisted iron wire double tangs hold masher to black painted wooden handle, 9½".................**$22.00**

Mayonnaise maker, clear glass base w/whipping mechanism attached to red metal top, crank handle.................**$15.00**

Mayonnaise maker, Wessen Oil **$75.00**

Measuring cup, tin, Rumford, w/cookie cutter that fits in the top.................**$45.00**

Melon baller/scoop, stainless steel, double-end style w/center wooden handle, ca 1940, 7½".................**$8.50**

Mixer, Borden's, clear base w/metal top, wire handle operates wire beater in base, Pat Mar 30, 1915.................**$22.00**

Mixer, Cross Cross on clear w/embossed baby's face on side, red metal top w/wire handle that controls mixing device.................**$50.00**

Mixer, Kamkap, INC, USA, clear class w/fired-on bands at 4, 8-, & 12-oz marks, metal top **$10.00**

Mixer, Lightning, 1-qt glass jar.................**$265.00**

Mixer, Super Whipper, rotary crank, attaches to jar.....**$150.00**

Mixer/churn, Ladd #2, clear base w/metal crank top ..**$100.00**

Mold, A&J, gray tin, fluted skirt, oval or diamond shaped..**$12.50**

Mold, pudding; Kreamer, tin, 2-pc **$35.00**

Pastry blender, nickel-plated iron w/green painted wood handle, 9½" **$18.00**

Pot holder, crocheted, blue & white, octagonal.................**$2.00**

Pot holder, crocheted, doll-dress shape (sometimes found w/its own crocheted hanger), from $3 to.................**$5.00**

Pot holder, crocheted w/applied rose in center, $3 to .**$4.00**

Scales, Hanson, white enameled w/black metal tray & fixtures, spring action, 25-lb capacity.................**$28.00**

Strainer, fine mesh wire in footed metal frame, 1930s, 4x7¼" **$22.00**

Strainer, fine wire mesh in metal frame w/tin color, original red painted wooden handle, 1930s, 8½" dia.................**$25.00**

Thermometer, Kitchen Aid, w/baster, MIB **$22.50**

Glassware

Angel food cake pan, Glasbake, crystal.................**$12.00**

Bake pan, Glasbake, white w/decal, 8x8".................**$8.00**

Baker, pearlware, oval, Fry, 6".................**$25.00**

Baker, sapphire blue, round or square, Fire-King, 1-pt ..**$6.00**

Batter bowl, yellow opaque, Hocking **$85.00**

Batter jug, forest green, New Martinsville.................**$75.00**

Batter pitcher, red w/metal top, matching red undertray ..**$175.00**

Bean pot, pearlware, w/lid, Fry, 1-pt.................**$50.00**

Beater bowl, green w/measures along sides, metal beater top w/green handle.................**$25.00**

Beater jar, red, 24-oz, Hocking.................**$45.00**

Bowl, batter; milk glass w/fired-on fruit (peaches, grapes & pears).................**$28.00**

Bowl, Butter Print, Pyrex, 2½-qt.................**$8.00**

Bowl, clear w/red ring & rim, faint embossed vertical ribs, 10¼".................**$15.00**

Bowl, coupe soup; Princess, white, oven-proof, Pyrex, 1952, 7½".................**$6.00**

Bowl, custard w/green or black fired-on dots, scalloped rim, 9".................**$35.00**

Bowl, Delphite blue, horizontal ribs, Jeannette, 5½"..**$60.00**

Bowl, Dots, orange on clear, Pyrex, 1968, 1½-pt.........**$3.00**

Bowl, drippings; milk glass w/red fired-on ships, McKee, 8-oz.................**$40.00**

Bowl, green w/Diamond Crystal Salt embossed on side, Hocking, 8½".................**$20.00**

Bowl, green w/handle & side spout, w/lid, US Glass ...**$35.00**

Bowl, ivory or w/fired-on design, beaded rim, Fire-King, 6".................**$14.00**

Bowl, milk glass w/red fired-on dots, Hazel Atlas, 9" ..**$20.00**

Bowl, mixing; Crisscross, crystal, Hazel Atlas, 7⅝".....**$10.00**

Bowl, mixing; Delphite blue, Pyrex, Corning Glass Works, 6½", 1 from set of 3.................**$9.00**

Bowl, mixing; Hex Optic, pink, flat rim, 9".................**$25.00**

Bowl, mixing; milk glass w/fired-on dots, McKee, 9".**$15.00**

Bowl, mixing; milk glass w/red fired-on ships, McKee, 9" ..**$20.00**

Bowl, mixing; pink, paneled bowl & flared rim, Hazel Atlas, 10⅝".................**$25.00**

Bowl, mixing; pink, Rest-Well, Hazel Atlas, 9½".........**$20.00**

Bowl, mixing; sapphire blue, Fire-King, sm **$16.00**

Bowl, mixing; Skating Dutch, milk glass w/red fired-on Dutch skaters, 9".................**$18.00**

Bowl, mixing; yellow, Rest-Well, Hazel Atlas, 8¾" **$40.00**

Bowl, mixing; yellow opaque, McKee, 9¼" **$25.00**

Bowl, Modern Tulip, black trim, Fire-King, 4-qt.........**$32.00**

Bowl, pink, no spout, 2 handles, 9".................**$20.00**

Bowl, splashproof mixing; ivory w/fired-on fruit, Fire-King, 1-qt.................**$14.00**

Butter box, pink w/embossed B, Jeannette, 2-lb.................**$160.00**

Butter dish, amber, embossed ribs on rectangular shape, Federal Glass, 1-lb **$35.00**

Butter dish, Block Optic, green, Hocking.................**$45.00**

Butter dish, Butter Print, Pyrex, design on lid.................**$8.00**

Butter dish, Crisscross, green, Hazel Atlas, 1-lb **$40.00**

Butter dish, pink, rectangular w/bow-handled lid.................**$60.00**

Butter dish, red ships on milk glass, rectangular, McKee...**$25.00**

Butter dish, Seville yellow, rectangular, McKee **$65.00**

Cake pan, Glasbake, heart shape, sm, med & lg, 3-pc set..**$25.00**

Cake pan, Glasbake, white w/decal, round **$8.00**

Cake pan, ivory, Fire-King, 9" dia **$14.00**

Cake pan, ivory w/fired-on fruit, square, Fire-King....**$20.00**

Cake plate, white, pedestal foot, Fire-King.................**$8.00**

Canister, clear w/embossed 'Coffee' label & vertical ribs, round w/metal lid..**$20.00**

Canister, clear w/multicolor fired-on rings, 64-oz.......**$17.50**

Canister, clear w/multicolor fired-on rings, 8-oz...........**$6.00**

Canister, clear w/multicolor tulips, round w/clear lid...**$15.00**

Canister, clear w/red Flour & checkerboard on square shape, black metal lid..**$22.50**

Canister, Coffee in black letters w/in multicolor floral stencil on clear square shape, red metal lid, sm, 16-oz....**$8.00**

Canister, custard w/blue or red fired-on dots, metal screw-on lid, 48-oz..**$28.00**

Canister, Flour & fleur-de-lis painted in black on clear square shape, black metal lid......................................**$22.50**

Canister, forest green w/silver paper label, diagonal ribs, Owens-Illinois, 40-oz..**$25.00**

Canister, green painted 'Taverne' scene on clear, green metal lid, lg..**$30.00**

Canister, milk glass w/black lettering on square shape, metal lid, McKee, 48-oz..**$50.00**

Canister, Sugar in black painted letters on caramel, square w/rounded corners & black metal lid, McKee, 48-oz..................**$100.00**

Carafe, clear w/gold star decor, black plastic handle, Pyrex, 8-cup..**$5.00**

Casserole, Glasbake, white decaled base, oval, w/clear lid, from $6 to..**$8.00**

Casserole, Glasbake, white w/design, round, w/lid, from $6 to..**$8.00**

Casserole, ivory w/fired-on fruit, oval w/clear lid, Fire-King..**$16.00**

Casserole, milk glass w/primrose decal, Fire-King, 1-qt...**$12.00**

Casserole, pearlware, w/lid, Fry, 6" dia......................**$25.00**

Casserole, pearlware, w/lid, Fry, 7" square, metal holder...**$55.00**

Casserole, pearlware w/green trim, oval, w/lid, Fry, 7"..**$50.00**

Casserole, sapphire blue, Fire-King, 1½-qt..................**$25.00**

Casserole, sapphire blue, Fire-King, 1-pt....................**$15.00**

Casserole, white opaque, oval, Pyrex..........................**$12.50**

Casserole, yellow, rectangular, clear lid w/black needlepoint design, cradled space-saver, Pyrex Gift Ware, 1957..**$12.00**

Cheese dish, Jennyware, ultramarine, rectangular, Jeannette..**$150.00**

Chip & dip set, white balloon design on turquoise, Pyrex, 1958..**$10.00**

Churn, green barrel-shaped container w/original churn top..**$285.00**

Coffeepot, red glass w/metal fittings & lid, Silex......**$200.00**

Cookie jar, green barrel shape w/matching green glass lid..**$60.00**

Cookie jar, green frosted, vertical ribs & painted decoration, matching green frosted lid......................................**$45.00**

Cookie jar, Party Line, pink, Paden City......................**$70.00**

Creamer & sugar bowl, pink, stacking set w/lid.........**$50.00**

Cup, soup; fired-on color, square sides & handle.........**$4.00**

Cup & saucer, Classic, w/or w/out floral decor, creamy ivory, Pyrex..**$9.00**

Custard, sapphire blue, deep, Fire-King, 6-oz..............**$4.00**

Custard cup, pearlware, no engraving, Fry, 4- or 6-oz..**$10.00**

Custard cup, sapphire blue, Fire-King, 6-oz..................**$4.00**

Decanter, yellow opaque w/pinched sides, McKee..**$100.00**

Funnel, canning; yellow, CW Hart, Troy NY..............**$45.00**

Gravy boat, pink, pouring spout each side, 2 handles, Cambridge..**$30.00**

Grease jar, decal decoration, Fire-King......................**$28.00**

Grease jar, milk glass w/red fired-on dots, Hocking..**$18.00**

Grease jar, Red Tulips on white opaque, Vitrock.......**$25.00**

Ice bucket, pink, w/lid, Fry......................................**$200.00**

Ladle, amber...**$35.00**

Ladle, amber w/shell bowl & crisscross handle, sm...**$12.00**

Ladle, blue, pan-shaped bowl, straight handle, Cambridge, sm..**$25.00**

Ladle, clear w/red handle..**$50.00**

Ladle, crystal w/side spout, sm..................................**$12.00**

Ladle, milk glass, Imperial..**$45.00**

Loaf pan, ivory w/fired-on fruit, deep, Fire-King........**$20.00**

Loaf pan, white w/design, Glassbake............................**$5.00**

Measuring cup, blue, 3-spout, Fire-King, 1-cup..........**$20.00**

Measuring cup, clear, 2-spout, Pyrex, 1-cup..............**$25.00**

Measuring cup, crystal, dry measure, 1-cup..............**$15.00**

Measuring cup, Delphite blue, Jeannette, ½-cup........**$45.00**

Measuring cup, green, embossed Armour advertising on side..**$25.00**

Measuring cup, green, no handle, 3 pouring spouts, Federal Glass..**$28.00**

Measuring cup, green, Paden City............................**$125.00**

Measuring cup, green, 1- or 3-spout, Hazel Atlas, 1-cup...**$25.00**

Measuring cup, sapphire blue, Fire-King, 3-spout......**$25.00**

Measuring cup, sapphire blue, 1-spout, Fire-King, 8-oz..**$20.00**

Measuring cup, ultramarine, 1-cup............................**$50.00**

Measuring pitcher, custard, McKee, 4-cup..................**$35.00**

Measuring pitcher, Delphite blue, McKee, 2-cup, minimum value..**$100.00**

Measuring pitcher, Diamond Check, red or black fired-on color on milk glass, McKee, 2-cup..........................**$30.00**

Measuring pitcher, green fired-on color, McKee, 2-cup..**$15.00**

Measuring pitcher, red or green fired-on dots on milk glass, McKee, 2-cup..**$28.00**

Measuring pitcher, white opaque w/red fired-on bands, Hazel Atlas, 2-cup..**$25.00**

Measuring pitcher, white Vitrock, w/lid, 2-cup..........**$40.00**

Meat loaf pan, pearlware, rectangular, w/lid, Fry, 9"..**$55.00**

Mug, chicken decal on white opaque, Anchor Hocking..**$6.00**

Mug, Terra, brown swirls etched on charcoal, Pyrex, 1964, 12-oz..**$3.00**

Mustard, Twist, pink, w/spoon, Heisey......................**$80.00**

Napkin holder, green, Fan Fold (no other embossing)...**$120.00**

Napkin holder, milk glass, Nar-O-Fold......................**$45.00**

Napkin holder, Party Line, green, Paden City..........**$125.00**

Napkin holder, Party Line, pink, Paden City............**$135.00**

Oil/vinegar cruet, amber, sm....................................**$27.50**

Oil/vinegar cruet, green, Paden City..........................**$60.00**

Pie plate, Delphite blue, Pyrex, Corning Glass Works, 10"..**$20.00**

Pie plate, pearlware, engraved, Fry, 9½", in holder...**$35.00**

Pie plate, sapphire blue, Fire-King, any size..............**$8.00**

Pie plate, sapphire blue, juice saver, Fire-King.........**$115.00**

Pitcher, green w/diagonal swirls along body, smooth at rim & lip, Rena Line, Paden City..................................**$40.00**

Pitcher, utility; pink, horizontal ribs, Hazel Atlas........**$60.00**

Plate, dinner; Bluebelle on blue opaque, Pyrex, late 1950s..**$8.50** late, dinner; Oxford, ivory, Pyrex, Macbeth-Evans, 1940s, 9¼" **$4.00**

late, Terra, brown swirls etched on charcoal, Pyrex, 1964, 12" **$6.00**

Pretzel jar, pink, embossed horizontal lids Hocking...**$75.00**

Punch ladle, green w/side spout, curved green handle ..**$45.00**

Ramekin, pearlware or lime glass, Fry, each..............**$10.00**

Refrigerator bowl, Crisscross, pink, w/lid, Hazel Atlas, 4x4" **$20.00**

Refrigerator dish, cobalt blue, Hazel Atlas, 5¾".........**$75.00**

Refrigerator dish, Delphite blue, w/lid, McKee, 4x5" .**$40.00**

Refrigerator dish, milk glass w/green fired-on dots, w/lid, McKee, 4x5" **$18.00**

Refrigerator dish, pink, horizontal ribs, w/legs, Federal, 3¾x5¾"..**$20.00**

Refrigerator dish, pink, tab handle, round, w/lid **$30.00**

Refrigerator dish, yellow fired-on color, clear lid, Pyrex, 3½x4¾"..**$4.00**

Refrigerator jar, Hex Optic, green, w/lid, Jeannette, 4½x5" ...**$22.00**

Rolling pin, white clambroth w/wooden handles.....**$125.00**

Salad fork & spoon, clear w/forest green handles......**$45.00**

Salad fork & spoon, clear w/twist handles & red teardrop finials **$60.00**

Salt & pepper shakers, cattails on white opaque, black metal lids, pr..**$15.00**

Salt & pepper shakers, Delphite blue w/black lettering, embossed ribs on lower body, tin lids, Jeannette, 8-oz, pr **$100.00**

Salt & pepper shakers, forest green, pr **$20.00**

Salt & pepper shakers, green w/embossed letters on front, square w/round metal lids, pr **$70.00**

Salt & pepper shakers, red, Hocking, ca 1960s, pr.....**$45.00**

Salt & pepper shakers, red, Wheaton Nuline, pr **$50.00**

Salt & pepper shakers, Skating Dutch, milk glass w/red fired-on Dutch skaters, pr **$20.00**

Salt & pepper shakers, white opaque w/black letters, square, Mckee, 8-oz, pr **$30.00**

Salt & pepper shakers, yellow opaque w/black lettering, black metal lids, Hocking, pr..............................**$35.00**

Salt & pepper shakers, yellow opaque w/black lettering, square, metal lids, McKee, pr **$20.00**

Server, sapphire blue, tab handles, Fire-King.............**$18.00**

Skillet, clear, McKee Range Tec...................................**$10.00**

Spoon, yellow, salad size...**$35.00**

Sugar shaker, crystal, Hazel Atlas, sm........................**$12.50**

Sugar shaker, crystal, marked Sugar & Cinnamon, metal lid, sm **$20.00**

Sugar shaker, custard w/black or green fired-on dots, McKee **$25.00**

Sugar shaker, red w/metal top, Gemco **$20.00**

Syrup pitcher, amber, Paden City #198, 8-oz..............**$45.00**

Syrup pitcher, dark amber shaded to pale yellow, matching dark amber lid..**$45.00**

Syrup pitcher, green w/metal top, square handle, Paden City **$35.00**

Syrup pitcher, pink, Paden City..................................**$50.00**

Syrup pitcher, pink w/floral cutting, Imperial **$45.00**

Teakettle, clear w/embossed horizontal ribs, red metal trim & metal 'whistle' top, Glasbake **$30.00**

Tray, green, Not Heat Resisting Glass, well-in-tree type, footed, Fry..**$80.00**

Tumbler, pink, embossed Mission Juice **$30.00**

Water bottle, clear flattened circle shape w/GE embossed on sides w/vertical ribs, blue metal cap....................**$10.00**

Water bottle, clear w/Water embossed on side..........**$12.00**

Water bottle, cobalt blue, shouldered form w/metal cap, Hazel Atlas, 10", 64-oz....................................**$60.00**

Water bottle, forest green w/embossed ribs on lower half, w/lid, Hocking..**$30.00**

Water bottle, red, plain or ribbed, Hocking **$85.00**

Syrup pitcher, amber with metal lid, Cambridge, $50.00.

Kitchen Prayer Ladies

The Enesco importing company of Elk Grove, Illinois, distributed a line of kitchen novelties during the 1960s that they originally called 'Mother in the Kitchen.' Today's collectors refer to them as 'Kitchen Prayer Ladies.' The line was fairly extensive — some pieces are common, others are very scarce. All are designed around the figure of 'Mother' who is wearing a long white apron inscribed with a prayer. She is more commonly found in a pink dress. Blue is harder to find and more valuable. Where we've given ranges, pink is represented by the lower end, blue by the higher. If you find her in a white dress with blue trim, add another 10% to 20%. For a complete listing and current values, you'll want to order *Prayer Lady Plus+* by April and Larry Tvorak. This line is pictured in *The Collector's Encyclopedia of Cookie Jars, Volume 1 and 2*, by Joyce and Fred Roerig.

Advisor: April Tvorak (See Directory, Kitchen Prayer Ladies)

Napkin holder, from $25.00 to $35.00.

Air freshener, from $125 to..**$145.00**

Bank, from $145 to..**$175.00**

Bell, from $75 to **$90.00**
Candle holders, pr, from $95 to **$110.00**
Canister, pink, each, from $200 to **$250.00**
Cookie jar, blue...**$495.00**
Cookie jar, pink **$185.00**
Crumb brush, from $150 to **$175.00**
Egg timer, from $135 to **$145.00**
Instant coffee jar, spoon-holder loop on side, from $85 to ..**$95.00**
Mug, from $100 to..**$125.00**
Picture frame, from $100 to **$125.00**
Planter, from $65 to **$75.00**
Plaque, full figure, from $45 to **$55.00**
Ring holder, from $40 to **$50.00**
Salt & pepper shakers, pr, from $12 to.......................**$20.00**
Scissors holder, wall mount, from $135 to **$145.00**
Soap dish, from $35 to **$45.00**
Spoon holder, upright, from $45 to............................**$50.00**
Spoon rest, from $50 to...**$80.00**
Sprinkler bottle, blue, from $300 to **$400.00**
Sprinkler bottle, pink..**$200.00**
String holder, from $135 to **$145.00**
Tea set, pot, sugar & creamer, from $175 to.............**$275.00**
Vase, bud; from $95 to..**$110.00**

Toothpick holder, from $20.00 to $25.00.

Kreiss & Co.

Collectors are hot on the trail of figural ceramics, and one of the newest areas of interest are those figurines, napkin holder dolls, salt and pepper shakers, etc., imported from Japan during the 1950s by the Kreiss company. It's so new, in fact, that we're not even sure if it's pronounced 'kriss' or 'kreese,' and dealer's asking prices also suggest an uncertainty. But there's one thing we are sure of, there's lots of activity here, and in case you haven't noticed as yet, we wanted to clue you in. There are several lines. One is a totally off-the-wall group of caricatures called Psycho Ceramics. There's a Beatnick series, Bums, and Cave People (all of which are strange little creatures), as well as some that are very well done and tasteful. Others you find will be inset with colored 'jewels.' Many are marked either with an ink stamp or an in-mold trademark (some are dated), so you'll need to start turning likely-looking items over to check for the Kreiss name just like you did last year for Holt Howard!

See also Napkin Ladies.

Advisors: Phil and Nyla Thurston (See Directory, Figural Ceramics)

Ashtray, man w/tomahawk **$35.00**
Ashtray, Wild Man head...**$18.00**
Bank, Beatnik Santa...**$75.00**
Bank, Christmas pig..**$85.00**
Bank, poodle..**$65.00**
Bank, poodle bust, 'Poodle Bank' on front...............**$25.00**
Bank/dresser caddy, skunk..**$85.00**
Bookends, good monk/bad monk, pr **$75.00**
Candle holder, angel..**$45.00**
Creamer & sugar bowl, Santa **$30.00**
Egg cup, I'm an Egghead...**$65.00**
Egg cup, Mrs Claus...**$35.00**
Figurine, Beatniks, from $85 to **$165.00**
Figurine, Christmas Party..**$85.00**

Figurine, Cinderella look-alike, $85.00. (Photo courtesy of Phil and Nyla Thurston.)

Figurine, clown w/umbrella...**$50.00**
Figurine, convict w/ball & chain **$85.00**
Figurine, devil, 5"..**$32.00**
Figurine, elephant w/drunk **$125.00**
Figurine, flamenco dancers, 8", pr **$125.00**
Figurine, flapper girl (several variations), 9", each, from $55 to **$75.00**

Figurines, harlequin dancers, $125.00 for the pair. (Photo courtesy of Phil and Nyla Thurston.)

Figurine, Hawaiian dancer, female, 6" **$55.00**
Figurine, Japanese lady in kimono w/lantern, 8".......**$95.00**
Figurine, Psycho Ceramics, each, from $85 to **$225.00**
Hors d'oeuvre, 3 Santas..**$65.00**
Mug, bum in garbage can **$65.00**
Mug, female bum in garbage can..................................**$85.00**
Pencil holder, Psycho Ceramics man's head...............**$85.00**

alt & pepper shakers, bear cubs, pr **$35.00**
alt & pepper shakers, bluebirds, pr **$35.00**
alt & pepper shakers, Christmas pigs, pr **$45.00**
alt & pepper shakers, monks w/hair, pr **$35.00**
helf sitters, Oriental couple, pr **$30.00**

L.E. Smith Glass

Originating just after the turn of the century, the L.E. Smith company continues to operate in Mt. Pleasant, Pennsylvania, at the present time. In the 1920s they introduced a line of black glass that they are famous for today. Some pieces were decorated with silver overlay or enameling. Using their own original molds, they made a line of bird and animal figures in crystal as well as in colors. The company is currently producing these figures, many in two sizes. They're one of the main producers of the popular Moon and Star pattern which has been featured in their catalogs since the 1960s in a variety of shapes and colors.

If you'd like to learn more about their bird and animal figures, *Glass Animals of the Depression Era* by Lee Garmon and Dick Spencer has a chapter devoted to those made by L.E. Smith.

See also Eyewinker; Moon and Stars.

Advisor: Ruth Grizel (See Directory, Westmoreland)

Newsletter: *The Glass Post*
P.O. Box 205
Oakdale, IA 52319-0205; Subscription: $25 per year for 12 issues

Figurine, Goose Girl, amber, 6", $40.00.

Animal dish, rooster, white carnival, 2-pc, tall **$45.00**
Animal dish, turkey, amethyst, 2-pc, med **$35.00**
Animal dish, turkey, crystal, 2-pc, med **$35.00**
Animal dish, turkey, white carnival, 2-pc, lg **$79.00**
Basket, Fine Cut/Button/Leaves pattern, clear, 12½" .. **$75.00**
Bookend, rearing horse, slag, each, from $50 to **$60.00**
Bowl, berry; robin blue, ftd, 4" **$16.00**
Bowl, Doily, red carnival **$38.00**
Bowl, fruit; topaz carnival, heavy, lg **$45.00**
Candle holder, kneeling angel, slag, each **$25.00**
Candle holders, kneeling angel, green, pr **$26.00**
Candy box, marigold iridescent, heart shape **$27.00**
Candy nappy, Almond Nouveau slag, heart shape, 6" . **$25.00**
Canoe, Daisy & Button, purple carnival **$25.00**
Creamer & sugar bowl, Hobstar, amethyst carnival **$25.00**

Figurine, bird, frosted w/red & green painted flowers & buds,
8½" **$25.00**
Figurine, camel, recumbent, amber, 4½x6" **$60.00**
Figurine, camel, recumbent, cobalt, 4½x6" **$65.00**
Figurine, camel, recumbent, crystal, 4½x6" **$45.00**
Figurine, cow, crystal, miniature **$10.00**
Figurine, elephant, crystal, 1¾" **$12.00**
Figurine, Goose Girl, crystal frosted w/pink, yellow & green
stain, 5½" **$18.00**
Figurine, Goose Girl, ice green carnival, 5½" **$40.00**
Figurine, Goose Girl, red, 5½" **$40.00**
Figurine, horse, recumbent, amberina, 9" long **$125.00**
Figurine, horse, recumbent, blue, 9" long **$115.00**
Figurine, horse, recumbent, green, 9" long **$100.00**
Figurine, horse, standing, crystal satin, pr **$75.00**
Figurine, Praying Madonna, crystal **$35.00**
Figurine, rabbit, crystal, miniature **$10.00**
Figurine, swan, crystal lustre, limited edition, w/certificate,
lg **$55.00**
Figurine, swan, ice pink carnival, 2" **$15.00**
Figurine, swan, light blue, Levay, 2" **$20.00**
Figurine, swan, light green carnival, Levay, 2" **$20.00**
Figurine, swan, milk glass w/decoration, 8½" **$45.00**
Figurine, unicorn, pink **$10.00**
Lamp, fairy; turtle figural, green **$25.00**
Novelty, boot on pedestal, amber **$12.00**
Novelty, boot on pedestal, green **$12.00**
Novelty, hat, amberina carnival **$17.50**
Novelty, shoe skate, ice blue, limited edition, 4" **$15.00**
Novelty, slipper, Daisy & Button, amber **$8.00**
Novelty, slipper, Daisy & Button, purple carnival **$25.00**
Pitcher, water; gold carnival **$50.00**
Pitcher, water; Heritage, red carnival **$40.00**
Pitcher, water; Hobstar, ice green, w/6 tumblers **$125.00**
Pitcher, water; Near-Cut, amber **$40.00**
Pitcher, water; Tiara Eclipse, green **$69.00**
Plate, Abraham Lincoln, purple carnival, lg **$40.00**
Plate, Herald, Christmas 1972, purple carnival, lg **$40.00**
Plate, Jefferson Davis, purple carnival, 1972, lg **$40.00**
Plate, John F Kennedy, purple carnival, lg **$45.00**
Plate, Robert E Lee, purple carnival, 1972, lg **$40.00**
Plate, Silver Dollar Eagle, purple carnival, 1972, lg **$40.00**
Punch bowl, Grape, amethyst, w/12 cups & ladle ... **$150.00**
Soap dish, swan figural, clear, 8½" **$22.50**
Toothpick holder, Daisy & Button, amberina **$12.50**
Toothpick holder, Daisy & Button, light green carnival,
Levay **$15.00**
Tumbler, Bull's Eye, red carnival **$22.00**
Vase, corn, crystal lustre, very lg **$37.00**

L.G. Wright

The L.G. Wright Glass Company is located in New Martinsville, West Virginia. Mr. Wright began business as a glass jobber and then began buying molds from defunct glass companies. He never made his own glass, instead many companies pressed his wares, among them the Fenton Art Glass Company, Imperial Glass Corporation,

Viking Glass Company, and the Westmoreland Glass Company. Much of L.G. Wright's glass were reproductions of Colonial and Victorian glass and lamps. Many items were made from the original molds, but the designs of some were slightly changed. His company flourished in the 1960s and 1970s; it remains open today under new ownership.

Advisor: Ruth Grizel (See Directory, Westmoreland)

Newsletter: *The Glass Post*
P.O. Box 205
Oakdale, IA 52319-0205; Subscription: $25 per year for 12 issues

Ashtray, Daisy & Button, ruby, 5½" **$20.00**
Basket, Daisy & Button, amber, flat bottom, 4½x7½" .**$35.00**
Bell, Daisy & Button, 6½" **$30.00**
Bowl, Daisy & Button, amber, 5" dia **$25.00**
Bowl, Daisy & Button, milk glass, w/handles, fluted rim, 9x12" **$40.00**
Candy dish, Paneled Grape, amber, footed, w/lid, 6½x4" ..**$45.00**
Candy dish, Paneled Grape, ruby, footed, 6½x4" **$45.00**
Compote, Palm Beach, apple green, ca 1930, 8½" **$95.00**
Covered dish, Atterbury Duck, any color, unmarked, 11" .**$70.00**
Covered dish, flatiron, amber, w/lid, 5x8½" **$50.00**
Covered dish, hen on nest, red slag, 5½" **$95.00**
Covered dish, lamb on basketweave base, amber, 5½"...**$35.00**
Covered dish, owl on basketweave base, amber, 5½" .**$65.00**
Covered dish, owl on basketweave base, blue slag, 5½" ..**$75.00**
Covered dish, owl on basketweave base, custard, caramel slag, or purple slag, 5½", each **$65.00**
Covered dish, owl on basketweave base, dark blue satin, 5½" **$50.00**
Covered dish, owl on basketweave base, red slag, 5½" ...**$95.00**
Covered dish, rooster on nest, red slag, 5½" **$95.00**
Covered dish, turkey on woven base, lilac mist, 5½"...**$40.00**

Covered dish, turtle, 'Knobby Back,' amber, lg, $95.00.

Covered dish, turtle, 'Knobby Back,' dark green, lg.**$125.00**
Covered dish, turtle, 'Knobby Back,' milk glass, lg ..**$135.00**
Covered dish, turtle on basketweave base, amber **$20.00**
Creamer & sugar bowl, Paneled Grape, amber, 2½"..**$45.00**
Cruet, Thumbprint, fluted **$85.00**
Goblet, Paneled Grape, amber, 8-oz....................**$20.00**
Goblet, wine; Paneled Grape, ruby, 2-oz **$15.00**

Oil lamp, Daisy & Button, ruby, 12" **$85.00**
Pitcher, Cherries, med green, 3x5" **$25.00**
Pitcher, Cherries, ruby, 3x5", from $45 to...................**$50.00**
Plate, log cabin, crystal mist, 1971, 9" **$45.00**
Plate, Paneled Grape, ruby, 7½" **$35.00**
Sugar bowl, Paneled Grape, amber, sm......................**$10.00**
Swan, lavender, 3½" **$35.00**
Swan, med or dark green, 3½".....................................**$30.00**
Swan, milk glass, 3½" **$35.00**
Toothpick holder, Cherries, red slag, 2x2½" **$30.00**
Tray, Daisy & Button, light blue, 3-part, 7½x4½".......**$35.00**

Labels

Each one a work of art in miniature, labels of all types appeal to collectors through their colorful lithography and imaginative choice of graphics representative of the product or the producer. Before cardboard boxes became so commonplace, wooden crates were used to transport everything from asparagus to yams. Cigar boxes were labeled both on the outside and in the lid. Tin cans had wonderful labels with Black children, luscious fruits and vegetables, animals, and birds. Some of the better examples are listed here. Many can be bought at much lower prices.

Crate, Champ Brand, Louisiana Sweet Potatoes and Yams, 1930s, 9x9", $4.00.

Can, Bert Marshall Grapefruit, grapefruit half & glass of juice, M **$3.00**
Can, Blackhoof, 2 lg tomatoes, M **$1.00**
Can, Buffalo Barlet Malt Syrup, blue & orange Deco image of buffalo heads, 1930, EX....................................**$8.00**
Can, Campus Peaches, college buildings & pennant, 1936, EX **$15.00**
Can, Cherry Hill, Indian holding arrows, tepees, M......**$8.00**
Can, Cobut Corn, hand cutting corn from ear onto plate, 1930, M **$10.00**
Can, Crest Sauerkraut, head of cabbage, EX **$4.00**
Can, Deer Head Apples, 10-point buck & 2 apples, M ..**$3.00**
Can, Del-Rose, 2 ears of corn, G...................................**$2.00**
Can, Domko's Pride Peaches, image of lg peach, 1930, EX .**$6.00**
Can, East Point Oysters, 3 oysters on a plate, M...........**$5.00**
Can, Excelsior Malt Syrup, dried barley on yellow background, 1930, EX **$4.00**
Can, Fountain Oysters, image of fountain & basket of oysters, 1930, EX..**$20.00**
Can, Fresh Asparagus, image of 2 bears, can & bald eagle, EX **$15.00**

Can, Golden Sheaf Pineapple, plate of pineapple & embossed wheat, 1931, M...$15.00

Can, Home Canned String Beans, country scene & pile of beans, M $6.00

Can, Isaacs June Peas, country lake scene & pods, M .$2.00

Can, Lucky Dutchman, smiling Dutchman holding can, 1930, EX...$2.00

Can, Marshall Pumpkin, seal on pumpkin, EX..............$3.00

Can, Mi-Boy Cut Wax beans, smiling young boy, M $3.00

Can, Orion Russian Fruit Drops, Art Deco image of woman & fruit, G $15.00

Can, Poppy Pineapple Chunks, bowl of fruit, bird & flowers, M $25.00

Can, Quaker Brand Pears, image of young Quaker woman & pear, VG $20.00

Can, Round Town Sugar Corn, morning-glories & country stream, M $8.00

Can, South Shore Peaches, golfers at country club & golf bag, 1934, EX...$30.00

Can, Sun-Lite Tomatoes, tomato w/jars & bottles, EX ..$15.00

Can, Traver's Ship Loganberries, image of the Union Jack & Lady Britannia w/berries, VG $12.00

Can, United Prunes, 3 prunes on a branch, M.............$1.00

Can, White Pigeon Sweet Corn, pigeon in flight & corn, G...$6.00

Cigar box, inner lid; Absaroka, portrait of Indian chief w/arrows & peace pipe, 6x9"...............$65.00

Cigar box, inner lid; Bantam, 'Worth Fighting For,' 2 cocks ready to fight, 6x9", EX $45.00

Cigar box, inner lid; Best Value, gold scales weighing box of cigars & pile of gold, 6x9", M....................$30.00

Cigar box, inner lid; Biscops, goat portrait encircled by flags, 6x9", M..$10.00

Cigar box, inner lid; Bumper, goat on hind legs embellished by scrolled banners, 6x9", M.....................$7.00

Cigar box, inner lid; Chief Joseph, name above portrait flanked by Indian & explorer, 6x9", EX...............$75.00

Cigar box, inner lid; College Ribbon, gold medals & red ribbons on green, M................................$2.00

Cigar box, inner lid; Gallus, rooster portrait in embellished horizontal oval, 6x9", EX.....................$30.00

Cigar box, inner lid; General Almonte, Mexican General & flag, M..$7.00

Cigar box, inner lid; Greetings to Dad, golf & fishing gear below man, M................................$2.00

Cigar box, inner lid; Havana Inn, name lettered diagonally across scene w/car parked next to inn, 6x9", M..$20.00

Cigar box, inner lid; Illinois Automobile Club, red embossed lettering, M................................$4.00

Cigar box, inner lid; Little Dan O'Brien, oval portrait of cigar maker, green, 6x9", M........................$2.00

Cigar box, inner lid; Lord Brown, man in red coat reading book, M..$10.00

Cigar box, inner lid; Majestic, ocean liner, 6x9", M $60.00

Cigar box, inner lid; Old Abe, Merit-Quality, oval portrait of President Lincoln, 6x9", M...................$35.00

Cigar box, inner lid; Red Head, smiling redheaded boy, 6x9", M $4.00

Cigar box, inner lid; Rofelda, lady's portrait encircled by stemmed roses, 6x9", M........................$7.00

Cigar box, inner lid; The Havana Post, 1904 Cuban newspaper of Morro Castle, 6x9", M...................$9.00

Cigar box, outer; Abraham Lincoln, profile portrait, canted corners, 4½" square, M........................$40.00

Cigar box, outer; Ben Franklin (Benja), portrait encircled by leaves, rounded corners, 4½" square, M..............$18.00

Cigar box, outer; Concordia, 2 women shaking hands, 4½" square, M..$4.00

Cigar box, outer; El Escudero, green & gold star, M $4.00

Cigar box, outer; Florita, woman w/gold flowers, M....$6.00

Cigar box, outer; Georgia Senator, image of man & coins, 4½" square, EX..$9.00

Cigar box, outer; Gold Hunter, Klondike prospector on railroad tracks, 4½" square, EX........................$50.00

Cigar box, outer; Great Talker, colorful parrot on a branch, canted corners, 4½" square, EX....................$75.00

Cigar box, outer; High Art, boy & bird flying, oval, EX...$75.00

Cigar box, outer; Key West Extras, views of cigar production, canted corners, 4½" square, M...................$40.00

Cigar box, outer; La Flora De Alfonso, roses & coins, 4½" square, M..$3.00

Cigar box, outer; La Fuga, Indian holding flag, M......$10.00

Cigar box, outer; Lady Cleveland, oval portrait surrounded by vine, canted corners, 4½" square, M....................$20.00

Cigar box, outer; Lillian, Lillian Russel framed in flowers, EX..$25.00

Cigar box, outer; Lulu, Deco image of man in chair enjoying cigar w/Black waiter, 4½" square, M $20.00

Cigar box, outer; Manobra, profile image of Indian chief holding hatchet, 4½" square, M.........................$17.00

Cigar box, outer; Morning Star, woman w/cherubs, crest & cornucopia, M..$8.00

Cigar box, outer; Old Judge, old man reading the newspaper, M..$40.00

Cigar box, outer; Pengo, Black natives dancing in jungle, M..$15.00

Cigar box, outer; Red Cap, image of lady dressed in red, 4½" square, G $3.00

Cigar box, outer; Rip Van Winkle, young man drinking wine, M..$10.00

Cigar box, outer; Ripple, image of yacht on open seas, canted corners, 4½" square, M........................$35.00

Cigar box, outer; Shetland Ponies, 2 ponies close together, 1931, 4½" square, M........................$30.00

Cigar box, outer; Taft, portrait of President Taft, 4½" square, EX..$20.00

Cigar box, outer; Vaudeville Sports, boys in tuxedos facing each other in boxing pose, canted corners, 4½" square, EX..$20.00

Crate, apple, Apple Kids, 2 boys pushing & pulling an apple, 1940, M..$12.00

Crate, apple, Bird Valley, image of lg crow, 1920, M...$4.50

Crate, apple, Chalet Apples, image of mountain-top chalet & apple orchards, M........................$60.00

Crate, apple, Kentucky Cardinal, image of red bird perched on branch, M..$35.00

Crate, apple, Pioneer Special Pack, 2 lg apples, 1930, M ..$2.00

Crate, apple, Sebastopol Queen, crowned apple queen holding wand, 1950, M........................$2.00

Crate, California Orange, Brownies, brownies juicing giant orange, 1930, M **$7.00**

Crate, California Orange, Memory, silhouette of woman in frame w/rose, 1920, M...**$9.00**

Crate, California Orange, Sun Garden, lg tree & rising sun, 1930, M **$12.00**

Crate, California Orange, Unicorn, image of unicorn running through field, 1930, M **$15.00**

Crate, California Orange, Yo-Semi-Te, forest scene, 1920, M.**$65.00**

Crate, Florida Citrus, Justice, statue of Lady Justice, 1940, M.**$4.00**

Crate, Florida Citrus, Kiss-Me, image of 2 children, 1940, M..**$8.00**

Crate, Florida Citrus, Right-O-Way, image of high-speed train & oranges, 1949, M..**$55.00**

Crate, Florida Citrus, Sunset Hill, orchard w/oranges, 1940, M...**$3.00**

Crate, lemon, Bridal Veil, Bridal Veil Falls, Yosemite Valley, 1927, M **$12.00**

Crate, lemon, Harmony, girl leading a group of circus toys, 1920, M **$85.00**

Crate, lemon, Onward, rear view of Statue of Liberty, 1930, EX **$60.00**

Crate, lemon, Paula, senorita w/fan, green background, 1930, EX...**$18.00**

Crate, lemon, Southern Beauties, colorful rosebuds, 1940, M **$3.00**

Crate, pear, B-Wise, image of owl, blue background, 1930, M...**$16.00**

Crate, pear, Blue Goose, image of goose on deep orange background, 1948, M...**$1.00**

Crate, pear, Our Pick, image of rooster & basket of fruit, 1930, M **$5.00**

Crate, pear, Quercus Ranch, lake scene w/orchard & lg tree, 1927, M **$4.00**

Crate, pear, Top Card, ace of spades on top of 3 cards, 1940, M **$3.00**

Crate, Safe Hit Brand, Texas Vegetables, 1940s, 9x7", $3.00.

Lamps

Aladdin Electric Lamps

Aladdin lamps have been made continually since 1908 by the Mantle Lamp Company of America, now Aladdin Industries Inc. in Nashville, Tennessee. Their famous kerosene lamps are highly collectible, and some are quite valuable. Most were relegated to the storage shelf or thrown away after electric lines came through the country, but today many people keep them on hand for emergency light.

Few know that Aladdin was one of the largest manufacturers of electric lamps from 1930 to 1956. They created new designs, colorful glass, and unique paper shades. These are not only collectible but are still used in many homes today. Many Aladdin lamps, kerosene as well as electric, can be found at garage sales, antique shops, and flea markets. You can learn more about them in the book *Aladdin Electric Lamps* written by J.W. Courter, who also periodically issues updated price guides for both kerosene and electric Aladdins.

Advisor: J.W. Courter (See Directory, Lamps)

Newsletter: *Mystic Lights of the Aladdin Knights*
J.W. Courter
3935 Kelley Rd.
Kevil, KY 42053; Subscription: $20 (6 issues, postpaid 1st class) per year with current buy-sell-trade information. Send SASE for information about other publications

Bed lamp, Whip-o-lite shade, #2010-SS or #2021-SS, from $50 to **$75.00**

Bedroom, ceramic, P-51, from $20 to **$25.00**

Boudoir lamp, Alacite, G-49 or G-50, from $30 to **$40.00**

Figurine, lamp, pheasant, G-234, from $175 to.........**$200.00**

Glass urn lamp, Alacite, closed urn, G-213A, from $175 to..**$225.00**

Magic Touch table lamp, ceramic base, MT-507 or MT-508, from $300 to...**$300.00**

Pinup lamp, Gun 'N Holster, ceramic, P-57, from $100 to ..**$125.00**

Ranch house lamp, Alacite Bullet, illuminated urn, w/decal, G-378C, from $175 to **$225.00**

Table lamp, Alacite, illuminated base, G-206, from $60 to .**$75.00**

Table lamp, Alacite, illuminated base, tall harp, G-325, from $30 to **$40.00**

Table lamp, ceramic, P-409, from $25 to....................**$40.00**

Table lamp, ceramic w/black iron base, contemporary style, M-475, from $35 to **$50.00**

Table lamp, figural, G-44, from $175 to **$225.00**

Table lamp, M-3, metal, from $75 to.........................**$100.00**

Table lamp, metal figurine, M-123, from $100 to......**$200.00**

Table lamp, Opalique, G-179, from $80 to................**$100.00**

TV lamp, shell, ceramic, TV-384, from $40 to.............**$50.00**

Aladdin Kerosene Mantle Lamps

Caboose lamp Model #23, aluminum, w/shade, B23000, from $50 to...**$75.00**

Model B, Simplicity, green, table lamp, B-29, 1948-53, EX finish, from $100 to...**$150.00**

Model B, Treasure, chromium, table model, 1937-53, EX finish, from $175 to...**$200.00**

Model B, Washington Drape, clear crystal, filigree stem, table lamp, B-50, 1940, from $80 to **$100.00**

Model B floor lamp, gold plated & ivory lacquer, B-425, 1941-42, 1946-51, from $150 to **$200.00**

Model C hanging, aluminum hanger & font (B-223), white paper shade, from $50 to.................................**$100.00**

Model C table lamp, font lamp w/no base, aluminum font, B-165, from $35 to...**$45.00**

Model 21C table lamp, aluminum font, B-139, from $25 to ...**$45.00**

Model 23 table lamp, Regency, brass shelf font, walnut base, B-2402, 1980 to present, from $40 to....................**$60.00**

Model 23 table lamp, Short Lincoln Drape, red carnival, no shade, Aladdin/Fenton, 1993, from $150 to **$275.00**

Figural Lamps

Many of the figural lamps on the market today are from the 1930s, forties and fifties. You'll often see them modeled as matching pairs, made primarily for use in the boudoir or the nursery. Many were made of glass, and *Bedroom and Bathroom Glassware of the Depression Years* by Margaret and Kenn Whitmyer (Collector Books) will prove to be an invaluable source of further information, if you're primarily interested in the glass variety. Unless another medium is mentioned in our descriptions, assume that all our figural lamps are glass.

See also Occupied Japan.

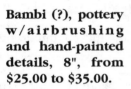
Bambi (?), pottery w/airbrushing and hand-painted details, 8", from $25.00 to $35.00.

Ballerina, porcelain, w/shade **$95.00**

Bear, lamb, or other nursery figural, pottery w/airbrushed colors, each, from $12 to **$18.00**

Birds, ceramic, multicolor w/blue lustre tree trunk, Japan, 5½", from $60 to...**$80.00**

Blackamoor head, porcelain, pr **$65.00**

Cat seated on flower-strewn mound, pottery, airbrushed colors, 7"..**$25.00**

Clown, frosted crystal, carousel shade w/embossed animals, from $30 to...**$35.00**

Colonial couple, ceramic, painted florals w/gold trim & glossy white glaze, Japan, 6½", pr, from $30 to...**$55.00**

Dancing couple, frosted crystal, matching glass pleated-look shade, from $35 to...**$40.00**

Delilah II, frosted pink or green, reclining lady, from $50 to **$60.00**

Dreamer, fired-on pink or blue, lady w/head tilted, head resting on her hand, floral shade, from $60 to **$80.00**

Harpist, slag glass, lady in flowing gown playing harp, later shade, from $30 to...**$35.00**

Humpty Dumpty on wall, ceramic, air-brushed multicolors, from $40 to **$50.00**

Lovebirds, red or green, US Glass (Tiffin), lg, from $200 to .**$225.00**

Lovers, frosted pink or green, couple in amorous embrace, 4 sm feet, from $65 to **$75.00**

Organ grinder, fired-on pink or blue, monkey on his shoulder, glass shade, from $40 to **$50.00**

Oriental girl, fired-on pink or blue, seated, arms at her side, basket in left hand, glass shade, from $45 to.......**$55.00**

Oriental lady, fired-on pink or blue, weighted nodder head, hands hold fan behind her head, glass shade, from $125 to...**$135.00**

Pierrot w/lady, ceramic, marked w/black Japan stamp, 7", from $20 to...**$35.00**

Scottie, fired-on pink or blue, paws up begging, glass shade w/embossed Scotties, from $95 to **$125.00**

Scotty pups in a basket, fired-on pink or blue, original glass shade, from $75 to..**$95.00**

Southern Belle, fired-on blue or pink, lady in hoop dress & bonnet, bouquet in hand, shells form shade, from $45 to **$55.00**

Southern Belle, frosted crystal, lady in hoop dress & bonnet, bouquet in hand, shells form shade, from $25 to.**$30.00**

Spanish dancer, painted pottery, 8"............................**$15.00**

Spring Nymph, frosted crystal, nymph figure atop urn form, from $100 to...**$125.00**

Tara, fired-on pink or blue, Southern lady in full skirt, glass shell shade, from $50 to...**$60.00**

Victorian lady, frosted pink or green, metal base & shade, from $75 to..**$85.00**

Motion Lamps

Though some were made as early as 1920 and as late as the seventies, motion lamps were most popular during the fifties. Most are cylindrical with scenes such as waterfalls and forest fires and attain a sense of motion through the action of an inner cylinder that rotates with the heat of the bulb. Linda and Bill Montgomery have written a book called *Motion Lamps, 1920s to the Present*, containing full-page color photographs and lots of good information if you'd like to learn more about these lamps.

Advisors: Jim and Kaye Whitaker (See Directory, Lamps)

Airplanes, Econolite, plastic, 1958, 11", from $100 to ..**$125.00**

Antique Cars, Econolite, plastic, 1957, 11", from $100 to ...**$140.00**

Christmas Tree, Econolite, many colors, paper, 1951, 15", from $75 to...**$120.00**

Church in snow scene, Econolite, plastic, 1957, 11"...**$90.00**

Fire fighters, LA Goodman, plastic, 1947, 11" **$175.00**

Fireplace, Econolite, gold wire base, 1958, 11".........**$120.00**

Forest fire, Econolite, gold wire base, 1955, 11", from $80 to **$120.00**

Forest fire, LA Goodman, plastic, 1856, 11" **$75.00**

Forest fire, Scene in Action, glass & pot metal, 1931, 10".....**$195.00**

Fountain of Youth, Econolite, boy, 1950, 10", from $90 to...**$130.00**

Hopalong Cassidy, Econolite (Roto-Vue Jr), red, 1949, 10"...**$600.00**

Marine scene, Scenes in Action, ship & lighthouse, glass, 1930s, from $150 to...**$175.00**

Merry-Go-Round, Econolite, Disney, red plastic, 1955, from $200 to...**$225.00**

Mill scene, Econolite, plastic, 1956, 11", from $90 to .**$100.00**

Miss Liberty, Econolite, 1957, 11".............................**$125.00**

Mountain waterfall & campers, LA Goodman, gold wire base, 1956, 11"...$130.00

Niagara Falls, Econolite, plastic, 1955, 11", from $70 to..$110.00

Niagara Falls, Econolite (Roto-Vue Jr), gold, 1950, 10"....$115.00

Niagara Falls, LA Goodman, plastic, 1957, 11"...........$70.00

Niagara Falls, SIA, glass & metal, 1930s, 10".............$150.00

Ocean creatures, LA Goodman, plastic, 1955, 11", from $100 to...$125.00

Oriental fantasy, LA Goodman, plastic, 1957, 11", from $90 to...$115.00

Santa & reindeer, LA Goodman, plastic, 1955, 11", from $100 to...$130.00

Seattle World's Fair, Econolite, plastic, 1962, 11", from $100 to $150.00

Serenader, Scene in Action, glass & pot metal, 1932, 13"...$225.00

Ships, Rev-O-Lite, bronze & plastic, 1930s, 10", from $110 to $125.00

Steamboats or riverboats, Econolite, gold wire base, 1957, 11" $130.00

Tropical fish, Econolite, plastic, 1954, 11" $70.00

Truck & bus, Econolite, gold wire base, 1955, 11"...$140.00

Water-skiers, Econolite, plastic, 1957, 11", from $125 to ..$150.00

Perfume Lamps

One catalog from the 1950s states that a perfume lamp 'precipitates and absorbs unpleasant tobacco smoke in closed rooms; freshens air in rooms, and is decorative in every home — can be used as a night lamp or television lamp.' An earlier advertisement reads 'an electric lamp that breathes delightful, delicate fragrance as it burns.' Perfume-burner lamps can be traced back to the earliest times of man. There has always been a desire to change, sweeten, or freshen air. Through the centuries the evolution of the perfume-burner lamp has had many changes in outer form, but very little change in function. Many designs of incense burners were used not only for the reasons mentioned here, but also in various ceremonies — as they still are to this day. Later, very fine perfume burners were designed and produced by the best glasshouses in Europe. Other media such as porcelain and metal also were used. It was not until the early part of the twentieth century that electric perfume lamps came into existence. Many lamps made by both American and European firms during the twenties and thirties are eagerly sought by collectors.

From the mid-1930s to the seventies there seems to have been an explosion in both the number of designs and manufacturers. This is especially true in Europe. Nearly every conceivable figure has been seen as a perfume lamp. Animals, buildings, fish, houses, jars, Oriental themes, people, and statuary are just a few examples. American import firms have purchased many different designs from Japan. These lamps range from replicas of earlier European pieces to original works. Except for an occasional article or section in reference books, very little has been written on this subject. The information contained in each of these articles generally covers only a specific designer, manufacturer, or country. To date, no formal group or association exists for this area of collecting.

Advisors: Tom and Linda Millman (See Directory, Lamps)

Bambi, standing on floral & grassy base, Goebel, marked TMK3 DIS 150, 6½"................................$350.00

Boy, Hummel-like figure w/musical instrument, standing against wall, Irice, 5½"..............................$40.00

Buddha, bright paint with gold highlights, Aerozon, #783, 8¾", $330.00. (Photo courtesy of Tom and Linda Millman.)

German Shepard, lay-down/stay position, realistic paint, Goebel, marked TMK3 ET 41, 4¼"..............$340.00

German Shepard, sitting, realistic paint, Goebel, marked TMK3 ET 34, 9"................................$340.00

Girl, Hummel-like figure w/accordion, standing against wall, Irice, 5½".......................................$40.00

Hyacinth bloom in fluted pot, Norcrest, 7" $45.00

Lady, basket on arm, 3 lg applied bows on skirt, gold trim, 6¼".......................................$45.00

Lady, basket on left arm, dog tucked under right arm, wears green hat & jacket, wide skirt w/pink bow, Irice, 6¾".......................................$60.00

Lady, holds bouquet w/right hand at waist, blue dress w/gold trim, Irice, 7¼".......................$45.00

Lady, holds fan in right hand, Colonial-style dress w/painted florals & silver trim, marked Made in Japan, 7" .$100.00

Lady, seated & reading to child on her lap, gold trim on base, Ardalt, 7¼".......................................$65.00

Lady with basket on right arm, Ardalt, 5¾", $65.00. (Photo courtesy of Tom and Linda Millman.)

Man, holding bouquet at waist front, wearing top hat w/flower, bow tie & shoes w/spats, Goebel, marked TMK6 58-071, 9"................................$380.00

Night watchman, carrying weapon & box lantern, multicolor paint, Goebel, marked TMK6 58-050-22, 8¼" $370.00

Oriental ginger jar, water lilies on red background w/gold trim, Aerozon, #734, 7⅜" $275.00

Penguin, standing pose w/realistic paint, Goebel, marked TMK3 ET 67, 7¼".......................................$355.00

Swans, 2 on wave base, Irice, 4¼"..........................$20.00

Table lamp, cone-shaped shade w/antique auto decoration, stepped circular base w/green band trim, Irice, 5"..$20.00

Table lamp, fluted shade w/yellow flowers & gold trim, bulbous base, circle foot w/gold trim, Irice, 5¼"......**$20.00**

Table lamp, white w/blue florals & gold trim, brass band around burner area, Irice, 5½" **$25.00**

TV Lamps

By the 1950s, TV was commonplace in just about every home in the country but still fresh enough to have our undivided attention. Families gathered around the set together and for the rest of the evening were entertained by Ed Sullivan or stumped by the $64,000 Question. Pottery producers catered to this scenario by producing TV lamps by the score, and with the popularity of anything from the 'fifties' being what it is today, suddenly these lamps are making an appearance at flea markets and co-ops everywhere.

See also Maddux of California.

Flamingos, Lane, 11", $65.00.

Black panther, Royal Hickman, 28"..............................**$35.00**

Flowers, multicolored glass & beads, lg center blossom w/light, plaster base **$35.00**

Galleon, brn onyx...**$37.50**

Horse, black w/gold mane, planter behind, red shade ..**$55.00**

Horse, running, green gloss...**$32.00**

Horses, gold lustre on black gloss, sm **$35.00**

Horses, running pr, black w/gold trim & saddles, lg..**$45.00**

Indian on horseback chasing 2 deer, naturalistic colors, Holland Mold, 9½" **$65.00**

Indian rider, metal figure in shell desert scene, marked souvenir of Michigan Indian Reservation on plaster base........**$50.00**

Mallard duck, natural colors, well done, 20" long **$65.00**

Owl, naturalistic, spread wings, Morton Pottery, marked Kran, lg..**$57.50**

Panther atop rocky ledge, Lane, 12x16", $75.00.

Panther, recumbent, olive green...................................**$35.00**

Roman warrior, kneeling behind panther, white foamy brown glaze **$35.00**

Seashells on plaster base, lg center shell w/light, 8", from $12 to **$18.00**

Shell, dark green glaze...**$24.00**

Shell, lg natural conch on round fluted plastic base ..**$11.00**

Lefton China

China, porcelain, and ceramic items with that now familiar mark, Lefton, have been around since the early 1940s and are highly sought after by collectors in the secondary marketplace today. The company was founded by Mr. George Zoltan Lefton, an immigrant from Hungary. In the 1930s he was in the designing and manufacturing of sportswear, and his hobby of collecting fine china and porcelain led him to the creation of his own ceramic business.

When the bombing of Pearl Harbor occurred on December 7, 1941, Mr. Lefton came to the aid of a Japanese-American friend and helped him protect his property from anti-Japanese groups. After this event, Mr Lefton was introduced to a Japanese factory owned by Kowa Koki KK. Up until 1980 this factory produced thousands of pieces that were marketed by the Lefton company with the initials KW preceding the item number. Figurines and animals plus many of the whimsical pieces such as Bluebirds, Dainty Miss, Miss Priss, Cabbage Cutie, Elf Head, Mr. Toodles, and Dutch Girl are eagerly collected today. As with any antique or collectible, the prices vary depending on location, condition, and availability. For the history of Lefton China, information about Lefton factories, marks, and other identification methods, we highly recommend the *Collector's Encyclopedia of Lefton China*, Volumes I and II, by our advisor, Loretta DeLozier.

See also Birthday Angels; Cookie Jars.

Advisor: Loretta DeLozier (See Directory, Lefton)

Club: National Society of Lefton Collectors

Newsletter: *The Lefton Collector*
c/o Loretta DeLozier
1101 Polk St.
Bedford, IA 50833; 712-523-2289 (Mon.-Fri. 9:00-4:00); Dues: $25 per year (includes quarterly newsletter)

Angel, Naughty Girls, #10297, 5".................................**$48.00**

Angel, pearl lustre, #1478, 4¼"....................................**$15.00**

Angel, sitting in flower playing instrument, #1699, 3¼", set of 3 ....**$150.00**

Angel, tumbling, #80159, 2¾", set of 4.....................**$140.00**

Ashtray, leaf shaped in violet design, 3934, set of 3 ..**$45.00**

Bank, Globe, For My Trip, #1309, 6½" **$30.00**

Bank, Howdy Doody sitting on barrel, #7411...........**$200.00**

Bank, Kewpie, #145, 6¾"..**$42.00**

Bank, Uncle Sam, Saving for My Income Tax, #882, 6½".**$40.00**

Bottles, oil & vinegar; Celery Line, #1306.................**$65.00**

Box, Heavenly Hobos, musical, plays Little Drummer Boy, #04650, 6".................**$60.00**

Candy box, antique ivory bisque, pedestal foot, w/lid, #906, 7¼".................**$45.00**

Candy box, To a Wild Rose, #2722, 4½".................**$32.00**

Coffeepot, Blue Paisley, #1972 ....**$90.00**

Coffeepot, Brown Heritage, Floral, #1866 ....**$135.00**

Coffeepot, Brown Heritage, Fruit, #20591 ....**$160.00**

Coffeepot, Fleur-de-Lis, #2910 ....**$65.00**

Coffeepot, Green Heritage, #3065 ....**$125.00**

Cookie jar, Bloomer Girl, #3966 ....**$250.00**

Cookie jar, Cabbage Cutie, #2130, 7".................**$225.00**

Cookie jar, Dainty Miss, #040, 7½".................**$200.00**

Cookie jar, Miss Priss, #1502, 7½".................**$135.00**

Creamer and sugar bowl, Miss Priss, #1508, $55.00.

Cookie jar, mushroom w/window & doors, #130 ....**$40.00**

Creamer & sugar bowl, black & white roosters, #2460....**$55.00**

Creamer & sugar bowl, Dainty Miss, #322.................**$60.00**

Creamer & sugar bowl, Sweet Lil, #1425, 4" **$40.00**

Cup & saucer, Blue Paisley, #2133 ....**$25.00**

Cup & saucer, Brown Heritage, floral, #1883 ....**$45.00**

Cup & saucer, Christmas, holly w/candy cane border, #026.................**$25.00**

Cup & saucer, jumbo; Good Morning Darling, #061 ..**$28.00**

Cup & saucer, Roses, black, #2042.................**$45.00**

Dish, Classic Elegance, #4808, 8½".................**$40.00**

Dish, Eastern Star, leaf shape, #20225.................**$22.00**

Dish, serving; candy cane pattern, leaf shape, #1294, 8"..**$22.00**

Egg cup, Bluebird, #286.................**$40.00**

Figurine, Bloomer Girl, bisque, #3080, 4".................**$50.00**

Figurine, Colonial man & woman, #1705, 10", pr.....**$300.00**

Figurine, Colonial man & woman, #2256, 10½", pr..**$275.00**

Figurine, deer, #521, 5⅝", pr **$28.00**

Figurine, duck, #7555, 11½" **$95.00**

Figurine, eagle, #802, 11".................**$100.00**

Figurine, long-tail rooster, #1528 ....**$175.00**

Figurine, man w/walking stick, #2349, 6¼" **$40.00**

Figurine, Persian cat, #1513, 3½".................**$8.00**

Figurine, Provincial boy & girl w/dogs, #5642, 8½".**$200.00**

Figurine, Provincial man & woman carrying flowers, #7223, 7".................**$100.00**

Figurine, quail, #760, 5¾", pr **$55.00**

Figurine, Six Little Adorables, limited edition, #326, set..**$125.00**

Figurine, Victorian lady w/umbrella, porcelain, #3585, 7½".................**$125.00**

Figurines, Colonial man and woman, #3658, 10", $250.00 for the pair. (Photo courtesy of Loretta DeLozier.)

Jam jar, Brown Heritage, floral, w/tray & spoon, #2761 ....**$38.00**

Jam jar, Fruits of Italy, #623, 4¼" **$25.00**

Jam jar, Grape Line, #2023, 4" **$28.00**

Jam jar, Green Heritage, #1152, 4½" **$35.00**

Jam jar, Pear 'N Apple, w/tray, #4255 ....**$22.00**

Lipstick holder, cherubs, bisque, #1063 ....**$35.00**

Nappy, Green Heritage, #1860 ....**$25.00**

Nappy, Misty Rose, leaf shape, #5724, 6½" **$12.00**

Nappy, Poinsettia, #4394, 7" **$22.00**

Pitcher & bowl, Christmas holly, #1970/71, 7½", 5" ...**$28.00**

Planter, Bluebird, #288 ....**$85.00**

Planter, book shape w/green holly, #5185, 4¾" **$20.00**

Planter, kitten, 5", $20.00.

Planter, dog, #167, 6" opening.................**$12.00**

Planter, lady, #3188, 7".................**$36.00**

Planter, pheasant, #904, 5½".................**$45.00**

Plaque, boy & girl in relief, ornate frame, #350, 8½", pr..**$60.00**

Plaque, dog's head, #7437, 5".................**$15.00**

Salt & pepper shakers, Dainty Miss, #439.................**$35.00**

Salt & pepper shakers, Miss Priss, #521.................**$35.00**

Salt & pepper shakers, To a Wild Rose, #2584 ....**$28.00**

Sleigh, Green Holly, #2637, 10½".................**$60.00**

Snack set, Eastern Star, #907.................**$22.00**

Snack set, Oriental design, #20402.................**$35.00**

Switch plate, single w/floral design, #077 ....**$20.00**

Teapot, Bluebird, #438 ....**$250.00**

Teapot, Green Holly, #1357 ....**$80.00**

Teapot, Miss Priss, #1502 ....**$145.00**

Tray, Rose Garden, 2-tier, #6587.................**$65.00**

Tumble-up, Misty Rose, #5697.................**$55.00**

Vase, Humpty Dumpty, #5881, 5".................**$75.00**

Vase, lady's head, #1736, 5½".................**$35.00**

Vase, lily shape w/hand-applied roses, #7093, pr.....**$195.00**

Vase, Only a Rose, #382, 5½".................................**$75.00**

Vase, tree trunk w/cherub, pastel gray, green, bisque, #970 ....**$95.00**

Wall pocket, boy w/basket, #2628, 7"..........................**$95.00**

Wall pocket, girl, Dainty Miss, #6767, 5".....................**$75.00**

Letter Openers

If you're cramped for space but a true-blue collector at heart, here's a chance to get into a hobby where there's more than enough diversification to be both interesting and challenging, yet requires very little room for display. Whether you prefer the advertising letter openers or the more imaginative models with handles sculpted as a dimensional figure or incorporating a penknife or a cigarette lighter, you should be able to locate enough for a nice assortment. Materials are varied as well, ranging from silverplate to wood. For more information, we recommend *Letter Openers, Advertising and Figural* (L&W Book Sales).

Advertising, brass, Henry Sears Co., Chicago, and Chas Munson Belting C., 9", $25.00 each.

Advertising, brass, Argenzio Brothers Fine Jewelers, marked Made in Japan, 8" **$10.00**

Advertising, bronze, Auto Compressor Co, Wilmington, Ohio, 7" **$15.00**

Advertising, bronze, Cadillac emblem at handle, G Fox Co, Cincinnati, Ohio, 9¼" **$100.00**

Advertising, bronze, HH Baumgartner Mfg Co on wide scroll at handle, JE Mergott Co, ca 1930, 8¾" **$15.00**

Advertising, bronze, Lincoln National Bank & Trust Co, Ft Wayne Indiana stamped on handle, 8¼" **$5.00**

Advertising, bronze, Metropolitan Life Insurance Co stamped emblem on handle, 8¾".....................................**$20.00**

Advertising, bronze, Order of the Eastern Star, American Art Works, ca 1937, 7" **$10.00**

Advertising, chromed steel, paper & plastic, Electrolux/Servel Inc, 9" **$25.00**

Advertising, copper, Art Type Co, Brown & Bigelow, St Paul, Minnesota, 8"..**$15.00**

Advertising, plastic, advertising w/calendar on opposing side of handle, 1940s, 8¾" **$20.00**

Advertising, plastic, Bank Americard, 1965, 7¼"..........**$5.00**

Advertising, plastic, Burdsal-Haffner Paint Co, 1955, 10" ..**$15.00**

Advertising, plastic, Fuller Brush Co, salesman as handle, 7¼" **$1.00**

Advertising, plastic, Greenwich Savings Bank, New York, 7" **$5.00**

Advertising, stainless steel, Pfizer Rondomycin, 7¼" **$20.00**

Aluminum, Art Nouveau mermaid as handle w/long sweeping blade, heavy, 9½"..**$40.00**

Aluminum, nude as handle, stamped Naples 1945 on blade, 10⅜"...**$30.00**

Brass, Charles Dickens bust on handle, marked Made in Austria, 8" **$45.00**

Brass, painted Birds of Paradise on handle, stainless steel blade, 6⅞" **$10.00**

Bronze, open-cutwork framed peacock as handle, embossed design on tapering blade, 8¾"...............................**$10.00**

Celluloid, full-figure elephant as handle w/wide blade, marked Made in Germany, 7½" **$30.00**

Celluloid, full-figured owl w/acanthus leaf trim as handle, 11¼"..**$60.00**

Copper, Abraham Lincoln, 11"....................................**$35.00**

Copper, full-figure American Indian, on handle, 7¼".**$50.00**

Copper, ship's anchor as handle, long thin blade, 9".**$15.00**

Copper, slim lady college graduate on handle, 7½"...**$30.00**

Ivory, full-figured Egyptian as handle, 10¾" **$60.00**

Metal w/copper-painted finish, Indian chief bust in profile on handle, marked Made in Japan, 7½" **$10.00**

Souvenir, bronze, Cheyenne, Wyoming, cowboy on bucking bronco w/open work at handle, 7¾"...................**$10.00**

Souvenir, bronze, Great Smoky Mountains w/bear on handle, 6" **$10.00**

Souvenir, metal & plastic, Kennedy Space Center, Florida, 7⅜" **$15.00**

Souvenir, plastic, Souvenir of Hotel Filipinas, Manila, Phillipines, 8"..**$5.00**

Steel, Middle Eastern sword w/jewel, w/leather scabbard, 9½"...**$25.00**

Sterling, French floral designed handle w/tapered & hilted blade, 7"..**$50.00**

Sterling, tapered oval handle w/thin triangular blade, monogram design, S Kirk & Sons, 1927-161, 5⅞" **$40.00**

Wood, hand carved & painted gypsy bust handle w/wide blade, 4½" **$10.00**

Wood, hand-carved squirrel handle w/short wide blade, 5" **$10.00**

Liberty Blue

'Take home a piece of American history!,' stated an ad from the 1970s for this dinnerware made in Staffordshire, England. Blue and white depictions of George Washington at Valley Forge, Paul Revere, Independence Hall — fourteen historic scenes in all — were offered on different place-setting pieces. The ad goes on to describe this 'unique...truly unusual...museum-quality...future family heirloom.'

For every five dollars spent on groceries you could purchase a basic piece (dinner plate, bread and butter plate, cup, saucer, or dessert dish) for fifty-nine cents on alternate weeks of the promotion. During the promotion, completer pieces could also be purchased. The soup tureen was the most expensive item, originally selling for $24.99. Nineteen completer pieces in all were offered along with a five-year open stock guarantee.

For more information we recommend Jo Cunningham's book, *The Best of Collectible Dinnerware*.

Advisor: Gary Beegle (See Directory, Dinnerware)

Bowl, cereal; from $10 to.................................**$12.50**
Bowl, flat soup; 8¾", from $15 to **$18.00**
Bowl, fruit; 5", from $4.50 to **$5.50**
Bowl, vegetable; oval **$40.00**
Bowl, vegetable; round **$35.00**
Butter dish, w/lid, ¼-lb, from $20 to **$35.00**
Casserole, w/lid, from $65 to.........................**$75.00**
Coaster, from $8 to **$10.00**
Creamer **$15.00**
Creamer & sugar bowl, w/lid, original box...............**$60.00**
Cup & saucer, from $7 to................................**$9.00**
Gravy boat, from $30 to **$35.00**
Gravy boat liner...**$15.00**
Mug, from $10 to **$12.00**
Pitcher, water **$95.00**
Plate, dinner; 10", from $7 to **$9.00**

Plate, Independence Hall, 10", from $7.00 to $9.00.

Plate, luncheon; scarce, 8¾" **$12.00**
Plate, scarce, 7" **$9.50**
Plate, 6", from $3 to **$4.50**
Platter, 12", from $35 to.................................**$45.00**
Platter, 14" **$65.00**
Salt & pepper shakers, pr **$25.00**
Soup ladle, plain white, no decal, from $30 to...........**$35.00**
Soup tureen, w/lid, from $250 to.....................**$300.00**
Sugar bowl, no lid **$15.00**
Sugar bowl, w/lid **$25.00**
Teapot, w/lid, from $95 to...............................**$125.00**

License Plates

Some of the early porcelain license plates are valued at more than $500.00. First-year plates (the date varies from state to state, of course) are especially desirable. Steel plates with the aluminum 'state seal' attached range in value from $150.00 (for those from 1915 to 1920) down to $20.00 (for those from the early forties to 1950). Even some modern plates are desirable to collectors who like those with special graphics and messages.

Our values are given for examples in good or better condition, unless noted otherwise. For further information see *License Plate Values* distributed by L-W Book Sales.

Advisor: Richard Diehl (See Directory, License Plates)

Newsletter: *Automobile License Plate Collectors*
Gary Brent Kincade
P.O. Box 712
Weston, WV 26452; 304-842-3773

Magazine: *License Plate Collectors Hobby Magazine*
Drew Steitz, Editor
P.O. Box 222
East Texas, PA 18046; Phone or FAX 610-791-7979; e-mail: PL8Seditor@aol.com or RVGZ60A@prodigy.com; Issued bimonthly; $18 per year (1st class, USA). Send $2 for sample copy

Arizona, 1969, w/'72 sticker, pr **$6.00**
1910, New Jersey..**$150.00**
1911, Iowa..**$95.00**
1912, Connecticut, porcelain..........................**$50.00**
1914, Missouri, repainted **$40.00**

1915, Colorado, $250.00 each.

1915, Maine, porcelain **$50.00**
1916, New Hampshire, porcelain **$50.00**
1918, Iowa, repainted.....................................**$10.50**
1919, Kansas, G-..**$12.50**
1920, New Jersey **$28.00**
1921, Connecticut **$18.50**
1921, Iowa, VG, pr **$40.00**
1922, Nebraska, repainted..............................**$13.50**
1923, Idaho..**$40.00**
1925, Minnesota...**$15.50**
1926, Rhode Island **$20.00**
1927, Delaware **$40.00**
1928, Kentucky, repainted **$25.00**
1929, North Dakota **$15.50**
1930, Montana..**$25.00**
1931, Arkansas, pr **$70.00**
1932, Mississippi **$30.00**
1933, Arizona, copper **$100.00**
1934, Tennessee..**$40.00**
1935, New Jersey **$15.50**
1936, New Hampshire, touched up.................**$5.50**
1937, New Mexico **$30.00**

1938, Pennsylvania	$10.50
1939, Michigan	$8.50
1940, Pennsylvania	$10.50
1941, Pennsylvania, porcelain, VG	$50.00
1941, Rhode Island	$18.00
1942, Oklahoma	$25.00
1943, California	$20.00
1945, Colorado	$8.50
1946, Hawaii	$75.00
1947, Missouri	$10.50
1948, Maryland	$20.00
1949, Iowa, only year for checkerboard aluminum, VG/EX, pr	$20.00
1949, Minnesota, centennial	$25.00
1950, Colorado	$10.50
1951, Louisiana	$35.00
1952, Kansas, tab	$3.50
1953, Louisiana, G-	$15.50
1954, Alabama	$15.50
1954, Arizona, w/'55 metal tag, pr, NM	$45.00
1955, Florida	$17.50
1955, Illinois, VG, pr	$15.00
1956, Alaska	$40.00
1957, Washington DC, inaugural, M, pr	$350.00
1958, Texas, pr	$18.50
1959, Washington	$14.50
1960, Vermont	$6.00
1961, Iowa	$4.50
1962, Illinois	$3.50
1963, North Carolina	$8.50
1964, Ohio	$4.50
1965, South Carolina	$5.50
1966, Idaho	$5.25
1967, Wisconsin	$4.50
1968, Wyoming	$5.50
1969, Florida	$5.50
1970, Rhode Island	$16.00
1971, Tennessee	$5.50
1972, Georgia	$5.00
1973, Utah	$2.75
1974, Oregon	$4.00
1975, California	$5.50
1976, Michigan, Bicentennial, single	$5.00
1976, Wisconsin	$3.00
1977, Delaware	$8.50
1978, Delaware	$8.50
1979, Virginia	$4.00
1980, California	$5.50
1981, South Dakota	$3.00
1982, Alaska	$9.50
1983, Connecticut	$9.00
1984, Alabama	$4.50
1985, West Virginia, map	$7.50

Little Red Riding Hood

This line of novelty cookie jars, canisters, mugs, teapots, and other kitchenware items was made by both Regal China and Hull. Any piece today is expensive. There are several variations of the cookie jars. The Regal jar with the open basket marked 'Little Red Riding Hood Pat. Design 135889' is worth about $300.00. The same with the closed basket goes for a minimum of $50.00 more. An unmarked Regal variation with a closed basket, full skirt, and no apron books at $600.00. The Hull jars are valued at about $350.00 unless they're heavily decorated with decals and gold trim, which can add as much as $250.00 to the basic value.

The complete line is covered in *The Collector's Encyclopedia of Cookie Jars* by Joyce and Fred Roerig, and again in *Little Red Riding Hood* by Mark E. Supnick.

Bank, standing, from $600 to	$635.00
Bank, wall hanging, from $1,500 to	$1,700.00
Batter pitcher, from $425 to	$450.00
Butter dish, from $395 to	$425.00
Canister, cereal; from $850 to	$900.00

Canister, flour; $800.00.

Canisters, coffee, sugar, tea or flour; each	$800.00
Cookie jar, closed basket, minimum value	$350.00
Cookie jar, open basket, red shoes	$575.00
Cracker jar, skirt held wide, unmarked	$900.00
Creamer, top pour, tab handle	$350.00
Match holder, wall hanging	$800.00
Mug, embossed figure, white, minimum value	$650.00
Mustard, w/spoon, from $375 to	$400.00
Salt & pepper shakers, lg, 5½", pr	$175.00
Salt & pepper shakers, standing, 3¼", or	$125.00
Spice jar, square base, from $650 to	$750.00
String holder, from $2,800 to	$3,000.00
Sugar bowl, crawling, unmarked	$275.00
Sugar bowl lid	$225.00
Teapot	$365.00
Wolf jar, red	$1,200.00
Wolf jar, yellow	$950.00

Little Tikes

For more than twenty-five years, this company (a division of Rubbermaid) has produced an extensive line of toys and playtime equipment, all made of heavy-gauge plastic, sturdily built and able to stand up to the rowdiest children and the most inclement weather. As children usually outgrow these items well before they're worn out, you'll often see them at garage sales, priced at a fraction of their original cost. We've listed a few below, along with what we feel would be a high average for an example in very good condition. Since there is no established secondary market pricing system, though, you can expect to see a wide range of asking prices.

Basketball goal, indoor/outdoor, adjust from 4' to 6', ball included, #4803, from $12 to **$15.00**

Car, Grand Coupe, optional doll seat or lift-lid trunk in back, #4458, from $10 to **$14.00**

Doll stroller, built-in tray, high back, for up to 20" dolls, #4478, from $5 to **$7.00**

Dump truck, deep red bed, helmet included, #6653, 19" long, from $4 to **$5.00**

Easel, Super Storage, takes roll paper, features chalkboard & storage tray, #4418, from $8 to **$12.00**

Picnic table, attached bench seats, for older children, 37x40x22", #4668, from $12 to **$15.00**

Play house, 2 windows w/opening shutters, drop-leaf table & phone inside, #4697, 46x44x41", from $35 to .. **$40.00**

Rocking chair, #7250, 25x23x15", from $6 to **$8.00**

School bus, Toodle Tots, roof doubles as handle, 5 'kids' included, 12" long, from $3 to **$4.00**

Shopping cart, lower storage shelf, solid walls, #4444, from $5 to **$7.00**

Slide, 2-in-1, features sprinkler & puddle area, indoor/outdoor, #4551, 77" long, from $18 to **$22.00**

Table w/2 chairs, 21" wide, #4230, from $8 to **$12.00**

Toy box, lift-off lid, 7 cubic ft, #7515, from $10 to **$15.00**

Tractor, toddler, no pedals, walk-along type, #4032, from $5 to **$8.00**

Tunnel, Peek-A-Boo, for babies & toddlers, #1553, from $9 to **$12.00**

Wagon, Explorer, extra lg, #4405, from $15 to **$20.00**

Workshop, Deluxe, w/tools & hardware, combination desk w/drawing surface, #4601, from $12 to **$15.00**

Lladro Porcelains

These porcelains are being produced in Labernes Blanques, Spain, and their retired and limited edition figurines are commanding high prices on the secondary market. They're distinctively styled and glazed, with long sleek lines and cool color schemes usually of dusty blue, ivory and grays. Look for their mark, though, since they have been widely copied.

Aggressive Goose, 6", $120.00.

All Aboard	**$225.00**
Boy From Madrid, #4898	**$120.00**
Can I Play?	**$300.00**
Cinderella	**$150.00**
Cow w/Pig, #4640	**$425.00**
Fall Cleanup, #5286	**$475.00**
Flower Song, from $475 to	**$525.00**
Girl w/Cat, #1187	**$400.00**
Girl w/Sheep, #4584, 1971	**$135.00**
Going Fishing, #4809	**$125.00**
Little Pals	**$1,800.00**
My Buddy	**$300.00**
Peace Offering	**$450.00**
Picture Perfect	**$385.00**
Shepherd w/Lamb, #4676	**$85.00**
Shepherdess w/Basket, #4676	**$75.00**
Shepherdess w/Rooster, #4677	**$75.00**
Summer Stroll	**$295.00**
Tree Toppers, #5830	**$125.00**
Voyage of Columbus	**$950.00**

Lu Ray Pastels

This was one of Taylor, Smith, and Taylor's most popular lines of dinnerware. It was made from the late 1930s until sometime in the early fifties in five pastel colors: Windsor Blue, Persian Cream, Sharon Pink, Surf Green, and Chatham Gray.

If you'd like more information, we recommend *Collector's Guide to Lu Ray Pastels* by Kathy and Bill Meehan (Collector Books).

Bowl, coupe soup; flat	**$13.00**
Bowl, fruit; 5"	**$5.00**
Bowl, mixing; 7"	**$70.00**
Bowl, salad	**$42.00**
Bowl, vegetable; oval, 9½"	**$16.00**
Bowl, 7"	**$75.00**
Cake plate	**$63.00**
Casserole	**$70.00**
Coffee cup, AD	**$18.00**
Coffeepot, AD	**$135.00**
Creamer	**$8.00**
Creamer, AD, individual	**$40.00**

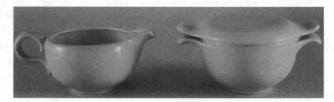

Creamer and sugar bowl, $20.00 for the set.

Egg cup, double	**$15.00**
Gravy boat	**$13.00**
Jug, water; footed	**$60.00**
Nappy, vegetable; round, 8½"	**$13.00**
Pitcher, bulbous w/flat bottom	**$45.00**

Plate, chop; 15"	$25.00
Plate, 10"	$16.00
Plate, 6"	$4.00
Plate, 8"	$15.00
Plate, 9"	$10.00
Platter, oval, 13"	$16.00
Salt & pepper shakers, pr	$13.00
Saucer, coffee	$8.50
Saucer, cream soup	$22.50
Sugar bowl, w/lid	$11.00
Teacup	$8.00
Teapot, flat spout, w/lid	$68.00
Tray, pickle	$24.00
Tumbler, juice	$35.00
Tumbler, water	$50.00

Lunch Boxes

Character lunch boxes made of metal have been very collectible for several years, but now even those made of plastic and vinyl are coming into their own.

The first lunch box of this type ever produced featured Hopalong Cassidy. Made by the Aladdin company, it was constructed of steel and decorated with decals. But the first fully lithographed steel lunch box and matching thermos bottle was made a few years later (in 1953) by American Thermos. Roy Rogers was its featured character.

Since then hundreds have been made, and just as is true in other areas of character-related collectibles, the more desirable lunch boxes are those with easily recognizable, well-known subjects — western heroes; TV, Disney, and cartoon characters; and famous entertainers.

Values hinge on condition. Learn to grade your lunch boxes carefully. A grade of 'excellent' for metal boxes means that you will notice only very minor defects and less than normal wear. Plastic boxes may have a few scratches and some minor wear on the sides, but the graphics are completely undamaged. Vinyls must retain their original shape; brass parts may be tarnished, and the hinge may show signs of beginning splits. If the box you're trying to evaluate is in any worse condition than we've described, to be realistic, you must cut these prices drastically. Values are given for boxes without matching thermoses, unless one is mentioned in the line. If you'd like to learn more, we recommend *A Pictorial Price Guide to Metal Lunch Boxes and Thermoses* by Larry Aikins, and *Schroeder's Collectible Toys, Antique to Modern* (Collector Books).

Metal

A-Team, 1970, VG	$12.00
Adam-12, 1972, EX, from $50 to	$75.00
Airline, 1968, VG+, from $40 to	$50.00
America on Parade, 1976, EX	$50.00
Annie, 1981, VG-	$8.00
Apple's Way, 1975, VG	$57.00
Archies, 1969, VG+	$63.00
Auto Race, 1967, VG+	$50.00

Battle of the Planets, 1979, VG	$28.00
Battlestar Galactica, 1978, VG+	$35.00
Bedknobs & Broomsticks, 1972, EX-, from $15 to	$20.00
Berenstein Bears, 1983, VG+	$21.00
Black Hole, 1979, VG-	$15.00
Bonanza, 1965, Aladdin, w/thermos, EX/NM	$200.00
Bugaloos, 1971, VG+	$58.00
Campus Queen, 1967, VG	$20.00
Chan Clan, 1973, VG+	$59.00

**Charlie's Angels, blue rim, NM, $65.00.
(Photo courtesy of June Moon.)**

Chitty-Chitty Bang-Bang, 1968, VG+	$95.00
Christmas Carousel, 2-handle, 1990s, EX	$9.00
Clash of the Titans, 1980, VG+	$25.00
Coca-Cola, 2-handle, 1980s, M	$28.00
Cracker Jack, 1979, VG+	$39.00
Curiosity Shop, 1972, VG+	$45.00
Cyclist, 1979, VG	$28.00
Dick Tracy, 1967, EX, from $125 to	$145.00
Disco, w/thermos, 1980, VG+	$37.00
Disco, 1980, VG+	$28.00
Disco Fever, 1979, VG+	$35.00
Disney Express, 1979, w/plastic thermos, EX+	$22.00
Doctor Dolittle, 1967, VG+	$65.00
Double Deckers, 1970, EX	$98.00
Dragon's Lair, 1983, VG	$13.00
Drummer Boy, 1970, EX+	$46.00
Dukes of Hazzard, 1980, VG	$8.00
Dukes of Hazzard, 1980, w/thermos, EX	$35.00
Dynomutt, 1976, G	$12.00
ET, 1982, w/thermos, NM+	$49.00
Evel Knievel, 1974, G	$15.00
Fall Guy, w/thermos, 1981, VG+	$29.00
Felix the Cat, 1988, 3x5x9", EX	$300.00
Flag, 1973, VG+	$20.00
Flintstones, 1964, yellow, VG	$79.00
Flipper, 1967, VG+	$135.00
Floral, 1970, M	$35.00
Fonz, 1976, VG+	$35.00
Fraggle Rock, 1984, VG	$10.00
Ghostland, 1977, EX	$49.00
GI Joe, 1982, VG	$18.00
Goober & Ghost Chasers, 1974, EX	$39.00
Gremlins, 1984, w/thermos, NM	$35.00
Grizzly Adams, 1977, w/thermos, EX+	$125.00

Hair Bear Bunch, w/plastic thermos, 1971, EX...........**$50.00**
Hansel & Gretel, 1982, EX...**$79.00**
Happy Days, 1976, VG+..**$45.00**
Hardy Boys, 1977, G+...**$12.00**
Harlem Globetrotters, 1971, VG+ **$35.00**
He-Man & Masters of the Universe, w/thermos, 1984, VG+ .**$12.00**
Heathcliff, 1982, NM..**$20.00**
Hee Haw, 1970, VG..**$39.00**
Holly Hobbie, flowers, w/thermos, 1981, VG+ **$15.00**
Hong Kong Phooey, 1974, VG, from $25 to **$30.00**
Howdy Doody, 1954, EX..**$400.00**
Huckleberry Hound & Friends, 1961, VG...................**$79.00**
Incredible Hulk, w/thermos, 1978, EX+.....................**$49.00**
Incredible Hulk, 1978, VG+..**$32.00**
Indiana Jones, 1984, VG..**$14.00**
Indiana Jones, 1984, w/thermos, NM.........................**$50.00**
Johnny Lightning, 1970, EX- **$34.00**
Julia, 1969, VG **$50.00**
Knight Rider, 1981, EX-..**$14.00**
Kung Fu, 1974, VG...**$23.00**
Lamb w/Red Bow, 2-handle, 1980s, EX......................**$12.00**
Land of the Giants, 1968, VG- **$38.00**
Land of the Lost, 1975, EX...**$75.00**
Lassie, 1978, VG+...**$35.00**
Lawman, 1961, VG...**$59.00**
Legend of the Lone Ranger, 1990, VG **$22.00**
Magic Kingdom, 1979, VG+..**$12.00**
Miss America, 1972, VG+..**$39.00**
Monroes, 1967, EX...**$150.00**
Mr Merlin, 1981, VG **$14.00**

Munsters, King Seeley, 1965, black rim, VG, $195.00. (Photo courtesy of June Moon.)

Muppet Babies, 1985, VG+ **$12.00**
Muppet Movie, 1979, VG **$30.00**
Pac Man, w/thermos, 1980, M, from $30 to **$40.00**
Partridge Family, 1971, VG-.......................................**$25.00**
Peanuts, tan rim, 1966, VG+.......................................**$24.00**
Peanuts, 1980, w/thermos, M......................................**$49.00**
Pebbles & Bamm-Bamm, 1971, w/thermos, EX..........**$75.00**
Play Ball, 1969, VG..**$28.00**
Popeye, 1964, EX..**$150.00**
Popeye, 1980, VG+...**$30.00**
Racing Wheels, 1977, VG+..**$25.00**
Return of the Jedi, w/thermos, 1983, EX, from $35 to...**$40.00**
Return of the Jedi, 1983, VG+ **$20.00**
Rifleman, 1960, VG+, from $200 to............................**$235.00**
Road Runner, 1970, G **$14.00**

Ronald McDonald, 1982, VG+ **$18.00**

Ronald McDonald Sheriff of Cactus Canyon, Aladdin, 1982, with thermos, EX, $28.00.

Rough Rider, 1972, VG+...**$45.00**
Satellite, 1958, VG+..**$45.00**
Secret Wars, 1984, VG **$12.00**
See America, 1972, VG+..**$50.00**
Sesame Street, 1983, green, VG+................................**$17.00**
Six Million Dollar Man, 1974, EX................................**$39.00**
Six Million Dollar Man, 1974, VG-..............................**$19.00**
Skateboarder, 1978, VG+..**$50.00**
Snow White, 1977, VG+..**$25.00**
Space Shuttle Orbiter Enterprise, 1977, VG, from $20 to...**$25.00**
Speed Buggy, 1973, VG, from $15 to..........................**$18.00**
Sports Afield, 1957, EX+...**$150.00**
Street Hawk, w/thermos, 1984, VG+...........................**$175.00**
Superman, 1978, EX **$45.00**
Thundercats, w/thermos, 1985, M..............................**$45.00**
Transformers, 1986, EX-...**$18.00**
US Mail, dome top, 1969, VG.....................................**$22.00**
Valentine, 2-handle, 1980s, EX...................................**$16.00**
Wagon Trail, 1964, EX+..**$175.00**

Walt Disney School Bus, Aladdin, dome top, EX, $60.00.

Walt Disney World, 1972, VG+ **$15.00**
Washington Redskins, 1970, VG+................................**$265.00**
Weave Pattern, 1972, EX-..**$15.00**
Weave Pattern, 1972, M..**$35.00**
Welcome Back Kotter, 1976, VG+ **$39.00**
Wild Frontier, 1977, VG+..**$30.00**
Wonderful World, 1980, EX...**$20.00**
Yankee Doodle, w/thermos, 1975, VG+ **$32.00**
Zorro, black, 1958, VG+..**$125.00**
18 Wheeler, 1978, VG+...**$38.00**

Plastic

Astrokids, w/robot thermos, 1988, M...........................$26.00
Atari Missile Command, dome shape, 1980, VG+.......$20.00
Back to the Future, 1989, VG+......................................$8.00
Batman, dark blue, no gloves, w/thermos, 1982, VG...$14.00
Batman, gray w/no gloves, 1982, VG+.......................$30.00
Bee Gees, 1978, VG+..$15.00
Benji, 1974, EX..$20.00
Bozostuffs, w/thermos, 1988, M.................................$29.00
California Raisins, w/thermos, M................................$20.00
Capt Planet, w/thermos, 1990, M...............................$20.00
Chiclets, w/thermos, 1987, M.....................................$50.00
Cinderella, w/thermos, 1992, EX................................$25.00
Colonial Bread Van, 1984, G+....................................$20.00
DEKA 4x4 Truck, w/thermos, 1988, M.......................$35.00
Dr Pepper, 1982, VG+...$20.00

Duck Tales, Aladdin, 1986, decal on blue, NM, $8.00.

Dukes of Hazzard, dome shape, 1980, VG.................$16.00
Dynosaurs, dome shape, thin, 1986, EX.....................$20.00
Ecology, dome shape, w/thermos, 1980, EX..............$35.00
Elephant, Hippo, Lion, 1986, EX................................$20.00
Flash Gordon, dome shape, w/thermos, 1979, NM....$95.00
Flav-O-Rich Milk, Atlantic Braves, 1990, EX..............$20.00
Gumby, 1986, VG+..$25.00
Here's Boomer, yellow, 1980, EX...............................$25.00
Hot Wheels, 1984, VG+..$15.00
Jabberjaw, w/thermos, 1977, EX................................$30.00
Jetsons: The Movie, w/thermos, 1990, M..................$25.00
Keebler, w/thermos, 1984, NM...................................$40.00
Kellogg's Corn Flakes, w/thermos, 1985, EX+...........$50.00
Looney Tunes, Taz Devil, w/thermos, 1988, M..........$20.00
Looney Tunes, w/thermos, 1989, VG+.......................$32.00
Lunch n' Tunes, bear on bench, radio works, 1986, EX...$40.00
Mickey & Donald, 1984, EX..$20.00
Mickey Mouse Mobile, 1978, VG+.............................$25.00
Minnie Mouse Head, thick, EX, from $20 to..............$30.00
Mork & Mindy, 1978, VG..$20.00
Muppet School Bus, 1989, VG+.................................$11.00
My Child, w/thermos, 1986, VG+...............................$15.00
Peanuts Wienie Roast, blue, 1985, EX.......................$10.00
Penguins, w/thermos, 1986, VG+..............................$20.00
Pepsi-Cola, red, w/thermos, 1980, VG+....................$20.00
Pup Named Scooby Doo, w/thermos, 1988, M..........$23.00
Return of the Jedi, red, 1983, EX...............................$20.00
Rock Lords, 1987, VG...$12.00

Rocky Roughneck, 1977, VG+....................................$20.00
Scooby Doo, 1984, VG+..$15.00
Sky Sox, black, 7 different ads on it, 1977, EX...........$20.00
Snoopy & Woodstock, dome shape, w/thermos, 1970, VG+...........$20.00
Snow White, blue, w/thermos, 1988...........................$15.00
Sport Billy, w/thermos, 1982, VG+............................$20.00
Star Trek: The Next Generation, w/thermos, 1988, M ..$20.00
StarCom US Space Force, w/thermos, 1987, M..........$20.00
Superman, dome shape, w/thermos, 1980, EX..........$40.00
Tom & Jerry: The Movie, 1992, VG+...........................$20.00
Wizard of Oz, w/thermos, 1989, VG+........................$25.00
Wuzzles, dome shape, w/generic thermos, 1985, VG+ ..$21.00
Yogi's Treasure Hunt, w/thermos, 1987, NM..............$28.00
101 Dalmatians, 1990, EX...$9.00

Vinyl

Annie, 1981, VG..$20.00
Ballerina on Lily Pad, pink, 1960s, VG+...................$125.00
Barbie, pink, w/thermos, 1971, EX............................$65.00
Barbie & Francie, w/metal thermos, 1965, EX..........$100.00
Barbie & Midge, black, 1963, EX................................$75.00
Boston Red Sox, 1960, EX, from $60 to......................$70.00
Capt Kangaroo, 1964, EX..$300.00
Challenger, green, softee, 1986, M...........................$200.00
Corsage, 1970, VG+..$99.00
Don't Bug Me (Ladybugs), drawstring, 1978, EX.......$39.00
Donny & Marie Osmond, long hair, 1976, VG+.........$50.00
Hawaiian Islanders, zippered, 1980s, VG+................$20.00
Junior Nurse, 1963, EX..$160.00
Leo Lion, drawstring, 1978, NM.................................$75.00
Li'l Jodie, softee, 1978, M...$100.00
Lion in the Cart, puffy, 1985, VG+.............................$40.00
Lion in the Van, 1978, M...$120.00
Little Old Schoolhouse, softee, 1974, EX...................$75.00
Pepsi, yel, softee, 1980, EX.......................................$39.00
Picadilly, 1971, VG+...$49.00
Pink Panther, 1980, VG+..$65.00
Sabrina, 1972, EX+...$200.00
Sesame Street, w/thermos, 1979, VG+......................$30.00
Speedy Turtle, drawstring, 1978, EX..........................$39.00
Strawberry Shortcake, w/thermos, 1980, EX..............$35.00
Swan Lake, blue, 1960s, VG+....................................$100.00
Tic Tac Toe, red, 1970, VG+.......................................$35.00
Tropical Swim Club, red, EX+....................................$59.00
Winston Cigarettes, drawstring, 1974, M...................$18.00
Wise Old Owl, drawstring, 1978, NM.........................$75.00
Wizard in the Van, 1978, VG......................................$45.00
1910 Ford, 1974, EX-..$80.00

Thermoses

Values are give for thermoses in excellent condition; all are made of metal unless noted otherwise.

Adam-12, Aladdin, 1973...$20.00
Astrokids, Brazil, plastic, 1988.................................$15.00
Auto Race, King Seeley Thermos, 1967....................$30.00

Benji, Thermos, plastic, 1980 ....$10.00

Beverly Hillbillies, Aladdin, metal with plastic cup, EX, $60.00.

Boston Red Sox, Ardee, vinyl, 1960s $12.00
Bozostuffs, Deka, plastic, 1988....................................$20.00
Camera, Taiwan, plastic, 1986......................................$5.00
Dark Crystal, King Seeley Thermos, 1982...................$10.00
Denim, King Seeley Thermos, vinyl, 1970s $20.00
Dinosaur, Taiwan, plastic, 1988 ....$10.00
Disco Fever, Aladdin, 1980 ....$30.00
Duck Tales (game), Aladdin, 1986 ....$8.00
Dune, Aladdin, plastic, 1984..$20.00
Ed Grimley, Aladdin, plastic, 1988 ....$8.00
Empire Strikes Back, swamp pictorial, King Seeley Thermos,
    1981 ....$10.00
Food Fighters, Aladdin, plastic, 1988 ....$10.00
Fox & the Hound, Aladdin, 1981 ....$10.00
GI Joe, King Seeley Thermos, 1982 ....$10.00
Go Bots, Thermos, plastic, 1984....................................$8.00
Gremlins, Aladdin, 1984 ....$8.00
Holly Hobbie, Aladdin, 1979...$5.00
Hot Wheels, King Seeley Thermos, 1969.....................$25.00
Karate, Taiwan, plastic, 1980...$8.00
Kid Power, American Thermos, 1974............................$20.00
Knight Rider, King Seeley Thermos, 1984....................$12.00
Land of the Lost, Aladdin, 1975....................................$35.00
Lassie, Ardee, vinyl, 1960s $12.00
Lone Ranger, Aladdin, 1980 ....$20.00
Lunch Break, Taiwan, plastic, 1986...............................$15.00
Mad Balls, Aladdin, plastic, 1986...................................$8.00
Magic Kingdom, Aladdin, 1980 ....$5.00
Masters of the Universe, Aladdin, 1983.........................$5.00
Mickey & the Gang, Taiwan, plastic, 1989 ....$10.00
Mork & Mindy, American Thermos, 1979....................$15.00
NFL, King Seeley Thermos, 1978.................................$25.00
Nosey Bears, Aladdin, plastic, 1988...............................$8.00
Picadilly, Aladdin, vinyl, 1971..$20.00
Pink Panther & Sons, King Seeley Thermos, 1984........$8.00
Polly Pal, King Seeley Thermos, 1975...........................$15.00
Rambo, King Seeley Thermos, 1985...............................$5.00
Return of the Jedi, King Seeley Thermos, 1983..............$5.00
Rocky, Thermos, plastic, 1977 ....$10.00
Roller Games, Thermos, plastic, 1989 ....$10.00
Rose Petal Place, Aladdin, 1983...................................$10.00
Sesame Street, Aladdin, 1983 ....$5.00
Sizzlers, King Seeley Thermos, vinyl, 1971...................$30.00
Smurfette, Thermos, plastic, 1984..................................$8.00
Sport Goofy, Aladdin, 1983...$12.00
Star Trek, Thermos, plastic, 1988...................................$5.00

Strawberry Shortcake, Aladdin, 1980...........................$5.00
Taxi, Taiwan, plastic, 1985 ....$5.00
Thundercats, Aladdin, 1985...$5.00
Transformers, Aladdin, 1986...$6.00
Wrinkles, Thermos, plastic, 1984 ....$7.00

Yellow Submarine, metal with plastic cup, NM, $140.00. (Photo courtesy of June Moon.)

MAD Collectibles

MAD, a hotly controversial and satirical publication that was first published in 1952, spoofed everything from advertising and politics to the latest movies and TV shows. Content pivoted around a unique mix of lofty creativity, liberalism, and the ridiculous. A cult-like following has developed over the years. Eagerly sought are items relating to characters that were developed by the comic magazine such as Alfred E. Neuman or Spy Vs Spy.

Advisor: Jim McClane (See Directory, MAD Collectibles)

Bendable figure, Alfred E Neuman, 1989 ....$15.00
Books, hardcover: MAD For Keeps, Forever MAD, Golden
    Trashery of MAD, or Ridiculously Expensive MAD,
    each..$150.00
Bust, bisque, sold through MAD magazine, early 1960s,
    3¾"...$300.00
Bust, bisque, sold through MAD magazine, early 1960s,
    5½"...$400.00
Calendar, any dated 1976 through 1981, each $12.00
Calendar, any dated 1989 through 1991, each $10.00
Campaign kits, 1960, 1964 or 1968 issue, complete, each,
    from $150 to..$400.00
Charm bracelet, sold through MAD magazine, ca late
    1950s $250.00
Coffee mug, MAD, 1988, any 1 of 6 styles.................$15.00
Computer game, MAD's Spy Vs Spy $20.00
Cuff links, Alfred E Neuman, 1950s $200.00
Denim jacket, MAD, 1993 ....$75.00
Disguise kit, Imagineering Corp, 1987 ....$20.00
Doll, Alfred E Neuman, What Me Worry tie, 1961, 20",
    rare $350.00
Game, Parker Brothers, card type, 1980 ....$15.00
Halloween costume, tuxedo style, plastic mask, Collegeville,
    1960, MIB $250.00
Hand puppet, Alfred E Neuman, rare.......................$250.00
Necktie, Watson Brothers, 1992.................................$35.00
Pen, Spy Vs Spy, Applause, 1988...............................$20.00

Postcard, Alfred E Neuman, pre-MAD, from $5 to......**$20.00**

Record, Fink Along w/MAD, 33⅓ rpm 1963, original sleeve, M **$80.00**

Record, Musically MAD, 33⅓ rpm, 1959, original sleeve, M **$50.00**

Record album, MAD Twists, Rock 'n Roll, 33⅓ rpm, M.....**$50.00**

Skateboard, MAD, 1988...**$50.00**

Squirt toy, any of 8 variations, Imagineering Corp, 1987, each **$20.00**

Sunglasses, any of 4 versions, Imagineering Corp, 1989, each **$30.00**

Sweatshirt, MAD, 1993..**$25.00**

T-Shirt, various styles, 1980s, each............................**$15.00**

T-Shirt, What Me Worry? I Read MAD!, late 1950s....**$400.00**

Tie bar, Alfred E Neuman, late 1950s **$200.00**

Watch, various styles, limited edition, Applause, 1988, each **$65.00**

Watch, various styles, regular edition, Applause, 1988, each...**$25.00**

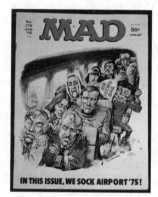

Magazine, July 1975, No. 176, EX, $8.00.

Maddux of California

Founded in Los Angeles in 1938, Maddux not only produced ceramics but imported and distributed them as well. They supplied chainstores nationwide with well-designed figural planters, TV lamps, novelty and giftware items, and during the mid-1960s their merchandise was listed in every major stamp catalog. Because of an increasing amount of foreign imports and an economic slowdown in our own country, the company was forced to sell out in 1976. Under the new management, manufacturing was abandoned, and the company was converted solely to distribution. Collectors have only recently discovered this line, and prices right now are affordable though increasing.

Ashtray, red or yellow, metal caddy w/6 individual trays.**$20.00**

Cats, Deco-style, black matt, facing, 12½", pr.............**$45.00**

Console bowl (set), shell; pink, 16" **$15.00**

Console bowl (set), swan, porcelain white, #1019, 11½"..**$20.00**

Figurine, Chinese pheasants, air-brushed colors, #912/#913, 11", pr **$30.00**

Figurine, deer & doe, stylized, elongated, 12", pr.......**$35.00**

Figurine, doe, walnut, white porcelain, tangerine, #907, 12½"...**$15.00**

Figurine, Early Birds, black matt, tangerine, #969, 14½", pr ..**$25.00**

Figurine, flamingo, #400/#401, pr............................**$35.00**

Figurine, flamingo, flying, natural, #970, 11" **$45.00**

Figurine, flamingo, winging, natural, #971, 12"..........**$45.00**

Figurine, horses, rearing & charging, #925/#926, pr..**$20.00**

Figurine, stag, standing, natural colors, #914, 12½"...**$15.00**

Figurines, bull, red, head up/head down, #972/#973, 11", pr...**$150.00**

Figurines, Chinese pheasants, 13", pr.........................**$45.00**

Planter, pink flamingo, #515, 10½", $45.00. (Photo courtesy of Lee Garmon.)

Planter, swan; black, #510, 11" **$18.00**

TV lamp, Colonial ship, #892, 10½"...........................**$30.00**

TV lamp, Malibu shell, Pearltone, #889, 10¼".............**$20.00**

TV lamp, mare & foal, white porcelain, #897 ....**$35.00**

TV lamp, Persian Glory (horse head), #887, 11½".....**$20.00**

TV lamp, shell, Pearltone, #809, 13" **$20.00**

TV lamp, stallion, prancing, on base, 12"...................**$30.00**

TV lamp, swan, white porcelain, #828, 12½", $20.00. (Photo courtesy of Lee Garmon.)

TV lamp, Toro (bull), foot on mound, #859, 11½".....**$20.00**

TV lamp, w/3-D planter, head of Christ, #841 ....**$25.00**

Vase, double; Flamingo Line, 5" **$40.00**

Vase, horse's head top, straight-sided body, aqua, 12" ...**$18.00**

Magazines

There are lots of magazines around today, but unless they're in fine condition (clean, no missing or clipped pages, and very little other damage); have interesting features (cover illustrations, good advertising, or special-interest stories); or deal with sports greats, famous entertainers, or world-renowned personalities, they're worth very little, no matter how old they are. Address labels on the front are acceptable, but if you find one with no label, it will be worth about 25% more than our listed values. For further information see *Old Magazines Price Guide* by L-W Book Sales and *Life Magazines, 1898 to 1994,* by one of our our advisors, Denis C. Jackson.

See also TV Guides.

Advisor: Denis C. Jackson (See Directory, Magazines)

Advisor: Don Smith, Rare National Geographics (See Directory, Magazines)

Newsletter: *The Illustrator Collector's News*
Denis C. Jackson, Editor
P.O. Box 1958
Sequim, WA 98328; Phone: 360-683-2559 or FAX 360-683-9708; e-mail ticn@daka.com

Agricultural Digest, 1934, November, Maxfield Parrish cover **$50.00**
Agricultural Digest, 1934, November, Parrish cover, NM .**$60.00**
Air Travel News, 1928, December, Graf Zeppelin article, NM..**$8.00**
Alaska Sportsman, 1940, October, VG....................**$7.50**
American, 1916, January, Armstrong cover..................**$25.00**
American Chauffeur, The; 1916, August, new auto article, NM **$16.00**
American Druggist, 1928, October, 1,000 drinks **$7.00**
American Heritage, 1970, December, Parrish illustration, NM **$40.00**
American Legion, 1927, February, HC Christy cover ..**$15.00**
American Legion, 1931, April, Ty Cobb article, NM......**$9.00**
Appleton's Magazine, 1905, December, Rose O'Neil illustration, NM **$16.00**
Arizona Highways, 1935, March, turquoise article, NM ..**$7.00**
Art Photography, 1956, April, Sophia Loren cover, NM..**$10.00**
Atlantic Monthly, 1973, August, Marilyn Monroe cover, NM **$5.00**
Avante Garde, 1969, #8, Picasso, NM.........................**$35.00**
Aviation Week & Space Technology, 1963, July 22, Manned Space Flight, NM...**$20.00**
Bachelor, 1937, April, VG.......................................**$30.00**
Baseball, 1920, October, Babe Ruth cover, NM...........**$80.00**
Baseball Illustrated, 1975, Reggie Jackson cover, EX..**$14.00**
Bewitch, 1966, VG **$35.00**
Blast, 1960, February, VG **$20.00**
Bohemian, The; 1908, January, postcard issue, NM....**$35.00**
Broadway Follies, 1933, October, VG **$30.00**
Cad, 1965, June, VG...**$20.00**
Century, The; 1884, January, Palmer Cox illustrations, EX..**$12.00**
Chain Store Age, 1954, March, Howdy Doody ad, NM ..**$15.00**
Click, 1938, March, Charlie Chaplin cover, EX **$22.00**
Collectibles Illustrated, 1982, November/December, Marilyn Monroe cover, EX **$7.00**
College Humor, 1932, February, Armstrong cover, NM ..**$40.00**
Collier's, 1928, November 10, G+ **$5.00**
Collier's, 1947, January, L Wood cover, NM................**$10.00**
Collier's, 1953, October 16, Marilyn Monroe cover, NM ..**$45.00**
Collier's, 1955, November 11, Agatha Christie stories, VG ..**$10.50**
Complete Baseball, 1953, December, Campanella cover, NM..**$18.00**

Correct Eating, 1927, September, Lindbergh article, NM...**$4.00**
Cosmopolitan, 1886, June, Buffalo Bill, EX **$25.00**
Cosmopolitan, 1905, Ethel Barrymore article, NM **$12.00**
Cosmopolitan, 1934, June, Harrison Fisher cover, G ..**$18.00**
Country Song Roundup, 1957, August, Elvis cover, NM..**$15.00**
Cue, 1953, June 27, Marilyn Monroe cover, NM **$30.00**
DISCoveries, 1989, September, Marty Robbins & Randy Travis, EX..**$3.00**
Ebony, 1967, January, Star Trek cover, NM **$5.00**
Eerie, 1974, April, Ken Kelly cover, EX......................**$4.00**
Esquire, 1960, November, Lenny Bruce article, EX.......**$6.00**
Etude, 1919, June, Rose O'Neill illustration, Jell-O ad, NM...**$20.00**
Family Circle, 1943, March 12, Ray Milland cover, VG .**$5.00**
Family Circle, 1944, January 21, Frank Sinatra cover, VG ..**$5.00**
Family Circle, 1945, January 19, Shirley Temple cover, VG **$15.00**
Family Circle, 1946, January 25, Bob Hope cover, VG .**$7.00**
Family Circle, 1946, July 26, Susan Hayward cover, VG ..**$7.00**
Family Circle, 1948, June, June bride cover, Gary Cooper article, VG **$3.00**
Family Circle, 1968, June, Ann Landers cover, NM **$4.50**
Favorite Westerns, 1960, August, John Wayne cover, EX..**$8.00**
Flair, 1950, Volume 1, #1, NM.................................**$18.00**
Good Housekeeping, 1914, August, nurse article, M..**$25.00**
Good Housekeeping, 1914, September, woman playing tennis, M **$25.00**
Good Housekeeping, 1969, February, Paul Newman cover, VG **$6.50**
Guns, 1956, February, VG+.....................................**$5.00**
Harper's Weekly, 1862, August 30, Stonewall Jackson, EX.**$35.00**
Heart Throbs, 1952, March, Jane Russell & Robert Mitchum cover, VG...**$12.50**
Ice Capades, 1945, G Petty cover, EX........................**$35.00**
Jack & Jill, 1961, May, Roy Rogers cover, EX..............**$10.00**
Ladies' Home Journal, 1911, April 1, flying pigeons, M..**$28.00**
Ladies' Home Journal, 1912, April, bluebirds, M.........**$18.00**
Ladies' Home Journal, 1921, February, Valentine bride, M..**$40.00**
Liberty, 1925, May 2, woman, chair & book, M..........**$25.00**
Liberty, 1933, February 18, Norman Guthrie Rudolph cover, EX **$15.00**
Liberty, 1940, June 15, Going Fishing by Tomde, EX.**$15.00**
Liberty, 1940, November 30, Sax Rohmer, G..............**$12.50**
Liberty, 1940, September 11, Election Time: Roosevelt & Willkie, EX **$15.00**
Life, 1908, February 20, Valentine couple, M **$40.00**
Life, 1909, July 29, cooking lady, M..........................**$30.00**
Life, 1911, August 24, Net Results, M........................**$25.00**
Life, 1921, December 15, Bag & Baggage, M..............**$30.00**
Life, 1926, December, There Is a Santa Claus, M........**$30.00**
Life, 1937, September 6, Harpo Marx, VG...................**$18.00**
Life, 1940, September 2, Dionne Quintuplets cover, EX..**$35.00**
Life, 1946, August 12, Loretta Young cover, VG+..........**$7.00**
Life, 1946, November 25, 10th Anniversary, VG+ **$6.00**
Life, 1947, September 29, Notre Dame football star Johnny Lujack cover, VG+...**$9.00**
Life, 1948, April 19, Winston Churchill cover, VG+ **$7.00**
Life, 1950, August 28, Gen Douglas MacArthur cover, VG+..**$10.00**
Life, 1951, April 16, Esther Williams cover, VG.............**$4.00**

Life, 1951, August 13, Dean Martin & Jerry Lewis cover, EX.**$18.00**

Life, 1951, May 7, Phyllis Kirk cover, EX **$7.00**

Life, 1951, September 3, Gina Lollobrigida cover, EX...**$10.00**

Life, 1953, July 20, Senator John F Kennedy cover, EX.**$10.00**

Life, 1954, May 31, William Holden, VG+ **$14.00**

Life, 1955, August 22, Sophia Loren cover, VG+.........**$15.00**

Life, 1956, April 23, Jayne Mansfield cover, VG+ **$28.00**

Life, 1956, April 9, Grace Kelly cover, VG+ **$8.00**

Life, 1957, February 4, Audrey Hepburn cover, NM...**$12.00**

Life, 1958, April 28, Willie Mays cover, VG+ **$15.00**

Life, 1958, December 1, Ricky Nelson cover, VG **$15.00**

Life, 1958, March 10, Yul Brynner cover, VG+ **$6.00**

Life, 1959, May 18, Jimmy Hoffa cover, VG+ **$4.00**

Life, 1959, November 9, Marilyn Monroe cover, VG...**$15.00**

Life, 1962, September 28, Don Drysdale cover, VG....**$12.50**

Life, 1963, December 6, Jackie Kennedy & children wait to join funeral procession cover, G...........................**$5.00**

Life, 1963, November 29, John F Kennedy cover, VG ..**$12.00**

Life, 1965, May 7, John Wayne cover, EX, $30.00.

Life, 1965, July 16, John F Kennedy cover, EX...........**$10.00**

Life, 1966, March 11, Adam West as Batman cover, NM..**$15.00**

Life, 1967, November 17, Jackie Kennedy cover, EX..**$12.00**

Life, 1969, July 4th, Neil Armstrong Off to the Moon cover, EX...**$12.00**

Life Story, 1944, October, Donna Reed cover, EX.......**$11.00**

Look, 1946, October 15, Ted Williams cover, NM.......**$50.00**

Look, 1955, July 25, Walt Disney article, Fess Parker as Davy Crockett at Disneyland cover, EX.....................**$12.00**

Look, 1963, December 3, John F Kennedy & John Jr cover, VG...**$7.50**

Look, 1963, January 9, Beatles article, EX **$25.00**

Look, 1964, February 11, NY World's Fair preview, VG.**$3.50**

Look, 1966, November 5, Honeymooners cover, NM.**$16.00**

McCall's, 1918, June, war bride & soldier, M..............**$25.00**

McCall's, 1937, October, Helen Hayes cover, VG.........**$8.00**

McCall's, 1951, June, Greta Garbo cover, VG.............**$10.00**

McCall's, 1952, March, Edgar Bergen article, VG **$8.00**

McCall's, 1955, October, Rosalind Russell article, VG...**$8.00**

McCall's, 1959, April, Fred Astaire article, Betsy McCall cut-out doll page, VG **$8.00**

Modern Screen, 1961, June, Elizabeth Taylor cover, G.**$7.50**

Movie Life, 1949, February, Alan Ladd cover, NM **$15.00**

Muscle Power, 1953, October, Mr America, NM...........**$4.00**

National Geographic Magazine, 1911, July, Reptiles of All Lands, VG **$40.00**

National Geographic Magazine, 1914, May, Birds of Town & Country, VG **$25.00**

National Geographic Magazine, 1915, May, America's Wild Flowers, VG...**$15.00**

National Geographic Magazine, 1921, March, America in the Air, VG...**$12.00**

National Geographic Magazine, 1927, May, Wild Flowers of the West, VG **$12.00**

National Geographic Magazine, 1929, July, Insects, VG ..**$12.00**

National Geographic Magazine, 1936, February, Man's Oldest Ally the Dog, VG...**$10.00**

National Geographic Magazine, 1947, July, The World in Your Garden, VG **$8.00**

National Geographic Magazine, 1948, February, Indians of the Far West, VG...**$8.50**

National Geographic Magazine, 1950, December, Gems, VG...**$9.50**

National Geographic Magazine, 1955, May, Grand Canyon, VG **$7.50**

National Geographic Magazine, 1958, December, Dead Sea Scrolls, VG **$7.50**

National Geographic Magazine, 1964, January, The Nation's Capitol, VG **$7.00**

National Geographic Magazine, 1969, December, Apollo 11, VG **$5.50**

National Geographic Magazine, 1975, December, The Maya: Children of Time, VG **$5.00**

National Geographic Magazine, 1976, September, Exploring the New Biology **$5.00**

National Geographic Magazine, 1981, January, Mount St Helens, VG **$4.00**

National Geographic Magazine, 1985, May, The Vietnam Memorial, VG **$4.00**

National Geographic Magazine, 1988, September, 100 Years of the Geographic, VG **$3.00**

National Geographic Magazine, 1993, January, Dinosaurs, VG **$2.00**

National Geography, 1963, August, Walt Disney issue, EX **$10.00**

National Lampoon, 1971, Back-to-School issue, VG **$4.00**

Newsweek, 1939, March 27, Secretary Douglas, named to the Supreme Court, EX..**$5.00**

Newsweek, 1941, September 8, Hitler cover, VG **$10.00**

Newsweek, 1953, January 19, Lucille Ball cover, EX+ ..**$25.00**

Newsweek, 1970, December, Jack Nicholson cover, EX..**$3.00**

Outdoor America, 1947, June, Gene Porter article, NM..**$5.00**

Peek, 1940, July, Betty Grable cover, EX....................**$10.00**

People Digest, 1951, August 15, Ava Gardner cover, NM ...**$7.00**

Photoplay, 1959, October, Doris Day cover, G **$10.00**

Playboy, 1955, September, Anne Fleming, Marilyn Monroe, VG..**$125.00**

Playboy, 1956, November, Betty Blue, VG **$70.00**

Playboy, 1959, January, Virginia Gordon, VG **$40.00**

Playboy, 1961, May, Susan Kelly, VG **$28.00**

Playboy, 1963, November, Terre Tucker, Jimmy Hoffa, VG ..**$36.00**

Playboy, 1965, April, Sue Williams, VG **$22.00**

Playboy, 1966, October, Linda Moon, Ann Margret, VG.**$15.00**

Playboy, 1974, July, Carole Vitale, VG **$14.00**

Playboy, 1976, March, Ann Pennington, VG **$6.00**

Playboy, 1977, November, Rita Lee, VG **$5.00**

Playboy, 1979, August, Dorothy Stratten, VG.............**$15.00**

Police Gazette, 1940, April, Carol Landis cover, EX......**$7.00**

Punch, 1946, November 27, Disney spoof, NM.............**$7.00**
Red Cross, 1918, January, nurse in white, M...............**$24.00**
Redbook, 1989, December, Sally Field & Dolly Parton cover, VG...**$2.50**
Ring Magazine, 1976, June, Latin Connection, EX **$15.00**
Rolling Stone, 1967, #1, John Lennon, NM.................**$60.00**
Saturday Evening Post, 1920, November 6, lady crying, M..**$26.00**
Saturday Evening Post, 1921, January 22, lady in snow, M..**$30.00**
Saturday Evening Post, 1938, August 20, cowboys & calves, NM **$12.00**
Saturday Evening Post, 1946, April 6, Norman Rockwell cover, article on Hawaii becoming a state, EX.....**$10.00**
Saturday Evening Post, 1956, October 13, Dwight D Eisenhower cover by Norman Rockwell, VG **$15.00**
Saturday Evening Post, 1960, February 13, Rockwell Painting Rockwell cover, VG **$12.50**
Saturday Evening Post, 1960, October 29, John F Kennedy cover by Norman Rockwell, VG.....................**$15.00**
Saturday Evening Post, 1961, April 1, Rockwell cover, EX...**$10.00**
Screenland Magazine, 1939, May, Betty Davis cover, EX+ ...**$15.00**
Sports Illustrated, 1956, April 23, Billy Martin cover, EX...**$15.00**
Sports Illustrated, 1958, September 29, World Series, NM...**$6.00**
Sports Illustrated, 1972, March 13, Johnny Bench, EX.....**$10.00**
Sports Illustrated, 1974, March 18, Babe Ruth cover, EX.**$45.00**
Sports Illustrated, 1975, August 11, Baseball Boom cover, EX **$15.00**
Sports Illustrated, 1976, November 22, Walter Payton cover, VG+...**$20.00**
Sports Illustrated, 1976, October 11, George Foster cover, VG+...**$20.00**
Sports Illustrated, 1977, January 17: Oakland Bowls 'Em Over cover, EX **$20.00**
Sports Illustrated, 1977, January 3, Clarence Davis cover, VG+...**$15.00**
Sports Illustrated, 1977, January 9, Terry Eurick cover, EX **$10.00**
Sports Illustrated, 1977, May 2, Reggie Jackson cover, EX ...**$20.00**
Sports World, 1983, June, Carlton cover, EX.................**$4.00**
Street & Smith Basketball, 1974, Dr J Erving, EX **$26.00**
This Week Magazine, 1954, September 14, Walt Disney's New $10,000,000 Toy article, VG.....................**$8.00**
Time, 1935, April 15, Dizzy Dean cover, NM..............**$60.00**
Time, 1941, January 6, Winston Churchill, Man of the Year, EX **$10.00**
Time, 1954, April 12, H-Bomb Over Pacific Ocean cover, EX **$12.00**
Time, 1954, July 26, Willie Mays cover, EX **$3.00**
Time, 1954, June 7, Humphrey Bogart cover, EX **$5.00**
Time, 1965, December, 31, John Maynard Keynes cover, EX **$5.00**
Time, 1971, March 8, Ali–Frazer cover, EX.................**$12.00**
True Confessions, Claudette Colbert cover, EX **$8.00**
True Confessions, 1938, February, Carole Lombard cover, EX **$12.00**
True Confessions, 1945, September, Marie Denham cover, EX **$5.00**
True Crime, May, 1955, VG...................................**$5.00**

True Story, 1934, December, Heather Angel cover, EX...**$7.00**
True Story, 1936, July, Clark Gable & Jeanette MacDonald cover, EX **$10.00**
True Story, 1936, October, Norma Shearer & Leslie Howard cover, EX **$8.00**
True Story, 1937, April, Carole Lombard cover, EX **$10.00**
True Story, 1938, April, Jean Rogers cover, EX **$6.00**
TV & Movie Play, 1968, February, Lee Majors cover, G+ .**$5.00**
TV-Radio Mirror, 1956, March, Steve Allen & Jane Meadows cover, VG **$7.50**
Vogue, 1940, January, swimsuit cover, EX...................**$8.00**
Walt Disney Magazine, 1958, February, Funicello cover, NM...**$15.00**

Woman's Day, 1946, January, EX, $4.00.

Pulp Magazines

As early as the turn of the century, pulp magazines were beginning to appear, but by the 1930s, their popularity had literally exploded. Called pulps because of the cheap wood-pulp paper they were printed on, crime and detective stories, westerns, adventure tales and mysteries were the order of the day. Crime pulps sold for as little as 10¢; some of the westerns were 15¢. Plots were imaginative and spicy, if not downright risque. The top three publishers were Street and Smith, Popular, and the Thrilling Group. Some of the more familiar pulp-magazine authors were Agatha Christy, Clarence E. Mulford, Erle Stanley Gardner, Ellery Queen, Edgar Rice Burroughs, Louis L'Amour, and Max Brand. Until the 1950s when slick-paper magazines signed their death warrant, they were published by the thousands. Because of the poor quality of their paper, many have not survived. Those that have are seldom rated better than very good. A near-mint to mint example will bring a premium price, since it is almost impossible to locate one so well preserved. Except for a few very rare editions, many are in the average price range suggested below — some much lower.

Advisor: J. Grant Thiessen (Pandora's Books Ltd.), Pulp Magazines (See Directory, Magazines)

Ace G-Man Stories, 1938, November–December, VG .**$30.00**
Adventure, 1939, April, VG.....................................**$20.00**
Amazing Stories, 1933, December, VG.......................**$35.00**
Amazing Stories, 1937, October, VG **$15.00**
Amazing Stories, 1944, December, VG.......................**$25.00**
Amazing Stories Quarterly, 1950, Fall, VG..................**$20.00**
Argosy, 1932, March 26, VG **$25.00**
Argosy All-Story, 1927, February 19, VG....................**$20.00**

Astounding, 1936, August, VG..............................**$35.00**
Avenger, 1940, May, VG.....................................**$40.00**
Black Mask, 1937, April, VG...............................**$35.00**
Dare-Devil Aces, 1933, June, G/VG........................**$22.00**
Dime Mystery, 1939, May, VG...............................**$25.00**
Dime Western, 1940, July, VG..............................**$15.00**
Doc Savage, 1935, September, G/VG.........................**$50.00**
Doc Savage, 1937, August, VG..............................**$65.00**
Doc Savage, 1940, October, VG.............................**$50.00**
Dusty Ayres & His Battle Birds, 1934, July, VG........**$100.00**
Exciting Western, 1947, September, VG.....................**$10.00**
Famous Fantastic Mysteries, 1943, March, VG.............**$15.00**
Fantastic Adventures, 1942, May, VG.......................**$15.00**
Fantastic Story, 1951, Summer, VG..........................**$8.00**
Fantastic Universe, 1949, November, VG.....................**$8.00**
G-Men, 1937, April, G/VG..................................**$20.00**
G-8 & His Battle Aces, 1931, October, VG.................**$80.00**
Great Detective, 1933, October, G/VG......................**$30.00**
Horror Stories, 1938, August–September, no cover, G-...**$20.00**
Jungle Stories, 1954, Winter, G...........................**$15.00**
Lone Eagle, 1934, May, VG.................................**$60.00**
Masked Rider, 1951, January, VG...........................**$15.00**
Operator #5, 1937, May-June, VG...........................**$80.00**
Planet Stories, 1944, Fall, VG............................**$35.00**
Popular Detective, 1943, June, VG.........................**$18.00**
Ranch Romances, 1939, April 2, VG.........................**$10.00**
Science Fiction Quarterly, 1953, May, VG..................**$10.00**
Shadow, 1933, May 1, G/VG.................................**$90.00**
Shadow, 1938, June 15, VG.................................**$75.00**
Short Stories, 1936, January, G/VG........................**$10.00**
Sky Birds, 1934, March, G/VG..............................**$20.00**
Sky Fighters, 1936, August, VG............................**$25.00**
Spicy-Adventure Stories, 1935, January, VG/EX...........**$60.00**
Spider, 1938, January, G..................................**$60.00**
Startling Stories, 1948, May, VG..........................**$10.00**
Super Science Stories, 1942, May, VG......................**$18.00**
Thrilling Wonder, 1939, February, VG......................**$15.00**
Top-Notch, 1912, July, G..................................**$15.00**
Top-Notch, 1933, June, G/VG...............................**$15.00**
Unknown, 1940, February, VG...............................**$45.00**
War Birds, 1936, August, VG...............................**$25.00**
Weird Tales, 1927, November, G............................**$80.00**
Weird Tales, 1928, October, G/VG..........................**$75.00**
Weird Tales, 1934, July, VG...............................**$75.00**
Weird Tales, 1938, October, VG............................**$65.00**
Weird Tales, 1943, March, VG..............................**$30.00**
Weird Tales, 1945, July, VG...............................**$25.00**
Western Story, 1928, June 6, VG...........................**$20.00**
Western Story, 1931, March 28, VG.........................**$18.00**
Western Story, 1941, June 28, VG..........................**$15.00**
Whisperer, 1941, June, G/VG...............................**$30.00**

Match Safes

Match safes or vesta boxes, as they are known in England, evolved to keep matches dry and to protect an individual from unintentional ignition. These containers were produced in enormous quantities over a 75-year period from various materials including silver, brass, aluminum, and gold, and their shapes and designs were limitless. They can usually be recognized by the presence of a small, rough area, which is actually a striking surface. Collectors should be cautious of numerous sterling reproductions currently on the market.

Advisor: George Sparacio (See Directory, Match Safes)

Advance Thresher, multicolor graphics, celluloid wrapped, 2¾x1½", EX...**$165.00**
Agate, book shape w/brass trim, 1¾x1¼", EX.........**$110.00**

Bird and flower motif, mother-of-pearl, with cigar cutter, 2¼x¾", EX, $150.00. (Photo courtesy of George Sparacio.)

Biscuit, figural brass, advertising Huntley & Palmer, 2⅛" dia, VG...**$165.00**
Bryant & May Wax Vesta/1893 Chicago World's Fair, tin w/lithograph design, 1¾x6¼", VG....................**$65.00**
Columbian Expo, medallion on ear of corn, figural, plated brass, 2½x1", EX....................................**$275.00**
Dangerfield, igniting safe, nickel silver, 1¾x3¼", EX.**$70.00**
Edgeworth Tobacco, lithographed tin, striker on bottom, 2½x3⅛", EX...**$5.00**
Filigree, floral motif on silver, 2½x1½", EX.............**$135.00**
Gladstone bust, figural, plated brass, 2½x1¼", EX...**$195.00**
Guide, leather-wrapped book form, lady on chamber pot on inside, 1⅝x1¼", VG.....................................**$325.00**
International Tailoring, Indian on lid, striker at both ends, plated brass, 2⅞x1⅜", EX.......................**$37.00**
Ivory, book form w/applied sterling initial, 1⅞x1⅛", EX..**$135.00**
Lady in boat motif, stamped Sterline, 2¼x1¾", EX..**$130.00**
Love's Flight, celluloid wrapped w/multicolor graphics, Whitehead & Hoag, 2¾x1½", EX....................**$135.00**
National Lead, celluloid wrapped w/multicolor graphics, 2⅝x1½", VG..**$45.00**
Oriental dragon, domed lid, quasi-figural, brass, 2½x1¼", EX..**$245.00**
Pen box, embossed D Leonardt on brass, 2⅛x2⅝x¾", EX.**$50.00**
Red Top Rye, thermoplastic w/slip top, 2⅞x1⅛", EX...**$65.00**
Schlitz Beer, leather wrapped w/cigar cutter, 2¾x1½", EX...**$85.00**
Shoe, figural, aluminum, flat type w/striker on heel, 2⅞x1¼", EX..**$75.00**
Shoe, figural, plated silver w/glass stones in sole & wire laces, 1⅜x2⅝", EX.....................................**$265.00**
Slide, embossed Dutch tavern motif on 830 silver, 1⅜x1⅞", EX..**$87.00**
Superdux, cylindrical, hard rubber, 3¼x1¼", EX.......**$25.00**
Union Cigar Makers, celluloid wrapped w/blue graphics, 2½x1½", EX..**$70.00**
US Arms w/bullet & target, silverplate, 2⅝x1½", EX.**$125.00**

McCoy Pottery

This is probably the best-known of all American potteries, due to the wide variety of goods they produced from 1910 until the pottery finally closed only a few years ago.

They were located in Roseville, Ohio, the pottery center of the United States during the first half of the century. They're most famous for their cookie jars, of which were made several hundred styles and variations. (For a listing of these, see the section entitled Cookie Jars.) McCoy is also well known for their figural planters, novelty kitchenware, and dinnerware.

They used a variety of marks over the years, but with little consistency, since it was a common practice to discontinue an item for awhile and then bring it out again decorated in a manner that would be in sync with current tastes. All of McCoy's marks were 'in the mold.' None were ink stamped, so very often the in-mold mark remained as it was when the mold was originally created. Most marks contain the McCoy name, though some of the early pieces were simply signed 'NM' for Nelson McCoy (Sanitary and Stoneware Company, the company's original title). Early stoneware pieces were sometimes impressed with a shield containing a number. If you have a piece with the Lancaster Colony Company mark (three curved lines — the left one beginning as a vertical and terminating as a horizontal, the other two formed as 'C's contained in the curve of the first), you'll know that your piece was made after the mid-seventies when McCoy was owned by that group. Today even these later pieces are becoming collectible.

If you'd like to learn more about this company, we recommend *The Collector's Encyclopedia of McCoy Pottery* and *The Collector's Encyclopedia of Brush-McCoy Pottery*, both by Sharon and Bob Huxford, and *McCoy Pottery, Collector's Reference & Value Guide*, by Bob and Margaret Hanson and Craig Nissen. All are published by Collector Books.

A note regarding cookie jars: beware of *new* cookie jars marked McCoy. It seems that McCoy never registered their trademark, and it is now legally used by a small company in Rockwood, Tennessee. Not only do they use the original mark, but they are reproducing some of the original jars as well. If you're not an experienced collector, you may have trouble distinguishing the new from the old. Some (but not all) are dated #93, the '#' one last attempt to fool the novice, but there are differences to watch for. The new ones are slightly smaller in size, and the finish is often flawed. They are also using the McCoy mark on jars never produced by the original company, such as Little Red Riding Hood and the Luzianne mammy.

See also Cookie Jars.

Newsletter: *The Nelson-McCoy Express*
Carol Seman, Editor
7670 Chippewa
Brecksville, OH 44141; 303-469-2310

Ashtray/novelty, 2 open hands form tray, tan............	**$30.00**
Bank, Happy Face	**$20.00**
Bank, Woodsey Owl..	**$75.00**
Basket, embossed leaves, metallic glaze, 1970...........	**$50.00**

Basket, green & cream basketweave look w/cream interior, marked, 1957...**$75.00**
Bean pot, painted apple on tan, similar to Purinton Apple in appearance, marked Heinz by McCoy, 1960s, w/lid...**$75.00**
Beer stein, Schlitz, 1971 ....**$30.00**
Bookends, lilies & green leaves, marked, 1948, pr...**$125.00**
Bowl, centerpiece, leaf form w/sm feet, brown, late 1960s.**$18.00**
Cache pot, double; bird between 2 flower-form pots, marked, 1948..**$35.00**
Coffee server, conical shape, turquoise, marked Eastman USA, late 1950s **$45.00**

Cornucopia vase, pink, marked, 1947, $24.00; Vase with arrowhead leaf, turquoise, marked, early 1940s, $22.00; Cornucopia vase, yellow, marked, early 1940s, $20.00.

Custard cup, embossed decoration along rim on tan, marked..**$8.00**
Dog dish, To Man's Best Friend, His Dog, marked **$60.00**
Flowerpot & saucer, melon ribs, pink, marked, 1959........**$12.00**
Jardiniere, embossed flowers along body, zig-zag borders at rim & base, dark green, marked, 1954..................**$28.00**
Jardiniere, Rustic, embossed pine cones, brown & green tones, marked, 1945 ....**$35.00**
Jardiniere, Springwood, white flowers w/black trim on green, marked, 1961...**$35.00**
Novelty, pelican, white w/painted details, no mark ...**$50.00**
Pillow vase, Jewell line, applied dragonfly w/jewels, marked, 1956 ....**$40.00**
Pitcher/vase, fish figural, detailed molding, green, minimum value **$350.00**
Pitcher/vase, parrot figural, multicolor wings, marked, 1952..**$175.00**
Planter, butterfly figural, creamy pastel green, unmarked, 1940 ....**$50.00**
Planter, conch shell, creamy white w/pink shading along edge, unmarked, 1954...**$30.00**
Planter, convertible auto, wire windshield, marked USA, 1954 ....**$35.00**
Planter, cradle, many embossed details, blue, marked.**$22.00**
Planter, lamb, white w/blue bow, unmarked, lg........**$30.00**
Planter, Liberty Bell, 8th of July embossed on base, marked, 1954..**$200.00**
Planter, pheasant, naturalistic colors, marked, 1959 ...**$35.00**
Planter, poodle w/head up, black w/red collar, marked, 1956...**$80.00**
Planter, rooster, gray w/red comb & waddle, marked, 1951...**$35.00**
Planter, twin shells, dark green, marked, 1953 ....**$15.00**
Planter, white w/central band that resembles stained glass, rectangular, marked, 1950s **$150.00**

Planter, zebra mother & baby, black & white stripes, marked, 1956, scarce..**$225.00**

Planter, 5 Scotties embossed across front, marked, 1949 ..**$30.00**

Planter/bookends, spaniel w/game bird in mouth, marked, 1955, pr **$100.00**

Salt & pepper shakers, head of cabbage is formed when shakers are placed together, dark green, pr.........**$60.00**

Tea set, Ivy, embossed ivy on tan, twig handles, marked, 1950, 3-pc...**$100.00**

Teapot, cat figural, paw spout & tail handle, black & white w/pink bow, 1971 ....**$85.00**

Teapot, Sunburst Gold, marked, 1957.........................**$65.00**

Vase, Antique Rose, pink roses on white, bulbous, flared neck w/scalloped rim, marked, 1959 ....**$25.00**

Vase, classic form w/embossed leaf decor, ornate handles, tan, marked, 1946, 9"...**$25.00**

Vase, English Ivy, green ivy on cream, brown handles & trim at rim & base, marked, 1953............................**$50.00**

Vase, Ripple Ware, green w/red at rippled rim, handles, 1950, 7"...**$20.00**

Vase, scrolling feather form, black & white, unmarked, 1950s **$40.00**

Vase, wheat embossed on 6-sided shape w/handles, dark green, marked, 1953...**$35.00**

Vase, Wild Rose, pink roses on pale yellow, marked, 1952, 6" **$40.00**

Wall pocket, leaf shape, marked, 1950, $28.00.

Wall pocket, orange & leaves, 1953 ....**$65.00**

Wall pocket, Sunburst Gold on fan, marked, 1957 .....**$60.00**

Wall pocket, 3 bananas & leaves, 1953.......................**$80.00**

Window box, Brocade line, pink w/green splotches, green interior, rectangular, marked, 1956.....................**$154.00**

Window box, embossed stone shapes form rectangle, dark green, marked, 1954, lg.......................................**$20.00**

Brown Drip Dinnerware

One of McCoy's dinnerware lines that was introduced in the 1960s is beginning to attract a following. It's a glossy brown stoneware-type pattern with frothy white decoration around the rims. Similar lines of brown stoneware were made by many other companies, Hull and Pfaltzgraff among them.

Advisor: Jo-Ann Bentz (See Directory, Hull)

Baker, oval, 10½"...**$12.00**

Baker, oval, 12½", from $18 to....................................**$22.00**

Baker, oval 9"...**$10.00**

Bean pot, individual; 12-oz...**$4.00**

Bean pot, 1½-qt, from $15 to **$20.00**

Bean pot, 3-qt, from $25 to **$30.00**

Bowl, cereal; 6"...**$6.00**

Bowl, lug soup; 12-oz...**$8.00**

Bowl, lug soup; 18-oz...**$10.00**

Bowl, spaghetti or salad; 12½"....................................**$15.00**

Bowl, vegetable; divided..**$15.00**

Bowl, vegetable; 9"...**$12.00**

Butter dish, ¼-lb...**$20.00**

Candle holders, pr, from $18 to....................................**$22.00**

Canister, Coffee..**$45.00**

Casserole, 2-qt..**$15.00**

Casserole, 3½-qt...**$20.00**

Casserole, 3-qt, w/hen on nest lid, from $45 to.........**$50.00**

Corn tray, individual; from $10 to **$14.00**

Creamer..**$4.00**

Cruet, Oil or Vinegar, each, from $12 to **$15.00**

Cup, 8-oz..**$5.00**

Custard cup, 6-oz...**$4.00**

Gravy boat, from $12 to...**$15.00**

Mug, pedestal base, 12-oz...**$7.50**

Mug, 12-oz...**$6.50**

Mug, 8-oz...**$5.00**

Pie plate, 9", from $15 to...**$18.00**

Pitcher, jug style, 32-oz..**$20.00**

Pitcher, jug style, 80-oz..**$30.00**

Plate, dinner; 10"..**$10.00**

Plate, salad; 7"...**$6.50**

Plate, soup & sandwich; w/lg cup ring **$10.00**

Platter, fish form, 18"..**$32.00**

Platter, oval, 14"...**$15.00**

Saucer...**$3.00**

Souffle dish, 2-qt...**$9.50**

Teapot, 6-cup..**$20.00**

Metlox Pottery

Founded in the late 1920s in Manhattan Beach, California, this company initially produced tile and commercial advertising signs. By the early thirties, their business in these areas had dwindled, and they began to concentrate their efforts on the manufacture of dinnerware, figurines, and kitchenware. Carl Gibbs has authored *Collector's Encyclopedia of Metlox Potteries* published by Collector Books, which we recommend for more information.

Carl Romanelli was the designer responsible for modeling many of the figural pieces they made during the late thirties and early forties. These items are usually imprinted with his signature and are very collectible today. Coming on strong is their line of 'Poppets,' made from the mid-sixties through the mid-seventies. There were eighty-eight in all, whimsical, comical, sometimes grotesque. They represented characters ranging from the seven-piece Salvation Army Group to royalty, religious figures, policemen, and professionals. They came with a nametag, some had paper labels, others backstamps.

Poppytrail was the trade name for their kitchen and dinnerware lines. Among their more popular patterns were California Ivy, Red Rooster, Homestead Provincial, and the later embossed patterns, Sculptured Grape, Sculptured Zinnia, and Sculptured Daisy.

Some of their lines can be confusing. There are two 'rooster' lines, Red Rooster (red, orange, and brown) and California Provincial (this one is in dark green and burgundy), and two 'homestead' lines, Colonial Homestead (red, orange, and brown like the Red Rooster line) and Homestead Provincial. Just remember the Provincial patterns are done in dark green and burgundy.

See also Cookie Jars.

Animal Keeper, Burrito the Burro	**$30.00**
Ashtray, California Provincial, 1950, 10"	**$40.00**
Ashtray, Colonial Heritage, 1956, 4½"	**$18.00**
Ashtray, Mosaic, 1950s, 4"	**$25.00**
Ashtray, Owl Line, 1960s, 6"	**$20.00**
Au Gratin, American Heritage (Vernon), 1980s	**$22.00**
Baker, Gold Dahlia, 1974, oval, 11"	**$25.00**
Baker, Vernon Della Robbia, 1965, oval, 12⅛"	**$50.00**
Bowl, Aztec, vegetable, 9⅜"	**$50.00**
Bowl, cereal; Colonial Heritage, 1956	**$16.00**
Bowl, cereal; Vernon Pacific Blue, 1971, 6¼"	**$10.00**
Bowl, Daisy, mid-1960s, footed, w/lid, 4¾"	**$40.00**
Bowl, fruit; California Strawberry, 1961, 5⅜"	**$12.00**
Bowl, fruit; Colonial Garden, 1967, 5½"	**$12.00**
Bowl, salad; Red Rooster (Decorated or Red), 1955/1956, 11"	**$80.00**
Bowl, soup; Colonial Heritage, 1956	**$20.00**
Bowl, soup; Sonoma, 1988, 8"	**$20.00**
Bowl, vegetable; Provincial Blue, 1950, 12"	**$65.00**
Bowl, vegetable; Tropicana, 1960, round, divided, 9"	**$25.00**
Bowl, vegetable; Vernon Antiqua, divided, round	**$45.00**
Bowl, vegetable; 1942 Series, 1985, round, med	**$25.00**
Butter dish, California Spatterware, 1987, w/lid	**$28.00**
Butter dish, Capistrano (Vernon), 1978, w/lid	**$35.00**
Butter dish, Tradition White, 1967, w/lid	**$55.00**
Cake plate, Daisy, mid-1960s, 13"	**$55.00**
Candle holder, Mosaic, 1950s, 6"	**$45.00**
Canister, Daisy, mid-1960s, 3-qt	**$45.00**
Canister, flour; Provincial Blue, 1950, w/lid	**$85.00**
Canister, Owl Line, 1960s, 1½-qt	**$35.00**
Canister, Strawberry (Shape), 1960s, 2½-qt	**$40.00**

Canisters, flour; Red Rooster (Red or Decorated), from $75.00 to $80.00 each.

Casserole, Mission, 1988, w/lid, 2-qt	**$95.00**
Celery dish, California Freeform, 1954	**$55.00**

Celery dish, California Ivy, 1946	**$40.00**
Chip & dip, Daisy	**$55.00**
Chip & dip, Pineapple (White)	**$22.00**
Chip & dip, Sombrero	**$45.00**
Chip & dip, Watermelon, sm	**$25.00**
Coaster, Colonial Heritage, 1956	**$20.00**
Coaster, Provincial Blue, 1950, 3¾"	**$22.00**
Coffeepot, California Provincial, 1950, 7-cup	**$125.00**
Coffeepot, Rattan (Vernon), 1979, w/lid, 44-oz	**$75.00**
Creamer, California Contempora, 1955	**$30.00**
Creamer, Golden Garden, 1967, 9-oz	**$22.00**
Creamer, Red Rooster (Decorated or Red), 1955/1956, 6-oz	**$25.00**
Cruet, vinegar; Provincial Blue, 1950, w/lid	**$38.00**
Cup & saucer, California Aztec, 1955	**$23.00**
Cup & saucer, California Ivy, 1946	**$14.00**
Cup & saucer, Galaxy (First Series), 1985	**$10.00**
Cup & saucer, Red Rooster (Decorated), 1955	**$16.00**
Cup & saucer, Vernon Tulips, 1971	**$12.00**
Egg cup, California Ivy, 1946	**$25.00**
Egg cup, Colonial Heritage, 1956	**$28.00**
Figurine, deer, Carl Romanelli, 7"	**$100.00**
Figurine, fawn, Miniature Series, 4¼"	**$40.00**
Figurine, horse, saddle bred, 6x6"	**$95.00**
Figurine, large circus/draft horse, Nostalgia line, 11x8"	**$135.00**
Figurine, rooster, Carl Romanelli, 8¼"	**$90.00**
Gravy boat, California Aztec, 1955	**$45.00**
Gravy boat, California Ivy, 1946, 12-oz	**$30.00**
Jam jar, Strawberry (shape), 1960s, w/lid, 6-oz	**$25.00**
Lazy susan, Homestead Provincial, 1950, complete 7-pc set	**$200.00**
Leaf dish, Ivy, late 1950s, 9x7"	**$25.00**
Leaf dish, Strawberry (Second Series), 1980s, w/applied fruit	**$28.00**
Leaf dish, Tonga Pod, late 1950s, 13x4"	**$28.00**
Mug, California Rose, 1959, 8-oz	**$15.00**
Mug, La Mancha White, 1971, 10-oz	**$20.00**
Mug, Strawberry (Shape), 1960s, footed, 6-oz	**$22.00**
Pepper mill, Homestead Provincial, 1950	**$50.00**
Pitcher, Colonial Heritage, 1956, sm	**$45.00**
Pitcher, Holstein Herd, 1988, 2-qt	**$60.00**
Pitcher, Homestead Provincial, 1950, 1½-pt	**$50.00**
Pitcher, water; Galaxy (Second Series), 1988, 2-qt	**$45.00**
Planter, Owl Line, 1960s, w/3 owl figures, 5¾"	**$50.00**
Plate, bread & butter; Brookside (Vernon), 1976, 6⅞"	**$9.00**
Plate, bread & butter; California Ivy, 1946, 6½"	**$8.00**
Plate, bread & butter; Colonial Heritage, 1956	**$8.00**
Plate, bread & butter; La Mancha White, 1971, 6½"	**$8.00**
Plate, bread & butter; Spring Garland (Vernon), 1979, 6⅞"	**$7.00**
Plate, buffet; Sonoma, 1988, 12"	**$75.00**
Plate, dinner; Blue Bird (Vernon), 1980s, 10¼"	**$10.00**
Plate, dinner; California Freeform, 1954	**$25.00**
Plate, dinner; Galaxy (Second Series), 1988, 10½"	**$10.00**
Plate, dinner; Holstein Herd, 1988, 10½"	**$14.00**
Plate, dinner; Provincial Blue, 1950, 10"	**$18.00**
Plate, dinner; Vernon Calypso, 1971, 10¼"	**$9.00**
Plate, luncheon; Strawberry (Shape), 1960s, 9⅜"	**$22.00**
Plate, luncheon; Vernon Antiqua, 1966	**$18.00**

Plate, salad; Morning Glory (Vernon), 1980, 8" **$9.00**
Plate, salad; Woodland Gold, 1959, 8" **$10.00**
Platter, Colonial Garden, 1967, oval, 14¼" **$40.00**
Platter, Mesa (Vernon), 1976, oval, 13" **$30.00**
Platter, Red Rooster (Decorated), 1955, oval, 9½" **$35.00**
Platter, Traditions, 1985, oval, lg...............................**$30.00**
Poppet, Alaskan Girl, 5" **$35.00**
Poppet, Arnie w/4" bowl **$55.00**
Poppet, Chester, saxophone man, Salvation Army Group,
    8" **$55.00**
Poppet, Joy, bell ringer, 6½"......................................**$35.00**
Poppet, Lorna, standing girl, 8" **$45.00**
Poppet, Salty the Sea Captain, 5¼" **$45.00**
Poppett, Emma the Cook, 8" **$45.00**

Provincial Blue: Teapot, $85.00; Pepper mill, $45.00; Ashtray, $15.00.

Quiche server, American Heritage (Vernon), 1980s, 10½"....**$32.00**
Salt & pepper shakers, California Spatterware, 1985, pr..**$16.00**
Salt & pepper shakers, Homestead Provincial, 1950, pr..**$30.00**
Salt & pepper shakers, Mission Verde, 1966, pr..........**$18.00**
Salt & pepper shakers, Vernon Florence, 1969, pr......**$13.00**
Salt & pepper shakers, Woodland Gold, 1959, pr.......**$24.00**
Sauce boat, California Strawberry, 1961, 1¼-pt...........**$40.00**
Sugar bowl, Golden Garden, 1967, w/lid, 12-oz.........**$25.00**
Sugar bowl, Red Rooster (Decorated or Red), 1955/1956,
    w/lid **$30.00**
Sugar canister, Colonial Heritage, w/lid.....................**$70.00**
Teapot, Blue Dahlia, 1974, 6-cup **$50.00**
Teapot, La Mancha Green, 1968, w/lid, 6-cup **$95.00**

Vase, angelfish, Carl Romanelli, 8½", $90.00.

Vase, bud; Mosaic, 1950s, 6" **$40.00**
Vase, swordfish, Carl Romanelli, 9"...........................**$125.00**

Model Kits

By and far the majority of model kits were vehicular, and though worth collecting, especially when you can find them still mint in the box, the really big news are the figure kits. Most were made by Aurora during the 1960s. Especially hot are the movie monsters, though TV and comic strip character kits are popular with collectors too. As a rule of thumb, assembled kits are priced about half as much as conservatively priced mint-in-box kits. The condition of the box is just as important as the contents, and top collectors will usually pay an additional 15% (sometimes even more) for a box that retains the factory plastic wrap still intact. For more information, we recommend *Aurora History and Price Guide* by Bill Bruegman and *Classic Plastic Model Kits* by Rick Polizzi. *Schroeder's Toys, Antique to Modern,* contains prices and descriptions of hundreds of models by a variety of manufacturers.

Club: *International Figure Kit Club*

Magazine: *Kit Builders* Magazine
Gordy's
P.O. Box 201
Sharon Center, OH 44274-0201; 216-239-1657 or FAX 216-239-2991

Magazine: *Model and Toy Collector Magazine*
137 Casterton Ave.
Akron, OH 44303; 216-836-0668 or Fax 216-869-8668

AEF Design, Aliens, Burke #AC-4, 1980s, 1/35 scale, MIB..**$20.00**
Airfix, High Chaparral Set #38, 1/75 scale, MIB **$8.00**
Airfix, Moonraker James Bond, 1979, M (VG+ box)...**$35.00**
AMT, Flintstones Rock Cruncher, 1974, MIB (sealed).**$45.00**
AMT, Pacer Wagon Kit #T484, NMIB **$25.00**
AMT, Star Trek, Klingon Battle Cruiser, 1968, MIB (sealed)...**$60.00**
AMT, 1949 Ford Coupe #T290, white, 1/25 scale, MIB..**$25.00**
AMT, 1953 Corvette T-310, M (VG box) **$25.00**
AMT, 1962 Corvette, NMIB..**$20.00**
AMT/Ertl, Deep Space 9, Runabout, MIB **$15.00**
AMT/Ertl, Dick Tracy Coupe #6107, 1/25, 1989, 1990, MIB.**$10.00**
AMT/Ertl, Robo 1 Police Car, MIB (sealed) **$10.00**
Aurora, Cave, Prehistoric Scenes, 2nd issue, 1972, M (NM
    sealed box)...**$45.00**
Aurora, Chinese Junk, 1962, M (EX+ box) **$35.00**
Aurora, Corsair American Privateer, 1959, M (G box) ..**$20.00**
Aurora, Cro-Magon Man, Prehistoric Scenes, 1971, M (M
    sealed box)...**$35.00**
Aurora, Dr Jekyll, Monsters of the Movies, MIB (sealed)..**$100.00**
Aurora, Dracula, Glow-in-the-Dark, assembled, 1972,
    NM **$35.00**
Aurora, Giant Wooly Mammoth, 1972, M (EX+ box)..**$100.00**
Aurora, Hunchback of Notre Dame, Glow-in-the-Dark, 1972,
    MIB **$150.00**
Aurora, Neanderthal Man, Prehistoric Scenes, 1st issue, EX+
    (EX+ box) **$55.00**
Aurora, Pendulum, Monster Scenes, M (NM box) **$125.00**
Aurora, Rat Patrol, 1967, M (EX+ box) **$100.00**
Aurora, Robin, Comic Scenes, MIB (sealed).............**$125.00**

Aurora, Robin the Boy Wonder, original issue, MIB, $150.00.

Aurora, Russian Stalin Tank #323, 1972, M (G box) ...**$35.00**

Aurora, Superman, Comic Scenes, 1974, MIB (sealed) .**$60.00**

Aurora, Viking Ship #230, 1/80, 1962, MIB **$60.00**

Aurora, Witch #470, Glow-in-the-Dark, 1972, MIB ...**$200.00**

Bachmann, Animals of the World, Lion #7101, 1959, 1/12, MIB **$40.00**

Bachmann, Birds of the World, Bohemian Waxwing #9011, 1/1, 1959, MIB...**$35.00**

Bachmann, Storytown USA, Humpty Dumpty, 1950s, M (VG box) **$70.00**

Bandai, Godzilla #0003526, 1990, 1/350, MIB **$55.00**

Bandai, Star-Blazers, Space Cruiser #0031235, 1/500, MIB **$75.00**

Billiken, Creature From the Black Lagoon, MIB **$120.00**

Billiken, Frankenstein, MIB....................................**$110.00**

Dark Horse, King Kong #K1092, 1992, MIB.................**$75.00**

Dark Horse, Predator, MIB......................................**$225.00**

Fun Dimensions, Colossal Mantis, MIB.....................**$100.00**

Graphitti, Superman Statue, MIB..............................**$110.00**

Halcyon, Alien, Alien Face Hugger #V02, vinyl, 1/1, 1991, MIB **$110.00**

Hawk, Explorer 18 Earth Satellite, NMIB....................**$35.00**

Hawk, Frantic Cats, Frantics, 1965, M (EX+ box)........**$75.00**

Hawk, Weird-Ohs, Drag Hag #536, 1960s, MIB (sealed) .**$150.00**

Horizon, Bride of Frankenstein #003, 1988, MIB **$50.00**

Horizon, Mole People, Mole Man #002, 1988, MIB **$40.00**

Hubley, Model A Roadster, MIB, $55.00.

Hubley, 1930 Packard Roadster #4800-500, metal, sealed contents, M (EX box)..**$60.00**

Imai, Batmobile, TV version, MIB **$75.00**

Imai, Speed Racer Mach 5, MIB **$65.00**

Imai, UFO, Sky #1241, 1983, MIB **$45.00**

ITC, US Coast Guard Rescue Boat, 1950s, M (EX+ box)...**$60.00**

Kaiyodo, Aliens, Queen, MIB **$275.00**

Kaiyodo, Aliens, Warrior, MIB **$200.00**

Lifelike, The General, 1971, M (EX box) **$75.00**

Lindberg, Flying Saucer, assembled, EX.......................**$30.00**

Lindberg, Ryan Navion Airplane, 1956, MIB................**$35.00**

Lodela (Revell of Mexico), Lost in Space, Cyclops Diorama #F820, MIB **$135.00**

Lunar, 2001: Space Odyssey, Discovery, MIB..............**$60.00**

Merit, 1949 Alfa Romeo Car #4601, red, 1/24, MIB **$25.00**

Monogram, Classic 1930 Packard Boattail Speedster, 1975, MIB (sealed)..**$25.00**

Monogram, First Lunar Landing, 1970, NMIB.............**$35.00**

Monogram, Invaders, UFO #6012, 1979, 1/72, MIB....**$75.00**

Monogram, Tyrannosaurus Rex, 1987, M (VG box) ...**$35.00**

Monogram, Voyage to the Bottom of the Sea, Flying Sub #86011, 1/60, 1979, MIB (sealed) **$100.00**

Monogram, 1957 Corvette, 1977, NMIB **$15.00**

MPC, Beverly Hillbillies TV truck, 1968, NMIB........**$100.00**

MPC, Cannonball Run, Countach #0682, 1/25, 1981, MIB ..**$40.00**

MPC, Walt Disney's Pirates of the Caribbean, Dead Men Tell No Tales, MIB, $120.00. (Photo courtesy of John and Sheri Pavone.)

MPC, Disney's Pirates of the Caribbean, Hoist High the Jolly Roger, 1972, M (EX+ box)....................................**$35.00**

MPC, Dukes of Hazzard, Daisy's Jeep CJ #0662, 1/25, 1980, MIB **$50.00**

MPC, Knight Rider, Knight 2000-KITT #6377, 1/25, 1988, MIB **$50.00**

MPC, Star Wars, C-3PO, 1977, MIB............................**$30.00**

MPC, Star Wars, Darth Vader Bust Action Model, 1978, MIB (sealed) **$55.00**

MPC, Star Wars (Return of the Jedi), C-3PO, 1983, MIB (sealed) **$25.00**

MPC, 1976 Corvette, NMIB **$30.00**

Multiple, Rube Goldberg's Signal for Shipwrecked Sailor #957, 1965, MIB **$75.00**

Nitto, SF3D, Armored Fighting Suit #23072, 1/20, 1980s, MIB **$20.00**

Palmer, Animals of the World, Atlantic Sailfish, 1950s, M (EX+ box) **$25.00**

Palmer, Gatling Gun, MIB..**$15.00**

Parks, Born Losers, Fidel Castro, MIB......................**$100.00**

Parks, Born Losers, Napoleon, 1965, MIB **$75.00**

Pyro, Ankylosaurus #D277, 1/24, 1968, MIB **$25.00**

Pyro, Gladiator Three-Wheeled Motorcycle #175, 1970, M (EX box) **$35.00**

Pyro, Gladiator Three-Wheeled Motorcycle #175, 1970, MIB (sealed) **$70.00**

Pyro, Ring Necked Pheasant, Mark Trail Series, M (EX+ box) **$35.00**

Raven Hood, Vampirella (Jim Fawkes) #JF, 1/16, MIB .**$145.00**

Renwal, Botany Science, 1964, MIB (sealed)...............**$45.00**

Renwal, Visible Horse #807, 1/3, 1960s, MIB...........**$145.00**

Revell, Beatles, Ringo, M (VG+ sealed box) **$200.00**

Revell, Billy Carter's Redneck-Power Pick-Up, 1978, MIB (sealed)...**$200.00**

Revell, Chicken Little, Miracle of Life in an Eggshell, 1976, M (EX box) **$60.00**

Revell, Deal's Wheels, Glitter Bug #1352, 1970, MIB (sealed) **$75.00**

Revell, Disney, Perri the Squirrel #1900, 1/1, 1956, MIB..**$100.00**

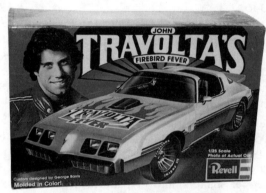

Revell, John Travolta's Firebird Fever, 1979, M in sealed box, $42.00. (Photo courtesy of June Moon.)

Revell, Dune Ornithopter #1775, 1/50, 1985, MIB **$50.00**

Revell, Grummen F4F-4 Wildcat, 1971, MIB (sealed) .**$25.00**

Revell, Magnum PI, TC's Helicopter #4416, 1/32, 1981, MIB.**$50.00**

Revell, Magnum PI 308 GTS Ferrari, 1982, MIB (sealed) ..**$35.00**

Revell, Moonraker, James Bond Space Shuttle #4306, 1/14, 1979, MIB (sealed)...**$20.00**

Revell, Robotech, Garton, 1984, MIB (sealed)............**$25.00**

Revell, Shuttle Challenger #4526, 1/144, 1982, MIB....**$16.00**

Revell, 1965 Ford Mustang Fastback #H-1286, yellow, 1/16, MIB **$65.00**

Screamin', Flash Gordon, 1/4, 1993, NM (EX+ box) **$35.00**

Screamin', Tales From the Crypt, Cryptkeeper #1300, 1994, 1\4, MIB **$50.00**

Superior Plastics, Deep Sea Lobster, 1962, M (G box)..**$40.00**

Testors, Grodies, Killer McBash #539, MIB.................**$30.00**

Testors, Silly Surfers, Beach Bunny Catchin' Rays, 1990, MIB.**$15.00**

Testors, Weird-Ohs, Freddie Flameout #733, 1990s, MIB (sealed) **$15.00**

Tsukuda, Batman Returns, Penguin #07, vinyl, 1/6, 1992, MIB **$85.00**

Tsukuda, Ghostbusters, Stay Puft Man #15, vinyl, 1/90, 1984, MIB **$125.00**

Union, Shuttle Challenger #15, 1/288, 1980s, MIB......**$20.00**

Moon and Star

Moon and Star (originally called Palace) was first produced in the 1880s by John Adams & Company of Pittsburgh. But because the glassware was so heavy to transport, it was made for only a few years. In the 1960s, Joseph Weishar of Wheeling, West Virginia, owner of Island Mould & Machine Company, reproduced some of the original molds and incorporated the pattern into approximately forty new and different items. Two of the largest distributors of this line were L.E. Smith of Mt. Pleasant, Pennsylvania, who pressed their own glass, and L.G. Wright of New Martinsville, West Virginia, who had theirs pressed by Fostoria, Fenton, and Westmoreland. Both companies carried a large and varied assortment of shapes and colors. Several other companies were involved in its manufacture as well, especially of the smaller items. All in all, there may be as many as one hundred different pieces, plenty to keep you involved and excited as you do your searching.

The glassware is already very collectible, even though it is still being made on a limited basis. Colors you'll see most often are amberina (yellow shading to orange-red), green, amber, crystal, light blue, and ruby. Pieces in ruby and light blue are most collectible and harder to find than the other colors, which seem to be abundant. Purple, pink, cobalt, amethyst, tan slag, and light green and blue opalescent were made, too, but on a lesser scale.

Current L.E. Smith catalogs contain a dozen or so pieces that are still available in crystal, pink, cobalt (lighter than the old shade), with an iridized finish. A new color was introduced in 1992, teal green, and at the water set in sapphire blue opalescent was pressed in 1993 by Weishar Enterprises. They are now producing limited editions in various colors and shapes, but they are marking their glassware 'Weishar,' to distinguish it from the old line. Cranberry Ice (light transparent pink) was introduced in 1994.

Our values are given for ruby and light blue. For amberina, green, and amber, deduct 30%. These colors are less in demand, and unless your prices are reasonable, you may find them harder to sell. Read *Mysteries of the Moon and Star* by George and Linda Breeze for more information.

Newsletter: *National Moon & Star News*
George and Linda Breeze
4207 Fox Creek
Mt. Vernon, IL 62864

Ashtray, allover pattern, moons form scallops along rim, 4 rests, 8" dia...**$25.00**

Ashtray, patterned moons at rim, star in base, 6-sided, 5½" **$18.00**

Ashtray, patterned moons at rim, star in base, 6-sided, 8½" **$25.00**

Banana boat, allover pattern, moons form scallops along rim, 9", from $28 to **$32.00**

Banana boat, allover pattern, moons form scallops along rim, 12" **$45.00**

Basket, allover pattern, moons form scallops along rim, footed, incurvate upright handles, 4", from $12 to.....**$15.00**

Basket, allover pattern, moons form scallops along rim, solid handle, 9", from $30 to...**$35.00**

Bell, pattern along body of bell w/plain rim & handle, 6", from $25 to...**$30.00**

Bowl, allover pattern, footed, crimped rim, 7½" **$35.00**

Butter dish, allover pattern, scalloped foot, patterned lid & finial, 6x5½" dia, from $45 to **$50.00**

Butter dish, allover pattern, stars form scallops along rim of base, star finial, oval, ¼-lb, 8½" **$45.00**

Butter/cheese dish, patterned lid, plain base, 7" dia ..**$40.00**

Cake plate, allover pattern, low collared base, 13".....**$50.00**

Cake salver, allover pattern w/scalloped rim, raised foot w/scalloped edge, 5x12" **$50.00**

Cake stand, allover pattern, plate removes from standard, 2-pc, 11"..**$65.00**

Candle bowl, allover pattern, footed, 8", from $28 to ..**$32.00**

Candle holder, allover pattern, bowl style w/ring handle, 2x5½" **$18.00**

Candle holders, allover pattern, flared base, 4½", pr .**$25.00**

Candle holders, allover pattern, flared foot w/scalloped edge, 6", pr..**$35.00**

Candle lamp, allover pattern, candlestick base, matching shade, 3-pc **$50.00**

Candle lamp, patterned shade, clear base, 2-pc, 7½"..**$25.00**

Candy dish, allover pattern on base & lid, footed ball shape, 6" **$25.00**

Canister, allover pattern, 1-lb or 2-lb, from $12 to......**$15.00**

Canister, allover pattern, 3½-lb or 5-lb, from $18 to ..**$22.00**

Chandelier, dome shape w/allover pattern **$100.00**

Cheese dish, patterned base, clear plain lid, 9½", from $65 to **$70.00**

Compote, allover pattern, footed, flared crimped rim, 5"...**$22.00**

Compote, allover pattern, raised foot, patterned lid & finial, 7½x6"..**$40.00**

Compote, allover pattern, raised foot on stem, patterned lid & finial, 10x8"..**$65.00**

Compote, allover pattern, raised foot on stem, patterned lid & finial, 12x8"..**$75.00**

Compote, allover pattern, scalloped foot on stem, patterned lid & finial, 8x4", from $35 to **$40.00**

Compote, allover pattern, scalloped rim, footed, 5½x8"..**$35.00**

Compote, allover pattern, scalloped rim, footed, 5x6½", from $18 to **$20.00**

Compote, allover pattern, scalloped rim, footed, 7x10"..**$45.00**

Console bowl, allover pattern, scalloped rim, flared foot w/flat edge, 8" dia **$25.00**

Creamer, allover pattern, raised foot w/scalloped edge, 5¾x3"..**$35.00**

Creamer & sugar bowl (open), disk foot, sm, from $25 to.**$28.00**

Cruet, vinegar; 6¾", from $40 to **$45.00**

Decanter, bulbous w/allover pattern, plain neck, foot ring, original patterned stopper, 32-oz, 12", from $50 to **$60.00**

Epergne, allover pattern, 2-piece, 9", $65.00.

Epergne, allover pattern, 1-lily, flared bowl, scalloped foot...**$65.00**

Goblet, water; plain rim & foot, 4½" **$12.00**

Goblet, water; plain rim & foot, 5¾" **$15.00**

Jardiniere, allover pattern, patterned lid & finial, 9¾" ..**$85.00**

Jardiniere/cracker jar, allover pattern, patterned lid & finial, 7¼"..**$50.00**

Jardiniere/tobacco jar, allover pattern, patterned lid & finial, 6"...**$35.00**

Jelly dish, allover pattern, patterned lid & finial, stemmed foot, 10½"..**$45.00**

Jelly dish, patterned body w/plain flat rim & disk foot, patterned lid & finial, 6¾x3½" dia **$35.00**

Lamp, oil; allover pattern, all original, 10", from $100 to ..**$125.00**

Lamp, oil or electric; allover pattern, all original, 24", from $200 to...**$250.00**

Lighter, allover patterned body, metal fittings.............**$35.00**

Nappy, allover pattern, crimped rim, 2¾x6" dia........**$18.00**

Pitcher, water; patterned body, ice lip, straight sides, plain disk foot, 1-qt, 7½"...**$65.00**

Plate, patterned body & center, smooth rim, 8"..........**$25.00**

Relish bowl, 6 lg scallops form allover pattern, 1½x8" dia **$25.00**

Relish dish, allover pattern, 1 plain handle, 2x8" dia .**$18.00**

Relish tray, patterned moons form scalloped rim, star in base, rectangular, 8" long..**$25.00**

Salt & pepper shakers, allover pattern, metal tops, 4x2" dia, pr..**$25.00**

Salt cellar, allover pattern, scalloped rim, sm flat foot..**$8.00**

Sherbet, patterned body & foot w/plain rim & stem, 4¼x3¾"..**$15.00**

Soap dish, allover pattern, oval, 2x6" **$12.00**

Spooner, allover pattern, straight sides, scalloped rim, raised foot, 5¼x4" dia, from $30 to................................**$35.00**

Sugar bowl, allover pattern, patterned lid & finial, sm flat foot, 5¼x4" dia, from $35 to................................**$40.00**

Sugar bowl, allover pattern, straight sides, patterned lid & finial, scalloped foot, 8x4½", from $35 to.............**$40.00**

Sugar shaker, allover pattern, metal top, 4½x3½" dia ..**$40.00**

Syrup pitcher and cheese shaker, allover pattern, metal tops, $40.00 each.

Toothpick holder, allover pattern, scalloped rim, sm flat foot..**$10.00**

Tumbler, iced tea; no pattern at flat rim or on disk foot, 11-oz, 5½" **$20.00**

Tumbler, juice; no pattern at rim or on disk foot, 5-oz, 3½", from $12 to...**$14.00**

Tumbler, no pattern at rim or on disk foot, 7-oz, 4¼", from $12 to...**$15.00**

Mortens Studio

During the 1940s, a Swedish sculptor by the name of Oscar Mortens left his native country and moved to the United States, settling in Arizona. Along with his partner, Gunnar Thelin, they founded the Mortens Studios, a firm that specialized in the manufacture of animal figurines. Though he preferred dogs of all breeds, horses, cats, and wild animals were made, too, but on a much smaller scale.

The material he used was a plaster-like composition molded over a wire framework for support and reinforcement. Crazing is common, and our values reflect pieces with a moderate amount, but be sure to check for more serious damage before you buy. Most pieces are marked with either an ink stamp or a paper label.

**Dog, yellow with black muzzle, #841, 3¼",
$45.00; Collie, #826, 2½", $50.00.**

Afghan dog, tan w/charcoal face, 7x7".........................**$90.00**

Boston Terrier dog, ivory markings on black, standing, 6x6"..**$75.00**

Boxer dog, standing, 5½x5½"..**$80.00**

Boxer pup, scratching, #508, from $55 to...................**$65.00**

Cocker Spaniel dog, black & white, #763...................**$60.00**

Cocker Spaniel pup w/paw up, #841.........................**$55.00**

Dalmatian pup, sitting, #812.......................................**$55.00**

Doberman Pinscher dog, 6x7", from $70 to...............**$85.00**

Horse, rearing, 9"...**$95.00**

Pekinese dog, standing, #740, 3½x4½"......................**$85.00**

Pointer dog, sitting, ivory w/black spots, 4x4¾"........**$65.00**

Spaniel puppy, ivory w/black spots, 3¾x3"................**$40.00**

Wall plaque, sea gull, 12x8".......................................**$150.00**

Morton Pottery

Morton, Illinois, was the location for six potteries that operated there at various times over the course of nearly a hundred years. The first was established by six brothers by the name of Rapp, who immigrated to America from Germany. Second- and third-generation Rapps followed in

the tradition that had been established by their elders in the late 1870s.

The original company was titled Morton Pottery Works and was later renamed Morton Earthenware Co. It was in business from 1877 until 1917. The second to be established was Cliftwood Art Potteries, Inc. (1920–1940). The Morton Pottery Company opened in 1922 and became the longest running of the six, having operated for more than fifty-four years by the time Midwest Potteries incorporated in 1940. They were in business for only four years. The last to open was the American Art Pottery who operated from 1947 until 1961. Various types of pottery were made by each — Rockingham and yellow ware in the early years, novelties and giftware from the 1920s on.

To learn more about these companies, we recommend *Morton's Potteries: 99 Years,* by Doris and Burdell Hall.

American Art Potteries

Figurine, deer, leaping, brown w/green spray, 6"......**$18.00**

Figurine, wild horse, brown spray, 11½"....................**$35.00**

Planter, bunny at stump, natural colors......................**$16.00**

Planter, quail, natural colors......................................**$25.00**

TV lamp, birds on branch, planter base, mauve & blue spray, 11"..**$30.00**

TV lamp, conch shell, yellow & brown......................**$22.00**

Vase, ostrich feathers on cornucopia, multicolor spray, 10½"..**$30.00**

Wall pocket, apple on leaf, red & green...................**$18.00**

Wall pocket, pear shape, purple w/blue interior........**$15.00**

Cliftwood Art Potteries, Inc.

Bookends, tree trunk w/applied birds, brown drip, pr..**$90.00**

Bowl, batter; pink & orchid on white, ribbed, handled.**$45.00**

Compote, pink, applied dolphin base, 6x8"...............**$85.00**

Figurine, Billikin, brown, 8"......................................**$55.00**

Figurine, bulldog, gray, seated, 11"...........................**$80.00**

Flower frog, lily pad, blue, 4"....................................**$14.00**

Lamp, boudoir; cobalt, #16, 6½".................................**$24.00**

Matchbox holder, pink & turquoise over white, wall mount...**$50.00**

Planter, cat sitting, yellow, 5½"..................................**$35.00**

Pointer, 9½", $25.00.

Vase, Grecian Urn, Old Rose, 6"................................**$35.00**

Wall pocket, tree trunk form, brown drip...................**$65.00**

Midwest Potteries Inc.

Figurine, camel, tan, 8½" **$20.00**
Figurine, cow creamer, white & gold, 5" **$20.00**
Figurine, Irish setter, natural colors, 5" **$35.00**
Figurine, lady dancer, white w/gold, 8½" **$28.00**
Figurine, spaniel, white w/gold, 4" **$16.00**
Figurine, tiger, yellow w/brown stripes, 6x10"............**$40.00**
Figurine, wild turkey, brown & tan spray, 12"............**$30.00**
Miniature, polar bear, white, 1¾" **$8.00**
Miniature, squirrel, brown, 2" **$10.00**
Miniature, swan, white matt, 2" **$12.00**

Planter, blue bird, $18.00.

Planter, mountain goat, green...**$9.00**
TV lamp, Siamese cats, brown & white, 13¼" adult & 8" kitten **$50.00**

Morton Pottery Works–Morton Earthenware Co.

Bean pot, yellowware, individual, ¼-pt.......................**$20.00**
Cuspidor, brown, 7"...**$50.00**
Jardiniere, green, 5"..**$20.00**
Mug, banded yellowware, 1-pt......................................**$85.00**
Nappy, yellowware, plain, 10"......................................**$45.00**
Nappy, yellowware, plain, 6"...**$36.00**
Pie baker, brown Rockingham, 6"................................**$65.00**
Pie baker, brown Rockingham, 9"................................**$95.00**
Pitcher, cobalt, mini, 3¼"...**$55.00**
Teapot, restaurant, brown, nesting, individual, set of 2 ..**$40.00**

Morton Pottery Co. (1922–1976)

Santa plate, $45.00.

Bank, bulldog, green..**$20.00**

Bank, pig, black w/white stripe **$40.00**
Christmas mug, natural colors **$15.00**
Custard cup, green, brown & white spatterware, 5-oz.**$20.00**
Figurine, John Kennedy Jr, age 3, saluting, rare **$35.00**
Flowerpot soaker, bird, blue & yellow **$18.00**
Grass grower, Christmas tree **$15.00**
Grass grower, Jiggs...**$30.00**
Head vase, 1940s style w/pillbox hat, white matt, #406.**$45.00**
Lamp, Davy Crockett, boy figure w/bear, green, brown & gray **$100.00**
Syrup, floral w/gold decor..**$40.00**
TV lamp, buffalo, natural colors...................................**$100.00**
TV lamp, horse head, brown...**$40.00**
Wall plaque, fruit cluster, natural colors **$20.00**
Wall plaque, shoe house, yellow, green & brown......**$20.00**

Moss Rose

Though the Moss Rose pattern has been produced by Staffordshire and American pottery companies alike since the mid-1800s, the line we're dealing with here was primarily made between the late 1950s into the 1970s by Japanese manufacturers. Even today you'll occasionally see a tea set or a small candy dish for sale in some of the chain stores. The collectors who are already picking this line up refer to it as Moss Rose, but we've seen it advertised under the name 'Victorian Rose.' The pattern consists of a briar rose with dark green mossy leaves on stark white glaze. Occasionally an item is trimmed in gold. In addition to dinnerware, many accessories and novelties were made as well.

Refer to *Schroeder's Antiques Price Guide* for information on the early Moss Rose pattern.

Advisor: April Tvorak (See Directory, Fire-King)

Ashtray and cigarette box, $15.00. (Photo courtesy of April Tvorak.)

Bowl, sauce **$4.00**
Bowl, soup **$6.00**
Butter dish..**$15.00**
Cottage cheese dish...**$10.00**
Cup & saucer...**$6.00**
Cup & saucer, demitasse **$8.00**
Egg cup, sm..**$6.00**
Plate, dinner **$5.00**
Plate, salad...**$4.00**
Platter...**$12.00**
Teapot...**$20.00**

Teapot, demitasse $25.00
Teapot, electric..$22.00

Motorcycle Collectibles

At some point in nearly anyone's life, they've experienced at least a brief love affair with a motorcycle. What could be more exhilarating than the open road — the wind in your hair, the sun on your back, and no thought for the cares of today or what tomorrow might bring. For some, the passion never diminished. For most of us, it's a fond memory. Regardless of which description best fits you personally, you will probably enjoy the old advertising and sales literature, books and magazines, posters, photographs, banners, etc., showing the old Harleys and Indians, and the club pins, dealership jewelry and clothing, and scores of other items of memorabilia such as collectors are now beginning to show considerable interest in. For more information and lots of color photographs, we recommend *Motorcycle Collectibles With Values* by Leila Dunbar (Schiffer Publishing).

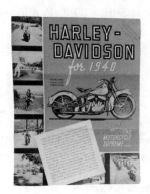

Handbill, Harley-Davidson for 1940, EX, $65.00. (Photo courtesy of Dunbar Gallery.)

Banner, Harley-Davidson Drop-Forged Forks, paper, image of 1930 cycle, EX...$525.00
Bolo tie, 1956 AMA/Gypsy Tour, replaced black cord....$50.00
Book, Harley-Davidson, by Maurice Hendry, softcover, Ballantine, 1972..$25.00
Book, The Story of Harley-Davidson, published by H-D, softbound, late 1960s, M $35.00
Booklet, Indian Riders Instruction Book, 1934, VG....$65.00
Brochure, Harley-Davidson for 1940, photo images & motorcycle on front, EX...$65.00
Brochure, Indian Commercial Motorcycles, More Business at Less Expense above encircled image of 2 men, 1930s, EX $60.00
Brochure, Indian Motorcycles, 40th Anniversary, 1941, EX...$90.00
Can, Harley-Davidson Chain Saver Lubricant, rectangular w/screw cap, 1950s, 8-oz, NM............................$150.00
Can, Harley-Davidson Gunk Cleaner, gold, yellow & black, 1-pt, full, VG..$95.00
Can, Harley-Davidson Leather Lacquer, paper label, pry lid, 1940s, ¼-qt, 2" dia, EX+..$25.00
Catalog rack, Indian, metal ring binder w/script lettering, red & black, old, rare, VG...$180.00

Clock, Indian Motorcycles, round metal frame w/glass lens, black numbers & red lettering on white, 18½" dia, NM+..$1,700.00
Decanter, Del Webb Mint 400, 1972 off-road motorcycle race, empty..$15.00
Hat, Indian Motorcycles, knitted cloth w/vinyl bill, red, black & yellow patch w/Indian in profile (no lettering), EX $325.00
Helmet & goggles, fitted leather hat w/metal goggles #AN6530, EX...$200.00
Jacket, child's, Harley-Davidson, black leather, zippered front, 1960s, EX...$85.00
Kidney belt, brown leather, older style, 6" at widest point, 40" long, VG...$25.00
Kidney belt, incised on leather: dice, club name, 40"...$50.00
Match holder, Indian Motorcycle/The New Indian Motor Power Plus, embossed brass rectangular container, 2¼x1½", EX+...$300.00
Oil can, Harley-Davidson Pre-Lux Premium Deluxe Motorcycle Oil, orange, black & white, 1-qt, full, NM................$90.00
Oil can, Harley-Davidson Racing Motorcycle Oil, black & orange on white, 1-qt, full, NM.........................$100.00
Oil can, Harley-Davidson Two-Cycle Motor Oil, For Use in Scooters/Motorcycles, cone-top w/screw lid, 5¾", full, NM $60.00
Oil can, Indian Motorcycle Oil, red, orange, black & cream, 1-qt, VG+..$300.00
Patch, Americana Motorcycle Association, wool triangular shape w/embroidered initials around swirled center, 5½", EX..$160.00
Pin, AMA Member, 1950s, each...................................$10.00
Pin, AMA Membership, clasp back, 1st through 9th year, each $15.00
Pin, AMA Membership, 2-yr, all gold, tiepin back $10.00
Pin, club event; Norwalk Centaurs MC 1973 Yuma Prison Run, brass..$5.00
Pin, Harley-Davidson, 2" wings, sterling, minor wear.....$50.00
Pin, Harley-Davidson, winged emblem, red on gold, 2", EX+ $55.00
Pin, various motorcycle clubs ca 1970s through 1980s, each.$5.00
Pin, 1962, AMA/Gypsy Tour Award, MOC....................$25.00
Pin-back button, Indian Cycles, Indian head in profile encircled by bands w/lettering, ¾" dia, EX+................$90.00
Pin-back button, Indian Motorcycles, Indian head in profile encircled by bands w/lettering, ¾" dia, EX.........$80.00
Plate holder, Harley-Davidson, brass, eagle atop company name, Made in USA at bottom, EX $20.00
Police lamp, Harley-Davidson, red rotating 12-volt, 7", NMIB..$225.00
Postcard, Indian Motorcycle advertising, linen, EX.....$20.00
Sign, Harley-Davidson, neon, eagle atop emblem, yellow & white, 24x34", new, NM......................................$300.00
Sign, Harley-Davidson, self-framed tin, Insist on Genuine Parts & Accessories above & below logo, red ground, 29x16", NM...$200.00
Sign, Harley-Davidson Cigarettes, tin, smiling couple on motorcycle behind product name, 1984, 17x21", M..........$55.00
Siren cover, Harley-Davidson, stainless steel, 1958, 5½" dia, NM $60.00

Tie bar, AMA Gypsy Tour Award, brass w/AMA logo **$20.00**

Tin, Harley-Davidson Fork Oil, red, white & blue, 1-pt, EX **$15.00**

Toy, Auburn Rubber, police cycle, red w/white rubber tires, blue officer rider, EX **$50.00**

Toy, Cragstan Harley-Davidson, mostly plastic, yellow w/black-suited rider, made in Hong Kong **$20.00**

Toy, Japanese tin litho motorcycle racer w/driver, friction, 4" **$20.00**

Trophy, Security Motorcycle Club Egg Hunt, 1967, 3" wings on marble base, 12" wood shaft holds gold-tone motorcycle **$15.00**

Trophy, 1967 Baymare, 1st place, motorcycle on top, wood w/gold-tone plaque **$15.00**

Window ventilators, Indian Motorcycle Co, black metal w/logos, 1920s, 27", EX, pr **$160.00**

Movie Posters

Although many sizes of movie posters were made and all sizes are collectible, the most collected size today is still the one-sheet, 27" wide and 41" long. Movie-memorabilia collecting is as diverse as films themselves. Popular areas include specific films such as *Gone With the Wind, Wizard of Oz*, and others; specific stars — from the greats to character actors; directors such as Hitchcock, Ford, Spielberg, and others; specific film types such as B-Westerns, all-Black casts, sports related, Noir, fifties teen, sixties beach, musicals, crime, silent, radio characters, cartoons, and serials; specific characters such as Tarzan, Superman, Ellery Queen, Blondie, Ma and Pa Kettle, Whistler, and Nancy Drew; specific artists like Rockwell, Davis, Frazetta, Flagg, and others; specific art themes, for instance, policeman, firemen, horses, attorneys, doctors or nurses (this list is endless). And some collectors just collect posters they like. In the past twenty years, movie memorabilia has steadily increased in value, and in the last few years the top price paid for a movie poster has reached $200,000.00. Movie memorabilia is a new field for collectors. In the past, only a few people knew where to find posters. Recently, auctions on the East and West coasts have created much publicity, attracting many new collectors. Many posters are still moderately priced, and the market is expanding, allowing even new collectors to see the value of their collections increase.

Advisors: Cleophas and Lou Ann Wooley, Movie Poster Service (See Directory, Movie Posters)

Alice in Wonderland, 1951, 1-sheet, linen backed, 41x27", NM, $975.00.

Alamo, John Wayne, 1960, 27x41", from $225 to **$325.00**

Apartment, Jack Lemmon & Shirley Maclaine, 1960, 27x41", from $75 to **$125.00**

Aristocats, Disney animation, 1971, 27x41", from $65 to... **$95.00**

Beach Blanket Bingo, Annette Funicello, 1965, 27x41", from $50 to **$75.00**

Bladerunner, Harrison Ford, 1982, 27x41", from $50 to.. **$95.00**

Blondie's Anniversary, Penny Singleton, 1947, 22x28", from $45 to **$75.00**

Call Me Madam, Merman & O'Connor, 1953, 22x28", from $45 to **$65.00**

Challenge of the Range, Starrett, 1949, 27x41", from $50 to **$85.00**

Chinatown, Nicholson & Dunaway, 1974, 27x41", from $175 to **$235.00**

Clambake, Elvis Presley, 1967, 14x36", from $45 to ... **$65.00**

Daisy Kenyon, Joan Crawford, 1947, 27x41", from $125 to **$165.00**

Dead Ringer, Bette Davis, 1964, 22x28", from $40 to .. **$60.00**

Exorcist, Blair & Burstyn, 1974, 14x36", from $40 to.. **$60.00**

Far Country, James Stewart, 1955, 14x22", from $20 to.. **$40.00**

Father's Little Dividend, Elizabeth Taylor, 1951, 14x36", from $75 to **$125.00**

Fear Strikes Out, Perkins & Malden, 1957, 27x41", from $40 to **$65.00**

First Men in the Moon, Harryhausen, 1964, 14x36", from $65 to **$95.00**

Flame & Flesh, Lana Turner, 1954, 27x41", from $40 to ... **$60.00**

Forever Darling, Lucy & Desi Arnez, 1956, 27x41", from $125 to **$165.00**

Fort Worth, Randolph Scott, 1951, 27x41", from $85 to.. **$135.00**

Four Sons, Don Ameche, 1940, 27x41", from $85 to.. **$125.00**

Fox & Hound, Disney animation, 1981, 27x41", from $40 to **$65.00**

French Connection, Gene Hackman, 1971, 27x41", from $40 to **$65.00**

Fuller Brush Man, Red Skelton, 1949, 22x28", from $35 to. **$60.00**

Gidget Goes Hawaiian, Walley, 1961, 14x22", from $20 to **$30.00**

Girl Said No, Armstrong, 1937, 27x41", from $135 to. **$185.00**

Gone With the Wind, Clark Gable & Vivien Leigh, 1939, 14x22", from $700 to **$950.00**

Gone With the Wind, Clark Gable & Vivien Leigh, 1980 reissue, 27x41", from $35 to **$55.00**

Grand Prix, James Garner, 1967, 22x28", from $45 to .. **$65.00**

Great Locomotive Chase, Disney, 1956, 27x41", from $45 to **$75.00**

Greatest, Ali, 1977, 27x41", from $45 to **$75.00**

Guys & Dolls, Marlon Brando & Frank Sinatra, 1955, 22x28", from $100 to **$150.00**

Hard Day's Night, Beatles, 1964, 22x28", from $175 to **$250.00**

Hell Bent for Leather, Murphy, 1960, 27x41", from $40 to **$55.00**

Hell Up in Harlem, all Black cast, 1974, 27x41", from $35 to **$50.00**

Hellcats of the Navy, Reagan & Davis, 1957, 14x36", from $70 to **$100.00**

How the West Was Won, all-star cast, 1962, 27x41", from $65 to **$95.00**

I Remember Mama, Irene Dunne, 1948, 22x28", from $65 to..**$85.00**

I'll See You in My Dreams, Day, 1951, 27x41", from $85 to..**$125.00**

If a Man Answers, Sandra Dee & Bobby Darin, 1962, 27x41", from $30 to..**$50.00**

Indiscreet, Cary Grant & Ingrid Bergman, 1958, 27x41", from $145 to..**$175.00**

Inherit the Wind, Tracy, March & Kelly, 1960, 27x41", from $40 to..**$65.00**

Jesse James at Bay, Roy Rogers, 1941, 27x41", from $550 to..**$850.00**

Johnny Angel, George Raft, 1945, 27x41", from $100 to.**$150.00**

Johnny Belinda, Jane Wyman, 1948, 14x36", from $75 to .**$100.00**

Julius Caesar, Marlon Brando & James Mason, 1953, 27x41", from $125 to..**$175.00**

Khartoum, Heston & Oliver, 1966, 27x41", from $65 to .**$90.00**

Kill the Umpire, William Bendix, 1950, 22x28", from $50 to..**$85.00**

Killers, Lee Marvin & Angie Dickinson, 1964, 27x41", from $45 to..**$65.00**

King Kong Vs Godzilla, director Honda, 1963, 27x41", from $150 to..**$200.00**

Kissing Bandit, Frank Sinatra, 1948, 27x41", from $100 to **$150.00**

Kitten With a Whip, Ann-Margret, 1964, 27x41", from $40 to..**$65.00**

Kitty, Paulette Goddard & Ray Milland, 1945, 27x41", from $125 to..**$150.00**

Lady Gambles, Barbara Stanwyck & Robert Preston, 1949, 27x41", from $75 to..**$125.00**

Last of the Pony Riders, Gene Autry, 1953, 27x41", from $85 to..**$125.00**

Lemon Drop Kid, Bob Hope & Marilyn Maxwell, 1951, 27x41", from $50 to..**$75.00**

Let's Make Love, Marilyn Monroe pictured, 1960, 11x14", from $40 to..**$65.00**

Life With Father, William Powell & Irene Dunn, 1947, 27x41", from $100 to..**$150.00**

Lion in Winter, Kathryn Hepburn & Peter O'Toole, 1968, 22x28", from $45 to..**$85.00**

Little Shop of Horrors, Nicholson, 1960, 14x36", from $65 to..**$95.00**

Living It Up, Martin & Lewis, 1954, 14x36", from $50 to ..**$75.00**

Loving You, Elvis Presley, 1957, 14x22", from $285 to ...**$325.00**

Mame, Lucille Ball, 1974, 27x41", from $30 to **$40.00**

Monsieur Beaucaire, Bob Hope, 1947, 27x41", from $65 to **$95.00**

Mr Winkle Goes to War, EG Robinson, 1944, 27x41", from $65 to **$95.00**

North by Northwest, Alfred Hitchcock, 1959, 41x81", from $475 to..**$650.00**

On Golden Pond, Kathryn Hepburn & Henry Fonda, 1981, 27x41", from $20 to **$40.00**

Paris Blues, Newman & Armstrong, 1961, 27x41", from $40 to..**$75.00**

Pink Panther, Peter Sellers & David Niven, 1964, 27x41", from $75 to..**$125.00**

Pursued, Mitchum & Wright, 1947, 22x28", from $150 to.**$180.00**

Quo Vadis, Kerr & Taylor, 1951, 27x41", from $100 to..**$150.00**

Raiders of the Lost Ark, Ford & Allen, 1981, 27x41", from $55 to..**$80.00**

Requiem for a Heavyweight, Anthony Quinn, 1962, 27x41", from $35 to..**$50.00**

Return of the Jedi, Ford & Hamill, 1983, 14x36", from $35 to.**$50.00**

Rich, Young & Pretty; Powell & Lamas, 1951, 27x41", from $40 to..**$60.00**

Riding High, Crosby & Hamilton, 1951, 27x41", from $50 to..**$80.00**

Ring-a-Ding Rhythm, Chubby Checker, 1962, 27x41", from $65 to..**$100.00**

Satchmo the Great, Louis Armstrong, 1957, 27x41", from $250 to..**$350.00**

Somewhere in Time, Christopher Reeve, 1980, 27x41", from $65 to..**$90.00**

Song of the South, Disney animation, 1946, 14x36", from $100 to..**$150.00**

Song of the Thin Man, Loy & Powell, 1947, 81x81", from $550 to..**$700.00**

Star Trek, William Shatner & Leonard Nimoy, 1979, 27x41", from $30 to..**$50.00**

State Fair, Pat Boone & Ann-Margret, 1962, 27x41", from $45 to..**$65.00**

Take the Money & Run, Woody Allen, 1969, 27x41", from $60 to..**$100.00**

Tea & Sympathy, Kerr, 1956, 27x41", from $55 to **$85.00**

Thelma Jordan, Barbara Stanwyck, 1949, 27x41", from $100 to..**$150.00**

There's Always a Woman, Blondell, 1938, 27x41", from $125 to..**$165.00**

Three Stooges in Orbit, Three Stooges, 1962, 22x28", from $50 to..**$85.00**

Thunder Road, Robert Mitchum, 1958, 27x41", from $100 to..**$150.00**

True Grit, John Wayne, 1969, 27x51", from $100 to .**$150.00**

Twelve Angry Men, Fonda & Cobb, 1957, 14x36", from $50 to..**$85.00**

Valley of the Headhunters, Johnny Weismuller, 1953, 14x36", from $50 to..**$85.00**

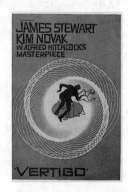

Vertigo, Paramount, 1958, NM, $515.00.

War of the Worlds, Barry & Pal Effects, 1953, 27x41", from $950 to..**$1,250.00**

Where Eagles Dare, Clint Eastwood, 1968, 14x36", from $45 to..**$75.00**

Wizard of Oz, Judy Garland, 1939, 22x28", minimum value **$8,000.00**

Wizard of Oz, Judy Garland, 1949 reissue, 22x28", minimum value **$450.00**

Wizard of Oz, Judy Garland, 1970s reissue, 27x41", from $65 to **$100.00**

Words & Music, Judy Garland & Mickey Rooney, 1948, 27x41", from $100 to **$150.00**

Napkin Dolls

Cocktail, luncheon, or dinner..., paper, cotton, or damask..., solid, patterned, or plaid — regardless of size, color, or material, there's always been a place for napkins. In the late 1940s and early 1950s, buffet-style meals were gaining popularity. One accessory common to many of these buffets is now one of today's hot collectibles — the napkin doll. While most of the ceramic and wooden examples found today date from this period, many homemade napkin dolls were produced in ceramic classes of the 1970s and eighties.

Advisor: Bobby Zucker Bryson (See Directory, Napkin Dolls)

Kreiss and Co., ladies with fruit baskets, pink, yellow or blue, candle holder in top of hats, from $45.00 to $60.00 each. (Photo courtesy of Bobbie Zucker Bryson.)

Betson's, yellow Colonial lady, bell clapper, marked Hand Painted Japan, 8½" **$55.00**

California Originals, pink Spanish dancer, splits in rear only, foil label, 13" **$95.00**

California Originals, toothpick holder basket over head, foil label, 13¾" **$70.00**

Enesco, Genie at Your Service, holding lantern, paper label, 8" **$80.00**

Goebel, half doll on wire frame, marked Goebel, W Germany, ca 1957, 9" **$175.00**

Holland Mold, Daisy, No 514, 7¼" **$60.00**

Holland Mold, Rosie, No H-132, 10¼" **$45.00**

Holt Howard, pink Sunbonnet Miss, marked Holt Howard, 1958, 5" **$60.00**

Japan, lady in green w/pink umbrella, bell clapper, unmarked, 9" **$55.00**

Japan, lady in pink & blue, unglazed, marked Japan, 9¼" **$50.00**

Kreiss & Co, blue doll w/yellow toothpick tray, candle holder in hat, marked Kreiss & Co, +pr 4¾" 'tip in' shakers **$125.00**

Kreiss & Co, green doll w/poodle, jeweled eyes, necklace & ring, candle holder behind hat, marked Kreiss & Co, 10¾"**$65.00**

Kreiss & Co, green lady holding fan, candle holder behind fan, marked Kreiss & Co, 8¾" **$55.00**

Kreiss & Co, yellow doll w/gold trim holding muff, jeweled eyes, candle holder in top of hat, marked Kreiss & Co, 10" **$75.00**

Man (bartender) holding tray w/candle holder, 8¾" ..**$85.00**

Servy Etta, wood w/marble base, marked USD Patent No 159,005, 11½" **$45.00**

Swedish doll, wooden, musical base, marked Patent No 113861, 12", MIB **$45.00**

Wooden Jamaican lady, movable arms, paper label: Ave 13 Nov 743, A Sinfonia, Tel 2350 Petropolis, 6"........**$85.00**

Newspapers

The two most important factors that determine the collectiblity of an old newspaper is historic content and condition. If you can recall studying the headlined event when you were back in school, you can be sure the newspaper is collectible. Papers that deal with other topics such as the death of Elvis or the capture of 'Machine Gun' Kelley, for instance, will also be interesting to a newspaper collector. It's been estimated, though, that only about 2% of all papers ever printed are worth more than a few dollars. The remainder fall into the category called 'atmosphere' editions, which include topics on local events, weather, etc. Some of the more valuable papers have been reproduced, and there are many subtle points you should be aware of if you're going to pursue the hobby. For more information, we recommend you order a copy of the booklet published by the NCSA (Newspaper Collectors Society of America). Send a large SASE and $2.00 to the address listed below. The NCSA also has an extensive web site on the Internet. The site contains over 200,000 words of information and is a treasure trove for those conducting historic research. The web address is: http://www.serv.com/ephemera/historybuff.html. Their e-mail address is: ephemera@mail.serv.com.

Club: NCSA (Newspaper Collectors Society of America)
Box 19134-S
Lansing, MI 48901

1931, Al Capone found guilty, from $25 to **$40.00**

1932, FDR elected 1st term, from $15 to **$25.00**

1934, Pretty Boy Floyd killed, from $20 to................**$40.00**

1936, Jessie Owens at Berlin Olympics, from $10 to..**$20.00**

1937, Hindenburg explodes, 1st reports, from $40 to .**$100.00**

1939-45, major battles in WWII, from $15 to **$40.00**

1941, Pearl Harbor attacked, December 8 issues, 1st reports, from $20 to...**$40.00**

1945, 1st atomic bomb dropped, from $20 to............**$40.00**

1950, John F Kennedy elected, from $10 to...............**$20.00**

1950, US enters Korean War, from $15 to...................**$30.00**

1951, Truman relieves MacArthur of command, from $10 to..**$20.00**

1957, Soviets launch Sputnik, from $5 to **$15.00**

1959, Hawaii joins the Union, from $10 to.................**$20.00**
1962, John Glenn orbits Earth, from $10 to.................**$15.00**
1962, Marilyn Monroe dies, from $20 to......................**$40.00**
1967, Super Bowl I, from $10 to **$25.00**
1968, assassination of Martin Luther King, from $10 to ..**$25.00**
1969, moon landing, from $10 to **$25.00**
1974, Nixon resigns, from $10 to **$20.00**
1977, death of Elvis, Memphis title, from $20 to........**$40.00**
1986, Challenger explodes, from $5 to **$10.00**

Niloak Pottery

The Niloak Pottery company was the continuation of a quarter-century-old family business in Benton, Arkansas. Known as the Eagle Pottery in the early twentieth century, its owner was Charles Dean Hyten who continued in his father's footsteps making utilitarian wares for local and state markets. In 1909 Arthur Dovey, an experienced potter formerly from the Rookwood Pottery of Ohio and the Arkansas-Missouri based Ouachita Pottery companies, came to Benton and created America's most unusual art pottery. Introduced in 1910 as Niloak (kaolin clay spelled backwards), Dovey and Hyten produced art pottery pieces from swirling clays with a wide range of artificially created colors including red, blue, cream, brown, gray and later green. Connected to the Arts & Crafts Movement by 1913, the pottery was labeled as Missionware (probably due to its seeming simplicity in the making). Missionware (or swirl) production continued alongside utilitarian ware manufacturing until the 1930s when economic factors led to the making of another type of art pottery and later to (molded) industrial castware. In 1931 Niloak Pottery introduced Hywood Art Pottery (marked as such), consisting of regular glaze techniques including overspray, mottling, and drips of two colors on vases and bowls that were primarily hand thrown. It was short-lived and soon replaced with the Hywood by Niloak (or Hywood) line to increase marketing potential through the use of the well-recognized Niloak name. Experienced potters, designers, and ceramists were involved at Niloak; among them were Frank Long, Paul Cox, Stoin M. Stoin, Howard Lewis, and Rudy Ganz. Many local families with long ties to the pottery included the McNeills, Rowlands, and Alleys, By the mid-1930s, Niloak, experiencing tremendous financial woes, came under new management led by Hardy L. Winburn of Little Rock. To compete better, the production focused primarily on industrial castware such as vases, bowls, figurines, animals, and planters. Niloak survived into the late 1940s when it became the Winburn Tile Company of Little Rock, which still exists today.

Virtually all of Niloak Missionware/swirl pottery is marked with die stamps. The exceptions are generally fan vases, wall pockets, lamp bases, and whiskey jugs. Be careful when you buy unmarked swirl pottery — it is usually Evans pottery (made in Missouri) which generally has either no interior glaze or is chocolate brown inside. Moreover, Evans made swirl wall pockets, lamp bases, and even hanging baskets that find their way on to today's market and are sold as Niloak. Niloak stickers are often placed on these unmarked Evans pieces — closely examine the condition of the sticker to determine if it is damaged or mutilated from the transfer process.

For more information, we recommend *The Collector's Encyclopedia of Niloak Pottery* by our advisor David Edwin Gifford, a historian of Arkansas pottery.

Advisor: David Edwin Gifford (See Directory, Niloak)

Club: National Society of Arkansas Pottery Collectors (for those interested in learning more about Niloak as well as Camark and Ouachita Potteries)
c/o David Edwin Gifford
P.O. Box 7617
Little Rock, Arkansas 72217; (Please send large SASE with inquiries.)

Castware

Ashtray, blue, marked w/block letter, 1½x3½"...........**$20.00**
Bowl, petal design, molded mark, 8x3½"....................**$75.00**
Cannon, blue, molded mark, 3¼".................................**$60.00**
Canoe planter, brown, marked w/block letter, 11".....**$75.00**
Duck planter, pink, molded mark, 4"...........................**$30.00**
Elephant planter, pink, marked w/block letter, 4½"...**$50.00**
Elephant planter on base, blue, molded mark, 6" **$75.00**
Parrot planter, brown, 4½"...**$30.00**
Pitcher, flying eagles, green, molded mark, 9½".........**$50.00**
Pitcher, w/stopper, blue, Potteries sticker, 7" **$85.00**

Planter, deer, shades of brown and green, low relief mark, 7", $40.00. (Photo courtesy of David Edwin Gifford.)

Polar bear planter, white, molded mark, 3½" **$30.00**
Rabbit planter, white, molded mark, 3½"....................**$30.00**
Salt & pepper shakers, bird shape, burgundy, Potteries sticker, pr **$45.00**
Salt & pepper shakers, green, ball shape, Potteries sticker, 2½", pr...**$30.00**
Southern Belle, yellow, Potteries sticker, 10" **$150.00**
Squirrel planter, brown, molded mark, 6" **$35.00**
Sugar bowl & creamer, blue, marked w/block letter, 4"..**$50.00**
Swan planter, white, molded mark, 6"........................**$35.00**
Vase, green, marked w/block letter, 4" **$40.00**
Vase, pink, w/wing handles, molded mark, 6" **$25.00**
Vase, yellow, marked w/block letter, 3" **$30.00**
Wishing well planter, green, molded mark, 8"...........**$50.00**

Hywood Art Pottery/Hywood by Niloak

Bowl, blue, incised Hywood (print), 4" **$45.00**
Vase, blue & white mottled, applied handles, stamped Hywood by Niloak, 6"...**$75.00**

Vase, blue & white mottled, incised Hywood in script, 7½" **$100.00**

Vase, burgundy, marked w/art letter, 7" **$75.00**

Vase, green & burgundy drip, applied handles, stamped Hywood Art Pottery, 6" **$100.00**

Vase, green & white mottled, applied handles, stamped Hywood Art Pottery, 6" **$100.00**

Vase, green w/mustard overspray, stamped Hywood by Niloak, 4" **$50.00**

Vase, green w/pink overspray, ribbed, 6" **$75.00**

Vase, green w/pink overspray, stamped Hywood by Niloak, 5" **$60.00**

Missionware Swirl

Ashtray, red, blue, white & brown, marked w/art letter, 4½x2½" **$200.00**

Bowl, brown & white, marked w/block letter, 3¼"..**$200.00**

Bowl, flower; red, blue, white & brown, marked w/art letter, 4x4" **$200.00**

Bowl, red, blue, white & brown, marked w/art letter, 5"...**$200.00**

Bowl, red, blue, white & brown, marked w/art letter, 6"...**$250.00**

Bowl, red, blue & white, marked w/art letter, 4" **$175.00**

Bud vase, red, blue, white & brown, marked w/art letter, 6"...**$175.00**

Bud vase, red, blue, white & brown, marked w/art letter, 8"...**$250.00**

Candlestick, red, blue, white & brown, marked w/art letter, 10"..**$300.00**

Candlestick, red, blue, white & brown, marked w/art letter, 6"...**$200.00**

Candlestick, red, blue & white, marked w/art letter, 8"..**$250.00**

Chamberstick, red, blue, white & brown, marked w/art letter, 5"...**$225.00**

Chamberstick, red, blue & white, marked w/art letter, 4" **$175.00**

Decanter, red, blue, white & brown, rare form, marked w/art letter, 6" **$600.00**

Humidor, red, blue & white, marked w/art letter, 4x5" ..**$250.00**

Humidor, red, blue & white, marked w/art letter, 5x7" ..**$500.00**

Jug, red, blue, white & brown, no mark, 6"..............**$400.00**

Match holder, red, blue, white & brown, marked w/art letter, 2½"..**$125.00**

Stein, red, blue & white, marked w/art letter, 4" **$200.00**

Vase, blue & white, marked Pat Pend'g block letter, 10"..**$500.00**

Vase, brown & cream, marked w/block letter, 8".....**$400.00**

Vase, rare exterior glaze, brown, gray & cream, Benton Ark mark, 7" **$500.00**

Vase, red, blue, white & brown, fan shape, no mark, 7"..**$300.00**

Vase, red, blue, white & brown, marked w/art letter, 10"..**$400.00**

Vase, red, blue, white & brown, marked w/art letter, 12"..**$500.00**

Vase, red, blue, white & brown, marked w/art letter, 2"...**$150.00**

Vase, red, blue, white & brown, marked w/art letter, 4"...**$125.00**

Vase, red, blue, white & brown, marked w/art letter, 6" .**$175.00**

Vase, red, blue & white, marked w/art letter, 8".......**$300.00**

Wall pocket, red, blue, white & brown, no mark, 6"..**$300.00**

Wall pocket, red, blue & white, no mark, 8" **$400.00**

Water bottle, w/cup, red, blue, white & brown, marked w/art letter, 8" **$500.00**

Noritake

Before the government restricted the use of the Nippon mark in 1921, all porcelain exported from Japan (even that made by the Noritake Company) carried the Nippon mark. The company that became Noritake had its beginning in 1904, and over the years experienced several changes in name and organization. Until 1941 (at the onset of WWII) they continued to import large amounts of their products to America. (During the occupation, when chinaware production was resumed, all imports were to have been marked 'Occupied Japan,' though because of the natural resentment on the part of the Japanese, much of it was not.)

Many variations will be found in their marks, but nearly all contain the Noritake name. Reproductions abound, be very careful. If you'd like to learn more about this subject, we recommend *The Collector's Encyclopedia of Noritake* (there are two books in the series) by Joan Van Patten; and *The Collector's Encyclopedia of Early Noritake* by Aimee Neff Alden. All are published by Collector Books.

Ashtray, figural white & brown dog sitting on rim of blue octagon w/tan kidney-shaped bowl, black trim, red mark, 2¾"..**$175.00**

Ashtray, round w/straight sides, no rests, 2 figural kittens at play on rim, tan w/blue bowl, lustre, green mark, 4" dia **$200.00**

Ashtray, round w/straight sides, 4 indented rests, demure girl & bird in white center, blue lustre sides, red mark, 5"..**$210.00**

Ashtray, round w/straight sides, 4 indented rests, queen-of-clubs playing card in center, orange & tan, green mark, 5"..**$80.00**

Bowl, figural owls (2) on edge of round dish w/acorn decor, white, tan & blue w/black trim, lustre, green mark, 5½"..**$175.00**

Bowl, figural toucan perched on edge of round bowl w/scalloped rim, blue w/tan interior, red trim, lustre, red mark, 7"..**$150.00**

Bowl, parallelogram w/2 square corner handles, stylized house & lake scene w/golden sky, gold trim, green mark, 8" **$65.00**

Bowl, round w/single open handle, peanut & leaves motif on white zigzagging w/brown, black border, red mark, 6¼"...**$90.00**

Bowl, 6-sided w/multicolored stylized floral motif on tan lustre, purple border, green mark, 7½" **$90.00**

Cake plate, round w/scalloped rim & scrolled handles, house in landscape against blue lustre sky, green mark, 10½"..**$80.00**

Cake plate, square w/blue scalloped border & open handles, kaleidoscopic floral design on round center, red mark, 10"..**$55.00**

Candlesticks, flat-rimmed cup on pedestal w/2 looped handles, pink rose & decor on blue lustre, red mark, 2", pr ...**$80.00**

Candy dish, stylized figure-8 w/pointed ends & handle twisted across center, ship at sea on lustre, green mark, 7" **$65.00**

Candy dish, white heart shape w/loop handle, single tree landscape in center, gold trim, green mark, 4½" .**$30.00**

Candy dish, 8-point star w/green airbrushing on sides, stylized multicolored floral center, gold trim, red mark, 7¼" **$105.00**

Chip & dip set, round bowl & plate, white w/Japanese decor, gold rims, red mark, 11½" **$80.00**

Cigarette box, square, Deco lady smoking & reclining w/book on lid, red & black w/gold trim, red mark, 3¾" **$250.00**

Cigarette holder, dome shape w/bird atop, tan lustre w/black base, red mark, 4¾" **$125.00**

Cigarette/playing card holder, rectangular container on pedestal base, silhouette image of Arab on camel, red mark, 4" **$110.00**

Comport, octagon on short pedestal base, Arab-type city-scape against blue & white, black trim, red mark, 6"........**$90.00**

Creamer & sugar bowl (open), flared zigzag rim w/angled handles, stylized floral design, yellow trim, red mark, 3¼" **$70.00**

Creamer & sugar bowl (open), flat sided w/triangular handle on sugar, black w/Japanese lantern motif, red mark, 3½" **$90.00**

Cruet set, conjoined egg shapes w/single center handle, light green shamrock design on tan lustre, red mark, 6½" **$80.00**

Dish, figural peacock w/tail forming oval-shaped bowl, green head & body w/lavender & tan tail, green mark, 6½" **$225.00**

Dresser tray, rectangular w/handles, blue w/white dot design on rim & around lady in center, gold trim, red mark, 11" **$65.00**

Flower frog, figural yellow & blue fish atop round fluted orange base w/holes, red mark, 4½" **$250.00**

Honey jar, dome-shaped hive w/3 applied bees, made in various motifs, green or red mark, 4½" **$80.00**

Honey jar, white dome-shaped beehive w/3 applied gold bees, pink china-painted roses, blue leaves, red mark, 4½" **$80.00**

Lemon dish, round w/off-center black handle, multicolored fruit w/blue leaves on white-veined tan lustre, red mark, 6" **$60.00**

Perfume bottle, handled urn w/lid & short pedestal base, floral design on white w/blue, gold & black, red mark, 6" **$150.00**

Pin dish, figural girl clown leaning back w/hands on knees, made in various colors, lustre finish, red mark, 4" .**$310.00**

Pin dish, round, figural girl in red center w/hands crossed under chin, green sides, black trim, red mark, 5" dia **$300.00**

Pin dish, round aqua dish w/figural tan dog w/black spots sitting at side, lustre finish, red mark, 2¾" dia.....**$60.00**

Pipe & match holder, figural orange elephant & tan pipe-shaped rest on white & green base, black trim, red mark, 3½" **$300.00**

Plate, Deco lady holding strand of beads against white background, gold-banded rim, red mark, 6¾" **$215.00**

Potpourri jar, blue & purple 3-footed squatty urn w/grape & leaf decor on dome lid, dark blue finial, green mark, 4¼" **$85.00**

Powder puff box, octagon, bird on flowering branch against light blue sky on lid, orange & black trim, red mark, 4¾" **$200.00**

Powder puff box, round, basket of flowers on cream backgound w/orange border, black trim, red mark, 3½" **$175.00**

Powder puff box, round, Spanish lady w/castanets against green background, red mark, 3½" **$225.00**

Relish dish, elongated oval, tan lustre w/pink & green floral decor at corners & in center, red mark, 7½"........**$35.00**

Sandwich plate, octagon w/center handle, stylized floral design against patterned background, red mark, 8¾" **$75.00**

Sandwich plate, round w/center handle, Japanese mountain & lake scene w/geisha, brown rim, gold trim, red mark, 8" **$80.00**

Sandwich tray, elongated w/open handles, inverted corners, multicolored pansies on white, green border, red mark, 18" **$60.00**

Spooner, elongated w/angled handles, various motifs & colors, green or red mark, 8"............................**$50.00**

Sugar shaker, stylized owl in blue, tan & white lustre w/black trim, green mark...**$140.00**

Vase, cornucopia applied to bell-shaped base, bird & floral motif on white w/blue shading, red mark, 7¾".**$160.00**

Vase, orange bird on bar between double white cornucopias w/fluted rims & floral decor, tan & black trim, green mark, 7" **$225.00**

Vase, tall white basket w/Japanese lantern on flowering branch w/birds, applied red flowers, silver trim, red mark, 7" **$135.00**

Wall pocket, mamma bird perched on edge of nest w/3 baby birds, tan lustre w/pink & green floral decor, green mark, 7"..**$275.00**

Wall pocket, white & blue cone shape w/stylized Spanish lady holding fan, gold trim, red mark, 8"..........**$160.00**

Azalea

The Azalea pattern was produced exclusively for the Larkin Company, who offered it to their customers as premiums from 1916 until the thirties. It met with much success, and even today locating pieces to fill in your collection is not at all difficult. The earlier pieces carry the Noritake M-in-wreath mark. Later the ware was marked Noritake, Azalea, Hand Painted, Japan.

Casserole, $125.00.

Bowl, #12, 10"...**$42.50**
Bowl, oatmeal; #55, 5½" **$28.00**

Bowl, vegetable; oval, #172, 9¼" **$58.00**
Butter tub, w/insert, #54 .... **$48.00**
Cake plate, #10, 9¾".. **$40.00**
Compote, #170 .... **$98.00**
Creamer & sugar bowl, #7 .... **$45.00**
Cup & saucer, #2 .... **$17.50**
Gravy boat, #40.. **$48.00**
Mustard jar.. **$55.00**
Pitcher, milk; #100, 1-qt **$195.00**
Plate, dinner; #13, 9¾" **$28.00**
Plate, soup; #19, 7⅛".. **$25.00**
Platter, #56, 12" **$58.00**
Salt & pepper shakers, bell form, #11, pr.................. **$30.00**
Salt & pepper shakers, bulbous, #89, pr.................... **$30.00**
Teapot, #15.. **$110.00**

Tree in the Meadow

Made by the Noritake China Company during the 1920s and thirties, this pattern of dinnerware is beginning to show up more and more at the larger flea markets. It's easy to spot; the pattern is hand painted, so there are variations, but the color scheme is always browns, gold-yellows, and orange-rust, and the design features a large dark tree in the foreground, growing near a lake. There is usually a cottage in the distance.

Basket, Dolly Varden, from $95 to **$125.00**
Bowl, berry; individual..**$12.00**
Bowl, cream soup; 2 handles **$35.00**
Bowl, oatmeal, from $10 to **$15.00**
Bowl, soup, from $15 to **$20.00**
Bowl, vegetable; 9"..**$35.00**
Butter pat..**$15.00**
Butter tub, open, w/drainer..**$35.00**
Celery dish, from $30 to..**$40.00**
Cheese & cracker..**$90.00**
Coffeepot, from $160 to **$200.00**
Condiment set, 5-pc.. **$45.00**
Creamer & sugar bowl, from $65 to **$70.00**
Cup & saucer, breakfast **$25.00**
Cup & saucer, demitasse; from $25 to **$35.00**
Egg cup, from $25 to.. **$30.00**
Gravy boat, from $40 to **$50.00**

Jam jar and underplate, green mark, 4¾", from $65.00 to $70.00.

Lemon dish, from $15 to..**$20.00**
Mayonnaise set, 3-pc, from $40 to **$50.00**
Mustard jar w/lid & spoon, from $30 to **$40.00**
Plate, bonbon..**$35.00**

Plate, dinner; from $25 to **$30.00**
Plate, grill **$40.00**
Plate, luncheon; square, from $25 to **$35.00**
Plate, 6¼" **$10.00**
Plate, 7½", from $12 to **$15.00**
Platter, 12", from $40 to..**$45.00**
Platter, 14", from $45 to..**$50.00**
Relish, divided, from $30 to **$40.00**
Salt & pepper shakers, individual, pr......................**$15.00**
Spoon holder, from $40 to **$50.00**
Sugar shaker & cream pitcher, from $75 to **$80.00**
Syrup jug, w/underplate, from $50 to........................**$55.00**
Tea tile, from $50 to **$55.00**
Teapot, demitasse; from $35 to **$45.00**
Teapot, strap handle..**$50.00**
Waste bowl, from tea set, from $35 to......................**$40.00**

Various Dinnerware Patterns, ca. 1930s to Present

So many lines of dinnerware have been produced by the Noritake company that to list them all would require a volume in itself. In fact, just such a book is available — *The Collector's Encyclopedia of Early Noritake* by Aimee Neff Alden (Collector Books). And while many patterns had specific names, others did not, so you'll probably need the photographs this book contains to help you identify your pattern. Contained herein is only a general guide for the more common pieces and patterns. The low side of the range will represent more current lines, while the high side can be used to roughly evaluate lines from about 1933 until the mid-sixties.

Newsletter: *Noritake News*
David H. Spain
1237 Federal Ave. E
Seattle, WA 98102; 206-323-8102

Bowl, berry; individual, from $8 to............................**$10.00**
Bowl, soup; 7½", from $10 to **$15.00**
Bowl, vegetable; round or oval, ca 1945 to present, from $25
    to **$35.00**
Bowl, vegetable; w/lid, ca 1933-1940 ....**$40.00**
Butter dish, 3-pc, ca 1933-1964, from $35 to..............**$50.00**
Creamer, from $15 to..**$25.00**
Cup, demitasse; w/saucer, from $10 to......................**$17.50**
Gravy boat, from $35 to..**$45.00**

Plate, dinner; Dresdlina (ca 1940 to 1955), from $20.00 to $30.00. (Photo courtesy of Aimee Neff Alden.)

Pickle or relish dish, from $15 to **$25.00**
Plate, bread & butter; from $8 to **$12.00**
Plate, dinner; from $15 to **$30.00**
Plate, luncheon; from $10 to **$18.00**
Plate, salad; from $10 to..................................**$15.00**
Platter, 12", from $25 to...................................**$40.00**
Platter, 16" (or larger), from $40 to **$60.00**
Salt & pepper shakers, pr, from $15 to...............**$25.00**
Sugar bowl, w/lid, from $15 to **$30.00**
Tea & toast set (sm cup & tray), from $15 to.........**$25.00**
Teapot, demitasse pot, chocolate pot, or coffeepot, from $45
  to..**$60.00**

Novelty Clocks

Novelty clocks with some type of motion or animation were popular in spring-powered or wind-up form for hundreds of years. Today they bring thousands of dollars when sold. Electric-powered or motor-driven clocks first appeared in the late 1930s and were produced until quartz clocks became the standard, with the 1950s being the era during which they reached the height of their production.

Four companies led their field. They were Mastercrafters, United, Haddon, and Spartus in order of productivity. Mastercrafters was the earliest and longest-lived, making clocks from the late forties until the late eighties. (They did, however, drop out of business several times during this long period.) United began making clocks in the early fifties and continued until the early sixties. Haddon followed in the same time frame, and Spartus was in production from the late fifties until the mid-sixties.

These clocks are well represented in the listings that follow; prices are for examples in excellent condition and working. With an average age expectancy of forty years, many now need repair. Dried-out grease and dirt easily cause movements and motions not to function. The other nemesis of many motion clocks is deterioration of the fiber gears. Originally intended to keep the clocks quiet, fiber gears have not held up like their metal counterparts. For fully restored clocks, add $50.00 to $75.00 to our values. (Full restoration includes complete cleaning of motor and movement, repair of same; cleaning and polishing face and bezel; cleaning and polishing case and repairing if necessary; and installing new line cord, plug, and light bulb if needed.) Brown is the most common case color for plastic clocks. Add 10% to 20% or more for cases in onyx (mint green) or any light shade. If any parts noted below are missing, value can drop one-third to one-half. We must stress that 'as is' clocks will not bring these prices. Deteriorated, non-working clocks may be worth less that half of these values.

Note: When original names are not known, names have been assigned. Assigned names are given in parentheses.

Advisors: Sam and Anna Samuelian (See Directory, Novelty Clocks)

Haddon

Based in Chicago, Illinois, Haddon produced an attractive line of clocks. They used composition cases that were hand painted, and sturdy Hansen movements and motions. This is the only company from whom new replacement motions are still available.

Granny rocking (Home Sweet Home), composition, electric, from $75 to....................................**$100.00**
Rocking Horse (Rancho), composition, electric, from $125
  to...**$175.00**
Teeter Totter, children on seesaw, electric, from $100 to..**$125.00**

Mastercrafters

Based in Chicago, Illinois, this company produced many of the most appealing and popular collectible motion clocks on today's market. Cases were made of plastic, with earlier examples being a sturdy urea plastic that imparted quality, depth and shine to their finishes. Clock movements were relatively simple and often supplied by Sessions Clock Company, who also made many of their own clocks.

Airplane, Bakelite & chrome, electric, from $175 to.**$225.00**
Blacksmith, plastic, electric, from $75 to **$100.00**
Carousel, plastic, carousel front, from $175 to to **$200.00**
Church, w/bell ringer, plastic, electric **$115.00**
Fireplace, plastic, electric, from $50 to **$75.00**
Girl swinging, plastic, electric, from $100 to............**$125.00**
Swinging Bird, plastic, w/cage front, from $125 to ..**$150.00**
Swinging Playmates, plastic, w/fence, electric, from $100
  to..**$125.00**
Waterfall, plastic, electric...................................**$115.00**

Spartus

This company made clocks well into the eighties, but most later clocks were not animated. Cases were usually plastic, and most clocks featured animals.

Cat w/flirty eyes, plastic, electric, from $25 to............**$40.00**
Panda bear, plastic, eyes move, electric, from $25 to..**$40.00**
Water wheel (lg style), plastic, electric, from $20 to...**$30.00**
Waterfall & wheel, plastic, electric, from $50 to **$75.00**

United

Based in Brooklyn, New York, United made mostly cast-metal cases finished in gold or bronze. Their movements were somewhat more complex than Mastercrafters'. Some of their clocks contained musical movements, which while pleasing can be annoying when continuously run.

Ballerina, wooden, electric, from $75 to...................**$100.00**
Bobbing chicks, metal case, various colors, electric, from $35
  to...**$50.00**
Bobbing chicks, wooden house, green & red, electric, from
  $40 to...**$60.00**
Cowboy w/rope, metal, wood base, electric, from $100
  to **$125.00**
Dancers, metal w/square glass dome, electric, from $100
  to **$150.00**

Fireplace, metal, gold, electric, from $50 to **$75.00**
Fishing boy, metal, fishing pole & fish move, electric, from
    $100 to..**$125.00**
Hula girl & drummer, wooden, electric, from $200 to..**$250.00**
Majorette w/rotating baton, electric, from $75 to **$100.00**
Owl, metal owl on wooden base, eyes move, electric, from
    $50 to..**$75.00**
Windmill, pink plastic case, electric, minor cracks in plastic,
    from $75 to...**$100.00**

Miscellaneous

God Bless America, flag waves, electric, from $75 to..**$100.00**
Klocker Spaniel, electric, from $50 to **$75.00**
Poodle, various colors, electric, from $75 to.............**$100.00**

Novelty Radios

Novelty radios come in an unimaginable variety of shapes and sizes from advertising and product-shapes, character forms, and vehicles to anything the producer might dream up. For information on this new, fun collectible read *Collector's Guide to Novelty Radios* by Marty Bunis and Robert Breed and *Schroeder's Collectible Toys, Antique to Modern* (Collector Books).

Advisor: Marty and Sue Bunis (See Directory, Novelty Radios)

Atlas Red Brute Car Battery, red w/white lettering.....**$35.00**
Avon Skin-So-Soft Bottle & Box, China, 1990, 7½".....**$35.00**
Bart Simpson clock radio, Bart riding his skateboard on base
    next to alarm clock, JPI/China, 6½x8" **$50.00**
Batman, blue case w/blue molded Batman figure against red
    circle on front, Vanity Fair & DC Comics/Hong Kong,
    1978, 7"..**$150.00**
Big Bird Head, yellow molded face w/red & white striped bow
    tie, hand strap, Jim Henson Prod Inc/China, 4x5" ..**$25.00**
Blinking Cat, gray & white w/2 red hearts embossed on
    chest, flashing LEDS for eyes, 6½" **$25.00**

Bozo the Clown, plastic, 6x7", EX, $85.00. (Photo courtesy of Sue and Marty Bunis.)

Burger King, Aren't You Hungry w/Burger King emblem on
    white pocket radio w/Whopper headphones, Talbot
    Toys, 1983 ....**$35.00**
Calculator, pocket size w/hand strap, Stewart/Hong Kong,
    5x3" **$45.00**
Camel Cigarette Pack, w/hand strap, 4".......................**$65.00**
Campbell's Cup Chicken Noodle w/White Meat Box, red on
    white, 2 Minute Soup Mix, PRI/China...................**$35.00**

Campbell's Soup Can, M...**$35.00**
Casper the Friendly Ghost, white Casper figure against yellow round case w/black outline, Sutton/Hong Kong,
    1972, 6½"...**$75.00**
Champion Spark Plug Box, M.......................................**$50.00**
Charlie Tuna, figure standing upright on base, red hat
    w/white name **$100.00**
Chevy Impala SS (1966), red, 2x8⅜"...........................**$75.00**
Cinnamon Toast Crunch 3-Ring Binder w/built-in radio,
    cover shows 3 chefs dancing to the music, Radioart/
    Taiwan **$50.00**
Combination Lock, marked Solid State, combination wheel in
    tuning knob, 6½x4"..**$75.00**
Coronet Paper Towels, M..**$32.00**
Del Monte Pineapple Chunks Can, replica label w/In It's
    Own Juice No Sugar Added on red dot.................**$75.00**
Delco Voyager Car Battery, black w/yellow & white lettering
    & trim...**$35.00**
Disco Sound Hi Fi, Art Deco styling w/couple dancing on
    disco dance floor, Hong Kong, 7x8" **$55.00**
Duracell Alkaline Battery, black & gold.....................**$40.00**
Dutch Boy Dirt Fighter Interior Latex Flat Wall Paint Can,
    w/plastic lid & bail handle..................................**$50.00**
EXXON Steel Belted Radial 78 T, black tire w/white lettering
    & stripe, chrome & black wheel, beveled stand ..**$45.00**
Faberge Brut Bottle, Industrial Contacts/New York, made in
    Japan, 8" **$60.00**
Flashlight, blue disk on key chain, Admiral, 3¾" dia ..**$45.00**
Ghostbusters, green Slimer figure on yellow base w/No
    Ghost symbol & Dancing Slimer FM Radio, Justin Toys,
    1984/1988 ....**$30.00**
Ghostbusters, The Real Ghostbusters lettered around No
    Ghost symbol on square case, Concept 2000/China,
    1986/1989, 4"...**$30.00**
Good News/Bad News, white pocket size, red smiling lips
    w/frowning lips & blue teardrop on reverse, Concept
    2000 ....**$50.00**
Hair Dryer, #2401-H, marked AirWaves 2000, black w/white
    lettering & trim, J&D Brush Co/China, 9" **$50.00**
Havoline Supreme Motor Oil Can, black & red on white
    Texaco emblem w/red & black lettering on gold ..**$35.00**
Hires Root Beer Can, image of frothy mug on wood-grain
    background **$30.00**
Hubba Bubba Soda Can, reads Original Bubble Gum .**$60.00**
Incredible Hulk, green 2-D crouching figure w/black outline,
    Marvel Comics/Amico Inc, 1978, 7".....................**$75.00**
Jerky Treats Box, white w/heart emblem above Beef Flavor
    lettered on diagonal red band, hungry pup looking up,
    Hong Kong **$35.00**
Keebler Animal Crackers Box, Uncommonly Good, multi-colored animals on white background, red handle,
    Taiwan **$45.00**
Kool-Aid Kool Bursts Bottle, replica w/shoulder strap, Kraft
    General Foods, 1992...**$35.00**
Lipton Cup-A-Soup, MIB...**$55.00**
Lunch Box, gold w/clown decals on ends, front panel
    w/dials & multicolored dots on white, Midland/Taiwan,
    5x6" **$35.00**
Marathon Ultra D Oil Can, M **$32.00**

Master Padlock, silver-tone w/Master lettered in black on red base, Hong Kong, 4½"...$75.00

Mr Peanut, MIB...$75.00

Nacho 'N Corn Thins Box, Nabisco, PRI/Hong Kong...$50.00

Oscar the Grouch, AM, MIB, $42.00.

Parking Meter, #131, black full-size replica on short round base, buffalo nickel displayed in sm window, Thomas, 17"...$75.00

Pepperidge Farm Distinctive Stuffing Box, China.......$50.00

Pink Panther, dark gray case outlined around gray & white image, marked The Pink Panther, Amico/Hong Kong, 1978, 9"...$100.00

Planet of the Apes, pendant style w/gold chain, Introport Development Co/Hong Kong, 1974, 3½" dia.......$45.00

Planters Cocktail Nuts Can..$55.00

Popeye, Olive Oyl, Sweet Pea & Wimpy, yellow fish-shaped case w/image of characters in sailboat, King Features/Minizoo...$50.00

RC (Royal Crown Cola) Can, Me & My RC, blue w/red & white lettering...$35.00

Robt E Lee Riverboat, red, white & blue w/brass trim, 9x16"...$75.00

Salem Filter Cigarette Pack, green & white on green, w/hand strap, 4...$75.00

Scott Towels Roll, gold seal reading 1931-1991 60 Years Of Value, blue floral design, w/antenna, Scott Paper Co, 1985..$60.00

Seven-Up #2001 Vending Machine, green w/red & white square 7-Up emblem on green & white vertical stripes, Hong Kong...$100.00

Shell SU 2000 Gas Pump, white w/black, red & yellow trim, Hong Kong...$50.00

Smiley Face, w/shoulder strap, Stewart, 3½" dia.......$45.00

Snapple Badge, I'm Tuned To Snapple/Pure — Natural Juice & Soda, red & black on white................................$55.00

Snoopy, figure sitting upright on round black pillow-type base, Determined Products/Hong Kong, 7".........$45.00

Spider-Man, red plastic disk shape w/Spider-Man signal design on front, w/strap & stand, unused, M......$20.00

Touring Car, red (ca 1917) model w/fixed roof, black fenders & running boards, gold-tone spoked wheels & trim, 5x9"...$75.00

Toy Soldier, red cylinder body w/blue hat, round white base, General Electric/Hong Kong, 7"............................$75.00

Twix Cookies-n-Creme/Chocolate Fudge, white w/replica label, white handle, rectangular, China................$75.00

UCAR Heavy Duty Anti-Freeze & Summer Coolant Can, red w/red, white & blue label, PRI/Hong Kong.........$50.00

Veryfine Apple Juice, M...$35.00

Video Camera, Accent, China, 4½x7"............................$50.00

Welch's Grape Juice Can, M..$32.00

Yoo-hoo Chocolate Flavored Drink Box, w/antenna & hand strap, China $45.00

Novelty Telephones

Novelty telephones modeled after products or advertising items are popular with collectors. Those that are cartoon or advertising character related are highly desired by collectors. For further information we recommend *Schroeder's Collectible Toys, Antique to Modern* (Collector Books).

Alf, plush figure w/phone, Hong Kong, NM...............$80.00

Bart Simpson, MIB...$35.00

Baseball Bat, M...$80.00

Batmobile (First Movie), MIB..$65.00

Beatle Bailey, 1983, MIB..$95.00

Bozo the Clown, Telemania, MIB..................................$80.00

Budweiser Beer Can, M...$30.00

Cabbage Patch Girl, 1980s, EX+....................................$85.00

Charlie Tuna, MIB...$60.00

Crest Sparkle Guy, M..$25.00

Garfield, eyes open & close, 1980s, EX.......................$40.00

Gumby, Perma Toys, 1985, MIB, $70.00.

Heinz Ketchup Bottle, MIB..$70.00

Inspector Gadget, 1984, MIB $65.00

Keebler Elf, figure stands beside receiver, M $50.00

Keebler Elf, NM $100.00

Kermit the Frog, push-button style, EX+ $225.00

Little Green Sprout, EX+ $75.00

Little Orphan Annie, 1983, M...$85.00

Mario Brothers, 1980s, MIB...$50.00

Mickey Mouse, ATC, NM..$100.00

Mickey Mouse, Unisonic, NM $70.00

Pizza Hut Pete, 1980s..$60.00

Poppin' Fresh, extended arm holds receiver, M $250.00

Raid Bug, EX+...$125.00

Seven-Up Can, EX+ $35.00

Snoopy, reclining figure w/push buttons, wall-mount, M..**$30.00**

Snoopy & Woodstock, extended arm holds receiver, M..**$60.00**

Snoopy & Woodstock, rotary dial, American Telephone, EX...**$125.00**

Snoopy & Woodstock, touch-tone, American Telephone, 1970s, EX...**$100.00**

Star Trek Enterprise Spaceship, MIB **$80.00**

Tang Lips, #1, MIB...**$100.00**

Tetley Tea Man, man on round base marked Tetley, Canadian premium, M................................**$200.00**

Tyrannosaurus Rex, MIB...**$80.00**

Winnie the Pooh, square base, M **$250.00**

Ziggy, 1989, MIB..**$80.00**

Eagle head, cast iron, 1860s, 4⅛x10¾".....................**$125.00**

Enterprise, cast iron, clamp-on, lever action, ca 1914...**$30.00**

Fish, olive wood, Greek, 1950s, 2¼x8" **$25.00**

Home, cast iron, screws to table, long lever, 1800s....**$40.00**

Lady's legs, cast brass, ca 1900s, 5½" **$55.00**

Lion, aluminum, on base, reproduction, 1900s, 5⅜x10" ...**$40.00**

Naughty Nellie, brass, unmarked, 6".........................**$35.00**

Punch & Judy, full figure, brass, 5" **$75.00**

Skull & cross bones, nickel-plated cast iron, English, 1928, 2x6"..**$100.00**

Whale, hand-wrought brass, marked HA PIND, 1900s, 1x6¼"...**$110.00**

Wolf's head, nickel-plated cast iron, marked Pat 1920, 4⅞x10"..**$125.00**

Nutcrackers

Many nutcrackers are figurals — squirrels and dogs are probably the easiest to find — and many are made of cast iron; but you'll also find hand-carved wood examples as well as brass and aluminum. The more imaginative the better. A maker's mark or a patent date adds to their worth. If you'd like more information, refer to *Ornamental and Figural Nutcrackers* by Judith A. Rittenhouse (Collector Books).

Advisor: Earl MacSorley (See Directory, Nutcrackers)

Club/Newsletter: Nutcracker Collectors' Club
Susan Otto, Editor
12204 Fox Run Dr.
Chesterland, OH 44026; 216-792-2686; $10.00 annual dues, quarterly newsletters sent to members, free classifieds

Alligator, cast brass, mounted to base, ca 1890s, 7½"...**$90.00**

Alligator, painted aluminum, John Wright, 1960s........**$20.00**

Antelope head, carved wood, glass eyes, ca 1890s, 9".**$150.00**

Anvil & blacksmith's hammer, black-painted cast iron, Wright, 1960s, 4" **$15.00**

Arcade, cast iron, lever action, ca 1920 ....**$30.00**

Bearded man's face, carved wood, $100.00.

Boxer (dog), wooden, glass eyes, probably Swiss, early 1900s, 7" **$135.00**

Clamp-on style, cast iron, mechanical, marked Enterprise Pat 1914 ....**$30.00**

Dog, black-painted cast iron, marked 24H on handle, ca 1900, 10½"..**$65.00**

Dog, cast iron w/tail handle, rectangular base, 13" **$95.00**

Occupied Japan Collectibles

Some items produced in Japan during the period from the end of WWII until the occupation ended in 1952 were marked Occupied Japan. No doubt much of the ware from this era was marked simply Japan, since obviously the 'Occupied' term caused considerable resentment among the Japanese people, and they were understandably reluctant to use the mark. So even though you may find identical items marked simply Japan or Made in Japan, only those with the more limited Occupied Japan mark are evaluated here.

Assume that the items described below are ceramic unless another material is mentioned. For more information, we recommend *The Collector's Encyclopedia of Occupied Japan* (there are five in the series) by Gene Florence.

Newsletter: *The Upside Down World of an O.J. Collector*
The Occupied Japan Club
c/o Florence Archambault
29 Freeborn St.
Newport, RI 02840; Published bimonthly. Information requires SASE

Ashtray, Colorado, embossed metal **$5.00**

Ashtray, knight's head w/shield-shaped bowl, 2 rests, gray & green w/gold trim, Lenwile China #6332..............**$10.00**

Ashtrays w/holder, figural elephant on holder w/5 ashtrays, glossy brown **$20.00**

Ashtrays w/holder, 3 figural elephants (trunks up) on triangular holder w/ashtray, glossy brown, 5½"..........**$15.00**

Bookends, wood, masted ships on L-shaped bases, dark brown stain, pr..**$75.00**

Boot, white w/blue flower & leaf design on top & upper sides, blue-trimmed sole, 3½"................................**$6.00**

Boot, white w/tan 'tooled' scroll design at calf, multicolored flowers & leaves on top, tan sole & heel, 6½" **$15.00**

Boutonniere, red, white & blue plastic on paper backing, marked OJ...**$4.00**

Bowl, salad; hand-turned wood, black lacquer, Karavan, 4x11½"..**$18.00**

Celluloid dog, down on front paws w/rear up, tongue out, white w/airbrushed brown spots, red collar **$15.00**

Celluloid doll, standing w/stationary legs, articulated arms, green 'crocheted' hat, top & pants w/booties **$30.00**

Celluloid lamb, standing, embossed, white w/pastel purple airbrushing on back.................................**$10.00**

Celluloid tiger, standing & roaring, embossed, airbrushed in natural colors......................................**$12.00**

Cigarette lighter, figural hand holding lighter, silver-plated metal **$15.00**

Coaster, papier-mache, round, floral decor..................**$5.00**

Condiment set, chicken nodders w/center well..........**$35.00**

Creamer, figural lemon......................................**$10.00**

Cup, Father lettered in gold, multicolored floral & scroll spray, 3½x3¾" dia **$15.00**

Cup & saucer, demitasse; slightly scalloped rim, black w/1-sided muted flower & leaf decor w/gold trim, Lenwile #6195..**$25.00**

Cup & saucer, demitasse; swirled pattern w/flared foot, rust w/gold handle & decor **$10.00**

Cup & saucer, demitasse; white w/allover red maple leaf design inside & out, gold trim, flared foot **$12.00**

Fan, silk w/bamboo sticks, hand-painted flowers on dark blue, 7" **$16.00**

Figurine, ballerina, blue-bodiced tutu, gold shoes & trim, pedestal base, 4¾"..**$40.00**

Figurine, bisque, bride & groom on round base, he in black tux, she in white w/multicolored flowers, New Star, 4" **$22.00**

Figurine, bisque, girl w/donkey cart, pastel colors w/gold trim, 3" **$65.00**

Figurine, bisque, man w/hands in pockets, whittled look, brown jacket w/blue pants, black hat, 2½" **$8.00**

Figurine, boy skier, green pants, orange shirt, on brown base, 2" **$5.00**

Figurine, boy violinist sitting on wall, brown shorts, blue jacket & green pointed hat, 4" **$10.00**

Figurine, colonial couple, 7½", $40.00 for the pair.

Figurine, colonial couple standing on base, he in blue coat, she in black & pink dress, gold trim, 4¾" **$15.00**

Figurine, Delft Blue, lady dancing & playing tambourine, hat in hand, pink ruffled hem, 5½"...........................**$25.00**

Figurine, Dutch couple holding baskets, he in yellow shirt w/red tie & blue pants, she in red & green dress, 4⅛", pr ..**$25.00**

Figurine, elf positioned on feet & hands looking forward, pink top, white ruffled collar, green pants & hat...........**$15.00**

Figurine, girl w/basket, standing in pink dress w/white pinafore & turquoise bandana, round base, gold trim, 4" **$10.00**

Figurine, pastoral lady holding jug, green hat, blue bodice, yellow bustle, orange ruffled skirt, red shoes, 6½".....**$25.00**

Lamp, courting couple, 6½", pr...................................**$60.00**

Lamp, pink-hatted lady, 8⅛".......................................**$35.00**

Leaf dish, cut-out handle, pastel floral decor on white, gold trim..**$5.00**

Leaf dish, cut-out handle, white sunflower w/blue leaves & stem on brown, embossed MIOJ.........................**$10.00**

Leaf dish, 1 lg w/2 sm oak leaves & 3 acorns embossed at stem, airbrushed green & tan w/painted veins, Ucagco China **$5.00**

Miniature cup & saucer, 4-footed square shape w/scalloped rims, floral decor on white w/black bands, gold handle & trim...**$10.00**

Miniature milk bottle, white w/gold trim......................**$5.00**

Miniature table lamp, pleated shade on white flared base w/red-lined trim...**$15.00**

Miniature teapot w/creamer & sugar bowl, multicolored floral decor on white w/tan lustre lids & handles....**$25.00**

Napkin, linen damask, paper label, 11¾" square **$12.00**

Parasol, tissue paper & bamboo, 4" **$6.50**

Party blowouts, colorful paper w/feather at end, whistle-type end **$1.00**

Perfume bottle, glass, canteen shape w/impressed Deco design, 2¾"...**$18.00**

Pincushion, heart-shaped metal holder w/fuchsia cushion, fancy textured design on metal **$8.00**

Pincushion, 10 Oriental babies hug rose cookie, 2" ...**$30.00**

Planter, applied angelfish on blue seaweed, 5x3x3"...**$12.00**

Planter, cucumber shape, green...................................**$8.00**

Planter, donkey pulling cart, small, $10.00.

Planter, donkey w/green cart, lg **$15.00**

Planter, Nubian in white turban & costume w/red accents, and gold shoes, earrings, holding white basket...**$25.00**

Planter, Oriental girl w/pink parasol seated between 2 baskets on base, rust top, blue pants, gold trim, 5" **$18.00**

Planter, Oriental pulling rickshaw, red mark...............**$18.00**

Planter, wicker-look baby buggy w/baby looking out, hand-painted flowers, brown trim, 3½".........................**$12.00**

Plaques, bisque, framed raised bust images of colonial lady & gent, pastel colors w/fabric lace, gold trim, 4½x4", pr...**$45.00**

Plate stand, wood, SS diamond mark **$15.00**

Rooster, inflatable rubber, purple ink stamp **$20.00**

Sewing kit, metal box w/thread & needles, red velvet mirrored top..**$20.00**

Shoe, rust-colored high-heel w/white dots, applied pink & green flower & leaves, bow at heel, 2½" **$8.00**

Shoe, white high-heel w/head image of George Washington on toe, red mark #02027 ....**$14.00**

Souvenir ashtray, Florida, shaped like the state, white w/black block lettering & colorful images, gold trim, Burger **$16.00**

Souvenir dish, General View of Niagara Falls, ivory band, gold trim, 3½" square **$5.00**

Souvenir pitcher, Lookout Mountain Tennessee, china, white ball shape w/circular image, gold trim, sm **$5.00**

Souvenir plate, Will Rogers Memorial/Claremore Oklahoma, 3½" dia...**$5.00**

Sugar bowl (open), figural tomato **$12.00**

Toby mug, black straw bonnet tied to head w/white kerchief, umbrella handle, 2⅜" **$22.00**

Toby mug, cross-eyed man, 2½" **$10.00**

Toby mug, man's head w/pursed lips, black hat, brown hair, green collar, red tie, blue front, 2½" **$12.00**

Tray, papier-mache, multicolored hand-painted flowers w/brown scrolls on mustard, 8x4¼" **$6.50**

Vase, tankard shape, cobalt bamboo reeding & handle, molded hand-painted leaf spray, 3½" **$8.00**

Window box, basketweave w/hand-painted floral swags, blue rope trim, 6x3" **$8.00**

Wishing well, brown w/yellow bucket........................**$12.50**

Old MacDonald's Farm

This is a wonderful line of novelty kitchenware items fashioned as the family and the animals that live on Old MacDonald's Farm. It's been popular with collectors for quite some time, and prices are astronomical, though they seem to have stabilized, at least for now.

These things were made by the Regal China Company, who also made some of the Little Red Riding Hood items that are so collectible, as well as figural cookie jars, 'hugger' salt and pepper shakers, and decanters. The Roerig's devote a chapter to Regal in their book *The Collector's Encyclopedia of Cookie Jars* and, in fact, show the entire Old MacDonald's Farm line.

Advisor: Rick Spencer (See Directory, Regal China)

Butter dish, cow's head..**$220.00**

Canister, flour, cereal or coffee, med, each..............**$220.00**

Canister, pretzels, peanuts, popcorn, chips or tidbits, lg, each **$300.00**

Canister, salt, sugar or tea; med, each **$220.00**

Canister, soap or cookies; lg, each............................**$300.00**

Cookie jar, barn **$275.00**

Creamer, rooster **$110.00**

Grease jar, pig..**$175.00**

Pitcher, milk **$400.00**

Shakers, boy & girl, pr **$75.00**

Shakers, churn, gold trim, pr **$90.00**

Shakers, feed shacks w/sheep, pr.............................**$195.00**

Spice jar, assorted lids, sm, each **$100.00**

Sugar bowl, hen...**$125.00**

Teapot, duck's head **$250.00**

Paden City Pottery

Founded in 1907, this company produced many dinnerware and kitchenware lines until they closed in the 1950s. Many were decaled; in fact, this company is credited with originating the underglaze decal process.

One of their most collectible lines is called Caliente. It was Paden City's version of the solid-color dinnerware lines that became so popular in the thirties and forties. Caliente's shapes were simple and round, but its shell-like finials, handles, and feet did little to enhance its Art Deco possibilities, which the public seemed to prefer at that time. As a result, it never sold in volume comparable to Fiesta or Bauer's Ring, but you should be able to rebuild a set eventually, and your efforts would be well worthwhile. If you'd like to see photographs of this line and many others produced by Paden City, see *The Collector's Encyclopedia of American Dinnerware* by Jo Cunningham.

Candle holder, ball form on square base, from $15 to..**$20.00**

Casserole, Floral, w/lid, from $15 to **$18.00**

Casserole, Patio decal, w/lid, round, from $20 to.......**$25.00**

Creamer, Far East on Shell-Crest shape, from $8 to....**$10.00**

Creamer, Yellow Rose on Minion shape, from $6 to **$8.00**

Cup & saucer, AD; American Beauty, from $12 to **$15.00**

Cup & saucer, Caliente, from $12 to **$16.00**

Cup & saucer, Paden Rose, from $6 to **$8.00**

Cup & saucer, Posies, from $4 to **$6.00**

Cup & saucer, Yellow Rose on Minion shape, from $8 to ...**$10.00**

Gravy boat, Nasturtium, from $12 to **$17.00**

Plate, Caliente, tangerine, 6", from $4 to **$6.00**

Plate, Far East on Shell-Crest shape, 9", from $4 to......**$6.00**

Plate, Paden Rose, 7", from $2 to **$3.00**

Plate, Patio decal, lg, from $8 to **$10.00**

Plate, Poppy, 7", from $2 to.......................................**$4.00**

Plate, serving; American Beauty on Minion shape, from $8 to...**$12.00**

Plate, Strawberry, Shenandoah Ware, 8", from $2 to **$4.00**

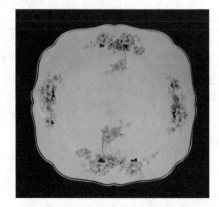

Plate, Touch of Black, $8.00.

Plate, Wild Rose on Princess line, 9", from $6 to.........**$8.00**

Platter, Patio decal on Shell-Crest shape, oval, from $15 to **$20.00**

Salt shaker, rose decal, from $4 to **$6.00**

Sugar bowl, Acacia Flowers, w/lid, from $12 to **$14.00**

Sugar bowl, Caliente, w/lid, from $15 to....................**$20.00**

Sugar bowl, Jonquil, from $4 to **$6.00**

Sugar bowl, Nasturtium decal on Shell-Crest shape, w/lid, from $12 to..**$14.00**

Teapot, Caliente, from $45 to **$50.00**

Paper Dolls

One of the earliest producers of paper dolls was Raphael Tuck of England, who distributed many of their dolls in the United States in the late 1800s. Advertising companies used them to promote their products, and some were often included in the pages of leading ladies' magazines.

But over the years, the most common paper dolls have been those printed on the covers of a book containing their clothes on the inside pages. These were initiated during the 1920s and because they were inexpensive retained their popularity even during the Depression years. They peaked in the 1940s, but with the advent of television in the fifties, children began to loose interest. Be sure to check old boxes and trunks in your attic, you just may find some waiting for you.

But what's really exciting right now are those from more recent years — celebrity dolls from television shows like 'The Brady Bunch' or 'The Waltons,' the skinny English model Twiggy, and movie stars like Rock Hudson and Debbie Reynolds. Just remember that cut sets (even if all original components are still there) are worth only about half the price of dolls in mint, uncut, originial condition.

If you'd like to learn more about them, we recommend *Collector's Guide to Paper Dolls* (there are two in the series) and *Collector's Guide to Magazine Paper Dolls,* all by Mary Young. Other references: *Collecting Toys #6* by Richard O'Brien; *Schroeder's Collectible Toys, Antique to Modern;* and *Toys, Antique and Collectible,* by David Longest.

Advisor: Mary Young (See Directory, Paper Dolls)

Newsletter: *Paper Dolls News*
Ema Terry
P.O. Box 807
Vivian, LA 71082; Subscription: $12 per year for 6 issues; want lists, sale items and trades listed

Newsletter: *Paper Doll and Doll Diary*
Mary Longo
P.O. Box 12146
Lake Park, FL 33403; Subscription: $12 per year for 6 issues

Circus Paper Dolls, Saalfield #2610, 1952, uncut, $35.00. (Photo courtesy of Mary Young.)

Annette Funicello, Walt Disney, 1950s, uncut, M........**$55.00**
Archies, Whitman #1987, 1969, 5 dolls, uncut, M (EX folder) **$30.00**

Babes in Toyland, 1961, uncut, M................................**$35.00**
Baby Sparkle Plenty, Saalfield, 1963, NM **$50.00**
Barbie's Quick Curl, Whitman #1984, 1973, incomplete ..**$10.00**
Barbie's Jewel Secrets, Whitman #1537, 1987, EX.........**$5.00**
Belles of the Civil War, Costume Dolls #226A, Platt & Munk, 1962, EX (VG+ box) **$12.00**
Beverly Hillbillies, Whitman #1955, 1964, 4 dolls, EX+ ..**$40.00**
Blondie (TV show), Saalfield #4434, 1968, uncut, M ..**$40.00**
Bozo the Clown Circus, 1966, unused, M....................**$25.00**
Cabbage Patch Deluxe Paper Dolls, Avalon, 1983, NM **$10.00**
Chuck & Di Have a Baby, Simon & Schuster, 1982, uncut, M **$15.00**
Debbie Reynolds Cut-Outs, Whitman #1970, 1959, EX....**$30.00**
Dinah Shore & George Montgomery Cut-Outs, Whitman #1970, 1959, EX..**$30.00**
Dodie, Saalfield #6044, 1971, unused, MIB **$35.00**
Dolly Darlings, Whitman #1963, 1966, G (original folder) **$20.00**
Donnie & Marie Osmond, Whitman #1991, uncut, M....**$22.00**
Family Affair's Buffy, Whitman #1985, 1968, uncut, M ..**$25.00**
Family Affair's Mrs Beasley Paper Doll Fashions, Whitman 1972, NM (NM folder) **$25.00**
Faye Emerson, Saalfield #2722, 1952, uncut, NM........**$85.00**
Finger Ding Paper Dolls, Whitman #1993, 1971, uncut, M..**$15.00**
Flying Nun, Saalfield #5121, 1968, M........................**$40.00**
Grace Kelly Cut-Out Dolls, Whitman #2069, 1956, uncut, NM (EX folder)..**$110.00**
Green Acres, Whitman #1979, 1967, EX+ (EX+ folder) .**$30.00**
Green Acres Magic Stay-On Dolls, Whitman #4773, 1968, EXIB..**$25.00**
Happy Days, Fonzie, Toy Factory #105, 1976, MIP (sealed) **$25.00**
Hayley Mills 'Moon Spinners' Cut-Out Doll, Whitman #1960, 1965, VG+..**$30.00**
Hayley Mills Summer Magic Cut-Outs, Whitman #1966, 1963, M..**$35.00**
Howdy Doody Puppet Show, 1952, VG **$25.00**
Jaclyn Smith, Charlie's Angels Kelly, Toy Factory, 1977, NRFB **$45.00**

Jane Russell Paper Dolls and Coloring Book, Saalfield #4328, 1955, uncut, $95.00. (Photo courtesy of Mary Young.)

Julia, Saalfield, #6055, 1968, MIB................................**$45.00**
Kiddle Kolognes, Whitman #1992, 1969, M................**$25.00**
Laugh-In Paper Doll & Punch-Out Book, Saalfield #1325, 1969, NM **$45.00**

Mary Poppins, Jane & Michael, Strathmore #1892-6, 1964, uncut, M **$35.00**

Mary Poppins, Whitman #1967, 1973, uncut, M.......... **$25.00**

Mary Poppins, Whitman #1982, 1966, M **$40.00**

Mickey & Minnie Steppin' Out, Whitman #1979, 1977, M. **$15.00**

My Fair Lady, Columbia Broadcasting, 1965, M **$35.00**

Nanny & the Professor, Artcraft, 1970, M (NM folder). **$35.00**

National Velvet, Whitman #1958, 1961, EX+ (EX folder) . **$25.00**

Oklahoma, A Golden Paper Doll Story Book, Simon & Schuster, 1956, M **$85.00**

Partridge Family, Artcraft #5137, 1971, M (NM folder). **$40.00**

Pat Boone Cut-Outs, Whitman #1968, 1959, M **$50.00**

Petal People Paper Dolls, Whitman #1980, 1969, incomplete, w/folder **$10.00**

Playhouse Kiddles Paperdolls, Whitman #1954, 1971, M. **$30.00**

Princess Di Paper Doll Book, Whitman #1985-50, M . **$15.00**

Raggedy Ann & Andy, Whitman #1713-B, 1978, uncut, MIB **$20.00**

Raggedy Ann & Andy, Whitman #1979, 1966, uncut, M. **$25.00**

Ricky Nelson, Whitman #2081, 1959, uncut, M **$65.00**

Rock Hudson, Whitman #2087, 1957, uncut, NM **$65.00**

Roy Rogers & Dale Evans, Whitman #1950, 1954, EX (EX folder) **$40.00**

Shirley Temple, Saalfield #1715, uncut, M................. **$200.00**

Shirley Temple, Saalfield #290, uncut, M................... **$135.00**

Shirley Temple, Whitman #4388, 1976, MIB, $25.00.

Sid & Marty Krofft's Kaleidoscope Puppets, Hemisphere/ Coca-Cola, 1968, uncut, M **$30.00**

Storybook Kiddles Sweethearts Paper Dolls, Whitman #1956, 1969, uncut, M **$30.00**

Tammy & Her Family, Whitman #1997, 1964, uncut, VG+ .. **$30.00**

That Girl, Saalfield #4479, 1967, uncut, M................... **$40.00**

Twiggy, Whitman #1499, 1967, M **$35.00**

Walter Lantz Cartoon Stars, Saalfield #1344, 1963, uncut, M.. **$30.00**

Welcome Back Kotter, Toy Factory, 1976, MIB (sealed) .. **$25.00**

Pencil Sharpeners

The whittling process of sharpening pencils with pocketknives was replaced by mechanical means in the 1880s. By the turn of the century, many ingenious desk-type sharpeners had been developed. Small pencil sharpeners designed for the purse or pocket were produced in the 1890s. The typical design consisted of a small steel tube containing a cutting blade which could be adjusted by screws. Mass-produced novelty pencil sharpeners became popular in the late 1920s. The most detailed figurals were made in Germany. These German sharpeners that originally sold for less than a dollar are now considered highly collectible!

Disney and other character pencil sharpeners have been produced in Catalin, plastic, ceramic, and rubber. Novelty battery-operated pencil sharpeners can also be found. For over fifty years pencil sharpeners have been used as advertising giveaways — from Baker's Chocolates and Coca-Cola's metal figurals to the plastic 'Marshmallow Man' distributed by McDonald's. As long as we have pencils, new pencil sharpeners will be produced, much to the delight of collectors.

Advisor: Phil Helley (See Directory, Pencil Sharpeners)

Plastic, Goofy clinging to side, marked WDP, ca 1980, $20.00. (Photo courtesy of Martha Hughes.)

Bakelite, airplane, from $40 to **$45.00**

Bakelite, baby chick, 1⅜" **$55.00**

Bakelite, Br'er Bear, WDP, round, fluted, 1⅜".............. **$45.00**

Bakelite, Charley McCarthy, from $45 to **$50.00**

Bakelite, Cinderella, decaled, round, from $55 to **$65.00**

Bakelite, Donald Duck, long-billed, 1" **$65.00**

Bakelite, elephant, 1⅝" **$40.00**

Bakelite, G-man gun, 2" **$30.00**

Bakelite, Joe Carioca, WDP, square, 1½" **$75.00**

Bakelite, Keep 'em Flying, round, 1" **$50.00**

Bakelite, Mickey Mouse, from $70 to.......................... **$80.00**

Bakelite, pig, 1⅜" **$65.00**

Bakelite, Popeye, decaled, rectangular **$40.00**

Bakelite, Scottie dog, from $20 to **$25.00**

Bakelite, tank, Keep 'Em Rolling, from $35 to **$40.00**

Bakelite, 1939, New York World's Fair **$50.00**

Celluloid, Japan, Black bride w/bouquet of flowers, 2¼" .. **$175.00**

Celluloid, Japan, elephant, 2" **$140.00**

Metal, Germany, dog... **$50.00**

Metal, Germany, drummer, from $35 to **$40.00**

Metal, Germany, elephant, ⅞" **$50.00**

Metal, Germany, grandfather clock, 1½" **$125.00**

Metal, Germany, magnifying glass w/3 kittens............ **$65.00**

Metal, Germany, nude boy w/silver cap **$50.00**

Metal, Germany, Statue of Liberty, 3" **$185.00**

Metal, Germany, typewriter **$75.00**

Metal, Occupied Japan, armored car, w/whistle & rubber wheels, from $75 to.. **$80.00**

Metal, Occupied Japan, bulldog head, 1½"................. **$65.00**

Metal, Occupied Japan, clown head w/bow tie, 1¾". **$50.00**
Metal, Occupied Japan, Indian chief bust....................**$85.00**
Metal, Occupied Japan, smiling pig face w/hat, 1¾"..**$70.00**

Pennsbury Pottery

From the 1950s throughout the sixties, this pottery was sold in gift stores and souvenir shops along the Pennsylvania Turnpike. It was produced in Morrisville, Pennsylvania, by Henry and Lee Below. Much of the ware was hand painted in multicolor on caramel backgrounds, though some pieces were made in blue and white. Most of the time, themes centered around Amish people, barber shop singers, roosters, hex signs, and folky mottos.

Much of the ware is marked, and if you're in the Pennsylvania/New Jersey area, you'll find lots of it. It's fairly prevalent in the Midwest as well and can still sometimes be found at bargain prices. If you'd like to learn more about this pottery, we recommend *Pennsbury Pottery Video Book* by Shirley Graff and BA Wellman.

Advisor: Shirley Graff (See Directory, Pennsbury)

Ashtray, Doylestown Trust..............................**$25.00**
Ashtray, Fairless Works, gray.........................**$30.00**
Ashtray, Outen the Light.................................**$20.00**
Ashtray, Rotary Club, Levittown, 8"................**$15.00**
Ashtray, Schmootzer's....................................**$30.00**
Bowl, Reverse, footed, 9"...............................**$35.00**
Butter dish, Folkart, w/lid, 5x4".....................**$45.00**
Cake stand, Black Rooster..............................**$85.00**
Candlesticks, hummingbird, #117, 5", pr.........**$250.00**
Candy dish, Hex, 6"..**$35.00**
Canister set, tea, coffee, flour & sugar, Black Rooster..**$550.00**

Casserole, Red Rooster, with lid, $75.00.

Coaster, Fish, pretzel form.............................**$20.00**
Coffeepot, Red Rooster, 2-cup, 6"...................**$40.00**
Creamer & sugar bowl, Red Rooster................**$45.00**
Cruets, Gay Nineties, pr.................................**$160.00**
Cruets, Pennsylvania Dutch, pr.......................**$120.00**
Cup & saucer, Hex..**$20.00**
Dealer sign, featuring birds............................**$150.00**
Desk basket, eagle..**$45.00**
Figurine, bluebird, 4".....................................**$125.00**

Figurine, bunny on gourd...............................**$150.00**
Figurine, cardinal, #120, 6½"..........................**$200.00**
Figurine, goldfinch, 4"....................................**$200.00**
Figurine, hummingbird, #119, 3½"...................**$200.00**
Figurine, magnolia warbler.............................**$135.00**
Figurine, redstart, 3".....................................**$135.00**
Figurine, scarlet tananger, 5½".......................**$250.00**
Figurine, Slick Chick.......................................**$150.00**
Figurine, wren, white, sm...............................**$75.00**
Gravy boat, Black Rooster...............................**$30.00**
Mug, Amish Couple...**$25.00**
Mug, beer; Gay Nineties..................................**$20.00**
Mug, Black Rooster...**$22.00**
Mug, Here's Looking at You..............................**$35.00**
Pie plate, Black Rooster, #1045........................**$85.00**
Pie plate, boy & girl, 9"...................................**$80.00**
Pitcher, Amish, 2½"...**$30.00**
Pitcher, Amish man, 5"....................................**$35.00**
Pitcher, Black Rooster, 4"................................**$22.00**
Pitcher, Folkart, 3¾"..**$25.00**
Pitcher, Tulip, 4"..**$40.00**
Plaque, Bucks Country Week commemorative...........**$40.00**
Plaque, eagle, 12½"...**$70.00**
Plaque, National & Newark Banking Co..............**$50.00**
Plaque, Pennsylvania family wagon, 8"..............**$45.00**
Plaque, Toleware, brown, 5x7".........................**$40.00**
Plate, Chistmas, 1970, w/angel.......................**$40.00**
Plate, Courting Buggy, 8"................................**$25.00**
Plate, Daily Bread..**$60.00**
Plate, Mother's Day, 1971, from $30 to.............**$35.00**
Plate, Red Rooster, 10"...................................**$40.00**
Pretzel bowl, Amish couple.............................**$75.00**

Pretzel bowl, Amish family and red barn, 12", from $75.00 to $80.00.

Pretzel bowl, Barber Shop Quartet.........................**$70.00**
Stein, Looking at You......................................**$24.00**
Teapot, Red Rooster, 4-cup..............................**$70.00**
Tile, basket of flowers, 6"................................**$35.00**
Tile, Hex, 6"..**$30.00**
Tile, Picking Apples, 6"...................................**$40.00**
Vase, Dartmouth insignia, 10".........................**$30.00**
Wall pocket, clown & donkey, 6½"....................**$95.00**

Pepsi-Cola

People have been enjoying Pepsi-Cola since before the turn of the century. Various logos have been registered over the years; the familiar oval was first used in the early 1940s. At about the same time, the two 'dots' between the words Pepsi and Cola became one, though more recent items may carry the double-dot logo as well, especially when they're designed to be reminiscent of the old ones. The bottle cap logo came along in 1943 and with variations was used through the early sixties.

Though there are expensive rarities, most items are still reasonable, since collectors are just now beginning to discover how fascinating this line of advertising memorabilia can be. There are three books in the series called *Pepsi-Cola Collectibles* written by Bill Vehling and Michael Hunt, which we highly recommend. Another good reference is *Introduction to Pepsi Collecting* by Bob Stoddard.

Note: In the descriptions that follow, the double-dot logo is represented by the equal sign.

Advisor: Craig and Donna Stifter (See Directory, Pepsi-Cola)

Newsletter: *Pepsi-Cola Collectors Club Express*
Bob Stoddard, Editor
P.O. Box 1275
Covina, CA 91723; Send SASE for information

Belt buckle, embossed Pepsi-Cola above Hits The Spot, NM **$15.00**
Book cover, Think Young- Say Pepsi Please above basketball player talking to girl, list of referee signals below, NM **$8.00**
Bottle opener, metal triangular shape w/Drink Pepsi-Cola engraved on handle, 1950s, EX+ **$18.00**
Calendar, 1947, Paintings Of The Year, complete, EX+ ..**$45.00**
Calendar, 1960, Pepsi-Cola Bottling Co, art by Lawson Wood, complete, EX+...**$110.00**
Can, flat top, Pepsi & bottle cap against blue background w/white diagonal lines, 1950s, 12-oz, EX+ **$50.00**
Clock, light-up, Pepsi logo at 12 w/lines between numbers 3-6-9, 1969, square, VG+ **$60.00**
Clock, light-up, Pepsi over bottle-cap logo right of clock w/numbers & dots, horizontal rectangle, 1960s, EX+ **$100.00**
Clock, light-up counter-top, Thank You Call Again, square clock left of Pepsi logo, 1967, 8x13", NM............**$45.00**

Clock, light-up, plastic bottle cap, 1950s, 12" dia, VG, $175.00. (Photo courtesy of Gary Metz.)

Coaster, Ask For Pepsi=Cola The Perfect Mixer, contour logo, 1940, 4¼" dia, EX+ **$15.00**
Cooler bag, vinyl, Disneyland Fun/NY World's Fair, round w/straps & zipper top, NM **$30.00**

Dispenser, cylinder w/front shaped like Pepsi=Cola bottle cap, NM+ **$300.00**
Display, diecut cardboard w/3-D plastic bottle, New Single Drink Size on triangle behind bottle & cap, 10x14", M **$250.00**
Display rack, 2-sided sign w/slanted bottle cap above Take Home... atop rack w/4 shelves, folds up, 65x18", NM **$150.00**
Door push bar, porcelain, Have a Pepsi in black flanked by logo, yellow background, 3x30", EX+ **$125.00**
Door push plate, tin, Pick a Pepsi in black on yellow, Pepsi=Cola bottle cap above & below, 13½x3½", EX.................**$165.00**
Drinking glass, oval Pepsi=Cola logo, white syrup line, NM **$15.00**
Game, Big League Baseball, 1950s-60s, EX...............**$100.00**
Handkerchief, allover bottle-cap design, M.................**$25.00**
Matchbook, Pepsi=Cola 5¢ contour logo, 1930s, EX+ ..**$8.00**
Menu board, tin, Have a Pepsi & bottle cap above chalkboard, yellow border, 1950s, 30x20", NM+.........**$175.00**
Menu board, tin, Say Pepsi Please & slanted bottle cap on yellow above chalkboard, rounded corners, 1950s, 30x19", G **$60.00**
Miniature bottle, clear swirl w/red & white label, 4½", NM **$12.00**
Miniature bottle, Pepsi=Cola paper label, NM............**$25.00**
Paperweight, glass, round w/Pepsi-Cola in center, decorative rim, M **$40.00**
Pocketknife, Pepsi-Cola 5¢ in blue on bone handle, 3", EX **$60.00**
Recipe booklet, Hospitality Recipes, shows tilted bottle on contour band, 1940, NM.......................................**$25.00**
Salt & pepper shakers, clear swirl bottles w/red & white applied label, blue & yellow screw caps, 5½", NM...............**$30.00**
Sign, cardboard, Here's Energy says man w/bottle left of oval Pepsi=Cola logo, 1940s, 11x28", VG **$135.00**
Sign, cardboard, Hot Popcorn at left of slanted bottle cap, embossed, foil back, NM **$125.00**
Sign, cardboard, Pepsi-Cola Hits the Spot at left of oval Pepsi=Cola logo, 4 ladies singing, 1940s, 11x28", G.**$155.00**
Sign, cardboard, 2-sided, Be Sociable... Serve.../Have a Pepsi, shows bottle cap & lady/6-pack, 1960s, 26x37", EX+...............**$130.00**
Sign, cardboard, 3-D, New Single Drink Size on yellow emblem at left of Pepsi bottle & cap, foil back, 1960s, NM+ **$250.00**
Sign, celluloid, Now It's Pepsi... Perfect Any Time! above Black couple, oval hanger or stand-up, 1960, 12x8", M.....**$100.00**
Sign, celluloid, Pepsi=Cola crown, 1945, 9" dia, NM ..**$275.00**
Sign, light-up, Drink Pepsi-Cola Ice Cold, molded plastic bottle cap, 1950s, 16" dia, EX **$500.00**
Sign, plastic, ...Say Pepsi Please, 3-D Pepsi-Cola glass in snow mound at left of Pepsi bottle cap, 1970s, VG.........**$65.00**
Sign, porcelain, Drink upper left of bottle cap, Iced lower right on yellow, curved corners, 1949, 12x30", EX+.......**$150.00**
Sign, porcelain, Enjoy Pepsi on bottle cap, 12x29", M..**$275.00**
Sign, porcelain, 2-sided, Have a Pepsi right of slanted bottle cap on yellow, curved corners, 1950s, 26x28", VG/VG+...**$60.00**
Sign, tin, diecut, slanted bottle cap on yellow circle atop white & gray courtesy panel, 1950s, 56x42", EX+ **$260.00**

Sign, tin, Drink Pepsi=Cola, Double Size 5¢, A Nickel Drink Worth a Dime, embossed, 28x20", EX+ **$250.00**

Sign, tin, Have a Pepsi & slanted bottle cap inset left of bottle, beveled edge, 1940s, 9x11", EX+ **$40.00**

Sign, tin, Say Pepsi Please, pictures bottle & cap, 1965, 46x17", M...**$150.00**

Stadium seat cushion, blue w/Pepsi logo, M **$30.00**

Thermometer, tin, Any Weather's Pepsi Weather on card w/ribbon, bottle cap above, 1950s, 25x9", NM ..**$250.00**

Thermometer, tin, Pepsi-Cola bottle cap above & below tube, red stepped sides, curved ends, 1950s, 27", EX **$90.00**

Thermometer, tin, Say Pepsi Please, stylized Pepsi bottle cap logo, yellow, square corners, 1967, 28", EX **$75.00**

Tip tray, Compliments of Pepsi-Cola in center, banded rim, rectangular, NM.......................................**$35.00**

Tip tray, Pepsi=Cola lettered in red on white milk glass, serrated edges, NM+......................................**$200.00**

Toy truck, Marx, plastic flatbed w/wood wheels, no cases, bottle cap decals on doors, EX+..........................**$75.00**

Trash can, shaped like a Pepsi can, early 1970s, 16", EX .**$20.00**

Tray, Pepsi=Cola bottle cap in center, round w/straight deep sides, 12" dia, EX..................................**$150.00**

Sign, die-cut cardboard easel-back, 1930s-40s, 8", $350.00.

Perfume Bottles

Here's an area of bottle collecting that has come into its own. Commercial bottles, as you can see from our listings, are very popular. Their values are based on several factors, for instance: is it sealed or full, does it have its original label, and is the original package or box present.

Figural bottles are interesting, especially the ceramic ones with tiny regal crowns as their stoppers.

Club: International Perfume and Scent Bottle Collectors Association
c/o Phyllis Dohanian
53 Marlborough St.
Boston, MA 02116-2099; 617-266-4351

Club: Perfume and Scent Bottle Collectors
Jeane Parris
2022 E Charleston Blvd.
Las Vegas, NV 89104; Membership: $15 USA or $30 foreign (includes quarterly newsletter); Information requires SASE

April Showers cologne, hand lotion & soap, MIB **$10.00**

Babe, Faberge, glass stopper, 2½", w/gold metal case.**$20.00**

Beloved, Matchabelli, clear glass crown w/blue & gold enameling, crown stopper, empty, 2¼" **$165.00**

Blue Carnation, Roger & Galet, square w/original paper label, 3"..**$5.00**

Blue Waltz, heart shape w/original label, 4½" **$5.00**

Breathless, Charbert, glass drum form, 3"...................**$10.00**

Buddha, Vantines, Buddha figural, caramel-colored stopper, 7"...**$100.00**

Chanel #5, clear square w/original label, 2"..................**$7.50**

Chanel #5 factice, all glass, 8½" **$65.00**

Crepe de Chine, Milot, clear 6-sided shape, white lid, 6¼"..**$10.00**

Crepe de Chine, Milot, short 6-sided shape w/metal lid, 1¾", MIB **$12.00**

Desert Flower, cologne & mini, Leigh, etched flowers & lg bottle, both 1½", M in G box **$25.00**

Desert Flower cologne & lotion, 4", MIB....................**$10.00**

Directoire, Charles of the Ritz, clear pyroform w/enameling, 4¾"...**$7.50**

Divine, D'Orsay, stylized shape w/clear Lucite top, 6½" ..**$80.00**

Duchess of York, Matchabelli, clear glass crown form w/gold & black enameling, crown stopper, 1¾".............**$45.00**

Dutchess of York, Matchabelli, clear crown w/gold enameling & label, crown stopper, 2½"..........................**$95.00**

Estee Lauder, fish figural, holds solid perfume, 3"......**$25.00**

Flambeau perfume whistle, Faberge, full, w/tag, 3", MIB..**$47.50**

Fleurs des Monde, Faberge, clear w/orange bouquet-shaped Bakelite stopper, 1½" **$50.00**

Forever Amber, mini in Lucite cube, EX labels, 1⅞" ..**$35.00**

Gardenglo, Solon Palmer, metal label, long dauber, 3½"...**$40.00**

Golden Autumn, Prince Matchabelli, 2" crown form on original black presentation stand, w/original cover .**$125.00**

Indescrete, Lucien Lelong, clear & frosted, sealed, 3½"..**$90.00**

Jasmine, Duret, clear w/embossed decor, ornate stopper, 4¼", MIB **$100.00**

Knowing, Estee Lauder, black kitten on gold pillow, jeweled collar, 1⅛x2", M in gold box **$150.00**

L'Interdit, Givenchi, mini, 1⅛", MIB.........................**$10.00**

Lanvin, gold metal, purse size, 2½" **$10.00**

Le French Rose, clear shouldered form w/faceted stopper, metal tag, 3" **$15.00**

Le Parfum Ideal, Houbigant, clear glass decanter shape resembling a Baccarat original, gold label, 2¼", w/floral box...**$110.00**

Lucky Lady cologne cream, Alleged, clear w/ivory-colored lady on front, red label, 2½"................................**$15.00**

Maderas de Orient, Myrugia, clear cylinder w/M label, full, 4½", MIB w/bright tassel......................................**$75.00**

Magie, Lancome, clear w/frosted stars, metal top, 5" .**$60.00**

Mais Quis, Bourjois, black enamel label, 3½"............**$40.00**

Maja cologne & soaps, Myrugia, 6-sided bottle, 2½", w/2 wrapped soaps, MIB...**$15.00**

Marjoram, Herbisimo, bright green glass, full, 3¾"......**$7.50**

Meteor, Coty, green stain at base on clear, white lid, full, 3"...**$45.00**

Mitsouko, Guerlain, crystal w/round label, flip-top, 4", MIB **$50.00**

My Jerrycah, Marc Fael, molded to resemble emergency gasoline can, brass stopper, empty, 1⅞" **$45.00**

My Sin, Lanvin, metal & glass cylinder, 2½".................**$10.00**

Narcisse, Richard Hudnut, gold lines, gold & green stopper, 2"..**$110.00**

Narcisse, shouldered bottle w/M label, ornate stopper, 2¾", MIB **$50.00**

Nina Ricci, clear and frosted glass heart shape with flowers, Lalique France etched on bottom, sealed, $175.00. (Photo courtesy of Monsen and Baer Auctions.)

Nuit de Noel, Caron, black glass, 2¾", MIB................**$20.00**

Number Please, white telephone holds perfume in center of dial **$15.00**

Obelisque, Nettie Rosenstein, clear ovoid w/fancy gold label, 4"..**$15.00**

Old South, slim inverted cylinder w/green glass stopper, 2½", w/trunk-shaped box **$25.00**

Orchid, Yardly, flower label, ball-shaped lid, 3", MIB ..**$30.00**

Passionment, Lucien Lelong, octagonal bottle & lid, sealed, 2¾", MIB...**$15.00**

Polo factice, Ralph Lauren, rider on bright green square bottle, gold lid, 11"...**$40.00**

Private Collection Estee Lauder, frosted glass w/plastic cap, label on bottom, 1¾", w/porcelain gold & white box **$90.00**

Quelque Fleurs, Houbigant, clear w/2 M labels, gray-stained flower stopper, 5½" **$45.00**

Renoir, clear w/gold vertical stripes, clear glass stopper, 4¼"...**$65.00**

S, Schiaparelli, frosted w/molded cursive S on front, pink metallic ball cap, ¼-oz, M in pink & white box.............**$220.00**

Samsara factice, Guerlain, ruby glass w/gold enamel label, 11x12" **$225.00**

Scandal, My Sin & Rumeur, Lanvin, 3 square bottles, each 2", in flip-front box...**$65.00**

Sculptura, Jovan, black glass torso w/gold cap, ⅛-oz, 2¾", MIB **$55.00**

Sculptura, Jovan, black plastic base, frosted glass figure, 4".**$45.00**

Sleeping, Schiaparelli, clear candlestick form w/red Bakelite cap, gold details & label, empty, 3" **$275.00**

Splash, Kaskot Interplanetary Inc, golden spaceship, sealed, 2", MIB..**$10.00**

Tabu, slim ribbed form w/gold lid, 5" **$5.00**

Tweed, Lentheric, clear shouldered shape w/black enameling & gold label, brass metal cap, 1⅝", NMIB **$35.00**

Un Air Embaume, Regaud, round black bottle w/gold stopper, 4" **$60.00**

White Diamonds, white bow-shaped stopper, mini, w/original tag, 2", MIB **$20.00**

Wind Song cream sachet, Prince Matchabelli, green crown form w/gold top, original label, 2¼"......................**$7.50**

Wind Song perfume, cologne & cream sachet, Prince Matchabelli, all full on presentation stage, 2".......**$50.00**

Wings, bulbous glass bottle w/ball stopper, 2½", ¼-oz, MIB **$30.00**

Worth, smoky blue glass with vertical ribs, turquoise stopper, Lalique molded in bottom, 3", MIB, $60.00. (Photo courtesy of Monsen and Baer Auctions.)

Pez Candy Dispensers

Though Pez candy has been around since the late 1920s, the dispensers that we all remember as children weren't introduced until the 1950s. Each had the head of a certain character — a Mexican, a doctor, Santa Claus, an animal, or perhaps a comic book hero. It's hard to determine the age of some of these, but if yours have tabs or 'feet' on the bottom so they can stand up, they were made in the last ten years. Though early on, collectors focused on this feature to evaluate their finds, now it's simply the character's head that's important to them. Some have variations in color and design, both of which can greatly affect value. For instance, Batman may have a blue hood and a black mask, or both his mask and his hood may match; sometimes they're both black and sometimes they're blue. (The first one is the most valuable, but not much more than the all-black variation.)

Condition is important; watch out for broken or missing parts. If a Pez is not in mint condition, most are worthless. Original packaging can add to the value, particularly if it is one that came out on a blister card. If the card has special graphics or information, this is especially true. Early figures were sometimes sold in boxes, but these are hard to find. Nowadays you'll see them offered 'mint in package,' sometimes at premium prices. But most intense Pez collectors say that those cellophane bags add very little if any to the value.

For more information, refer to *A Pictorial Guide to Plastic Candy Dispensers Featuring Pez* by David Welch; *Schroeder's Collectible Toys, Antique to Modern;* and *Collecting Toys #6* by Richard O'Brien.

Advisor: Richard Belyski (See Directory, Pez)

Newsletter: *Pez Collector's News*
Richard and Marianne Belyski, Editors
P.O. Box 124
Sea Cliff, NY 11579; 516-676-1183; Subscription: $19 for 6 issues)

Angel, no feet, 1970s...**$25.00**

Barney Bear, no feet..$35.00
Barney Bear, w/feet..$20.00
Bouncer Beagle, w/feet..$6.00
Bugs Bunny, w/feet, from $1 to............................$3.00
Charlie Brown, w/feet, from $1 to.......................$3.00
Charlie Brown, w/feet, frown..............................$6.00
Chick in Egg, no feet..$12.00
Chick in Egg, no feet, w/hair $50.00
Cockatoo, no feet, blue face, red beak................$35.00
Daffy Duck, no feet..$10.00
Daffy Duck, w/feet, from $1 to...........................$3.00
Donald Duck, no feet..$15.00
Donald Duck, no feet, diecut.............................$115.00
Dumbo, w/feet, blue head...................................$20.00

Fireman, no feet, $25.00; Policeman, no feet, $25.00. (Photo courtesy of June Moon.)

Gonzo, w/feet, from $1 to $3.00
Goofy, no feet, old...$10.00
Goofy, no feet, removable nose & teeth $30.00
Incredible Hulk, no feet, dark green....................$20.00
Incredible Hulk, no feet, light green....................$10.00
Incredible Hulk, w/feet, light green, remake $3.00
Indian Brave, no feet, reddish............................$150.00
Indian Chief, no feet, marbleized........................$65.00
Indian Chief, no feet, yellow headdress...............$45.00
Indian Maiden, no feet, w/headband....................$70.00
Kermit the Frog, w/feet, from $1 to......................$3.00
Mickey Mouse, w/feet, from $1 to........................$3.00
Mimic Monkey, no feet, w/ball cap, different colors, each
    from $25 to..$35.00
Monkey Sailor, no feet, w/white cap....................$25.00
Nurse, no feet, brown hair...................................$75.00
Orange, no feet..$75.00
Pebbles Flintstone, w/feet, from $1 to..................$3.00
Penguin (Batman), no feet, soft head...................$75.00
Pilgrim, no feet..$100.00
Pluto, no feet, red..$10.00
Pluto, w/feet, from $1 to......................................$3.00
Practical Pig (B), no feet $30.00
Rooster, w/feet, whistle head..............................$25.00
Rooster, w/feet, white or yellow head..................$25.00
Santa Claus (C), no feet, from $5 to....................$15.00
Scrooge McDuck (A), no feet...............................$20.00
Scrooge McDuck (B), w/feet $6.00
Smurfette, w/feet, blue..$5.00
Snoopy, w/feet, from $1 to...................................$5.00
Snowman (A), no feet, from $5 to $10.00
Snowman (B), w/feet, from $1 to $5.00

Space Gun, orange $75.00
Thor, no feet..$150.00
Tinkerbell, no feet..$100.00
Uncle Sam, no feet...$65.00
Wile E Coyote, w/feet...$25.00
Woodstock, w/feet, painted feathers.....................$10.00

Zorro, no feet, with Zorro logo, $75.00; no logo, $45.00; King Louie, no feet, orange, $20.00.

Pfaltzgraff Pottery

Pfaltzgraff has operated in Pennsylvania since the early 1800s making redware at first, then stoneware crocks and jugs, yellow ware and spongeware in the twenties, artware and kitchenware in the thirties, and stoneware kitchen items through the hard years of the forties. In 1950 they developed their first line of dinnerware, called Gourmet Royale (known in later years as simply Gourmet). It was a high-gloss line of solid color accented at the rims with a band of frothy white, similar to lines made later by McCoy, Hull, Harker and many other companies. Although it also came in pink, it was the dark brown that became so popular. Today these brown stoneware lines are among the newest interests of young collectors as well as those more seasoned, and they all contain more than enough unusual items to make the hunt a bit of a challenge and loads of fun.

The success of Gourmet was just the inspiration that was needed to initiate the production of the many dinnerware lines that have become the backbone of the Pfaltzgraff company.

A giftware line called Muggsy was designed in the late 1940s. It consisted of items such as comic character mugs, ashtrays, bottle stoppers, children's dishes, a pretzel jar, a cookie jar, etc. All of the characters were given names. It was very successful and continued in production until 1960. The older versions have protruding features, while the later ones were simply painted on.

Because of the popularity of the brown-glazed dinnerware, other Pfaltzgraff lines are becoming very collectible as well. We've featured several in our listings. To calculate the values of Yorktowne, Heritage, and Folk Art items not listed below, use Village prices.

For further information, we recommend *Pfaltzgraff, America's Potter,* by David A. Walsh and Polly Stetler, published in conjunction with the Historical Society of York County, York, Pennsylvania.

Advisor: Jo-Ann Bentz (See Directory, Pfaltzgraff)

Ashtray, brown drip glaze, 4" dia, from $8 to............**$10.00**

Folk Art, jar lamp, #787, 19", from $35 to **$40.00**

Folk Art, jug lamp, #785, 16", from $25 to **$30.00**

Gourmet Royale, ashtray, #321, 7¾", from $10 to **$12.00**

Gourmet Royale, baker, #321, oval, 7½", from $17 to..**$20.00**

Gourmet Royale, baker, #323, oval, 9½", from $20 to..**$22.00**

Gourmet Royale, bean pot, #11-3, 3-qt, w/warmer, from $48 to...**$50.00**

Gourmet Royale, bean pot, #11-1, 1-qt, from $20 to..**$22.00**

Gourmet Royale, bean pot, #11-2, 2-qt, from $28 to..**$30.00**

Gourmet Royale, bean pot, #30, w/lip, lg, from $45 to....**$50.00**

Gourmet Royale, bowl, #241, oval, 7x10", from $15 to..**$17.00**

Gourmet Royale, bowl, cereal; #934SR, 5½", from $6 to..**$8.00**

Gourmet Royale, bowl, mixing; 10", from $15 to **$17.00**

Gourmet Royale, bowl, mixing; 6", from $8 to **$10.00**

Gourmet Royale, bowl, mixing; 8", from $12 to **$14.00**

Gourmet Royale, bowl, salad; tapered sides, 10", from $25 to...**$28.00**

Gourmet Royale, bowl, soup; 2¼x7¼", from $6 to **$8.00**

Gourmet Royale, bowl, spaghetti; #319, straight sides, 14", $30 to...**$35.00**

Gourmet Royale, bowl, vegetable; #0314, divided, from $20 to...**$24.00**

Gourmet Royale, bowl, vegetable; 9¾" **$15.00**

Gourmet Royale, butter dish, #394, ¼-lb stick-type, from $12 to...**$14.00**

Gourmet Royale, butter warmer, #0301, stick handle, double spout, 9-oz, w/stand, from $18 to **$20.00**

Gourmet Royale, casserole, hen on nest, 2-qt, from $70 to...**$90.00**

Gourmet Royale, casserole, individual; #399, stick handle, 12-oz, from $10 to **$12.00**

Gourmet Royale, casserole, stick handle, 1-pt, from $12 to **$14.00**

Gourmet Royale, casserole, stick handle, 1-qt, $18.00.

Gourmet Royale, casserole, 2-qt, from $20 to **$22.00**

Gourmet Royale, casserole warming stand..................**$10.00**

Gourmet Royale, chafing dish, w/handles, lid & stand, 8x9", from $30 to...**$32.00**

Gourmet Royale, cheese shaker, bulbous, 5¾", from $18 to..**$22.00**

Gourmet Royale, chip 'n dip, #0306, 2-pc set, w/stand, from $28 to...**$30.00**

Gourmet Royale, chip 'n dip, #311, 1-pc, 12", from $18 to..**$20.00**

Gourmet Royale, coffee server, on metal & wood stand, 10¾", from $100 to...**$125.00**

Gourmet Royale, corn tray, individual; molded as ear of corn, scarce, from $12 to...**$14.00**

Gourmet Royale, creamer, #382, from $5 to.................**$7.00**

Gourmet Royale, cruet, coffeepot shape, fill through spout, 5", from $20 to..**$22.00**

Gourmet Royale, cup, from $2 to.................................**$3.00**

Gourmet Royale, flour scoop, sm, from $12 to..........**$15.00**

Gourmet Royale, fondue pot, w/holder & wood trim, from $35 to..**$40.00**

Gourmet Royale, gravy boat, #426, double spout, lg, +underplate, from $14 to **$16.00**

Gourmet Royale, jug, #382, 10-oz, from $14 to **$16.00**

Gourmet Royale, jug, #384, 32-oz, from $32 to **$36.00**

Gourmet Royale, ladle, sm, from $12 to......................**$15.00**

Gourmet Royale, ladle, 3½" dia bowl w/11" handle, from $18 to..**$20.00**

Gourmet Royale, Lazy Susan, #308, 3 sections w/center bowl, 14", from $32 to...**$36.00**

Gourmet Royale, marmalade, from $18 to...................**$20.00**

Gourmet Royale, mug, #391, 12-oz, from $6 to **$8.00**

Gourmet Royale, mug, #392, 16-oz, from $12 to.......**$14.00**

Gourmet Royale, pitcher, w/ice lip, #415 ....**$18.00**

Gourmet Royale, plate, dinner; #88R, 10", from $6.50 to...**$8.00**

Gourmet Royale, plate, egg; holds 12 egg halves, 7¾x12½", from $20 to...**$22.00**

Gourmet Royale, plate, grill; #87, 3-section, 11", from $18...**$20.00**

Gourmet Royale, plate, salad; 6¾", from $3 to **$4.00**

Gourmet Royale, plate, steak; 12", from $15 to **$20.00**

Gourmet Royale, platter, #320, 14", from $20 to.........**$25.00**

Gourmet Royale, platter, #337, 16", from $25 to.........**$30.00**

Gourmet Royale, rarebit, #330, w/lug handles, oval, 11", from $15 to...**$18.00**

Gourmet Royale, rarebit, w/lug handles, oval, 8½", from $10 to...**$12.00**

Gourmet Royale, rarebit w/lug handles, oval, 8", from $6 to.**$8.00**

Gourmet Royale, relish dish, #265, 5x10", from $15 to..**$17.00**

Gourmet Royale, roaster, #325, oval, 14", from $30 to ..**$35.00**

Gourmet Royale, roaster, #326, oval, 16", from $50 to ..**$60.00**

Gourmet Royale, salt & pepper shakers, #317/318, 4½", pr, from $12 to...**$14.00**

Gourmet Royale, salt & pepper shakers, bell shape, pr, from $25 to...**$35.00**

Gourmet Royale, salt & pepper shakers, owl shape, pr, from $25 to...**$35.00**

Gourmet Royale, saucer, #89R, from $3 to **$4.00**

Gourmet Royale, serving tray, stick handle, 4-part, $20.00.

Gourmet Royale, shirred egg dish, #360, 6", from $10 to.**$12.00**

Gourmet Royale, souffle dish, #398, ribbed exterior, 1-qt, 8½", from $20 to...**$22.00**

Gourmet Royale, soup tureen, #393, 5-qt, +underplate, from $65 to..**$70.00**

Gourmet Royale, sugar bowl, from $5 to **$7.00**
Gourmet Royale, teapot, #0381, 6-cup, from $18 to...**$22.00**
Gourmet Royale, tray, snack; 8⅜x11⅝", from $17 to........**$20.00**
Gourmet Royale, tray, tidbit; 2-tier, from $15 to **$18.00**
Heritage, demitasse cup & saucer, #283.......................**$4.50**
Heritage, quiche, #233, pinched rim, from $8 to **$10.00**
Heritage, teapot, #555, 24-oz, from $10 to **$14.00**
Muggsy, ashtray **$125.00**
Muggsy, bottle stopper, head, ball shape **$85.00**
Muggsy, canape holder, Carrie, lift-off hat pierced for tooth-picks, from $125 to...**$150.00**
Muggsy, cigarette server......................................**$125.00**
Muggsy, clothes sprinkler bottle, Myrtle, Black, from $225 to...**$260.00**
Muggsy, clothes sprinkler bottle, Myrtle, white, from $195 to...**$225.00**
Muggsy, cookie jar, character face, minimum value.**$250.00**
Muggsy, mug, action figure (golfer, fisherman, etc), any, from $65 to **$80.00**
Muggsy, mug, Black action figure............................**$125.00**
Muggsy, shot mug, character face, from $45 to **$50.00**
Muggsy, tumbler **$60.00**
Muggsy, utility jar, Handy Harry, hat w/short bill as flat lid, from $175 to...**$200.00**
Planter, donkey, brown drip glaze, 10", from $15 to..**$20.00**
Planter, elephant, brown drip glaze, from $90 to **$110.00**
Village, baker, #024, oval, 7¾" **$4.00**
Village, baker, #236, rectangular, 2-qt, from $10 to **$12.00**
Village, baker, #237, square tab handles, 9", from $8 to...**$11.00**
Village, baker, #42, oval, 10¼" **$5.00**
Village, beverage server, #490, lighthouse shape, dome lid, from $15 to...**$20.00**
Village, bowl, fruit; #008, 5", from $2 to......................**$3.00**
Village, bowl, mixing; 1-qt, 2-qt, 3-qt, 3-pc set, from $18 to **$22.00**
Village, bowl, rim soup; #012, 8½", from $3.50 to........**$4.50**
Village, bowl, serving; #010, 7", from $4 to..................**$5.50**
Village, bowl, soup/cereal; #009, 6" **$2.50**
Village, bowl, vegetable; #011, 8¾", from $6 to............**$9.00**
Village, butter dish, #028, ¼-lb, from $6 to..................**$8.00**

Village, butter dish, ½-lb, from $6.00 to $8.00.

Village, candlestick lamp, #559, spool-shaped base, w/pleated shade, sm, from $10 to **$12.00**
Village, candlesticks, #564, spool shaped, 3¾", pr, from $8 to...**$10.00**
Village, canister set, 4-pc, from $35 to.........................**$40.00**
Village, casserole, #315, w/lid, 2-qt, from $15 to........**$18.00**
Village, clock, #925, round, from $20 to.....................**$25.00**
Village, coffee mug, #89F, 10-oz, from $5 to.................**$7.00**
Village, cookie jar, #540, 3-qt, from $12 to..................**$15.00**

Village, corn dish, #046, 8½" long..............................**$3.00**
Village, creamer & sugar bowl, #020, lighthouse shape, from $10 to...**$12.00**
Village, cup, #001, 8-oz, from $1.50 to **$2.50**
Village, dessert server (footed custard cup), 10-oz, from $6 to...**$8.00**
Village, glassware, rocks/juice tumbler **$2.00**
Village, glassware, water goblet....................................**$3.00**
Village, glassware, wine goblet....................................**$2.50**
Village, gravy boat, #433, 16-oz, w/underplate, from $8 to...**$11.00**
Village, mug, pedestal; #90F, 10-oz, from $3.50 to **$4.50**
Village, napkin holder, #086, from $4 to **$6.00**
Village, onion soup crock, #295, w/stick handle, sm, from $4 to...**$6.00**
Village, pepper mill, from $6 to **$8.00**
Village, picture frame, #352, from $7 to.......................**$9.00**
Village, pitcher, #416, 2-qt, from $12 to......................**$15.00**
Village, plate, dinner; #004, 10¼", from $2 to..............**$3.00**
Village, plate, luncheon; #005, 8¾", from $2 to **$3.00**
Village, plate, salad; #113, 8¼" **$2.00**
Village, platter, #016, 14", from $8 to.........................**$11.00**
Village, potpourri simmerer, #251, from $5 to..............**$7.00**
Village, salt & pepper shakers, #025, lighthouse shape, pr, from $5 to...**$7.00**
Village, saucer, #002, 6¼"..**$1.00**
Village, spoon rest, #515, 9" long, from $3 to **$4.00**
Village, table light, #620, w/glass hurricane shade **$6.00**
Village, thermal carafe, 1-litre....................................**$15.00**
Village, trivet, #615, 7½" square, from $5 to **$7.00**
Village, tureen, soup; #160, 3½-qt, from $30 to.........**$35.00**
Village, utensil crock, #500, 6½", from $5 to..............**$7.00**
Yorktowne, jar lamp, #787, 19", from $35 to..............**$40.00**
Yorktowne, jug lamp, #189, 21", from $35 to..............**$40.00**

Photographica

A photograph is a moment in time caught on copper, glass, tin or paper. Since the Parisian artist Daugerre perfected the first practical photographic process in 1839, countless images have been produced.

Paper images were first introduced by W.H. Talbot in 1841. Since then, numerous processes have been developed. By the 1860s the wet-plate albumen print process (paper coated with egg white mixture) was being widely employed by traveling photographers across our country and the world. The Civil War was our first widely photographed historical event. Civil War images are constantly increasing in value. Snapshots, however, are of little value unless they are of high quality and of an extremely rare subject. Content and condition are two vital considerations in determining the value of a photograph. Even a rare image is of little value if it is in poor condition.

Early cases are collectible in their own right; often the case is worth more than the image. Cased images are fragile and extreme caution must be used when examining them. In addition to studying the case, mat shape and preserver style, be sure to look for hallmarks, imprints and production information. The size of a cased image is determined according to the size plate used to produce it (there is no agreement on the exact measurements): Full plate, ½ plate, ¼ plate, ⅙ plate, ⅑ plate, and 1⁄16 plate.

Though made well before the time frame we've established for this book, old photographs are so plentiful both at yard sales and flea markets as well (often preserved above even the family silver or jewelry!), we wanted to include some guidelines to help you evaluate them.

Advisor: Betty Davis (See Directory, Photographica)

Ambrotype: (1855–1865) - Black negative image on glass; its black backing produces positive view

Civil War infantryman, ⅙ plate, ruby	**$350.00**
Common image, 1⁄16 plate	**$35.00**

First Congregational Church, Harwich, Massachusetts, ½ plate, $715.00.

Girl on horse, 1⁄16 plate	**$35.00**

Daguerreotype: (1893–1865) - Copper plate coated with silver

Family portrait, ½ plate, ca 1851	**$85.00**
Girl in bonnet, 1⁄16 plate, common case, ca 1845	**$45.00**
Postmortem, 1⁄16 plate, ca 1853	**$110.00**
Young couple, ⅑ plate, piece of hair attached to case, early	**$110.00**

Tintype: (1856–1867) - Image on tin, cased until ca 1860s; sold in paper mats at fairs until ca 1930

Couple on bike at carnival, ⅑ plate, ca 1900	**$35.00**
Enlisted man in US Colored Regiment, ⅙ plate	**$275.00**
Occupational, 1⁄16 plate, ca 1890	**$65.00**
Postmortem of child, ⅙ plate, full case	**$125.00**

Wet Plate and Albumen Prints (1860–1880s) - Glass plate process used to produce most paper prints

Albumen on mat, girl w/doll	**$38.00**
Albumen on mat, Indian man & woman, ca 1880	**$120.00**
Albumen on mat, Missouri street scene, ca 1880	**$45.00**
Albumen on mat, 1904 fireman w/pumper	**$175.00**
Cabinet card, Black policeman	**$55.00**
Cabinet card, circus fat man	**$40.00**
Cabinet card, railroad worker	**$45.00**
Cartes de viste, Civil War soldier	**$45.00**
Cartes de viste, PT Barnum, autographed	**$200.00**
Catres de viste, little girl w/doll	**$25.00**

Albumen on board, little girl w/large doll in doorway, 8x10", $45.00. (Photo courtesy of Betty Davis.)

Pie Birds

Pie birds were known as pie funnels in the 1800s in England and Wales. They originated as center supports for top crusts on meat pies and were used to prevent sogginess. Meat pies did not have bottom crusts. There was also a second purpose — to vent the steam and prevent juice/gravy overflow. There are many new pie birds on the US market. Bascially, the new pie birds are figural and, most importantly, they're hand painted, not airbrushed like the old ones were! The older figural pie vents were the black-faced chefs with airbrushed smocks (not bright colors), an elephant with CCC embossed on the back of his drum, Benny the Baker holding a pie crimper and a cake tester marked Pat. Pend. As we know, most of the new designs are original — just don't be fooled into buying them for old ones. There are new black birds everywhere, though. They'll have yellow beaks and protruding white-dotted eyes. If they're on a white base and have an orange beak, they're old. There were no old holiday-related pie vents, these are all new. You'll find Santas, pilgrims, pumpkins, rabbits, holiday trees, posies, and leprechauns. New figural pie vents are sold from $6.50 to $30.00 by the original designer/potter.

Advisor: Lillian M. Cole (See Directory, Pie Birds)

Newsletter: *Pie Birds Unlimited*
Lillian M. Cole
14 Harmony School Rd.
Flemington, NJ 08822

Advertisement, TG Green, on pie funnel, England, 1993 to present	**$10.00**
Benny the Baker, Cardinal China	**$85.00**
Bird, black & white on white base, marked Royal Worcester, 2-pc	**$65.00**

Bird, cobalt, stoneware, New Hampshire pottery, new, 4¼" $10.00
Black chef, full-figure, airbrushed $75.00
Black chef, half-figure, England, new $39.00
Black chef, yellow, red & white attire, brown spoon, Taiwan, 4½" $10.00
Black clown, hat, striped shirt & pants w/suspenders, England $39.00
Black snowman, w/hat & scarf, England, new $35.00
Blackbird on log, marked Artone Pottery England $50.00
Blackbird w/pointed light caramel beak & eyes (sm), England..$23.00
Bluebirds on nest, 1950s, USA, copyright on back...$100.00
Boy w/'Pie Boy' painted down leg, USA....................$85.00
Canary, yellow w/pink lips, Josef Originals $22.00
Chef w/pan, no arches, Josef or Lorrie Originals, imported $40.00
Crow dressed as chef, holds pie, marked SB, England, new...$30.00
Dragon, tin w/spines & horns, marked SB England, new ..$30.00

Duck with long neck, blue, pink or yellow, USA, 1940s-50s, $25.00.

Elephant, Cardinal China, CCC on bk, USA $65.00
Funnel, Pyrex glass...$30.00
Funnels, plain, white, England, from $15 to $25.00
Granny Pie Baker, Lorrie Design, Japan $28.00
Green Willow, decaled, new $15.00
Ireland, green stoneware funnel, marked Cork, from 1988 to present, each..$30.00
Mammy, airbrushed, brown skin tone, 1940s $110.00
Morton 'patches' pie bird, USA..................................$18.00
Rooster, Blue Willow...$20.00

Rooster, thin ceramic (unusual), multicolored details, USA, 5", $50.00. (Photo courtesy of Lillian Cole.)

Rooster, multicolored, marked Cleminson or incised Cb ..$25.00
Royal Commemorative pie funnel, England $35.00
Songbirds, blue or pink, 1940s-50s, USA, each..........$18.00
Songbirds, gold beaks & feet, 1950s, USA, each........$65.00

Pierce, Howard

In Howard Pierce's early pieces such as high-gloss bowls and vases, one can see the William Manker influence. Pierce had worked with Manker before beginning his own business in Claremont, California, in 1941. However, it is the wildlife and animals that brought forth Howard's enormous talent. So varied were his abilities that during his career, he produced models made from polyurethane (a medium quickly discontinued when Howard discovered he was allergic to it); Wedgwood-type Jasper ware with matte pink or light green; Mt. St. Helens ash which created a sandy, rough-textured glaze; gold leaf; experimental glazes; lava treatment; and cement for small items as well as commissioned pieces sometimes as tall as fifteen to twenty feet.

Several marks were used during Pierce's almost fifty-five year career. The earliest mark was the in-relief underglaze Pierce name, usually accompanied by a stock number and 'Claremont, Calif.' Collectors have dubbed this the 'Claremont' mark. The next mark was a 'Howard Pierce Porcelains' stamp; in later years, the word 'Porcelain' was removed. When Howard and Ellen Pierce destroyed the molds in 1992 due to Howard's health, the creativity of the man mandated that he continue to work, albeit on a limited basis. A smaller kiln was purchased, and items were made on a miniature scale with a stamp mark, simply 'Pierce.' Collectors should note that not all pieces are marked. Howard Pierce passed away in February, 1994.

Advisor: Susan Cox (See Directory, California Pottery)

Bowl, gloss burgundy, 2½x4½".................................$30.00
Figurine, cat, seated, brown & white, 14" $50.00
Figurine, hippo, brown bottom, gray top, 1950s, 3¾x9¾".$75.00
Figurine, hippo, Mt St Helens ash brown, 6" $40.00
Figurine, partridge, stylized, brown, 1950s, lg............$55.00

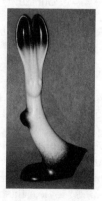

Figurine, rabbit, #102-P, 10½", $85.00. (Photo courtesy of Pat and Kris Secor.)

Figurine, roadrunner, polyurethane w/wire legs, tail up..$215.00
Figurine, rooster & hen, brown & white, 1950s, 9"/8", pr..$175.00
Figurine, squirrel, gray, 4"..$25.00
Figurine, turtle, speckled brown & white, 1950s, 5"...$25.00

Figurine, water bird, white & brown bill & feet, 14"..**$65.00**

Flower frog, hummingbird figural, satin brown & white, stamped mark, 5½"...**$75.00**

Magnet, turtle, blue, 2¼"...**$35.00**

Vase, creche style w/Deco girl in circular cutout, lime green, square **$65.00**

Vase, creche style w/fish, dark green, 8"...................**$95.00**

Vase, flamingo inset, white satin on dark green, #P300, 9", $165.00; Vase, horse and tree inset, white satin on dark green, #P500, 7x10", $165.00. (Photo courtesy of Pat and Kris Secor.)

Vase, girl reading book, brown agate high gloss, stamped mark, 6½" **$75.00**

Wall pocket, matt green & white, 3x2½" **$35.00**

Whistle, bird shape, brown, 3½" **$20.00**

Whistle, snake crawling, gray, 4"..............................**$30.00**

Pin-Back Buttons

Literally hundreds of thousands of pin-back buttons are available; pick a category and have fun! Most fall into one of three fields — advertising, political, and personality related, but within these three broad areas are many more specialized groups. Just make sure you buy only those that are undamaged, are still bright and unfaded, and have well-centered designs and properly aligned printing. The older buttons (those from before the 1920s) may be made of celluloid and the cardboard backing printed with the name of a company or a product.

See also Political.

Newsletter: *The Button Pusher*
P.O. Box 4
Coopersburg, PA 18036; Subscriptions: 1 yr - $19.94 US.

A Day To Remember, June 8, 1969, Mickey Mantle photo, multicolor celluloid, 4" **$25.00**

A&P, Growing w/America, For 75 Years, men standing w/1859 sign & 1934 sign flank A&P logo, red, white & blue, 1930s, NM **$20.00**

Aerosmith, Done w/Mirrors, M...............................**$12.00**

All of Me (Movie), flashes from Lily Tomlin to Steve Martin, NM **$8.00**

Archie Club, Member arched above head image w/dotted bow tie, Archie Club below, red, white & blue, 1950s, NM **$20.00**

Astronaut John Glenn, America's First Orbital Spaceman, image in space helmet, red & blue on white, 1962, 3½", NM **$30.00**

Astronaut Neil Armstrong, The First Man on the Moon, July 19-20 1969..., head image w/rocket & lunar module, 4", NM **$20.00**

Bart Simpson, Under Achiever & Proud of It Man, green, 6", MIP **$4.00**

Beatles, flashes from I Like Beatles w/first names to faces, blue, Vari-Vue, 2½", EX...**$25.00**

Beatles, I Love the Beatles, blue & red on white w/musical notes, 3", EX..**$25.00**

Beatles, I Still Love the Beatles, blue & red on white, 3", NM **$30.00**

Beatles, I'm An Official Beatles Fan, black & white faces & autographs on red & white, 4", VG+ **$25.00**

Beatles, The Beatles, black & white photo under clear plastic w/green border, 3", EX **$25.00**

Black Hills, black & white hilltop photo image of the State Game Lodge, oval, EX..**$15.00**

Boy Scouts, portrait image, multicolor on red, white & blue, 1¼", VG **$10.00**

Buster Brown & Tige, Member Brownbilt Club, multicolored, ⅞", EX..**$25.00**

Captain Kirk & Mr Spock, black & white photo images, 1976, 2¼", M **$8.00**

Chicago Member, Centennial Dental Congress, American Dental Assn over World's Fair logo, 1933, blue on white, oval, EX **$36.00**

Chicago Scout Camps, I Am Going To Camp, evergreen tree flanked by 1933 date, red & green on white, EX ..**$18.00**

Chip & Dale Rescue Rangers, multicolored, 1994, NM.**$3.00**

Dad's Root Beer, Have You Had It?, logo & white lettering on blue, VG **$10.00**

Dale Evans, black & white photo on green, 1950s, 1¼", VG .**$8.00**

Davy Crocket, Indian Fighter, yellow & red, 1940s, 1½", EX **$18.00**

Dick Tracy, Home of Dick Tracy, Woodstock Illinois, profile image talking on wrist radio, 2¼", M.....................**$20.00**

Dick Tracy Detective, profile w/gun, multicolored, 1¼", EX **$45.00**

Dorothy Hart, Sunbrite Junior Nurse Corps, black, red & white, 1", EX **$25.00**

Dr Pepper, w/bottle & 10-2-4 clock, blue & white, ¾", VG..**$20.00**

Elvis, Don't Be Cruel, broken heart & 2 guitars, red, white & blue, ⅞", EX..**$18.00**

Elvis, I Like Elvis in red lettering on white center band, red above & below, 1950s, 1¾", NM **$30.00**

ET & Elliot, multicolored photo, Universal Studios, 1982, 6", NM **$3.00**

Everly Brothers Fan Club, black & white photo image, 1950s, 1½", NM **$30.00**

Fonzie, Fonz Is Cool, multicolored thumbs-up image, 1976, 3½", EX **$10.00**

Gene Autry, face image on white, 1¼", VG **$15.00**

Goofy Movie, video release promo, 1995, NM...........**$10.00**

Green Hornet, Official Green Hornet Agent, green, blue & black, 1966, 4", NM **$40.00**

Hank Aaron 715 Home Run, April 8, 1974, Atlanta Braves, 2¼"...$12.00

Hopalong Cassidy, Best Wishes From Hoppy, photo bust image w/script lettering below, 1950s, 1¾", NM..$30.00

I Love Mickey w/Teresa Brewer & Mickey Mantle photo, names at bottom, 1960s.........................$40.00

Indiana Lumbermen's Mutual Insurance Company, logo & maroon lettering on wood-grain background, 3½", EX+ $12.00

Jackie Gleason, Joe the Bartender or the Bus Driver, 1950s, EX...$25.00

Jetsons, Kool-Aid giveaway at movie theatres, oval, EX..$5.00

Joe DiMaggio, photo w/name at bottom, celluloid, 1¾".....$18.00

John Wayne, late 1940s, photo image, 1¼", EX, $45.00.

Knott's Berry Farm, Friendliest Place in the West, white & gold litho tin, 2", M.................................$12.00

Lion King, features characters, 1993, 3", NM.................$5.00

Lion King, Simba, I'm Gonna Be King, 1993, 2½", NM..$4.00

Little Mermaid, white or purple lettering, 1980s, 3", NM, each...$4.00

Lou Gehrig, sepia-colored celluloid, 1¾" $35.00

Lucy (Peanuts), Gal Friday, litho tin, 2", EX.................$3.00

Michael Jackson, Beat it, MOC $8.00

Mickey Mantle, photo w/name at bottom, celluloid, 1¾".$20.00

Mickey Mouse, Follow My Adventures, Buy Coats Master Loaf, image of Mickey on off-white, 1¼", EX+ $50.00

Mickey Mouse, Sixty Years w/You Mickey, 1988, 2¼", NM..$4.00

Mickey Mouse Globe Trotters Member, issued by various bread companies, 1930s, black, red and white, 1¼", EX, $75.00.

Miller High Life Open Golf Tournament Press, Blue Mound Golf & Country Club, July 13-17, 1955, white on red, 2½", EX+...$40.00

Pepsi=Cola, Bigger/Better lettered above & below, Pepsi=Cola, red on white, 1940s, NM.................$20.00

Pinocchio, Walt Disney's..., Gepetto working Pinocchio's puppet strings while the rest watch, multicolor, 3½", NM $20.00

Rescuers Down Under, w/map background, 1980s, NM $5.00

Roy Rogers, black & white photo image on gray, name in lg letters below, 1940s, 1¼", VG+............................$25.00

Roy Rogers, Nellybelle (jeep), multicolored, Post Grape Nuts, 1953, ⅞", EX...$20.00

Roy Rogers, Post Grape Nuts, multicolored, 1953, ⅞", EX $25.00

Shirley Temple Club, Chicago Times, blue & white litho tin, ⅞", VG...$50.00

Smurfs, as rollerskater, soccer player or trumpet player, 1½", EX, each...$5.00

Snoopy, Happy Birthday, Hallmark, 1990, 1½", MOC..$5.00

Snoopy Fan Club, litho tin, 2¼", EX $6.00

Superman Club, 1960s, 3", EX $25.00

Ted Williams, black & white photo w/name at bottom, 1¾" $18.00

Tennessee Gater Bowl, celluloid, 2¼", w/attached molded plastic troll figure...$30.00

This Pin Certifies I Shook Hands With Babe Ruth on baseball background $55.00

Tom & Jerry Go for Sunbeam Bread, red, white & black, litho tin, 1⅛", EX...$20.00

Tom Mix for Sheriff, close-up image w/lettering on outer band, 1930s, 1½", NM $160.00

Universal Monsters, Wolf Man, Mummy or Frankenstein, 1960s, ⅞", $10.00 each.

Woodstock, Party Animal, Hallmark, 1990, MOC.........$4.00

101 Dalmatians, puppies on red background, 3", NM..$3.00

Kellogg's Pep Pins

Chances are if you're over forty, you remember them, one in each box of PEP (Kellogg's wheat-flake cereal that was among the first to be vitamin fortified). There were eighty-six in all, each carrying the full-color image of a character from one of the popular cartoon strips of the day — Maggie and Jiggs, the Winkles, Dagwood and Blondie, Superman, Dick Tracy and many others. Very few of these cartoons are still in print.

The pins were issued in five sets, the first in 1945, three in 1946, and the last in 1947. They were made in Connecticut by the Crown Bottle Cap Company, and they're marked PEP on the back. You could wear them on your cap, shirt, coat, or the official PEP pin beenie, a orange and white cloth cap made for just that purpose.

The Superman pin — he was the only D.C. Comics Inc. character in the group — was included in each set.

Not all are listed below. These are the most valuable. If you find an unlisted pin, it will be worth from $10.00 to $15.00. Values are given for pins in near mint condition.

Advisor: Doug Dezso (See Directory, Candy Containers)

Bo Plenty, NM	$30.00
Corky, NM	$16.00
Dagwood, NM	$30.00
Dick Tracy, NM	$30.00
Early Bird, NM	$6.00
Fat Stuff, NM	$15.00

Felix the Cat, NM, $75.00. (Photo courtesy of Doug Dezso.)

Flash Gordon, NM	$30.00
Flat Top, NM	$30.00
Goofy, NM	$10.00
Gravel Gertie, NM	$15.00
Harold Teen, NM	$15.00
Inspector, NM	$15.00
Jiggs, NM	$25.00
Judy, NM	$10.00
Kayo, NM	$20.00
Little King, NM	$15.00
Little King, NM	$15.00
Little Moose, NM	$15.00
Maggie, NM	$25.00
Mama De Stross, NM	$30.00
Mamie, NM	$15.00
Navy Patrol, NM	$6.00
Olive Oyl, NM	$30.00
Orphan Annie, NM	$25.00
Pat Patton, NM	$10.00
Perry Winkle, NM	$15.00
Pop Jenks, NM	$15.00
Popeye, NM	$30.00
Rip Winkle, NM	$20.00
Skeezix, NM	$15.00
Superman, NM	$38.00
Toots, NM	$15.00
Uncle Walt, NM	$20.00
Uncle Willie, NM	$12.00
Winkles Twins, NM	$75.00
Winnie Winkle, NM	$15.00

Pinball Machines

Coin-op machines, pinballs in particular, are finding their way into more and more private homes, as collectors re-create fifties and sixies ambience in their basement rec rooms. Unless you're good at electronics, be sure the machine you buy is in working condition. It's often difficult to find someone locally who is capable of doing repair work, especially on the older machines.

ABT Billiard Practice, resembles pool table, 1931, G	$500.00
American Amusement Super Flipp, 1 player, flippers, 1987, VG	$125.00
Bally Ballyhoo, 1 player, countertop, 7 balls/1¢, 1932, G	$375.00
Bally Bumper, 1 player, no flippers, 5 balls/5¢, 1936, VG	$250.00
Bally Goofy, 1 player, countertop, 7 balls/5¢, 1932, VG	$225.00
Bally Triumph, 1 player, no flippers, 5 balls/5¢, 1940, VG	$225.00
Chicago Coin Rapid Transit, 1 player, no flippers, 1935, VG	$300.00
Exhibit Golden Gate, 1 player, no flippers, 1934, VG	$175.00
Golden Official, countertop, 7 shots/1¢, 1933, VG	$100.00
Gottlieb Caveman, 4 players, flippers, 3 shots/25¢, G	$135.00
Gottlieb Eclipse, 4 players, 3 balls/25¢, 71x55x25", G	$350.00
Gottlieb Humpty Dumpty, 1 player, flippers, 5 balls/5¢, VG	$850.00
Gottlieb Sinbad, 4 players, flippers, 3 balls/25¢, 1970s, VG	$225.00
Mills Golden Official, 1 player, countertop, 1933, G-	$125.00
Mills Official Pin Table, 1 player, no flippers, 1932, VG	$175.00

Mills Owl, 1 player, no flippers, 5 balls/5¢, 1941, VG+, $500.00.

Mills Wow, 1 player, countertop, 10 balls/1¢, 1932, G	$175.00
Peo Daisy, square countertop, 7 balls/1¢, 1932, rare, VG	$250.00
Richard Loony, 1 player, no flippers, 7 balls/1¢, 1932, G	$300.00
Stoner Beacon, 1 player, no flippers, 10 shots/5¢, 1935, G	$175.00
Stoner Top Hat, 1 player, no flippers, 5 balls/5¢, 1935, G	$100.00
Tivoli-Jr, 1 player, countertop, no flippers, 1933, VG	$200.00

Pinup Art

Some of the more well-known artists in this field are Vargas, Petty, DeVorss, Elvgren, Moran, Ballantyne, Armstrong, and Phillips, and some enthusiasts pick a favorite and concentrate their collections on only his work. From the mid-thirties until well into the fifties, pinup art was extremely popular. Female movie stars from this era were ultra-glamorous, voluptous, and very sensual creatures, and this type of media influence naturally impacted the social and esthetic attitudes of the period. As the adage goes, 'Sex sells.' And well it did. You'll find calendars, playing cards, magazines, advertising, and merchandise of all types that depict these unrealistically perfect ladies. Though not all items will be signed, most of these artists have a distinctive, easily identifiable style that you'll soon be able to recognize.

Unless noted otherwise, values listed below are for items in at least near-mint condition; blotters are unusued.

Advisor: Denis Jackson (See Directory, Pinup Art)

Newsletter: *The Illustrator Collector's News*
Denis Jackson, Editor
P.O. Box 1958
Sequim, WA 98382; 206-683-2559; Subscription: $17 per year

Ad for Old Gold, Petty, Wearied by a Windbag, Old Gold Girl & Windbag on a couch, color, 1935, 10x14", NM ..**$12.00**
Blotter, Armstrong, Queen of Hearts, 1948, 4x9", NM ..**$15.00**
Blotter, Elvgren, Flying High, jet blows redhead's skirt up, Brown & Bigelow, 4x9", NM......................................**$8.00**
Blotter, Elvgren, I Barely Made It!, girl wading through stream, July 1949, NM **$12.00**
Blotter, Frush, magician's assistant pulling handkerchief out of hat, w/1-month calendar, January, 1956, 4x9", NM......**$6.00**
Blotter, Moran, Do You Still Prefer Blonds?, brunette in red top, 1948, 4x9", NM...................................**$11.00**
Calendar, DeVorss, Blue Belle, 1943, 34x16", EX.....**$100.00**
Calendar, Erbit, Reflections, 33x16", EX...................**$45.00**

Calendar, Mac Therson, 1948, various pinup girls, 12½x9½", $35.00.

Calendar, Mozert, A Good Deal, 1955, 17x10" **$50.00**
Calendar, Otto, Bubbles, 1946, 10x8", EX...................**$25.00**
Calendar, Vargas, Esquire, 1944, verses by Phil Stack, EX+ **$65.00**
Calendar, Vargas, Esquire, 1947, w/envelope, EX.....**$100.00**
Calendar, Vargas, Esquire 40th Anniversary, glossy reproductions of centerfolds from 1940-45, NM................**$12.00**
Calendar print, Elvgren, Bubbling Over, girl bathing in wooden tub, 11x8", EX...**$27.00**
Cartoon, Petty, I Said No, Esquire, July 1937, NM......**$13.00**
Cartoon, Petty, Oh! You Would, Would You?, Esquire, April 1939, NM **$13.00**

Cigarette pack sleeve, Elvgren, EX............................**$12.00**
Date book, Bill Randall, 12 pages, 1954, 9½x16", NM..**$55.00**
Drinking glasses, set of 4, each w/different pinup girl, 1940, M..**$15.00**
Gatefold, Chiriaka, The Lady's Unstrung, redheaded showgirl reclining, ca 1950s, 16½x13", EX.............................**$6.00**
Gatefold, Moore, Checkermate, blond in polka-dot bikini, full color, early 1950s, 17x13¼", VG.........................**$6.00**
Gatefold, Vargas, Exit, reclining blond in blue negligee, Esquire, November 1940, NM **$60.00**
Gatefold, Vargas, To Mary From Keith, Red Cross nurse on orange background, Esquire, April 1941, NM.......**$40.00**
Greeting card, Dancer, Deco dancing girl in yellow dress, Japanese lanterns, folded, NM **$5.00**
Magazine print, Petty, full page, blond on phone, March, 1947, NM **$25.00**
Magazine print, Vargas, starlett Autumn Rice sitting in 2-pc swimsuit, True, January, 1952, 8x11", VG+...........**$15.00**
Matchbook, Petty, unused, M **$3.00**
Memo pad, Ballantyne, Behind in Her Packing, 1955, 3½x6½"..**$9.00**
Mutoscope card, Armstrong, girl in yellow sarong & floral lea w/guitar, M...**$10.00**
Playing cards, Elvgren, double deck, complete, EXIB (plastic box) **$80.00**
Playing cards, Elvgren, Esso giveaway, incomplete, VG (fair box) **$40.00**
Playing cards, MacPherson, double deck, complete, deluxe British case w/unused score pads, M **$100.00**
Playing cards, Vargas, complete w/2 jokers, purple card backs & box, 1950s, NM (VG box) **$125.00**
Postcard, Vargas, Yearning, published by Tale of Two Cities, NM..**$3.00**
Print, Armstrong, All My Love, brunette's face through torn letter, 8x10½" **$25.00**
Print, Armstrong, Betty, girl in ornate silk headdress, 1925, 8x10" (1970s B&B repro valued at $15)................**$60.00**
Print, Armstrong, Dreamy Eyes, 10x11½" **$40.00**
Print, Armstrong, Let's Get Together, girl in swimsuit w/dog on a leash, 5x7" **$12.00**
Print, Armstrong, Sailor Beware, brunette in sailor's outfit on ropes, 21x28"..**$205.00**
Print, DeVorss, Alluring, girl in low-cut gown on bed, 1951, 16x32" **$65.00**
Print, DeVorss, Easy To Look At, redhead in violet ruffled negligee, 1948, 8x10"......................................**$32.00**
Print, DeVorss, Good Evening, girl in long gloves, 11x22"...**$35.00**
Print, DeVorss, Happy Landing, blond in pink ski suit, 1944, 16x20" **$60.00**
Print, Elvgren, French Dressing, girl w/black hair in black heels putting on red skirt, 1940s-50s, 9½x7½".....**$22.00**
Print, Elvgren, In the Dough, brunette in apron & hose w/bread dough, 9½x7½" **$13.00**
Print, Elvgren, Modern Venus, nude, 1951, 3½x2½".....**$7.00**
Print, Moran, Delighted, Girl in Mexican fiesta costume, 1950, 16x20" **$65.00**
Print, Moran, Follies of 1937, dancing redhead in top hat, 15x11" **$45.00**
Print, Moran, Goodbye I'm Taking Off Now, 1944, 5¼x4¼"..**$45.00**

Print, Moran, Remember Me?, redhead seated in red gown w/green phone, 27x22" **$90.00**

Print, Mozert, Anytime, girl in white strapless gown w/flower, Brown & Bigelow, 11x23" **$50.00**

Print, Mozert, How's This?, girl in swimsuit, 1948, 11x8" ..**$80.00**

Print, Mozert, Moonglow, seated blond nude, 6x4½"...**$13.00**

Print, Mozert, Thoroughbred, girl in riding outfit, 1949, 14½x11" **$55.00**

Print, Petty, blond in negligee lying on stomach w/phone & address book on white background, ca 1945, 12¼x18¾", NM **$85.00**

Print, Radiant, salesman's sample #7266, redhead in satin gown w/glove in 1 hand & lace fan in other, 1951, 6x8", NM **$10.00**

Print, Vargas, Diana the Huntress, 1920s, 24x30"......**$395.00**

Print, Vargas, Scheharazade, Deco girl dressed in blue w/jeweled turban, 24x30"...............................**$300.00**

Print, Vargas, World War II, redhead lying in see-through skirt & holding purple heart, limited edition, 1975, 25x37", M **$175.00**

Program, Petty, As the Girls Go By, 2 girls on phone, VG ..**$15.00**

Program, Petty, Ice Capades, Girl in Marine uniform skating w/baton, 1944, 8½x11", VG+...........................**$25.00**

Program, Vargas, Skating Vanities, blond skater in pink dress, 1947, 11x8" **$35.00**

Record sleeve, Candy-O, The Cars, redhead on hood of car, EX..**$15.00**

Record sleeve, Vargas, Gee Whiz, Bernadette Peters topless w/orchids over breasts, 1980, 7x7", EX+ (NM record)..**$25.00**

Restaurant reservation punch-out place card, Moran, EX ..**$35.00**

Trading cards, Vargas, reproductions of classic images, 51 cards, MIB (sealed)...............................**$25.00**

Playing Cards

Here is another collectible that is inexpensive, easy to display (especially single cards), and very diversified. Among the endless variations are backs that are printed with reproductions of famous paintings and pinup art, carry advertising of all types, and picture tourist attractions and world's fair scenes. Early decks are scarce, but those from the forties on are usually more attractive anyway, so pick an area that interests you most and have fun! Though they're usually not dated, you may find some clues that will help you to determine an approximate date. Telephone numbers, zip codes, advertising slogans, and patriotic messages are always helpful.

Everett Grist has written an informative book, *Advertising Playing Cards*, which we highly recommend to anyone interested in playing cards with any type of advertising.

Club/Newsletter: American Antique Deck Collectors; 52 Plus Joker Club
Clear the Decks, quarterly publication
Ray Hartz, President
P.O. Box 1002
Westerville, OH 43081; 614-891-6296

Aircraft Spotters #1, USPC, 1942, 52+Joker+information card, NM in EX box **$25.00**

Alaska, narrow, totem pole backs, 52 photos, 1950s, 52+Joker, M **$20.00**

American Air, light blue backs, special Aces, 1962, 52 complete, EX in box **$10.00**

American Contract Bridge League, Fall Nationals, picture backs form San Diego Bridge, USPC, 52+2 Jokers, NMIB **$6.00**

Amtrack, logo w/blue border, 1975, 52+2 Jokers, NMIB ..**$5.00**

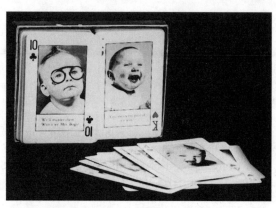

Babies, Constance Bannester photographs, double-deck, 1951, $50.00.

Bodega Casino, Deadwood SD, by Gemaco, white & green backs, 2 decks, sealed in celluloid wrapper w/casino chip **$22.50**

Caesar's Palace, Las Vegas NV, hole-punched cards, red & blue backs, 2 decks, sealed w/casino chip **$12.00**

Can-Can, wide, blue w/gold, Philibert, 1956, 52+extra card, M in vinyl case **$60.00**

Chicago, 54 scenes, lakefront on backs, color, photo face cards, black & white, 52+Joker, VG+ in G box......**$8.00**

Congress, Independence Hall, celu-tone, ca 1941, M in torn wrapper **$10.00**

Congress #606, USPC, Mildred, 1930s, gold edge, M, sealed in paper wrapper....................................**$40.00**

Cowboy, Centaur, pinochle deck, 48 complete, ca 1940, EX in box **$7.50**

Dallas Cheerleaders, 52 action photos, 1981, 52+Joker+2 extra cards, VG in box **$2.50**

Death on Drugs, Weedon Enterprises, 52 reasons not to abuse drugs, 1985, 52, M in EX box **$18.00**

Fairchild Semiconductor, wide, prosaic nonstandard, 1968, 52+2 Jokers+2 extra cards, M in EX box.............**$14.00**

General Tire, Gemaco, double deck, 52+Joker, EX **$10.00**

Gerber, Gerber doll w/cereal backs, 1950s, MIB **$22.50**

Goldwater, Art Deco-style courts, red & blue border, 1966, 52+2 Jokers, EX in G box **$26.00**

Grand Prix, wide, Lirola designs, Grimaud, 1973, 52+2 Jokers+extra card, MIB **$15.00**

Green Hornet, TV photos on pips, special courts & Jokers, 52+2 Jokers, MIB...**$20.00**

Harlem Globetrotters, 50th Year, 1972, double deck, MIB, sealed..**$15.00**

Harold Lloyd Estate, narrow, by Liberty, USA, modern, 52+2 Jokers, NM in paper box.....................................**$10.00**

Helmsley Hotels, nonstandard pictorial w/Leona Helmsley in color on 36 cards, 1986, 52+4 extra cards, gold edges, MIB **$65.00**

Hollywood, Aces & Jokers as star caricatures, 52+3 Jokers+extra card, M in G box **$17.50**

Homes of Henry Wadsworth Longfellow and Ralph Waldo Emerson, 2 complete decks, EX in VG box, $15.00.

Illinois Central, Panama Ltd, narrow, yellow border, ca 1953, 52+Joker, NM in EX box **$12.00**

Kennedy Kards, Kennedy family courts, 1963, M in cellophane wrapper..**$32.00**

Laugh-In, jokes on courts & pips, 1969, 52+2 Jokers, MIB **$45.00**

Moth, Waddington, gold edges, 52+Joker, NMIB **$32.00**

New England Transportation, bus & truck backs on double deck, 104 complete, G **$12.50**

Paris Story, Philibert, color photo on each card, 52+2 Joker, MIB **$20.00**

Party Pack, naughty cartoons, oversize, 1953, 52+Joker, NMIB...**$22.50**

Personalities souvenir, photo cards w/many personalities, white backs, 1970s, 52 on cheap paper, 1⅝x2¼", EX **$12.50**

Polar bear/panther, Waddington, double deck, 104+2 Jokers, MIB **$56.00**

Qantas, triangles w/blue Roo, 1985, MIB **$12.00**

Rickey's Town House, complete, $10.00.

Rockwell International, nonstandard astronaut courts, robot Jokers, 1980, 52+2 Jokers, NM in EX box..............**$55.00**

Sailing ship, Western Playing Cards, double deck, gold edges, M in sealed wrapper..**$22.00**

Sandusky Cement, wide, Medusa logo backs, worn gold edge, 52+Joker, VG in broken box **$32.50**

Santa Fe, tiered trains, desert & trestle, double deck, 1972, M, sealed in paper box...**$10.00**

Shakespeare, wide, character courts, Waddington, 32+2 Jokers+book, MIB **$17.50**

Shriner-Mason, narrow, logo on black, 1930s, MIB **$32.50**

Southern Pacific, western scenes, ca 1935, 52+2 Jokers, EX+ in EX box **$12.50**

Survival, wide, survival tips, Environs, 1974, 52, M....**$10.00**

Tee-Up, Creative Card Co Sports Series, golf cartoons, 1963, 52+2 Jokers, MIB..**$15.00**

Texas Centennial, 100th Anniversary, 1936, 52+Joker+extra card, MIB **$28.00**

Thunderbird, Whitman, black w/sketch of Thunderbird, gold edge, 52+2 Jokers, M...**$3.00**

Time Magazine, oversize, 1962, 52 complete, NMIB ..**$50.00**

Trans Caribbean, purple-tone photo of DC-8, 1960s, EX in box..**$38.00**

TWA, Collector Series, Lockheed 1049, 1952, 52+2 Jokers, EX in box **$10.00**

Union Pacific, First Spike Centennial 1869-1969, narrow, special Ace of Spades, 52+Joker+extra card, MIB........**$6.00**

USA Air, horizontal red US and brown Air, MIB **$6.00**

Victory, Arrco, Chicago, courts are Uncle Sam, Liberty, soldiers, Hitler-Mussolini Joker, 1945, 52+2 Jokers, EX in box..**$65.00**

Western Printing, plant on backs, 52+special Jokers, VG in box..**$15.00**

Worldways Canada, wide, logo Aces, 52+2 Jokers, MIB...**$20.00**

Zulu, John Waddington Ltd, London, African shield shapes, 1960s?, 52+Joker, NMIB...**$20.00**

3 dogs in a basket, Arrco, pinochle, 48 complete, G ...**$5.00**

Political Memorabilia

Political collecting is one of today's fastest-growing hobbies. Between campaign buttons, glassware, paper, and other items, collectors are scrambling to aquire these little pieces of history. Before the turn of the century and the advent of the modern political button, candidates produced ribbons, ferrotypes, stickpins, banners, and many household items to promote their cause. In 1896 the first celluloid (or cello) buttons were used. Cello refers to a process where a paper disc carrying a design is crimped under a piece of celluloid (now acetate) and fastened to a metal button back. In the 1920s the use of lithographed (or litho) buttons was introduced.

Campaigns throughout the 1930s until today have used both types of buttons. In today's media-hyped world, it is amazing that, in addition to TV and radio commercials, candidates still use some of their funding to produce buttons. Bumper stickers, flyers, and novelty items also still abound. Reproductions are sometimes encountered by collectors. Practice and experience are the best tools in order to be aware.

One important factor to remember when pricing buttons is that condition is everything. Buttons with any cracks, stains, or other damage will only sell for a fraction of our suggested values. Listed below are some of the items one is likely to find when scrutinizing today's sales.

For more information about this hobby, we recommend you read Michael McQuillen's monthly column 'Political Parade' in *Antique Week* newspaper.

Advisor: Michael McQuillen (See Directory, Political)

Club: A.P.I.C. (American Political Items Collectors)
Michael McQuillen
P.O. Box 11141
Indianapolis, IN 46201-0141; National organization serving needs of political enthusiasts; send SASE for more information

Bandanna, Win w/Ike for President, portrait, red, white, blue & black, 26" square, EX...**$50.00**

Bank, John F Kennedy, 1917-1963, bust figural, Banthrico, bronze color, 5", EX...**$30.00**

Bumper sticker, Goldwater in '64, red & yellow, EX....**$3.00**

Button, All the Way w/Adlai, single portrait, flasher, black & white, 2¼", EX **$15.00**

Button, America's First Lady Jacqueline Kennedy, single portrait, celluloid, multiple colors, EX **$70.00**

Button, Bush-Quayle '88, jugate, celluloid, multiple colors, 2¼", EX...**$4.00**

Button, Clinton-Gore '92, picture of oval office, oval, celluloid, blue, yellow, white & red, 2¼", EX.............**$75.00**

Button, Dan Quayle for Congress, picture of a quail, celluloid, white & green, 1¼", EX...................................**$20.00**

Button, Dewey-Warren in '48, jugate pictures in reverse order, celluloid, red, white & blue, scarce, ⅞", EX.........**$750.00**

Button, Dukakis, Bentsen, Winners for 1988, jugate, oval, celluloid, multiple colors, 2¼", EX..............................**$4.00**

Button, Ferraro for Vice-President, portrait, celluloid, multiple colors, 2¼", EX **$4.00**

Button, For the Love of Ike, Vote Republican, portrait, celluloid, red, white, blue & black, 6", EX **$40.00**

Button, Go Forward w/Stevenson-Sparkman, jugate, lithographed metal, multiple colors, 1¾", EX **$30.00**

Button, Goldwater-Miller, jugate, rectangular, celluloid, red, white, blue & black, 2x3", EX................................**$10.00**

Button, I Like Ike, celluloid, red, white & blue, 3", EX..**$10.00**

Button, I'm a Michigan Republican From Ford Country, portrait, celluloid, red, white & blue, 2¼", EX..........**$12.00**

Button, I'm for Barry Goldwater for Vice-President, celluloid, yellow & blue, 3", EX...**$15.00**

Button, Inauguration Day...Man of the '60s, Kennedy, celluloid, multiple colors, 6", EX **$25.00**

Button, Joe & I for Willkie, Joe Louis portrait, celluloid, black & white, 1¼", EX..**$475.00**

Button, Kennedy (Robert) for US Senator, portrait, celluloid, red, white, blue & black, 3", EX..........................**$22.00**

Button, Landon-Knox, picture of elephant, lithographed metal, brown & yellow, ⅝", on felt sunflower, EX.............**$4.00**

Button, Leadership for the '60s, Kennedy-Johnson, jugate, lithographed metal, multiple colors, 2¼x3½", EX.......**$40.00**

Button, Minnesota Truman Club, celluloid, gold & brown, 2", EX **$200.00**

Button, Nixon, celluloid, red & white, 4", EX **$6.00**

Button, Nixon in November, portrait, celluloid, red, white, blue & black, 6", EX..**$125.00**

Button, Our Nation Needs Nixon & Lodge, jugate, oval, lithographed metal, red, white, blue & black, 2¼x3", EX..**$18.00**

Button, Reagan in 1980, celluloid, red, white & blue, 1¼", EX..**$4.00**

Button, Robin McGovern, McGovern pictured as Robin Hood, celluloid, black, white & green, 4", EX **$70.00**

Button, Roosevelt-Wallace, jugate, lithographed metal, red, white & blue, 1", EX..**$18.00**

Button, Rosalyn Carter for First Lady, 1980, portrait, celluloid, multiple colors, 2¼", EX....................................**$5.00**

Button, Truman-Barkley, picture of Capitol Dome, lithographed metal, red, white & blue, ⅞", EX **$22.00**

Button, We Want Pat Too, portrait, celluloid, red, white, blue & black, 1¼", EX..**$10.00**

Button, Wings for Willkie, America, picture of airplane, lithographed, red, white & blue, 1¼", EX.................**$15.00**

Can, Gold Water, The Right Taste for the Conservative Taste, tall tin can, gold, white & green, 5", EX.............**$15.00**

Cigarette pack, I Like Ike, portrait, red, white & blue, unopened, EX **$25.00**

Cigarette pack, Stevenson for President, portrait, red, white & blue, unopened, EX..**$25.00**

Clock, FDR The Man of the Hour, FDR figural (at ship's wheel), bronze, working, 13", EX **$125.00**

Convention badge, 1984 Democratic National Convention Delegate, red, white & blue ribbon w/Liberty Bell medal, EX..**$40.00**

License plate attachment, Wallace for President, portrait, metal, multiple colors, 6x11", EX...........................**$18.00**

Medal, 1961 Kennedy Inauguration, bronze, 3", EX...**$30.00**

Mug, 1969, Nixon-Agnew GOP, pottery, Frankoma, 5x3x4", EX...**$65.00**

Neck tie, Taft for President, portrait, cotton, blue & white, EX **$40.00**

Paper-doll book, First Family, The Reagans, cut-out book, Dell, 9x12", EX...**$10.00**

Pennant, Barry Goldwater for President, felt, blue & white, 1964, 15" long, EX...**$30.00**

Pennant, Win w/Willkie, portrait, felt, red, white, blue & black, EX **$45.00**

Postcard, LBJ for the USA, portrait, multiple colors, EX ..**$4.00**

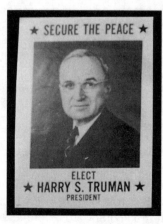

Poster, Harry S. Truman, black, white and red paper, 1948, 22x16", EX, $100.00. (Photo courtesy of Michael McQuillen.)

Poster, Mondale for President, paper, white on blue, 16x24", EX...**$6.00**

Record, Nixon's the One, portrait, cardboard 45 rpm, black & white, 6x6", EX..**$10.00**

Salt shakers, Kennedy in his rocking chair, china, 4", EX..**$45.00**

Sheet music, Hello Jimmy, portrait, red, white & blue, 9x12", EX..**$8.00**

Wendell Willkie's campaign of 1940 provides collectors with a wide spectrum of buttons to search for. Items shown range in price from $15.00 to $750.00 each. (Photo courtesy of Michael McQuillen.)

Porcelier China

The Porcelier Manufacturing Company began in East Liverpool, Ohio, in 1926. It moved to Greensburg, Pennsylvania, in 1930, where it continued to operate until its closing in 1954. They are best known for their extensive line of vitrified china kitchenware, but it should also be noted that they made innumerable lighting fixtures.

They used many different methods of marking their ware, and each mark included the name Porcelier, usually written in script. With the exception of sugar bowls and creamers, most pieces are marked. The mark can be an ink stamp in black, blue, brown, or green; engraved into the metal bottom plate (as on electrical pieces); on a paper label (as found on lighting fixtures); incised block letters; or raised block letters.

The values below are suggested for pieces in excellent condition. Our advisor for this category, Susan Grindberg, has written the *Collector's Guide to Porcelier China, Identification and Values.*

Advisor: Susan Grindberg (See Directory, Porcelier)

Club/Newsletter: Porcelier Collectors Club
21 Tamarac Swamp Rd.
Wellingford, CT 06492; *Porcelier Paper* Newsletter, $2.50 for sample copy

Ashtray, 1939 New York World's Fair, unmarked, from $120 to..**$150.00**

Boiler, Sprig..**$35.00**

Canister, Serv-All, w/platinum trim............................**$40.00**

Canister, sugar; Country Life Series **$45.00**

Casserole, Country Life Series, w/lid, 9½"................**$90.00**

Cookie jar, Serv-All, w/platinum trim.......................**$80.00**

Creamer, Beehive Crisscross **$15.00**

Creamer, Country Life Series................................**$15.00**

Creamer, Double Floral **$12.00**

Creamer, Hearth **$10.00**

Creamer, Nautical..**$25.00**

Creamer, Pink Flower Platinum **$10.00**

Creamer, Tomato..**$18.00**

Creamer, Tulips..**$25.00**

Electric percolator, Basketweave Wild Flowers........**$125.00**

Electric percolator, Double Floral **$90.00**

Electric percolator, Pink Flower Platinum.................**$70.00**

Electric percolator, Tulips...............................**$125.00**

Hostess set, Field Flowers, complete w/electric urn, sugar bowl & creamer......................................**$140.00**

Mug, Ringed, solid color **$20.00**

Mug set, Wildlife, gold trim, MIB, from $180.00 to $240.00. (Photo courtesy of Susan Grindberg.)

Percolator set, Miniature Rose, complete w/electric percolator, sugar bowl & creamer................................**$145.00**

Pitcher, Flight, disc form **$90.00**

Pitcher, Ribbed Band, 2-cup **$27.00**

Pitcher, 1939 New York World's Fair, disc form, 5", from $125 to..**$150.00**

Pitcher, 1939 New York World's Fair, disc form, 7", from $150 to..**$225.00**

Powder jar...**$80.00**

Salt & pepper shakers, Oriental Deco, each...............**$15.00**

Sandwich grill, Scalloped Wild Flowers, from $280 to **$325.00**

Sandwich grill, Serv-All, w/platinum trim, from $175 to.**$250.00**

Standard ink stamp mark. (Photo courtesy of Susan Grindberg.)

Sugar bowl, Beehive Crisscross	$15.00
Sugar bowl, Country Life Series	$15.00
Sugar bowl, Double Floral	$12.00
Sugar bowl, Hearth	$10.00
Sugar bowl, Nautical	$25.00
Sugar bowl, Pink Flower Platinum	$10.00
Sugar bowl, Tomato	$18.00
Sugar bowl, Tulips	$25.00
Teapot, American Beauty Rose, 6-cup	$45.00
Teapot, Beehive Crisscross, 4-cup	$42.00
Teapot, Beehive Crisscross, 6-cup	$37.00
Teapot, Blue Roses, 6-cup	$45.00
Teapot, Colonial, Silhouette decal, 6-cup	$95.00
Teapot, Colonial, undecorated, 6-cup	$35.00
Teapot, Country Life Series, 2-cup	$45.00
Teapot, Country Life Series, 4-cup	$42.00
Teapot, Country Life Series, 6-cup	$45.00
Teapot, Country Life Series, 8-cup	$55.00
Teapot, Diamond Leaf, 2-cup	$40.00
Teapot, double; Basketweave Wild Flowers, 8-cup	$90.00
Teapot, double; Colonial, Black-Eyed Susan decal, 6-cup	$95.00
Teapot, Flight, 4-cup	$45.00
Teapot, Flight, 6-cup	$45.00
Teapot, Harlequin, 4-cup	$35.00
Teapot, Harlequin, 6-cup	$42.00
Teapot, Hearth, 6-cup	$30.00
Teapot, Hearth, 8-cup	$32.00
Teapot, Leaves, 2-cup	$37.00
Teapot, Magnolia, 6-cup	$35.00
Teapot, Nautical, 2-cup	$40.00
Teapot, Nautical, 6-cup	$35.00
Teapot, Oriental Deco, 6-cup	$45.00
Teapot, Paneled Orb, 6-cup	$40.00
Teapot, Pears, 2-cup	$30.00
Teapot, Pears, 4-cup	$30.00

Teapot, Rooster, 6-cup, $60.00. (Photo courtesy of Susan Grindberg.)

Teapot, Scalloped Wild Flowers, 6-cup	$55.00
Teapot, Serv-All, red & black	$45.00
Teapot, Southern Belle, 6-cup	$40.00
Teapot, Tomato, 6-cup	$40.00
Teapot, Tree Trunk, 4-cup	$45.00
Teapot, Tree Trunk, 6-cup	$35.00
Teapot, Tree Trunk, 8-cup	$40.00
Teapot, Trellis Bottom, 6-cup	$32.00

Teapot, Trellis Top, 6-cup	$32.00
Teapot, 1939 New York World's Fair, 4-cup, from $250 to	$300.00
Teapot, 1939 New York World's Fair, 8-cup, from $225 to	$260.00
Waffle iron, Scalloped Wild Flowers, from $250 to	$325.00
Waffle iron, Serv-All, w/gold trim, from $175 to	$225.00

Postcards

There are now more postcard collectors in America than there are for any other collectible. The golden age of cards was between 1900 to 1920. From that era came excellent examples of art, signed, poster, and advertising cards. Worldwide view cards have been made for one hundred years, and while some have little or no value, a rare real photo with social, historical, or political significance may be worth several hundred dollars. Condition is very important, and a bent corner or tear is viewed just as a chip or crack is when judging the condition of a piece of glass. This is an area of collecting where much research and documentation is needed. Signed postcards of major artists such as Mucha, Kirchner, Colombo, Drayton, O'Neill, etc., are rapidly increasing in price because of investor speculation. View cards are the bread and butter of postcard collecting and are being used for historical research. The possibilities of collecting are limitless. Certain cards, for instance WWI devastation scenes, are almost valueless, whereas chromolitho cards of diners or car races are desirable. Postcard collecting makes a great family hobby because of its inclusiveness of subjects.

Advisor: Pamela E. Apkarian-Russell (See Directory, Postcards)

Holiday, Christmas, Santa holding doll, $16.00; Santa delivering toys, $15.00. (Photo courtesy of Pamela Apkarian-Russell.)

Anti-Axis, Hitler's face in toilet bowl	$15.00
Anti-Axis, Quick Get Cohen My Lawyer, shows Hitler in jail	$15.00
Birthday, child w/puppies & roses, French	$4.00
Comic, Bonzo dressed as a caveman	$16.00
Comic, suffrage parade of chickens, owl above	$25.00
Fantasy, Midsummer Dreams, illustrated by Thomas Maybank, Tuck	$25.00

Fantasy, photo image of aviator in biplane within flower cameo in sky, tinted **$14.00**

Fantasy, 2 dogs in boxing ring, Dutch.........................**$20.00**

Holiday, Christmas, child giving Santa letter, Clapsaddle ..**$10.00**

Holiday, Christmas, Dicken's Christmas Carol, Valentine, set of 6 ....**$100.00**

Holiday, Christmas, image of Nimble Nicks in car w/Santa, Whitney **$15.00**

Holiday, Christmas, image of Santa reading street sign ..**$14.00**

Holiday, Easter, dressed rabbit couple on seesaw, he w/bouquet of flowers, Easter Greetings, early **$14.00**

Holiday, Easter, elves & giant Easter egg, French.........**$6.00**

Holiday, Easter, embossed image of 2 rabbits w/elf in front of egg house, A Happy Easter **$14.00**

Holiday, Easter, 4 realistic rabbits w/decorative Easter-egg bodies running across field, Easter Greetings.......**$12.00**

Holiday, Halloween, boy & girl w/jack-o'-lantern, illustrated by Mary Evans Price **$7.00**

Holiday, Halloween, boys stealing gate, Tuck **$25.00**

Holiday, Halloween, cat on orange background, invitation, Whitney **$25.00**

Holiday, Halloween, pumpkin boy hugs owl in tree, Whitney **$14.00**

Holiday, New Year's, girl throwing snowball, Schmucker/ Winch..**$25.00**

Holiday, St. Patrick's Day, couple dancing, $7.00; Girl in front of shamrock and bagpipes, signed SLS (Samuel L. Shucher), $25.00. (Photo courtesy of Pamela Apkarian-Russell.)

Linen, Anderson's Pea Soup Restaurant **$5.00**

Linen, Citation running at Hialeah race track, Miami....**$7.00**

Linen, fisherman w/mermaid, comic image..................**$5.00**

Linen, Florida, state flower & bird..............................**$1.00**

Linen, Miami Parrot Jungle...**$5.00**

Photo, actress Anna May Wong, tinted **$14.00**

Photo, Amtrack, interior view of dining car **$6.00**

Photo, Ceylon, view of elephants................................**$8.00**

Photo, Charlie Chaplin **$15.00**

Photo, child on carousel horse...................................**$40.00**

Photo, child w/teddy bears & dolls **$15.00**

Photo, Daytona Beach, shows 2 cars racing **$35.00**

Photo, fantasy image of lady w/champagne & a fan in the sky...**$8.00**

Photo, Hitler & Mussolini, side view............................**$28.00**

Photo, Josephine Baker in banana costume.............**$200.00**

Photo, Michigan hunters w/bird kill **$12.00**

Photo, miner in mine, tinted......................................**$14.00**

Photo, Pittsburgh PA, interior view of airport...............**$5.00**

Photo, Shirley Temple in blue-tinted dress.................**$22.00**

Photo, South American monkey climbing tree **$1.00**

Photo, Stonehenge, close-up view **$8.00**

Photo, Thomaston GA, shows Main Street & roses **$12.00**

Photo, Toy Town Tavern, Winchendon MA, tinted **$5.00**

Photo, woman & Borzoi, sepia..................................**$15.00**

Photo, 2 people playing table tennis **$20.00**

Poster Art, Air France, shows Paris & Eiffel Tower.....**$18.00**

Scenic, Alaska, view of totem pole **$5.00**

Scenic, Jacksonville FL, alligator border....................**$25.00**

Scenic, lighthouse in Portland ME.............................**$4.00**

Scenic, town view, lighthouse border.........................**$10.00**

Scenic, town view, lobster border...............................**$20.00**

Scenic, town view, shell border **$10.00**

Wedding, bride & groom #6949, embossed, marked PFB .**$10.00**

Wedding, bride & groom in carriage, Rose O' Neill, Kewpie **$45.00**

3-D, roses **$4.00**

Powder Jars

Glassware items such as powder jars, trays, lamps, vanity sets, towel bars, and soap dishes were produced in large quantities during the Depression era by many glasshouses who were simply trying to stay in business. They used many of the same colors as they had in the making of their colored Depression glass dinnerware that has been so popular with collectors for more than twenty years.

Some of their most imaginative work went into designing powder jars. Subjects ranging from birds and animals to Deco nudes and Cinderella's coach can be found today, and this diversity coupled with the fact that many were made in several colors provides collectors with more than enough variations to look for to keep them interested and challenged.

For more information we recommend *Bedroom and Bathroom Glassware of the Depression Years* by Margaret and Kenn Whitmyer (published by Collector Books).

Advisor: Sharon Thoerner (See Directory, Powder Jars)

Cinderella's Coach, pink frosted with black lid, small size, from $110.00 to $140.00.

Annette w/2 dogs, crystal **$75.00**

Babs II, cobalt, 3-footed, smaller version, very rare ..**$565.00**

Babs II, pink frost, 3-footed, smaller version **$155.00**
Basset hound, pink frost, from $145 to **$165.00**
Carrie, black, draped nude figural stem **$215.00**
Carrie, pink frost w/painted flowers, draped nude figural
    stem **$155.00**
Cinderella's Coach, pink frost w/black lid, rectangular body,
    sm footrest for coachman, lg **$195.00**
Cleopatra II, crystal, shallow base, deep lid, 4¾" **$95.00**
Court Jester, pink frost, figural finial **$135.00**
Crinoline Girl, crystal, off-the-shoulder gown, flowers in right
    hand, embossed bows on skirt **$40.00**
Crinoline Girl, pink frost, off-the-shoulder gown, flowers in
    right hand, embossed bows on skirt **$120.00**
Dancing Girl, blue transparent, feminine features, rope trim
    at top of base **$480.00**
Dancing Girl, green frost, feminine features, rope trim at top
    of base **$120.00**
Elephant w/carousel base, green frost **$255.00**
Elephants battling, crystal **$45.00**
Elephants battling, pink frost **$85.00**
Godiva, satin, nude seated on diamond-shaped base ..**$185.00**
Lillian II, satin, overall ripples **$55.00**
Lillian III, crystal, stippled lid, base w/hexagonal band .**$50.00**
Lillian VII, milk glass, cone-shaped base....................**$175.00**
Lillian VII, pink frost, cone-shaped base **$250.00**
Liz, satin top, green satin base **$120.00**
Lovebirds, green frost..**$120.00**
Martha Washington, crystal, Colonial lady between boy &
    girl **$60.00**
Martha Washington, pink frost, Colonial lady between boy &
    girl..**$115.00**
Military Hat, stippled visor, lines encircling crown, amber..**$27.00**
Minstrel, crystal **$50.00**
Minstrel, crystal w/green paint **$75.00**
My Pet, 3 Scotties on lid, crystal................................**$75.00**

Pandora, green frosted, from $175.00 to $225.00.

Parrots, satin...**$40.00**
Penguins, pink frost, dome top **$300.00**
Spike Bulldog, green frost **$155.00**
Spike Bulldog, pink frost **$125.00**
Terrier, pink frost, sm..**$155.00**
Three Birds, crystal...**$65.00**
Three Birds, green frost **$95.00**
Vamp, pink frost, flapper's head forms finial **$155.00**
Wendy, satin, flapper girl w/arms outstretched, beaded neck-
    lace **$65.00**

Purinton Pottery

The Purinton Pottery Company moved from Ohio to Shippenville, Pennsylvania, in 1941 and began producing several lines of dinnerware and kitchen items hand painted with fruits, ivy vines, and trees in bold brush strokes of color on a background reminiscent of old yellow ware pieces. The company closed in 1959 due to economic reasons.

Purinton has a style that's popular today with collectors who like the country look. It isn't always marked, but you'll soon recognize its distinct appearance. Some of the rarer designs are Palm Tree and Peasant Lady, and examples of these lines are considerably higher than the more common ones. You'll see more Apple and Fruit pieces than any, and in more diversified shapes.

For more information we recommend *Purinton Pottery, An Identification and Value Guide,* by Susan Morris.

Newsletter: *Purinton Pastimes*
P.O. Box 9394
Arlington, VA 22219; Subscription: $10 per year

Apple, ashtray, wire holder, 5½" **$40.00**
Apple, bean pot, 3¾" **$50.00**
Apple, bowl, dessert; 4" **$8.00**
Apple, bowl, salad; 11" **$50.00**
Apple, candle holder, 2x6"...**$45.00**
Apple, canister set, oval shaped, cobalt trim, 9" **$75.00**
Apple, coffeepot, 8-cup, 8" **$90.00**
Apple, cup, 2½" **$10.00**
Apple, dish, jam & jelly; 5½" **$45.00**
Apple, dish, pickle; 6" **$30.00**
Apple, dish, vegetable; divided, 10½"........................**$35.00**
Apple, jar, grease; w/lid, 5½" **$85.00**
Apple, jug, Kent-style, 1-pt, 4½" **$35.00**
Apple, mug, beer; 16-oz, 4¾".......................................**$55.00**
Apple, mug, juice; 6-oz, 2½" **$15.00**
Apple, night bottle, 1-quart, 7½" **$55.00**

Apple, pitcher, 2-pint, 6¼", $75.00.

Apple, plate, chop; scalloped decorated border, 12"..**$40.00**
Apple, plate, dinner; 9¾" **$15.00**
Apple, plate, salad; 6¾" **$10.00**
Apple, platter, grill; indented, 12".................................**$45.00**

Apple, platter, meat; 11" or 12", each $30.00
Apple, saucer, 5½" $3.00
Blue Pansy, planter, basket, 6¼" $65.00
Cactus Flower, bowl, fruit; 12" $85.00
Chartreuse, creamer, 3½" $20.00
Chartreuse, plate, chop; 12" $25.00
Chartreuse, wall pocket, 3½" $35.00
Cook Forest, ewer, souvenir, 9" $150.00
Creasant Flower, coaster, 3½" $40.00
Creasant Flower, plate, lap; 8½" $35.00
Creasant Flower, tumbler, 12-oz, 5" $30.00
Daisy, grease jar, w/lid, 5½" $60.00
Daisy, jug, Rebecca; 7½" $50.00
Feather Flower, teapot, 2-cup, 4" $55.00
Fruit, bowl, range; w/lid, red trim, 5½" $45.00
Fruit, creamer & sugar bowl, miniature, 2", set..........$30.00
Fruit, cruet, oil & vinegar; square, solid apple & purple
    grapes, 5" $50.00
Fruit, jug, Kent; 1-pt, 4½" $30.00
Fruit, plate, breakfast; 1 of 4 different fruits, 8½", each...$30.00
Fruit, saucer, 5½" $3.00
Fruit, storage jar, stacking, 8¾" $85.00
Fruit, teapot, 4-cup, 5" $55.00
Fruit, tumbler, 12-oz, 5" $20.00
Half-Blossom, planter, rum jug; 6½" $55.00
Heather Plaid, canister, coffee; square, 7½" $40.00
Heather Plaid, creamer, 3" $20.00
Heather Plaid, mug, handled, 8-oz, 4" $25.00
Heather Plaid, plate, chop; 12" $25.00
Heather Plaid, plate, dinner; 9¾" $15.00
Heather Plaid, sugar bowl, w/lid, 4" $30.00
Heather Plaid, teapot, 6-cup, 6" $65.00
Intaglio, butter dish, 6½" $55.00

Intaglio: dinner plate, $20.00; Coffee mug, 4", $60.00; Beer mug, 5", $60.00.

Intaglio, pitcher, beverage; 2-pt, 6¼" $55.00
Intaglio, saucer, 5½" $3.00
Ivy-Red Blossom, biscuit jar, 8" $55.00
Ivy-Red Blossom, coffeepot, 8" $65.00
Ivy-Red Blossom, pitcher, beverage; 2-pt, 6¼" $55.00
Ivy-Yellow Blossom, jug, Kent; 1-pt, 4¼" $30.00
Ivy-Yellow Blossom, sugar bowl, w/lid, 5" $25.00
Maywood, pickle dish, 6" $15.00
Maywood, platter, grill; 12" $25.00
Maywood, roll tray, 11" $20.00

Ming Tree, jardiniere, 5" $40.00
Ming Tree, plate, dinner; 9¾" $20.00
Ming Tree, platter, meat; 12" $40.00
Mountain Rose, decanter, 5" $45.00
Mountain Rose, marmalade jar, 4½" $65.00
Mountain Rose, plate, chop; 12" $50.00
Mountain Rose, tumbler, 12-oz, 5" $35.00
Normandy Plaid, bowl, dessert; 4" $8.00
Normandy Plaid, bowl, range; w/lid, 5½" $50.00
Normandy Plaid, bowl, vegetable; open, 8½" $20.00
Normandy Plaid, grease jar, w/lid, 5½" $60.00
Normandy Plaid, mug, beer; 16-oz, 4¾" $40.00
Normandy Plaid, pitcher, beverage; 2-pt, 6¼" $55.00
Normandy Plaid, roll tray, 11" $35.00
Normandy Plaid, saucer, 5½" $3.00

Palm Tree: Canister, $200.00; Matching range shakers, $75.00.

Palm Tree, plate, dinner; 9¾" $125.00
Palm Tree, vase, 5" $75.00
Peasant Garden, plate, chop; 12" $150.00
Peasant Garden, plate, lap; indent for cup, 8½" $90.00
Peasant Garden, salt & pepper shakers, jug-style, 2½", pr..$65.00
Pennsylvania Dutch, jug, Dutch; 2-pt, 5¾" $100.00
Pennsylvania Dutch, planter, basket; 6¼" $85.00
Pennsylvania Dutch, platter, meat; 12" $50.00
Pennsylvania Dutch, relish tray, 3-part, pottery handle,
    10" $75.00
Pennsylvania Dutch, wall pocket, 3½" $65.00
Petals, baker, 7" $35.00
Petals, honey jug, 6¼" $45.00
Petals, saucer, 5½" $6.00
Provincial Fruit, tumbler, 12-oz, 5" $20.00
Red Feather, TV lamp, 8½" $75.00

Ribbon Flower: Fruit bowl, 12", $50.00; Dutch jug, $45.00.

Saraband, candle holder, 2x6" $20.00
Saraband, cruets, oil & vinegar; square, 5", pr............$25.00
Saraband, plate, chop; 12" $15.00
Seaform, coffee server, w/lid, 9" $125.00
Seaform, platter, meat; 12" $50.00
Shooting Star, honey jug, 6¼"................................$35.00
Shooting Star, vase, 5" $25.00
Sunflower, tumbler, 12-oz, 5"................................$30.00
Sunny, wall pocket, 3½" $40.00
Tea Rose, planter, 5"..$65.00
Tea Rose, roll tray, 11" $50.00
Windflower, jardinere, 5"......................................$30.00
Woodflowers, sugar bowl, w/lid, 4" $45.00

Puzzles

The first children's puzzle was actually developed as a learning aid by an English map maker, trying to encourage the study of geography. Most 19th-century puzzles were made of wood, rather boring, and very expensive. But by the Victorian era, nursery rhymes and other light-hearted themes became popular. The industrial revolution and the inception of color lithography combined to produce a stunning variety of themes ranging from technical advancements, historical scenarios, and fairy tales. Power saws made production more cost effective, and wood was replaced with less expensive cardboard.

As early as the twenties and thirties, American manufacturers began to favor character-related puzzles, the market already influenced by radio and the movies. Some of these were advertising premiums. Die-cutters had replaced jigsaws, cardboard became thinner, and now everyone could afford puzzles. During the Depression they were a cheap form of entertainment, and no family get-together was complete without a puzzle spread out on the card table for all to enjoy.

Television and movies caused a lull in puzzle making during the fifties, but advancements in printing and improvements in quality brought them back strongly in the sixties. Unusual shapes, the use of fine art prints, and more challenging designs caused sales to increase.

If you're going to collect puzzles, you'll need to remember that unless all the pieces are there, they're not of much value, especially those from the 20th century. The condition of the box is important as well. Right now there's lots of interest in puzzles from the fifties through the seventies that feature popular TV shows and characters from that era. Remember, though a frame-tray puzzle still sealed in its original wrapping may be worth $10.00 or more, depending on the subject matter and its age, a well-used example may well be worthless as a collectible.

To learn more about the subject, we recommend *Character Toys and Collectibles* and *Toys, Antique and Collectible*, both by David Longest; *Toys of the Sixties, A Pictorial Guide,* by Bill Bruegman; and *Schroeder's Toys, Antique to Modern* (Collector Books).

Newsletter: *Piece by Piece*
P.O. Box 12823
Kansas City, KS 66112-9998; Subscription: $8 per year

Barney Google & Snuffy Smith, frame-tray, Jaymar, 1940s-50s, NM..$35.00
Barney Google & Snuffy Smith, jigsaw, Jaymar, 1963, EX+ (EX+ box)..$15.00
Bat Masterson, jigsaw, Colorforms, 1960s, set of 2, NMIB ..$35.00
Beany & Cecil, frame-tray, thick wood, Cecil in ocean, Playskool, 1961, 11x13", EX+ $25.00
Beverly Hillbillies, jigsaw, group posing for family portrait, Lamar, 1963, M (EX box) $28.00
Black Hole, frame-tray, astronaut & Maximillian, Whitman, 1979, NM...$5.00
Bonanza, jigsaw, On the Trail, Milton Bradley, 100 pcs, NM (EX+ box)..$30.00
Broken Arrow, frame-tray, Chochise & others in horse-drawn wagon, EX $20.00
Broken Arrow, jigsaw, Built-Rite, 1958, NMIB $25.00
Brownies & Cubies, jigsaw, Jaymar, 1962, NM (EX+ box).$20.00
Bugs Bunny, frame-tray, Bugs selling carrot burgers from Elmer Fudd's garden, Jaymar, 1950s, VG+...........$15.00
Bullwinkle, jigsaw, Western Publishing/Whitman, 1976, 100 pcs, EXIB $5.00
Buzzy the Crow, jigsaw, shows Buzzy popping out of pie before Ole King Cole, 70 pcs, unused, MIB.........$25.00
Captain Kangaroo, Mr Green Jeans & Teddy, jigsaw, Fairchild, 1971, M (NM box)............................$25.00
Cheyenne, jigsaw, Milton Bradley, 1957, set of 3, NMIB .$50.00
Cisco Kid, frame-tray, Cisco w/horse, Doubleday, VG+.$25.00
Combat, frame-tray, Jaymar, 1950s, 11x14", EX+.........$12.00
Creature From the Black Lagoon, jigsaw, Golden, 1990, 200 pcs, MIB..$6.00
Daktari, jigsaw, Whitman, 1967, 100 pcs, EXIB $15.00
Davy Crockett, jigsaw, Indian Attack, Jaymar, EX+ (VG+ box) $65.00
Deputy Dawg, jigsaw, Fairchild, 1977, M (NM box)...$15.00
Dick Tracy, jigsaw, Dick Tracy at office party w/Crime Does Not Pay on wall, Jaymar, EX+ (EX box)..............$40.00
Dick Tracy, jigsaw, Manhunt for Mumbles, Jaymar, 1950s-60s, NM+ (EX box)..$65.00
Dino (Flintstones), frame-tray, shows Dino doing housework w/elephant vacuum & speaking on phone, 8x10", EX $15.00

Disney Movie Classics, jigsaw, Jaymar, 100 pieces, MIB, $10.00.

Dr Doolittle, frame-tray, #4568, Doctor testing horse's eyes, 1967, NM $45.00

Dudley Do-Right, jigsaw, Dudley takes Snydley's clothes, Whitman, 1975, 100 pcs, M (EX sealed box)........**$25.00**

Farrah Fawcett, jigsaw, wearing swimsuit, 1977, 405 pcs, NM+ (EX box)...**$32.00**

Flintstones, frame-tray, Pebbles on stuffed Dino toy, Whitman, 1963, 11x14", EX+ **$15.00**

Flipper, jigsaw, Whitman, 1967, NMIB.....................**$30.00**

Frankenstein, jigsaw, Golden, 1990, 200 pcs, MIB........**$6.00**

Frankenstein, jigsaw, Jaymar, 1963, 60 pcs, NMIB.....**$40.00**

Frankenstein Jr, jigsaw, shows Frankenstein Jr & child flying over countryside, 99 pcs, Whitman, 1968, EXIB ..**$15.00**

Gabby Gator, frame-tray, shows Gabby conducting a group of singing frogs, Preskool, 1963, VG+.................**$10.00**

Gumby, frame-tray, Whitman, 1968, 11x14", EX+ **$15.00**

Gunsmoke, jigsaw, Jr Jigsaw, NM.............................**$35.00**

Hair Bear Bunch, jigsaw, Birthday for Hair Bear in cave, Whitman, 1972, EX+ **$20.00**

Herman & Katnip, frame-tray, Herman w/Katnip in ice-cream cone, EX+ **$5.00**

How the West Was Won, jigsaw, HG Toys, 1978, MIB (sealed) **$30.00**

Howdy Doody, frame-tray, Howdy skiing w/Clarabell, Whitman, 1950s, 12x9", VG.................................**$35.00**

King Leonardo, jigsaw, The Hunter Is Knighted, Jaymar, 1962, EX (VG+ box) **$15.00**

KISS, jigsaw, APC, 1977, 200 pcs, EXIB......................**$15.00**

Lady & the Tramp, jigsaw, Jaymar, 1955, 11x14", EX .**$12.00**

Land of the Giants, jigsaw, Whitman, 1969, 125 pcs, 20" dia, EX+ (EX box) **$45.00**

Lariat Sam, jigsaw, Fairchild, 1977, EX+.....................**$15.00**

Lassie, jigsaw, Whitman, 1971, 14x18", NMIB **$12.00**

Little Lulu, jigsaw, Whitman, 1950s, EX+ (EX+ box)...**$20.00**

Lone Ranger, jigsaw, Lone Ranger & Tonto leaving town, Jaymar, 1947, EX+ (VG+ box)...............................**$50.00**

Love Bug, frame-tray, M (sealed) **$18.00**

Man From UNCLE, jigsaw, Micro Film Affair, Milton Bradley, 1965, NM (EX+ box)..**$50.00**

Marlin Perkins Wild Kindom, jigsaw, 1971, MIB (sealed) ..**$20.00**

Maverick, jigsaw, Jigsaw Jr, EX+................................**$35.00**

Mickey Mouse Club, frame-tray, Jaymar, 1950s, EX....**$10.00**

Mighty Mouse, jigsaw, shows Mighty holding up a collapsed building, Whitman, 1967, EXIB............................**$15.00**

Mighty Mouse Playhouse, jigsaw, scene of Mighty & friends playing homemade instruments on stage, Fairchild, 1956, EXIB..**$20.00**

Milton the Monster, frame-tray, 1966, NM **$25.00**

Milton the Monster, jigsaw, Whitman, 1967, NMIB.....**$45.00**

Mister Bug, frame-tray, Milton Bradley, 1955, EX **$15.00**

Monkees, jigsaw, Speed Boat, Fairchild, 1967, NMIB.**$38.00**

Mother Goose Comic Picture Puzzles, Parker Brothers, 1950s, set of 4, MIB, $45.00. (Photo courtesy of June Moon.)

Munsters, jigsaw, family in car, Whitman, 1965, EXIB ...**$45.00**

Pinocchio, frame-tray, Whitman, 1973, 8x11", M (sealed)...**$18.00**

Popeye, frame-tray, shows Popeye & friends fishing while Brutus attaches bomb to line, Gund, 1950s, 10", VG+...........**$25.00**

Popeye, jigsaw, Sunday comic scene, 1942, 9x14", EX+ ..**$75.00**

Raggedy Ann & Andy, frame-tray, Milton Bradley, 1955, EX+...**$18.00**

Road Runner, jigsaw, Whitman, 1972, MIB (sealed) ...**$30.00**

Robin Hood's Merry Men, jigsaw, Built Rite, 1956, NMIB...**$20.00**

Rocketeer, jigsaw, #5151, Golden Book Co, 300 pcs, MIB .**$25.00**

Rocky & Bullwinkle, frame-tray, posed for 2 Martians taking photo, Whitman, 1960, EX.................................**$25.00**

Rookies, jigsaw, 1975, EX (original canister)...............**$10.00**

Roy Rogers, frame-tray, Roy about to mount Trigger, 11x14", EX...**$45.00**

Santa Claus, frame-tray, Whitman, 1966, 11x14", EX+ ..**$10.00**

Shotgun Slade, jigsaw, Milton Bradley, 1960, 100 pcs, 10x18", NMIB...**$30.00**

Simpsons, jigsaw, Milton Bradley, 250 pcs, MIB.........**$10.00**

Six Million Dollar Man, jigsaw, Steve throwing oil drum at crooks, APC, 1975, NM (EX+ can).........................**$25.00**

Sky Hawks, frame-tray, Whitman, 1970, EX+ **$15.00**

Space Kidettes, frame-tray, shows Space Kidettes landing spacecraft on a planet, Whitman, 1967, 11x14", EX **$18.00**

Space Kidettes, jigsaw, Whitman, 1968, VG **$18.00**

Star Trek, frame-tray, Whitman, 1978, 8x10", M (sealed)......**$12.00**

Superman, jigsaw, Christopher Reeve, 1979, NMIB **$15.00**

Superman, jigsaw, Saalfield, 1940, set of 3, MIB, $330.00.

Superman, jigsaw, Whitman, 1965, 150 pcs, EX+ **$25.00**

Tennessee Tuxedo, jigsaw, Fairchild, 1971, 100 pcs, MIB (sealed) **$25.00**

Tommy Tortoise & Moe Hare, jigsaw, shows Tommy & Moe in a race, 70 pcs, Built-Rite, 1961, unused, MIB ..**$25.00**

Topcat, frame-tray, shows Topcat reading newspaper in trash can as Officer Dibble approaches, Whitman, 1961, 11x14", EX+ **$15.00**

Underdog, jigsaw, steps on body of Simon & brings flowers to Sweet Polly, Whitman, 1973, NM (EX+ box) ...**$15.00**

Welcome Back Kotter, frame-tray, Whitman, M (sealed).....**$15.00**

Woody Woodpecker, frame-tray, shows Woody tied to a batch of helium balloons, Whitman, 1954, 11x14", EX+ ...**$25.00**

Woody Woodpecker, jigsaw, shows Woody hanging from side of a ship fending off a swordfish, Whitman 1960, VG+ (w/box)...**$25.00**

Yogi Bear & Boo Boo, jigsaw, shows Yogi & Boo Boo bouncing on pogo sticks, 63 pcs, Whitman, 1960, EXIB ..**$25.00**

Zorro, jigsaw, Garcia & Diego, MIB............................**$55.00**

Razor Blade Banks

Razor blade banks are receptacles used to store used razor blades for disposal. While the double-edged disposable razor blades date back as far as 1903, ceramic and figural razor blade safes most likely only date as far back as the late 1920s and early 1930s. The invention of the electric razor and later disposable razors did away with the need for these items, and their production ended in the 1950s.

Shapes can include barber chairs, barbers, animals and, more popular, barber poles. Listerine produced a white donkey and elephant in 1936 with political overtones. They also made a white ceramic frog. These were used as promotional items for shaving cream. All prices reflect near-mint to excellent condition and are based on availability.

Advisor: Debbie Gillham (See Directory, Razor Blade Banks)

Barber bust, in coat and tie, from $55.00 to $65.00. (Photo courtesy of Debbie Gillham.)

Barber chair, lg, from $125 to.....................................$175.00
Barber chair, sm, from $95 to.....................................$150.00
Barber holding pole, Occupied Japan, 4", from $45 to...$55.00
Barber shop quartet, from $95 to.............................$125.00
Barber standing in blue coat & stroking chin, from $65 to $75.00
Box w/policeman holding up hand, metal, from $50 to ..$65.00
Cleminson barber head, different colors on collar, from $25 to...$30.00
Cleminson man shaving, mushroom shape, from $25 to..$30.00
Dandy Dans, plastic w/brush holders, from $40 to....$50.00
Frog, marked For Used Blades, from $65 to $75.00

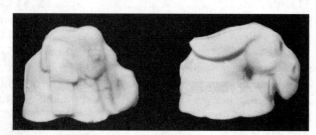

Listerine elephant, from $30.00 to $40.00; Listerine donkey, from $20.00 to $30.00. (Photo courtesy of Debbie Gillham.)

Listerine frog, from $15 to...$20.00
Pudgy barber w/buggy eyes, full-figure, from $65 to ..$75.00
Safe, green, marked Razor on front, from $45 to $65.00
Shaving brush, ceramic, possibly American Bisque, from $50 to...$60.00

Shaving cup, hangs on wall, marked Gay Blades, floral design, from $50 to..$65.00
Tony the barber, Ceramic Arts, from $65 to $75.00
Wooden barber, gay blade bottom unscrews, Woodcroft, 1950, 6", from $65 to..$75.00
Wooden barber, w/key & metal holders for razor & brush, 9", from $85 to...$95.00

Reamers

Reamers were a European invention of the late 1700s, devised as a method of extracting liquid from citrus fruits, which was used as a medicinal remedy. Eventually the concept of freshly squeezed juice worked its way across the oceans. Many early U.S. patents (mostly for wood reamers) were filed in the mid-1880s, and thanks to the 1916 Sunkist 'Drink An Orange' advertising campaign, the reamer soon became a permanent fixture in the well-equipped American kitchen. Most of the major U.S. glass companies and pottery manufacturers included juicers as part of their kitchenware lines. However, some of the most beautiful and unique reamers are ceramic figures and hand-painted, elegant china and porcelain examples. The invention of frozen and bottled citrus juice relegated many a reamer to the kitchen shelf. However the current trend for a healthier diet has garnered renewed interest for the manual juice squeezer.

Most of the German and English reamers listed here can be attributed to the 1920s and thirties. Most of the Japanese imports are from the 1940s.

Advisor: Bobby Zucker Bryson (See Directory, Reamers)

Newsletter: *National Reamer Association Quarterly Review*
c/o Larry Branstad
R.R. 3, Box 67
Frederic, WI 54837; 715-327-4365

Ceramic Reamers

Child's, lustre w/red & yellow flowers, Japan, child's, 2", 2¾" from $95 to...$125.00
Child's, 2-pc, orange lustre w/red, blue & yellow flowers, 2"..$95.00
Clown, brown body & hat, blue button & collar, 6" ..$85.00
Clown, saucer, orange & white, Germany/Goebel, 5" dia...$250.00

Clown, white with black, orange and red details, Japan/Sigma, 2-piece, 6½", $95.00. (Photo courtesy of Bobbie Zucker Bryson.)

Clown, 2-pc, white, black, red & orange, Japan, 6½" ..**$95.00**

Dog, 2-pc, beige w/red & black trim, 8" **$225.00**

Elephant, 2-pc, white w/red & blue trim, 4¼", from $150 to **$200.00**

House, 2-pc, beige w/green trees w/tan branches, blue door & windmill, Japan, 4½" **$150.00**

House, 2-pc, beige w/tan & orange trim, Japan, 5½"..**$100.00**

Lemon, 2-pc, Germany, 3" **$55.00**

Orange, 2-pc, Orange For Baby, yellow w/blue flowers, Goebel, 3½" **$150.00**

Pear, 3-pc, orange w/green leaves & gold trim, Japan, 4¾" **$55.00**

Pitcher, beige with multi-colored flowers and black trim, Japan, 2-piece, 8¾", $50.00. (Photo courtesy of Bobbie Zucker Bryson.)

Pitcher, 2-pc, black w/gold wheat, 8" **$45.00**

Pitcher, 2-pc, cream w/red & black cattails, Universal Potteries, 9" **$125.00**

Rose, pink w/green leaves, Germany, 1¾" **$225.00**

Saucer, cream, tan & maroon w/blue trim, England, 3¼" dia **$90.00**

Saucer, cream w/yellow bees, Japan, 3¾" dia **$45.00**

Saucer, white w/pink flowers & green leaves, Germany, 4½" dia **$75.00**

Saucer, 2-pc, France, Ivoire Corbelle, Henriot Quimper #1166, 4¼" dia **$350.00**

Swan, 2-pc, cream w/rose flowers & green base, Japan, 4¼" **$60.00**

Teapot, 2-pc, yellow, tan & white, England/Shelley, 3½" ..**$95.00**

Teapot style, 2-pc, white w/blue sailboat, Germany, 3¼"..**$65.00**

Teapot style, 2-pc, white w/red flowers & trim, Prussia/Germany/Royal Rudolstadt, 3¼" **$150.00**

Teapot style, 2-pc, white w/yellow & maroon flowers, Nippon, 3¼" **$90.00**

Teapot style, 2-pc, yellow, tan & white, England/Shelley, 3½" **$95.00**

Toby-style man, gray hair, green jacket, lavender hat, 4¾" **$175.00**

USA, Ade-O-Matic Genuine Coorsite Porcelain, green, 9", $150.00. (Photo courtesy of Bobbie Zucker Bryson.)

USA, Jiffy Juicer, US Pat 2,130,755, Sept 2, 1928, 5¼" ...**$85.00**

Glass

Amber, paneled sides, Westmoreland, lg.................**$275.00**

Amber, 2-cup measure w/reamer top, US Glass......**$275.00**

Amber (dark), Indiana Glass, loop handle **$275.00**

Clear, baby's, notched top **$50.00**

Clear frosted, Baby's Orange **$65.00**

Clear w/elephant-decorated base, baby's, Fenton **$75.00**

Clear w/flower decal, baby's, Westmoreland............**$40.00**

Crystal, embossed ASCO, Good Morning, Orange Juice .**$20.00**

Crystal, Jennyware **$85.00**

Crystal, spout opposite handle, Indiana Glass **$12.00**

Custard, embossed McK, 6" **$25.00**

Custard, Sunkist...**$30.00**

Delphite blue, Jeannette, sm......................................**$75.00**

Emerald green, straight sides, Fry **$30.00**

Green, Orange Juice Extractor....................................**$50.00**

Green, paneled sides, loop handle, Federal Glass......**$25.00**

Green, Party Line, 4-cup pitcher w/reamer top **$95.00**

Green, pointed cone, Federal Glass............................**$15.00**

Green, slick handle, insert near top of cup, graduated measurements on side, US Glass................................**$35.00**

Green, tab handle, Hazel Atlas....................................**$10.00**

Green, 2-cup pitcher w/reamer top, Hazel Atlas **$30.00**

Green, 4-cup pitcher marked A&J w/reamer top, Hazel Atlas **$35.00**

Green, 4-cup pitcher w/reamer top, Hocking............**$35.00**

Green custard, embossed Sunkist...............................**$85.00**

Jad-ite, grapefruit, McKee..**$150.00**

Jad-ite, Sunkist...**$25.00**

Jad-ite (light), 2-cup measure w/reamer top **$22.50**

Milk glass, embossed Valencia..................................**$100.00**

Milk glass, McKee, sm...**$20.00**

Pearl opalescent, fluted sides, Fry **$35.00**

Pearl opalescent, straight sides, Fry **$25.00**

Pink, baby's, Westmoreland, 2-pc **$165.00**

Pink, Federal, sm..**$100.00**

Pink, Hex Optic, bucket container w/reamer top......**$45.00**

Pink, Orange Juice Extractor, unembossed **$200.00**

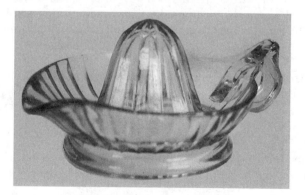

Pink, Jennyware, $90.00.

Pink, ribbed sides, loop handle, Federal Glass..........**$30.00**

Seville Yellow, embossed Sunkist...............................**$55.00**

Tufglas, light or dark...**$85.00**

Ultramarine, Jennyware..**$110.00**
Vitrock, orange, loop handle, Hocking.......................**$20.00**
Yellow, 2-cup measure w/reamer top, Hazel Atlas.....**$35.00**
Yellow opaque, Sunkist..**$55.00**

Records

Records are still plentiful at flea markets and some antique malls, but albums (Rock, Jazz, and Country) from the fifties and sixties are harder to find in collectible condition (very good or better). Garage sales are sometimes a great place to buy old records, since most of what you'll find there have been stored more carefully by their original owners.

There are two schools of thought concerning what is a collectible record. While some collectors prefer the rarities — those made in limited quantities, by an unknown who later became famous, or those aimed at a specific segment of music lovers — others like the vintage Top-10 recordings. Now that they're so often being replaced with CDs, we realize that even though we take them for granted, the possibility of their becoming a thing of the past may be reality tomorrow.

Whatever the slant your collection takes, learn to visually inspect records before you buy them. Condition is one of the most important factors to consider when assessing value. To be judged as mint, a record may have been played but must have no visual or audible deterioration — no loss of gloss to the finish, no stickers or writing on the label, no holes, no skips when it is played. If any of these are apparent, at best it is considered to be excellent and its value is at least 50% lower. Many of the records you'll find that seem to you to be in wonderful shape would be judged only very good, excellent at the most, by a knowledgeable dealer. Sleeves with no tape, stickers, tears, or obvious damage at best would be excellent; mint condition sleeves are impossible to find unless you've found old store stock.

Be on the lookout for colored vinyl or picture discs, as some of these command higher prices; in fact, older Vogue picture disks commonly sell in the $50.00 to $75.00 range, some even more. It's not too uncommon to find old radio station discards. These records will say either 'Not for Sale' or 'Audition Copy' and may be worth more than their commercial counterparts. Our values are based on original issue.

If you'd like more information, we recommend *American Premium Record Guide* by L.R. Docks.

Advisor: Dave Torzillo, 45 rpms and LPs (See Directory, Records)

45 rpm

Values for 45 rpms are 'with dust jacket'; if no jacket is present, reduce these prices by at least 50%.

Allen Ronnie; High School Love, San 209, EX **$20.00**
Anka, Paul; Puppy Love, Paramount 10082, from $3 to.**$5.00**
Ball, Earl; Party of One, Pathenon 101, EX **$10.00**
Beatnicks, Blue Angel, Key-Lock 913, EX...................**$15.00**
Berry, Chuck; Maybellene, Chess 1604 ....**$15.00**

Blake, Tommy; Freedom, RCA Victor 6925, EX............**$8.00**
Bread, Any Way You Want Me, Electra 45666, from $5 to..**$7.00**
Breedlove, Jimmy; Jealous Fool, Diamond 144, EX....**$10.00**
Burke, Eddie; Rock Mop, D 1063, EX.........................**$10.00**
Carter, Bill; Cool Tom Cat, Ozark 1234, EX.................**$30.00**
Charmers, Magic Rose, Allison 921, EX **$12.00**
Cline, Patsy; Turn the Cards Slowly, Coral 61523, EX ..**$20.00**
Coasters, Searchin', Atco 6087 ....**$20.00**
Copeland, Ken; Fanny Brown, Lin 5017, EX...............**$20.00**
Dale, Jimmie; Emma Lee, Drew-Blan 1003, EX..........**$12.00**
Day, Jack; Rattle Bone Boogie, Arcade 155, EX...........**$35.00**
Dixon, Floyd; Time & Place, Aladdin 3101, EX **$30.00**
Douglas, Mel; Cadillac Boogie, San 1506, EX.............**$30.00**
Edwards, Jimmy; Love Bug Crawl, Mercury 71209, EX .**$10.00**
Evergreens, Ever Truly Yours, Chart 605, EX...............**$30.00**
Five Chords, Red Wine, Cuca 1031, EX.......................**$20.00**
Fleetwoods, Mr Blue, Dolton 2001, EX.......................**$20.00**
Four Sons, Little Rock, Linco 1316, EX **$15.00**
Gent, JC; Bad Girl Blues, Marlo 1501, EX..................**$10.00**
Guitar Frank, Wild Track, Bridges 2203/2204, EX.......**$20.00**
Harpo, Slim; I'm a King Bee, Excello 2113, EX **$12.00**
Hess, Bennie; Wild Hog Hop, Major 1001, EX............**$75.00**
Hornets, Crying Over You, Flash 125, EX....................**$40.00**
Jack & Jill, Party Time, Caddy 110, EX **$10.00**
Jackson, Lee; Fishin' in My Pond, Cobra 5007, EX **$15.00**
Jive Bombers, Bad Boy, Savoy 1508, EX **$8.00**
Kilgore, Merle; Hang Doll, Imperial 5555, EX.............**$15.00**
Lillie, Lonnie; Truck Driver's Special, Marathon 5003, EX..**$75.00**
Loudermilk, John D; Rhythm & Blues, RCA Victor 8308, EX..**$8.00**
Louise, Paul; Cock-A-Doodle, Eko 502, EX **$30.00**
Marigolds, Rollin' Stone, Excello 2057, EX **$15.00**
McKown, Gene; Rock-A-Billy Rhythm, Aggie 101, EX...**$50.00**
Mitchell, Billy; Bald Headed Woman, Atlantic 974, EX..**$20.00**
Monkees, I'm a Believer, Colgems 1002, from $5 to.....**$7.00**
Murphy, Don; Mean Mama Blues, Cosmopolitan 2264, EX.**$40.00**
Nelson, Ricky; Be Bop Baby, Imperial.........................**$35.00**
Orbison, Roy; Sweet & Innocent, RCA Victor 7381, EX..**$15.00**
Pennington,Ray; Boogie Woogie Country Girl, Lee 502, EX..**$25.00**
Popeye's Pollution Solution, Peter Pan, 1970s, Popeye sleeve, VG+ **$6.00**
Pratt, Lynn; Tom Cat Boogie, Hornet 1000, EX..........**$30.00**
Prophets, Stormy, Atco 6078, EX................................**$12.00**
Ritter, Tex; Sunday School Songs, Capital, 1960s, set of 2 in fold-out sleeve, NM **$15.00**
River of No Return/I'm Gonna File My Claim, Marilyn Monroe picture sleeve, M.......................................**$12.50**
Rodgers, Buck; Little Rock Rock, Starday 245, EX **$20.00**
Rogers, Roy; & Dale Evans, Cowboys Never Cry/I Love The Outdoors, Little Golden, ca 1950s, EX+ ...**$22.00**
Sam the Sham & the Pharaohs, Wooly Bully, XL 906, EX..**$20.00**
Shutters, Harold; Rock & Roll Mr Moon, Golden Rod 204, EX **$100.00**
Simon & Garfunkel, Bridge Over Troubled Water, Columbia 45079, from $3 to...**$5.00**
Snappers, The; If There Were, 20th Fox 148, EX........**$15.00**
Springsteen, Bruce; Born To Run, Columbia 10209, from $5 to..**$7.00**

Tate, Joe; Satellite Rock, Roulette 4059, EX................$10.00

Tillis, Mel; Juke Box Man, Columbia 40944, EX..........$12.00

Vincent, Darryl; Daddy's Gone Batty, Sandy 1016, EX.$20.00

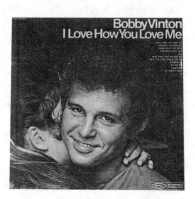

Vinton, Bobby; I Love How You Love Me, Epic, $6.00.

Wayne, Scott; Roobie Doobie, Talent 1011, EX...........$12.00

Williams, Lew; Bop Bop Ba Doo Bop, Imperial 5411, EX...$20.00

Young, George; Can't Stop Me, Mercury 71259, EX ...$20.00

78 rpm

Andrews, Mose; Ten Pound Hammer, Decca 7338, EX..$25.00

Ashley, Clyde; Down in Arkansas, Superior 2558, EX..$25.00

Baldwin, Luke; Travelin' Blues, Champion 16343, EX..$25.00

Barnes, Frankie; Hokey Pokey, Champion 16366, EX..$10.00

Beverly Hill Billies, Prairie Skies, Brunswick 519, EX...$8.00

Big Boy Knox, Texas Blues, Bluebird 6904, EX..........$30.00

Big Sister, Pig Meat Mama, Varsity 6063, EX...............$15.00

Brooks, Bob; Red River Valley, Columbia 15689-D, EX.$12.00

Cadillac, Bobby; Carbolic Acid Blues, Columbia 14413-D, EX $100.00

Card, Ken; The Last Flight of Wiley Post, Champion 45128, EX $10.00

Carter, Floyd; Flemington Kidnap Trial, Oriole 8847, EX..$10.00

Carter, Harry; Letter From Texas, Bluebird 6009, EX..$40.00

Clifford, Bob; Hobo Jack's Last Ride, Vocalion 5499, EX..$20.00

Country Paul, Side Walk Boogie, King 4573, EX.........$12.00

Davenport, Emmett; Virginia Moonshiner, Supertone 9539, EX $12.00

Delaney, Tom; Bow Legged Mama, Columbia 14122-D, EX $20.00

Duncan Sisters, Dusty Roads, Columbia 15745-D, EX..$10.00

Egbert the Easter Egg/Peter Cottontail, RCA, 1950s, w/multi-color sleeve, EX $28.00

Florida Kid, The; Lazy Mule Blues, Bluebird 8625, EX..$15.00

Frazier, Lee; Ice Man Blues, Champion 16626, EX......$80.00

Gilmore, Gene; Brown Skin Woman, Decca 7661, EX .$12.00

Groovy Five, The; Wrong Love Blues, Groovy 103, EX..$10.00

Hail to Princess Aurora, Little Golden/Disney, 1959, w/Disney-illustrated sleeve, EX+ $9.00

Hall Brothers, Hitch-Hike Blues, Bluebird 7801, EX...$10.00

Hogg, Andrew; Dark Clouds, Crown 122, EX.............$10.00

Houston Boines, Monkey Motion, RPM 364, EX.........$15.00

Hunty, Dave; Katy Lee, Champion 15565, EX............$15.00

Hutto, JB; Dim Lights, Chance 1165, EX....................$25.00

I Wonder, Little Golden/Disney, 1959, w/Disney-illustrated sleeve, NM $15.00

Jenkins, Robert; Steelin' Boogie, Parkway 103, EX.....$15.00

Junior Blues, Whiskey Head Woman, RPM 320, EX ...$15.00

Justice, Dick; Cocaine, Brunswick 336, EX.................$20.00

Lewis, Archie; Miss Handy Hanks, Champion 16677, EX...$30.00

Locks, James (Blazer Boy); Blazer Boy Blues, Regal 3231, EX $15.00

Martin, John; The Hobos Pal, Superior 2658, EX........$30.00

McCoy, Robert/Lee; Mean Black Cat, Bluebird 7303, EX..$30.00

Meyers, Hazel; Plug Ugly, Banner 1358, EX...............$15.00

Miller, Stanley; Lost Train Blues, Champion 15315, EX..$40.00

Monkey Joe & His Grinders; Sweet Petunia Stomp, Bluebird 6061, EX $50.00

Newman, Fred; San Antonio, Paramount 3267, EX.....$15.00

Nugrape Twins, The Road Is Rough & Rocky, Columbia 14251-D, EX $30.00

Once Upon a Dream, Little Golden/Disney, 1959, w/Disney-illustrated sleeve, EX+ $9.00

Patrick, Luther; Cornbread, Gennett 6448, EX............$20.00

Pollyanna, Golden, 1960, Halley Mills photo cover, NM .$18.00

Powell, Louis; Mushmouth Blues, Vocalion 0404, EX.$15.00

Prescott, Charlie; The Dixie Cowboy, Challenge 335, EX ...$30.00

Rodgers, Jessie; Rattlesnake Daddy, Bluebird 5839, EX..$10.00

Short Brothers, Whistling Corn, Okeh 45206, EX........$15.00

Sing a Smiling Song, Little Golden/Disney, 1959, w/Disney-illustrated sleeve, EX+ $9.00

Skumps, Little Golden/Disney, 1949, w/Disney-illustrated sleeve, NM $15.00

Sleeping Beauty Song, Little Golden/Disney, 1959, w/Disney-illustrated sleeve, EX+ $12.00

Smith, Clara; Shipwrecked Blues, Columbia 14077-D, EX...$50.00

Spencer, Mamie; Scrubbin' Blues, Oriole 795, EX.......$30.00

St Louis Jimmy, Florida Hurricane, Aristocrat 7001, EX ..$25.00

Stone, Jimmy; Midnight Boogie, Imperial 8137, EX...$10.00

Sykes, Roosevelt; Drivin' Wheel, Regal 3286, EX........$15.00

Thomas, Earl; Rent Day Blues, Decca 7221, EX..........$30.00

Thompson, Ernest; Little Brown Jug, Columbia 147-D, EX $12.00

Toby Tyler, Little Golden/Disney, 1959, Toby Tyler in the Circus movie scene on sleeve, NM $10.00

Uncle Jim Hawkins, Arkansas Traveler, Challenge 301, EX...$8.00

Walker, William; I'll Remember You, Columbia 14578-D, EX $50.00

Weaver, Sylvester; Polecat Blues, Okeh 8608, EX.......$60.00

West, Ed 'Jake'; Waiting for the Train, Challenge 813, EX...$8.00

Williams, Bilye; Disgusted Blues, Acorn 310, EX........$10.00

Wooten, Kyle; Choking Blues, Okeh 45526, EX..........$50.00

Young, Man; Let Me Ride Your Mule, Old Swing Master 19, EX $30.00

LP Albums

$64,000 Question, Jazz Record, Columbia, 1955, photo of game show set on sleeve, EX+..............................$25.00

Alamo, Columbia, 1960, stereo, John Wayne as Davy Crockett sleeve, NM $25.00

Alisha $15.00

Bay City Rollers, Wouldn't You Like It, Bell, SYBEL 8002, from $3 to..$5.00

Beach Boys, Surfer Girl, Pickwick, common reissue $8.00

BJ Thomas, ABC Records, ABDP-858...........................$5.00

Bobby Darin, If I Were a Carpenter, Atlantic SD 8135, NM, from $10 to...**$15.00**

Bobby Vee, Just Today, Liberty LST-7554, from $15 to...**$20.00**

Bobby Vinton, Serenade of Love, ABCD957, 1976 ....**$6.00**

Captain Beefheart, Trout Mask Replica......................**$30.00**

Coasters, Coast Along With the Monoral 135, from $20 to **$40.00**

Connie Francis, More Greatest Hits, MGM E-3893, VG, from $10.00 to $15.00.

Connie Francis, Songs to a Swinging Band, MGM E3893, VG, from $10 to...**$15.00**

Davy Crockett, King of the Wild Frontier, Columbia, 1950s, monoral, Fess Parker & Buddy Ebsen sleeve, EX..**$30.00**

Dean Martin, Gentle on My Mind, Reprise RS 6330, VG, from $10 to...**$12.00**

Dean Martin, Houston **$10.00**

Ellington Jazz Party in Stereo, Columbia CS8127, from $15 to **$20.00**

Etta James, from $20 to sometimes more than...........**$40.00**

Everly Brothers, Chained to a Memory, Columbia HS11388, reprint **$5.00**

Everly Brothers Featuring Wake-Up Little Susie, Harmony HS11304, reissue, from $4 to **$8.00**

Fleetwood Mac, very common **$10.00**

Four Seasons at the Hop...**$20.00**

Frampton Comes Alive!, picture disc.........................**$25.00**

Frank Zappa, interviews, picture disc, from $20 to **$30.00**

Gene Pitney's Big Sixteen, Musicar, copyright 1964 ...**$15.00**

Gentlemen Prefer Blondes, soundtrack, marked Made in Spain, Marilyn Monroe sleeve, M **$50.00**

Glen Campbell, Rhinestone Cowboy, Capital SW-11430 ..**$6.00**

Grateful Dead, Go to Heaven, from $8 to..................**$10.00**

Hank Snow, Big Country Hits, RCA LSP-2458, from $6 to.**$10.00**

Hawaiian Eye, Warner Brothers, 1960, cast photo sleeve, EX+ **$28.00**

Hollywood — Basie's Way......................................**$15.00**

Hurray for Hollywood, Marilyn Monroe cover, 12 stars featured on sleeve back, M...**$25.00**

James Brown, Please Please Please, King 610.............**$45.00**

Jerry Lewis Just Sings, Decca, 1960s, 12 popular songs, EX+ **$25.00**

Jimmy Clanton...**$20.00**

Jimmy Durante in Person, MGM, 1950s, 12 humorous songs, VG+ **$15.00**

Johnny Cash, Live at Folsom, Columbia Stereo...........**$15.00**

Kenny Rogers, Liberty/United Records LWAK979, 1979..**$4.00**

Love Andy, Columbia CS9566.....................................**$5.00**

Meet the Monkees, Colgems 101, from $15 to...........**$20.00**

Misfits, Limited Edition Collector's Series, original movie soundtrack, photo sleeve, G **$20.00**

Mommy, Gimmie a Drinka Water, Capital, 1950s, Danny Kaye, cover, w/13 children's songs, EX+.............**$15.00**

Mr Arcker Bilk, Strangers on the Shore **$8.00**

One Step Beyond, Decca, 1960, 11 tracks of music from TV series, EX+...**$48.00**

Otis Redding, Dictionary of Soul, from $40 to **$50.00**

Paul Anka, Paramount Monoral 240, from $30 to.......**$35.00**

Peter Gunn, RCA, 1959, music composed by Henri Mancini, EX...**$18.00**

Pure Delight, Harmony, 1960s, Danny Kaye cover, humorous songs, EX+...**$15.00**

R Dean Taylor, Indiana Wants Me.............................**$12.00**

Raspberries, diecut raspberry cover **$20.00**

Ray Price Greatest Hits, Columbia CL1566....................**$5.00**

Rick Nelson Sings for You **$25.00**

Ricky Nelson, Album Seven, Imperial IR, Stereo 12082, VG, $25.00.

Righteous Brothers, Just Once in My Life, Philles Records PHLP 4008, NM...**$25.00**

Rolling Stones, Made in the Shade............................**$15.00**

Rudolph...& Other Christmas Favorites, 1960s, Gene Autry cover, 10 Christmas songs, EX+.......................**$12.00**

Shari (Lewis) in Storyland, RCA, 1962, 8-page fold-out sleeve of photos, EX...**$15.00**

Simon & Garfunkel, Hit Sounds, Pickwick 3059, from $40 to **$45.00**

The American Breed, Bend Me, Shape Me.................**$25.00**

The Cars **$15.00**

The Chiffons, One Fine Day.....................................**$35.00**

The Girl Who Came to Supper, Columbia, 1963, fold-out sleeve w/photos of Florence Henderson, NM......**$35.00**

The Long Riders Soundtrack **$5.00**

The Magic of Judy Garland......................................**$20.00**

The Ventures, Walk, Don't Run, Volume II.................**$20.00**

Three Stooges' Nonsense Songbook, Coral, 1960s, stereo, color photo sleeve, NM.......................................**$55.00**

TV Western Themes, RCA, 1950s, w/sleeve, EX **$18.00**

Twilight Zone, Stereo, 1961, w/sleeve, NM...............**$75.00**

Victor Borge, Caught in the Act, 1950s, live recording, w/sleeve, NM **$12.00**

77 Sunset Strip Soundtrack, WB 1289 ....**$15.00**

Red Wing Potteries, Inc.

For almost a century, Red Wing, Minnesota, was the center of a great pottery industry. In the early 1900s, several local companies merged to form the Red Wing Stoneware Company. Until they introduced their dinnerware lines in 1935, most of their production centered around stoneware jugs, crocks, flowerpots, and other utilitarian items. To reflect the changes made in 1935, the name was changed to Red Wing Potteries, Inc. In addition to scores of lovely dinnerware lines, they also made vases, planters, flowerpots, etc., some with exceptional shapes and decoration.

Some of their more recognizable lines of dinnerware and those you'll most often find are Bob White (decorated in blue and brown brush strokes with quail), Tampico (featuring a collage of fruit including watermelon), Random Harvest (simple pink and brown leaves and flowers), and Village Green (or Brown, solid-color pieces introduced in the fifties). Often you'll find complete or nearly complete sets, and when you do, the lot price is usually a real bargain.

If you'd like to learn more about the subject, we recommend *Red Wing Stoneware, An Identification and Value Guide,* and *Red Wing Collectibles,* both by Dan and Gail DePasquale and Larry Peterson and *Red Wing Art Pottery* by B.L. Dollen.

Advisors: Wendy and Leo Frese, Artware (See Directory, Red Wing)

Club/Newsletter: *Red Wing Collectors Newsletter*
Red Wing Collectors Society, Inc.
Doug Podpeskar, membership information
624 Jones St.
Eveleth, MN 55734-1631; 218-744-4854; Please include SASE when requesting information.

Art Ware

Ash receiver, #880, pelican, light green **$100.00**
Ashtray, M-1472, horse head, Fleck Zephyr Pink (pink speckled) **$60.00**
Bowl, B-2013, Belle, white w/light green interior, 13"..**$30.00**
Bowl, console; #1014, magnolia, ivory w/brown antiquing, 12½" **$50.00**
Candle holder, #980, Dutch Blue **$75.00**
Candle holder, #981, 'polka-dot' Dutch Blue, ca late 1930s **$75.00**
Horn of Plenty, #442, white w/green interior, 1950s..**$35.00**

Planter, #439, duck, $50.00.

Planter, #1087, seashell shape..................................**$50.00**

Shoe, #651, white w/light green interior, sm..............**$50.00**

Vase, #797, Deco style, blue over white, 11", $50.00.

Vase, #1120, deer, tan w/no hand-painted details **$40.00**
Vase, #1143, turquoise & white **$60.00**
Vase, #1359, 'stacking teacups,' gray w/pink interior, w/original sticker **$25.00**
Vase, #144-8", Brush Ware, crane, no mark................**$40.00**
Vase, #157-9", green & white, early.............................**$65.00**
Vase, #776, lady on a swing w/pr of cupids, 12"........**$60.00**
Vase, #794, Prismatique, modern styling, 11" **$60.00**
Vase, H511, Lotus, hand painted, 10".........................**$75.00**
Vase, M-3007, Murphy, Decorator Line, Orange Crystalline, elongated neck, 12" **$100.00**
Wall planter, M-1484, guitar, Fleck Pink Zephyr **$35.00**

Dinnerware

Blossom Time, bowl, divided vegetable.....................**$35.00**
Blossom Time, cup & saucer, from $7 to **$9.00**
Blossom Time, nappy...**$28.00**
Blossom Time, plate, dinner..**$12.00**
Bob White, bowl, cereal; from $18 to........................**$22.00**
Bob White, bowl, fruit; from $12 to...........................**$15.00**
Bob White, bowl, salad; bird interior, 12", from $60 to..**$70.00**
Bob White, bowl, divided vegetable...........................**$35.00**
Bob White, butter dish, ¼-lb, from $65 to..................**$75.00**
Bob White, casserole, 2-qt **$45.00**
Bob White, casserole, 4-qt **$50.00**
Bob White, cookie jar **$125.00**
Bob White, creamer, from $20 to **$25.00**
Bob White, cup & saucer, from $15 to **$20.00**
Bob White, gravy boat, stick handle...........................**$45.00**
Bob White, hors d'oeuvres holder **$50.00**
Bob White, pitcher, water; 60-oz................................**$50.00**
Bob White, plate, 10½" **$12.50**
Bob White, plate, 6½", from $5 to **$6.00**
Bob White, plate, 8" **$8.00**
Bob White, salt & pepper shakers, bird shape, pr......**$40.00**
Bob White, salt & pepper shakers, hourglass shape, 6", pr .**$24.00**
Bob White, sugar bowl, w/lid, from $25 to................**$30.00**
Bob White, teapot & stand **$120.00**
Brittany, bowl, cream soup; w/lid...............................**$40.00**
Brittany, teapot **$100.00**
Capistrano, bowl, berry; 5½" **$8.00**
Capistrano, bowl, divided vegetable; from $25 to **$30.00**
Capistrano, bowl, salad; 12".......................................**$45.00**

Capistrano, casserole, lg	$65.00
Capistrano, creamer	$10.00
Capistrano, cup & saucer	$9.00
Capistrano, plate, salad; 8", from $6 to	$8.00
Capistrano, plate, 10½"	$10.00
Capistrano, plate, 6½"	$5.00
Capistrano, platter, 13", from $30 to	$40.00
Capistrano, platter, 15", from $35 to	$45.00
Capistrano, sugar bowl, w/lid	$15.00
Chevron, coffeepot	$65.00
Chevron, plate, 10"	$12.50
Chevron, platter, oval, 14", from $20 to	$25.00
Chevron, teapot, 6-cup, from $55 to	$65.00
Country Garden, bread tray	$50.00
Country Garden, gravy boat	$22.00
Country Garden, nappy	$20.00
Country Garden, plate, 10½"	$15.00
Country Garden, plate, 8"	$10.00
Country Garden, sauce dish	$12.50
Driftwood, boat, divided vegetable	$25.00
Driftwood, cup & saucer	$12.00
Driftwood, plate, bread & butter	$7.00
Driftwood, plate, dinner	$10.00
Driftwood, platter, 15"	$45.00
Kashmir, butter dish	$35.00
Lexington Rose, bowl, berry; 5⅛"	$7.00
Lexington Rose, bowl, cream soup	$17.00
Lexington Rose, cup & saucer	$11.00
Lexington Rose, pitcher, water	$65.00
Lexington Rose, plate, dinner; 10¼"	$11.00
Lexington Rose, plate, 6"	$5.50
Lotus, casserole	$30.00
Lotus, creamer	$12.00
Lotus, cup & saucer	$10.00
Lotus, plate, 7½"	$7.00
Lotus, relish, 3-part	$22.00
Lotus, sugar bowl	$15.00
Lute Song, beverage server	$55.00
Lute Song, bowl, salad; 5x11"	$30.00
Lute Song, bowl, 5", from $7 to	$8.50
Lute Song, butter dish	$38.00
Lute Song, casserole	$35.00
Lute Song, creamer, from $10 to	$12.00
Lute Song, cup & saucer, from $10 to	$13.00
Lute Song, gravy, stick handle, w/lid	$35.00
Lute Song, plate, 10"	$13.00
Lute Song, plate, 7"	$7.50
Lute Song, sugar bowl	$14.00
Lute Song, teapot	$65.00
Magnolia, bowl, rim soup	$15.00
Magnolia, cup & saucer	$10.00
Magnolia, gravy boat, fast stand, from $25 to	$30.00
Magnolia, plate, 10"	$12.00
Morning Glory, chop plate	$35.00
Navajo, bowl, divided vegetable	$28.00
Navajo, chop plate, 12"	$24.00
Navajo, jam & jelly, footed	$55.00
Pepe, bowl, divided vegetable	$25.00
Pepe, plate, salad	$6.50

Plum Blossom, cup & saucer, demitasse	$60.00
Random Harvest, bowl, salad; lg	$85.00
Random Harvest, coffeepot, tall	$45.00
Random Harvest, creamer	$12.00
Random Harvest, cup & saucer	$12.50
Random Harvest, gravy boat	$35.00
Random Harvest, plate, 10"	$12.50
Random Harvest, platter, 13"	$18.00
Random Harvest, sugar bowl, w/lid	$15.00
Round-Up, bowl, divided vegetable	$95.00
Round-Up, bowl, salad; 10"	$95.00
Round-Up, creamer	$50.00
Round-Up, cruets, pr	$275.00
Round-Up, cup & saucer, from $55 to	$60.00
Round-Up, plate, 10½", from $35 to	$40.00
Round-Up, plate, 7½"	$20.00
Round-Up, relish, 3-part	$95.00
Round-Up, salt & pepper shakers, pr, from $125 to	$150.00
Round-Up, teapot	$275.00
Smart Set, casserole, 2-qt	$70.00
Smart Set, cocktail tray	$48.00
Smart Set, creamer, from $22 to	$30.00
Smart Set, cup & saucer	$38.00
Smart Set, plate, 10"	$35.00
Smart Set, plate, 6"	$12.00
Smart Set, sugar bowl, w/lid, from $22 to	$30.00
Smart Set, tray, bread; 24"	$100.00
Tampico, bowl, cereal	$15.00
Tampico, bowl, divided vegetable; from $35 to	$45.00
Tampico, bowl, fruit	$10.00
Tampico, bowl, salad; 12"	$85.00
Tampico, cake plate, footed	$85.00
Tampico, coffee mug, from $45 to	$50.00
Tampico, cup & saucer, from $12 to	$15.00
Tampico, gravy boat, w/stand	$50.00
Tampico, plate, 10½", from $12 to	$15.00
Tampico, plate, 6½"	$5.00
Tampico, plate, 8½"	$9.50
Tampico, platter, 13", from $25 to	$30.00
Tampico, relish	$35.00

Tampico, water pitcher, 13", from $75.00 to $85.00.

Trio, bowl, divided vegetable	$28.00
Trio, bowl, rectangular	$26.00
Trio, creamer	$14.00
Trio, cup & saucer, from $15 to	$18.00
Trio, plate, 10", from $15 to	$20.00

Trio, sugar bowl...$18.00
Village Green, bean pot, 2-qt $28.00
Village Green, bowl, salad; individual, 6".....$15.00
Village Green, bowl, sauce $9.00
Village Green, butter dish, w/lid.................$45.00
Village Green, casserole, lg.............................$28.00
Village Green, casserole, sm...........................$15.00
Village Green, coffee server, 1-gal, w/metal stand, from $60
   to...$65.00
Village Green, gravy boat w/tray $40.00
Village Green, marmite......................................$8.00
Village Green, salt & pepper shakers, pr...................$22.50
Village Green, warmer $18.00

Stoneware

Bean pot, Albany slip, Boston style, marked RWUS,
   ½-gal $110.00

Bean pot, Broderick Company, Advertising Specialties, St. Paul, Minn., from $65.00 to $85.00.

Bowl, nappy, embossed knotch-like decoration along rim,
   light blue, unmarked, from $150 to $175.00
Bowl, paneled w/sponging on white, 5", from $400 to..$500.00
Bowl, Red & Blue Banded, sm.......................$35.00
Casserole, Saffron, brown & white bands on cream,
   embossed ribs, handles, w/lid, marked RWU, med & lg,
   each from $100 to..$150.00
Churn, red wing, union oval & #2 on white, 2-gal, from $225
   to...$275.00
Cock, target & #2, cobalt on salt glaze, marked RW, 2-
   gal $115.00
Cooler, birch leaf & #10, cobalt on salt glaze, marked MN, 10-
   gal $385.00
Crock, butter; Albany slip, high style, marked MN, 1-gal .$70.00
Crock, double P & #3, cobalt on salt glaze, marked M, 3-gal,
   from $500 to..$600.00
Crock, flower & #6, cobalt on salt glaze, unsigned, 6-gal,
   from $150 to..$200.00
Jar, preserve/snuff; Albany slip, marked MN, 1-gal $55.00
Jug, bail handle, Albany slip, marked M, 1-gal, from $200
   to...$250.00
Jug, bail handle, white, marked M, 1-qt, from $100 to ...$125.00
Jug, bail handle, white, molded seam, marked RW, ½-gal,
   from $75 to...$100.00
Jug, bail handle, white w/molded seam, marked MN, ½-gal ..$90.00

Jug, bail handle, white w/molded seam, marked RW, 1-qt ..$130.00
Jug, beehive; birch leaves, union oval & #4 on white, 4-gal,
   from $500 to..$600.00
Jug, common, Albany slip, ball top, marked MN, 1-gal ..$165.00
Jug, common, white, dome top, marked MN, ½-gal ..$55.00
Jug, fancy, Albany slip & white, unsigned, 1-pt, from $25
   to...$50.00
Jug, fancy; Albany slip & white, marked RW, 2-gal, from $225
   to...$275.00
Jug, shoulder; Albany slip top, red wings on white, 2-gal,
   from $400 to..$500.00
Jug, shoulder; birch leaves & #5 on white, marked RW, 5-gal,
   from $125 to..$175.00
Jug, shoulder; white w/standard top, marked MN, 1-qt ..$85.00
Jug, syrup; white w/shoulder, identified by pour spout,
   marked M, ½-gal, from $40 to.............................$60.00
Jug, wide mouth, white w/molded seam, marked RW, 1-qt,
   from $50 to...$70.00
Jug, wide shoulder; red wing, union oval & #3 on white,
   marked RWU, 3-gal, from $75 to.........................$100.00
Pan, milk; white, marked MN, 7" $55.00
Pitcher, Albany slip w/embossed decorative band along rim,
   from $325 to..$375.00
Pitcher, Cherryband, blue on white $200.00
Pitcher, mustard; Albany slip, marked NS $200.00
Pitkin, Albany slip & white, marked M, 1-pt to 4-pt, from $250
   to...$300.00
Spittoon, salt glaze, unmarked $200.00

Regal China

Perhaps best known for their Beam whiskey decanters, the Regal China company (of Antioch, Illinois) also produced some exceptionally well-modeled ceramic novelties, among them their 'hugger' salt and pepper shakers, designed by artist Ruth Van Telligen Bendel. Facing pairs made to 'lock' together arm-in-arm, some huggies are signed Bendel while others bear the Van Telligen mark. Another popular design is her Peek-a-Boo Bunny line, depicting the coy little bunny in the red and white 'jammies' who's just about to pop his buttons.

See also Cookie Jars; Old MacDonald's Farm.

Advisor: Rick Spencer (See Directory, Regal China)

Bendel Shakers

Bears, white w/pink & brown trim, pr.....................$100.00
Bunnies, white w/black & pink trim, pr...................$135.00
Kissing pigs, gray w/pink trim, pr $375.00
Love bugs, burgundy, lg, pr $165.00
Love bugs, green, sm, pr...$65.00

Van Telligen Shakers

Bears, brown, pr...$20.00
Boy & dog, black, pr...$95.00
Boy & dog, white, pr $60.00
Bunnies, solid colors, pr $22.00

Ducks, pr..**$30.00**
Dutch boy & girl, pr...**$40.00**
Mary & lamb, pr...**$55.00**
Peek-a-Boo, solid white, lg, pr................................**$400.00**
Peek-a-Boo, solid white, sm, pr...............................**$200.00**
Peek-a-Boo, white w/burgundy trim, rare, sm, pr...**$350.00**
Peek-a-Boo, white w/gold trim, lg, pr.....................**$450.00**

**Peek-a-Boo with red dots, small, $220.00
for the pair.**

Sailor & mermaid, pr...**$195.00**

Miscellaneous

Creamer & sugar bowl, cat form, each.....................**$100.00**
Creamer & sugar bowl, Tulip **$100.00**
Salt & pepper shakers, A Nod to Abe, 3-pc set **$225.00**
Salt & pepper shakers, cat, pr **$225.00**
Salt & pepper shakers, FiFi, pr **$450.00**
Salt & pepper shakers, tulips, pr **$50.00**
Salt & pepper shakers, Vermont Leaf People, 3-pc ..**$125.00**
Sugar bowl, White Rabbit (from Wonderland), w/lid ...**$600.00**

Rock 'n Roll Memorabilia

Ticket stubs and souvenirs issued at rock concerts, posters of the artists that have reached celebrity status, and merchandise such as dolls, games, clothing, etc., sold through retail stores during the heights of their careers are just the thing that interests collectors of rock 'n roll memorabilia. Some original, one-of-a-kind examples — for instance, their instruments, concert costumes, and personal items — often sell at the large auction galleries in the East where they've realized very high-dollar hammer prices. Greg Moore has written *A Price Guide to Rock and Roll Collectibles* which is distributed by L-W Book Sales.

See also Beatles Collectibles; Elvis Presley Memorabilia; Magazines; Pin-Back Buttons; Records.

Bee Gees, guitar, plastic, 1979, 29½", EX...................**$60.00**
Bill Haley & the Comets, songbook, photo cover, 1954,
  EX+..**$20.00**
Black Sabbath, frisbee, promo for tour, 1979, EX.......**$20.00**
Blondie, ashtray, promo for Parallel Lines, acrylic hexagon
  w/color LP photo, EX...**$35.00**

Blondie, International Fan Club Book, #2, 1981, EX ..**$10.00**
Bruce Springsteen, poster, Cover Me, EX **$25.00**
Cars, matchbook, Candy-o promo, Elektra, unused, EX ...**$12.00**
Cheap Trick, bow tie, black w/white Cheap Trick lettering,
  EX...**$28.00**
Culture Club, cup, plastic, white w/black & white image of
  Boy George & logo, 5¼", EX.....................................**$20.00**
Dave Clark Five, tour book, lg format, 1964, EX........**$40.00**

**David Cassidy, Colorforms
Dress-Up Set, 1972, from
$25.00 to $35.00.**

Def Leppard, pencil holder, metal, Pyromania, 1984, EX...**$18.00**
Donny & Marie Osmond, Dress-Up Kit, Colorforms, 1977,
  NMIB..**$35.00**
Donny & Marie Osmond, record player, Sing Along Radio...,
  MIB **$60.00**
Donny & Marie Osmond, TV Show Playset, MIB **$50.00**
Donny Osmond, Keepsake Photo & Activity Book, Artcraft,
  1973, NM **$20.00**
Ed 'Cookie' Burns, comb, 1959, MOC........................**$60.00**
Elton John, tour book, 28 pages, 1975, EX+ **$18.00**
Fabian, pillow, black & white printed cloth w/blue back,
  1950s, 11x11", EX..**$75.00**
Jackson Five, pennant, felt, We Love the Jacksons w/black &
  white group photo, 1970s, 11x29", EX..................**$60.00**
Jackson Five, pillow, VG..**$35.00**

**KISS, Colorforms Set,
1979, EX in EX box,
$85.00. (Photo cour-
tesy of June Moon.)**

KISS, eraser, MIP...**$12.00**
KISS, music book, Rock 'n Roll Over, 64 pages of music w/6
  color photos, Almo Publications, EX.....................**$10.00**
KISS, necklace, Peter Criss autograph in gold-tone, 78",
  MIP **$35.00**
KISS, pencils, set of 4, MIP (sealed)..........................**$45.00**
KISS, pendant, silver-tone V-shape w/head of Gene Simmons
  & logo, NM...**$35.00**

KISS, poster, Put-Ons, Bi-Rite Enterprises, 1976, 9½x9½", MOC...**$18.00**

KISS, puffy stickers, set of 4, Rocksticks, MOC..........**$60.00**

KISS, tour program, Lick It Up, 1984 World Tour, 24 pages, VG+..**$45.00**

KISS, View-Master reels, set of 3, w/booklet, MIP......**$35.00**

KISS, wastebasket, lithographed metal, P&K products, 1978, 19x11" dia, NM...**$225.00**

Led Zeppelin, patch, Song Remains the Same, 4x3½", NM **$8.00**

Madonna, notebook, Desperately Seeking Susan, 1985, EX **$20.00**

Michael Jackson, Colorforms, 1984, MIB (sealed).......**$25.00**

Michael Jackson, slipper socks, 1984, EX **$20.00**

Monkees, bracelet, color head images in gold-tone disk, MIB **$30.00**

Monkees, dolls, Show Biz Baby, set of 4, 4", EX......**$300.00**

Monkees, flasher ring, changes from 2 portraits to other 2 portraits, chrome, VG **$20.00**

Monkees, mobile, diecast figures, 3", VG+ **$75.00**

Monkees, tablet, photo cover, unused, M....................**$40.00**

Monkees, tambourine, EX, $85.00. (Photo courtesy of Bob Gottuso.)

Monkees, tour program, summer, 1987, EX...................**$8.00**

New Kids on the Block, fashion plates, Hasbro, 1990, EXIB.**$5.00**

New Kids on the Block, figures, Danny or Jordan, poseable, 6", MIB, each..**$8.00**

Paul McCartney & Wings, card set, Back to the Egg, set of 5 black & white photos, EX **$15.00**

Prince, Graffiti, double-sided, EX **$12.00**

Ricky Nelson, photo, facsimile signature, sent to studio by fan, 1958, 5x7", NM **$30.00**

Rolling Stones, fan club kit, EX **$12.00**

Rolling Stones, puffy stickers, 1983, MOC **$8.00**

Shawn Cassidy, scrapbook, w/photos, 187 pages, 1978, EX **$50.00**

U2, poster, Hamburg Germany Live tour, EX..............**$10.00**

Van Halen, program & ticket, 1980 concert tour, EX..**$35.00**

Van Halen, puffy stickers, 3 different sets w/David Lee Roth, EX, each..**$5.00**

Van Halen, scarf, black, EX...**$5.00**

Rookwood

Although this company was established in 1879, it continued to produce commercial artware until it closed in 1967.

Located in Cincinnati, Ohio, Rookwood is recognized today as the largest producer of high-quality art pottery ever to operate in the United States.

Most of the pieces listed here are from the later years of production, but we've included some early pieces as well. With few exceptions, all early Ohio art pottery companies produced an artist-decorated brown-glaze line — Rookwood's was called Standard. Among their other early lines were Sea Green, Iris, Jewel Porcelain, Wax Matt, and Vellum.

Virtually all of Rookwood's pieces are marked. The most familiar mark is the 'reverse R'-P monogram. It was first used in 1886, and until 1900 a flame point was added above it to represent each passing year. After the turn of the century, a Roman numeral below the monogram indicated the current year. In addition to the dating mark, a die-stamped number was used to identify the shape.

The Cincinnati Art Galleries held two large and important cataloged auctions in 1991. The full-color catalogs contain a comprehensive history of the company, list known artists and designers with their monograms (as well as company codes and trademarks), and describe each lot thoroughly. Collectors now regard them as an excellent source for information and study.

Ashtray, #1139, 1946, rook figural, white matt, 6½" wide..**$175.00**

Ashtray, #1139, 1966, rook figural, light blue gloss, 6½" wide **$250.00**

Ashtray, #2890, 1925, triangular w/butterfly, blue matt .**$145.00**

Bookends, #2275, 1945, rook figural, light brown gloss, 5½", pr...**$375.00**

Bookends, #2655, 1946, owl figural, yellow-green gloss, 6", pr...**$250.00**

Bookends, #2836, 1946, artichoke form, brown gloss, 3½", pr...**$250.00**

Bowl, #6424, 1953, flower shape, light green gloss, 8" dia.**$145.00**

Bowl, #6459, 1945, bird & floral embossed on blue, 4½".**$170.00**

Candlestick, #1635, 1919, blue & green, Eiffel tower shape **$395.00**

Font, #6975, 1947, St Francis Holy Water, brown gloss, 10" **$225.00**

Jar, #6221, 1943, beige gloss, w/lid, 6½" **$325.00**

Jar, peanut; 1949, 6-sided, blue gloss, w/lid, 4½".....**$325.00**

Lamps, 1948, freesias on green gloss, all original fittings & shades, 26" overall, pr.....................................**$3,000.00**

Paperweight, 1928, rooster, $300.00.

Paperweight, #2711, 1965, pelican figural, mottled mustard gloss, 6" long...**$450.00**

Paperweight, #6020, 1928, fruit basket, multicolored, 3½" **$210.00**
Paperweight, 1940, Potter at the Wheel on black, 3½"..**$175.00**
Pin tray, #6391, 1946, pink porcelain, 7" **$150.00**
Pitcher, #6795, 1944, blue, 4"......................................**$100.00**
Pitcher, #774, 1966, blue gloss, 5¼".........................**$135.00**
Plate, #7222, 1963, Central Life, uranium orange gloss, 7½" **$150.00**
Plate, #7224, 1965, Whittier College, yellow gloss, 7½".**$145.00**
Plate, #7239, 1965, Summit Country Day, white gloss, 7¼" **$115.00**
Platter, #6986, 1947, fish form, yellow-green gloss, 12½" long..**$145.00**
Rose tray, #6989, ca 1940, blue gloss, 5½" dia **$80.00**
Tile, #442, parrot among blossoms, 6" square+frame .**$350.00**
Tray, 1946, red fish...**$295.00**
Urn, #6010C, 1944, white matt, 2 handles, 12½" **$465.00**

Vase, 1927, green glaze with embossed geometrics, 20", $600.00.

Vase, #1642, 1942, maroon porcelain w/blue highlights, footed, 4½" **$250.00**
Vase, #2075, 1918, blue w/handles, 4 sm feet, 7".....**$350.00**
Vase, #2207, 1943, Deco design on blue-gray matt, 5".**$145.00**
Vase, #2500C, 1946, light green gloss w/dolphin handles, signed KS, 13"...**$175.00**
Vase, #2591, 1952, banded daisies on brown gloss, 6".**$125.00**
Vase, #2592, 1946, cattails embossed on blue glossy, 5½"...**$250.00**
Vase, #2816, 1948, cattails on blue-gray matt, 5" **$145.00**
Vase, #6204C, 1949, charcoal w/turquoise gloss, 7"....**$300.00**
Vase, #6219, 1939, florals embossed on green gloss, 7"...**$300.00**
Vase, #6331, 1938, red over caramel crystalline, 7½x7½"..**$550.00**
Vase, #6363, 1946, floral decor on brown gloss, 6"..**$140.00**
Vase, #6510, 1949, leaves on light brown gloss, 5" ..**$120.00**
Vase, #6614, 1960, black bisque w/thick white glossy drip, 4" **$70.00**
Vase, #6762, 1949, Mexican & donkey on green gloss, 5½" **$145.00**
Vase, #6833, 1948, water lilies on turquoise gloss, 6"..**$175.00**
Vase, #778, 1964, speckled blue-green, fluted neck, 10"..**$175.00**

Rooster and Roses

Back in the 1940s, newlyweds might conceivably have received some of this imported Japanese-made kitchenware as a housewarming gift. They'd no doubt be stunned to see the prices it's now bringing! Rooster and Roses (Ucagco called it Early Provincial) is one of those lines of novelty ceramics from the forties and fifties that are among today's hottest collectibles. Ucagco was only one of several importers whose label you'll find on this pattern; among others are Py, ACSON, Norcrest and Lefton. The design is easy to spot — there's the rooster, yellow breast with black crosshatching, brown head and, of course, the red crest and waddle, large full-blown roses with green leaves and vines, and a trimming of yellow borders punctuated by groups of brown lines. (You'll find another line having blue flowers among the roses; this is not considered Rooster and Roses by purist collectors.) The line is fun to collect, since shapes are so diversified. Even though there has been relatively little networking among collectors, more than seventy-five items have been reported.

Advisor: Jacki Elliott (See Directory, Rooster and Roses)

Ashtray, rectangular, 3x2" **$9.50**
Ashtray, round or square, sm, from $15 to.................**$25.00**
Ashtray, square, lg, from $25 to **$35.00**
Basket, flared sides, 6", from $35 to **$45.00**
Bell, from $25 to..**$35.00**
Biscuit jar, w/wicker handle, from $50 to...................**$65.00**
Bowl, cereal; from $10 to...**$14.00**
Bowl, rice; on saucer, from $25 to **$35.00**
Bowl, 8"...**$25.00**
Box, trinket; w/lid, round, from $25 to **$35.00**
Box, 4½x3½", from $25 to..**$35.00**
Butter dish, ¼-lb, from $20 to **$25.00**
Candle warmer (for tea & coffeepots), from $15 to ...**$25.00**
Candy dish, flat chicken-shaped tray w/3 dimensional chicken head, made in 3 sizes, from $30 to **$40.00**
Candy dish, w/3-D leaf handle, from $17 to...............**$25.00**
Canister set, round, 4-pc, from $150 to **$175.00**
Canister set, square, 4-pc, from $100 to **$150.00**
Carafe, w/stopper lid, 8", from $55 to **$65.00**
Casserole dish, w/lid **$65.00**
Castor set in revolving wire rack, 2 cruets, mustard jar & salt & pepper shakers, from $65 to.............................**$75.00**
Chamberstick, saucer base, ring handle, from $20 to..**$25.00**
Cheese dish, slant lid, from $40 to..............................**$55.00**
Cigarette box w/2 trays, from $30 to **$40.00**
Coffee grinder, rare, from $75 to.................................**$85.00**
Coffeepot, 'Coffee' in neck band, w/creamer & sugar bowl, both w/appropriately lettered neck bands, 3 pcs, from $75 to...**$85.00**

Condiment set, mustard jar and salt and pepper shakers on tray, miniature, $40.00 to $50.00.

Condiment set, 2 cruets, salt & pepper shakers, & mustard jar on tray, miniature, from $40 to.............................**$50.00**

Cookie jar, ceramic handles, from $85 to.................**$100.00**

Creamer & sugar bowl, w/lid, lg.............................**$25.00**

Creamer & sugar bowl on rectangular tray, from $35 to ..**$40.00**

Cruets, cojoined w/twisted necks, sm.........................**$20.00**

Cruets, oil & vinegar, flared bases, pr, from $25 to **$30.00**

Cruets, oil & vinegar, square, lg, pr, from $30 to........**$35.00**

Cruets, oil & vinegar; w/salt & pepper shakers in shadow box, from $55 to..**$75.00**

Cup & saucer, from $15 to.......................................**$25.00**

Demitasse pot, w/4 cups & saucer, from $85 to.......**$100.00**

Demitasse pot, w/6 cups & saucers, from $100 to ...**$125.00**

Egg cup, from $20 to..**$25.00**

Egg cup on tray, from $25 to **$35.00**

Egg plate..**$28.00**

Flowerpot, buttress handles, 5", from $35 to.............**$45.00**

Instant coffee jar, spoon-holder tube on side, from $20 to **$30.00**

Jam & jelly containers, cojoined, w/lids & spoons, from $25 to **$35.00**

Jam jar, attached underplate, from $25 to..................**$35.00**

Ketchup or mustard jar, flared cylinder w/lettered label, each, from $25 to **$30.00**

Lamp, pinup, made from either a match holder or a salt box, each **$75.00**

Match holder, wall mount, from $40 to **$45.00**

Measuring cup set, 4 pcs w/matching ceramic rack, from $35 to **$45.00**

Measuring spoons on 8" ceramic spoon-shaped rack, from $35 to **$40.00**

Mug, rounded bottom, med, from $12 to...................**$15.00**

Mug, straight upright bar handle, lg, from $15 to......**$25.00**

Napkin holder, from $30 to **$40.00**

Pipe holder/ashtray, from $30 to..............................**$40.00**

Pitcher, bulbous, 5", from $18 to..............................**$22.00**

Pitcher, neck band lettered 'Milk'.............................**$22.50**

Pitcher, 3½", from $12 to **$14.00**

Plate, dinner; from $25 to **$35.00**

Plate, luncheon; from $15 to....................................**$25.00**

Platter, 12", from $30 to..**$35.00**

Recipe box, from $25 to...**$35.00**

Recipe box & salt & pepper shakers in wall-hanging shadow box, from $45 to..**$55.00**

Relish tray, 2 round wells w/center handle, 12", from $22 to **$28.00**

Relish tray, 3 wells w/center handle............................**$45.00**

Salad fork & spoon w/wooden handles on ceramic wall-mount rack, from $35 to **$40.00**

Salt box, wooden lid, from $45.00 to $55.00.

Salt & pepper shakers, drum shape w/long horizontal ceramic handle, lg, pr, from $30 to.................................**$40.00**

Salt & pepper shakers, w/applied rose, square, pr.....**$23.00**

Salt & pepper shakers, w/handle, pr, from $15 to......**$20.00**

Salt & pepper shakers, w/lettered neck band, pr.......**$25.00**

Salt & pepper shakers, 4", pr, from $15 to.................**$20.00**

Salt box, wooden lid, from $45 to **$55.00**

Shaker, cheese or sugar; 7", from $20 to **$30.00**

Skillet, 4"..**$18.00**

Slipper, applied rose to toe......................................**$28.00**

Snack tray w/cup, oval, from $45 to.........................**$55.00**

Snack tray w/cup, square, from $45 to.......................**$55.00**

Spice rack, 3 rows of 2 curved-front containers, together forming half-cylinder shape w/flat back, from $60 to ...**$70.00**

Spice set, 9 square containers in wood frame w/pull-out ceramic tray in base, from $75 to........................**$85.00**

Spoon holder, w/lg salt shaker in well on side extension, from $20 to..**$25.00**

Stacking tea set, teapot, creamer & sugar bowl, from $70 to..**$80.00**

Syrup pitcher on tray (comes in 3 sizes), from $65 to..**$95.00**

Tazza (footed tray), 3x6" dia, from $35 to.................**$45.00**

Tea set, stacking pot, creamer & sugar bowl, from $85 to ...**$125.00**

Teapot, from $55 to...**$65.00**

Tray, closed tab handles each end, 11", from $25 to .**$30.00**

Tray, round w/chamberstick-type handle on 1 side, 5½", from $15 to..**$20.00**

Tumbler, from $15 to...**$20.00**

Vase, round w/flat sides, 6", from $20 to **$30.00**

Wall hanger, teapot shape, pr, from $75 to **$90.00**

Wall pocket **$45.00**

Watering can, from $25 to..**$30.00**

Roselane Pottery

Beginning as a husband and wife operation in the late 1930s, the Roselane Pottery Company of Pasadena, California, expanded their inventory from the figurines they originally sold to local florists to include a complete line of decorative items that eventually were shipped to Alaska, South America, and all parts of the United States.

One of their lines was the Roselane Sparklers. Popular in the fifties, these small animal and bird figures were airbrush decorated and had rhinestone eyes. They're fun to look for and not at all expensive.

If you'd like to learn more, there's a chapter on Roselane in *The Collector's Encyclopedia of California Pottery* by Jack Chipman.

Bowl, Chinese Modern, square, pedestal, 2½x6¼".....**$20.00**

Bowl, console; pink & gray, A-20, 20" long...............**$40.00**

Bowl, rectangular w/3 sections, footed, pink, 14x7" ..**$95.00**

Candle holders, Chinese Modern, dove gray gloss, pr ..**$75.00**

Dealer sign, deep aqua high glaze, 3x12½"............**$275.00**

Figurine, angelfish, sparkler eyes, California USA, 4½" ..**$14.00**

Figurine, Bali dancers, male, 11"; female 11¼", each.**$65.00**

Figurine, boy w/dog, 5½"..**$30.00**

Figurine, cat, sitting, Siamese w/sparkler eyes & collar, unmarked, 7"...**$15.00**

Figurine, cat, sitting, slanted sparkler eyes, C in circle USA mark, 4½", from $8 to **$10.00**

Figurine, cat, sitting, sparkler eyes, amber collar, California USA, 6¾", from $12 to...**$15.00**

Figurine, cat, standing, sparkler eyes, wearing collar, 5½" **$15.00**

Figurine, cocker spaniel, sparkler eyes, Roselane C in circle USA, 4½"...**$9.00**

Figurine, deer, standing, pink sparkler eyes, unmarked, 5½", from $10 to...**$14.00**

Figurine, deer, upturned head, satin-matt brown on white, plastic sparkler eyes, 4x3½", from $12 to **$14.00**

Figurine, deer w/antlers, standing, sparkler eyes & collar, no mark, 4½" **$9.00**

Figure, elephant, modern, brown lustre glaze, logo burnt into wooden base, early 50s, 8"................................**$150.00**

Figurine, elephant, sparkler eyes & headpiece, 6", from $15 to...**$20.00**

Figurine, giraffe, sitting, light gray high glaze, ca 1960, 5½"...**$35.00**

Figurine, girl w/bouquet, in-mold mark, 5"................**$30.00**

Figurine, hound dog, sitting, sparkler eyes, 4"...........**$12.00**

Figurine, hound dog w/pup, sparkler eyes, 4" & 2", pr.....**$20.00**

Figurine, kitten, sitting, aqua sparkler eyes, 1¾" **$7.00**

Figurine, mama kangaroo with babies, amber sparkler eyes, $25.00.

Figurine, pouter pigeon, pink sparkler eyes, 3½", from $15.00 to $18.00.

Figurine, owl, baby; sparkler eyes, 2¼"......................**$12.00**

Figurine, owl, sparkler eyes, modern, black, 5¼".......**$18.00**

Figurine, raccoon, standing, sparkler eyes, from $10 to.**$12.00**

Figurine, roadrunner...**$60.00**

Figurine, whippet dog, sparkler eyes, sitting, California USA, 7½"...**$14.00**

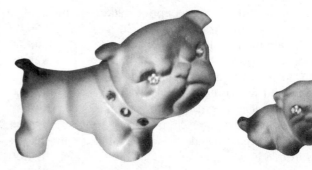

Figurines, bulldogs, blue sparkler eyes, amber stones on collar, large: from $15.00 to $18.00; small: from $6.00 to $8.00.

Figurines, pheasants, stylized, brown on white glaze, male & female (tail up), ceramic seed pearl eyes, 7¾", set..**$55.00**

Planter, Chinese Coolie atop rectangular form............**$22.50**

Vase, Chinese Modern, square, raised design, 8"........**$35.00**

Vase, Chinese Modern, square, raised design, 9¾".....**$40.00**

Rosemeade

The Wahpeton Pottery Company of Wahpeton, North Dakota, chose the trade name Rosemeade for a line of bird and animal figurines, novelty salt and pepper shakers, bells, and many other items which were sold from the 1940s to the sixties through gift stores and souvenir shops in that part of the country. They were marked with either a paper label or an ink stamp; the name Prairie Rose was also used. See *Collector's Encyclopedia of the Dakota Potteries* by Darlene Hurst Dommel for more information.

Advisor: Bryce Farnsworth (See Directory, Rosemeade)

Bank, Jamestown buffalo, $320.00.

Creamer & sugar bowl, embossed corn decor, 2½" ...**$40.00**

Creamer & sugar bowl, turkey figural, 3¾x4½"........**$180.00**

Figurine, pheasant rooster, tail up, on base, 3¾"........**$95.00**

Pin, Prairie Rose..**$500.00**

Pitcher, advertising, Ewald Bros Dairy, 6" **$180.00**

Pitcher, pink, braided handle, 3¾"...............................**$85.00**

Salt & pepper shakers, black bears, sitting, pr...........**$55.00**

Salt & pepper shakers, Bob White quail, pr...............**$50.00**

Salt & pepper shakers, brussel sprouts, 1½", pr **$40.00**

Salt & pepper shakers, dolphins, green, w/tails up, resting on fins, pr **$55.00**

Salt & pepper shakers, gophers, sm, pr......................**$50.00**

Salt & pepper shakers, greyhound dog heads, pr.......**$40.00**
Salt & pepper shakers, oxen, red, pr.........................**$130.00**
Salt & pepper shakers, quail, w/feather top knots, pr..**$80.00**
Salt & pepper shakers, rabbits, running, 2½", pr........**$90.00**
Salt & pepper shakers, raccoons, pr **$90.00**
Salt & pepper shakers, skunks, lg, pr **$50.00**
Salt & pepper shakers, swans, blk, pr **$70.00**
Salt & pepper shakers, tulips, pink w/green leaves, 2¼",
   pr **$45.00**
Spoon rest, cactus shape...**$85.00**
Spoon rest, chicken embossed on spoon shape.........**$80.00**
Spoon rest, Minnesota Centennial...............................**$50.00**
Spoon rest, pansy shape, 3¾" **$125.00**
Spoon rest, sunflower shape **$180.00**
TV lamp, Palomino horse against foliage, 9½" **$500.00**
Vase, swan figural...**$35.00**
Wall pocket, deer in foliage, 5" **$60.00**
Watering can, rose, molded rabbit design, 4"..............**$75.00**

Flower frog, pheasant, 4¾", $85.00.

Roseville Pottery

This company took its name from the city in Ohio where they operated for a few years before moving to Zanesville in the late 1890s. They're recognized as one of the giants in the industry, having produced many lines of the finest in art pottery from the beginning to the end of their production. Even when machinery took over many of the procedures once carefully done by hand, the pottery they produced continued to reflect the artistic merit and high standards of quality the company had always insisted upon.

Several marks were used over the years as well as some paper labels. The very early art lines often carried an applied ceramic seal with the name of the line (Royal, Egypto, Mongol, Mara, or Woodland) under a circle containing the words Rozane Ware. From 1910 until 1928 an Rv mark was used, the 'v' being contained in the upper loop of the 'R.' Paper labels were common from 1914 until 1937. From 1932 until they closed in 1952, the mark was Roseville in script, or R USA. Pieces marked RRP Co Roseville, Ohio, were not made by the Roseville Pottery but by Robinson Ransbottom of Roseville, Ohio. Don't be confused. There are many jardinieres and pedestals in a brown and green blended glaze that are being sold at flea markets and antique malls as Roseville that were actually made by Robinson Ransbottom as late as the 1970s and eighties. That

isn't to say they don't have some worth of their own, but don't buy them for old Roseville.

Most of the listings here are for items produced from the 1930s on — things you'll be more likely to encounter today. If you'd like to learn more about the subject, we recommend *The Collector's Encyclopedia of Roseville Pottery, Vols 1 and 2*, and *The Catalog of Early Roseville*, all by Sharon and Bob Huxford.

Newsletter: *Rosevilles of the Past*
Jack Bomm, Editor
P.O. Box 656
Clarcona, FL 32710-0656; Subscription: $19.95 per year for 6 to 12 newsletters

Apple Blossom, vase, #388-10, pink, 10"....................**$160.00**
Apple Blossom, vase, #390-12, pink, 12½" **$250.00**
Apple Blossom, wall pocket, #366-8, blue, 8½" **$200.00**
Apple Blossom, window box, #368-8, pink, 2½x6½"..**$85.00**
Artwood, planter, #1055-9, green, 7x9½"....................**$70.00**
Artwood, planter, 3-pc set, #1050/#1051, yellow & brown,
   4"/6" **$100.00**
Artwood, vase, #1057-8, blue, 8".................................**$85.00**

Autumn, shaving mug, no mark, 4", $275.00.

Baneda, candlestick, red, label, 4½" **$275.00**
Baneda, vase, footed & shouldered cylinder w/sm scrolled
   handles at neck, green, no mark, 7"....................**$275.00**
Baneda, vase, footed teardrop shape w/plain rim, long
   curved handles, embossed floral band on mottled pink,
   label, 9"..**$500.00**
Bittersweet, candlestick, #851-3, pink & white, 3"......**$60.00**
Bittersweet, cornucopia, #857-4, pink & white, 4½" ..**$75.00**
Bittersweet, vase, #809-8, 8" **$165.00**
Bittersweet, wall pocket, #866-7, green, 7½" **$135.00**
Blackberry, basket, 6½" **$500.00**
Blackberry, jardiniere, sm curved handles, label, 4".**$250.00**
Blackberry, vase, shouldered w/plain rim tapering to flat bot-
   tom, sm half-ring handles, label, 6" **$325.00**
Bushberry, bowl, #411-6, blue, 6".............................**$150.00**
Bushberry, bud vase, #152-7, tan, 7½" **$125.00**
Bushberry, mug, #1-3½, green, 3½" **$135.00**
Bushberry, vase, #32-7, green w/hint of tan, 7".......**$120.00**
Capri, ashtray, #599-3, maroon, 13" **$40.00**
Capri, basket, #510-10, green, 9" **$95.00**
Capri, planter, #C-1010-10, light tan, 5x10½" **$75.00**
Clemana, flower frog, #23, tan, 4"............................**$125.00**

Clemana, vase, #754-8, green, 8½" $225.00

Clemana, vase, #756-9, green, 9½" $245.00

Clematis, candlesticks, #1155-2, green, 2½", pr $65.00

Clematis, flower arranger, #102-5, green, 5½" $65.00

Clematis, vase, #102-6, green & tan, 6½" $65.00

Clematis, wall pocket, #1295-8, 8½" $165.00

Columbine, cornucopia, #149-6, green & tan, 5½" $75.00

Columbine, hanging basket, 8½" $200.00

Columbine, vase, #17-7, blue, 7½" $125.00

Cosmos, flower frog, ball shape w/handle, blue, 3½" ..$80.00

Cosmos, vase, #134-4, bluish green, 4" $60.00

Cosmos, vase, #375-4, gold & green, 4" $125.00

Dawn, console bowl, #318-14, yellow, 16" $150.00

Earlam, vase, ovoid w/slightly lipped rim, curved handles, variegated turquoise w/hint of tan, 6" $160.00

Earlam, vase, teardrop shape, rimless, variegated turquoise & tan, no mark, 9" $250.00

Falline, bowl, low & round, ear-shaped handles, pea-pod decor on tan, no mark, 11" $300.00

Falline, vase, trumpet shape w/curved handles, shades of green & blue w/tan interior, label, 8" $425.00

Ferella, candlestick, cut-out shell design on flared base, mottled tan & blue, 4½" $200.00

Ferella, vase, bulbous, cut-out shell design at rim & flared base, angled handles, mottled tan & blue, 6" $350.00

Foxglove, flower frog, #46, blue, 4" $75.00

Foxglove, vase, #47, green & pink, 8½" $165.00

Foxglove, wall pocket, #1292-8, blue, 8" $275.00

Freesia, basket, #390-7, deep tan & brown, 7" $120.00

Freesia, console bowl, #469-14, blue, 16½" $185.00

Freesia, wall pocket, #1296-8, tan & brown, 8½" $200.00

Freesia, window box, #1392-8, green, 10½" $100.00

Fuchsia, candlestick, #1132, green & tan, 2" $70.00

Fuchsia, console bowl w/frog, #353-14/#37, green & tan, 4x15½" $260.00

Fuchsia, vase, #898-6, blue, 8" $225.00

Futura, vase, pillow form, black paper label, 5x6", $300.00.

Futura, vase, stacked-ring neck on angled body tapering to rimmed base, long angled handles, green & tan, no mark, 7" $200.00

Gardenia, bowl, #626-6 ....$75.00

Gardenia, tray, #631-14, gray & taupe, 15" $140.00

Gardenia, vase, #658-10, green, 10" $135.00

Hyde Park, ashtray, sm $10.00

Iris, basket, #355-10, pink & green, 9½" $335.00

Iris, bowl, #360-6 ....$120.00

Iris, hanging basket, bulbous, angled handles, pink, 8"...$250.00

Iris, jardiniere, #647-3, tan, 3½" $65.00

Iris, wall pocket, #1284-8, pink & green, 8" $385.00

Ivory II, candlestick, ball-shaped cup on flat saucer base, 2½" $35.00

Ivory II, hanging basket, 7" $100.00

Ivory II, jardiniere, #574-4, 4" $50.00

Ixia, candlestick/bud vase, #1128, yellow & gold, 5" $100.00

Ixia, console bowl, #330, green, 3½x10½" $120.00

Ixia, vase, #858-8, pink, 8½" $100.00

Jonquil, flowerpot, 5½" $135.00

Jonquil, vase, sm curved handles at neck, no mark, 4" ..$125.00

Laurel, bowl, widely fluted rim w/closed angled handles, gold background, no mark, 3½" $125.00

Laurel, vase, closed angle handles, gold background, 9½".$200.00

Lotus, bowl, #L6-9, green & ivory, 3x9" $70.00

Lotus, pillow vase, #L4-10, blue & ivory, 10½" $150.00

Luffa, jardiniere, 6" $175.00

Luffa, vase, 6" $175.00

Magnolia, ashtray, #28, blue, 7" $100.00

Magnolia, cornucopia, #184-6, blue, 6" $75.00

Magnolia, planter, #183-6, blue, 6" $90.00

Mayfair, jardiniere, #1109-4, brown, 4" $40.00

Mayfair, wall pocket, corner type, #1014-8, 8" $120.00

Ming Tree, bowl, #526-9, green, 4x11½" $90.00

Ming Tree, conch shell, #563, blue, 8½" $50.00

Ming Tree, vase, #572-6, white, 6½" $110.00

Mock Orange, pillow vase, #930-8, pink, 7" $100.00

Mock Orange, planter, #931-8, gold, 3½x9" $65.00

Mock Orange, vase, #973-8, green, 8½" $95.00

Moderne, comport, #297-6, ivory, 6" $150.00

Moderne, triple candlestick, #1112, aqua, 6" $150.00

Moderne, urn, #299, ivory, 6½" $150.00

Montacello, vase, w/handles, 6" $400.00

Montacello, vase, 4" $200.00

Morning Glory, candlestick, tall cup on flared base, angled handles, green, no mark, 5" $250.00

Morning Glory, pillow vase, handles at bottom, ivory, label, 7" $365.00

Moss, triple bud vase, #1108, shades of green & pink on white, 7" $200.00

Moss, vase, #290-6, 6" $150.00

Moss, vase, #776-7, 7½", from $150.00 to $200.00.

Orian, candlestick, handles, rose, no mark, 4½".........$90.00

Orian, comport, #272-10, blue w/peach interior, 4½x10½" dia $150.00

Peony, bowl, #430-10, gold, 11".................**$100.00**
Peony, mug, #2-3½, gold, 3½".....................**$100.00**
Peony, planter, #387-8, blue, 10".................**$100.00**
Peony, wall pocket, #1293-8, green & tan, 8"..........**$200.00**
Pine Cone, boat dish, #427-8, blue, 9"...........**$325.00**
Pine Cone, candlestick, #112-3, tan, 2½"...........**$75.00**

Pine Cone, pitcher, #708-9, blue, impressed mark, 9½", $850.00.

Pine Cone, planter, #124, blue, 5"...............**$200.00**
Pine Cone, tumbler, #414, blue, 5"...............**$250.00**
Poppy, bowl, #336-10, green, 12"................**$150.00**
Poppy, jardiniere, #642-4, 5".....................**$100.00**
Poppy, vase, #346-6, pink & yellow, 6"..........**$125.00**
Primrose, vase, #760-6, blue, 7".................**$150.00**
Raymor, bean pot, #194, black, from $60 to.............**$70.00**
Raymor, bean pot, #195, gray, from $50 to.................**$60.00**
Raymor, bowl, divided vegetable; #165, 13"..............**$55.00**
Raymor, bowl, salad; #161, 11½"....................**$40.00**
Raymor, bowl, vegetable; #160, 9".................**$40.00**
Raymor, butter dish, #181, w/lid, 7½".............**$100.00**
Raymor, casserole, #183, w/lid, 11", from $60...........**$80.00**
Raymor, casserole, #185, w/lid, 13½", from $90 to...**$115.00**
Raymor, casserole, individual; #199, 7½"............**$40.00**
Raymor, casserole w/hot plate, #84/#198, from $75 to...**$85.00**
Raymor, coffee tumbler, w/handle, 4".............**$50.00**
Raymor, coffeepot, swinging; #176, from $300 to.....**$350.00**
Raymor, coffeepot stand (for #176)............**$175.00**
Raymor, condiment cruet, 5½", from $35 to.............**$50.00**
Raymor, condiment mustard, 3½"..............**$75.00**
Raymor, condiment tray, 8½".....................**$30.00**
Raymor, cookie jar, #20, 10".....................**$175.00**
Raymor, corn server, individual; #162, 12½"..............**$25.00**
Raymor, cup & saucer, #151, from $25 to.................**$30.00**
Raymor, gravy boat, #190, 9½"....................**$35.00**
Raymor, plate, dinner; #152, from $20 to.................**$30.00**
Raymor, plate, luncheon; #153, from $15 to.............**$20.00**
Raymor, plate, salad; #154, from $12 to.................**$18.00**
Raymor, ramekin, individual; #156, w/lid, 6½"..........**$45.00**
Raymor, salt & pepper shakers, 3½", pr, from $50 to.**$75.00**
Raymor, shirred egg, #200, 10", from $35 to.............**$45.00**
Raymor, tea set, #157/158, 3 pcs, from $250 to.......**$300.00**
Raymor, teapot, #14, 6½", from $65 to.................**$80.00**
Rozane, bowl, #8-8, blue, 7½"....................**$125.00**
Rozane, vase, #102-12, green, 12"................**$165.00**
Silhouette, box, #740, tan, 4½"....................**$125.00**
Silhouette, double planter, #757-9, aqua, 5½"...........**$90.00**
Silhouette, ewer, #716-6, white, 6½"...............**$75.00**
Snowberry, flowerpot, #1PS-5, rose, 5½".................**$120.00**

Snowberry, tray, #1BL-12, blue, 14".................**$185.00**
Snowberry, vase, #IRB-6, blue, 6"................**$100.00**
Snowberry, vase, #1V1-12, blue, 12½"...............**$200.00**
Sunflower, candlestick, no mark, 4"...............**$165.00**
Sunflower, console bowl, elongated w/ear-shaped handles, 3x12½"................................**$325.00**
Sunflower, vase, 6"...............................**$450.00**
Teasel, vase, #881-6, tan & ivory, 6"............**$80.00**
Teasel, vase, #887-10, pale green, 10".............**$225.00**
Thorn Apple, triple bud vase, #1120, blue, 6"..........**$150.00**
Thorn Apple, vase, #305-6, pink & green, 6½"...........**$175.00**
Thorn Apple, vase, #816-8, tan, 8½"...............**$225.00**
Topeo, vase, blue, no mark, 9"....................**$265.00**
Topeo, vase, red, ball shape, silver paper label, 6"..**$250.00**
Tourmaline, vase, bulbous, curved handles, mottled tan, sm silver label, 5"................................**$90.00**
Velmoss, bowl, w/handles, rose, no mark, 3x11"......**$120.00**
Water Lily, flower frog, #48, tan, 4½"............**$95.00**
Water Lily, hanging basket, w/handles, pink, 9".......**$225.00**
White Rose, basket, #362-8, green & rose, 7½".........**$175.00**
White Rose, double bud vase, #148, green & rose, 4½"..**$110.00**
White Rose, double candlestick, #1143, green & rose, 4"..**$110.00**
White Rose, vase, #388-7, green & rose, 7"...............**$175.00**
Wincraft, cornucopia, #221-8, apricot, 5x9"................**$80.00**
Wincraft, ewer, #218-18, blue, 19"................**$325.00**
Wincraft, vase, #274-7, chartreuse, 7"............**$90.00**
Windsor, bowl, angled handles, variegated brown & green, silver paper label, 3x10"...................**$175.00**
Windsor, vase, curved handles at plain short neck, variegated blue, 6"...................................**$185.00**
Wisteria, vase, angled handles at neck, silver paper label, 8½"..**$450.00**
Zephyr Lily, cornucopia, #204-8, blue, 8½"...........**$100.00**
Zephyr Lily, fan vase, #205-6, green, 6½"...............**$120.00**
Zephyr Lily, tray, curved heart shape, embossed white floral decor on tan & brown, 14½"...................**$175.00**

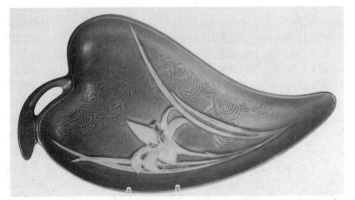

Zephyr Lily, tray, leaf shape, blue, impressed mark, 14½", $175.00.

Royal China

The dinnerware made by Royal China of Sebring, Ohio, is becoming very collectible, the lines mentioned here in particular. All are found on the same standard company shapes. The most popular are their Currier and Ives and Blue Willow patterns, both decorated with blue transfers on white backgrounds, but interest in the other patterns is growing all the time. Memory Lane is decorated with red transfers of rural life, Colonial Homestead and Old Curiosity Shop both have green transfer prints, and Fair Oaks has brown with multicolor accents. Buck's County is decorated in golden tan on a yellow ground. Each line has a distinctive border design that will help you identify the pattern on unmarked pieces. Of the two green lines, Old Curiosity Shop's border depicts hinges and pulls, while Colonial Homestead's represents wooden frames with nailed joints. The Willow pattern was made in both blue and pink, but pink is hard to find and not as collectible. Tradition is an allover Jacobean-type floral, and though it's often found in the pink transfer, it comes in other colors as well.

Advisor: BA Wellman (See Directory, Dinnerware)

Blue Willow, ashtray, 5½"...$12.00
Blue Willow, bowl, cereal; 6¼"....................................$12.00
Blue Willow, bowl, fruit nappy; 5½"..............................$4.50
Blue Willow, bowl, soup; 8¼".......................................$10.00
Blue Willow, bowl, vegetable; 10"................................$18.00
Blue Willow, butter dish, ¼-lb......................................$35.00
Blue Willow, cake plate, w/handles, 10½".....................$20.00
Blue Willow, casserole..$30.00
Blue Willow, creamer...$6.00
Blue Willow, cup & saucer..$6.00
Blue Willow, gravy boat...$15.00
Blue Willow, patter, 13"...$28.00
Blue Willow, pie plate, 10", from $12 to.......................$15.00
Blue Willow, plate, bread & butter; 6¼"..........................$3.00
Blue Willow, plate, chop; 10".......................................$20.00
Blue Willow, plate, dinner; 10".......................................$6.00
Blue Willow, plate, salad; 7¼".......................................$7.00
Blue Willow, salt & pepper shakers, pr.........................$18.00
Blue Willow, sugar bowl, w/lid......................................$10.00
Blue Willow, teapot...$65.00
Blue Willow, tray, tidbit; 2-tier.....................................$35.00
Buck's County, ashtray, 5½"...$7.00
Buck's County, bowl, fruit nappy; 5½"............................$3.00
Buck's County, bowl, soup; 8½".....................................$7.00
Buck's County, bowl, vegetable; 10"..............................$15.00
Buck's County, cake plate, w/handles, 10½"..................$12.00
Buck's County, casserole, w/lid.....................................$65.00
Buck's County, creamer..$5.00
Buck's County, cup & saucer..$4.00
Buck's County, gravy boat..$10.00
Buck's County, plate, bread & butter; 6¼".......................$1.50
Buck's County, plate, dinner; 10"....................................$4.00
Buck's County, salt & pepper shakers, pr......................$10.00
Buck's County, sugar bowl, w/lid....................................$7.50
Buck's County, teapot..$65.00
Colonial Homestead, bowl, cereal; 6¼"..........................$10.00
Colonial Homestead, bowl, fruit nappy; 5½".....................$3.00
Colonial Homestead, bowl, soup; 8¼"..............................$7.50
Colonial Homestead, bowl, vegetable; 10".....................$20.00
Colonial Homestead, cake plate, tab handles, 10½"........$12.00
Colonial Homestead, casserole, angle handles, w/lid.$50.00

Colonial Homestead, chop plate, 12"..............................$18.00
Colonial Homestead, creamer..$5.00
Colonial Homestead, cup & saucer....................................$5.00
Colonial Homestead, gravy boat.....................................$12.00
Colonial Homestead, pie plate.......................................$15.00
Colonial Homestead, plate, bread & butter; 6"..................$1.50
Colonial Homestead, plate, dinner; 10".............................$4.00
Colonial Homestead, plate, salad; rare, 7¼".....................$6.00
Colonial Homestead, plate, tab handles, 10½".................$12.00
Colonial Homestead, platter, oval, 13"............................$18.00
Colonial Homestead, salt & pepper shakers, pr...............$12.00
Colonial Homestead, sugar bowl, w/lid............................$10.00
Currier & Ives, ashtray, 5½"..$13.00
Currier & Ives, bowl, cereal; tab handles, 6¼"................$30.00
Currier & Ives, bowl, cereal; 6¼"...................................$10.00
Currier & Ives, bowl, fruit nappy; 5½", from $3.50 to..$5.00
Currier & Ives, bowl, vegetable; 10"...............................$25.00
Currier & Ives, bowl, vegetable; 9".................................$20.00
Currier & Ives, butter dish, Fashionable.........................$38.00
Currier & Ives, butter dish, ¼-lb, from $30 to.............$35.00
Currier & Ives, casserole, angle handles, w/lid...........$95.00
Currier & Ives, casserole, tab handles.........................$150.00
Currier & Ives, creamer, angle handle.............................$6.00
Currier & Ives, creamer & sugar bowl, w/handles......$20.00
Currier & Ives, cup, angle handle, tall, 9".......................$3.50
Currier & Ives, gravy boat, tab handle...........................$30.00
Currier & Ives, lamp, candle; w/globe...........................$125.00
Currier & Ives, pie plate, 10"...$28.00
Currier & Ives, plate, bread & butter; 6¼".......................$4.00
Currier & Ives, plate, calendar; ca 1970s-85, each, from $15
   to...$20.00
Currier & Ives, plate, chop; marked, 12¼".......................$28.00
Currier & Ives, plate, dinner; 10"....................................$6.00
Currier & Ives, plate, luncheon; 9".................................$15.00
Currier & Ives, plate, salad; 7¼"....................................$12.00
Currier & Ives, plate, snack; w/cup & well, 9"...............$25.00
Currier & Ives, platter, oval, 13"....................................$30.00
Currier & Ives, platter, tab handles, 10½".......................$28.00
Currier & Ives, salt & pepper shakers, pr.......................$30.00
Currier & Ives, spoon rest, wall hanging........................$30.00

Currier and Ives: Soup bowl, $10.00; Gravy boat, $15.00; Cup and saucer, $6.00.

Currier & Ives, sugar bowl, no handles, w/lid............$25.00
Currier & Ives, teapot...$125.00

Currier & Ives, tidbit tray, 3-tier............................$75.00
Currier & Ives, tray, gravy boat; like 7" plate.............$35.00
Currier & Ives, tray, gravy boat; 7¼"....................$18.00
Currier & Ives, tumbler, iced tea; glass, 5½"..........$16.50
Currier & Ives, tumbler, juice; glass, 3½"..............$16.50
Currier & Ives, tumbler, old-fashioned; glass, 3¼".....$16.50
Currier & Ives, tumbler, water; glass, 4¾".............$16.50
Fair Oaks, bowl, 9"..$15.00
Fair Oaks, cake plate, w/handles, 10"...................$9.00
Fair Oaks, casserole.....................................$22.00
Fair Oaks, creamer...$4.50
Fair Oaks, cup & saucer..................................$5.00
Fair Oaks, plate, bread & butter........................$2.00
Fair Oaks, plate, dinner; 10"............................$4.00
Fair Oaks, salt & pepper shakers, pr....................$8.00
Fair Oaks, sugar bowl, w/lid.............................$8.00

**Memory Lane:
Ashtray, $10.00;
Dinner plate, 10",
$4.00; Cup and
saucer, $5.00.**

Memory Lane, bowl, cereal; 6¼"...........................$9.00
Memory Lane, bowl, fruit nappy; 5½".....................$3.00
Memory Lane, bowl, soup; 8¼"............................$7.50
Memory Lane, bowl, vegetable; 10".......................$20.00
Memory Lane, butter dish, ¼-lb..........................$30.00
Memory Lane, cake plate, w/handles, 10"................$12.00
Memory Lane, chop plate, 12"............................$20.00
Memory Lane, creamer......................................$6.00
Memory Lane, gravy boat liner, from $12 to..............$15.00
Memory Lane, plate, bread & butter; 6¼"................$2.00
Memory Lane, plate, luncheon; rare, 9¼"................$8.00
Memory Lane, plate, salad; rare, 7¼"...................$7.00
Memory Lane, platter, 13"...............................$25.00
Memory Lane, salt & pepper shakers, pr.................$12.00
Memory Lane, sugar bowl, w/lid..........................$9.00
Memory Lane, tumbler, iced tea; glass..................$12.00
Memory Lane, tumbler, juice; glass......................$8.00
Old Curiosity Shop, bowl, cereal; 6½"...................$5.00
Old Curiosity Shop, bowl, fruit nappy; 5½".............$4.00
Old Curiosity Shop, bowl, vegetable; 9".................$18.00
Old Curiosity Shop, bowl, vegetable; 10"................$18.00
Old Curiosity Shop, cake plate, w/handles, 10".........$15.00
Old Curiosity Shop, creamer.............................$6.00
Old Curiosity Shop, cup & saucer........................$5.00
Old Curiosity Shop, plate, bread & butter; 6¼".........$2.50
Old Curiosity Shop, plate, dinner; 10"..................$4.00
Old Curiosity Shop, salt & pepper shakers, pr..........$15.00
Old Curiosity Shop, sugar bowl, w/lid...................$9.00
Tradition, bowl, fruit nappy; 5½".......................$3.00

Tradition, bowl, vegetable; 10".........................$15.00
Tradition, cake plate, 10"..............................$20.00
Tradition, creamer.......................................$4.00
Tradition, cup & saucer..................................$4.00
Tradition, gravy boat...................................$15.00
Tradition, plate, dinner; 10"............................$6.00
Tradition, sugar bowl....................................$8.00

Royal Copley

This is a line of planters, wall pockets, vases, and other novelty items, most of which are modeled as appealing animals, birds, or human figures. They were made by the Spaulding China Company of Sebring, Ohio, from 1942 until 1957. The decoration is underglazed and airbrushed, and some pieces are trimmed in gold (which can add 25% to 50% to their values). Not every piece is marked, but they all have a style that is distinctive. Some items are ink stamped; others have (or have had) labels.

Royal Copley is really not hard to find, and unmarked items may often be had at bargain prices. The more common pieces seem to have stabilized, but the rare and hard-to-find examples are showing a steady increase. Your collection can go in several directions; for instance, some people choose a particular animal to collect. If you're a cat lover, they were made in an extensive assortment of styles and sizes. Teddy bears are also popular; you'll find them licking a lollipop, playing a mandolin, or modeled as a bank, and they come in various colors as well. Wildlife lovers can collect deer, pheasants, fish, and gazelles, and there's also a wide array of songbirds.

If you'd like more information, we recommend *Royal Copley* written by Leslie Wolfe, edited by Joe Devine.

Advisor: Joe Devine (See Directory, Royal Copley)

Ashtray, leaf shape w/lg flower, rose-colored w/yellow bloom, green mark, 5"............................$8.00
Ashtray, square w/sides curved inward, gold w/incised stylized rooster & hen, 2 rests on each side, marked USA, 7x7"............................$35.00
Ashtray, straw hat w/ribbon, gray & pink, raised lettering, rare, 5"............................$25.00
Ashtray, triangular w/3 holders on 1 side, blue, 5½x4½"..$15.00
Bank, pig standing upright & dressed in blue & white striped shirt & blue pants, paper label or green mark, 7½".$55.00
Bank, rooster, multicolor, slot at top of trail, paper label, 7½"............................$65.00
Bank, teddy bear sitting upright, white w/black ears, features & paws, red neck bow, paper label, 7½"............$85.00
Boot, white w/multicolored floral decor, 6"...............$18.00
Creamer, chick dressed in rose-colored hat & cape w/blue bow, found w/Pat Pending or Spaulding Pat #113724, 4¾"............................$18.00
Creamer & sugar bowl (open), flower petals form bowls w/leaf handles, gray w/pink, 3", each.................$18.00
Figurine, lark on stump w/flowers, blue w/yellow breast & head, paper label, 5"............................$15.00
Figurine, mallard duck, standing, gray w/dark green & deep rose, yellow bill, paper label, 7"...................$20.00

Figurine, mutt dog sitting upright with head cocked, brown w/black ears, white chest & paws, paper label, 8"..**$25.00**

Figurine, sea gull in flight, multicolored, paper label, 8".**$30.00**

Figurine, spaniel, brown tones, collar around neck, paper label, 6"..**$18.00**

Figurine, swallow w/wings spread on stump, multicolored, paper label, 8"..**$22.00**

Figurine, thrush on stump, brown w/rose-colored breast & neck, paper label, 6½"..**$18.00**

Figurine, 2 birds on a stump, blue w/black on tails & wings, yellow breasts w/touch of pink, paper label, 6"..**$30.00**

Figurines, Oriental boy or girl, both holding jugs & swaying, rose & blue, paper labels, 7½", each....................**$18.00**

Lamp, bamboo base w/bamboo design on shade, red, black & gold..**$50.00**

Lamp, Oriental, swaying & holding jug, original gathered cloth shade w/ribbon & lace **$50.00**

Lamp base, clown figure, smiling w/hands in pocket, paper label, 7¼" **$75.00**

Lamp base, cocker spaniel, begging, brown & white, very rare, 10" **$50.00**

Pitcher, Floral Beauty, 2 lg rose-colored flowers w/blue centers & green leaves on blue, green stamp, 8" **$40.00**

Planter, boat shaped, footed, light turquoise w/brown speckles, paper label, 3½"..**$12.00**

Planter, bowl on 3-footed branch base, white w/green philodendron leaves, paper label, 4¼"......................**$10.00**

Planter, bust of old colonial man, black hat, raised lettering, 8" **$50.00**

Planter, clown figure w/lg round backside, yellow & white, brown dots, 8¼" **$50.00**

Planter, cocker spaniel head, 5" **$15.00**

Planter, deer & fawn heads, taupe & white, raised lettering, 9" **$25.00**

Planter, dog beside suitcase, rare, $45.00.

Planter, dog, brown tones, right paw raised, paper label, 7½" **$50.00**

Planter, farm boy or girl, standing, yellow & blue, 6½", each **$20.00**

Planter, flower blooms & leaves form boat-shaped bowl & base, airbrushed yellow, pink & green, green stamp, 7".....**$12.00**

Planter, girl's head w/eyes closed in pigtails & wearing bonnet, white w/black hair & pink bows, raised letters, 7"..**$35.00**

Planter, kitten & boot, kitten along side of brown & white cowboy boot, paper label only, scarce, 7½" **$45.00**

Planter, kitten in cradle, bow around neck, pink blanket, blue cradle, paper label only, 7½" **$70.00**

Planter, kitten with ball of yarn, 8", $22.00.

Planter, Madonna bust, praying, blue & white, 9" **$38.00**

Planter, mailbox w/duck, tan mailbox marked US Mail on brown stump, rare, 6¾" **$50.00**

Planter, mallard duck, gray w/dark green & deep rose, yellow bill, paper label, 7¾"..**$22.00**

Planter, open book on base, Season's Greetings, decal on white w/gold trim, 5" **$20.00**

Planter, Oriental boy or girl sitting next to & leaning on container, deep rose & blue, raised letters, 5½" **$14.00**

Planter, Oriental fish in blue & pink on 1 side only of footed flat-sided container, paper label, 5½"....................**$12.00**

Planter, pillow-type w/molded brown deer head on gray & dark orange airbrushing, paper label, 7½" **$22.00**

Planter, pillow-type w/open center, blue & pink Oriental fish decor, paper label, 5¼" **$15.00**

Planter, poodle upright w/square black container, 7"...**$35.00**

Planter, puppy seated in front of wagon, brown w/white chest & paws, 1 black ear, light green wagon, 5¾".........**$35.00**

Planter, Riddle, round foot, 5" **$18.00**

Planter, rooster, multicolor, raised letters on base, paper label, common, 7¼"..**$25.00**

Planter, rooster w/head down, multicolor on white, paper label or raised letters, 7"..**$20.00**

Planter, salt box, cream & tan w/Salt lettered within scrolled border, raised lettering, 5½"................................**$30.00**

Planter, Siamese cats before basketweave planter, 9".**$95.00**

Planter, Spooks, black & white, 4" **$16.00**

Planter, stuffed elephant w/trunk up, white w/green dots, paper label, 6½"..**$65.00**

Planter, teddy bear w/concertina, brown & black-toned bear w/pink & black instrument, paper label, 7½" **$70.00**

Planter, teddy bear with mandolin, 7", $45.00.

Planter & candle holder, star shape, white w/vertical ribs, paper label, 4¾"..**$24.00**

Planter plaque, plate shape w/rooster or hen, multicolored, raised letters, 6¾", each **$38.00**

Planter plaque, plate w/Dutch windmill scene, white scalloped border w/blue-green rim, script mark, 8" ..**$60.00**

Razor blade receptacle, red & white striped barber's pole w/white or gold-tone dome top, 6¼", each **$50.00**

Tray, rectangular w/incised stylized fruit design, ribbed tab handles, deep golden brown, paper label, 4½" ...**$25.00**

Vase, Carol's Corsage, 2 lg yellow flowers w/blue leaves on airbrushed green, green stamp, 7" **$18.00**

Vase, cornucopia upright on base, white w/decaled pink floral motif, gold trim, raised lettering or gold stamp, 8¼"..**$30.00**

Vase, cylindrical w/white stylized leaf & vine decor dividing pink & black, paper label, 8½" **$18.00**

Vase, cylindrical w/2 embossed green & light brown fish on brown swirled water effect, gold trim, raised letters, 5½"..**$20.00**

Vase, ivy, green on cream, round pillow w/curved top, green base, gold trim, paper label, 6¼" **$20.00**

Vase, leafy branch, white on black, tall oval, 8¼" **$15.00**

Vase, mare & foal heads, brown w/black mane, paper label, 8½"..**$30.00**

Vase, rose decal on white, bulbous w/fluted & flared neck & base, bead trim, scrolled handles, gold stamp, 6¼" ...**$12.00**

Vase/planter, deer, open style, 7½" **$30.00**

Royal Haeger

Many generations of the Haeger family have been associated with the ceramic industry. Starting out as a brickyard in 1871, the Haeger Company (Dundee, Illinois) progressed to include artware in their production line as early as 1914. That was only the beginning. In the thirties they began to make a line of commercial artware so successful that as a result a plant was built in Macomb, Illinois, devoted exclusively to its production.

Royal Haeger was their premium line. Its chief designer was Royal Arden Hickman, a talented artist and sculptor who worked in mediums other than pottery. For Haeger he designed a line of wonderfully stylized animals and birds, high-style vases, and human figures and masks with extremely fine details.

Paper labels were used extensively before the mid-thirties. Royal Haeger ware has an in-mold script mark, and their Flower Ware line (1954–1963) is marked 'RG' (Royal Garden).

For those wanting to learn more about this pottery, we recommend *Collecting Royal Haeger* by Lee Garmon and Doris Frizzell.

Ashtray, boomerang shape, #1006, 12" **$4.00**

Ashtray, free-form, #1273, 8"...**$6.00**

Bookend, ram figure, #R-132, 9", each **$30.00**

Bowl, console; beaded, #R-467, 15" **$8.00**

Bowl, pedestal, octagon shape, #3002, 8½" **$12.00**

Bowl, S-curved shape, white, #RG-73, 14" **$8.00**

Bowl, w/lg reclining mermaid, #505, 21" **$75.00**

Bowl/planter, violin shape; #R-293, 17" **$35.00**

Candle holder, cornucopia; #R-312, 5½", each.............**$9.00**

Candle holders, upright, flower & candle combo, #R-485, 7½", pr..**$18.00**

Candle holders, 2-block style, #R-579, 5", pr............**$18.00**

Candlesticks, double branch, #3232, 7", pr..............**$45.00**

Cigarette box, turtle w/snail on back, #R-684, 9¼" **$30.00**

Dealer's sign, antique gold, Deco styling **$50.00**

Decanter, dolphin shape, AMVETS, #1974..................**$25.00**

Figurine, cocker pup, sleeping, #R-776, 6" **$12.00**

Figurine, dachshund, #R-736, 14½" **$45.00**

Figurine, Egyptian cat, head down, #R-493, 6½" **$30.00**

Figurine, fighting cock, #R-791, 11½" **$40.00**

Figurine, girl sitting w/2 bowls, #R-1225, 13" **$35.00**

Figurine, panther, black, #R-683, 18" **$35.00**

Figurine, pheasant, #R-130, 12" **$24.00**

Figurine, prospector w/burros, #R-479, 11½"............**$55.00**

Figurine, Russian Wolfhound, white, #R-319, 8½", $75.00.

Figurine, tigress on rock, #R-313, 9" **$95.00**

Lamp, cabbage rose, #5174, 24", complete..................**$75.00**

Lamp, table; ginger, fluted, #5362, 28", complete **$55.00**

Lamp, table; mermaid on seashell, #5398, 26", complete .**$85.00**

Lamp, TV; bronco, #6105, 11½" **$75.00**

Lamp, TV; leaping gazelle, 13½"..................................**$45.00**

Pitcher, Ebony Cascade, #R-1619S, 16" **$18.00**

Planter, double racehorse, #R-883, 11"........................**$45.00**

Planter, fawn, white w/turquoise interior, #R-1913 .....**$35.00**

Planter, fawn shape, #617, 6½"......................................**$8.00**

Planter, gondolier shape, w/inserts, #R-657, 19½" **$30.00**

Planter, horse w/peg mane, 10" **$40.00**

Planter, stag figure, Art Deco, #R-1146, 5½"..............**$12.00**

Planter, tiny cow, label, 4½" **$15.00**

Planter, window; #3422, 18"..**$12.00**

Planter/bookend, moon fish, #1240, 10"....................**$35.00**

Plate, leaf shape, #R-286, 12"......................................**$20.00**

Platter, fish shape, stoneware, #854-H, 18"................**$18.00**

Urn, squat shape, white neck, light blue body, black base, #R-351, 10"..**$18.00**

Vase, pillow; #R-651, 8"..**$20.00**

Vase, swan shape, #R-430, 8"......................................**$15.00**

Vase/planter, conch shell; #R-322, 7½" **$35.00**

Wall pocket/hanging planter, fish shape, #R-1627, 13"......**$18.00**

RumRill

RumRill-marked pottery was actually made by other companies who simply provided the merchandise that George Rumrill marketed from 1933 until his death in 1942. Rumrill designed his own lines, and the potteries who filled the orders were the Red Wing Stoneware Company, Red Wing Potteries, Shawnee (but they were involved for only a few months), Florence, and Gonder. Many of the designs were produced by more than one company. Examples may be marked RumRill or with the name of the specific pottery.

Advisors: Wendy and Leo Frese, Three Rivers Collectibles (See Directory, RumRill)

Ashtray, #549, Dutch Blue, Art Deco styling **$45.00**
Bowl, #690, light green, 4x9½" **$35.00**
Bowl, console; #338, Pompeian, Continental Group, ftd, w/handles, 13" **$65.00**
Bowl, console; #612, light green w/brown antiquing, Vintage Group **$50.00**
Candle holder, #539, Eggshell, Manhattan Group, 14½" long...**$90.00**
Cornucopia, double; #685, pink gloss w/Seal Brown interior..**$50.00**
Ewer, #207, Scarlet & Bay **$25.00**
Ivy ball, #600-6", orange gloss, closed top w/3 openings **$100.00**

Ivy ball, #600-10, Dutch blue, $150.00. (Photo courtesy of Wendy and Leo Frese.)

Pitcher, ball shape, blended yellow, brown & orange..**$25.00**
Planter, #274, Goldenrod...**$25.00**
Planter, #306, Apple Blossom **$40.00**
Planter, #500, Dutch Blue, Classic Group **$50.00**
Vase, #C-5, blended yellow, orange & brown, 4" **$20.00**

Vase, green shading to brown, 4 handles, 9½", $75.00.

Vase, #M-4, w/handles, made in Minnesota, lg...........**$40.00**
Vase, #294, Goldenrod, Fluted Group, 5½" **$35.00**
Vase, #356, white, 7"...**$40.00**
Vase, #587, light green, w/handles..............................**$40.00**
Vase, blue, swirled, w/handles, made in Ohio, 9" **$40.00**
Water jug, #A50, w/corked cap, Scarlet & Bay, ca 1930s..**$60.00**

Russel Wright Designs

One of the country's foremost industrial designers, Russel Wright, was also responsible for several dinnerware lines, glassware, and aluminum that have become very collectible. American Modern, produced by the Steubenville Pottery Company (1939–1959) is his best known dinnerware and the most popular today. It had simple, sweeping lines that appealed to tastes of that period, and it was made in a variety of solid colors. The most desirable are: Cantaloupe, Glacier, Bean Brown, and White. Double our values for these colors. Chartreuse is represented by the low end of our range, Cedar, Black Chutney, and Seafoam by the high end, and Coral and Gray near the middle.

Iroquois China made his Casual line, and because it was so serviceable, it's relatively easy to find today. It will be marked with both Wright's signature and 'China by Iroquois.' To price Brick Red and Aqua Casual, double our values; for Avocado, use the low end of the range. Cantaloupe, Oyster, and Charcoal are valued at 50% more than prices listed.

Wright's aluminum ware is highly valued by today's collectors, even though it wasn't so well accepted in its day, due to the fact that it was so easily damaged.

If you'd like to learn more about the subject, we recommend *The Collector's Encyclopedia of Russel Wright Designs* by Ann Kerr.

American Modern

Baker, sm, 10¾", from $25 to **$30.00**
Bowl, lug soup..**$15.00**
Celery dish **$25.00**
Coffeepot, AD **$75.00**
Cup & saucer **$15.00**
Mug (tumbler), from $55 to **$60.00**
Pickle dish..**$16.00**
Plate, dinner; 10" **$10.00**
Ramekin, individual, w/lid...**$150.00**
Relish rosette...**$150.00**
Salt & pepper shakers, pr **$14.00**
Sugar bowl, w/lid **$14.00**
Teapot, 6x10" **$75.00**

Casual

Bowl, fruit; redesigned, 5¾" **$8.00**
Bowl, salad; 10" **$30.00**
Butter dish, ½-lb...**$75.00**
Casserole, open, 10" **$40.00**
Coffeepot, w/lid..**$85.00**

Creamer and sugar bowl, stack set, $30.00.

Creamer, redesigned **$15.00**
Cup & saucer, coffee **$12.00**
Lid for gravy bowl, ladle slot, 6¾" **$20.00**
Mug, redesigned, 9-oz **$75.00**
Percolator **$175.00**
Plate, dinner; 10" **$10.00**
Plate, luncheon; 9½" **$8.00**
Platter, oval, 14½" **$30.00**
Salt & pepper shakers, stacking, pr **$12.00**
Sugar bowl, lg family sz **$18.00**

Glassware

American Modern, cordial, 2" **$38.00**
American Modern, dessert dish, 2" **$40.00**
American Modern, sherbet, 2½" **$25.00**
American Modern, tumbler, juice; 4" **$30.00**
Eclipse, shot glass **$10.00**
Iroquois Pinch, tumbler, juice or water; 6- or 14-oz, each ..**$35.00**

Highlight

Bowl, oval vegetable; from $55 to **$60.00**
Creamer, from $25 to **$30.00**
Mug, from $30 to **$35.00**
Plate, bread & butter; from $8 to **$10.00**
Platter, round, sm, from $55 to **$60.00**
Sugar bowl, from $25 to **$30.00**

Knowles

Cup, 7½-oz, from $8 to **$10.00**
Lid, for round serving bowl, from $18 to **$20.00**
Plate, salad; 8¼", from $8 to **$10.00**
Platter, oval, 13", from $16 to **$18.00**
Platter, oval, 16", from $25 to **$30.00**
Sauce boat, from $25 to **$30.00**
Teapot, from $100 to **$125.00**

Plastic

Black Velvet, bowl, vegetable; w/lid, from $30 to **$35.00**
Black Velvet, lug soup, from $12 to **$15.00**
Copper Penny, plate, dinner; from $5 to **$6.00**
Copper Penny, platter, from $19 to **$22.00**
Flair, bowl, oval vegetable; deep, from $12 to **$13.00**

Flair, plate, salad; from $4 to **$5.00**
Home Decorator, cup & saucer, from $7 to **$9.00**
Home Decorator, lug soup, from $10 to......................**$12.00**
Meladur, bowl, fruit; 6-oz, from $7 to **$8.00**
Meladur, plate, dessert; 6¼", from $4 to **$5.00**
Meladur, plate, dinner; 9", from $6 to **$8.00**
Residential, bowl, oval vegetable; shallow, from $10 to..**$12.00**
Residential, creamer, from $8 to **$10.00**
Residential, tumbler, from $13 to **$15.00**

Spun Aluminum

Bowl..**$75.00**
Casserole **$85.00**
Cheese board **$85.00**
Gravy boat..**$125.00**
Ice bucket **$75.00**
Pitcher, sherry **$250.00**
Vase, lg, 12"..**$110.00**

Sterling

Ashtray, $75.00; Relish, 4 compartment, 16½", $55.00.

Celery tray, 11¼", from $15 to...................................**$18.00**
Cup, 7-oz, from $8 to **$10.00**
Pitcher, water; redesigned, from $55 to **$60.00**
Plate, dinner; 10¼", from $10 to................................**$12.00**
Sugar bowl, w/lid, 10-oz, from $15 to **$17.00**

White Clover (for Harker)

Bowl, divided vegetable; clover decorated, from $35 to...**$40.00**
Bowl, vegetable; 8¼", from $22 to **$25.00**
Casserole, clover decorated, w/lid, 2-qt, from $45 to.**$50.00**
Creamer, clover decorated, from $12 to......................**$14.00**
Plate, bread & butter; color only, 6", from $5 to...........**$6.00**
Plate, salad; color only, 7⅝", from $7 to **$9.00**
Sugar bowl (individual ramekin), w/lid, from $18 to .**$20.00**

Salt Shakers

Probably the most common type of souvenir shop merchandise from the twenties through the sixties, salt and pepper shaker sets can be spotted at any antique mall or flea market today by the dozens. Most were made in Japan and imported by various companies, though American manufacturers made their fair share as well.

'Miniature shakers' are hard to find and their prices have risen faster than any others. They were made by Arcadia Ceramics (probably an American company). They're under 1½" tall, some so small they had no space to accommodate a cork. Instead they came with instructions to 'use Scotch tape to cover the hole.'

Advertising sets and premiums are always good, since they appeal to a cross section of collectors. If you have a chance to buy them on the primary market, do so. Many of these are listed in the Advertising Character Collectibles section of this guide.

There are several good books on the market. We recommend *Salt and Pepper Shakers, Identification and Values, Vols I, II, III and IV*, by Helene Guarnaccia; and *The Collector's Encyclopedia of Salt and Pepper Shakers, Figural and Novelty, First and Second Series*, by Melva Davern.

See also Advertising Character Collectibles; Breweriana; Condiment Sets; Holt Howard; Occupied Japan; Regal China; Rosemeade; Vandor and other specific companies.

Advisor: Judy Posner (See Directory, Salt and Pepper Shakers)

Club: Novelty Salt and Pepper Club
c/o Irene Thornburg, Membership Coordinator
581 Joy Rd.
Battle Creek, MI 49017; Publishes quarterly newsletter and annual roster. Annual dues: $20 in USA, Canada, and Mexico; $25 for all other countries

Advertising

AO Smith Harvestore System, ceramic, dark blue silos w/white lettering, pr..**$25.00**
Bromo Seltzer, cobalt blue glass bottles w/black stoppers, embossed lettering, pr..**$12.00**
Campbell's Barbecue, red & white can w/white lid, marked Salt Shaker & Pepper Shaker, 1980s (?), pr...........**$35.00**
Greyhound Bus Line, silver bus w/black wheels, lettering on sides, pr **$85.00**
Heinz, clear glass teardrop shape w/flat front, back & bottom, chrome top, name on red emblem, pr...........**$8.00**
Luzianne Coffee, plastic, Mammys standing w/serving trays, brown skin w/gold shirts & green skirts, F&F Die Works, pr **$175.00**
Precision Sweepers, plastic, 1 red & 1 white canister-type sweeper w/name, pr (w/box marked A Gift For You)..**$20.00**
Samovar Dry Vodka, clear glass bottles w/paper labels, gold screw caps, pr...**$18.00**
Stokley's Kissin' Strawberries, plastic, red strawberries w/facial features, 1 w/eyes open & 1 w/eyes closed, pr (w/box)...**$10.00**
Tappan, plastic, Harvest Gold stove w/black trim, 1976, 1-pc...**$28.00**
Tipo Sherry & Ruby Port, clear glass bulbous bottles on round plastic bases, screw caps, paper labels, pr **$10.00**

Animals, Birds and Fish

Bear holding 2 fish, ceramic, dark brown bear w/light accents seated w/2 bright blue fish, 3-pc **$15.00**

Bird-on-nest holder w/2 egg shakers, ceramic, lift bird from nest to reveal eggs, shades of brown, yellow & red, 4-pc..**$12.00**
Birds, ceramic, lg round heads & bodies w/flat bottoms, lg eyes w/black painted lashes, blue & yellow airbrushing, pr..**$8.00**
Birds, lustre, tan w/black wings, long yellow beaks & green topknots, flat bottoms, pr..**$15.00**
Birds in eggshells, lustre, white birds w/gold beaks, white & gold eggshells, center handle, 3-pc.....................**$12.00**
Buffalo, ceramic, realistic stride w/heads down, black & gray airbrushing, black horns & eyes, scarce, pr..........**$15.00**
Bulls, ceramic, realistic walking pose, brown & gray airbrushing on white, pr...**$12.00**
Butterflies on flowers, ceramic, pink butterflies w/black trim on double yellow flowers w/green leaves, pr......**$12.00**
Camel w/cargo, porcelain, resting, realistic color w/black hooves, multicolored cargo shakers, 3-pc **$18.00**
Cat minstrels, ceramic, standing upright, she w/bow on head & playing flute, he in black top hat & playing accordion, pr..**$20.00**
Cat sitting atop eight ball, ceramic, deep tan w/pink ears & neck bow, blue eyes, pr **$10.00**
Cat w/ball of yarn, ceramic, yellow & white cat sitting upright hugging pink ball of yarn, pr...................**$12.00**
Cat watching fish in bowl, ceramic, white cat on yellow plaid base eyeing fish in round globe on yellow plaid base, pr **$25.00**

Cats, green plastic with white ears, paws and bows, 2¾", $22.00.

Cats w/neck bows, ceramic, sitting upright, yellow w/black trim, pink bow w/eyes closed, blue bow w/eyes open, pr...**$8.00**
Cats w/neck bows, pot metal, sitting upright, 1 white w/pink ears & blue bow, 1 black w/pink ears & red bow, pr **$12.00**
Cats w/umbrellas & sunglasses, ceramic, white w/black, yellow & maroon trim, blue eyes, pr........................**$15.00**
Choosie in doghouse, ceramic, others in series are: Sad Sack; Weary; Happy; Grouchy; Dreamie; Shootie, pr....**$25.00**
Clams, ceramic, open shells, painted shades of brown, cream & black, pr..**$8.00**
Cow holding milk can, ceramic, lime green cow w/blue eyes holding white milk can w/facial features, pr........**$10.00**
Cows, ceramic, standing w/heads turned to the side, white w/black spots, light brown hooves, pr **$8.00**

Crow & scarecrow, ceramic, free-standing black crow w/scarecrow in airbrushed tattered clothes, pr....**$22.00**

Dog w/bone, ceramic, beige dog w/lg blue eyes sitting upright holding white bone w/facial features, pr...............**$12.00**

Donkey cart w/jugs, ceramic, amber cart & donkey w/exaggerated features, 2 amber jugs marked Little Brown Jugs, 3-pc..**$10.00**

Donkeys, ceramic, seated w/heads up, cartoon-like features w/pink airbrushing & lg black eyes, pr **$15.00**

Duck couple, ceramic, black w/yellow bills & feet dressed in red & white hats, neckties & bows, pr **$20.00**

Duck couple kissing, ceramic, dressed wearing hats, flat bottoms, solid white, 1-pc.............................**$12.00**

Elephants, ceramic, dressed in circus attire, 1 w/raised trunk & the other w/raised foot, dark gray airbrushing, pr...**$18.00**

Elephants, ceramic, playing baseball, white w/multicolored trim, catcher seated w/trunk up, batter on grassy base, pr **$45.00**

Elephants, ceramic, standing upright, cartoon-like w/dark gray airbrushing on white, closed eyes, red smile, pr........**$8.00**

Fish, ceramic, exaggerated features, 1 green w/brown top fin, 1 yellow w/green top fin, black eyes looking up, pr **$8.00**

Fish in a creel holder, ceramic, dark multicolored fish shakers upright in caramel-colored wicker basket, 3-pc.....**$15.00**

Foxes w/long sleek bodies, ceramic, brown over white airbrushing, pr................................**$15.00**

Frogs smoking pipes, ceramic, dressed seated upright w/pipes in mouths, pr............................**$18.00**

Gorillas, ceramic, 1 waving w/pink open-mouth smile & the other frowning, white w/black trim, pr **$10.00**

Hippos, ceramic, seated w/mouths open, light beige w/pink tongues, black hooves, eyes looking up, pr.........**$12.00**

Hippos, ceramic, standing w/mouths closed, dark gray airbrushing on white, black eyes, red nostrils & mouths, pr..**$12.00**

Kangaroo mother w/twins in pouch, ceramic, reddish brown on white, lg black & blue eyes w/painted lashes, 3-pc ..**$18.00**

Leopards, bone china, resting female & standing male w/realistic features, yellow & white w/black spots, Relco, pr.....**$15.00**

Lions, bone china, realistic, resting female & standing male, brown & black airbrushing over tan, Relco, pr....**$15.00**

Lions w/fur trim, ceramic, cartoon-like seated male & female, brown & tan airbrushing, blue eyes, Norcrest Furland, pr.....................................**$15.00**

Monkey hanging from palm tree, ceramic, white monkey w/dark brown airbrushing hanging by 1 arm, pr ..**$12.00**

Monkey in car, ceramic, gray & white w/green hat & green & yellow vest, green airbrushed car, pr...................**$25.00**

Monkey lying on banana, ceramic, baby monkey w/lg blue eyes & brown airbrushing on yellow & brown banana, pr...**$24.00**

Mouse couple, ceramic, fully clothed in Beatrix Potter style, he seated & she standing w/basket, pr..................**$25.00**

Owls on a tray, ceramic, black & yellow w/multicolored accents, round fruit-type tray w/leaves, 3-pc **$8.00**

Ox pulling hay wagon on tray, ceramic, brown & white ox w/black hip straps, yellow hay in tan wagon w/black trim, 3-pc...**$15.00**

Parakeets on a branch, plastic, shades of green, 3-pc..**$12.00**

Penguins, wood, Salty & Peppy, bowling-pin type natural bodies w/flat bottoms, painted features, applied beaks, hats, pr..**$8.00**

Pig couple, wood, sitting upright, natural w/painted features, applied ears, snouts & legs, pr.............................**$10.00**

Pigs playing leapfrog, ceramic, white pigs w/pink airbrushed ears dressed in multicolored clothes, yellow neck bows, pr...**$12.00**

Pigs sleeping, ceramic, 1 draped over the other, solid pink w/black trim, pr..............................**$10.00**

Rabbit heads in garden, ceramic, white heads w/brown features positioned in holes on green garden napkin holder, 3-pc.................................**$18.00**

Rabbits, wood, flat-sided, natural w/black painted features, pr..**$8.00**

Rattlesnake nodder, head & tail shakers sit in coiled body, pink, blue & teal design, 3-pc **$18.00**

Scottie dogs, ceramic, sitting upright, 1 dark gray & 1 reddish brown airbrushing on white, glancing eyes, 1-pc..**$12.00**

Sea horses, ceramic, metallic gold, pr.......................**$15.00**

Seal balancing ball on nose, ceramic, black seal w/red & white ball, 2-pc.......................................**$18.00**

Seals, metal, metallic gold, pr........................**$12.00**

Squirrels, ceramic, long sleek bodies, brown airbrushing on white, yellow eyes, pink ears, pr **$15.00**

Starfish, ceramic, yellow & blue w/dark red, pr.........**$10.00**

Tigers performing on circus balls, ceramic, tigers on red, white & blue striped balls, pr................**$20.00**

Toucans, ceramic, black & white w/yellow beaks, wings partially spread, pr..**$12.00**

Turkeys, ceramic, soft shades of airbrushed brown, yellow & green on white w/deep rose waddles, black painted trim, pr..**$10.00**

Vulture & cactus, ceramic, black, white & caramel airbrushed vulture, green cactus on caramel base, pr............**$25.00**

Worm leaving pear, ceramic, pear w/realistic airbrushed colors, green leaf, gray worm w/head upright, pr....**$18.00**

Black Americana

Bald head w/slice of watermelon, ceramic, black skin w/black googly eyes, red smile, seedless watermelon, pr **$45.00**

Bellhop w/suitcase, ceramic, standing, black skin & suit w/red hat, mouth & trim, light caramel suitcase stands alone, pr.**$95.00**

Boy on whale, ceramic, brown-skinned boy in red shorts rides atop whale, 2-pc.............................**$90.00**

Boy seated on bale of cotton, ceramic, black skin w/white shirt & blue overalls, bale slightly airbrushed, 1955, pr **$95.00**

Boy w/watermelon slice, ceramic, seated w/lg slice in lap, reddish brown skin, watermelon w/red shaded to white, pr...**$40.00**

Chef couple, ceramic, standing holding spoons, black skin & clothing w/pink aprons & hats, side-glancing eyes, pr........**$35.00**

Chef couple, ceramic, whimsical standing pose w/cake & pie, black skin w/movable eyes, strong colors w/white, Enesco, pr..**$145.00**

Chefs, ceramic, figures shaped like clothespins w/flat bottoms, brown skin, white hats w/S&P, Napco #K2218 A, pr **$75.00**

Chefs, ceramic, 1 lifting tray, other w/bottle & mug, black skin, white uniforms, 1 red & 1 white hat, pr......**$95.00**

Clown & seal w/ball, ceramic, multicolored, pr..........**$80.00**

Couple, chalkware, standing, he w/cane & hand in pocket, she w/hand on hip & holding flower, white, yellow & blue, pr.............**$45.00**

Couple dancing, ceramic, dressed in colorful tropical attire, lady in fruit turban, he w/ruffled sleeves & pants, pr.............**$28.00**

Couple seated in peanut shell, ceramic, reddish brown skin w/white clothing, red dots on dress, white peanut shell, 3-pc.............**$125.00**

Couple seated on separate stumps, ceramic, Porgy & Bess type, she holding fan, he w/legs crossed, dark brown skin, pr.............**$125.00**

Couple standing under palm tree on tray, ceramic, she w/hands on hips, he showing open hands, brown skin, red lips, 3-pc.............**$115.00**

Gents in bowler hats, chalkware, standing w/hands in pockets, black-skinned w/multicolored clothing, newer, pr.....**$55.00**

Gents in fezes, wood, black bead heads & bodies wearing natural fezes w/stripes, white painted grass skirts, no arms, pr.............**$20.00**

Liza & Rastus, wood, flat-sided figures w/painted features, names lettered on front, pr.............**$25.00**

Mammy, ceramic, 1 standing w/bowl, other bent over/lifting bowl, white w/red aprons, yellow bandannas, Design 50, pr.............**$35.00**

Mammy, chalkware, standing w/hand on hip, black-skinned, red dress w/white apron, yellow bow on white head scarf, pr.............**$55.00**

Mammy & Chef, ceramic, he w/spoon & wearing hat, she w/hands on hips & no hat, pastel clothing, marked Salt & Pepper, pr.............**$90.00**

Mammy & chef, ceramic, standing, he holding spoon, she showing petticoat, black skin, white clothes w/red & blue trim, pr.............**$75.00**

Mammy & chef, ceramic, standing holding spoons, she w/hands on hips, solid black w/gold trim, pr.....**$45.00**

Mammy & chef heads, ceramic, airbrushed brown skin w/goggly eyes, red lips, she in red scarf, he in white hat, pr.............**$90.00**

Mammy & chef heads, ceramic, he winking, she sticking out tongue, reddish brown skin w/red airbrushing on hats, pr.............**$65.00**

Mammy & gent, ceramic, hugging, chubby figures w/reddish brown skin, multicolored clothing, pr.............**$70.00**

Mammy & gent, chalkware, standing, he holding hat, she w/hands folded in front, brown-skinned, yellow & red clothes, pr.............**$45.00**

Mammy carrying 2 baskets, ceramic, wicker baskets on shoulder carrier, brown skin, black dress w/red pinafore, 3-pc.............**$95.00**

Mammy sitting cross-legged, chalkware, hands behind hips, black skin, white dress w/orange or green dots & trim, pr.............**$45.00**

Minstrels, bisque, 1 seated w/guitar, other standing w/drum, black skin, no shirts, colorful tropical native garb, pr.............**$35.00**

Native & grass hut, ceramic, he standing in red cape & gold jewelry, white hut w/brown stripes & red shield, pr.............**$45.00**

Native boy & girl flirting, ceramic, he resting on elbows, she w/legs bent back, reddish brown skin, white lips, pr .**$55.00**

Native boy w/alligator, ceramic, brown-skinned boy standing w/hands on hips, green alligator w/mouth open looking up, pr.............**$65.00**

Pickaninny on potty, ceramic, Japan, 1930s, pr..........**$70.00**

Red-cap w/suitcases, ceramic, standing on oval base w/suitcase in each hand, brown skin, blue jacket & red pants, 3-pc.............**$95.00**

Winking chef and cook babies in basket, ceramic, $95.00.

Character

Andy Panda & Miranda, ceramic, characters carrying 6-sided shakers w/silver tops, names on bases, 1950s, pr ...**$200.00**

Barney Google and Snuffy Smith, chalkware, 1940s, $45.00.

Cat & the Fiddle, ceramic, gray cat w/black features holding brown oversized fiddle, pr.............**$20.00**

Charlie Brown & Lucy, ceramic, seated on blue sofa w/sandwich & cup, Willitts Design, newer, 3-pc.............**$65.00**

Cow & the moon, ceramic, yellow half-moon w/facial features, white cow w/black spots, standing, pr.......**$25.00**

Dish & the Spoon, ceramic, white dish head w/features & black lower body, white spoon w/features & yellow body, pr.............**$30.00**

Donald Duck, ceramic, seated w/head turned sideways, white w/red hat & trim, black eyes, yellow bill & feet, 1940s, pr.............**$45.00**

Donald Duck, ceramic, singing Donald on round marked bases, Dan Brechner, 1960s, pr, minimum value.**$100.00**

Donald Duck, porcelain, seated, pastel airbrushing w/black glancing eyes, Leeds China, 1940s, pr.................**$45.00**

Donald Duck & Goofy, ceramic, Donald w/carton of milk & Goofy w/yellow apple on round bases, newer, pr..**$25.00**

Donald Duck & Ludwig Von Drake, ceramic, multicolored figures on round bases w/names, Brechner, pr, minimum value **$100.00**

Donald Duck singing, ceramic, blue hat & jacket w/red bow tie, Brechner, 1960s, pr, minimum value **$100.00**

Dorothy & the Scarecrow w/Lion & the Tin Man from the Wizard of Oz, ceramic, 50th anniversary, Clay Art, 1989, pr..................**$25.00**

Dumbo, chalkware, seated looking up, pink w/features & trim, pr.................**$25.00**

Figaro the cat (Pinocchio), standing, black & white w/yellow eyes, red ears, nose & mouth, 4¾", pr **$125.00**

Garfield & Odie, ceramic, Garfield dressed as pilgrim w/musket, yellow Odie w/bug eyes, ears up & tongue out, w/box, pr **$95.00**

Goose & the golden egg, ceramic, white goose w/metallic gold trim, metallic gold egg, pr **$18.00**

Hare & the Tortoise, ceramic, white rabbit leaning sideways w/pink ears & black features, reddish brown turtle, pr **$15.00**

Hickory Dickory Dock mouse & clock, ceramic, gray mouse fits atop amber grandfather's clock w/black trim, pr **$20.00**

Humpty Dumpty, plastic, red w/yellow hat, pr **$25.00**

Humpty Dumpty, porcelain, seated on brick wall, white w/delicate facial features, blue & yellow clothes, Clay Art, pr **$25.00**

Jack & Jill, porcelain, Jill w/bucket & Jack standing at well, pr.................**$35.00**

Jonah & the Whale, ceramic, Jonah figure fits inside of gray whale, pr **$45.00**

King Kong holding airplane & Empire State Building, ceramic, black gorilla & white building, Sarsaparilla, pr **$18.00**

Knothead & Splinter, ceramic, carrying white 6-sided shakers, names on bases, Walter Lantz, 1950s, pr, minimum value.................**$200.00**

Little old lady & shoe, porcelain, lady in black hat w/rose jacket, brown dress & green apron, white & orange shoe, pr.................**$35.00**

Ma & Old Doc (Paul Webb cartoon characters), porcelain, she in white w/green dots, yellow scarf & apron, Imperial, pr **$110.00**

Mary & her lamb, porcelain, brown-haired Mary in green, white & pink pinafore w/basket, lamb kicking up hind legs, pr.................**$35.00**

Mickey & Minnie, ceramic, seated & appear to be in conversation, she in red w/white dots, he in red w/yellow shoes, pr.................**$95.00**

Mickey & Minnie chefs, ceramic, Mickey in blue shirt, white hat & apron, Minnie in pink dress & hat, white apron, pr **$45.00**

Mickey Mouse, ceramic, in yellow car waving, Good/WD, 1989, 2-pc.................**$20.00**

Mickey Mouse & Pluto, ceramic, Mickey standing in yellow shirt, red shorts & brown shoes, Pluto seated w/mouth open, pr.................**$25.00**

Miss Piggy & Kermit the Frog, ceramic, Kermit the magician ready to saw through Miss Piggy in trunk, 2-pc ..**$95.00**

Old King Cole, ceramic, multicolored king standing in gray stuffed chair, 2-pc **$35.00**

Pinocchio & girl, porcelain, pr **$100.00**

Pinocchio & Jiminy Cricket, ceramic, Pinocchio seated w/Jiminy Cricket standing & waving, pr...........**$125.00**

Pluto, ceramic, seated upright, white w/red ears & trim, black eyes, 1940s, pr **$55.00**

Pluto, ceramic, 1 upright w/bone & spoon w/other balancing plate & cup on nose, unauthorized, Japan, pr, minimum value **$100.00**

Pluto & doghouse, ceramic, yellow Pluto seated in front of blue dish w/white bone, white doghouse marked Pluto, pr.................**$22.00**

Princess & the Frog, ceramic, princess in blue w/yellow hair leans over to kiss frog on tree stump, Clay Art, pr..**$18.00**

Rabbit in the Hat, ceramic, white rabbit w/shades of pink & brown & brown trim atop black top hat, pr **$20.00**

Raggedy Ann & Andy, ceramic, seated w/legs apart, simplified style, white w/red hair, black & green trim, pr......**$32.00**

Red Riding Hood & Big Bad Wolf, porcelain, Red Riding Hood in red cape & blue dress, Wolf in bed, pr............**$18.00**

Robinson Crusoe, ceramic, multicolored figure seated on raft w/name, 2-pc **$25.00**

Sylvester & Tweety Bird, ceramic, Sylvester standing upright licking his chops & looking down on Tweety in nest, pr.................**$22.00**

Tasmanian Devil, ceramic, Taz's head on crate marked Danger, 2-pc.................**$35.00**

Thumper, chalkware, seated position w/hands on knees, white w/pink on ears, black features, pr.............**$25.00**

Wizard of Oz Witches, ceramic, Wicked Witch in black w/green face, Good Witch in pink, Clay Art, 1989, pr **$18.00**

Woody & Winny Woodpecker, ceramic, on lettered bases, carrying white shakers w/silver tops, 1958, pr, minimum value **$200.00**

Ziggy & his dog, ceramic, white Ziggy w/yellow shirt, white dog w/blue nose, Universal Press Syndicate, pr ..**$45.00**

Fruit, Vegetables and Other Food

Apples, ceramic, realistic w/red shading to white at bottom, brown stems, glossy, Kessler, pr **$12.00**

Banana bongo player & dancer, ceramic, tropical banana figures w/facial features peeled halfway down, pr..**$65.00**

Banana people, bisque, banana bunches w/facial features & green stems on blue seated bodies w/red shoes, pr.**$25.00**

Bananas in baskets, ceramic, bananas w/winking facial features & leaves for arms in wicker baskets, airbrushed, pr.................**$25.00**

Bananas on tree hanger, ceramic, airbrushed, satin finish, 3-pc **$10.00**

Celery people, ceramic, celery jeads w/cartoon features on human bodies w/yellow sweaters, brown pants & black shoes, pr.................**$25.00**

Corn, ceramic, chubby ears in upright position w/silks peeled away in front exposing pale yellow corn, newer, pr.................**$12.00**

Eggplant & cabbage football referees, ceramic, black & white striped shirts, whistles around neck, pr **$65.00**

Eggplants, ceramic, realistic looking in upright position, med purple w/lighter purple leaves & stems, Kessler, pr **$12.00**

French bread, ceramic, loaf torn in half, pr **$10.00**

Grape people, ceramic, purple grape clusters standing upright w/facial features, eyes glancing up, pr....**$15.00**

Grapes, colored glass, blue cluster & clear cluster w/brown plastic stems, inverted funnels inside, pr..............**$15.00**

Ice-cream cones, ceramic, chocolate, lying on sides, pr..**$10.00**

Latke people, ceramic, potatoes w/facial features & silver spoons & forks for arms, marked Latke Salt/Pepper, pr **$35.00**

Onion heads on a tray, ceramic, smiling faces w/big black eyes & green leaf tray, pr **$25.00**

Orange & lemon, colored glass, realistic versions w/green plastic leaves, inverted funnels inside, pr.............**$15.00**

Pea pods on leaf tray, ceramic, realistic open pods showing row of peas on green leaf & vine tray, 3-pc........**$15.00**

Pea-pod couple, ceramic, standing, closed pods w/cartoon features, wire stands are arms & legs, marked S/P, pr..**$35.00**

Pear & apple, colored glass, blue pear & red apple w/white plastic leaves, inverted funnels inside, pr.............**$15.00**

Pie a la mode, scoop of vanilla ice cream atop wedge of pie, 2-pc...**$15.00**

Pineapple heads, ceramic, pr...**$15.00**

Radishes, ceramic, 3 round bright red radishes w/2-tone green compacted tops, glossy, newer, pr **$10.00**

Red peppers, ceramic, realistic, standing upright, green leaves at bottom, pr..**$15.00**

Strawberries, ceramic, realistic, upright w/green stems at bottom, yellowish tops, pr **$15.00**

Toast & toaster, ceramic, slice of toast w/white toaster, pr **$12.00**

Tomato & green pepper baseball players, ceramic, 1 w/bat & 1 w/glove, pr **$65.00**

Tomatoes in basket, ceramic, $20.00.

Tomatoes on a tray, ceramic, realistic red tomatoes w/green stems on green & yellow handled tray, 3-pc **$18.00**

Turkey in pan, ceramic, golden brown turkey in yellow pan, 2-pc...**$12.00**

Watermelon & peach tennis players, ceramic, watermelon & peach heads on human bodies, Napco, 1956, pr.....**$65.00**

Watermelon halves, ceramic, upright w/flat bottoms, centers lightly airbrushed in red w/brown seeds, Kessler, pr **$12.00**

Holidays and Special Occasions

Birthday cake & slice of cake on plate, ceramic, white w/red & pink decoration, metallic gold server & fork, pr......**$16.00**

Christmas boots, ceramic, red w/white cuffs, gold stars atop turned-up toe, holly design on sides, gold heel, pr..**$10.00**

Christmas-caroling angels, ceramic, eyes closed, blue head scarf & red gloves, red neck scarf & green gloves, pr **$18.00**

Christmas choir children, porcelain, red robes & gold trim, she w/hymn book & he w/candle, pr **$16.00**

Christmas elephants standing upright in Santa hats, ceramic, 1 w/eyes closed & the other w/glancing eyes, pr.....**$15.00**

Christmas house & Santa, ceramic, red & white cartoon-type house w/curved sides & roof, sleek red & white Santa, pr **$15.00**

Christmas snowman couple, ceramic, she w/wreath & tipping yellow hat, he w/candy cane & tipping black hat, pr **$16.00**

Christmas snowman jack-in-the box, ceramic, white decorated snowman w/candy cane in white box w/blue edge trim, 2-pc **$20.00**

Christmas tree & gift, ceramic, green tree w/multicolored decorations, white box w/red splotches, pr.........**$20.00**

Christmas trees, ceramic, presents on white round bases beneath white stylized decorated trees w/garland, pr...**$18.00**

Easter bunny & egg, ceramic, white bunny seated upright w/side-glancing eyes, pink accents, white decorated egg, pr...**$12.00**

Halloween jack-o'-lanterns, ceramic, pumpkins w/black smiling features, black witches' hats w/green & yellow trim, pr **$12.00**

Halloween pumpkin & witch on broom, ceramic, bright orange pumpkin w/no features, green witch w/orange hat, pr **$15.00**

Halloween skull & hand, ceramic, white skull w/black accents, white hand standing upright w/black nails, pr...........**$22.00**

Mother's Day, ceramic, white cylinder shape w/Mother & floral decoration above verse, gold trim, pr **$10.00**

St Patrick's Day couple, ceramic, standing, dressed in green w/Hummel-type features, shamrocks on dress & base, pr...**$15.00**

Santa and Mrs. Claus, ceramic, $10.00.

Thanksgiving pilgrim children, ceramic, cartoon-like features w/girl waving & boy holding gun, pr.................**$18.00**

Thanksgiving turkey & pilgrim girl, ceramic, girl in white & orange, colorful turkey w/red head & waddle, Napco, pr..**$18.00**

Wedding couple on bench, porcelain, wooden bench, kissing pose, 3-pc..**$18.00**

Household Items

Alarm clocks, ceramic, round & footed, white w/red numbers & hands, pr..**$8.00**

Chair & fireplace, ceramic, black chair w/caramel-colored fireplace embossed God Bless Our House, pr **$8.00**

Coffee mills, pot metal, 1 white & 1 black w/painted decorations, pr **$12.00**

Coffeepot & teapot, porcelain, white hobnail w/applied red cherries & green leaves, gold trim, pr...................**$10.00**

Coffeepots, pot metal, 1 white & 1 black w/painted floral decorations, tall angled spouts, dome lids, pr......**$12.00**

Irons standing upright, pot metal, 1 black & 1 white w/painted Dutch designs on bottoms, pr..........................**$12.00**

Light bulbs, ceramic, resting on sides, pr **$6.00**

Rolling pin & scoop, ceramic, white w/floral decoration, pr..**$15.00**

Stove & refrigerator, ceramic, white w/red trim, 1940s, pr..**$15.00**

Stove w/coffeepot & teakettle, red clay, black cast-iron stove holder w/gold trim, black coffeepot & tea kettle, 3-pc..**$15.00**

Televisions, wood, early natural cabinet model w/black trim, pictures cowboy w/horse & ice skater, pr.............**$8.00**

Thimble & spool of thread, ceramic, black & white, pr.**$12.00**

Watering cans, porcelain, light beige w/pink & blue applied flowers, gold trim, pr..**$10.00**

Miniatures

Book & hurricane lamp, ceramic, black book w/maroon bookmark, hurricane lamp w/white chimney & maroon & gold base, pr..**$35.00**

Box of chocolates & flowers, ceramic, pr....................**$35.00**

Car & stop sign, ceramic, purple car w/red & white stop sign, pr..**$45.00**

Coffeepot & cup of coffee, ceramic, bulbous pot w/metallic gold handle, white cup & saucer, pr....................**$25.00**

Cowboy boots, ceramic, brown w/gold trim, pr........**$35.00**

Diary w/stack of letters, ceramic, pink diary w/gold trim, white lettered tied w/pink bow, pr.......................**$35.00**

Dog & dish of food, ceramic, white dog w/gold & brown dish, pr **$35.00**

Dustpan & whisk broom, ceramic, green dustpan & yellow whisk broom w/gold trim, pr **$30.00**

Fish & creel, ceramic, white fish w/dark gray airbrushing, caramel-colored creel w/closed lid & gold clasp, pr.................**$35.00**

Garden gate & hat, ceramic, rose-covered archway over open gate, white hat w/blue accents, pr........................**$35.00**

Graduate's cap & diploma, ceramic, black hat & white scroll w/gold trim, pr..**$30.00**

Ice skates & sled, ceramic, white w/brown airbrushing & gold trim, pr **$35.00**

Ice-cream maker & dish of ice cream, ceramic, brown bucket w/metallic gold crank & top, ice cream w/gold fork, pr..**$30.00**

Mouse & trap, ceramic, gray mouse w/pink ears, white trap w/yellow cheese, both w/metallic gold trim, pr ..**$30.00**

Outhouses w/antenna ceramic, brown & black w/half-moons on doors, only 1 w/antenna, pr **$30.00**

Pancakes & syrup, ceramic, plate of pancakes on white plate w/metallic fork & knife, syrup jar w/yellow top, pr ..**$30.00**

Pixies, porcelain, seated, 1 w/legs apart & 1 w/hands clasped around bent knee, green costumes w/red hats, pr..**$20.00**

Raccoon, ceramic, seated w/legs apart, dressed as bandits, pr **$20.00**

Raccoons, ceramic, in playful pose, realistic colors, pr .**$20.00**

Sausage & eggs on plate, ceramic, 2-pc **$30.00**

Shaving mug & brush, ceramic, speckled mug w/foaming top, upright brush, pr..**$30.00**

Sherlock Holmes' hat w/pipe & book w/magnifying glass, ceramic, pr..**$65.00**

Wedding ring & license, ceramic, ring in black box w/white interior & gold trim, white license w/black lettering, pr..**$35.00**

People

Alcatraz convict heads, ceramic, scruffy heads on black & white striped shoulders w/prisoner numbers & lettering, pr..**$25.00**

Amish couple, ceramic, standing, she w/basket, he w/rake, white w/light blue airbrushing, dark blue & black accents, pr **$10.00**

Angel & devil, ceramic, serene angel in white w/gold trim standing w/hands together, red devil w/gold trim standing, pr..**$20.00**

Angels, ceramic, standing, 1 dressed as chambermaid holding pitcher, soap & towel, 1 playing concertina, pr **$12.00**

Angels, ceramic, standing w/eyes closed, hands clasped, white w/blue wash over hair & gowns, white wings, black trim, pr..**$12.00**

Beach boy & girl, porcelain, standing w/balls, 1940s look w/1-pc suits, striped tops w/belted waists, brown bases, pr **$28.00**

Bellhop holder w/egg shakers on tray, porcelain, white eggs on blue tray held by bellhop in red suit & hat, 3-pc **$75.00**

Bellhops, porcelain, standing w/tilted heads & holding cards, red hats & green jackets w/white pants, Germany, pr......**$45.00**

Bowler & bowling pins, porcelain, bowler in black pants & pink shirt w/black ball, white w/black bowling pins, newer, pr **$25.00**

Boy & girl babies, bisque, seated in diapers w/outstretched arms & looking up, girl w/bow in hair, pr...........**$20.00**

Brewmeister w/2 kegs on tray, ceramic, he standing w/mug & towel over arm in front of 2 upright kegs, 3-pc **$15.00**

Bullfighter & bull, ceramic, red bull w/gold hooves charging red cape held by bullfighter in black & white, 2-pc..**$18.00**

Canadian Mounties, ceramic, standing w/arms behind back, tan hats, red jackets & blue pants, marked S&P, pr **$25.00**

Chef couple, porcelain, standing side by side, white w/multicolored trim, I'm Salt/I'm Pepper lettered on aprons, 1-pc **$22.00**

Chefs, ceramic, Salt w/hat over 1 eye & holding pan & spoon, Pepper holding pan w/both hands, white w/black shoes, pr **$20.00**

Civil War soldiers, wood, marked North & South, painted blue & gray, Japan, pr...............................**$15.00**

Clown on drum, ceramic, pink & blue clown in black hat lying on back w/feet up on tan & brown drum, pr.........**$22.00**

Clowns, ceramic, Emmet Kelly type standing w/cane & 1 arm behind back, red jackets, brown hats, plaid pants, pr ..**$28.00**

Clowns, ceramic, 1 dancing atop the other bent over w/flat back, white w/striped & dotted costumes, pr **$18.00**

Clowns, chalkware, heads on blue bulbous bodies w/white collars & buttons down front, red hats, pr **$18.00**

Colonial couple on base, porcelain, he in long coat & ruffled shirt, white w/brown hair & blue trim, ovoid base, 3-pc **$25.00**

Couple, wood, half figures w/cartoon-type painted features, he in black bowler hat & red bow tie, she in red hat, pr **$12.00**

Couple before & after, ceramic, cartoon-like, he reverses from smiling to frowning, she from smiling to scolding, pr **$25.00**

Couple before & after, ceramic, realistic, reverses from young bride & groom to elderly couple, pr.....................**$25.00**

Couple in roadster, lustre, she driving w/hand attached to steering wheel, he in back seat, pr **$55.00**

Couple kissing, ceramic, seated on wooden bench, he w/ankles crossed, she w/book, pastel colors w/black trim, 3-pc **$10.00**

Couple kissing, porcelain, seated, facing each other, he in red, she in blue & green, 1-pc **$22.00**

Couple w/baby, ceramic, standing in nightclothes appearing to have had little sleep, white w/blue & red trim, pr ..**$25.00**

Cowboy & horse, porcelain, cowboy standing in tan chaps, green vest & yellow scarf, white horse w/black & gold trim, pr...**$20.00**

Cowboy couple, ceramic, standing, he in chaps w/guns drawn, she w/whip, yellow & black, flat bottoms (no feet), pr..**$15.00**

Drunk & lamppost, ceramic, man wearing black top hat & jacket in drunken pose on base w/Say When sign on lamppost, 2-pc **$15.00**

Dutch couple, ceramic, standing, white w/black & metallic gold trim, pr **$15.00**

Dutch girls, lustre, standing w/hands under white aprons, red dresses w/yellow trim, metallic gold hats, pr.........**$45.00**

English couple, ceramic, standing, he in black & blue, she in black & yellow w/white apron & hat, Josef Originals, pr **$25.00**

Eskimo & igloo, ceramic, Eskimo w/allover rose glaze standing in front of white igloo, pr...............................**$15.00**

Eskimo couple, ceramic, standing, white chubby figures w/black hair showing around furry hoods, 1949, pr................**$10.00**

Farmer w/wheelbarrow, pot metal, red wheelbarrow w/black contents & white flower painted on side, red & black farmer, pr...**$8.00**

Fisherman, ceramic, English-type, standing, wearing yellow slicker & hat, w/pipe, fish on pole, restaurant name, pr **$45.00**

Fisherman & wife, porcelain, Old Salty standing w/pipe & other hand in pocket, wife standing w/hands on hips, Germany, pr...**$45.00**

Football & basketball players, ceramic, cartoon figures w/red noses on grassy bases, Napco, 1958, pr **$35.00**

Frontiersmen in canoe, ceramic, wearing coonskin caps & plaid shirts, reddish brown canoe w/airbrushing, 3-pc **$25.00**

Garden couple, ceramic, standing, he in black overalls & straw hat holding a trowel, she in pink dress w/red apple, pr..**$12.00**

Geisha girls, porcelain, half-figures w/green kimonos, multicolored trim, pr..**$18.00**

Gnomes, ceramic, 1 standing & waving, other lying on side & waving, brown clothing & hats, pink skin w/white beards, pr..**$20.00**

Grandma in rocking chair, pot metal, red chair w/grandma in blue robe w/white collar & hat, red knitting in lap, pr...**$8.00**

Hawaiian couple, ceramic, she dancing the hula, he seated playing the ukulele, pr...**$15.00**

Hawaiian girls, ceramic, 1 dancing while other is standing playing the ukulele, multicolored w/black hair, pr........**$18.00**

Hillbilly & jug, ceramic, leaning back on elbows, black pants & hat w/yellow shirt, white beard, brown & white jug, pr...**$12.00**

Hillbilly couple in barrels, ceramic, airbrushed colors, barrels marked Salt & Pepper, satin finish, pr **$12.00**

Hillbilly w/2 jugs, ceramic, standing w/jugs on arms, rose shirt w/blue pants, black hat & beard, grassy base, 3-pc ..**$18.00**

Indian busts, ceramic, Seminole couple w/realistic features, she w/long black braids, he w/yellow feathers, pr **$15.00**

Indian couple, ceramic, standing, cartoon-like, he w/potbelly, winking & w/thumb pointing at her, she w/eyes closed, pr **$12.00**

Indian couple kissing, ceramic, facing each other, tan outfits, he in full headdress, she in black pigtails, pr **$25.00**

John F Kennedy, ceramic, seated in rocking chair marked JFK, brown hair, gold trim, 2-pc...........................**$50.00**

Lady w/crooked smile, ceramic, matronly half-figure in green dress w/purse on arm, pr **$10.00**

Latin couple kissing, ceramic, seated on wooden bench, he in sombrero & serape, she w/yellow flower in black hair, 3-pc **$15.00**

Laurel & Hardy heads, ceramic, black hats w/gold trim, brown hair, rose-colored bow ties, pr **$95.00**

Laurel & Hardy heads on tray, composition, brown-tone w/black hats, black bow ties w/white dots on tray, Greece, 3-pc...**$95.00**

Mail couple, ceramic, boy & girl standing w/bags marked US Mail, gray & white, he w/black shoes, she w/red, pr **$18.00**

Mailman & mailbox, ceramic, he standing w/mail bag over shoulder, mailbox on post marked US Mail, blue uniform, pr **$15.00**

Mexican couple, hand-painted clay, seated, he in sombrero, drab shades of brown, green & tan, pr...................**$6.00**

Mexican couple, red clay, stylized standing figures w/holes for facial features, partially glazed, pr...................**$15.00**

Mexican w/baskets, ceramic, taking a siesta, yellow tones w/multicolored accents, 3-pc...............................**$25.00**

Milkman & cow, ceramic, milkman in red & blue holding a case of milk bottles while running from disgruntled cow, pr...**$35.00**

Oriental couple, ceramic, seated, she w/fan, he playing string instrument, white & black w/gold trim, pr...........**$12.00**

Oriental couple, ceramic, standing, she w/head tilted, he w/head turned, yellow & blue w/black accents, gold trim, pr...**$15.00**

Oriental man lifting urn, ceramic, man in black jacket & red pants looking up while lifting yellow & white urn, 1-pc...**$25.00**

Photographer w/camera, ceramic, boy looking through early camera on tripod, he in yellow vest & striped pants, pr..**$20.00**

Pirates, ceramic, $12.00.

Pixies on mushrooms, ceramic, 1 seated Indian style, the other seated in casual pose, black outfits w/yellow legs, pr...**$8.00**

Railroad conductors, ceramic, standing, 1 checking watch & the other w/hand on hip & holding towel, blue & white, pr...**$30.00**

Scarecrow couple kissing, ceramic, seated on wooden bench, yellow hats w/black trim, blue tattered clothing, 3-pc...**$15.00**

Spanish couple, ceramic, standing in black, red & yellow costumes, Josef Originals, pr.......................................**$25.00**

Street cleaner & 2-wheeled cart, ceramic, standing w/broom over shoulder, white w/black accents, pr.............**$15.00**

Sunbathing couple, ceramic, portly figures lying on rafts w/faces covered by newspaper & hat, newer, pr..**$18.00**

Will Rogers bust w/scrolls, ceramic, painted bust w/brown lettering on white scroll, pr....................................**$28.00**

Winking man, ceramic, round bald-headed cartoon head atop seated body in black jacket & brown pants & shoes, 2-pc...**$70.00**

Souvenir

Connecticut, ceramic, vertical containers w/split image of state showing points of interest & activities, pr ...**$10.00**

Disneyland, ceramic, Mark Twain & Columbia riverboats, 1950s, pr...**$45.00**

Florida, ceramic, alligators standing upright w/hands on hips in colorful T-shirts marked Florida, pr.................**$12.00**

Florida, ceramic, coconut heads w/cartoon facial features, white & black crossed eyes, Florida embossed on foreheads, pr...**$8.00**

Florida, ceramic, pink flamingos standing on green marked bases, 1 w/head down & the other w/head toward back, pr...**$20.00**

Hollywood, ceramic, famous white Hollywood letters on green & gold 2-pc hillside, Sarsaparilla, pr...........**$15.00**

Honolulu Hawaii, ceramic, white open book w/brown lettering & graphics, brown ukulele, pr.......................**$28.00**

Idaho, ceramic, potato heads w/smiling features wearing crowns marked Idaho, bases marked Spud Salt/Pepper, pr...**$10.00**

Kennebunkport Maine, ceramic, black locomotive & tender w/name in white script, glossy, lg, pr **$25.00**

Missouri, ceramic, light beige mule w/black trim, black Show Me & Missouri lettered on light beige state shape, pr **$15.00**

Mormon Temple & Tabernacle, ceramic, white buildings w/light gray & yellow airbrushing, names on bases, pr **$25.00**

Mount St Helen, ceramic, mountain before & after eruption, gray, Zoeller, 1980, pr **$40.00**

Niagara Falls, ceramic, newlyweds in car marked Just Married, Niagara Falls Canada, 2-pc.....................**$28.00**

Ottawa Canada, circular image of Mounty on leather-type die-cut leaf holder w/2 plastic shakers, 3-pc........**$35.00**

Pennsylvania, ceramic, waving teddy bears w/white neck bows seated on marked tree stumps, pr.................**$8.00**

San Francisco, ceramic, trolley cars marked San Francisco, yellow tops & bottoms w/blue-green sides, pr **$10.00**

Springfield Ill, ceramic, ax w/lettering on white handle, blue-gray head, brown airbrushed log, pr **$18.00**

Texas, porcelain, thimble shape w/Texas lettered over various points of interest, pr...**$8.00**

Toronto Canada, ceramic, white open book w/green lettering & graphics & blue maple leaf, pr......................**$28.00**

Washington DC, lustre, Washington Monuments on round grassy bases, name on side, pr............................**$18.00**

Yellowstone Park/Old Faithful, ceramic, tall square shapes marked S & P on tops, lettering & wildlife on front, pr...**$15.00**

Miscellaneous

Baseball & glove, ceramic, light green w/brown stitching, pr...**$15.00**

Boxing gloves, ceramic, brown, pr **$10.00**

Cigarette lighter & pack of cigarettes, ceramic, pr......**$20.00**

Confederate & Union officers' hats, ceramic, light blue Confederate & dark blue Union w/Stars & Stripes emblem, pr...**$12.00**

Cottages, ceramic, white w/blue roofs & shutters, painted-on tree & shrubs, Kessler, pr....................................**$12.00**

Dice, ceramic, black w/white spots, pr **$12.00**

Feet w/painted toenails standing upright, ceramic, white w/big toes spread apart, red nails, pr....................**$10.00**

Galleons, lustre w/metallic gold trim, pr....................**$15.00**

Golf balls on tees, ceramic, white balls on metallic gold tees, pr....................**$10.00**

Graters, ceramic, realistic versions w/handles atop, gray air-brushing w/red S&P, newer, pr **$18.00**

Gum-ball machines, plastic, realistic looking w/clear globes, red tops & bases w/black fronts, newer, pr **$18.00**

Gun & holster, ceramic, yellow 6-shooter w/yellow holster, newer, pr....................**$18.00**

Lock & key, ceramic, gray padlock w/yellow key, pr..**$15.00**

Mandolin & violin, ceramic, white fronts w/multicolored trim, brown sides, pr **$8.00**

Milk shake & milk shake maker, ceramic, Sarsaparilla, pr....................**$16.00**

S&P, ceramic, white letter figures w/gold outline trim, Camark Pottery, 1950s, pr **$18.00**

Spoon & fork couple dancing, pink spoon & fork heads w/facial features dressed in evening attire, pr **$40.00**

Stagecoach, ceramic, white passenger compartment sits atop brown wheel base w/driver's seat, 2-pc..............**$15.00**

Streetcars, ceramic, marked Desire, shades of green, gold & brown, pr....................**$10.00**

Tankards, ceramic, replicas of Bavarian tankards w/lids, natural w/blue & brown, partially lustered, pr............**$8.00**

Tire pump & flat tire, ceramic, brown pump & gray tire, pr **$25.00**

Toothbrush & tube of toothpaste, ceramic, pr **$15.00**

Trash cans w/clown faces, ceramic, white w/red knobs on lids, smiling faces w/red noses, bow ties, pr **$10.00**

Schoop, Hedi

One of the most successful California ceramic studios was founded in Hollywood by Hedi Schoop, who had been educated in the arts in Berlin, Germany. She had studied not only painting but sculpture, architecture, and fashion design as well. Fleeing Nazi Germany with her husband, the famous composer Frederick Holander, Hedi settled in California in 1933 and only a few years later became involved in producing novelty giftware items so popular that they were soon widely copied by other California companies. She designed many animated human figures, some in matched pairs, some that doubled as flower containers. All were hand painted and many were decorated with applied ribbons, sgraffito work and gold trim. To a lesser extent, she modeled animal figures as well. Until fire leveled the plant in 1958, the business was very productive. Nearly everything she made was marked.

If you'd like to learn more about her work, we recommend *The Collector's Encyclopedia of California Pottery* by Jack Chipman.

Advisors: Pat and Kris Secor (See Directory, California Pottery)

Candle holder, 2-sided lady, 1 side w/eyes open, 1 closed, incised mark, 1962, 12½" **$375.00**

Dish, leaf form w/angel figurine, maroon w/gold trim...**$75.00**

Figurine, ballet dancer, pink w/platinum mottling, 10", from $135 to....................**$150.00**

Figurine, German girl, light blue dress, holding skirt out, 11"....................**$110.00**

Figurine, girl, brunette, yellow & white dress w/blue flowers, holds yellow basket, w/sticker, 9½", EX+.............**$70.00**

Figurine, girl, short yellow dress, white apron, 2 baskets behind, flower-strewn base, 12" **$115.00**

Figurine, girl in blue, skirt to side, basket on head, 12" ..**$98.00**

Figurine, girl sitting before open book, yellow & white dress w/rose on front, 9" **$50.00**

Figurine, Hula girl, 11¾", $165.00. (Photo courtesy of Pat and Kris Secor.)

Figurine, lady in long pink & black dress w/umbrella, tall.**$90.00**

Figurine, lady sitting w/skirt that flares up to form bowl, aqua & pink w/silver trim, 10x13" **$225.00**

Figurine, Oriental boy w/basket, yellow & black w/dragon ..**$45.00**

Figurine/planter, Oriental boy & girl, he w/oboe, black & white, 10½", pr **$150.00**

Figurines, dancers, arms crossed above their heads, long white gowns w/gold trim, 11", pr, from $130 to **$145.00**

Figurines, Oriental couple with buckets, 11½" and 13", from $125.00 to $150.00 for the pair.

Flower holder/lamp base, Colbert, yellow dress, purple hat, necktie & baskets, underglazed painted mark, 1940s, 11½".....**$125.00**

Lamps, Oriental man & lady, gold trim, pr **$400.00**

Lamps, slender ladies (matching), green w/gold trim, pr .**$495.00**

Scouting Collectibles

Collecting scouting memorabilia has been a popular hobby for many years. Through the years, millions of boys and girls have been a part of this worthy organization founded in

England in 1907 by retired Major-General Lord Robert Baden-Powell. Scouting has served to establish goals in young people and help them to develop leadership skills, physical strength, and mental alertness. Through scouting, they learn basic fundamentals of survival. The scouting movement came to the United States in 1910, and the first World Scout Jamboree was held in 1911 in England. If you would like to learn more, we recommend *A Guide to Scouting Collectibles With Values* by R.J. Sayers (ordering information is given in the Directory).

Advisor: R.J. Sayers (See Directory, Scouting Collectibles)

Boy Scouts

Bank, scout w/staff, gold, standing pose w/coin & pack ..**$40.00**
Book, Boy Scout Handbook, August 1961, 6th edition, Norman Rockwell cover, 480 pages, VG **$10.00**
Book, Boy Scout Handbook, 1915-27, 2nd edition, VG ..**$20.00**
Book, Boy Scout Handbook, 1927-40, 3rd edition, VG ...**$12.00**
Book, Cub Scout Handbook, 1930-40, Wolf, Bear or Lion, VG, each..**$8.00**
Book, Patrol Leader Handbook, 1929-40, VG **$10.00**

Books, Bear Cub Scout and Lion Cub Scout, 1948, 2nd edition, $5.00 each.

Clutch pin, 1960 National Jamboree, Official, stick back..**$3.00**
Coin, Civic Good Turn, brass, 1974 ....**$2.00**
First Aid Kit, flat tin, Bauer & Black, 1930s **$7.00**
Game, The Game of Scouting, McLoughlin, 1912, set of 50 cards..**$30.00**
Medal, Explorer Silver Award, type 2, wings, gold ribbon, 1958-68 ....**$100.00**
Merit badge, Cooking, 6 variations, from $2 to..........**$10.00**
Neckerchief, 1937 Jamboree, Official, blue or red, VG, each...**$40.00**
Neckerchief, 1957 National Jamboree, cotton, 4 variations ..**$8.00**
Patch, Asst Scoutmaster, light green twill on tan, 1920, square **$40.00**
Patch, District Commissioner, gold wreath, 1960, 3" dia, VG .**$10.00**
Patch, jacket patch & neckerchief; 1960 Jamboree, Official, set of 3...**$30.00**
Patch, National Order of the Arrow Conference, 1969 .**$12.00**
Patch, Scoutmaster, type 1, brown eagle on tan, 1920, square **$75.00**
Patch, 1937 Jamboree, Official, felt, 3", not reproduction ..**$65.00**
Patch, 1950 Jamboree, Official, canvas, 3" dia, VG.....**$20.00**

Patch, 1953 National Jamboree, Official Issue, twill, 3" ..**$15.00**
Patch, 1960 National Staff, gold wreath, 3" dia, VG....**$15.00**
Patch, 1981 National Jamboree, Official, solid emblem ..**$4.50**
Patch, 1989 National Jamboree, Youth Services Staff....**$5.00**
Pocket watch, Waltham, scout scene on front, 1940, working...**$35.00**
Pocket watch, 1969 National Jamboree, 3 variations, 3" dia .**$6.00**
Pocketknife, Camillus, 2-blade fish fillet, stainless steel blade etched: American Wildlife, 1980-82, 11" long.........**$7.50**
Pocketknife, Imperial, 4-blade utility, 1940, VG..........**$15.00**
Pocketknife, Imperial Knife Associated Companies, 4-blade, standard w/shackle & metal shield, black plastic handle **$17.50**
Pocketknife, Remington #RS3333, 4-blade utility, 1930s, VG...**$50.00**
Pocketknife, Ulster, 1-blade, bone handle w/shield, 1937-41 ....**$15.00**
Pocketknife, Ulster, 4-blade utility, 1950-60, VG.........**$10.00**
Toy, lead scout figures, Barclay, set of 4.....................**$80.00**
Toy, lead scout figures, set of 5 w/mold.....................**$60.00**
Toy, Scout Machine Gun, gun on caisson w/wood wheels, 1915 ....**$75.00**
Watch, Timex, wind-up type, scout logo on front, 1940-60...**$14.00**
Watch fob, coin silver, scout & crossed rifles, 1930, VG..**$30.00**
Watch fob, First Class Scout, gold wash, 1920-30, VG...**$45.00**
Watch fob, Tenderfoot Scout, silver, 1930-40, VG.......**$30.00**

Girl Scouts

Blouse & skirt, white blouse w/printed design, brown skirt, M **$20.00**

Book, Girl Scout Handbook, 1955, hardcover, VG, $15.00.

Book, Girl Scout Handbook, 1963, new edition, hardcover, 510 pages, VG...**$12.50**
Bookends, Girl Scout, composition, 1940, pr..............**$15.00**
Calendar, 1959, color photos, complete, 16x10", EX ..**$20.00**
Camera, Kodak, bellows type, green, 1930s...............**$75.00**
Camera, Kodak, box type, 1930-40, VG......................**$35.00**
Camera, Kodak Official Instant-Load, 1968 ....**$15.00**
Camera, Senior Girl Scout, Imperial Mark 27, 3-way flash, molded plastic case, w/pocket viewer, neck strap, 1960s..**$45.00**
Card, 1916 Official GSA Membership, signed by Low, VG ..**$45.00**
Coin, Girl Scouts of America 60th Anniversary, golden finish, 1972...**$9.00**
Compass, Silva System, Official, 1950s-60s, MIB........**$25.00**

Cookie cutters, green handles, complete set, 1950.....**$20.00**

Doll, Girl Scout uniform, green shorts, Uneeda, 1960-64, 15" **$30.00**

Doll, Patsy Ann, Girl Scout uniform, fully jointed, Effanbee, 1959, 15" **$45.00**

Dress, green & white w/2 pockets, green plastic buttons, USA strip on sleeve, 1960s, EX............................**$20.00**

First-aid kit, Johnson & Johnson, Official, 3-color lithograph on tin, empty, EX...**$20.00**

Flashlight, Brownie Scout, metal w/chrome finish & Brownie logo, 1960s, 3" long, EX.......................................**$40.00**

Hat, gray-green w/emblem on front, MIB **$28.00**

Mess Kit, EX in worn box, $28.00.

Patch, GSA First Class, on tan square, VG..................**$40.00**

Patch, Merit Badge, uncut khaki cotton w/embroidered black border, red & green flower embroidered in center .**$22.00**

Pin, Eaglet, 10k gold, type 2, 1930s..........................**$150.00**

Pin, Tenderfoot, type 1, crude clasp, 1920, VG **$15.00**

Pocketknife, Kutmaster, green grips w/gold trefoil emblem, lanyard loop, 1950s, EX **$20.00**

Sash, 1970s era w/18 merit badges, 7 patches & 4 service stars **$28.00**

Sweater, Brownie, brown wool w/insignia patch, EX ..**$10.00**

Tin, GSA Peanut Brittle, tin top, 1930s **$30.00**

Uniform, light speckled-green top, skirt, belt & hat, 1930, set **$50.00**

Uniform, Mariner Girl Scout, blue, middy w/white braid, long sleeves w/cuffs, pleated skirt, 1953-60...............**$150.00**

Uniform, tan top & bloomers w/patches, 1920s, set...**$150.00**

Sebastians

These tiny figures were first made in 1938 by Preston W. Baston and sold through gift stores, primarily in the New England area. When he retired in 1976, the Lance Corporation chose one hundred designs which they continued to produce under Baston's supervision. Since then, the discontinued figures have become very collectible.

Baston died in 1984, but his son, P.W. Baston, Jr., continues the tradition.

The figures are marked with an imprinted signature and a paper label. Early labels (before 1977) were green and silver foil shaped like an artist's palette; these are referred to as 'Marblehead' labels (Marblehead, Massachusetts, being the location of the factory), and figures that carry one of these are becoming hard to find and are highly valued by collectors.

Newsletter: *Sebastian Miniatures Collectors Society News*
Cyndi Gavin McNally
c/o Lance Corp.
321 Central St.
Hudson, MA 01749; 508-568-1401 or FAX 508-568-8741

America Salutes Desert Storm, painted **$160.00**

America's Home Town, Smith's **$60.00**

Best in the Midwest, paperweight.............................**$85.00**

Charles Dickens, blue label **$35.00**

Christmas Morning..**$30.00**

Dachshund **$160.00**

Davy Crockett **$160.00**

Diedrich Knickerbocker, Marblehead era **$50.00**

First at Bat..**$35.00**

For You...**$40.00**

Gathering Tulips **$100.00**

House of 7 Gables, Marblehead era...........................**$60.00**

Jack & Jill, blue label..**$35.00**

John Smith & Pocahontas **$125.00**

Mr Sheraton..**$220.00**

Nathaniel Hawthorne **$160.00**

Oliver Twist and Beetle, Marblehead label, $50.00.

Paul Revere **$45.00**

Peace & Brotherhood **$45.00**

Phoebe **$135.00**

Pilgrims, Marblehead label **$50.00**

Scrooge **$25.00**

Scrooge, Marblehead **$50.00**

Soap Box Derby...**$45.00**

Son of the Desert..**$200.00**

Stagecoach, marblehead era **$65.00**

Statue of Liberty, AT&T **$85.00**

White House, gold...**$100.00**

Sewing Collectibles

Once regarded simply as a necessary day-to-day chore, sewing evolved into an art form that the ladies of the 1800s took much pride in. Sewing circles and quilting bees became popular social functions, and it was a common practice to take sewing projects along when paying a visit. As this evolution took place, sewing tools became more decorative and were often counted among a lady's most prized possessions.

Of course, 19th-century notions have long been collectible, but there are lots of interesting items from this century as well. When machine-made clothing became more readily available after the 1920s, ladies began to lose interest in home sewing, and the market for sewing tools began to drop off. As a result, manufacturers tried to boost lagging sales with novelty tape measures, figural pincushions, and a variety of other tools that you may find hard to resist.

Retail companies often distributed sewing notions with imprinted advertising messages; these appeal to collectors of advertising memorabilia as well. You'll see ads for household appliances, remedies for ladies' ills, grocery stores, and even John Deere tractors.

For further information (about figural pincushions) we recommend *Collector's Guide to Made in Japan Ceramics* by Carole Bess White; *Sewing Tools and Trinkets* by Helen Thompson, *Antique and Collectible Thimbles and Accessories* by Averil Mathis; *Advertising and Figural Tape Measures* by L-W Book Sales; and *Toy and Miniature Sewing Machines* by Glenda Thomas (Collector Books).

Advisor: Marge Geddes (See Directory, Sewing Collectibles)

Club: Thimble Collectors International
6411 Montego Rd.
Louisville, Ky 40228

Newsletter: *Thimbleletter*
Lorraine M. Crosby
93 Walnut Hill Rd.
Newton Hgts., MA 02161; Subscription: $12 per year, sample issue available for $2

Newsletter: *Thimble Guild*
Wynneth Mullins
P.O. Box 381807
Duncansville, TX 75138-1807

Charm, scissors, brass over base metal, stork figural, miniature, 1½" **$18.00**
Charm, sterling thimble w/gold wash **$12.50**
Crochet hook, covered metal, resembles fountain pen .**$65.00**
Darner, black egg w/sterling repousse handle, child size, 4½", VG **$50.00**
Darner, black glass egg w/sterling repousse handle, P&B mark, EX **$95.00**
Darner, blown milk glass, ball shape w/ridged handle, 6" **$68.00**
Darner, dark green blown glass, ball-shaped working end, 5¼", EX **$68.00**
Darner, glove; sterling w/rope pattern on handle, end removes to access needle compartment, VG **$140.00**
Darner, mold-blown blue glass foot form **$27.50**
Darner, wooden egg w/handle, opens for access to thread, 7" **$30.00**
Emery, red strawberry w/sterling leaf top **$60.00**
Emery, satin cat figural, red inside ears, marked Japan ..**$55.00**

Hem gauge, sterling heart at top w/open swirls & repousse roses, metal 3" ruler w/slide lock, 4½" **$80.00**
Kit, dark blue Bakelite w/rhinestone chips, bullet style w/thread reel **$20.00**
Knitting gauge, celluloid, Good Shepherd Yarns advertising, flat, 6½" **$15.00**
Knitting guards, celluloid, black hoof shapes w/fur trim, 1¾", pr **$55.00**
Knitting needles, unmarked sterling, 14", pr **$95.00**
Measure, brass, teapot form w/ornate handle, self-winding, 1½" **$200.00**
Measure, celluloid, basket of fruit, 1", Japan **$85.00**
Measure, celluloid, dog standing on log, black & gray, 2¼" **$70.00**
Measure, celluloid, dog w/front feet on ball, brown, white & pink, 2" **$78.00**
Measure, celluloid, pig in red boot figural **$50.00**

Measure, celluloid pig, 2½" long, $75.00.

Measure, celluloid, tan ship, 2¼" **$50.00**
Measure, celluloid, winking white pig, flowers painted on his back **$78.00**
Measure, plastic, Hoover advertising on gray, 1½" dia ...**$32.00**
Mending kit, Lydia Pinkham, light green cardboard tube, no portrait **$7.50**
Needle book, Army-Navy heroes, Teddy Roosevelt portrait **$25.00**
Needle book, paper coal bucket shape, Waltham Coal, VG **$20.00**
Needle book, Sewing Society, Victorian children **$12.50**
Needle book, Worcester Salt, salt-box form, 2½" **$15.00**
Needle case, celluloid, umbrella figural w/floral decor, top opens **$60.00**

Needle case, Piccadilly Imported Gold Eye, 3x5¼", $18.00.

Needle case, sterling w/engraving, narrow & flat, 2¼"...**$80.00**

Needle dispenser, green tube, marked Broadway **$25.00**

Needle packet box, leather w/gold tooling, Jos Rodgers advertising, pull-off cap.................................**$18.00**

Pin box, Fernware, sycamore wood w/pull-off cover, 1¼", EX **$85.00**

Pin holder, Mauchline ware, disk shape w/New Hampshire lighthouse, blue fabric center, VG.........................**$85.00**

Pincushion, bird perched beside cushion, tan lustreware with red and blue details, Japan, 3¼", $18.00.

Pincushion, brown fabric & white scalloped shell w/hand-painted florals, 1¼"...................................**$36.00**

Pincushion, brown velvet fabric between 2 shells, Shaker style, 1½"...**$65.00**

Pincushion, nodder turtle, base metal w/antique off-white finish, glass eyes **$25.00**

Pincushion, vegetable ivory base w/cushion top, ivory thread post, 3½"..**$57.50**

Pincushion on stand, Tunbridge ware, center post, 1¼"...**$80.00**

Scissors, base metal, stork figural, 3½"........................**$20.00**

Scissors, base metal w/lg loops & sm blades, marked China, early 20th century, 2¼"..................................**$35.00**

Scissors, gilt over metal, allover embossed decor, French style, M **$75.00**

Scissors, sterling, allover repousse swirls, 4½"...........**$55.00**

Scissors, sterling w/daisy at base of shanks & at base of tops **$90.00**

Scissors sharpener/pin holder, metal..........................**$20.00**

Silk winder, mother-of-pearl, flat square w/rounded corners, 1½"...**$85.00**

Tatting shuttle, mother-of-pearl, 2½x¾", EX **$85.00**

Tatting shuttle, sterling, engraved diamond & rays, marked Webster...**$145.00**

Tatting shuttle, Tartan ware, McFarlane, slender, 2¾x½" ..**$195.00**

Thimble, brass w/red enamel over engine-turned design, jade green stone top................................**$85.00**

Thimble, case, mahogany, acorn form w/grooves around a pull-off cap, 2¾"..**$65.00**

Thimble, sterling, anchor decor, Goldsmith, Stern Co ..**$85.00**

Thimble, sterling, Atlantic Cable style w/applied scalloped border, unmarked **$70.00**

Thimble, sterling, chased roses & leaves, unmarked..**$75.00**

Thimble, sterling, cherubs w/garlands, Simons........**$230.00**

Thimble, sterling, daisies overlapping, diagonal indentations **$50.00**

Thimble, sterling, diagonal indents on ten panels, Simons **$40.00**

Thimble, sterling, egg & dart pattern, Simons............**$25.00**

Thimble, sterling, farm scene, Simons **$75.00**

Thimble, sterling, fleur-de-lis, scrolled rim, Waite Thresher.**$65.00**

Thimble, sterling, heavy applied chased border, unmarked.**$48.00**

Thimble, sterling, horseshoes & 4-leaf clover **$175.00**

Thimble, sterling, linked circles, pie-crust rim **$45.00**

Thimble, sterling, Louis XV rim, Ketcham & McDougal ..**$45.00**

Thimble, sterling, orchid band, VG.............................**$80.00**

Thimble, sterling, plain band, scrolled rim, Simons....**$27.50**

Thimble case, silver, walnut figural, Unger Bros, unlined, chatelaine loops, 1", EX **$85.00**

Thimble holder, Mauchine ware, bottle form w/Catskill NY Mountain House scene, w/thimble post inside, 4" .**$175.00**

Thimble holder, sweet grass, EX **$30.00**

Thimble purse, brass, egg shaped w/embossed decor, 1¾", w/2" brass chain **$80.00**

Thimble stand, base metal, Deco-style standing lady, 2½"...**$75.00**

Thimble stand, base metal, elephant w/trunk up, w/post, 2x3"...**$68.00**

Thimble stand, porcelain, owl, painted flowers, 2½".**$25.00**

Thread holder, sterling w/applied fleur-de-lis on cover & lower portion, initials on top.............................**$165.00**

Thread winder, mother-of-pearl fish figural **$125.00**

Shawnee Pottery

In 1937, a company was formed in Zanesville, Ohio, on the suspected site of a Shawnee Indian village. They took the tribe's name to represent their company, recognizing the Indians to be the first to use the rich clay from the banks of the Muskingum River to make pottery there. Their venture was very successful, and until they closed in 1961, they produced many lines of kitchenware, planters, vases, lamps, and cookie jars that are very collectible today.

They specialized in figural items. There were 'Winnie' and 'Smiley' pig cookie jars and salt and pepper shakers; 'Bo Peep,' 'Puss 'n Boots,' 'Boy Blue,' and 'Charlie Chicken' pitchers; Dutch children; lobsters; and two lines of dinnerware modeled as ears of corn.

Values sometimes hinge on the extent of an item's decoration. Most items will increase by 50% to 200% when heavily decorated and gold trimmed.

Not all of their ware was marked Shawnee; many pieces were simply marked USA with a three- or four-digit mold number. If you'd like to learn more about this subject, we recommend *The Collector's Guide to Shawnee Pottery* by Duane and Janice Vanderbilt; *Shawnee Pottery, Identification & Value Guide,* by Jim and Bev Mangus; and *Collecting Shawnee Pottery* by Mark E. Supnick.

Advisor: Rick Spencer (See Directory, Shawnee)

Club: Shawnee Pottery Collectors' Club
P.O. Box 713
New Smyrna Beach, FL 32170-0713; Monthly nationwide newsletter. SASE (c/o Pamela Curran) required when requesting information. Optional: $3 for sample of current newsletter

Bank, bulldog, from $150 to..................................$175.00
Candle holders, cornucopia form, marked USA, 3½", pr....$15.00
Candle holders, embossed leaves, marked USA, pr....$24.00
Casserole, bowl w/basketweave, lid in form of fruit, gold trim, marked Shawnee 83 ....$135.00
Creamer, elephant, pink ears & mouth, marked Pat USA..$35.00
Creamer, Puss 'n Boots, green & yellow, marked Shawnee 85 ....$55.00
Creamer, Sunflower, lg flower on white, marked USA..$45.00
Figurine, bear, tumbling $60.00
Figurine, donkey, unmarked, 6½"..............................$12.00
Figurine, Pekingese..$60.00
Figurine, Scotty w/sling, unmarked, 5¼"....................$16.00
Figurine, squirrel..$60.00
Flowerpot, Bow Knot, w/saucer, marked USA, 4½"....$6.00
Flowerpot, embossed diamond decor, marked USA 484, 4" $8.00
Jardiniere, embossed lappets, marked, USA, 2½" $8.00
Jardiniere, embossed tulips, marked USA, 3½"..........$10.00
Lamp base, Champ the Dog $20.00
Lamp base, flamenco dancers, no mark $45.00
Match holder, Fern pattern, marked USA $80.00

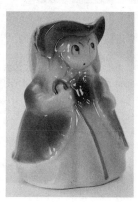

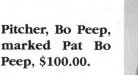

Pitcher, Bo Peep, marked Pat Bo Peep, $100.00.

Pitcher, Charlie Chicken, marked Pat Chanticleer, minimum value $80.00
Pitcher, Flower & Fern on jug shape $50.00
Pitcher, Pennsylvania Dutch, bright flowers on white ball form, marked USA 64 ....$95.00
Pitcher, Smiley the Pig, peach or red flower, marked Pat Smiley, minimum value..$90.00
Pitcher, Smiley the Pig, red flower w/gold, marked Pat Smiley USA, minimum value..$210.00
Pitcher, Tulip, bright tulip flowers on white ball form, marked USA $95.00
Planter, boy & stump, marked USA 533 ....$12.00
Planter, cat & saxophone, marked USA 729................$55.00
Planter, cat beside highchair, marked USA 727..........$55.00
Planter, deer & fawn beside stump, gold trim, marked Shawnee 669..$28.00
Planter, dog in boat, marked Shawnee 736................$22.00
Planter, donkey & basket, gold trim, marked USA 671...$35.00
Planter, donkey & cart, gold trim, #538, USA............$30.00
Planter, duckling, marked Shawnee USA 720..............$26.00
Planter, elephant w/basket on back, white w/blue trim, marked USA $20.00
Planter, elf shoe, gold trim, marked Shawnee 765......$20.00

Planter, embossed shells form scalloped rim, marked Shawnee USA 154, 6"..$10.00
Planter, fawn, open back, no mark, 9" $10.00
Planter, giraffe, marked Shawnee 521......................$30.00
Planter, girl standing beside urn, marked Shawnee 718..$30.00
Planter, goose, marked USA....................................$10.00
Planter, lamb, gold trim, marked USA 724 ....$35.00
Planter, mouse & cheese, gold trim, marked USA 705 ..$32.00
Planter, pixie beside lg open flower, unmarked $15.00
Planter, pony, curly mane & tail, marked Shawnee 506 ...$40.00
Planter, poodle on bicycle w/cart behind, marked USA 712 ....$32.00
Planter, rabbit, ears up, marked USA $16.00
Planter, rocking horse, marked USA 526 ....$24.00
Planter, Southern girl, marked USA, 6" $10.00
Planter, squirrel at stump, marked USA $10.00
Planter, stagecoach, marked USA J545P.....................$35.00
Planter, terrier & doghouse, marked Shawnee USA....$22.00
Salt & pepper shakers, Charlie Chicken, gold trim, sm, pr, from $60 to..$80.00

Salt and pepper shakers, chefs, from $20.00 to $25.00.

Salt & pepper shakers, cottages, marked USA 9, sm, pr..$250.00
Salt & pepper shakers, Dutch boy & girl, gold trim, lg, pr.$60.00
Salt & pepper shakers, Dutch boy & girl, lg, pr $50.00
Salt & pepper shakers, Farmer Pig, sm, pr..................$30.00
Salt & pepper shakers, flowerpots, gold trim, sm, pr.$45.00
Salt & pepper shakers, milk cans, gold w/decals, sm, pr ..$50.00
Salt & pepper shakers, Muggsy, blue bow, lg, pr.....$150.00
Salt & pepper shakers, Muggsy, sm, pr $65.00
Salt & pepper shakers, owls, green eyes, sm, pr........$30.00
Salt & pepper shakers, Smiley, blue bib, gold & decals, lg, pr $200.00
Salt & pepper shakers, Smiley, peach bib, gold trim, sm, pr $95.00
Salt & pepper shakers, Smiley & Winnie, clover bud decor, lg, pr, from $125 to..$140.00
Salt & pepper shakers, Smiley & Winnie, sm, pr $55.00
Salt & pepper shakers, Smiley Pig, pink, lg, pr..........$80.00
Salt & pepper shakers, Sunflower, flower on white, range size, pr $50.00
Sugar bowl, bucket w/lid form, marked Great Northern USA 1042 ....$55.00
Sugar bowl, Pennsylvania Dutch, jug form, open.......$65.00
Teapot, Blue Leaves, marked USA $45.00
Teapot, Clover Bud, marked USA $100.00

Teapot, embossed flower on green, marked USA **$35.00**
Teapot, Embossed Rose, solid gold, marked USA, minimum value **$200.00**
Teapot, Granny Ann, gold trim, marked Pat Granny Ann USA **$225.00**
Teapot, Granny Ann, marked USA **$100.00**
Teapot, Tom Tom, plain, marked Tom the Piper's Son Pat USA **$100.00**
Teapot, Tulip, bright flower on white, marked USA...**$45.00**
Vase, embossed cornucopia, marked USA, 5" **$14.00**
Vase, embossed floral decor, marked USA 592, 8"......**$14.00**
Vase, embossed flower, double handles, marked USA, 5" ..**$12.00**
Vase, embossed flowers, marked USA 1268, 5" **$24.00**
Vase, embossed iris on fan shape, marked USA, 6"....**$18.00**
Vase, embossed Oriental figure, paper label, 12" **$24.00**
Vase, embossed philodendrons w/gold, marked Shawnee 805, 6½" **$40.00**
Vase, ribbed pitcher form, marked USA, 9" **$14.00**
Vase, rope handles, marked USA, 5½" **$12.00**
Vase, Swirl, marked USA, 5" **$14.00**
Vase, wheat w/gold trim, flared foot, marked, USA, 5" ..**$20.00**
Vase/planter, fish, marked USA 717 ....**$55.00**
Wall pocket, bow w/gold trim, marked USA 434 ....**$35.00**
Wall pocket, star form, marked USA **$25.00**

Corn Ware

Bowl, fruit; marked #92 ....**$40.00**
Bowl, mixing; marked #5, 5" **$25.00**
Bowl, mixing; marked #8, 8" **$35.00**
Bowl cereal; marked #94 ....**$45.00**
Butter dish, marked #72 ....**$50.00**
Casserole, marked #73, individual, from $60 to **$75.00**

Casserole, marked #74, large, $60.00.

Cookie jar, marked #66, from $200 to **$250.00**
Corn holder, marked #79 ....**$32.00**
Creamer, gold trim, marked USA, from $65 to **$75.00**
Creamer, marked #70 ....**$25.00**
Mug, marked #69 ....**$45.00**
Pitcher, white corn, gold trim, marked USA **$135.00**
Plate, marked #68, 10" **$36.00**
Platter, marked #96, 12" **$52.00**
Salt & pepper shakers, lg, pr **$30.00**
Salt & pepper shakers, sm, pr **$20.00**

Snack set, 4 mugs & 4 plates, MIB **$435.00**
Sugar bowl, white corn, marked USA, from $35 to....**$42.00**

Lobster Ware

Bowl, salad/spaghetti; marked 922 ....**$46.00**
Butter dish, lobster finial, marked Kenwood USA 927 .**$65.00**
Creamer jug, marked 921 ....**$50.00**
French casserole, stick handle, lobster finial, marked 904, 2-qt **$40.00**

Hors d'oeuvres holder, marked USA, 7¼", from $225.00 to $250.00.

Mug, lobster's claw forms handle, marked Kenwood USA 911, 8-oz **$95.00**
Relish, lobster finial, marked Kenwood USA 936, 5½" ...**$65.00**
Salt & pepper shakers, full body, marked USA, pr...**$120.00**
Sugar or utility jar, marked 907 ....**$26.00**

Valencia

Ashtray **$17.00**
Bud vase **$22.00**
Coaster **$17.00**
Creamer & sugar bowl, w/lid **$35.00**
Egg cup, from $14 to **$17.00**
Mustard jar, w/lid **$45.00**
Nappie, 9½" **$25.00**
Pie plate, 10½" **$25.00**
Pitcher, ball jug, marked USA **$40.00**
Pitcher, water, w/lid **$55.00**
Plate, chop; 15" **$36.00**
Plate, deep, 8" **$20.00**
Plate, 10" **$17.00**
Plate, 7¾" **$14.00**
Plate, 9¾" **$16.00**
Salt & pepper shakers, pr **$24.00**
Syrup **$48.00**
Teacup & saucer **$25.00**
Teapot, regular **$55.00**
Tray, utility **$28.00**

Sheet Music

Flea markets are a good source for buying old sheet music, and prices are usually very reasonable. Most examples can be bought for less than $5.00. More often than not, it is collected for reasons other than content. Some of the cover art was done by well-known illustrators like Rockwell, Christy, Barbelle, and Starmer, and some collectors like to zero in on their particular favorite, often framing some of the more attractive examples. Black Americana collectors can find many good examples with Black entertainers featured on the covers and the music reflecting an ethnic theme.

You may want to concentrate on music by a particularly renowned composer, for instance George M. Cohan or Irving Berlin. Or you may find you enjoy covers featuring famous entertainers and movie stars from the forties through the sixties. At any rate, be critical of condition when you buy or sell sheet music. As is true with any item of paper, tears, dog ears, or soil will greatly reduce its value.

If you'd like a more thorough listing of sheet music and prices, we recommend *The Sheet Music Reference and Price Guide* by Anna Marie Guiheen and Marie-Reine A. Pafik and *The Collector's Guide to Sheet Music* by Debbie Dillon.

After All the Good Is Gone, Conway Twitty, Conway Twitty photo cover, 1975 ....**$5.00**

Ain't It Kind of Wonderful, Gene Wilder, Movie: The World's Greatest Lover, Gene Wilder photo cover, 1977.....**$5.00**

All I've Got To Get Now Is My Man, Cole Porter, Movie: Panama Hattie, 1942 ....**$8.00**

Amado, Allan Roberts & Doris Fisher, Movie: Gilda, Rita Hayworth photo cover, 1946 ....**$10.00**

America, Stephen Sondheim & Leonard Bernstein, Movie: West Side Story, 1957....................**$5.00**

And Mimi, Jimmy Kennedy & Nat Simon, Blue Baron photo cover, 1947 ....**$5.00**

And This Is My Beloved, Robert Wright & Chet Forrest, Musical: Kismet, 1953 ....**$5.00**

Arizona Waltz, Rex Allen, Movie: Arizona Cowboy, Rex Allen photo cover, 1949 ....**$3.00**

Around the Corner, Gus Kahn & Art Kassel, Art Kassel photo cover, 1930 ....**$5.00**

At the Flying 'W,' Allie Wrubel, Elliot Lawrence photo cover, 1948....................**$3.00**

Aurora Waltz, Barlow, Pfeiffer cover artist....................**$10.00**

Ballad of Davy Crockett, George Gruns, Fess Parker photo cover **$5.00**

Barking Dog, Al Stillman, Crew Cuts photo cover, 1954 ..**$5.00**

Beyond the Reef, Jack Pitman, Bing Crosby photo cover, 1949....................**$3.00**

Big Man, Glen Larson & Bruce Belland, Donny Osmond photo cover **$5.00**

Blue Gardenia, Bob Russell & Lester Lee, Movie: The Blue Gardenia, 1943 ....**$3.00**

Blue Shadows on the Trail, Eliot Daniel & Johnny Lange, Movie: Melody Time, Disney, 1948 ....**$15.00**

Brazil, Bob Russell, Movie: Saludos Amigos, Disney, 1939.**$15.00**

Bridge Over Troubled Waters, Simon & Garfunkel photo cover, 1970 ....**$3.00**

By Candle Light, Cole Porter, Movie: You Never Know ..**$5.00**

By the Time I Get to Phoenix, Jim Webb, Glen Campbell photo cover, 1967 ....**$6.00**

Can't You Just See Yourself, Sammy Cahn & Jules Styne, Musical: High Button Shoes, 1948 ....**$5.00**

Carlotta, Cole Porter, Movie: Can Can, 1943....................**$5.00**

Chase Me I'm Single, Bert Grant, Florence Tempest photo cover, 1913 ....**$10.00**

Chi-Baba Chi-Baba, Perry Como photo cover, EX......**$10.00**

Close, Cole Porter, Movie: Rosalie, 1937....................**$5.00**

Coconut Grove, Harry Owens, Movie: Coconut Grove, 1938.**$5.00**

Come Out, Come Out, Wherever You Are?, Sinatra photo cover, 1944 ....**$4.00**

Corn Silk, Irving Kahal, Wayne King & Hal Bellis, Wayne King photo cover, 1940 ....**$3.00**

Cossack Love Song, George Gershwin, 1926 ....**$10.00**

Cupid & the Moon, Ward, Pfeiffer cover artist, 1908..**$15.00**

Darling Sue, Sterling, Harry Von Tilzer photo cover.....**$3.00**

Dawn, Mack David & Jerry Livingston, Jaye P Morgan photo cover **$5.00**

Day by Day, Crosby photo cover, 1945 ....**$4.00**

Delicious, George Gershwin, Movie: Delicious, Janet Gaynor photo cover, 1931 ....**$10.00**

Dime a Dozen, Cindy Walker, Sammy Kaye photo cover, 1949 ....**$3.00**

Don't Cha Go 'Way Mad, Al Stillman & Jimmy Mundy, Harry James photo cover, 1945 ....**$2.00**

Don't Cry Joe, Joe Marsala, Nick cover artist, 1940 ......**$3.00**

Don't Drink the Water, Williams & Gordon, Movie: Don't Drink the Water, Jackie Gleason photo cover, 1969 ....**$5.00**

Down Among the Sheltering Palms, James Brockman & Abe Olman, Pied Pipers photo cover, 1915....................**$5.00**

Down in the Depths, Cole Porter, Movie: Red, Hot & Blue, 1936....................**$5.00**

Dreams, Never More Than Dreams, Jose Valdez & Wilbur Chenoweth, Rudy Vallee photo cover, 1929............**$5.00**

Dreams, Sinatra photo cover, 1945....................**$4.00**

Dreamy Old New England, Marty Beck, Frank Capano & Max C Freedman, Vaughn Monroe photo cover, 1948...**$2.00**

Either It's Love or It Isn't, Roberts & Fisher, Movie: Dead Reckoning, Humphrey Bogart & Lizabeth Scott, 1946..**$10.00**

Eleventh Hour Melody, King Palmer & Carl Sigman, Al Hibbler photo cover, 1956....................**$3.00**

Enjoy Yourself, Guy Lombardo cover, 1948, VG+........**$7.50**

Everybody's Talkin', Fred Neil, Movie: Midnight Cowboy, Harry Nilsson photo cover, 1968 ....**$2.00**

Eyes of Blue, Stone & Young, Movie: Shane, Alan Ladd, Jean Arthur & Van Heflin photo cover, 1953 ....**$5.00**

Fairy Moon, Charles K Harris, Grace Edmonds photo cover, 1911 ....**$10.00**

Faithful Forever, Robin & Rainger, Movie: Gulliver's Travels, 1939 ....**$5.00**

Fine Romance, Fields & Kern, Movie: Swing Time, Astaire & Rogers photo cover, 1936....................**$10.00**

Flea in Her Ear, Cahn & Kaper, Movie: A Flea in Her Ear, Rex Harrison photo cover, 1968....................**$3.00**

For You, For Me, For Evermore, George Gershwin, 1941 ..**$5.00**

Forever & Ever, Malia Roasa & Franz Winkler, Perry Como photo cover, 1947 ....**$3.00**

From This Moment, Cole Porter, Musical: Out of This World, 1950....................**$3.00**

Gideon Bible, Steve Allen, Steve Allen photo cover, 1954..**$5.00**

Girl Upstairs, Alfred Newman, Movie: The Seven Year Itch, Marilyn Monroe photo cover, 1955 ....**$20.00**

Go Away Little Girl, Carole King, Donny Osmond, photo cover, 1962 ....**$5.00**

Going My Way, Bing Crosby photo cover, 1944, G **$5.00**

Golden Years, Movie: Houdini, Tony Curtis & Janet Leigh photo cover, 1953 ....**$5.00**

Goodnight, Irene, Huddie Ledbetter & John Lomax, Gordon Jenkins & the Weavers photo cover, 1950 ....**$3.00**

Great Divide, Gimbel & Schifrin, Movie: Bullitt, McQueen & Bisset photo cover, 1969 ....**$5.00**

Green Leaves of Summer, Webster & Tiomkin, Movie: The Alamo, John Wayne & Linda Cristal, 1960 ....**$5.00**

Guitar Boogie, Arthur Smith, Arthur Smith photo cover, 1946 ....**$5.00**

Gypsy, Billy Reid, Sammy Kaye photo cover, 1947 .....**$5.00**

Have I Told You Lately That I Love You, Scott Wiseman, Bing Crosby & the Andrew Sisters photo cover, 1946 ....**$10.00**

He's Got Me Hook, Line & Sinker, Pearl King, Dorothy Collins photo cover, 1956 ....**$5.00**

He's in Love, Wright & Forrest, Musical: Kismet, 1953 .**$5.00**

Heart & Soul, Loesser & Carmichael, Movie: A Song Is Born, 1938 ....**$5.00**

Heat Wave, Irving Berlin, Musical: Easter Parade, 1933 ....**$10.00**

Heaven Is a Raft on a River, Robert & Helen Thomas, Jane Pickens photo cover, 1954 ....**$5.00**

Here, There & Everywhere, Lennon & McCartney, Beatles photo cover, 1966 ....**$25.00**

Here I'll Stay, Lerner & Weill, Movie: Love Life, 1948 ..**$5.00**

Ho Ho Song, Red Buttons & Joe Darion, Red Buttons photo cover, 1953 ....**$5.00**

Holiday in Venice, Frank Magine, LeRoy Maule photo cover, 1930 ....**$5.00**

Home Cookin', Livingston & Evans, Movie: Fancy Pants, Hope & Ball photo cover, 1950 ....**$10.00**

Home on the Range, Nick Manoloff, Jackie Heller photo cover, 1935 ....**$5.00**

Hooray for Love, Leo Robin & Harold Arlen, Movie: Casbah, 1948 ....**$5.00**

How About You?, Freed & Lane, Movie: Babes on Broadway, 1941 ....**$3.00**

I Always Knew, Cole Porter, Movie: Something To Shout About, 1943 ....**$5.00**

I Beg of You, Elvis Presley, 1957 ....**$20.00**

I Believe, Jane Froman photo cover, 1953 ....**$3.00**

I Close My Eyes, Kaye & Reed, Dinah Shore facsimile signed photo cover, 1945 ....**$3.00**

I Don't Care If the Sun Don't Shine, Mack David, Tony Martin photo cover, 1949 ....**$3.00**

I Don't Know How To Love Him, Rice & Webber, Musical: Jesus Christ Superstar, 1970 ....**$5.00**

I Double Dare You, Shand & Eaton, Jerry Freeman photo cover, cover artist Starmer, 1937 ....**$5.00**

I Hate Men, Cole Porter, Musical: Kiss Me Kate, 1948 ..**$5.00**

I Have Dreamed, Rodgers & Hammerstein, 1951 ....**$3.00**

I Hear a Dream, Robin & Rainger, Movie: Gulliver's Travel, 1939 ....**$5.00**

I Love You Honolulu, Harry Launder, Harry Launder photo cover, 1915 ....**$10.00**

I Saw Mommy Kissing Santa Claus, Tommie Conner, 1952 ....**$2.00**

I See the Moon, Meredith Wilson, The Mariners photo cover, 1953 ....**$3.00**

I Used To Be Colored Blind, Irving Berlin, Astaire & Rogers photo cover, 1938 ....**$15.00**

I Went to Your Wedding, Jessie Mae Robinson, Patti Page photo cover, 1952 ....**$5.00**

I Whistle a Happy Tune, Rodgers & Hammerstein II, Movie: The King & I, 1951 ....**$5.00**

I Wish I Knew, 1945, Betty Grable photo from Diamond Horseshoe movie, EX+ **$5.00**

I'd Give a Million Tomorrows, Milton Berle & Jerry Livingston, Arthur Godfrey photo cover, 1948 ....**$5.00**

I'll Dance at Your Wedding, Loesser & Carmichael, Movie: Mr Bug Goes to Town, 1941 ....**$5.00**

I'll Sing You a Thousand Love Songs, Clark Gable and Marion Davies photo cover, $10.00.

I'm a Indian Too, Irving Berlin, Movie: Annie Get Your Gun, 1946 ....**$5.00**

I'm a Little Teapot, Kelly & Sanders, Ronnie Kemper, 1941 ....**$3.00**

I'm Alright, Loggins, Movie: Caddyshack, Murray, Dangerfield & Chase photo cover, 1980 ....**$3.00**

I'm in the Mood for Love, Raft, Langford, Faye & Kelly photo cover, 1935 ....**$5.00**

I'm Not Your Steppin' Stone, Monkees, 1966 ....**$5.00**

I'm Shooting High, Jimmy McHugh, Lainie Kazan photo cover, 1963 ....**$3.00**

I've Got the Sun in the Morning, Irving Berlin, Movie: Annie Get Your Gun, 1946 ....**$5.00**

I've Gotta Be Me, Walter Marks, Musical: Golden Rainbow, Lawrence & Gorme photo cover, 1967 ....**$3.00**

If I Had a Wedding Ring, Skelton & Alter, Movie: Breakfast in Hollywood, 1945 ....**$5.00**

If I Had Never Loved You, Kusik & Becaud, Movie: The Deadly Trap, Faye Dunaway photo cover, 1972 ....**$3.00**

If You Could Care, Wimperis & Darewski, Movie: Task Force, Jane Wyatt & Gary Cooper photo cover, 1949 .....**$10.00**

If You Knew Suzie, Eddie Cantor, Movie: Eddie Cantor Story, Eddie Cantor photo cover, 1944 ....**$20.00**

In a World of My Own, Hillard & Fain, Musical: Alice in Wonderland, 1951 ....**$10.00**

Irish Soldier Boy, Lanyon & DeWitt, Connie Foley photo cover, 1950 ....**$3.00**

It Was Written in the Stars, Robin & Arlen, Movie: Casbah, 1948 ....**$5.00**

It's Impossible, A Manzanero & Sid Wayne, Perry Como photo cover, 1968 ....**$5.00**

It's My Lazy Day, Burnette, Movie: Bordertown Trails, Smiley Burnette photo cover, 1946......................**$3.00**

It's So Peaceful in the Country, Alec Wilder, Mildred Bailey photo cover, 1942 ....**$3.00**

Jean, Rod McKuen, Movie: Prime of Miss Jean Brodie, Oliver photo cover, 1969 ....**$5.00**

Johnny Is the Boy for Me, Paul, Stillman & Roberts, Les Paul & Mary Ford photo cover, 1953......................**$5.00**

Just Ask Your Heart, Joe Ricci, Frankie Avalon photo cover, 1959......................**$3.00**

Katrina, Raye & DePaul, Movie: Adventures of Ichabod Crane & Mr Toad, Dicney, 1949 ....**$10.00**

Kokomo, Love, Melcher, Phillips & McKenzie, Movie: Cocktail, Tom Cruise photo cover, 1988 ....**$3.00**

Last Waltz, Reed & Mason, Engelbert Humperdinck, 1967..**$3.00**

Lawrence of Arabia, Maurice Jarre, Movie: Lawrence of Arabia, 1962......................**$5.00**

Leaving on a Jet Plane, John Denver, Peter, Paul & Mary photo cover, 1969 ....**$3.00**

Let's Be Friendly, Webster & Fain, Movie: Hollywood or Bust, Martin & Lewis & Anita Ekberg, 1956 ....**$5.00**

Little Bit Independent, Edgar Leslie & Joe Burke, Ozzie & Harriet photo cover, 1935......................**$5.00**

Little White Gardenia, Sam Coslow, Movie: All the King's Horses, Carl Brisson & Mary Ellis photo cover, 1935......................**$5.00**

Look to the Rainbow, EY Harburg & Burton Lane, Movie: Finian's Rainbow, 1946......................**$5.00**

Lookin' Out My Back Door, John Fogerty, Creedence Clearwater Revival photo cover, 1970 ....**$3.00**

Lot of Livin' To Do, Adams & Strause, Movie: Bye Bye Birdie, 1960......................**$5.00**

Love Me Tender, WW Fosdick & George R Paulton, Elvis Presley photo cover, 1956......................**$25.00**

Love of My Life, Cole Porter, Movie: The Pirate, 1948...**$5.00**

Love Them All, Sandy Linzer, Nancy Sinatra photo cover, 1970......................**$3.00**

Lovelight in the Starlight, 1938, Bob Hope & Dorothy Lamour from Her Jungle Love, EX+ **$8.00**

Magic Mountain, Allen & George, Movie: The Magic Mountain, 1964......................**$5.00**

Man & His Dreams, Burke & Monaco, Movie: Star Maker, Bing Crosby photo cover, 1940 ....**$5.00**

Man From Laramie, Washington & Lee, Movie: The Man From Laramie, Stewart & O'Donnell, 1955 ....**$5.00**

Man I Love, Ira & George Gershwin, Movie: Strike Up the Band, 1945......................**$10.00**

Man That Got Away, Arlen & Gershwin, Movie: A Star Is Born, Judy Garland photo cover, 1954 ....**$10.00**

Mandy, Irving Berlin, Musical: Ziegfeld Follies, 1919.**$10.00**

Maybe This Time, Ebb & Kander, Movie: Cabaret, Liza Minelli photo cover, 1972 ....**$3.00**

Mexico, Wolcott & Gilbert, Movie: The Three Caballeros, Disney, 1945......................**$10.00**

Michelle, McCartney, Beatles photo cover, 1965..........**$5.00**

Mister Five by Five, Raye & DePaul, Movie: Behind the 8 Ball, Holley cover artist, 1942......................**$5.00**

Mister Sandman, Pat Ballard, Chordettes photo cover, 1954.**$3.00**

Mister Snow, Rodgers & Hammerstein, Movie: Carousel, Macrae, Jones & Mitchell photo cover, 1945 ....**$3.00**

Mockin' Bird Hill, Vaughn Horton, Les Paul & Mary Ford photo cover, 1949 ....**$3.00**

Moon River, Audrey Hepburn caricature photo cover, 1961 ....**$3.00**

Moonlight Serenade, Parish & Miller, Movie: Glen Miller Story, Stewart & June Allyson photo cover, 1939 ....**$10.00**

More, Glazer & Alstone, Perry Como photo cover, 1956..**$5.00**

Mutual Admiration Society, Dubey & Karr, Musical: Happy Hunting, 1956......................**$5.00**

My Heart Cries for You, Sigman & Faith, Dinah Shore photo cover, 1950 ....**$5.00**

My Love Song to You, Alfred & Firsch, Jackie Gleason photo cover, 1954 ....**$15.00**

My Mother Would Love You, Cole Porter, Movie: Panama Hattie, 1942......................**$5.00**

New O'leans, Kahn & Johnston, Movie: Thanks a Million, 1935......................**$5.00**

Nice To Be Around, Williams & Williams, Movie: Cinderella Liberty, James Caan & Marsha Mason photo cover, 1973 ....**$3.00**

Night & Day, Cole Porter, Movie: Night & Day, 1944...**$3.00**

No Other Love, Rogers & Hammerstein, Movie: Me & Juliet, 1953......................**$5.00**

No Two People, Loesser, Movie: Hans Christian Andersen, 1951 ....**$10.00**

Nobody's Heart, Hart & Rodgers, Movie: All's Fair, 1942..**$5.00**

Now Is the Hour, Crosby photo cover, 1946................**$5.00**

Okalehau, Robin & Rainger, Movie: Waikiki Wedding, 1937 ....**$5.00**

Old Before My Time, Karliski, Movie: A Time To Sing, Hank Williams Jr, Shelley Fabares & Ed Begley photo cover, 1968 ....**$3.00**

Old Glory, Mercer & Arlen, Movie: Star Spangled Rhythm, 1942 ....**$10.00**

On the Street Where You Live, Lerner & Lowe, Movie: My Fair Lady, 1956......................**$5.00**

One Song, Morey & Churchill, Movie: Snow White, Disney, 1937 ....**$10.00**

Only a Rose, Hooker & Friml, Movie: The Vagabond King, 1925 ....**$10.00**

Only for Americans, Irving Berlin, Musical: Miss Liberty, 1949......................**$10.00**

Only One, Croswell & Pochriss, Musical: Tovarich, 1963....**$3.00**

Oop Shoop, Shirley Gunter & the Queens, Crew Cut photo cover, 1954 ....**$3.00**

Oops, Mercer & Warren, Movie: The Belle of New York, 1952......................**$8.00**

Over & Over, Crawford, Movie: C'mon Lets Live a Little, 1965......................**$3.00**

Over Pine Mountain Trails, Sherwood & Ganz, Movie: Over Pine Mountain Trails, 1941......................**$3.00**

Over the Rainbow, EY Harburg & Harold Arlen, Movie: The Wizard of Oz, 1939......................**$35.00**

Paducah, Robin & Warren, Movie: The Gang's All Here, 1943......................**$5.00**

Painting the Rose Red, Hillard & Fain, Movie: Alice in Wonderland, Disney, 1951 ....**$10.00**

Pearly Shells, Edward & Pober, Billy Vaughn photo cover, 1964......................**$5.00**

Peddler Man, Lawrence & Brodszky, Movie: Flame & the Flesh, 1954..**$5.00**

Pennies From Heaven, Burke & Johnston, Movie: Pennies From Heaven, 1936.....................................**$5.00**

Pennsylvania Polka, Lester Lee & Zeke Manners, Movie: Give Out Sister, 1942.................................**$3.00**

People Will Say We're in Love, Rodgers & Hammerstein II, Musical: Oklahoma, 1943 ....**$5.00**

Perfect Song, Amos & Andy photo cover, ¾" tear, 1929..**$9.00**

Policeman's Ball, Irving Berlin, Musical: Miss Liberty, 1949...**$10.00**

Polka Dot Polka, Robin & Warren, Movie: The Gang's All Here, 1943 ....**$10.00**

Pretty Doll, Black & LeGrand, Movie: A Matter of Innocence, 1968..**$3.00**

Raindrops Keep Falling on My Head, Newman, Redford & Ross photo cover, 1969 ....**$3.00**

Ramblin' Rose, Noel & Joe Sherman, Nat King Cole photo cover, 1962 ....**$3.00**

Riders in the Sky, Stan Jones, Burl Ives photo cover, 1949..**$3.00**

Rio Rita, Tierney & McCarthy, Movie: Rio Rita, 1929..**$10.00**

River Kwai March, Arnold, Movie: The Bridge Over River Kwai, 1957 ....**$5.00**

Road to Morocco, Burke & Heusen, Movie: Road to Morocco, 1952..**$5.00**

Rock-A-Bye Your Baby With a Dixie Melody, 1960s, Jerry Lewis photo cover, NM **$15.00**

Rose of the Rancho, Robin & Rainger, Movie: Rose of the Rancho, 1935 ....**$5.00**

Scamp of the Campus, Greer & Klages, Movie: Cheer Up & Smile, 1930 ....**$3.00**

Sea of the Moon, Freed & Warren, Movie: Pagan Love Song, 1950..**$8.00**

Second Hand Rose, Clarke & Hanley, Barbara Streisand, 1965..**$3.00**

Secret Love, 1953, Doris Day cover, NM........................**$5.00**

Sew the Buttons On, John Jennings, Musical: Riverwind, 1963 ....**$3.00**

Shadows of Paris, Wells & Mancini, Movie: A Shot in the Dark, 1964..**$3.00**

Shall We Dance, Rodgers & Hammerstein II, Movie: The King & I, 1951 ....**$5.00**

She's a Lady, Cy Coben, Perry Como & Betty Hutton photo cover, 1950 ....**$3.00**

Shoo-Shoo Baby, Phil Moore, Movie: Beautiful but Broke, 1943..**$5.00**

Shot-Gun Boogie, Tennessee Ernie Ford, Tennessee Ernie Ford cover, 1951 ....**$3.00**

Sisters, Irving Berlin, Movie: White Christmas, 1942...**$10.00**

Sit Down You're Rocking the Boat, Jo Swerling, Abe Burrows & Frank Loesser, Musical: Guys & Dolls, 1950.................**$5.00**

Sixteen Going on Seventeen, Rodgers & Hammerstein II, Movie: Sound of Music, 1959.....................**$3.00**

Soliloquy, Rodgers & Hammerstein II, Movie: Carousel, 1945 ....**$3.00**

Someone Who Cares, Harvey, Movie: Fools, 1971.......**$3.00**

Son of a Sheik, Rudolph Valentino photo cover, 1926.**$15.00**

Sooner or Later, 1946, Song of the South's Uncle Remus & other characters on cover, NM..........................**$12.00**

Star Eyes, Raye & DePaul, Movie: I Dood It, Red Skelton & Eleanor Powell photo cover, 1943.........................**$5.00**

Summer Place, Steiner, Movie: A Summer Place, 1959 .**$3.00**

Sweet Dreams, Don Gibson, Patsy Cline photo cover, 1955 ....**$2.00**

Take It From There, Robin & Rainger, Movie: Coney Island, 1943..**$5.00**

That Silver Haired Daddy of Mine, Movie: Tumbling Tumbleweed, 1932...**$5.00**

That's Amore, 1953, Dean Martin & Jerry Lewis cover, NM **$35.00**

Three Coins in a Fountain, cast photo cover, 1954, 2 sm tears **$2.00**

Three Little Words, Amos 'n Andy cover, ca 1930, $30.00.

Thumper Song, Bliss, Sour & Manners, Movie: Bambi, Disney, 1942..**$10.00**

Till There Was You, Meredith Wilson, Movie: The Music Man, 1950..**$5.00**

Tulips & Heather, Milton Carson, Perry Como photo cover, 1950..**$3.00**

Ugly Duckling, Frank Loesser, Movie: Hans Christian Andersen, 1951...**$5.00**

Very Good Advice, Hillard & Fain, Movie: Alice in Wonderland, Disney, 1951 ....**$10.00**

Was It Rain, Hirsch & Handman, Movie: The Hit Parade, 1937 ....**$10.00**

We'll Make Hay While the Sun Shines, Arthur Freed and Nacio Herb Brown, Marion Davies and Bing Crosby photo cover, 1933, $10.00.

What Do You Do With a General, Irving Berlin, Movie: White Christmas, 1942..**$10.00**

Where or When, Rodgers & Hart, Movie: Babes in Arms, 1934..**$10.00**

Who Wants To Live Like That?, Foster Carling, Movie: Song of the South, Disney, 1946............................**$10.00**

Wild Is the Wind, Washington & Tiomkin, Movie: Wild Is the Wind, 1957 ....**$3.00**

Yellow Dog Blues, by W.C. Handy, 1919, $35.00.

You Are My Lucky Star, 1935, Jack Benny cover, EX+ ..**$8.00**
You're the Only Star, 1938, Gene Autry cover, EX+ ...**$24.00**
Young at Heart, Sinatra photo cover, 1954 ....**$4.00**

Shell Pink Glassware

Here's something new to look for this year — lovely soft pink opaque glassware made by the Jeannette Glass Company for only a short time during the late 1950s. Prices, says expert Gene Florence, have been increasing by leaps and bounds! You'll find a wide variance in style from piece to piece, since the company chose shapes from several of their most popular lines to press in the satiny shell pink. Refer to *Collectible Glassware from the 40s, 50s, and 60s,* by Mr. Florence for photos and more information.

Advisors: April and Larry Tvorak (See Directory, Fire-King)

Bowl, fruit; footed, 9" high **$35.00**
Bowl, holiday bow design, footed, 10½" dia **$35.00**
Bowl, Lombardi, 4-toe, floral-designed center, 11" **$45.00**
Bowl, Lombardi, 4-toe, plain center, 11" **$28.00**
Bowl, pheasants at base (beaks break very easily), 8" dia ...**$48.00**
Bowl/planter, gondola shape, 4¼x17½x5" **$25.00**
Cake stand, footed...**$25.00**

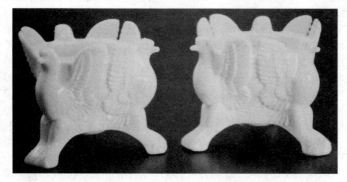

Candle holders, eagle figures, $70.00 for the pair.

Candlesticks, 2-light, pr...**$65.00**
Candy dish, acorn design, w/lid, 6½x5½" square **$35.00**
Candy dish bottom, National, produced for Napco....**$12.00**

Candy jar, grape design, w/lid, ½-lb..........................**$25.00**
Celery/relish dish, beaded edge, 3 compartments **$45.00**
Cigarette set, butterfly design, box w/butterfly knob, 2 ash-trays, from $100 to..**$125.00**
Compote (most common piece made), 6"..................**$12.00**
Cookie jar, w/lid, 6½x5¾", from $90 to **$125.00**
Creamer **$10.00**
Dish, diamond shape, florentine footed, 10x7¾".......**$35.00**
Goblet, Thumbprint, 8-oz...**$12.00**
Grape dish, octagonal w/partitions, 2x12"..................**$50.00**
Honey jar, beehive form, w/lid & clear plastic spoon **$55.00**
Juice set, Thumbprint, pitcher & 4 tumblers **$75.00**
Nut/candy dish, footed, 3½x5¼".....................................**$22.00**
Powder jar, rose design, w/lid...**$38.00**

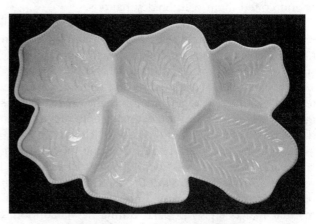

Relish tray, 6-part, 16", $38.00.

Sherbet, Thumbprint, 5-oz **$15.00**
Snack set, feather design, plate w/cup **$15.00**
Sugar bowl, w/lid **$20.00**
Tray, beverage; handles, 12½x9¾".................................**$55.00**
Tray, feather design, handles, oval, compartmented, 15¾" long **$65.00**
Tray, Venetian leaf form w/feather design, 6 compartments..**$45.00**
Vase, cornucopia form, pr...**$38.00**
Vase, diamond design, 7x5½"..**$28.00**
Vase, diamond design w/tiny flowers on base, produced for Napco **$18.00**
Vase, grape design, produced for Napco....................**$15.00**
Vase, heavy beaded bottom, 9" **$85.00**

Vase, ribbed body and beaded foot, 9", $85.00.

Vase, sawtooth rim, produced for Napco **$18.00**
Wedding bowl, w/lid, 6½" high **$25.00**
Wedding bowl, w/lid, 8" high.................................**$32.00**

Shirley Temple

Born April 23, 1928, Shirley Jane Temple danced and smiled her way into the hearts of America in the movie *Stand Up and Cheer.* Many, many successful roles followed and by the time Shirley was eight years old, she was #1 at the box offices around the country. Her picture appeared in publications almost daily, and any news about her was news indeed. Mothers dressed their little daughters in clothing copied after hers and coifed them with Shirley hairdos.

The extent of her success was mirrored in the unbelievable assortment of merchandise that saturated the retail market. Dolls, coloring books, children's clothing and jewelry, fountain pens, paper dolls, stationery, and playing cards are just a few examples of the hundreds of items that were available. Shirley's face was a common sight on the covers of magazines as well as in the advertisements they contained, and she was featured in hundreds of articles.

Though she had been retired from the movies for nearly a decade, she had two successful TV series in the late fifties, *The Shirley Temple Story-Book* and *The Shirley Temple Show.* Her reappearance caused new interest in some of the items that had been so popular during her childhood, and many were reissued.

Always interested in charity and community service, Shirley became actively involved in a political career in the late sixties, serving at both the state and national levels.

If you're interested in learning more, we recommend *Shirley Temple Dolls and Collectibles* by Patricia R. Smith; *Toys, Antique and Collectible,* by David Longest; and *Shirley in the Magazines* by Gen Jones.

Note: All of the pinback buttons we describe below have been reproduced, so has the cobalt glassware with Shirley's likeness. Beware!

Advisor: Gen Jones (See Directory, Character and Personality Collectibles)

Newsletter: *The Shirley Temple Collectors News*
8811 Colonial Rd.
Brooklyn, NY 11209; Dues: $20 per year; checks payable to Rita Dubas

Autograph, as adult, common **$10.00**
Book, Captain January, by Laura Richards, w/photos from movie, Random House, 1st printing, EX, from $25 to...**$30.00**
Book, Films of Shirley Temple, by R Windeler, lg soft cover, M **$10.00**
Book, Heidi, Random House, Shirley Temple edition, 1st printing, EX, from $25 to **$30.00**
Book, Little Colonel, by Anne Fellows Johnston, w/photos from movie, Random House, 1st printing, EX, from $25 to...**$30.00**

Book, Little Colonel, Little Big Book, Saalfield, 1935, EX...**$35.00**
Book, Shirley Temple's Favorite Tales of Long Ago, Random House, 1958, lg, VG **$12.00**
Book, Susannah of the Mounties, by Muriel Denison, w/photos from movie, Random House, 1936, EX, from $25 to **$30.00**
Book, The Littlest Rebel, by Edward Peple, w/photos from movie, Random House, 1st printing, EX, from $25 to **$30.00**
Book, Those Endearing Young Charms, by Marc Best, hardcover w/dust jacket, EX **$18.00**
Book, 20th Century Fox Presents Shirley Temple in Heidi, #337, 10x10", EX, minimum value.........................**$30.00**
Bust, green chalkware, 12", minimum value.............**$500.00**
Cereal bowl, white portrait on cobalt glass, 1930s, original only..**$60.00**
Cereal box backs, 1930s, set of 12............................**$150.00**
Christmas card, Hallmark, 1935, M............................**$30.00**
Cigar bands, ca 1980s, set of 10 ....**$15.00**
Cigarette card, Famous Film Stars, Shirley Temple & Cooper, Now & Forever, Gallaher Ltd #39, EX..................**$10.00**
Coloring book, Shirley Temple Crossing the Country, M, minimum value...**$35.00**
Coloring set, Saalfield, 1930s, EXIB.........................**$100.00**
Doll, plastic & vinyl, 1982-83, 12", M.........................**$35.00**
Doll, plastic & vinyl, 1982-83, 8", M...........................**$30.00**

Doll, Shirley in Wee Willie Winkie, vinyl, missing original jacket, 12", $190.00. (Photo courtesy of Cindy Sabulis.)

Doll, vinyl, ca 1950s, 12", M......................................**$165.00**
Doll, vinyl, Montgomery Ward, 1972, 17", M **$165.00**
Doll, vinyl, 1950s, 12", M..**$165.00**
Doll, vinyl, 1950s, 15", M..**$265.00**
Doll, vinyl, 1950s, 15", played with...........................**$85.00**
Doll, vinyl, 1950s, 17", M..**$325.00**
Doll, vinyl, 1950s, 17", MIB.......................................**$400.00**
Doll, vinyl, 1950s, 19", M..**$400.00**
Doll, vinyl, 1950s, 36", M.......................................**$1,600.00**
Doll, vinyl, 1972, reissue, Montgomery Ward, 17", M...**$165.00**
Doll, vinyl, 1972, reissue, Montgomery Ward, 17", played with, EX...**$45.00**
Doll, vinyl, 1973, 16", M...**$125.00**
Drawing book, Saalfield #1725, 1935, EX, minimum value...**$35.00**
Figurine, salt, 1930s, 4", EX......................................**$75.00**
Figurine, Stand Up & Cheer, Nostalgia, MIB **$80.00**
Lobby card, Bachelor & Bobby Soxer, #8 in series, scene at picnic **$15.00**
Lobby card, The Blue Bird (Mexican), set of 5...........**$75.00**

Lobby card, Young People, group cast scene of George Montgomery carrying injured child, EX, minimum value **$25.00**

Magazine, Life, November 1, 1937, Shirley & stand-in cover, EX...**$8.00**

Magazine, Movie Mirror, March 1939, Shirley With a Difference, 2-page layout, 5 sepia photos, VG+, minimum value....**$20.00**

Magazine, Woman's Home Companion, August 1942, Shirley Temple Presents Junior Miss, EX **$5.00**

Magazine ad, How Shirley Temple Spends Her Vacation, Country Gentleman, August 1937, ½-page **$4.00**

Magazine ad, Shirley in pink dress w/blue Dodge car, 1936, full page...**$10.00**

Magic slate, Shirley Temple Treasure Board, Saalfield #8806, 1959, EX..**$25.00**

Mug, cobalt glass, mug....................................**$40.00**

Pamphlet, Story of My Life, giveaway in 1935, M.......**$25.00**

Paper dolls, Saalfield #1715, Shirley Temple Standing Dolls, 1935, uncut, minimum value **$150.00**

Paper dolls, Saalfield #1739, Shirley Temple & Dresses, 1959, uncut, minimum value..................................**$25.00**

Paper dolls, Saalfield #2112, Shirley Temple & Dresses, 1934, uncut, minimum value **$150.00**

Pen & pencil set, 1930s, minimum value....................**$75.00**

Photo, vintage black & white glossy of Shirley celebrating New Years, posed w/clock, 8x10", EX **$8.00**

Pin-back button, My Friend Shirley, original **$40.00**

Pin-back button, My Friend Shirley on red background, 1935 ....**$40.00**

Pin-back button, Shirley Temple & Chicago Sun Times, 1930s **$100.00**

Pitcher, cobalt glass **$40.00**

Plate, Poor Little Rich Girl, Nostalgia, MIB.................**$40.00**

Playing cards, 1930s, MIB **$65.00**

Pocket mirror, Shirley as Heidi, 1937, NM.................**$40.00**

Postcard, Home of Shirley Temple w/insert photo of Shirley, Western Publishing #810, unused...........................**$4.50**

Postcard, Shirley in pjs w/rabbit applique, Ludlow #FC-149-050, EX..**$1.00**

Postcard, To All Little Girls & Boys, Merry Xmas, Shirley Temple, sepia photo...................................**$1.00**

Poster, Miss Annie Rooney, 27x41", reissue, G **$40.00**

Poster, Susannah of the Mounties, reissue, 1958, 27x41", G **$150.00**

Program, Since You Went Away, Danish text, 8 pages w/3 Shirley photos, EX **$15.00**

Program, Tournament of Roses, 1939, 38 pages, 11x8½" ..**$20.00**

School tablet, 1935, M......................................**$40.00**

Sheet music, Shirley's Favorite Songs From Her Newest Pictures, 40 pages, EX..**$50.00**

Sheet music, The Good Ship Lollipop, Bright Eyes, EX .**$15.00**

Sheet music, Together, Since You Went Away, EX........**$5.00**

Soap, Shirley figural, Kirk Guild, 1930s, MIB............**$150.00**

Song album, Shirley Temple Song Album #2, EX.......**$30.00**

Spoon, likeness in bowl & on handle, modern manufacture.**$10.00**

Tea set, Ideal, pink plastic, original box....................**$235.00**

Teddy bear, Bearly Temple, EX+ **$50.00**

Video, Kiss & Tell, EX...................................**$25.00**

Shot Glasses

Shot glasses come in a wide variety of colors and designs. They're readily available, inexpensive, and they don't take lots of room to display. Most sell for $5.00 and under, except cut glass, for which you would probably have to pay $100.00. Carnival glass examples go for about $50.00, pressed glass for about $75.00. Colored glass, those with etching or gold trim, or one that has an unusual shape — squared or barrel form, for instance — fall into the $3.00 to $7.00 range. Several advertising shot glasses, probably the most common type of all, are described in our listings. Soda advertising is unusual and may drive the value up to about $12.00 to $15.00.

Both new and older glasses alike sell for a little more in the Western part of the country. One-of-a-kind items or oddities are a bit harder to classify, especially sample glasses. Many depend on the elaborateness of their designs as opposed to basic lettering. These values are only estimates and should be used as a general guide. The club welcomes your suggestions and comments. For more information, we recommend *Shot Glasses: An American Tradition*, by Mark Pickvet.

Note: Values for shot glasses in good condition are represented by the low end of our ranges, while the high end reflects estimated values for examples in mint condition.

Advisor: Mark Pickvet (See Directory, Shot Glasses)

Club: The Shot Glass Club of America
Mark Pickvet, Editor
P.O. Box 90404
Flint, MI 48509; Non-profit organization publishes 12 newsletters per year; Subscription: $6; sample: $1

Callum Shot, Havre, Montana, red on frosted glass, $4.00.

Scrapbook, Saalfield, 1936, EX, $45.00.

Frosted w/gold designs, $6 to **$8.00**

General, w/enameled design, $2 to **$3.00**

General advertising, $3 to................................**$4.00**
General etched designs, $5 to.........................**$7.50**
General porcelain, $4 to.................................**$6.00**
General tourist, $2 to....................................**$3.00**
General w/frosted designs, $3 to....................**$4.00**
General w/gold designs, $6 to........................**$8.00**
Inside eyes, $5 to...**$7.50**
Mary Gregory, $100 to **$150.00**
Nudes, $20 to...**$25.00**
Plain, w/or w/out flutes, 50¢ to.....................**$1.00**
Pop or soda advertising, $12.50 to...............**$15.00**
Rounded European designs w/gold rims, $4 to **$5.00**

Roy's Liquor, fired-on green, $5.00.

Ruby flashed, $30 to...................................**$40.00**
Square, general, $5 to....................................**$7.50**
Square w/etching, $7.50 to **$10.00**
Square w/pewter, $12.50 to **$15.00**
Square w/2-tone bronze & pewter, $15 to **$17.50**
Standard glass w/pewter, $7.50 to..................**$10.00**
Taiwan tourist, $1 to.......................................**$2.00**
Tiffany, Galle, fancy art, $500 to **$750.00**
Turquoise & gold tourist, $5 to.......................**$7.50**
Whiskey or beer advertising, modern, $4 to **$5.00**
Whiskey sample, $25 to...............................**$250.00**
19th-century cut patterns, $25 to..................**$35.00**

Silhouette Pictures

These novelty pictures are familiar to everyone. Even today a good number of them are still around, and you'll often see them at flea markets and co-ops. They were very popular in their day and never expensive, and because they were made for so many years (the twenties through the fifties), many variations are available. Though the glass in some is flat, others were made with curved glass. Backgrounds may be foil, a scenic print, hand tinted, or plain. Sometimes dried flowers were added as accents. But the characteristic common to them all is the subject matter reverse painted on the glass. People (even complicated groups), scenes, ships, and animals were popular themes. Though quite often the silhouette was done in solid black to create a look similar to the 19th-century cut silhouettes, colors were sometimes used as well.

In the twenties, making tinsel art pictures became a popular pastime. Ladies would paint the outline of their subjects on the back of the glass and use crumpled tinfoil as a back-

ground. Sometimes they would tint certain areas of the glass, making the foil appear to be colored. This type is popular with with today's collectors.

If you'd like to learn more about this subject, we recommend *The Encyclopedia of Silhouette Collectibles on Glass* by Shirley Mace.

Advisor: Shirley Mace (See Directory, Silhouette Pictures)

Convex Glass

Boy & girl w/burro, full-color background, Benton Glass, 8x6"......................................**$45.00**
Boy shows his catch of fish to lady, full-color background, Benton Glass, 5x4"................**$32.00**
Couple dancing, pink, blue, white & yellow details, Peter Watson's Studio, 6" dia **$25.00**
Couple in theatre balcony, Benton Glass, 5x4"..........**$32.00**
Courting couple in garden, full-color scene w/black garden details, Benton Glass, 5x4"...............**$18.00**
Courting couple in garden, red on white, Benton Glass, 8x6"......................................**$60.00**
Indian in long headdress stands by horse, colorful western scene w/covered wagons forms background, Benton Glass, 5x4" **$35.00**

Lady handing a drink to man on horse surrounded by colorful leaves and birds, Benton Glass, 5x4", $30.00. (Photo courtesy of Shirley and Ray Mace.)

Lady looking into hand mirror, maid kneels at her feet, Benton Glass, 4½x3½" **$25.00**
Lady's full-color portrait, white lace painted on glass surrounds her, Donald Art Co, New York, 1941, 8x6".............**$30.00**
Man pulls lady in sled, full-color winter scene forms background, Benton Glass, 8x6" **$38.00**
Man returning handkerchief to lady in bustle, advertising & thermometer, CE Erickson, 5x4" **$30.00**
Masted sailing ship on white-capped ocean, Benton Glass, 5x4" **$25.00**
Scotty dog trying to reach bird on branch, Benton Glass, 5x4" **$30.00**

Flat Glass

Bird on branch, black w/multicolor details on cream, titled The Cardinal, Reliance, 10x7" **$22.00**
Boy fishing w/dog beside him, dried flowers pressed into background, Fisher & Flowercraft, 4½" square **$18.00**
Colonial couple in courting scene, she is seated on garden bench, Art Publishing Co, 1930s.................**$23.00**

Couple at gate surrounded by flowers, titled At the Garden Gate, pink & white details, Buckbee-Brehm, 1931, 5½x4½"...**$35.00**

Couple in garden about to kiss, flowers pressed into the background, marked Fisher Hand Painted Silhouettes, 4½" square **$22.00**

Couple kissing at gate, titled Good Night, Buckbee-Brehm, dated 1932, 5½x4½"................................**$24.00**

Couple w/2 children at home before fireplace, red & white details, Newton Manufacturing **$18.00**

Courting couple beside tree, from When Love Was Young series, C&A Richards Boston Mass, 3½" dia **$15.00**

Dancing figures (2 draped nudes) at seashore, signed Ellery Friend, Volland, 9x6½" **$50.00**

Dancing figures (4 nudes), black on gold background, titled Springtime of Life, Gleam O' Gold, 6x5" **$35.00**

Double Dutch, Dutch boy and girl holding hands, Reliance, 10x8", $30.00. (Photo courtesy of Shirley and Ray Mace.)

Dutch boy, colorful tinsel colors figure, Tinsel Art, 10x8"...**$18.00**

Dutch boy & girl w/tulip, windmill beyond, titled Tulip Time, Reliance, 11x7"...**$30.00**

Exotic bird on branch, colorful tinsel complete figure & flowers, black background, Tinsel Art, 16x12" **$25.00**

Flowers in vase, multicolor details on cream, titled Phlox & Asters, Reliance, 11x7"....................................**$30.00**

Girl & wolf in woods, titled, Little Red Riding Hood, black on silver foil, Reliance, 10x8" **$35.00**

Head & shoulders of a gentleman & a lady, Buckbee-Brehm Company, Minneapolis Minn, 5½x4½", pr **$30.00**

Lady at desk kissing letter, titled The Love Letter, Buckbee-Brehm, 5½x4½" **$23.00**

Lady at spinning wheel, black silhouette w/gold foil background, Art Publishing Co, 1930s.........................**$25.00**

Lady at spinning wheel, multicolor details, advertising at bottom of picture, Newton Manufacturing.................**$20.00**

Lady in ornate gown at dressing table, Reliance NRA stamp 12-33, 9x12"..**$40.00**

Lady's portrait, black on silver background, Reliance, 5x4" **$20.00**

Man bringing flowers to lady w/parasol, titled Courtship, Reliance, 4x4"..**$15.00**

Man on horse, colorful canyon w/waterfall beyond, Souvenir-Yellowstone Park, Wyoming-Haynes Inc, Newton Manufacturing...**$18.00**

Man tips his hat to lady, titled Gallant, black on gold foil, Deltes, 1933, 10x8" **$22.00**

Mother greeting children at steps of porch, titled Home From School, Reliance, 7x5" **$18.00**

Nude child playing triangle, titled Kinder Music, KW Diefenbach, Tallimit Art, C&A Richards, 9x7".......**$60.00**

Roses in vase, black & multicolor on cream, titled Florals, noted Hand Colored on Glass, C&A Richards, oval, 5x4" **$15.00**

Sailing ships on blue water, colorful sky, marked Guaranteed...real exotic butterfly wings, Made in London, 4½" square **$40.00**

Spanish lady in arch, titled Senorita, black on silver foil, Deltex, 1933, 10x8" **$30.00**

Silverplated Flatware

When buying silverplated flatware, avoid pieces that are worn or have been monogrammed. Replating can be very expensive. Matching services often advertise in certain trade papers and can be very helpful in helping you locate the items you're looking for. One of the best sources we are aware of is *The Antique Trader*, they're listed with the trade papers in the back of this book.

If you'd like to learn more about the subject, we recommend *Silverplated Flatware, Revised Fourth Edition*, by Tere Hagan.

Advisor: Rick Spencer (See Directory, Regal China)

Adoration, 1930, berry spoon, International................**$24.00**

Adoration, 1930, dessert place spoon, International.....**$6.00**

Adoration, 1930, dinner knife, hollow handle, International **$7.00**

Adoration, 1930, master butter knife, International......**$4.00**

Adoration, 1930, salad fork, International....................**$6.00**

Ambassador, 1919, ice cream fork, International **$16.50**

Ambassador, 1919, iced tea spoon, International..........**$8.50**

Ambassador, 1919, round soup spoon, International....**$7.00**

Ambassador, 1919, salad fork, International **$6.00**

Ambassador, 1919, tomato server, International.........**$14.00**

Anniversary, 1923, cold meat fork, 1847 Rogers **$13.00**

Anniversary, 1923, sugar tongs, 1847 Rogers **$12.00**

Anniversary, 1923, teaspoon, 1847 Rogers....................**$2.00**

April, 1950, cold meat fork, Rogers & Bros...................**$9.00**

April, 1950, dessert place spoon, Rogers & Bros **$4.00**

April, 1950, dinner knife or fork, $12.00 each; teaspoon, $7.00.

April, 1950, master butter spreader, Rogers & Bros **$4.50**

Caprice, 1937, cocktail fork, Oneida **$5.00**

Caprice, 1937, cold meat fork, Oneida **$12.00**

Caprice, 1937, pierced dessert server, Oneida............**$16.00**

Cedric, 1906, beef fork, Wm Rogers............................**$8.00**

Cedric, 1906, bouillon spoon, Wm Rogers **$6.00**

Cedric, 1906, seafood fork, Wm Rogers........................$7.00
Century, 1923, cream ladle, Holmes & Edwards.........$14.00
Century, 1923, dessert knife, hollow handle, Holmes & Edwards $7.00
Century, 1923, jelly slice, Holmes & Edwards............$10.00
Century, 1923, round soup spoon, Holmes & Edwards..$5.00
Century, 1923, sugar spoon, Holmes & Edwards..........$7.00
Century, 1923, tomato server, Holmes & Edwards.....$25.00
Continental, 1914, gravy ladle, 1847 Rogers $8.00
Continental, 1914, iced tea spoon, 1847 Rogers............$3.00
Continental, 1914, sugar spoon, 1847 Rogers...............$3.00
Coronation, 1936, casserole spoon, Oneida Community ..$16.00
Coronation, 1936, master butter knife, Oneida Community $3.00
Coronation, 1936, salad fork, Oneida Community $6.00
Coronation, 1936, viande dinner knife, hollow handle, Oneida Community...$10.00
Daffodil, 1950, covered vegetable dish, International.$55.00
Daffodil, 1950, pickle fork, 2 tines, International..........$9.00
Daffodil, 1950, well & tree platter, footed, International, 18x13" $95.00
Danish Princess, 1938, baby spoon, Holmes & Edwards....$7.00
Danish Princess, 1938, gravy ladle, Holmes & Edwards ...$24.00
Danish Princess, 1938, round soup spoon, Holmes & Edwards $7.00
Danish Princess, 1938, tablespoon, Holmes & Edwards..$6.00
Dolly Madison, 1911, cocktail fork, Holmes & Edwards..$6.00
Dolly Madison, 1911, fruit spoon, Holmes & Edwards.$4.00
Dolly Madison, 1911, sauce ladle, Holmes & Edwards..$16.00
Dolly Madison, 1911, 3-pc carving set, Holmes & Edwards $45.00
Evening Star, 1950, berry spoon, Oneida Community ..$25.00
Evening Star, 1950, jelly knife, Oneida Community $7.00
Evening Star, 1950, tablespoon, Oneida Community $6.00
Evening Star, 1950, teaspoon, Oneida Community $2.00
First Love, 1930, ice cream fork, 1847 Rogers.............$19.00
First Love, 1930, iced tea spoon, 1847 Rogers $15.00
First Love, 1930, individual butter spreader, 1847 Rogers ...$6.00
First Love, 1930, pickle fork, 1847 Rogers..................$12.00

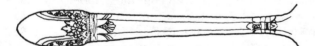

First Love, 1937, dinner knife or fork, $20.00 each; teaspoon, $8.00.

Grecian, 1915, cold meat fork, 1881 Rogers..................$8.00
Grecian, 1915, fruit spoon, 1881 Rogers $5.00
Grecian, 1915, iced tea spoon, 1881 Rogers................$15.00
Grecian, 1915, luncheon fork, 1881 Rogers..................$5.00
Heritage, 1953, nut scoop, 1847 Rogers.......................$5.00
Heritage, 1953, pierced relish spoon, 1847 Rogers.......$6.00
Heritage, 1953, punch ladle, hollow handle, 1847 Rogers..$120.00
Heritage, 1953, stuffing spoon, 1847 Rogers $40.00
Joan, 1896, lettuce fork, Wallace $35.00
Joan, 1896, nut pick, Wallace......................................$7.00
Joan, 1896, oyster ladle, Wallace $35.00
Joan, 1896, pie server, hollow handle, Wallace...........$18.00

Lady Hamilton, 1932, dessert place spoon, Oneida Community $5.00
Lady Hamilton, 1932, dinner fork, Oneida Community $6.00
Lady Hamilton, 1932, luncheon knife, hollow handle, Oneida Community $5.00
Milady, 1940, cake serving fork, Oneida Community $16.00
Milady, 1940, cucumber server, Oneida Community ..$12.00
Milady, 1940, dinner knife, hollow handle, Oneida Community $6.00

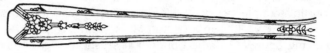

Milady, 1940, teaspoon, $7.00.

Old Colony, 1911, bouillon spoon, 1847 Rogers $12.00
Old Colony, 1911, cake serving fork, 1847 Rogers.....$22.00
Old Colony, 1911, demitasse spoon, 1847 Rogers......$11.00
Old Colony, 1911, ice cream fork, 1847 Rogers..........$26.00
Old Colony, 1911, pickle fork, long handle, 1847 Rogers.$18.00
Old Colony, 1911, soup ladle, 1847 Rogers $80.00
Patrician, 1914, bouillon spoon, Oneida Community ...$6.00
Patrician, 1914, pastry server, hollow handle, Oneida Community $15.00
Patrician, 1914, pie/pastry fork, Oneida Community $8.00
Patrician, 1914, sauce ladle, Oneida Community $12.00
Patrician, 1914, teaspoon, Oneida Community.............$3.00
Sheraton, 1910, berry spoon, Oneida Community $24.00
Sheraton, 1910, demitasse spoon, Oneida Community $5.50
Sheraton, 1910, dinner fork, hollow handle, Oneida Community $10.00
Sheraton, 1910, punch ladle, hollow handle, Oneida Community $125.00
South Seas, 1955, baby fork, Oneida Community.........$6.00
South Seas, 1955, oval soup spoon, Oneida Community....$5.00
South Seas, 1955, pastry server, Oneida Community..$15.00
South Seas, 1955, salad set, hollow handles, Oneida Community, 2-pc..$35.00

Southern Mansion, 1980, dinner knife or fork, $12.00 each; teaspoon, $7.00.

White Orchid, 1953, sugar spoon, Oneida Community.......$5.00

Soda-Pop Memorabilia

A specialty area of the advertising field, soft-drink memorabilia is a favorite of many collectors. Now that vintage Coca-Cola items have become rather expensive, interest is expanding to include some of the less widely known sodas — Grapette, Hires Root Beer, and Dr Pepper, for instance.

If you want more pricing information, we recommend *Huxford's Collectible Advertising* by Sharon and Bob Huxford.

See also Coca-Cola; Pepsi-Cola.

Advisors: Craig and Donna Stifter (See Directory, Soda-Pop Collectibles)

Newsletter: National Pop Can Collectors
P.O. Box 7862
Rockford, IL 61126; Send for free information

Ashtray, Canada Dry, green glass, logo & ...For the Sake of Your Scotch in center, Emigrate To... on rim, 8" dia, NM..**$20.00**

Ashtray, Hires, glass bottle shape, EX+......................**$15.00**

Ashtray, Seven-Up, brown glass w/white lettering, Fresh Up With Seven-Up, It Likes You, 3 rests, 5½" dia, NM..**$15.00**

Blotter, Chero-Cola, Drink...There's None So Good on oval within 8-sided border on rectangle, VG+.............**$15.00**

Bottle opener, Chero-Cola, metal girl figure, Drink Chero-Cola 5¢, G+..**$25.00**

Bottle opener, Dr Pepper, wall mount, embossed lettering, NM..**$25.00**

Bottle opener, NuGrape, shows bottle, EX+................**$12.00**

Bottle opener, Orange-Crush, metal Crushy figure, NM+ .**$25.00**

Bottle opener w/tag, Moxie, name embossed on key opener, tag features pointing Moxie man & Drink Moxie, G **$25.00**

Bottle topper, Ma's Old Fashion Root Beer, diecut cardboard, Demand the Best on blue arrow encircling Ma, 9x9", EX+ **$10.00**

Bottle topper, Seven-Up, Enjoy a 7-Up Float on curved banner w/logo in center, 7-Up With Your Favorite Ice Cream, NM **$10.00**

Calendar, Clicquot Club Ginger Ale, 1942, complete, 24x14", EX **$100.00**

Calendar, Dr Pepper, 1951, complete, 21x13", NM, $100.00.

Calendar, Hires, 1957, hand-held frothy mug in front of 8-pack carton, Number One in More Ways..., complete, M **$25.00**

Calendar, Nehi, 1935, Rolf Armstrong girl standing in yellow gown w/white fur cape, dark background, 24x12", EX+..**$75.00**

Calendar, Royal Crown Cola, 1953, features Arlene Dahl w/bottle, complete, 24x11", EX+........................**$210.00**

Clock, Dr Pepper, Drink Dr Pepper on center band encircled by numbers w/enlarged 10-2-4, 14" dia, VG **$250.00**

Clock, NuGrape, w/black numbers around yellow logo over tilted bottle, light-up, metal frame, 15" dia, NM.**$275.00**

Clock, Royal Crown Cola, RC above Royal Crown Cola on red emblem, reverse-painted glass light-up, 15x15", NM **$200.00**

Clock, Seven-Up, light-up, You Like It...It Likes You!, square w/wooden frame, EX+ **$100.00**

Clock, Seven-Up, plastic, 7-Up logo in center, numbered 12-3-6-9, vertical, G..**$50.00**

Clock, Sun Crest, light-up, image of bottle surrounded by black numbers, 1950s, round, NM **$300.00**

Clock, Whistle, diecut masonite & wood, Golden Orange Refreshment Time on dial flanked by bottle & cartoon face, EX **$550.00**

Decal, Hires, Drink Hires Root Beer on bottle cap, EX..**$15.00**

Door push bar, Nesbitt's, porcelain, bottle cap at right of ...Take Home a Carton, yellow background, 32½", EX+ **$150.00**

Door push bar, Seven-Up, porcelain, Fresh Up Seven-Up flanked by logo on white background, 3x30", EX ...**$50.00**

Door push plate, Canada Dry, embossed tin, The Best of Them All, emblem above & behind hand-held bottle, vertical, NM **$100.00**

Door push plate, Mission Orange, tin, Drink & bottle cap above bottle, Naturally Good! below, orange & blue, 1950s, NM+......................................**$150.00**

Door push plate, Pal Ade, tin, Drink lettered diagonally above unopened bottle, stripes above & below, vertical, NM **$75.00**

Drinking glass, Double Cola, red & white logo, 4", M ..**$20.00**

Ice-cream scoop, Hires, plastic, Only One Taste Says Hires to You lettered on handle, EX.............................**$12.00**

Lighter, Diet-Rite Cola, aluminum w/flip top, Sugar-Free in script above product name in lower-case lettering, VG...**$15.00**

Menu board, Cloverdale Soft Drinks, framed border w/Drink...Soft Drinks on white panel above 7 menu inserts, 20x10", EX..................................**$110.00**

Menu board, Double Cola, tin, red & white oval logo & starbursts on blue above chalkboard, 28x20", M **$75.00**

Menu board, Hires, tin, Hires Root Beer in red on white above board, 27x19", EX+..................................**$100.00**

Menu board, Nehi, Drink... on yellow panel above Special Today in yellow script on chalkboard, 1930s-40s, 28x20", EX+ **$125.00**

Menu board, Seven-Up, wood, First Against Thirst & 7-Up logo above 3 rows of menu spaces, EX **$50.00**

Menu board, Squirt, tin, Switch To on circle pointing to bottle & Squirt boy above chalkboard, 27x19", NM+ **$75.00**

Menu board, Whistle, Thirsty? Just Whistle above board w/elves in each corner, embossed, 27x20", NM ..**$260.00**

Mug, Buckeye Root Beer, black logo, tail of Y forms circle around Buckeye Root Beer, regular handle, footed, M **$45.00**

Mug, Buckeye Root Beer, black logo, tail of Y forms circle around Buckeye Root Beer, V-shaped handle, footed, NM **$30.00**

Mug, Dad's Root Beer, glass barrel shape w/applied logo, red & yellow rectangular logo, 5x3", NM...................**$25.00**

Mug, Dad's Root Beer, glass barrel shape w/embossed lettering, M..**$20.00**

Mug, Frostop Root Beer, glass, Icy Cold Frostop Root Beer, yellow logo, 6", M....................$15.00

Mug, Hires, ceramic, Drink Hires It Is Pure on red diamond, 5½", NM....................$50.00

Mug, Hires, plastic, brown & red logo, Hires Root Beer, 5", NM....................$5.00

Mug, Howel's Root Beer, glass, embossed script lettering on oval, fluted sides, 5", NM....................$45.00

Picnic cooler, Seven-Up, vinyl, Fresh Up With 7-Up, white w/green straps, EX+....................$15.00

Plate, Moxie, china, logo & pointing Moxie man in center, gold rim, 6", M....................$45.00

Postcard, Cherry Smash, name lettered on George Washington's Mount Vernon lawn w/Black man serving him & Martha, NM....................$100.00

Salt & pepper shakers, Seven-Up, plastic bottles w/applied 7-Up label w/bubbles, M, pr....................$40.00

Sign, cardboard, Dr Pepper, Smart Lift above Dr Pepper sign, fishing girl at right, self-framed, 1940s-50s, 15x25", NM....................$275.00

Sign, cardboard, Grape Smack, Drink Grape Smack above bottle flanked by Always & Good, Ice Cold..., vertical, EX....................$125.00

Sign, cardboard, Grapette, Thirsty or Not! in upper left corner, girl w/bottle & flowers in lower right, 28x24", NM+....................$165.00

Sign, cardboard, Hires, Enjoy in script at left of girl w/glass & Hires Delicious... sign, 1950s, 13" dia, EX....................$125.00

Sign, cardboard, Kist Beverages, I Want To Get Kist..., Kist lips above bottle & girl w/lips puckered, 18x12", EX+....................$50.00

Sign, cardboard, Royal Crown Cola, Take Home RC for Your Family!, shows mom & kids in store, 1950s, 11x28", NM....................$110.00

Sign, cardboard, Squeeze, Had Your Squeeze Today? left of bathing beauty leaning on diving board, 24x18", EX+....................$150.00

Sign, cardboard diecut, Chero-Cola, Drink Chero-Cola, There's None So Good 5¢ on oval above fountain scene, 15x12", NM....................$175.00

Sign, cardboard diecut, Lucky Club Cola, Ace for Thirst, comical image of cowboy w/horseshoe-shaped limbs, 24x12", EX....................$100.00

Sign, cardboard diecut, Moxie, hand-held bottle, 20x10", NM....................$75.00

Sign, cardboard hanger, Cherry Smash, Always Drink Cherry Smash, Pleases Everybody Everywhere 5¢, w/logo, 5x11", VG....................$175.00

Sign, cardboard hanger, Cherry Smash, Drink Cherry Smash above logo & text, recipes on reverse, EX+....................$35.00

Sign, cardboard stand-up, Dr Swett's Root Beer, lady in fitted sweater holding up glass, product name below, 17x10", NM....................$100.00

Sign, cardboard stand-up, Eze-Orange, ...Appetizing Refreshing above bottle & 5¢ East To Serve East To Drink, 10x5", EX+....................$15.00

Sign, cardboard stand-up, Orange Kist, Drink...Ice Cold..., elves working hard-to-fill bottle, diecut, 11x9", NM....................$65.00

Sign, neon counter-top, Grapette, name on oval w/encased yellow panel surrounded by white tube, 1930s-40s, 13x22", NM....................$700.00

Sign, porcelain, Canada Dry, logo at left of Canada Dry Beverages, 7x24", M....................$70.00

Sign, porcelain, Kist Beverages, Drink..., red lips on white w/black & white lettering, red border, 1950s, 17x23", NM+....................$145.00

Sign, tin, Chocolate Crush, Drink...A Rich Creamy Chocolate Soda in a Bottle, brown & white on yellow, 1930s, 14x20", EX....................$180.00

Sign, tin, Clem's Cola, embossed Drink in diagonal letters above bottle cap & bottle on oval, red & yellow, 24x36", NM....................$200.00

Sign, tin, Cloverdale Soft Drinks, Cloverdale above 4-leaf clover & Soft Drinks on white oval inset on green, 9x13", EX....................$40.00

Sign, tin, Crush Carbonated Beverage, Ask for a..., Natural Flavor! Natural Color!, yellow & white on red, 4x26", EX+....................$100.00

Sign, tin, Dad's Root Beer, 30" dia, NM, $300.00.

Sign, tin, Diet-Rite Cola, Sugar-Free Diet-Rite Cola, w/bottle image, bordered, 1960s, 18x54", EX....................$45.00

Sign, tin, Grape Smash, Better Than Straight... above grape cluster & name, 5¢ Carbonated/In Bottles 5¢, 10x14", EX....................$325.00

Sign, tin, Jumbo Cola, Drink Jumbo, A Super Cola above bottle on yellow background, 1940s, 35x14", EX....................$245.00

Sign, tin, June Kola, Now in Quarts, 6 Full Glasses left of tilted bottle, 30x20", NM+....................$175.00

Sign, tin, Lemon Kola, name & 5¢ below lady in hat & draped shawl holding glass, 9x6", EX+....................$475.00

Sign, tin, Nesbitt's, name on orange above tilted bottle on blue, curved corners, 26x7", NM....................$110.00

Sign, tin, Nichol Kola, America's Taste Sensation, long-legged waiter w/5¢ bottle, red, black on cream, 1936, 36x12", EX....................$100.00

Sign, tin, Orange Squeeze, With the True Fruit Flavor, tilted bottle flanked by product name, yellow ground, 12x28", NM....................$150.00

Sign, tin, 7-Up, 28x20", VG, $65.00.

368

Sign, tin, Seven-Up, Real 7-Up Sold Here, round, 1930s, 14" dia, VG...**$80.00**

Sign, tin, Sun Crest, for drink rack, Drink... It's Best in black & white over white sun on red ground, 9x17", EX....**$50.00**

Sign, tin, Triple AAA Root Beer, Just Say Triple AAA Root Beer on emblem left of bottle, self-framed, 19x28", NM+......**$200.00**

Sign, tin, Triple Cola, It's Bigger It's Better at left of tilted bottle, 16 Ounces lower right, 32x12", NM+..............**$75.00**

Sign, tin diecut, Cleo Cola, Drink Cleo Cola for Goodness Sake, 26x28", EX+...**$200.00**

Sign, tin diecut, Dad's Root Beer, Original Dad's Draft Root Beer on bottle cap, 30" dia, NM..........................**$300.00**

Sign, tin diecut, Hires, bottle shape, 1950s, 58", NM ..**$425.00**

Sign, tin diecut, Orange-Crush, Enjoy Orange-Crush on bottle cap, 18" dia, EX+...**$225.00**

Syrup dispenser, Buckeye Root Beer, tree stump, ceramic, NM+ **$500.00**

Syrup dispenser, Grape-Julep, ceramic potbelly shape, Drink Grape-Julep, gold trim on base, original pump, 14x9", VG...**$750.00**

Syrup dispenser, Ward's Orange-Crush, ceramic orange shape w/embossed lettering, original pump, 15", VG ..**$550.00**

Thermometer, Crystal Club Pale Dry Ginger Ale, metal, logo & product name above bottle w/dial in center, 27", EX+ **$100.00**

Thermometer, Dr Pepper, tin, Dr Pepper Hot or Cold, canted corners, 1960s, 27x8", NM...................................**$100.00**

Thermometer, Frostie Root Beer, tin, figure behind bottle cap above tube, 6-pack carton below, 30", EX **$125.00**

Thermometer, Grapette, tin, Remember To Buy Grapette above bottle & tube, 15", EX **$100.00**

Thermometer, Hires, diecut tin bottle, 27", NM **$125.00**

Thermometer, Ma's Old Fashion Root Beer, Ma's on red oval above bottle w/dial face, Ma Knows Best below, yellow, 24", NM...**$130.00**

Thermometer, Orange-Crush, dial type, Taste Orange-Crush & daisies on orange background, 12" dia, NM+ **$125.00**

Thermometer, Orange-Crush, tin, Naturally It Tastes Better & product name above bottle & tube, rounded ends, 15", EX **$300.00**

Thermometer, Royal Crown Cola, blue, name on diamond above tube on arrow pointing up, vertical, rounded corners, VG+ **$75.00**

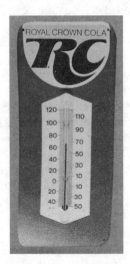

Thermometer, Royal Crown Cola, tin, 1960s, 14x6", NM, $75.00. (Photo courtesy of Dunbar Gallery.)

Thermometer, Seven-Up, dial type, logo on green background, 12" dia, NM+ **$100.00**

Thermometer, Squirt, tin, Put a Little Squirt in Your Life, Squirt on band above bottle & tube, 15", NM......**$65.00**

Tip tray, Moxie, Moxie Makes You Eat, Drink & Feel Better on label in center, simulated wood-grain ground, 6" dia, NM **$225.00**

Soda Bottles with Painted Labels

The earliest type of soda bottles were made by soda producers and sold in the immediate vicinity of the bottling company. Many had pontil scars, left by a rod that was used to manipulate the bottle as it was blown. They had a flat bottom rather than a 'kick-up,' so for transport, they were laid on their side and arranged in layers. This served to keep the cork moist, which kept it expanded, tight, and in place. Upright the cork would dry out, shrink, and expel itself with a 'pop,' hence the name 'soda pop.'

Until the thirties, the name of the product or the bottler was embossed in the glass or printed on a paper label (sometimes pasted over reused returnable bottles). Though a few paper labels were used as late as the sixties, nearly all bottles produced from the mid-thirties on had painted-on (pyroglazed) lettering, and logos and pictures were often added. Imaginations ran rampant. Bottlers waged a fierce competition to make their soda logos eyecatching and sales inspiring. Anything went! Girls, airplanes, patriotic designs, slogans proclaiming amazing health benefits, even cowboys and Indians became popular advertising ploys. This is the type you'll encounter most often today, and collector interest is on the increase. Look for interesting, multicolored labels, rare examples from small-town bottlers, and those made from glass other than clear or green. If you'd like to learn more about them, we recommend *The Official Guide to Collecting Applied Color Label Soda Bottles* by Thomas E. Marsh.

Advisor: Thomas Marsh, Painted-Label Soda Bottles (See Directory, Soda-Pop Collectibles)

A&W Root Beer, clear glass, 10-oz.............................**$10.00**

Abenakis, green glass, 7-oz.......................................**$10.00**

American Beverages, clear glass, 12-oz **$10.00**

Big Boy, clear glass, 32-oz..**$25.00**

Big Chief, clear glass, any size **$20.00**

Big Cola, clear glass, 13-oz......................................**$25.00**

Big Dot, clear glass, 10-oz **$10.00**

Big Red, clear glass, 10-oz **$10.00**

Bonnie Miss, clear or green glass, 8-oz **$15.00**

Buffalo Rock Ginger Ale, clear glass, 7-oz **$15.00**

Canfield's Beverages, clear glass, 9-oz......................**$10.00**

Chex, green glass, 7-oz **$10.00**

Clicquot Club Beverages, green glass, 32-oz..............**$15.00**

Clicquot Club Quality Flavors, green glass, 12-oz.......**$10.00**

Cott Nectar Beverages, clear glass, 12-oz **$15.00**

Cow Boy, clear glass, 6-oz..**$15.00**

Double Cola Jr, clear glass, 7½-oz **$10.00**

Dr Pepper, clear glass, 10-oz **$45.00**

Dr Swett's Early American Root Beer, 12-oz...............**$10.00**

Dr Swett's Original Root Beer, clear glass, 12-oz **$15.00**
Fanta, clear glass, 10-oz **$10.00**
Fresca, green glass, 1-pt 12-oz...............................**$15.00**
Fresca, green glass, 10-oz **$10.00**
Gold Dot, clear glass, 12-oz **$10.00**
Golden Age, clear glass, 12-oz **$20.00**
Good Guy, clear glass, 12-oz **$25.00**

Hi-Ho, 7-oz, $15.00; Holly Beverages, 7-oz, $15.00; Hornet Brand Beverages, 10-oz, $25.00. (Photo courtesy of Tom Marsh.)

Hillbilly, green glass, 10-oz...................................**$10.00**
Icy, clear glass, 10-oz **$15.00**
Jack Frost, clear glass, 1-qt...................................**$15.00**
Jumbo, clear glass, 10-oz.......................................**$10.00**
Lazy-B Beverages, clear glass, 10-oz......................**$20.00**
Liberty Bottling Co, clear glass, 8-oz.....................**$25.00**
Like, green glass, throwaway, 10-oz **$10.00**
Mini Pop, clear glass, 4-oz.....................................**$10.00**
Miscoe Orange Dry, amber glass, 7½-oz.................**$15.00**
Mission Beverage, clear glass, 1-qt........................**$15.00**
Moxie, aqua glass, 7-oz..**$20.00**
Mrs Warner's Old Fashioned Root Beer, amber glass, 12-oz **$35.00**
Nectar Sparkling Beverages, green glass, 7-oz...........**$10.00**
Neeco, amber glass, 6-oz..**$25.00**
Nehi, clear glass, 10-oz **$10.00**
O'Joy, clear glass, 7-oz...**$20.00**
Orange-Crush, clear glass, 10-oz **$10.00**
Par-T-Pak Pale Dry Ginger Ale, 1-qt **$15.00**
Peppo, aqua glass, 10-oz..**$10.00**
Pepsi (Diet), clear glass, 8-oz or 10-oz..................**$5.00**
Pepsi-Cola, clear glass, 1-qt **$25.00**
Pepsi-Cola, clear glass, 8-oz..................................**$5.00**
Purity's Ginger Ale, green glass, 1-qt.....................**$15.00**
Rex Quality Beverage, clear glass, 1-qt...................**$45.00**
Rose, clear, glass, 1-qt **$15.00**
Set Up, green glass, dice labels, 1-qt......................**$20.00**
Set Up, green glass, playing-card label, 1-qt **$15.00**

Sky High Beverages, 20-oz, $20.00; Tico, 1-qt, $8.00. (Photo courtesy of Tom Marsh.)

Seven-Up, green glass, 7-oz....................................**$15.00**
Ski-Club, clear glass, 1-qt......................................**$25.00**
Skipper, green glass, 1-qt.......................................**$15.00**
Sprite, green glass, 7-oz...**$10.00**
Squeeze, clear glass, 7-oz or 8-oz..........................**$10.00**
Squirt (Low Calorie), green glass, 10-oz.................**$10.00**
Up Town, green glass, 1-qt......................................**$15.00**
Vino Punch, amber glass, 7-oz................................**$25.00**
Walker's Root Beer, amber glass, 1953, 1-qt............**$125.00**
Walker's Root Beer, amber glass, 1954, 7-oz............**$125.00**
Wise-Up, green glass, 1-qt......................................**$20.00**
Yoo Hoo Chocolate, clear glass, 8-oz......................**$10.00**
Zeps Sparkling Pale Dry Ginger Ale, green glass, 1-qt..**$20.00**

Sporting Goods

Catalogs and other items of ephemera distributed by sporting good manufacturers, ammunition boxes, and just about any other item used for hunting and fishing purposes are collectible. In fact, there are auctions devoted entirely to collectors with these interests.

One of the most well-known companies specializing in merchandise of this kind was the gun manufacturer, The Winchester Repeating Arms Company. After 1931, the mark was changed from Winchester Trademark USA to Winchester-Western. Remington, Ithaca, Peters and Dupont are other manufacturers whose goods are especially sought after.

Ammo box, Clinton Cartridge Comp Pointer 10 ga, #4 shot, red, yellow & blue 2-pc box, full, labels intact, G........**$175.00**
Ammo box, Eley .375-caliber H&H Magnum, green w/black print, 10 per case, EX....................................**$40.00**
Ammo box, Federal Monarch 12-gauge, #8 shot, mk US Property, full, VG..**$26.00**
Ammo box, John Rigby .416 metal-covered solid bullets, black & yellow, full box, scarce, G+...................**$55.00**
Ammo box, Kynoch .404-caliber, Nitro-Express metal-covered soft nose, 5 per box, 2⅞" case, VG.............**$30.00**
Ammo box, Kynoch .470-caliber, metal-covered solid bullets, 5 per box, red & yellow w/black print, 3¼" case, G..**$40.00**
Ammo box, Peters High Velocity 28-gauge, #4 shot, red, blue & yellow box, full, NM...**$75.00**
Ammo box, Savage .250-300 caliber, red & yellow w/Indian Chief, EX, from $40 to....................................**$45.00**
Ammo box, Spanish .43-caliber, green label w/black print, 2-pc box, G **$25.00**
Ammo box, Western .35 Remington, red, blue & yellow, NM..**$30.00**
Ammo box, Western .38-40 Smokeless, buff box w/white labels & red & black print, 2-pc box, VG.............**$70.00**
Ammo box, Western X-Pert 12 ga, #2 shot, red, yellow & blue 2-pc box, empty, G **$30.00**
Ammo box, Winchester .40-82 caliber, orange label w/black print on 2-pc box, VG+ (sealed box) **$265.00**
Ammo box, Winchester Repeater 12-gauge, red, blue & yellow 2-pc box, VG **$25.00**
Book, Complete Book of Rifles & Shotguns, by Jack O'Conner, 1961, G **$30.00**

Book, Game Laws Directory, 1909, Remington/UMC, 122 pages, VG.................................$16.00

Book, Gun Digest, 2nd edition, 1946, EX..................$50.00

Book, Gun Digest, 8th Annual Edition, 1954, EX.......$26.00

Book, Sportman's Hunting Digest, Sports Afield, 1956, 31 pages, EX.................................$5.00

Book, Stoeger's Shooters Bible, #32, 1940, 508 pages, VG+ $34.00

Book, Winchester, The Gun That Won the West, by Harold Williamson, 1952, G.................................$17.00

Book, Winchester Ammunition Handbook, 4th edition..$15.00

Calendar, CG Store Frewsburg, NY, Phillip R Goodwin print of hunter w/horses crossing stream, complete, 15½x8", VG.................................$60.00

Calendar, LC Chase Co, 1914, untitled Phillip R Goodwin, linen paper, incomplete, 36x18", EX+.................$420.00

Calendar, Peters Cartridge Co, 1933, mallards flying over marsh, reproduction, 33x16", M (shrink wrapped)..............$20.00

Calendar, Phillip R Goodwin's 'Timberline Drama,' hunters watching grizzly, color, complete, 16½x9", VG+...$105.00

Calendar, Wheelers Fertilizer, 1918, lg moose in lily pads, complete, 20x12", VG.................................$60.00

Calendar, Winchester, 1977, featuring Bill Images, 21x13", NM.................................$15.00

Can, Winchester New Gun Oil, tin, red and yellow, 1968, NM, $45.00.

Caps, UMC, Expressly for Colt Belt & Pocket Pistols, beige-colored tin, EX.................................$70.00

Catalog, Smith & Wesson, 1930, 48-pages, NM...........$57.00

Catalog, Story of Ammo & Its Uses, Peters Ammo Co, 20 pages, colored cover, VG+.....................................$40.00

Cleaning kit for shotgun, Ward's Western Field, tin case w/cardboard sleeve, complete, VG+.....................$41.00

Counter felt, Dead Shot Smokeless Powder, dark blue & yellow print w/soft blue background, 21x8", G+ ...$265.00

Counter felt, Peters Shells & Cartridges, moose in center, maroon & white, 11½x10½", EX.........................$480.00

Counter felt, Remington-UMC, Big Game Cartridges, ram's head & rifle shell, brown, yellow & red, 14¼x11¾", EX $305.00

Counter felt, Shoot Dupont Powders, green & faded yellow, 10x8½", G.................................$100.00

Counter felt, UMC, quail sitting on top of Nitro Club shot shell, red, black & yellow, framed, 13¼x11", EX..........$505.00

Dynamite box, Austin Powder, wooden, dovetailed, stenciled in red, VG.................................$40.00

Fish creel, willow weave, unused, EX.........................$50.00

Order blanks, Ithaca Gun Co, 17 pcs, 1930s, 6x3½", NM..$10.00

Plate, Winchester, US Bicentennial, pewter, NM.........$21.00

Poster, Hintermeister, 2 men in canoe shooting at moose, color, 12x10", EX.................................$20.00

Poster, Mason City Coca-Cola Bottling Co, Off Guard, shows bear & hunter, Phillip R Goodwin, oak frame, 26½x28", NM.................................$890.00

Poster, Remington, framed, 22x16", EX, $225.00.

Poster, The Warning, moose at stream w/ducks in flight, Edwards, color, 1921, 29½x16½", EX.................$675.00

Poster, US Cartridge Co, shows the entire line of shells & testimonials, 23x34", VG.................................$90.00

Poster, Western/Winchester, pheasant hunt, 1955, 42x28", EX.................................$85.00

Poster, Winchester, Duck Camp, 1954, 23x16", EX...$155.00

Poster, Winchester, hunter watching squirrel in tree, 1955, 42x28", EX.................................$55.00

Poster, Winchester, man shooting flying pheasant, 1955, 42x28", EX+.................................$85.00

Poster, Winchester Golden Spike Commemorative, 14x27½".................................$16.00

Primers, Berdan Co, English, full sealed tube of 250, VG+.................................$35.00

Sign, Ithaca Guns, Hammer & Hammerless, Every Gun Warranted, brown lettering on cream background, 6x14", VG.................................$1,100.00

Targets, Winchester, air rifle, bull's-eye on front, tubes of shot on back, buff w/black print, 12 pcs, G+ $5.00

Targets, Winchester, Ranger Targets, for .22 caliber, packet of 12, VG (original folder).................................$35.00

Sports Collectibles

When the baseball card craze began sweeping the country a decade ago, memorabilia relating to many types of sports began to interest sports fans. Today ticket stubs, uniforms, autographed baseballs, sports magazines, and game-used bats are prized by baseball fans, and some items, depending on their age or the notoriety of the player or team they represent, may be very valuable. Baseball and golfing seem to be the two sports most collectors are involved with, but hockey and auto racing are gaining ground. There are several books on the market you'll want to read if you're interested in sports:

Value Guide to Baseball Collectibles by M. Donald Raycraft and R. Craig Raycraft, *Collector's Guide to Baseball Memorabilia* by Don Raycraft and Stew Salowitz, and *The Encyclopedia of Golf Collectibles* by John M. Olman and Morton W. Olman.

Game-used equipment is sought out by collectors, and where once they preferred only items used by professionals, now the sports market has expanded, and collectors have taken great interest in the youth equipment endorsed by many star players now enshrined in their respective Halls of Fame. Some youth equipment was given as advertising premiums and bear that company's name or logo. Such items are now very desirable collectibles.

See also Autographs; Indianapolis 500 Memorabilia; Magazines; Pin-Back Buttons; Puzzles.

Advisors: Don and Anne Kier (See Directory, Sports Collectibles)

Almanac, 1955 Baseball..............................**$20.00**
Ashtray, Bobby Orr, plastic w/photo scene of play action, marked, MB-Italy, 5x5", M...........................**$6.00**
Baseball glove, Rawlings, w/facsimile Billy Williams signature, Hall of Fame 1965-74, EX+ **$30.00**

Baseball glove, Robin Roberts, MacGregor, 1950s, EX in VG box, $100.00.

Baseball glove, Spalding, model MS-12L, Mel Stottlemyre facsimile signature, EX **$20.00**
Baseball glove, Wilson, facsimile George Kell signature, Hall of Fame 1945-1948, EX..........................**$30.00**
Basketball, Indiana University, 1975-76, signed by 12 team members & Bobby Knight, EX+ **$75.00**
Bat, Adirondack, Dave Parker store model, 36", NM..**$25.00**
Bat, Adirondack, Jackie Robinson Little League model, 30", NM **$100.00**
Bat, Hanna Baltrite, Chuck Klein model, block letters, VG+ **$45.00**
Bat, Hillerich & Bradsby, Jackie Robinson model, 34", VG..................................**$150.00**
Bat, Hillerich & Bradsby, Jimmie Foxx gold signature model, 16", EX+..................................**$300.00**
Bat, Hillerich & Bradsby, Little League model, 29", VG..**$10.00**
Bat, Louisville Slugger, Play Ball With Atlantic, 16"..**$30.00**
Book, Kellogg's Sports Library Blue Book, 1934, 4½x6½", EX+ **$25.00**
Book, Vince Lombardi on Football, hardcover, color illustrations, Gallahad Books, NM **$15.00**

Booklet, Wheaties Sports Library of Football, copyright 1945, 30 pages, 5x7"..................................**$4.00**
Catcher's mask, Rawlings, Stan Lopata model, 1950s, VG+ **$30.00**
Catcher's mitt, Sears, Ted Williams model, EX...........**$50.00**
Coaster, New York Yankees & Schaefer Beer, M **$3.50**

Doll, Detroit Tigers, stuffed cloth, 1977, 12", EX, $40.00.

Doll, Pittsburgh Steelers, molded vinyl head, stuffed plush body w/fabric feet, Gund, 1967, 18"....................**$12.50**
First day cover, Tom LaSorda, National Sports Collector's Convention, July 8, 1983, 7x4"..................**$25.00**
First day cover, 1932 Olympics, 3rd Olympic Winter Games at Lake Placid, NY, 3½x6½", EX+..........................**$15.00**

Glasses, Wilson Tennis Balls, set of 5, $65.00.

Helmet, New York Jets, used in game.......................**$225.00**
Magazine, Boxing, 1936, Joe Lewis cover....................**$32.00**
Magazine, Life, May 2, 1949, Arnold Galiffa cover **$10.00**
Magazine, Life, May 5, 1972, Cathy Rigby cover.........**$10.00**
Magazine, Sports Illustrated, April 4, 1976, Hank Aaron cover **$12.50**
Magazine, Sports Illustrated, December 10, 1979, Sugar Ray Leonard cover..................................**$6.00**
Magazine, Sports Illustrated, September 20, 1954, bulldogging scene on cover **$15.00**
Magazine, Sports Illustrated, 1955, Hialeah Horserace cover.**$8.00**
Magazine, Sports Illustrated, 1973, Miami Dolphins cover **$8.00**
Magazine, Wrestling Magazine, March 1951, NM **$12.50**
Matchcover, Joe Louis & Max Schmeling boxing, Buick/NBC, 1936, 3½x9½", EX+ **$12.00**
Medal, United States Lawn Tennis Association Bronze Medal, w/ribbon, Robbins Co, 1930, EX..........................**$65.00**

Media Guide, Denver Broncos, 1970, w/information on players, teams, statistics & ads..**$15.00**

Mug, Saratoga Race Course, frosted clear glass w/horses crossing finish line, 1950s, 5½", M **$10.00**

Newspaper, LA Times, October 16, 1989, Gretzky Becomes the Greatest One headline, complete.....................**$8.00**

Newspaper, The Baltimore Sun, September 7, 1995, Immortal Cal (Cal Ripkin Jr) headline, complete.................**$25.00**

Pamphlet, Body Builder Magazine, 1948, EX **$6.00**

Paperback book, Football Rules in Pictures, by Schiffer & Durosha, 1969 ....**$4.00**

Paperback book, Strange but True Basketball Stories, by Howard Liss, 1972...**$5.00**

Patch, Chicago Cubs, embroidered twill, souvenir style, ca 1960s, 7"...**$8.00**

Patch, 50th Anniversary 1933-1983 All-Star Game, cloth, M **$10.00**

Pencil, wood bat form, Baseball's 100th Anniversary Your Advertisement Neatly Displayed in This Space, 6"...**$28.00**

Pennant, American League Baseball Champions, 1944, Compliments of St Louis Browns w/photo...........**$30.00**

Pennant, 1966 World Series, LA Dodgers vs Baltimore Orioles, blue felt w/silkscreen design & letters, 29".............**$20.00**

Photo, Don Mattingly, 4x5" **$7.50**

Photo, Ivan Putski, glossy black & white, 8x10" **$5.00**

Photo, Larry Bird, color, 8x10"...................................**$4.00**

Pocketknife, bat form, 2 blades, marked Fairmount Cutlery Co, 1960s, 2½", w/attached chain & ¾" plastic baseball ..**$75.00**

Poker chip, clay w/embossed golfer, 1930s, 1½".........**$8.00**

Postcard, Boston Braves, 1948, color, unused.............**$20.00**

Postcard, Joe Di Maggio's restaurant, real color photo, unused **$20.00**

Program, New York Mets, 1989 ....**$5.00**

Program, New York Yankees & Milwaukee Braves, 1957 World Series **$100.00**

Program, 1948 US Olympic Weightlifting Trials, w/photos & text **$7.50**

Program, 1967 ABA Basketball All-Stars, EX+ **$75.00**

Program w/scorecard, New York Yankees, 1987, Catfish Hunter cover **$10.00**

Record, Great Moments in Sports, Autolite Records, 1965, 33⅓ rpm, VG+..**$25.00**

Scorecard, Brooklyn Dogers, 1941 ....**$45.00**

Scorecard, New York Mets, 1972 Spring Training, w/4 autographs: Berra, Garrett, Rauch & Harrelson **$45.00**

Scorecard, skeet, marked Western World's Champion Ammunition, 1960s, 8x9", EX.............................**$6.00**

Scorecard, St Louis Cardinals, 1962, color cover w/mascot, unused **$7.50**

Sign, Dallas Cowboys, Big Signs series, Fleer Gum, 1968, cardboard w/hole at top, 7¾x11½".....................**$6.00**

Sunday supplement magazine, 1956, Richie Ashburn & Robin Roberts, EX+ **$4.50**

Ticket, Baltimore vs Texas at Memorial Stadium, April 8, 1985, unused **$5.00**

Ticket, NBA All-Star Game, February 3, 1976, East vs West, unused **$25.00**

Ticket, 1972 World's Series, unused **$50.00**

Tie tack, Brooklyn Dodgers World Champions 1955 on pennant-shaped enameled metal.......................**$28.00**

Trading card, Brooklyn Dodgers, 1988 series, set of 12....**$35.00**

Trading card, Gene Tunney, Lambert & Butler Cigarettes..**$22.00**

Trading card, Jack Dempsey, Churchman's Cigarettes, 1½x3"...**$30.00**

Willie Mays, black & white photo on red background, celluloid, 1½"...**$14.00**

Yearbook, Buffalo Bills, 1971, staff & player biographies, historical highlights, 100 pages.................................**$40.00**

St. Clair Glass

Since 1941, the St. Clair family has operated a small glasshouse in Elwood, Indiana. They're most famous for their lamps, though they've also produced many styles of toothpick holders, paperweights, and various miniatures as well. Though the paperweights are usually stamped and dated, smaller items may not be marked at all. In addition to various colors of iridescent glass, they've also made many articles in slag glass (both caramel and pink) and custard. For more information, we recommend *St. Clair Glass Collector's Book* by Bonnie Pruitt (see Directory, St. Clair).

Animal dish, dolphin covered bowl, green carnival, Joe St Clair...**$45.00**

Animal dish, horse covered bowl, cobalt carnival, Joe St Clair...**$45.00**

Bowl, sauce; Paneled Grape, ice blue carnival, 1968...**$35.00**

Candy dish, Inverted Fan & Feather, cobalt carnival, w/lid, unmarked (Joe St Clair)....................................**$35.00**

Creamer, Paneled Grape, purple carnival, unmarked (Joe St Clair), 1968 ....**$45.00**

Frame, floral, Made for International Carnival Glass Assn, 10th Anniversary, Indianapolis, Ind 1976, Joe St Clair **$95.00**

Goblet, Holly, blue carnival, unmarked (Joe St Clair) ..**$25.00**

Goblet, Paneled Thistle, blue carnival, unmarked (Joe St Clair) **$25.00**

Goblet, Strawberry & Currant, flared, white carnival, Joe St Clair...**$40.00**

Kewpie doll, chocolate, solid, Joe St Clair.................**$30.00**

Paperweight, Bicentennial, red, white & blue flowers, bell shape, Bob & Maude St Clair, 1976.....................**$75.00**

Paperweight, blue & white flowers, Bob & Maude St Clair, 1975, med..**$50.00**

Paperweight, Henry Sears, Christmas 1977, $65.00.

Plate, Liberty Bell Centennial, cobalt carnival, 1976, Joe St Clair...**$30.00**

Plate, Paneled Grape, purple carnival, unmarked (Joe St Clair), 1968 ....**$45.00**

Toothpick holder, Bi-Centennial, blue carnival, Joe St Clair..**$30.00**

Toothpick holder, Dog's Head, cobalt carnival, Joe St Clair..**$25.00**

Toothpick holder, Floral, dark amber carnival, Joe St Clair..**$35.00**

Toothpick holder, Ford, Rockefeller, Washington, Liberty Bell shape, cobalt carnival............................**$35.00**

Toothpick holder, Hanging Cherries, white carnival...**$30.00**

Toothpick holder, Heron in Rushes, custard, unmarked (Joe St Clair)..**$22.00**

Toothpick holder, Heron in Rushes, custard iridescent, unmarked (Joe St Clair)....................................**$25.00**

Toothpick holder, Indian Head, green & white, Joe St Clair..**$20.00**

Toothpick holder, Indian Head, vaseline iridescent....**$25.00**

Toothpick holder, S Repeat, amber carnival, Joe St Clair..**$25.00**

Tumbler, Cactus, red/amberina, Joe St Clair, rare.......**$35.00**

Tumbler, Floral, purple carnival, unmarked...............**$30.00**

Tumbler, Wildflower, deep purple carnival.................**$27.00**

Wheelbarrow, jade slag, Joe St Clair..........................**$25.00**

Stanford Corn

Teapots, cookie jars, salt and pepper shakers, and other kitchen and dinnerware items modeled as ears of yellow corn with green shucks were made by the Stanford company, who marked most of their ware. The Shawnee company made two very similar corn lines; just check the marks to verify the manufacturer.

Butter dish..**$45.00**

Casserole, 8" long **$35.00**

Cookie jar..**$85.00**

Creamer & sugar bowl **$45.00**

Pitcher, 7½" **$55.00**

Plate, 9" long **$30.00**

Relish tray..**$35.00**

Salt & pepper shakers, sm, pr **$35.00**

Salt & pepper shakers, 4", pr......................................**$25.00**

Spoon rest..**$25.00**

Teapot...**$60.00**

Stangl Birds

The Stangl Pottery Company of Flemington and Trenton, New Jersey, made a line of ceramic birds which they introduced in 1940 to fulfill the needs of a market no longer able to access foreign imports, due to the onset of WWII. These bird figures immediately attracted a great deal of attention. At the height of their production, sixty decorators were employed to hand paint the birds at the plant, and the overflow was contracted out and decorat-ed in private homes. After WWII, inexpensive imported figurines once again saturated the market, and for the most part, Stangl curtailed their own production, though the birds were made on a very limited basis until as late as 1977.

Nearly all the birds were marked. A four-digit number was used to identify the species, and some pieces were signed by the decorator. An 'F' indicates a bird that was decorated at the Flemington plant.

Club: Stangl/Fulper Collectors Club
P.O. Box 64
Changewater, NJ 07831; Yearly membership: $25 (includes quarterly newsletter)

Allen Hummingbird, #3634 ....**$80.00**

Audubon Warbler, #3755, 4¼", from $150 to **$175.00**

Audubon Warbler, #3756D, 7¾", pr, from $365 to....**$385.00**

Black Poll Warbler, #3819 ....**$150.00**

Black-Throated Green Warbler, #3814 ....**$125.00**

Blue-Headed Vireo, #3448 ....**$70.00**

Bluebird, #3276..**$70.00**

Broadbill Hummingbird, #3629, from $100 to...........**$125.00**

Cardinal, pink, #3444...**$85.00**

Cerulean Warbler, #3456..**$65.00**

Chestnut-Backed Chickadee, #3811 ....**$120.00**

Chickadees on branch, #3581, $225.00.

Cockatoo, #3405, 6½", from $48 to **$52.00**

Cockatoo, #3580, 9", from $125 to **$150.00**

Cockatoo, #3584, 11⅜", from $225 to.......................**$250.00**

Cockatoos, #3405D, old, pr **$190.00**

Duck (flying), #3443, from $225 to **$250.00**

European Finch, #3922, from $850 to.........................**$950.00**

Evening Grosbeak, #3813 ....**$125.00**

Golden-Crowned Kinglet, #3848 ....**$100.00**

Golden-Crowned Kinglets, #3853, group, from $575 to..**$600.00**

Goldfinch, #3849..**$100.00**

Goldfinches #3635, group from $175 to **$200.00**

Hen, shaker, #3286, late **$45.00**

Hen Pheasant, Antique Gold, #3491 ....**$100.00**

Indigo Bunting, #3589 ....**$70.00**

Kentucky Warbler, #3598..**$60.00**

Kingfisher, #3406, from $65 to...................................**$75.00**

Kingfishers, #3406D, pr, from $115 to **$130.00**

Nuthatch, #3593, 2½", from $55 to............................**$65.00**

Oriole, #3402...**$65.00**

Orioles, #3402D, revised, pr, from $100 to................**$125.00**

Owl, #3407...**$350.00**

Parula Warbler, #3583...**$50.00**
Prothonotary Warbler, #3447.......................................**$75.00**
Red-Breasted Nuthatch, #3851, from $75 to **$85.00**
Red-headed Woodpecker, #3751, pink glossy..........**$145.00**
Red-headed Woodpecker, #3752D, pink glossy, 7¾", pr, from
   $235 to **$255.00**
Redstarts, #3490D, pr..**$245.00**
Rieffers Hummingbird, #3628, from $100 to **$125.00**
Rooster, #3445, gray **$225.00**
Rufous Hummingbird, #3585, 3"..................................**$60.00**
Scarlet Tanager, #3750D, pink, 8", pr, from $435 to ..**$355.00**
Titmouse, #3592..**$55.00**
Western Bluebird, #3815, from $425 to.....................**$465.00**
Western Tanager, #3749, red matt, 4¾", from $200 to ..**$235.00**
Wilson Warbler, #3597, from $50 to **$60.00**
Wren, #3401, revised, from $50 to **$60.00**
Yellow-Headed Verdin, #3921, minimum value.....**$1,250.00**
Yellow-Throated Warbler, #3924, from $425 to........**$450.00**

Stangl Dinnerware

The Stangl Company of Trenton, New Jersey, grew out of the Fulper company that had been established in Flemington early in the 1800s. Martin Stangl, president of the company, introduced a line of dinnerware in the 1920s. By 1954, 90% of their production centered around their dinnerware lines. Until 1942, the clay they used was white firing, and decoration was minimal, usually simple one-color glazes. In 1942, however, the first of the red-clay lines that have become synonymous with the Stangl name was created. Designs were hand carved into the greenware, then hand painted. More than one hundred different patterns have been cataloged. From 1974 until 1978, a few lines previously discontinued on the red clay were reintroduced with a white clay body. Soon after '78, the factory closed.

If you'd like more information on the subject, read *The Collector's Encyclopedia of American Dinnerware* by Jo Cunningham.

Amber Glo, coffee server..**$50.00**
Amber Glo, creamer & sugar bowl, individual **$25.00**
Amber Glo, gravy boat, w/undertray **$20.00**
Amber Glo, plate, 10", from $10 to **$12.00**
Antique Gold, compote, lace edge, footed, 4x9½"....**$20.00**
Antique Gold, cornucopia, #5066, 11" **$40.00**

Antique Gold, leaf bowl, basket handle, #5137, 13¼" **$35.00**
Black Gold, apple tray, #3546, 13"............................**$55.00**
Black Gold, heart dish, #3797....................................**$30.00**
Blueberry, bowl, salad; 12", from $50 to **$60.00**
Blueberry, butter dish, from $30 to...........................**$40.00**
Blueberry, cup **$10.00**
Blueberry, pitcher, 1-pt, from $25 to.........................**$30.00**
Blueberry, relish, from $25 to....................................**$28.00**

Blueberry, teapot, $65.00.

Country Garden, bowl, divided vegetable..................**$35.00**
Country Garden, casserole, w/handle, 8" **$40.00**
Country Garden, coffeepot, 8-cup, from $50 to..........**$60.00**
Country Garden, cup & saucer....................................**$16.00**
Country Garden, lug soup **$12.00**
Country Garden, plate, 10" **$18.00**
Country Life, bowl, fruit; w/rooster, 5½", from $35 to **$45.00**
Country Life, bread tray, w/hen & chicks **$265.00**
Country Life, chop plate, farmhouse behind garden,
   12½" **$450.00**
Country Life, chop plate, 12"....................................**$225.00**
Festival, bowl, cereal..**$12.00**
Festival, bowl, divided vegetable **$30.00**
Festival, bowl, lug soup **$12.00**
Festival, casserole, w/serving lid **$42.00**
First Love, bowl, salad; 10", from $30 to **$35.00**
First Love, casserole, stick handle, 6"........................**$12.50**
First Love, plate, 8", from $6 to **$8.00**
Florette, bowl, flat soup **$10.00**
Florette, gravy boat...**$10.00**
Florette, plate, 11"..**$14.00**
Florette, plate, 6"...**$5.00**
Florette, salt & pepper shakers, pr............................**$12.00**
Florette, stacking mug & saucer **$18.00**
Fruit, bowl, coupe soup...**$22.00**
Fruit, bowl, salad; Terra Rose, 12"............................**$45.00**
Fruit, pitcher, ½-pt..**$15.00**
Fruit, relish...**$36.00**
Garden Flower, casserole, 8", from $50 to..................**$60.00**
Garden Flower, creamer, individual, from $12 to **$18.00**
Garden Flower, plate, 10", from $15 to.......................**$18.00**
Garden Flower, teapot, from $50 to **$55.00**
Golden Blossom, bowl, vegetable; w/lid, 8" **$38.00**
Golden Blossom, egg cup, from $8 to.........................**$10.00**
Golden Blossom, mug..**$10.00**

Golden Blossom, plate, 10", from $10 to....................**$12.00**
Golden Harvest, ashtray, rectangular, from $18 to......**$22.50**
Golden Harvest, bowl, divided vegetable...................**$38.00**
Golden Harvest, bread tray....................................**$28.00**
Golden Harvest, chop plate, 14½" **$50.00**
Golden Harvest, egg cup **$10.00**

Golden Harvest, Salt and pepper shakers, $15.00; Gravy boat, $18.00.

Golden Harvest, sugar bowl, from $12.50 to **$15.00**
Granada Gold, cornucopia, brown & blue, #3675, 10x12" .**$55.00**
Granada Gold, double pear dish, center basket handle, #3782, 7½" square **$20.00**
Kiddieware, Barnyard Friends, dish & cup **$175.00**
Kiddieware, Barnyard Friends, 3-part dish...............**$175.00**
Kiddieware, Five Little Pigs, dish **$165.00**
Kiddieware, Humpty Dumpty, plate, pink rim.........**$150.00**
Kiddieware, Mary Quite Contrary, cup & bowl, from $200 to...**$225.00**
Kiddieware, Ranger Boy, cup, from $100 to **$125.00**
Kiddieware, Wild Animals, cup, from $135 to **$150.00**
Kiddieware, Woman in the Shoe, cup, from $80 to .**$120.00**
Laurel, carafe...**$110.00**
Magnolia, chop plate, 14½", from $30 to **$35.00**
Magnolia, coffeepot, 8-cup, from $40 to.....................**$45.00**
Magnolia, cup & saucer......................................**$15.00**
Magnolia, plate, 10", from $10 to **$12.50**
Magnolia, teapot **$48.00**
Orchard Song, bowl, lug soup **$12.50**
Orchard Song, bread tray....................................**$23.00**
Orchard Song, plate, 9", from $10 to **$12.00**
Orchard Song, server, center handle, 10".....................**$6.00**
Orchard Song, teapot, 6-cup, from $35 to...................**$45.00**
Provincial, bowl, lug soup **$12.00**
Provincial, bowl, salad; 10" **$35.00**
Provincial, candle warmer...................................**$22.00**
Provincial, creamer & sugar bowl **$20.00**
Provincial, cup & saucer **$13.00**
Provincial, pitcher, ½-pt......................................**$20.00**
Provincial, plate, 10" **$15.00**
Provincial, plate, 6" **$5.00**
Provincial, plate, 8" **$10.00**
Starflower, coaster/ashtray.....................................**$7.50**
Starflower, mug, 2-cup, from $20 to **$25.00**
Starflower, plate, 8", from $6 to...............................**$8.00**
Thistle, bowl, fruit **$12.00**
Thistle, bowl, salad; 12" **$50.00**
Thistle, bowl, vegetable; divided............................**$35.00**
Thistle, casserole, w/lid, ind **$15.00**
Thistle, chop plate, 12½" **$28.00**
Thistle, coaster **$15.00**
Thistle, cup & saucer..**$12.00**

Thistle, egg cup **$15.00**
Thistle, plate, 10" **$15.00**
Thistle, plate, 8" **$10.00**
Thistle, salt & pepper shakers, pr **$16.00**
Town & Country, coffeepot, blue **$100.00**
Tropic Isle, carafe **$135.00**
White Dogwood, bowl, 8"....................................**$30.00**
Yellow Tulip, coffeepot, 8-cup, from $35 to **$40.00**
Yellow Tulip, plate, 11", from $12 to **$15.00**

Star Trek Memorabilia

Trekkies, as fans are often referred to, number nearly 40,000 today, hold national conventions, and compete with each other for choice items of Star Trek memorabilia, some of which may go for hundreds of dollars.

The Star Trek concept was introduced to the public in the mid-1960s through a TV series which continued for many years in syndication. An animated cartoon series (1977), the release of six major motion pictures, and the success of 'Star Trek, The Next Generation,' television show (Fox network, 1987) all served as a bridge to join two generations of loyal fans.

Its success has resulted in the sale of vast amounts of merchandise, both licensed and unlicensed, such as clothing, promotional items of many sorts, books and comics, toys and games, records and tapes, school supplies, and party goods. Many of these are still available at flea markets around the country. An item that is 'mint in box' is worth at least twice as much as one in excellent condition but without its original packaging. For more information, refer to *Modern Toys, American Toys, 1930-1980,* by Linda Baker and *Schroeder's Collectible Toys, Antique to Modern* (Collector Books).

Advertising premium, USS Enterprise, inflatable, Kraft, 24", M **$15.00**
Bank, figural Captain Kirk standing in front of console, painted vinyl, Play Pal, 1975, 11", EX..................**$45.00**
Book, Mission to Horatius, TV Authorized Edition, Whitman, 1968, NM **$30.00**
Bookmark, Captain Kirk, Antioch, EX..........................**$1.00**
Bowl, plastic, 1975, EX......................................**$15.00**
Calendar, Star Date 1979, EX **$20.00**
Coloring book, Rescue to Raylo, Whitman, 1978, EX+..**$10.00**
Cups, paper, w/Captain Kirk, Mr Spock, Dr McCoy & Enterprise, 1976, 8-count, NM (sealed package)..**$15.00**
Curtains, blue w/Star Trek characters & Enterprise, 1970s, 60x24", EX **$25.00**
Doll, Mr Spock, plush body w/vinyl head, Knickerbocker, 1972, 12", NM (EX box) **$40.00**
Eraser, Mr Spock, 1983, EX **$10.00**
Figure, Ertl, Captain Kirk, Star Trek III, 3¾", MOC.....**$25.00**
Figure, Ertl, Scotty, Star Trek III, 3¾", MOC.............**$25.00**
Figure, Galoob, Captain Piccard, Next Generation, 3¾", MOC...**$15.00**
Figure, Galoob, Commander Riker, Next Generation, 3¾", MOC..**$15.00**
Figure, Galoob, Georgi La Forge, Next Generation, 3¾", MOC...**$15.00**

Figure, Galoob, Lt Commander Data, Next Generation, 3rd series, flesh face, 3¾", MOC **$30.00**

Figure, Galoob, Lt Tasha Yar, Next Generation, 3¾", MOC...**$30.00**

Figure, Galoob, Lt Worf, Next Generation, 3¾", MOC..**$15.00**

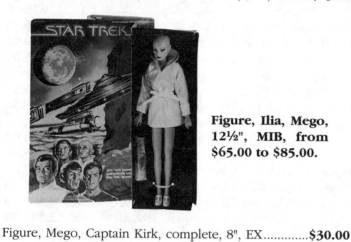

Figure, Ilia, Mego, 12½", MIB, from $65.00 to $85.00.

Figure, Mego, Captain Kirk, complete, 8", EX.............**$30.00**

Figure, Mego, Captain Kirk, The Motion Picture, 3¾", MOC **$35.00**

Figure, Mego, Captain Kirk, 12", NMIB.......................**$80.00**

Figure, Mego, Dr McCoy, no accessories, 8" **$35.00**

Figure, Mego, Dr McCoy, The Motion Picture, 3¾", MOC (unpunched), minimum value **$35.00**

Figure, Mego, Ilia, 12", MIB **$75.00**

Figure, Mego, Klingon, complete, 8", EX....................**$25.00**

Figure, Mego, Klingon, 8", MOC **$55.00**

Figure, Mego, Mr Spock, complete, 8", EX..................**$25.00**

Figure, Mego, Mr Spock, The Motion Picture, 3¾", M (EX card) **$35.00**

Figure, Mego, Mr Spock, 12", NMIB............................**$75.00**

Figure, Mego, Mr Spock, 8", MOC................................**$50.00**

Game, Star Trek, Ideal, 1967, EX+ (EX box) **$60.00**

Greeting cards, Captain Kirk, 6 different, M, each........**$2.00**

Gun, dart/cap; blue plastic w/black grips & muzzle, diecast works, Remco, 1966-67, 12½", G **$50.00**

Gun, water; black plastic phaser, AHI, 5", MOC.........**$45.00**

Kite, plastic, Mr Spock, Hi-Flier, 1975, MOC (sealed).**$45.00**

Magic Slate, w/stylus, 1978, EX+ **$26.00**

Mug, Mr Smock or Sulu, photo image, MIB, each.....**$18.00**

Napkins, paper, w/Captain Kirk, Mr Spock, Dr McCoy & Enterprise, 1976, 20-count, M (sealed package)...**$10.00**

Photograph, black & white publicity shot of William Shatner as Captain Kirk w/facsimile signature, 5x4", 1965, VG+...**$5.00**

Play putty, w/print fluid & sponge, NMOC (Kirk & Spock on card)...**$10.00**

Playset, Inter-Space Communicator Set, Lone Star, 1974, MIB **$55.00**

Playset, Star Trek USS Enterprise Bridge, The Motion Picture, for 3¾" figures, white plastic, MIB.....................**$135.00**

Postcard book, set of 48 cards, M **$35.00**

T-shirt, gold, 1990, EX...**$20.00**

Vehicle, Corgi, Klingon Warship, Star Trek II, M (NM card)..**$25.00**

Vehicle, Corgi, USS Enterprise, Star Trek II, MOC.......**$25.00**

Vehicle, Dinky, Klingon Warship, diecast, MIB...........**$85.00**

Vehicle, Ertl, USS Enterprise, Star Trek III, MOC........**$25.00**

Vehicle, Galoob, USS Enterprise, Next Generation, 1988, NMOC **$35.00**

Vehicle, USS Enterprise, The Motion Picture, Dinky, diecast, 4", MOC **$30.00**

Walkie talkies, Star Trek Communicators, Mego, 1974, plastic, MIB, $150.00. (Photo courtesy of June Moon.)

Star Wars

In the late seventies, the movie 'Star Wars' became a box office hit, most notably for its fantastic special effects and its ever-popular theme of space adventure. Two more movies followed, 'The Empire Strikes Back' in 1980 and 'Return of the Jedi' in 1983. After the first movie, an enormous amount of related merchandise was released. Most of these items were action figures, made by the Kenner company who included the logo of the 20th Century Fox studios (under whom they were licensed) on everything they made until 1980. Just before the second movie, Star Wars creator, George Lucas, regained control of the merchandise rights, and items inspired by the last two films can be identified by his own Lucasfilm logo. Since 1987, Lucasfilm, Ltd., has operated shops in conjunction with the Star Tours at Disneyland theme parks.

What to collect? First and foremost, buy what you yourself enjoy. But remember that condition is all important. Look for items still mint in the box. Using that as a basis, if the box is missing, deduct at least half. If a major accessory or part is gone, the item is basically worthless. Learn to recognize the most desirable, most valuable items. There are lots of Star Wars bargains yet to be had!

Original packaging helps date a tag, since the package or card design was updated as each new movie was released. Naturally, items representing the older movies are more valuable than later issues.

For more coverage of this subject, refer to *Schroeder's Collectibles Toys, Antique to Modern* (Collector Books).

Bank, Chewbacca, ceramic, Sigma, MIB.....................**$25.00**

Bank, Darth Vader, plastic, EX+...................................**$18.00**

Belt, Return of the Jedi, elastic, w/Darth Vader buckle, EX...**$12.00**

Boots, Star Wars, Darth Vader pictured, EX................**$75.00**

Case, Chewbacca, bandolier strap, MIB......................**$30.00**

Case, Laser Rifle, NM (EX box) **$45.00**

Costume, R2-D2, Ben Cooper, NMIB **$12.00**

Figure, Action Masters, 4-pack, scarce, MIP **$60.00**

Figure, Admiral Ackbar, Return of the Jedi, 3¾", MOC ..**$18.00**

Figure, Anakin Skywalker, Tri-Logo, 3¾", MOC..........**$45.00**

Figure, At-At Commander, Empire Strikes Back, 3¾", MOC ...**$22.00**
Figure, B-Wing Pilot, Return of the Jedi, 3¾", MOC...**$16.00**
Figure, B-Wing Pilot, Return of the Jedi, 3¾", w/accessories, M **$5.00**
Figure, Bib Fortuna, Return of the Jedi, 3¾", MOC....**$16.00**
Figure, Biker Scout, Return of the Jedi, MOC **$28.00**

Figure, Boba Fett, 3¾", M on 21-back card, $485.00. (Photo courtesy of June Moon.)

Figure, Boba Fett, Return of the Jedi, 3¾", MOC.......**$40.00**
Figure, Darth Vader, 12", EX..............................**$85.00**
Figure, Darth Vader, Star Wars, 3¾", w/accessories, M ..**$15.00**
Figure, Death Squad Commander, Empire Strikes Back, 3¾", MOC..........**$75.00**
Figure, Dulok Scout, Ewoks, 3¾", MOC..............**$15.00**
Figure, Emperor, Return of the Jedi, 3¾", MOC..........**$20.00**
Figure, Emperor, Tri-Logo, 3¾", MOC.........................**$20.00**
Figure, Ewok, plush, 15", NM.............................**$25.00**
Figure, Ewok, plush, 8", NM.............................**$18.00**
Figure, FX-7, Empire Strikes Back, 3¾", w/accessories, M..........**$10.00**
Figure, Gammorean Guard, Return of the Jedi, 3¾", MOC.............**$15.00**
Figure, Han Solo, Empire Strikes Back, 3¾", Hoth Gear, MOC..........**$35.00**
Figure, Han Solo, Return of the Jedi, 3¾", Bespin outfit, sm head, MOC..........**$50.00**
Figure, IG-88, Empire Strikes Back, 3¾", MOC..........**$50.00**
Figure, Imperial Commander, Empire Strikes Back, 3¾", w/accessories, MOC..............**$8.00**
Figure, Imperial Commander, Return of the Jedi, 3¾", MOC..........**$30.00**

Figure, Imperial Dignitary, Power of the Force, 3¾", MOC, from $60.00 to $75.00. (Photo courtesy of June Moon.)

Figure, Jawa, Empire Strikes Back, 3¾", MOC...........**$80.00**
Figure, Jawa, 12", MIB (sealed) **$300.00**

Figure, King Gorneesh, Ewoks, 3¾", MOC **$15.00**
Figure, Klaatu, Return of the Jedi, 3¾", MOC............**$15.00**
Figure, Lobot, Empire Strikes Back, 3¾", MOC..........**$28.00**
Figure, Luke Skywalker, Empire Strikes Back, 3¾", Bespin fatigues, complete, M......................**$15.00**
Figure, Luke Skywalker, 12", VG **$85.00**
Figure, Lumat, Power of the Force, 3¾", MOC...........**$50.00**
Figure, Lumat, Return of the Jedi, 3¾", MOC.............**$25.00**
Figure, Princess Leia Organa, Empire Strikes Back, Bespin gown, MOC......................**$100.00**
Figure, Princess Leia Organa, 12", MIB, from $235 to ..**$275.00**
Figure, Rebel soldier, Empire Strikes Back, 3¾", Hoth gear, MOC......................**$30.00**
Figure, R2-D2, Star Wars, 3¾", MOC.....................**$135.00**
Figure, Snaggletooth, Return of the Jedi, 3¾", MOC ..**$55.00**
Figure, Stormtrooper, Empire Strikes Back, 3¾", MOC...**$75.00**
Figure, Walrus Man, Empire Strikes Back, 3¾", MOC...**$80.00**
Figure, Yoda, Return of the Jedi, 3¾", MOC **$40.00**
Game, Battle at Sarlacc's Pit, Return of the Jedi, 3-D, EX (EX box).......................**$12.00**
Game, Escape From Death Star, EX **$18.00**
Kite, Luke Skywalker, Spectra, MIP **$12.00**
Mask, Boba Fett, full head, Don Post, M....................**$75.00**
Mask, Yoda, full head, Don Post, M **$35.00**
Paint kit, Luke or Han Solo, Craft Master, M (EX card) ..**$10.00**
Pendant, C-3PO, Darth Vader, Yoda or R2-D2, MOC, each...**$25.00**
Picture frame, C-3PO, ceramic, Sigma, MIB **$30.00**
Place mats, R2-D2 & C-3PO, 2-pc set, NMIP **$25.00**
Plate, R2-D2 & Wicket, limited edition, Hamilton, 8½", MIB.......................**$25.00**
Playset, Darth Vader's Star Destroyer, VG..................**$75.00**

Playset, Death Star Compactor, Micro Collection, MIB, from $70.00 to 85.00. (Photo courtesy of June Moon.)

Playset, Ewok Assault Catapult, Return of the Jedi, MIB...**$25.00**
Playset, Imperial Attack Base, EX..............................**$35.00**
Playset, Imperial Attack Base, EXIB **$65.00**
Poster, Procter & Gamble premium, 1978, EX, any **$6.00**
Puffy stickers, Empires Strikes Back, 1980, MIP.........**$10.00**
Puppet, Yoda, vinyl, Kenner, 1981, EX+.....................**$10.00**
Puzzle, frame-tray, Darth Vader, EX **$15.00**
Toothbrush, Oral B, MIB (sealed) **$8.00**
Tote Bag, Return of the Jedi, canvas, w/hang tag, NM...**$15.00**
Vehicle, At-At, VG+...**$80.00**
Vehicle, Ewok Combat Glider, MIB.............................**$25.00**

Vehicle, Millennium Falcon, Micro Collection, Sears Exclusive, 1982, scarce, MIB, $600.00. (Photo courtesy of June Moon.)

Vehicle, Mobile Laser Cannon (MLC-S), EX **$10.00**
Vehicle, Personnel Deployment Transport, EX **$10.00**
Vehicle, Speeder Bike, Return of the Jedi, VG **$15.00**
Vehicle, Twin Pod Cloud Car, EX **$22.00**
Vehicle, Y-Wing Fighter, NM **$85.00**
Vehivle, TIR Bomber diecast, EX **$250.00**
Waste can, Return of the Jedi, Cheinco, litho tin, VG+ ... **$22.00**

Steiff Animals

These stuffed animals originated in Germany around the turn of the century. They were created by Margaret Steiff, whose company continues to operate to the present day. They are identified by the button inside the ear and the identification tag (which often carries the name of the animal) on their chest. Over the years, variations in the tags and buttons help collectors determine approximate dates of manufacture.

Teddy bear collectors regard Steiff bears as some of the most valuable on the market. When assessing the worth of a bear, they use some general guidelines as a starting basis, though other features can come into play as well. For instance, bears made prior to 1912 that have long gold mohair fur start at a minimum of $75.00 per inch. If the bear has dark brown or curly white mohair fur instead, that figure may go as high as $135.00. From the 1920 to 1930 era, the price would be about $50.00 minimum per inch. A bear (or any other animal) on cast-iron or wooden wheels starts at $75.00 per inch; but if the tires are hard rubber, the value is much lower, at $27.00 per inch.

It's a fascinating study which is well covered in *Teddy Bears and Steiff Animals, First, Second and Third Series,* by Margaret Fox Mandel. Also see Cynthia Powell's *Collector's Guide to Miniature Teddy Bears.*

Club: Steiff Collectors Club
Beth Savino
c/o The Toy Store
7856 Hill Ave.
Holland, OH 43528; 419-865-3899 or 800-862-8697

Alligator, ca 1950, 15½" long, NM **$85.00**
Badger, Diggy, chest tag, ca 1950, 6", EX **$65.00**

Bear, caramel mohair, original ribbon, 1950s raised script button, stock tag, 5", NM **$250.00**
Bear, gold mohair, no identification, ca 1950, 9", NM **$265.00**
Bear, Original Teddy, light golden beige, original ribbon, all identification, ca 1960, 6", M **$165.00**
Bear, Zotty, original ribbon, all identification, ca 1960, 9", M **$135.00**
Bird, wooly w/metal feet, no identification, 2", EX **$65.00**
Bison, all identification, 6½", M **$325.00**
Camel, airbrushed details, 1950s raised script button, stock tag, 6" **$125.00**
Cat, black & white, wooly, 1950s raised script button, stock tag, 2½", M **$100.00**
Cat puppet, Tabby, 1950s ribbon button, M **$95.00**
Dog, Basset puppy, sitting, no identification, 4", EX .. **$60.00**
Dog, Biggie beagle, brown & white, w/chest tag & incised button, 7" **$128.00**
Dog, Boxer, standing, original collar, no identification, ca 1950, 6½", NM **$75.00**

Dog, Cocker Spaniel, brown and white mohair, glass eyes, all identification, 4", $200.00.

Dog, Dalmatian, raised script button & tag, 11", M .. **$625.00**
Dog, Ginny's Pup, original blanket, leash, ribbon & bell, 1950s raised script button, 3½", M **$235.00**
Dog, Molly, original ribbon, 1950s raised script button, 9½", EX **$275.00**
Dog, Mopsy, seated, no identification, ca 1950, 5", EX .. **$55.00**
Dog, wooly, incised button, ca 1960, 2", NM **$40.00**
Dormouse, Dormy, 1950s raised script button & stock tag, 5", NM **$90.00**
Dormouse, no identification, ca 1960, 5", NM **$75.00**
Elephant, Jumbo, sitting, incised button, all identification, 9" **$235.00**
Fawn, mohair, all identification, 5½", M **$125.00**
Fox, Xorry, sitting, 1950s raised script button, 6", EX ... **$85.00**
Fox, Xorry, standing, 6", NM **$80.00**
Goat, Snucki, all identification, 6", M **$140.00**
Goat, Snucki, chest tag, 5" **$60.00**
Goat, Zicky, w/ribbon & bell, 4", EX **$35.00**
Hamster, Goldy, chest tag, ca 1950, 4", M **$85.00**
Hamster, Woolie, incised button, stock tag, ca 1960, 3" long, M **$75.00**
Hedgehog, Joggy, down on all fours, all identification including incised button, 5" long, M **$70.00**
Hen, mohair w/metal feet, 1950s raised script button, chest tag & partial stock tag **$99.00**
Lamb, black, 1950s raised script button, 5½", EX **$110.00**

Lion, Leo, mohair, no identification, 4".......................**$48.00**

Llama, plush, glass eyes, all identification, 1964, 6", $95.00.

Lobster, felt, 1950s raised script button, stock tag, 4½" long, M...**$250.00**
Mole, Maxi, w/shovel, chest tag, 5", M.....................**$75.00**
Monkey, Mungo, all identification, ca 1950, 10", NM .**$165.00**
Mouse, white, incised button, stock tag, 3½", M **$65.00**
Owl, incised button, stock tag, 1960s, 6", M **$65.00**
Pelican, Piccy, airbrushed details, all identification, 6" .**$325.00**
Pig, Jolanthe, all identification, original braid, ca 1950, 10", M...**$225.00**
Polar bear, collar & bell, chest tag, 5".......................**$200.00**
Rabbit, begging, original ribbon & bell, chest tag, ca 1950, 4"...**$115.00**
Rabbit, hide-a-gift, red & white felt dress, raised script button, chest & stock tags, 1960s, 5", M **$195.00**
Rabbit, Niki, gray, 1950s raised script button, zone tag, 8"...**$195.00**
Rabbit, Ossi, original ribbon, all identification, ca 1950, 6", M..**$85.00**
Rabbit, running, original ribbon & bell, all identification, ca 1950, 9½", M...**$185.00**
Rabbit, running, 1950s raised script button, chest & stock tags, original ribbon & bell, 4½" long, M **$125.00**
Rabbit, skiing, Lulac face, original clothes, skis, etc, incised button, stock tag, ca 1972, 13½", M....................**$250.00**
Rabbit, Sonny, incised button, chest & stock tags, original ribbon, ca 1960, 8"...**$150.00**
Rabbit, Sonny, seated, original ribbon, all identification, 1960s, 6", NM...**$135.00**
Rabbit, Sonny, seated, original ribbon, all identification, ca 1960, 8", M...**$175.00**
Ram, Wotan, all identification, 4½", M......................**$235.00**
Rooster, chest tag, 7", M...**$135.00**

Rhinoceros Nosy, mohair with braided tail, original stock tag and button, 5½" long, $135.00.

Rooster, 1950s raised script button, remnant of stock tag, 7", EX...**$95.00**
Seal, Robby, all identification, ca 1950, 10", M **$195.00**
Turkey, 1950s raised script button, 4¼", NM **$195.00**
Zebra, wool plush, 1950s raised script button fragment, US Zone tag, 8½", EX **$120.00**

String Holders

Today we admire string holders for their decorative nature. They are much sought after by collectors. However, in the 1800s, they were strictly utilitarian, serving as dispensers of string used to wrap food and packages. The earliest were made of cast iron. Later, advertising string holders appeared in general stores. They were made of tin or cast iron and were provided by companies pedaling such products as shoes, laundry supplies, and food. These advertising string holders command the highest prices.

These days we take cellophane tape for granted. Before it was invented, string was used to tie up packages. String holders became a staple item in the home kitchen. To add a whimsical touch, in the late 1920s and 1930s, many string holders were presented in human shapes, faces, animals, and fruits. Most of these novelty string holders were made of chalkware (plaster of Paris), ceramics, or wood fiber. If you were lucky, you might have won a plaster of Paris 'Super Hero' or comic character string holder at your local carnival. These prizes were known as 'carnival chalkware.' The Indian string holder was a popular giveaway, so was Betty Boop and Superman.

Our values reflect string holders in excellent condition.

Advisor: Ellen Bercovici (See Directory, String Holders)
Apple, many variations, chalkware, from $20 to **$35.00**

Cherries, chalkware, from $95.00 to $115.00. (Photo courtesy of Ellen Bercovici.)

Apple & berries, apple in shades of red & yellow, berries & leaves in shades of red, green, & black, ceramic, 8"...............**$40.00**
Apple w/face, ceramic, Py, from $100 to **$125.00**
Babies, 1 happy, 1 crying, ceramic, Lefton, pr, from $200 to **$250.00**
Bananas, chalkware, from $85 to **$95.00**
Bird, 'String Nest Pull,' ceramic, from $25 to...............**$35.00**
Bird in birdcage, chalkware, from $85 to **$95.00**

Bird on branch, scissors in head, ceramic, from $75 to..**$85.00**

Bonzo (dog) w/bee on chest, ceramic, from $100 to...**$125.00**

Boy, top hat & pipe, eyes to side, chalkware, from $50 to..**$60.00**

Butler, Black man w/white lips & eyebrows, ceramic, minimum value **$250.00**

Chef, chalkware, from $35 to **$50.00**

Chef, Rice Crispy, chalkware, from $100 to **$125.00**

Chef, white head w/black mustache & red mouth, Whiteware, marked Plasto Mfg Co, 7½" **$45.00**

Chef w/rolling pin, full figure, chalkware, from $50 to..**$60.00**

Clown w/string around tooth, chalkware, from $85 to...**$95.00**

Dog, Schnauzer, ceramic, from $100 to **$125.00**

Dutch girl's head w/green hat, chalkware, 7¼"..........**$45.00**

Elephant, yellow, England, ceramic, from $50 to **$60.00**

Girl in bonnet, eyes to side, chalkware, from $50 to.**$60.00**

Granny in rocking chair, Py, ceramic, from $100 to..**$125.00**

Heart, puffed, Cleminson, ceramic, from $40 to **$50.00**

House, Cleminson, ceramic, from $75 to....................**$85.00**

Iron w/flowers, ceramic, from $70 to **$80.00**

Jester, chalkware, from $85 to **$95.00**

Kitten w/ball of yarn, white head w/blue eyes & black accents, pale yellow yarn, ceramic, 5½"..............**$40.00**

Kitten w/ball of yarn, yellow & black striped head w/smiling features, red yarn, chalkware, 6¾".........................**$45.00**

Kitten w/ball of yarn, yellow face & black accents, red yarn, chalkware, 6½" **$45.00**

Little Red Riding Hood, chalkware, minimum value .**$200.00**

Maid, Sarsaparilla, ceramic, 1984, from $50 to **$60.00**

Mammy, full figure w/black skin, white head scarf & apron over print dress, ceramic, 7" **$150.00**

Mammy, full figured, plaid & polka-dot dress, ceramic, from $100 to...**$125.00**

Mammy face, many variations, chalkware, from $200 to...**$250.00**

Man in top hat, head w/airbrushed accents, chalkware, 9"..**$45.00**

Mouse, Josef Originals, ceramic, from $80 to..............**$90.00**

Penguin, ceramic, from $50 to.....................................**$60.00**

Penguin, pottery, w/scissor holder, marked England .**$55.00**

Pirate & gypsy, wood fiber, pr, from $100 to............**$125.00**

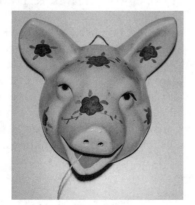

Pig with flowers, ceramic, from $100.00 to $125.00. (Photo courtesy of Ellen Bercovici.)

Rooster, Royal Bayreuth, ceramic, from $300 to **$400.00**

Rose, chalkware, from $100 to **$125.00**

Rosie the Riveter, chalkware, from $100 to...............**$125.00**

Sailor boy, chalkware, from $100 to **$125.00**

Senor, chalkware, from $40 to....................................**$50.00**

Senora, chalkware, from $65 to **$75.00**

Soldier, head w/tan cap, chalkware, 7¾" **$45.00**

Southern belle, lady in full white skirt & bonnet holding basket of flowers, Japan, ceramic, 6¼" **$45.00**

Southern gentleman w/2 belles, Japan, ceramic, 6¼"...**$50.00**

Witch in pumpkin, winking, ceramic, from $125 to.**$150.00**

Woman w/turban, chalkware, from $125 to.............**$150.00**

Swanky Swigs

These glass tumblers ranging in size from 3¼" to 4¾" were originally distributed by the Kraft company who filled them with their cheese spread. They were primarily used from the 1930s until sometime during the war, but they were brought out soon after and used to some extent until the late 1970s. Many were decorated with fired-on designs of flowers, 'Bustling Betty' scenes (assorted chores being done by a Gibson-type Betty), 'Antique' patterns (clocks, coal scuttles, lamps, kettles, coffee grinders, spinning wheels, etc.), animals (in their 'Kiddie Cup' line), or solid colors of red, yellow, green, and blue (Fiesta ware look-alikes).

Even the lids are collectible and are valued at a minimum of $3.00, depending on condition and the advertising message they convey.

For more information we recommend *Collectible Glassware of the 40s, 50s, and 60s* and *The Collector's Encyclopedia of Depression Glass,* both by Gene Florence; and *Collectible Drinking Glasses* by Mark Chase and Michael Kelly.

Antique #1, any color, from $2 to **$4.00**

Bands, colors & numbers of bands vary, ca 1933, from $2 to **$4.00**

Bachelor's Buttons, ca 1955, from $2 to **$4.00**

Bustling Betsy, any color, from $2 to............................**$4.00**

Checkerboard, any color combination w/white, ca 1936, from $15 to..**$20.00**

Circles, any color, ca 1934, from $3 to.........................**$5.00**

Cornflower #1, light blue w/green leaves, from $3 to..**$5.00**

Cornflower #2, dark blue, light blue, red or yellow (leaves are same color), ca 1947, from $2 to **$4.00**

Fired-on opaque color, blue, green, orange or yellow, ca 1939, from $4 to..**$6.00**

Forget-Me-Nots, any color, ca 1948, from $2 to **$4.00**

Jonquils, yellow w/green leaves, from $3 to.................**$5.00**

Sailboat #2, any color, ca 1936, from $8 to **$10.00**

Kiddie Cups, animals or flowers, from $2.00 to $4.00 each.

Stars, any color, ca 1935, from $3 to............................**$5.00**
Texas Centennial, any color, ca 1936, from $8 to......**$10.00**
Tulips, blue or green, ca 1937, from $3 to....................**$6.00**
Tulips, red w/green leaves, from $3 to.........................**$5.00**
Tulips #3, any color w/dark green leaves, ca 1950, from $2
   to...**$4.00**
Violets, purple w/green leaves, from $3 to **$5.00**

Syroco

Syroco Inc. originated in New York in 1890 when a group of European woodcarvers banded together to produce original hand carvings for fashionable homes of the area. Their products were also used in public buildings throughout upstate New York, including the state capitol. Demand for those products led to the development of the original Syroco reproduction process that allowed them to copy the original carvings with no loss of detail. They later developed exclusive hand-applied color finishes to further enhance the product, which they continued to improve and refine over ninety years.

Syroco's master carvers use tools and skills handed down from father to son through many generations. Woods used, depending on the effect called for, include Swiss pear wood, oak, mahogany, and wormy chestnut. When a design is completed, it is transformed into a metal cast through their molding and tooling process. A compression mold system using wood fiber was used from the early 1940s to the 1960s. Since 1962 a process has been used where pellets of resin are injected into a press, heated to the melting point, and then injected into the mold. Because the resin is liquid, it fills every crevice, thus producing an exact copy of the carver's art. It is then cooled, cleaned, and finished.

Other companies have produced similar items, among them are Multi Products, now of Erie, Pennsylvania. It was incorporated in Chicago in 1941 but in 1976 was purchased by John Hronas. Multi Products hired a staff of artists, made some wood originals and developed a tooling process for forms. They used a styrene-based material, heavily loaded with talc or calcium carbonate. A hydraulic press was used to get excess material out of the forms. Shapes were dried in kilns for seventy-two hours, then finished and, if the design required it, trimmed in gold. Items made included bears, memo pads, thermometers, brush holders, trays, plaques, nut bowls, napkin holders, etc., which were sold mainly as souvenirs. The large clocks and mirrors were made before the 1940s, and may sell for as much as $100.00 and more, depending on condition. Syroco used gold trim, but any other painted decoration you might encounter was very likely done by an outside firm. Some collectors prefer the painted examples and tend to pay a little more to get them. You may find similar products also stamped 'Ornawood,' 'Decor-A-Wood,' and 'Swank.'
See also Novelty Clocks.

Advisor: Doris J. Gibbs (See Directory, Syroco)

Ashtray, white, yellow & pink painted roses at side, 2 rests,
   4x4½", from $10 to...**$15.00**
Bookends, mare & colt, pr, from $7 to......................**$15.00**
Bookends, Mount Rushmore, pr, from $7 to..............**$15.00**
Bookends, ships, pr, from $7 to...............................**$15.00**

Box, deer & trees on lid, 4½x6", from $8 to...............**$10.00**
Box, ship on lid, 4x6", from $7 to.............................**$10.00**
Box, white, yellow & red painted roses on lid, Syroco, 4x6",
   from $10 to...**$15.00**
Box, white dog on lid, 4x6", from $8 to....................**$10.00**
Brush holder, double horse heads, 9", w/7" whisk brush,
   from $8 to...**$18.00**
Brush holder, pirate, 6", from $12 to **$15.00**
Brush holder, ship, Ornawood, 5", from $10 to.........**$15.00**
Brush holder, 9", w/7" whisk brush, from $8 to **$18.00**

Clock, #4580, gold-painted floral frame, marked Syrocco, Inc. made in USA, 15x15", minimum value $100.00. (Photo courtesy of Lee Garmon.)

Crucifix, white paint, 8½", from $6 to **$10.00**
Desk set, hinged top, divided box, Syroco, 6½x9½", from $8
   to...**$10.00**
Figurine, bear, from 1½" to 5½", each, from $2 to.....**$10.00**
Figurine, guitar player, from 3½" to 7", each, from $2 to...**$10.00**
Picture frame, florals at top, oval, 8x5½"......................**$6.00**
Plate, cabin in woods, pine cones, 6", from $2 to........**$5.00**
Plate, openwork, leaves & flowers, Syrocowood, 8½", from
   $5 to..**$10.00**
Thermometer, horseshoe, cap & quirts, wall plaque style, 5",
   from $5 to...**$10.00**
Thermometer, owl, painted, 5", from $8 to **$12.00**
Tie rack, bartender, painted, 6x10", from $15 to.........**$25.00**
Tie rack, bartender, standing, 8½", from $15 to..........**$25.00**
Tie rack, Indian in full headdress, wall-hanging type, from
   $10 to...**$20.00**
Tie rack, pointer dog, wall-hanging type, from $10 to...**$15.00**
Tray, openwork, leaves & flowers, Syrocowood, 12x7½",
   from $2 to...**$7.00**
Wall plaque, dog head, black or brown, 3" pr, from $3 to.**$5.00**
Wall plaque, flowers, 10", pr, from $10 to..................**$15.00**
Wall plaque, man & woman on oval background, 4x6", pr,
   from $5 to...**$10.00**
Wall plaque, squirrel, 4½", pr, from $6 to...................**$10.00**
Wall plaque, The Lord Knoweth Them That Are His prayer,
   marked Pressed Artwood **$3.00**
Wall shelf, vase form, floral decor, Multi Products, 9x7", from
   $12 to...**$15.00**

Taylor, Smith and Taylor

Though this company is most famous for their pastel dinnerware line, Lu Ray, they made many other patterns, and some of them are very collectible. They were located in the East Liverpool area of West Virginia, the 'dinnerware capitol' of the world. Their answer to HLC's very successful Fiesta line was Vistosa. It was made in four primary colors and though quite attractive, the line was never developed to include any more than twenty items. Other lines/shapes that collectors especially look for are Coral-Craft (having white designs inlaid on pink Lu-Ray, 1939 only), Conversation (a shape designed by Walter Dorwin Teague, 1950 to 1954), and Pebbleford (a textured, pastel line on the Versatile shape, 1952 to 1960).

For more information we recommend *Collector's Guide to LuRay Pastels* by Bill and Kathy Meehan (Collector Books).

Note: To evaluate King O'Dell, add 15% to the values we list for Conversation. For Boutonniere, add 15% to our Ever Yours values; and for Dwarf Pine, add the same amount to the values suggested for Versatile.

See also LuRay Pastels.

Conversation, bowl, vegetable; oval, sm...........................**$5.00**
Conversation, butter dish **$9.00**
Conversation, coffee server....................................**$20.00**
Conversation, cup & saucer **$3.50**
Conversation, plate, dinner; 1950-54............................**$2.50**
Conversation, salt & pepper shakers, pr.......................**$5.00**

Conversation, platter, King O' Dell pattern, $10.00.

Conversation, sugar bowl, w/lid.................................**$5.00**
Ever Yours, cake plate...**$6.00**
Ever Yours, creamer..**$2.50**
Ever Yours, plate, salad...**$1.50**
Ever Yours, platter, oval **$3.00**
Ever Yours, tea tile **$20.00**

Pebbleford, casserole, with lid, $30.00.

Pebbleford, coupe soup **$3.00**
Pebbleford, creamer...**$5.00**
Pebbleford, cup & saucer..**$5.00**
Pebbleford, plate, dinner.......................................**$3.00**

Pebbleford, salt & pepper shakers, pr **$5.00**
Taverne, bowl, oval, 9¼" **$24.00**
Taverne, bowl, round vegetable; 8¾".............................**$23.00**
Taverne, bowl, soup; 7¾".......................................**$15.00**
Taverne, creamer, footed **$14.00**
Taverne, cup & saucer **$15.00**
Taverne, plate, 10" **$25.00**
Taverne, plate, 8"..**$20.00**
Taverne, plate, 9"..**$10.00**
Taverne, teacup & saucer..**$12.00**
Taylorstone, casserole, w/lid **$10.00**
Taylorstone, cup & saucer.......................................**$2.00**
Taylorstone, plate, dinner......................................**$1.50**
Taylorton, cup & saucer...**$3.00**
Taylorton, dessert dish **$1.50**
Taylorton, plate, dinner **$2.00**
Taylorton, platter..**$4.00**
Taylorton, salt & pepper shakers, pr............................**$5.00**
Versatile, chop plate **$6.00**
Versatile, cup & saucer **$3.00**
Versatile, divided baker **$15.00**
Versatile, egg cup, double......................................**$10.00**
Versatile, plate, bread & butter **$1.50**
Versatile, plate, luncheon **$1.75**
Versatile, platter, 13"...**$4.00**
Versatile, sauce boat **$4.00**
Vistosa, bowl, salad; footed....................................**$160.00**
Vistosa, bowl, 5¾"..**$8.00**
Vistosa, bowl, 8½"..**$24.00**
Vistosa, cake plate **$25.00**
Vistosa, chop plate, 13" **$18.00**
Vistosa, chop plate, 15" **$35.00**
Vistosa, creamer **$20.00**
Vistosa, cup & saucer **$15.00**
Vistosa, egg cup **$22.50**
Vistosa, gravy boat **$90.00**
Vistosa, pitcher..**$75.00**
Vistosa, plate, 7"..**$8.00**
Vistosa, plate, 9"..**$10.00**
Vistosa, salt & pepper shakers, pr..............................**$32.00**
Vistosa, sugar bowl, w/lid......................................**$25.00**
Vistosa, teapot...**$95.00**
Vogue, bowl, fruit..**$2.00**
Vogue, casserole, handles, w/lid **$27.00**
Vogue, plate, 10"...**$3.00**
Vogue, plate, 7" **$2.50**
Vogue, sauce boat...**$7.50**
Vogue, teacup & saucer..**$4.50**

Tiara Exclusives

Collectors are just beginning to take notice of the glassware sold through Tiara in-home parties, their Sandwich line in particular. Several companies were involved in producing the lovely colored glassware they've marketed over the years, among them Indiana Glass, Fenton, Dalzell Viking and L.E. Smith. In the late 1960s, Tiara contracted with Indiana to produce their famous line of Sandwich dinnerware (a staple at Indiana Glass since the late 1920s). Their catalogs continue to carry this pattern, and over the years, it has been offered in many colors: ruby, teal, crystal, amber, green, pink, blue and others in limited amounts. We've listed a few pieces of Tiara's Sandwich below, and though the market is unstable, our values will serve to offer an indication of current values. Unless you're sure of what you're buying, though, don't make the mistake of paying 'old' Sandwich prices for Tiara. To learn more about the two lines, we recommend *Collectible Glassware from the 40s, 50s, and 60s*, by Gene Florence (Collector Books).

Ashtray, Sandwich, 4 rests, 7⅜", from $5 to **$7.00**
Basket, Sandwich, footed, 10", from $25 to...............**$32.50**
Bowl, salad; Sandwich, 5", from $2 to **$3.50**
Bowl, salad; Sandwich, 6 crimps at top edge, 10", from $14 to **$16.00**
Bowl, vegetable; Sandwich, deep & round w/flared sides, 8" dia, from $10 to **$12.00**
Butter dish, Sandwich, w/high domed lid, 6", from $18 to..**$25.00**

Butter dish, Sandwich, green, 1970s,
from $18.00 to $25.00.

Candle holder, Sandwich, 8½", pr, from $15 to **$18.00**
Candle lamp, Sandwich, egg-shaped top w/footed base, 5¾", from $8 to...**$10.00**
Canister, Sandwich, 5⅝", from $6 to **$8.00**
Canister, Sandwich, 7½", from $8 to **$10.00**
Canister, Sandwich, 8⅞", from $10 to **$12.00**
Clock, Sandwich, traditional metal face w/wide glass rim, battery-operated, 12", from $18 to.........................**$20.00**
Creamer, Sandwich, footed, 5", from $4 to....................**$5.00**
Cruet, Sandwich, crimped top, w/stopper, 6", from $7 to...**$9.00**
Cup, Sandwich, 9-oz, from $2.50 to **$3.50**
Decanter, Sandwich, hand blown w/hand-ground stopper, 10", from $12 to **$18.00**
Dish, relish; Sandwich, 3-compartment, 12", from $10 to ..**$12.00**
Egg tray, Sandwich, 12", from $10 to **$14.00**
Goblet, wine; Sandwich, from $3 to **$6.00**
Pitcher, Sandwich, 68-oz, from $20 to **$25.00**
Plate, dinner; Sandwich, 10", from $6 to **$8.00**
Plate, salad; Sandwich, 8", from $3 to...........................**$5.00**
Platter, Sandwich, footed, from $12 to.........................**$15.00**
Platter, Sandwich, 12", from $9 to **$12.00**
Platter, Sandwich, 16" dia, from $10 to **$15.00**

Platter, Sandwich, 8½", from $6 to **$8.00**
Salt & pepper shakers, Sandwich, 4¾", pr, from $12 to .**$15.00**
Saucer, Sandwich, 6", from $1 to....................................**$2.00**
Sugar bowl, footed, 2-handled, open, Sandwich, 5", from $4 to **$5.00**
Tray, serving; Sandwich, high rim edge, 10", from $9 to..**$12.00**
Tumbler, Sandwich, footed, 10-oz, 6½", from $4 to **$6.00**
Vase, Sandwich, footed, 3¾", from $6 to.......................**$8.00**

Pitcher, Sandwich, amber, 68-oz, from $20.00 to $25.00.

Tire Ashtrays

Manufacturers of tires issued miniature versions that contained ashtray inserts that they usually embossed with advertising messages. Others were used as souvenirs from World's Fairs. The earlier styles were made of glass or glass and metal, but by the early 1920s, they were replaced by the more familiar rubber-tired variety. The inserts were often made of clear glass, but colors were also used, and once in awhile you'll find a tin one. The tires themselves were usually black; other colors are rarely found. Hundreds have been produced over the years; in fact, the larger tire companies still issue them occasionally, but you no longer see the details or colors evident in the pre-WWII tire ashtrays. Although the common ones bring modest prices, rare examples sometimes sell for up to several hundred dollars. For ladies or non-smokers, some miniature tires contained a pin tray.

For more information we recommend *Tire Ashtray Collector's Guide* by Jeff McVey.

Advisor: Jeff McVey (See Directory, Tire Ashtrays)

Allstate SR Balloon, w/green 'disc wheel' insert, EX ..**$80.00**
Armstrong Air Coaster 6.00-16 Deluxe Streamline, white tire w/clear insert **$100.00**
Armstrong Miracle SD, clear insert w/manufacturer's imprint **$25.00**
Atlas 5.50-17 4-Ply, clear insert embossed Atlas..........**$50.00**
BF Goodrich Comp T/A, clear imprinted insert..........**$30.00**
BF Goodrich Silvertown Lifesaver Radial HR70-15, clear insert w/100th Anniversary 1970 imprint, in original box **$50.00**
Bridgestone Radial RD-201 165SR13 (Japan), clear insert w/manufacturer's imprint **$35.00**

Bridgestone RD-207, clear insert w/Bridgestone imprint $30.00

Co-op Agri-Radial, tractor tire w/clear imprinted insert ..$35.00

Cooper Cobra Radial GT 75th Anniversary, clear insert w/manufacturer's imprint $25.00

Dayton Thorobred Heavy Duty Six Ply 7.50-18, green insert w/2 rests embossed 'D' $100.00

Diamond Balloon 33 X 6.00, blue insert embossed Diamond $80.00

Dominion Royal Heavy Duty 7.00-19 (Canada), amber insert embossed w/'castle' logo $100.00

Dominion Royal Tires, clear insert, Canadian $50.00

Dunlop Generation IV Radial, clear imprinted insert $25.00

Firestone (plastic tire), red & black mottled plastic insert w/3 rests $15.00

Firestone GSR Giant Steel Radial, clear imprinted insert ...$35.00

Firestone Heavy Duty High Speed Gum-Dipped Balloon 6.00-18, embossed amber insert, 1936 ......$125.00

Firestone Hi-Type Cushion, metal insert embossed Firestone Truck Tires Cushion-Traction-Mileage $100.00

Firestone Transport 110 Tubeless, clear insert embossed Firestone $35.00

Firestone 40x12 (steel rim inside), bronze insert w/2 rests embossed Firestone Truck Tires Cushion Traction Mileage $150.00

Fisk Glider 6.00-16, clear insert embossed Fisk $125.00

Fisk Tuf-Lug, clear insert embossed Fisk w/image of 'bedtime boy' $150.00

General Ameri*Steel, clear imprinted insert $25.00

General Streamline Jumbo, clear or green insert embossed The General Tire/Goes Along Way To Make Friends $70.00

General XP 2000H HR, clear insert w/manufacturer's imprint $25.00

Goodrich Euzkadi (Mexico), clear insert embossed Goodrich Duran Mas! Euzkadi $45.00

Goodrich Silvertown Heavy Duty Cord 36 X 6, clear insert w/Goodrich Zipper Boot advertising label $50.00

Goodrich Silvertown Skid-Ring Tractor Type, front tractor tire w/clear insert embossed Goodrich Tires $75.00

Goodrich Silvertown the Safest Tire Ever Built, blue-gray Akro Agate insert embossed Goodrich Tires $50.00

Goodyear Double Eagle 6.00-21, green insert w/Goodyear Tires sticker $125.00

Goodyear Double Eagle 6.00-21, green insert w/1 rest & matchbox holder $125.00

Goodyear Eagle VR50, wide Corvette tire w/clear imprinted insert $30.00

Goodyear Vector, clear imprinted insert $20.00

Hood Arrow Heavy Duty 6-Ply 6.00-20, clear insert w/advertising label or embossed Hood Tires $75.00

Kelly Springfield 6.00-16, green insert w/advertising sticker $50.00

Kelly-Springfield Aramid Belted Radial Voyager 1000, clear insert w/manufacturer's imprint $20.00

Miller Deluxe Long Safe Mileage Geared-to-the-Road, clear insert embossed Miller Tires $80.00

Mohawk Super Chief, clear imprinted insert $40.00

Mohawk Ultissimo, clear insert w/dealer's imprint $35.00

Olympic Air-Ride Tubeless Airtite 6.40-13 (Australia), clear insert w/manufacturer's imprint $70.00

Pirelli SN55 Cinturato (Italy), aluminum insert $40.00

Remington Cushion-Aire '78' Dual Belt, clear imprinted insert $35.00

Seiberling All-Tread, clear insert w/advertising sticker $25.00

Thompson Aircraft Tire Corporation, clear insert w/manufacturer's imprint $75.00

Tyer Rubber Co Andover, Mass, clear insert w/manufacturer's imprint $100.00

US Royal Master (red & white sidewall stripes), clear insert w/manufacturer's imprint $60.00

Vogue Miracle Ride Tyre (white tire), clear insert w/manufacturer's imprint $75.00

Western Auto (plastic tire), red & black mottled plastic insert w/3 rests $35.00

Miller Tires, 8 rests, 7" dia, EX, $45.00. (Photo courtesy of Henry Hain.)

Tobacco Collectibles

Until lately, the tobacco industry spent staggering sums on advertising their products, and scores of retail companies turned out many types of smoking accessories such as pipes, humidors, lighters, and ashtrays. Even though the smoking habit isn't particularly popular nowadays, collecting tobacco-related memorabilia is! See *Huxford's Collectible Advertising* by Sharon and Bob Huxford for more information.

See also Cigarette Lighters; Labels.

Club: Tobacciana
Chuck Thompson and Associates
P.O. Box 11652
Houston, TX 77293; Send SASE for free list of publications

Club/Newsletter: *Tobacco Jar*
Society of Tobacco Jar Collectors
Charlotte Tarses, Treasurer
3011 Fallstaff Road #307
Baltimore, MD 21209; Dues: $30 per year ($35 outside of U.S.)

Ad, Lucky Strike, Her Singing Coach Advises a Light Smoke, features Carole Lombard in pink gown, 1937, VG ..$25.00

Ashtray, Carter Hall Tobacco, tin, round w/embossed image of tobacco, 3½" dia, NM $5.00

Box, Pall Mall Cigarettes, red w/Christmas motif left of name, 2x8½x7", EX..**$60.00**

Bridge pad, Chesterfield Cigarettes, cameo image of woman above lit cigarette, They Satisfy, 1930s, EX...........**$30.00**

Canister, Velvet Tobacco, red emblem on square shape w/beveled corners, flared bottom, slip lid w/knob, NM...**$145.00**

Cigar box, Charles the Great, 5x10", VG **$15.00**

Cigar box, Just It, 4x8", EX **$15.00**

Cigarette carton, Lucky Strike, image of man reading paper & smoking, It's Toasted, EX+................................**$45.00**

Cigarette carton, Philip Morris, cardboard carton w/Johnny calling for Philip Morris, America's Finest..., brown, EX **$45.00**

Cigarette papers, Buffalo Tobacco, NM...........................**$7.00**

Cigarette papers, Bull Durham, EX+ **$5.00**

Display, cardboard stand-up, Philip Morris, Johnny w/pack of cigarettes standing atop as panel, 5-ft, NM....**$165.00**

Fan, Lucky Strike, tobacco-leaf shape w/product lettering & open pack around image of Frank Sinatra, EX+..**$250.00**

Game, Sarony Roulette, w/game pcs, held 200 cigarettes, EX...**$45.00**

Humidor, Bagdad Tobacco, ceramic canister w/Bagdad above portrait of man in red fez, shaded blue glaze, 6½", EX...**$85.00**

Insert cards, Cope's Cigarettes, British Dickens Characters series, set of 25, 1939, M.......................................**$35.00**

Lunch box, George Washington, clasp closure, red, white & blue w/oval image of George, EX.........................**$65.00**

Lunch box, Just Suits, bail handle, red w/black & gold, EX+...**$75.00**

Lunch box, Main Brace Cut Plug, rounded corners, swing handles, yellow w/red lettering on basket-weave design, EX+...**$100.00**

Match holder, Kool Cigarettes, metal, Matches (blank price space) ¢ Light Up a Kool & penguin on box back panel, green & white 8x7x4", VG+ **$30.00**

Mug, Winston Cigarettes, red plastic w/logo on 2 sides, 8x4" dia, NM **$5.00**

Pocket container, Half & Half/Burley & Bright, cardboard, 1943, EX...**$12.00**

Pocket mirror, Mascot Crushed Cut Tobacco, 2" dia, EX+ ..**$55.00**

Pocket tin, Bagley's Old Colony Mixture, vertical, concave, gold w/red oval profile portrait of lady in bonnet, EX **$135.00**

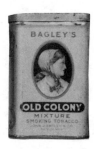

Pocket tin, Bagley's Old Colony Mixture, white background, VG, $100.00.

Pocket tin, Forest & Stream, vertical (tall), red w/oval image of duck in flight, EX+..**$100.00**

Pocket tin, Lucky Strike, flat, rounded corners, red logo on green w/decorative gold border, NM+...................**$50.00**

Pocket tin, Lucky Strike, vertical, green, Genuine above red logo, It's Toasted, Roll Cut for Pipe or Cigarettes, NM **$95.00**

Pocket tin, Peachy Double Cut Tobacco, vertical, pictures peach, EX+...**$125.00**

Pocket tin, Picobac, vertical (short), tobacco plant (hand-held) above name on diagonal band, Very Mild below, NM **$85.00**

Pocket tin, Picobac, vertical (tall), tobacco plant (hand-held) above name on diagonal band, Very Mild (no 10¢), NM..**$95.00**

Pocket tin, Union Leader Redi Cut Tobacco, vertical, red w/oval bust image of Uncle Sam, NM.................**$150.00**

Postcard, Bull Durham, Panama, from the Trip Around the World series of 33, NM...**$65.00**

Sign, Black Cat Cigarettes, paper, Give Me Black Cat Every Time!, woman w/cat & cigarette, 1950s, framed, 32x22", EX..**$200.00**

Sign, Camel Cigarettes, paper, Smoke Camels above pack of cigarettes flanked by So Mild & So Good, red ground, 24x30", M...**$25.00**

Sign, Camel Cigarettes, tin, Smoke Camel Cigarettes lettered diagonally above open pack on circle, 18x12", NM **$60.00**

Sign, Chesterfield Cigarettes, porcelain, 1950, 17x11", EX, $125.00. (Photo courtesy of Dunbar Gallery.)

Sign, Chesterfield Cigarettes, diecut tin flange, Buy Here on red oval above pack, Regular & King-Size, 17x12", EX+ **$40.00**

Sign, Lucky Strike, cardboard stand-up, carton above Give a Christmas Carton... & open pack, 1936, 30x20", EX..**$235.00**

Sign, Lucky Strike, tin, open pack & lady in circle, embossed, 1950s-60s, 24x17", EX+...**$300.00**

Sign, Velvet Tobacco, diecut cardboard stand-up, Joy Ride above 2 men in car w/product name & pipe on front, 9x7", VG **$175.00**

Store bin, Mail Pouch Tobacco, dark blue w/yellow & white lettering, Always Fresh, Chew..., 10x3½x11", VG+ **$225.00**

Thermometer, Mail Pouch Tobacco, porcelain, Treat Yourself to the Best, Chew... below, white, blue & yellow, 8", VG...**$75.00**

Tin, Big Ben Chewing Tobacco, round, key-wind, red w/silhouette image of Big Ben & black lettering on yellow label, EX+ **$30.00**

Tin, Carmen Cigarettes, flat, photo image of Carmen w/walking stick under arm, holds 20 cigarettes, VG+ **$40.00**

Tin, Dan Patch, rectangular w/rounded corners, yellow w/black image & lettering, red border & trim, 4x6", VG+ **$50.00**

Tin, Hiawatha, rectangular w/rounded corners, green, EX+ **$130.00**

Tin, Kool Cigarettes, flat, Season Greetings, Arctic scene w/penguins, holds 50 cigarettes, EX+.................**$240.00**

Tin, Lucky Strike, round, green, red logo above Cigarettes in gold, holds 100 cigarettes, 4", EX+........................**$85.00**

Tin, Old Bond, oval portrait of George Washington flanked by As Good & As a Bond, Now 2 for 5¢ below, slip lid, 6", G+..**$35.00**

Tin, Webster, 3½x5", VG, $45.00.

Tip tray, Chesterfield Cigarettes, They Satisfy & The Blend Can't Be Copied, blue w/gold lettering & pack, 6x4", EX.**$115.00**

Tip tray, Cortez Cigars, For Men of Brains on black above red Cortex in diagonal script, red border, rectangular, EX ..**$45.00**

Tobacco pouch, Buffalo Tobacco, cloth w/paper label, 1-oz, NM **$20.00**

Tobacco pouch, Bull Durham, cloth w/paper label, draw-string closure, NM (sealed) **$15.00**

Tumbler, Camel Cigarettes, plastic, colorful images of Camel Joe at Joe's Place, 1994, 4½", M **$5.00**

Watch fob, Velvet Tobacco, enamel, shows pipe w/smoke forming the word Velvet, Tobacco lettered below, 1¼x1", VG...**$50.00**

Whetstone, Bagley's Old Colony Tobacco, celluloid, multicolored tobacco tin in center, oval, EX+..............**$40.00**

Toothbrush Holders

Novelty toothbrush holders have been modeled as animals of all types, in human forms, and in the likenesses of many storybook personalities. Today all are very collectible, especially those representing popular Disney characters. Most are made of bisque and are decorated over the glaze. Condition of the paint is an important consideration when trying to arrive at an evaluation.

For more information, refer to *Pictorial Guide to Toothbrush Holders* by Marilyn Cooper.

Advisor: Marilyn Cooper (See Directory, Toothbrush Holders)

Annie Oakly, standing in orange hat & neckerchief holding gun, 2 holes, Japan, 5¾".....................................**$100.00**

Bellhop w/bouquet of flowers, multicolored, 1 hole, Japan, 5¼"..**$75.00**

Betty Boop, bust form holding glass & toothbrush, 4 holes, KFS, 1983, 4¾"...**$85.00**

Big Bird, sitting, yellow w/orange feet, 2 holes, Taiwan, 4½"...**$80.00**

Bonzo, standing, blue lustre body w/red paw, 2 holes, Japan, 5x3"...**$90.00**

Boy brushing teeth, standing on stool at sink, multicolored, 2 holes, Japan, 6½"..**$90.00**

Boy playing violin w/dog watching, multicolored, 2 holes, Goldcastle/Japan, 5½"..**$80.00**

Candlestick Maker, standing in striped apron on marked base, 1 hole, Goldcastle/Japan, 5¼".....................**$80.00**

Cat on pedestal, green cat (winking) atop green airbrushed pedestal w/center floral design, 2 holes, 6" **$150.00**

Clown w/ruffled collar, standing w/open pockets, white upper body w/orange trim, blue lustre pants, TRICO/Japan, 6½" **$85.00**

Dutch boy, standing w/hands on hips & open pockets on blue overalls, 3 holes, Japan, 5¼" **$75.00**

Dutch boy & girl, kissing, shades of purple, green & yellow, 2 holes, Japan, 6¼"..**$65.00**

Flapper girl, half figure w/blond hair & side glance, silver lustre coat w/white fur trim, black purse, 2 holes, 4¼" **$120.00**

Giraffe, standing, yellow w/orange dots on back, 3 holes, Japan, 6"...**$125.00**

Mexican taking a siesta, multicolored, 1 hole, Japan, 6"...**$90.00**

Minnie Mouse, 4", $425.00. (Photo courtesy of Dunbar Gallery.)

Peter Rabbit, side-view of dressed rabbit walking, marked base, Germany, 6¼" **$375.00**

Sailors on anchor, facing each other, white w/orange & black trim, 2 holes, Japan, 5½".......................................**$70.00**

Three Bears, 3 brown bears standing on white rectangular base holding 3 white bowls w/gold trim, 3 holes, Japan, 4" **$95.00**

Tom Tom the Piper's Son, holding 2 pigs, 2 holes, Japan, 5¾" **$100.00**

Toys

Toy collecting has long been an area of very strong activity, but over the past decade it has really expanded. Many of the larger auction galleries have cataloged toy auctions, and it isn't uncommon for scarce 19th-century toys in good condition go for $5,000.00 to $10,000.00 and up. Toy shows are popular, and there are clubs, newsletters, and magazines that cater only to the needs and wants of toy collectors. Though once buyers ignored toys less than thirty years old, in more recent years, even some toys from the eighties are sought after.

Condition has more bearing on the value of a toy than any other factor. A used toy in good condition with no major flaws will still be worth only about half (in some cases much less) as much as one in mint (like new) condition. Those mint and in their original boxes will be worth considerably more than the same toy without its box (sometimes twice as much).

There are many good toy guides on the market today including: *Modern Toys, American Toys, 1930 to 1980,* by Linda Baker; *Collecting Toys* and *Collecting Toy Trains* by Richard O'Brien; *Schroeder's Collectible Toys, Antique to Modern; Elmer's Price Guide to Toys* by Elmer Duellman; *Toys of the Sixties, A Pictorial Guide,* by Bill Bruegman; *Occupied Japan Toys With Prices* by David C. Gould and Donna Crevar-Donaldson; *Toys, Antique and Collectible, Antique and Collectible Toys, 1870 — 1950,* and *Character Toys and Collectibles,* all by David Longest; and *Collector's Guide to Tinker Toys* by Craig Strange. More books are listed in the subcategory narratives that follow. With the exception of O'Brien's (Books Americana) and Bruegman's (Cap't Penny Productions), all previous titles are published by Collector Books.

See also Advertising Character Collectibles; Breyer Horses; Bubble Bath Containers; Character Collectibles; Disney Collectibles; Dolls; Fast-Food Collectibles; Fisher-Price; Halloween; Hartland Plastics, Inc.; Model Kits; Paper Dolls; Games; Puzzles; Star Trek; Star Wars; Steiff Animals; Trolls.

Action Figures and Accessories

Back in 1964, Barbie dolls were sweeping the feminine side of the toy market by storm. Hasbro took a risky step in an attempt to capture the interest of the male segment of the population. Their answer to the Barbie craze was GI Joe. Since no self-respecting boy would admit to playing with dolls, Hasbro called their boy dolls 'action figures,' and to the surprise of many, they were phenomenally successful. Today action figures generate just as much enthusiasm among toy collectors as they ever did among little boys.

Action figures are simply dolls with poseable bodies. The original GI Joes were 12" tall, but several other sizes were made over the years, too. Some are 8" to 9", others 6", and 3¾" figures have been favored in recent years. GI Joe was introduced in the 3¾" size in the eighties and proved to be unprecedented in action figure sales. (See also GI Joe.)

In addition to the figures themselves, each company added a full line of accessories such as clothing, vehicles, play sets, weapons, etc. — all are avidly collected. Be aware of condition! Original packaging is extremely important. In fact, when it comes to the recent issues, loose, played-with examples are seldom worth more than a few dollars.

For more information, refer to *Collectible Action Figures* by Paris and Susan Manos, *Mego Toys* by Wallace M. Chrouch, and *Collector's Guide to Dolls in Uniform* by Joseph Bourgeois.

Club: The Classic Action Figure Collector Club
Old Forest Press, Inc.
P.O. Box 2095
Halesite, NY 11743; Send SASE for information about club and official club magazine, *Collect 'Em All*

Action Jackson, figure, Action Jackson, Mego, 1974, 8", M (NM box)..**$32.00**
Action Jackson, outfit, Western #1108, Mego, 1974, NMIB...**$8.00**
Advanced Dungeons & Dragons, figure, Elkhorn, Kelek, Mericon, Strongheart, Warduke or Zarak, LJN, 1983-84, NM, each..**$18.00**
Advanced Dungeons & Dragons, figure, Strongheart or Warduke, LJN, 1983-84, MOC, each **$45.00**
Advanced Dungeons & Dragons, figures, BowMarc, Grimsword, Morthlord, LJN, 1983-84, NM, each...**$25.00**
Advanced Dungeons & Dragons, figures, Stalwart Men-At-Arms, LJN, 1983-84 ....**$25.00**
Adventures of Indiana Jones, accessory, Map Room Playset, Kenner, 1982-83, MIB (minor wear).....................**$35.00**
Adventures of Indiana Jones, accessory, Streets of Cairo Adventure Set, Kenner, 1982-83, MIB **$65.00**
Adventures of Indiana Jones, figure, Belloq in Ceremonial Robe or Cairo Swordsman, complete, Kenner, 1982-83, NM..**$8.00**
Adventures of Indiana Jones, figure, German Mechanic, Kenner, 1982-83, MOC **$25.00**
Adventures of Indiana Jones, figure, Toht, Kenner, 1982-83, MOC..**$15.00**
Adventures of Indiana Jones, horse, Arabian, Kenner, 1982-83, MOC...**$95.00**

Batman, figure, Man-Bat, Kenner, MOC, $22.00.

Battlestar Galactica, figure, Commander Adama, Apollo or Starbuck, Mattel, 1978, 3¾", MOC, each...............**$22.00**
Battlestar Galactica, figure, Commander Adama, Mattel, 1978, 3¾", no weapon o/w EX **$10.00**
Battlestar Galactica, figure, Cylon Centurian, w/cloth jacket, Mattel, 1978, 12", EX...**$25.00**
Battlestar Galactica, figure, Cylon Warrior, silver, w/weapon, Mattel, 1978, 3¾", EX **$15.00**
Battlestar Galactica, figure, Daggit, Mattel, 1978, 3¾", EX..**$15.00**

Battlestar Galactica, figure, Imperious Leader, Mattel, 1978, 3¾", M (EX unpunched card)......................**$15.00**

Best of the West, accessory, Circle X Ranch, Marx, 1965-76, MIB......................**$175.00**

Best of the West, accessory, Johnny West Travel Case (for figures & accessories), Marx, 1965-76, VG+..............**$22.00**

Best of the West, dogs, Flack (English setter) or Flick (German Shepherd), Marx, 1965-76, NM, each....**$60.00**

Best of the West, figure, Captain Maddox, Marx, 1965-76, few pcs missing o/w EX......................**$50.00**

Best of the West, figure, Chief Cherokee, Marx, 1965-76, few pcs missing o/w EX (NM box) **$70.00**

Best of the West, figure, Geronimo, rare orange body, w/accessories, Marx, 1965-76, NM (NM Johnny West Adventure box)......................**$100.00**

Best of the West, figure, Geronimo & Pinto, Marx, 1965-76, EXIB......................**$130.00**

Best of the West, figure, Jaimie West, Marx, 1965-76, MIB..**$75.00**

Best of the West, figure, Jane West, Marx, 1965-76, NMIB..**$70.00**

Best of the West, figure, Johnny West, Marx, 1965-76, NMIB......................**$125.00**

Best of the West, figure, Josie West, Marx, 1965-75, MIB..**$75.00**

Best of the West, figure, Sheriff Garrett, royal blue, Marx, 1965-76, VG+......................**$20.00**

Best of the West, figure, Sheriff Garrett w/Thunderbolt, M (M box) **$125.00**

Big Jim, figure, Josh, nude, Mattel, 1973-76, VG.........**$20.00**

Big Jim, outfit, Skin Diving #8855, Action Adventure Series, Mattel, 1973-76, MOC **$10.00**

Black Hole, figure, Booth, Durant, Holland, McCray or Reinhardt, Mego, 1980, 3¾", MOC, each **$18.00**

Black Hole, figure, Captain Dan Holland, Mego, 1980, 12", M (NM box) **$55.00**

Black Hole, figure, Dr Kate McCray, Mego, 1980, 12", M (EX+ box) **$60.00**

Black Hole, Sentry Robot, Mego, 1980, 3¾", M (EX+ card)...**$50.00**

Bonanza, coyote, American Character, 1966, EX.........**$15.00**

Bonanza, figure, Ben Cartwright, w/horse & accessories, American Character, 8", NM......................**$180.00**

Bonanza, figure, Hoss, w/stallion, American Character, 1966, 8", M (stable box) **$200.00**

Bonanza, mountain lion, American Character, 1966, EX..**$15.00**

Buck Rogers, accessory, Laserscope Fighter (for sm figures), Mego, 1979, M (EX+ box) **$45.00**

Buck Rogers, figure, Adrella, Draco, Killer Kane or Tiger Man, Mego, 1979, 3¾", MOC, each......................**$28.00**

Buck Rogers, figure, Buck, Twiki, Wilma or Vincent, Mego, 1979, 3¾", NM, each......................**$25.00**

Buck Rogers, figure, Buck Rogers, Mego, 1979, 12", MIB...**$45.00**

Buck Rogers, figure, Draco, Draconian Guard, Kane, Tiger Man, Mego, 1979, 3¾", NM, each......................**$15.00**

Buck Rogers, figure, Draco, Mego, 1979, 12", M (EX+ box).**$60.00**

Buck Rogers, figure, Draconian Guard, Mego, 1979, 12", M (EX box) **$60.00**

Buck Rogers, figure, Killer Kane, Mego, 1979, 12", MIB...**$55.00**

Buck Rogers, figure, Tiger Man, Mego, 1979, 12", M (EX+ box) **$60.00**

Buck Rogers, figure, Walking Twiki, Mego, 1979, 7½", M (EX box) **$50.00**

Captain Action, accessory, belt, Spider-Man, Ideal, 1966-68, NM **$40.00**

Captain Action, accessory, belt w/holster, Flash Gordon, Ideal, 1966-68, NM......................**$75.00**

Captain Action, accessory, boots, Batman, Ideal, 1966-68, NM **$10.00**

Captain Action, accessory, jet pack helmet w/strap, Captain Action, Ideal, 1966-68, EX......................**$10.00**

Captain Action, accessory, shirt, Tonto, Ideal, 1966-68, NM.**$25.00**

Captain Action, figure, Action Boy, w/accessories, Ideal, 1967, 8", EX......................**$325.00**

Captain Action, figure, Dr Evil, w/original shirt & pants, Ideal, 1967, ...**$190.00**

Captain Action, outfit, Aquaman, w/accessories, Ideal, 1966, EX......................**$95.00**

Captain Action, outfit, Superman, on original mannequin, complete, Ideal, 1966, EX **$130.00**

CHiPs, figure, Jimmy Squeaks, Ponch or Wheels Willy, Mego, 1978-81, 3¾", MOC, each......................**$10.00**

CHiPs, figure, Jon, Mego, 1978-81, 8", MOC **$35.00**

CHiPs, figure, Ponch, Mego, 1978-81, 8", MOC **$25.00**

CHiPs, figure, Sarge, Mego, 1978-81, 8", MOC...........**$40.00**

Crash Dummies, figure, Larry or Vince, MOC, each...**$12.00**

Dark Knight Collection, figure, Bruce Wayne, Kenner, 1990, MOC......................**$15.00**

Dark Knight Collection, figure, Iron-Winch Batman or Shadow-Wing Batman, Kenner, 1990, MOC, each.................**$15.00**

DC Comics Super Heroes, figure, Aquaman, green arm version, Toy Biz, 1989-90, MOC **$20.00**

DC Comics Super Heroes, figure, Green Lantern, Toy Biz, 1989-90, MOC......................**$25.00**

DC Comics Super Heroes, figure, The Flash, Toy Biz, 1989-90......................**$10.00**

Dick Tracy, figure, Al 'Big Boy' Caprice, Dick, Itchy, Lips Manlis, Pruneface or Sam Catchem, Playmates, 1990, MOC, each......................**$12.00**

Dukes of Hazzard, figure, Bo or Luke, Mego, 1981, 3¾", MOC, each from $18 to......................**$25.00**

Dukes of Hazzard, figure, Bo or Luke, Mego, 1981, 8", MOC, each from $22 to......................**$30.00**

Dukes of Hazzard, figure, Boss Hogg, Mego, 1981, 8", M (EX+ card) **$20.00**

Dukes of Hazzard, figure, Daisy, Mego, 1981, 3¾", MOC...**$25.00**

Dukes of Hazzard, figure, Daisy, Mego, 1981, 8", MOC..**$40.00**

Dune, figure, Baron Harkonnen, Feyd, Rubban or Sardaukan Warrior, no accessories, LJN, 1984, EX, each.........**$8.00**

Dune, figure, Feyd, complete, LJN, 1984, EX.............**$15.00**

Flash Gordon, accessory, Ming's Space Shuttle, Mattel, 1979, EX (VG box) **$30.00**

Flash Gordon, figure, Dr Zarkov, Mego, 1976, 9", M (EX+ box) **$80.00**

Flash Gordon, figure, Flash Gordon or Ming, Mattel, 1979, MOC, each......................**$25.00**

Flash Gordon, figure, Ming the Merciless, Mego, 9", M (EX box) **$60.00**

Grizzly Adams, figure, Grizzly Adams, Mattel, 1978, 9", MIB (minor wear) **$45.00**

Grizzly Adams, figure, Nakoma, Mattel, 1978, 9", M (EX box)......................**$35.00**

Happy Days, figure, Fonzie, Mego, 1978, 8", MIB **$50.00**
Happy Days, figure, Potsie, Mego, 1978, 8", MOC **$60.00**
Happy Days, figure, Ralph, Mego, 1978, 8", MOC......**$45.00**
Happy Days, figure, Richie, Mego, 1978, 8", MOC **$50.00**

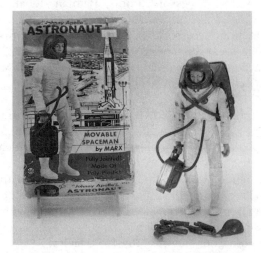

Johnny Apollo, figure, Johnny Apollo Astronaut, Marx, missing few accessories otherwise NMIB, $75.00.

Lone Ranger Rides Again, accessory, Apache Buffalo Hunt, Gabriel, 1979, VG **$12.00**
Lone Ranger Rides Again, accessory, Hidden Silver Mine, Gabriel, 1979, MIB..................................**$40.00**
Lone Ranger Rides Again, accessory, Landslide Adventure, Gabriel, 1979, MIB **$35.00**
Lone Ranger Rides Again, figure, Butch Cavendish or Little Bear, Garbiel, 1979, 9", VG+, each....................**$18.00**
Lone Ranger Rides Again, horse, Scout, Gabriel, 1979, M (EX box) **$40.00**
Lone Ranger Rides Again, horse, Smoke, Gabriel, 1979, M (VG+ box) **$35.00**
M*A*S*H, accessory, jeep, w/figure, Tri-Star International, NM (EX box) **$36.00**
M*A*S*H, figure, Hawkeye, Klinger, Macahy or Winchester, Tri-Star International, sm, MOC, each **$18.00**
Mad Monster Series, figure, Dracula, complete, Mego, 1974, 8", EX **$60.00**
Mad Monster Series, figure, Frankenstein or Wolfman, complete, Mego, 1974, 8", EX, each............................**$35.00**
Mad Monster Series, figure, Mummy, Mego, 1974, 8", MIB **$55.00**
Major Matt Mason, accessory, Cat Trak, red or white, Mattel, 1966-68, EX, each **$10.00**
Major Matt Mason, accessory, communicator, Mattel, 1966-68, EX...**$6.00**
Major Matt Mason, accessory, laser rifle, Mattel, 1966-68, EX...**$10.00**
Major Matt Mason, accessory, Space Probe Pack, complete, Mattel, 1966-68, EX **$22.00**
Major Matt Mason, figure, Captain Laser, complete, Mattel, 1966-68, EX **$60.00**
Major Matt Mason, figure, Matt Mason, Mattel, 1966-68, EX ..**$45.00**
Major Matt Mason, figure, Sgt Storm, Mattel, 1966-68, VG.**$28.00**
Marvel Super Heroes Secret Wars, accessory, Tower of Doom, Mattel, 1984, M (EX+ sealed box).............**$36.00**

Marvel Super Heroes Secret Wars, figure, Baron Zemo, Mattel, 1984, VG **$12.00**
Marvel Super Heroes Secret Wars, figure, Dr Octopus, Kang or Magneto, Mattel, 1984, MOC, each...................**$15.00**
Marvel Super Heroes Secret Wars, figure, Wolverine, Mattel, 1984, MOC..**$50.00**
Masters of the Universe, accessory, Castle GreySkull, Dragon Walker or Munstroid, Mattel, 1984, NM, each **$25.00**
Masters of the Universe, figure, Skeletor (battle armor), Stratus or Terror Claw Skeletor, Mattel, 1974, MOC, each **$50.00**
Maxx FX, figure, Freddy Kruger, Matchbox, NRFB..**$40.00**
Moonraker, figure, Drax, Mego 1979, 12", NMIB......**$130.00**
Moonraker, figure, Holly, Mego, 1979, 12", M (EX+ box).**$135.00**
Moonraker, figure, James Bond, Mego, 1979, 12", M (NM+ box) **$90.00**
Nobel Knights, figure, Eric the Viking, Marx, 1968-72, no accessories o/w EX...**$30.00**
Nobel Knights, figure, Sir Gordon the Gold Knight, w/most accessories & full armor, Marx, 1968-72, NM+ **$135.00**
Nobel Knights, figure, Sir Stuart the Silver Knight, w/most accessories & armor, Marx, 1968-72, G.................**$50.00**
Nobel Knights, horse, Valor, Marx, 1968-72, unused, MIB...**$135.00**
Official Scout High Adventure, accessory, Balloon Race to Devil's Canyon, Kenner, 1974-75, M (EX box).....**$22.00**
Official Scout High Adventure, accessory, Lost in the High Country, Kenner, 1974-75, EX............................**$12.00**
Official Scout High Adventure, figure, Craig Cub Scout, Kenner, 1974-75, M (EX box) **$30.00**
Official Scout High Adventure, figure, Steve Scout, complete, Kenner, 1974-75, EX **$20.00**
Official Scout High Adventure, figure, Steve Scout, Kenner, 1974-75, MIB **$30.00**
Official World's Greatest Heroes, figure, Aqualad, complete, Mego, 1976, EX **$140.00**
Official World's Greatest Super Heroes, figure, Aquaman, complete, Mego, 1972, 8", EX **$45.00**
Official World's Greatest Super Heroes, figure, Batman, Mego, 1978, 12", MIB **$75.00**
Official World's Greatest Super Heroes, figure, Batman, w/removable cowl, Mego, 1972, 8", VG **$100.00**
Official World's Greatest Super Heroes, figure, Penguin, Mego, 1973, 8", EXIB...**$80.00**
Official World's Greatest Super Heroes, figure, Penguin, Mego, 1973, 8", M (EX card)................................**$60.00**
Official World's Greatest Super Heroes, figure, Spider-Man, Mego, 1972, 8", EX (VG+ box) **$75.00**
Official World's Greatest Super Heroes, figure, Spider-Man, Mego, 1978, MIB..**$80.00**
Pee-Wee's Playhouse, accessory, Magic Screen, wind-up, Matchbox, 1988, MOC **$8.00**
Pee-Wee's Playhouse, figure, Pee-Wee, Matchbox, 1988, MOC **$15.00**
Pee-Wee's Playhouse, figure, Reba or Ricardo, Matchbox, 1988, MOC, each..**$20.00**
Planet of the Apes, accessory, Battering Ram, Mego, 1973-75, M (VG box)..**$35.00**
Planet of the Apes, accessory, Village Playset, Mego, 1973-75, unused, (M (EX box)..**$50.00**

Planet of the Apes, figure, Cornelius or Zira, complete, Mego, 1973-75, 8", EX, each........................**$30.00**

Planet of the Apes, figure, Peter Burke, complete, Mego, 1973-75, 8", EX........................**$40.00**

Planet of the Apes, figure, Soldier Ape, rare all-brown version w/gloves, Mego, 1973-75, 8", EX........................**$70.00**

Pocket Super Heroes, figure, Batman, Mego, 1979, MOC...**$40.00**

Pocket Super Heroes, figure, Hulk, Mego, 1979, EX..**$20.00**

Pulsar, accessory, Pulsar Life Systems Center, Mattel, 1977-78, EXIB........................**$22.00**

Pulsar, figure, Pulsar, Mattel, 1977-78, 13", NMIB.......**$30.00**

Robotech, figure, Dana Sterling, Lisa Hayes or Lynn Minmei, Matchbox, 1986, 12", MIP, each........................**$25.00**

Rocky, figure, Apollo Creed, Phoenix Toys, 1983, 8", MOC........................**$40.00**

Rocky, figure, Clubber Lang, Phoenix Toys, 1983, 8", MOC........................**$40.00**

Space: 1999, figure, Commander Koenig, Mattel, 1976-77, 9", M (VG+ card)........................**$50.00**

Space: 1999, figure, Dr Russel or Professor Bergman, Mattel, 1976-77, 9", MOC, each........................**$45.00**

Super Powers, accessory, carrying case for figures, Kenner, 1984-86, NM........................**$25.00**

Super Powers, accessory, Hall of Justice, Kenner, 1984-86, MIB........................**$90.00**

Super Powers, accessory, Supermobile, Kenner, 1984-86, M (VG box)........................**$15.00**

Super Powers, figure, Darkside, Kenner, 1984-86, M (VG card)........................**$15.00**

Super Powers, figure, Flash or Kalibak, Kenner, 1984-86, MOC, each........................**$10.00**

Super Powers, figure, Superman, complete, Kenner, 1984-86, NM **$20.00**

Super Powers, figure, Wonder Woman, Kenner, 1984-86, M (NM card) **$30.00**

Thundercats, accessory, Luna-Laser, LJN, 1985-87, MIB..**$18.00**

Thundercats, figure, Captain Cracker, Safari Joe or Snowman of Hook Mountain, LJN, 1985-87, MOC, each......**$25.00**

Thundercats, figure, Lion-O, LJN, 1985-87, MOC........**$35.00**

Universal Monsters, figure, Creature From the Black Lagoon, Remco, 1980, MOC........................**$25.00**

Universal Monsters, figure, Dracula, Remco, 1980, NM..**$12.00**

Wizard of Oz, accessory, Munchkinland Playset, complete, Mego, 1974, VG........................**$150.00**

Wizard of Oz, figure, Cowardly Lion, Mego, 1974, 8", M.**$25.00**

Wizard of Oz, figure, Dorothy w/Toto, Mego, 1974, 8", MIB.**$28.00**

Wizard of Oz, figure, Wizard, Mego, 1974, 8", M (brown mailer box)........................**$15.00**

Wizard of Oz, figure, Wizard, Multi-Toy, 1989, 12", MIB..**$30.00**

World's Greatest Super Knights, figure, King Arthur or Sir Lancelot, Mego, 1975-76, 8", EX, each **$45.00**

WWF, World Wrestling Federation, Crush (Series 4), Hasbro, MOC........................**$25.00**

WWF, World Wrestling Federation, figure, British Bulldog (Series 3), Hasbro, MOC........................**$35.00**

WWF, World Wrestling Federation, figure, El Matador (Series 4), Hasbro, MOC........................**$10.00**

WWF, World Wrestling Federation, figure, Skinner, Hasbro, M........................**$10.00**

WWF World Wrestling Federation, figure, Nasty Boys (Tag Team), Hasbro, MOC........................**$45.00**

Zeroid, accessory, Robot Zogg Commander Set, complete, Ideal, 1970, EX........................**$90.00**

Zeroid, figure, Robot from Star Raiders, Ideal, 1970, M..**$45.00**

Zeroid, figure, Zintar Robot, gray, Ideal, 1970, EX.....**$65.00**

Marvel Super Heroes Secret Wars, figure, Baron Zemo, Mattel, MOC, $25.00.

Battery Operated

It is estimated that approximately 95% of the battery-operated toys that were so popular from the forties through the sixties came from Japan. The remaining 5% were made in the United States by other companies. To market these toys in America, many distributorships were organized. Some of the largest were Cragstan, Linemar, and Rosko. But even American toy makers such as Marx, Ideal, Hubley, and Daisy marketed them as well. After peaking in the sixties, the Japanese toy industry began a decline, bowing out to competition from the cheaper die-cast and plastic toy makers.

Remember that it is rare to find one of these complex toys that have survived in good, collectible condition. Batteries caused corrosion, lubricants dried out, cycles were interrupted and mechanisms ruined, rubber hoses and bellows aged and cracked, so the mortality rate was extremely high. A toy rated good, that is showing signs of wear but well taken care of, is generally worth about half as much as the same toy in mint (like new) condition. Besides condition, battery-operated toys are rated on scarcity, desirability, and the number of 'actions' they perform. A 'major' toy is one that has three or more actions, while one that does only one or two is considered 'minor.' The latter, of course, are worth much less.

In addition to the books we referenced in the beginning narrative to the toy category, you'll find more information in *Collecting Battery Toys* by Don Hultzman (Books Americana).

AI, Traffic Policeman, cop blows whistle & turns as light changes, 13", NM (EX box)........................**$310.00**

Alps, Airport Service Bus, door opens, NMIB..........**$125.00**

Alps, Balloon Blowing Teddy, bear seated in chair kicks & raises balloon, litho tin & plush w/light-up eyes, 11", VG+........................**$65.00**

Alps, Bongo the Drumming Monkey, MIB...............**$250.00**

Alps, Bubble Blowing Monkey, monkey dips wand in solution & blows bubbles, plush w/light-up eyes, 10", NMIB **$150.00**

Alps, Busy Housekeeper Bear, moves forward & backward w/vacuum, tin & plush, 8", NM (EX+ box) **$235.00**

Alps, Chimpanzee the One-Man Drummer, plush monkey in yellow hat playing drums, 6 actions, 1950s, 9", NMIB **$110.00**

Alps, Clown the Magician, leans, tips hat & flips stack of cards, nose lights up, tin, cloth & vinyl, 12", EX (VG box) **$175.00**

Alps, Daisy the Drumming Duck, 9", MIB **$375.00**

Alps, Dandy the Happy Drumming Pup, plays drum & cymbals w/moving head & light-up eyes, tin & plush, 9", EX (VG+ box) **$110.00**

Alps, Fido the Xylophone Player, dog plays xylophone & sways, tin & plush, 9", scarce, NM (VG+ box)...**$250.00**

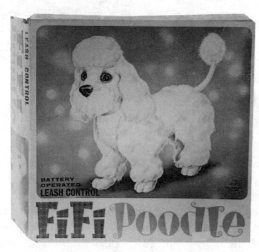

Alps, Fifi Poodle, leash control, MIB, $45.00.

Alps, Fishing Polar Bear, bear pulls fish out of pond, throws it in basket & squeals, plush & tin, 10", NM (EX box)..**$255.00**

Alps, Gooney Car, 3-way mystery action w/blowing horn, mustached driver in black hat, white tin w/gold trim, EXIB **$55.00**

Alps, Hooty the Happy Owl, 9", MIB **$185.00**

Alps, Hot Rod Custom T Ford, 10½", MIB **$200.00**

Alps, Indian Joe, plays war-dance tune on drum & moves head side to side, 12", EX+ (VG box)..................**$80.00**

Alps, Jolly Santa on Snow, remote control, skates & skis while ringing bell, 1950s, 12", NM (EX box)......**$285.00**

Alps, Mary's Little Lamb, advances w/nodding head, stops & speaks, plush & tin, 10", EX+ (EX+ box)............**$125.00**

Alps, Pet Turtle, 7", NM **$125.00**

Alps, Picnic Bunny, pours carrot juice into cup & drinks it, plush over tin, NMIB..**$75.00**

Alps, Ski Lift, goes to end of cable & changes direction, tin, 7", NM **$150.00**

Alps/Cragston, Dishwasher, complete w/accessories, tin, 1950s, 9", MIB **$130.00**

Bandai, Cycling Daddy, rides tricycle, vinyl figure w/cloth clothes, 10", MIB..**$225.00**

Bandai, Harbor Patrol, 9", EX+..**$160.00**

Bandai, Old Fashioned Hot Rod, bump-&-go action, tin w/vinyl driver, 6", EXIB **$110.00**

CK, Musical Jolly Chimp, 10½", MIB........................**$100.00**

Cragston, Shuttling Train Set, railroad car w/dog travels track, many actions, tin, 38", MIB........................**$215.00**

Daishin, Happy Naughty Chimp, 1960, MIB **$100.00**

Daiya, Army Tank, brown w/USA decal, tin, working, VG+ **$30.00**

Diva, Green Caterpillar, 20", EX **$185.00**

Haji, Strutting My Fair Dancer, sailor girl does jig on platform, tin & celluloid, 12", NM (EX box) **$135.00**

Ideal, Smarty Bird, 1964, EX **$60.00**

Illco/WDP, Minnie Mouse Shopping Cart, bump-&-go action, plastic, 1960s-70s, 10", EX+ (EX box) **$65.00**

Linemar, Jocko the Drinking Monkey, 11", VG+.......**$100.00**

Linemar, Jungle Trio, monkey w/cymbals sits on elephant while other beats drum, round base, tin & vinyl, 9", NM **$260.00**

Linemar, Sparking Bear, 9", NMIB **$475.00**

Linemar, Telephone Bear, bear sits at desk & writes, picks up phone & chatters, litho tin & plush, 8", EXIB **$200.00**

Linemar, Traffic Light, lights change from green to red on all 4 sides, 18", EX+ (EX+ box) **$145.00**

Linemar, Walking Cat, remote control, advances & moves head, eyes light up & meows, plush & tin, 6", EX+ (VG box) **$60.00**

Marusan (SAN), Smoky Bear, remote control, 5 actions, 1950s, 8½", NMIB **$75.00**

Marusan (SAN), Smoky Joe Car, bump-&-go action, driver smokes pipe that lights up & blows smoke, tin & vinyl, 8½", EX **$100.00**

Marx, Agent .012 Car, 1966, MIB........................**$125.00**

Marx, Amphibious Military Vehicle w/Soldiers, forward & reverse action, plastic, complete, 9", EX+ (EX+ box)............**$145.00**

Marx, Buttons the Puppy w/the Brain, nonworking o/w VG **$110.00**

Marx, Clang-Clang Locomotive, advances w/light & sound, early 1960s, 13", MIB..**$85.00**

Marx, Marx-A-Copter, circles pylon, bombs submarine & rescues men, plastic, 1958, NMIB........................**$50.00**

Marx, Mickey Mouse on Big Wheel, advances w/sound, NMIB **$275.00**

Mattel, Surfing Snoopy, #3477, M........................**$60.00**

Mattel, Vroom Cement Mixer, EX+ (partial box)......**$125.00**

Modern Toys, M-81 Tank, remote control, 8½", EX .**$100.00**

MT, Bing Ring Circus Truck, bump-&-go action w/whistle sound, tin w/vinyl clown driver, 12", scarce, NM **$200.00**

MT, Father Bear, sits in rocker & lifts book & glass, head moves & eyes light up, tin & plush, 9", NM+ (EX+ box)..**$200.00**

MT, Good Time Charlie, man sitting by street lamp w/cigar & flask, 1960s, 12", EX (G box)........................**$165.00**

MT, Loop Plane, remote control, advances & loops, prop spins, tin w/vinyl-headed pilot, 9", NM (EX box)............**$155.00**

MT, Sparky the Seal, walks & balances ball in stream of air above nose, plush over tin, 8", M **$100.00**

MT, Telephone Rabbit, sits in rocking chair & picks up phone, plush & tin, MIB **$275.00**

MT, Tinkling Trolley, 10½", MIB $200.00

Palitoy, Talking Batmobile, press roof to play phrases, 1977, unused, M (NM box)...............................$300.00

Remco, Movieland Drive-In Theater, plastic w/double-feature film strips & 4 tin cars, NMIB $200.00

S&E, Drinking Captain, 1950, MIB $175.00

Sonsco, Walking-Climbing Fireman, fireman climbs up & down ladder w/hose, tin, 7", NM (G- box)........$280.00

Taiyo, Highway Patrol, tin, 7½", EX...............$30.00

Thomas Toys, Mobile Searchlight Unit, blue & yellow truck w/attached wagon & searchlight, 1950s, 16", EX+ (EX box) $165.00

TN, Brave Eagle, beats drum, sways & makes war-whoop sound, tin & plastic w/cloth clothes, 12", NM+ (EX+ box)...$125.00

TN, Charlie Weaver Bartender, makes drink, smacks lips while face turns red & ears smoke, 12", MIB.....$130.00

TN, Chimp & Pup Rail Car, 8", MIB $375.00

TN, Circus Elephant, moves legs & balances ball, plush over tin, 10", NM (EX box)...............................$175.00

TN, Cragston Circus Jet, NMIB $250.00

TN, Dolly Dressmaker (Dolly Seamstress), at sewing machine, 10 actions, 7", NMIB...........................$200.00

TN, Fire Chief Mystery Car, tin, 10", EX...................$145.00

TN, Jolly Penguin, 7", MIB...............................$175.00

TN, Knitting Grandma, 8½", M...............................$250.00

TN, McGregor, eyes roll & smoke emits from cigar-smoking man as he rises from suitcase, tin & cloth, 11", NM (EX box) $165.00

TN, Miss Friday the Typist, tin & vinyl, 7", EX (VG box).$165.00

TN, Multi-Action Electra-Jet, lithographed tin, 16" long, NMIB, $185.00.

TN, Piano Pooch, plays piano w/sound, tin & plush, 7", NM (EX box)...$135.00

TN, Roaring Gorilla, remote control, plush & tin, 1950s, 9½", EX+ (VG+ box)...................................$300.00

TN, Roaring Lion, remote control, mane puffs out as he walks & roars, 12", NM (EX box)...................$130.00

TN, Shaking Antique Car, 7", MIB...........................$125.00

TN, Turn-O-Matic Gun Jeep, 10", NMIB $175.00

TN, Windy the Juggling Elephant, waves feet while spinning umbrella or blows ball, plush & tin, 10½", MIB.......$325.00

TN, Worried Duck, 11", MIB...............................$225.00

TPS, Dune Buggy, tin & plastic, EX+...................$100.00

TPS, Ferris Wheel, nonstop action & sound as pigs revolve w/balls inside drum, tin & plastic, 9", NM (EX box)...............$120.00

Y, Bubble Blowing Musician, man at podium blowing bubbles w/trumpet, 1950s, 11", NMIB...................$120.00

Y, Burger Chef, plush dog flipping food in skillet on tin brick grill, 9", MIB...............................$220.00

Y, Captain Blushwell, 11", MIB...................$165.00

Y, Drinking Dog, 1950s, M...............................$125.00

Y, Hungry Baby Bear, mama bear feeds baby bear, several actions, tin & plush w/cloth clothes, 9½", NM (EX box) $175.00

Y, Mac the Turtle, rolls over barrel w/several actions, 7", NM (EX box) $285.00

Y, Magic Bulldozer, bump-&-go, w/driver, tin, 5".....$175.00

Y, Piggy Cook, 9½", MIB $275.00

Yonezawa, Jumbo the Bubble Blowing Elephant, plush and lithographed tin, 1950, 7", MIB, $185.00.

Guns

One of the bestselling kinds of toys ever made, toy guns were first patented in the late 1850s. Until WWII, most were made of cast iron, though other materials were used on a lesser scale. After the war, cast iron became cost prohibitive, and steel and diecast zinc were used. By 1950, most were made either of diecast material or plastic. Hundreds of names can be found embossed on these little guns, a custom which continues to the present time. Because of their tremendous popularity and durability, today's collectors can find a diversity of models and styles, and prices are still fairly affordable.

See also Western Heroes.

Newsletter: *Toy Gun Collectors of America*
Jim Buskirk, Editor and Publisher
175 Cornell St.
Windsor CA 95492; 707-837-9949; Published quarterly, covers both toy and BB guns. Dues: $15 per year

American Silent Ray Gun, black, 11", EX...................$75.00

Atom Buster Air Blaster, w/atomic target, 1950s, NMIB..$100.00

Belco Gun, Made in USA, solid metal, 3½", NM.........$18.00

Daisy Bull's Eye, blue frame, wood grips, no bullets, EX.$95.00

Daisy Model A BB Gun, break action, wood stock, EX .$125.00

Daisy Model H BB Gun, lever action, wood stock, EX......$75.00

Daisy No 101 BB Gun, Model 36, lever action, wood stock, EX......**$25.00**

Daisy No 104 BB Gun, double-barrel, wood stock, EX..**$450.00**

Daisy No 105 BB Gun, Junior Pump Gun, wood stock, EX......**$90.00**

Daisy No 195 BB Gun, Buzz Barton, lever action, wood stock, EX......**$65.00**

Daisy Rocket Dart Pistol, tin, 1950s, 7½", VG......**$100.00**

Daisy Spittin' Image Six-Gun, bronze finish w/plastic wood-grain grips, EX......**$45.00**

Elvin Space Universe Sparking Ray Gun, blue, white & yellow tin, marked T, Japan, 1960s, NMIP......**$45.00**

Esquire Action Miniatures No 10 Authentic Derringer, bronze diecast, fires caps, 1960s, 2", MOC......**$15.00**

Halco Texan Holster Set w/Cap Pistols, diecast w/plastic grips, NMOC......**$75.00**

Hamilton Invaders Pistol, w/2 grenades, EX......**$75.00**

Hubley Army .45 Repeater Cap Gun, metal w/plastic grips, nickel-plated cast-iron trigger, unused, 6½", M (G box)......**$125.00**

Hubley Colt .38 Cap Pistol w/Chest Holster & Suspenders, diecast, 1959, unused, NM (VG card)......**$85.00**

Hubley Cowboy Gold Cap Pistol No 275, diecast, swing-out revolving cylinder, black plastic grips, 1950s, 12", VG......**$125.00**

Hubley Dagger Derringer, metal w/slide-out plastic dagger, barrel rotates, 7", NMOC......**$140.00**

Hubley Flintlock Jr Pistol, unused, NMIB......**$45.00**

Hubley Remington .36 Cap Pistol, diecast w/black plastic grips, revolving cylinder w/6 2-pc bullets, 1959, 8", VG......**$75.00**

Hubley Sharp Shooter Rifle, nickel-plated w/green plastic stock, bolt action, roll caps, not a repeater, 1965, 37", NMIB......**$150.00**

J Rosenthal Toys Thunderbird 100-Shot Variable Direction Water Pistol, bright orange w/swivel nozzle, 1966, 8", MIP......**$65.00**

Kilgore Avenger Cap Pistol, diecast pistol in plastic shell, complete w/ammo, 3", NMOC......**$25.00**

Kilgore Border Patrol Cap Pistol, nickel-plated cast iron, side-loading automatic, 1935, 4½", VG......**$45.00**

Kilgore Captain 50-Shot, 4¼", MIB......**$75.00**

Kilgore Dude Derringer Cap Pistol, silver diecast single shot, black plastic grips, Italy, 1974, 4", MOC......**$25.00**

Kilgore Eagle, set of 2 w/double holster, plastic grips, EX+......**$165.00**

Kilgore Mountie Cap Pistol, black metal w/silver trim, black grips, lever-release pop-up cap magazine, 1950, 6", MIB....**$45.00**

King No 0005 BB Gun, pump action, wood stock, EX .**$65.00**

King No 0017 BB Gun, break action, wood stock......**$65.00**

King No 2136 BB Gun, lever action, wood stock, EX..**$20.00**

King No 2236 BB Gun, lever action, wood stock, EX..**$20.00**

KO Mars Rifle, tin w/red plastic barrels, sparking action & sound, VG (original box)......**$65.00**

KO Space Jet Friction Ray Gun, Japan, litho tin & plastic, sparks, reciprocating rocket in green barrel, 1957, 9", VG...**$50.00**

Kusan Western Heritage Texan, diecast, MOC......**$25.00**

Langston Super Nu-Matic Paper Buster Gun, diecast w/plastic nose extension, 5", NM (EX box)......**$35.00**

Leslie-Henry Matt Dillon Cap Pistol, nickel-plated diecast with steer on copper grips, 1950, 10", M, $225.00.

Leslie-Henry Smoky Joe Texas Longhorn Cap Pistol, coppered metal, lever release, break-to-front, 1950s, 9", VG......**$65.00**

Leslie-Henry Texas Cap Pistol, diecast, extra-long barrel, white grips, unused, M......**$65.00**

Lido Cosmo Pistol in Space No 891, Hong Kong, plastic w/battery-op lights & laser sound, 1970s, 10", MIB......**$45.00**

Lone Star Space Ranger Cap Pistol, blue-painted diecast w/red & white trim, pop-up magazine, 1960s, VG......**$200.00**

Marx Blue & Gray Shell Shooting Civil War Cavalry Pistol, plastic w/diecast works, plastic bullets, 1960, 10", MOC......**$75.00**

Marx Desert Patrol Lugar Pistol & Silencer, plastic w/diecast works, dark gray w/brown grips, 1960s, 10", MOC...**$30.00**

Marx Security Pistol, 1970s, MOC......**$20.00**

Marx Tommy Gun, 24", EX......**$50.00**

Mattel Agent Zero-M Rifle, EX......**$35.00**

Mattel Burp Gun, pressed steel & plastic, fires perforated roll caps, ca 1955, 23" w/stock extended, NMIB......**$100.00**

Mattel Shootin' Shell Snub-Nose .38 Cap Pistol, diecast w/revolving cylinder, brown plastic grips, 1960s, 7", VG......**$45.00**

Mini-Mag X-200 Multi-Matic Spy Rifle, NMOC......**$30.00**

New King BB Gun, repeater, break action, wood stock, EX......**$80.00**

Nichols Buccaneer Shell-Firing Flintlock Pistol No 210, diecast, red plastic bullets, 1958, 3½", MOC......**$25.00**

Nichols Dyno-Mite Derringer Cap Gun, EX (EX box)..**$60.00**

Park Plastics Squirt Ray Atomic Repeater Water Gun, brass nozzle w/solid rubber plug, 1950s-60s, 5½", M...**$20.00**

Playcraft Co Atom-Matic Water Rocket Gun, pressed aluminum, brass & plastic, rubber stopper, ca 1949, 7", VG......**$75.00**

Remco Electronic Space Gun, gray plastic w/red trim, battery-op light w/4-color wheel, 1950s, MIB......**$175.00**

Remco Jupiter 4-Color Signal Gun No 600, black plastic w/red trim, internal color wheel, 1950s, 9", MIB......**$65.00**

Renwal .38 Military & Police Automatic Revolver No 265, gray plastic, spring-loading w/12 bullets, 1960s, NMIB......**$65.00**

Stevens Ranger, cast aluminum w/black grips, single shot, w/holster marked Cowboy, ca 1946, 7½", NMIB...**$75.00**

Tigrett Atom Flash Zoomeray Space Gun, red plastic, wrist motion fires rolled paper wad w/message, 1950s, 7", NMIB ..**$45.00**

Tim-Mee Laser Ray Gun, plastic, 10", MIB......**$55.00**

TN Flashy-Ray Gun, multicolored tin w/space graphics, pull trigger & battery-op light flashes, 18½", MIB.....**$150.00**

Topper/Deluxe-Reading Multi-Pistol 09, NMIB......**$75.00**

Twentieth Century Products Super Site Magic Bullet Gun, plastic, telescopic sight, whistle in grip, 1950s, 9", VG .**$20.00**

US Plastic Flying Saucer Space Gun, 1950s, EX+ (EX+ box)..**$110.00**

US Plastic Space Patrol Dart Gun, red plastic w/raised design on handle, 10", EX+................................**$95.00**

WF Friction Ray Gun, Hong Kong, blue transparent plastic, sparks, 1970s, 7", M..............................**$25.00**

Wham-O Air Blaster, black plastic w/rubber diaphragm, w/original gorilla target, 1960s, 10", EX..............**$75.00**

Wyandotte Dart Pistol, 1950s, MIB..............................**$75.00**

Ramp Walkers

Though ramp-walking figures were made as early as the 1870s, ours date from about 1935 on. They were made in Czechoslovakia from the twenties through the forties and in this country during the fifties and sixties by Marx, who made theirs of plastic. John Wilson of Watsontown, Pennsylvania, sold his worldwide. They were known as 'Wilson Walkies' and stood about 4½" high. But the majority has been imported from Hong Kong.

Advisor: Randy Welch (See Directory, Toys)

Alice in Wonderland's Mad Hatter & White Rabbit, plastic, Marx, 1951, 3", NM..............................**$75.00**

Astro & George Jetson, Hanna-Barbera, NM..............**$90.00**

Baby Walk-A-Way, Marx, NM..............................**$40.00**

Baseball Player w/Bat & Ball, NM..............................**$40.00**

Big Bad Wolf & Three Little Pigs, NM..............**$125.00**

Brontosaurus w/Monkey, Marx, NM..............**$25.00**

Chicks w/Easter Egg, NM..............................**$30.00**

Chilly Willy, penguin on sled pulled by parent, NM..**$25.00**

Chipmunks w/Acorns, NM..............................**$30.00**

Cowboy on Horse, metal legs, NM..............................**$20.00**

Cowboy on Horse, plastic w/metal legs, sm, NM......**$20.00**

Dachshund, NM..............................**$15.00**

Dancing Boy & Girl, NM..............................**$40.00**

Dog, standing, NM..............................**$20.00**

Donald Duck & Goofy, riding go-cart, NM..............**$40.00**

Donald Duck Pulling Nephews in Wagon, NM..........**$35.00**

Dutch Boy & Girl, NM..............................**$30.00**

Elephant, plastic w/metal legs, sm, NM..............**$20.00**

Eskimo, Wilson, NM..............................**$75.00**

Fiddler & Fifer Pigs, NM..............................**$40.00**

Figaro the Cat w/Ball, NM..............................**$30.00**

Firemen, $30.00.

Fred Flintstone & Barney Rubble, NM..............**$40.00**

Fred Flintstone on Dino, NM..............................**$70.00**

Goofy, riding hippo, NM..............................**$45.00**

Hippo w/Native, Animals w/Riders Series, Marx, NM........**$25.00**

Horse, plastic w/yellow rubber ears & string tail, lg, NM..**$30.00**

Indian Chief, Wilson, NM..............................**$45.00**

Jiminy Cricket w/Cello, NM..............................**$30.00**

Lion w/Clown, Animals w/Riders Series, Marx, NM...**$25.00**

Little Red Riding Hood, Wilson, $40.00; Clown, Wilson, $30.00; Nurse, Wilson, $30.00. (Photo courtesy of Randy and Adrienne Welch.)

Mickey Mouse, pushing lawn roller, NM..............**$35.00**

Mickey Mouse & Minnie, plastic w/metal legs, sm, NM..**$40.00**

Mickey Mouse & Minnie w/basket of food, NM.........**$40.00**

Mickey Mouse & Pluto, hunting, NM..............**$40.00**

Milking Cow, Marx, lg, NM..............................**$40.00**

Monkeys w/Bananas, NM..............................**$50.00**

Olive Oyl, Wilson, NM..............................**$175.00**

Pig, wood & composition, NM..............................**$20.00**

Pluto, plastic, NM..............................**$20.00**

Pluto, plastic w/metal legs, NM..............................**$30.00**

Policeman, wood & composition, EX..............**$40.00**

Popeye, celluloid, Erwin, lg, NM..............................**$60.00**

Popeye, pushing spinach-can wheelbarrow, NM.......**$40.00**

Rabbit, Wilson, NM..............................**$40.00**

Reindeer, NM..............................**$35.00**

Sailor, Wilson, NM..............................**$30.00**

Santa, w/white sack, NM..............................**$40.00**

Santa & Mrs Claus, faces on both sides, NM..............**$40.00**

Sheriff & Outlaw, NM..............................**$65.00**

Teeny Toddler, walking baby girl, plastic, Dolls Inc, lg, NM..............................**$40.00**

Top Cat & Benny, NM..............................**$65.00**

Walking Baby, plastic w/moving eyes & cloth dress, lg, NM..............................**$50.00**

Yogi Bear & Huckleberry Hound, NM..............**$50.00**

Zebra w/Native, Marx, NM..............................**$25.00**

Robots and Space Toys

As early as 1948, Japanese toy manufacturers introduced their robots and space toys. Some of the best examples were made in the fifties, during the 'golden age' of battery-operated toys. They became more and more complex, and today some of these in excellent condition may bring well over $1,000.00. By the sixties, more and more plastic was used in their production, and the toys became inferior.

Airport Saucer, battery-op, MT, MIB.........................**$125.00**
Apollo X Moon Challenger, battery-op, TN, EX........**$185.00**
Atom Boat, friction, w/animated Oriental astronaut, China, 1960s, VG+ (G box) **$250.00**
Attacking Martian, battery-op, advances as chest guns fire, w/flashing lights & sound, tin & plastic, SH, 9", MIB...**$135.00**

Big Max Electronic Conveyor Robot, battery-operated, Remco, 1958, complete with truck and metal discs, EX, $265.00. (Photo courtesy of June Moon.)

Big Max Robot, battery-op, Remco, 8", NMIB...........**$200.00**
Busy Robot, battery-op, tin, SH/Japan, EX+..............**$150.00**
Cape Canaveral Mobile Satellite Tracking Station, EX .**$185.00**
Countdown Launcher, Ideal, EX+.................................**$65.00**
Cragston Astronaut, battery-op, holds ray gun, blue tin w/yellow striping, 11", EX **$175.00**
Cragston Flying Saucer, battery-op, girl in clear dome, bump-&-go action w/lights & noise, KO, 8" dia, EX (G+ box) **$150.00**
Cragston Mr Robot, battery-op, bump-&-go action, advances w/spinning devices, head lights up, tin, 11", EX .**$385.00**
Cragston Satellite, battery-op, mystery action w/flashing lights, tin w/diecut floating astronaut, 9", NM....**$155.00**
Earth Satellite, battery-op, remote control, flies in different directions, tin, EX+ (EX+ box)..............................**$580.00**
Engine Robot, battery-op, SH/Japan, 9½", MIB **$150.00**
Fighting Spaceman, battery-op, tin w/plastic chest cover, SH/Japan, 12", EX...**$150.00**
Fire Rocket X-007, battery-op, advances w/siren, pilot pops out when it hits an object, tin, Yonezawa, 14" long, EXIB...**$225.00**
Flying Saucer Space Patrol 3, battery-op, advances w/lights & sound, w/astronaut, tin, KO, 7½", NM (EX box)........**$260.00**
Friendship 7 Space Capsule, friction, capsule rolls w/rocking action, revolving astronaut, SH/Japan, 1960s, 10", VG+..**$100.00**
Getta-1 Robot, wind-up, movable limbs, tin, 7½", M .**$175.00**

Golden Sonic Spaceship, Bizarre Toy, 19", MIB **$150.00**
H2O Missile, Mattel, 1959, EXIB.................................**$125.00**
Interplanetary Space Saucer, flies & makes siren noise when cord is pulled, plastic, Merit, 7" dia, EXIB..........**$185.00**
Jumping Rocket, wind-up, robot pilot in rocket w/hopping & bucking motion, tin, SY/Japan, 6", VG+ (EX box)..**$100.00**
Kiddy Rocket, wind-up, advances w/U-turn action, tin w/vinyl figure, Yonezawa, 6", NM (EX box) **$100.00**
Lighted Space Vehicle, battery-op, bump-&-go w/floating ball, lights & sound, MT/Japan, 1950s, 8", NM...**$275.00**
Looping Space Tank, battery-op, moves w/flashing lights & firing guns, tin w/clear plastic dome, Daiya, NM (G+ box).**$200.00**
Luna Hovercraft, battery-op, remote control, TPS/Japan, 8", MIB **$325.00**
M-18 Space Tank, battery-op, EXIB **$125.00**

Man in Space, lithographed tin with celluloid head and arms, Alps, EX in box, $300.00.

Mars King, battery-op, advances, stops & screeches, chest lights up & shows Mars landscape, tin, 10", VG+ (G box) **$100.00**
Mini Robotank TR2, battery-op, MIB **$325.00**
Mini-Martians Jet Car, bright plastic spacecraft w/clear plastic dome & decal, Ideal, 1967, 8", EXIB...................**$150.00**
Missile Robot, wind-up, advances w/sparking chest, shoots missiles, chrome-plated plastic, TPS/Japan, 5", NM (EX+ box) **$140.00**
Moon City, battery-op, Cragstan, 1970, MIB..............**$260.00**
Moon Globe Orbiter, battery-op, moon orbiter on track rotates & makes moon globe spin, plastic & tin, Mego, 10", NMIB **$175.00**
New Astronaut, battery-op, SH/Japan, 9½", MIB **$130.00**
New Space Capsule, battery-op, SH/Japan, NMIB....**$250.00**
Nike Rocket, friction, advances, hits object & lifts to vertical position, tin, Masuya, 7", NM (EX+ box) **$125.00**
Pete the Spaceman, battery-op, Bandai, 5", MIB **$200.00**
Planet-Y Space Station, battery-op, bump-&-go w/lights & sound, TN/Japan, NM (VG box)........................**$200.00**
Radar Tank, battery-op, TN/Japan, 8", EX+..............**$125.00**
Robby (Robot Bulldozer), friction, robot driver on yellow dozer w/treads, tin, Marusan (SAN), 6", VG+ (G box).....**$175.00**
Robot Tractor, battery-op, robot on treaded tractor moves back & forth w/lighted moving pistons, Showa/Japan, 9½", G **$150.00**

Robot w/Ultra Spark, wind-up, metal & plastic, 6", MIB ..**$20.00**

Rotate-O-Matic Super Giant Robot, battery-op, walks & rotates upper body, tin w/plastic arms, SH/Japan, 16", EXIB.**$150.00**

S-61 Space Explorer, friction, tin, Japan, 13", EX+ **$65.00**

Satellite Barometer, 1950s, EX+ **$40.00**

Solar-X Rocket Ship, battery-op, tin & plastic w/rubber wheels, 15", EX **$55.00**

Space Capsule, friction, realistic NASA-type vehicle, astronaut inside, tin, SH/Japan, 9½", VG+ **$10.00**

Space Capsule w/Floating Astronaut, battery-op, marked Apollo, bump-&-go w/lights & sound, tin, MT/Japan, M (EX box) **$125.00**

Space Car, battery-op, nonfall action w/blinking lights, vinyl-headed driver in tin space car, MT/Japan, 10", EXIB **$175.00**

Space Fighter, battery-op, bounces, walks & stops, chest door opens to expose guns, SH/Japan, 10", NM (EX box)..**$150.00**

Space Frontier Rocket, battery-op, hatch opens to expose astronaut w/camera, tin & plastic, KY/Japan, 18", EX (G box) **$100.00**

Space Helmet with Radar Goggles, Banner Plastics, 1950s, NM in EX box, $400.00.

Space Model QX-2 Walkie-Talkies, Remco, 1950s, NMIB .**$90.00**

Space Navigator Pin & Compass Set, WSNY/Japan, ca 1955, MOC...**$50.00**

Space Patrol 3 Saucer, KO, 7½" dia, EX **$125.00**

Space Robot, friction, rocket w/swinging-arm robot moves w/space noise, tin, SY/Japan, 6", VG+ (G box).**$150.00**

Space Scout, battery-op, tin, 1960s, EX+ **$200.00**

Space Skooter, battery-op, tin, TN/Japan, 8", EXIB ..**$225.00**

Space Vehicle, battery-op, space tank w/bump-&-go action & floating ball, tin, MT/Japan, 8", EXIB **$150.00**

Sparking Robot, wind-up, tin, N/Japan, 6½", NMIB .**$210.00**

Sparky Robot, wind-up, tin, 8", EX+ **$250.00**

Star Defender Playset, complete, Woolworth/Woolco, 1970s, EX (EX card) **$100.00**

Super Robot, wind-up, advances w/sparking chest, tin & plastic, N/Japan, 5", EX (VG box) **$275.00**

Super Space Commander, battery-op, advances w/lighted space scene in chest, SH/Japan, 9½", M (EX+ box) **$65.00**

Talking Robot, battery-op, talks & fires rockets from head w/push-button action, plastic, Y/Japan, 12", MIB..**$250.00**

USA-NASA Apollo, battery-op, piloted ship moves w/nonfall action, astronaut rotates above, tin, MT/Japan, 7", M (EX box) **$185.00**

Walking Robot, wind-up, walks w/swinging arms & antennas, w/chest gun, rests on wire easel back, tin, Linemar, 6", VG+ **$200.00**

Winner Space Rocket, battery-op, rocket moves along track, tin, Exelo/Japan, 5½", EXIB **$250.00**

X-09 Space Survey, battery-op, triangular space vehicle w/bump-&-go action, astronaut w/animated arm, 9", EX (G box)..**$125.00**

X-10 Space Vehicle, battery-op, MIB..........................**$375.00**

X-107 Satellite w/Astronaut in Orbit, painted tin, Modern Toys, 7½" dia, VG (original box) **$125.00**

X-12 Moon Crawler, battery-op, M.............................**$100.00**

X-15 Flying Saucer, wind-up, 1950s, 6" dia, EX+ **$200.00**

X-5 Spaceship, battery-op, bump-&-go action w/flashing lights, tin & plastic, TM/Japan, 8½", NM (VG box)............**$85.00**

X-6 Rocket, friction, tin, MT/Japan, 1950s, 4", scarce, NM (EX box) **$350.00**

X-70 Astronaut, wind-up, advances w/sound, holds walkie-talkie, plastic, Hong Kong, EXIB **$185.00**

XB-115 Rocket, friction, advances w/sparks & space noise, nose cone spins, tin & plastic, SH/Japan, 11½", MIB **$150.00**

Zoomer Robot, battery-op, diamond-shaped antenna & coiled metal hair atop head, holds wrench, tin, Japan, 9", EX.........**$230.00**

Slot Car Racers

Slot cars first became popular in the early 1960s. Electric raceways set up in retail storefront windows were commonplace. Huge commercial tracks with eight and ten lanes were located in hobby stores and raceways throughout the United States. Large corporations such as Aurora, Revell, Monogram, and Cox, many of which were already manufacturing toys and hobby items, jumped on the bandwagon to produce slot cars and race sets. By the end of the early 1970s, people were losing interest in slot racing, and its popularity diminished. Today the same baby boomers that raced slot cars in earlier days are revitalizing the sport. Vintage slot cars are making a comeback as one of the hottest automobile collectibles of the 1990s. Want ads for slot cars appear more and more frequently in newspapers and publications geared toward the collector. As you would expect from their popularity, slot cars were generally well used, so finding vintage cars and race sets in like-new or mint condition is difficult. Slot cars replicating the 'muscle' cars from the sixties and seventies are extremely sought after, and clubs and organizations devoted to these collectibles are becoming more and more commonplace. Large toy companies such as Tomy and Tyco still produce some slots today, but not in the quality, quantity or variety of years past.

Aurora AFX: Furious Fueler Dragster, HO scale, yellow and white, MOC, $20.00; Magna Traction Corvette GT, HO scale, white with red, yellow and orange front, MOC, $20.00. (Photo courtesy of Gary Pollastro.)

AC Gilbert, Ford (1940), #19090, 1/32 scale, VG **$75.00**

AC Gilbert, Sulky #1, w/black horse, 1/32 scale, M ...**$60.00**

AMT, Mercury Comet, 1/24 scale, EX **$150.00**

Aurora, AFX, Autoworld McClaren XJR #54, orange, NM....**$12.00**

Aurora, AFX, Chevelle Stockcar #17, orange & white, EX ..**$12.00**

Aurora, AFX, Dodge Charger, blue, NM **$20.00**

Aurora, AFX, Ford Baja Bronco, red, NM **$14.00**

Aurora, AFX, Pontiac Grand Am, red, white & blue, NM ..**$15.00**

Aurora, AFX, Revamatic Slot Car Set, EXIB **$50.00**

Aurora, AFX Magna-Traction, Custom Van, orange, red & black, NM **$14.00**

Aurora, AFX Magna-Traction, Firebird Formula, red, orange & black, NM **$22.00**

Aurora, AFX Magna-Traction, Grand Am Funny Car, red, white & blue, NM **$16.00**

Aurora, AFX Magna-Traction, Porsche #16, red, white & blue, NM **$12.00**

Aurora, Batmobile, #1385, black, rare, EX..................**$50.00**

Aurora, G-Plus, Monza GT #0, white & green stripe, NM...**$15.00**

Aurora, Pickup Hot Rod, O scale, EX+ **$100.00**

Aurora, Thunderjet, Camero, EX **$30.00**

Aurora, Thunderjet, Corvette, turquoise, NM..............**$45.00**

Aurora, Thunderjet, Dune Buggy, white w/red striped roof, EX..**$30.00**

Aurora, Thunderjet, Ford GT, #1374, yellow w/black stripe, M **$25.00**

Aurora, Thunderjet, Lola GT, #1378, green w/white stripe, NM **$20.00**

Aurora, Thunderjet, Mustang 2+2 Fastback, #1373, yellow & black & red stripes, EX+ **$35.00**

Aurora, Thunderjet, Thunderbird (1967), #1379, EX...**$40.00**

Aurora, Ultra-5, Shadow Can-Am #3, white, red, orange & yellow, NM...**$10.00**

Aurora, Ultra-5, Matador Stocker #1, white, yellow & red, NM **$16.00**

Aurora, Vibrator, International Pickup Truck, #1580, dark gray & black, EX...**$150.00**

Eldon, Chevy Impala, 1/32 scale, NM.........................**$45.00**

Eldon, Pontiac Bonneville, white, 1/32 scale, NM **$50.00**

Ideal, Dukes of Hazzard Racing Set, MIB, $85.00. (Photo courtesy of June Moon.)

Ideal, Motorific Giant Detroit Race Track, w/Corvette, EX+ (EX+ box)...**$85.00**

Motorific, Grand Prix, NMIB **$35.00**

Remco, Mighty Mike Race Track, complete set, NMIB ...**$100.00**

Strombecker, Cheetah, 1/32 scale, EX......................**$35.00**

Strombecker, Ford GT, 1/32 scale, EX **$35.00**

Strombecker, Pontiac Bonneville, 1/32 scale, EX........**$40.00**

TCR, Jam Car, yellow & black, NM **$14.00**

TCR, Mercury Stock Car, purple w/chrome, NM.........**$18.00**

Tyco, A-Team Van, black w/red stripe, NM **$38.00**

Tyco, Bandit Pickup, black & yellow, NM **$12.00**

Tyco, Blazer, red & black, EX...................................**$10.00**

Tyco, Chevy (1957), red w/orange & yellow stripes, NM..**$18.00**

Tyco, Funny Mustang, orange w/yellow flame, NM...**$25.00**

Tyco, Jam Car, yellow & black, w/lights, NM **$10.00**

Tyco, Lamborghini, red, EX **$12.00**

Tyco, Mack Truck, dark blue & black, NM **$22.00**

Tyco, Porsche Carrera, #8527, yellow & black, NM....**$25.00**

Tyco, Turbo Firebird, black & gold, NM **$12.00**

Tyco, Van-Tastic, #8539, blue & white, EX................**$20.00**

Vehicles

These are the types of toys that are intensely dear to the heart of many a collector. Having a beautiful car is part of the American dream, and over the past eighty years, just about as many models, makes, and variations have been made as toys for children as the real vehicles for adults. Novices and advanced collectors alike are easily able to find something to suit their tastes as well as their budgets.

One area that is right now especially volatile covers those fifties and sixties tin scale-model autos by foreign manufacturers — Japan, U.S. Zone Germany, and English toy makers. Since these are relatively modern, you'll still be able to find some at yard sales and flea markets at reasonable prices.

There are several good references on these toys: *Collecting Toy Cars and Trucks* by Richard O'Brien; *Hot Wheels, A Collector's Guide* by Bob Parker; *Collector's Guide to Tootsietoys* by David Richter; *Collector's Guide to Tonka Trucks, 1947 — 1963,* by Don and Barb deSalle; *Collectible Coca-Cola Toy Trucks* by Gael de Courtivron; *Matchbox Toys, 1948 to 1996,* and *Collector's Guide to Diecast Toys and Scale Models* by Dana Johnson; and *Motorcycle Toys, Antique and Contemporary,* by Sally Gibson-Downs and Christine Gentry.

Newsletter: *The Ertl Replica*
Mike Meyer, Editor
Highways 136 and 20
Dyersville, IA 52040; 319-875-2000

Newsletter: *Matchbox USA*
Charles Mack
62 Saw Mill Rd.
Durham, CT 06422; 203-349-1655

AC Williams, Lincoln Sedan, cast iron, green w/metal spoked wheels, rear spare, 9", G.....................................**$255.00**

Arcade, bus, cast iron, silver & red, 7½", replaced white rubber tires, VG...**$120.00**

Arcade, Century of Progress Greyhound Bus, cast iron, 1933, 7½", EX...**$175.00**

Bandai, Cadillac Roadster (1933), friction, olive brown w/tan simulated soft top, whitewall tires, 8½", EXIB **$95.00**

Bandai, Cadillac Sedan (1960), friction, dark red w/CADDY license plate, whitewall tires, 11¼", NM (EX box) ...**$300.00**

Bandai, Chevrolet Impala 4-Door (1961), battery-op, travels in 5 patterns, white, 11", EX+ (EX box) **$475.00**

Bandai, Lincoln (1958), friction, red w/black top, 11½", VG **$150.00**

Bandai, Oldsmobile Toronado (1966), battery-op, red w/black tires, NM **$200.00**

Bandai, Rambler Classic Station Wagon (1961), friction, blue & white, 7½", NM (VG box).............................**$100.00**

Banner, Fuel Oil Tanker Truck, pressed steel, green w/yellow tires, 1950s, 7", EX **$25.00**

Banner, Jewel Tea Van, pressed steel, brown, G+....**$135.00**

Champion, Mack Dump Truck, cast iron, red C-style cab w/blue dump bed, nickel-plated tires, 7¾", G...**$175.00**

Champion, Motorcycle, cast iron, w/integral driver, blue w/white rubber tires, 7", EX **$180.00**

Corgi, Corvette Stingray, yellow w/black rubber tires, 1967, NM+ **$26.00**

Corgi, Inter-City Mini-Bus, orange w/whitewall tires, 1973, NM+ **$15.00**

Corgi, Lotus-Climax Racing Car, green w/black rubber tires, original driver, 1964, NM......................................**$20.00**

Corgi, Superman Police car, #260, Metropolis Buick, MIB, $60.00.

Courtland, Dump Truck, pressed steel, 5½", EX.......**$100.00**

Courtland, Stake Truck, pressed steel, yellow & white, VG **$125.00**

Dinky, Cadillac El Dorado, #175, NM **$100.00**

Dinky, Ford Cortina Mk II, #159, NM **$100.00**

Dinky, Ford Cotina, #133, NM..................................**$110.00**

Dinky, Merryweather Fire Engine, Falck, NM **$150.00**

Dinky, Merryweather Fire Engine, NM.......................**$80.00**

Dinky, Plymouth Fury, #115, NM..............................**$125.00**

Dinky, Police Range Rover, #254, NM........................**$50.00**

Dinky, Rolls Royce Phantom V, #124, NM..................**$90.00**

Dinky, Rolls Royce Phantom V, #152, NM..................**$65.00**

Dinky, Sam's Car, #108, silver, NM..........................**$120.00**

Dinky, Volvo 256 Estate Car, #122, NM **$50.00**

Dinky, 3-Ton Army Wagon, #621, NM......................**$100.00**

Girard, Delivery Truck, pressed steel, white w/black rubber tires, side-dump action, 11", EX **$155.00**

Girard, Dump Truck, white, black rubber tires, 1930s, 11", EX **$155.00**

Haiji, 1958, Edsel Convertible, friction, turquoise w/red and white interior, 11", VG...................................**$450.00**

Hot Wheels, American Hauler, blue, red-line tires, 1976, EX+ **$12.00**

Hot Wheels, Backwoods Bomb, green, red-line tires, 1975, G **$4.00**

Hot Wheels, Chaparral 2G, ice blue, red-line tires, 1969, NM **$22.00**

Hot Wheels, Chevy Convertible (1957), brown, black tires, 1990, MIP...**$5.00**

Hot Wheels, Classic Cobra, Real Rider, red, 1986, MIP....**$18.00**

Hot Wheels, Custom Firebird, blue w/blue interior, red-line tires, EX **$14.00**

Hot Wheels, Ford Delivery Truck (1934), yellow, black tires, 1986, MIP...**$10.00**

Hot Wheels, Funny Money, gray, red-line tires, complete, 1972, NM **$45.00**

Hot Wheels, Grand Prix Series Indy Eagle, red-line tires, in common colors MIP, from $30.00 to $40.00; in Gold Chrome MIP, from $150.00 to $200.00.

Hot Wheels, GT Racer, purple, black tires, 1989, MIP....**$5.00**

Hot Wheels, Heavy Weights, Moving Van, green, red-line tires, 1970, NM **$22.00**

Hot Wheels, Letter Getter, red, white & blue, black tires, 1979, NM..**$8.00**

Hot Wheels, Minitrek, white, black tires, 1983, MIP...**$10.00**

Hot Wheels, Mutt Mobile, metallic aqua w/black interior, red-line tires, complete, 1971, EX+ **$36.00**

Hot Wheels, Mutt Mobile, purple, red-line tires, 1970, G+ **$20.00**

Hot Wheels, Porsche 917, magenta, red-line tires, 1970, EX+ **$14.00**

Hot Wheels, Thunder Burner, white, black tires, 1987, MIP **$20.00**

Hot Wheels, Turismo #10, red, black tires, 1981, NM...**$10.00**

Hot Wheels Rumblers, Devil's Duce, yellow, w/original driver, 1972, EX+ **$50.00**

Hot Wheels Rumblers, Road Hog, orange or dark blue, 1971, NM **$20.00**

Hot Wheels Rumblers, 3-Squealer, metallic green, 1971, NM **$30.00**

Hot Wheels Sizzlers, Anteater, metallic pink, EX+ **$20.00**

Hot Wheels Sizzlers, Hot Head, metallic green, NMIB . **$22.00**

Hot Wheels Sizzlers, Live Wire, metallic gold, NMIB . **$25.00**

Hubley, Airflow Sedan, cast iron, pink w/nickel-plated grill & rear bumper, rear spare, rubber tires, 1930s, 4½", VG **$145.00**

Hubley, Coupe, cast iron, green w/white rubber tires, 1930, 6", EX **$160.00**

Ichiko, Cadillac (1967), friction, red w/black tires, 28", VG **$400.00**

Ichiko, Fire Chief Car, friction, advances w/warning light, red tin, 6", NM (EX box) **$75.00**

Kingsbury, Zypher Coupe & Boat Trailer, pressed steel, orange w/rubber wheels, 1936, 20½", no boat o/w EX **$345.00**

Marx, Earth Hauler w/Scoop, pressed steel, ca 1964, EX... **$100.00**

Marx, Garbage Truck, pressed steel, white w/red & black lettering, sliding rear door, litho tin wheels, 13", VG+ **$220.00**

Marx, Lumar Contractors Load & Dump Truck, pressed steel, red, yellow & white, 1950s, 15", NM (VG+ box) .. **$250.00**

Matchbox King Size, Hoveringham Tipper Truck #K-1B, 1960, MIB **$45.00**

Matchbox King Size, Leyland Tipper Truck #K-4C, w/LE Transport labels, 1970, G+ **$5.00**

Matchbox King Size, Merryweather Fire Engine #K-15A, w/decals, 1964, VG+ **$15.00**

Matchbox King Size, Pipe Truck #K-10B, 1967, MIB .. **$40.00**

Matchbox, Models of Yesteryear, 1911 Daimler #Y-13B, yellow with red seats, 4-spoke steering wheel, open spare recess, MIB, $50.00. (Photo courtesy of Dana Johnson.)

Matchbox Regular Wheels, Aveling Barford Road Roller #1-A, 1962, NM **$15.00**

Matchbox Regular Wheels, Aveling Barford Road Roller #1-D, 1962, EX+ **$10.00**

Matchbox Regular Wheels, Cat D8 Bulldozer #18-D, 1964, NM+ **$10.00**

Matchbox Regular Wheels, Dodge Crane Truck #63-C, red hook, black wheels, 1968, MIB **$15.00**

Matchbox Regular Wheels, Dodge Stake Truck #4-D, 1967, M **$10.00**

Matchbox Regular Wheels, Dodge Wrecker #13-D, 1965, NM+ **$13.00**

Matchbox Regular Wheels, Foden Concrete Truck #21-D, 1968, NM+ **$12.00**

Matchbox Regular Wheels, Ford Anglia #7-B, gold wheels, 1961, NM **$28.00**

Matchbox Regular Wheels, Ford Pickup #6-D, 1968, M..... **$16.00**

Matchbox Regular Wheels, Ford Pickup #6-D, 1968, MIB. **$26.00**

Matchbox Regular Wheels, Ford Zodiac Convertible #39-A, turquoise interior, metal wheels, complete, 1957, M (EX box) **$40.00**

Matchbox Regular Wheels, Mercedes Ambulance #3-C, 1968, NM+ **$6.00**

Matchbox Regular Wheels, Mercedes Trailer #2-D, orange canopy, 1968, MIB **$8.00**

Matchbox Regular Wheels, Prime Mover #15-A, 1956, MIB **$21.00**

Matchbox Superfast, Baja Dune Buggy #13-F, green, 1971, MIB **$6.00**

Matchbox Superfast, Ford Mustang #8-F, orange w/ivory interior, 1970, EX+ **$30.00**

Matchbox Superfast, Kenworth Cab-Over Semi #45-E, white, 1982, M **$2.00**

Matchbox Superfast, Land Rover Safari #12-D, gold w/tan luggage, 1970, NM+ **$20.00**

Matchbox Superfast, Mercedes Truck #1-F, olive w/tan canopy, blue windows, 5-spoke wheels, 1970, NM. **$3.00**

Matchbox Superfast, Mercedes Truck #1-F, 1970, NM... **$4.00**

Matchbox Superfast, Pony Trailer #43-D, yellow w/light or dark green base, w/original horses, 1970, M **$14.00**

Matchbox Superfast, Snorkel Fire Engine #63-H, red w/painted base insert, 1982, M **$5.00**

Matchbox Superfast, US Mail Jeep #38-F, blue w/white roof & base, silver hubs, 1976, M **$15.00**

Matchbox Superfast, Zoo Truck #35-E, red w/black base, gray cage, tan lions, 5-arch wheels, complete, 1982, NM **$12.00**

Minic, Ford Saloon, blue, 3½", NM (EX+ box) **$150.00**

Minic, Royal Mail Van, red tin w/decals, 3½", EX **$110.00**

Minic, Transport Van, blue w/decals, 3½", NM from $80 to **$125.00**

MSK, Buick, friction, working windshield wipers & searchlight, 7", NM (EX box) **$150.00**

Nylint, Aerial Ladder Fire Truck, pressed steel, 1970s, VG+ **$40.00**

Nylint, Dinty Moore 4x4 Explorer, pressed steel, 1992, M (NM box) **$20.00**

Nylint, NAPA 18-Wheeler, pressed steel, 1983, MIB ... **$50.00**

Structo, Cadillac (1957), pressed steel, 7", EX+ **$25.00**

Structo, End Loader, pressed steel, orange, 1950s, 15½", VG **$110.00**

Structo, Scout Wrecker, pressed steel, red & white, NMIB **$160.00**

Structo, Structo 66 Tanker Truck, pressed steel, red, VG .. **$150.00**

Tonka, Army Jeep, 1964, EX **$140.00**

Tonka, Dump Truck, red cab w/yellow dump bed, 13½", EX **$150.00**

Tonka, Farm Stake Truck, #4, green w/white stake sides, VG+ **$125.00**

Tonka, Marine Boat Service Truck, 1961, G **$130.00**

Tonka, Pickup Truck, blue, 1958, VG+ **$115.00**

Tonka, Pickup Truck, Hi-Way Dually, 1959, VG+.....**$140.00**
Tonka, Road Grader, orange, 1959, G.........................**$60.00**

Tonka Stables truck with horse carrier and two horses, 1960s, EX, $75.00. (Photo courtesy of June Moon.)

Tonka, Tanker Truck, Starkist Orange, plastic, 1981, 10", EX...**$30.00**
Tonka Jeepster, late version, 13", VG+.........................**$30.00**
Wyandotte, Cattle Truck, pressed steel, red, yellow & blue, 23", VG+ **$100.00**
Wyandotte, Tanker Truck, pressed steel, red w/black rubber wheels, w/rear door, 1935, 10½", VG+...............**$115.00**
Wyandotte, Tow Truck, pressed steel, red & blue, 1940s, VG **$65.00**

Y, 1962 Ford Sunliner, red with lithographed interior, friction powered, 1962, 10", NM in EX box, $355.00.

Yonezawa, Buick Sedan (1959), friction, tan over brown w/chrome fins, whitewall tires, 8", EXIB **$250.00**
Yonezawa, Cadillac Police Car (1960), battery-op, 18", G .**$115.00**

Wind-Ups

Wind-up toys, especially comic character or personality-related, are greatly in demand by collectors today. Though most were made through the years of the thirties through the fifties, they carry their own weight against much earlier toys and are considered very worthwhile investments. Mechanisms vary, some are key wound while others depended on lever action to tighten the mainspring and release the action of the toy. Tin and celluloid were used in their manufacture, and although it is sometimes possible to repair a tin wind-up, experts advise against putting your money into a celluloid toy whose mechanism is not working, since the material may be too fragile to tolerate the repair.

Alps, Bar-X Cowboy, twirls lariat on horse, 6", EXIB ..**$225.00**
Alps, Carnival Man, clown holding cane, tin w/cloth costume, 9", MIB...**$210.00**

Alps, Drinking Sam, tin w/cloth clothing, 8", NMIB.**$150.00**
Alps, Gay Cabellero, Mexican in sombrero on vibrating donkey w/spinning tail, celluloid, 6", NM (EX box).**$200.00**
Alps, Happy Life, girl rocks in beach chair as umbrella spins & goose rotates, tin & celluloid, 9", NM (EX+ box) **$350.00**
Alps, Honey Bear, plush bear licks beehive while bee flies overhead, 7", EXIB **$250.00**
Alps, Ice Cream Monkey, vibrates & licks ice-cream cone, plush over tin, 6", NM (EX box).........................**$125.00**
Alps, Little Shoemaker, hammers nail in shoe, tin w/cloth shirt & original hat, 6", EX+ (EX+ box) **$175.00**
Automatic Toy, Hoppo the Mechanical Rabbit, advances w/cart, tin & plastic, 9", NM (EX+ box), from $50 to.............**$85.00**
Automatic Toy, Spiral Speedway, 2 buses travel on track that loops on overpass, 1950s, MIB.........................**$200.00**
Baldwin, Little Red Hen, lays wooden eggs & cackles, tin, crank action, 5", EX (G box) **$175.00**
Billiken, Batman, advances w/swinging arms, litho tin w/vinyl cape, 1989, 9", MIB...**$145.00**

Brimtoy, Santa Claus, 1940s, 4", EX in worn box, from $350.00 to $375.00. (Photo courtesy of Dunbar Gallery.)

Cragstan, Rock 'N Roll Monkey, tin w/vinyl face, NM..**$225.00**
Cragstan, Rock 'N Roll Pluto, advances w/gyro-power swaying motion, plastic, 1969, 5", EXIB.....................**$100.00**
Emporium Specialties, Monkey Shines, goes up & down palm tree, tin w/paper leaves, 1950, 18", MIB.............**$300.00**
Gosco, Traffic Policeman, trolley car & automobile travel in & out of garages, tin, 9½", EX...........................**$400.00**
Haji, Clever Monkey, monkey holds sign, peddles drum & turns, tin, 7", EXIB..**$175.00**
Ideal, Mystery Gas Station, cars travel around station, tin & plastic, complete, 1950s, 18", EX.........................**$275.00**
Irwin Toys, Cinderella, connected figures of Cinderella & the Prince dancing, 1950s, MIB................................**$225.00**
Joustra, Circus Boy, clown boy turns head as he rings bell & waves, tin, 6", EX+ **$350.00**
K, Donald Duck Waddler, advances side to side, celluloid, 3", EXIB...**$650.00**
K, Monkey & Seal, monkey rides unicycle & pulls seal, many actions, tin w/cloth costume, 7", EXIB **$175.00**
KO, Bobby's Crazy Car, clown in bumper car, litho tin & vinyl, early 1950s, 8", NM (EX box)...................**$350.00**

Kraemer, Sparking Choo Choo, friction, tin, complete w/tracks, 1950s, 17", M (VG box) **$160.00**

KT, Soldier on Motorcycle, camouflage motorcycle, 5½", G **$175.00**

Lindstrom, Climbing Monkey, monkey goes up & down rope, G (G box)..**$55.00**

Lindstrom, Dancing Dutch Boy, boy w/concertina vibrates around, tin, 1930s, 8", NM (EX box)....................**$300.00**

Lindstrom, Dancing Indian, Indian w/ax & knife vibrates around, tin, 5½", EX..**$100.00**

Lindstrom, Dancing Lassie, girl in plaid vibrates around, tin, 8", EX+...**$155.00**

Lindstrom, Sweeping Mammy, vibrates around while sweeping, 1930s, 8", NM (EX+ box).....................**$400.00**

Linemar, Donald Duck Dipsy Doodle, Donald on tractor-type vehicle, metal body, 1950s, 6", EX......................**$675.00**

Linemar, Donald Duck Drummer, advances & rocks while beating drum, tin, 6", NM **$675.00**

Linemar, Ferdinand the Bull, advances with twirling tail & head movement, tin, 1950s, 5½", scarce, EX (VG box)..**$500.00**

Linemar, Honeymoon Cottage, train circles under 3 tunnels, gate rises & lowers, 7x7", NM..............................**$200.00**

Linemar, Howdy Doody's Pal Clarabell, cable control, 1950s, 7", NM (EX box) **$650.00**

Linemar, Huckleberry Hound Aeroplane, friction, tin w/vinyl figure, 1961, 10", NMIB................................**$675.00**

Linemar, Huckleberry Hound Go-Mobile, friction, tin w/rubber tires, 6½", NM (EX box)................................**$500.00**

Linemar, Jocko the Climbing Monkey, jockey climbs up & down string, tin, 6½", NM (EX box)..................**$125.00**

Linemar, Mickey Mouse Motorcyclist, friction, tin, 3½", EX **$350.00**

Linemar, Olive Oyl Ballet Dancer, friction, put blade in slot & pull base, tin, 6", NMIB.............................**$450.00**

Linemar, Pluto (Walking), advances in realistic motion, tin & plush, 5", VG+...**$246.00**

Linemar, Pluto on Motorcycle, friction, tin, 3½", EX+..**$450.00**

Linemar, Popeye in Roadster, friction, 8", EX............**$650.00**

Linemar, Superman Rollover Tank, advances as Superman forces tank to flip over, tin, 4", VG.....................**$450.00**

Martin, Rabbit in Cage, rabbit in exercise wheel attached to rabbit house, hand-painted tin, 8", G................**$150.00**

Marx, Army Staff Car, early 1950s, EX, $85.00. (Photo courtesy of June Moon.)

Marx, Honeymoon Express, train circles track, 1950s, 9" dia, NMIB..**$225.00**

Marx, Hop-a-Long Cassidy, rider w/lariat on rocking base, arms move suggesting bucking horse, 10", VG..**$400.00**

Marx, Huckleberry Hound Car, friction, litho tin w/vinyl figure, 1962, 4", NM (EX box) **$300.00**

Marx, Milton Berle Car, head spins as car travels in crazy motion, tin w/plastic hat, 1950s, 6", EXIB **$450.00**

Marx, Tricky Taxi, travels to end of table & turns around, tin, 1940, 5", NM+ (EX+ box)................................**$325.00**

Marx, Tumbling Monkey, circus monkey flips between 2 chairs, tin, 1942, 6", NM (EX box)......................**$300.00**

Mattel, Action Clown Mobile, #463, friction, plastic, 1952, 6x7", NMIB **$85.00**

Mattel, Dancing Dude & Music Box, cowboy does jig on stage, hand crank, NMIB.................................**$130.00**

Mikuni, Dog Chasing Puppy, mother hops along w/flapping ears trying to get puppy, tin, 8", EXIB...............**$175.00**

MM, Easter on Parade, rabbit pulls sled w/3 chicks in basket, celluloid & pressed steel, 8", NMIB....................**$225.00**

MT, 101 Dalmatians Bus, friction, tin, 16", NM (EX box) **$575.00**

Nosco, Doodle-Bug, plastic w/full-figure driver, 1950, 10", MIB **$230.00**

Nylint, Elgin Street Sweeper, yellow tin w/plastic driver, turning brushes, rubber wheels, 8½", EX, from $160 to...**$175.00**

Ohio Art, Alpine Cable Car, 2 cable cars travel up & down 3-level slope, tin, NM **$125.00**

Ohio Art, Giant Ferris Wheel, spins w/bell noise, tin, 1950s, 17", NM+ (EX+ box) **$600.00**

Ohio Art, Musical Merry-Go-Round, airplanes & horses spin, tin, 9", NM (EX+ box)..**$525.00**

Ohio Art, Toe Joe, MIB, from $150.00 to $175.00. (Photo courtesy of June Moon.)

P&F, Perpetual Motion Acrobat, composition clown w/interconnecting metal rods, 16", VG (original box).....**$220.00**

Plaything, Hula-Hoop Monkey, monkey stands on barrel & hula-hoops, tin, 1950s, 10", NM (EX box) **$100.00**

Renewal, Fire Truck, friction, white plastic w/black rubber tires, complete w/ladder, hose & fireman, 1950s, 11", NM..**$250.00**

Rico, Rodeo Joe, jeep travels in circular motion as vaquero jumps up & down, 4½", EX..............................**$400.00**

Schuco, Donald Duck, vibrates around while opening & closing his bill, tin & plastic, 1960, 6", M (EX+ box) ..**$700.00**

Schuco, Drinking Mouse, raises ceramic beer mug, tin w/cloth clothing, 4", EX **$200.00**

Schuco, Girl w/Baby, tin w/cloth clothing & hat, NM, from $145 to..**$185.00**

Schuco, Scottie Dog, advances w/moving legs, tin & plush, 4½", NM, from $160 to.................................**$185.00**

Schuco, Solisto Clown Drummer, vibrates while beating snare drum, tin w/cloth clothing, 4½", NM (EX box) **$500.00**

Schuco, Solisto Monkey Violinist, vibrates while playing, tin w/cloth clothing, 4½", EX+.........................**$275.00**

Schuco, Traveler, clown w/suitcase, 1940s, EX........**$350.00**

Technofix, Cable Car, #303, car travels from station house up mountain as 2 others travel road, 18", NMIB, from $250 to...**$300.00**

Technofix, Touchdown Chimp, holds ball & moves legs rapidly, tin w/celluloid ball, 3", EX....................**$250.00**

TM, Turntable Railway, train engine pushes coach then returns to pick it up, tin, 12", EX (worn box)......**$65.00**

TN, Bobo the Magician, lifts hat as egg & chick appear, tin, 9", NM...**$400.00**

TN, Grasshopper, advances & turns w/moving legs, tin w/plastic wings, 6", MIB **$125.00**

TN, Ironing Monkey, moves iron across cloth on ironing boars, tin & plush, 6½", NM (EX box)................**$100.00**

TN, Percy Penguin, advances on skis w/flapping arms, friction, tin, 5", NM (EX box).....................................**$200.00**

TN, Santa Claus, rings bell & waves Merry Christmas sign, tin, 6", NM (EX+ box) **$250.00**

TPS, Animal's Playland, treehouse w/rotating animals, others on seesaw & swing, tin, NMIB............................**$325.00**

TPS, Bear Golfer, hits ball across ramp into net, tin, 4½", NM (EX box)...**$250.00**

TPS, Circus Clown, advances in erratic motion on unicycle, 6", NM (EX box) **$450.00**

TPS, Clown w/Lion, lion jumps through red felt hoop, tin, 6", NM (EX+ box)..**$350.00**

TPS, Fishing Bear, fish bounces in & out of bear's net, tin, 7", NM (EX box)...**$300.00**

TPS, Jolly Snake, wiggles as head turns side to side, tin, 7½", NM (EX box)...**$125.00**

TPS, Magic Circus, monkey & seal dance & shake w/magnetic action on platform, tin & plastic, 6", NMIB **$200.00**

TPS, Magic Tunnel & Dream Land Bus, bus travels around carnival base, tin, NM (EX box) **$175.00**

Unique Art, Artie Car, smiling clown in dunce-type hat rides crazy car w/dog on hood, 7", VG, from $200 to ..**$250.00**

Unique Art, Baggage Cart w/Operator, operator on front platform guides 4-wheeled flat cart w/baggage, 14", VG+ **$175.00**

Unique Art, Gertie the Galloping Goose, pecks & bounces, tin, 1930s, 9½", EX (G box)................................**$175.00**

Unique Art, GI Joe & His Jouncing Jeep, forward & reverse action, tin, 1941, 8", MIB..................................**$300.00**

Unique Art, Rodeo Joe, jeep travels w/crazy action as figures bounce in seat, tin, 1930s, 7", VG **$225.00**

Wyandotte, Red Ranger Ride 'Em Cowboy, cowboy on horse mounted on rocking platform, tin, 1930s, 7", EX..**$175.00**

Y, Boxing Dog, staggers side to side while boxing, tin & plush, 6", MIB **$85.00**

YH, Texas Ranger Horse Carrier, advances as horses bob their heads up & down, friction, tin, 9", EXIB ...**$150.00**

Wolverine, No. 31 Merry-Go-Round, 1950s, MIB, $500.00. (Photo courtesy of June Moon.)

Transistor Radios

Introduced during the Christmas shopping season of 1954, transistor radios were at the cutting edge of futuristic design and miniaturization. Among the most desirable is the 1954 four-transistor Regency TR-1 which is valued at a minimum of $750.00 in jade green. Black may go for as much as $300.00, other colors from $350.00 to $400.00. The TR-1 'Mike Todd' version in the 'Around the World in Eighty Days' leather book-look presentation case goes for $4,000.00 and up! Some of the early Toshiba models sell for $250.00 to $350.00, some of the Sonys even higher — their TR-33 books at a minimum of $1,000.00, their TR-55 at $1,500.00 and up! Certain pre-1960 models by Hoffman and Admiral represented the earliest practical use of solar technology and are also highly valued. Early collectible transistor radios all have civil defense triangle markings at 640 and 1240 on the frequency dial and nine or fewer transistors. Very few desirable sets were made after 1963.

Values in our listings are for radios in at least very good condition — not necessarily working, but complete and requiring very little effort to restore them to working order. Cases may show minor wear. All radios are battery-operated unless noted otherwise. For more information we recommend *Collector's Guide to Transistor Radios* by Marty and Sue Bunis (Collector Books.)

Advisors: Marty and Sue Bunis (See Directory, Radios)

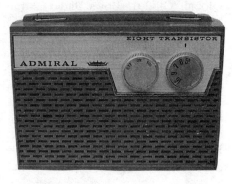

Admiral, YD242, 8-transistor, red plastic, fold-down handle, made in Japan, 1965, 2⅜x7¼", $10.00. (Photo courtesy of Marty and Sue Bunis.)

Acme, CH620, Tops All, 1961, horizontal, 6-transistor, AM..**$35.00**

Admiral, #221, 1958, black, 6-transistor, stylized 'A' logo, antenna in handle, AM **$45.00**

Admiral, #703 or #708, Super 7, 1960, 7-transistor, crown logo, AM **$30.00**

Admiral, YK327, Bolero, 12-transistor, AFC/FA/AM switch, antenna **$15.00**

Admiral, Y2303GPN, Starfire, 1963, 6-transistor, AM...**$30.00**

Admiral, Y821 & Y822, Holiday, 1960, clock radio, 8-transistor, crown logo, AM, each **$15.00**

Admiral, 7L12, 1956, 1st solar-powered radio, horizontal red case, 6-transistor, AM, complete w/Sun Power Pak..........**$350.00**

Air Chief, #4-C-69, 1963, 14-transistor, 3-band slide rule dial, 2 antennas, AM/FM.................................**$25.00**

Airline, GEN-1257A, 1965, 8-transistor, leather case & handle, AM **$10.00**

Aiwa, AR-751, 1965, 7-transistor, see-through dial w/horizontal bars, AM **$25.00**

Arvin, #62R19, 1962, 6-transistor, black plastic case w/textured grill area, crown logo, AM **$15.00**

Automatic, PTR-15B, 1958, leather case, lg grill w/rectangular cutouts, AM **$25.00**

Cameo, #64N06-03, 1964, 6-transistor, upper right round window dial, lg perforated grill, AM **$15.00**

Channel Master, #6506, Cordless, 1962, 5-transistor, caramel & white plastic, checkered grill, AM **$30.00**

Continental, TFM-1090, 1964, 10-transistor, right front 2-band dial, lg grill, AM/FM **$15.00**

Crosley, JM-8BK, Enchantment, 1956, book-shaped novelty, leather cover, 2-transistor, AM **$150.00**

Daltone, Royal #400, 2-transistor, see-through panel, rounded top right corner, made in Japan, AM **$60.00**

Deluxe, TRS-6, 1959, 6-transistor, right front window dial, lg grill w/vertical slots, AM..............................**$30.00**

Elgin, TR-4, vertical plastic case, see-through panel w/right round dial, metal grill, made in Japan, AM **$80.00**

Emerson, #31P56, 8-transistor, lg left metal perforated grill area w/G clef logo, AM.............................**$20.00**

Emerson, #843, Transistor III, leather case, swing handle, lg metal grill w/G clef logo, AM **$60.00**

Falcon, #6THK, 1964, 6-transistor, diamond-shaped dial, metal grill, made in Hong Kong, AM.................**$20.00**

General Electric, P765B, 1957, 6-transistor, metal & leatherette, pull-up handle, rechargeable, AM......**$40.00**

General Electric, P796B, 1958, light blue leather, plastic lattice grill, AM **$20.00**

General Electric, P809C, 1961, 5-transistor, green plastic, woven grill, pull-up handle, AM.................**$20.00**

Global, GR-201, Boy's Radio, 2-transistor, right front see-through panel, left grill w/horizontal bars, Japan made, AM...**$85.00**

GMK, TN201, 2-transistor, blue & white plastic, rounded upper right corner w/dial, made in Japan, AM **$60.00**

Grundig, #302, Ocean-Boy, 1965, 17-transistor, 9 push buttons, long/short wave, FM **$50.00**

Halex, Transworld Ambassador, 4-band dial, push buttons on top, 2 antennas, long/short wave, FM **$35.00**

Hitachi, WH-999, Hiphonic, 1965, 9-transistor, 3-band slide rule dial, short wave, AM........................**$35.00**

Jade, J-162, 6-transistor, upper right round window dial, lower grill w/horizontal bars, AM.......................**$10.00**

Jefferson-Travis, JT-204, Long Distance, 1961, 7-transistor, upper front see-through panel, AM.................**$135.00**

Juliette, TR-91M, 1968, 9-transistor, front grill w/horizontal bars & center logo, chain on left side, AM..........**$45.00**

Lamie, TR-1660, 1964, 6-transistor, upper right front window dial, lower horizontal grill bars, AM.....................**$10.00**

Linmark, T-61, 1959, 6-transistor, left front rectangular window dial, round grill, AM.........................**$45.00**

Lloyd's, TR-6Ka, 1964, 6-transistor, round window dial over grill w/vertical slots, AM.................................**$15.00**

Magnavox, #2AM-70, 1964, 7-transistor, off-center window dial over perforated grill w/logo lower left, AM..**$20.00**

Magnavox, AM-82, Envoy, 1964, 8-transistor, 2 right knobs, perforated grill w/logo on left, AM **$15.00**

Matsushita, DT-495, 1962, 6-transistor, upper right thumb-wheel dial knob, left grill w/horizontal bars, AM ..**$25.00**

Melodic, GT-586, 1961, 6-transistor, upper left front dial knob over perforated grill, AM...........................**$30.00**

Mitsubishi, #6X-720, recessed window dial w/thumb-wheel tuning over lg vertical metal textured & perforated grill, AM **$55.00**

MMA, #602, 1963, 6-transistor, thumb-wheel dial over perforated grill, AM **$20.00**

Motorola, #6X28P, 1959, 6-transistor, pink plastic case, jet plane design molded into front panel, AM..........**$95.00**

Motorola, #8X26E, Power 10, 8-transistor, charcoal plastic case, horizontal grill bars w/logo, AM **$45.00**

Motorola, X26W, 1961, 7-transistor, white plastic case w/lg checkered grill area, rear fold-out metal stand, AM..**$25.00**

Motorola, X37S, 1962, 6-transistor, tan leather, window dial over perforated grill, AM **$25.00**

National AB-210, 9-transistor, 2-band slide rule dial, lg metal grill w/logo lower left, band switch, short wave, AM **$35.00**

Norwood, MN-1000, 1965, 10-transistor, 2-band slide rule dial over perforated grill, telescoping antenna, AM/FM..**$15.00**

Orion, JT-602, Signal-Radio, upper left dial knob, plastic case w/metal perforated grill, AM.................................**$25.00**

Panasonic, #12RT1, 1964, 12-transistor, horizontal 2-band slide rule dial w/3 knobs, lower grill, AM/FM **$15.00**

Panasonic, T-22M, 1962, 8-transistor, blue plastic case, w/2-band slide rule dial, band switch & battery meter in grill...**$35.00**

Petite, NTR-150, 1961, 6-transistor, window dial w/thumb-wheel tuning, Oriental design grill, AM................**$50.00**

Philco, NT-1004, 1965, 10-transistor, leather case w/3 right knobs, checkered grill w/lower left logo, AM/FM ..**$15.00**

Philco, T-902-124, 9-transistor, leather case w/3 knobs, upper metal perforated grill, AM **$15.00**

Philips, L1D90T, Fanette 190, 1959, 7-transistor, diagonally divided front w/lower perforated grill, W Germany, AM..**$45.00**

Raytheon, #8TP-2, 1955, 8-transistor, brown leather w/front & rear metal perforated grills, AM........................**$175.00**

RCA, #1-BT-32, Transicharg Deluxe, 1958, 7-transistor, for use w/battery charger unit, white & pink plastic, w/charger........**$100.00**

RCA, #1-T-5J, New Globe Trotter, 1959, 8-transistor, charcoal w/horizontal slide rule dial, horizontal grill bars, AM...**$25.00**

RCA, #4RG12, 1963, plastic case w/upper front dial knob over lattice grill, AM **$20.00**

RCA, RLG, blue plastic w/upper right window dial over lower grill w/horizontal bars, made in Hong Kong, AM..**$10.00**

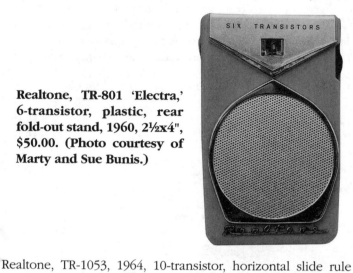

Realtone, TR-801 'Electra,' 6-transistor, plastic, rear fold-out stand, 1960, 2½x4", $50.00. (Photo courtesy of Marty and Sue Bunis.)

Realtone, TR-1053, 1964, 10-transistor, horizontal slide rule dial over vertical grill bars, AM.............................**$15.00**

Regency, TR-4, 1957, 4-transistor, ebony or ivory plastic case w/lg round dial perforated grill, AM, each.........**$150.00**

Rhapsody, FA-101, 1964, 10-transistor, 2 slide rule dials (1 AM, 1 FM), lg perforated grill **$20.00**

Ross, RE-101, Dynamic, 1964, 10-transistor, round dial knob over lattice grill, AM **$20.00**

Seimens, RT-10, 1960, 8-transistor, soft plastic, 3-band slide rule dial, rectangular cutouts in grill, W Germany.**$25.00**

Seminole, #1011, 1964, 10-transistor, recessed/perforated oval panel w/cat's eye dial, AM...................................**$35.00**

Sharp, FX-495, 1963, 10-transistor, 2-band slide rule dial over perforated grill w/center logo, AM/FM **$25.00**

Silvertone, #1023, 1961, 6-transistor, mint green plastic case w/thumb-wheel dial, metal perforated grill, AM..**$30.00**

Silvertone, #226, 1962, 10-transistor, 2-band slide rule dial, 2 knobs, lg perforated grill, AM/FM **$20.00**

Silvertone, #9204, 1959, 6-transistor, gray plastic case, thumb-wheel dial on side, metal perforated grill, AM.....**$50.00**

Sony, #3F-66W, round 2-band dial over perforated metal grill, telescoping antenna, made in Japan, AM/FM.......**$25.00**

Sony, TR-63, 1957, 6-transistor, made in red, black, green, or yellow plastic, Sony's 1st import to USA, AM **$500.00**

Soundesign, #1276, Mini, 2 knobs on top, front grill w/horizontal bars, strap on side, AM **$15.00**

Standard, SR-J715F, 1964, 10-transistor, horizontal FM slide rule dial, thumb-wheel knob on right..................**$25.00**

Sylvania, #5P10, 5-transistor, left window dial over horizontal grill bars w/right logo, AM....................................**$50.00**

Symphonic, S-62, 1963, 6-transistor, round window dial over lg perforated grill, AM **$15.00**

Tonecrest, #1889, 1965, 8-transistor, right window dial w/thumb-wheel tuning, vertical bars over grill, AM **$10.00**

Toshiba, #TP-345, 1960, 6-transistor, right thumb-wheel dial, plastic w/metal perforated grill, AM......................**$90.00**

Toshiba, #6TC-485, 1963, 6-transistor, vertical/folding clock radio, AM...**$75.00**

Trancel, #6TP-348, see-through panel w/horizontal slide rule dial, metal perforated grill, fold-out stand, AM ..**$125.00**

Trav-ler, TR-286-B, Power Mite, 1958, 6-transistor, red & ivory plastic w/metal perforated grill, swing handle, AM.........**$100.00**

Truetone, DC3090, 1960, 3-transistor, window dial w/thumb-wheel tuning, round perforated grill, swing handle, AM **$75.00**

Truetone, DC3612, 1965, 12-transistor, round dial knob, perforated grill, AM...**$15.00**

Valiant, AM1400, Hi Power, round dial knob, vertical bars over grill, AM **$30.00**

Viscount, #601, 1965, 6-transistor, window dial w/thumb-wheel tuning, horizontal grill bars, AM.................**$10.00**

Vista, G-1050, 1964, 10-transistor, 2-band thumb-wheel dial, horizontal grill slots, telescoping antenna, AM/FM........**$20.00**

Westinghouse, H-588P7, 1957, 7-transistor, round dial knob, checkered grill area, AM **$85.00**

Westinghouse, H-699P7, 1959, 7-transistor, green & white plastic case w/lower round dial knob, checkered grill above, AM **$35.00**

Windsor, #15066, Boy's Radio, 2-transistor, plastic w/metal textured & perforated logo, made in Japan, AM..**$65.00**

Zenith, Royal 100 Zenette, 1961, 6-transistor, round dial knob overlaps lg crisscross grill w/logo, fold-out stand, AM..**$40.00**

Zenith, Royal 1000-D Trans-Oceanic, 1958, leatherette, metal & plastic, fold-down front w/world map, 9-band.....**$100.00**

Zenith, Royal 13, window dial over vertical grill bars, made in Hong Kong, AM **$20.00**

Trolls

The legend of the troll originated in Scandinavia. Ancient folklore has it that they were giant, supernatural beings, but in more modern times, they're portrayed as dwarfs or imps who live in underground caverns. During the seventies there was a TV cartoon special called *The Hobbit* and a movie, *The Lord of the Rings*, based on J.R.R. Tolkien's books, that caused them to become popular. As a result, books, puzzles, posters, and dolls of all types were available on the retail market. In the early eighties, Broom Hilda and Irwin Troll were featured in a series of books as well as Saturday morning cartoons, and in the early ninties, trolls enjoyed a strong comeback.

The three main manufacturers of the 'vintage' trolls are Dam Things (Royalty Des. of Florida), Uneeda (Wishniks), and A/S Nyform of Norway. Some were made in Hong Kong and Japan as well, but generally these were molded of inferior plastic.

The larger trolls (approximately 12") are rare and very desirable to collectors, and the troll animals, such as the giraffe, horse, cow, donkey, and lion made by Dam, are bringing premium prices.

For more information, refer to *Collector's Guide to Trolls* by Pat Peterson.

Advisor: Roger Inouye (See Directory, Trolls)

Ark animals, Troll Family, Europe, MOC, each...........**$12.00**

Bamboozle bear, white mohair, yellow felt bow around neck, rare..**$28.00**

Batman, no hood, normal-size eyes, Wishnik, 5" **$15.00**

Caveman, green eyes, yellow hair, leopard-skin outfit, Dam, 12"...**$150.00**

Cow, limited edition, short brown hair, dark amber eyes, green felt tie, Dam, 7" **$75.00**

Cowboy, long yellow hair, red hat, Wishnik, 3½" **$15.00**

Doll face, petal-shaped red & white costume, Wishnik, 7" **$20.00**

Donkey, dark brown mohair, Dam, lg.....................**$145.00**

Girl w/accordion, plastic amber eyes, brown & gray hair, molded clothes, 6" **$50.00**

Good-night, pink hair, black eye, yellow nightshirt, Wishnik, 5"...**$20.00**

Here Comes the Judge, gold eyes, light orange hair, black gown w/white letters, Wishnik, 6" **$50.00**

Hobbit, yellow mohair, nude, gloved hands, 2½" **$8.00**

Indian girl, long black hair, red headband w/yellow feather, belt, Dam..**$50.00**

Mouse, bank, Norfin, MIP **$60.00**

Pixie face, nude, yellow molded hair, painted eyes, Wishnik, 7" **$20.00**

Playboy bunny, light blue eyes, yellow hair, black ears & outfit, Dam, 5½"...**$55.00**

Rock-nik, amber eyes, black hair, 1-pc red & blue costume w/sequins, guitar glued to costume, Wishnik, 6"..**$15.00**

Santa, bank, 7", M...**$68.00**

Sea Captain, pencil holder, blue w/gold-trimmed uniform, gray string beard, wooden, 4"................................**$2.00**

Seal, bank, w/key, M..**$48.00**

She-nik, white mohair to the floor, yellow eyes, S on front of dress, 5" **$14.00**

Smart-Nik, graduation gown & hat, amber inset eyes, Wishnik, 6" **$20.00**

Sock-it-to-Me, Laugh-In jokes all over, white hair, 6" ..**$50.00**

Thumbsucker, long white mohair, purple felt dress, Norfin, 18" **$85.00**

Turtle, green shell, chin in hands, feet in air, resting on elbows & body, bank slot, Dam, 4" **$50.00**

Viking, Dam, white mohair, brown eyes, blue felt dress, silver belt and helmet, NM, from $150.00 to $200.00. (Photo courtesy of Roger Inouye.)

Viking, wooden body, black rabbit fur, holds spiked mace, tin shield painted gold, 2½"......................................**$5.00**

Whale, blue eyes, grayish-white chest, coin slot in head, Dam, 5"...**$50.00**

TV Guides

This publication goes back to the early 1950s, and granted, those early issues are very rare. But what an interesting, very visual way to chronicle the history of TV programming!

Values in our listings are for examples in fine to mint condition. For insight into *TV Guide* collecting, we recommend *The TV Guide Catalog* by Jeff Kadet, the *TV Guide* Specialist.

Advisor: Jeff Kadet (See Directory, TV Guides)

1953, July 3, Perry Como **$35.00**
1953, May 1, Eve Arden **$45.00**

1953, May 15, David and Ricky Nelson, $90.00.

1954, Jan 1, Bing Crosby..**$50.00**
1954, June 25, Howdy Doody & Buffalo Bob..........**$150.00**
1954, June 4, Arthur Godfrey.......................................**$20.00**
1955, February 12, Cast of Hit Parade **$30.00**
1955, January 1, Loretta Young **$20.00**
1955, July 2, Lassie & Rin-Tin-Tin **$70.00**
1955, October 1, Mickey Mouse & His Club **$95.00**
1956, April 14, Grace Kelly Coronation Issue.............**$20.00**
1956, June 30, Robert Cummings of Love That Bob!..**$32.00**
1956, October 6, Gale Storm **$42.00**
1957, April 27, Groucho Marx **$12.00**
1957, August 31, Clint Walker as Cheyenne **$35.00**
1957, February 9, Hugh O'Brian as Wyatt Earp **$18.00**
1958, August 2, Walter Brennan of The Real McCoys...**$12.00**
1958, January 18, John Payne of The Restless Gun....**$40.00**
1958, March 15, James Arness & Amanda Blake........**$20.00**
1958, May 17, Danny Thomas & TV family.................**$15.00**
1958, November 22, Ronald & Nancy Reagan............**$22.00**
1959, April 11, Ward Bond of Wagon Train................**$15.00**
1959, August 22, Cast of I've Got a Secret **$10.00**
1959, February 21, Cast of Perry Mason **$25.00**
1959, July 11, Cast of Peter Gun **$15.00**
1959, May 30, Steve McQueen.....................................**$75.00**
1959, October 24, Jay North as Dennis the Menace ...**$62.00**
1960, August 13, Nick Adams as The Rebel **$25.00**
1960, December 24, Merry Christmas...........................**$18.00**
1960, February 20, Red Skelton **$15.00**
1960, June 11, Cast of Bachelor Father **$8.00**

1960, March 12, Chuck Conners as The Rifleman.......**$60.00**
1961, January 28, Ron Howard & Andy Griffith..........**$65.00**
1961, July 1, The Flintstones.......................................**$50.00**
1961, June 3, Cast of Naked City...............................**$15.00**
1961, March 4, Raymond Burr as Perry Mason...........**$15.00**
1962, February 24, Troy Donahue.............................**$10.00**
1962, January 13, Cast of Hazel................................**$25.00**
1962, May 5, Cast of Dobie Gillis.............................**$10.00**
1962, November 24, Mrs John F Kennedy..................**$12.00**
1962, September 29, Lucille Ball...............................**$40.00**
1963, January 19, Cast of Car 54 Where Are You?......**$35.00**
1963, June 29, Donna Reed & Carl Betz.....................**$10.00**
1963, November 2, Cast of My Favorite Martian.........**$50.00**
1963, September 7, Irene Ryan & Donna Douglas **$12.00**
1964, February 22, David Janssen as The Fugitive......**$90.00**
1964, January 4, Cast of The Dick Van Dyke Show....**$25.00**
1964, July 25, Fred McMurray....................................**$12.00**
1964, March 14, Cast of The Beverly Hillbillies...........**$15.00**
1964, May 30, Cast of McHale's Navy **$8.00**
1964, October, Robert Vaughn of The Man From UNCLE...**$20.00**
1965, August 21, Fess Parker as Daniel Boone...........**$10.00**
1965, July 31, Cast of My Three Sons **$10.00**
1965, June 5, Flipper & Brian Kelly **$20.00**
1965, May 15, Robert Lansing of 12 O'Clock High **$18.00**
1966, January 8, Ava Gabor & Eddie Albert of Green Acres.**$35.00**
1966, June 18, Cast of Bewitched..............................**$28.00**
1966, March 26, Adam West as Batman.....................**$140.00**
1966, November 12, Marlo Thomas of That Girl...........**$8.00**
1967, February 18, Dean Martin & Friends..................**$10.00**
1967, March 25, Robert Culp & Bill Cosby of I Spy ...**$10.00**
1967, May 27, Cast of F Troop by Searle.....................**$8.00**
1967, May 6, Harry Morgan & Jack Webb of Dragnet ..**$10.00**

1968, August 24, cast of Star Trek, $95.00.

1968, January 20, Cast of High Chaparral....................**$25.00**
1968, March 16, Sally Field as The Flying Nun **$6.00**
1968, November 2, The Mod Squad............................**$15.00**
1969, April 5, Smothers Brothers **$6.00**
1969, January 4, Cast of Here Come the Brides............**$20.00**
1969, July 26, Cast of Petticoat Junction....................**$10.00**
1969, March 8, Laugh-In's Dingalings..........................**$8.00**

1970, July 4, Cast of Eddie's Father.............................**$5.00**
1970, March 7, Cast of Hee Haw...............................**$10.00**
1970, September 26, Cast of Room 222 ....**$8.00**
1971, February 20, Doris Day....................................**$18.00**
1971, February 6, The Cast of The Odd Couple **$16.00**
1971, March 27, Cast of Bonanza **$15.00**
1971, May 22, David Cassidy of The Partridge Family...**$32.00**
1972, January 22, Cast of Mission Impossible **$12.00**
1972, June 3, Rod Serling of Night Gallery.................**$10.00**
1972, March 11, Marcus Welby MD **$6.00**
1973, August 25, Buddy Ebsen of Barnaby Jones.........**$5.00**
1973, February 24, Cast of M*A*S*H.........................**$15.00**
1973, March 31, Lucille Ball & Desi Arnez Jr **$25.00**
1973, May 19, Mary Tyler Moore................................**$15.00**

1974, August 31, Telly Savalas as Kojak, $5.00.

1974, December 7, Michael Landon of Little House on the Prairie...**$18.00**
1974, January 26, David Carradine of Kung Fu...........**$10.00**
1974, March 16, Carol Burnett & Vicki Lawrence **$5.00**
1975, April 12, Cher..**$8.00**
1975, January 4, Angie Dickenson of Police Woman..**$12.00**
1975, March 8, Chad Everett of Medical Center **$5.00**
1975, September 6, Special Fall Preview **$25.00**
1976, August 21, Cast of the Waltons...........................**$6.00**
1976, February 14, Red Foxx of Sanford & Son............**$6.00**
1976, January 10, Ron Howard & Henry Winkler of Happy Days **$20.00**
1976, March 13, Cast of Chico & the Man **$8.00**
1977, January 15, Jimmy Carter Inauguration...............**$5.00**
1977, March 19, Last Mary Tyler Moore Show **$28.00**
1977, March 26, Jack Klugman of Quincy **$5.00**
1980, December 27, Tom Selleck of Magnum PI **$8.00**
1980, February 2, Cast of Different Strokes **$5.00**
1980, July 19, Cast of The Love Boat **$5.00**
1981, April 25, Alan Alda by Hirschfeld........................**$5.00**
1981, October 31, Cast of Hill Street Blues....................**$5.00**
1982, January 30, Cast of CHiPS **$5.00**
1982, July 10, Cast of Facts of Life **$5.00**
1982, May 8, Goldie Hawn **$5.00**
1983, April 9, Elvis Presley...**$10.00**
1983, David Hasselhoff & KITT of Knight Rider **$8.00**
1984, February 11, Cast of Scarecrow & Mrs King........**$8.00**
1984, July 21, Cast of Knots Landing............................**$5.00**
1984, July 7, Valerie Bertinelli......................................**$5.00**
1985, February 2, Cagney & Lacey by Amsel **$5.00**
1985, March 2, Michael Landon **$8.00**
1985, November 9, Charles & Diana **$5.00**
1986, April 5, Cast of Family Ties.................................**$6.00**

1986, August 16, Suzanne Sommers.............................**$5.00**
1986, December 6, Delta Burke of Designing Women..**$5.00**
1986, January 11, Cast of Night Court.........................**$5.00**
1987, April 4, Susan Dey & Harry Hamlin of LA Law...**$5.00**
1987, August 15, Alf..**$10.00**
1987, March 28, Kirk Cameron of Growing Pains.........**$4.00**
1987, March 7, Justine Bateman & Michael J Fox.........**$5.00**
1988, January 2, Cast of Falcon Crest..........................**$4.00**
1988, June 11, Cast of Thirtysomething.......................**$5.00**
1988, October 8, Brandon Tartikoff & Stars...............**$10.00**
1989, March 11, What's In...**$6.00**
1989, May 20, Rosanne..**$6.00**
1989, October 7, Delta Burke & Gerald McRaney........**$8.00**
1990, June 9, Bart Simpson/Ninja Turtles..................**$10.00**
1990, March 31, Bob Saget of Funniest Home Videos..**$5.00**
1990, May 5, Oprah Winfrey.......................................**$5.00**
1991, August 31, It's Kirk Vs Picard...........................**$10.00**
1991, January 19, 60 Minutes' Best Stories..................**$4.00**
1991, November 30, The Judds....................................**$4.00**
1992, April 18, Cast of Home Improvement.................**$5.00**
1992, December 12, Katey Sagal of Married With Children..**$5.00**
1992, June 6, Grant Show of Melrose Place.................**$4.00**
1992, May 30, Cast of The Wonder Years.....................**$8.00**
1993, July 24, Summer Sci-Fi Issue............................**$8.00**
1993, May 15, Closing Time at Cheers..........................**$5.00**
1993, Mike Wallace: Inside 60 Minutes.......................**$10.00**
1994, February 26, Whitney Houston...........................**$10.00**
1994, January 1, Tim Allen..**$8.00**
1994, July 2, Reba McIntire.......................................**$10.00**
1995, April 15, Fran Drescher as The Nanny.................**$4.00**
1995, October 14, George Clooney & Julianne Margulies of
ER...**$5.00**
1995, September 23, Cast of Friends............................**$7.00**

TV Shows and Movies

Since the early days of TV and the movies right up to the present time, hit shows have inspired numerous toys and memorabilia. If they were well established, manufacturers often cashed in on their popularity through the sale of more expensive items such as toys and dolls; but more often than not, those less established were promoted through paper goods such as books, games, and paper dolls, just in case their fame turned out to be short lived.

Already in some of the newsletters specializing in toys, you see dealers offering Roger Rabbit memorabilia for sale, and the same is true of Indiana Jones, The Equalizer, and Ninja Turtles. So with an eye to the future (possibly the *near* future), see if you can pick the shows that will generate the collectibles you need to be hanging on to.

See also Beatles Collectibles; Character and Promotional Drinking Glasses; Character Collectibles; Cowboy Character Collectibles; Disney Collectibles; Dolls (Celebrity); Elvis Presley Memorabilia; Games; Halloween; Magazines; Movie Posters; Paper Dolls; Puzzles; Rock 'n Roll Memorabilia; Shirley Temple; Star Trek; Star Wars; Toys; TV Guides.

Club: Barbara Eden's Official Fan Club
P.O. Box 556
Sherman Oaks, CA 91403; 818-761-0267

Club: Dionne Quint Collectors
Jimmy Rodolfos
P.O. Box 2527
Woburn, MA 01888; 617-933-2219

Club: *The Baum Bugle*
The International Wizard of Oz Club
Fred M. Meyer
220 N 11th St.
Escanaba, MI 49829

Club: *Beyond the Rainbow Collector's Exchange*
P.O. Box 31672 St.
St. Louis, MO 63131

Newsletter: *Dark Shadows Collectibles Classified*
Sue Ellen Wilson
6173 Iroquois Trail
Mentor, OH 44060; 216-946-6348; For collectors of both old and new series

Newsletter: *Quint News*
Dionne Quint Collectors
P.O. Box 2527
Woburn, MA 01888, 617-933-2219

A-Team, air freshener, Mr T figure, 1983, MIP.............**$8.00**
A-Team, dinnerware set, plastic, 1983, MIB (sealed)...**$25.00**
A-Team, party hats, set of 4 different, EX...................**$10.00**
A-Team, tray, 1983, metal, 12x17", EX........................**$15.00**
Addams Family, hand puppet, Gomez, vinyl head w/cloth
body, 1960s, EX...**$50.00**
All in the Family, doll, Joey Stivic, Ideal, 1976, NMIB..**$45.00**
Annie, belt, leather, 1981, EX.....................................**$8.00**
Annie, doll, Knickerbocker, 1982, 6", MIB...................**$20.00**
Annie, napkins, Happy Birthday, 1980s, MIP (sealed)..**$6.00**
Annie, tray, litho metal, 1982, 17x12", EX...................**$15.00**
Arachnophobia, Big Bob Spider, Remco, 1990, MOC...**$8.00**
Batman (1st Movie), display figure, cardboard stand-up, 60",
EX..**$45.00**
Batman Forever, roll of tape, printed w/action scenes featuring 13 characters, Creative Plastics, 1995, MIB.......**$4.00**
Batman Returns, pillow, 18x18", NM..........................**$10.00**
Battlestar Galactica, activity book, Grosset & Dunlap, 1979,
NM...**$15.00**
Battlestar Galactica, Colorforms Adventure Set, deluxe version, 1978, NM (EX+ box).....................................**$35.00**
Battlestar Galactica, Poster Art Set, 2 posters, 6 pens & instructions, 1978, MIP (sealed).................................**$30.00**
Battlestar Galactica, wall plaque, EX..........................**$20.00**
Ben Casey, charm bracelet, steel w/plastic pearls, Sears,
1962, NMOC...**$25.00**
Ben Casey, coloring book, Saalfield, 1963, EX+.........**$15.00**
Ben Casey, nodder, 1960s, NM, from $100 to..........**$125.00**
Bewitched, tablet, 1964, 8x10", unused, M.................**$15.00**

Bionic Woman, paint-by-number set, MIB..................$45.00

Bionic Woman, tattoo & sticker set, 8 stickers & 1 sheet of 28 tattoos, Kenner, 1976, MIB........................$8.00

Bonanza, coloring book, Artcraft, 1960, NM $25.00

Bonanza, hat, Little Joe, EX $55.00

Brady Bunch, coloring book, Whitman, 1974, partially colored o/w EX+ $35.00

Brady Bunch, Fishing Fun Set, 1973, MOC $40.00

Burns & Allen, Coffee Servers, 2 glass pots w/2 plastic coasters, Pyrex/Motorola TV, 1950s, NMIB.................$130.00

Candid Camera, coloring book, Lowe, 1963, partially colored o/w EX+ $25.00

Captain Kangaroo, coloring book, 1977, M..................$10.00

Captain Kangaroo, doll, talker, Mattel, 1967, 20", non-working o/w EX.......................................$55.00

Car 54 Where Are You?, hand puppets, Toddy & Muldoon, soft vinyl heads w/cloth bodies, Eurolis, 1962, 9", EX, pr...$100.00

Charlie's Angels, Colorforms, 1978, NM (EX box) $30.00

Charlie's Angels, cosmetic kit, w/mirror & bag, 1970s, MIB $65.00

Charlie's Angels, jewelry set, Fleet, M (NM card) $50.00

Charlie's Angels, necklace, Farrah, 1977, MOC $30.00

Charlie's Angels, purse, vinyl box style, beige w/names in black lettering, 8", NM..$20.00

Charlie's Angels, 3-D viewer, w/4 strips, Fleet, 1974, M (NM card)..$45.00

Child's Play, doll, Chucky, 1991, 18", M $20.00

CHiPS, Emergency Medical Kit, complete w/case, 1980, MIB $35.00

Combat, paint-by-number, Hasbro, 1963, unused, NMIB..$175.00

Creature From the Black Lagoon, 3-D viewing glasses, unused, M..$15.00

Dr Doolittle, card game, Post premium, 1967, NM.....$20.00

Dr Doolittle, Fun Sponge Bath Toy, Amsco #1591, NMIB$30.00

Dr Doolittle, hand puppet, vinyl head w/cloth body, talker, Mattel, 1967, working, EX..$55.00

Dr Doolittle, jack-in-the-box, working, NM.................$85.00

Dr Doolittle, lawn sprinkler toy, Sea Snail, pink, AJ Renzi Plastic Corp, 1975, NMIB..$50.00

Dr Doolittle, party plates, w/animals & their names, Hallmark, MIP..$15.00

Dr Doolittle, tablet, NMIP $15.00

Dr Kildare, coloring & activity book, Lowe, 1963, NM...$35.00

Dragnet, badge, Sergeant Los Angeles Police #714, EX....$20.00

Dukes of Hazzard, bowl, EX $12.00

Dukes of Hazzard, Etch-A-Sketch Fun Screens, 1981, MIP..$15.00

Dukes of Hazzard, guitar, metal, 1981, EX $45.00

Dukes of Hazzard, tray, metal, 1981, 17x12", EX........$20.00

Fall Guy, truck, motorized break-apart model, Fleetwood, 1981, MOC..$8.00

Family Affair, activity book, Mrs Beasley Color & Read, unused, M..$35.00

Family Affair, coloring book, Mrs Beasley, 1975, unused, M..$30.00

Family Affair, doll, Mrs Beasley, stuffed body, Mattel, 1976, 10", EX..$20.00

Family Affair, hat box, features Buffy, 1969, EX $50.00

Family Matters, doll, Steve Urkel, Hasbro, 1991, 18", MIB.$32.00

Flipper, coloring book, Whitman, 1965, EX.................$15.00

Fugitive, 'Wanted' poster, reproduction, 17x11", EX...$20.00

Full House, doll, Michelle, talker, Meritus, 1991, 15", MIB $40.00

Get Smart, coloring book, Artcraft, 1965, partially colored o/w EX+ $50.00

Ghostbusters, figure, Sta-Puft, vinyl w/movable arms & legs, 1984, 7", EX+..$10.00

Ghostbusters, iron-on transfers, 1984, MOC...............$10.00

Ghostbusters, patch, cloth, 1986, MOC.......................$4.00

Gilligan's Island, coloring book, Whitman, 1964, scarce, EX+ $60.00

Gilligan's Island, tablet, 1965, unused, NM.................$18.00

Godzilla, bop bag, inflatable, 1985, 48", MIB.............$18.00

Good Times, doll, JJ, talker, Shindana, 23", nonworking o/w NM (EX box)..$120.00

Green Hornet, balloons, 20th Century Fox, 1960s, MOC..$175.00

Green Hornet, spoon, 1966, NM $25.00

Gremlins, figure, hard rubber, 1984, 4", EX................$8.00

Gremlins, night light, EX..$10.00

Gremlins, sticker book, 1984, unused, M $8.00

Hardcastle & McCormick, handcuffs, JaRu, 1983, MOC..$18.00

Harry & the Hendersons, figure, Harry, bendable, 8", MOC $8.00

Hawaii Five-O, binoculars, Larami, MIB, $25.00.

Hogan's Heroes, Signal Sender & Compass, 1977, MOC..$25.00

Hogan's Heroes, tablet, 1965, unused, 8x10", NM $20.00

I Love Lucy, hat, w/original tag, NM $50.00

In Living Color, doll, Homey the Clown, Acme, 1992, 24", MIP..$20.00

James Bond, beach towel, portrait & facsimile signature of Sean Connery as James Bond, 1964, M $85.00

James Bond, press book for Thunderball, NM...........$75.00

Joe Palooka, figure, bisque, Germany, 7", NM...........$65.00

Laugh In, Button Kit, 72 round stickers w/sayings & 8 photo stickers of the cast, Schlatter, 1968, EXIB $20.00

Laugh In, punch-out & paste book, 1968, unused, EX..$15.00

Little House on the Prairie, paint-by-number set, 1979, MIB..$45.00

Little Lulu, bank, Play Pal Plastics, 7½", NM $45.00

Little Orphan Annie, charm, celluloid, 1930s, NM $20.00

Little Orphan Annie and Sandy, wall pocket, lustre finish, marked Licensed by Famous Artists Syndicate, Made in Japan, 5½", $150.00.

Love Boat, barber kit, MOC $15.00
M*A*S*H, wallet, MOC $20.00
Magnum PI, tray, 1982, metal, 17x12", EX $15.00
Man From UNCLE, Secret Cap Shooting Lighter, EX... $45.00
Mork & Mindy, activity book, Mork From Ork, 1978, unused, EX $12.00

Mork and Mindy, doll, Mork, talker, stuffed cloth, Mattel, 1979, 16", EX, $35.00. (Photo courtesy of June Moon.)

Mork & Mindy, Magic Show, Colorforms, MIB $30.00
Mr Ed, hand puppet, talker, Mattel, 1962, VG $110.00
Munsters, gift bag, M $20.00
Munsters, hand puppet, Grandpa, vinyl head w/cloth body, 1960s, EX $50.00
Munsters, hand puppet, Herman, vinyl w/cloth body, 1960s, EX $50.00
Munsters, hand puppet, Lily, vinyl head w/cloth body, 1960s, VG $45.00
My Favorite Martian, coloring book, Whitman, 1964, partially colored o/w EX $25.00
My Favorite Martian, coloring book, Whitman, 1964, unused, M $50.00

Nanny & the Professor, coloring book, Artcraft, 1971, partially colored o/w EX $25.00
Partridge Family, coloring & activity book, Artcraft, 1973, unused, M, from $30 to $35.00
Pee-Wee's Playhouse, Pee-Wee Ball Darts, w/balls & foam board, etc, Herman Toys/Hong Kong, 1987, MIB (sealed) $35.00
Planet of the Apes, bank, plastic, M $45.00
Planet of the Apes, coloring book, 1974, unused, M.. $30.00
Planet of the Apes, plaque, 3-D, Milton Bradley, 1975, EXIB $75.00
Punky Brewster, doll, Punky, Galoob, 1984, MIB $40.00
Punky Brewster, pendant w/pearls, MOC $8.00
Rat Patrol, hat, red w/logo, 1966, EX $85.00
Rocky, doll, Rocky, stuffed body w/vinyl extremities, w/sweat suit & accessories, United Artists, 1980s, 18", EX $18.00
Romper Room, jack-in-the-box, 1970, EX $20.00
Romper Room, tambourine, Mr Doo Bee, 1960s, EX . $25.00
Rookies, Crime Buster Set, 1975, MOC $30.00
Rookies, movie viewer w/film, 1975, MOC $40.00
Six Million Dollar Man, Bionic Video Center, w/2 movie cartridges, EX (EX box) $50.00
Six Million Dollar Man, Give-A-Show Projector, 1977, MIB. $25.00
Smokey & the Bandit, figure, Bandit, diecast metal, Ertl, 1982, M (EX+ card) $12.00
Soupy Sales Show, activity book, Treasure Books, 1965, NM $18.00
Space: 1999, bank, Commander Koenig figure, vinyl, 11", EX+ $50.00
Space: 1999, Sonic Powered Megaphone, battery-operated, Vanity Fair, 1970s, VG (original box) $25.00
Sugarfoot, coloring book, 1959, unused, M $65.00
Superman, wastebasket, lithographed tin w/photo image of Christopher Reeve, EX $35.00
SWAT, bullhorn, 1975, EX $12.00
That Girl, coloring book, Saalfield, 1967, NM $50.00
Wagon Train, playset, Marx, 1950s, NMIB $500.00
Welcome Back Kotter, desk calendar, features Horshack, 1977, EX $35.00
Welcome Back Kotter, greeting cards, set of 6, MIB (sealed) $25.00
Wheel of Fortune, wristwatch, gold-tone case w/animated disk, black leather band, Sharp/Merv Griffin Ent, 1990, M. $45.00
Wizard of Oz, doll, Dorothy, Presents, 14", MIB $35.00
Wizard of Oz, doll, Scarecrow, premium, 1960s, 16", NM.. $25.00
Wizard of Oz, doll, Wicked Witch, Presents, 14", MIB. $40.00
Wizard of Oz, figure, bendable, Justoys, MOC $6.00
Wizard of Oz, pressbook, for 3rd release, 12 pages w/sample herald, 1955, NM $80.00

Wizard of Oz, sand pail, Swift's Oz Peanut Butter, 1950s, red and yellow lithographed tin, 6½", EX, $125.00.

Twin Winton

A California-based company founded by twins Ross and Don, the company called Twin Winton Ceramics had its beginnings in the mid-thirties. The men remained active in the ceramic industry until 1975, designing and producing animal figures, cookie jars and matching kitchenware items.

One of their most successful concepts was their Hillbilly line — mugs, pitchers, bowls, lamps, ashtrays, and novelty items modeled after the mountain boys in Paul Webb's cartoon series. Don Winton was its designer, and over the years he designed for other companies as well — Disney, Brush-McCoy, Ronald Reagan Foundation, and many more. In 1952 the twins' older brother Bruce bought out the company, and it was he that developed the famed wood stain finish for which the Twin Winton cookie jars, salt and pepper shakers, etc., are famous. When the company closed in the mid-1970s, the molds were sold to Treasure Craft, who used some of them in their own production.

If you'd like more information, read *The Collector's Encyclopedia of California Pottery* by Jack Chipman and *The Collector's Encyclopedia of Cookie Jars, Vol I and II,* by Joyce and Fred Roerig.

Note: Color codes in the listings below are as follows: A — avocado green; CS — Collectors Series, fully painted; G — gray; O — orange; P — pineapple yellow; R — red; and W — wood stain with hand-painted detail. Values are based on actual sales as well as dealer's asking prices.

See also Cookie Jars.

Advisor: Mike Ellis (See Directory, California Pottery)

Accent lamps, any of 11 different designs, W...........$150.00
Ashtrays, poodle, kitten, elf or Bambi, W, each..........$40.00
Bank, cop, W, G..$50.00
Bank, Dobbin, W, G..$50.00
Bank, Dutch girl, W, G..$60.00
Bank, elf on stump, W, G......................................$40.00
Bank, foo dog, W, G...$50.00
Bank, Friar, W, G...$40.00
Bank, happy bull, W, G..$40.00
Bank, Hotei, W, G...$40.00
Bank, lamb, W, G..$50.00
Bank, nut w/squirrel, W, G....................................$50.00
Bank, owl, W, G...$50.00
Bank, Persian cat, W, G.......................................$50.00
Bank, pig, W, G...$40.00
Bank, pirate fox, W, G..$50.00
Bank, poodle, W, G..$40.00
Bank, rabbit, W, G..$50.00
Bank, Ranger bear, W, G.......................................$50.00
Bank, sailor elephant, W, G...................................$40.00
Bank, shack, W, G...$50.00
Bank, shoe, W, G..$50.00
Bank, squirrel, W, G..$40.00
Bank, teddy bear, W, G..$40.00
Bronco Group, ashtray, cowboy on saddle.................$65.00
Bronco Group, mug, cowboy handle $25.00

Bronco Group, pitcher, bronco on side, cowboy handle ..$85.00
Bronco Group, pouring spouts, head & hat, each......$30.00
Bronco Group, stein, steer opposite cowboy handle .$50.00
Candy jar, bear w/lollipop on stump, W, G $45.00
Candy jar, Candy House, W, G................................$45.00
Candy jar, elephant w/lollipop, W, G $50.00
Candy jar, elf in stump, W, G..............................$45.00
Candy jar, nut w/squirrel finial, W, G.....................$55.00
Candy jar, old shoe, W, G....................................$45.00
Candy jar, Pot O' Candy, W, G...............................$30.00
Candy jar, train, W, G.......................................$50.00
Candy jar, turtle w/hare finial, W, G......................$65.00
Canister set, Barn, Cookies, Flour, Sugar, Coffee & Tea, W, A, P, O, R, G, 5 pcs...$275.00
Canister set, House, Cookies, Flour, Sugar, Coffee & Tea, 5 pcs...$450.00
Canister set, Pot O' Canister, Cookies, Flour, Sugar, Coffee & Tea, W, A, P, O, G, 5 pcs..........................$175.00
Canister set, Ye Olde Bucket, Cookies, Flour, Sugar, Coffee, Tea & Salt, W, 6 pcs...................................$250.00
Figurines, animal miniatures, green, brown or black gloss, marked Winton & # (some are unmarked), 4" to 8", from $15 to...$140.00
Figurines, children series, marked Twinton (rarely marked Twin Winton), from 3" to 7", each, from $125 to $175.00
Hillbilly Line (Ladies of the Mountains), mug w/lady handle...$25.00
Hillbilly Line (Ladies of the Mountains), pouring spouts, heads, each..$30.00
Hillbilly Line (Ladies of the Mountains), salt & pepper shakers, pr..$35.00
Hillbilly Line (Ladies of the Mountains), stein w/lady handle...$50.00
Hillbilly Line (Men of the Mountains), ashtray, Clem on his back...$50.00
Hillbilly Line (Men of the Mountains), bowl, bathing hillbilly..$40.00
Hillbilly Line (Men of the Mountains), cigarette box outhouse...$75.00
Hillbilly Line (Men of the Mountains), cookie jar, outhouse, minimum value...$350.00
Hillbilly Line (Men of the Mountains), lamp, Clem w/jug on barrel...$275.00
Hillbilly Line (Men of the Mountains), mug w/hillbilly handle...$20.00
Hillbilly Line (Men of the Mountains), pitcher w/hillbilly handle...$75.00
Hillbilly Line (Men of the Mountains), pouring spout dealer plaque...$350.00
Hillbilly Line (Men of the Mountains), pouring spouts, heads & hats, each...$25.00
Hillbilly Line (Men of the Mountains), pretzel bowl bathtub..$40.00
Hillbilly Line (Men of the Mountains), punch bowl, hillbilly chasing lady, minimum value..........................$350.00
Hillbilly Line (Men of the Mountains), punch cup w/hillbilly-handle..$15.00
Hillbilly Line (Men of the Mountains), salt & pepper shakers, pr...$35.00

Hillbilly Line (Men of the Mountains), stein w/hillbilly handle $40.00

Hillbilly Line, stein, $40.00; mug, $20.00. (Photo courtesy Jack Chipman.)

Ice bucket, bathing in barrel, W $250.00
Ice bucket, bottoms up on barrel, W........................$250.00
Ice bucket, Clem w/jug sitting on barrel, W $200.00
Ice bucket, Clem w/suspenders holding barrel, W...$200.00
Mugs, puppy, kitten, elephant, owl, bear or lamb, W, each...$35.00
Napkin holder, Bambi, W $50.00
Napkin holder, butler, W $100.00
Napkin holder, cocktail; elephant holding bottle, W..$100.00
Napkin holder, cocktail; horse sitting down holding bottle, W $100.00
Napkin holder, cocktail; rabbit holding bottle, W.....$100.00
Napkin holder, cocktail; St Bernard head, W............$100.00
Napkin holder, cow, W $85.00
Napkin holder, Dobbin, W $50.00
Napkin holder, Dutch girl, W $50.00
Napkin holder, elephant, W $50.00
Napkin holder, elf on stump, W, A, P, O.....................$85.00
Napkin holder, goose, W $50.00
Napkin holder, Hotei, W, A, P, O, each $60.00
Napkin holder, kitten, W $85.00
Napkin holder, lamb, W $50.00
Napkin holder, owl, W, A, P, O, each $85.00
Napkin holder, pig, W $85.00
Napkin holder, poodle, W $60.00
Napkin holder, potbellied stove, W $50.00
Napkin holder, Ranger bear, W $85.00
Napkin holder, shack, W, A, P, O, R, each..................$85.00
Napkin holder, squirrel, W $60.00
Planter, Bambi deer, W..$45.00
Planter, cat & boat, W $45.00
Planter, dog & drum, W $45.00
Planter, elephant & drum, W $45.00
Planter, Ranger bear, W...$45.00
Planter, squirrel & stump, W..$45.00
Salt & pepper shakers, barrel, W, pr............................$50.00
Salt & pepper shakers, bucket, W, A, P, O, pr $30.00
Salt & pepper shakers, butler, W, G, pr........................$50.00
Salt & pepper shakers, cat w/churn, W, pr $40.00
Salt & pepper shakers, cop, W, G, pr...........................$40.00

Salt & pepper shakers, cow, W, G, pr $40.00
Salt & pepper shakers, dinosaur, W, pr.....................$200.00
Salt & pepper shakers, Dobbin, W, G, pr......................$45.00
Salt & pepper shakers, dog, W, pr.................................$45.00
Salt & pepper shakers, duck, W, pr...............................$45.00
Salt & pepper shakers, Dutch girl, W, G, pr..............$35.00
Salt & pepper shakers, elephant, W, G, pr...............$30.00
Salt & pepper shakers, elf on stump, W, A, P, O, G, pr ..$40.00
Salt & pepper shakers, Friar, W, G, pr......................$35.00
Salt & pepper shakers, frog, W, pr.............................$50.00
Salt & pepper shakers, goose, W, G, pr.....................$45.00
Salt & pepper shakers, happy bull, W, G, pr $40.00
Salt & pepper shakers, hen on nest, W, pr...............$50.00
Salt & pepper shakers, Hotei, W, A, P, O, pr $30.00
Salt & pepper shakers, Indian, W, pr.........................$60.00
Salt & pepper shakers, Jack-in-the-Box, W, pr...........$75.00
Salt & pepper shakers, kangaroo, W, pr.....................$100.00
Salt & pepper shakers, kitten, W, pr $40.00
Salt & pepper shakers, lamb, W, G, pr $30.00
Salt & pepper shakers, lion, W, A, P, O, pr................$45.00
Salt & pepper shakers, mouse (sailor), W, A, P, O, G, pr ..$30.00
Salt & pepper shakers, mouse (w/tie), W, pr..............$40.00
Salt & pepper shakers, owl, W, G, pr..........................$30.00
Salt & pepper shakers, Persian cat, W, G, pr $50.00
Salt & pepper shakers, pig, W, G, pr...........................$50.00
Salt & pepper shakers, pirate fox, W, pr.....................$45.00
Salt & pepper shakers, rabbit, W, G, pr......................$45.00
Salt & pepper shakers, raccoon, W, G, pr $45.00
Salt & pepper shakers, Ranger bear, W, G, pr $40.00
Salt & pepper shakers, Robin Hood & Maid Marion, hand painted, pr...$95.00
Salt & pepper shakers, rooster, W, G, pr....................$30.00
Salt & pepper shakers, squirrel w/cookies, W, G, pr .$30.00
Salt & pepper shakers, turtle, W, G, pr $40.00
Salt & pepper shakers, W, G, pr....................................$40.00
Salt & pepper shakers donkey, W, G, pr.....................$40.00
Spoon rests, any of 14 different designs, W, each......$35.00
Sugar bowl & creamer, cow & bull, W......................$100.00
Sugar bowl & creamer, hen & rooster, W.................$100.00
Talking picture frames, any of 10 different designs, W ..$95.00
Wall pocket/planter, bear, rabbit, elephant, lamb or puppy, W, each..$35.00

Universal Dinnerware

This pottery incorporated in Cambridge, Ohio, in 1934, the outgrowth of several smaller companies in the area. They produced many lines of dinnerware and kitchenware items, most of which were marked. They're best known for their Ballerina dinnerware (simple modern shapes in a variety of solid colors) and Cat-Tail (See Cat-Tail Dinnerware). The company closed in 1960.

Bittersweet, bowl, mixing; 3-qt, from $18 to..............$20.00
Bittersweet, casserole, pedestal foot, 5-pt, from $27.50 to.$32.50
Bittersweet, cup & saucer, from $10 to.......................$12.00
Bittersweet, drip jar, w/lid, flat back..........................$18.00
Bittersweet, salt & pepper shakers, pr $12.50
Calico Fruit, bowl, mixing; w/lid, 8¾".........................$40.00

Calico Fruit, bowl, utility; w/lid, 5" $28.00
Calico Fruit, bowl, 9"...$18.00
Calico Fruit, jug, w/lid..$35.00
Calico Fruit, pepper shaker...$20.00
Laurella, bowl, soup; 8" $10.00
Laurella, cake plate, 11", from $10 to $12.50
Laurella, cup & saucer, from $5 to $8.00
Laurella, sugar bowl $10.00

Mixed Fruit, refrigerator jar, 4", $12.00.

Mount Vernon, creamer, from $7 to............................$10.00
Mount Vernon, plate, 9", from $10 to $12.00
Mount Vernon, salt & pepper shakers, pr...................$12.50
Mount Vernon, sugar bowl, from $10 to......................$12.50
Orchid, bowl, soup; 8"...$12.50
Orchid, bowl, vegetable; 9⅝", from $12.50 to $15.00
Orchid, plate, 9", from $8 to.......................................$10.00
Orchid, teapot, from $28 to $32.00
Oxford, bean pot, individual, restyled, from $6 to $8.00
Oxford, casserole, old style, 4½-pt, from $22.50 to....$25.00
Oxford, custard, restyled...$5.00
Oxford, jug, old style, 2-pt, 6" $20.00
Oxford, teapot, restyled, 2-cup $25.00
Poppy, bowl, soup; 8"..$12.00
Poppy, butter dish, from $22.50 to $25.00
Poppy, gravy boat $15.00
Poppy, teacup & saucer, from $5 to............................$8.00
Upico, butter dish, 1-lb, from $70 to...........................$75.00
Upico, casserole, tab handled, 7½", from $28 to $32.00
Upico, plate, 9¼", from $10 to $12.50
Upico, salt & pepper shakers, pr, from $18 to...........$20.00

Valentines

Valentines that convey sentimental messages are just the type of thing that girls in love tuck away and keep. So it's not too hard to find examples of these that date back to the early part of the century. But there are other kinds of valentines that collectors search for too — those with Black themes and Disney characters, advertising and modes of transportation, 3-dimensionals, and mechanicals. Look for artist-signed cards; these are especially prized.

Advisor: Katherine Kreider (See Directory, Valentines)

Newsletter: *National Valentine Collectors Bulletin*
Evalene Pulati
P.O. Box 1404
Santa Ana, CA 92702; 714-547-1355

Big-eyed children hiding behind stuffed chair, 3½x2¾", EX $3.00
Clockwork, heart, USA, 1958, 5½x4", NM $15.00
Diorama, Disney, 1938, 4¾x7x1", EX..........................$35.00
Easel back, diecut kaleidoscope style, 1927, 7x4".........$5.00
Flat, attorney, comic, 1930s, 8x7½", EX....................$5.00
Flat, Flintstones, 1962, 4¾x3", EX...............................$5.00
Flat, Henry, USA, 4x4", EX...$5.00
Flat, Oriental, USA, 4x3½, VG $1.00
Flat, troll, USA, 1960s, 5x4¾", EX..............................$5.00
Flat, young lady watering garden, original rubber hose, 5¼x8½", EX...$10.00

Fold-out, cupid on heart above bouquet of roses, EX, $8.00.

Gift-Giving, lollipop, 1930s, 4¾x3¾", EX $3.00

Honeycomb fold-out, boy and girl peeking at each other, 1936, EX, $20.00.

Little Jack Horner, USA, 1940s, 6½x3¾", EX **$5.00**
Mechanical-flat, ace of hearts, MIG, 7X5¼", EX............**$5.00**
Mechanical-flat, lobster, initials HB, MIB, 7x5", NM....**$10.00**
Mechanical-flat, movie director w/easel back, MIG, 7½x4¼" .**$5.00**
Mechanical-flat, polo pony, MIG, 1940s, 9x7½", EX.....**$5.00**
Popeye, 1930s, 5x3½", EX.................................**$5.00**
Tute Fruite, 1930, 6x4½", EX **$10.00**

Vallona Starr

Triangle Studios opened in the 1930s, primarily as a ceramic gift shop that sold the work of various California potteries and artists such as Brad Keeler, Beth Barton, Cleminsons, Josef Originals, and many others. As the business grew, Leona and Valeria, talented artists in their own right, began developing their own ceramic designs. In 1939 the company became known as Vallona Starr, a derivation of the three partners' names — (Val)eria Dopyera de Marsa, and Le(ona) and Everett (Starr) Frost. They made several popular ceramic lines including Winkies, Corn Design, Up Family, Flower Fairies and the Fairy Tale Characters salt and pepper shakers. There were many others. Vallona Starr made only three cookie jars: Winkie (beware of any jars made in colors other than pink or yellow); Peter, Peter, Pumpkin Eater (used as a TV prize-show giveaway; and Squirrel on Stump (from the Woodland line). For more information we recommend *Vallona Starr Ceramics* by Bernice Stamper.

See also Cookie Jars.

Advisor: Bernice Stamper (See Directory, Vallona Starr)

Bowl, cereal; Corn, single green ear along rim on yellow, from $20 to...**$25.00**
Bowl, Humpty Dumpty, white & pink head on square brick wall base, minimum value...............................**$125.00**
Butter dish, Corn, green & yellow, rectangular base w/lid, from $35 to...**$40.00**
Creamer & sugar bowl set, Corn, ear tab handles on sugar, green & yellow, 4½", pr, from $35 to...................**$40.00**
Figurine, Indian boy kneeling in canoe, green & brown, 2-pc set, minimum value **$75.00**
Marmalade, Corn, green & yellow, w/lid, from $25 to..**$30.00**

Pitcher, Corn, green and yellow, 1-qt, from $50.00 to $55.00. (Photo courtesy of Bernice Stamper.)

Pitcher, Winkie, pink & yellow w/blush, minimum value .**$100.00**
Plate, dinner; Corn, green & yellow, single ear at rim, 10", from $25 to..**$30.00**
Salt & pepper shakers, Aladdin & lamp, white w/heavy gold trim, pr, minimum value...............................**$95.00**
Salt & pepper shakers, Bears Eating (adapted from fairy tale), pr, from $35 to.......................................**$40.00**
Salt & pepper shakers, Couple of Bad Eggs, tan egg form w/frown & black patch over eye, pr, from $15 to.....**$20.00**
Salt & pepper shakers, Drip & Drop, marked w/name, pr, from $18 to...**$20.00**
Salt & pepper shakers, Earth, w/yellow orb marked ?, pr, from $30 to...**$35.00**
Salt & pepper shakers, Flying Saucer, silver saucer w/red pilot, pr, minimum value.................................**$350.00**
Salt & pepper shakers, Flying Saucer, yellow saucer w/green pilot, pr, minimum value.............................**$250.00**
Salt & pepper shakers, Gingham Dog & Calico Cat, pr, from $45 to...**$50.00**
Salt & pepper shakers, Glumm (undertaker) & Glee (clown), black & white w/gold trim, pr, minimum value...**$75.00**
Salt & pepper shakers, In the Doghouse, man in doghouse & wife w/rolling pin, pr, minimum value...............**$125.00**
Salt & pepper shakers, Indian woman grinding corn, red, blue or yellow dress, 2-pc style, pr, from $40 to .**$45.00**
Salt & pepper shakers, Little Miss Muffet, in yellow & white dress w/spider, w/spilled porridge, pr, minimum value **$125.00**

Salt and pepper shakers, Little Miss Muffet, minimum value $125.00. (Photo courtesy of Bernice Stamper.)

Salt & pepper shakers, prospector & jug, multicolor miner w/silver pan & gold nuggets, jug marked XXX, pr, minimum value...**$95.00**
Salt & pepper shakers, Tortoise & Hare (nursery rhyme theme), pr, minimum value.................................**$55.00**
Salt & pepper shakers, World War II Block Wardens, lg bodies w/wide black belt, shoes & hat, pr, minimum value **$125.00**
Salt & pepper shakers, Turnip & Lettuce, natural colors w/gold trim, pr, from $45 to...............................**$50.00**
Spoon rest, Corn, green & yellow, single ear on oval form, from $20 to...**$25.00**
Spoon rest, Winkie, pink & yellow w/blush, Winkie base w/honeymoon design handle, minimum value....**$30.00**

Vandor

For more than thirty-five years, Vandor has operated out of Salt Lake City, Utah. They're not actually manufacturers, but distributors of novelty ceramic items made overseas. Some pieces will be marked 'Made in Korea,' while others are marked 'Sri Lanka,' 'Taiwan,' or 'Japan.' Many of their best things have been made in the last few years, and already collectors are finding them appealing — anyone would. They have a line of kitchenware designed around 'Cowmen Mooranda' (an obvious take off on Carmen), another called 'Crocagator' (a darling crocodile modeled as a teapot, a bank, salt and pepper shakers, etc.), character-related items (Betty Boop and Howdy Doody, among others), and some really wonderful cookie jars reminiscent of fifties radios and jukeboxes.

For more information, we recommend *The Collector's Encyclopedia of Cookie Jars, Vol II*, by Joyce and Fred Roerig.

Advisor: Lois Wildman (See Directory, Vandor)

Baseball, bank, from $25 to $35.00
Baseball, mug...$40.00
Beethoven, bank...$20.00
Betty Boop, ashtray, reclining on piano, 1981 ....$55.00
Betty Boop, bank, Bank & Trust, 1981 ....$150.00
Betty Boop, bookends, jukebox, 1981, pr................$165.00
Betty Boop, box, bust, 1985 ....$60.00
Betty Boop, box, T-Bird, 1986....................................$85.00
Betty Boop, chalkboard $30.00
Betty Boop, clock, bed of roses $65.00
Betty Boop, clock, Betty & Bimbo $65.00
Betty Boop, clock, Covered Wagon, KS, 1985, rare, from $350
  to..$400.00
Betty Boop, clock, face $45.00
Betty Boop, clock, full figure, from $48 to $50.00
Betty Boop, creamer & sugar bowl, 'Tropico,' w/lids, set..$75.00
Betty Boop, egg cup..$30.00
Betty Boop, figurine, hula girl, 1984, rare $350.00
Betty Boop, hand mirror, 1983, rare $150.00
Betty Boop, mask, head, 1981.....................................$65.00
Betty Boop, mug, bust, 1981 ....$35.00
Betty Boop, music box, jukebox, 1985.......................$125.00
Betty Boop, music box, piano, 4-pc $125.00
Betty Boop, picture frame..$45.00
Betty Boop, salt & pepper shakers, car hop, 1985, pr..$45.00
Betty Boop, salt & pepper shakers, wooden boat, 2nd series,
  pr $40.00
Betty Boop, utensil holder, from $15 to $35.00
Betty Boop, vase, moon, 1983.....................................$85.00
Betty Boop, wall hook, figural, 1984, rare $125.00
Cow, salt & pepper shakers, w/beach ball..................$30.00
Cow, salt & pepper shakers, w/inner tube, pr............$30.00
Cowboy, salt & pepper shakers, 1991, pr....................$20.00
Crocagator, bank...$18.00
Crocagator, salt & pepper shakers, w/parasol, pr.......$20.00
Crocagator, soap dish, in boat $20.00
Crocagator, teapot...$30.00
Flintstones, bank, Bamm-Bamm & Dino, from $85 to..$90.00

Flintstones, bank, Fred Flintstone standing, from $65 to...$85.00
Flintstones, bank, Pebbles on Dino, 1989, from $45 to.....$60.00
Flintstones, mug, Barney Rubble.................................$20.00
Flintstones, mug, Fred Flintstone, 1989, from $15 to..$20.00
Flintstones, salt & pepper shakers, Pebbles & Bamm-Bamm,
  1989, pr...$40.00
Howdy Doody, bank, bust $125.00
Howdy Doody, bank, TV..$145.00
Howdy Doody, bookends, sitting pose holding book on
  knees, marked Vandor, pr, minimum value........$100.00
Howdy Doody, box, in car, 2-pc..................................$65.00
Howdy Doody, face mask $130.00
Howdy Doody, picture frame.......................................$45.00
Howdy Doody, snow dome, #0572............................$50.00
Howdy Doody, spoon rest...$50.00
Jetsons, mug, George, #2233, 1990, from $20 to........$30.00
Miss Piggy, candy box, heart shape $65.00

Mona Lisa, bank, 1992, $25.00.

Mona Lisa, mug..$85.00
Mona Lisa, salt & pepper shakers, 1992, pr.................$20.00
Mona Lisa, teapot...$40.00
Popeye, bank, Popeye bust w/pipe, 1980..................$125.00
Popeye, bank, Popeye sitting on pile of rope, 1980....$125.00
Popeye, bank, Swee' Pea, unmarked.........................$150.00
Popeye, egg cup, Swee' Pea $45.00
Popeye, mug, Olive Oyl...$38.00
Popeye, mug, Popeye, 1980 ....$38.00
Popeye, mug, Wimpy, 1990..$25.00
Popeye, music box, Olive Oyl, 1980 ....$145.00
Popeye, music box, Wimpy on hamburger..............$110.00
Popeye, plate, Olive Oyl head, 1980 ....$65.00
Popeye, salt & pepper shakers, Popeye & Olive Oyl, 1980,
  pr $125.00

Vernon Kilns

Founded in Vernon, California, in 1930, this company produced many lines of dinnerware, souvenir plates, decorative pottery, and figurines. They employed several well-known artists whose designs no doubt contributed substantially to their success. Among them were Rockwell Kent, Royal Hickman, and Don Blanding, all of whom were responsible for creating several of the lines most popular with collectors today.

In 1940, they signed a contract with Walt Disney to produce a line of figurines and several dinnerware patterns that were inspired by Disney's film *Fantasia*. The figurines were made for a short time only and are now expensive.

The company closed in 1958, but Metlox purchased the molds and continued to produce some of their bestselling dinnerware lines through a specially established 'Vernon Kiln' division.

Most of the ware is marked in some form or another with the company name and, in some cases, the name of the dinnerware pattern.

If you'd like to learn more, we recommend *The Collector's Encyclopedia of California Pottery* by Jack Chipman and *Collectible Vernon Kilns, An Identification and Value Guide,* by Maxine Feek Nelson.

Newsletter: *Vernon Views*
P.O. Box 945
Scottsdale, AZ 85252; Published quarterly

Anytime, bowl, soup	**$8.00**
Anytime, creamer & sugar bowl	**$15.00**
Anytime, plate, salad	**$3.00**
Ashtray, Boulder Dam, maroon on white, 5½"	**$10.00**
Barkwood, bowl, salad; 10½", from $25 to	**$35.00**
Barkwood, creamer, regular	**$12.00**
Barkwood, pitcher, 1-qt	**$25.00**
Barkwood, plate, dinner	**$15.00**
Barkwood, teacup & saucer	**$12.00**
Barkwood, teapot, 8-cup, from $25 to	**$35.00**
Beverly, chop plate, 12"	**$30.00**
Brown-Eyed Susan, bowl, chowder; from $10 to	**$12.00**
Brown-Eyed Susan, bowl, serving; oval, 10", from $18 to	**$22.00**
Brown-Eyed Susan, chop plate, 12", from $18 to	**$25.00**
Brown-Eyed Susan, creamer, regular	**$18.00**
Brown-Eyed Susan, egg cup	**$28.00**
Brown-Eyed Susan, mug, applied handle, 8-oz, from $18 to	**$25.00**
Brown-Eyed Susan, platter, 10½"	**$20.00**
Brown-Eyed Susan, salt & pepper shakers, pr	**$10.00**
Brown-Eyed Susan, syrup, drip-cut top	**$65.00**
Brown-Eyed Susan, teapot, w/lid	**$65.00**
Calico, plate, dinner	**$20.00**
Chintz, bowl, fruit	**$8.00**
Chintz, coffeepot, 8-cup	**$65.00**
Chintz, egg cup	**$20.00**
Chintz, platter, 14"	**$35.00**
Coral Reef, butter dish	**$65.00**
Coral Reef, cup & saucer	**$26.00**
Coral Reef, plate, 8½"	**$22.00**
Delores, bowl, serving; oval	**$25.00**
Delores, plate, bread & butter; 6½"	**$6.00**
Desert Bloom, bowl, rim soup; 8"	**$10.00**
Dolores, chop plate, 12"	**$30.00**
Fantasia, bowl, Sprite, solid color, 3x10½", from $250 to	**$265.00**
Fantasia, figurine, elephant standing, #24, Disney, from $350 to	**$375.00**
Fantasia, figurine, hippo in tutu, #34, Disney, 1940, from $350 to	**$375.00**
Fantasia, salt & pepper shakers, Hop & Lo mushrooms, pr, from $125 to	**$150.00**
Gingham, bowl, serving; 8½"	**$15.00**
Gingham, casserole, round, from $40 to	**$45.00**

Gingham, cup & saucer, demitasse	**$22.00**
Gingham, egg cup, double	**$18.00**
Gingham, plate, luncheon; from $8 to	**$12.00**
Gingham, salt & pepper shakers, regular, pr	**$10.00**

Harvest, plate, 12", $30.00.

Hawaiian Flowers, bowl, coupe soup; 7½"	**$18.00**
Hawaiian Flowers, bowl, serving; 8"	**$22.00**
Hawaiian Flowers, cup & saucer	**$25.00**
Hawaiian Flowers, pickle dish, tab handles, 6"	**$30.00**
Hawaiian Flowers, plate, dinner; from $25 to	**$30.00**
Hawaiian Flowers, plate, 6¼", from $10 to	**$12.00**
Hawaiian Flowers, plate, 7½"	**$20.00**
Hawaiian Flowers, salt & pepper shakers, pr	**$35.00**
Hawaiian Flowers, sugar bowl, w/lid, individual	**$30.00**
Homespun, bowl, fruit; 5½", from $5 to	**$7.00**
Homespun, bowl, rim soup; 8½"	**$15.00**
Homespun, jam jar, notched lid, 5"	**$60.00**
Homespun, muffin tray, tab handles, dome lid, 9"	**$75.00**
Homespun, pitcher, 1-qt, from $35 to	**$40.00**
Homespun, plate, luncheon	**$12.00**
Homespun, platter, 14", from $30 to	**$35.00**
Homespun, salt & pepper shakers, lg, pr, from $15 to	**$20.00**

Homespun: Vegetable bowl, $15.00; Cup and saucer, $12.00; Tumbler, $15.00.

Lei Lani, bowl, salad; 11" **$75.00**
Lei Lani, butter tray & lid, oblong **$50.00**
Lei Lani, chop plate, 12".....................................**$50.00**
Lei Lani, egg cup **$20.00**
Lei Lani, mug, 3½" **$30.00**
Lei Lani, pitcher, jug style, w/lid, 1-pt **$20.00**
Lei Lani, salt & pepper shakers, pr, from $30 to........**$40.00**
Lei Lani, sugar bowl, demitasse; w/lid......................**$65.00**
May Flower, butter tray & lid, oblong.....................**$45.00**
May Flower, chop plate, 14" **$50.00**
May Flower, egg cup..**$20.00**
May Flower, relish, leaf shape, 12".....................**$25.00**
Melinda, sugar bowl, pink, w/lid **$15.00**
Moby Dick, chop plate, blue, 12" **$175.00**
Moby Dick, cup & saucer, brown **$25.00**
Moby Dick, plate, bread & butter **$15.00**
Native California, bowl, rim soup **$18.00**
Native California, casserole, w/lid, 4¾" **$35.00**
Native California, chop plate, 14".......................**$40.00**
Native California, cup & saucer, AD **$27.00**
Native California, platter, 16" **$40.00**
Native California, teapot, 6-cup, from $55 to **$65.00**
Orchard Ware, creamer **$18.00**
Orchard Ware, salt & pepper shakers, pr **$30.00**
Organdie, bowl, chowder; 6", from $8 to.................**$12.00**
Organdie, bowl, rim soup **$12.50**
Organdie, bowl, serving; 7½" **$15.00**
Organdie, bowl, 9" **$18.00**
Organdie, coaster, 4½", from $18 to **$22.00**
Organdie, cup & saucer, colossal.........................**$135.00**
Organdie, jam jar, notched lid, 5" **$65.00**
Organdie, pitcher, disk, w/decor, 2-qt **$75.00**
Organdie, pitcher, ½-pt **$25.00**
Organdie, plate, dinner; from $12 to **$18.00**
Organdie, platter, relish or pickle; sm.................**$17.00**
Organdie, salt & pepper shakers, pr **$20.00**
Organdie, sugar bowl, angular, individual.................**$20.00**
Organdie, tumbler..**$14.00**
Our America, plate, brown, Rockwell Kent, 9" **$75.00**
Rio Verde, bowl, salad; 11" **$75.00**
Santa Barbara, chop plate, 14".............................**$60.00**
Sherwood, bowl, divided vegetable **$12.50**
Sherwood, bowl, 10" **$9.00**
Sherwood, bowl, 9" **$10.00**
Sherwood, creamer **$6.00**
Sherwood, cup & saucer **$3.75**
Sherwood, plate, salad **$6.00**
Sherwood, relish, 3-part **$16.00**
Tam O'Shanter, bowl, divided vegetable; from $28 to..**$32.00**
Tam O'Shanter, butter dish, ¼-lb, from $28 to...........**$32.00**
Tam O'Shanter, platter, 14"...................................**$30.00**
Trade Winds, syrup...**$45.00**
Ultra California, bowl, cereal; 6"..........................**$15.00**
Ultra California, egg cup **$20.00**
Ultra California, pitcher, jug form, 4½" **$32.00**
Ultra California, plate, luncheon..........................**$15.00**
Ultra California, teapot, 6-cup.............................**$70.00**
Wheat, bowl, lug chowder.....................................**$12.00**
Wheat, egg cup..**$18.00**

Wheat, plate, dinner...**$15.00**
Wheat, salt & pepper shakers, pr.........................**$20.00**
Winchester '73, bowl, chowder; tab handle **$30.00**
Winchester '73, platter, 12" **$125.00**
Winchester '73, tumbler..**$45.00**

Souvenir plate, Knott's Berry Farm, 1949, blue transfer, $25.00.

View-Master Reels and Packets

View-Master, the invention of William Gruber, was introduced to the public at the 1939–1940 New York World's Fair and the Golden Gate Exposition in California. Since then, View-Master reels, packets and viewers have been produced by five different companies — the original Sawyers Company, G.A.F. (1966), View-Master International (1981), Ideal Toys and Tyco Toys (the present owners). Because none of the non-cartoon single reels and three-reel packets have been made since 1980, these have become collectors' items. Also highly sought after are the 3-reel sets featuring popular TV and cartoon characters. The market is divided between those who simply collect View-Master as a field all its own and collectors of character-related memorabilia who will often pay much higher prices for reels about Barbie, Batman, The Addams Family, etc. Our values tend to follow the more conservative approach.

The first single reels were dark blue with a gold sticker and came in attractive gold-colored envelopes. They appeared to have handwritten letters. These were followed by tan reels with a blue circular stamp. Because these were produced for the most part after 1945 and paper supplies were short during WWII, they came in a variety of front and back color combinations, tan with blue, tan with white, and some were marbleized. Since print runs were low during the war, these early singles are much more desirable than the printed ones that were produced by the millions from 1946 to 1957. Three-reel packets, many containing story books, were introduced in 1955, and single reels were phased out. Nearly all viewers are very common and have little value except for the very early ones, such as the Model A and Model B. Blue and brown versions of the Model B are especially rare. Another desirable viewer, unique in that it is the only focusing model ever made, is the Model D. For more information we recommend *View-Master Single Reels, Volume I,* by Roger Nazeley.

ABC Circus, B-411, MIP (sealed) **$18.00**
Adam 12, 1972, MIP **$30.00**
Alice in Wonderland, B-360, MIP **$15.00**
America's Man in Space, B-657, MIP........................**$18.00**
Apple's Way, B-558, MIP (sealed) **$25.00**
Archie, 1975, MIP (sealed) **$30.00**
Aristocats, B-365, MIP..**$10.00**
Babes in Toyland, 1961, NMIP **$35.00**
Bambi, B-400, MIP (sealed) **$18.00**
Batman, B-492, MIP (sealed) **$38.00**
Beep Beep the Roadrunner, B-538, MIP (sealed) **$20.00**
Big Blue Marble, B-587, MIP (sealed)......................**$20.00**
Birth of Jesus, B-875, MIP **$12.00**
Bonanza, MIP..**$35.00**
Buck Rogers, 1980, MIP (sealed)..............................**$12.00**
Buck Rogers in the 25st Century, MIP **$25.00**
Bugs Bunny, B-531, MIP **$15.00**
Bugs Bunny in Big Top Bunny, B-549, MIP (sealed) .**$22.00**
Captain America, H-43, MIP (sealed) **$25.00**
Captain Kangaroo, A-C755, MIP **$25.00**
Casper's Ghostland, B-545, MIP (sealed)..................**$20.00**
Cat From Outer Space, 1978, NMIP **$20.00**
Charlotte's Web, B-321, MIP....................................**$15.00**
Children's Zoo, B-617, MIP (sealed)........................**$18.00**
CHiPs, 1980, MIP (sealed) **$22.00**
Cinderella, B-318, MIP **$12.00**
City Beneath the Sea, B-496, MIP............................**$30.00**
Civil War, 1960s, NMIP..**$45.00**
Close Encounters of the Third Kind, 1977, NMIP **$20.00**
Conquest of Space, 1968, complete, MIP **$12.00**
Dark Shadows, 1968, NM (EX package)....................**$70.00**
Dennis the Menace, B-539, MIP (sealed)..................**$28.00**
Dinosaurs, #4138, TV show, MIP (sealed)..................**$8.00**
Disney World Liberty Square, A-950, MIP (sealed) **$18.00**
Donald Duck, B-525, MIP **$15.00**
Dr Strange, 1979, MIP (sealed) **$18.00**
Eight Is Enough, 1980, MIP (sealed) **$20.00**
Emergency!, B-597, MIP (sealed) **$22.00**
Fangface, 1980, NMIP..**$15.00**
Fantastic Voyage, 1983, M (EX package) **$42.00**
Flash Gordon on the Planet Mongo, 1976, MIP (sealed) ..**$18.00**
Flipper, B-485, MIP **$35.00**
For the Love of Benji, H-54, NMIP **$12.00**
Frankenstein, 1976, MIP (sealed)..............................**$20.00**
Golden Book Favorites, H-14, MIP (sealed)................**$30.00**
Green Hornet, MIP **$95.00**
Hair Bear Bunch, B-552, MIP (sealed) **$25.00**
Happy Days, 1974, MIP (sealed) **$15.00**
Hare & the Tortoise, B-309, MIP (sealed)..................**$20.00**
Harlem Globetrotters, 1977, MIP (sealed)................**$25.00**
Hearst Castle, A-190, MIP..**$18.00**
Horses, H-5, MIP (sealed) **$18.00**
Huckleberry Hound & Yogi Bear, B-512, NM (EX package) **$15.00**
It's a Bird, Charlie Brown, B-556, MIP......................**$12.00**

James Bond Moonraker, 1979, MIP **$25.00**
King Kong, B-392, MIP (sealed) **$35.00**

KISS, Canadian issue, GAF, 1978, 3-reel set, MIP, $85.00. (Photo courtesy of June Moon.)

Lassie & Timmy, B-474, MIP......................................**$20.00**
Laverne & Shirley, 1978, MIP (sealed) **$25.00**
Little Drummer Boy, B-871, MIP (sealed)..................**$18.00**
Little Orphan Annie, 1978, MIP **$28.00**
Lost in Space, 1967, NMIP **$80.00**
M*A*S*H, 1978, M (NM package)..............................**$25.00**
Man From UNCLE, B-484, MIP **$40.00**
Mary Poppins, NMIP..**$15.00**
Million-Dollar Duck, B-506, MIP (sealed)..................**$30.00**
Mod Squad, B-478, MIP (sealed) **$35.00**
Moon Rockets & Guided Missiles, B-656, MIP **$20.00**
Niagara Falls, A-655, MIP **$15.00**
Night Before Christmas, B-382, MIP **$15.00**
Partridge Family, B-569, MIP **$35.00**
Peanuts, B-536, MIP (sealed) **$15.00**
Pink Panther, J-12, MIP **$15.00**
Planet of the Apes, 1974, NMIP................................**$35.00**
Pluto, 1980, MIP (sealed) **$12.00**
Popeye, B-516, MIP **$12.00**
Prehistoric Animals, B-619, MIP................................**$22.00**
Project Apollo, B-658, MIP **$25.00**
Rin-Tin-Tin, Sawyer's, 1955, VG (VG package)............**$22.00**
Rookies, BB-452, MIP (sealed) **$25.00**
Rookies, 1975, MIP (sealed) **$12.00**
Rudolph the Red-Nosed Reindeer, B-870, MIP (sealed)...**$18.00**
San Francisco Sight-Seeing, A-167, MIP **$15.00**
Six Million Dollar Man, B-559, MIP (sealed) **$30.00**
Sleeping Beauty, B-308, MIP......................................**$15.00**
Snoopy the Red Baron, B-544, MIP (sealed)..............**$20.00**
Snow White & the Seven Dwarfs, 1980, NMIP............**$12.00**
Space 1999, BB-451, MIP **$28.00**

Star Trek, B-499, 1968, MIP, $30.00.

Statue of Liberty, A-648, MIP $18.00
Sub-Mariner, 1978, NMIP.............................$25.00
Superman the Movie, 1979, NMIP................$25.00

Talking View-Master Gift Pak III, GAF, #2275, NM in EX canister, $30.00.

Tarzan, Sawyers, 1950, NM (EX+ package) $45.00
Time Tunnel, NM (EX package)......................$45.00
UFO, MIP...$25.00
Voltron, Defenders of the Universe, #1055, MIP (sealed) ..$8.00
White House, A-793, MIP.............................$20.00
Winnie the Pooh & the Honey Tree, B-362, MIP........$15.00
Wizard of Oz, 1962, NM (EX package).......................$25.00
Wonders of the Deep, B-612, M (EX package) $18.00
Woody Woodpecker, 1964, complete w/booklet, NMIP ..$25.00
X-Men, Captive Hearts, #1085, MIP (sealed) $8.00

Viking Glass

Located in the famous glassmaking area of West Virginia, this company has been in business since the 1950s, most recognized for their glass animals and birds. Their Epic Line (circa 1950s–'60s) was innovative in design and vibrant in color. Rich tomato-red, amberina, brilliant blues, strong greens, black, amber and deep amethyst were among the rainbow hues in production at that time. During the 1980s, the company's ownership changed hands, and the firm became known as Dalzell-Viking (indicated by D-V in our descriptions). Some of the Epic Line animals were reissued in crystal, crystal frosted, and black. If you're interested in learning more about these animals, refer to *Glass Animals of the Depression Era* by Lee Garmon and Dick Spencer (Collector Books).

Advisor: Ruth Grizel (See Directory, Westmoreland)

Ashtray, duck, dark blue, 9" $45.00
Ashtray, M monogram, crystal, 8" dia $45.00
Ashtray, pear w/leaf, vaseline, rare, 6" $35.00
Ashtray, plain, orange, 9" dia.......................$35.00
Ashtray, R monogram, crystal, 9" dia $45.00
Ashtray, ruby, 9" dia.....................................$55.00
Bell, orange, no ringer, 6"...........................$35.00
Bookends, Wise Old Owl, green, pr..........................$30.00

Bowl, Della Robbia, vaseline, footed, 5x10"..............$65.00
Bowl, Della Robbia, vaseline, 4x12"............................$65.00
Bowl, swan figural, amber, 6" dia $45.00
Candle holders, dolphin standard, pink, hexagonal foot, 9½", pr $150.00
Candy dish, Ashley, bright red, round, w/lid, D-V $35.00
Candy dish, bird form, lid w/long tail only, amber $50.00
Candy dish, long-tailed bird on lid, amber, 11½x6" ...$95.00
Candy dish, long-tailed bird on lid, dark blue or ruby, 11½x6" $125.00
Candy dish, 25th Anniversary, birds & flowers, crystal, w/lid.................$45.00
Dish, divided; butterflies, pink opaque, 4-footed, 6x4" ..$75.00
Dish, duck figural, dark blue, 9x4" $45.00
Figurine, angelfish, amber, 7x7" $125.00
Figurine, angelfish, black, 6½" $150.00
Figurine, bear baby, black, D-V $45.00
Figurine, bear mama, black, D-V.............................$65.00
Figurine, bird, long tail, orange, 10" $45.00
Figurine, bird, short tail, crystal, 7" $35.00

Figurine, cat, green, 1960s, 8", $55.00.

Figurine, cat, Epic Series, black, D-V $45.00
Figurine, cat, sitting, crystal w/Crystal Mist, 6½".........$55.00
Figurine, dog, Epic Series, black, D-V $45.00
Figurine, duck, footed, amber, 5" dia.......................$45.00
Figurine, duck, footed, green, 5" dia $45.00
Figurine, duck, footed, orange, 5" dia......................$45.00
Figurine, duck, footed, ruby, rare, 5".......................$65.00
Figurine, hound dog, crystal & frost, 6x5½"...............$50.00
Figurine, Jesus, crystal w/Crystal Mist, 6x5" $65.00
Figurine, lovebirds, crystal & frost, 5½x4"..................$45.00
Figurine, mouse, Crystal Mist, 4" $35.00
Figurine, penguin, crystal, 7" $25.00
Figurine, pig, black, D-V...$75.00
Figurine, polar bear, black, D-V $60.00

Figurine, seal, persimmon, 9¾", $15.00.

Figurine, swan, fluted, green or orange, 6½x4" **$45.00**
Figurine, swan, Pink Mist, paper label, 6x3½" **$45.00**
Figurine, swan, Yellow Mist, paper label, 6" **$50.00**
Figurine, wolfhound, black, D-V **$75.00**
Plate, free-form, ruby, 19x12" **$95.00**
Salver, Ashley, bright red, footed, lg, D-V **$55.00**
Vase, fluted, crystal w/flowers, 8" **$35.00**
Vase, ribbed, ruby, 12" **$35.00**

Wade Porcelain

If you've attended many flea markets, you're already very familiar with the tiny Wade figurines, most of which are 2" and under. Wade made several lines of them, but the most common were made as premiums for the Red Rose Tea Company. Most of these sell for $3.50 to $7.00 or so. Some of the animals are much larger and may sell for more than $100.00.

The Wade company dates to 1810. The original kiln was located near Chesterton in England. The tiny pottery merged with a second about 1900 and became known as the George Wade Pottery. They continued to grow and to absorb smaller nearby companies and eventually manufactured a wide range of products from industrial ceramics to Irish porcelain giftware. In 1990 Wade changed its name to Seagoe Ceramics Limited.

If you'd like to learn more, we recommend *The World of Wade* by Ian Warner and Mike Posgay.

Advisor: Ian Warner (See Directory, Wade)

Newsletter: *The Wade Watch*
The Collector's Corner
8199 Pierson Ct.
Arvada, CO 80005; 303-421-9655 or 303-424-4401 or Fax 303-421-0317; Subscription: $8 per year (4 issues)

Premiums

Circus Animal, Elephant, Tom Smith, 1978-79, molded-in mark Wade England on drum-type base, 1¼" **$14.00**
Circus Animal, Seal, Tom Smith, 1978-79, molded-in mark Wade England on drum-type base, 1⅝" **$14.00**
Circus Animal, Tiger, Tom Smith, 1978-79, molded-in mark Wade England on drum-type base, 1⅝" **$12.00**
Farmyard, Bull, Tom Smith, 1982-83, molded-in mark Wade England around base, 1⅛", from $10 to **$12.00**
Farmyard, Dog, Tom Smith, 1982-83, molded-in mark Wade England around base, 1", from $8 to **$10.00**
Farmyard, Duck, Tom Smith, 1982-83, molded-in mark Wade England around base, 1", from $12 to **$14.00**
Farmyard, Goat, Tom Smith, 1982-83, molded-in mark Wade England around base, 1½", from $8 to **$10.00**
Mini-Nursery Rhyme & Fairy Tale, Dr Foster, Canadian Red Rose Tea, 1971-79, 1¾", from $5 to **$8.00**
Mini-Nursery Rhyme & Fairy Tale, Gingerbread Man, Canadian Red Rose Tea, 1971-79, 1⅝", from $26 to **$30.00**
Mini-Nursery Rhyme & Fairy Tale, Goosey Gander, Canadian Red Rose Tea Promotion, 1971-79, 1⅜" **$5.00**

Mini-Nursery Rhyme & Fairy Tale, Humpty Dumpty, Canadian Red Rose Tea, 1971-79, 1½" **$4.00**
Mini-Nursery Rhyme & Fairy Tale, Jack (Jack & Jill), Canadian Red Rose Tea, 1971-79, 1¼" **$8.00**
Mini-Nursery Rhyme & Fairy Tale, Little Bo-Peep, Canadian Red Rose Tea, 1971-79, 1¾" **$4.00**
Mini-Nursery Rhyme & Fairy Tale, Little Jack Horner, Canadian Red Rose Tea, 1971-79, 1⅜", from $4 to **$6.00**
Mini-Nursery Rhyme & Fairy Tale, Mother Goose, Canadian Red Rose Tea, 1971-79, 1⅝" **$12.00**
Mini-Nursery Rhyme & Fairy Tale, Old King Cole, Canadian Red Rose Tea, 1971-75, 1½" **$6.00**
Mini-Nursery Rhyme & Fairy Tale, Old Woman Who Lived in a Shoe, Canadian Red Rose Tea, 1971-79, 1⅜" **$5.00**
Mini-Nursery Rhyme & Fairy Tale, Puss in Boots, Canadian Red Rose Tea, 1971-79, 1¾" **$7.00**
Mini-Nursery Rhyme & Fairy Tale, Queen of Hearts, Canadian Red Rose Tea, 1971-79, 1¾", from $12.50 to **$15.00**
Mini-Nursery Rhyme & Fairy Tale, The Pied Piper, Canadian Red Rose Tea, 1971-79, 1¾" **$8.00**
Mini-Nursery Rhyme & Fairy Tale, Wee Willie Winkie, Canadian Red Rose Tea, 1971-79, 1¾" **$5.00**

Piggy bank family, Annabel, $50.00.

Safari, Kangaroo, Tom Smith, 1967-77, molded-in mark Wade England around base, similar to Whimsie model, 1⅝"...**$10.00**
Safari, Koala bear, Tom Smith, 1976-77, molded-in Wade England around base, 1¼" **$15.00**
Safari, Lion, Tom Smith, 1976-77, molded-in mark Wade England around base, 1⅛", from $10 to **$12.00**
Safari, Walrus, Tom Smith, 1976-77, molded-in mark Wade England around base, 1¼" **$10.00**
Survival, Golden Eagle, Tom Smith, 1984-85, molded-in mark Wade England around base, 1¾" **$12.00**
Survival, Green Turtle, Tom Smith, 1984-85, molded-in mark Wade England around base, 1¼" **$12.00**
Survival, North American Bison, Tom Smith, 1984-85, molded-in mark Wade England around base, 1⅛" **$5.00**
Survival, Polar Bear, Tom Smith, 1984-85, molded-in mark Wade England around base, 1" **$12.00**
Whimsie, Alligator, Canadian Red Rose Tea, 1967-73, molded-in mark, ½x1 1½" **$7.00**
Whimsie, Butterfly, Canadian Red Rose Tea Promotion, 1967-73, multicolored, full-flight pose, ½x1x1¾" wingspan **$7.00**

Whimsie, Camel, USA Red Rose Tea, 1985-86, single glaze, 1⅜" **$4.00**

Whimsie, Frog, Canadian Red Rose Tea, 1967-73, green & yellow, marked Wade England, ⅞x1⅛" **$7.00**

Whimsie, Giraffe, USA Red Rose Tea, 1985-86, single glaze, 1½" **$4.00**

Whimsie, Gorilla, USA Red Rose Tea, 1985-86, single glaze, 1½" **$4.00**

Whimsie, Pine Marten, USA Red Rose Tea, 1985-86, single glaze, 1⅜" **$4.00**

Whimsie, Poodle, Canadian Red Rose Tea, 1967-73, white standard, molded-in mark, 1⅝x1⅝" **$7.00**

Whimsie, Seal, USA Red Rose Tea, 1983-85, single glaze, 1½x1¼" **$5.00**

Whimsie, Terrapin, Canadian Red Rose Tea Promotion, 1967-73, molded-in mark, ⅜x1⅝" **$7.00**

Whimsie, Turtle, USA Red Rose Tea, 1983-1985, single glaze, 1⅞" long **$5.00**

Whimsie, Wild Boar, USA Red Rose Tea, 1983-85, single glaze, 1⅛x1" **$5.00**

Whoppas, Bison, Canadian Red Rose Tea, 1981, 1¾x2¼" ..**$15.00**

Whoppas, Bobcat, Canadian Red Rose Tea, 1981, 1½x1⅞", from $20 to...**$25.00**

Whoppas, Brown Bear, Canadian Red Rose Tea, 1981, 1½x1¾", from $12 to..**$15.00**

Whoppas, Elephant, Canadian Red Rose Tea, 1981, 2⅛x2" ..**$20.00**

Whoppas, Hippo, Canadian Red Rose Tea, 1981, 1⅜x2¼" ...**$20.00**

Whoppas, Polar Bear, Canadian Red Rose Tea, 1981, 1½x2¼" **$20.00**

Wildlife, Fieldmouse, Tom Smith, 1980-81, molded-in mark Wade England around base, 1", from $10 to........**$12.00**

Wildlife, Partridge, Tom Smith, 1980-81, molded-in Wade England around base, 1⅛", from $10 to **$12.00**

Wildlife, Weasel, Tom Smith, 1980-81, molded-in mark Wade England around base, 1⅜", from $10 to **$12.00**

Wall Pockets

A few years ago there were only a handful of really avid wall pocket collectors, but today many are finding them intriguing. They were popular well before the turn of the century. Roseville and Weller included at least one and sometimes several in many of their successful lines of art pottery, and other American potteries made them as well. Many were imported from Germany, Czechoslovakia, China, and Japan. By the 1950s, they were passé.

Some of the most popular today are the figurals. Look for the more imaginative and buy the ones you like — these are light-hearted collectibles! If you're buying to resell, look for those designed around animals, large exotic birds, children, lucious fruits, or those that are especially eye-catching. Appeal is everything. For more information, refer to *Collector's Guide to Wall Pockets, Affordable and Others,* by Marvin and Joy Gibson; *Wall Pockets of the Past* by Fredda Perkins; and *Collector's Encyclopedia of Wall Pockets* by Betty and Bill Newbound.

Apron, white pinafore-type w/red trim & flower at waist w/green leaves, marked Conrad, 5½"....................**$15.00**

Basket, brown w/yellow band of multicolored fruit & flowers w/green leaves, bamboo handle, Japan, 8".........**$30.00**

Bird on tree trunk, yellow breasted w/blue head & rose accents, blue tree trunk w/rose-colored flowers, Japan, 6¼"...**$25.00**

Bird on tree trunk, yellow head & wings w/red tail & green breast on white tree trunk w/flowers, gold trim, Japan, 8"...**$25.00**

Coffeepot, white w/3 applied red cherries w/green leaves & thin-painted on branches, unmarked, 6"..............**$15.00**

Creamer & sugar bowl, conjoined, white w/multicolored free-hand flower & leaf design, brown-sponged handle & rims, 8"...**$15.00**

Duck in flight, frontal view appearing to swoop out of sky, black, gray & yellow, molded-feather detail, Japan, 7"...**$45.00**

Duck in flight, side view w/wings down, airbrushed colors w/white neck band, gold bill, unmarked, 8¼" **$20.00**

Dutch girl carrying lg green lustre basket over her shoulder, Japan, 5½"...**$35.00**

Elf on front of bucket, green w/pink skin tone, Treasure Craft, 5½"...**$15.00**

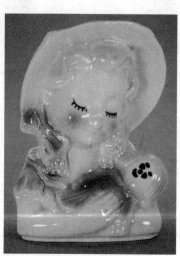

Girl holding doll, marked USA 810, 6", from $35.00 to $40.00.

Glamour girl, head turned to 1 shoulder, eyes closed, white w/airbrushed shoulder & hair flower, gold trim, USA.........**$22.00**

Iron, white w/green leaves & brown scrolled detail around base, green zigzag design w/brown trim on handle, 6"......**$14.00**

Japanese man w/basket on back, multicolored costume, Japan, 8" **$75.00**

Macaw, black & yellow w/orange beak, yellow grapes w/green leaves, lustre finish, Japan, 5½".............**$30.00**

Oil lamp, w/chimny & single-handled base, green w/gold accents, unmarked, 7½" **$20.00**

Parakeet pair perched on branch, airbrushed colors, unmarked, 7¼"...**$15.00**

Parrot on a perch, side view w/black & yellow head looking down, yellow breast w/orange, green & brown wings, Japan, 9" **$40.00**

Parrot w/grape cluster, leaves fanned out behind yellow bird w/aqua & rose accents, deep blue grapes, unmarked, 8½"...**$30.00**

Peacock, white w/multicolored accents on tan lustre tree trunk, Japan, 6" **$30.00**

Rolling pin, horizontal w/double openings, white w/green accents, unmarked, 11½" **$12.00**

Siamese cat w/brown fish atop yellow creel w/brown trim, 5½" **$20.00**

Swan & cattails, red & blue w/green leaves embossed on V-shaped vase, Japan, 6½" **$20.00**

Tulips, muted yellow & red tones, tied together w/blue bow, Japan, 7" **$25.00**

Parrot and flowers, 7½" dia, $24.00.

Watt Pottery

The Watt Pottery Company operated in Crooksville, Ohio, from 1922 until sometime in 1935. The ware they produced is easily recognized and widely available today. It appeals to collectors of country antiques, since the body is yellow ware and its decoration simple.

Several patterns were made: Apple, Autumn Foliage, Cherry, Dutch Tulip, Morning-Glory, Pansy, Rooster, Tear Drop, Starflower, and Tulip among them. All were executed in bold brush strokes of primary colors. Some items you'll find will also carry a stenciled advertising message, made for retail companies as premiums for their customers.

For further study, we recommend *Watt Pottery, An Identification and Price Guide* by our advisors, Sue and Dave Morris

Advisors: Sue and Dave Morris (See Directory, Watt Pottery)

Apple, baker, lg handle, w/lid, #96 ....**$125.00**
Apple, bowl, cereal; #52 or #94, each **$35.00**
Apple, bowl, mixing; ribbed, #6, #7 or #8, each **$45.00**
Apple, bowl, mixing; ribbed, #9 ....**$55.00**
Apple, bowl, ribbed, #602, #603 or #604, each **$45.00**
Apple, bowl, ribbed, w/lid, #600 ....**$125.00**
Apple, bowl, spaghetti; #44, individual **$100.00**
Apple, casserole, tab handled, #18, individual **$200.00**
Apple, creamer, #62 ....**$75.00**
Apple, divided plate **$800.00**
Apple, Dutch oven casserole, #73 ....**$200.00**
Apple, French casserole, stick handle, #18 ......**$225.00**

Apple, ice bucket...**$225.00**
Apple, mug, #121, each **$175.00**
Apple, mug, #501 ....**$225.00**
Apple, pie plate, #33 ....**$150.00**

Apple, pitcher, #17, ice lip, 8", $225.00; Mug, #701, $200.00.

Apple, plate, dinner; 9½" **$400.00**
Apple, platter, #49, 12" **$275.00**
Apple, salt & pepper shakers, barrel shape, pr **$245.00**
Apple, salt & pepper shakers, hourglass shape w/raised S&P letters, pr **$225.00**
Apple (Double), bowl, #73 ....**$85.00**
Apple (Double), bowl, mixing; #5 or #6, each **$75.00**
Apple (reduced decoration), bowl, mixing.................**$65.00**
Autumn Foliage, bowl, #73 ....**$45.00**
Autumn Foliage, bowl, cereal; #94 ....**$25.00**
Autumn Foliage, creamer, 362 ....**$55.00**
Autumn Foliage, mug, #121 ....**$175.00**
Autumn Foliage, pitcher, #16 ....**$70.00**
Banded, (Blue & White or Green & White), bowl, mixing; various sizes, each **$25.00**
Banded (Blue & White), pitcher.........................**$45.00**
Banded (Brown), sugar bowl, w/lid **$150.00**
Banded (Brown), teapot, #112 ....**$375.00**
Banded (Light Blue & White), cookie jar **$65.00**
Banded (Light Blue & White), pitcher **$45.00**
Banded (White), pitcher....................................**$45.00**
Basketweave (Brown), bean pot, handles.................**$50.00**
Basketweave (Brown), mug, #801 or #806, each......**$10.00**
Basketweave (multicolored), bowl, varied sizes, each .**$25.00**
Brown Glaze, bean pot **$25.00**
Brown Glaze, electric warmer **$125.00**
Cherry, bowl, cereal; #23 ....**$35.00**
Cherry, bowl, spaghetti; #39 ....**$100.00**
Cherry, pitcher, #15 ....**$65.00**
Cherry, pitcher, #17 ....**$125.00**
Cherry, platter, #31 ....**$145.00**
Cherry Berry, bowl, #4 ....**$25.00**
Daisy (White), casserole, stick handle, individual **$125.00**
Daisy (White), cup & saucer **$75.00**
Daisy (White), plate, salad **$65.00**
Dogwood, platter...**$55.00**
Dutch Tulip, bowl, #6, #7 or #8, each **$70.00**

Dutch Tulip, bowl, mixing; #63.........................$65.00
Dutch Tulip, bowl, w/lid, #67..........................$175.00
Dutch Tulip, creamer, #62..............................$95.00
Dutch Tulip, French casserole, stick handle, w/lid, #18, individual...$245.00

Dutch Tulip, pitcher, #15, $95.00.

Dutch Tulip, pitcher, #16 ....$125.00
Eagle, bowl, cereal $55.00
Eagle, bowl, mixing; #6, #7 or #8, each $65.00
Esmond, bean pot, handles $135.00
Esmond, pitcher, shaded black to brown, ice lip $95.00
Esmond, platter...$125.00
Kathy Kale, bowl, oval serving..........................$45.00
Kitch-N-Queen, bowl, mixing; ribbed, #5-#9, each....$30.00
Kitch-N-Queen, salt & pepper shakers, hourglass shape, pr $135.00
Kla Ham'rd, pitcher $55.00
Kla Ham'rd, stacking refrigerator jar $55.00
Morning Glory, cookie jar, #95.........................$275.00
Morning Glory, creamer, #97 ....$100.00
Morning Glory, pitcher, ice lip, #96 ....$300.00
Pansy (Cut-Leaf w/Bull's Eye), bowl, serving; 15"......$80.00
Pansy (Cut-Leaf), bowl, mixing; each $35.00
Pansy (Cut-Leaf), bowl, serving; individual $25.00
Pansy (Cut-leaf), casserole, stick handle, individual.$125.00

Pansy (Cut-Leaf), cup and saucer, #612, $225.00.

Pansy (Cut-Leaf), creamer & sugar bowl $100.00
Pansy (Old), casserole, w/lid...........................$55.00

Pansy (Old), pitcher, #15 ....$55.00
Pansy (Old), pitcher, #17 ....$125.00
Pansy (Old), platter, #49 ....$100.00
Raised Pansy, pitcher $200.00
Rooster, bowl, #58 ....$90.00
Rooster, bowl, w/lid, #05 ....$135.00
Rooster, creamer, #62 ....$85.00
Rooster, ice bucket $185.00

Rooster, pitcher, #16, 6½", $150.00.

Rooster, refrigerator pitcher, #69 ....$275.00
Rooster, sugar bowl, w/lid, #98.........................$275.00
Shaded Brown, mug......................................$10.00
Shaded brown, pitcher $40.00
Speckled Ware, bowl, slad; #106 ....$25.00
Speckled Ware, vinegar & oil set $100.00
Starflower, bean pot, handles, #76 ....$90.00
Starflower, bowl, cereal; #74...........................$25.00
Starflower, bowl, mixing; #5 ....$55.00
Starflower, bowl, mixing; #6, #7 or #8, each.............$35.00
Starflower, creamer, #62................................$75.00
Starflower, grease jar, #47 ....$175.00
Starflower, ice bucket..................................$185.00
Starflower, mug, #121 ....$195.00
Starflower, pie plate, #33 ....$125.00
Starflower, pitcher, #15................................$45.00
Starflower, platter, #31................................$140.00
Starflower, salt & pepper shakers, barrel shape, pr.$160.00
Starflower (Green on Brown), bowl, spaghetti; #39...$90.00
Starflower (Green on Brown), platter, #31 ....$110.00
Starflower (Green on Brown), tumbler....................$150.00
Starflower (Pink on Black), cup & saucer $85.00
Starflower (Pink on Black), sugar bowl..................$75.00
Starflower (Pink on Green), casserole, stick handle, individual $125.00
Starflower (Pink on Green), casserole, w/lid $125.00
Starflower (Pink on Green), cup & saucer $65.00
Starflower (White on Blue), bowl, spaghetti; #39.....$175.00
Starflower (White on Red), mug, #121 ....$225.00
Tear Drop, bowl, mixing; #6.............................$40.00
Tear Drop, cheese crock, #80...........................$275.00
Tear Drop, creamer $75.00
Tear Drop, French casserole, w/lid, #18, individual ..$200.00

Tear Drop, pitcher, #16 ....**$75.00**
Tulip, bowl, mixing; #600 or #601, each **$85.00**
Tulip, bowl, mixing; #63 ....**$60.00**
Tulip, bowl, ribbed, w/lid, #600 ....**$200.00**
Tulip, cookie jar, #503 ....**$300.00**
Tulip, creamer, #62 ....**$95.00**
Tulip, pitcher, #15 ....**$225.00**
Tulip, pitcher, ice lip, #17 ....**$300.00**

Weeping Gold

In the mid- to late 1950s, many American pottery companies produced lines of 'Weeping Gold.' Such items have a distinctive look and appear to be covered with irregular droplets of lustrous gold. In fact, real gold was used; however, there is no known successful way of separating the gold from the pottery. You'll see similar pottery covered in 'Weeping Silver.' Very often, ceramic whiskey decanters made for Beam, McCormick, etc., will be trimmed in 'Weeping Gold.' Among the marks you'll find on these wares are 'McCoy,' 'Kingwood Ceramics,' and 'USA,' but most items are simply stamped '22k (or 24k) gold.'

Apple wall pocket, marked 24k gold, USA, 5", $20.00.

Basket, Dixon Art Studios 22k gold, 8½x5" **$25.00**
Bowl, flattened ball form, footed, Swetye Salem O, 3x5½" .**$9.00**
Bowl, leaf shape w/scalloped inverted rim, stem handle, 24k gold, Made in USA, 9¾x4¾" **$9.00**
Figurine, rooster, well detailed, lg **$28.00**
Planter/vase, lobed oval, swirls in gold, 3x10½x4¾" .**$10.00**

Teapot, marked McCoy, circa 1957, $65.00.

Tidbit tray, 2-tier **$20.00**
Tray, elongated diamond shape w/triangular handles, inverted rim, Savoy Fine China 24k gold, 11" long **$9.00**

Vase, pleated fan form, 10-point rim, chevron design in gold, footed, 7x7" **$15.00**
Vase, scalloped fan form, 3 low angled handles each side, footed, Antique Reproduction, 22k gold #903, 6½" **$10.00**
Vase, scalloped square, 22k gold, 3x4½" **$6.00**

Weil Ware

Though the Weil company made dinnerware and some kitchenware, their figural pieces are attracting the most collector interest. They were in business from the 1940s until the mid-fifties, another of the small but very successful California companies whose work has become so popular today. They dressed their 'girls' in beautiful gowns of vivid rose, light dusty pink, turquoise blue and other lovely colors enhanced with enameled 'lacework' and flowers, sgraffito, sometimes even with tiny applied blossoms. Both paper labels and ink stamps were used to mark them, but as you study their features, you'll soon learn to recognize even those that have lost their labels over the years. Four-number codes and decorators' initials are usually written on their bases.

If you want to learn more, we recommend *The Collector's Encyclopedia of California Pottery* by Jack Chipman.

Advisors: Pat and Kris Secor (See Directory, California Pottery)

Ashtray, Bamboo, 5" **$7.50**
Bottle, violin shape, 9" **$28.00**
Bowl, cream soup; Rose **$6.00**
Bowl, salad; Rose, sm **$4.00**
Bowl, shell form, pink w/pale green interior.............**$12.00**
Butter dish, Rose **$13.50**
Cigarette box & ashtray, Ming Tree............................**$36.00**
Coffeepot, Bamboo, w/lid...**$75.00**
Cup & saucer, Rose **$6.00**
Dish, Dogwood, divided, square, 10½" **$15.00**
Figurine, boy w/wheelbarrow, #4005 ....**$45.00**
Figurine, Buddy, boy, 7" **$15.00**
Figurine, girl, lifted chin, sgraffito floral on skirt, lg ...**$50.00**
Figurine, girl in blue gown w/pink shawl, 10½" **$45.00**
Figurine, girl in loose dress, hands to hair, vase behind, 11".**$42.00**
Figurine, girl seated on square planter well holds guitar, 6".**$42.00**
Figurine, sailor boy w/flowers before white vase, 10¾" ...**$40.00**
Plate, Bamboo, 10" **$10.00**
Plate, Rose, 10" **$17.50**
Platter, Blossom, 13" **$22.00**

Vase, lady with two vases, 11½", $50.00.

Vase, Ming Tree, green & white, 10"............................$60.00
Vase, Ming Tree, w/coralene, 8½"...............................$40.00
Wall pocket, lady's head w/fan, hand-painted flowers, 8"..$50.00
Wall pocket, Oriental girl...$40.00

Weller

Though the Weller Pottery has been closed since 1948, they were so prolific that you'll be sure to see several pieces anytime you're 'antiquing.' They were one of the largest of the art pottery giants that located in the Zanesville, Ohio, area, using locally dug clays to produce their wares. In the early years, they made hand-decorated vases, jardinieres, lamps, and other decorative items for the home, many of which were signed by notable artists such as Fredrick Rhead, John Lessell, Virginia Adams, Anthony Dunlavy, Dorothy England, Albert Haubrich, Hester Pillsbury, E.L. Pickens, and Jacques Sicard, to name only a few. Some of their early lines were First and Second Dickens, Eocean, Sicardo, Etna, Louwelsa, Turada, and Aurelian. Portraits of Indians, animals of all types, lady golfers, nudes, and scenes of Dickens stories were popular themes, and some items were overlaid with silver filigree. These lines are rather hard to find at this point in time, and prices are generally high; but there's plenty of their later production still around, and most pieces are relatively inexpensive.

If you'd like to learn more, we recommend *The Collector's Encyclopedia of Weller Pottery* by Sharon and Bob Huxford.

Alvin, double bud vase, 2 tree-trunk forms connected by branches w/fruit, no mark, 6"................................$55.00
Alvin, vase, tree-trunk form w/embossed leaves, no mark, 8½"...$75.00
Arcadia, fan vase, lg leaves form bowl, blue, in-mold script mark, 8x15"...$60.00

Arcadia, vase, #A-11, green, 8½", $60.00.

Ardsley, bud vase, embossed cattails & leaves on trumpet-shaped vase w/white flowers at base, ink stamp, 7½"..$75.00
Ardsley, corner vase, 3-footed w/embossed iris decor at corners, paper label & ink stamp, 7"..................$125.00
Atlas, bowl, #C-3, round w/star-shaped rim, flat bottom, cream, in-mold script mark, 4".....................$45.00
Atlas, candlesticks, #C-12, blue star shapes w/cream trim, no mark, pr...$50.00

Baldin, bowl, embossed ivory apple decor on blue ground, no mark, 4"...$225.00
Baldin, vase, long plain neck w/embossed apple decor on low bulbous body, no mark, 7"........................$50.00
Barcelona, ewer, bulbous body, painted floral medallion on amber, ink stamp, 9½"....................................$225.00
Barcelona, vase, tumbler form w/lipped rim, painted floral design on amber, hand marked, 7"..................$150.00
Blossom, double cornucopias, blue w/embossed white floral spray, in-mold script mark, 6½"...................$40.00
Blossom, vase, bulbous w/trumpet neck & intricate handles, blue w/white embossed flower & branch decor, marked, 9½"..$100.00
Blue Drapery, bowl, pink rose decor on deep blue 'drapery' background, no mark, 3"...............................$40.00
Blue Drapery, fan vase, pink rose decor on deep blue 'drapery' background, no mark, 4"...........................$35.00
Blue Ware, jardiniere, footed, dancing classical figures & trees, no mark, 8½"......................................$275.00
Blue Ware, vase, tumbler shape w/high-stepping classical figure holding grape cluster, sm die-impressed mark, 8½"..$250.00
Bonito, bowl, free-hand floral design on ivory, marked & initialed CF, 3½"...$135.00
Bonito, vase, footed heart shape w/scrolled handles, free-hand floral design on ivory, marked, 5"............$125.00
Bouquet, pitcher, #B-18, blue w/embossed jonquil & leaf decor, in-mold mark, 9½".............................$80.00
Bouquet, vase, #B-15, handled teardrop form w/wavy rim, dogwood decor, in-mold script mark, 5"........$30.00
Bouquet, vase, #B-3, bowl shape w/incurvate scalloped rim, green w/white floral decor, in-mold mark, 4½"...$30.00
Breton, bowl, floral band on incurvate rim, reddish tan, hand marked, 4"...$85.00
Breton, vase, bulbous w/thick rim, embossed floral band on reddish tan, no mark, 7".............................$65.00
Cactus, figurine, duck, turquoise, hand marked, 4½"..$110.00
Cactus, figurine, resting camel, brown, hand marked, 4".$100.00
Cameo, basket, green footed ball shape w/embossed white floral design, fancy handle, in-mold script mark, 7½".........$45.00
Candis, ewer, white w/embossed floral decor, in-mold script, 11"..$70.00
Candis, vase, white floral panels alternating w/aqua stepped panels, in-mold script, 11".............................$70.00
Classic, plate, cut-out scalloped design around rim, white, paper label & in-mold script mark, 4"..............$70.00
Classic, wall pocket, fan shape w/cut-out scalloped design around rim, paper label & in-mold script mark, 6"..$125.00
Claywood, spittoon, incised floral design on panels, no mark, 4½"..$150.00
Claywood, vase, bulbous w/incised floral design on panels, no mark, 3½"...$65.00
Claywood, vase, cylindrical incised floral design on panels, no mark, 8½"...$90.00
Cornish, bowl, footed w/incurvate rim, scrolled handles, berry & leaf design w/ribbed band on cream & brown, marked, 4"..$35.00
Cornish, jardiniere, blue w/incised & embossed berry & leaf design on ribbed band, scrolled handles, in-mold script, 7"..$30.00

Creamware, bowl, straight-sided & footed w/horizontal handles, dark blue cameo decor, no mark, 2½" **$40.00**

Darsie, flowerpot, ivory w/embossed swag & tassel design at scalloped rim, in-mold script mark, 9½"...............**$65.00**

Darsie, vase, embossed swag & tassel design on turquoise footed ovoid, flared rim, in-mold script mark, 9½"........**$65.00**

Delsa, basket, footed w/ribbon-&-bow-form handle, green w/embossed pastel flower & leaf decor, marked, 7".**$50.00**

Delsa, ewer, #10, blue w/blue, yellow & pink flower & green leaf decor on textured ground, marked, 7" **$30.00**

Dupont, bowl, straight-sided, ivory w/pink potted flower & swag decor on grid panels, 3"......................**$50.00**

Dupont, planter, square, ivory w/doves & flower tree on grid panels, die-impressed mark, 5"..............................**$60.00**

Elberta, cornucopia, shades of brown & amber, hand marked, 8" **$45.00**

Elberta, 3-part bowl, shades of amber & green, hand marked, 3½"..**$50.00**

Ethel, Creamware, fan vase, die-impressed mark, 6"..**$55.00**

Evergreen, console bowl, footed w/flared scalloped rim, die-impressed mark, 5" **$65.00**

Evergreen, planter, pelican, $80.00.

Evergreen, triple candle holder, fluted cups staggered on scrolled base, in-mold script mark, 7½" **$75.00**

Fairfield, bowl, green & brown w/band of embossed cherubs, no mark, 4½"..**$90.00**

Flemish, comport, ivory bowl w/pink rose finial on lid, rose decor around pedestal base, die-impressed mark, 8½" **$175.00**

Flemish, jardiniere, stemmed 3-leaf decor over floral band on light brown wash, die-impressed mark, 7½"......**$125.00**

Florala, console bowl, multicolored floral band on ivory, no mark, 11" **$75.00**

Florala, wall pocket, multicolored floral decor on ivory panels, die-impressed mark, 10"................................**$150.00**

Florenzo, basket, fan shape w/fluted rim, embossed rose decor on handle & down sides, ivory & green, marked, 5½" **$100.00**

Forest, basket, embossed, die-impressed mark, 8½" ..**$225.00**

Forest, tub planter, handled, embossed, no mark, 4".**$100.00**

Fruitone, bud vase, bulbous body w/long tapered neck, reddish brown, die-impressed mark, 11½" **$85.00**

Fruitone, vase, ovoid shape w/short neck & lipped rim, dark brown to amber, no mark, 6" **$75.00**

Glendale, double bud vase, unmarked, 7", $275.00.

Gloria, ewer, tan w/embossed blue & white floral & branch decor, in-mold script mark, 9" **$50.00**

Ivoris, footed w/deeply scalloped rim, floral design at end of handles, ivory, hand marked, 5"...........................**$50.00**

Ivoris, ginger jar, tab handles, etched berry & leaf design, hand marked, 8½" **$75.00**

Ivoris, vase, flared rim on plain ivory bulbous shape w/fancy cut-out & scrolled handles, hand marked, 6".......**$35.00**

Ivory (Clinton Ivory), jardiniere, bowl shape, decorated w/squirrels in tree, no mark, 6½".....................**$150.00**

Ivory (Clinton Ivory), vase, cylindrical, oak-leaf design on vertical panels, die stamp, 10".........................**$95.00**

Klyro, candlestick, brown footed pyramid w/pink & blue floral & berry design, cut-out arched bars at base, 9½ "...**$65.00**

Klyro, planter, 4 footed fence-like panels w/cut-out vertical bars & an embossed floral swag on each side, die stamp, 4"...**$60.00**

Knifewood, bowl, white embossed daisy pattern on brown, die-impressed mark, 3"..**$100.00**

Knifewood, vase, cylinder flared & lipped at top & bottom w/embossed peacock design, die-impressed mark, 9" **$225.00**

Loru, bowl, footed round shape w/fluted rim, deep red w/embossed leaf decor around base, in-mold script mark, 4" **$40.00**

Loru, vase, footed cylinder w/slightly flared & fluted rim, green w/brown shading around base, in-mold script mark, 10" **$45.00**

Malverne, boat bowl, bud & leaf decor on textured drab green & yellow ground, stem handles, half-kiln ink stamp, 11"...**$80.00**

Malverne, vase, bulbous body, neck w/plain rim, embossed bud & leaf decor on textured ground, hand marked, 5½".**$50.00**

Manhattan, pitcher, green cylinder w/curved handle at plain rim, embossed dark green flower & leaf decor, marked, 10" **$100.00**

Manhattan, vase, cylinder tapering to footed base, plain rim, green w/embossed vertical leaf decor, hand marked, 9" **$85.00**

Marbleized, bowl, brown, tan & ivory swirls, die-impressed mark, 1½x5½".................................**$45.00**

Marbleized, comport, w/thick pedestal base, med brown swirl, sm die-impressed mark, 8" **$110.00**

Marbleized, vase, trumpet shape w/dark brown & ivory swirls, hand marked, 7½" **$100.00**

Marvo, hanging basket, bowl w/rounded bottom & lipped rim, green w/allover embossed floral & leaf design, ink stamp, 5"...**$150.00**

Marvo, vase, cylindrical w/allover embossed floral & leaf design, green, ink stamp, 8½" **$75.00**

Melrose, basket, w/embossed grape & rose design, die-impressed mark, 10"..**$175.00**

Melrose, vase, taupe cylinder w/ruffled rim & swirl marks, embossed apples & applied branches, die-impressed mark, 7" **$160.00**

Mirror Black, bud vase, trumpet shape, no mark, 5½"..**$40.00**

Mirror Black, strawberry jar, no mark, 6½" **$85.00**

Montego, vase, ovoid w/closed handles, reddish brown w/aqua drip at rim & handles, ink stamp, 5".......**$50.00**

Muskota, bowl w/goose, die-impressed mark, 4½"..**$325.00**

Muskota, flower frog, frog on lily pad, 4½"............**$230.00**

Muskota, gate w/2 flowerpots & 2 cats, die-impressed mark, 7"..**$550.00**

Noval, bowl, white w/black fluting, applied multicolored fruit handles, no mark, 3½x9½" **$75.00**

Noval, vase, white ball shape w/trumpet neck, black rim, bottom & handles, red rose decor (no leaves) around middle, 6" **$65.00**

Oak Leaf, basket, #G-1, ball shaped w/twig handle, deep tan w/embossed acorn & leaf decor, in-mold script mark, 7½"...**$100.00**

Oak Leaf, ewer, green w/embossed oak leaf decor, in-mold script mark, 14"...**$125.00**

Panella, bowl, 3-footed w/incurvate rim, tan & peach w/embossed yellow & green flower & leaf decor, 3½".....................**$25.00**

Panella, cornucopia, gray & green w/embossed yellow & green flower & leaf decor, marked, 5½"...............**$20.00**

Paragon, bowl, allover etched design on blue ball shape, lipped rim, in-mold script mark, 4½"....................**$55.00**

Paragon, vase, allover floral on tan ovoid, footed, in-mold script mark, 7½"......................................**$85.00**

Parian, vase, trumpet shape w/geometric diamond-shaped floral design, no mark, 13"...................................**$175.00**

Pastel, candlestick, hole in domed base w/scalloped edge, peach, no mark, 1½"......................................**$20.00**

Pastel, circle vase, pale aqua w/embossed decor, in-mold script mark, 6" **$45.00**

Patra, basket, footed, light brown textured ground w/etched green rim, stylized floral handle, hand marked, 5½"............**$125.00**

Patra, bowl, #3, 3-footed w/green indented rim, stylized floral design on light brown textured ground, hand marked, 3"..**$65.00**

Patricia, bowl, squatty round shape w/4 duck heads adorning rim, ivory, in-mold script mark, 3"...................**$40.00**

Patricia, planter, ivory pelican form, in-mold script mark, 5" **$90.00**

Pearl, bud vase, cylindrical, ivory w/embossed swagged pearl & rose design, die-impressed mark, 7"........**$50.00**

Pumila, bowl, water-lily form on pad, shades of green w/golden tan interior, foil label, 4" **$35.00**

Pumila, console plate, layered lily pads as edge w/flower in center, brown w/golden undertones, no mark, 3x12"..**$50.00**

Raydance, vase, footed bulbous shape w/flared neck, scrolled handles, yellow w/embossed vining leaf design, marked, 8" **$35.00**

Roba, cornucopia, light & dark tan w/embossed white flower & branch decor, in-mold script mark, 5½" **$35.00**

Roba, ewer, embossed flower & branch decor on white w/green shading, in-mold script mark, 11" **$135.00**

Roba, vase, #R-20, 13", $150.00.

Roma, ashtray, bowl shape w/4 rests, ivory w/green & pink floral band above vertical ribs, no mark, 2½".................**$60.00**

Roma, bowl, 4-footed w/twig handles, ivory w/band of pink rose & green leaf decor, die-impressed mark, 3" **$80.00**

Roma, bud vase, 4-sided w/4-sided base, lipped rim, ivory w/colorful scrolled grape decor, no mark, 6½" ...**$50.00**

Roma, triple candlestick, ivory w/vertical green leaf & pink floral decor, no mark, 9" **$175.00**

Rudlor, console bowl, footed boat shape w/4-bead handles, white w/embossed flower & branch decor, marked, 17½"..**$50.00**

Sabrinian, bud vase, twisted vertical shell w/flared, 7"..**$100.00**

Silvertone, double bud vase, embossed floral decor w/brown twig handle, kiln stamp, 6"..................................**$150.00**

Silvertone, fan basket, embossed grape decor w/twig handle, ink stamp, 13" **$300.00**

Softone, candlestick, draped linear design on cup w/disk base, pink, hand marked, 2½"..............................**$25.00**

Sydonia, cornucopia, mottled green, hand marked, 8"..**$60.00**

Sydonia, double candlestick w/bud vase, 2 fluted cups & cone-shaped vase on scrolled base, blue, hand marked, 11½"..**$135.00**

Tivoli, vase, ivory trumpet shape w/black rim on black footed base w/multicolored floral band, die-impressed mark, 6"..**$75.00**

Tutone, candlesticks, green & gold 3-footed triangles w/flower & berry decor, half-kiln ink stamp, 2½", pr...........**$125.00**

Tutone, planter, 5½", $65.00.

Tutone, vase, 3-footed bulbous shape, embossed arrowhead leaf & flower decor, red w/green shading at base, ink stamp, 4"..$45.00

Velva, bowl, reddish brown w/leaf & berry design on center panel, tab handles, footed, hand marked, 3½x12½"..$65.00

Velva, vase, footed ovoid shape w/tab handles & lipped rim, green w/floral design on center vertical panel, 6"...$50.00

Voile, fan vase, embossed apple-tree decor, handled, no mark, 7"..$45.00

Voile, jardiniere, scalloped rim, footed, embossed multicolored apple-tree decor on ivory, no mark, 6"........$75.00

Warwick, jardiniere, bud & branch decor on brown textured ground, half-kiln ink stamp, 7"............................$150.00

Warwick, pillow vase, footed, bud & branch decor on brown textured ground w/branch handles, half-kiln ink stamp, 4½"...$60.00

Wild Rose, vase, footed cone shape w/scalloped tab handles, green w/embossed white flower & branch decor, marked, 7½"..$30.00

Woodcraft, ashtray, tree stump form w/leaf decor, no mark, 3"...$90.00

Woodcraft, basket, acorn form w/twig handle, die-impressed mark, 9½"...$250.00

Woodcraft, bowl, 4-footed wood-look w/cut-out branch design, die-impressed mark, 3½"........................$90.00

Woodcraft, bud vase, brown tree trunk w/limbs turned down as handles, apple decor, no mark, 6½".................$50.00

Woodcraft, fan vase, apple-tree decor, no mark, 7"....$50.00

Woodcraft, hanging basket, trumpet shape w/berry decor, fluted rim, no mark, 6"...$125.00

Woodrose, jardiniere, brown oaken bucket w/handles & black bands, embossed rose design, die-impressed mark, 3½"...$60.00

Woodrose, wall pocket, white fan-shaped oaken bucket w/embossed yellow rose & leaf design, no mark, 6"...$120.00

Zona, bowl, ivory w/embossed brown rabbit & blue bird decor, in-mold mark, 5½"..$40.00

Zona, comport, lg incised flower design repeated around bowl on green textured ground, plain ivory pedestal base, 5½"..$70.00

Western Collectibles

Although the Wild West era ended over one hundred years ago, today cowboy gear is a hot area of collecting. Prices have soared over the last five years, and the market is growing steadily stronger. Evidence of this is the seventy-five plus shows and auctions specializing in this field that are held annually across the nation.

These historic collectibles are not just found out West. Some of the most exceptional pieces have come from the East Coast states and the Midwest. But that should come as no surprise when you consider the that the largest manufacturer of bits and spurs was the August Buemann Co. of Newark, NJ (1868–1926).

Until now, the only thing lacking in this growing market was a good reference to identify and evaluate these treasures. That gap has been filled with the publication of *Old West Cowboy Collectibles Auction Update and Price Guide*, which lists auction-realized prices of more than 650 lots, with complete descriptions and numerous photos. You can obtain a copy from our advisor, Dan Hutchins.

Advisor: Dan Hutchins (See Directory, Western Collectibles)

Bit, half-bred; lg sterling silver conchos, fancy-style cheeks & slobber bars, ca 1940s...$550.00

Bit, spade; att Eduardo Grigalva, high spade, silver inlay, snake pattern, ca 1930s...$175.00

Bit, spade; Garcia Saddlery, silver-inlaid stars, ca 1935...$400.00

Bit, space; Wall Walla WA prison-made, spoonless, 1930s..$400.00

Book, *Young Cowboy,* by Will James, 2nd edition, 1936..$95.00

Boots, child's; black leather w/white overlay & blue inlay, ca 1940s, 6x6"...$185.00

Branding irons, early, set of 3.....................................$210.00

Calendar, McCabe Silversmiths, print of Will Rogers, 1945..$325.00

Chaps, Al Funstnow, white wooly, exceptional condition...$1,200.00

Chaps, batwing style, ca 1930.....................................$100.00

Chaps, Hamley, batwing style, 2-color.......................$725.00

Chaps, HH Heiser, batwing style, plain......................$400.00

Chaps, shotgun style, fringed.....................................$375.00

Chaps, working, brass studded, #6 slotted conchos, 1935..$245.00

Cuffs, child's; nickel-studded star pattern, ca 1940s...$80.00

Cuffs, studded, Lone Star pattern, ca 1930s................$65.00

Hat, Stetson, 8" crown, 2" ribbon, 5" pencil roll band edge, includes box w/roundup scene, 1920s, M.......$1,700.00

Longhorns, ca 19th century, 67" long.......................$3,300.00

Saddle, child's; nickel-over-brass spots, 1940s..........$275.00

Saddle, Denver Dry Goods, Powder River trademark, Mother Hubbard style, minor splits on padded seat, 1930s.$770.00

Saddle, Edward H. Bohlin, pleasure type, very plain, ca 1940s...$1,000.00

Saddle, Nobby Harness Co, well tooled, silver mounted on corners of side-skirt jockeys & fenders, ca 1940........$3,500.00

Saddle, RT Frazier, good color w/floral tooling, original saddlebags & tapaderos, 1930s.............................$2,200.00

Saddlebags, leather, 3" eagle & snake conchos, ca 1960....$465.00

Satchel, floral-tooled leather, ca 1930s.....................$400.00

Scarf, Cheyenne Frontier Days 1938 rodeo, silk.........$95.00

Spurs, att Crockett, Eagle pattern, original leathers, minor pitting on back side, 1940s, pr..............................$385.00

Spurs, child's; early leathers, silver conchos, ca 1920s, pr.$770.00

Spurs, Don Ricardo, nickel silver w/horse heads, ca 1950, pr...$300.00

Spurs, double mounted, sterling w/Garcia's pattern #28, floral-tooled leathers, silver buckles & conchos, 1958, pr...$1,320.00

Spurs, Mexican, double-mounted silver, 1⅝" rowels, tooled straps & conchos, ca 1940s, pr............................$192.50
Spurs, Mexican, iron, very plain, pr............................$45.00
Spurs, Oscar Crockett, silver-overlaid iron, 2½" 21-point rowels, no leathers, ca 1940s, pr $550.00
Spurs, Oscar Crockett, stainless steel mounted w/silver star & quarter moon, unusual chap guard, ca 1940s, pr ..$600.00
Spurs, parade; Oscar Crockett, fully overlaid sterling silver, ca 1950, pr $675.00
Spurs, Spanish/Moorish style, ornate repros, ca 1930s, pr.$165.00

Westmoreland Glass

The Westmoreland Specialty Company was founded in 1889 in Grapeville, Pennsylvania. Their mainstay was a line of opalware (later called milk glass) which included such pieces as cream and sugar sets, novel tea jars (i.e., Teddy Roosevelt Bear Jar, Oriental Tea Jars, and Dutch Tea Jar), plus a number of covered animal dishes such as hens and roosters on nests. All of these pieces were made as condiment containers, which originally held baking soda and Westmoreland's own mustard recipe. By 1900 they had introduced a large variety of pressed tablewares in clear glass and opal, although their condiment containers were still very popular. By 1910 they were making a large line of opal souvenir novelties with hand-painted decorations of palm trees, Dutch scenes, etc. They also made a variety of decorative vases painted in the fashion of Rookwood Pottery, plus sprayed finishes with decorations of flowers, fruits, animals, and Indians. Westmoreland gained great popularity with their line of painted, hand-decorated wares, and they also made many fancy-cut items.

These lines continued in production until 1939, when the Brainard family became full owners of the factory. The Brainards discontinued the majority of patterns made previously under the West management and introduced dinnerware lines, primarily made of milk glass, with limited production of black glass and blue milk glass. Colored glass was not put back into full production until 1964 when Westmoreland introduced Golden Sunset, Avocado, Brandywine Blue and ruby glass.

The company made only limited quantities of carnival glass in the early 1900s and then re-introduced it in 1972 when most of their carnival glass was made in limited editions for the Levay Distributing Company. J.H. Brainard, president of Westmoreland, sold the factory to Dave Grossman in 1981, and he, in turn, closed the factory in 1984. Westmoreland first used the stamped W over G logo in 1949 and continued using it until Dave Grossman bought the factory. Mr. Grossman changed the logo to a W with the word Westmoreland forming a circle around the W.

Milk glass was always Westmoreland's main line of production and in the 1950s, they became famous for their milk glass tableware in the #1881 'Paneled Grape' pattern. It was designed in 1950 by Jess Billups, the company's mold maker. The first piece he made was the water goblet. Items were gradually added until a com-

plete dinner service was available. It became their most successful dinnerware, and today it is highly collectible, primarily because of the excellence of the milk glass itself. No other company has been able to match Westmoreland's milk glass in color, texture, quality, or execution of design and pattern.

For more information we recommend *Welcome Home, Westmoreland; Westmoreland Glass: Our Children's Heirlooms;* and *The Westmoreland Glass Collector's Kit,* all by our advisor Ruth Grizel, and *Westmorland Glass Identification and Value Guide* by Charles West Wilson.

Advisor: Ruth Grizel (See Directory, Westmoreland)

Club: Westmoreland Glass Society
Jim Fisher, President
513 5th Ave
Coralville, IA 52241; 319-354-5011

Newsletter: *The Original Westmoreland Glass Collector's Newsletter*
c/o Ruth Grizel, Editor
P.O. Box 205
Oakdale, IA 52319-0205

Animals and Birds

Bird, pipe holder, green mist, #10.............................$20.00
Bulldog, black, #75...$30.00
Bulldog, crystal mist, painted collar, rhinestone eyes, 2½" ...$35.00
Butterfly, green mist, #1, sm...................................$15.00
Butterfly, pink mist, #2, med $20.00
Cardinal, green mist, #11 ....$25.00
Cardinal, ruby, #11 ....$30.00
Lovebirds on nest, mint green, #20.........................$70.00
Owl, toothpick holder, milk glass, #62 ....$20.00
Owl, toothpick holder, purple marble, #62 ....$30.00
Owl, toothpick holder, white carnival, #62 ....$50.00
Owl on books, dark blue mist, #10 ....$25.00
Owl on books, electric blue carnival, #10, 1977, rare ..$38.00
Owl on books, light blue mist, #10..........................$20.00
Owl on books, pink carnival, #10.............................$20.00
Owl on books, purple marble, #10..........................$30.00
Pound Owl, mother-of-pearl, #1...............................$40.00
Robin, crystal, 3¼" long $20.00
Swan, raised wings, cobalt carnival, limited edition, made for Levay...$225.00
Swan on nest, milk glass, closed neck, 5½"...............$75.00
Wren, no perch, almond, #5....................................$20.00
Wren, no perch, soft mist blue, #5..........................$20.00
Wren on perch, green mist, #5................................$55.00

Covered Animal Dishes

Cat on rectangular lacy base, milk glass, #1 ....$125.00
Cat on ribbed base, milk glass, #18, 5"....................$35.00
Chick, salt dish, milk glass w/yellow paint, #3, 1" $24.00
Dog on wide-rib base, amber, Westmoreland Specialty Co, 5½"...$75.00

Dog on ribbed base, milk glass with blue body, Westmoreland Specialty, $65.00.

Duck on wavy base, blue opaque, #10 ....**$75.00**
Duck on wavy base, milk glass, #10 ....**$75.00**
Eagle mother, lacy base, milk glass..........................**$125.00**
Eagle mother on basket, milk glass, #21 ....**$100.00**
Fox on lacy base, milk glass, #1 ....**$150.00**
Hand & dove on lacy base, milk glass, #1 ....**$150.00**
Hen on basket, milk glass w/blue head, #2, Westmoreland
    Specialty Co, 5½" **$70.00**
Hen on nest, milk glass w/red trim, #4, 3"..................**$20.00**
Lovebirds on nest, almond, #20 ....**$65.00**
Lovebirds on nest, clear moss green, #20...................**$45.00**
Lovebirds on nest, crystal satin, #20 ....**$45.00**
Mule-eared rabbit, blue opaque, on picket-fence base, 5½".**$95.00**
Robin on pedestal base, marked WG **$60.00**
Robin on twig nest, antique blue, #7.........................**$65.00**
Robin on twig nest, milk glass, #7 ....**$50.00**
Rooster, blue opaque w/white head, #2, Westmoreland
    Specialty Co, 5½" **$85.00**
Rooster, milk glass, #2, Westmoreland Specialty Co, 5½"...**$65.00**
Rooster on basketweave base, milk glass, #1, 8" **$50.00**
Rooster on lacy base, milk glass, #1, 8"....................**$85.00**
Santa on sleigh, milk glass w/hand-painted details, #1872,
    5½" **$95.00**
Swan on rectangular lacy base, milk glass, #1873 ....**$150.00**

Turtle, Thousand Eye, clear, $45.00.

Lamps

Boudoir lamp, English Hobnail/#555, milk glass, stick type
    w/flat base...**$45.00**

**Candle mini lamp, frosted green shade
with flowers, milk glass base, 8", $48.00.**

Candle mini lamp, blue mist shade w/daisy decal, milk glass
    base, #1972, from $30 to **$35.00**
Candle mini lamp, brown mist w/floral bouquet shade,
    almond base, #1972.................................**$35.00**
Candle mini lamp, crystal mist w/Roses & Bows shade, milk
    glass base, #1972 ....**$55.00**
Candle mini lamp, crystal w/25th Anniversary decor on
    shade, crystal mist base, #1972....................**$25.00**
Candle mini lamp, green mist shade, milk glass base,
    #1972..**$20.00**
Candle mini lamp, ruby shade w/hand-painted rose, milk
    glass base, #1972 ....**$55.00**
Electric mini lamp, ruby w/ruby floral, #1976, 6½" **$95.00**
Fairy lamp, frosted shade w/pink flowers, milk glass base,
    #1972..**$35.00**

Fairy lamp, #1932, ruby stain on crystal, $65.00.

Votive candle holder, crystal mist w/flower decor, flat, #1976,
    2½" **$18.00**

Modern Giftware

Basket, purple slag, #750 ....**$50.00**
Bell, almond w/rose, fluted rim, #1902, 5"..................**$35.00**

Bell, crystal mist w/colored Christmas wreath, fluted rim, #1902 ....**$35.00**

Bell, crystal w/holly, fluted rim, #1902 ....**$25.00**

Bell, milk glass w/beaded bouquet, plain rim, #1902, 5"..**$30.00**

Bell, milk glass w/butterfly, ruffled rim, #1902, 5"......**$30.00**

Bell, milk glass w/strawberries, plain rim, #1902, 5"..**$30.00**

Bell, ruby w/floral, ruffled rim, #1902, 5" **$45.00**

Bowl, wedding; milk glass, #1874, 10", +pr candle holders, 3-pc set **$65.00**

Bowl, wedding; milk glass w/blue grapes & leaves, #1874, 10" **$70.00**

Box, heart shape, milk glass w/Roses & Bows, #1902 .**$55.00**

Candle holders, Dolphin, milk glass, #1049, 9", pr.....**$85.00**

Candle holders, Dolphin, milk glass, 3½", pr.............**$25.00**

Candle holders, wedding; milk glass w/Roses & Bows, #1874, 4½" square, pr...**$85.00**

Candy dish, Seashell & Dolphin, milk glass, #1048....**$40.00**

Compote, Dolphin/#1049, milk glass, 13"...................**$95.00**

Compote, Seashell & Dolphin, milk glass, #1048, 8"..**$35.00**

Cookie jar, Cherry/#109, milk glass.............................**$90.00**

Covered egg trinket box, almond w/beaded flowers, #1..**$30.00**

Covered egg trinket box, blue opaque w/beaded bouquet, #1 ....**$30.00**

Cup, punch; Multi-Fruit, milk glass, #81 ....**$10.00**

Egg cup, chick, milk glass w/red trim, #602 ....**$20.00**

Grandma's slipper, milk glass w/Christmas decor, #1900...**$35.00**

Napkin rings, milk glass w/holly decor, #1900, set of 4 ..**$150.00**

Pansy basket, green marble, #757 ....**$35.00**

Pansy basket, milk glass, #757.....................................**$15.00**

Plate, leaf, blue opaque, #1923, 6" **$25.00**

Puff box, almond w/beaded bouquet, #1902..............**$35.00**

Puff box, green mist w/daisies, #1902 ....**$30.00**

Puff box, ruby w/ruby floral, #1902............................**$35.00**

Salt & pepper shakers, Pansy, milk glass, #757, pr.....**$50.00**

Salt & pepper shakers, Pansy, mother-of-pearl, #757, pr ..**$50.00**

Salt & pepper shakers, Pansy, mother-of-pearl w/pastel flowers & leaves, #757, pr...**$75.00**

Straw jar, crystal mist w/blue china rose, #1813 ....**$45.00**

Tray, sandwich; Dolphin, almond, central dolphin handle, #1212..**$65.00**

Urn, Roses and Bows, milk glass, #1943, 12½", $125.00.

Vase, Seashell & Dolphin, electric blue opal, #1048...**$89.00**

Vase, Swan, electric blue carnival opalescent, #115, 6½"...**$55.00**

Vase, Swan, milk glass, #115, 6½"................................**$25.00**

Plates

Christmas, black glass, #1802, 1972, 1973, 1974, or 1975 (series), MIB, each...**$75.00**

Contrary Mule, milk glass, #17 ....**$35.00**

Eagle Cup Plate, milk glass, #507................................**$20.00**

Fleur-de-Lis, milk glass, #4...**$10.00**

Forget-Me-Not, black glass, Mary Gregory-style boy w/rake, #2 ....**$55.00**

Forget-Me-Not, black glass, Mary Gregory-style running deer, #2 ....**$65.00**

Forget-Me-Not, milk glass, #2 ....**$10.00**

George Washington, purple carnival, limited edition .**$50.00**

Heart, Beaded Bouquet on almond, #32 ....**$35.00**

Heart, green mist, #32 ....**$20.00**

Heart, ruby w/white dogwood, #32 ....**$35.00**

Indian Head & Beaded Loop Border, purple carnival, #10, limited edition **$45.00**

National, milk glass, #15, 7"...**$22.00**

One Hundred & One, crystal w/ruby & ruby floral, #101 ....**$55.00**

S Border, milk glass, #23, square..................................**$12.50**

Wicket, Battle of Bunker Hill decor, milk glass, #30 ..**$60.00**

Wicket, green mist, #30 ....**$20.00**

Wicket, Washington Crossing the Delaware decor, milk glass, #30 ....**$60.00**

Woof-Woof, milk glass, Westmoreland Specialty Co...**$50.00**

Zodiac, crystal w/blue, red, ruby or yellow stain, #25, 15", each **$95.00**

Zodiac, milk glass w/hand-painted fruit, #25, 15" **$85.00**

3 Kittens, purple carnival, 1974 limited edition...........**$50.00**

3 Owls, purple carnival, 1974 limited edition **$50.00**

Tableware

Ashtray, Ball & Swirl/#1842, green marble **$30.00**

Ashtray, Beaded Grape/#1884, milk glass, 4".............**$12.00**

Ashtray, English Hobnail/#555, milk glass, lg **$10.00**

Basket, Ball & Swirl/#1842, Golden Sunset, split handle ..**$24.00**

Basket, Panelled Grape/#1881, milk glass, split handle..**$30.00**

Basket, Thousand Eye/#1000, crystal w/stain, flat, 8".**$95.00**

Bottle, cologne; Panelled Grape/#1881, milk glass, gold decor...**$55.00**

Bowl, Beaded Grape/#1884, milk glass, w/lid, footed, 9".**$60.00**

Bowl, console; Doric/#3, mint green, lacy edge, w/matching pr of candle holders, 3-pc set................................**$45.00**

Bowl, Della Robbia/#1058, milk glass w/gold trim, 4".**$20.00**

Bowl, divided serving; Beaded Edge/#22, hand-painted fruit on milk glass...**$65.00**

Bowl, fruit; Old Quilt/#500, milk glass, footed, 9"......**$45.00**

Bowl, Lotus/#1921, Flame, cupped, 9".........................**$90.00**

Bowl, Lotus/#1921, Flame, flared rim, 12"...................**$95.00**

Bowl, Lotus/#1921, milk glass, oval, lg........................**$50.00**

Bowl, Old Quilt/#500, milk glass, flat, low, 9"............**$65.00**

Bowl, Old Quilt/#500, milk glass, footed, 4½"...........**$20.00**

Bowl, Panelled Grape/#1881, milk glass, cupped, 9".**$45.00**

Bowl, Ring & Petal/#1875, milk glass, bell form, 10". **$30.00**

Bowl, Ring & Petal/#1875, milk glass, low foot, 4½x8½" .. **$35.00**

Bowl, Ring & Petal/#1875, milk glass, square **$30.00**

Bowl, Rose Trellis/#1967, decorated milk glass, crimped rim **$40.00**

Bowl, Rose Trellis/#1967, milk glass (plain), crimped rim .. **$25.00**

Bowl (Grandfather), Sawtooth/#556, Golden Sunset, w/lid, footed **$75.00**

Bowl (Grandfather), Sawtooth/#556, milk glass, w/lid, footed, 13½" **$85.00**

Box, chocolate; Maple Leaf/#1928, ruby **$45.00**

Box, Old Quilt/#500, milk glass, square, w/lid **$35.00**

Butter dish, Old Quilt/#500, milk glass, ¼-lb **$25.00**

Cake salver, Beaded Grape/#1884, milk glass, square, footed, 11" **$85.00**

Cake salver, Ring & Petal/#1875, milk glass, footed, 11" ... **$45.00**

Candelabra, Lotus/#1921, milk glass, 3-tier, pr **$85.00**

Candle holders, Beaded Grape/#1884, milk glass, pr. **$25.00**

Candle holders, Lattice Edge/#1890, milk glass, pr **$25.00**

Candle holders, Lotus/#1921, Flame, pr **$55.00**

Candle holders, Maple Leaf/#1928, milk glass, flat tops, 9", pr **$55.00**

Candle holders, Ring & Petal/#1875, green mist, pr ... **$22.00**

Candle holders, Spiral/#1710, green marble, pr **$55.00**

Candy dish, Ball & Swirl/#1842, milk glass **$20.00**

Candy dish, Beaded Grape/#1884, milk glass, pedestal foot, 4" **$20.00**

Candy dish, Della Robbia/#1058, milk glass w/Roses & Bows, w/lid **$65.00**

Candy dish, Octagon/#1211, green marble **$65.00**

Celery dish, American Hobnail/#77, milk glass, oval . **$11.00**

Celery vase, Old Quilt/#500, milk glass **$20.00**

Cheese/butter dish, Colonial/#1776, blue moonstone (rare color), round, w/lid **$85.00**

Coffee/punch cup, Thousand Eye/#1000, crystal **$8.00**

Compote, Beaded Grape/#1884, milk glass w/blue grapes & leaves, footed, 7" square **$45.00**

Compote, Della Robbia/#1058, painted fruit on mother-of-pearl finish, w/lid **$50.00**

Compote, mint; Irish Waterford/#1932, crystal w/ruby stain **$35.00**

Compote, Panelled Grape/#1881, milk glass, footed, lipped, 9" **$50.00**

Compote, Panelled Grape/#1881, mint green, ruffled .. **$65.00**

Compote, Princess Feather/#201, Golden Sunset, footed, ruffled **$75.00**

Cookie jar, Maple Leaf/#1928, milk glass, rare **$100.00**

Cordial, Thousand Eye/#1000, crystal, 2-oz **$10.00**

Covered dish, Sawtooth/#556, purple slag, 5½" **$75.00**

Creamer, American Hobnail/#77, milk glass **$12.00**

Creamer & sugar bowl, Cherry/#109, milk glass, w/lid .. **$30.00**

Creamer & sugar bowl, Maple Leaf/#1928, milk glass .. **$35.00**

Creamer & sugar bowl, Old Quilt/#500, milk glass, 3½" ... **$25.00**

Creamer & sugar bowl, Panelled Grape/#1881, milk glass, w/lid, sm **$25.00**

Cruet, Panelled Grape/#1881, milk glass **$25.00**

Cup & saucer, Della Robbia/#1058, dark stain **$35.00**

Cup & saucer, English Hobnail/#555, milk glass (rare) ... **$20.00**

Decanter, wine; Panelled Grape/#1881, milk glass ... **$150.00**

Decanter and wine goblets, Panelled Grape, #1881, $185.00 for the set. (Photo courtesy of Frank J. Grizel.)

Dresser set, Panelled Grape/#1881, milk glass, 4-pc .. **$200.00**

Egg cup, double; American Hobnail/#77, milk glass .. **$18.00**

Epergne, Panelled Grape/#1881, milk glass, smallest of 3 sizes, 2-pc **$100.00**

Epergne, Panelled Grape/#1881, milk glass, 12" bowl w/8" vase, 2-pc **$165.00**

Epergne, Panelled Grape/#1881, milk glass, 12" bowl w/8" vase, footed **$250.00**

Finger bowl, American Hobnail/#77, milk glass, footed, 4½" **$12.00**

Goblet, water; Colonial/#1776, Golden Sunset **$20.00**

Goblet, water; Della Robbia/#1058, milk glass **$14.00**

Goblet, water; Della Robbia/#1058, milk glass w/gold trim, 8-oz **$18.00**

Goblet, water; Princess Feather/#201, crystal, footed, 8-oz .. **$12.00**

Gravy boat & plate, Panelled Grape/#1881, milk glass ... **$65.00**

Heart w/handle, Irish Waterford/#1932, crystal w/ruby stain, 8" **$45.00**

Heart w/handle, Irish Waterford/#1932, crystal w/ruby stain, 6" **$35.00**

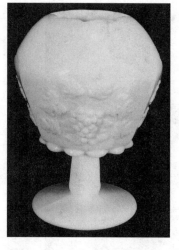

Ivy ball, Panelled Grape, #1881, milk glass, $45.00. (Photo courtesy of Frank J. Grizel.)

Honey dish, Cherry/#109, green marble, w/lid **$45.00**

Jardiniere, Panelled Grape/#1881, milk glass, straight sides, 5" **$28.00**

Mayonnaise bowl, American Hobnail/#77, milk glass, belled rim, 4½"...**$18.00**

Mayonnaise bowl, Lotus/#1921, milk glass, 4"............**$20.00**

Mayonnaise bowl, Lotus/#1921, pink, 4", w/7" underplate..**$25.00**

Mayonnaise bowl, Thousand Eye/#1000, milk glass w/stain, footed, w/ladle..**$50.00**

Mayonnaise set, Panelled Grape/#1881, milk glass, 3-pc set...**$40.00**

Nappy, Beaded Edge/#22, milk glass, oval.................**$10.00**

Pitcher, juice; Panelled Grape/#1881, purple carnival, 1975, +6 tumblers...**$250.00**

Pitcher, water; High Hob/#550, electric blue opal, w/6 tumblers..**$335.00**

Pitcher, water; Old Quilt/#500, honey amber carnival, w/6 9-oz tumblers..**$150.00**

Pitcher, water; Old Quilt/#500, milk glass, w/6 9-oz tumblers..**$120.00**

Plate, Beaded Edge/#22, milk glass, cherries, 7"..........**$8.00**

Plate, Beaded Edge/#22, milk glass, Christmas decor, 7"..**$25.00**

Plate, Beaded Edge/#22, milk glass, peaches, 7"..........**$8.00**

Plate, Beaded Edge/#22, milk glass, 2 red poppies, 7"..**$20.00**

Plate, Beaded Edge/#22, milk glass, 2 yellow daffodils, 7"...**$10.00**

Plate, Beaded Edge/#22, strawberries, 4½"................**$10.00**

Plate, Della Robbia, #1058, 14", $95.00.
(Photo courtesy of Frank J. Grizel.)

Plate, Irish Waterford/#1932, crystal w/ruby stain, rare, 8½"..**$65.00**

Plate, Old Quilt/#500, milk glass, 10".......................**$55.00**

Plate, Old Quilt/#500, milk glass, 8".........................**$50.00**

Plate, Panelled Grape/#1881, milk glass, 10½"...........**$45.00**

Plate, Princess Feather/#201, Golden Sunset, 8".........**$30.00**

Platter, Thousand Eye/#1000, crystal, 18"..................**$65.00**

Powder jar, American Hobnail/#77, milk glass............**$25.00**

Puff box, Beaded Grape/#1884, milk glass, square.....**$20.00**

Puff box, Panelled Grape/#1884, mint green, w/lid...**$45.00**

Punch ladle, Panelled Grape/#1881, milk glass, from $55 to..**$60.00**

Punch set, English Hobnail/#555, crystal, bowl & lg underplate, w/12 cups..**$450.00**

Relish, Old Quilt/#500, milk glass, 3-part..................**$35.00**

Rose bowl, American Hobnail/#77, milk glass, footed, 4½"..**$20.00**

Rose bowl, Doric/#3, milk glass, low foot, cupped, 6"..**$25.00**

Rose bowl, Doric/#3, milk glass, pinched, flared rim, 6½"..**$21.00**

Salt & pepper shakers, American Hobnail/#77, milk glass, chrome lids, pr...**$22.00**

Salt & pepper shakers, High Hob/#550, milk glass, pr..**$20.00**

Salt & pepper shakers, Lotus/#1921, pink, blue, green or amber, pr..**$50.00**

Salt & pepper shakers, Panelled Grape/#1881, milk glass, blown, 4½", pr...**$50.00**

Salt cellar, English Hobnail/#555, milk glass.................**$6.00**

Saucer, Princess Feather/#201, Golden Sunset............**$15.00**

Sherbet, Della Robbia/#1058, dark stain.....................**$30.00**

Sherbet, Old Quilt/#500, milk glass............................**$20.00**

Sherbet, Princess Feather/#201, crystal........................**$9.00**

Sherbet, Thousand Eye/#1000, crystal (plain), low.....**$12.00**

Sherbet, Thousand Eye/#1000, crystal w/stain, low....**$20.00**

Shot glass/toothpick holder, American Hobnail/#77, milk glass, 2½"...**$12.50**

Soap dish, Panelled Grape/#1881, milk glass.............**$50.00**

Sugar bowl, American Hobnail/#77, milk glass, 3½"..**$12.00**

Sweetmeat, Colonial/#1776, green marble..................**$32.00**

Sweetmeat, Doric/#3, almond, beaded........................**$30.00**

Syrup pitcher, Old Quilt/#500, milk glass, 3-oz..........**$25.00**

Tidbit tray, Panelled Grape/#1881, milk glass, 2-tier..**$75.00**

Toothpick holder, Panelled Grape/#1881, milk glass.**$35.00**

Tray, celery; Old Quilt/#500, milk glass, footed, 6"....**$35.00**

Tumbler, iced tea; American Hobnail/#77, milk glass, low foot..**$15.00**

Tumbler, iced tea; Old Quilt/#500, milk glass, 11-oz.**$16.00**

Tumbler, iced tea; Princess Feather/#201, crystal, flat 12-oz...**$20.00**

Tumbler, juice; Panelled Grape/#1881, milk glass......**$25.00**

Tumbler, water; American Hobnail, low foot, 11-oz, from $12 to...**$15.00**

Tumbler, water; Panelled Grape, milk glass, flat, 4¼"..**$20.00**

Tumbler, water; Thousand Eye, crystal, flat, 8-oz.......**$12.00**

Vase, Ball & Swirl/#1842, milk glass, bell form w/crimped rim, 9"..**$25.00**

Vase, Beaded Grape/#1884, milk glass, crimped edge, 6"..**$25.00**

Vase, Colonial/#1776, yellow mist, footed..................**$30.00**

Vase, Drape & Tassel/#1861, milk glass......................**$75.00**

Vase, Old Quilt/#500, milk glass, fan form.................**$15.00**

Vase, Panelled Grape/#1881, milk glass w/green & gold decor, bell form, 9"...**$38.00**

Vase, swung; Colonial/#1776, dark blue mist.............**$40.00**

Wine, Irish Waterford/#1932, crystal w/ruby stain, footed, 2-oz, rare...**$30.00**

Wine, Panelled Grape/#1881, milk glass, 2-oz, from $18 to..**$20.00**

Vases

Buzz Star, ruby, #224..**$95.00**

Lily of the Valley, blue opal, #241..............................**$55.00**

Lily of the Valley, milk glass, #241.............................**$20.00**

Lily of the Valley, white carnival, #241......................**$50.00**

Mary Gregory-style boy fishing, dark blue mist, blown, #78...**$65.00**

Tear Drop, milk glass, #231..**$75.00**

Wheaton

Though the Wheaton Company of Millville, New Jersey, made several series of bottles (examples of which are listed below), those with portraits of our country's presidents are the most collectible. Many colors have been used, including iridescents.

Bottle, Andrew Jackson, from $30 to $35.00
Bottle, Apollo II, 1st Man on the Moon, 4 astronauts, 1969 ....$25.00
Bottle, Benjamin Franklin..$25.00
Bottle, Calvin Coolidge, from $20 to...........................$25.00

Bottle, Clark Gable, $12.00.

Bottle, Douglas MacArthur..$35.00
Bottle, Dr Chandler Jamaica Ginger Root Bitters $15.00
Bottle, Franklin Pierce, second or corrected version, from $30 to $35.00
Bottle, Gerald R Ford, from $10 to..............................$15.00
Bottle, Herbert Hoover, from $10 to $15.00
Bottle, Horseshoe Bitters...$40.00
Bottle, James K Polk, from $30 to $35.00
Bottle, John Adams, from $20 to $25.00
Bottle, John Tyler, from $15 to $25.00
Bottle, RDR (Franklin Delano Roosevelt), from $20 to.$25.00
Bottle, Rutherford B Hayes, from $35 to $40.00
Bottle, Rutherford B Hayes, second or corrected version, from $30 to...$35.00
Bottle, Ulysses S Grant, from $15 to $20.00

Bottle, Union, $10.00.

Bottle, William Howard Taft, from $20 to $25.00
Bottle, Zachary Taylor, second or corrected version, from $30 to $35.00
Doll, Colonial lady w/basket, teal blue carnival.........$30.00
Doll, Southern Belle, butterscotch carnival $30.00
Figurine, bull frog, emerald carnival, lg.....................$25.00
Figurine, bull frog, emerald carnival, sm...................$15.00
Paperweight, shark, teal carnival, lg $40.00
Plate, Spirit of 75, teal carnival, 1976........................$30.00

World's Fairs and Expositions

Souvenir items have been issued since the mid-1800s for every world's fair and exposition. Few fairgoers have left the grounds without purchasing at least one. Some of the older items were often manufactured right on the fairgrounds by glass or pottery companies who erected working kilns and furnaces just for the duration of the fair. Of course, the older items are usually more valuable, but even souvenirs from the past fifty years are worth hanging on to.

Newsletter: *Fair News*
World's Fair Collectors' Society, Inc.
Michael R. Pender, Editor
P.O. Box 20806
Sarasota, FL 34238; Dues: $12 (12 issues) per year in USA; $13 in Canada; $20 for overseas members

St. Louis 1904

Book, Uncle Jeremiah at the Great Exposition, CM Stevens, hardcover, 332-page, 5½x7½", EX.......................$17.50
Box, brass, shield, stars, laurel wreath, etc, 1¼" dia, EX...$30.00

Collapsible cup, nickel with embossed design of Palace of Mines and Metallurgy on lid, EX, $30.00.

Cup, collapsible, nickel w/embossed design of Palace of Mines & Metallurgy, EX.......................................$30.00
Dresser jar, milk glass w/gold trim, US Government Building decal (worn) on lid, 3½x3"...................................$20.00
Medal, aluminum, design of German Heater stove, EX..$12.50

Paperweight, ruby-flashed glass w/etched rose & bird, World's Fair 1904 & name, 2½x4" $60.00

Pocket mirror, multicolor picture of Palace of Transportation on celluloid, 2" dia, NM $75.00

Pocketknife, celluloid handles w/multicolor fair designs, Germany, 1 blade broken, VG $45.00

Toothpick holder, ruby-flashed top half w/gold lettering: Louisiana Purchase Exposition....1904, 2¼x1½" $10.00

Tray, metal w/central scene of US Government Building & floral border, 12" dia, EX............................$30.00

Tumbler, milk glass w/embossed designes of Cascade Gardens, Palace of Machinery, florals, etc, 5x3½" .$20.00

Tumbler, silverplate w/scenes in relief, 3½"...............$32.00

Panama-Pacific, 1915

Book, Panama-Pacific International Exposition, San Francisco 1915, 2nd edition, hardcover, 56-page, 7x10", EX....$20.00

Book, San Francisco Standard Guide Including the Panama-Pacific Exposition, hardcover, about 180 pages, 6x9¼", EX..$30.00

Booklet, California and the Expositions, Union Pacific System, 64 pages, $20.00.

Box, metal w/embossed design of Service Building, open-work on sides, 2x4½x2¼", EX....................$17.50

Cloth, orange silk w/Tower of Jewels design & poppy border, minor damage at folds, 12x14"..................$7.50

Folder, illustrations & information about San Diego & exposition, 4x9", EX....................................$10.00

Napkin ring, celluloid w/cut-out design, Tower of Jewels in center, 2x2", EX....................................$20.00

Pin-back button, lady above 2 continents on multicolor celluloid, exposition mark, Whitehead & Hoag paper label, 1¼"..$30.00

Pin-back button, milk maid w/cow, celluloid, 1¾", w/5" ribbon (tattered) marked: Banner Butter Section......$27.50

Postcard, Palace of Varied Industries, multicolor, Pacific Novelty Co, EX.......................................$3.00

Postcard album, Official Souvenir, 10 detachable postcards by Cardinell-Vincent, 9 in full color, EX....................$20.00

Sesqui-Centennial, 1926

Book, Flags of America Compliments of John Wanamaker Store, soft cover, 32-page, 5½x8", NM.................$12.50

Brooch, oval copper-colored medallion w/Liberty bell, etc, designs, in green frame set in brass, 1x1¼", EX..$20.00

Key, metal Liberty Bell shape, marked Sesqui-Centennial 1776-1926 Phila PA on each side, 2¼" long, NM.$15.00

Medallion/fob, copper-colored medal w/stamped design of Liberty Bell, flags, rifles, etc, 1½x1½", EX............$12.50

Paperweight, heavy metal, 3-D shape of Liberty Bell, well marked, 3x3x1½", NM................................$22.50

Pin-back button, Liberty Bell in multicolor on celluloid, dates of 1776 & 1926, 150 Years of Independence, 1" dia, NM...$12.50

Program, Official Daily (Ohio Day), listing of events, advertising, 32-page, 6x9", NM.....................................$12.50

Chicago, 1933

Ashtray, copper, embossed design of Chrysler Building, dated 1933, EX...$7.50

Book, Official Book of the Fair, pre-fair publication, w/many illustrations, 96-page, 6½x9½", EX.......................$25.00

Book, Souvenir Book 1934, Curt Teich, Kaufmann & Fabry photos, color covers, 64 pages of views, 1934, 6½x9½", EX..$25.00

Booklet, Durkee Famous Foods, multicolor overview of the fair on cover, recipes for Durkee products, 16-page, EX...$4.00

Booklet, Romance of Steel, information & illustrations of US Steel, designed to be mailed, EX......................$3.00

Booklet, Wings of a Century, modes of transportation through the years, 12-page+covers, 8½x11½", EX................$15.00

Bracelet, silver-colored metal, comet logo & 6 other designs, dated 1933 in center, NM................................$15.00

Elongated cent, Sky Ride World's Fair Chicago 1933, EX..$10.00

Folder, Official View Book, 20 full-color postcard size views, designed for mailing, 6x4", EX..........................$12.50

Komic Kamera, Chicago's 1934 World's Fair Viewer, 1934, litho tin, w/strips of cartoon characters, NMIB...$145.00

Medal, brass, Indian in full headdress, Century of Progress Exposition, Fort Dearborn on reverse, 1¼" dia....$12.50

Medal, bronze, Ford in script across a car radiator, V-8 emblem in wreath & Thirty Years of Progress, 1⅜" dia...........$20.00

Medal, bronze, Official Medal, male in loincloth w/arms outstretched, Research Industry, 1½" dia $30.00

Medal, silver-colored metal w/comet design, 1933, A Century of Progress, 1" dia, EX.............................$7.50

Notebook, Compliments of Chicago & Northwestern Railway, EX, $5.00

Pin-back button, comet design, I Was There, ¾" dia, EX. **$5.00**

Plate, Carillon Tower, black on white china, urns & floral design on border, dated 1934, 8¼" **$40.00**

Playing cards, Official Souvenir, backs marked A Century...Chicago 1934, multicolor backs, complete deck w/joker, NMIB.. **$37.50**

Program, Opening Day, special events of the day, illustrations, ads, etc, 24-page, 8x11", EX **$22.50**

Spoon, Comet design & building-form handle, marked Official A Century of Progress 1933, view in bowl, silver-plated.. **$10.00**

Ticket, black on green, 4x2½", NM.......................... **$12.50**

Tray, silver-colored metal w/Fort Dearborn, Chicago Sky Line, plane & blimp, floral border, 7½x5", lt wear.......... **$15.00**

Watch fob, brass, overview of the fair, marked Leonard Refrigeration for the Home, cutout for strap, 1¼" dia, EX **$25.00**

California-Pacific, 1935

Book, Official Guide, illustrated, map, much information, Wolcott, 84-page, 6x8½", EX................................ **$22.50**

Booklet, Official Guide (1 day), activities & times, much information, 5½x8½", EX **$5.00**

Folder, painted Desert Exhibit, illustrated, 3¼x6", EX.. **$5.00**

Medal, brass, embossed buildings, exposition mark & state seal of CA, marked State of CA Souvenir, EX................ **$10.00**

Medal, brass w/CA Pacific International Exposition 1935 & embossed state seal, exposition mark, 1" dia, EX.. **$7.50**

Golden Gate Exposition, 1939–1940

Crumb set, embossed metal, EX, $18.00.

Map, San Francisco, aerial view of expo, dated 1939, unfolds to about 20x20" **$5.00**

Map folder, Plan To Visit the Golden Gate International Exposition, Standard Oil Co of CA, missing cover..... **$5.00**

Sticker, embossed metallic, Junket Food Products, blue & silver w/red lettering, 1½x2½", EX **$5.00**

Ticket, souvenir; 1940 stub still attached, 5x2½" **$10.00**

New York, 1939

Ashtray, silver-colored metal w/embossed lettering & Trylon & Perisphere in center, 5 cigarette rests, light wear, 4½" dia **$22.50**

Book, For the Visitor in NY City, fair information, fold-out map in back, Guaranty Trust Co, 88-page, 1939, 4½x7".... **$15.00**

Book, New Hampshire Troubadour, World's Fair Edition, illustrated by Maxfield Parrish, 96 pages, NM **$115.00**

Book, The Story of Lucky Strike, fair logo embossed on cover, 94 pages, NM **$15.00**

Bottle, milk glass with metal cap, 9", NM, $28.00.

Card, Frank Buck's Jungleland, Buck & animals pictured, 1940, 5½x3½", EX.. **$5.00**

Diary, simulated leather cover w/Trylon & Perisphere design in orange on brown background, zipper closure, 4x5", EX.. **$20.00**

Folder, Brazilian Exhibit, marked NY World's Fair 1939, lists products of Brazil, NM **$1.50**

Folder, Routes to the World's Fair, Trylon & Perisphere design, map of NY, tunnel & bridge info, EX **$7.50**

Fountain pen/automatic pencil combination, Trylon & Perisphere, NY World's Fair 1939, Durium 14k Gold Plated, EX **$45.00**

Hot pad, silvery metallic finish w/embossed Administration Building design, 8x6", EX.................................... **$20.00**

Lapel pin, view of Trylon & Perisphere, dated 1939 under clear glass, mounted on brass backing, VG **$30.00**

Pin, Heinz Pickles.. **$10.00**

Playing cards, Trylon & Perisphere in blue & white on maroon, NY World's Fair in blue letters, sealed in wrapper, +case **$40.00**

Playing cards, Trylon & Perisphere on each card, set of 52, NM **$38.00**

Polaroid view, shaped like front of Chrysler auto, used in Chrysler Motors theater, EX.................................... **$35.00**

Postcard, Bridge of Tomorrow, Colortint view, Grinnell Litho, NM.. **$3.00**

Postcard, Section of the Court of States, Tichnor Quality Views, NM **$3.00**

Salt & pepper shakers, heavy metal, Trylon & Perisphere shapes, fair marks, wear to finish, 4" & 2" dia, pr .**$25.00**

Statuette, Statue of Liberty, dark bronze-colored metal, Trylon & Perisphere design at base, 5½x2", NM..**$50.00**

Ticket, Press, red serial number on green background, Trylon & Perisphere design on corners, 1940 .... **$1.50**

Ticket envelope, Pennsylvania Railroad w/ad for fair, EX+...**$10.00**

Tumbler, rose & yellow Music Building graphics **$12.00**

Vase, Jasperware w/Trylon & Perisphere, shoulder handles, 2¾".. **$18.00**

San Francisco, 1939

Comb case, metal w/red enameled buildings, bridges, etc, gold-colored date, w/amber-colored comb, 4½x1¼", NM..**$22.50**

Medal, aluminum w/2 embossed locomotives of the Union Pacific, clipper ship flying over covered wagon, NM ..**$7.50**

Medal, bird's-eye view of expo & 1939 on gold or copper-colored finish, 2¾", NM **$20.00**

Medal, brass, Petroleum Exhibit & 1939, bright finish, 1⅜" dia......**$7.50**

Postcard, Triumphal Arch, multicolor, HS Crocker Co, Official Postcard, EX **$2.50**

Seattle, 1962

Catalog, Masterpieces of Art, exhibits in Fine Arts Pavilion, soft cover, 160-page, EX......**$10.00**

Cuff links, Monorail, Space Needle, etc on light blue w/gold lettering, MIB......**$7.50**

Handkerchief, bird's-eye view of fair on cotton, 12½" square, NM......**$5.00**

Pamphlet, 8th Annual Regional Gem & Mineral Show, World's Fair Seattle 1962, NM **$4.00**

Pennant, red & black felt w/Space Needle design, 7¾", EX..**$3.00**

Pin tray, ceramic w/Space Needle in center, fair mark, 3" dia **$2.50**

Plate, coppertone chalkware w/aerial view of fairgrounds in relief, Century 21 logo, w/hanger, 12¾" **$15.00**

Record, Rhapsody 21, conducted by Paul Whitman, official theme of expo, original sealed package......**$20.00**

Tray, black lacquer w/US Science Building, Space Needle, Monorail, etc, 10¾" dia, M......**$10.00**

Tumbler, red Space Needle graphics, 4¾"......**$9.00**

Tumbler, World of Art on clear, 6½" **$7.00**

New York, 1964

Book, Official Guide Book, many illustrations, Time-Life, 312 pages, NM......**$12.50**

Bowl, multicolor scene on clear glass, 4x4½"......**$12.50**

Brochure, Magic Skyways, Ford/Disney, Wonder Rotunda exhibit souvenir, 8 pages, 9x4", EX+......**$22.00**

Bumper sticker, I've Seen NY State at the Fair, Theaterama, 4x8", NM......**$15.00**

Cigarette lighter, enameled Unisphere & flags on chrome, MIB **$12.00**

Coaster, Lowenbrau Beer w/fair logo & dates, EX......**$8.00**

Envelope, from GM, 2 imprints regarding Futurama Exhibit, mailed **$3.00**

Folder, Fall In, Continental Insurance Pavilion, multicolor, 3½x8½", NM......**$3.50**

Folder, Styling X-Cars, experimental designs by Ford, Allegro, Cougar II, & Mustang II, NM **$5.00**

Folder, World's Fair, colorful, fair information, ticket prices, etc, 4x9", NM......**$3.00**

Game, Official NY World's Fair, complete w/cards, markers, instructions, etc, Milton Bradley, colorful box cover, EX......**$35.00**

Map, Seagrams World Fair Map & NY City Guide, NY map & colorful fair map, opens to 18x32", NM......**$7.50**

Medal, bronze, Unisphere w/lettering, OK at the World's Fair on reverse, 1½" dia......**$15.00**

Metal, brass, Unisphere design, etc, 1⅛" dia **$5.00**

Newspaper, New York News, Special World's Fair section, much color, many ads, April 12, 1964, EX **$15.00**

Patch, Armored Car Service/NY World's Fair, 3" dia **$3.00**

Postcard, Riding the Swiss Sky Ride, Colorpicture publisher, NM......**$2.50**

Snow dome, 3-D Unisphere in white against blue background on 3" square orange plastic base, 3" dia, M......**$35.00**

Timetable, Pennsylvania Railroad service to fair, EX+ ..**$9.50**

Tray, metal w/multicolor scene of Unisphere, 12" dia, NM .**$15.00**

Tumbler, frosted glass w/multicolor scenes, fair marks, dates, etc, 7x3"......**$10.00**

Spokane, 1974

Ashtray, white ceramic w/fair vignettes & gold lettering, 4½", M......**$6.50**

Card, to order admission tickets in advance of fair opening, prices shown, M......**$1.00**

Folder, United States Pavilion, drawing & description of exhibit......**$2.00**

Pamphlet, Celebrating Tomorrow's Fresh New Environment, M......**$3.00**

Plate, colorful aerial view of fair in center on ceramic, 10½", M......**$15.00**

Tumbler, Expo '74 logo, Land's End Tavern, Spokane WA on clear, pedestal ft, 5⅛"......**$7.00**

Knoxville, 1982

Mug, white ceramic w/multicolor Sunsphere & 3 arches, 2½"......**$4.50**

T-shirt, blue w/red sunburst logo of fair, 1982 World's Fair May-October, Knoxville TN, USA, M **$15.00**

Tray, aluminum w/silver & black US Pavilion & World's Fair 1982, Knoxville TN, 4¾x7"......**$7.00**

Tray, metal, Stroh's the Official Beer at the Fair, 10⅝x13¼", M......**$8.00**

Tumbler, Sunsphere w/rainbow on clear glass, pedestal foot, 6½"......**$10.00**

Tumbler, Wendy's & red fair logo on clear glass, 5¾" .**$10.00**

New Orleans, 1984

Book, Official World's Fair Pictorial Book, color views, soft cover, 48 pages, M......**$10.00**

Booklet, 10 views of fairgrounds & pavilions, mini, M...**$2.50**

Box, porcelain, fair dates & logo, footed, w/lid, M **$8.00**

Charm, gold-plated pelican, fair marks, sm disk, M **$5.00**

Cookbook, Official...of the 1984 Louisiana World Exposition, hardcover, 284 pages, M **$20.00**

Cup & saucer, white ceramic w/gold trim, gold fair logo, 4⅝" dia **$7.50**

Hurricane glass, recipe for cocktail on back, fair dates, 1984 logo, 8⅝"......**$9.00**

Magazine, Louisiana Life World's Fair Commemorative Issue, M **$7.50**

Auction Houses

Many of the auction galleries we've listed here have appraisal services. Some, though not all, are free of charge. We suggest you contact them first by phone to discuss fees and requirements.

Aston Auctioneers & Appraisers
2825 Country Club Rd.
Endwell, NY 13760-3349
Phone or FAX 607-785-6598
Specializing in and appraisers of Americana, folk art, other primitives, furniture, fine glassware and china

Bill Bertoia Auctions
2413 Madison Ave.
Vineland, NJ 08630
609-692-4092 or FAX 609-692-8697
Specializing in antique toys and collectibles

Cincinnati Art Gallery
635 Main St.
Cincinnati, OH 45202
513-381-2128
Specializing in American art pottery, American and European fine paintings, watercolors

Collectors Auction Services
326 Seneca St.
Oil City, PA 16301
814-677-6070
Specializing in advertising, oil and gas, toys, rare museum and investment-quality antiques

David Rago
9 S Main St.
St. Lambertville, NJ 08530
609-397-9374
Gallery:
17 S Main St.
Lambertville, NJ 08530
Specializing in American art pottery and Arts & Crafts

Don Treadway Gallery
2128 Madison Rd.
Cincinnati, OH 45208
513-321-6742 or FAX 513-871-7722
Member: National Antique Dealers Association, American Art Pottery Association, International Society of Appraisers, and American Ceramic Arts Society

Dynamite Auctions
Franklin Antique Mall & Auction Gallery
1280 Franklin Ave.
Franklin, PA 16323
814-432-8577 or 814-786-9211

Early Auction Co.
123 Main St.,
Milford, OH 45150

Garth's Auctions, Inc.
2690 Stratford Rd.
Box 369
Delaware, OH 43015
614-362-4771

Hake's Americana & Collectibles
Specializing in character and personality collectibles along with all artifacts of popular culture for over 20 years. To receive a catalog for their next 3,000-item mail/phone bid auction, send $5 to:
Hake's Americana
P.O. Box 1444M
York, PA 17405

James D. Julia
P.O. Box 210
Showhegan Rd.
Fairfield, ME 04937

Kerry and Judy's Toys
7370 Eggleston Rd.
Memphis, TN 31825-2112
901-757-1722
Specializing in 1920s through 1960s toys; Consignments always welcomed

L.R. 'Les' Docks
Box 691035
San Antonio, TX 78269-1035
Providing occasional mail-order record auctions, rarely consigned (the only consignments considered are exceptionally scarce and unusual records)

Lloyd Ralston Toys
447 Stratford Rd.
Fairfield, CT 06432

Manion's International Auction House, Inc.
P.O. Box 12214
Kansas City, KS 66112
913-299-6692 or FAX 913-299-6792

Michael Verlangieri, California Pottery
P.O. Box 844
W Cambria, CA 93428-0844
Phone or FAX 805-927-4428

e-mail verlangieri@thegrid.net
http://www.thebook.com/verlangieri

Noel Barrett Antiques & Auctions
P.O. Box 1001
Carversville, PA 18913
215-297-5109

Richard Opfer Auctioneering, Inc.
1919 Greenspring Dr.
Timonium, MD 21093
301-252-5035

Smith House
P.O. Box 336
Eliot, ME, 03903
207-439-4614 or FAX 207-439-8554
Specializing in toys

Clubs

There are hundreds of clubs and newsletters mentioned throughout this book in their respective categories. There are many more available to collectors today, some are generalized and cover the entire realm of antiques and collectibles, while others are devoted to a specific interest such as toys, coin-operated machines, character collectibles, or railroadiana. We've listed several below. You can obtain a copy of most newsletters simply by requesting one. If you'd like to try placing a 'for-sale' ad or a mail bid in one of them, see the introduction for suggestions on how your ad should be composed.

AB Bookman's Weekly
P.O. Box AB
Clifton, NJ 07015
201-772-0020 or FAX 201-772-9281
$80 per year bulk mail USA ($80 per year Canada or Foreign). $125 per year 1st class mail (USA, Canada, and Mexico). Foreign Air Mail: Inquire. Sample copies: $10. AB Bookman's Yearbook: $25. All advertising and subscriptions subject to acceptance

Antique Advertising Association of America (AAAA)
P.O. Box 1121
Morton Grove, IL 60053
708-446-0904
Also *Past Times* newsletter for collectors of popular and antique advertising. Subscription: $35 per year

Antique and Collectible News
P.O. Box 529
Anna, IL 62906
Monthly newspaper for auctions, antique shows, collectibles and flea markets for the Midwest USA. Subscription: $12 per year

Antique and Collectors Reproduction News
Mark Cherenka, Circulation Dept.
P.O. Box 12130
Des Moines, IA 50312-9403
800-227-5531
Monthly newsletter showing differences between old originals and new reproductions. Subscription: $32 per year

Antique Gazette
6949 Charlotte Pk. #106
Nashville, TN 37209
Monthly publication covering the antique and collectibles market. Subscription: $16.95 per year

Antique Monthly magazine
Stephen C. Croft, Publisher
2100 Powers Ferry Rd.
Atlanta, GA 30339
404-955-5656 or FAX 404-952-0669
Subscription: $19.95 per year (11 issues)

The Antique Trader Weekly
P.O. Box 1050 CB
Dubuque, IA 52004-1050
319-588-2073
Subscription: $35 (52 issues) per year;

Antique Week
P.O. Box 90
Knightstown, IN 46148
Weekly newspaper for auctions, antique shows, antiques, collectibles and flea markets. Write for subscription information.

Antiques and Collecting
1006 S Michigan Ave.
Chicago, IL 60605
800-221-3148
Monthly magazine with a wide variety of information and an extensive classified section. Subscription: $28 per year; $50 for two years

Arts and Crafts Quarterly
P.O. Box 3592, Sta. E
Trenton, NJ 08629
800-541-5787

Ashtray Journal
Chuck Thompson, Editor Publisher
Box 11652
Houston, TX 77293
Subscription $14.95 a year (6 issues); sample $3.95

Auction Opportunities, Inc.
Doyle Auctioneers and Appraisers
109 Osborne Hill Rd.
Fishkill, NY 12524
800-551-5161
Subscription: $25 per year

Bojo
P.O. Box 1403
Cranberry Township, PA 16066-0403
412-776-0621 (9 am to 9 pm EST)
Issues fixed-price catalog containing Beatles and Rock 'n Roll memorabilia

Bookmark Collector
Joan L. Huegel
1002 W. 25th St.
Erie, PA 16502
Quarterly newsletter: $5.50 per year ($6.50 in Canada); sample copy: $1 plus stamp or LSASE

California Pottery Newsletter
c/o Verlangieri Gallery
816 Main St.
W Cambria, CA 93428
800-292-2153

Chicagoland Antique Advertizing
Slot Machine and Jukebox Gazette
Ken Durham, Editor
P.O. Box 2426
Rockville, MD 20852
20-page newsletter published twice a year. Subscription: 4 issues for $10; Sample: $5

Clear the Decks
52 Plus Joker
Bill Coomer, Secretary
1024 S Benton
Cape Girardeau, MO 63701
For collectors of playing cards, unusual and antique decks

Coin-Op Newsletter
Ken Durham, Publisher
909 26th St., NW
Washington, DC 20037
Subscription (10 issues): $24;
Sample: $5

The Collector
Box 158
Heyworth, IL 61745
309-473-2466
Newspaper published monthly

Collectors' Classified
William Margolin
P.O. Box 347
Hollbrook, MA 02343-0347
617-961-1463
Covers collectibles in general; 4 issues: $1

Collector's Digest
P.O. Box 23
Banning, CA 92220
714-849-1064
Subscription: $11 (6 issues) per year

Collector's Mart magazine
P.O. Box 12830
Wichita, KS 67277
Subscription: $23.95 per year; Add $15 in Canada

Deco Echoes Publications
The Echoes Report
P.O. Box 2321
Mashpee, MA 02649
508-428-2324 or FAX 508-428-0077
Quarterly publication focusing on 20th-century designs and styles with classified ad section

Depression Glass Daze
Teri Steel, Editor/Publisher
Box 57
Otisville, MI 48463
810-631-4593
The nation's marketplace for glass, china, and pottery

Dunbar's Gallery
76 Haven St.
Milford, MA 01757
508-634-8697 or FAX 508-634-8698
Specializing in quality advertising, Halloween, toys, coin-operated machines; holding cataloged auctions occasionally, lists available

Ephemera News
The Ephemera Society of America, Inc.
P.O. Box 37
Schoharie, NY 12157
518-295-7978

The Front Striker Bulletin
Bill Retskin
P.O. Box 18481
Asheville, NC 28814
704-254-4487 or FAX 704-254-1066
Quarterly newsletter for matchcover collectors, $17.50 per year for 1st class mailing + $2 for new member registration

GAB! (Glass Animal Bulletin!)
P.O. Box 143
N Liberty, IA 52317
Subscription: $16 for 12 monthly issues; free ads to subscribers

Glass Collector's Digest
P.O. Box 553
Marietta, OH 45750-0553
800-533-3433
Subscription: $22 (6 issues) per year; Add $8 for Canada and foreign

The Glass Post
P.O. Box 205
Oakdale, IA 52319-0205
FAX 319-626-3216
Subscription: $25 per year. All ads are free to subscribers.

Gonder Pottery Collectors' Newsletter
c/o John and Marilyn McCormick
P.O. Box 3174
Shawnee, KS 66203

Morgantown Newscaster
Morgantown Collectors of America
Jerry Gallagher and Randy Supplee
420 1st Ave. NW
Plainview, MN 55964
Subscription: $15 per year; SASE required for answers to queries

Newspaper Collectors Society of America
P.O. Box 19134
Lansing, MI 48901
517-887-1255 or FAX 517-887-2194

Old Stuff
Donna and Ron Miller, Publishers
336 N Davis
P.O. Box 1084
McMinnville, OR 97128
Published 6 times annually; Copies by mail: $3 each; Annual subscription: $12 ($20 in Canada)

Paper Collectors' Marketplace
470 Main St.

P.O. Box 128
Scandinavia, WI 54977
715-467-2379 or FAX 715-467-2243
Subscription: $19.95 (12 issues) per year in USA; Canada and Mexico add $15 per year

Paper Pile Quarterly
P.O. Box 337
San Anselmo, CA 94979-0337
415-454-5552 or FAX 415-454-2947
Subscription: $20 per year in USA and Canada

Phillips Archives
Robert W. Phillips
1703 N Aster Pl.
Broken Arrow, OK 74012
918-254-8205 or FAX 918-252-9362
e-mail: rawhidebob@aol.com
Author and leading authority on western genre and Roy Rogers. Current books include *Western Comics Journal*, *Bob Wills Journal* and *Singing Cowboy Stars*

The Pokey Gazette
Steve Santi
19626 Ricardo Ave.
Hayward, CA 94541
510-481-2586
A *Little Golden Book* collector newsletter

Pottery Collectors Express
Paradise Publications
P.O. Box 221
Mayview, MO 64071-0221

Salt and Pepper Illustrated Sales List
Judy Posner
May–Oct: RD 1, Box 273SC
Effort, PA 18330
717-629-6583 or
Nov–April: 4195 S Tamiami Trail, #183SC
Venice, FL 34293
941-497-7149
e-mail: Judyandjef@aol.com.
Send $2 and LSASE. Buy-Sell-Collect

Southern Oregon Antiques and Collectibles Club
P.O. Box 508
Talent, OR 97540
503-535-1231
Meets 1st Wednesday of the month; Promotes 2 shows a year in Medford, OR

Stanley Tool Collector News
c/o The Old Tool Shop
208 Front St.

Marietta, OH 45750
Features articles of interest, auction results, price trends, classified ads, etc.; Subscription: $20 per year; Sample: $6.95

Statue of Liberty Collectors' Club
Iris November
P.O. Box 535
Chautauqua, NY 14722
216-831-2646

Thimble Collectors International
6411 Montego Rd.
Louisville, KY 40228

Three Rivers Depression Era Glass Society
Meetings held 1st Monday of each month at DeMartino's Restaurant, Carnegie, PA.
For more information call:
Edith A. Putanko
John's Antiques & Edie's Glassware
Rte. 88 & Broughton Rd.
Bethel Park, PA 15102
412-831-2702

Tiffin Glass Collectors
P.O. Box 554
Tiffin, OH 44883
Meetings at Seneca Cty. Museum on 2nd Tuesday of each month

Tobacciana
Chuck Thompson and Associates
P.O. Box 11652
Houston, TX 77293
Send SASE for free list of publications

Tobacco Jar Newsletter
Society of Tobacco Jar Collectors
Charlotte Tarses, Treasurer
3011 Fallstaff Road #307
Baltimore, MD 21209
Dues: $30 per year ($35 outside of US)

Toy Gun Collectors of America Newsletter
Jim Buskirk, Editor and Publisher
175 Cornell St.
Windsor CA 95492
707-837-9949
Published quarterly, covers both toy and BB guns. Dues: $15 per year

Toys and Prices magazine
700 E State St.
Iola, WI 54990-0001
715-445-2214 or FAX 715-445-4087
Subscription: $14.95 per year

The Upside Down World of an O.J.Collector
The Occupied Japan Club
c/o Florence Archambault
29 Freeborn St.
Newport, RI 02840
Published bimonthly. Information requires SASE

Vernon Views
P.O. Box 945
Scottsdale, AZ 85252.
Published quarterly beginning with the spring issue, $6 per year

View-Master Reel Collector
Roger Nazeley
4921 Castor Ave.
Philadelphia, PA 19124

Vintage Paperback Collecting Guide
Black Ace Books
1658 Griffith Park Blvd.
Los Angeles, CA 90026
213-661-5052
Information about terms, book fairs, auctions, and references; Available for $2 postpaid

Watt's News
c/o Susan Morris and Jan Seeck
P.O. Box 708
Mason City, IA 50401
Subscription: $10 per year

The Wrapper
Bubble Gum and Candy Wrapper Collectors
P.O. Box 573
St. Charles, IL 60174
708-377-7921

The 50s Flea
April and Larry Tvorak
P.O. Box 126
Canon City, CO 81215-0126
719-269-7230
Published once a year, $4 postpaid; Free classified up to 30 words.

Special Interests

In this section of the book we have listed hundreds of dealers/collectors who specialize in many of the fields this price guide covers. Many of them have sent information, photographs, or advised us concerning current values and trends. This is a courtesy listing, and they are under no obligation to field questions from our readers, though some may be willing to do so. If you do write to any of them, don't expect a response unless you include an SASE (stamped self-addressed envelope) with your letter. If you have items to offer them for sale or are seeking information, describe the piece in question thoroughly and mention any marks. You can sometimes do a pencil rubbing to duplicate the mark exactly. Photographs are still worth a 'thousand words,' and Xerox copies are especially good if for paper goods, patterned dinnerware, or even smaller 3-dimensional items.

It's a good idea to include your phone number if you write, since many people would rather respond with a call than a letter. And suggesting that they call back collect might very well be the courtesy that results in a successful transaction. If you're trying to reach someone by phone, always stop to consider the local time on the other end of your call. Even the most cordial person when dragged out of bed in the middle of the night will very likely *not* be receptive to you.

With the exception of the Advertising, Books, Bottles, Character Collectibles, and Toys sections which we've alphabetized by character or type, buyers are listed alphabetically under bold topics. A line in italics indicates only the specialized interests of the particular buyer whose name immediately follows it. Recommended reference guides not available from Collector Books may be purchased directly from the authors whose addresses are given in this section.

Advertising

Aunt Jemima
Lynn Burkett
P.O. Box 671
Hillsdale, MI 49242
517-437-2149

Big Boy
Steve Soelberg
29126 Laro Dr.
Agoura Hills, CA 91301
818-889-9909

Campbell's Soup
Dave and Micki Young
414 Country Ln. Ct.
Wauconda, IL 60084
847-487-4917

Cereal boxes and premiums
Scott Bruce
P.O. Box 481
Cambridge, MA 02140
617-492-5004

Gasoline globes, pumps, signs and promotional items
Author of book
Scott Benjamin
411 Forest St.
LaGrange, OH 44050
216-355-6608

Jewel Tea products and tins
Bill and Judy Vroman
739 Eastern Ave.
Fostoria, OH 44830
419-435-5443

Miniature oil-can banks
Peter Capell
1838 W Grace St.
Chicago, IL 60613-2724
312-871-8735
Also thermometers shaped like old gasoline station pole signs

Reddy Kilowatt and Bordon's Elsie
Lee Garmon
1529 Whittier St.
Springfield, IL 62704

Smokey Bear
Glen Brady
P.O. Box 3933
Central Point, OR 97502
503-772-0350

Aluminum
Author of book
Dannie Woodard
P.O. Box 1346
Weatherford, TX 76086
817-594-4680

American Bisque
Author of book
Mary Jane Giacomini
P.O. Box 404
Ferndale, CA 95536-0404
707-786-9464

Animal Dishes
Author of book
Everett Grist
6503 Slater Rd., Ste. H
Chattanooga, TN 37412-3955
615-855-4032

Also aluminum, advertising playing cards, and marbles

Appliances
Jim Barker
Toaster Master General
P.O. Box 41
Bethlehem, PA 10106

Autographs
Don and Anne Kier
2022 Marengo St.
Toledo, OH 43614
419-385-8211

Automobilia
General line; specializing in Chevrolet, hot rod and drag racing memorabilia, and toys
Jim and Nancy Schaut
P.O. Box 10781
Glendale, AZ 85318-0781
602-878-4293

Tire ashtrays; author of book
Jeff McVey
1810 W State St., #427
Boise, ID 83702

Autumn Leaf
Edits newsletter
Gwynneth Harrison
P.O. Box 1
Mira Loma, CA 91752-0001
909-685-5434
Buys and appraises

Aviation
Commercial items from the 1920s through the 1970s
John R. Joiner
52 Jefferson Pky., Apt. D
Newnan, GA 30263
404-502-9565

Airline memorabilia, chrome ashtrays with airplanes on pedestals
Dick Wallin
P.O. Box 1794
Springfield, IL 62705
217-498-927

Avon Collectibles
Author of book
Bud Hastin
P.O. Box 43690
Sal Vegas, NE 89116

Tammy Rodrick
Stacey's Treasures
1509 N 300 St.
Sumner, IL 62466
Also character toys, glasses, cereal boxes and premiums; beer steins, Blue Willow, head vases, and trolls

Banks
Modern mechanical banks
Dan Iannotti
212 W Hickory Grove Rd.
Bloomfield Hills, MI 48302-1127

Barware
Especially cocktail shakers
Arlene Lederman Antiques
150 Main St.
Nyack, NY 10960

Specializing in vintage cocktail shakers
Stephen Visakay
P.O. Box 1517
W Caldwell, NJ 07707-1517

Beer Cans and Breweriana
Steve Gordon
P.O. Box 632
Olney, MD 20830-0632
301-439-4116

Bells
Unusual; no cow or school
Author of book
Dorothy Malone Anthony
802 S Eddy
Ft. Scott, KS 66701

Birthday Angels
Jim and Denise Atkinson
555 East School St.
Owatonna, MN 55060
507-455-3340

Black Americana
Buy, sell and trade; lists available
Judy Posner
May-Oct: RD 1, Box 273SC
Effort, PA 18330
717-629-6583 or
Nov-April: 4195 S Tamiami Trail, #183SC
Venice, FL 34293
914-497-7149
e-mail: Judyandjef@aol.com

Pre-1950s items
Jan Thalberg
23 Mountain View Dr.
Weston, CT 06883

Black and golliwog items of all types
The Butler Did It!
Catherine Saunders Watson
P.O. Box 302
Greenville, NH 03048-0302
Phone or FAX: 603-878-2171

Black Glass
Author of book
Marlena Toohey
703 S Pratt Pkwy.
Longmont, CO 80501
303-678-9726

Blue Ridge
Author of several books; Columnist for The Depression Glass Daze
Betty Newbound
4567 Chadsworth
Commerce, MI 48382
Also milk glass, wall pockets, figural planters, collectible china and glass

Blue Willow
Author of several books
Mary Frank Gaston
Box 342
Bryan, TX 77806
Also china and metals

Bobbin' Heads by Hartland
Author of guide; newsletter
Tim Hunter
1668 Golddust
Sparks, NV 89436
702-626-5029

Books
Big Little Books
Ron and Donna Donnelly
P.O. Box 7047
Panama City Beach, FL 32413

Children's
My Bookhouse
27 S Sandusky St.
Tiffin, OH 44883
419-447-9842

Children's illustrated
Noreen Abbott Books
2666 44th Ave.
San Francisco, CA 94116

Children's illustrated, Little Golden, etc.
Ilene Kayne
1308 S Charles St.
Baltimore, MD 21230
410-685-3923

Fine books and antique toys
Bromer Booksellers, Inc.
607 Boylston St., on Copley Sq.
Boston, MA 02116

Little Golden Books, Wonder and Elf
Author of book on Little Golden Books,
Steve Santi
19626 Ricardo Ave.
Hayward, CA 94541

Paperback originals
For Collectors Only
2028B Ford Pkwy #136
St. Paul, MN 55116

Paperback originals, TV and movie tie-ins, etc.
Tom Rolls — Books
640 E Seminary #2
Greencastle, IN 46135

Bottle Openers
Charlie Reynolds
2836 Monroe St.
Falls Church, VA 22042
703-533-1322

Bottles
Bitters, figurals, inks, barber, etc.
Steve Ketcham
P.O. Box 24114
Minneapolis, MN 55424
612-920-4205
Also advertising signs, trays, calendars, etc.

Dairy and milk
Author of book
John Tutton
R.R. 4, Box 929
Front Royal, VA 22630
703-635-7058

Painted-label soda
Author of books
Thomas Marsh
914 Franklin Ave.
Youngstown, OH 44502
216-743-8600 or 800-845-7930 (book orders)

Boyd
Joyce M. Pringle
Chip and Dale Collectibles
3708 W Pioneer Pky.
Arlington, TX 76013
Also Summit and Mosser

Breweriana
DLK Nostalgia and Collectibles
P.O. Box 5112
Johnstown, PA 15904
Also Art Deco, novelty clocks, toys and football cards

Breyer
Author of book
Carol Karbowiak Gilbert
2193 14 Mile Rd. 206
Sterling Hts., MI 48310

British Royal Commemoratives
Audrey Zeder
6755 Coralite St. S
Long Beach, CA 90808

Brush-McCoy Pottery
Authors of book
Steve and Martha Sanford
230 Harrison Ave.
Campbell, CA 95008
408-978-8408

Bubble Bath Containers
Matt and Lisa Adams
1234 Harbor Cove
Woodstock, GA 30189
770-516-687

Calculators
Guy Ball
14561 Livingston St.
Tustin, CA 92780

California Perfume Company
Not common; especially items marked Goetting Co.
Dick Pardini
3107 N El Dorado St., Dept. G
Stockton, CA 95204-3412
Also Savoi Et Cie, Hinze Ambrosia, Gertrude Recordon, Marvel Electric Silver Cleaner, and Easy Day Automatic Clothes Washer

California Pottery
Susan N. Cox
Main Street Antique Mall
237 East Main Street
El Cajon, CA 92020
619-447-0800
Want to buy: California pottery, especially Brayton, Catalina, Metlox, Kay Finch, etc.; Also examples of relatively unknown companies. Must be mint. (Susan Cox has devoted much of the past 15 years to California pottery research which caught her interest when she was the editor and publisher of the *American Clay Exchange.* She would appreciate any information collectors might have about California pottery companies and artists.)

Pat and Kris Secor
P.O. Box 3367
Rock Island, IL 61204-3367
309-786-4870
Especially Hedi Shoop, Brad Keeler, Howard Pierce, Kay Finch, Matthew Adams, Marc Bellaire, Twin Winton, Sascha Brastoff; Many others

Michael John Verlangeri Gallery
P.O. Box 844
W Cambria, CA 93428-0844
Editor of *The California Pottery Trader* newsletter; Holds cataloged auctions

Cleminson
Robin Stine
P.O. Box 6202
Toledo, OH 43614
419-385-7387

Twin Winton
Mike Ellis
266 Rose Ln.
Costa Mesa, CA 92627
714-645-4697 or FAX 714-645-4697

Vallona Starr
Author of book
Bernice Stamper
7516 Elay Ave.
Bakersfield, CA 93308-7701
805-393-2900

Camark Pottery
Author of book, historian on Arkansas pottery
David Edwin Gifford
P.O. Box 7617
Little Rock, AR 72217

Cameras
Classic, collectible and usable
Gene's Cameras
2603 Artie St., SW Ste. 16
Huntsville, AL 35805
205-536-6893

Wooden, detective and stereo
John A. Hess
P.O. Box 3062
Andover, MA 01810
Also old brass lenses

Harry Poster
P.O. Box 1883
S Hackensack, NJ 07606
201-410-7525
Also accessories and 3-D projectors

Candlewick
Has matching service
Joan Cimini
63680 Centerville-Warnock Rd.
Belmont, OH 43718

Candy Containers
Glass
Jeff Bradfield
90 Main St.
Dayton, VA 22821
703-879-9961
Also advertising, cast-iron and tin toys,
postcards and Coca-Cola

Glass
Doug Dezso
864 Paterson Ave.
Maywood, NJ 07607
Author of book on candy containers;
other interests: Tonka Toys, Shafford
black cats, German bisque comic character nodders, Royal Bayreuth creamers, and Pep pins

Carnival Chalkware
Author of book
Thomas G. Morris
P.O. Box 8307
Medford, OR 97504
541-779-3164
Also Devil and Cards, Disney, slot
machines, Ginger Rogers memorabilia

Cast Iron
Door knockers, sprinklers, figural paper-
weights and marked cookware
Craig Dinner
P.O. Box 4399
Sunnyside, NY 11104
718-729-3850

Cat Collectibles
Marilyn Dipboye
33161 Wendy Dr.
Sterling Hts., MI 48310
810-264-0285

Ceramic Arts Studio
BA Wellman
P.O. Box 673
Westminster, MA 01473-1435

Cereal Boxes and Premiums
Author of book
Scott Bruce; Mr. Cereal Box
P.O. Box 481
Cambridge, MS 02140
617-492-5004
Editor of magazine *Flake;* Buys, sells,
trades, appraises

Character and Personality Collectibles
Author of books
Bill Bruegman
Toy Scouts, Inc.
137 Casterton Ave.
Akron, OH 44303
330-836-0668 or FAX 330-869-8668
e-mail: toyscout@salamander.net
Dealers, publishers and appraisers of
collectible memorabilia from the '50s
through today

Any and all
Terri Ivers
Terri's Toys
419 S First St.
Ponca City, OK 74601
405-762-8697 or 405-762-5174
FAX 405-765-2657
e-mail: ivers@pcok.com

Any and all
John Thurmond
Collector Holics
15006 Fuller
Grandview, MO 64030
816-322-0906

Any and all
Norm Vigue
62 Barley St.
Stoughton, MA 02072
617-344-5441

Batman, Gumby and Marilyn Monroe
Colleen Garmon Barnes
114 E Locust
Chatham, IL 62629

Beatles
Bojo
Bob Gottuso
P.O. Box 1403
Cranberry Twp., PA 16066-0403
Phone or FAX 412-776-0621

Beatles
Rick Rann, Beatelist
P.O. Box 877

Oak Park, IL 60303
708-442-7907

Betty Boop
Leo A. Mallette
2309 Santa Anita Ave.
Arcadia, CA 91006-5154

Bubble Bath Containers
Matt and Lisa Adams
1234 Harbor Cove
Woodstock, GA 30189
770-516-6874

California Raisins
Ken Clee
Box 11412
Philadelphia, PA 19111
215-722-1979

California Raisins
Larry De Angelo
516 King Arthur Dr.
Virginia Beach, VA 23464

Dick Tracy
Larry Doucet
2351 Sultana Dr.
Yorktown Hts., NY 10598

Disney, Western heroes, Gone With the
Wind, character watches ca 1930s to
mid-1950s, premiums and games
Ron and Donna Donnelly
Saturday Heroes
P.O. Box 7047
Panama City Beach, FL 32413
904-234-7944

Disney, buy, sell and trade; lists available
Judy Posner
May-October: RD 1, Box 273
Effort, PA 18330
717-629-6583 or
Nov-April: 4195 S Tamiami Trail, #183SC
Venice, FL 34293
941-497-7149
e-mail: Judyandjef@aol.com

Disney, especially Roger Rabbit
Allen Day
P.O. Box 525
Monroe, NC 28810

Elvis Presley
Author of book
Rosalind Cranor
P.O. Box 859
Blacksburg, VA 24063

Elvis Presley
Lee Garmon
1529 Whittier St.
Springfield, IL 62704

Garfield
Adrienne Warren
1032 Feather Bed Ln.
Edison, NJ 08820
908-381-7083 (EST)
Also Smurfs and other characters, dolls, monsters, premiums; Lists available

I Dream of Jeannie, Barbara Eden
Richard D. Barnes
1520 W 800 N
Salt Lake City, UT 84116
801-521-4400

Lil' Abner
Kenn Norris
P.O. Box 4830
Sanderson, TX 79848-4830

The Lone Ranger
Terry and Kay Klepey
c/o The Silver Bullet Newsletter
P.O. Box 553
Forks, WA 9833

Peanuts and Schulz Collectibles
Freddi Margolin
P.O. Box 5124P
Bay Shore, NY 11706

Roy Rogers and Dale Evans
Author of books
Robert W. Phillips
1703 N Aster Pl.
Broken Arrow, OK 74012-1308
One of the most widely-published writers in the field of cowboy memorabila; Research consultant for TV documentary *Roy Rogers, King of the Cowboys* (AMC-TV/Repbulic Pictures/Galen Films)

Shirley Temple
Gen Jones
294 Park St.
Medford, MA 02155

Smokey Bear
Glen Brady
P.O. Box 3933
Central Point, OR 97502
503-772-0350

Star Trek and Star Wars
Craig Reid

1911 E Sprague Ave.
Spokane, WA 99202
509-536-8489

Star Wars
Jim and Brenda Roush
739 W Fifth St.
Marion, IN 46953
317-662-6126

Three Stooges
Harry S. Ross
Soitenly Stooges Inc.
P.O. Box 72
Skokie, IL 60076

Tom Mix
Author of book
Merle 'Bud' Norris
1324 N Hague Ave.
Columbus, OH 43204-2108

TV and movie collectibles
TVC Enterprises
P.O. Box 1088
Easton, MA 02334
508-238-1179

Wizard of Oz
Bill Stillman
Scarfone & Stillman Vintage Oz
P.O. Box 167
Hummelstown, PA 17036
717-566-5538

Character and Promotional Drinking Glasses
Mark Chase and Michael Kelly
Collector Glass News
P.O. Box 308
Slippery Rock, PA 16057
412-946-2838 or 412-794-6420

Character Clocks and Watches
Author of book
Howard S. Brenner
106 Woodgate Terrace
Rochester, NY 14625

Bill Campbell
1221 Littlebrook Ln.
Birmingham, AL 35235
205-853-8227 or FAX 405-658-6986
Also character collectibles, advertising premiums

Character Mugs
Plastic, also advertising
Cheryl and Lee Brown

7377 Badger Ct.
Indianapolis, IN 46260
317-253-4620

Character Nodders
Matt and Lisa Adams
1234 Harbor Cove
Woodstock, GA 30189
770-516-6874

Chintz
Marge Geddes
P.O. Box 5875
Aloha, OR 97007
503-649-1041

Mary Jane Hastings
310 West 1st South
Mt. Olive, IL 62069
Phone or FAX 217-999-7519

Author of book
Joan Welsh
7015 Partridge Pl.
Hyattsville, MD 20782
301-779-6181

Christmas Collectibles
Especially from before 1920 and decorations made in Germany
J.W. 'Bill' and Treva Courter
3935 Kelley Rd.
Kevil, KY 42053
Phone or FAX 502-488-2116

Clocks
All types
Bruce A. Austin
40 Selborne Chase
Fairport, NY 14450
716-223-0711

Clothes Sprinkler Bottles
Ellen Bercovici
5118 Hampden Ln.
Bethesda, MD 20814
301-652-1140

Clothing
Blue Denim Clothing Co.
3213 Jeannie Ln.
Muskogee, OK 74453
918-683-1589

Coca-Cola
Also Pepsi-Cola
Terri Ivers
419 S First St.
Ponca City, OK 74601

405-762-8697 or 405-762-5174
FAX 405-765-2657
e-mail: ivers@pcok.com

Also Pepsi-Cola and other brands of soda
Craig and Donna Stifter
P.O. Box 6514
Naperville, IL 60540
630-717-7949

Coin-Operated Vending Machines
Ken and Jackie Durham
909 26th St., NW
Washington, DC 20037

Colorado Pottery (Broadmoor)
Carol and Jim Carlton
8115 S Syracuse St.
Englewood, CO 80112
303-773-8616
Also Coors, Lonhuda, and Denver White

Comic Books
Avalon Comics
Larry Curcio
P.O. Box 821
Medford, MA 02155
617-391-5614

Compacts
Author of book; unusual shapes, also vanities and accessories
Roselyn Gerson
P.O. Box 40
Lynbrook, NY 11563

Cookbooks
Author of book; also advertising leaflets
Col. Bob Allen
P.O. Box 85
St. James, MO 65559

Cookie Cutters
Author of book and newsletter
Rosemary Henry
9610 Greenview Ln.
Manassas, VA 22100

Cookie Jars
Joe Devine
1411 3rd St.
Council Bluffs, IA 51503
712-232-5233 or 712-328-7305
Also Russel Wright

Buy, sell and trade; lists available
Judy Posner
May-October: RD 1, Box 273
Effort, PA 18330

717-629-6583 or
Nov-April: 4195 S Tamiami Trail, #183SC
Venice, FL 34293
941-497-7149
e-mail: Judyandjef@aol.com

Phil and Nyla Thurston
82 Hamlin St.
Cortland, NY 13045
607-753-6770
Other interests listed under Figural Ceramics

Corkscrews
Antique and unusual
Paul P. Luchsinger
1126 Wishart Pl.
Hermitage, PA 16148

Coors
Rick Spencer
3953 S Renault Cir.
W Valley, UT 84119

Cowan
Author of book
Mark Bassett
P.O. Box 771233
Lakewood, OH 44107

Cracker Jack Items
Phil Helley
Old Kilbourn Antiques
629 Indiana Ave.
Wisconsin Dells, WI 53965
Also banks, radio premiums and wind-up toys

Wes Johnson, Sr.
106 Bauer Ave.
Louisville, KY 40207

Crackle Glass
Authors of book
Stan and Arlene Weitman
101 Cypress St.
Massapequa Park, NY 11758
516-799-2619 or FAX 516-797-3039

Credit Cards and Related Items
Walt Thompson
Box 2541
Yakima, WA 98907-2541

Cuff Links
National Cuff Link Society
Eugene R. Klompus
P.O. Box 346
Prospect Hts., IL 60070

Phone or FAX 847-816-0035
Also related items

Dakins
Jim Rash
135 Alder Ave.
Pleasantville, NJ 08232
609-646-4125

Decanters
Homestead Collectibles
Art and Judy Turner
R.D. 2, Rte. 150
P.O. Box 173
Mill Hall, PA 17751
717-726-3597 or FAX 717-726-4488

deLee
Joanne and Ralph Schaefer
3182 Williams Rd.
Oroville, CA 95965-8300
916-893-2902 or 800-897-6263

Depression Glass
Also Elegant glassware
John and Shirley Baker
673 W Township Rd. #118
Tiffin, OH 44883
Also Tiffin glassware

Dinnerware
Cat-Tail
Ken and Barbara Brooks
4121 Gladstone Ln.
Charlotte, NC 28205

Fiesta, Franciscan, Russel Wright, Lu Ray, and Metlox
Fiesta Plus
Mick and Lorna Chase
380 Hawkins Crawford Rd.
Cookeville, TN 38501
615-372-8333
Also other Homer Laughlin patterns

Mary Frank Gaston
P.O. Box 342
Bryan, TX 77806

Homer Laughlin China, author of book
Darlene Nossaman
5419 Lake Charles
Waco, TX 76710

Liberty Blue
Gary Beegle
92 River St.
Montgomery, NY 12549
914-457-3623

Also most lines of collectible modern American dinnerware as well as character glasses

Royal China
BA Wellman
88 State Rd. W
Homestead Farms #2
Westminster, MA 01473-1435

Russel Wright, Eva Zeisel, Homer Laughlin
Charles Alexander
221 E 34th St.
Indianapolis, IN 46205
317-924-9665

Dolls
Annalee Mobilitee Dolls
Jane's Collectibles
Jane Holt
P.O. Box 115
Derry, NH 03038
Extensive lists sometimes available

Boudoir dolls
Bonnie M. Groves
402 N Ave. A
Elgin, TX 78621
512-281-9551

Betsy McCall and friends
Marci Van Ausdall
P.O. Box 946
Quincy, CA 95971
e-mail: DREAMS707@aol.com

Celebrity and character dolls
Henri Yunes
971 Main St., Apt. 2
Hackensack, NJ 07601
201-488-2236

Chatty Cathy; authors of book
Don and Kathy Lewis
187 N Marcello Ave.
Thousand Oaks, CA 91360
805-499-7932

Dolls from the 1960s–70s, including Liddle Kiddles, Barbie, Tammy, Tressy, etc.; Co-author of book on Tammy
Cindy Sabulis
P.O. Box 642
Shelton, CT 06484
203-926-0176

Liddle Kiddles and other small dolls from the late '60s and early '70s
Dawn Parrish
9931 Gaynor Ave.

Granada Hills, CA 91343-1604
818-894-8964

Strawberry Shortcake
Geneva D. Addy
P.O. Box 124
Winterset, IA 50273

Dollhouse Furniture and Accessories
Renwal, Ideal, Marx, etc.
Judith A. Mosholder
R.D. #2, Box 147
Boswell, PA 15531
814-629-9277

Renwal, Plasco, Marx, etc.
Marian Schmuhl
7 Revolutionary Ridge Rd.
Bedford, MA 10730
617-275-2156

Door Knockers
Craig Dinner
Box 4399
Sunnyside, NY 11104
718-729-3850

Egg Beaters
Author of Beat This: The Egg Beater Chronicles
Don Thornton
Off Beat Books
1345 Poplar Ave.
Sunnyvale, CA 94087

Egg Cups
Joan George, Editor
Egg Cup Collectors Corner
67 Stevens Ave.
Old Bridge, NJ 08857

Author of book
Brenda Blake
Box 555
York Harbor, ME 03911
207-363-6566

Egg Timers
Ellen Bercovici
5118 Hampden Ln.
Bethesda, MD 20814
301-652-1140

Jeannie Greenfield
310 Parker Rd.
Stoneboro, PA 16153

Elegant Glass
Cambridge, Fostoria, Heisey

Deborah Maggard Antiques
P.O. Box 211
Chagrin Falls, OH 44022
216-247-5632
Also china and Victorian art glass

Ertl Banks
Homestead Collectibles
P.O. Box 173
Mill Hall, PA 17751
Also decanters

Eyewinker
Sophia Talbert
921 Union St.
Covington, IN 47932
317-793-325

Farm Collectibles
Farm Antique News
Gary Van Hoozer, Editor
812 N Third St.
Tarkio, MO 64491-0812
816-736-4528

Fast-Food Collectibles
Author of book
Ken Clee
Box 1142
Philadelphia, PA 19111
215-722-1979

Authors of several books
Joyce and Terry Losonsky
7506 Summer Leave Ln.
Columbia, MD 21046-2455
Illustrated Collector's Guide to McDonald's® Happy Meal® Boxes, Premiums and Promotions ($9 plus $2 postage), *McDonald's® Happy Meal® Toys in the USA* and *McDonald's® Happy Meal® Toys Around the World* (both full color, $24.95 each plus $3 postage), and *Illustrated Collector's Guide to McDonald's® McCAPS®* ($4 plus $2) are available from the authors.

Bill and Pat Poe
220 Dominica Cir. E
Niceville, FL 32578-4068
904-897-4163 or FAX 904-897-2606
Also cartoon and character glasses, Pez, Smurfs and California Raisins; Send $3 (US delivery) for 70-page catalog

Fenton Glass
Ferill J. Rice
304 Pheasant Run
Kaukauna, WI 54130

Figural Ceramics

Especially cookie jars, California pottery, Prayer Lady, Fitz & Floyd, and Kreiss as well as other imports; Also American pottery
Phil and Nyla Thurston
82 Hamlin St.
Cortland, NY 13045
607-753-6770

Especially Kitchen Prayer Lady, Enesco and Holt Howard
April and Larry Tvorak
P.O. Box 126
Canon City, CO 81215-0126
719-269-7230

Fire-King

Authors of book
April and Larry Tvorak
P.O. Box 126
Canon City, CO 81215-0126
719-269-7230

Fishing Collectibles

Publishes fixed-price catalog
Dave Hoover
1023 Skyview Dr.
New Albany, IN 47150
Also miniature boats and motors

Randy Hilst
1221 Florence #4
Pekin, IL 61554
309-346-2710

Flashlights

Editor of newsletter
Bill Utley
P.O. Box 4094
Tustin, CA 92681
714-730-1252 or FAX 714-505-4067

Florence Ceramics

Author of book
Doug Foland
1811 NW Couch #303
Portland, OR 97209

John and Peggy Scott
4640 S Leroy
Springfield, MO 65810

Flower Frogs

Nada Sue Knauss
12111 Potter Rd.
Weston, OH 43569
419-669-4735

Frankoma

Authors of books
Phyllis and Tom Bess
14535 E 13th St
Tulsa, OK 74108

Author of books
Susan N. Cox
Main Street Antique Mall
237 East Main St.
El Cajon, CA 92020
619-447-0800
Also unsharpened advertising pencils, complete matchbooks, Horlick's advertising, women's magazines from 1900 to 1950. (Susan Cox has written 3 books and 5 price guides on Frankoma pottery and is currently working on an updated price guide and a Frankoma advertising book. She has devoted much of the past fifteen years to California pottery research and welcomes any information collectors might have about California companies and artists.)

Fruit Jars

Especially old, odd or colored jars
John Hathaway
Rte. 2, Box 220
Bryant Pond, ME 04219
Also old jar lids and closures

Fulper

Douglass White
P.O. Box 5400672
Orlando, FL 32854
407-841-6681

Gambling and Related Items

Robert Eisenstadt
P.O. Box 020767
Brooklyn, NY 11202-0017

Games

Paul Fink's Fun and Games
P.O. Box 488
59 S Kent Rd.
Kent, CT 06757
203-927-4001

Paul David Morrow
1045 Rolling Point Ct.
Virginia Beach, VA 23456-6371

Geisha Girl Porcelain

Author of book
Elyce Litts
P.O. Box 394
Morris Plains, NJ 07950
Also ladies' compacts

Glass Animals

Author of book
Lee Garmon
1529 Whittier St.
Springfield, IL 62704

Glass Knives

Editor of newsletter
Adrienne Escoe
4448 Ironwood Ave.
Seal Beach, CA 90740-2926
e-mail: escoebliss@earthlink.net

Glass Shoes

Author of book
The Shoe Lady
Libby Yalom
P.O. Box 7146
Adelphi, MD 20783

Graniteware

Author of books
Helen Greguire
716-392-2704
Also carnival glass and toaster

Griswold

Buying catalogs and research materials only
Author of book
Bill and Denise Harned
P.O. Box 330373
Elmwood, CT 06133-0373

Halloween

C.J. Russell and Pamela Apakarian-Russell
Halloween Queen Antiques
P.O. Box 499
Winchester, NH 03470
Also other holidays and postcards

Hartland Plastics, Inc.

Specializing in Western Hartlands
Judy and Kerry Irwin
Kerry and Judy's Toys
7370 Eggleston Rd.
Memphis, TN 38125-2112

Specializing in sports figures
James Watson
25 Gilmore St.
Whitehall, NY 12887

Head Vases

Jean Griswold
701 Valley Brooks Rd.
Decatur, GA 30033
404-299-6606

Holt Howard
April and Larry Tvorak
P.O. Box 126
Canon City, CO 81215-0126
719-269-7230

Homer Laughlin
Author of book
Darlene Nossaman
5419 Lake Charles
Waco, TX 76710

Horton Ceramics
Darlene Nossaman
5419 Lake Charles
Waco, TX 76710

Hull
Mirror Brown, also Pfaltzgraff Gourmet Royal and other lines
Jo-Ann Bentz
Dealer at Shep's Grove, D15 & D16
P.O. Box 146AA, Beaver Rd. R.R. #3
Birdsboro, PA 19508-9107
610-582-0311

Brenda Roberts
R.R. #2
Marshall, MO 65340

Mirror Brown, also Pfaltzgraff Gourmet Royal; rare items only
Bill and Connie Sloan
4965 Valley Park Rd.
Doylestown, PA 18901

Imperial Glass
Joan Cimini
63680 Centerville-Warnock Rd.
Belmont, OH 43718
Also has Candlewick matching service

Editor of glass-oriented newsletter
Ruth Grizel
P.O. Box 205
Oakdale, IA 52319-0205

Imperial Porcelain
Geneva D. Addy
P.O. Box 124
Winterset, IA 50273

Indy 500 Memorabilia
Eric Jungnickel
P.O. Box 4674
Naperville, IL 60567-4674
630-983-8339

Insulators
Mike Bruner
6980 Walnut Lake Rd.
W Bloomfield, MI 48323
313-661-8241
Also porcelain signs, light-up advertising clocks, exit globes, lightening rod balls and target balls

Len Linscott
3557 Nicklaus Dr.
Tutusville, FL 32780

Jewel Tea
Products or boxes only; no dishes
Bill and Judy Vroman
739 Eastern Ave.
Fostoria, OH 44830
419-435-5443

Jewelry
Marcia Brown (Sparkles)
P.O. Box 2314
White City, OR 97503
503-826-3039

Men's accessories and cuff links only; edits newsletter
The National Cuff Link Society
Eugene R. Klompus
P.O. Box 346
Prospect Hts., IL 60070
Phone or FAX 847-816-0035

Josef Originals
Jim and Kaye Whitaker
Eclectic Antiques
P.O. Box 475, Dept. GS
Lynnwood, WA 98046

Kay Finch
Animals and birds, especially in pink with pastel decoration
Mike Drollinger
1202 Seventh St.
Covington, IN 47932
317-793-2392

Kentucky Derby and Horse Racing
B.L. Hornback
707 Sunrise Ln.
Elizabethtown, KY 42701

Kitchen Prayer Ladies
April and Larry Tvorak
P.O. Box 126
Canon City, CO 81215-0126
719-269-7230
Author of *Prayer Lady Plus*; to order

send $6.95 plus $1 postage and handling.

Labels
Cerebro
P.O. Box 1221
Lancaster, PA 17603
800-695-2235

Lamps
Specializing in Aladdin
Author of books
J.W. Courter
3935 Kelley Rd.
Kevil, KY 42053
502-488-2116

Motion lamps
Eclectic Antiques
Jim and Kaye Whitaker
P.O. Box 475, Dept. GS
Lynwood, WA 98046

Perfume Lamps
Tom and Linda Millman
231 S Main St.
Bethel, OH 45106
513-734-6884 (after 9 pm)

Law Enforcement and Crime-Related Memorabilia
Tony Perrin
1401 N Pierce #6
Little Rock, AR 72207
501-868-5005 or 501-666-6493 (after 5 pm)

Lefton
Author of book
Loretta De Lozier
1101 Polk St.
Bedford, IA 50833

License Plates
Richard Diehl
5965 W Colgate Pl.
Denver, CO 80227

Lunch Boxes
Norman's Ole and New Store
Philip Norman
126 W Main St.
Washington, NC 27889-4944
919-946-3448

Terri's Toys and Nostalgia
Terri Ivers
419 S First St.
Ponca City, OK 74601

405-762-8697 or 405-762-5174
FAX 405-765-2657
e-mail: ivers@pcok.com

MAD Collectibles
Jim McClane
232 Butternut Dr.
Wayne, NJ 07470

Magazines
Issues price guide to illustrations, old magazines and pinups
Denis C. Jackson
Illustrator Collector's News
P.O. Box 1958
Sequim, WA 98382
360-683-2559 or FAX 360-683-9708
e-mail: ticn@daka.com

Pre-1950 movie magazines, especially with Ginger Rogers covers
Tom Morris
P.O. Box 8307
Medford, OR 97504
503-779-3164

National Geographic
Author of guide
Don Smith's National Geographic Magazines
3930 Rankin St.
Louisville, KY 40214
502-366-7504

Pulps
J. Grant Thiessen
Pandora's Books Ltd.
Box 54
Neche, ND 58265-0054
FAX 204-324-1628 or
e-mail: jgthiess@mts.net
http://www.pandora.ca/pandora
Issues catalogs on various genre of hardcover books, paperbacks, and magazines of all types

Marbles
Author of books
Everett Grist
6503 Slater Rd., Ste. H
Chattanooga, TN 37412-3955
615-855-4032

Match Safes
George Sparacio
P.O. Box 791
Malaga, NJ 08328
609-694-4167

Matchcovers
Bill Retskin
P.O. Box 18481
Asheville, NC 2281

McCoy Pottery
Authors of book
Robert and Margaret Hanson, Craig Nissen
P.O. Box 70426
Bellevue, WA 98005

Motorcycles
Also related items and clothing
Bruce Kiper
Ancient Age Motors
2205 Sunset Ln.
Lutz, FL 33549
813-949-5060

Movie Posters
Movie Poster Service
Cleophas and Lou Ann Wooley
Box 517
Canton, OK 73724-0517
405-886-2248 or FAX 405-886-2249
In business full time since 1972; own/operate mail-order firm with world's largest movie poster inventory

Napkin Dolls
Bobbie Zucker Bryson
1 St. Eleanoras Ln.
Tuckahoe, NY 10707
914-779-1405

Niloak Pottery
Author of book; historian on Arkansas pottery
David Edwin Gifford
P.O. Box 7617
Little Rock, AR 72217
Autographed books available

Newspaper Collector Society
Rick Brown
P.O. Box 19134
Lansing, MI 19134

Novelty Clocks
Animated and nonanimated
Carole S. Kaifer
P.O. Box 232
Bethania, NC 27010
Also items of pressed wood and Syrocco

Electric motion clocks, buy, sell, trade and restore
Sam and Anna Samuelian
P.O. Box 504

Edgmont, PA 19028-0504
610-566-7248
Also motion lamps, transistor and novelty radios

Novelty Radios
Authors of several books
Sue and Marty Bunis
R.R. 1, Box 36
Bradford, NH 03221-9102

Nutcrackers
Earl MacSorley
823 Indian Hill Rd.
Orange, CT 06477

Orientalia and Dragonware
Susie Hibbard
2570 Walnut Blvd. #20
Walnut Creek, CA 94596

Paper Dolls
Author of books
Mary Young
P.O. Box 9244
Wright Bros Branch
Dayton, OH 45409

Pencil Sharpeners
Phil Helley
629 Indiana Ave.
Wisconsin Dells, WI 53965
608-254-8659

Advertising and figural
Martha Hughes
4128 Ingalls St.
San Diego, CA 92103
619-296-1866

Pennsbury
Author of price guide; video book available
BA Wellman
88 State Rd. W
Homestead Farms #2
Westminster, MA 01473-1435

Joe Devine
1411 3rd St.
Council Bluffs, IA 51503
712-232-5322 or 712-328-7305

Shirley Graff
4515 Graff Rd.
Brunswick, OH 4421

Pepsi-Cola
Craig and Donna Stifter
P.O. Box 6514

Naperville, IL 60540
630-717-7949
Other soda pop memorabilia as well

Perfume Bottles
Especially commercial, Czechoslovakian, Lalique, Baccarat, Victorian, crown top, factices, miniatures
Monsen and Baer
Box 529
Vienna, VA 22183
703-242-1357
Buy, sell and accept consignments for auctions

Pez
Richard Belyski
P.O. Box 124
Sea Cliff, NY 11579
516-676-1183

Pfaltzgraff
Gourmet Royal as well as other dinnerware lines
Jo-Ann Bentz
Dealer, Shupp's Grove, D15 & D16
Adamstown, PA or
Box 146 AA, Beaver Rd., R.R. 3
Birdsboro, PA 19508
610-582-0311

Gourmet, Gourmet Royal
Bill and Connie Sloan
4965 Valley Park Rd.
Doylestown, PA 18901

Photographica
Antique photography and paper
Betty Davis
5291 Ravenna Rd.
Newton Falls, OH 44444
FAX 216-872-0386

Any pre-1900
John A. Hess
P.O. Box 3062
Andover, MA 01810

Pie Birds
Also funnels
Lillian M. Cole
14 Harmony School Rd.
Flemington, NJ 08822
908-782-3198
Also old ice cream scoops

Pinup Art
Issues price guides to pinups, illustrations and old magazines

Denis C. Jackson
Illustrator Collector's News
P.O. Box 1958
Sequim, WA 98382
360-683-2559 or FAX 360-683-9708
e-mail: ticn@daka.com

Pocket Calculators
International Assn. of Calculator Collectors
Guy D. Ball
14561 Livingston St.
Tustin, CA 92680-2618
714-759-2116 or FAX 714-730-6140

Political
Michael and Polly McQuillen
McQuillen's Collectibles
P.O. Box 11141
Indianapolis, IN 46201-0141
317-322-8518

Before 1960
Michael Engel
29 Groveland St.
Easthampton, MA 01027

Pins, banners, ribbons, etc.
Paul Longo Americana
Box 490
Chatham Rd., South Orleans
Cape Cod, MA 02662
508-255-5482

Porcelier
Jim Barker
Toaster Master General
P.O. Box 41
Bethlehem, PA 10106

Author of book
Susan Grindberg
6330 Doffing Ave. E
Inner Grove Hts., MN 55076
612-450-6770 or FAX 612-450-1895
e-mail: Porcelier@visi.com
http://www.visi.com/Porcelier/
Specializing in Porcelier China; Author of *Collector's Guide to Porcelier China*; Autographed copies available from the author for $18.95 + $2.05 postage & handling (Minnesota residents add $1.23 sales tax)

Postcards
C.J. Russell & Pamela Apakarian-Russell
Halloween Queen Antiques
P.O. Box 499
Winchester, NH 03470
Also Halloween and other holidays

Powder Jars
John and Peggy Scott
4640 S Leroy
Springfield, MO 65810

Sharon Thoerner
15549 Ryon Ave.
Bellflower, CA 90706
310-866-1555
Also slag glass

Purinton Pottery
Susan Morris
P.O. Box 656
Panora, IA 50216
515-755-3161

Purses
Veronica Trainer
P.O. Box 40443
Cleveland, OH 44140

Puzzles
Wooden jigsaw type from before 1950
Bob Armstrong
15 Monadnock Rd.
Worcester, MA 01609

Especially character related
Norm Vigue
62 Bailey St.
Stoughton, MA 02072
617-344-5441

Radio Premiums
Bill Campbell
1221 Littlebrook Ln.
Birmingham, AL 35235
205-853-8227 or FAX 405-658-6986

Radios
Antique Radio Labs
James Fred
Rte. 1, Box 41
Cutler, IN 46920
Buy, sell and trade; Repairs radio equipment using vacuum tubes

Authors of several books on antique, novelty and transistor radios
Sue and Marty Bunis
R.R. 1, Box 36
Bradford, NH 03221-9102

Author of book
Harry Poster
P.O. Box 1883
S Hackensack, NJ 07606
201-410-7525

Also televisions, related advertising items, old tubes, cameras, 3-D viewers and projectors, View-Master and Tru-View reels and accessories

Railroadiana

Any item; especially china and silver
John White, 'Grandpa'
Grandpa's Depot
1616 17th St., Ste. 267
Denver, CO 80202
303-628-5590 or FAX 303-628-5547
Also related items; Catalogs available

Also steamship and other transportation memorabilia
Fred and Lila Shrader
Shrader Antiques
2025 Hwy. 199
Crescent City, CA 95531
707-458-3525
Also Buffalo, Shelley, Niloak and Hummels

Razor Blade Banks

David Geise
1410 Aquia Dr.
Stafford, VA 22554
703-569-5984

Reamers

Bobbie Zucker Bryson
St Eleanoras Ln.
Tuckahoe, NY 10707
914-779-1405

Debbie Gillham
47 Midline Ct.
Gaithersburg, MD 20878
301-977-5727

Records

45 rpm and LPs
Mason's Bookstore, Rare Books, and Record Albums
Dave Torzillo
115 S Main St.
Chambersburg, PA 17201
717-261-0541

Picture and 78 rpm kiddie records
Peter Muldavin
173 W 78th St.
New York, NY 10024
212-362-9606

Especially 78 rpms
L.R. 'Les' Docks
Box 691035

San Antonio, TX 78269-1035
Write for want list

Red Wing Artware

Wendy and Leo Frese
Three Rivers Collectibles
P.O. Box 551542
Dallas, TX 75355
214-341-515
e-mail: rumrill@ix.netcom.com

Regal China

Van Telligen, Bendel, Old MacDonald's Farm
Rick Spencer
3953 S Renault Cir.
West Valley, UT 84119
801-973-0805
Also Silverplated Flatware, Coors, Shawnee, Watt, Silverplate (especially grape patterns)

Rooster and Roses

Jacki Elliott
9790 Twin Cities Rd.
Galt, CA 95632
209-745-3860

Roselane Sparklers

Lee Garmon
1529 Whittier St.
Springfield, IL 62704

Rosemeade

NDSU research specialist
Bryce Farnsworth
1334 14½ St. S
Fargo, ND 58103
701-237-3597

Royal Bayreuth

Don and Anne Kier
2022 Marengo St.
Toledo, OH 43614
419-385-8211

Royal Copley

Author of books
Joe Devine
1411 3rd St.
Council Bluffs, IA 51503
712-323-5233 or 712-328-7305
Buy, sell or trade; Also pie birds

Royal Haeger and Royal Hickman

Author of books
Lee Garmon
1529 Whittier St.
Springfield, IL 62704

RumRill

Wendy and Leo Frese
Three Rivers Collectibles
P.O. Box 551542
Dallas, TX 75355
214-341-5165
e-mail: rumrill@ix.netcom.com

Ruby Glass

Author of book
Naomi L. Over
8909 Sharon Ln.
Arvada, CO 80002
303-424-5922

Russel Wright

Author of book
Ann Kerr
P.O. Box 437
Sidney, OH 45365

Salt and Pepper Shakers

Figural or novelty; buy, sell and trade; lists available
Judy Posner
May-October: RD 1, Box 273
Effort, PA 18330
717-629-6583 or
Nov.-April: 4195 S Tamiami Trail, #183SC
Venice, FL 34293
941-497-7149
e-mail: Judyandjef@aol.com

Scottie Dog Collectibles

Donna Palmer
2446 215th Ave. SE
Issaquah, WA 98027

Scouting Collectibles

Author of books
R.J. Sayers
P.O. Box 629
Brevard, NC 28712
Book available by sending $24.94 plus $4 for shipping and handling

Sebastians

Blossom Shop Collectibles
Jim Waite
112 N Main St.
Farmer City, IL 61842
800-842-259

Sewing Collectibles

Marge Geddes
P.O. Box 5875
Aloha, OR 97007
503-649-1041

Sewing Machines
Toy only; authors of book
Darryl and Roxana Matter
P.O. Box 65
Portis, KS 67474-0065

Shawnee
Rick Spencer
3953 S Renault Cir.
West Valley, UT 84119
801-973-0805

Shot Glasses
Author of book
Mark Pickvet
P.O. Box 90404
Flint, MI 48509

Silhouette Pictures (20th Century)
Author of book
Shirley Mace
Shadow Enterprises
P.O. Box 1602
Mesilla Park, NM 88047
505-524-6717 or 505-523-0940
e-mail: Shmace@nmsu.ed

Snow Domes
Author of book and newsletter
Nancy McMichael, Editor
P.O. Box 53310
Washington, DC 20009

Soda Fountain Collectibles
Harold and Joyce Screen
2804 Munster Rd.
Baltimore, MD 21234
410-661-6765

Soda-Pop Memorabilia
Craig and Donna Stifter
P.O. Box 6514
Naperville, IL 60540
630-717-7949

Painted-label soda bottles; author of books
Thomas Marsh
914 Franklin Ave.
Youngstown, OH 44502
216-743-8600 or 800-845-7930 (order line)

Sports Collectibles
Equipment and player-used items
Don and Anne Kier
2022 Marengo St.
Toledo, OH 43614
419-385-8211

Bobbin' head sports figures
Tim Hunter
1668 Golddust
Sparks, NV 89436
702-626-5029

Paul Longo Americana
Box 490
Chatham Rd., South Orleans
Cape Cod, MA 02662
508-255-5482
Also stocks and bonds

Golf collectibles
Pat Romano
32 Sterling Dr.
Lake Grove, NY 11202-0017

Sports Pins
Tony George
22431-B160 Antonio Pky. #252
Rancho Santa Margarita, CA 92688
714-589-6075

St. Clair Glass
Ted Pruitt
3382 W 700 N
Anderson, IN 46011
Book available ($15)

Stangl
Birds, dinnerware, artware
Popkorn Antiques
Bob and Nancy Perzel
P.O. Box 1057
4 Mine St.
Flemington, NJ 08822
908-782-9631

Statue of Liberty
Mike Brooks
7335 Skyline
Oakland, CA 94611

String Holders
Ellen Bercovici
5118 Hampden Ln.
Bethesda, MD 20814
301-652-1140

Swanky Swigs
Joyce Jackson
900 Jenkins Rd.
Aledo, TX 76008
817-441-8864

Syroco and Similar Products
Doris J. Gibbs
3837 Cuming #1

Omaha, NE 68131
402-556-4300

Teapots and Tea-Related Items
Author of book
Tina Carter
882 S Mollison
El Cajon, CA 92020

Tire Ashtrays
Author of book
Jeff McVey
1810 W State St., #427
Boise, ID 83702-3955
Book available ($12.95 postpaid)

Toothbrush Holders
Author of book
Marilyn Cooper
8408 Lofland Dr.
Houston, TX 77055
713-465-7773

Toys
Any and all
June Moon
245 N Northwest Hwy.
Park Ridge, IL 60068
847-825-1411 or FAX 847-825-6090

Aurora model kits, and especially toys from 1948-1972
Author of books
Bill Bruegman
137 Casterton Dr.
Akron, OH 44303
330-836-0668 or FAX 330-869-8668
e-mail: toyscout@salamander.net
Dealers, publishers and appraisers of collectible memorabilia from the '50s through today

Building blocks and construction toys
Arlan Coffman
1223 Wilshire Blvd., Ste. 275
Santa Monica, CA 90403
310-453-2507

Die-cast vehicles
Mark Giles
P.O. Box 821
Ogallala, NE 69153-0821

Fisher-Price pull toys and playsets up to 1986
Brad Cassidy
1350 Stanwix
Toledo, OH 43614
419-385-9910

Games and general line
Phil McEntee
Where the Toys Are
45 W Pike St.
Canonsburg, PA 15317

Hot Wheels
D.W. (Steve) Stephenson
11117 NE 164th Pl.
Bothell, WA 98011-4003

Model kits other than Aurora; edits publications
Gordy Dutt
Box 201
Sharon Center, OH 42274-0201

Puppets and marionettes
Steven Meltzer
670 San Juan Ave. #B
Venice, CA 90291
310-396-6007

Sand toys
Authors of book
Carole & Richard Smyth
Carole Smyth Antiques
P.O. Box 2068
Huntington, NY 11743

Slot race cars from 1960s-70s
Gary T. Pollastro
4156 Beach Dr. SW
Seattle, WA 98116
206-935-0245

Tin litho, paper on wood, comic character, penny toys and Schoenhut
Wes Johnson, Sr.
106 Bauer Ave.
Louisville, KY 40207

Tootsietoys; author of books
David E. Richter
6817 Sutherland
Mentor, OH 44060
216-255-6537

Tops and Spinning Toys
Bruce Middleton
5 Lloyd Rd.
Newburgh, NY 12550
914-564-2556

Toy soldiers, figures and playsets
The Phoenix Toy Soldier Co.
Bob Wilson
P.O. Box 26365
Phoenix, AZ 85068
602-863-2891

Transformers and robots
David Kolodny-Nagy

3701 Connecticut Ave. NW #500
Washington, DC 20008
202-364-8753

Trolls
Roger Inouye
765 E Franklin Ave.
Pomona, CA 91766
909-623-1368

Walkers, ramp-walkers, and wind-ups
Randy Welch
Raven'tiques
27965 Peach Orchard Rd.
Easton, MD 21601-8203
410-822-5441

TV Guides
Price guide available
TV Guide Specialists
Jeff Kadet
P.O. Box 20
Macomb, IL 61455

Valentines
Author of book
Katherine Kreider
Kingsbury Productions
P.O. Box 7957
Lancaster, PA 17604-7957
717-892-3001 or
4555 N Pershing Ave., Ste. 33-138
Stockton, CA 95207
209-467-8438

Vallona Starr
Author of book
Bernice Stamper
7516 Elay Ave.
Bakersfield, CA 93308-7701

Van Briggle
Dated examples, author of book
Scott H. Nelson
Box 6081
Santa Fe, NM 87502
505-986-1176
Also UND (University of North Dakota),
other American potteries

Vandor
Lois Wildman
175 Chick Rd.
Camano Island, WA 98282

Vernon Kilns
Maxine Nelson
873 Marigold Ct.
Carlsbad, CA 92009

View-Master and Tru-View
Roger Nazeley

4921 Castor Ave.
Philadelphia, PA 19124
Harry Poster
P.O. Box 1883
S Hackensack, NJ 07606
201-410-7525

Walter Sigg
3-D Entertainment
P.O Box 208
Swartswood, NJ 07877

Wade
Author of book
Ian Warner
P.O. Box 93022
Brampton, Ontario
Canada L6Y 4V8

Watt Pottery
Author of book
Susan and Dave Morris
P.O. Box 656
Panora, IA 50216
515-755-3161

Western Collectibles
Author of books
Warren R. Anderson
American West Archives
P.O. Box 100
Cedar City, UT 84720
801-586-9497
Also documents, autographs, stocks and
bonds, and other ephemera

Author of books
Dan Hutchins; Hutchins Publishing Co.
P.O. Box 529
Marion, IA, 52302
505-425-3387

Western Heroes
*Author of books, ardent researcher and
guest columnist*
Robert W. Phillips
Phillips Archives of Western Memorabilia
1703 N Aster Pl.
Broken Arrow, OK 74012
918-254-8205 or FAX 918-252-9363

Westmoreland
Author of books; newsletter editor
Ruth Grizel
P.O. Box 205
Oakdale, IA 52319-0205

World's Fairs and Expositions
D.D. Woollard, Jr.
11614 Old St. Charles Rd.
Bridgeton, MO 63044
314-739-4662

Index

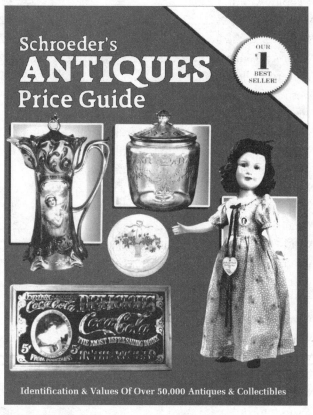